Lecture Notes in Computer Science 3032

Commenced Publication in 1973
Founding and Former Series Editors:
Gerhard Goos, Juris Hartmanis, and Jan van Leeuwen

Springer-Verlag Berlin Heidelberg GmbH

Minglu Li Xian-He Sun
Qianni Deng Jun Ni (Eds.)

Grid and Cooperative Computing

Second International Workshop, GCC 2003
Shanhai, China, December 7-10, 2003
Revised Papers, Part I

Volume Editors

Minglu Li
Qianni Deng
Shanghai Jiao Tong University
Department of Computer Science and Engineering
Shanghai 200030, P.R. China
E-mail: {li-ml, deng-qn}@cs.sjtu.edu.cn

Xian-He Sun
Illinois Institute of Technology
Department of Computer Science
Stuart Building, Chicago, IL 60616, USA
E-mail: sun@iit.edu

Jun Ni
University of Iowa
Department of Computer Science
Iowa City, IA 52242, USA
E-mail: jun-ni@uiowa.edu

Library of Congress Control Number: 2004104848

CR Subject Classification (1998): C.2, D.4, D.2, H.4, H.3, H.5.2-3, I.2

ISSN 0302-9743
ISBN 978-3-540-21988-0 ISBN 978-3-540-24679-4 (eBook)
DOI 10.1007/978-3-540-24679-4

springeronline.com

Originally published by Springer-Verlag Berlin Heidelberg New York in 2004

Typesetting: Camera-ready by author, data conversion by PTP-Berlin, Protago-TeX-Production GmbH
Printed on acid-free paper SPIN: 10999318 06/3142 5 4 3 2 1 0

Preface

Grid and cooperative computing has emerged as a new frontier of information technology. It aims to share and coordinate distributed and heterogeneous network resources for better performance and functionality that can otherwise not be achieved. This volume contains the papers presented at the 2nd International Workshop on Grid and Cooperative Computing, GCC 2003, which was held in Shanghai, P.R. China, during December 7–10, 2003. GCC is designed to serve as a forum to present current and future work as well as to exchange research ideas among researchers, developers, practitioners, and users in Grid computing, Web services and cooperative computing, including theory and applications.

For this workshop, we received over 550 paper submissions from 22 countries and regions. All the papers were peer-reviewed in depth and qualitatively graded on their relevance, originality, significance, presentation, and the overall appropriateness of their acceptance. Any concerns raised were discussed by the program committee. The organizing committee selected 176 papers for conference presentation (full papers) and 173 submissions for poster presentation (short papers). The papers included herein represent the forefront of research from China, USA, UK, Canada, Switzerland, Japan, Australia, India, Korea, Singapore, Brazil, Norway, Greece, Iran, Turkey, Oman, Pakistan and other countries. More than 600 attendees participated in the technical section and the exhibition of the workshop.

The success of GCC 2003 was made possible by the collective efforts of many people and organizations. We would like to express our special thanks to the Ministry of Education of P.R. China and the municipal government of Shanghai. We also thank IBM, Intel, Platform, HP, Dawning and Lenovo for their generous support. Without the extensive support from many communities, we would not have been able to hold this successful workshop. Moreover,our thanks go to Springer-Verlag for its assistance in putting the proceedings together.

We would like to take this opportunity to thank all the authors, many of whom traveled great distances to participate in this workshop and make their valuable contributions. We would also like to express our gratitude to the program committee members and all the other reviewers for the time and work they put into the thorough review of the large number of papers submitted. Last, but not least, our thanks also go to all the workshop staff for the great job they did in making the local arrangements and organizing an attractive social program.

December 2003

Minglu Li, Xian-He Sun
Qianni Deng, Jun Ni

Conference Committees

Honorary Chair

Qinping Zhao (MOE, China)

Steering Committee

Guojie Li (CCF, China)
Weiping Shen (Shanghai Jiao Tong University, China)
Huanye Sheng (Shanghai Jiao Tong University, China)
Zhiwei Xu (IEEE Beijing Section, China)
Liang-Jie Zhang (IEEE Computer Soceity, USA)
Xiaodong Zhang (NSF, USA)

General Co-chairs

Minglu Li (Shanghai Jiao Tong University, China)
Xian-He Sun (Illinois Institute of Technology, USA)

Program Co-chairs

Qianni Deng (Shanghai Jiao Tong University, China)
Jun Ni (University of Iowa, USA)

Panel Chair

Hai Jin (Huazhong University of Science and Technology, China)

Program Committee Members

Yaodong Bi (University of Scranton, USA)
Wentong Cai (Nanyang Technological University, Singapore)
Jian Cao (Shanghai Jiao Tong University, China)
Jiannong Cao (Hong Kong Polytechnic University, China)
Guo-Liang Chen (University of Science and Technology of China, China)
Jian Chen (South Australia University, Australia)
Xuebin Chi (Computer Network Information Center, CAS, China)
Qianni Deng (Shanghai Jiao Tong University, China)
Xiaoshe Dong (Xi'an Jiao Tong University, China)
Joseph Fong (City University of Hong Kong)
Yuxi Fu (Shanghai Jiao Tong University, China)
Guangrong Gao (University of Delaware, Newark, USA)
Yadong Gui (Shanghai Supercomputing Center, China)
Minyi Guo (University of Aizu, Japan)
Jun Han (Swinburne University of Technology, Australia)
Yanbo Han (Institute of Computing Technology, CAS, China)
Jinpeng Huai (Beihang University, China)
Weijia Jia (City University of Hong Kong)
ChangJun Jiang (Tongji University, China)
Hai Jin (Huazhong University of Science and Technology, China)
Francis Lau (University of Hong Kong)
Keqin Li (State University of New York, USA)
Minglu Li (Shanghai Jiao Tong University, China)
Qing Li (City University of Hong Kong)
Xiaoming Li (Peking University, China)
Xinda Lu (Shanghai Jiao Tong University, China)
Junzhou Luo (Southeast University, China)
Fanyuan Ma (Shanghai Jiao Tong University, China)
Dan Meng (Institute of Computing Technology, CAS, China)
Xiangxu Meng (Shandong University, China)
Jun Ni (University of Iowa, USA)
Lionel M. Ni (Hong Kong University of Science & Technology)
Yi Pan (Georgia State University, USA)
Depei Qian (Xi'an Jiao Tong University, China)
Yuzhong Qu (Southeast University, China)
Hong Shen (Advanced Institute of Science & Technology, Japan)
Xian-He Sun (Illinois Institute of Technology, USA)
Huaglory Tianfield (Glasgow Caledonian University, UK)
Weiqin Tong (Shanghai University, China)
Cho-Li Wang (University of Hong Kong)
Frank Wang (London Metropolitan University, UK)
Jie Wang (Stanford University, USA)
Shaowen Wang (University of Iowa, USA)
Xingwei Wang (Northeastern University, China)

Jie Wu (Florida Atlantic University, USA)
Zhaohui Wu (Zhejiang University, China)
Nong Xiao (National University of Defense Technology, China)
Xianghui Xie (Jiangnan Institute of Computing Technology, China)
Chengzhong Xu (Wayne State University, USA)
Zhiwei Xu (Institute of Computing Technology, CAS, China)
Guangwen Yang (Tsinghua University, China)
Laurence Tianruo Yang (St. Francis Xavier University, Canada)
Qiang Yang (Hong Kong University of Science & Technology)
Jinyuan You (Shanghai Jiao Tong University, China)
Haibiao Zeng (Sun Yat-Sen University, China)
Ling Zhang (South China University of Technology, China)
Xiaodong Zhang (NSF, USA and College of William and Mary, USA)
Wu Zhang (Shanghai University, China)
Weimin Zheng (Tsinghua University, China)
Aoying Zhou (Fudan University, China)
Wanlei Zhou (Deakin University, Australia)
Jianping Zhu (University of Akron, USA)
Hai Zhuge (Institute of Computing Technology, CAS, China)

Organization Committee

Xinda Lu (Chair) (Shanghai Jiao Tong University, China)
Jian Cao (Shanghai Jiao Tong University, China)
Ruonan Rao (Shanghai Jiao Tong University, China)
Meiju Chen (Shanghai Jiao Tong University, China)
An Yang (Shanghai Jiao Tong University, China)
Zhihua Su (Shanghai Jiao Tong University, China)
Feilong Tang (Shanghai Jiao Tong University, China)
Jiadi Yu (Shanghai Jiao Tong University, China)

Will Globus dominate Grid computing as Windows dominated in PCs? If not, what will the next Grid toolkits looks like?

Panel Chair

Hai Jin, Huazhong University of Science and Technology, China
hjin@hust.edu.cn

Panelists

Wolfgang Gentzsch, Sun Microsystems, Inc., USA
wolfgang.gentzsch@sun.com

Satoshi Matsuoka, Tokyo Institute of Technology, Japan
matsu@is.titech.ac.jp

Carl Kesselman, University of Southern California, USA
carl@isi.edu

Andrew A. Chien, University of California at San Diego, USA
achien@ucsd.edu

Xian-He Sun, Illinois Institute of Technology, USA
sun@iit.edu

Richard Wirt, Intel Corporation, USA
Richard.Wirt@intel.com

Zhiwei Xu, Institute of Computing Technology, CAS, China
zxu@ict.ac.cn

Francis Lau, University of Hong Kong
fcmlau@csis.hku.hk

Huaglory Tianfield, Glasgow Caledonian University, UK
H.Tianfield@gcal.ac.uk

Table of Contents, Part I

Session 1: Grid Application

Session 2: Peer to Peer Computing

Session 3: Grid Architectures

Session 4: Grid Middleware and Toolkits

Session 5: Web Security and Web Services

Table of Contents, Part II

Session 6: Advanced Resource Management, Scheduling, and Monitoring

Session 7: Network Communication and Information Retrieval

Session 8: Grid QoS

Session 9: Algorithm, Economic Model, Theoretical Model of the Grid

Session 10: Semantic Grid and Knowledge Grid

Session 11: Data Remote Access, Storage, and Sharing

Session 12: Computer-Supported Cooperative Work and Cooperative Middleware

Vega Grid: A Computer Systems Approach to Grid Research

Zhiwei Xu

Institute of Computing Technology, CAS, China

Abstract. As grid computing gains support and popularity, the needs grow for studying computer science and technology problems arising from grid systems and applications. In this talk, the speaker will present an organization of grid computing problems into a metaphor of man-computer society, and pose several computer science questions. He will then highlight a computer systems approach used by the Vega Grid research team at Institute of Computing Technology, Chinese Academy of Sciences. This approach helps the Vega Grid team understand grid computing machine models, grid address space, grid subject space, and grid programming models, as well as generate promising research results.

M. Li et al. (Eds.): GCC 2003, LNCS 3032, p. 1, 2004.

Problems of and Mechanisms for Instantiating Virtual Organizations

Carl Kesselman

University of Southern California

Abstract. In the past, significant accomplishments in science, engineering or business were the product of the work of an individual, or a small, tightly knit work group. However, today accomplishments of merit are often produced within the context of dynamic, distributed, multi-organizational collaborations whose participates are drawn from different, autonomously operated "physical" organizations. We call these collaborations virtual organizations, or VOs.

By sharing the resources and capabilities of its participants with other members of the collaboration, a VO provides value not found in traditional organizational structures. However, the dynamic and multi-institutional nature of a VO creates unique challenges to resource sharing. We require mechanisms for formulation and enforcement of VO wide security, usage policies, resource management, and a means of mapping these mechanisms into the corresponding policies and mechanisms of the physical organizations from which the virtual organization draws resources and services.

M. Li et al. (Eds.): GCC 2003, LNCS 3032, p. 2, 2004.

Grid Computing: The Next Stage of the Internet

Irving Wladawsky-Berger

Vice President, Technology and Strategy
IBM Corporation

Abstract. Grid computing is the next wave of distributed computing based on open standards and using commercial-off-the-shelf building blocks. It is becoming the new economy and
major forces propelling the IT industry. In the emerging world of the virtual Internet, grids will provide instant global access to innovative services that deliver the power of the entire Internet to mobile users anywhere, any time, via any device, online or offline.

Grid computing is a continuing advances in technology, which is base on open standards-based integration. As grid computing gains support and popularity, the needs grow for studying computer science and technology problems arising from grid systems and applications. Grid computing is supported by many countries and governments. Government plays a very important role in the development of Grid. The ministry of education of China has issued the ChinaGrid project.

Currently, Grid technologies are extending to commercial applications. It has a significant influence on human society and various activities.

M. Li et al. (Eds.): GCC 2003, LNCS 3032, p. 3, 2004.

Making Grid Computing Real for High Performance and Enterprise Computing

Richard Wirt

Intel Senior Fellow, Enterprise Platforms Group

General Manager, Software and Solutions Group, INTEL CORPORATION

Abstract. Grid computing, whether used in enterprise or research/academia deployments, is the next wave of distributed computing based on open standards and using commercial-off-the-shelf building blocks. In the emerging world of the virtual Internet, grids will provide instant global access to innovative services that deliver the power of the entire Internet to mobile users anywhere, any time, via any device, online or offline. This presentation will focus on how the industry is coming together to make Grid computing the future of distributed computing, removing barriers to unbounded, unlimited interactions over the network.

M. Li et al. (Eds.): GCC 2003, LNCS 3032, p. 4, 2004.

Grid Computing for Enterprise and Beyond

Songnian Zhou

CEO, Platform Computing Inc.

Abstract. Grid is emerging as the infrastructure software that integrates widely dispersed IT resources and organizations to support resource sharing and collaboration. In this talk, we discuss the development of Grid technology and its application to enterprises in a variety of industries over the past 10 years, based on Platform Computing's experience as a Grid computing pioneer and market leader. We then look at the road forward for Grid adoption by the broad IT market.

M. Li et al. (Eds.): GCC 2003, LNCS 3032, p. 5, 2004.

Semantic Grid: Scientific Issues, Methodology, and Practice in China

Hai Zhuge

Institute of Computing Technology, Chinese Academy of Sciences

Abstract. The future interconnection environment will be a platform-irrelevant Virtual Grid consisting of requirements, roles and resources. With machine-understandable semantics, a resource can actively and dynamically cluster relevant resources to provide on-demand services by understanding requirements and functions each other. Versatile resources are encapsulated to provide services in the form of Single Semantic Image by using the uniform resource model. A resource can intelligently assist people to accomplish complex task and solve problems by participating versatile resource flow cycles through virtual roles to use proper knowledge, information, and computing resources.

M. Li et al. (Eds.): GCC 2003, LNCS 3032, p. 6, 2004.

Grid Computing, Vision, Strategy, and Technology

Wolfgang Gentzsch

Sun Microsystems, Inc.

Abstract. Recent advances in networking, hardware and software provide a powerful 'Grid' infrastructure for computing, communication and collaboration. Sun's grid software stack enables users to build grid environments in an evolutionary way, starting with Cluster Grids on a departmental level, to Enterprise Grids, and eventually to Global Grids as part of the Internet. In the presentation, we outline Sun's grid computing strategy, describe the grid technology, and present some customer solutions.

M. Li et al. (Eds.): GCC 2003, LNCS 3032, p. 7, 2004.

Towards a Petascale Research Grid Infrastructure

Satoshi Matsuoka

Global Scientific Information and Computing Center
Tokyo Institute of Technology / National Institute of Informatics

Abstract. Grid computing will not only allow researchers to tackle large problems not possible with current computing infrastructures, but also will make available large, collaborative virtual computing environments throughout within organizations as well as across organizations, in some cases on a global scale. The talk will cover our ongoing R&D efforts to effectively implement such infrastructures that surmount to facilitating multi-teraflops to petaflops of computing power and multi-petabytes of storage in an ubiquitous fashion, namely (1) The Titech Campus Grid project, an experimental Grid deployment project within the Titech campus, consisting of over 1000 processors of various GSIC resources, (2) The KEK-AIST-KEK Gfarm project that is developing a middleware and a testbed to allow petascale processing of large-volume instrumentation data ranging up to over petabytes of storage requirements, and (3) the latest Japanese National Research Grid Initiative (NAREGI) that aims to build the next generation Grid middleware intended to be used throughout the research Grids in Japan as well as other in other countries, and structured to be a triage of Grid middleware R&D, Grid enabling of Nanoscience Applications, as well as facilitating of 100Teraflops scale testbed and demonstration of grand-challenge Nanoscince applications thereof.

M. Li et al. (Eds.): GCC 2003, LNCS 3032, p. 8, 2004.

The Microgrid: Enabling Scientific Study of Dynamic Grid Behavior

Andrew A. Chien

Science Applications International Corporation
University of California at San Diego

Abstract. A fundamental property of Grids is the dynamic sharing of resources, and the adaptation of application behavior in resource use to dynamic attributes of the resource environment. Such dynamism poses interesting challenges in communication, resource scheduling, and system stability.

To study network, compute resource, and application properties in support of developing appropriate protocols, we have designed, built, and validated a set of grid modelling tools called the MicroGrid. These tools enable entire, unmodified Grid applications to be run against arbitrary network, compute, and storage resource environments, enabling study of these issues of dynamism software in a broad and thorough fashion. We describe the design of the MicroGrid system, its capabilities, and how we solved a number of interesting challenges in its design, including resource virtualization, scalable network emulation, and background workload generation. We describe some studies which use the MicroGrid to study the behavior of dynamic Grid applications and Grid resources.

The MicroGrid is part of the NSF funded Virtual Grid Application Development Software (VGrADS) research project.

M. Li et al. (Eds.): GCC 2003, LNCS 3032, p. 9, 2004.

On-Demand Business Collaboration Enablement with Services Computing

Liang-Jie (LJ) Zhang

IBM T. J. Watson Research Center

Abstract. In this talk, I will introduce a model for on-demand business process based collaboration, namely, Extended Business Collaboration (eBC), and its major characteristics: modeling, solution stack, configurable business protocol enabling framework, on-demand services deployment, as well as monitoring and analytical control. Then we present a few major research issues associated with facilitating extended business collaboration, followed by our proposed Annotated Business HyperChain technology leveraging Services computing and semantic annotation model. Services computing is the evolution of Internet computing by leveraging services oriented architecture. Services computing is mainly targeting for a new ground break technology suite – Web services and services oriented Grid/Utility Computing, Business Computing, and Autonomic Computing. A research prototype is illustrated at the end of the talk followed by some observations and discussion of open research issues requiring further exploration.

M. Li et al. (Eds.): GCC 2003, LNCS 3032, p. 10, 2004.

Multidisciplinary Design Optimization of Aero-craft Shapes by Using Grid Based High Performance Computational Framework[1]

Hong Liu [1], Xi-li Sun [2], Qian-ni Deng [2], and Xin-da Lu [2]

[1] Department of Engineering Mechanics, Shanghai Jiao Tong University
hongliu@sjtu.edu.cn
[2] Department of Computer Science, Shanghai Jiao Tong University, 200030, Shanghai, P. R. China

Abstract. This paper presents a novel high performance computational (HPC) framework for multidisciplinary design optimization (MDO) of aero-craft shapes by using "Grid computing" technology. In this HPC framework, MDO computation is completed by using a genetic algorithm based optimization code and some performance evaluation codes. All those codes in the HPC system are named as "Grid Services" independently. The HPC framework can run on various computers with various platforms, through which computer resources are provided to the designers in the form of services, no matter where those computers are located. Based on this HPC framework the MDO process can be performed interactively. To demonstrate the ability of this HPC framework, a conceptual aero-craft optimization case was described.

1 Introduction

Multidisciplinary Design Optimization (MDO) is highly required in the development of novel high-performance aero-crafts, including flight performance, aerodynamic performance etc. Therefore, for many years MDO of aero-crafts has been a significant challenge for scientists and designers. MDO is a methodology for design and analysis of complex engineering systems and subsystems that coherently exploit the synergism of mutually interacting phenomena [1]. Many research works also have shown that MDO is a systematic methodology and focuses on the interactive relationship between many disciplines for a system [2],[3],[4].

Generally, Multidisciplinary Design Optimization of a complex system, especially an aero-craft system, usually involves many scientists from various disciplines. The design results from each discipline are finally grouped into a single designer-in-chief.

[1] This research is supported by the National Natural Science Foundation of China (Grant number: 90205006, 60173103) and Shanghai Rising Star Program (Grant number: O2QG14031).

M. Li et al. (Eds.): GCC 2003, LNCS 3032, pp. 11–18, 2004.

requirement for a complex system is increased. MDO problems become more complex. Advances in disciplinary analysis in resent years have made those problems worse and those analysis model restricted to simple problems with very approximate approaches can not been used again. As those analysis codes for MDO of flight vehicles have grown larger and larger, it is indeed too incomprehensible and difficult for a designer-in-chief to maintain, since few know clearly what is included in the code and few can explain clearly the results from those codes. Therefore, the role of disciplinary scientist increases and it becomes more difficult for a designer-in-chief to manage the design process. To complete the design process smoothly, the designer-in-chief must joint all specialists from their own disciplines in a collaborative optimization process. Thus, a need exists, not simply to increase the speed of those complex analyses, but rather to simultaneously improve optimization performance and reduce complexity [2].

However, high performance computing based on parallel computing technology can only increase the speed of those analysis codes, one will wonder whether there is a high performance system that can lessen the complexity or improve optimization performance for collaborative works. As the Grid technology developed, there appears a new way to solve the problem. Recently, significant progress has been made on the computational grid technology. The goal of the Grid computing is to share computing resources globally. The problem underlies of Grid concept is coordinated resource sharing and problem solving in dynamic, multi-institutional virtual organizations. In Grid computing environment, the computing resources are provided as Grid service. Then, we can construct a Grid based HPC framework, to improve the performance of the MDO algorithms and gain many new characteristics that is impossible in traditional means for MDO of a large aero-craft system. This grid based HPC framework for MDO can make the design process be easily controlled and monitored and can be conducted interactively, and through this computing Grid system many specialists in various disciplines can be easily managed in one MDO group.

In the following section, the HPC framework based on Grid technology will be described in details, and an optimization of aero-craft shape is discussed.

2 Grid Based HPC Framework for MDO

2.1 Procedure for MDO of Aero-crafts

Procedure for Multidisciplinary Design Optimization of aero-crafts by using genetic algorithms (GA) can be shown from figure 1. The basic idea of the GA is to simulate the evolution of the nature to find an optimized solution for a given problem or a set of Pareto optimal solution for a MDO problem. When conduct Optimization of the aero-craft shapes using GA, we will follow the steps listed below. Firstly, set the range of a set of given parameters that we called designing parameters. Secondly, use a random algorithm to select a specific value for each parameter from the given range. Thirdly, use the analysis code, such as CFD module and CFM module to compute each child task and get the result set. Fourthly, use a comparison algorithm to select the best result. Fifthly, use the best result as the "seeds" to generate the next generation.

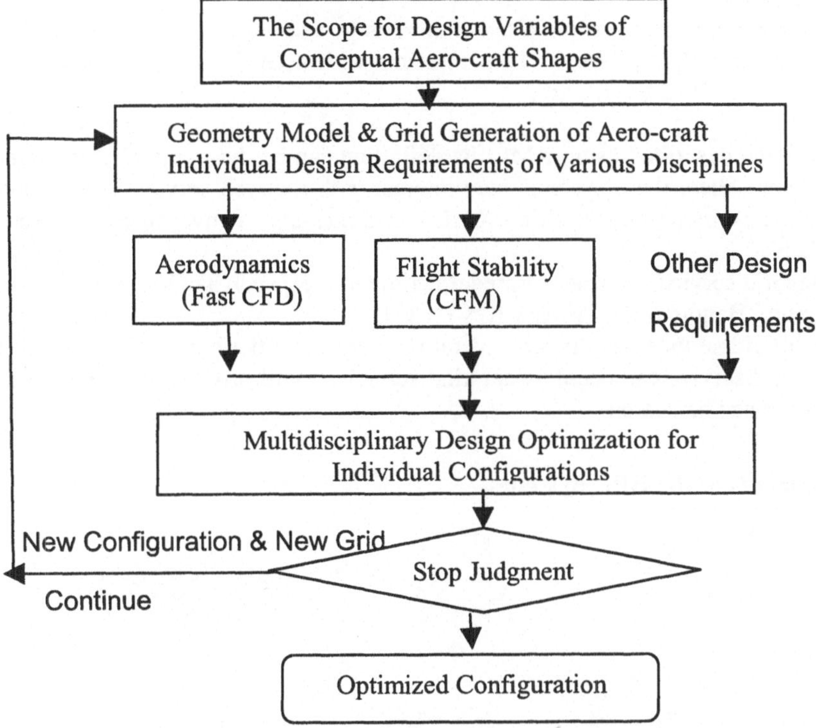

Fig. 1. Flowchart of the Optimization Procedure.

2.2 Grid Based HPC Framework

It is easy to see that the GA has parallel computation nature. Each child task can be allocated to a single CPU and executed independently. Traditionally, we can use a Parallel Virtual Machine (PVM) or Message Passing Interface (MPI) to finish this work. The program may run on a super computer with many CPUs. However, high performance computing based on PVM or MPI can only increase the speed of those analysis codes. By using the grid computing technology, a novel high performance framework that can lessen the complexity or improve optimization performance for collaborative works is proposed. How the system has been constructed will be briefly described.

The Grid based HPC framework for MDO is composed of many Grid services. Each Grid service is built on the web and grid technology. Each service has some standard interfaces to support the registering of service, the querying of service, the communication and the interacting between the client and the service provider. Then, we will discuss the Grid Service features of the HPC framework firstly. Secondly we will discuss all the components of the HPC framework.

Grid Service

A Grid service is a web service that conforms to a set of conventions (interfaces and behaviors) that define how a client interacts with a Grid service [5]. Some general features of the Grid service are:

1. Every Grid service is a web service, whose public interfaces and bindings are defined and described using XML. Its definition can be discovered by other software systems. Then, these systems may interact with the web service in a manner prescribed by its definition, using XML based messages conveyed by internet protocols [6].
2. The Grid service has a set of predefined interfaces, such as Grid Service, Registry, Factory, Handle Map, Primary Key etc [5].
3. Each Grid service has the responsibility to maintain the local policy, which means the Grid service can decide what kind services it will provide and what kind of resources can be shared.

Components of the HPC System

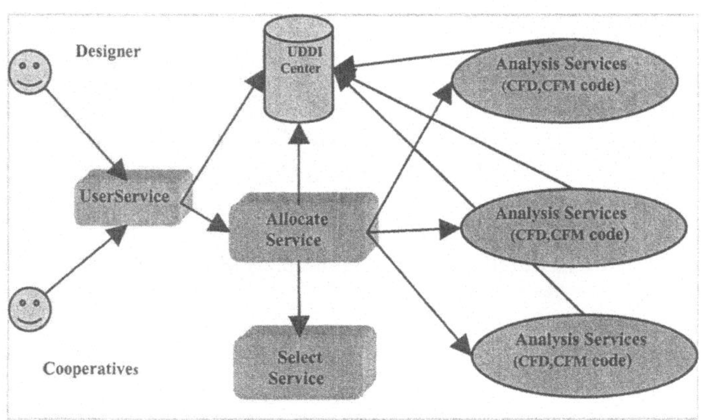

Fig. 2. System Framework.

The system is composed of three modules as shown in figure 2. The first part is User service module. From figure 2, the executor and the co-designer are the specific users of this system. The user can submit the tasks, monitor the computing progress and get the middle and final results via the web pages. When received the requests from the users, the User service can query the UDDI center to find what kinds of services available now. The User service can supports the user accounts management, supports the task submitting and parameter adjusting. It can interact with other services to finish the computing work. The second part is the UDDI center module. The responsibility of this module is acting as an information exchange center. The third part is the Application services, including Allocate service, Select service and Analysis service including CFD service, CFM service and other Analysis services.

The Allocate service is a service to control process. It accepts the requests from the User service. Then the control process will find the available Select and Analysis computing services. Then the connections are built among the Allocate service, Select service and Analysis services. The parameters are conveyed to the Select service to generate the specific child tasks distributed to the analysis computing services.

The Analysis computing service is the computing part of this HPC framework. The executable codes are named as solvers. In this paper, CFD, CFM and other solvers are adopted in the analysis module for Grid service. CFD (computational fluid dynamics) code is a 3-D explicit flow solver in which three-dimensional Navier-Stokes equations are solved by employing a central difference and artificial dissipation finite volume scheme [7]. CFM (computational flight mechanics) code is a code developed to analyze the stability of aircraft or aerospace craft In order to run all those analysis codes, an automatic grid generation code is required. In the analysis service, we adopt our 3-D overlapping (Chimera) grid generation code [8] to generate computational grids for CFD and CFM solver. After the results are returned, the Select service is called and selects the best one from them.

3 Application on Aero-craft Shape Optimization Design

3.1 Hardware Architecture

To construct the basic hardware environment for our Grid system, we connect most of computer resources in our university, including a SGI Onyx3800 (64CPUs, 64 Gflops) supercomputer, four set of IBM-1350 Clusters (86 Gflops), Sun E-450 & Series Ultra workstations and many PC connected to our Campus network. The maximum speed of data-flow of our campus network between those computers can reach 1 Gb/s. The connection work for our final computing environment is in construction.

3.2 Demonstration of the Web Service in the Grid System

The Grid based HPC system finally works well by connecting users and the Grid services. For users, if they want to start a new design, he only need submit their tasks through the web. To complete a MDO (Multidisciplinary Design Optimization) task, the designer-in-chief also can communicate with other designers from various disciplines through the web. There is a billboard on the web page. The task executor and the co-designers exchange information by it. When the co-designer finds some parameters are not suitable for the task, he leaves messages on the billboard. The task executer can adjust the parameters. Web services will help any designers complete their whole designing tasks mutually and interactively.

When an authenticated user submits a task, the tasks control process will allocate a sequence number for that task and generate a record in the database. All the information of the task including the parameters, the results and the interaction messages between the executor and co-designers can be record in the database as needed. After the user's identity has been identified, users may query how many analysis services are available in the UDDI center. Then the user may set the task's initial parameters, send the parameters and the compute task to the User service. The User service then looks up the Allocate service and Select service in the UDDI center and then uses the connection model to build connections with them.

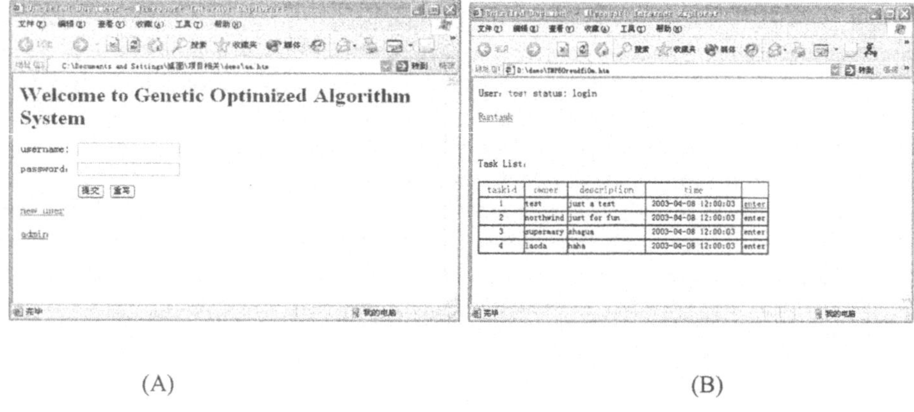

Fig. 3. The demonstration of the Web services of the optimization Grid system, (A) is the First Web Page for Register and (B) is the Second Web Page for Task Running.

Figure 3 illustrates the first and second web page entering the Grid system and running an optimization design task. After the results are returned to the User service, the User service puts that information on the user's browser, so the user can monitor the design process dynamically. It is clearly that what a designer to do is obtain all his requirements from a special Web.

3.3 Application of the Grid System for Aero-craft Shape Optimization

As a demonstration case for the Grid system, a conceptual aero-craft deign is conducted. In the aero-craft conceptual design process, we only consider two basic performances, including aerodynamic high ratio of lift to drag and flight stability. The performances can be computed by CFD solver and CFM solver respectively. To complete this optimization design, we define an objective function is a function of L/D (ratio of lift to drag) maximization, and set the flight stability as constrain to the optimization problems. For this aero-craft conceptual design, there are 11 design variables to be optimized. The size of population, the mutation rate and crossover rate are the basic control parameters to the GA, which can be changed interactively from the web page of the Grid system. Then we can obtain results, as shown from figure 4 and figure 5.

Figure 4 shows all of the optimization process and illustrates that with the generation increasing, Lift/Drag Ratio and the fitness of the evaluation is become larger. Figure 5 is the aero-craft shape of Generation 500 and Generation 3000. As the generation increased, more optimized aero-craft shape can be obtained before the optimal is reached. The designer-in-chief also can joint two scientists from aerodynamics and flight mechanics. They can exchange their advices through the web of the Grid System.

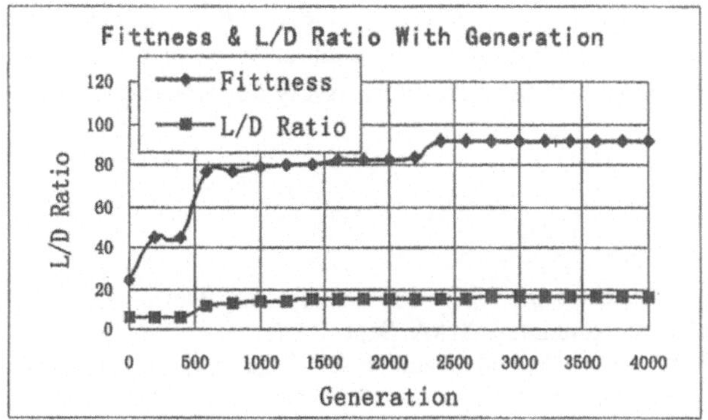

Fig. 4. The Optimization Process: Lift/Drag Ratio with the generation increasing.

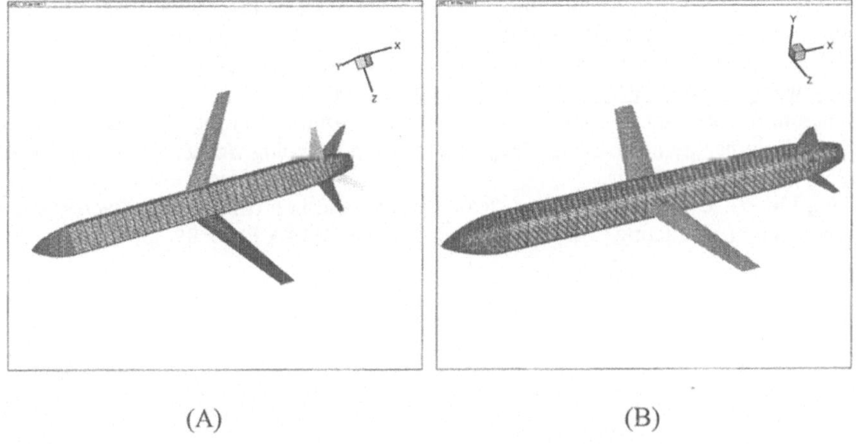

(A) (B)

Fig. 5. The aero-craft shape of Generation 500 and Generation 3000, (A) is the shape for 500 generation and (B) is the shape for 3000 generation.

4 Conclusion

A Grid based HPC framework for MDO of aero-crafts is described and by using this computing grid an application case for a conceptual aero-craft design is completed. The advances of this HPC framework over the traditional parallel computing means can be clearly shown. Firstly, it presents a new framework for the applications of MDO of aero-crafts, which can utilize the computing power over a wide range, and in which the number of analysis service is dynamically changed. Secondly, it is a great improvement in the optimization design method for the aero-craft shapes. By using this HPC system, designers can control the parameters during the progress and can also check the middle results. The designer and the co-designers can exchange their points of view about the designing. This enables scientists from various disciplines to complete collaborative design work interactively all over the world.

References

1. Anon., "Current State off the Art in Multidisciplinary Design Optimization," prepared by the MDO Technical Committee, AIAA, Sept. 1991.
2. Kroo, Ilan., Steve Altus, Robert Braun, Peter Gage, and Ian Sobieski, "Multidisciplinary Optimization Methods For Aircraft Preliminary Design," AIAA paper 94-4325-CP, 1994.
3. Giesing, J. P. and Barthelemy, J. M. , "A Summary of Industry MDO Applications and Needs," AIAA paper 98-4737, 1998.
4. Balling, R.J., Sobieszczanski-Sobieski, J., "Optimization of Coupled Systems: A Critical Overview of Approaches," AIAA Journal Vol. 34., No.1, 1996, pp6-17.
4. Ian Foster, Carl Kesselman, Jeffrey Nick and Steven Tuecke. , "The Physiology of the Grid: An Open Grid Services Architecture for Distributed Systems Integration," 2002.2 http://www.globus.org/research/papers/ogsa.pdf.
6. Web Service Architecture, W3C Working Draft , 14 November 2002., URL: http://www. w3 .org/TR/2002/WD-ws-arch-20021114/
7. Jameson, A., Schmidt, W. and Turkel, "Numerical Solutions of the Euler Equations by the Finite Volume Methods Using Runge-Kutta Time Stepping Schemes," AIAA Paper 81-1259, 1981.
8. Hong Liu, W. Dong, and H.T. Fan, "Conservative and non-conservative Overlapping Grid Generation in Simulating Complex Supersonic Flow," AIAA Paper 99-3305, 1999.

A Research on the Framework of Grid Manufacturing

Li Chen [1], Hong Deng [1], Qianni Deng [2], and Zhenyu Wu [1]

[1] Shanghai Jiao Tong University, School of Mechanical and Power Engineering, Shanghai 20 00 30,
69042 Heidelberg, Germany62932905 Shanghai, China
chen_li@sjtu.edu.cn
[2] Shanghai Jiao Tong University, Department of Computer and Science, Shanghai 20 00 30,
69042 Heidelberg, Germany62932905 Shanghai, China
deng-qn@cs.sjtu.edu.cn

Abstract. This paper presents firstly in the world the framework of Grid manufacturing, which neatly combines Grid technology with the infrastructure of advanced manufacturing technology. It studies the Grid-oriented knowledge description and acquisition, and constructs the distributed Knowledge Grid model. It also deals with the protocol of node description in collaborative design, and builds up the distributed collaborative design model. And the research on the protocol and technology of node constructing leads to the collaborative production model of Grid manufacturing.

1 Introduction

With the rapid technological innovations of the networked manufacturing, much more is learned about the inherent limitations of the network technology.[1-4] Grid is regarded as the next generation Internet as well as Grid manufacturing is then presented as an advanced solution for the bottleneck of networked manufacturing. The research on Grid will build up solid theoretical and technological fundaments to realize a great stride in manufacturing. Fig. 1 shows the evolution of networked manufacturing.

2 About Grid

The prototype of Grid is the Meta Computing sponsored by US government during the past decade. Now the modes of Grid include: Computational Grid, Data Grid, Knowledge Grid, and Information Grid. Grid technology features in: heterogeneity distribution and sharing, scalability, adaptability and dynamic, structural unpredictability, multi-level management domain. The hourglass structure of Grid is illustrated as in Fig.2.

M. Li et al. (Eds.): GCC 2003, LNCS 3032, pp. 19–25, 2004.

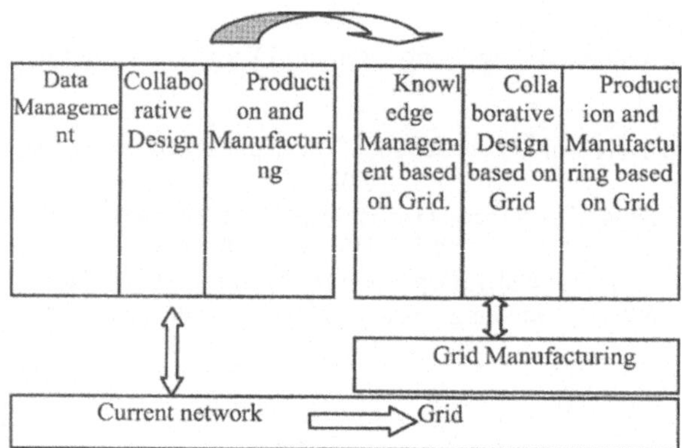

Fig. 1. Grid manufacturing and the evolution from Network to Grid

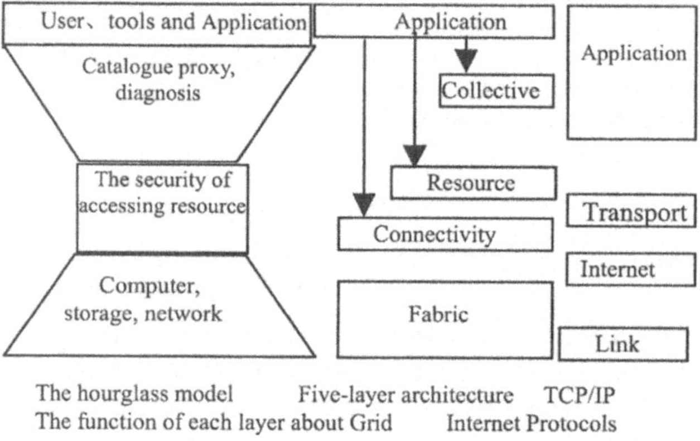

Fig. 2. The layered Grid architecture and its relationship to the Internet protocol architecture[5]

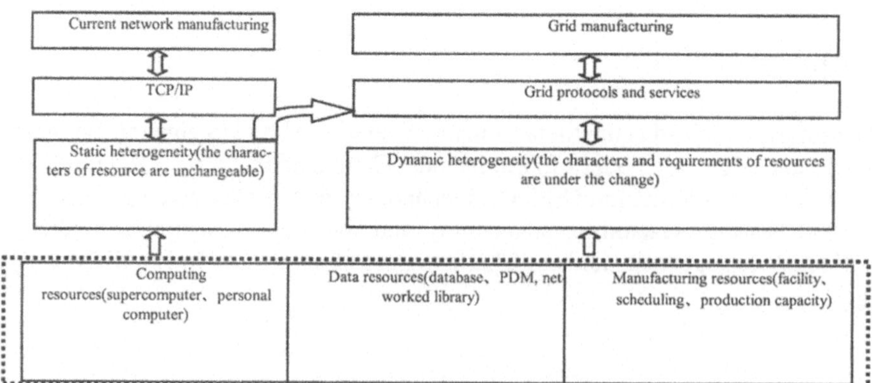

Fig. 3. The integration and usage of heterogeneous resources in Grid manufac-

3 The Concept of Grid Manufacturing

Based on Grid technology, Grid manufacturing focuses on the whole product life-cycle of design, manufacturing and service, trying to upgrade the entire manufacturing practice. The supporting technologies include: System Integrated Model based on interaction of manufacturing resources, Standard Encapsulation Interface and Protocol of manufacturing resources, Knowledge-based Data Management Model and Active Knowledge Supply and Acquisition System, and so on.[6] The Grid manufacturing calls for many design and manufacturing resources which are featuring in their notably general heterogeneity in the computer system. In fact, with all the design and manufacturing resources encapsulated onto the Grid, it involves many new issues such as the heterogeneous coordination of different resources in collaborative project, the real-time heterogeneous coordination within the same resources (the performance like business competition, service need and supply may change over time and working status, which brings about the real-time problem). Benefited from the Grid technology, a Grid model will constitute uniformly the static-dynamic interactive protocols of Grid nodes and data, and integrate various manufacturing resources, thus push forward the development of modern manufacturing. The model is as shown in Fig.3.

4 Data and Knowledge Management of Grid Manufacturing

First analyze the storage mode and structure of heterogeneous data on the Grid nodes; then build up the general and open knowledge description, internal encapsulation protocol and exchange standard, and various information and knowledge required in Grid manufacturing encapsulation (including the heterogeneous database, design and operating know-how, thinking process on various nodes, etc.); finally display these knowledge by the uniform external interactive protocols and interfaces.

a. To establish the Grid-manufacturing-Oriented (GMO) agent mechanism of automatic search and acquisition for knowledge sources ,which includes agent-based intellectual knowledge acquisition, multi-agent collaborative knowledge search and GMO multi-agent interactive knowledge protocol.

b. To establish the GMO active knowledge supply mechanism, which includes Knowledge Grid-based scheduling mechanism of distributed data management and dynamic model of GMO knowledge acquisition and supply

The rules of Grid manufacturing determine the association of knowledge acquisition and the algorithm of knowledge search, and based on these technologies problems in Grid manufacturing are readily provided with solutions by collaborations of active agents, which is a strong and active replacement for the traditional data acquisition.

5 Collaborative Design of Grid Manufacturing

The distributed design mechanism based on Grid manufacturing technology is seeking to enhance the interactions of collaborative design between the dynamic union of enterprises to the level of high efficiency, high speed, large scale, and massive data traffic.

The various collaborative design teams are distinct in their specialty, research direction, personnel and computational method. What is more, these teams are joining and quitting at any time, with individual difference of their attributions to the group. To construct such a sophisticated dynamic system, the key job is to define precisely the function, operation flow, communication protocol of the Grid nodes, then build up the dynamic permission mechanism for the design units as technical support of the collaborative design.[7]

5.1 Grid Design Nodes Description

A uniform description for the design nodes is very important for the collaborative design, which lies in: the description provides a uniform infrastructure and an open participation protocol; it encapsulates the design nodes to endow every individual node with similarity to the group. Considering more compatibility, a uniform protocol description emphasizes the external part, standard service (such as the access to the design nodes, data storage, adding resources and experts participation) with those resources-relevant details abstracted:

- Self-extension capability of internal nodes and collaborative design group;
- Open course management;
- Interactive collaboration
- Dynamic task solving with the changes of nodes status. (The design nodes description includes Protocol description, Fundamental design service ,Standard information of design model and Definition of Grid interfaces.)

5.2 Constructing Permission Mechanism

The permission mechanism is supporting the dynamic Grid design nodes by:

(1) Grid collaboration information base

(2) Grid protocols

(3) nodes permission regulation

(4) feedback and monitor of nodes permission

(5) detecting and solving the nodes conflicts

The permission mechanism is based on the fundamental service and relating protocols, and mainly concerns about the protocols of Connectivity Level and Resource Level.

5.3 Interactions of Collaborative Design

When the design teams connect the Grid through their own nodes, they are allowed to control and modify the design models of other teams. Such interactions is under the operating authority control, and based on the service and protocols of Grid, also requiring the customization on the Grid platform by the design teams.

6 Collaborative Production Model of Grid Manufacturing

6.1 Construction of the Model

The construction protocol and technology of manufacturing nodes is to realize the high performance scheduling and dynamic collaboration of Grid manufacturing resources.

The structure of manufacturing nodes is very complicated in that every node is composed of many design elements such as computing, communication and storage as well as manufacturing elements such as equipment, technique, and transportation. The uniform protocol and interface technology based on Grid call for the uniform integrated operation system of heterogeneous nodes, uniform network interface protocols, and concerted regulation of the network infrastructure. The nodes have uniform external operation protocols and real-time working status and results sharing protocols, which involve data transfer, flow, group communication, distributed object protocols. These protocols build up the connections between resources and support the Grid management and applications.

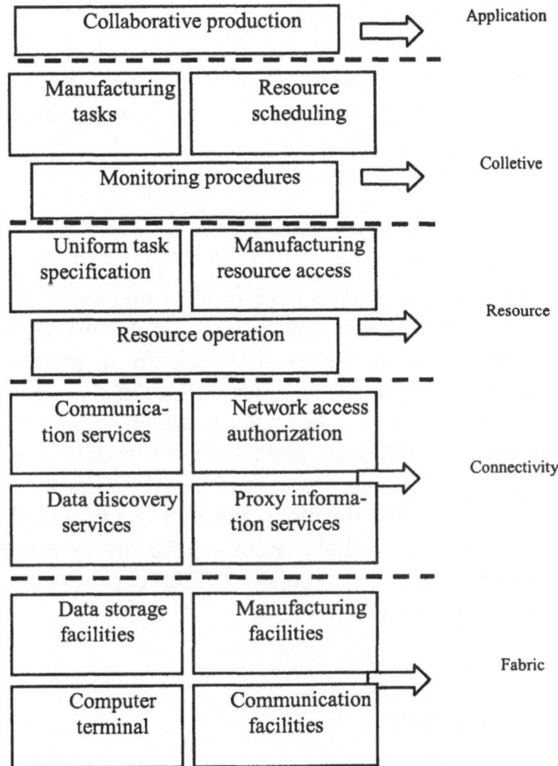

Fig. 4. Collaborative production model

The resources scheduling is based on the traditional high performance computing but even more sophisticated. Due to the general heterogeneity of the resources, a time-dependent performance prediction model is needed. Considering various environments and conditions, the dynamic Grid information diagram is used to illustrate the performance fluctuations of the manufacturing nodes. At the same time, the Grid theory is applied to improving the transplantability, scalability, efficiency and repeatability of manufacturing nodes resources, as well as the combination of local and inter-nodes scheduling. The scheduling work has two parts: one is to perform the computation and data distribution of design and manufacturing nodes on the physical position; another is to arrange the task of Grid manufacturing nodes along the time axis.

After the manufacturing task is submitted and the order confirmed by the scheduling model, a collaborative distributing mechanism is responsible for the interactions between the manufacturing resources by taking three steps:

(1) To process the resources description and distribute the tasks to every node;

(2) To process the infrastructure resources description, analyze the tasks and send them to the related Grid nodes;

(3) To confirm that all the subtask is distributed successfully, run the distributed simulation solving program, perform simultaneously the parallel subtasks of manufacturing and production service, trace the task status and give feedback to the scheduling mechanism in time.

6.2 Realization of the Model

The kernel of the collaborative production model, the resources scheduling and manufacturing collaboration will be realized by the five-level Grid structure and related functional modules. The resources scheduling process can be subdivided into: uniform resources description, resources accessing, resources operating and scheduling performance evaluation. The manufacturing collaboration can be subdivided into task planning, task analyzing, and progress scheduling. With the subdivisions the collaborative manufacturing model can be decomposed into many sub-models or subprocesses. With the functions and services provided by the five-level Grid structure, the manufacturing collaboration can be finally achieved when these sub-models are realized by the technical support of the corresponding level. The production collaboration model is shown in Fig.4.

7 Conclusion

This research presents the concept of Grid manufacturing in the world, which is the next-generation technology subsequent to the networked manufacturing. Along with more work done on the Grid manufacturing, the defects with networked manufacturing will get improved. The Grid manufacturing framework will push forward greatly the development of advanced manufacturing technology.

References

1. Xingjun Chu, Yuqing Fan: The research of PDM based on Web. Journal of Beijing Aeronautics and Astronauts University 2(1999) 205–207
2. Xucan Chen, Yuxing Peng, Sikun Li: PDM of CAD Collaborative Design based on C-S. Computer Engineering and Design (1998) 53
3. Dan Wu, Xiankui Wang, Zhiqiang Wei et al.: The Distributed PDM based on Collaborative Service Environment. Journal of Tsinghua University (Science and Technology) 6 (2002) 791–781
4. Zhiqiang Wei, Xiankui Wang, Chengyin Liu et al.: The Distributed PDM under the Environment of Agile Manufacturing. Journal of Tsinghua University(Science and Technology), 8 (2000) 45
5. I. Foster, Carl Kesselman, Steven Tuecks: The anatomy of the grid-Enabling scalable virtual organizations. http://www.globus.org/research/papers/
6. H.Zhuge: A Knowledge Grid Model and Platform for Global Knowledge Sharing. Expert System with Applications, Vol. 22. no.4,(2002)
7. G. von Laszewski, I. Foster, J. Gawor et al.: Designing Grid-based problem solving environments and portals. Proceedings of the 34th Annual Hawaii International Conference on System Sciences, IEEE Press (2001)

Large-Scale Biological Sequence Assembly and Alignment by Using Computing Grid

Wei Shi and Wanlei Zhou

School of Information Technology, Deakin University
221 Burwood Hwy, Burwood, VIC 3125, Australia
{shiwei, wanlei}@deakin.edu.au

Abstract. Large-scale sequence assembly and alignment are fundamental parts of biological computing. However, most of the large-scale sequence assembly and alignment require intensive computing power and normally take very long time to complete. To speedup the assembly and alignment process, this paper parallelizes the Euler sequence assembly and pair-wise/multiple sequence assembly, two important sequence assembly methods, and takes advantage of Computing Grid which has a colossal computing capacity to meet the large-scale biological computing demand.

1 Introduction

The research on Human Genome Project[1] has been gradually diverted to the post-processing of the biological data. Computer technologies are widely used to analyse these data. Sequence assembly[2], which is also called fragment assembly, is to recover the fragments into the original sequences. These fragments are broken from DNA sequences using some method such as the commonly used shotgun[3] method. Sequence alignment[4] is to compare a known sequence with one or more than one other sequences to get the homology relationship among these sequences. According to the number of sequences to be compared, sequence alignment can be classified into pair-wise sequence alignment and multiple sequence alignment.

Sequence assembly and alignment are computing-intensive. It often costs a long time to calculate median-size or even small-size biological data, not mentioning the large-size data. However, sequence assembly and alignment have exposed good parallelism, and good speedup can be achieved by data distribution, i.e. distributing the biological data onto multiple computing machines which will compute their own data independently and gathering all the results from all the machines involved to obtain the final result.

Computing grid is an emerging large-scale computing technology in recent years, which aims to couple geographically distributed resources and offer consistent and inexpensive access to resources irrespective of their physical location or access point. To carry out large-scale sequence assembly and alignment, it often requires setting up big computing centres with powerful computing capacity. This will need a large amount of investment and the cost of maintenance for such centres is not trivial.

M. Li et al. (Eds.): GCC 2003, LNCS 3032, pp. 26–33, 2004.

Using a computing grid will enable scientists to acquire much more computing capacity without the need to invest on big computing centres whose performance/price ratio will decline rapidly with time.

This paper is organised as follows. In section 2, we introduce the basic ideas of Euler sequence assembly algorithm, Smith-Waterman pair-wise sequence assembly algorithm and Clustal W multiple sequence assembly algorithm. Then in section 2 we present the parallelization of these algorithms. And the implementation of these algorithms on computing grid is given in section 4. The last section, section 5, concludes the paper.

2 Biological Sequence Assembly and Alignment

2.1 Euler Sequence Assembly

The traditional paradigm for sequence assembly is overlap-layout-consensus[2]. The weakness of this paradigm is that it can not effectively solve the notorious "repeat" problem[3]. Sequence assembly algorithms under this paradigm includes Phrap[5], Cap4[6], Celera Assembler[7] and so on. An Euler sequence assembly algorithm, proposed by Pavel A. Pevzner[8], abandons this paradigm and gives a better resolution. This algorithm generates l-tuples from reads(fragments of the sequence), l is the length of the tuple, and the number of the tuples generated is n-l+1(is the length of the read). A l-tuple consists of l continuous letters of a read. All the tuples will be used to generate a deBruijn graph G. The vertices of G are l-tuples. And there will be a directed edge between two vertices if the suffix of l-1 length of source vertex is the same with the prefix of the sink vertex. The multiplicity of one edge represents the times of the edge appearing in the original sequence, which is greater than 1 if the edge connects more than one pair of vertices. Euler sequence assembly algorithm finds Euler paths in graph G by consistency analysis which determines how the Euler path is extended. These paths are in fact the contigs. Consistency analysis is the essential and most computing intensive part of the algorithm.

In this algorithm the sequence assembly is cast as finding a path visiting every edge of the graph exactly once, an Eulerian Path Problem. There exists a linear-time solution in contrast to the NP complexity of other algorithms.

2.2 Pair-Wise Sequence Alignment

Smith-Waterman algorithm[9] is the optimal algorithm for pair-wise biological sequence alignment, which gives the optimal local alignment of two sequences in mathematical sense. Two sequences to be compared are placed on the top of and at the left of a similar matrix SM, and each element of SM is calculated by formula (1):

$$SM[i,j] = \begin{cases} SM[i,j-1] + gp \\ SM[i-1,j-1] + ss \\ SM[i-1,j] + gp \\ 0 \end{cases} \quad (1)$$

The value of one element of *SM* is determined by the left element, left upper and upper elements. *gp* is the gap penalty for inserting a space into the sequence and *ss* is the value obtained from comparing two letters which is often negative if the two letters are different. *gp* and *ss* can be reset by users. There will be one or more than one elements with the maximal value after calculating all the values of elements. Tracing back the path of each element which it follows to get the maximal value, the algorithm gives one or more than one optimal local alignments between these two sequences.

2.3 Multiple Sequence Alignment

Clustal W[10] is the most popular MSA (multiple sequence alignment) software which is to align multiple sequences. Clustal W has three main stages. The first stage is to align every two sequences in the sequence set to calculate their similarity distance. The guide tree is constructed according to the similarity distance between each pair of sequence in the second stage. And in the last stage, all sequences are progressively aligned according to the similarities among sequences, i.e. the sequences with more similarity will be aligned with priority.

3 Parallel Sequence Assembly and Alignment

There is an increasing demand for faster sequence analysis with the rapidly increasing amounts of genomic sequence data available. For the effective parallel processing of the biological data, good parallel algorithms and softwares are required. This section addresses the parallelization of sequence assembly and alignment, which will in turn bring the speedup of other applications in biological computing because many of them are built upon sequence analysis.

3.1 Parallel Euler Sequence Assembly

For the parallelization of the sequence assembly one major innovation is that in our algorithm all the biological data generated by the whole genome shotgun method for some organism will be loaded into the computing grid at one time and processed as a whole. For existing sequence assembly methods, they usually partition the data into different groups according to their similarity, then assemble the data in each group separately on individual computers and finally merge the partial results. The determination of the similarity of different fragment is approximate, which will usually result in errors that some fragments with less similarity are assigned to the same group and fragments with more similarity to the different group. So the partial result of assembly will potentially be incorrect and the final result will be incorrect as well. By means of parallelization which can take advantage of more storage capacity and computing power, the data will not have to be partitioned. So the sequence assembly is conducted from a global view, not being constricted to a single group. The idea for parallelizing the Euler sequence assembly approach is introduced as followings. And more details can be found in section 4.1.

We use a hash table to represent the deBruijn graph. Each element in the hash table represents a vertex of the deBruijn graph, i.e. a l-tuple. The hash table is distributed onto different computing node of the computing grid. Sequence assembly can be started from any element in the hash table. In our algorithm on each computing node the element with the smallest index in the hash table whose multiplicity is greater than 0 is selected to be the first element in the assembly process, which is the initial path. Then the algorithm extends the path in both directions to incorporate more l-tuple on each computing node. Once an l-tuple is incorporated its multiplicity would be decreased by 1. When the l-tuple to be incorporated is owed by another computing node, the node which extends current path to include this l-tuple will have to send a request to that node. The node received the request will acknowledge the incorporation and decrease the multiplicity of that l-tuple by 1 if the multiplicity is greater than 0, otherwise it will reply the requesting node that the l-tuple is not available. When there is no more l-tuples available the node will stop assembling in this direction and will continue to assemble in the opposite direction. If the assembly has been finished in both directions, the node will try to find another element in the hash table to start to assemble another Euler path. The assembly on one computing node finishes when the multiplicities of all the elements in the hash table on the node have become 0. When all the computing nodes finish assembly, they will send the partial assembly results (paths) to the master node which will be responsible for assembling them further to form the final result. The consistency analysis would still be carried out in the final stage. And the calculation in this stage has to be conducted sequentially.

Each computing node extends the Euler path as long as possible in both directions and determines the path it should follow by consistency analysis when there is more than one candidate. It is very time-consuming to make such decisions for each computing node because it will consult with the reads to judge which is the next tuple to be added to the current sequence using consistency rule. To speedup the decision process we copy all the reads to all the computing nodes so that they can make the decision by themselves, rather than consulting other computing nodes which will cause overhead.

In summary, the parallelization of the sequence assembly uses the master/slaves method. A master computing node generates l-tuples stored into a hash table from all the reads and distributes them onto slave computing nodes. These slave nodes assemble the l-tuples simultaneously and send the partial assembly result to the master node after all the l-tuples have been assembled. The final assembly result will be produced by the master node, which receives the partial results from all the slave nodes and assembles them further by similar approach.

3.2 Parallel Pair-Wise Sequence Alignment

The approach to parallelize the pair-wise sequence alignment is to distribute the computation along the diagonals of the similarity matrix because the computation of element values along one diagonal is independent. But there is dependency between neighbouring diagonals because the calculation of one element value is relied on the values of its left element, upper element and left-upper element. So the parallel alignment is executed in a wave-front way that computing nodes first calculate the values along the first diagonal in parallel, then along the second diagonal in parallel, … …, until the last diagonal in parallel.

And the computing granularity can be changed to achieve the best performance according to the number of the size of the similarity matrix and number of computing nodes available in a computing grid. There will be a trade-off between the granularity and load balancing. Larger granularity will reduce the communication overhead which will improve the performance, but at the same time it is more likely to incur load imbalance which will degrade the performance. The detailed discussion can be found in section 4.2.

3.3 Parallel Multiple Sequence Alignment

The parallelization of Clustal W is conducted on all its three stages. For the first stage, we will have two levels of parallelization. The first level of parallelization lies in the calculation conducted on the whole $n(n\text{-}1)$ pairs of sequences. Because the calculation on different sequence pair is completely independent we get a very high degree of parallelism. The second level of parallelization lies in the pair-wise sequence alignment. For achieving load balancing across all the computing nodes, we will partition all the computing nodes into some groups with similar computing capacity. In the first level of parallelization, all the sequence pair will be distributed into the computing groups according to each pair's computing load which can be estimated in terms of the length of each sequence in the pair. The second level of parallelization will be achieved in each group, i.e. parallel pair-wise sequence alignment for each pair which would be conducted in the group the pair of sequences belongs to.

For the second stage, the calculation of the minimal value of each row in the distance matrix can be parallelized. And then the minimal value of the matrix can be calculated according to each computing node's result. And for the third stage, we exploit the parallelism existing in the iterative loops.

4 Large-Scale Sequence Assembly and Alignment Using Computing Grid

Grid computing provides a computing platform with huge computing capacity which potentially can be much more powerful than any current parallel computing system. Biological computing is to address the biological problems by taking advantage of modern computing technologies. The combination of biological computing and Grid technology will promote biological computing to a new level by exploiting almost unlimited Grid resources. This section explains how to implement the parallel algorithms we have proposed for sequence assembly and alignment on a computing grid.

4.1 Implementation

4.1.1 The Implementation of Parallel Sequence Assembly on a Computing Grid

Hash table is the most important data structure used by the sequence assembly. The *l*-tuple to be accessed can be rapidly located by using the hash table. The *djb2* function, one of the best string hash functions, is used here. The hash table is evenly distributed onto each computing node. Assuming that the size of the hash table is *n* and the number of computing nodes available in the computing grid is *p* (the computing nodes are numbered 0,1,2,…,p-1), the size of partial hash table on each node is $\lceil n/p \rceil$. For some *l*-tuple generated from some read its hash value *h* can be calculated by the hash function with the string of *l*-tuple as input. This *l*-tuple will be assigned to the computing node numbered $h\%\lceil n/p \rceil$. Linear list is used to deal with the hash conflict. Hash table also contains the multiplicity of each *l*-tuple which determines how many times the *l*-tuple would appear in the assembly result. The repeat and non-repeat *l*-tuples will be assembled at the same time. And the parallel assembly will finish when the multiplicities of all the *l*-tuples are decreased to zero.

4.1.2 The Implementation of Parallel Pair-Wise Sequence Alignment on a Computing Grid

Assuming we align sequence *X* and *Y* with the length of *m* and *n* respectively, we partition the similarity matrix into blocks as shown in Table 1. The number of columns of each block is *k* and the number of rows is *l*. Each block will be assigned to a computing node. The blocks on different nodes will be calculated in parallel. A computing node needs to get k+l+1 elements from left, left upper and upper blocks when it calculates some block. And k+1 elements are needed to get from another node. By partitioning the matrix into blocks, each computing node will calculate more data (a block) after receiving the adjacent elements at one time. So the granularity is increased and communication frequency is reduced. The value of *k* and *l* should be set according to the network bandwidth available. But the granularity should not be too big otherwise the parallelism would be damaged.

4.1.3 The Implementation of Parallel Multiple Sequence Alignment on a Computing Grid

Different computing granularity can be adopted at different stages of the Clustal W algorithm in its implementation on a computing grid. All the sequence alignments conducted in the first stage of Clustal W are independent. So they can be parallelized in smaller granularity so as to achieve maximal parallelism. But for the second and third stages the granularity should be bigger because there are more dependency among the computing nodes. Smaller granularity will bring more communication overhead which will offset the benefit gained from parallelism.

4.2 Load Balancing and Communication Overhead

Load balancing is a big problem for parallel computing, and grid computing is not an exception. More load on the computing nodes with less computing power will make others wait for them, thus resources are wasted and performance are degraded. And since the communication overhead is relatively high in a computing grid, the interaction frequency among the computing nodes should be as low as possible.

As for the parallel sequence assembly and alignment on computing grid, load distribution algorithms developed before can still be used to improve their performance. But they should be modified so as to be as effective as possible for load balancing in biological Grid computing. Factors which should be considered by these algorithms include more communication overhead, heterogeneity and so on.

The interaction among the computing nodes in a parallel sequence assembly algorithm is not trivial. Computing nodes have to request the *l*-tuples from other nodes. If one request per *l*-tuple is sent, there will be too many communication requests which will bring a large amount of overhead incurred mainly by communication startup. So these single requests should have to be incorporated to a request set which will be sent once. The similar situation occurs in the sequence alignment and the similar approach can be applied.

Table 1. The distribution of similarity matrix onto computing nodes

	Sequence X					
Sequence Y	0	1	2	...	$\lceil m/k \rceil$-1	P_1
	$\lceil m/k \rceil$	$\lceil m/k \rceil$+1	$\lceil m/k \rceil$+2	...	2$\lceil m/k \rceil$-1	P_2
	2$\lceil m/k \rceil$	2$\lceil m/k \rceil$+1	2$\lceil m/k \rceil$+2	...	3$\lceil m/k \rceil$-1	P_3
	...	...	...	...	...	...
	(t-1) $\lceil m/k \rceil$	(t-1) $\lceil m/k \rceil$+1	(t-1) $\lceil m/k \rceil$+2	...	t$\lceil m/k \rceil$-1	P_t
	t$\lceil m/k \rceil$	t$\lceil m/k \rceil$+1	t$\lceil m/k \rceil$+2	...	(t+1) $\lceil m/k \rceil$-1	P_1
	...	...	...	...	...	...
	($\lceil n/l \rceil$-1) $\lceil m/k \rceil$	($\lceil n/l \rceil$-1) $\lceil m/k \rceil$+1	($\lceil n/l \rceil$-1) $\lceil m/k \rceil$+2	...	$\lceil n/l \rceil \lceil m/k \rceil$-1	$P_{\lceil n/l \rceil \% t}$

5 Conclusion

It is a very promising way to conduct large-scale biological sequence assembly and alignment by using computing grid to take advantage of its giant storage and computing capacity. This paper gives the strategy on parallelization of the Euler sequence assembly, pair-wise sequence assembly and multiple sequence assembly and their implementation on a computing grid. Effective task scheduling and good computing granularity will boost the performance of biological applications running on a computing grid. Good experimental result has been achieved when conducting parallel sequence assembly and alignment on clusters. But we should do more to take advantages of grid computing. The load balancing discussed in this paper is static, i.e. load distribution taking place at the beginning of calculation. In the future work we will investigate dynamic load balancing to adjust the load assigned to the computing nodes dynamically to be adaptable to the fluctuation of the Grid computing environment.

References

1. Carol, A., Robert, D., Strausberg, R.L.: Human Genome Project: Revolutionizing Biology Through Leveraging Technology. Proceedings of SPIE - The International Society for Optical Engineering. California (1996) 190–201
2. Eugene, W.M.: Toward Simplifying and Accurately Formulating Fragment Assembly. J. Comp. Bio. 2(1995) 275–290
3. James, L.W., Gene, M.: Whole Genome Shotgun Sequencing. Geno. Res. 7(1997) 401–409
4. Liming, C., David, J., Evgueni, L.: Evolutionary Computation Techniques for Multiple Sequence Alignment. Proceedings of the IEEE Conference on Evolutionary Computation. San Diego 7(2000) 829–835
5. Phil, G.: Documentation for Phrap. http://www.genome.washington.edu/ UWGC/analysis-tools/phrap.html. (1994)
6. Xiaoqiu, H., Anup, M.: CAP3: A DNA Sequence Assembly Program. Geno. Res. 9(1999) 868–877
7. James, K.B., Ken, F.S., Rodger, S.: A New DNA Sequence Assembly Program. Nucl. Acids Res. 23(1995) 4992–4999
8. Pavel, A.P., Haixu, T., Smith, W.: An Eulerian Path Approach to DNA Fragment Assembly. Proceedings of National Academy of Sciences of the United States of America. 98(2001) 9748–9753
9. Temple, F.S., Michael, S.W.: Identification of Common Molecular Subsequences. J. Mol. Bio. 147(1981) 195–197
10. Julie, D.T., Desmond, G.H., Toby, J.G.: Clustal W: Improving the Sensitivity of Progressive Multiple Sequence Alignment Through Sequence Weighting, Position-Specific Gap Penalties and Weight Matrix Choice. Nucl. Acid Res. 22(1994) 4673–4680

Implementation of Grid-Enabled Medical Simulation Applications Using Workflow Techniques

Junwei Cao, Jochen Fingberg, Guntram Berti, and Jens Georg Schmidt

C&C Research Laboratories, NEC Europe Ltd., Germany
cao@ccrl-nece.de

Abstract. GEMSS is a European project that aims at providing high performance medical simulation services in a distributed and grid computing environment. The GEMSS grid middleware is designed using web services technologies and standards and provides support for authorization, workflow, security, Quality of Service aspects. In this work, one of the GEMSS applications, maxillo-facial surgery simulation, is described, which includes a complete chain of tools necessary for the entire process from geometric model generation from scan data to computer simulation and visualization. The Triana workflow environment is utilized to implement the application for uniform access of local processes (e.g. image pre-processing and meshing), interactive tools (e.g. mesh manipulation) and grid-enabled remote services (e.g. HPC finite element simulation). It is concluded that workflow provides benefits to flexibility, reusability and scalability and is potential to become a mainstream grid application enabling technology.

1 Introduction

The grid builds on the accessibility of the Internet to allow effective use of geographically distributed resources [13, 1]. Grid computing technologies will provide the basis for the next generation of Internet-enabled HPC solutions. GEMSS (Grid Enabled Medical Simulation Services) [14] is a European project that aims to create a grid testbed for medical computing.

In GEMSS a grid middleware will be developed that can be used to provide medical practitioners and researchers with access to advanced simulation and image processing services for improved pre-operative planning and near real-time surgical support. The grid architecture is designed based on Web Services technologies and standards and supposed to meet various requirements from business, legal and social, security, performance and application aspects. Workflow specification, enactment and execution are essential supports of the GEMSS grid middleware for business process management, QoS negotiation and application enabling.

Maxillo-facial surgery simulation [12] is one of the medical service applications included in the GEMSS test-bed, which provides a virtual try-out space for the pre-operative planning of maxillo-facial surgery. The implementation of the maxillo-facial surgery simulation requires a chain of tools necessary for the entire process

M. Li et al. (Eds.): GCC 2003, LNCS 3032, pp. 34–41, 2004.

from geometric model generation from scan data to computer simulation and visualization.

The work presented in this paper takes maxillo-facial surgery simulation as an example application and provides an initial demonstration of using workflow techniques to enable the application for uniform access of local processes (e.g. image segmentation and mesh generation), interactive tools (e.g. mesh manipulation) and remote web services for large-scale simulation (e.g. HPC finite element simulation). An existing open source problem solving environment, Triana [24], is utilized as a workflow manager for the application. Triana is written in Java and provides abundant graphical user interfaces for both toolbox implementation and workflow construction. In this work, several Triana toolboxes and an example workflow model are developed and detailed information is provided on how to develop Java wrappers for various binaries and scripts, turn them into Triana toolboxes using the Triana unit, and set up web services for remote access of HPC resources.

2 GEMSS

The GEMSS middleware is built on existing web services technologies and standards and provides support for authorization, workflow, security, Quality of Service aspects. This section provides brief information on the GEMSS architecture and one of the six GEMSS applications, maxillo-facial surgery simulation.

2.1 GEMSS Architecture

The GEMSS architecture, shown in Fig. 1, uses a client/server topology employing a service-oriented architecture. Detailed information on individual modules is not provided below and can be found in [14].

The GEMSS client architecture is mainly a pluggable component framework, which aims to provide flexible support to various application scenarios by placing minimal demands upon the components themselves and providing sufficient means for them to interact. The component framework is used by applications as the entry point into the GEMSS grid middleware and hides the details of the grid as far as possible.

A GEMSS service can be implemented using existing web services technologies. Application services provide generic interfaces for starting application, uploading and downloading files. Resource manager and data storage provide interfaces for services to access actual HPC resources.

2.2 Maxillo-Facial Surgery Simulation

One of the GEMSS target applications deals with computing pre-operative simulations for maxillo-facial surgeries. In clinical practice treatment of patients with in-born deformations of the mid-face is performed by cutting ill-formed bones and pulling them into the "right" position.

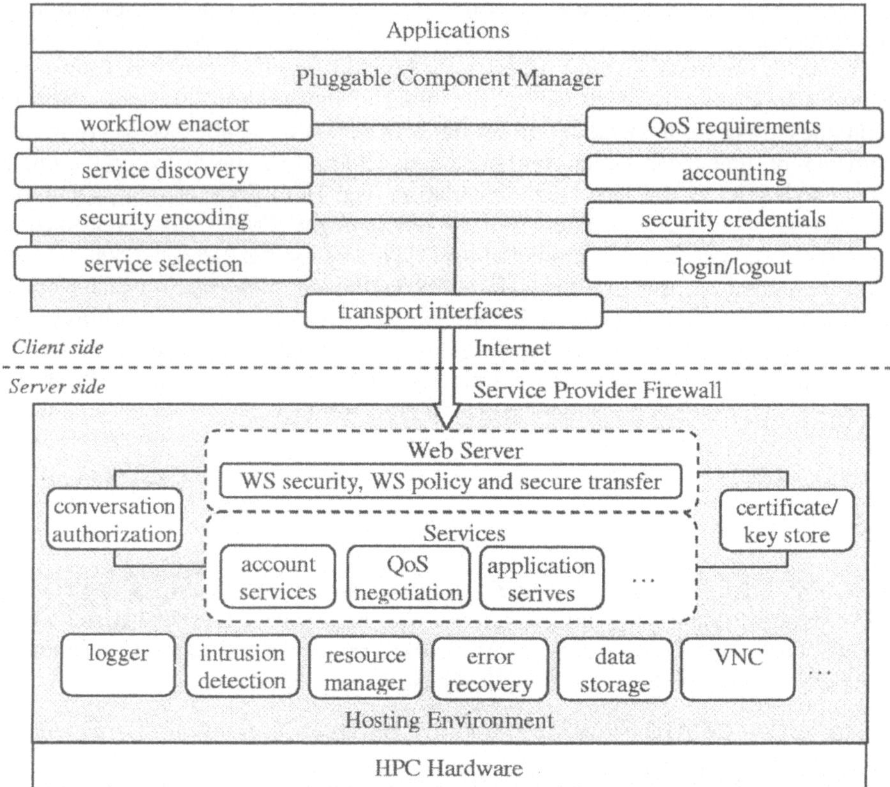

Fig. 1. The GEMSS architecture is composed with the client side architecture and service provider architecture, which plays as middleware between grid applications and resources.

A halo frame is mounted to the patient's skull (see Fig. 2a). Distractors, mounted to the halo fixed at certain points in the midface, exert a force on a midface region, gently pulling it to a pre-defined position in order to achieve a medically and cosmetically pleasing result. The simulation of the process includes a complete chain of tools [12], which are partly described below.

- *Image segmentation.* As shown in Figs. 2b, 2c and 2d, bone and soft tissue parts can be identified from the original CT image. This can be performed at the client as an image pre-processing step.
- *Mesh generation.* The process allows the generation of meshes suitable for Finite Element simulation (see an example in Fig. 2e) and could be computation intensive if the mesh size is very large. In our initial implementation, this step is also considered as a client side process.
- *Mesh manipulation.* This process provides the meshing model with initial and boundary conditions for simulation using a user friendly tool. An example of virtual bone cutting is shown in Fig. 2f. This is an interactive process and can be only carried out at the client side.

- *Finite Element analysis*. The Finite Element simulation capability is provided by a fully parallel program linked with a load balancing library. Example visualizations of simulation results are illustrated in Figs. 2g and 2h. In this case the simulation result shows that a better bone position can be achieved after the surgery. This is the part that required grid enabling to access remote HPC resources.

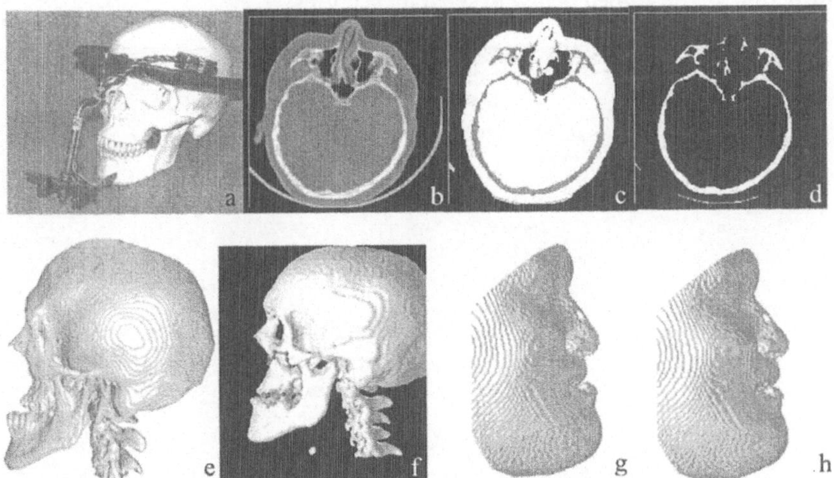

Fig. 2. Maxillo-facial surgery simulation. (a) The halo device mounted on the head; (b) CT images; (c) Identification of substructures (bone, soft tissue and background); (c) Selection of bones from others; (e) Mesh of a skull; (f) Virtual bone cutting; (g) Visualization of the geometric face change I (before the surgery); (h) Visualization of the geometric face change II (after the surgery).

3 Application Workflow

Workflow techniques are utilized in the GEMSS project for multiple purposes. In this work, only application workflow is implemented using an existing workflow tool.

3.1 Triana Environment

The Triana software environment is intended to be flexible and can be used in many different scenarios and at many different levels. One of the Triana applications is described in [23], where Triana is equipped with P2P computing mechanisms for galaxy visualization. In another European grid project GridLab [17], Triana is integrated with grid environments via grid application toolkit (GAT) interfaces

In this work, Triana is used as a management environment for the simulation application workflow. It provides an effective wizard to build high level toolboxes in a semi-visual way so that workflow activities are uniformly encapsulated and handled by the Triana workflow. The Triana unit is the base class on which that all of toolboxes are built. The unit class provides abundant methods for each toolbox to handle inputs, outputs, parameters and even corresponding graphical input interfaces in a standard way. Fig. 3 provides a screenshot of the Triana implementation of maxillo-facial surgery simulation. Toolbox implementation and workflow construction are described below in separate sections.

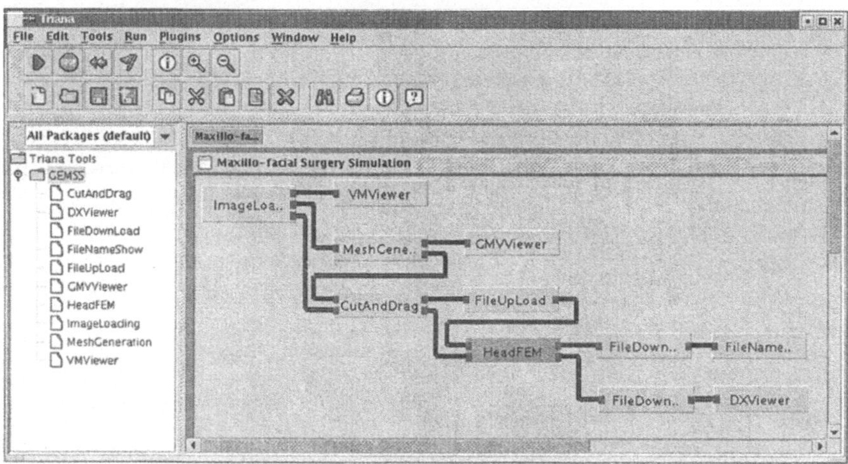

Fig. 3. Triana implementation of maxillo-facial surgery simulation, with a complete list of the GEMSS toolboxes in the left column and the example workflow in the main window.

3.2 Toolbox Implementation

There are three types of toolboxes used for building the maxillo-facial surgery simulation workflow: input, processing and output. The only input toolbox shown in Fig. 3 is the image loading toolbox. Main processing toolboxes include those for mesh generation, bone cutting and dragging, and Finite Element analysis. Output toolboxes are implemented for result visualization.

- *ImageLoading*. This is the entry point of the simulation workflow. The user is required to input the image file name to start the workflow execution.
- *MeshGeneration*. Since image processing and meshing described in Section 2.2 are both client-side local processes, a shell script is developed to describe the whole chain of the process. The toolbox is implemented via a Java wrapper to the script execution. The mesh generation toolbox takes input from the image loading and outputs a result mesh file for mesh manipulation.
- *Cut&Drag*. The activity allows the user to define initial and boundary conditions for simulation via virtual bone cutting and dragging operations. The toolbox implements an iterative process so that the user can repeat the activity until a satisfying result is obtained. It takes inputs from both the mesh file and the original image file and outputs an all-in-one model file ready for simulation.

- *HeadFEM.* The Finite Element simulation takes two inputs from the *Cut&Drag* toolbox and outputs two sets of files, one including detailed simulation data and the other including a ready input for visualization. In order to implement the toolbox, the HeadFEM service has to be set up for remote access of HPC resources. This is implemented using the Apache Tomcat and Axis. In the client side toolbox implementation, the JAX-RPC call provided by the Apache Axis library is used to access the HeadFEM service.
- *FileUpload and FileDownload.* These two toolboxes are necessary before and after the simulation activity and temporarily implemented using FTP. In the later GEMSS implementation, these will be supported by application services as well.
- *VMViewer, GMVViewer and DXViewer.* These output toolboxes are used in the workflow for result visualization. As shown in Fig. 3, the VM tool is used to display the original image file, the GMV tool for mesh visualization and the DX tool for the visualization of simulation results. The use of these tools during workflow execution is also illustrated in Fig. 4.
- *FileNameShow.* This is an output toolbox that can be used to pop up a window and display the input file name.

3.3 Workflow Construction

Workflow construction is straightforward in the Triana environment given all toolboxes ready. The developer can drag and link toolboxes to directly construct a workflow ready for execution. The workflow developed for maxillo-facial surgery simulation is shown in Fig. 3. The screenshot of an example workflow execution is illustrated in Fig. 4. In this case the input is a CT image file shown in Fig. 4b. Output toolboxes in the workflow invoke different tools to visualize results (see Figs. 4b-4e).

4 Related Work

Apart from the GEMSS project, there are some other projects that are using grid computing for medical or biological application. These include European MammoGrid project for breast cancer screening [21], UK e-Science Programme MyGrid [22] and Swiss BioOpera [5] projects for bioinformatics, Japan BioGrid project [3], Singapore BioMed grid [4], and so on.

Workflow techniques are also used in many other grid projects. Pioneering WebFlow project [2] uses workflow as high level mechanism for high performance distributed applications. Early grid projects Condor [8] and UNICORE [25] provide workflow capability to manage task dependencies. The Globus project [15] is also developing a grid service flow language (GSFL). Current other projects that involve workflow development include USA ASCI grid [6], UK MyGrid [22], European projects GRASP [16] and CrossGrid [9].

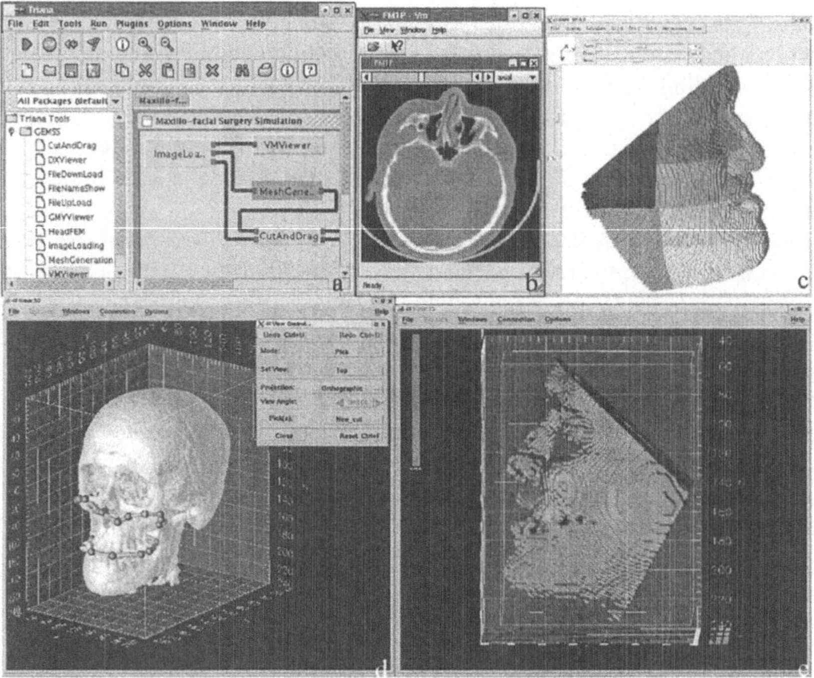

Fig. 4. An example workflow execution given a CT image file. (a) The Triana software environment; (b) The VM tool for browsing the input image file; (c) The GMV tool for browsing the mesh file; (d) The DX tool for interactive virtual bone cutting and dragging; (e) The DX tool for simulation result visualization. (Note: The data set and guidance for placing the bone cuts was kindly provided by Dr. T. Hierl, University Clinic Leipzig.)

There are also many grid-aware workflow environments and tools under development. IBM BPWS4J is a web services flow execution engine designed for BPEL4WS [10]. Symphony [20] focuses more on security issues. GridFlow [7] focuses more on workflow simulation and scheduling. In several most recent work, workflow techniques are used to address various interesting issues in grid environments, including failure handling [18], authorization [19], automatic workflow generation and grid mapping [11].

5 Conclusions

There are many discussions in grid computing community on programming models for grid application development. According to our experiences on using the Triana workflow for building GEMSS applications described in this work, advantages of using workflow techniques are summarized as follows:

- *Flexibility*. The application can be constructed at different levels easily and quickly using workflow mechanisms.
- *Reusability*. A toolbox once developed can be reused in multiple applications.

- *Scalability*. Workflow-based applications can be constructed in a hierarchical way, which provides possibilities for applications to scale up in a grid environment.

It is expected that workflow will become one of mainstream programming models for future grid application development.

References

1. F. Berman, A. J. G. Hey, and G. Fox, Grid Computing: Making The Global Infrastructure a Reality, John Wiley & Sons, 2003.
2. D. Bhatia, V. Burzevski, M. Camuseva, G. Fox, etc., "WebFlow – a Visual Programming Paradigm for Web/Java Based Coarse Grain Distributed Computing", Concurrency: Practice and Experience, Vol. 9, No. 6, pp. 555-577, 1997.
3. BioGrid. http://www.biogrid.jp/.
4. BioMed. http://bmg.bii.a-star.edu.sg/.
5. BioOpera. http://www.inf.ethz.ch/personal/bausch/bioopera/main.html.
6. H. P. Bivens, "Grid Workflow", GGF Working Document, 2001.
7. J. Cao, S. A. Jarvis, S. Saini, and G. R. Nudd, "GridFlow: Workflow Management for Grid Computing", in Proc. of 3rd IEEE Int. Symp. on Cluster Computing and the Grid, Tokyo, Japan, pp. 198-205, 2003.
8. Condor. http://www.cs.wisc.edu/condor/.
9. CrossGrid. http://www.crossgrid.org/.
10. F. Curbera, Y. Goland, J. Klein, F. Leymann, D. Roller, S. Thatte, S. Weerawarana, "Business Process Execution Language for Web Services, Version 1.0", July 2002. http://www.ibm.com/developerworks/library/ws-bpel/.
11. E. Deelman, J. Blythe. Y. Gil, C. Kesselman, et. al., "Mapping Abstract Complex Workflows onto Grid Environments", J. Grid Computing, Vol. 1, No, 1, pp. 25-39, 2003.
12. J. Fingberg, G. Berti, U. Hartmann, and A. Basermann, "Head-Mechanical Simulations with SimBio", NEC Research & Development, Vol. 43, No. 4, 2002.
13. I. Foster, and C. Kesselman, The Grid: Blueprint for a New Computing Infrastructure, Morgan-Kaufmann, 1998.
14. GEMSS. http://www.ccrl-nece.de/gemss/.
15. Globus. http://www.globus.org/.
16. GRASP. http://eu-grasp.net/.
17. GridLab. http://www.gridlab.org/.
18. S. Hwang, and C. Kesselman, "Grid Workflow: a Flexible Failure Handling Framework for the Grid", in Proc. of 12th IEEE Int. Symp. on High Performance Distributed Computing, Seattle, USA, pp. 126-137, 2003.
19. S. Kim, J. Kim, S. Hong, and S. Kim, "Workflow-based Authorization Service in Grid", in Proc. of 4th IEEE Int. Workshop on Grid Computing, Phoenix, USA, 2003.
20. M. Lorch, and D. Kafura, "Symphony – A Java-based Composition and Manipulation Framework for Computational Grids", in Proc. of 2nd IEEE/ACM Int. Symp. on Cluster Computing and the Grid, Berlin, Germany, pp. 136-143, 2002.
21. MammoGrid. http://www.healthgrid.org/.
22. MyGrid. http://www.mygrid.info/.
23. I. Taylor, M. Shields, I. Wang, and R. Philp, "Distributed P2P Computing within Triana: A Galaxy Visualization Test Case", in Proc. of 17th IEEE Int. Parallel & Distributed Processing Symp., Nice, France, 2003.
24. Triana. http://www.triana.co.uk/; http://trianacode.org/.
25. UNICORE. http://www.unicore.de/.

C^2: A New Overlay Network Based on CAN and Chord*

Wenyuan Cai, Shuigeng Zhou, Linhao Xu, Weining Qian, and Aoying Zhou

Dept. of Computer Sci. and Eng., Fudan University, Shanghai, 200433, China
{wycai,sgzhou,xulh,wnqian,ayzhou}@fudan.edu.cn

Abstract. In this paper, we present C^2, a new overlay network based on CAN and Chord. For an n-peer C^2 system, each peer maintains only about $O(\log n)$ other peers' information, and achieves routing within $O(\log n)$ hops. For each peer's join or departure, C^2 can update the routing table within $O(\log n)$ messages with high probability. What distinguish C^2 from many other peer-to-peer data-sharing systems are its low computation cost and high routing efficiency in dynamic environment. In the case that considerable peers fail simultaneously (*i.e.*, quite a lot other peers' routing tables are out of date), the average hop number of successful routings does not increase obviously.

1 Introduction

Although they came into being only a few years ago, Peer-to-Peer data-sharing systems have become one of the most prevalent Internet applications. It is crucial for P2P systems to design a scalable overlay structure and apply a deterministic routing mechanism to locate the desired resources. Roughly, there are two types of data-sharing P2P systems — unstructured and structured P2P systems. As far as routing efficiency is concerned, structured P2P systems are generally superior to unstructured P2P systems. Although current structured P2P systems, such as Chord[7], CAN[4], Tapestry[8], Pastry[6], and Viceroy[2], have been proved to possess features of deterministic location, load balance and dynamic membership etc, each of which shows unique merits of its own. In this paper, we present a new overlay network C^2, which integrates merits of resource locating of both Chord[7] and CAN[4].

Compared with CAN and Chord, C^2 boasts of lower computation cost, higher routing efficiency and better fault tolerance. In steady state, for an n-peer C^2 system, each peer maintains about $O(\log n)$ other peers' information, and achieves routing within $O(\log n)$ hops. For each peer's join or departure, C^2 can update the routing table within $O(\log n)$ messages with high probability. To locate a key, C^2 needs $O(\log n)$ hops at most, and the computation cost for each hop is quite lower than other algorithms. In dynamic environment where peers join and depart the system unpredictably, C^2 can still run smoothly.

* This work was supported by the Natural Science Foundation of China (NSFC) under grant no. 60373019, and Fudan University Innovation Foundation for Graduate Students.

M. Li et al. (Eds.): GCC 2003, LNCS 3032, pp. 42–50, 2004.

2 The C^2 Network

C^2 network is a kind of combination of CAN and Chord. Peers' identifiers and resources are mapped onto a discrete d-dimensional Cartesian coordinate space by uniform hash function as in CAN and Chord. Each dimension is a circle from 0 to 2^m-1 (m is a predefined system parameter), *i.e.*, there are totally 2^m valid coordinate points on each dimension. Thus the entire space can be (but not necessarily) partitioned into at most $2^{m\times d}$ unit hypercubes. Considering that each of these $2^{m\times d}$ unit hypercubes can represent one peer, the entire space can hold at most $2^{m\times d}$ peers. However, one peer may cover more than one unit hypercube. In what follows, we denote the number of peers in C^2 network $n = \alpha \times 2^{m\times d}$($\alpha$ is a constant, satisfying $\alpha\in(0,1)$).

Definition 1. ***maximal point (MaxP):*** *the maximal point of a hypercube zone is the point whose coordinate value is the maximal one in every dimension.*

Definition 2. ***minimal point (MinP):*** *the minimal point of a hypercube zone is the point whose coordinate value is greater than the minimal coordinate value by 1 in every dimension.*

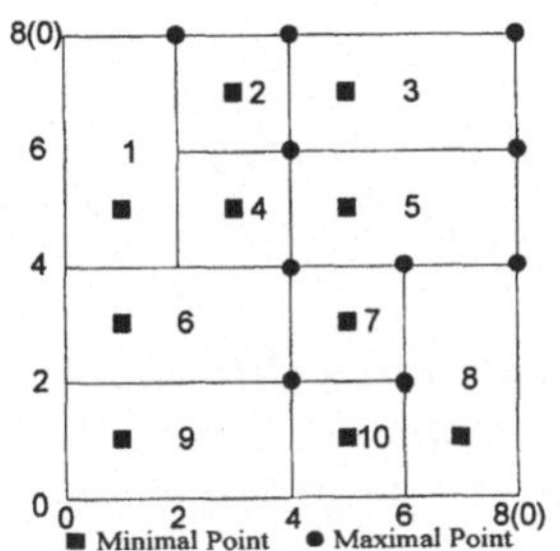

Fig. 1. A 2-dimensional C^2 with 10 peers

Example 1. Figure 1 shows a 2-dimensional $[0,2^3\text{-}1]\times[0,2^3\text{-}1]$ coordinate space partitioned among 10 C^2 peers. The $MaxP$ of a zone is presented by a circular dot, and the $MinP$ by a square dot. The keys in the zone of peer 10 is (5,1),(5,2),(6,1),and(6,2).

2.1 Routing Table

Each peer maintains a routing table which is organized into $d \times m$ entries.

Definition 3. ***neighbor point (NbP):*** *For each peer, P, there is a point Q whose coordinate value succeeds P's MaxP by* $2^j (0 \leq j \leq m-1)$ *in the r-th dimension* $(1 \leq r \leq d)$ *and shares the same value with P's MinP in all the other dimensions. Point Q is the j-th neighbor point of P in the r-th dimension.*

The j-th entry at row r of P's routing table corresponds to the peer whose zone covers P's j-th NbP in the r-th dimension. Each entry in the routing table consists of the IP address, the $MaxP$ and the $MinP$ of the corresponding peer.

Theorem 1. *For an n-peer C^2 system, the number of entries in the routing table of any peer is $O(\log n)$.*

Proof. As we have seen, the number of entries in every peer's routing table is $d \times m$. And the number of peers in C^2 network $n = \alpha \times 2^{m \times d} (\alpha \in (0,1))$. Thus, the number of entries in the routing table of any peer is $O(\log n)$.

2.2 Routing in C^2

In this subsection, we will introduce the routing scheme of C^2, that is, how a query message is routed to the destination peer.

Definition 4. ***maximal difference dimension (MaxDD):*** *the maximal difference dimension of a peer P with regard to a key K, is the dimension in which the difference between the peer's MaxP and the key is the largest in all dimensions, that is,*

$$MaxDD = \arg\max_{i=1}^{d} Dif_i(P, K) \tag{1}$$

Above,

$$Dif_i(P, K) \begin{cases} K_i - MaxP_i & K_i \geq MaxP_i \\ K_i - MaxP_i + 2^m & K_i < MaxP_i \end{cases} \tag{2}$$

Definition 5. ***minimal difference dimension (MinDD):*** *the minimal difference dimension of a peer P with regard to a key K, is the dimension in which the difference between the peer's MaxP and the key is the least in all dimensions, that is,*

$$MinDD = \arg\min_{i=1}^{d} Dif_i(P, K) \tag{3}$$

Lemma 1. *In logical overlay, given a peer P and a key K, P's farthest legal*[1] *NbP in its MaxDD has the maximal hop distance towards K in the routing table.*

Proof. Let a key $K(K_1, K_2, \cdots, K_d)$ and a peer P whose $MaxP$ is $(P_1, P_2, \cdots, P_d)$ in d-dimensional coordinate space, and $2^j \leq Dif_{MaxDD}(P, K) < 2^{j+1} (0 \leq j < m)$. Then, the farthest legal NbP in $MaxDD$ is $Q(P_1, P_2, \cdots, P_{MaxDD} + 2^j, \cdots, P_d)$, the hop distance in logical overlay is 2^j.

If $\exists h$ *and* $s(h \neq MaxDD, 1 \leq s < m)$(without loss of generality, we assume $h > MaxDD$), the hop distance of legal NbP $Q'(P_1, P_2, \cdots, P_{MaxDD}, \cdots, P_h + 2^s, \cdots, P_d)$ is bigger than that of Q, that is $2^j < 2^s$. Then $2^j \leq Dif_{MaxDD}(P, K) < 2^{j+1} \leq 2^s \leq Dif_h(P, K) < 2^{s+1}$ $(0 \leq j < s < m)$, which contradicts with the fact that $MaxDD = \arg\max_{i=1}^{d} Dif_i(P, K)$.

Thus, 2^j is the maximal distance of legal hop.

[1] **legal** means that the NbP of the hop should not exceed the key in any dimension

Theorem 2. *In logical overlay, given a peer P and a key K, P's farthest legal NbP in its MaxDD has the minimal hop distance towards K in the routing table.*
Proof. Let a key $K(K_1, K_2, \cdots, K_d)$ and a peer $P(P_1, P_2, \cdots, P_d)$ in d-dimensional coordinate space, and $2^j \leq Dif_{MaxDD}\ (P, K) < 2^{j+1}$ $(0 \leq j < m)$. $Q(P_1, P_2, \cdots, P_{MaxDD}+2^j, \cdots, P_d)$ is the farthest legal NbP in P's $MaxDD$. For any legal NbP $Q'(Q_1, Q_2, \cdots, Q_{MaxDD}, \cdots, Q_h+2^s, \cdots, Q_d)$, in the h-th dimension ($h \neq MaxDD$, without loss of generality, we assume $h > MaxDD$), according to Lemma 1, $s \leq j$. Then,
$D^2_{Q',K} - D^2_{Q,K} = \sum_{i=1}^{d} Dif_i^2(Q', K) - \sum_{i=1}^{d} Dif_i^2(Q, K)$
$= [Dif^2_{MaxDD}(P, K) + (Dif_h(P, K) - 2^s)^2] - [Dif_{MaxDD}(P, K) - 2^j)^2 + Dif_h(P, K)^2]$
In the case of $s = j$,

$$D^2_{Q',K} - D^2_{Q,K} = 2^{s+1} \times [Dif_{MaxDD}(P, K) - Dif_h(P, K)] \geq 0.$$

In the case of $s < j$, that is $s + 1 \leq j$,

$$D^2_{Q',K} - D^2_{Q,K} = 2^s \times [2^{j-s}(2Dif_{MaxDD}(P, K) - 2^j) - (2Dif_h(P, K) + 2^s]$$
$$\geq 2^s(2^{2j-s} - 2^{s+2} + 2^s) \geq 2^s(2^{s+2} - 2^{s+2} + 2^s) = 2^{2s} > 0.$$

Thus, $D_{Q',key} > D_{Q,key}$.
Therefore, P's farthest legal NbP in its $MaxDD$ has the minimal hop distance towards K in the routing table.

Algorithm 1 P.Route(key)

```
if key is in P's zone then
    Return RouteSucceeded;
else
    Compute the differences between MaxP and key in all dimensions
    Sort the dimensions by the differences
    for r = MaxDD to MinDD do
        Choose the farthest legal entry Q on the r-th row of the routing table;
        if Q is available then
            Return Q;
        end if
    end for
    Return RouteFailed
end if
```

Algorithm 1 is the pseudocode of the routing strategy in C^2. The input of the algorithm is the key, the output is the identifier of the peer to which the message will be forwarded. When a peer P receives a lookup message, it first checks whether the key locates in its own zone. If its own zone covers the key, then the routing succeeds; Otherwise, P computes its $MaxDD$ with regard to the key, then tries to forward the message to the peer Q covering its farthest legal NbP in the $MaxDD$. If Q is available, the algorithm will return Q; otherwise, P will try in the second $MaxDD$(the dimension which has the second maximal difference between P's $MaxP$ and the key in all dimensions), and so on.
Example 2. Figure 2 is the example of peer 10 to locate the key (4, 7).

Theorem 3. *Suppose the number of peers in C^2 network is n, for any given peer P, the number of hops to locate a key K is $O(\log n)$.*

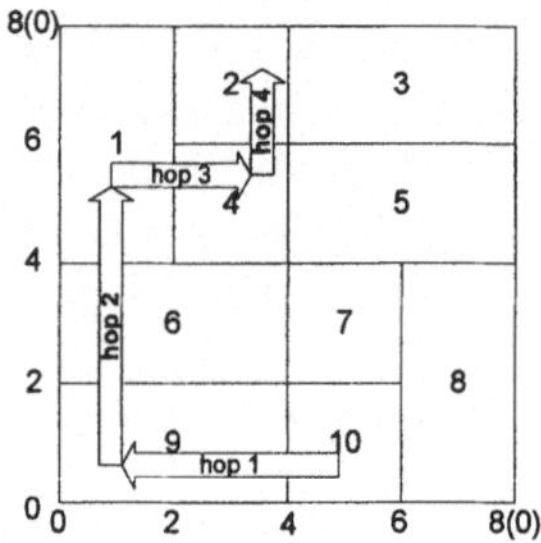

Fig. 2. Example of routing

Proof. Let the key K is managed by peer Q. Recall that if $P \neq Q$, then P forwards the message to a peer T, whose zone covers the farthest legal NbP in the $MaxDD$ of P. Suppose T is in the j-th entry of the r-th row. The distance between P's $MaxP$ and its NbP, which is covered by T's zone, is 2^{j-1}. Since P choose the j-th entry but not the (j+1)-th entry, the distance between P's $MaxP$ and K is less than 2^j, so the distance between T's $MaxP$ and K on dimension r is not more than the distance between T and P. Therefore, T halves the distance between P and key on the r-th dimension. Considering the range of every dimension is 2^m, then within m steps the distance will reduce to 0. Since there are d dimensions, the total step will be $d \times m$ which is $O(\log n)$.

2.3 Join C^2

In a dynamic network, peers can join and leave the system at any time. In this subsection, we will introduce how the system handling the join of a new peer. The method to manipulate the departure of an existing peer will be introduced in next subsection.

When a new peer arrives, it needs to initialize its routing table, and then informs some other peers of its presence. In order to balance the workload, a new peer must be allocated its own zone, which is generated by splitting the zone of an existing peer in half or taking over a zone from an existing peer. The join process takes six steps:

1. Find a peer already in C^2 by some external mechanism
2. Generate a point in the coordinate space by using hashing method;
3. Route to the existing peer whose zone cover the point;
4. Choose the peer responsible for the biggest zone in the routing table;
5. Split the zone, the new coming peer manages the smaller half.
6. Update routing table of both peers and inform other peers of their presence.

In order to simplify the join and departure scheme, each peer P maintains d predecessor pointers and a routed table which is a list of peers satisfying that P is in these peers' routing table. When peers join and leave, maintaining predecessor pointers and routed table can facilitate the update of routing tables.

Example 3. Figure 3 shows an example of join of peer 11, which randomly generates the point valued (1,5), via peer 10.

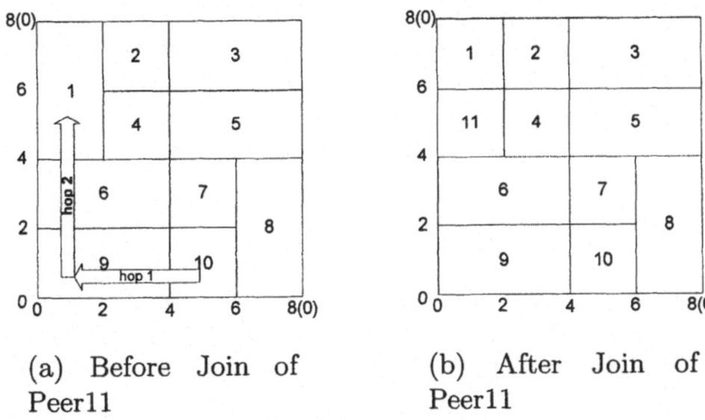

(a) Before Join of Peer11

(b) After Join of Peer11

Fig. 3. Example of Join

2.4 Departure from C^2

When peers leave C^2, It is necessary that their zones be taken over by an existing peer. And the routing table of existing peers should also be updated.

In the case of normal departure, the depart peer P should find an existing peer to take over its zone. In order to balance the workload, the P chooses the most lightly loaded peer Q in its routing table, and then notifying Q to take over the zone. Q can download the routing table from P without any modification. Then, Q will download the routed table from P and notify the peers, in whose routing table P exists, to change their routing tables by substituting Q for P. After P's departure, Q will act as two peers and be responsible for two zones.

In the case of failure departure, the peer, which is the predecessor on the first dimension will take over the zone. By using the method similar to Chord, the routing table can be rehabilitated within $O(\log n)$ messages. However, it is very difficult to inform the peer whose routing table contains the failure peer instantaneously. Thus, it is quite possible that not all the information in the routing table is correct. One of the recuperative methods is that every peer contacts the peers in its routing table periodically. When some of the peers in the routing table are unavailable, they will update these entries by re-locating the *NbP*s using the routing scheme mentioned in subsection 2.2.

Example 4. Figure4 shows an example of peer 8's departure.

2.5 Fault Tolerance

In dynamic environment, peers' departure and failure are unpredictable. Thus, it is quite possible that some routing tables are out-of-date. Even with some out-dated routing tables in the network, the routing scheme of C^2 can still reach the destination with little additional overhead.

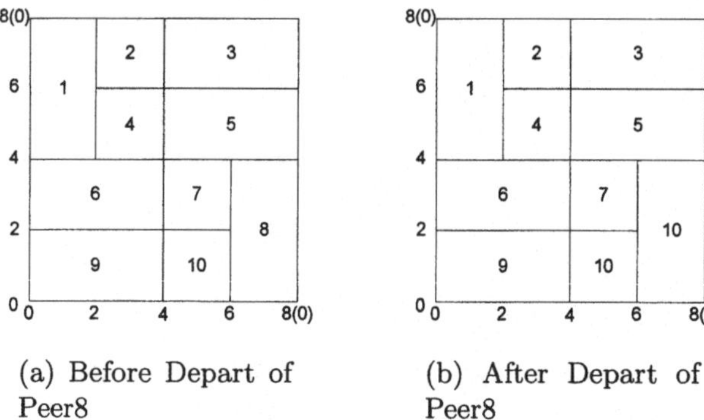

(a) Before Depart of Peer8

(b) After Depart of Peer8

Fig. 4. Example of Departure

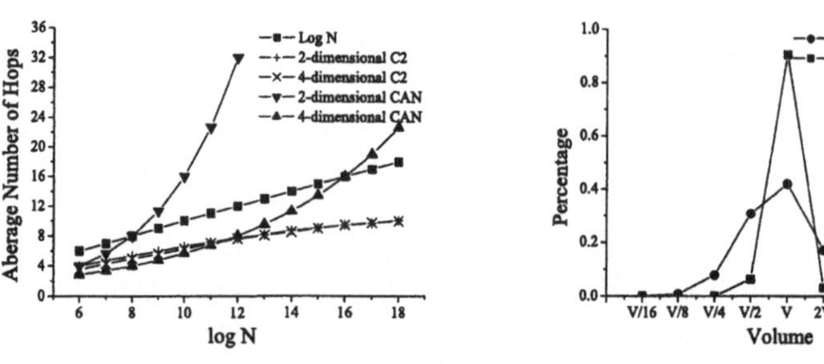

Fig. 5. Scalability

Fig. 6. Workload Balancing

Thanks to its unique routing scheme, C^2 is quite fault tolerant. Suppose peer P wants to route a message to the peer whose zone covers key K. It computes the differences between its $MaxP$ and K in all dimensions, and sorts the dimensions by their differences. Then, it chooses the farthest legal entry in $MaxDD$. If the peer corresponding to the entry is available, P forwards the message to it; otherwise, the second $MaxDD$ will be used, and so on. Therefore, in most cases, it can find a way out to reach the destination peer, unless all the d dimensions have no way out, which rarely happens in practice.

3 Performance Evaluation

In this section, we present simulation results to demonstrate the performance of C^2. We implement an experimental C^2 platform in Java, which can deploy up to 2^{18} peers. First, we examine the association between routing efficiency and network scale, and compare C^2 with CAN. Second, the workload distribution of C^2 network is also investigated. Finally, we study the trend of routing performance changing with failure ratio of peers in the network.

In the first simulation experiment, we vary the number of peers from 2^6 to 2^{18} in networks with d=4, m=6 and d=2, m=12 respectively. In each of

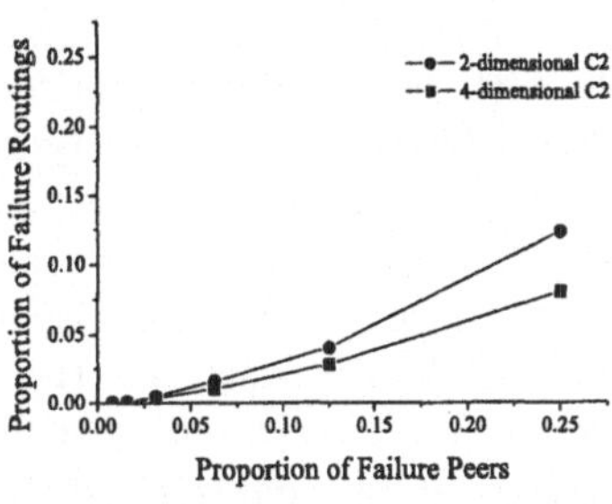

(a) Failure Routing vs. Failure Peer

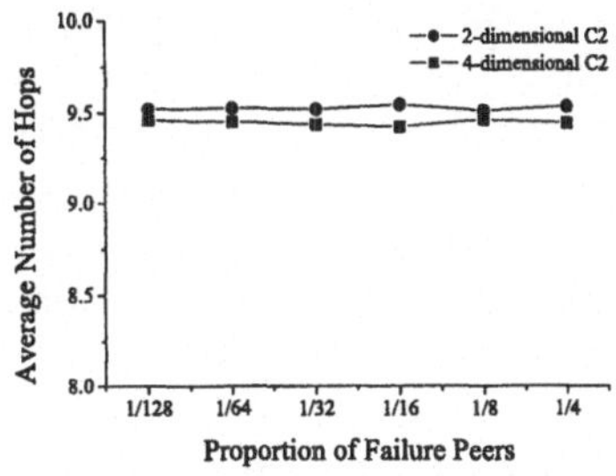

(b) Performance in Failure

Fig. 7. Fault Tolerance of C^2

the total 10000 trials, two peers are chosen randomly and a message is routed between them, and the average hop number is recorded. The results are showed in Figure 5, where the "Log N" and "CAN" curves show the values of $\log n$ and the average hop numbers in CAN respectively. The experiment result shows that the average number of hops in an n-peer C^2 network is about $\frac{1}{2}\log n$. Obviously, as the network scale increases, the hop number of routing in CAN grows more rapidly than in C^2, which means that C^2 is more scalable than CAN.

Figure 6 shows workload distribution of peers in C^2. Here, V represents the average workload.We can see that without checking the routing table to choose the biggest zone, only about 40% peers' workload is V, and the heaviest workload is $8V$. However, by checking the routing table locally, the workload balancing has been ameliorated significantly: more than 90% peers' workload is the average workload, and the heaviest workload is only $2V$. This experiment shows that the join and departure strategy of C^2 is favorable for workload balance.

Figure 7 illustrates the fault tolerance feature of C^2. We implement this experiment by varying the proportion of failed peers from $\frac{1}{128}$ to $\frac{1}{4}$ in a C^2 network with 2^{16} peers. In each of the total 10000 trials, two online peers are chosen randomly and a message is routed between them. The ratio of failed routing and the average hops of successful routing are recorded. Simulation shows that only a small fraction of routing failed even in the case that considerable peers are off-line simultaneously and subsequently some peers' routing tables are outdated, while the average hops of successful routings will not increase.

4 Conclusion

In this paper, we present and evaluate C^2, a new overlay network based on CAN and Chord. C^2 is decentralized, scalable, and fault-tolerant. We show how a C^2

overlay network can be efficiently and reliably constructed to support resource sharing in dynamic environment.

Each C^2 peer maintains a routing table with only $O(\log n)$ entries, and a message can be routed to its destination within $O(\log n)$ hops. In dynamic environment, C^2 gains high fault tolerance with two merits. First, the system is resilient to failure by updating the information within $O(\log n)$ messages. Second, even information in the routing table is outdated, the routing scheme can still bypass the failed peers to the target with moderate overhead. Hence, even with coinstantaneous failure of considerable peers, the system is still reliable and the performance can be guaranteed. Our theoretical analysis and simulation results validate the scalability and fault tolerance of C^2.

References

1. J. Kubiatowicz, D. Bindel, Y. Chen, S. Czerwinski, P. Eaton, D. Geels, R. Gummadi, S. Rhea, H. Weatherspoon, W. Weimer, C. Wells, and B. Zhao. Oceanstore: An architecture for global-scale persistent storage. In *Proc. of ASPLOS 2000.*
2. D. Malkhi, M. Naor, and D. Ratajczak. Viceroy: A scalable and dynamic emulation of the butterfly. In *Proc. of the 21st ACM PODC*, 2002.
3. C. Plaxton, R. Rajaram, and A. W. Richa. Accessing nearby copies of replicated objects in a distributed environment. In *Proc. of SPAA*, 1997.
4. S. Ratnasamy, P. Francis, K. Handley, R. Karp, and S. Shenker. A scalable content-addressable network. In *Proc. of ACM SIGCOMM 2001*, 2001.
5. S. Ratnasamy, S. Shenker, and I. Stoica. Routing algorithms for DHTs: Some open questions. In *Proc. of IPTPS'2002.*
6. A. Rowstron and P. Druschel. Pastry: Scalable, distributed object location and routing for large-scale peer-to-peer systems. In *Proc. of ACM International Conference on Distributed Systems Platforms (Middleware)*, 2001.
7. I. Stoica, R. Morris, D. Karger, M. F. Kaashoek, and H. Balakrishnan. Chord: a scalable peer-to-peer lookup service for internet applications. In *Proc. of ACM SIGCOMM 2001*, pages 149–160. ACM Press, 2001.
8. B. Zhao, J. Kubiatowicz, and A. Joseph. Tapestry: An infrastructure for fault-tolerant wide-area location and routing. Technical report, Tech. Rep. USB/CSD-01-1141, University of California at Berkeley, Computer Science Department, 2001.

An Engineering Computation Oriented Visual Grid Framework

Guiyi Wei[1,2,3], Yao Zheng[1,2], Jifa Zhang[1,2], and Guanghua Song[1,2]

[1] College of Computer Science, Zhejiang University, Hangzhou, 310027, P. R. China
[2] Center for Engineering and Scientific Computation, Zhejiang University, Hangzhou, 310027, P. R. China
[3] Hangzhou Institute of Commerce, Hangzhou, 310035, P. R. China

Abstract. Grid computing technology is a focused field in high performance computing. This paper describes an engineering computation oriented visual grid framework VGrid, which is capable to bridge the gap between currently deployed grid services and the computational applications. Based on the Globus toolkit, and coupled with a client component, a services pool and a server component, VGrid visually performs resource discovery, task schedule, and result processing. VGrid improves the efficiency of utilization of resources by introducing a logical resource concept. VGrid applications of numerical simulations in engineering sciences are demonstrated.

1 Introduction

Computer simulations become increasingly more important in studying physical systems and engineering designs. However, even today's most powerful supercomputers were utilized, the scope and accuracy of these simulations are still severely limited by the available computational power. When we endeavor to simulate the true complexity of nature and engineering process, we will require much larger scale calculations than those are possible at present. We can break through these limits by simultaneously harnessing multiple networked supercomputers, running a single massively parallel simulation to numerically model the problems of more complexity and high fidelity [1].

In order to solve these engineering and scientific computing problems, grid computing has emerged as a new infrastructure, distinguished from conventional distributed computing since that it focuses on large-scale resource sharing, innovative applications, and, in some cases, high-performance orientation [2]. The sharing that we are concerned with is not primarily file exchange but rather direct access to computers, software, data, and other resources, as is required by a range of collaborative problem-solving and resource brokering strategies emerging in industry, science, and engineering. The shared resources are autonomous, distributed, heterogeneous and dynamic. At the present time, there are at least two available pieces of grid middleware, such as Globus [3] from Argonne National Laboratory, and Legion [4] from University of Virginia. The Globus adopts OGSA [5] architecture. There are many successful

M. Li et al. (Eds.): GCC 2003, LNCS 3032, pp. 51–58, 2004.

applications based on the Globus, such as Cactus, OVERFLOW-D2, X-ray CMT, SFExpress, MM5, and Nimrod [6]. The Legion uses the object-oriented technology [9]. There exist many successful applications based on the Legion, such as NAS, DSMC, and NPACI [7].

Although grid computing achieved great successes in many fields, it still needs to be improved in some aspects. That is due to the facts:

1. The emergence of standards in grid technologies needs more scientists' efforts in various fields. Their efforts make grid technology meet the requirements in these fields.
2. The gap between currently deployed grid services and the would-be user community has been largely stretched.

2 VGrid Framework

VGrid locates between grid middleware (such as Globus and Legion) and engineering applications as shown in Figure 1. It provides an integrated development environment, abstracts basic grid services (such as authorization, authentication, MDS, GRAM, GASS, and etc.) empowered by grid middleware, and provides high level VGrid services oriented to engineering applications. Using VGrid services through their APIs, applications can be developed and deployed more efficiently under grid computing environment. VGrid framework consists of client component, application middleware component and server component, as shown in Figure 2.

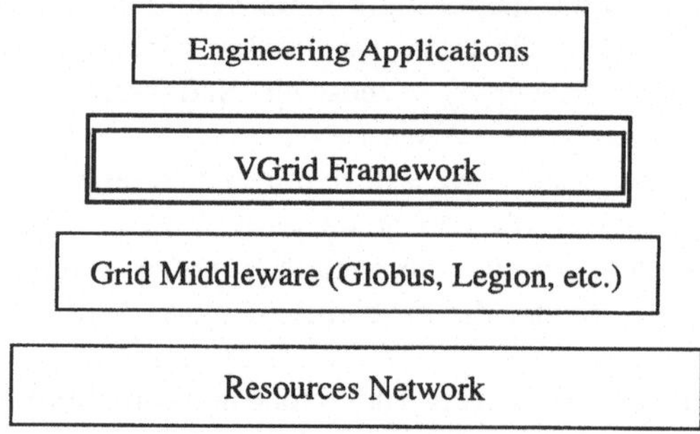

Fig. 1. Location of VGrid in the grid environment

The client component is a portal of VGrid and provides a graphical user interface for development and execution of grid-based applications. It comprises a VGrid system manager, a services manager, an application development environment, a task manager and a result manager.

Application middleware component is actually a hierarchical services pool. All services in the pool are based on the Grid Security Infrastructure supplied by the Globus Toolkit. Taking consideration of resources security, the using of each service must base on a success of authentication and authorization.

Server component is composed of distributed resources manager in the virtual organizations. This resources manager communicates with local hosts through the network. They provide resources such as computer power, storage, software, data, and visualization devices.

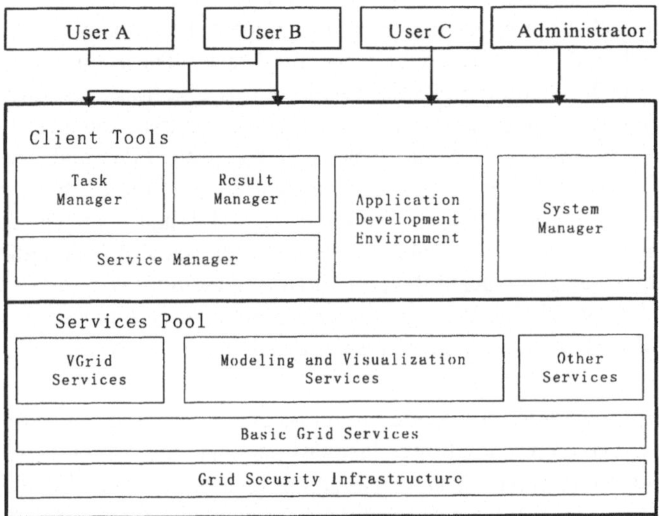

Fig. 2. VGrid architecture

In order to satisfy different requirements, VGrid users are classified into three levels,that is User A, User B, and User C, according to their motivation. User A has some developed application programs, but does not know about grid technologies. He only wants to find out proper resources to execute his programs. User B also has some developed application programs, and has some acquaintance with grid technologies and utilization of the grid-based distributed resources. He wants to choose the proper resources to deploy his programs and to monitor the processes of submission, execution and result processing. User C wants to develop applications in the grid or to upgrade an existing program to make it fit with the grid environment. He is very familiar with grid technologies, and wants to take full advantage of grid services to develop and to deploy his applications in order to utilize use resources more efficiently.

VGrid provides three type services VS (VGrid services), GS (grid services), and MVS (geometry modeling and visualization services):

1. **GS:** Provided by the Globus Toolkit, it includes MDS (Metacomputing Directory Service), GRAM (Globus Resource Allocation Manager), and GridFTP [8].
2. **VS**: It includes virtual organization register, user manager, resource information services, task definition, task import and export, task submission, task scheduling, task monitor, and file transfer. A VGrid user can accomplish resources discovering, information transfer and task running by using these services in a visual fashion.
3. **MVS**: It is oriented to engineering computation and scientific visualization. It includes geometry modeling, geometry meshing, data format conversion, local visualization, remote visualization, and distributed visualization.

3 Implementation of VGrid Framework

3.1 Visual Resources Discovery in the VGrid

The execution of a computing task needs a lot of resources. The resources are distributed, dynamic and autonomous in a grid environment. How many resources are available? Which should be allocated to a specified task? These questions must be answered during task scheduling. To answer these two questions, resources information services provide two interfaces, a hierarchical resources tree, and a resources list. The content of this tree is detailed information of the hosts in virtual organizations, to which the local host registered. It also shows the architecture of those virtual organizations. Each item in the list is information of an individual host. The information on the list can be customized for display. Generally it consists of host name, node count, CPU count, speed and free percentage of CPU, free memory size, free secondary storage, network bandwidth and latency. A user can get enough information from this tree and the list for task schedule. The resources a task needs can be allocated through this interface.

In the VGrid, resources are divided into two classes, computing power and visualization devices. The computing power includes personal computers, PC clusters, workstations and supercomputers. The visualization devices are special distributed display devices, and are used to display high fidelity images and sophisticated graphical results of engineering computations.

VGrid adopts object-oriented technology to describe resources. Each attribute item in a resource object is stored by a couple of value as <attribute, value>. All information in a virtual organization is encapsulated as <node_id, res_info>, where the "node_id" is a host name or IP address of the host, and the "res_info" is an instance of class "MdsResult", which is used to describe the information of a resource in detail.

3.2 Definition of a VGrid Task and Dynamic Resource Allocation

A session for each user is defined in the VGrid. The session is created when one logs in, and destroyed after one logs out. In the session, a user defines computation task, possesses resources, monitors task execution, collects results, and does post-process for the results. In the VGrid, the session is described as a SCB (session control block), which includes user information, identification of the user for each task.

The VGrid provides a graphical user interface as depicted in Figure 3, to input a new task or to update an existing task. The data include executable program, resources requirements, and schedule requirements. When VGrid accepts the data, an instance of task class is initialized and added to logical resources allocation queue. The task's state is initialized to value "WAITING". The C++ definition of VGrid task class is defined as follows:

```
class VTask{
  public:
    enum TaskType { Single = 0, Mpi = 1,
                    Multiple = 2 };
    enum TaskStyle { CpuBusy = 0, IOBusy = 1};
    enum TaskState { Scheduling = 0, Scheduled= 1,
                     Finished = 2 };
    enum InTaskQueue { ScheduleQueue = 0,
                       SubmitedQueue = 1,
                       FinishedQueue = 2 };
  private:
    struct Sid          sessionid;
    Qstring             taskname;
    Qstring             jobidstring;
    struct JobRsl       jobrslstring;
    TaskState           taskstate;
    struct TaskQueue    taskqueue;
    struct QTime        starttime;
    QString             finishtime;
    int                 priority;
    QString             jobcontact;
    ...
};
```

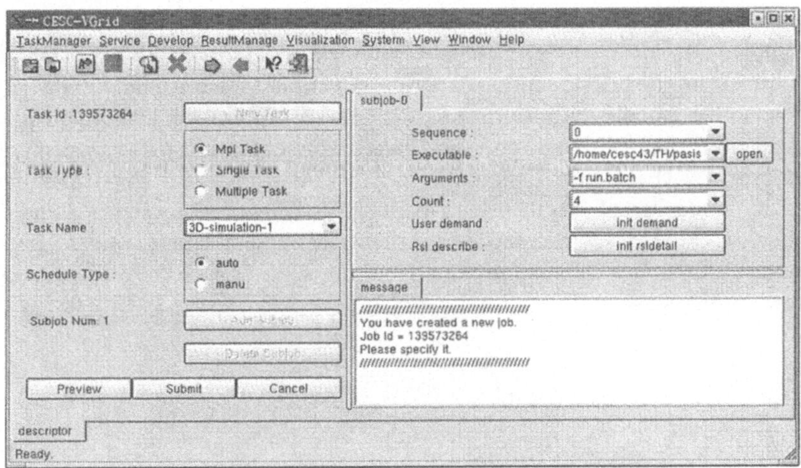

Fig. 3. A snapshot of defining a task in the VGrid

The dynamic resource allocation includes two steps, that is logical resources allocation and physical resources allocation. During the logical resources allocation, tasks in the queue possess logical resources by the FIFO algorithm. Logical resource is a type of virtual resource defined by the VGrid. It includes resource name, node count, and CPU count. The physical resources are not allocated until the task is scheduled to execute, because resources in the grid are dynamic. The performance of VGrid can be improved by introducing the concept of logical resource. The next step of this phase is task schedule, which maps logical resources to physical resources. A task is added to ASQ (Auto Schedule Queue) or ISQ (Interactive Schedule Queue), according to its attribute of schedule control after logical resources allocation. Tasks in ASQ will be scheduled automatically. But tasks in ISQ should be scheduled manually, that is, a user can filter and select resources from available list manually as he needs in a graphical interface.

After the task gets enough resources, its state is changed to "READY", then it will be add to EQ (execute queue). Tasks in the EQ state are actual executable jobs and will be submitted using the FIFO algorithm by VGrid executor, which is a daemon named Vexecutor.

4 Engineering Computational Applications with the VGrid

Engineering sciences (such as solid mechanics, fluid mechanics, and thermodynamics) and most physical sciences allow physical systems to be described in a form of Partial Differential Equations (PDE). Due to their complexities, most of these equations could not be solved analytically. With the advances of computer technology, numerical methods become preferred. Finite Element Method (FEM) is a popular approach among these methods. The method, coupled with the development in computer technology, has been successfully applied to the solution of these problems in a nonlinear manner for all spatial domains.

The process of FEM analysis includes three steps: 1) discretization of the domain, which transforms the PDEs into algebraic equations; 2) formulating the algebraic equations to the global equilibrium equations; and 3) solving the algebraic equations. In this section, two use cases of VGrid-based applications are to be presented. The first case is a 2-D numerical simulation for a safe factor of a slope under its self-weight in geotechnical engineering. Four grid computation nodes (single CPU, 2.0GHz) are utilized for the pre-process, computing, and post-process during the simulation. It takes 7.6 seconds in the computing stage. The results of the simulation are shown in Figure 4.

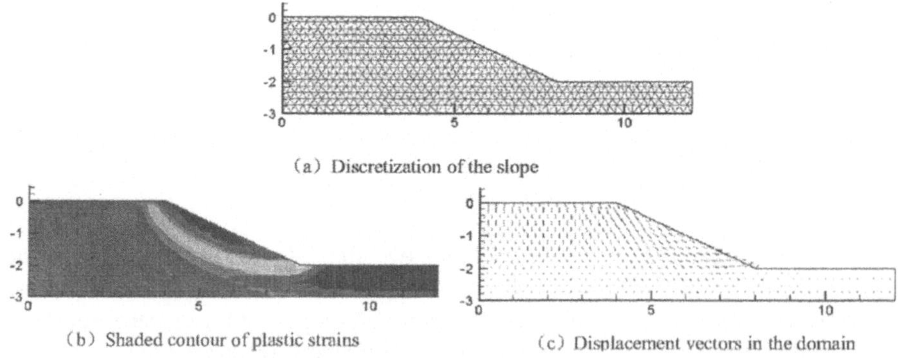

Fig. 4. The simulation results of the first case

The second case is a 3-D numerical simulation of the deformation of a mechanical device under a surface pressure. It is more intricate than the first case. To test the speedup and scalability, the VGrid runs the simulation program with the same parameters for two times using different number of computational nodes networked with 100M bandwidth. The types of the computation resources used and the time consumed in this case are shown in Table 1, the results of the simulation are shown in Figure 5.

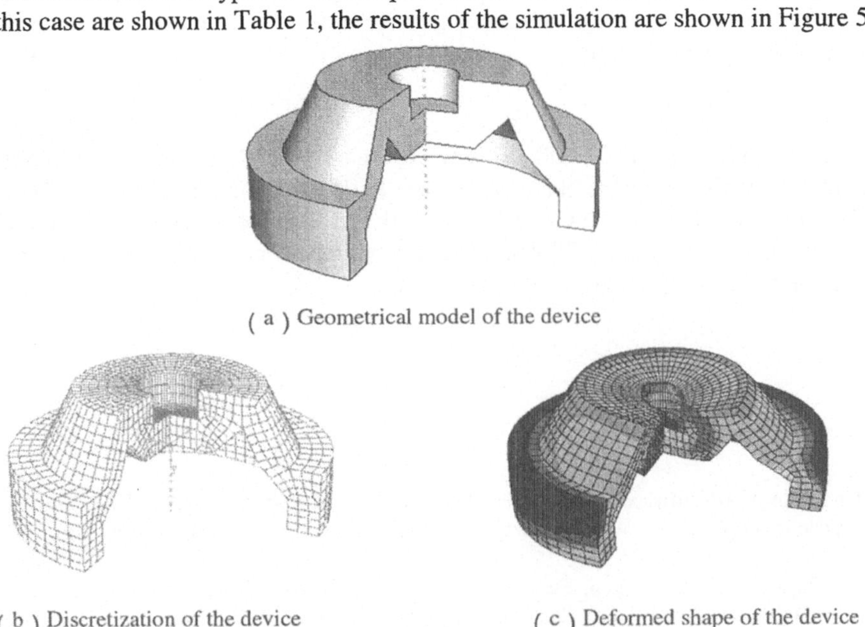

(a) Geometrical model of the device

(b) Discretization of the device

(c) Deformed shape of the device

Fig. 5. The simulation results of the second case

Table 1. Used computation resources and consumed time of the second case

Runs	Types of Machines	Nodes	Time Consumed
1	Intel Pentium IV PCs (P4 2.0G Hz)	3	87.3 sec
	Intel Pentium IV PCs (P4 1.8G Hz)	1	
2	Intel Pentium IV PCs (P4 2.0G Hz)	6	61.4 sec
	Intel Pentium IV PCs (P4 1.8G Hz)	2	

5 Conclusions

An ideal application oriented grid computing framework should have a friendly user interface, and provide a virtual computing environment composed of many heterogeneous resources. Users are enabled to develop and to deploy applications easily with the computing power, provided in the grid environment, just like using a supercomputer. The VGrid supplies the users with a graphical grid-enabled application development and deployment environment for engineering computation. It hides detailed complex processes of grid middleware. Users are able to use all kind of resources in the virtual organizations transparently. The VGrid improves the efficiency of development and speed up the execution of engineering applications in grid computing environment by using VGrid services. Therefore, it is an efficient environment for engineering computation.

Acknowledgements. The authors wish to thank the National Natural Science Foundation of China for the National Science Fund for Distinguished Young Scholars under grant Number 60225009. We would like to thank the Center for Engineering and Scientific Computation, Zhejiang University, for its computational resources, with which the research project has been carried out.

References

1. Gabrielle Allen, Edward Seidei, John Shalf: Scientific Computing on the Grid: Tomorrow's Dynamic Applications Will Require Computational Grids, *Scientific Computing*, Springer, 2002
2. Ian Foster, Carl Kesselman, Steven Tuecke: The Anatomy of the Grid: Enabling Scalable Virtual Organizations, *Int. J. Supercomputing Applications*, 2001, 15(3)
3. I. Foster, and C. Kesselman (eds.): The Grid: Blueprint for a New Computing Infrastructure, Morgan Kaufmann, 1999
4. Anh Nyguyen-Tuong, Steve Chapin, Andrew Grimshaw, Charlie Viles: Using Reflection for Flexibility and Extensibility in a Metacomputing Environment, *Technical Report CS-98-33*, Department of Computer Science, University of Virginia, 1998
5. J. Nick, I. Foster, C. Kesselman and S. Tuecke: The Physiology of the Grid: An Open Grid Services Architecture for Distributed Systems Integration, *Open Grid Service Infrastructure WG*, Global Grid Forum, 2002
6. Globus Alliance, URL: http://www.globus.org/research/applications/default.asp (Current September 14, 2003)
7. Legion: A Worldwide Virtual Computer, URL: http://legion.virginia.edu/overview.html (Current September 14, 2003)
8. I. Foster, J. Insley, G. von Laszewski, C. Kesselman, and M. Thiebaux: Distance Visualization: Data Exploration on the Grid, *Computer*, 32(12): 36-43, 1999
9. Andrew S. Grimshaw, Michael J. Lewis, Adam J. Ferrari, John F. Karpovich: Architectural Support for Extensibility and Autonomy in Wide-Area Distributed Object Systems1, *Technical Report CS-98-12,* June 3, 1998

Interaction Compatibility: An Essential Ingredient for Service Composition

Jun Han

School of Information Technology
Swinburne University of Technology
John Street, Hawthorn, Vic. 3122, Australia
jhan@it.swin.edu.au

Abstract. Common to Grid services, Web Services, software agents and software components is that they are independently built and provide services aimed for composition. A key issue is whether or not the services in a composite system can interact with each other ``sensibly'' and as orchestrated by the enclosing composition. In this paper, we introduce an approach where we can specify individual services' interaction intentions, and check their compatibility in a composite system. We discuss the use of the approach, the specification language, and the compatibility checking tool in the context of software components. They are equally applicable to other service frameworks mentioned above.

1 Introduction

In recent years there has been great interest in service-oriented systems. These include systems built from Grid services, Web services, software agents or software components. The key driving force behind all these efforts is the potential to deliver systems with resource sharing/reuse, higher quality, lower cost and shorter time-to-market. This potential rests on the ability of assembling composite systems from independently developed services.

While having their own specific issues to address, the above mentioned service frameworks share many common features and challenges. One of the key challenges is how to ensure that the services used in a system can work together effectively to achieve the system goals. In particular, there are two specific issues of concern:

1. Are services are compatible with each other when they interact in the composite system?
2. How to ensure that the services work collaboratively towards the overall system goals.

The first issue is about whether or not the interacting services inherently satisfy (i.e., are *compatible* with) each other in terms of functionality, interaction and quality of service. The second issue is about how to *coordinate* the various services to meet the system requirements. The two issues are inter-related. This paper concerns the first issue, *service compatibility*.

M. Li et al. (Eds.): GCC 2003, LNCS 3032, pp. 59–66, 2004.

Without compatibility, the services involved in a composite system can not work together properly (if at all), not to mention achieving system goals. In general, services play provider and consumer roles relative to each other in the composite system. Compatibility exists at different levels. First, the service providers should have the *functionality* that the service consumers require. This requires that the corresponding required and provided services "match" syntactically and semantically. Second, a service provider usually requires and provides a number of operations and has a particular intention implemented in regards to how the operations interleave to effect the services it provides. We refer to the intended (partial) order of operation invocations (or events) as the service's *interaction protocols*. The interaction protocols of related service providers and consumers should also match. Third, a service consumer may demand a service provider to guarantee certain qualities in providing a service while the provider requires the consumer to satisfy certain obligations. For example, a tax lodgement service (as a service consumer) may require that the tax calculation service (as a service provider) to encrypt the tax calculation results while the calculation service requires the lodgement service to encrypt the tax return data in the first place. The *quality of service* may concern security, reliability, performance, etc. In general, service compatibility at all levels is essential. This paper is particularly concerned with compatibility in service interaction protocols.

To facilitate interaction compatibility, we need to be able (1) to specify clearly the interaction intentions of individual services -- *specification*, (2) to check statically at assembly/composition time the compatibility of the related services' interaction protocols -- *verification*, and (3) to check dynamically at run-time that the actual service interactions conform to the interaction protocols -- *validation*. In this paper, we introduce a notation for specifying service interaction protocols and a validation tool for checking run-time conformance of service interactions against predefined protocols, using the CORBA object platform as an example service framework. They can be equally applied to other service frameworks. The specification of interaction protocols takes the form of temporal constraints, and the run-time validation is fully automatic.

The paper is organized as follows. Section 2 examines the requirements for interaction compatibility in service composition. Section 3 introduces our approach to interaction compatibility, including the specification and run-time validation of service interactions. The service interaction protocols are specified as temporal constraints. The run-time validation involves the interception of service interactions, the FSM-based internal representation of temporal constraints, and the conformance checking of service interactions against the temporal constraints. Section 4 discusses related work before section 5 summarises the key contributions and future directions.

2 Requirements for Interaction Compatibility

Service-oriented computing involves (1) independently developed services and (2) compositions of these services to form systems of specific purposes. The services used in a given composite system interact with each other to achieve system goals. It is important that the services used in the system are compatible with each other. To gain proper understanding of the services and facilitate system composition, the commonly adopted approach is to publish or specify the externally observable properties of the services in their interfaces and check their compatibility in the context of a given composite system. In general, the interface properties of a service should include those about its functionality, interaction and quality. Only through the publication, understanding and checking of these properties can a service be possibly used properly, especially in the context of dynamic composition.

The existing models for service interface specification, such as those of CORBA, EJB, COM/.NET and WSDL, have mainly focused on specifying the syntax and types of service operations. More recently, we have seen increased interest in interface specification and checking for interaction and quality properties of services.

In the context of a composite system, the interaction compatibility between the services involved is critical to the proper functioning of the system. Even if the services provide each other with expected functionality and quality of service, the system may still not function as required. For example, an on-line auction system may involve three types of services: the auctioneer service, the bidder service, and the banking service. A bidder interacts with the auctioneer to bid for items on sale, and both the auctioneer and the bidders interact with the banking service to open accounts and settle financial transactions. The banking service naturally requires that an account be set up before any operations on the account. The auctioneer service requires that a bidder first register with the auctioneer, including the account details as opened with the banking service, before accepting any of its bids. Furthermore, the auctioneer checks with the banking service that a bidder has sufficient fund in its nominated account before acknowledging a bid. While having the functionality of lodging bids, the bidder service may or may not be able to conform to the auctioneer's requirements of registration and sufficient fund. If not, the auctioneer and the bidder services are not compatible, which will result in system error or even system failure.

The above example has clearly shown that

1. the interaction protocols or the partial ordering of operations that a service assumes and implements need to be clearly specified for understanding and use at the time of service composition --- *specification*;
2. at the time of composition (static or dynamic), the compatibility between the interaction protocols of the related services needs to be checked to avoid system error and failure --- *verification*;
3. after service composition, tests can be further conducted to validate the actual service interactions against the relevant protocol specifications --- *validation*.

To provide practical support for service composition, a simple specification notation and automatic verification and validation tools are required for specifying and checking service interaction protocols.

3 An Approach to Interaction Compatibility

In this section, we introduce an approach to the specification and compatibility checking of service interaction protocols. We illustrate its use regarding interaction specification and validation in the context of software components with CORBA as the service platform (see [8] and [9] for further details). The approach is equally applicable to other service frameworks like Web services and Grid services.

3.1 Specifying Service Interactions

Realising the limitations of current commercial approaches to service interface definition, we have proposed a comprehensive framework for rich interface definition in the context of software components in [7]. It deals with service functionality, interaction and quality. In this paper, we focus on the issue of component interaction protocols and their compatibility. In specifying the interaction protocols of a component, we have adopted a temporal logic based approach, where we use well-known temporal operators to define the temporal relationships between operation invocations. As such, the interaction protocols of a component are defined as a set of *temporal constraints*.

A temporal relationship between operation invocations is expressed in terms of the relative order between them. In general, the definition of a temporal constraint takes the following form

action tr action;

where *action* can be an operation, an event, a get or set operation on an attribute, or the creation of a component; *tr* is a temporal operator identifying the temporal relationship between the actions concerned. Some of the temporal operators are `PRECEDES`, `BEFORE`, `LEADSTO`, `PAIRWISEBEFORE` and `PAIRWISELEADSTO`.

In incorporating interaction constraints into CORBA, we have chosen to define interaction constraints separately from existing CORBA interface definitions for simplicity. For each CORBA interface definition, we have a `COMPONENT` definition containing all the constraints on the corresponding type of objects. Figure1 shows a component definition for `Auctioneer`. The `Auctioneer` provides the `register` and `bid` operations, and requires an `acknowledge` operation from the `Bidder` components and an `enoughFund` operation from the `Bank` component. The `Auctioneer` interface/component has three interaction constraints. The first constraint states that for a given bidder, the `register` operation should be invoked before any of the other operations (and not after them). The second constraint states that a `bid` must be immediately followed by a call to the `bank's enoughFund` operation to check if there is sufficient fund. The third constraint states that each bid invocation must lead to an acknowledge operation on the bidder.

3.2 Validating Service Interactions

Explicit specification of component interaction constraints helps the component developer and user to implement and use a component properly. Whether or not the component services are *actually* used properly at run-time is a different question. Validation or testing is often required. In this regard, we have implemented a validation tool for checking the run-time interactions of a component against its defined interaction constraints. The tool RIDLMON (Rich IDL Monitor) adopts a *monitoring* approach, and achieves protocol validation by

- translating the constraint specifications into extended finite state machines (eFSMs) that serve as the constraints' internal representation in the monitoring tool for easy processing;
- identifying and intercepting the run-time interactions needed for validation;
- checking the intercepted interactions against the constraints' internal representation, and reporting violations (if any).

RIDLMON is written entirely in Java using JDK 1.4 for the CORBA product ORBacus 4.0.5. For the purpose of intercepting run-time interactions between components, we have used CORBA portable interceptors [11].

```
COMPONENT Auctioneer {
  register(bidder) BEFORE
           (bid(bidder, ...),
            bidder.acknowledge (...),
            bank.enoughFund(bidder, ...));
  bid(bidder, ...) PRECEDES
            bank.enoughFund(bidder, ...);
  bid(bidder, ...) PAIRWISELEADSTO
            bider.acknowledge(...);
};
```

Fig. 1. Interaction constraints for `Auctioneer`

Constraint Representation. The use of temporal constraints in specifying component interaction protocols has proved to be *intuitive* and *incremental*, and is well suited to the needs of system designers [8]. However, they are not easy to use in the run-time automatic checking of interaction constraints. As such, we choose to use an extended form of finite state machines (eFSMs) as the internal representation of temporal constraints. In general, each binary temporal relationship (operator) has a corresponding eFSM representation. In particular, `PAIRWISEBEFORE` and `PAIRWISELEADSTO` require the extended form of FSM as they need explicit assertion checking at certain state transitions. For example, Figure 2 presents the eFSM representation of "`A PAIRWISELEADSTO B`", where `O` stands for any operation other than `A` or `B`. Note that the matching process discards the excessive `B`'s in every maximal sub-sequence starting with `A` and ending with `B` or `O`, by setting the number of `B`'s to the number of `A`'s minus one at the reset point. At the end, the number of `A`'s must be less than or equal to the number of `B`'s.

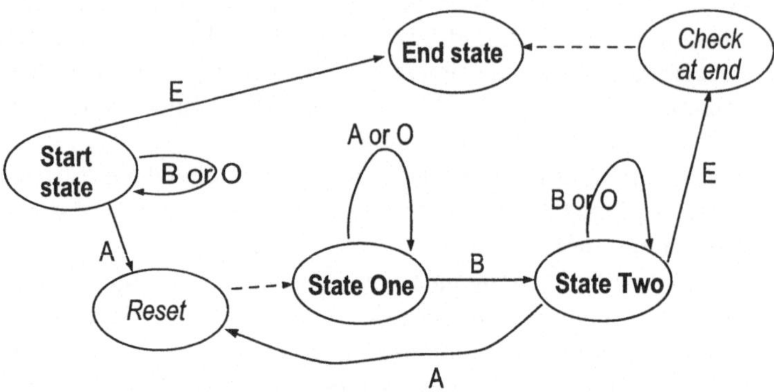

Fig. 2. eFSM representation of "`A PAIRWISELEADSTO B`"

Violation Checking. As discussed above, the interaction constraints are internally represented as eFSMs in RIDLMON. When a component is created, the relevant eFSMs for it are initialised. When an operation invocation is captured by the interceptors attached to the component, it is forwarded to RIDLMON to advance the eFSMs. In advancing the eFSMs, violations to the constraints can be determined. In general, a constraint violation occurs when one of the following situations is present:

- *The captured operation or event does not represent a valid transition of an eFSM.* For example, `B` is received at the start of the `BEFORE` machine.
- *The captured operation or event causes a matching process to fail.* For instance, the number of `A`'s is more than the number of `B`'s when `PAIRWISELEADSTO` machine transits to the "`End state`" (see Figure 2). This is applicable only to liveness constraints like `PAIRWISEBEFORE` and `PAIRWISELEADSTO`. These liveness constraints can only be fully checked at the end of interactions.

We note that an operation invocation is usually relevant to two components: the caller (as outgoing call) and the callee (as incoming call). Therefore, it can be captured at multiple intercepting points as actions of different components. This is so, because our approach to monitoring is component specific and at a given moment the monitoring may focus on only the component at one end and not the component at the other end.

4 Related Work

There have been a number of other efforts in introducing interaction protocols into component interface descriptions. These include the use of finite state machines [16], process algebras [5, 2], regular expressions [12], Petri nets [3], description logics [4], and temporal descriptions [10]. These approaches all have their limitations (see [9] for a detailed discussion).

Work in the area of object-based coordination and synchronisation also concerns interactions between objects. But, it takes a prescriptive approach, i.e., enforcing interaction requirements between objects from a system design perspective, instead of checking their compatibility. Typical efforts include composition filters [1] and coordination languages [6, 13].

More recently, there has been much interest in the area of Web service composition, concerning interactions of Web services. Example efforts include the Web Service Choreography Interface (WSCI) [15] and the Business Process Execution Language for Web Services (BPEL4WS) [14]. From the viewpoint of service interaction, these approaches essentially apply existing techniques to the Web service context.

5 Conclusions

The proper use of services in a composite service-based system is critical to the correct functioning of the system. This is particularly so when the services are developed by third parties or different teams, and calls for richer interface description than that allowed by the interface definitions in the current standards such as CORBA IDL and WSDL. In this paper, we have analysed the requirements for interaction compatibility, and introduced an approach to describing and validating the interaction protocols of individual services. The service interaction protocols are described as interaction constraints, using a small set of temporal operators. This allows intuitive and incremental description of interaction protocols, and is easy for practitioners to learn and use. The validation tool RIDLMON monitors the run-time interactions between the services in a composite system, and checks them against the predefined interaction constraints of the services. Any violation to the constraints represents misuse of the relevant services, and can be identified by the validation tool. We note that while our approach has been implemented using the CORBA object platform, it is equally applicable to any other IDL-based service frameworks.

We are currently investigating a number of improvements to our approach and the validation tool RIDLMON. One issue is to allow the specification of finer-grained interaction constraints involving operation parameters. Another issue is to deal explicitly with concurrency of components and synchronisation modes of component interactions. Furthermore, we are also investigating static compatibility checking for service interaction protocols at composition-time.

Acknowledgment. I would like to thank Ksze Kae Ker for his effort in implementing the validation tool RIDLMON.

References

1. M. Aksit et al. Abstracting object interactions using composition filters. In *Proceedings of 1993 European Conference on Object-Oriented Programming*, pages 152–184, Kaiserslautern, Germany, July 1993.

2. R. Allen and D. Garlan. A formal basis for architectural connection. *ACM Transactions on Software Engineering and Methodology*, 6(3):213–249, July 1997.
3. R. Bastide, O. Sy, and P. Palanque. Formal specification and prototyping of CORBA systems. In *Proceedings of the 13th European Conference on Object-Oriented Programming*, pages 474–494, Lisbon, Portugal, June 1999.
4. A. Borgida and P. Devanbu. Adding more "DL" to IDL: Towards more knowledgeable component inter-operability. In *Proceedings of the 21th International Conference on Software Engineering*, pages 378–387, Los Angeles, USA, May 1999.
5. C. Canal, E. Pimentel, J.M. Troya, and A. Vallecillo. Extending CORBA interfaces with protocols. *The Computer Journal*, 44(5):448–462, October 2001.
6. S. Frolund and G.A. Agha. A language framework for multi-object coordination.In *Proceedings of 1993 European Conference on Object-Oriented Programming*, pages 346–340, Kaiserslautern, Germany, July 1993.
7. J. Han. A comprehensive interface definition framework for software components. In *Proceedings of the 1998 Asia-Pacific Software Engineering Conference*, pages 110–117, Taipei, Taiwan, December 1998. IEEE Computer Society.
8. J. Han. Temporal logic based specification of component interaction protocols. In *Object Interoperability : ECOOP'2000 Workshop on Object Interoperability*, pages 43–52, Sophia Antipolis, France, June 2000.
9. J. Han and K.K. Ker. Ensuring compatible interactions within component-based software systems. In *Proceedings of the 2003 Asia-Pacific Software Engineering Conference*, Chiangmai, Thailand, December 2003. IEEE Computer Society. To appear (10 pages).
10. X. Logean. *Run-time Monitoring and On-line Testing of Middleware Based Communication Services*. PhD thesis, Ecole Polytechnique Federale De Lausanne (Lausanne EPFL), 2000.
11. OMG. Portable interceptors. ftp://ftp.omg.org/pub/docs/orbos/99-12-02.pdf, December 1999.
12. F. Plasil and W. Visnovsky. Behaviour protocols for software components. *IEEE Transactions on Software Engineering*, 28(11):1056–1076, November 2002.
13. S. Ren and G.A. Agha. RTsynchronizer: Language support for real-time specifications in distributed systems. In *Proceedings of ACM SIGPLAN Workshop on Languages, Compilers, and Tools for Real-Time Systems*, pages 50–59, La Jolla, CA, USA, June 1995.
14. The BPEL4WS Team. Business Process Execution Language for Web Service (BPEL4WS). Project report, www-106.ibm/developerworks/library/ws-bpel/, May 2003.
15. The WSCI Team. Web Service Choreography Interface (WSCI) 1.0. Technical report, W3C, August 2002.
16. D.M. Yellin and R.E. Strom. Protocol specifications and component adaptors. *ACM Transactions on Programming Languages and Systems*, 19(2):292–333, March 1997.

A Distributed Media Service System Based on Globus Data-Management Technologies[1]

Xiang Yu, Shoubao Yang, and Yu Hong

Dept. of Computer Science,
University of Science and Technology of China, Hefei 230026, PR, China
xyu4@mail.ustc.edu.cn, syang@ustc.edu.cn

Abstract. Recently, emerging high performance applications require the ability to exploit diverse, geographically distributed resources, specifically, in a Grid environment. A collection of software, called the Globus grid toolkit, is developed to address related drawbacks. In this paper, we describe an application (we call it Distributed Media Service System, DMSS for short) developed in this toolkit: we present the features and physical infrastructure of the goal system, the effectiveness of the toolkit approach, our heuristic enhancements, and draw a conclusion regarding future work.

1 Introduction

Grid technology is deemed a critical element of future high performance computing environments that will enable entirely new classes of applications. We devised a media service system, called DMSS here, with the very prevalent Globus[1] toolkit. Basically, our DMSS system harnesses data management in the Globus toolkit, which enables various operations on files, namely, registration, publication, deletion, copy, inquiry, remote access, data transfer, security protection, etc, and effectively utilizes resources, avoiding the bottleneck caused by multiple users linked together in traditional central media service systems. The organization of this paper is as follows. In the next section, we describe the physical architecture and system functionalities of our DMSS. In section 3, we introduce the major technical supports from Globus. This is followed up by section 4, where we give a detailed explanation on the five modules of DMSS system. A brief conclusion and future work is presented in the remainder of this paper.

1 This paper is supported by the National Natural Science Foundation of China (Contract No. 60273041) and the National '863' High-Tech Program of China (Contract No. 2002AA104560).

M. Li et al. (Eds.): GCC 2003, LNCS 3032, pp. 67–74, 2004.

2 Physical Structure and Functionalities of DMSS

2.1 Physical Structure

Our DMSS system, a virtual organization, consists of a server and a host of nodes. The server's main duties are providing users with access to the DMSS system, and enabling them to publish, access and maintain data files. Each node stores some data files or offers logical management of Replica catalogs, and its location is distributed geographically. As per figure 1, host Pi (i=1,2......) beyond the dotted lines of each area does not belong to the effective member node set of the system (or rather, the DMSS virtual organization) . Take area 4 for example, nodes N1 and N2 are member nodes of the system, while hosts P1, P2 and P3 have no membership. However, P1, P2 and P3 can be members of other VOs. That is to say, if area 4 is a VO, then nodes N1 and N2 are the member nodes of not only the DMSS system, but also VO area 4, but P1, P2, and P3 are member nodes of only the VO area 4.

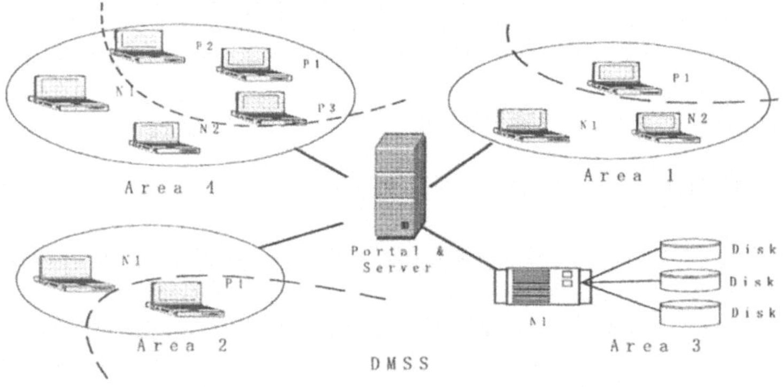

Fig. 1. Physical structure of DMSS system

Theoretically, any node can enter or quit the system randomly, which guarantees the scalability of the DMSS system. Illustrated below is the membership procedure of a host entering the DMSS system:

The node first obtains an effective certificate, whose publisher is a credential of DMSS system, so as to authenticate its legal identity.

Then, the node registers to the DMSS server, declaring that it wants to become a member of the VO, offering its remaining disk space or Replica catalogue service.

2.2 Functionalities

The DMSS system fully utilizes remaining resources in network, via the following:

1, Replica catalogs logically manage distributed media files. There are two sorts of nodes:

- A node has its own Replica catalog.
- A node can store files only, has no Replica catalog, so that its files are managed logically by Replica catalogs of other nodes.

2, When the user connects to the server, the server calls access function, and returns to the user the nearest download location of the file in question, or else, redirects the user to a nearest node, where the user directly gets the media service.

3, System evaluates the latency and checks if it has surpassed limitation. If so, the system searches for an effective node nearest to the user and stores a copy of the file. Next time, this very user or others near him would get faster service if they access the same file.

4, System is maintained periodically, deleting redundant replicas for optimal disk utilization.

3 Basic Globus Services Used in DMSS

We harness various Globus services in our implementation, specifically, MDS, Replica, GSI, GridFtp, GASS and GRAM[1-6], which are only basic services, therefore, we combine with them our original access selection algorithm plus the strategy of event-recording and redundancy maintenance.

MDS (Metacomputing Directory Service)[2] integrates LDAP (Lightweight Directory Access Protocol)[3] to construct its own schema and store static and dynamic information of Grid internal entities, then establishes a uniform namespace. We offer three MDS functions: 1) a unique global name for nodes 2) registration of legal member nodes 3) obtains host name, IP address and the volume of available disk space of effective nodes.

Replica Catalogs offer services like registration, publication, deletion, copy and facilitates relevant publication, mutual information access between entities, and the distribution of information resources and information services[4]. In our DMSS system, Replica serves these purposes: catalog creation, logical file management, file publication and file access.

GridFtp provides secure and effective data transfer[5]. In DMSS system, GridFtp provides three services: file upload, file download and physical storage of replicas.

GSI (Globus Security Infrastructure) locates resources with X.509 certificate information provided by MDS service[6] together with RSA encryption algorithm, to achieve mutual authentication between user and resources.

GRAM (Globus Resource Allocation Manager) handles resource requests, executes remote applications, allocates resources and manages system actions, computes and transmits information of resource updates to MDS. In DMSS, GRAM plays two roles via commands on the server's remote node: obtain latency by ping command and delete redundant copies by rm command.

GASS (Global Access to Secondary Storage) services, which interoperates with other Globus modules, mainly addresses the remote I/O problem in a Grid system.

4 DMSS System Architecture – The Five Modules

We assume that each node owns legal identity and credential, and is member node of the DMSS system to guarantee security for each node and its information access.

As shown in figure 2, the whole system is comprised of five modules: Portal, Replica generation, Replica selection, Event recording, and Replica management.

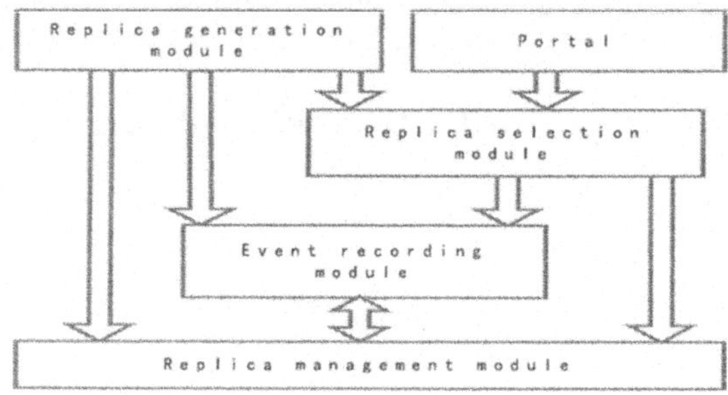

Fig. 2. Architecture of DMSS system

4.1 Portal – Streaming Media Service Entry

It provides users web-interface, and implements the redirection of users to optimized nodes for media services, or returns optimized node for the accessed files. Common Grid users need a GUI (graphic user interface) in grid application, which we call portal. We devised a user interface for implementation of the system, as in figure 3.

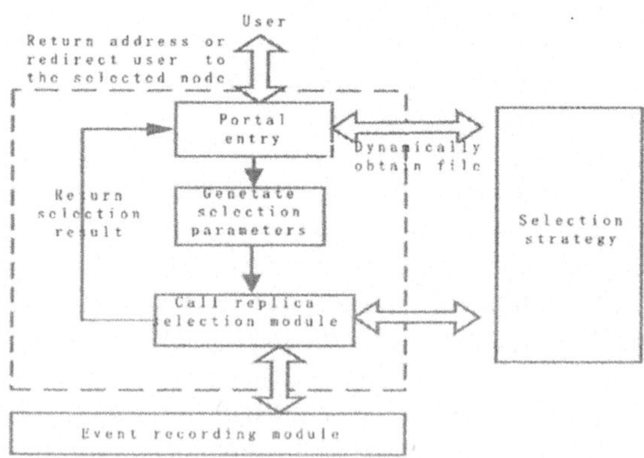

Fig. 3. Flowchart of Portal

JSP (Java Server Pages) and Java Servlet toolkits are adopted to implement the connection of user interface and back-platform. The critical problems are:

The media files are sorted into 3 categories in our DMSS system. Assume the system has got some audio files in storage, they can be categorized as such: catalog name (rc),set name (lc): lc represents the singer's name, file name (lf): lf represents the song's name.

When the user accesses a file, JSP page offers parameter description of accessed files. Then, JSP relays these parameters to Java Servlet, which calls the Replica selection module. The module consults the selection strategy and returns the most effective node address of accessed files.

4.2 Replica Generation Module

Although Globus provides file publication and registration, namely, media file catalogs, media file sets, logical media files and the mapping of logical location to physical location of media files, we must monitor the MDS information service to obtain optimal node for Replica generation, or else choose a node (with adequate physical space for the additional files) as the mapping from the additional logical file to a specific physical address. Replica generation includes replica catalog generation, logical set generation and file publication, as shown in figure 4.

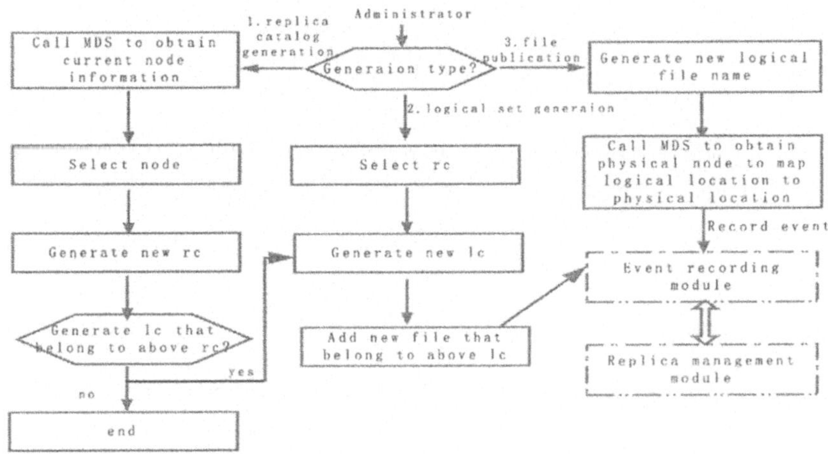

Fig. 4. Flowchart of Replica generation module

1, Replica catalog generation: System calls MDS service for current node information and selects the most suitable node for generating duplicate catalog with the specified heuristic.

2, Logical set generation: Intuitively, a logical set is generated when its parent replica catalog is in existence, then new attributes are added to files in the set.

3, File publication: We come up with two operations in the file addition: 1) generation of logical file, 2) mapping from logical address of the file to its physical address (generation of physical address). However, the Replica generation module doesn't guarantee the atomicity of the two operations, so we devised an Event recording module, which records current events with four different states. An event is in the finishing state only if all its operations are completed. The Event recording module addresses the atomicity problem, which is further examined in ensuing parts. Meanwhile, Replica management module reads information from the Event recording module, and completes the ultimate file addition job. Thus, we just need to select the physical node address of the file in question, and record its original storage address together with its logical address and its physical address in the Event recording module.

4.3 Replica Selection Module

It provides access to media files, selects optimal node for media files, checks the need for redundant replicas, and reports to the Event recording module related information.

Globus Replica catalog service simply accesses object file, however, when there are multiple copies of the file in the system, the module is not capable of selecting the most effective node for file storage. The Replica selection module integrates MDS services with the access-selection heuristic, optimizing its service.

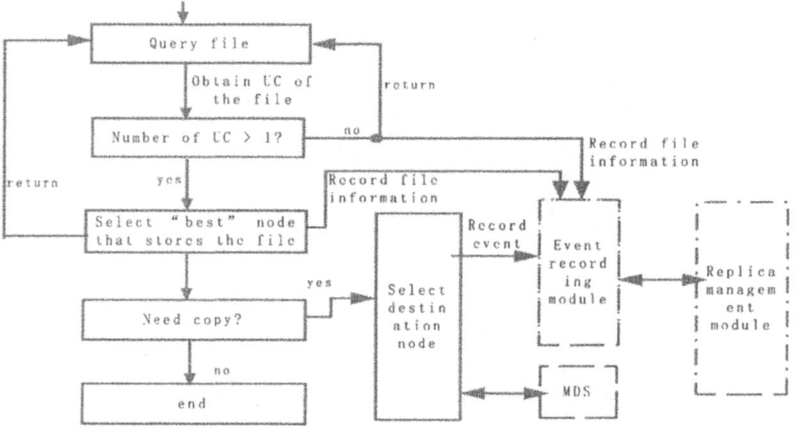

Fig. 5. Flowchart of Replica selection module

As shown in figure 5, when the Replica selection module receives an access request, it locates the file's logical address firstly, and subsequently physical address via the mapping. To speed up service, a file might have one or even multiple copies in the system, so DMSS system switches between two conditions:

When the file is stored in a single node, one uc value is returned, in this case, the system directly returns access results, and the Replica selection module decides whether to make redundant copies.

When the file is stored in multiple nodes, multiple uc values are returned, so the problem of how to select the node which can offer fastest service, is put to the Replica selection module, then, as in the first case the decision of redundant copies.

4.4 Event Recording Module

The essentiality of an event recorder for the DMSS system lies in the following points.

1) Either the file publication or redundancy copy (this is virtually file publication) needs to call the Replica management module.

2) Also, to maintain redundancy rate of system files and optimize disk space, we set a limit to the number of system file copies--a file can have at most one copy on each node in the system.

As shown in figure 6, two tables are maintained by Event management module:

1) Event recording table: records information about files to be published. State description is shown in table 1.

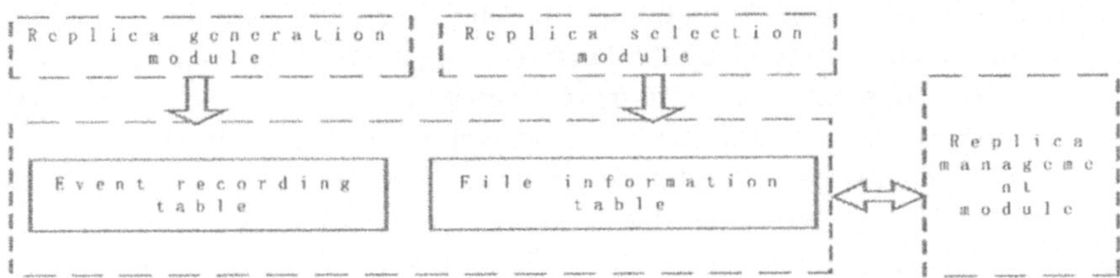

Fig. 6. Flowchart of Event recording module

2) File access information table: records file access information and provides information about the node storing the file, and the number of times each node is accessed in a period.

Table 1. State description

state	State value	Description
1	00	Event not completed
2	01	Event logically copied, but not physically submitted
3	10	Event physically copied, not logically configured
4	11	Event completed, can be deleted from record table

4.5 Replica Management Module

It maintains media files in the Grid, periodically updates file redundancy rate, and optimizes disk space to achieve optimal file storage. Data file maintenance jobs are:

The realistic file publication. When an event is in state 00, Replica management completes the file addition. File addition consists of two steps: Firstly, physical copy; the system modifies the event state to 01 or 10; secondly, logical configuration, event concludes and its state changes to 11.

Maintaining redundancy rate of data. The module reads internal information and periodically deletes redundant replica files in the system, avoiding too many identical replicas and reduces redundancy.

After system starts(timestamp=0), the Replica management module's first redundancy maintenance is after T=T1+T2, during which the module reads information from records of time slices T1 and T2, then maintenance is executed every other T.

5 Conclusion and Future Work

In this paper, we discussed the functionalities and features of a Distributed Media Service System based on Globus data-management; we provided further explanation on the design of its components.

The DMSS system applies the concept of data Grid, providing data files and services in a distributed manner (ubiquitous). In Media services, files are read-only, no consistency problem. Considering the latency brought about by security measures in Globus Grid environment (latency in mutual authentication can reach 7 seconds), we deploy an anonymous file access module. However, latency is inevitable.

In particular, the problem that the system needs file update as well as information pre-extraction of newly published files, is expected to be addressed in future work, by employing the up-to-date techniques---actively search and retrieve and then automatically publish files on the Internet.

References

1. Ian Foster, Carl Kesselman: The Globus Project: A Status Report. In Proc. Heterogeneous Computing Workshop, pages 4-18. IEEE Computer Society Press, 1998
2. MDS 2.1: Creating a Hierarchical GIIS, Available from http://www.globus.org/mds
3. Henze Johner, Larry Brown: Understanding LDAP. Available from http://www.redbooks.ibm.com
4. Byoungdai Lee, Jon B.Weissman: Dynamic Replica Management in the Service Grid. Available from http://www-users.cs.umn.edu/~jon/papers/hpdc_sg.pdf
5. W. Allcock, J. Bester, J. Bresnahan, A. Chervenak, I. Foster, C. Kesselman, S. Meder, V. Nefedova, D. Quesnel, and S. Tuecke: Data Management and Transfer in High-Performance Computational Grid Environments. Parallel Computing, 2001.
6. Ian Foster, Carl Kesselman, Gene Tsudik: "A Security Architecture for Computational Grids" 37-46 Electronic Edition(IEEE Computer Society DL), 2002.

Load Balancing between Heterogeneous Computing Clusters

Siu-Cheung Chau[1]* and Ada Wai-Chee Fu[2]

[1] Dept. of Physics and Computer Science, Wilfrid Laurier University, Waterloo, Ontario, Canada, N2L 3C5

[2] Dept. of Computer Science and Engineering, Chinese University of Hong Kong, Hong Kong, China

Abstract. More and more organizations have computing clusters located in different places. The distance between the computing clusters can be quite far away and the computing clusters can also differ in size. The load in one cluster may be very high while the other clusters may have nothing running on the system. A higher throughput can be achieved if load balancing is added. In this paper, we propose a simple and efficient load balancing method to balance loads for heterogeneous computing clusters of various sizes that are quite far away from each other. We assume that the computer clusters are connected in the form of a hypercube. We then use the load balancing method for hypercubes to balance the load between heterogeneous computing clusters. After applying the propose method, the maximum load difference between any two computing clusters can be at most one more than the optimal solution.

1 Introduction

In a computing cluster, time critical tasks can be executed quickly by splitting a task into sub-tasks. The sub-tasks are then executed in parallel in different processing nodes of a computing cluster. To maximize the benefit of computing clusters, the tasks assigned to each processing node should be roughly the same. Hence, load balancing is necessary to balance load between the processing nodes within a computing cluster. If an organization has more than one computing clusters and the computing clusters are located in different places, we also want to balance the load between the computing clusters to improve the overall throughput.

An example of such organization is Sharcnet. Sharcnet is a partnership between a number of universities and colleges in Canada. All the members of Sharcnet are located in southwestern Ontario, Canada. Currently, Sharcnet has five members with computing clusters. SHARCNET is structured as a "cluster of clusters".

* This research was supported by a research grant from the National Sciences and Engineering Research Council of Canada

M. Li et al. (Eds.): GCC 2003, LNCS 3032, pp. 75–82, 2004.

Built on the Alpha processors, SHARCNET clusters consist of four-processor, 833Mhz, Alpha SMP (symmetric multi-processors) systems connected via Quadrics interconnection technology. The Alpha SMP are then connected together through Gigabit ethernet. Clusters of 24 SMPs (96 processors) are deployed at McMaster University and 27 SMPs (108 processors) are deployed at the University of Guelph. At The University of Western Ontario, there are three clusters, one of 12 SMPs (48 processors), one of 36 SMPs (144 processors) and one of 64 HP processors are deployed. The two SMP clusters are also connected using Nortel's optical DWDM (Dense Wave Division Multiplexing). Smaller development clusters (8 processors) are deployed at the University of Windsor and at Wilfrid Laurier University. Depending on funding from the government, more computing clusters will be added to current member sites and to other universities such as the University of Waterloo, Brock University, and Trent University in the region.

The computing clusters within Sharcnet are quite far away from each other and not all of them are connected through dedicated fibre optic lines. In fact, only two computing clusters within Sharcnet are connected by fibre optics lines. The rest of them are connected through internet access line. For example, the distance between Wilfrid Laurier University and the University of Windsor is almost four hundred kilometers and there is no dedicated communication line between the two locations. Hence, the load balancing method to balance the load between computing clusters should have as few communications as possible.

Each computing cluster within Sharcnet is controlled by a master node that is outside of the cluster. The master node act as the scheduler for the cluster. We assume that the master node of each of the computing cluster are connected as a node of a hypercube. By making this assumption, we can group clusters that are connected directly through a high-speed link in the same sub cube to take advantage of their connections. We can also make use of the topology of a hypercube to reduce the amount of communications during load balancing.

With the above assumption, not only that we can reduce the communication cost, we can also achieve almost optimal load balancing quality between the computers within the computing clusters. To make things slightly simpler, initially, we assume that the computing clusters are homogeneous and each computing cluster is of the same size. We will relax these assumptions later.

A n-dimensional hypercube is a network with $N = 2^n$ nodes. Each node can be coded by a binary sequence of length n. Two nodes are connected if their binary sequences differ in exactly one position. Each node $v = v_1v_2...v_n$ is connected to n nodes. Node v is connected to node $u = u_1u_2...u_n$ if $v_i \neq u_i$ and $v_j = u_j$ for $j \in \{1..n\}$ and $j \neq i$. The link between v and u is also called the link of dimension i.

2 Previously Proposed Load Balancing Schemes for Hypercubes

If we can estimate the execution time of any task accurately and we also know the total number of tasks in advance, we can use a static load balancing method to assign balanced load to each of the processing nodes. Load balancing is not necessary. Unfortunately, there exists a large class of non-uniform problems with uneven and unpredictable computation and communication requirements. For these problems, we have to deal with the load imbalance dynamically.

Many load-balancing algorithms for hypercube have been proposed. Willebeek-Lamair and Reeves [2] showed that Receiver initiated diffusion method always outperforms the Sender initiated diffusion method. Cybenko [1] showed that the diffusion methods[4,5] are inferior to the dimension exchange method in terms of their efficiencies and balance qualities.

For the dimension exchange method (DEM) [7,1,2,3], all node pairs whose addresses differ only in the least significant bit, balance their load between themselves. Similarly, all node pairs whose addresses differ in only the second least significant bit, balance the load between themselves. The above process is repeated until each node has exchanged and balanced its load with its neighbors in all the dimensions. After execution of the DEM, the load difference between any pair of nodes is at most n.

Let w_u be the number of tasks in node u and $\oplus$ be the bitwise exclusive OR operator. Figure 1 shows the DEM algorithm for a hypercube.

DEM

for $k = 0$ to $n - 1$
node u exchange with node v the current value of w_u
and w_v, where $(u \oplus v) \oplus 2^k = 0$
if $(w_u - w_v) > 1$, send $\lfloor (w_u - w_v)/2 \rfloor$ tasks to node v
if $(w_v - w_u) > 1$, receive $\lfloor (w_v - w_u)/2 \rfloor$ tasks from node v
$w_u = \lceil (w_u + w_v)/2 \rceil$ if $w_u > w_v$
$w_u = \lfloor (w_u + w_v)/2 \rfloor$ otherwise

Fig. 1. The DEM algorithm for hypercubes.

The cube walking algorithm (CWA)[3] can balance the load better than the DEM. After applying the CWA to a hypercube, the load difference between any nodes is at most one which is optimal. The number of communication steps in the CWA is the same as DEM. However, CWA requires an additional $nN/2$ messages of size $O(n)$ to send the load information vectors where N is the number of nodes in an n-dimensional hypercube.

3 Improved Dimension Exchange Algorithm for Hypercubes

After the execution of the original DEM, the load difference between any two nodes is bounded by n. We can view the exchange of information and task migration in the least significant dimension of pairs of nodes as dividing the tasks among the two $(n-1)$-cubes roughly equally. However, the difference in the total number of task between the two $(n-1)$-cubes may be as high as $N/2$. This happens when the total number of tasks between every pair of nodes in the same dimension is an odd number and all the nodes in one sub-cube have one more task than the nodes in the other sub-cube.

Similarly, the exchange of load information and task migration in the second least significant dimension can be viewed as dividing tasks roughly equally between the two $(n-2)$-cubes in each of the $(n-1)$-cubes. The difference in the total number of tasks between two $(n-2)$-cubes in a $(n-1)$-cube is bounded by $N/4$. Using the above reasoning, after the execution of the DEM, the maximum load difference between any two nodes is at most n.

The maximum difference can be reduced by $n/2$ if we divide the tasks more carefully between the sub-cubes in the load exchange of each dimension. Consider two neighboring nodes u and v with tasks w_u and w_v. Suppose $(w_u - w_v) > 0$. Instead of simply sending $\lfloor (w_u - w_v)/2 \rfloor$ tasks to node v, we may want to send $\lceil (w_u - w_v)/2 \rceil$ tasks to node v. By having a better scheme on which node should send $\lfloor (w_u - w_v)/2 \rfloor$ tasks or $\lceil (w_u - w_v)/2 \rceil$ tasks to its neighboring nodes, we could get a tighter bound on the maximum task difference. The improved DEM[8] is shown in Figure 2.

Theorem 1. *After applying the improved DEM to an n-dimensional hypercube, the load difference between any two nodes u and v is at most $n/2$.*

From Theorem 1, the improved DEM has a better upper bound in load difference between any two nodes compared to the original DEM. Simulations were also done for both the DEM and the improved DEM for a hypercube from dimension 3 to dimension 12. The load are randomly assigned to each node of a hypercube and DEM or the improved DEM is applied to balance the load. The simulation is repeated 100,000 times. The results are listed in Table 1 and Table 2.

From the data listed in Table 1, after applying the original DEM to a hypercube, the expected load difference between any two nodes is roughly $n/2$. The difference is much lower than the upper bound of n. This can be explained by the fact that the upper bound can only happen for a special case.

From the data in Table 2, after applying the improved DEM, the expected load difference between any two nodes is always less than 2. If the dimension of the hypercube is less than or equal to 12, the maximum load difference for any two nodes is at most 2. This happens because the load in each sub-cube of the hypercube would be roughly the same after one step of load balancing. The load balancing quality of the improved DEM compares favorably with the CWA where the maximum load difference is at most one.

Improved DEM

Let node $u = u_1u_2...u_n$ and $v = v_1v_2...v_n$.

```
for k = 0 to n − 1
   node u exchange with node v the current value of w_u
   and w_v, where (u ⊕ v) ⊕ 2^k = 0
   if k ≠ n
     if (w_u − w_v) > 0 and u_{k+1} = 0,
       send ⌊(w_u − w_v)/2⌋ tasks to node v
       w_u = ⌈(w_u + w_v)/2⌉
     if (w_u − w_v) > 0 and u_{k+1} = 1,
       send ⌈(w_u − w_v)/2⌉ tasks to node v
       w_u = ⌊(w_u + w_v)/2⌋
     if (w_v − w_u) > 0 and u_{k+1} = 0,
       receive ⌈(w_v − w_u)/2⌉ tasks from node v
       w_u = ⌈(w_u + w_v)/2⌉
     if (w_v − w_u) > 0 and u_{k+1} = 1,
       receive ⌊(w_v − w_u)/2⌋ tasks from node v
       w_u = ⌊(w_u + w_v)/2⌋
   else
     if (w_u − w_v) > 1
       send ⌊(w_u − w_v)/2⌋ tasks to node v
       w_u = ⌈(w_u + w_v)/2⌉
     if (w_v − w_u) > 1
       receive ⌊(w_v − w_u)/2⌋ tasks from node v
       w_u = ⌊(w_u + w_v)/2⌋
```

Fig. 2. The improved DEM algorithm for hypercubes.

The improved DEM requires only nN communications between the computing clusters. The CWA requires $nN/2$ more messages of size $O(n)$ compared to the improved DEM. For distributed load balancing with global information about load in all the nodes, an all-to-all message exchange between the nodes requires $N(N-1)$ communications. If we want to minimize the communications between the nodes, the improved DEM would be a very good alternative and the resulting load balancing quality is almost as good as the CWA or the optimal solution. Hence, the improved DEM is a good candidate for load balancing between homogeneous computing clusters of the same size.

Table 1. The maximum load difference between any two nodes after applying DEM

n	Max load difference between any two nodes								Avg diff
	0	1	2	3	4	5	6	7	
3	780	49256	49170	793	0	0	0	0	1.50
4	0	12827	73855	13318	0	0	0	0	2.00
5	0	863	48776	49446	915	0	0	0	2.50
6	0	3	13053	73697	13237	10	0	0	3.00
7	0	0	864	48815	49461	860	0	0	3.50
8	0	0	9	14547	73490	11952	2	0	3.97
9	0	0	0	859	48865	49393	883	0	4.50
10	0	0	0	2	11820	73180	14991	7	5.03
11	0	0	0	0	905	49152	49024	919	5.50
12	0	0	0	0	4	13340	73414	13242	6.00

Table 2. The maximum load difference between any two nodes after applying the improved DEM

n	Max load difference between any two nodes								Avg diff
	0	1	2	3	4	5	6	7	diff
3	9375	87483	3142	0	0	0	0	0	0.94
4	2030	87595	10375	0	0	0	0	0	1.08
5	104	79546	20350	0	0	0	0	0	1.20
6	0	69903	30097	0	0	0	0	0	1.30
7	0	60765	39235	0	0	0	0	0	1.39
8	0	52938	47062	0	0	0	0	0	1.47
9	0	47435	52565	0	0	0	0	0	1.53
10	0	43649	56351	0	0	0	0	0	1.56
11	0	39580	60420	0	0	0	0	0	1.60
12	0	34671	65329	0	0	0	0	0	1.65

4 Load Balancing between Heterogeneous Computing Clusters

Unfortunately, not all computing clusters within an organization are of the same size and consist of the same processing nodes. For example, the computing clusters within Sharcent are of different size and consist of different processing nodes. With a little bit of adjustment, the Improved DEM would also work for computing clusters of various sizes and consist of different processing nodes.

Consider two nodes u and v within a hypercube. Let $w_u = 640$ tasks and $w_v = 960$ tasks. Suppose u is a computing cluster with $p_u = 64$ processing nodes and v has $p_v = 32$ processing nodes. Instead of sending (960-640)/2 tasks from v to u as indicated in the improved DEM, we should take into account the number of processing nodes in each computing clusters. After load balancing, the number of tasks that are assigned to each processing node in all the computing clusters should be roughly the same. The average load in each processing nodes in u, and v is $w_u/p_u = 640/64 = 10$ and $w_v/p_v = 960/32 = 30$ respectively. In order to balance the load between u and v, we should send $w_v - (w_u + w_v)/(p_u + p_v) * p_v = 427$ tasks from node v to node u. After the transfer, the average load in each processing nodes in u, and v will be around 17. Figure 3 lists the revised DEM that balances load between computing clusters of different size.

Revised DEM

Let node $u = u_1 u_2 ... u_n$ and $v = v_1 v_2 ... v_n$.

for $k = 0$ to $n - 1$
    node u exchange with node v the current value of w_u
    and w_v, where $(u \oplus v) \oplus 2^k = 0$,
    and the number of processing nodes p_u and p_v
    if $k \neq n$
      if $(w_u/p_u - w_v/p_v) > 0$ and $u_{k+1} = 0$,
        send $\lfloor w_u - (w_u + w_v)/(p_u + p_v) * p_u \rfloor$ tasks to node v
        $w_u = \lceil w_u - (w_u + w_v)/(p_u + p_v) * p_u \rceil$
      if $(w_u/p_u - w_v/p_v) > 0$ and $u_{k+1} = 1$,
        send $\lceil w_u - (w_u + w_v)/(p_u + p_v) * p_u \rceil$ tasks to node v
        $w_u = \lfloor w_u - (w_u + w_v)/(p_u + p_v) * p_u \rfloor$
      if $(w_v/p_v - w_u/p_u) > 0$ and $u_{k+1} = 0$,
        receive $\lceil w_v - (w_u + w_v)/(p_u + p_v) * p_v \rceil$ tasks from node v
        $w_u = \lceil w_v - (w_u + w_v)/(p_u + p_v) * p_v \rceil$
      if $(w_v/p_v - w_u/p_u) > 0$ and $u_{k+1} = 1$,
        receive $\lfloor w_v - (w_u + w_v)/(p_u + p_v) * p_v \rfloor$ tasks from node v
        $w_u = \lfloor w_v - (w_u + w_v)/(p_u + p_v) * p_v \rfloor$
    else
      if $(w_u/p_u - w_v/p_v) > 1$
        send $\lfloor w_u - (w_u + w_v)/(p_u + p_v) * p_u \rfloor$ tasks to node v
        $w_u = \lceil w_u - (w_u + w_v)/(p_u + p_v) * p_u \rceil$
      if $(w_v/p_v - w_u/p_u) > 1$
        receive $\lfloor w_v - (w_u + w_v)/(p_u + p_v) * p_v \rfloor$ tasks from node v
        $w_u = \lfloor w_v - (w_u + w_v)/(p_u + p_v) * p_v \rfloor$

Fig. 3. Revised DEM for Computing Cluster of various sizes.

The method listed above can also handle computing clusters with different processing nodes. We can assign a value s_u to represent the processing power of a processing nodes in u. The value s_u would be used as a factor in adjusting the value p_u. The value p_u would be calculated by multiplying the number of processing nodes in u by the processing power s_u. We can then use the load balancing method as listed in Figure 3.

5 Summary

A method to balance the load between heterogeneous computing clusters that are far apart is proposed. It is based on the improved dimension exchange method (DEM) for synchronous load balancing for hypercube architecture. Although, theoretically, the proposed method cannot provide the optimal load balancing quality, in practice, it is very close to the optimal if the number of computing clusters is less than 4096. In fact, the maximum load difference between any two computing clusters can be at most one more than the optimal solution. Furthermore, the proposed method requires a lot fewer communications between the computing clusters. In the near future, we will try to conduct simulation study of our load-balancing method and also try to conduct load balancing experiments between the computing clusters of Sharcnet.

References

1. G. Cybenko, Dynamic load-balancing for distributed memory multicomputers, Journal of Parallel and Distributed Computing, (7)2, October 1989, pages 279-301.
2. M. Willebeek-Lemair and A.P. Reeves, Strategies for dynamic load-balancing on highly parallel computers, IEEE Transcation on Parallel and Distributed Systems, (4)9, September 1993, Pages 979-993.
3. M. Wu and W. Shu, A load balancing algorithm for n-cube, Proceedings of the 1996 International Conference on Parallel Processing, IEEE Computer Society, 1996, Pages 148-155.
4. K.G. Shin and Y. Chang, Load sharing in distributed real-time system with state-change broadcasts, IEEE Transcation on Computers, (38)8, August 1989, Pages 1124-1142.
5. N.G. Shivaratri and P. Krueger, Load distributing for locally distributed systems, IEEE Computers, (25)12, December 1992, Pages 33-44.
6. C.Z. Xu and F.C.M. Lau, The generalized dimension exchange method for load balancing in k-ary n-cube and variants. Journal of Parallel and Distributed Computing, (24)1, January 1995, Pages 72-85.
7. S. Ranka, Y. Won, and S. Sahni, Programming a hypercube multicomputer, IEEE Software, (24)1, September 1988, Pages 69-77.
8. Siu-Cheung Chau and Ada Wai-Chee Fu, Load Balancing between Computing Clusters, Proceedings of the Fourth International Conference on Parallel and Distributed Computing, Applications and Technologies, IEEE press, August 2003, pages 548-551.

"Gridifying" Aerodynamic Design Problem Using GridRPC

Quoc-Thuan Ho, Yew-Soon Ong, and Wentong Cai*

Parallel & Distributed Computing Centre
School of Computer Engineering
Nanyang Technological University, Singapore 639798

Abstract. This paper presents a "gridifying" process for aerodynamic wing design as a case study of complex engineering design problems. In order to assist engineers and scientists to solve the problems on the Grid environment effectively, we developed an API based on GridRPC, a Remote Procedure Call standard interface for Grid-enabled applications. In this work, we also provide mechanisms to reduce communication cost and schedule GridRPC requests across multiple clusters on the Grid. These facilities are incorporated in our GridRPC API implementation.

Keywords: Aerodynamic design Grid computing GridRPC Composite service Metascheduling

1 Introduction

Thanks to the advent of more and more powerful computers and progress of discretization methods and iterative solution algorithms, paper-based engineering design has been transformed towards 3D solid models and computer simulations. The increasing use of computational power in the design process helps design engineers reduce the design cycle time, save costs, and at the same time assures the quality of the products.

A typical life cycle of the complex engineering design begins with Computer Aided Design (CAD) modelling, followed by pre-processing, optimization, and visualization phases. It is common in the present complex engineering design life cycle that the preprocessing and optimization take up the overwhelming bulk of the computation. As a result, bottleneck often happens at these phases. One way to mitigate the problem is to employ parallelism in the design process via multiple computing nodes.

Grid computing offers very powerful and inexpensive computational resources that can be pooled together to solve large problems. Recently, many computationally intensive applications in complex engineering design have been deployed successfully on the Grid. Employing Grid computing can help reduce the bottleneck problem in preprocessing and optimization phases by using clusters of computers to analyze and optimize different alternative designs in parallel . However, "gridifying" an application involves coping with many challenging issues,

* Contact Author: aswtcai@ntu.edu.sg

M. Li et al. (Eds.): GCC 2003, LNCS 3032, pp. 83–90, 2004.

for examples, programming cost, interoperability, resource discovery and selection, as well as attaining high performance.

Applications can be "gridified" using Globus API, MPICH/G2, CoG, etc. [4]. We propose an implementation of GridRPC API to "gridify" our application since GridRPC API is relatively simple, well-understood, and offers high-level abstraction whereby complexity of Grid environment are hidden from the users [6]. A successful example of using GridRPC can be found in [12]. Recently, GridRPC has also been implemented in NetSolve [14] and Ninf-G [7].

However, these current state-of-the-art GridRPC implementations lack the support for automatic resource discovery and selection on the Grid environment. As a result, users have to perform look-up and select resources that suit their needs manually before they can assign computing tasks to the respective resources. This leads to inefficiency since a large number of resources exist on the Grid and these resources are often dynamic. In addition, most optimization problems, for example, aerodynamic design problems, have a large number of evaluation tasks that requires many identical computations with different analysis parameter sets. Hence it is inefficient if interactions between clients and resources are repeated many times for the same remote procedure call.

In this paper, we present a GridRPC API implementation and the "gridifying" process that takes into account the above issues. Further, automatic resource discovery and selection are considered as basic functionalities of our GridRPC API implementation. In particular, a mechanism called *composite service* is introduced as an extension of the GridRPC API. It is employed as a means to reduce communication cost between clients and resources. In addition, a metascheduler that schedules GridRPC requests and balances workload across multiple clusters on the Grid is also introduced.

The rest of this paper is organized as follows. Section 2 briefly describes a general aerodynamic wing design problem and previous work deployed on NetSolve platform. In section 3, we present a "gridifying" process using the GridRPC API we have developed. Discussion on composite service and the metascheduler for load balancing in Grid environment are also presented in this section. Experimental results on aerodynamic wing design problem using the GridRPC API developed are discussed in section 4. Finally, section 5 draws conclusions and outlines future work.

2 Aerodynamic Wing Design Problem

Aerodynamic design, one of the most frequently tackled problems in aeronautics, is a computationally intensive application. Due to the large design spaces, usually stochastic optimization algorithms such as Genetic Algorithms (GA) are employed in the aerodynamic search in order to arrive at a near optimum design [15,11]. GAs typically require thousands of function evaluations and hence require excessive CPU time to locate a near optimal solution, where a single function evaluation involving high-fidelity analysis codes could take minutes or even hours of computation time. Hence, it is not uncommon that the design of an aircraft wing using evolutionary algorithms may take up several months of CPU time even on a supercomputer. This often poses a serious impediment to the practical application of evolutionary optimization to complex engineering design problems as the design process may prove to be computationally intractable if an optimal design is desired.

Since GAs are population-based technique, parallelizing the algorithm is easily achieved such that several designs in each generation can be evaluated simultaneously across the available machines. In a previous work [8], the problem was tackled by using a parallelized evolutionary algorithm for computationally expensive problems deployed on NetSolve platform [1]. Analysis codes are wrapped and deployed on multiple NetSolve servers. Then, a large number of evaluation tasks are farmed to NetSolve servers via the NetSolve agent. As a result, improvement of the design cycle has been attained.

Presently, engineers and scientists still desire to shorten the design cycle time and at the same time assure design quality. However, due to large search spaces in complex engineering design problems, in particular, in multidisciplinary design optimization, computational benefit using a single cluster may be limited. Therefore, migrating the most time consuming part of the design cycle to a Grid environment which has limitless computational resources will help shorten the entire design cycle time. In the subsequent section, we present the efforts required to deploy an aerodynamic wing design problem onto the Grid.

3 "Gridifying" the Problem Using GridRPC

3.1 Infrastructure for GridRPC

The GridRPC API was built on top of Globus [2] that represents the de-facto standard of Grid infrastructure and enables interoperability among various Grid resources. Many services provided by Globus such as Globus Monitoring and Discovery Service (MDS), Grid Resource Allocation Manager (GRAM), Grid Resource Information Service (GRIS), Grid Security Infrastructure (GSI), Global Access to Secondary Storage (GASS), and GridFTP were employed in our GridRPC API implementation. In particular, we consider resource discovery, selection and scheduling as basic functionalities in our implementation. They were incorporated in the implementation so that GridRPC clients can interact with Grid resources autonomically.

It is difficult for a GridRPC client program to know how many resources exist and where they are. Thus, the client needs a centralized like directory service to locate resources. Here, Lightweight Directory Access Protocol (LDAP) [3] is employed to query the MDS database for the resource and workload information. The GridRPC initialization function retrieves information from MDS on software (remote procedure and specialized libraries), hardware (platform, operating system, etc.), and the workload and checks whether or not these resources are capable of servicing further GridRPC requests. In order to monitor and provide information of clusters of computer, the Ganglia monitor toolkit [5] is employed.

3.2 Composite Services

Execution of a GridRPC request is done at the resources. When a resource is not a single computer, e.g., a clusters of computers, the remote invocation of a procedure is usually carried out using resource managers such as Condor [13], PBS [9], SGE [10], etc. All client requests must be submitted through the resource manager. Subsequently, the resource manager schedules these requests across several computing servers and then harvests the results obtained for the clients. The remote procedure calls are considered here as basic services. In an application that requires a large number of identical basic services with different parameter sets, invoking these basic services individually may prove to be inefficient. This is because the interactions between clients and resources would be intensively high. In particular, since Grid resources are geographically distributed across the Internet, performance of applications may decreases drastically due to the high communication latency involved.

In order to avoid the above mentioned disadvantages, we extend GridRPC API for composite services. An additional parameter that indicates the number of basic services will be carried out inside a composite service is introduced in GridRPC API. When the number is equal to one, the composite service becomes a basic service. Using composite service, a set of basic GridRPC requests can be bundled into one composite GridRPC request such that the amount of communications between clients and resources is reduced drastically. The complexity of communication is also hidden from the user.

NetSolve is used as the middleware to implement composite services. However, since NetSolve does not explicitly attempt to balance the workload across computing nodes [1], it cannot avoid overloading situation whereby a certain computing node is overloaded by multiple uncooperative clients. When a client sends multiple asynchronous requests within a short time, the NetSolve agent may fail to obtain up-to-date workload information on the computing nodes and thus provide inaccurate prediction. To tackle this issue, we modified the scheduler of NetSolve agent such that parallel tasks can be distributed fairly across different computing nodes.

Figure 1 presents the execution mechanism for the GridRPC systems. It is assumed that applications are developed using our extended GridRPC API. At the front-end, the GridRPC client activates several remote procedure calls. The metascheduler embedded in GridRPC API implementation then farms the requests to the available resources based on workload and resource information recorded in the Globus MDS. Hence, every time a new resource joins the Grid, it needs to register to the Globus MDS. In addition, its workload information obtained from Ganglia is also pushed onto Globus MDS. At the back-end, once the GRAM's gatekeeper of a cluster receives a composite service request, an instance of the composite service will be initialized on the master node of the cluster. Subsequently, the set of basic service requests will be farmed across multiple computing nodes in the cluster. The responsibility of the NetSolve agent is to perform local scheduling and resource discovery across computing nodes in the cluster for basic services.

3.3 Metascheduling

Resource selection and scheduling plays a critical factor on the performance of Grid applications. In order to effectively and efficiently schedule GridRPC

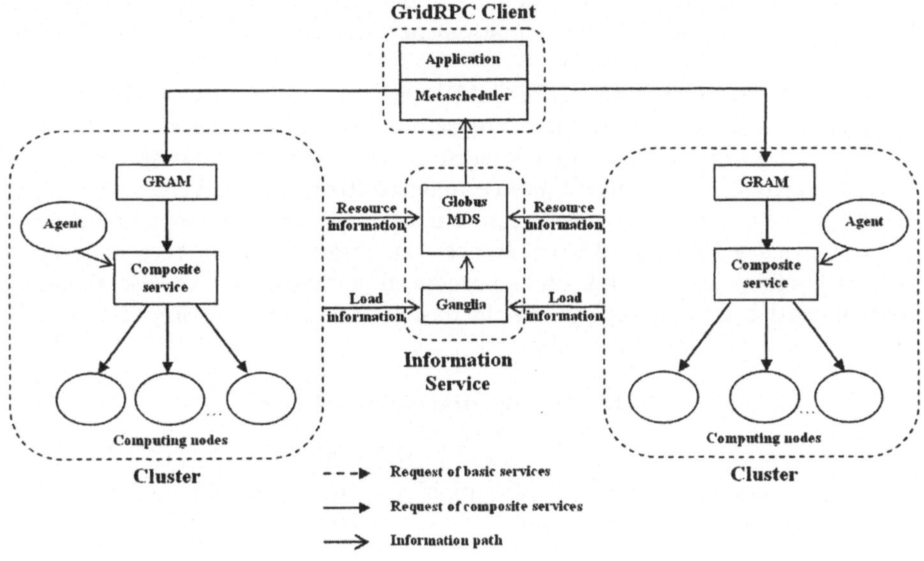

Fig. 1. GridRPC execution system

programs, the scheduler should possess ability to estimate the execution time of services on resources as well as workload increment of the resources during program execution. Scheduling mechanism has been incorporated into GridRPC API implementation such that each client has its own metascheduler. Upon initialization of a GridRPC-enabled client, the metascheduler obtains a list of available resources together with their status from Globus MDS. Whenever the GridRPC client makes a GridRPC call, the metascheduler selects the most suitable resource and submits the request to the resource.

The metascheduler not only performs match-making between the request's requirements and available resources but also predicts workload change of the resources once a request is submitted. Prediction is required since retrieving resource status from the resource monitor is time consuming and the information may not be up-to-date due to network latency. Especially, when asynchronous requests are produced in a loop, resource status cannot be updated as fast as the requests generated. Since the metascheduler is incorporated in the GridRPC API implementation and it schedules the requests online, the scheduling algorithm should not be complex. Hence, we use a heuristic algorithm with $O(nmlogm)$ complexity to schedule GridRPC requests.

4 Experimental Results

In this experiment, the design of airfoil for minimum drag was deployed on 3 clusters within the Nanyang Technological University Campus Grid. Their configuration and initial load are presented in Table 1. Each cluster has 10 computing nodes and 1 master node. 200 potential airfoil designs are analyzed in parallel. The analysis codes employed here are reduced version of 2D Euler codes.

We used our extended GridRPC API with composite services in our implementation. In the GridRPC client program, 200 evaluation tasks are submitted in a loop of 20 asynchronous calls, each of which invokes a composite service. Each instance of the composite service analyzes 10 designs on a cluster. Instead of using the basic service that needs 200 remote procedure calls, we employed composite service with only 20 calls. Hence, the communication cost between the GridRPC client and the resources is reduced significantly. We also minimized communication cost by replicating the design parameters on three clusters.

Table 1. Properties of three clusters

	HPC Cluster	HPC2 Cluster	Sun Cluster
Raw performance	480.943 MFLOPS	90.147 MFLOPS	85.833 MFLOPS
Initial workload	3.188	0.020	0.021

Upon receiving the analysis jobs submitted by the GridRPC client, the metascheduler distributed 13, 4, and 3 requests to HPC Cluster, HPC2 Cluster and Sun Cluster, respectively. The workload of three clusters servicing these service requests are presented in Figure 2. At the beginning of the experiment, HPC Cluster had the highest workload because of heavy local tasks. However, since the metascheduler takes into account both workload and raw performance on scheduling, it distributed more requests to HPC Cluster because it is the most powerful system. From the figure, it can be seen that although 13 requests were assigned to the HPC cluster, the load-one index did not increase much compared with the other two clusters. In contrast to HPC Cluster, Sun Cluster had the lowest performance since its average clock speed is the lowest. Therefore, it will take more time to finish a small number of composite requests.

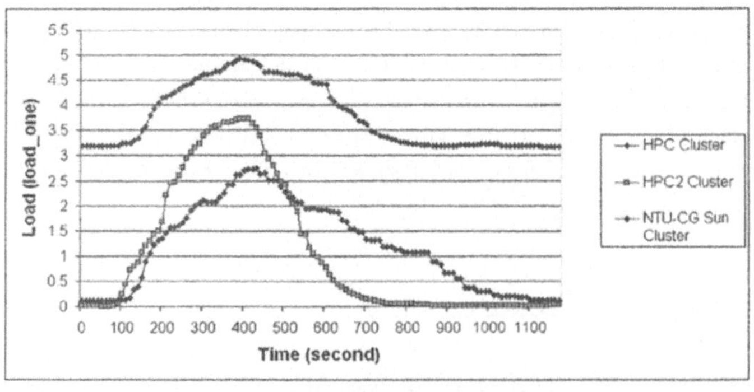

Fig. 2. Workload of three clusters

Load information shown in Figure 2 also implicitly presents the differences among computing platforms, for instances, between HPC2 Cluster, an Intel platform with Linux operating system and Sun Cluster, a Sun platform with Solaris operating system. Although both clusters started with the similar load and their raw performance values were approximately equal, the peak workload values and their changes looked different.

On the contrary, load balancing within a cluster is easier. A snapshot of workload of computing nodes inside HPC2 Cluster during execution grabbed from Ganglia Web monitoring page is shown in Figure 3. In this snapshot, 40 designs were analyzed from 18:40 to 19:00. Workload of the master node (*ec-pdccm* machine) differed from that of the computing nodes because it only performed scheduling computing tasks of composite services.

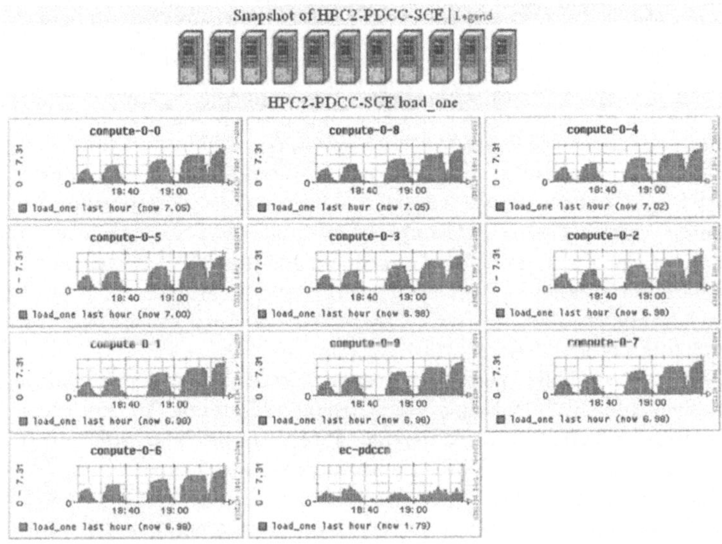

Fig. 3. Load characteristics of a cluster during optimization phase

5 Conclusions and Future Work

"Gridifying" an application over the Grid is still hindered by a lack of suitable middleware. In this paper, we present a design and implementation of the GridRPC API to attain a seamless and transparent access to Grid resources. How to "gridify" a problem in aerodynamic wing design using our GridRPC implementation is also discussed. Composite services in our implementation can hide complexity of underlying execution across multiple clusters of computers and reduce communication cost between GridRPC clients and Grid resources. Experimental results indicate that the metascheduler can successfully select the suitable resources for its requests according to the resource status and balance the workload among different heterogeneous resources of diverse capabilities. In our future work, we will look at dynamic approach to bundle GridRPC requests. The scheduling thus can be more adaptive to clusters of different sizes and workloads across multiple resources.

References

1. D. Arnold, et. al. Innovations of the NetSolve Grid Computing System. In *Concurrency: Practical and Experience 14(13-15): 1457-1479 (2002)*, 2002.
2. I. Foster and C. Kesselman. The Globus Project: A Status Report. In *Proc. IPPS/SPDP '98 Heterogeneous Computing Workshop, pp 4..18*, 1998.
3. I. Foster and G. von Laszewski. Usage of LDAP in Globus. Available at: `ftp://ftp.globus.org/pub/globus/papers/ldap_in_globus.pdf`
4. C. Lee, S. Matsuoka, D. Talia, M. Mueller, G. Allen, J. Saltz. A Grid Programming Primer. Advanced Programming Models Research Group, Global Grid Forum. Available at: `http://www.eece.unm.edu/~apm/docs/APM_Primer_0801.pdf`
5. M. L. Massie, B. N. Chun, and D. E. Culler. The Ganglia Distributed Monitoring System: Design, Implementation, and Experience. February 2003.
6. H. Nakada, S. Matsuoka, K. Seymour, J. Dongarra, C. Lee, and H. Casanova. GridRPC: A Remote Procedure Call API for Grid Computing. Advanced Programming Models Research Group, The Global Grid Forum, July 2002. Available at: `http://www.eece.unm.edu/~apm/docs/APM_GridRPC_0702.pdf`
7. H. Nakada, Y. Tanaka, S. Matsuoka, and S. Sekiguchi. Ninf-G: A GridRPC System on the Globus Toolkit. In *Grid computing: Making the Global Infrastructure a Reality*, John Wiley & Sons, March 2003.
8. Y. S. Ong, P. B. Nair, and A. J. Keane. Evolutionary Optimization of Computationally Expensive Problems via Surrogate Modeling. In *American Institute of Aeronautics and Astronautics Journal*, 40(4), pp. 687-696, 2003.
9. PBS Documentation Set. Available at: `http://www.pbspro.com`
10. Grid Engine Documentations. Available at: `http://gridengine.sunsource.net/project/gridengine/documentation.html`
11. D. Quagliarella, et. al. (Eds.). Genetic Algorithms and Evolution Strategies in Engineering and Computer Science. John Wiley & Sons, Chichester, 1998.
12. H. Takemiya, K. Shudo, Y. Tanaka, S. Sekiguchi. Development of Grid Applications on Standard Grid Middleware. In *Workshop on Grid Applications and Programming Tools*, GGF8, June 25, 2003
13. D. Thain, et. al. Condor and the Grid. In *Grid Computing: Making The Global Infrastructure a Reality*, John Wiley & Sons, March 2003.
14. S. Vadhiyar, K. Seymour, and M. Miller. Implementation of GridRPC over NetSolve. In *GGF5 APM Meeting*, Edinburgh, Scotland, July 22, 2002.
15. K. Yamamoto, O. Inoue. Applications of Genetic Algorithm to Aerodynamic Shape Optimization. In *Proceedings of the 12th AIAA Computational Fluid Dynamics Conference*, 1995.

A WEB-GIS Based Urgent Medical Rescue CSCW System for SARS Disease Prevention

Xiaolin Lu

School of Information Technology,
Zhejiang University of Finance & Economics
Hangzhou 310012, China
email@luxiaolin.com

Abstract. To enable public collaborate with the urgent medical rescue organization, exchange information, participate in activities of prevention against the dangerous epidemic disease like SARS disease happened recently, and rescue patients in shortest time, this paper proposed a framework for the Web-GIS based urgent medical rescue CSCW for SARS disease prevention. The Web-GIS, CSCW, java and multimedia technologies were adopted to construct an integrated collaborative environment. A Web-GIS java applet was used as geometric graphical user interface in web, which could make the public share the geo-referenced epidemic disease information. The CSCW technologies were used to enable the public collaborate with the relevant hygiene department, and medical rescue center. An architecture based on J2EE was applied to the system for expanding the system to large scale. The system can provide an efficient means for performing SARS condition analysis, isolating the area of the developing disease, and controlling the spreading of epidemic disease within shortest time. The system functions and some key technological issues were investigated in the paper. The system has very important practical value for SARS epidemic disease prevention.

1 Introduction

The incident of severe acute respiratory Syndrome (SARS) happened recently is a malignant epidemic disease calamity, a global public health crisis. It caused great danger to public health and security. At the same time, it caused enormous impact in the fields of transportation, education, industry and economics. Enormous direct and indirect losses have already posed the great threat to national security, social stability.

In the process of prevention against the SARS disease and reduction the natural disaster, many people in many difference places and fields involved to corroborate synchronously and asynchronously to fight the disease. The activities of SARS prevention include discovering SARS cases and suspected SARS cases, sending the information to the hospital to rescue the patients, isolating the patient's relevant SARS virus source area, and notifying and sending out the alarm information to the public. All those activities are needed to be managed and be treated by a CSCW system for preventing against SARS and reducing the natural disaster.

M. Li et al. (Eds.). GCC 2003, LNCS 3032, pp. 91–98, 2004

The GIS and CSCW technologies has been applied in the fields of preventing against epidemic disease and natural disaster. There are some research of using the GIS and CSCW in the fields of public health and urban planning [1-6]. In the field of applying GIS to public health, mach work has been carried out to display the epidemic situation to the public by providing a SARS map which enable public to get the information of the epidemic situation conveniently and visually. In urban planning and land administration, GIS-based CSCW system is a powerful assistant for communication, interactive collaborative work and geo-referenced information visualization [1].

Although many researches have been devoted to the SARS maps to enable public to get information of epidemic situation, little research work has been investigated on applying the Web-GIS based CSCW technologies to enable public participate in activities of prevention against SARS, such as the activities of reporting SARS information to public health department, collaborating with other medical workers, and sending the SOS signal for urgent medical rescue, etc.

This paper proposed an infrastructure for an urgent medical rescue CSCW system for public health and security based on WEB-GIS technology. The system aims to offer a new efficient means for preventing SARS and reducing the disaster and to enable public to participate the prevention activities against SARS, such as reporting the SARS information to the public health departments or hospitals, sending or reading the information for rescue, so that hygiene department workers and public could work together to fulfill the rescue work. It could be beneficial to hurry up the speed of the processes of urgent rescue and prevent the epidemic virus area from spreading to larger scale areas that enable more people out of the danger of being possibly affected by the epidemic diseases. This paper described our research work on the design of the system infrastructure, system functions, Web-GIS and CSCW integration, and some key technological issues of the system.

2 Related Works

The Web-GIS and CSCW technologies have extensive application prospects in the field of urgent medical reuse field for protecting the public health and security, exchanging the real time information, and enabling public participated in the collaborative works through Internet.

2.1 Web-GIS Technologies

Web-GIS is a technique that set up geographical information system on Web. User can get the geographical information mutually by Web-GIS application through Internet. It makes GIS functions expand to web site by web technology. Various kinds of geographical space data, attribute data, picture can be obtained through web. With the rapid development of Web-GIS technology, GIS based applications can be developed with low costs, little maintain work. Web-GIS based system has been popularizing in large scale [1][3].

2.2 Web-GIS Based CSCW System

Computer supported collaborative work (CSCW) system provide a means for people to collaboration [1]. It enables a group of people in different place share the environment and information, engage the common tasks, such as decision-making. With the development of web, networking and multimedia technologies, it can enable public to participate the group collaborative work over Internet.

The Web-GIS Based CSCW system is integrated the GIS tools and CSCW groupware tools together to support the collaborative work with spatial information [9][10]. In the Web-GIS based CSCW system, system information, especially the geographical messages are visualize visualized. It benefits from both GIS and CSCW system for supporting public participation in the collaborative work.

3 Web-GIS Based Urgent Medical Rescue CSCW System for SARS Disease Prevention

Web-GIS based CSCW systems are the most efficient means for public communication with the geo-referenced information. With the increase of the bandwidth, transmission speed of the Internet, the GIS applications in Internet have been promoted greatly.

In the processes of prevent SARS disease, many data contained the geo-reference information, such as the specific location or place, latitude and longitude, street address and other census and political boundaries. Web-GIS based CSCW systems have many practical applications in SARS disease prevention. They can be applied in epidemic disease surveillance and control, rapid communication of geo-reference information, etc. Following is the aspects of preventing epidemic disease and assuring public health and security.

1. Providing the geographic distribution of epidemic diseases.
2. Analyzing spatial and temporal trends of epidemic disease.
3. Alarm the risk area of epidemic disease.
4. Assessing resource allocation.
5. Decision-making supporting for prevention against epidemic disease.
6. Controlling and monitoring diseases.

There are many advantages in Web-GIS based CSCW system. Web-GIS offers the graphical user interface, mutual operation on map. All those function meet the demands of a CSCW system. Web-GIS also include useful additional functions to support CSCW system, such as to setup thematic map, analysis geographical information, edit map, draw and pursue layer, find special position in map, visit various kinds of data source, etc. The Web-GIS based CSCW utilizes interaction of computer, GIS, distribution of network and multimedia comprehensive, supports different place, different specialized colony members to finish task of cooperating together. The goal of Web-GIS based CSCW is to utilize the computer to overcome the obstacles of the time and space that the group works to make higher working efficiency. It is an idea solution to adopt the technologies of CSCW and Web-GIS to build an urgent medical rescue CSCW system for public health and security.

The goal of the WEB-GIS based urgent medical rescue CSCW System is to setup a visual collaborating work environment for government department, public and hygiene department to prevent against the epidemic disease such as the SARS disease. In the design for Web-GIS based CSCW system, the system architecture, personnel roles design and system functions and system security were investigated in this section.

3.1 System Architecture Design

The system aimed to be used by a group of people in different field, which include the public health relevant government department, hospitals, urgent medical rescue center, urgent rescue group and public. The all processes of SARS disease prevention would get many departments involved. The GIS-based computer supported collaborative work system was the assistant for achieving of communication, interactive operation, effective data processing and GIS data visualization. Figure 1 shows the system structure.

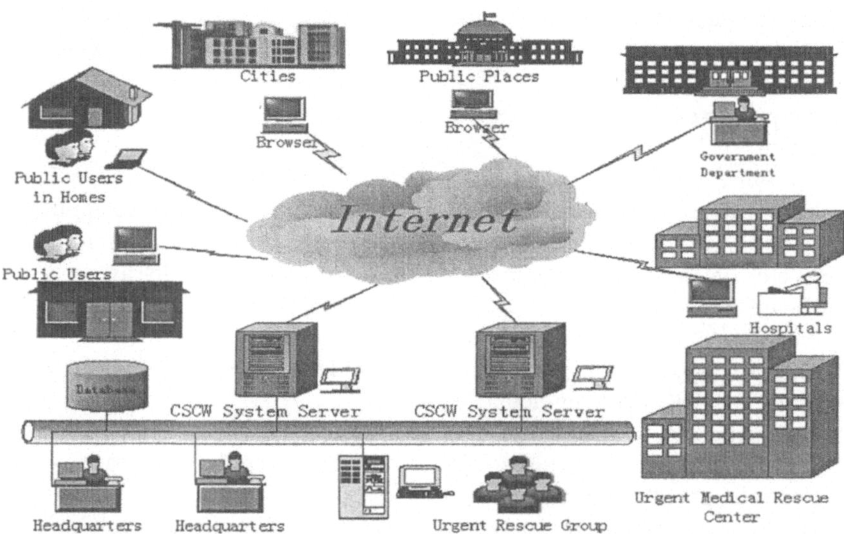

Fig. 1. System structure of the Web-GIS based urgent medical rescue CSCW system for SARS disease prevention

Because there were many computers with different kinds of operating system would work in coordination in the system, the distributed, platform independent system architecture were considered for adapting the change of future use. To meet the system requirement of integrated many computers with different operation system in network, we choice the J2EE and EJB technology to construct an enterprise level system. This is discussed in much more detail in ref. [7] and [8].

The system architecture was composed of three layers as showed figure 2. The first the layer of the system was the database layer. The database of the system included the geography data, SARS data, CSCW data, etc. the middle layer was the system transaction, which was consisted of the system function modules, such as the rescue management, users management, SARS information collection, Collaborative system functions, etc. The third layer was the user interface, which included the GIS applet, CSCW workspaces, etc.

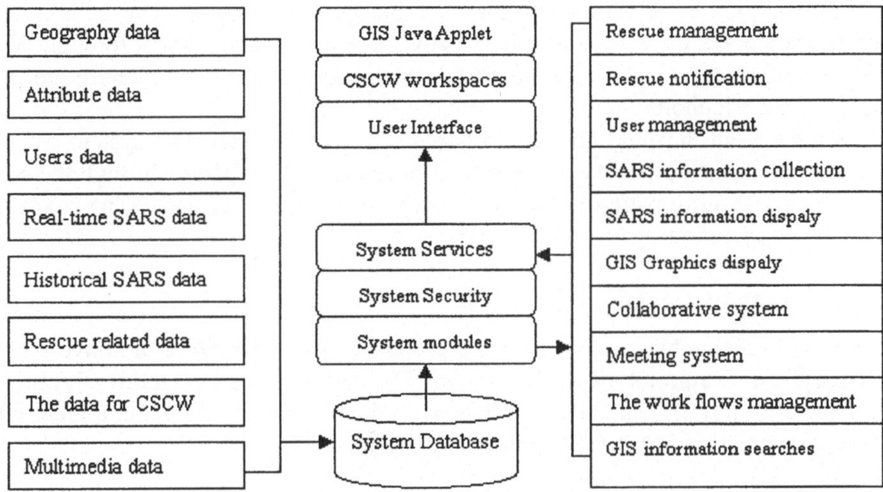

Fig. 2. System architecture of the Web-GIS based urgent medical rescue CSCW system

Web-GIS applet was the core component in the system to get and show the geographical information for public in web site. Also, public can use the GIS java applet in browser to reporting the most recent SARS case information to SARS cure headquarters. After the message from the public received by the headquarter, there will be a serious of immediate actions for SARS health cure center to take, such as confirming the information, notifying relevant department, rescue the SARS patient, isolating the epidemics disease area and broadcasting the information.

System architecture is platform independent, multi-layers and distributed structure. It can combine GIS database, CSCW database and lots of host computers together and share the system resource and data.

3.2 The Principle of System Functions Design

Web-GIS based CSCW system for SARS preventing, following basic functions were considered and realized.

1. Information Sharing. The databases of GIS, SARS and CSCW are the information center of the system. All the cooperating work and information sharing depend on the databases. For example, when the public report SARS epidemic situation through system, the information will be stored in the database and be shared by others.

2. Human computer interaction based on WEB-GIS. The Web-GIS is the basis graphical user interface of man-machine interface in the system. Based on WEBGIS, interoperable SARS information system obtains the geographical position simultaneity. The SARS information reporters, the information managers, the policymakers and headquarters can use the GIS geographical user interface to work together. The friendly interface and interactive system is essential and convenient for SARS information transmission in flexible way. It provides the basic functions in coordination work-ing environment.

3. SARS epidemic situation broadcast. In this system, every one participates in the activities to cooperate, broadcast the epidemic situation data of SARS through WEB-GIS. The information can be also broadcasted by other medias like text message, short massages and telephone.

4. Government, hospital and health cure center cooperation. The system can synchronize government; hospital and health cure center and cooperate through the center database. SARS information in the system can be used to share and exchanged information in cooperation.

3.3 System Implementation

According to the system analysis and the proposed system structure of above section, we have finished a prototype of the system. The system has adopted three layers system structure of J2EE. The GIS data stored in the databases, and geographical interface is shown with a JAVA GIS applet in the webpage.

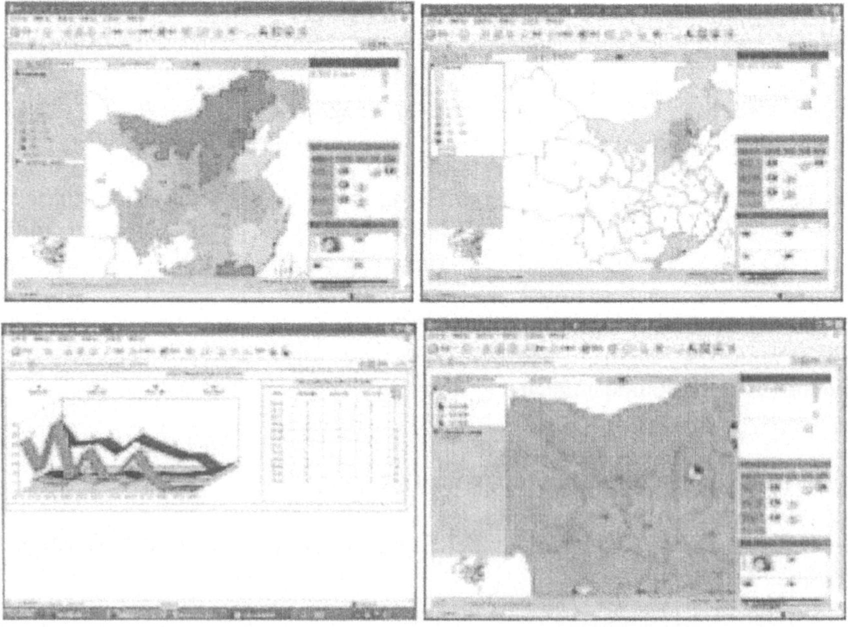

Fig. 3. Several pictures of the system shot screen to describe the factions of the system

Here are several pictures of the system interface screens to demonstrate the usage of the system. The system interface, shown in the top left picture in figure 3, is explained as following: In the center area of the picture is the SARS map with relevant SARS epidemic situation information. The legend figure of map is at the upper left corner. The lower left corner is a key map. The upper right corner is an online meeting chart room. Below the online meeting chart room is the online user lists of the system. The lower right corner is a visual teleconference.

There are four pictures in the figure 3. The left top picture showed a distribution map for the cumulated SARS cases. Right top picture showed the newly increased distribution of case of the recent day. The relevant information could be shown by simple clicking a special point or area in the map to inquire about detailed information. Left bottom picture expresses a certain tendency of a district through click in the map. The right bottom picture is SARS case reporting interface by clicking the place where the SARS cases happened to input the SARS case to the center database. All the users of the system can share the SARS information in real time and collaborate with each other by using the online meeting chart room and visual teleconference.

The system could provide a visual GIS and CSCW environment to meet the practical need in the processes of SARS patients urgent rescue and quickly control the epidemic disease. All the processes in urgent medical rescue could be don in real time. The system could be very useful in responding the sudden outbreak disease and controlling the disease condition in shortest time.

4 Discussions and Further Work

Though the prototype of the system has implemented. There are still lot works to research in the field of urgent medical rescue for SARS disease prevention. Following are some key technologies needed investigated in future work:

1. The Java GIS applet: the java GIS java applet is the key part in the system and it is used be to display the geometrical information in the web side. It supports the all the data formats of GIS data, which is stored in the databases that support the JDBC connection. Further research on the Java GIS applet is needed for more system functions.

2. GIS and SARS data construction: The basic GIS and SARS data are very important to the system. Because cost of the GIS data with high precise is to high for us to constructed a high precise map, in our work the some of GIS maps were constructed from the paper maps by using the map editing software. In the future research work, more precise map of 1:M format will be used in the system.

3. Model of SARS spreading: The model of SARS spreading development is one our future work. The model of epidemic disease spreading could be very important to justify the danger level in the area affected by SARS disease. More practical model could be investigated in the further work.

5 Conclusions

The Web-Based urgent medical rescue CSCW system for SARS disease prevention, combined the Web-GIS, CSCW, Internet, and java technologies together, could provide efficient means which not only enable public to get the geo-referenced information of most recent epidemic disease situation, but also enable the public to collaborate with the local government and medical workers to prevent the natural disaster together. The system can provide the geographic distribution of epidemic diseases, analyze spatial and temporal trends of epidemic disease, alarm the risk area, assess resource allocation, perform decision-making supporting for prevention against epidemic disease, and control and monitor SARS diseases, so that system could play a important role in enables the government department, medical workers and public collaboration for the prevention SARS disease.

References

1. Jiang, J., Jun, C.: A GIS—based computer supported collaborative work (CSCW) system for urban planning and land management. Phonograms metric Engineering & Remote Sensing, Vol. 68 (4). (2002) 353-359
2. Yingwei, L., Xiaolin, W., Zhuoqun, X.: Design of a Framework for Multi-User/Application Oriented WebGIS Services. 2001 International Conference on Computer Networks and Mobile Computing (ICCNMC'01), October 16 - 19, Beijing China (2001) 151-157
3. Shanzhen, Y., Lizhu, Z., Chunxiao, X., Qilun, L., Yong, Z.: Semantic and Interoperable WebGIS. International Conference on Web Information Systems Engineering (WISE'01), Vol.2, December 03 - 06, Kyoto Japan (2001) 42-48
4. Mennecke, B.E., Crossland, M.D.: Geographic Information Systems: Applications and Research Opportunities for Information Systems Researchers. 29th Hawaii International Conference on System Sciences (HICSS), Vol.3, January, Maui Hawaii (1996) 537-546
5. Selçuk Candan, K., Venkat Rangan, P.: Collaborative Multimedia Systems: Synthesis of Media Objects. IEEE Transactions on Knowledge and Data Engineering, May, New York(1998) 433-457.
6. Massimo Franceschetti, Jehoshua Bruck: A Group Membership Algorithm with a Practical Specification. IEEE Transactions on Parallel and Distributed Systems, November, New York (2001) 1190-1200
7. Xiaolin Lu: Symmetric Distributed Server Architecture for Network Management System. International Workshop on Advanced Parallel Processing Technology (APPT2003), Xiamen China, LNCS Vol. 2834, X. Zhou, S. Jahnichen, M. Xu and J. Cao, eds., Springer-verlag, New York (2003) 425-429
8. Xiaolin Lu: Infrastructure of Unified Network Management System Driven By Web Technology. The Fourth International Conference on Parallel and Distributed Computing, Applications and Technologies (PDCAT2003), Chengdu China, Pingzhi Fan and Hong Shen, eds., IEEE press, New York (2003) 111-115
9. Kingston, R., Carver, S., Evans, A. and Turton, I.: Web-Based Public Participation Geographical Information Systems: An Aid To Local Environmental Decision-Making. Computers, Environment and Urban Systems, Vol. 24, No. 2. (2000) 109-125
10. Massimo Franceschetti, Jehoshua Bruck: A Group Membership Algorithm with a Practical Specification. IEEE Transactions on Parallel and Distributed Systems, November, New York (2001) 1190-1200

MASON: A Model for Adapting Service-Oriented Grid Applications*

Gang Li[1], Jianwu Wang[1], Jing Wang[1], Yanbo Han[1], Zhuofeng Zhao[1], Roland M. Wagner[2], and Haitao Hu[1]

[1] Software Division, ICT, Chinese Academy of Science, PRC
[2] Fraunhofer Institute for Software and Systems Engineering, Dortmund, Germany
{ligang, wjw, wangjing, yhan }@ict.ac.cn

Abstract. Service-oriented computing, which offers more flexible means for application development, is gaining popularity. Service-oriented grid applications are constructed by selecting and composing appropriate services. They are one kind of promising applications in grid environments. However, the dynamism and autonomy of environments make the issues of dynamically adapting a service-oriented grid application urgent. This paper brings forward a model that supports not only monitoring applications through gathering and managing state and structure metadata of service-oriented grid applications, but also dynamic application adjustment by changing the metadata. Besides that, the realization and application of the model is presented also.

1 Introduction

In grid environments, services are important resources that can be viewed as a kind of grid application components[1]. A developer can quickly construct large-scale and distributed applications by selecting and composing appropriate services, resulting in so-called service-oriented grid applications (SOGA). However, due to independent evolution of services and dynamic changes of requirements, those applications encounter challenges of dynamic adaptation.

On one hand, services are locally autonomous. Service providers independently develop and maintain their services, and services can freely join or quit grid environment. The independent changes of services can make original services, which that compose an application, not meet users' requirements any more. On the other hand, problems due to requirement changes still exist and requirement changes are even more dynamic. So, dynamic adjustment of application structures and behaviors is needed. In addition, in order to adapt an application, states of application components should be known. So it is also necessary to monitor a SOGA on application level.

* This paper is supported by the National Natural Science Foundation of China under Grant No. 60173018, the Young Scientist Fund of ICT Chinese Academy of Science under Grant No. 20026180-22 and the Key Scientific and Technological Program for the Tenth Five-Year Plan of China under Grant No. 2001BA904B07.

M. Li et al. (Eds.): GCC 2003, LNCS 3032, pp. 99–107, 2004.

The composite service execution model of SWORD[2], proposed by Stanford University, is useful to gathering states of a SOGA. During the execution of a SOGA, each service is presented by an operation and the execution model is described as the connection of the related operations. The execution logic of the services is manifested in the execution model, but the execution logic in the application cannot be changed.

To adapt to changes in network environments, Israel Ben-Shaul etc. present a component model and a composition model for distributed application development and deployment[3]. The component model allows the modification of both structure and behavior of components, and the composition model enables to dynamically deploy components into remote sites and dynamically reconfigure the deployment. However, services are special components that are much more autonomous, which cannot be modified by users. Although the models benefit SOGA adaptation, there is still much work to be done in order to adjust a SOGA on application level.

Other typical research includes work related to BPEL4WS[4] and GSFL[5]. Currently, some execution environments for BPEL4WS can trace the execution by visible means. They offer the function of monitoring, but the monitoring granularity is very coarse. Among the service composition model supported by GSFL, there is a life cycle model for describing the life cycle of activities and services in a service composition, which enables to get application states. Although monitoring is a necessary part of dynamic adjustment, current work related to both BPEL4WS and GSFL does not support the adjustment of application.

Aiming at the special and open issues of adjusting a SOGA, we developed the CAFISE Framework[6]. CAFISE Framework is an environment that supports developing, running and adjusting a SOGA. In the CAFISE Framework, we bring forward a model for monitoring and adjusting a SOGA, which is named MASON (Model for Adapting a Service-Oriented Grid Application) model. It supports not only monitoring application through gathering and managing state and structure metadata of service compositions, but also dynamic adjustment by changing the metadata.

Our work benefits from architecture reflection[7,8]. Architecture reflection keeps software architecture as a meta description of software. Our work uses dynamic application structures as the meta description, which present a SOGA on implementation level from architecture angles, and are more concrete and helpful to adjusting. In addition, the MASON model supports gathering and showing the states of a SOGA on different levels, which cannot be achieved with architecture reflection.

The remainder of this paper is organized as follows. Before presenting the MASON model, concepts about the SOGA in the CAFISE Framework, which are related to the model, are briefly given in section 2. Section 3 presents the model in details. Section 4 describes the model realization in the CAFISE Framework. Section 5 gives a case study on how to adjust a SOGA through the model. Section 6 sums up with several concluding remarks.

2 The SOGA Specified with Darnel

In the CAFISE Framework, a SOGA is presented with Darnel (Dynamic Service Composition Description Language)[9], which is an executable service composition description language that uses the activities associated with services to organize the collaboration among services.

The application written in Darnel is mainly composed of coordination among services and its context. The *context* describes the situation and the target or intermediate results of the coordination. Thus, we can not only get the intermediate state of the coordination but also dynamically adjust the application by analyzing the deflection of the target and intermediate results. As a structure segment supporting modularization, a *coordination block* mainly includes coordination partners and their relations, sub-context and involved activities. Activities are structure units of the application, which include *structure activity* and *simple activity*. *Structure activities* define the control logic of the application and *simple activities* denote service placeholders. *Simple activities* dynamically associate with services that are basic function units and programming components of the SOGA. Services can be chained with *connectors*[10] that are referenced by *simple activities*. With the model presented in this paper, the SOGA in Darnel can be adjusted dynamically.

3 The Model for Dynamically Adapting a SOGA

To dynamically adapt a SOGA in Darnel, we present the MASON model. It depicts the dynamic structures and states of a SOGA, stores related metadata and specifies how to obtain state and structure data of an application. Referring to the model, software developers can design tools that support monitoring and dynamically adjusting a SOGA.

The model is based on the object-oriented notion, yet it is not a simple application of the object concepts. Services are basic function units of a SOGA. They are programming components on a higher abstract level and can evolve independently. In the MASON model, objects are abstract of services or service compositions. These objects are dynamically and locally created while the application is running, and do not need centralized management. Besides that, objects in the MASON model support dynamic and adaptive adjustment to a SOGA. With these objects, the structure and state metadata can be modified, and the service connections and member services can be changed. The adjustment capabilities enhance adaptability of a SOGA in volatile grid environments as well as the exception handling ability.

3.1 Model Definition

The MASON model includes a set of runtime objects, relationships among them and model interfaces. Runtime objects are objects that are created while a SOGA is running, and they contain data related to dynamic structures and states of the SOGA. Relationships among runtime objects include structure and behavior relationships, with which runtime objects are linked up as a whole. The model interfaces contain essential operations through which dynamic structures and states data can be gotten and changed. Some details about the primary runtime objects are presented in table 1.

In those runtime objects, a kind of important properties is related to application states. The runtime objects contain state related properties on different levels that describe states of services, activities and coordination blocks. The activity state properties of the simple activity object and the structure activity object describe the states of the relevant activities of a SOGA. There are five kinds of activity states: ready, running, suspended, completed and terminated. The simple activity object additionally contains a service state property that shows the state of the service bound with the activity. As a part of a SOGA, the service associated with an activity is not stateless, it has four kinds of states: ready, running, completed and terminated. The coordination object in the object coordination layer contains state information of a coordination block in a SOGA, which includes ready, running, terminated and completed state.

Table 1. Primary Runtime Objects of the MASON model

Runtime Objects	Main Properties	Main Operations	Remarks
App	application name, context and coordination module set	getX	It contains application global information.
Coordination	coordination block name, activity set, initial activities, current activities, current state	getX, setX, addX and deleteX	It can be used to get coordination block state and change its structure.
Structure activity	activity name, subset of activity, current activity, activity state	getX, setX, addX and deleteX	It can be used to get activity state and adjust the activity.
Simple activity	activity name, current state and service state	getX and setX	It can be used to get activity state and asso-ciated service, and to adjust a simple activity.
Connector	Ports, selection function, currently selected service, connection partners, candidate services	getX, setX, addX and deleteX	It specifies dynamic service connection and enabling connection re-configuration.

The runtime objects above-mentioned are not irrelevant. They compose a hierarchical structure, which mainly consists of elemental layer, object coordination layer and global object layer. With the three layers, the runtime objects are organized in different granularities. The elemental layer is the fundamental one of the three layers, and the objects in this layer are runtime images of *simple activities*, *structure activities* and *connectors* of the SOGA in Darnel language. The object coordination layer is in the middle tier, and is used to conglutinate and coordinate the objects of elemental layer. The coordination objects represent *coordination blocks* of the SOGA and contain references to runtime objects of elemental layer according to the coordination blocks' structures. Besides that, a coordination object marks the initial activities and current running activities in application execution. The global object layer is on top of the hierarchical structure and the App objects in this layer are used to get global information of an application, whose context properties record global data, intermediate and target results. An App object property, named coordination block set, contains references to coordination objects. The runtime objects and their structure relationships describe a SOGA structure on meta level.

The runtime objects have relationships not only in structure aspect, but also in behavior aspect. When an object property related to application state changes, the relevant objects may be infected due to the relationships among them. For example, when a service that is bound with a simple activity is available, the simple activity object's current state property is "ready" also. When the service is invoked, the simple activity object's current state property is changed into "running". The coordination object, which contains the simple activity object, will change its related property. These relationships are pictured in figure 1. Thus, runtime objects can influence each other at the behavior aspect.

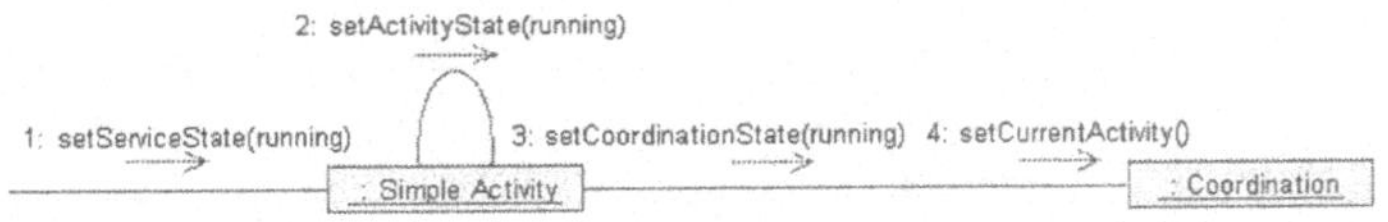

Fig. 1. Example of Behavior Relationships among Runtime Objects

With structure and behavior relationships, the runtime objects form an organic whole that interact with outside through model interfaces. Operations of the runtime objects, such as get, set, add and delete, compose interfaces of the model with which data of states and dynamic structures can be obtained and reconfigured. To prevent the security issues that arise from unlimited modification, the model interfaces put restrictions on accessing to the objects. For example, because services are autonomous, contrived modifications to service states are not permitted; only operations that adjust states of simple activities and service binding strategy of connectors are offered.

All in one word, those objects of the MASON model encapsulate operations and meta data of application structures and states, and the model contains structure and behavior relationships among the objects. By changing the meta data through the model interfaces, the model supports dynamically adjusting a SOGA.

3.2 Supports for Dynamic Adjustment

When a SOGA is dynamically adjusted, execution information like states should firstly be gotten. The MASON model supports monitoring a SOGA mainly through the introspection of structure and state. The runtime objects store relevant data, so with the model interfaces, application structure and state data can be gotten. Table 2 lists parts of contents that can be gotten and monitored with the model. It shows that through different operations of runtime objects, user can acquire application states information in different granularities. Other information, such as structure and context, can be gotten in similar way.

With the dynamic structure and state information gotten from the MASON model, the dynamic adjustment of a SOGA can be achieved through model interfaces on object coordination layer and elemental layer. These operations can modify the structure and state metadata. Table 3 lists parts of adjustments that the model supports.

Table 2. Parts of Monitored Contents and Related Runtime Objects

Monitoring type	Monitored contents	Runtime objects	Operation examples
monitoring application states	coordination block state	coordination	getCoordinationState
	activity state	structure/simple activity	getActivityState
	service state	simple activity	getServiceState

Table 3. Parts of Adjusted Contents and Related Runtime Objects

Adjustment type	Adjusted contents	Runtime objects	Operation examples
adjusting application structures	coordination block structure	coordination	addSimpleActivity
	service binding strategy	connector	setBindingType
adjusting application states	coordination state	coordination	setCoordinationState
	activity state	structure/simple activity	setActivityState

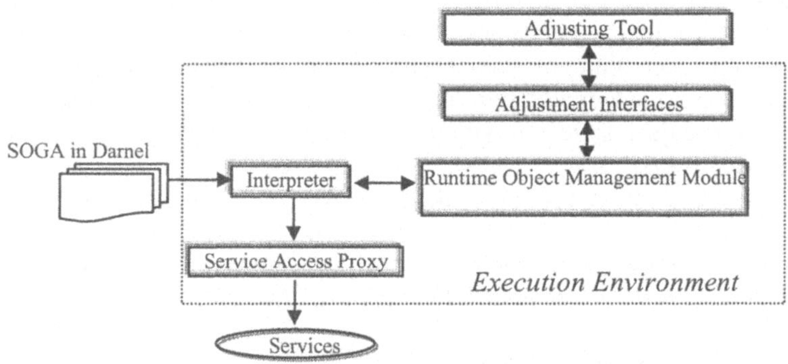

Fig. 2. Realization of the MASON model in the CAFISE Framework

4 Model Realization

The MASON model presents a reference for designing tools that support dynamic adjustment of a SOGA. Up to now, the model has been realized in CAFISE Framework. The realized modules are illustrated in figure 2.

In the framework, execution environment and adjusting tool are two key components. The MASON model is manifested by the execution environment, which interprets and executes a SOGA. The adjusting tool gets and changes needed data through model interfaces implemented by execution environment, through which user can make timely modification on running applications.

The execution environment of CAFISE Framework mainly includes Interpreter, Runtime Object Management Module (ROMM), Adjustment Interfaces and Service Access Proxy etc., among which the ROMM and Adjustment Interfaces are designed referring to the MASON model. When the interpreter interprets a SOGA, it invokes the system object factory. The factory creates runtime object App, which initiates other relevant runtime objects according to execution situations. The ROMM takes charge of managing these runtime objects. It chooses the ready activities in the coordination block and sends the result to the interpreter. If the activity is a structure one, the ROMM sets its activity state property. If the activity is a simple one, after setting the property, the ROMM determines whether it is necessary to create a connector object according to the situation of service connection. After the connection between activity and service is confirmed, the interpreter invokes the service access proxy and resets the properties of runtime objects through the ROMM. The Adjustment Interfaces realize the MASON model interfaces, which provide methods to access and manipulate runtime objects. Based on the Adjustment Interfaces, monitoring and adjusting tools can be designed by developers.

5 Case Study

In this section, a case study is presented in which the MASON model is applied to the project FLAME2008 in order to provide a flexible dynamic adjustment tool for the end user. The case contained in this case study relates to a journalist's travel plan. The journalist combines the services provided by diverse providers into a SOGA and executes it to get the expected results. But during the application running, he may want to change some parts of the SOGA so as to rearrange his plan. Therefore a tool that can adjust the SOGA during runtime is needed.

The MASON model is used in the system to dynamically adjust a SOGA. Firstly the user needs to monitor the application. As far as how to monitor a SOGA is concerned, the Adjustment Interfaces provide essential supports. In this case, the interface is implemented through observer pattern[11]. Taking monitoring a simple activity as an example, figure 3 illustrates how to use the realized MASON model to monitor with the pattern.

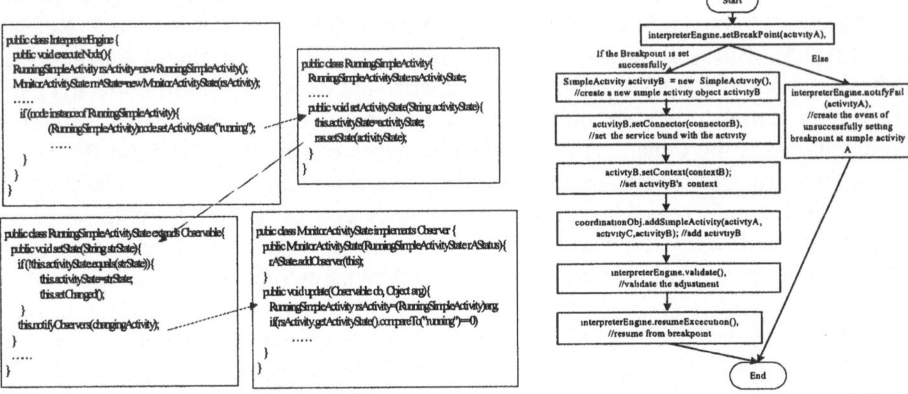

Fig. 3. Example of Monitoring

Fig. 4. Example of Adjusting

If user's demands change or services do not return expected results, a SOGA can be dynamically adjusted through the realized MASON model to adapt to those changes. Firstly, the structure and state data related to the application segments, which will be influenced by the changes, can be gotten through the runtime objects. With the data, the interpreter judges whether a breakpoint can be set at the affected activities. If the breakpoints are feasible, the affected running activities are suspended with methods of the Adjustment Interfaces. Then breakpoints are set and executing contexts are saved. Dynamic structures related to the adjustments are changed through runtime objects. After changing, the integrity and validity of changed application structure are checked. At last, breakpoints are cancelled and the application is resumed to execute. Taking adding a simple activity as an example, figure 4 presents the key steps of dynamic adjustments. activityA and activityC are runtime objects that represent simple activity A and C. IA new simple activity B bound with a service is added between simple activity A and C.

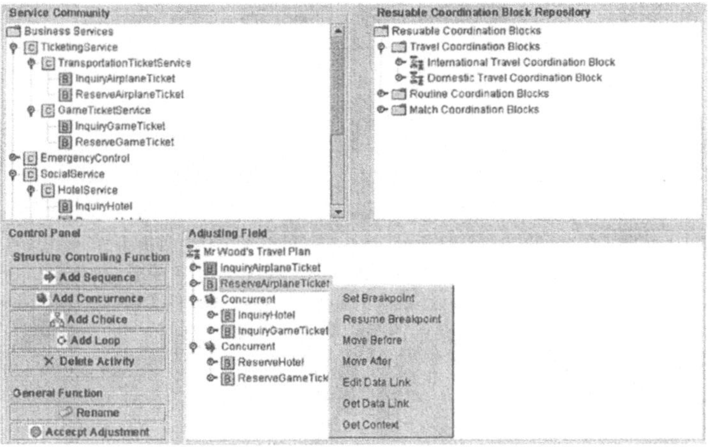

Fig. 5. The Adjusting Tool in the CAFISE Framework

Based on the forementioned, an adjusting tool has been implemented which is illustrated in figure 5. It is composed of Adjusting Field, Control Panel, Reusable Coordination Block Repository and Service Community. In the Adjusting Field, different states of a SOGA are marked with different colors. Monitoring details can be shown by doubly clicking on the monitored application components. When the application is to be dynamically adjusted, services can be dragged from the Service Community to create new simple activities; structure activities can be changed with the Control Panel; reusable coordination blocks can be gotten from the Reusable Coordination Block Repository. Other adjusting operations, such as setting breakpoints, are available through the right clicked menu (shown in figure 5).

Experiences of realizing and applying the MASON model in this case shows: 1) with the model, states of a SOGA can be gotten and shown conveniently; 2) dynamic and flexible adjustment of a SOGA, such as adding new simple activities and replacing existing services, can be achieved.

6 Conclusions

In grid environments, services evolve independently and requirements of users are volatile. Those factors bring adaptation requirements to service-oriented grid applications. To solve the problem, the MASON model for adapting service-oriented grid applications is presented in this paper. The model contains metadata of application states and dynamic structures. It can be created dynamically and locally. Through the model interfaces, the application states can be gathered and the application structures and behaviors can be dynamically adjusted. With the experiences of realizing and applying the model, we conclude:

1. The model supports not only monitoring through gathering and managing state and structure metadata of service-oriented applications, but also dynamic adjustment by changing the metadata.
2. By supporting adjustment, the model enables dynamic adaptation and on-line evolution of service-oriented grid applications.

References

1. I. Foster, C. Kesselman, J. Nick and S. Tuecke. Grid Services For Distributed System Integration. IEEE Computer. Vol. 35, no.6, 2002, pages 37-46.
2. S. R. Ponnekanti, A. Fox. SWORD: A Developer Toolkit for Web Service Composition. The Eleventh World Wide Web Conference (Web Engineering Track). Honolulu, Hawaii, May, 2002.
3. I. Ben-Shaul, O. Holder, and B. Lavva. Dynamic Adaptation and Deployment of Distributed Components in Hadas. IEEE Transactions on Software Engineering. Vol. 27, no.9, 2001, pages 769-787.
4. T. Andrews F. Curbera etc. Business Process Execution Language for Web Services Version 1.1. http://www-106.ibm.com/developerworks/webservices/library/ws-bpel/. May 2003.
5. S. Krishnan1, P. Wagstrom1 and G. Laszewski. GSFL: A Workflow Framework for Grid Services. http://www-unix.globus.org/cog/projects/workflow/. July 2002.
6. H. Yanbo, Z. Zhuofeng, L. Gang etc. CAFISE: An Approach to Enabling Adaptive Service Configuration of Service Grid Applications. Journal of Computer Science and Technology. Vol. 18, no.4, 2003, pages 484-494.
7. C. E. Cuesta, P. Fuente, and M. Barrio-Solárzano. Dynamic Coordination Architecture through the Use of Reflection. Proceedings of the 2001 ACM Symposium on Applied Computing (SAC), pages 134-140.
8. G. Blair, G. Coulson, P. Robin, and M. Papathomas. An Architecture for Next Generation Middleware. Proceedings of Middleware '98. Springer Verlag, September 1998, pages 191-206.
9. CAFISE group. Darnel Language Specification. Technical Report. Software Division, ICT, CAS, 2002.
10. L. Gang, H. Yanbo, Z. Zhuofeng, W. Jianwu and R. M. Wagner. An Adaptable Service Connector Model. Proceedings of VLDB'29 Workshop on Semantic Web and Databases. Berlin, Germany, 2003, pages 79-90.
11. E. Gamma, R. Helm, R. Johnson and J. Vlissides. Design Patterns: Elements of Reusable Software Architecture. Addison-Wesley, 1995.

Coordinating Business Transaction for Grid Service

Feilong Tang, Minglu Li, Jian Cao, and Qianni Deng

Department of Computer Science and Engineering,
Shanghai Jiao Tong University, Shanghai 200030, P.R. China
{tang-fl,li-ml}@cs.sjtu.edu.cn

Abstract. Grid service is next-generation computing platform. Transaction for Grid service is one of the key technologies. In heterogeneous, dynamical and autonomous Grid environment, however, traditional transaction technologies is unsuitable. And little attention has been paid to support transaction coordination for Grid service. In this paper[1], we propose a transaction framework that can coordinate atomic and cohesion transaction and recover system from various exceptions. The atomic transaction ensures the ACID properties while the cohesion transaction relaxes the atomicity and isolation properties. By generating and executing compensation transaction automatically, the framework can satisfy the requirements of business transactions for Grid service environment.

1 Introduction

The main goal of Grid computing is sharing large-scale resources and accomplishing collaborative tasks [1]. Owing to unreliability of Grid, transaction coordination is one of key technologies which decide whether Grid computing can be applied to practical applications, especially to commercial applications.

The traditional distributed transaction has the ACID properties, that is Atomicity, Consistency, Isolation and Durability. However, the strict ACID transaction must satisfy following conditions: (1) the transaction is short-lived, (2) coordinator has entire control power to participants, and (3) application systems are tightly coupled.

Transaction coordination for Grid service is extremely challenging because:

- Coordinating Grid services often takes a long time due to business latency or/and user interaction;
- Users may not be able to lock necessary resources because of the autonomy of Grid service;
- Communication is unreliable and transaction suffers from missing messages.
- Grid services are loosely coupled.

[1] This paper is supported by 973 project (No.2002CB312002), 863 project (No.2001AA415310) of China, grand project (No.03dz15027 and 03dz15026) and key project (No.025115033) of the Science and Technology Commission of Shanghai Municipality.

M. Li et al. (Eds.): GCC 2003, LNCS 3032, pp. 108–114, 2004.

2 Related Work

About traditional distributed transaction, there have been some standards and models. DTP [9](Distributed Transaction Processing) is a widely used model. It defines three roles (Application Program, Transaction Manager and Resource Manager) and two kinds of interfaces (TX interface and XA interface). OTS [2](Object Transaction Service) is a distributed transaction standard based on CORBA. However, it is infeasible to apply above schemes to Grid applications because they cannot effectively support long-lived transactions.

WS-Coordination and WS-Transaction [3,4], proposed by IBM, Microsoft and BEA, describe a Web services [12] transaction framework that can accommodate multiple coordination protocols. It classifies transaction in Web services environment into atomic transaction and business activity. However, it does not provide coordination scheme for business activity in detail.

Business Transaction Protocol (BTP)[5], proposed by OASIS, defines a set of messages exchanged between coordinator and participants. Although HP has issued its BTP product Web Services Transactions (HP-WST)[6], the complex structure of message and workflow management limits its comprehensive application. In addition, BTP lacks of flexible recovery mechanisms.

Based on Globus Toolkit [7,8] and agent technology, we propose a transaction framework that can simultaneously coordinate short-lived and long-lived transaction for Grid service and automatically recover from exceptions. Moreover, by means of compensation technology, it is unnecessary to lock resources in global transaction and undo the entire transaction when cancelling part of sub-transactions, which improves the application concurrency and system efficiency.

3 Framework of Coordination

Our transaction framework is shown in Fig. 1. Its core element Agent consists of following complements:

- Time Service, which generates driving signal to undo operations taken previously.
- Generator of compensation transaction, which automatically generates compensation transaction.
- Log Service, which records all transaction operations, states.
- Coordinator or Participant/Candidate, which is dynamically generated to coordinate transaction.

4 Coordination Mechanism

4.1 Transaction Type

In Grid environment, transaction coordination must have the abilities to handle both short-lived operations and long-lived business activities. We employ two types of transaction mechanisms to satisfy different application demands:

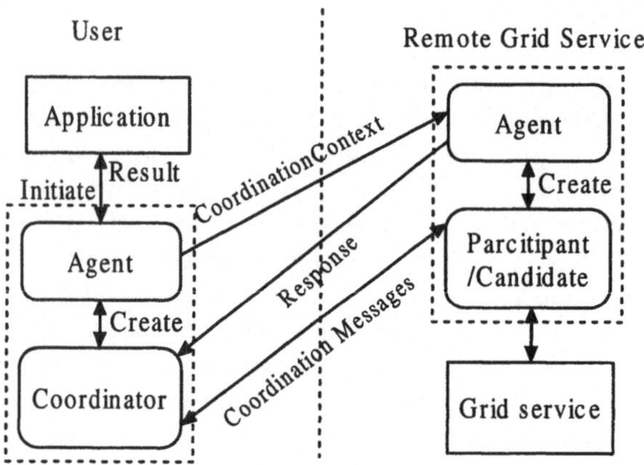

Fig. 1. A transaction framework for Grid service.

Definition 1. Atomic transaction (AT) is the transaction whose all participants have to commit synchronously or abort entirely, and the intermediate states of the transaction are invisible.

Definition 2. Cohesion transaction (CT) is the transaction that allows some candidates to abort while others to commit, where each action is executed independently and the results are visible to outside. In contrast to AT, CT has following new characteristics:

- Renegotiation. If some candidates are not ready for commit , a coordinator may renew to locate new candidates, which will continue until completing the transaction or attempting N times.
- Expiration. Each negotiation message contains timeout parameter. If the coordinator doesn't take further actions, the candidates will autonomously cancel previous actions by compensation transaction after timeout.

Atomic transaction is used to coordinate short-lived transaction and its exception is handled by rollback operation. Long-lived transaction is coordinated by cohesion transaction, where exception before commit is handled by rollback operations and recovery after commit is implemented by compensation transactions.

4.2 Coordination Mechanism

Different from traditional transaction, the transaction coordination for Grid environment focuses on how to coordinate sub-transactions rather than to handle inside of individual sub-transaction (see Fig. 2).

Coordination of atomic transaction. It includes following steps:

Initiation of an atomic transaction. For remote Grid service to join in an atomic transaction, the client-side agent sends CoordinationContext (CC) message to them and creates a Coordinator, which lives until end of the transaction.

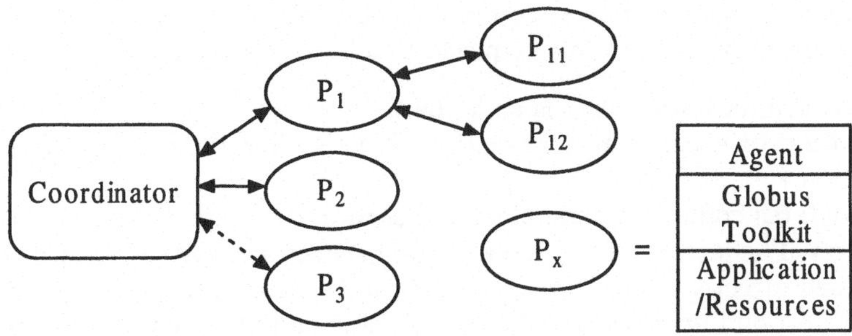

Fig. 2. An example of transaction process: dashed line refers to alternative candidate, which possibly occurs only in cohesion transactions.

The CC message includes necessary information to create a transaction, including transaction type AT, transaction identifier, coordinator address and expires. Participants return Response messages to Coordinator, indicating it agrees to join the transaction.

Preparation for the transaction. Coordinator sends Prepare messages to participants P_i (i=1, 2, . . . ,N). Each P_i reserves necessary resources and returns Prepared or NotPrepared message, depending on whether the reservation is successful or not.

Commit of the transaction. Within T_1, if Coordinator receives N Prepared messages, it sends Commit to all P_i and records the commit in log. Otherwise, it sends Abort to them, making them cancel the previous reservation. On receiving Commit message, each Participant: (a) requests for allocating the reserved resources, (b) records the transaction in log in order to recover later from possible failures, and (c) monitors the execution of corresponding task and report result to Coordinator.

Within T_2, if Coordinator receives N Committed messages, it judges the transaction is correctly completed. Otherwise, it reports failure to the user and sends Rollback messages to all P_i, making them recover to the previous states.

In execution of a transaction, if any P_i itself contains sub-transactions, it will apply above mechanism recursively. In this case, nested transactions form a tree structure, and the P_i not only is a participant but also serves as the sub-coordinator for its children P_{ij} (see Fig. 2).

Coordination of cohesion transaction. Owing to long lifetime, Compensation transaction cann't synchronously commit. We adopt following basic policies for cohesion transaction:

- Instead of reservation of resources, candidates immediately commit the transaction.
- In a given time T, coordinator can determine to confirm or cancel the committed transaction, according to the interest of user. But once the Confirm/Cancel message is sent within T, the result is unchangeable.

– If some candidates fail to commit or don't join, the entire transaction can carry on by initiating new requests to locate substitutes.

The coordination process is as follows.

Initiation of a cohesion transaction. It is similar to that in AT except the transaction type is CT.

Candidates commit independently. Coordinator sends Enroll messages to all candidates. The latter reserve and allocate necessary resources, record operations in log, then directly commit the transaction. If successfully, each candidate generates corresponding compensation transaction and returns Committed message, which contain execution results, to the Coordinator. Otherwise, it automatically rollbacks operations taken previously and returns Aborted messages. From then on, it is removed from the transaction.

Confirmation of user. According to the returned results, the user may take either action through the Coordinator:

– For candidates committing successfully, he confirms some and cancels the others by sending Confirm and Cancel messages to them respectively, within T.
– For failed candidates, he needn't reply them and may renew to send CoordinationContext messages to locate new candidates.

Confirmation of successful candidates. Within T, if a candidate receives a Confirm message, it responds a Confirmed message. Otherwise, it executes a compensation transaction to recover the state to one before commit.

5 Recovery

Recovery includes two ways: before and after commit, which are implemented by rollback and compensation respectively. Here, we focus on how to compensate sub-transactions of a cohesion transaction.

Compensation is the act of making amends when something has gone wrong or when plans are changed. To ensure data consistency, we combine relevant compensation operations into a transaction, namely compensation transaction.

Definition 3. Compensation transaction is the transaction that semantically undoes the partial effects of a sub-transaction without performing cascading abort of dependent sub-transactions.

Generation of compensation transaction adopts event-driven mechanism. Only operations that affect data value or states of an application system need to generate corresponding compensation operations.

Generation of compensation transaction involves following procedures (see Fig. 3):

– By Rule Pre-definition interface, providers of Grid services set up the generation rules of compensation operation.
– According to specified rules, which are stored in Rule Base, Compensation Generator automatically generates compensation operations in the execution of sub-transaction.

– When the sub-transaction commits, Compensation Generator encapsulates the compensation operations generated previously into a compensation transaction.

In a cohesion transaction, both Cancel message and timeout signal startup corresponding compensation transaction to undo the effect of committed sub-transaction.

Compensation operations are generated in the execution course of a sub-transaction. If the sub-transaction fails, all the compensation operations generated previously will be abandoned, which ensures a compensation transaction only undoes effects generated by its corresponding sub-transaction.

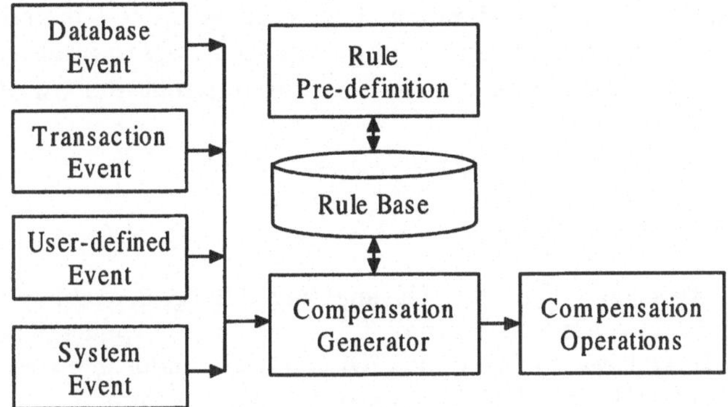

Fig. 3. Generation of compensation transaction.

6 Security Solution

Different from traditional distributed system, in the Grid service environment, a transaction may involve to access to many remote services, while different services often are controlled under different organizations and policies. To ensure the security of transaction, it is necessary to implement the mutual authentication in a convenient way, and then determine whether the user is authorized to request the resource based on some local policies. We use GSI [10,11] to address these issues. The security solution works like this:

– Authentication. It first creates a proxy credential signed by user's private key by using a user proxy. The GSI checks the user's identity using its authentication algorithm.
– Authorization. The factory service maps the proxy credential into local user name, then checks local policy to determine whether the user is allowed to access its local resources. If user is authorized, the factory allocates a credential C_p to create a process that accesses the resources.

- Delegation. For user to access other remote resources, it promulgates process credential C_p on behalf of user. By tracing back along the certificate chain to check the original user certificate, processes started on separate sites by the same user can authenticate one another, enabling user to sign once, run anywhere.
- Encryption. It implements communication protection by using SSL.

7 Conclusions and Future Works

We presented a business transaction coordination framework for Grid service. It has the abilities to manage short-lived operations and long-lived commercial activities. By rollback before commit and compensation after commit, the framework has reliable recovery mechanism. The complex process is invisible to users. The compensation rules may flexibly be set up according to practical demands so that it may adapt to unreliable Grid service environment and various application requirements.

References

1. I Foster, C Kesselman, S Tuecke. The anatomy of the grid: enabling scalable virtual organizations. International Journal of Supercomputer Applications, 2001, 15(3).
2. M Narita, H Arakawa, S Yagi et al. DOPG's cross-vendor interoperability tests of CORBA/OTS and EJB. The Distributed Object Promotion Group, 2002.
3. F Cabrera, G Copeland, T Freund et al. Web Services Coordination(WS-Coordination). 2002.
4. F Cabrera, G Copeland, B Cox et al. Web Services Transaction (WS-Transaction). 2002. 5
5. A Ceponkus, W Cox, G Brown et al. Business Transaction Protocol V1.0. 2002.
6. HP. HP Web Service Transactions 1.0 Tech Preview. 2002.
7. I Foster, C Kesselman. The Globus project: a status report. Heterogeneous Computing Workshop (HCW98) Proceedings, 1998. 4-18.
8. I Foster, C Kesselman. Globus: a metacomputing infrastructure toolkit. The International Journal of Supercomputer Applications, 1997,11(2). 115-128.
9. I. C. Jeong, Y. C. Lew. DCE (Distributed Computing Environment) based DTP (Distributed Transaction Processing). Information Networking, (ICOIN-12) Proceedings. Jan, 1998. 701 -704.
10. R. Butler, V.Welch, D. Engert, I. Foster, S.Tuecke, J. Volmer and C. Kesselman. A national-scale authentication infrastructure. Computer, December, 2000.
11. I. Foster, C. Kesselman, G. Tsudik, and S. Tuecke. A security architecture for computational Grids. ACM Conference on Computer and Communications Security.1998.
12. F. L. Tang, M. L. Li, J. Cao et al. Technology of Enterprise Application Integration Based on Web Services. Proceeding of International Workshop on Grid and Cooperative Computing (GCC 2002). December, 2002.

Conceptual Framework for Recommendation System Based on Distributed User Ratings

Hyun-Jun Kim[1], Jason J. Jung[1], and Geun-Sik Jo[2]

[1] Intelligent E-Commerce Systems Laboratory, School of Computer Science & Engineering, Inha University, Incheon, 402-751, Korea
{dannis,j2jung}@eslab.inha.ac.kr
[2] School of Computer Science & Engineering, Inha University, Incheon, 402-751, Korea
gsjo@inha.ac.kr

Abstract. A recommender system is an automated collaborative filtering system that helps users to decide what they are interested in by extracting their own preferences. Most studies related to recommendation system have focused on centralized environment causing several serious problems such as fraud rating and privacy issues. In this paper, however, we propose the distributed recommender system with FOAF on P2P environment. This system can recommend users without the centralized server, which keeps updating their profiles. In order to find out the most eligible users to be recommended, user grouping (selecting objects) is one of the most important processes in the whole recommendation. Thereby, we have exploited cosine-based similarity method to cluster the users in the same level. More importantly, RFR (Recommend-Feedback-Rerecommend) algorithm is suggested to improve the confidence of recommendation. For the experiment, we have used the *MovieLens* datasets and have tested the performance by using "F1-measure" and Mean Absolute Error (*MAE*). As a conclusion, we have improved the robustness of the system. Also, we have shown the possibility of distributed recommender system on semantic web.

1 Introduction

As the Internet infrastructure has been developed, recommender systems have been issued as one of solutions for information retrieval. A recommender system on E-commerce and Information retrieval has brought reduction of cost for searching by extracting information in which users are interested and listing the result that are likely to fit the user. The computation for recommendation is based on stochastic process which sparse and incomplete data, so that the result can be either correct or occasionally very wrong [1]. At the same time, in order to recommend some information to user, the system has to learn the user preference in advance [2] and this causes privacy issue. These conditions are regarded as a problem that should be solved for modeling recommender system more efficiently. To solve these problems and to increase the performance of the recommender system such as robustness, *MAE* and "F1-measure", researchers have suggested a number of alternative approaches using various techniques [3], [4]. We will present some of the researches in next section.

M. Li et al. (Eds.): GCC 2003, LNCS 3032, pp. 115–122, 2004.

In this paper, we propose a Peer-to-Peer recommender system based on FOAF ('Friend Of A Friend'). Due to the extensibility of the FOAF-based distributed environment, it is possible to aggregate information from other users who have the same interest. User preference is asserted as a property of the FOAF document format by learning user's behaviors. Once the system learns user preferences, it can classify users with respect to their own preferences on real time, and also, it can recommend items in which users are interested to the rest of them in the same group on P2P network. Furthermore, we can increase the robustness of recommendation using RFR algorithm that helps users to decide whether the recommendation is reliable or not by considering other user's rating results in the same group. Finally, we can get satisfactory result of robustness [5]. The outline of the paper is as follows. Section 2 concentrates on the recent and related researches, section 3 refers to the suggesting recommender system based on FOAF and we explain experimental result in section 4. We conclude this study with the future work in section 5.

2 Related Work

Recommender systems, regarded as a part of personalization technique [4], are mainly used in personal information systems and E-Commerce to recommend products to customers. *Tapestry* is one of the earliest systems of collaborative filtering-based recommender system [6]. The *GroupLens* system that developed by research group in University of Minnesota is based on rating for collaborative filtering of *netnews* in order to help people find relevant articles in the huge stream of available articles [7]. This system is also called ratings-based automated recommender system, because filtering is executed by the explicit opinions of people from a close-knit community [8]. There is an additional project, *MovieLens*, which is web-based recommender system for movies, based on *GroupLens* technology. They also offer an experimental data source and a framework for studying user interface issues related to recommender systems [9]. Meanwhile, there have been many studies to enhance privacy issues. In [10], John Canny tries to solve privacy problem with security technologies such as key sharing, encryption and decryption. [11] suggested *Local Profile Model* to protect personal profiles by separating personal profiles from centralized server to each user's PC. Although it can protect draining of personal profile, but the system is working on centralized server, so it is still weak in fraud rating and malicious server attack.

3 Distributed Recommender System Based on FOAF

Recently, information integration and standardization on Semantic web environment have been emerging important field [12]. Many studies have been developed using RDF and XML. FOAF [13] derived from RDFweb makes users possible to link themselves to friend of a friend by using RDF-based document for user profile. When a user publishes a document for some information with FOAF, machines are able to make use of that information, and also users can make their own friends' network by interlinking FOAF. Our recommender system is based on FOAF under distributed environment such as P2P to increase recommendation performance. The recommender system extracts each user's preference that is represented by FOAF document format. By the preferences of each user, recommender system groups users. And then, when a user evaluates an item m_i, the system determines whether m_i is good enough to recommend to another users in the same group or not. Once the system decides to recommend m_i to other users, the recommendation is only applied to level n. We can define the 'level' as the depth of friends to be known by the user directly.

3.1 Extracting User Preferences

Before grouping users according to their preferences, the system needs to know about each user's preferences. In this paper, as used in *MovieLens*, we have distinguished movie genres into 19 categories. Usually a movie can be comprised in more than one category, at the same time, a user can have more than one preference about movie genre. We used *MovieLens*-like strategy to collect users' taste. Each page shows a list that consists of movies selected randomly from an ad hoc manual list of popular movies and the rest randomly from all movies [2]. In order to extract accurate preferences from each user, we employed a probabilistic method as shown Eq.(1).

Assume there are the set of users $U=\{u_1,u_2,\ldots,u_i\}$, the set of movies that is rated by a user u_i is $M=\{m_1,m_2,\ldots,m_j\}$ and the set of genre is $G=\{g_1,g_2,\ldots,g_k\}$. The function $f(P_{ik})$ extracts i-th user's preference about a genre k. This function

$$f(P_{ik}) = \sum_{j=1}^{n} \frac{g_k(m_j)}{\mu} R_{ij} \qquad \mu = \sum_{m=1}^{n} C_m(u_i, m_j) \tag{1}$$

where C_m is a set of genres included in a movie m_j and R_{ij} means a rating value of i-th user about a movie m_j. Also μ means total count of genres that included in movies that are rated by a user u_i.

3.2 User Grouping on Distributed Environment (Object Selection Procedure)

Distributed recommender system is basically impossible to group users at once. To enhance this shortcoming, there have been many studies clustering users on real-time [14]. Because each user' profile is distributed, the grouping of users must be processed at the same time with the recommendation. Although it takes more time to group users compare with centralized system, we can overcome some drawbacks of the system. The user grouping (object selection procedure) is processed on real-time, so it can make distributed system more dynamically, for example, when a new friend is added on a user or when a user's preferences are changed, we do not need to update any part of the system. And the place where users' information is gathering does not exist. Therefore, the distributed recommender system is less dependent on environment than centralized system. It also guarantees users' privacy [10]. Grouping of users must be done before recommendation. For the grouping of users, we used cosine-based similarity that is the most common way to compute the similarity between two users. The similarity between A and B can be calculated with each vectors of A and B, $Sim(A, B) = cos(\vec{A} \cdot \vec{B})$.

$$f(G_i) = \sum_{i+1}^{n} S(\sum_{i}^{n-1} S(u_i)) \qquad S(u_i) \geq T_{optimal} \tag{2}$$

As shown in Eq.(2), the grouping is calculated by the function $f(G_i)$ and it is a summation of the function *S*. where, *S*(*a*) means a set of similar users of user *a* who has preference bigger than threshold $T_{optimal}$.

3.3 RFR (Recommend-Feedback-Re-recommend) Recommendation

On the process of a recommendation, a rating can be regarded as an essential factor for the quality of the system. But, although a user rates an item with good score, we cannot say the result is reliable, because it is just a user's subjective opinion. Therefore, for the quality of recommendation, we need to aggregate same group users' rating as many as possible. Therefore we focused on this level. We assume that a level is a group of a user who has known by a user directly.

$$Level_n = FriendOf(u_i) \qquad Level_{n+1} = FriendOf(Level_n) \tag{3}$$

Recommended user C_1 will take three pieces of information from recommender in $level_{n-1}$. They will be sent by FOAF document involved the name of an item m_j, rating result and the number of rater. The rating result is both a factor that can influence a recommended user to make their decision and a criterion that can compare with threshold for recommendation. Once a user rates an m_j, the rating result is also sent to members of $level_{n+1}$. We can consider three cases as shown in Fig. 1.

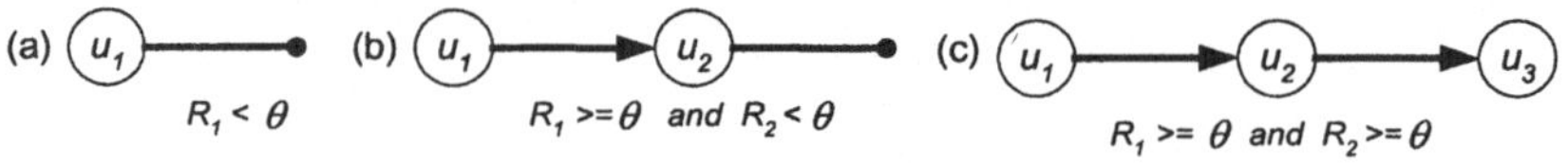

(a) u_1 — $R_1 < \theta$
(b) u_1 → u_2 — $R_1 >= \theta$ and $R_2 < \theta$
(c) u_1 → u_2 → u_3 — $R_1 >= \theta$ and $R_2 >= \theta$

Fig. 1. Three cases of recommendation process by rating.

In Fig. 1(a), R_1 is a rating result from the user C_1. If R_1 is less than threshold θ, no recommendation is being made. And in Fig. 1(b) and Fig. 1(c), there can be two actions from the user C_2 according to their actions; 1) *C2* rates m_j, 2) *C2* do not rates m_j.

In case of 1), the system needs to update the rating result. But the case of 2), the system only needs to recommend another level. To update rating result on real-time, we suggested RFR (Recommend-Feedback-Re-recommend) system.

If U_1 on level 1 rates an item m_j that satisfies with threshold, the system recommends the m_j with rating result to C_1, C_2, and C_n on level 2. Due to the independency between users, each user on the same level cannot recognize another's rating result.

To update summarized rating result from all users on P2P network feedback process is needed. By this process, U_1 will take rating results from users on level 2. Feedback is a set of rating result from users, $Feedback=\{Rate(C_1),\ldots,Rate(C_n)\}$. The first recommender, U_1 can calculate the updated rating result after feedback. Then, it will be re-recommended to C_1, C_2, and C_n, and these processes are applied to all levels (Eq.(4)). Therefore, as the level grows the rating result can be more reputable. The function *Re-recommend* is formulated as follows:

$$Re\text{-}recommend = \frac{Rate(User_i) + Feedback}{N+1} \tag{4}$$

where N is the number of set of feedback.

4 Experiment

In this section, we analyzed performance of proposed system using "F1-measure" and *MAE*. We also examined performance of robustness against malicious action as level increases. Experiments were carried out on Pentium 1 GHz with 256MB RAM, running MS-Windows 2000 Server. The recommender system was implemented by Visual Basic 6.0, Active Server Page (ASP), and IIS 5.0.

4.1 Data Sets

We used *MovieLens* data sets to experiment suggesting recommendation system. *MovieLens* is a web-based research recommender system. The data set contains 1,000,000 anonymous ratings of approximately 3,900 movies made by 6,040 users who joined the site in 2000. For the experiment, we selected 450 users to use only about 66,926 rating dataset [9]. By users' rating data, we can extract all users' preferences. After we got the preferences, we made a matrix of user-user similarity that has 450 rows and 450 columns. Then, we also made the Most Similar Users (MSU) set by cosine-based similarity method.

4.2 Performance Measure

In this experiment, first of all, we employ "F1-measure" widely used in information retrieval community to find the optimal threshold $T_{optimal}$ for user grouping procedure. As shown in Eq.(5), "F1-measure" is calculated by *precision* and *recall*. So we defined *precision* as the ratio of *hit set* size to the *prediction set* size, and *recall* as ratio of *hit set* size to the MSU set size. Whereas, *prediction* is defined as the set of recommendation generated by the system and *hit set* is defined as the intersection of prediction set and MSU set which can be written as '*hit set* = *prediction set* $\cap$ *MSU set*'. For example, if a user u_1 recommends an item m_j to u_2 and u_3, we can define *prediction set* as '$prediction\ (m_j) = \{u_1 \rightarrow u_2, u_1 \rightarrow u_3\}$'.

$$precision\ (P) = \frac{size\ of\ hit\ set}{size\ of\ prediction} \qquad recall\ (R) = \frac{size\ of\ hit\ set}{size\ of\ MSU\ set} \tag{5}$$

Also, for the measurement of the system's accuracy, we used *MAE* as shown in Eq.(6). Where N_p is defined as the number of *prediction*.

$$MAE = \frac{\sum |MSU - prediction|}{N_p} \tag{6}$$

4.3 Experimental Results

For the $T_{optimal}$ of user grouping procedure, we used "F1-measure" with 124 items. After we made FOAF network, recommended each items to users who are randomly selected. We carried out the experiment while changing threshold from 0.1 to 1.

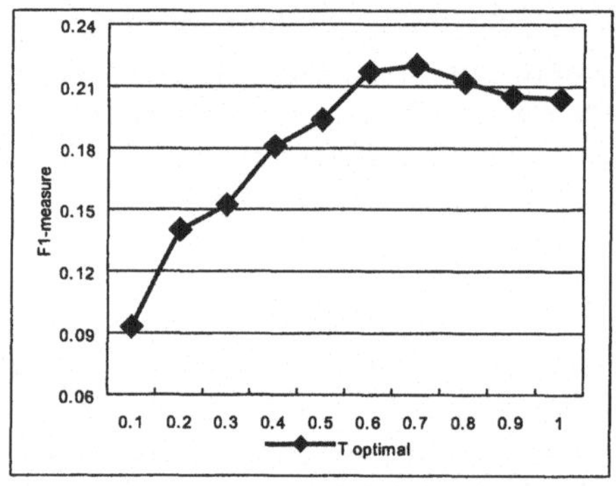

Fig. 2. Variation of the *F1-measure* as changing threshold, $T_{optimal.}$

In Fig. 2., when we set threshold to 0.7, it shows the best result, that is, this leads to the best performance for user grouping (object selection). When any users are recommended on FOAF network, the users propagate the recommendation to their friends who have similarity that is bigger than 0.7 of threshold.

Then, we have used *MAE* to show how the accuracy changes as level increase. In Fig. 3(a), we tested changing values through 6 levels. When we use a data set without any fraud rating, the result is continuously getting lower than former level, $level_{n-1}$. Since the number of users is exponentially increased as a level increase, the system can aggregate as many users' opinion. It means that even there are some of malicious ratings, users can take more accurate recommendation than centralized system as level increase. We have also shown the performance of the system in Fig. 3(b) using "F1-measure" to show robustness. As illustrated in graph, we involved some of malicious ratings in terms of 10%, 20%, and 30%. Generally, even when malicious ratings are included, system's performance is increased as level increase as we already show in Fig. 3(a). When there is no fraud rating, in Fig. 3(b), the performance evaluated by "F1-measure" is improved about 9.17%, and in case of 10%, 20%, and 30% of fraud ratings are included, the performance is improved by 8.02%, 11.35%, and 15.69% respectively.

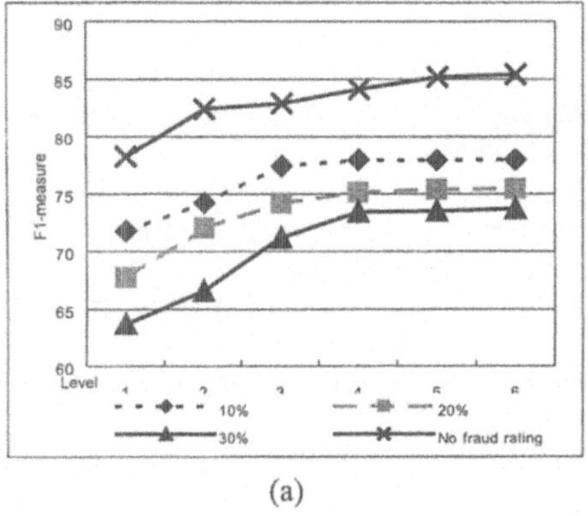

(a)

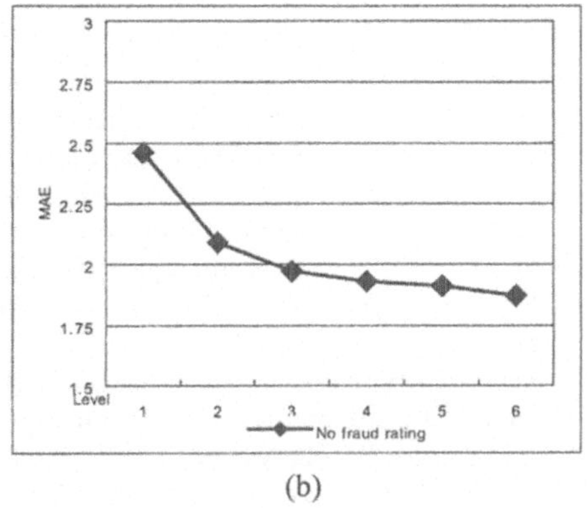

(b)

Fig. 3. Variant of *mean absolute error* (*MAE*) as level increase (a) and system performance measured by "F1-measure" in case of malicious ratings are included (b).

No matter how many fraud ratings are included in a rating data set, as level increase, the performance is improved 11.68% in terms of the three cases in average. Especially, when the percentage of fraud rating is increased, we can get more efficient improvement of the performance. As a result, these three fraud ratings brought only 9.71% of degradation of robustness, compared with original rating set (no fraud rating set).

5 Conclusions and Future Work

As a growing demand of distributed environment, we suggested P2P collaborative filtering system. The proposed system showed two major improvements. First, it can collect other user's ratings by RFR algorithm. So this helps users to make a decision effectively. Second, it is robuster than the centralized recommender system using clustering algorithms such as *k-NN*. When a malicious user tries to give wrong information to other users on the system, in fact, there has not been a way to protect. The proposed system, as shown in experiment Fig. 3(b), consists of P2P users can filter this malicious rating out. As increasing a level, users on the FOAF network can get filtered recommendation from their friends. Meanwhile, there still remain two major defects. First, we need to find a way to keep a consistency of the system. Because P2P is made of peer users, for the quality of performance, it needs as many users to rate items for recommendation. Second, *MAE* in single level is still bigger than the centralized system. Therefore we also need to improve this problem in future.

Acknowledgement. This research was supported by University IT Research Center Project (31152-01).

References

1. Herlocker, J. L., Konstan, J. A., Riedl, J.: Explaining Collaborative Filtering Recommendations. In Proc. of ACM 2000 Conf. on CSCW (2000)
2. Rashid, A. M., Albert, I., Cosley, D., Lam, S. K., McNee, S. M., Konstan, J. A., Riedl, J.: Getting to Know you: Learning New User Preferences in Recommender Systems. In Proc. of the 7th Int. Conf. on Intelligent User Interfaces (2002) 127–134
3. Resnick, P. and Varian, H.R.: Recommender Systems. Comm. of ACM 40, 3 (1997) 56–58
4. Schafer, J.B., Konstan, J.A., Riedl, J.: Recommender Systems in E-Commerce. In Proc. of the ACM Conf. on Electronic Commerce (1999)
5. O'Mahony, M., Hurley, N., Kushmerick, N., Silvestre, G.: Collaborative Recommendation: A Robustness Analysis. ACM Tran. on Internet Technology, Special Issue of Machine Learning for the Internet (2002)
6. D. Goldberg, D. Nichols, B. M. Oki, D. Terry.: Using collaborative filtering to weave an information tapestry. Comm. of the ACM, 35(12) (1992) 61–70
7. Rensnick, P., Iacovou, N., Suchak, M., Bergstrom, P., Riedl, J.: GroupLens : An open architecture for collaborative filtering of Netnews. In Proc. of ACM Conf. on Computer Supported Cooperative Work (1994)
8. Sarwar, B., Karypis, G., Konstan, J., Riedl, J.: Item-Based Collaborative Filtering Recommendation Algorithms. In Proc. of the 10th Int. World Wide Web Conference (2001)
9. Sarwar, B., Karypis, G., Konstan, J., Riedl, J.: Analysis of recommendation algorithms for E-commerce. In Proc. of ACM'00 Conf. on Electronic Commerce (2000) 158–167
10. Canny, J.: Collaborative filtering with privacy. In Proc. of the IEEE Sym. on Research in Security and Privacy (2002) 45–57
11. Sarwar, B. M., Konstan, J. A., Riedl, J.: Distributed Recommender Systems: New Opportunities for Internet Commerce. Chapter 20, Internet Commerce and Software Agents: Cases, Technologies and Opportunities. Idea Group Pubs (2001) 372–393
12. Davies, J., Fensel, D., Harmelen, F. A.: Towards the Semantic Web: Ontology-driven Knowledge Management. John Wiley & Sons, Ltd (2003)
13. http://rdfweb.org/foaf/
14. Nejdl, W., Wolpers, M., Siberski, W., Schmitz, C., Schlosser, M., Brunkhorst, I., Loser, A.: Super-Peer-Based Routing and Clustering Strategies for RDF-Based Peer-To-Peer Networks. In Proc. of the Twelfth International World Wide Web Conference (2003)

Grid Service-Based Parallel Finite Element Analysis

Guiyi Wei[1,2,3], Yao Zheng[1,2], and Jifa Zhang[1,2]

[1] College of Computer Science, Zhejiang University, Hangzhou, 310027, P. R. China
[2] Center for Engineering and Scientific Computation, Zhejiang University, Hangzhou, 310027, P. R. China
[3] Hangzhou Institute of Commerce, Hangzhou, 310035, P. R. China

Abstract. In this paper, we present our work on the integration of existing engineering applications using Grid Services. We address a visual grid framework that provides an integrated development environment for engineering computation applications. Furthermore, we demonstrate how such services can interact with each other. These interactions enable a level of integration that assists the scientific application architect in leveraging applications running in heterogeneous runtime environments. Our framework is implemented by using the existing infrastructures and middleware, the Globus Toolkit. We test our framework for computation solid mechanics applications that require large data transferring, interactive steering, using of multiple platforms, visualization, and access via a portal with graphic interface.

1 Introduction

The name "Finite Element Method" (FEM) appears for the first time in the open literature in an article by Clough [1], Turner, and etc. [2], who used the method in nonlinear structural analysis. Computerized nonlinear structural analysis has acquired full adult rights, but has not developed equally in all areas. FEM has various aspects. On a mathematical point of view, it is a scheme to produce an approximate solution, the accuracy of which can be increased as desired. The functional analysis theory is essential to understand this point. On a computational point of view, efficiency should be sought in solving actual problems which result in large degrees of freedom. Sophisticated algorithms need to be implemented in applying FEM, in particular, to non-linear problems. Parallel computing, which is naturally fit to FEM, is needed to solve large-scale problems.

As a new parallel computing infrastructure, the grid [3-5] enables flexible sharing among a collection of resources that is maintained as parts of different administrative domains. Providing the basic middleware infrastructure for bootstrapping sophisticated collaborative environment, the computational grid allows scientists to collaborate resources even controlled by different domains. Access to these resources is enabled through the use and creation of "virtual organizations".

To scientists in the area of engineering and scientific computing, what they need is a grid-enabled portal, by which they can deploy applications easily without concerning

M. Li et al. (Eds.): GCC 2003, LNCS 3032, pp. 123–130, 2004.

with complex details of grid technologies. With graphical user interfaces, the portal is an integrated development environment based on grid services. In this paper, we describe a multidisciplinary applications-oriented and visualization grid environment. It provides a development and deployment platform for geometrical modeling, discretization, scientific computing and visualization. Advanced services of it can be accessed easily in a visual mode. Their integration as a part of a workflow process enables the creation of services that can be easily reused by the community. Scientists are then in a position to concentrate on the science, while platform developers can focus on the delivery of services that can be assembled as building blocks to create more elaborate services.

2 Introduction to FEM

The term *Finite Element Method* actually identifies a wide range of techniques. A model-based simulation process using FEM involves several steps. These steps are illustrated in Figure 1.

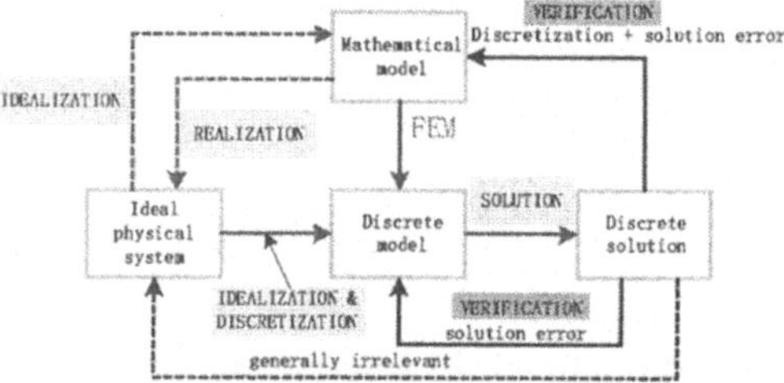

Fig. 1. The mathematical FEM [7]

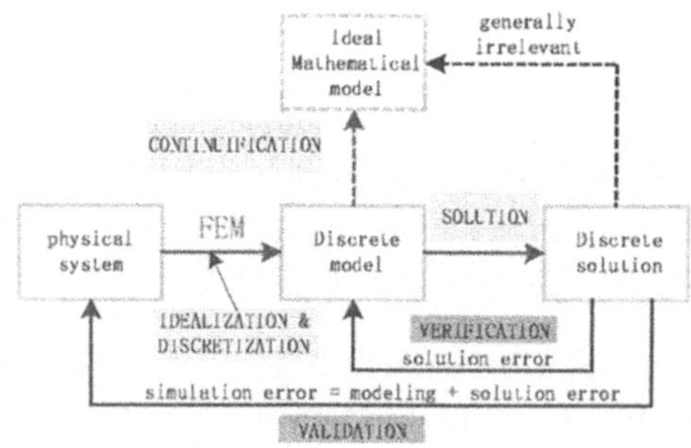

Fig. 2. The physical FEM [7]

In the *discretization* step, a discrete finite element model is generated from a variational or weak form of the mathematical model. The FEM equations are processed by an equation solver, which delivers a discrete solution (or solutions). This may be presented as a *realization* of the mathematical model. Indeed FEM discretizations may be constructed without any reference to physics. In the *mathematical FEM* this is largely irrelevant, however, since the ideal physical system is merely that: a figment of the imagination. The second way of using FEM is the process illustrated in Figure 3. The centerpiece is now the *physical system* to be modeled. Accordingly, this sequence is called the *Physical FEM*. The solution is computed as before. Figure 2 shows an ideal physical system, meanwhile Figure 1 depicts an ideal mathematical model.

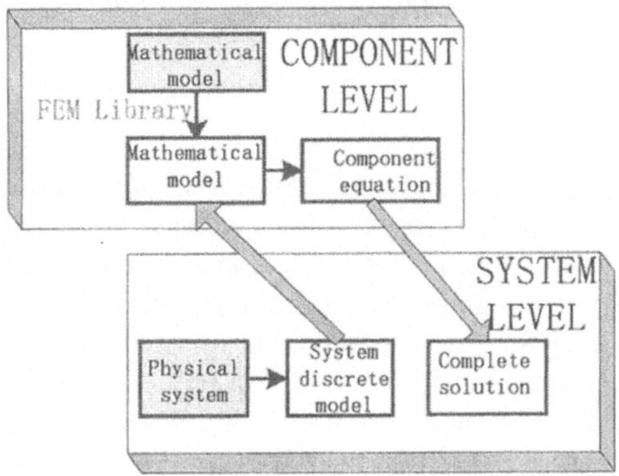

Fig. 3. Combining physical and mathematical modeling through multilevel FEM [7]

3 Application Requirements

To design a computational environment that supports our proposed algorithmic solution, we analyzed the requirements based on the modality of the scientific research to be performed, and concluded that the environment should be (1) a secure environment that protects from the loss of intellectual property and allows restricted access to the data and compute resources; (2) a visual environment that enables the scientist to use the tools in a straightforward fashion; (3) an adaptive environment that is flexible to future changes based on hardware and software; (4)and a dynamic environment that allows the creation of transient services to enable ad hoc collaboration and use of other application services.

We decided to base engineering applications on a framework that is centered on visualization and collaboration of grid services. Additionally, we need to develop advanced application specific services that build on the basic grid services provided by the grid middleware.

Further analysis of our problem domain revealed that it is beneficial to build the framework based on a service-oriented architecture. Such an environment includes flexible design while still being able to integrate sophisticated security solutions. Additionally, we can design services that interact with each other and may operate at geographically dispersed locations.

4 Engineering Computation Oriented Visual Grid Framework

This section describes an engineering computation oriented visual grid framework, which is capable to bridge the gap between currently deployed grid services and the computational applications. The framework is named as VGrid, and is a visual grid environment oriented to engineering computation. Based on the Globus, and coupled with a client component, a services pool and a server component, VGrid visually performs resources discovery, task schedule, and result processing. VGrid improves the efficiency of utilization of resources by introducing a logical resource concept.

4.1 VGrid Architecture

The VGrid is actually a bridge between engineering application and the grid middleware. It provides advanced grid services for developers in a visual fashion. The services include visual MDS, visual FTP service, task management service, dynamic resources dispatch service, geometry modeling and discretization service, result processing service, data format transformation service, parallel computation service, post-process service, and scientific visualization service. These services are integrated by a layered structure. All services are based on GSI service provided by the Globus. To insure security of resources, these services can be used only after authentication and authorization. Users call for services by using a GUI interface of VGrid. The VGrid architecture is shown in Figure 4.

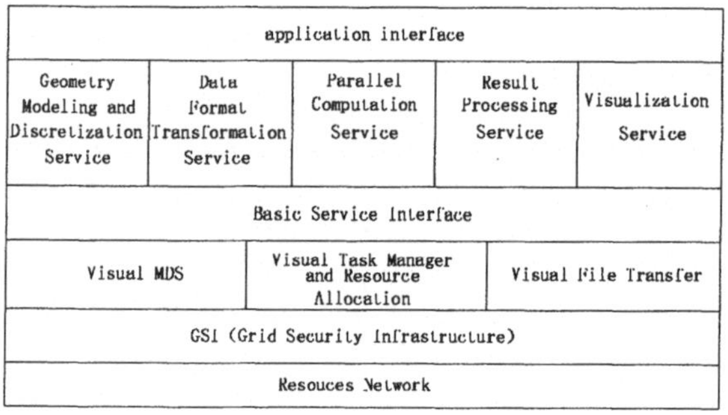

Fig. 4. VGrid architecture

4.2 Visual MDS

The execution of a computing task needs a lot of resources. The resources are distributed, dynamic and autonomous in a grid computation environment. How many resources are available? Which should be allocated to a specified task? These questions must be answered during task scheduling. To answer these two questions, resources information services provide two interfaces, a hierarchical resources tree, and a resources list. The content of this tree is detailed information regarding hosts in the virtual organizations, where local hosts are registered. It also shows the architectures of those virtual organizations.

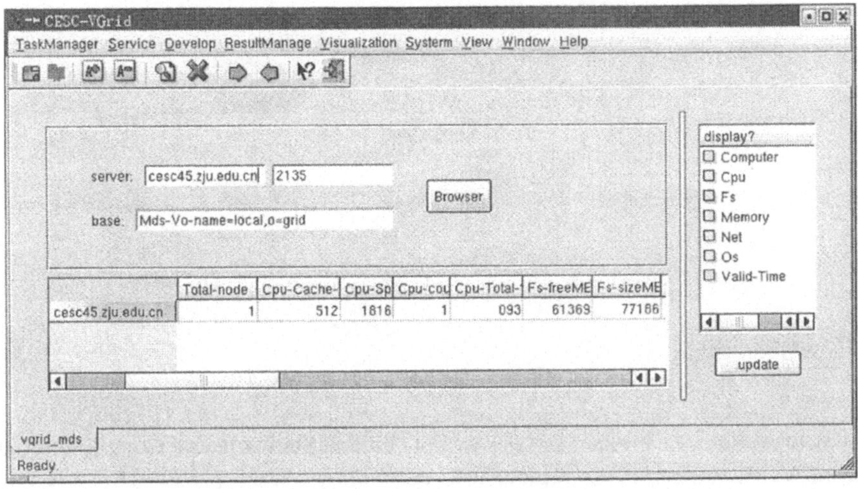

Fig. 5. The snapshot of MDS research result

Each item in the list is information of an individual host. The information on the list can be customized for display. Generally it consists of host name, node count, CPU count, speed and free percentage of CPU, free memory size, free secondary storage, network bandwidth and latency (as shown in Figure 5).

4.3 Visual File Transfer Service

To satisfy the requirement of engineering applications, VGrid integrates GASS [8] (Global Access to Secondary Storage) service and GridFTP service into a visual file transfer service. Visual file transfer service supports remote I/O in a grid environment and GSI and Kerberos security mechanism. Based on authentication, it also supported third-party controlled data transfer mode used for transferring large data set. The communities of researchers that need to access and to analyze this data are often geographically distributed, as are the computing and storage resources that these communities rely upon to store and to analyze their data. It is a time-consuming task to transfer these data. To save transfer time, VGrid visual file transfer service support parallel transfer, strip data transfer, and partial file transfer. In a wide area network, several parallel TCP streams are employed simultaneously to improve the bandwidth.

4.4 Implementation of Task Management and Dynamic Resource Allocation

The service of task manager and dynamic resource allocation in VGrid included task creation, logical resource allocation, physical resource allocation, task submission, task monitoring, and task execution. The workflow of the service is shown in Figure 6.

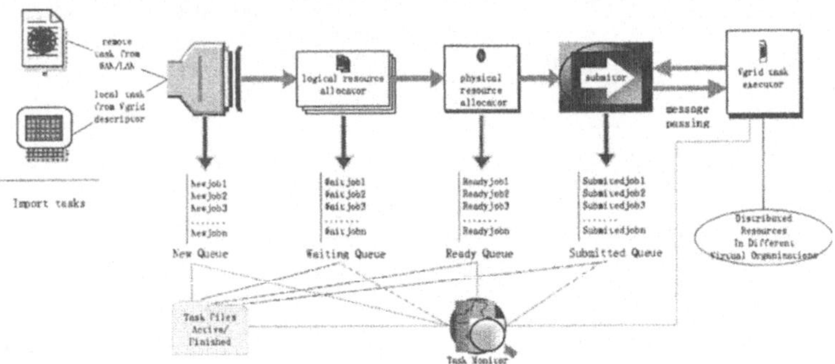

Fig. 6. VGrid task management and resource allocation

A new task can be created in two ways: (1) a local task created using graphic interface of VGrid client; (2) a remote task created by WAN and/or LAN user, which adopted VGrid GRAM protocol. After parsing, the legal tasks will be added to New Queue.

Logical resource allocator dispatches logical resource to tasks. Logical resource is a type of virtual resource defined by the VGrid. It includes resource name, OS type, node count, CPU count, memory size, and etc. Tasks occupies logical resources are moved to Waiting Queue from the New Queue.

Physical resource allocator dispatches physical resource to tasks in the Waiting Queue. During dispatching, visual MDS service is used to confirm resources available. A deadline and budget constrained cost-time optimization algorithm was use to automatically select resources among available resources. VGrid also supported dispatching physical resources through a graphical interface manually. By this way, users are able to setup a special constraint to filter and to get required resources. Tasks occupies physical resources are moved to Ready Queue from the Waiting Queue.

Tasks in the Ready Queue are submitted to task executor by task scheduler using the FIFO algorithm. Client/Server architecture and message passing mechanism are adopted to communicate between the task scheduler and the task executor. The task scheduler creates a new process for every task. This process would not exit until the task is completed. As a daemon program, the task executor provides task deliver service. It makes use of the multiple thread mechanism to accomplish tasks submission. When a message is received from the task scheduler, a thread is created. The thread submitted subtasks of the task to the specified distributed resource managers, receives "jobcontacts", and sends "jobcontacts" to the corresponding process of task scheduler. The task monitor needs the "jobcontacts" to handle the task.

5 An Illustrative Application

Within the VGrid framework, we choose a mechanical device as an illustrative case to examine the parallel finite element analysis in terms of its fitness with the framework, and provide a series of screenshots to illustrate the status of our implementation.

After the discretization by unstructured mesh (4-node tetrahedra), the model consists of 5941 nodes and 24806 elements. Eight grid computing nodes (single CPU, 2GHz, Linux platform, networked with 100M bandwidth) are utilized to carry out the analysis. The results are shown in Figure 7, and are combined from individual subdomains. The domain decomposition is implemented serially by a partitioning program named *Metis* [6].

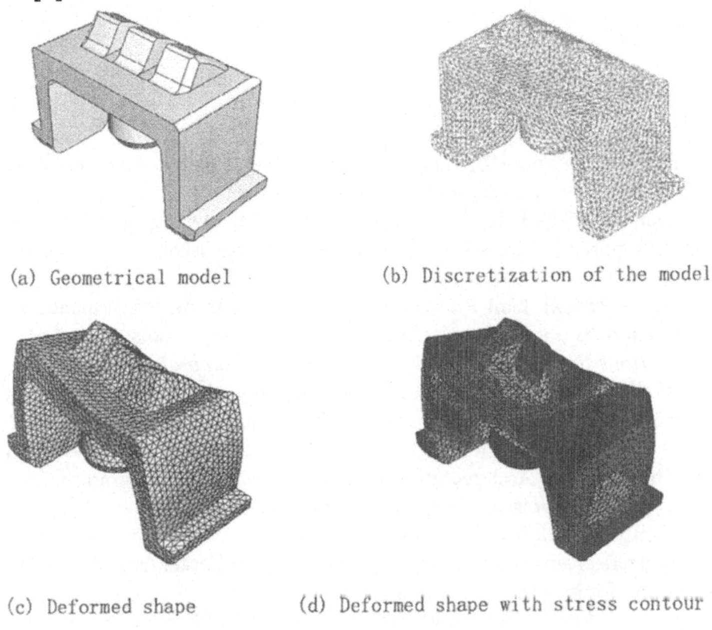

(a) Geometrical model (b) Discretization of the model

(c) Deformed shape (d) Deformed shape with stress contour

Fig. 7. Numerical simulation of a mechanical device

6 Conclusions

In this paper, we have shown that a visual grid framework can be used to provide efficient engineering computation environments. We have demonstrated this feature by prototyping an application-oriented portal usable for computation solid mechanics studies. We have developed an architecture that is flexible and open so that additional services can be integrated in our system. Because of the service-oriented design, it will be possible to replace our services in the future with more advanced ones and to customize the behavior of the system with the help of a workflow engine. Because we combine the use of standard commodity technologies with grid technologies, we are able to create a grid infrastructure using commodity tools. This initial application has already led to the modification and enhancement of toolkits such as the Globus toolkit providing access to the grid.

Acknowledgements. The authors wish to thank the National Natural Science Foundation of China for the National Science Fund for Distinguished Young Scholars under grant Number 60225009. We would like to thank the Center for Engineering and Scientific Computation, Zhejiang University, for its computational resources, with which the research project has been carried out.

References

1. R. W. Clough: The Finite Element Method in Plane Stress Analysis, *Proc. 2nd ASCE Conf. on Electronic Computation*, Pittsburgh, PA, 1960
2. M. J. Turner, E. H. Dill, H. C. Martin and R. J. Melosh: Large Deflection Analysis of Complex Structures Subjected to Heating and External loads, *J. Aerospace Sci.*, 27, 97-107
3. Gregor von Laszewski, Gail Pieper, and Patrick Wagstrom: Performance Evaluation and Characterization of Parallel and Distributed Computing Tools, *Chapter Gestalt of the Grid, Wiley Book Series on Parallel and Distributed Computing*, 2002.
4. I. Foster, C. Kesselman, and S. Tuecke: The Anatomy of the Grid: Enabling Scalable Virtual Organizations, *International Journal of Supercomputer Applications*, 15(3), 2001.
5. Ian Foster, Carl Kesselman, Jeffrey Nick, and Steven Tuecke: The Physiology of the Grid: An Open Grid Services Architecture for Distributed Systems Integration, http://www.globus.org/research/papers/ogsa.pdf, February 2002.
6. METIS: Family of Multilevel Partitioning Algorithms, URL: http://www-users.cs.umn.edu/~karypis/metis/ (Current September 26, 2003)
7. Introduction to Finite Element Methods http://titan.colorado.edu/courses.d/IFEM.d/IFEM.Ch01.d/IFEM.Ch01.pdf

The Design and Implementation of the GridLab Information Service

Giovanni Aloisio, Massimo Cafaro, Italo Epicoco, Daniele Lezzi, Maria Mirto, and Silvia Mocavero

Center for Advanced Computational Technologies
University of Lecce/ISUFI, Italy
{giovanni.aloisio,massimo.cafaro,italo.epicoco,
daniele.lezzi,maria.mirto,silvia.mocavero}@unile.it

Abstract. The grid computing paradigm emerged recently as a new field distinguished from traditional distributed computing because of its focus on large-scale resource sharing and innovative high-performance applications. The grid infrastructure ties together a number of Virtual Organizations, that reflect dynamic collections of individuals, institutions and computational resources. Flexible, secure and coordinated resource sharing among VOs requires the availability of an information rich environment to support resource discovery and decision making processes. The Globus Toolkit provides applications developers with the Monitoring and Discovery Service (MDS) to support development of grid-aware applications, able to exploit the knowledge about current grid status and configuration to adapt themselves to changes in heterogeneous, dynamic environments. In this paper we describe the design and implementation of the GridLab Information Service.

1 Introduction

The grid computing paradigm [1] emerged recently as a new field distinguished from traditional distributed computing because of its focus on large-scale resource sharing and innovative high-performance applications. The grid infrastructure ties together a number of Virtual Organizations (VOs) [2], that reflect dynamic collections of individuals, institutions and computational resources. Flexible, secure and coordinated resource sharing between VOs requires the availability of an information rich environment to support resource discovery and decision making processes. The Globus Toolkit [3] provides applications developers with the Monitoring and Discovery Service (MDS) to support development of grid-aware applications, able to exploit the knowledge about current grid status and configuration to adapt themselves to changes in heterogeneous, dynamic environments.

Currently, the MDS infrastructure is based on two kind of Information Services, the Grid Resource Information Service (GRIS) and the Grid Index Information Service (GIIS). The GRIS supplies information about a specific resource,

M. Li et al. (Eds.): GCC 2003, LNCS 3032, pp. 131–138, 2004.

while the GIIS can be thought of as an aggregate directory because a GIIS gathers information from multiple GRIS servers (belonging to the same VO or to multiple VOs) and supplies it as an aggregate collection of information. Thus the MDS is a hierarchical infrastructure with distributed services allowing for scalability and fault tolerance (a resource failure does not affect other resources).

The paper is organized as follows. Section 2 introduces the GridLab Project and Section 3 recalls GridLab MDS requirements. We present in Section 4 the details about the design and implementation of the GridLab MDS and conclude the paper in Section 5.

2 The GridLab Project

The GridLab project [4] is funded by the European Commission under the Fifth Framework Programme of the Information Society Technology. The GridLab project aims to allow the integration of applications with emerging Grid technologies, providing a Grid Application Toolkit (GAT) that can be used to develop grid-aware applications without having to understand, or even being aware of the underlying technologies. The project is grounded by two principles, (i) the co-development of infrastructure with real applications and user communities, leading to working scenarios, and (ii) dynamic use of grids, with self-aware simulations adapting to their changing environment. Central to the project are:

- **The design and development of a Grid Application Toolkit (GAT).** The main goal of the project is to provide a software environment for grid-enabled scientific applications. GridLab will provide a set of high-level APIs through which applications access and use available resources. The functionality of the APIs will be provided by several capabilities providers, which may be GridLab services or third-party services; where possible these will be Grid Services, i.e., services compliant with the Open Grid Service Architecture (OGSA) [5] [6] specification;
- **The implementation of dynamic simulation scenarios for the Grid.** The benefits of the GAT will be demonstrated by developing and implementing real application scenarios, exploiting to the fullest extent the power of the Grid. To this end, in the project we will utilize extensively specific application frameworks, namely Cactus [7] and Triana [8], which are Problem-Solving Environments (PSEs) for composing, compiling and running applications in specific areas;
- **The development of Grid applications on a real testbed.** GAT is accompanied by the establishment of a testbed constructed by linking heterogeneous collections of supercomputers and other resources spanning Europe and the USA, using and extending existing testbeds.

The GridLab project consists of twelve core workpackages, with additional workpackages covering exploitation, dissemination and project management; the University of Lecce leads the Information Services workpackage, whose purpose is to extend the existing Globus Toolkit Monitoring and Discovery Service to provide the information rich environment needed by grid-aware applications.

3 GridLab MDS Requirements

The goal of the GridLab Information Service is to provide a new set of Globus MDS extensions taking into account that the grid is inherently dynamic, i.e machine load and availability, network latency and bandwidth change continually, so MDS extensions need to be developed to address grid-aware application requirements. This functionalities will allow new uses of global computational resources. Limitations and capabilities of Globus MDS v2.2 have been used as a starting point to develop the needed extensions. The design of the Gridlab MDS has been strongly dependent on inputs from others Work Packages, and the information schema defined by the Globus Project has been used as a starting point.

The GridLab Project requirements can be classified as being *functional*, *not functional*, *technological* and *inverse*. Functional requirements describe the functionalities that the system must provide; usually they imply a certain degree of interaction between the user and the system. It is worth noting here that the user, in a grid context, need not be necessarily a person: often the user will be a software agent acting on behalf of a real user. Not functional requirements describe the services provided by the system as internal functionalities between software modules; they can also be used to express temporal constraints. These requirements are not directly concerned with the functionalities that the system will provide, however, their implementation is critical with respect to the correctness of the whole project. Technological requirements are strictly related to the hardware and software infrastructure on which the project will be based. Finally, inverse requirements are implicit requirements that must be correctly detected and stated explicitly. Often, inverse requirements are concerned with the security of the system. GridLab functional requirements include, to date, the following:

The Information Service provides information related to:

- Services;
- Web Services;
- Software;
- Users;
- Firewalls;
- Virtual Organizations;
- Certification Authorities;
- Clusters.

Not functional requirements include the following:

The Information Service must be accessed through a Web Service interface. The information providers for users, CA certificates and clusters retrieve the information directly. Information providers for services, web services, software, firewalls and VOs retrieve the information from an internally managed database, which is initially empty and must be populated through the GridLab MDS Web Service.

Technological requirements dictate the use of the Globus Toolkit MDS version 2.2, and the porting of the system to the architectures belonging to the GridLab testbed (linux, tru64, irix), while inverse requirements lead to the adoption of the Globus Security Infrastructure (GSI) [9] as the security mechanism.

4 The GridLab MDS

The design of the GridLab Information Service led to the attributes described in the next subsections. These attributes comes from a detailed comparison of attributes already available inside the Globus MDS and attributes needed for GridLab grid computing scenarios. Related information providers were implemented using the Perl scripting language, in order to simplify the porting process to other architectures. The front-end Web Service that provides read/write access to the MDS has been implemented in C using the gSOAP Toolkit [10] and the GSI plug-in for gSOAP [11].

The gSOAP Toolkit is a platform-independent development environment for C and C++ Web Services. The toolkit provides an easy-to-use RPC compiler that produces the stub and skeleton routines to integrate (existing) C or C++ applications into SOAP/XML Web Services. A unique aspect of the gSOAP toolkit is that it automatically maps native C/C++ application data types to semantically equivalent XML types and vice versa. This enables direct SOAP/XML messaging by C/C++ applications on the Web. As a result, full SOAP interoperability can be achieved with a simple API relieving the user from the burden of SOAP details, thus enabling him or her to concentrate on the application-essential logic. The toolkit uses the industry-standard SOAP 1.1/1.2 and WSDL 1.1 protocols and offers an extensive set of features that are competitive to commercial implementations, including stand-alone HTTP server capabilities, Zlib compression, SSL encryption and streaming Direct Internet Message Encapsulation (DIME) attachments.

We developed the GSI plug-in for gSOAP in the context of the GridLab project to build a GSI enabled front-end Web Service to MDS. The plug-in exploits the modular architecture of the gSOAP Toolkit allowing the development of GSI enabled Web Services and clients, with full support for mutual authentication/authorization, delegation of credentials and connection caching. It is worth noting here that both gSOAP and the GSI plug-in for gSOAP are open-source software and freely available.

The security policy adopted for the current prototype release of GridLab MDS is to deny anonymous binding to the MDS; MDS servers can be contacted directly only through GSI binding. Authorized users are actually allowed to read/write data through our MDS Web Service, and authentication/authorization is based on Globus GSI.

4.1 Information Related to Services and Web Services

During the course of the GridLab project, a number of services and Web Services will be developed by GridLab Work Packages. One of the most important requirements for GridLab grid computing scenarios is the ability to discover services dynamically. The MDS will provide GridLab developers with the following functionalities: registration, unregistration and lookup. More than one instance for each service or Web Service can be registered. In this category falls the following attributes:

- GridLab-Mds-Service-name: service logical name;
- GridLab-Mds-Service-port: service port;
- GridLab-Mds-Service-type: service protocol;
- GridLab-Mds-Service-description: service description;
- GridLab-Mds-Service-publisher: service publisher (X509v3 certificate distinguished name).

- GridLab-Mds-WebService-name: Web Service name;
- GridLab-Mds-WebService-WSDL-location: url where the WSDL document for the Web Service can be found;
- GridLab-Mds-WebService-publisher: Web Service publisher (X509v3 certificate distinguished name);
- GridLab-Mds-WebService-description: Web Service description.

4.2 Information Related to Installed Software

In order to submit jobs on grid resources, it is of crucial importance to know details related to the software packages that will be used in a run, may be a complex parallel simulation or a simple batch job. In this category falls the following attributes:

- GridLab-Mds-Software-name: name;
- GridLab-Mds-Software-version: version;
- GridLab-Mds-Software-path: pathname;
- GridLab-Mds-Software-totalLicences: number of total software licences;
- GridLab-Mds-Software-freeLicence: number of available software licences;
- GridLab-Mds-Software-licenceInfo: information about software licence;
- GridLab-Mds-Software-startupEnvironment: (multi-valued) software startup environmental variables;
- GridLab-Mds-Software-executable: software executable;
- GridLab-Mds-Software-arguments: (multi-valued) software arguments;
- GridLab-Mds-Software-description: software description;
- GridLab-Mds-Software-helpURL: software help URL;
- GridLab-Mds-Software-usage: software usage.

4.3 Information Related to Users

Information related to users allow complex brokering strategies: for instance, once the set of computing resources available to a user is known to a broker, it is then possible to choose carefully where to submit a user's job. The broker's decision will be based on the information gathered from the MDS and on the job's requirements. In this category falls the following attributes:

- GridLab-Mds-User-ID: user's login name on local resource;
- GridLab-Mds-User-Mapped-DN: (multi-valued) attribute representing the distinguished name mapped on the user;
- GridLab-Mds-User-homedir: user's home directory;
- GridLab-Mds-User-shell: user's shell;
- GridLab-Mds-User-UID: user's UID;
- GridLab-Mds-User-GID: user's GID;
- GridLab-Mds-User-comment: a short comment about the user.

4.4 Information Related to Firewalls

This kind of information is strictly related to service information. As a matter of fact, before registering a service, GridLab developers will query the MDS to know dynamically the range of open ports available on a specified computational resource. This is required to allow other people to connect to a service. In this category falls the following attributes:

- GridLab-Mds-Firewall-hostname: firewall hostname;
- GridLab-Mds-Firewall-ports: (multi-valued) represents open ports (range);
- GridLab-Mds-Firewall-validityTime: time frame during which open ports ranges are valid;
- GridLab-Mds-Firewall-adminDN: distinguished name of the firewall administrator.

4.5 Information Related to Virtual Organizations

The GridLab project will span multiple Virtual Organizations. Corresponding information will allow people to know, for instance, how to request an account on a machine belonging to a particular Virtual Organization, or the people to contact in case of trouble. In this category falls the following attributes:

- GridLab-Mds-Vo-name: Virtual Organization to which a specified computational resource belongs to;
- GridLab-Mds-Vo-helpDeskPhoneNumber: (multi-valued) help-desk phone;
- GridLab-Mds-Vo-helpDeskURL: URL pointing to a Virtual Organization's web page;
- GridLab-Mds-Vo-adminName: administrator name of the VO.

4.6 Information Related to Recognized Certification Authorities

This is a set of information about the certification authorities allowed to sign the user's certificates that can be used to access and use the resource; it is important to know which CAs must be contacted to obtain a valid certificate and which CAs are recognized on a given computational resource. In this category falls the following attributes:

- GridLab-Mds-Certificate-Subj: distinguished name of the recognized certification authority;
- GridLab-Mds-Certificate-version: CA's certificate version;
- GridLab-Mds-Certificate-serialNumber: CA's certificate serial number;
- GridLab-Mds-Certificate-signatureAlgorithm: CA's certificate signature algorithm;
- GridLab-Mds-Certificate-issuer: CA's certificate issuer;
- GridLab-Mds-Certificate-validity-from: beginning date of the CA's certificate validity;
- GridLab-Mds-Certificate-validity-to: end date of the CA's certificate validity;
- GridLab-Mds-Certificate-publicKeyAlgorithm: CA's certificate public key algorithm;
- GridLab-Mds-Certificate-RSAPublicKey: CA's certificate RSA public key;
- GridLab-Mds-Certificate-crlURL: url where the CA CRL can be found.

4.7 Information Related to Clusters

The information about Clusters include general information about nodes (number of CPUs, available memory etc), and detailed information about queues and jobs running. Accessing such information is crucial for resource management, brokering strategies etc. In this category we show here, due to space limitations, the most important attributes:

- GridLab-Mds-Cluster-cpudistribution: the cpu distribution of the nodes given in the form of "m cpu:n nodes";
- GridLab-Mds-Cluster-nodecpu: the cpu type of the nodes (model name and MHz);
- GridLab-Mds-Cluster-nodememory: the memory installed on the node in MB;
- GridLab-Mds-Queue-assignedcpunumber: the number of cpus assigned to the queue;
- GridLab-Mds-Queue-status: the queue status;
- GridLab-Mds-Queue-running: the number of running jobs in the cluster belonging to this queue;
- GridLab-Mds-Queue-maxwallclocktime: the maximum wall clock time allowed for jobs submitted to the queue in mins;
- GridLab-Mds-Queue-maxcputime: the maximum CPU time allowed for jobs submitted to the queue in mins;
- GridLab-Mds-Queue-job-total-count: the number of queue total jobs;
- GridLab-Mds-Job-status: the status of the job;

5 Conclusions

In this paper we described the requirements, design and implementation of the GridLab Information Service. The system allows flexible, secure and coordinated resource sharing between VOs and supports the development of grid-aware applications capable of adapting themselves to changes in heterogeneous, dynamic environments. Currently, the system leverages the Globus Toolkit MDS v2.2, however we plan to design and implement an OGSA compliant Information Service porting the system to Globus Toolkit v3. Additional work includes the use of security services, in particular for authorization, when these services will be released by the GridLab security Work Package. Of course, the current schema is not meant to be static, the schema will evolve and will be extended to support additional information that will be required by the GridLab project.

Acknowledgements. We gratefully acknowledge support of the European Commission 5th Framework program, grant IST-2001-32133, which is the primary source of funding for the GridLab project.

References

1. Foster, I., Kesselman C.: The Grid: Blueprint for a new Computing Infrastructure, Morgan Kaufmann, 1998
2. Foster, I., Kesselmann, C., Tuecke, S.: The Anatomy of the Grid: Enabling Scalable Virtual Organizations. International Journal Supercomputer Applications, Vol.15, 2001, No. 3, pp. 200–222
3. Foster, I., Kesselman C.: GLOBUS: a Metacomputing Infrastructure Toolkit, Int. J. Supercomputing Applications, 1997, pp. 115–28
4. The GridLab project. http://www.gridlab.org
5. Foster, I., Kesselmann, C., Nick, J., Tuecke, S.: Grid Services for Distributed System Integration. Computer, Vol. 35, 2002, No. 6, pp. 37–46
6. Foster, I., Kesselmann, C., Nick, J., Tuecke, S.: The Physiology of the Grid: An Open Grid Services Architecture for Distributed System Integration. Technical Report for the Globus project. http://www.globus.org/research/papers/ogsa.pdf
7. Goodale, T., Allen, G., Lanfermann, G., Massó, J., Radke, T., Seidel, E., Shalf, J.: The Cactus Framework and Toolkit: Design and Applications. Proceedings of *Vector and Parallel Processing – VECPAR'2002, 5th International Conference*, (Berlin, Germany),Lecture Notes in Computer Science, Springer-Verlag, 2003.
8. Triana. http://www.triana.co.uk
9. Foster, I., Kesselmann, C., Tsudik G., Tuecke, S.: A security Architecture for Computational Grids. Proceedings of 5th ACM Conference on Computer and Communications Security Conference, pp. 83-92, 1998.
10. Van Engelen, R.A., Gallivan, K.A.: The gSOAP Toolkit for Web Services and Peer-To-Peer Computing Networks. Proceedings of IEEE CCGrid Conference, May 2002, Berlin, pp- 128–135
11. Aloisio, G., Cafaro, M., Lezzi, D., Van Engelen, R.A.: Secure Web Services with Globus GSI and gSOAP. Proceedings of Euro-Par 2003, 26th - 29th August 2003, Klagenfurt, Austria, Lecture Notes in Computer Science, Springer-Verlag, N. 2790, pp. 421-426, 2003

Comparison Shopping Systems Based on Semantic Web – A Case Study of Purchasing Cameras

Ho-Kyoung Lee [1], Young-Hoon Yu [1], Supratip Ghose [1], and Geun-Sik Jo[2]

[1] Intelligent E-Commerce Systems Laboratory, School of Computer Science & Engineering, Inha University, Incheon, 402-751, Korea
{machi,yhyu,anik}@eslab.inha.ac.kr
http://eslab.inha.ac.kr/

[2] School of Computer Science & Engineering, Inha University, Incheon, 402-751, Korea
gsjo@inha.ac.kr

Abstract. A critical capability required for operating in today's information overload is the ability to aggregate information from disparate sources into a unified coherent form. To date, almost majority contents of shopping mall are built by technology that is not regarding as integration and extension. We need to make a meta-data and product lists additionally if we want to use comparison-shopping. However, this meta-data does not contain semantics, it can only serve text searching. For this reason, a buyer wastes time costs to get any information in which they are really interested. Moreover, comparison shopping malls are adapted by their own technology; therefore it is also impossible to share their products information. In this paper, we use semantic web technology DAML+OIL. By using this, we make ontology for each shopping mall, and we define concept and structure and we made DAML markup instance data, then extracted semantic factors using DAMLJessKB. We also used these extracted semantic factors as a fact for the JESS inference engine, so that we can make it possible to inference and provide reasoning in web data structures. Our approach allows inference to be carried out when a query is processed and done. Thereby, to validate our approach, we have implemented a working prototype based on and then used the above semantic web inference-system.

1 Introduction

By all measures, the Web is enormous and growing at a staggering rate. This growth has made it both increasingly difficult and increasingly important for humans and programs to quickly and accurately access Web information and services. Contents of existing shopping mall are composed of special product meta-data. Such built in meta-data is hard to offer more than simple text search because it is not retaining meaning and in real condition unnecessary search result is a wastage of time for many purchasers thereby. However it is possible to provide meaningful content for the machine. Ontology that is specification of concept can structure knowledge from data for sharing information among shopping malls such as comparison buyer systems in [3] [7]. That is why, we delve into making a system that can provide semantic web inferencing and can help us achieve flexible and precise information retrieval.

M. Li et al. (Eds.): GCC 2003, LNCS 3032, pp. 139–146, 2004.

2 Related Works

Comparison-shopping system refers to system that search shop which when user wishes to find specification goods and compare relevant goods for shopping. It has been said in the related literature [11] that there are several first generation comparison-shopping tools have been emerging in the last few year that encompass Cross-Merchant Product comparison as well as provide Price-comparison shopping Agents. So, currently there are several intelligent agents or wrapper online shopping services. The prominent of those are Bargain Finder, developed by Andersen Consulting, Firefly, From Firefly, Inc, and ShopBot, from the University of Washington.

However, shortcoming of those systems are that Web pages typically contain not only one or more product descriptions, but also information about the store itself, meta--information about the shopping process, headings, likes to related sites, and advertisements. Existing keyword-based search retrieves irrelevant information, writing wrappers for each on-line store is a time-consuming activity and changes in the outfit cause high maintenance efforts. The quality has also been affected with information source being incomplete and error prone. Extracting data from HTML coded webpages is difficult because there is no mechanical way to identify a useful pattern for extraction. XML provides essentially a mechanism to declare and use simple data structures and moreover it can express complex language but still does not an adequate language for representing and reasoning about the kind of knowledge essential to realizing the Semantic web vision. As our work related to the ontology-enhanced query engine we try to give a brief view to the related terminologies in the following discussion.

The central idea in Semantic Web is to develop and use machine-understandable instead of human-understandable language for the expression of the semantic content of Web pages to make the Web more intelligent, therefore, to help people find the right information on the web. Meta-data is there for the search engine to work with meaningful information.

DAMLJessKB [2] is a tool for reasoning with the Semantic web and DAML. DAMLJessKB maps DAML triples into facts in a production system and then applies rules implementing the relevant Semantic Web languages.

JESS [5] was initially developed as a Java version of the CLIPS (C Language Integrated Production System) expert system shell, but it has now grown into a complete, distinct, dynamic environment of its own. It provides a convenient way to integrate complex reasoning capabilities into Java-based software and makes it suitable for Semantic Web reasoning.

3 System Architecture

Our suggested comparative shopping system architecture based on Semantic Web is shown in Fig.1. Each domain generates ontology based on DAML+OIL for its products, and instance is being made from this ontology by DAML document.

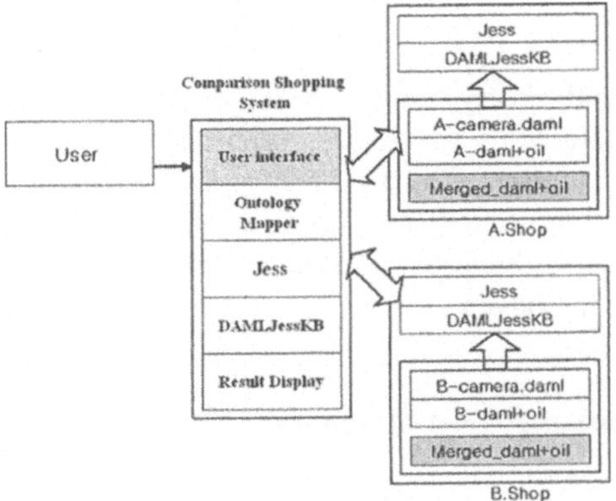

Fig. 1. System Architecture

When integrating information to semantic web based comparative shopping system, they use ontology mapper of the system, so that they can map ontologies from various domains. By doing this, the system can get merged ontology (Merged DAML+OIL) that define relations among products from various domains.

Buyer can search any product that interests him by using user interface. This process is done according to Fig.1. Any query that is made by a buyer is being sent to each domain, then it is inputted as a fact for JESS through Merged DAML+OIL and DAMLJessKB and the inference is being done based on DAML+OIL rules/domain rules. Last, DAMLJessKB transforms the result to DAML format.

The Semantic Web Search system accepts user queries by means of a Graphical User Interface (GUI). On initialization, the GUI loads the default ontology and displays the ontology classes and their respective property values respectively.

We utilized Jena toolkit [14] for this purpose. The toolkit includes an ARP (Another RDF Parser) to parse the RDF documents. It also contains a DAML API with classes to manipulate DAML ontologies and extract information from them. The Jena toolkit dynamically reads in the ontology and obtains the class-property information. This ensures that the application is domain neutral.

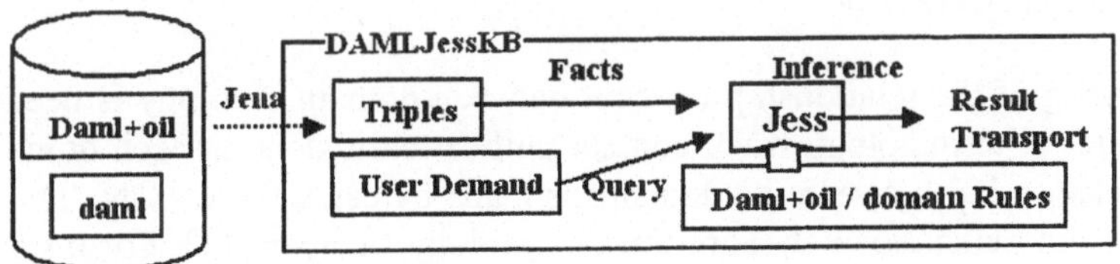

Fig. 2. *(JESS)* reasoning process through *(DAMLJessKB)*

Final result, which is processed from various domains, is being sent to final buyer by Result Display module on the system.

3.1 User Interface

The user interacts with the system by means of user interface that allows the user to make appropriate selections for classes, their properties, and properties of Object properties within the domain. Buyer puts information of detailed search information as well as purchasing item, and Search item through the user interface of the web or application. The Queries have been made and executed at JESS Query, and then the result is provided to the buyer.

3.2 Creation of Ontology and Metadata

The ontology based on DAML+OIL of camera as a comparison purchasing domain is provided in this paper. For example, SLR is defined as a subclass of camera. SLR class is a search object when camera class is selected at query. Therefore subclass of camera search as Digital large-format can be selected at the time of searching SLR. While all cameras have a viewfinder, a SLR has a viewfinder whose value is restricted to "Through the Lens".

```
<daml:Class rdf:ID="SLR">
 <daml:intersectionOf rdf:parseType="Collection">
   <daml:Class rdf:about="#Camera"/>
   <daml:Restriction>
     <daml:onProperty rdf:resource="#viewFinder"/>
     <daml:hasValue rdf:resource="#ThroughTheLens"/>
   </daml:Restriction>
 </daml:intersectionOf>
</daml:Class>
```

Fig. 3. Camera Ontology with DAML+OIL

DAML instance meta-data is made of based on concept structure of the ontology.

3.3 Ontology Metadata

The mapping of the relationship concept between domain ontology is needed to protect conflict of terminology when content unification is done in each domain. Terminology relationship between the domains is made by using the KAON (The Karlsruhe Ontology and Semantic Web Tool Suite) Ontology Mapper [11]. For instance, let us assume that "size" is used for the property as the size of camera lens in the domain A and at the same time, we can assume that "focal-length" is used for the same meaning in domain B. Then, these two properties must be considered as same concept by JESS inference process. "Focal-length" and "size" relationship equality be represented by using "samePropertyAS" in the DAML+OIL specification.

```
<daml:DatatypeProperty rdf:ID="focal-length">
    <daml:samePropertyAs rdf:resource="#size"/>
    <rdfs:domain rdf:resource="#Lens"/>
    <rdfs:range rdf:resource="&xsd;#string"/>
</daml:DatatypeProperty>
<daml:DatatypeProperty rdf:ID="f-stop">
    <daml:samePropertyAs rdf:resource="#aperture"/>
    <rdfs:domain rdf:resource="#Lens"/>
    <rdfs:range rdf:resource="&xsd;#string"/>
</daml:DatatypeProperty>
```

Fig. 4. Mapping Ontology

3.4 DAMLJessKB

JESS should be converted into rule through DAMLJessKB because it does not understand DAML+OIL syntax declaration.

DAMLJessKB provides JESS with meaning of ontology compared of daml+oil in the form of fact. The information can be achieved by *defquery* of JESS based on fact and rules. For example, with the JESS Query that is shown below in fig. 5, includes the camera body to the list of which the prize is over 2,000,000 korean won.

```
(defquery search2 (declare (max-background-rules 100))
 (PropertyValue &rdf;type ?n &machi;Body)
 (PropertyValue &machi;cost ?n ?res)
 (PropertyValue &rdf;value ?res
   ?s&:(or (integerp ?s) (floatp ?s))&:(>= (float ?s) 200000))
)
```

Fig. 5. JESS Query

4 Experimental Evaluation

4.1 Experimentation

To Date, through the implemented system the user can query with some of its specifications for purchasing camera. The user starts by entering several search terms to specify what he or she is looking for.

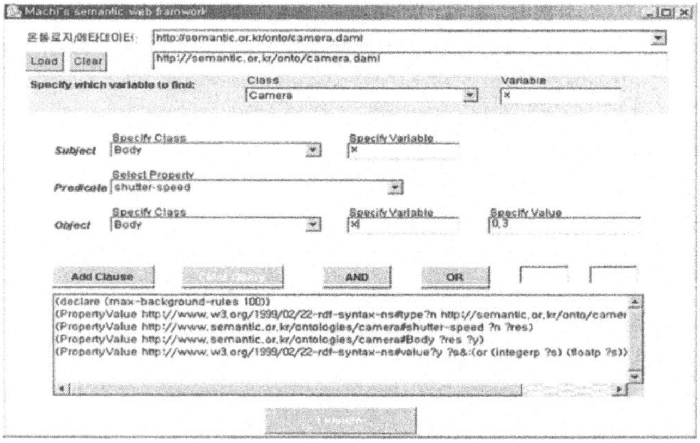

Fig. 6. Query interface

This figure depicted in Fig. 7 below is the result set of a particular relevant query entered by the user at query interface of Fig. 6. The relevant information of a product is shown in the right window in a tree structure upon selection of the particular product type from the left window. The interface produced a meaningful and intuitive display of search results by hierarchically displayed output. To give a precise meaning between a concept and its sub-concept in the concept hierarchy, our solution lies in producing a meaningful display of search results by moving away from the traditional ranked list of relevant documents and to instead generate hierarchically displayed output. This output visualizes the query results with numbers attached to the relevant fragments of the concept hierarchy, each number indicating the importance of the camera component level of a particular product type with respect to the particular component concept it is attached to.

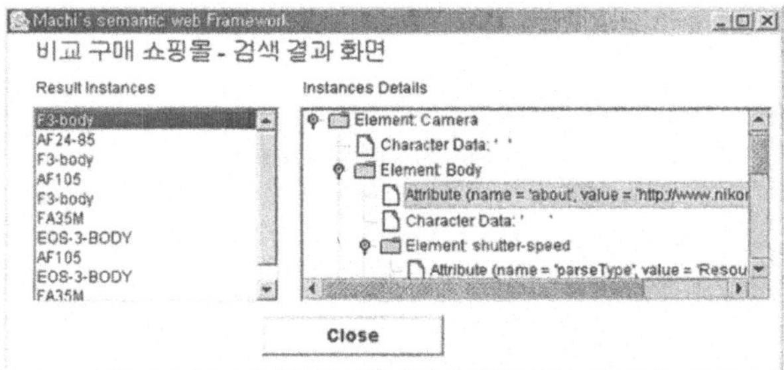

Fig. 7. Result display for Query interface

The advanced query interface is currently under development.

4.2 Evaluation

The system is evaluated based on recall and precision; the widely used metrics in the information retrieval [8]. Recall is the ratio of the number relevant documents retrieved to the total number of relevant documents. Precision is the ratio of relevant documents to the number of retrieved documents as defined in the Eq. (1).

$$\text{precision (P)} = \frac{\text{size of relevant set}}{\text{size of retrieved set}} \quad recall\,(R) = \frac{\text{size of relevent, retrieved set}}{\text{total size of relevent set}} \tag{1}$$

In this paper, we treat the camera data consisted of three types for making a comparison of them. The type **A** is based on the semantic web, the type **B** is RDBMS data based on the individual shopping malls, and the type **C** is the meta data that is made for integrating each RDBMS data.

We categorize each of 500 cameras' lenses & their own bodies to three types such as **A**, **B**, **C** and distribute those to three severs. Using this data set, we measure average of recall and precision about the result of fifty queries like the following

'Find cameras which the price is under *Ⅰ1,500,000, zoom lens is 75~300mm, shutter-speed is 1/500 sec~1.0 sec, and company of product is SAMSUNG'*

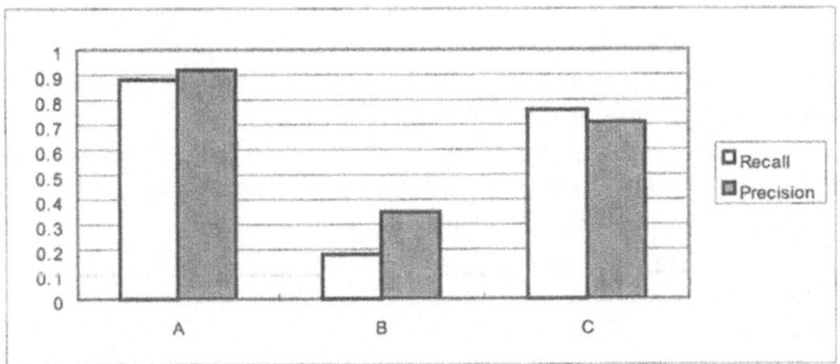

Fig. 8. Result Graph

As shown in Fig. 8, our experimental result shows that recall and precision of our system **A** are improved by 66% and 54% on those of **B** respectively, and 5% and 22% on those of **C** respectively. Moreover, we can convince that System **A** based on the Semantic web is more effective than others, which are not based on the Semantic web.

5 Conclusion and Future Work

The goal of our system is to demonstrate an e-commerce application enabled by the Semantic web techniques and to support purchase decisions by simplifying price comparisons. In this article, we use the DAML meta-data, DAML+OIL ontology and reasoning engine with JESS & DAMLJessKB. The main idea is there to marking up shopping web pages with Semantic Web languages and, based on their list prices, comparing the real end prices by applying various business rules. Because of the machine understandable and relation of a concept, we can express the specific detail of a product and using reasoning with DAML+OIL, will be the originator of accurate retrieval. Our system can be used to answer queries aout explicit and implicit knowledge specified by the ontology thus provide a query answering facility that performs deductive retrieval from knowledge represented in DAML+OIL.

In Future, we need to study on ontology mapping and merging among ontologies automatically so that heterogeneous agents system can interoperate rapidly and effectively. Moreover, using RuleML we will integrate some other domain that finds the application of the JESS for the rule empowered shopping agent. Effort is going on how to combine the notion of web services with the results of the Semantic web, Peer to Peer and Grid computing. Web services is a technological concept of linking applications to business partners and customers without having to change applications and therefore consequently turn the Internet into one single, unified computing platform providing further access to infrastructure with the aid of Grid computing. Finally, our aim is to build a system that will automate the management of quality metadata, address the problem of creating and managing ontologies that will ensure web shopping for a large scale distributed system.

References

1. Tim Berners-Lee, James Hendler and Ora Lasilla, "The Semantic Web", The Scientific American, May (2001)
2. Kopena, J. and Regli, W., 'DAMLJessKB: A tool for rea-soning with the Semantic Web.' IEEE Intelligent Systems18(3), May/June, (2003)
3. Cost, R. S., Finin, T., Joshi, A., Peng, Y., Nicholas, C.,Soboroff, I., Chen, H., Kagal, L., Perich, F., Zou, Y., and Tolia, S. 'ITTALKS: A Case Study in the Semantic Web and DAML+OIL.' IEEE Intelligent Systems 17(1):40-47,(2002)
4. Roger L. Costello,David B. Jacobs "OWL tutorial" http://www.xfront.com/owl/
5. E. Friedman-Hill, JESS: The Rule Engine for the Java Platform, 1995, http://herzberg.ca.sandia.gov/jess.
6. U. Shah et al., "Information Retrieval on the Semantic Web," Proc. ACM Conf. Information and Knowledge Management,ACM Press, (2002)
7. Kapil Rajendra Dukle. A Prototype Query-Answering Engine Using Semantic Reasoning.
8. Badrul Sarwar, George Karypis, Joseph Konstan, and John Riedl "Analysis of e-commendation Algorithms for E-Commerce" Minnesota, (2000)
9. R. Doorenbos, O. Etzioni, and D. Weld. A Scalable Comparison-Shopping Agent for the World-Wide Web. In Proceedings of the First Internation Conference on Autonomous Agents, (1997)
10. DAML+OIL, DARPA. (2001), www.daml.org/2001/03/daml+oil index
11. Robert H. Guttman and Pattie Maes Agent-Mediated Integrative Negotiation for Retail Electronic Commerce. First international workshop on Agent mediated Electronic Trading AMET-98-
12. KAON, http://kaon.semanticweb.org
13. AQSearch, http://www1.coe.neu.edu/~zqliu/mim3152/aqsearch.html
14. Jena toolkit, http://jena.sourceforge.net/

A New Navigation Method for Web Users

Jie Yang[1], Guoqing Wu[1], and Luis Zhu[2]

[1] State Key Lab of Computer Software Engineering, Wuhan University, Wuhan 430072, Hubei Province, China
clear1203@sina.com, clear1203@hotmail.com
[2] Qingdao R&D Department of LUCENT Co., Qingdao 266071, Shan dong Province, China
luiszhu@lucent.com

Abstract. Despite the growth of Internet and the advances in WWW technology, current methods for web users to make good use of information from so enormous web pages are not as efficient as we would like. After an algorithm is necessarily given for collecting desired data to gain top grade results, a modified Markov Chain Model is introduced which utilizes all group members' traces to recommend some potential sites and navigates them when browsing Web pages.

1 Introduction

The existing Web assisting techniques are usually sorted into search engine (among which the intelligent search engine based on agent is the most notable), bookmark distributed with some browser and some other ones as neuron network. However, none of the traditional navigation methods are satisfactory since the search key always must be precise so austere while the bookmark has passive nature rather than active one [1]. Web mining is categorized into Web content mining, Web structure mining and Web usage mining (pays close attention to the second data derived from the behavior of users). To establish a path towards higher efficiency in web pages mining, a model to analyze the log data of proxy server and forecast some potential popular Web pages is presented. Based on the history data, our prototype system is active and alternating. It gives a top list (hit parade) to users after calculation using our modified Markov Chain Model, which is fulfilled automatically after configuration.

2 Collecting Desired Data

It is anything but realistic to input the log data directly to our model without any preprocess carried on the original raw data. Redundant information and other dirty data should be discarded, and the over-detailed http addresses need extracted, rearranged, and synthesized. In our proxy server the size of everyday access log (all in text) is about 4M or 5M Bytes, so here is the inductive method and we reach that there is no same address in the final data set L and the translation T is subjection [2].

M. Li et al. (Eds.): GCC 2003, LNCS 3032, pp. 147–150, 2004.

3 New Associated Navigation Method

There are many methods used for social navigation as Markov Chain Model [3], decision tree, Bayes net, entropy, clustering, etc. To considerable degree users would browse the past web pages even the whole history and Markov Chain Model is a very classical probability model suitable for the no-memory situation where the next state only depends on the just previous one. Additionally, one parameter should be added to the model telling how many days should be considered when it makes a decision.

Def 1 Let M be a k*k matrix with elements $m_{i,j}$ (i , j = 1,2,…,k. $m_{i,j}$ means the probability that the next state (web page) will be s_j if the previous state is s_i). A random process (X_0, X_1, …) with finite space S=(s_1,s_2,…s_k) is said to be a Markov Chain with transition matrix M, if for all $i, j \in \{1,2,..., k\}$ and all $i_0,..., i_{n-1} \in \{1,2,..., k\}$ then

$$P(X_{n+1} = s_j \mid X_0 = s_{i_0}, X_1 = s_{i_1},..., X_{n-1} = s_{i_{n-1}}, X_n = s_i)$$. M satisfies:

$$= P(X_{n+1} = s_j \mid X_n = s_i) = m_{i,j}$$

$m_{i,j} \geq 0$ for all $i, j \in \{1,..., k\}$ (1) $\sum_{j=1}^{k} m_{i,j} = 1$ for all $i \in \{1,..., k\}$ (2)

Def 2 Let U be a vector with its dimension as the number of the states (web pages); (u_1,u_2,…,u_k) is the probability distribution(u_i = P(X=s_i)); U^{prev}, U^{next} represents previous and next probability distribution respectively; X is a random process and s_i, the i-th state. Then we come to two new properties:

$$\sum_{i=1}^{k} u_i = 1 \qquad (3) \qquad U^{next} = U^{prev} * M \qquad (4)$$

Def 3 Let k be a variable and M be a k*k matrix with elements $m_{i,j}$ and Random process (X, X') with state space S in new model. Then: $P(X' = s_j \mid X = s_i) = m_{i,j}$ (5)

Def 4 Let L be a k-dimension vector with elements l_i. L is said to be a data record if for all $i \in \{1,2,..., k\}$ and $l_i \geq 0$. L^n, L^{new} represents the n-th day's data and new data respectively. The new model will resume to the original Markov Chain Model if α(denotes data on which day are considered recent) is 1. And γ ranks data according to the frequency they were lastly used). When α is m and L^n is the visited times of some given page on the n-th day, L^{new} is weighted sum of the history data:

$$L^{new} = \sum_{i=n-m+1}^{n} l^i * \gamma^{n-i} \qquad (6)$$

M=($m_{i,j}$) where

$$m_{i,j} = \begin{cases} l_j / \sum_{k=1,k\neq i}^{n} l_k & i \neq j \\ 0 & i = j \end{cases} \qquad (7)$$

Th Let L=(l_1, l_2, …, l_n) where $l_k > 0$ ($1 \leq k \leq n$) then M_{nxn}=($m_{i,j}$) (7)satisfies (1)(2).

Proof Considering $l_1, l_2, \ldots, l_n > 0$, we have $m_{i,j} \geq 0$. Hence M_{nxn} satisfies (1).

$\sum_{j=1}^{n} m_{k,j} = \sum_{j=1,j\neq k}^{n} m_{k,j} + m_{k,k} = \sum_{j=1,j\neq k}^{n} (l_j / \sum_{l=1,l\neq k}^{n} l_l) + 0 = (\sum_{j=1,j\neq k}^{n} l_j)/(\sum_{l=1,l\neq k}^{n} l_l) = 1$ Therefore, M_{nxn} satisfies (2) □

On the above model, input of the data-mining algorithm consists of α(less than h, the length of history data), γ, today's data and corresponding history data($l^1=(l^1_1, l^1_2, \ldots, l^1_n), \ldots, l^h=(l^h_1, l^h_2, \ldots, l^h_n)$). Output is $U=(u_1, u_2, \ldots, u_n)$ where $u_i=P(X'=s_i)$(the probability that the user will browse web page s_i next time). We can also introduce a start page l^{init} as a 1-dimension matrix {1} if necessary

Table 1. Algorithm for data mining

```
for i=1 to n  l_i^new = 0
for j=1 to α l_i^new = l_i^new + l_i^(h-j+1) * γ^(j-1)  end (for j)
end (for i)
```

$$sum = \sum_{i=1}^{n} l_i^{new}$$

```
for i=1 to n
for j=1 to n  if i=j then {m_i,j=0;continue};  m_i,j=l_j/(sum-l_i)  end (for j)
end (for i)
```

$l^{output}=l^{new} * M_{nxn}(m_{i,j})$

$$U^{output}=(u_1, u_2, \ldots, u_n), \text{ where } u_i = l_i^{output} / (\sum_{j=1}^{n} l_j^{output})$$

4 Application Results and Conclusions

During applying the prototype system to evaluate the model, close attention was paid to whether it led to satisfactory results and the program ran with high performance [4]. The experiments were carried on a 4-CPU (296-MHz) computer with 2G RAM under SunOS 5.6. By modifying and compiling the source codes of proxy software, our new method worked. We downloaded continuous 10 days' log file from the proxy server at random. The system is divided into two parts and one (written in Perl) is responsible for collecting then analyzing data and providing the Top List while the other presents the list to users and displays the visited time of every hyperlink.

Table 2. Parameters in Our System

AddrLen	From where to obstruct the hyperlinks
HistoryDays (α)	Log data of how many days used for analysis
Affection (γ)	The factor to reduce the affection of history data
AutoDetection	Whether filtering hyperlinks automatically

The results are in Figure1,2,3,4(for limitation the latter three omitted). In every figure, there are two curves: "hit number for top list"(how many hyperlinks in our prediction are popular today) and "hit number for the whole data"(that are visited today). Figure 1 manifests that given fixed γ(=0.9), the bigger the α is, the higher the hit number is. Users' browsing activities have continuity that as the relationship between the coming pages and history data. Similarly, with fixed α(=2,3,4 respectively) the smaller the γ is, the lower the hit number is. At last as for the performance of the system, the most time-consuming job (calculate the prediction using the organized data) is done off line. With a big α, the data to be processed are huge and thus the processing time is long.

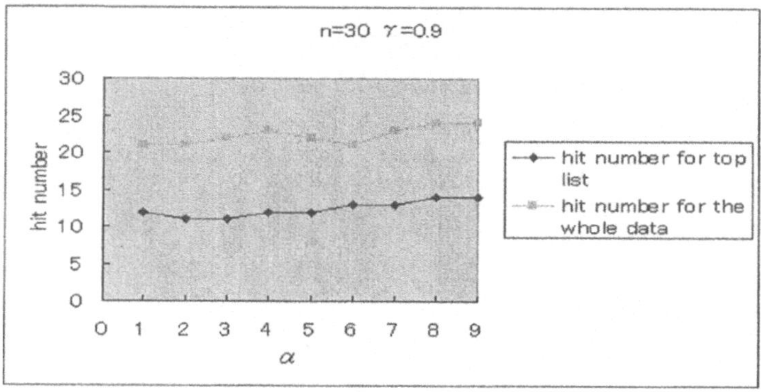

Fig. 1. (n=30,γ=0.9)

What we have presented is an intuitive, active method for associated navigation according to users' activities. It is attractive for its simplicity, traceability and accommodation of change. In our modified Markov Chain Model group data are used rather than private data as the input. Moreover, the model makes use of not only historic but also current people's activities to get results. However, like other navigation method, the modified model only work well when applied on small-sized system. The further efforts are still in need of carried out such as how to combine it with "smart" autonomous navigation like agent and other methods. The greatest chance brought out from the method may come in the virtues of the exacting and formal basis: the use of the model, whose effect and feasibility is verified and shown by the results of the analysis in our proxy server's access log.

References

1. R. Kosala, H. Blockeel: Web Mining Research: A Survey. SIGKDD Explorations, 2(1), July 2000.
2. J. Srivastava, R. Cooley, M. Deshpande, Pang-Ning Tan: Web Usage Mining: Discovery and Applications of Usage Patterns from Web Data. SIGKDD Explorations, 1(2), Jan 2000.
3. Olle Häggström: Finite Markov Chains and Algorithmic Applications. Cambridge Univ. Press.
4. M. Levene and G. Loizou: Web interaction and the navigation problem in hypertext. Encyclopedia of Microcomputers, Vol. 28, Supplement 7, Marcel Dekker, New York, pp. 381-398, 2002.

Application Availability Measurement in Computational Grid*

Chunjiang Li, Nong Xiao, and Xuejun Yang

School of Computer,
National University of Defense Technology,
Changsha, 410073 China, +86 731 4575984
chunjiangli@263.net

Abstract. The computational grid built on wide-area distributed computing systems is a more variable and unreliable computing environment, hence it is undoubtedly important to analyze its availability. In our opinion, the availability of such an open computing environment should be analyzed from the applications' perspective. In this paper, we propose an application specific availability analysis method for computational grid, then present a measurement model for the applications' availability. This model abstracts the key factors that affect the availability of applications in the computational grid.

1 Introduction

Computational Grids [1,2] enable the coupling and coordinated use of geographically distributed resources for such purposes as large-scale computation, distributed data analysis, and remote visualization. It is necessary to predict how well the computational grid serving the applications. Availability analysis is such a method. For computational grids, the availability analysis should be done from the point of view of applications. Because the computing grid is an open computing environment without boundary, and each application in the computational grid never use all resources in it, the application's availability totally depends on the resources it got and the recovery service provided by the grid service layer. In this paper, we proposed a measurement model for the application availability in computational grid.

This paper is organized as follows. The application availability is defined in section 2. In section 3, availability models in practice are reviewed. In section 4, our applications availability measurement model is presented. Conclusion and future work is presented in section 5.

* This work is supported by the National Science Foundation of China under Grant No.60203016 and No.69933030; the National High Technology Development 863 Program of China under Grant No.2002AA131010.

M. Li et al. (Eds.): GCC 2003, LNCS 3032, pp. 151–154, 2004.

2 Application Availability

Traditionally, availability is defined as:

$$p = \frac{uptime}{uptime + downtime}$$

It works well for defining the availability of a single processor, disk or other device, where devices are either "up" or down. The application availability, in our opinion, could be defined as:

$$A = \frac{t_{run}}{t_{run} + t_{stall}}$$

t_{run} is the time that application keep running, t_{stall} is the time to recover from resource failure.

3 Availability Models

Techniques to evaluate a system's availability can be broadly categorized as measurement-based and model-based. Measurement-based evaluation requires building a real system and taking measurements and then analyzing the data statistically, it is expensive. Model-based evaluation on the other hand is inexpensive and relatively easier to perform [3].

Model-based evaluation can be through discrete-event simulation, or analytic models, or hybrid models combining simulation and analytic parts. The main benefit of discrete-event simulation is the ability to depict detailed system behavior in the models. Its drawback is the long execution time, particularly when tight confidence bounds are required in the solutions obtained. Analytic models are more of an abstraction of the real system than a discrete-event simulation model. It is easier to develop and faster to solve. The main drawback is the set of assumptions that are often necessary to make analytic models tractable.

Analytic availability models can be categorized to non-state space models and state space models. The former includes reliability block diagram RBD and fault trees. The later includes Markovian model, Stochastic Petri nets and Reward Nets [4]. The two main assumptions used by non-state space models are statistically independent failures and independent repair units for components. Although these two assumptions made the non-state space model not exact enough, the non-state space model is easier to develop and solve, and can be evaluated to compute measures like system availability, reliability and system mean time to failure. On the contrary, in the state space models, when the number of the system components increases, the state space will explode. For example, the number of states in the exact Markov chain for an n-processor VAXcluster is $O(n^3)$ [5]. The computational complexity of the exact analysis depends on the solution method used. For instance, if a full storage iterative method is used, then the time complexity will be $O(n^6)$ [5]. So, some approximate method is used to reduce the complexity of state space models. The probabilistic model is a good approximate method for availability modeling [6].

Next section, we propose an approximate measurement model for the application availability in the computational grid.

4 Application Availability Model

Suppose a task set $GA = \{GT_1, GT_2, \cdots, GT_m\}$ composes a grid application. The tasks of GA are scheduled to k grid site, the number of tasks in each grid site is TN_i, and $\sum_{i=1}^{k} TN_i = m$. Then the availability of application GA can be described by a serial RBD built by C_i and GN_i, GN_i is grid site and C_i is the network connection between grid sites.

Only when all C_i and GN_i are available, the grid application GA could run smoothly. So the availability of GA is:

$$A(GA) = \prod_{i=1}^{k} A(C_i)A(GN_i)$$

$A(C_i)$ is the availability of C_i, suppose its failure rate is γ_i and repair rate is τ_i, then $A(C_i) = \frac{\tau_i}{\gamma_i+\tau_i}$. $A(GN_i)$ is the availability of TN_i tasks in the grid site GN_i, it can be measured by the probabilistic model.

Suppose the total resource number in grid site GN_i is RTN_i, and the number of resources allocated to the application is RN_i, each task mapping to a resource. The probability of a resource in "up" state is Pw_i, the probability of permanent failure for a single resource is Pe_i, and $Pw_i+Pe_i = 1$. RE_i is number of resources which is available.

In computational grid, the service layer support migrating tasks between grid sites. When $RE_i < TN_i$, the tasks which could not be served must migrate to other resources. Pt_i is the availability of such task. Suppose the total runtime of a task without failure is t_{run}, if its resource fails, the time to recovery is t_{rec}, then Pt_i can be defined by $\frac{t_{run}}{t_{rec}+t_{run}}$. In computational grid, the most costly recovery method for failed task is to restart it on a newly allocated resource. Here, for simplicity, we suppose each task in a grid site has the same Pt_i; in practice, this value for each failed task must be calculated by the recovery mechanism.

Then the availability of the TN_i tasks in grid site GN_i is:
$A(GN_i) \equiv P_r\{RE_i \geq TN_i\} + P_r\{RE_i < TN_i$ and the failed tasks migrated successfully$\}$

$$= \sum_{k=TN_i}^{RN_i} \binom{RN_i}{k} Pw_i^{\,k} Pe_i^{\,RN_i-k} + \sum_{j=0}^{TN_i-1} \binom{RN_i}{j} Pw_i^{\,j} Pe_i^{\,RN_i-j} Pt_i^{\,TN_i-j}$$

$$= (Pw_i + Pe_i)^{RN_i} - \sum_{j=0}^{TN_i-1} \binom{RN_i}{j} Pw_i^{\,j} Pe_i^{\,RN_i-j} + \sum_{j=0}^{TN_i-1} \binom{RN_i}{j} Pw_i^{\,j} Pe_i^{\,RN_i-j} Pt_i^{\,TN_i-j}$$

$$= 1 - \sum_{j=0}^{TN_i-1} \binom{RN_i}{j} Pw_i^{\,j} Pe_i^{\,RN_i-j} + \sum_{j=0}^{TN_i-1} \binom{RN_i}{j} Pw_i^{\,j} Pe_i^{\,RN_i-j} Pt_i^{\,TN_i-j}$$

In conclusion, the availability of application GA can be described as follows:

$$A(GA)=\prod_{i=1}^{k}A(C_i)\bullet\prod_{i=1}^{k}A(GN_i)$$

$$=\prod_{i=1}^{k}A(C_i)\bullet\prod_{i=1}^{k}(1-\sum_{j=0}^{TN_i-1}\binom{RN_i}{j}Pw_i^{\,j}Pe_i^{\,RN_i-j}+\sum_{j=0}^{TN_i-1}\binom{RN_i}{j}Pw_i^{\,j}Pe_i^{\,RN_i-j}Pt_i^{\,TN_i-j})$$

$$=\prod_{i=1}^{k}A(C_i)\bullet\prod_{i=1}^{k}(A_{ra}(GN_i)+A_t(GN_i))$$

$$A_{ra}(GN_i)=1-\sum_{j=0}^{TN_i-1}\binom{RN_i}{j}Pw_i^{\,j}Pe_i^{\,RN_i-j}$$

$$A_t(GN_i)=\sum_{j=0}^{TN_i-1}\binom{RN_i}{j}Pw_i^{\,j}Pe_i^{\,RN_i-j}Pt_i^{\,TN_i-j}$$

$A_{ra}(GN_i)$ is determined by resource allocation, we call it resource allocation availability; $A_t(GN_i)$ describes the availability of the tasks which suffered resource failure, we call it task migration availability.

5 Conclusion and Future Work

In computational grid, in order to provide high availability service for the applications, a measurement model for application availability is absolutely necessary. This paper presents such a model. We are concentrating on constructing the high availability service architecture in grid platform to make the computational grid more available for users. There are still much work has to be done in order to implement multiple recovery mechanisms in this architecture.

References

1. Foster, I., Kesselman, C.: The Grid: Blueprint for a New Computing Infrastructure. Morgan Kaufmann Publishers (1999)
2. Foster, I.: The grid: A new infrastructure for 21st century science. Physics Today **54** (2002)
3. Archana Sathaye, S.R., Trivedi, K.: Availability models in practice. In Proceedings of Int. Workshop on Fault-Tolerant Control and Computing (FTCC-1) (2000)
4. R. Sahner, A.P., Trivedi, K.S.: Performance and Reliability Analysis of Computer Systems: An Example-Based Approach Using the SHARPE Software Package. Kluwer Academic Publishers (1995)
5. Ibe, O.: Validation of the approximate availability analysis of vaxclusters. Internal Report, Digital Equipment Corporation (1988)
6. O. Ibe, R.H., Trivedi, K.S.: Approximate availability analysis of vaxcluster systems. IEEE Transactions on Reliability **38** (1989) 146–152

Research and Application of Distributed Fusion System Based on Grid Computing

Yu Su, Hai Zhao, Wei-ji Su, Gang Wang, and Xiao-dan Zhang

School of Information Science & Engineering
Northeastern University
110004 Shenyang, P.R. China
webants@163.com

Abstract. Grid computing is used to realize the connection of distributed, heterogeneous computing resources through grid, assist in accomplishing computing task. Focusing on the weakness of centralized information fusion, put forward the disturbed fusion model utilizing grid computing node to realize local decision fusion on the basis of distributing information fusion architecture, and transform the decision to global fusion center to make global decision, and achieve more exact situation assessment and trend estimate, and utilize this model to equipment fault diagnosis system as an attempt of grid computing.

1 Introduction

Fusion is the integrating and processing of multi-sensor information gathered which adopt the technology of the computer to obtain the integrating and processing of the observe technology information [1]. Adopt distributed multi-sensor fusion system can obtain more concrete and more accurate estimation and determination. Grid computing accomplish share by connecting many disturbed computing resource with high-speed network in order to accomplish compute task together [2]. For this reason, it is an effective attempt to utilize the sharing resource ability of grid computing to accomplish disturbed fusion technology.

In this paper using grid computing to accomplish disturbed fusion structure was discussed, and grid structure and disturbed fusion technology were researched.

2 Distributed Information Fusion Technology

Information fusion can integrate observed outside information and prophetic knowledge. Multi-sensor information fusion system fully utilized data gathered by sensors, through assembling mutually supplementary and redundant information on space and time according to the rule, and produce the intact coherence explanation and description to the observed target. Multi-sensor information fusion can improve the capability

M. Li et al. (Eds.): GCC 2003, LNCS 3032, pp. 155–158, 2004.

of the multi-source heterogenic sensor system, and can eliminate information losing caused by the single sensor's imperfect detection.

According to different structure, disturbed information system can be classified three sorts: centralized fusion system, layered fusion system and horizontal fusion system. In them, centralized fusion system could flexibly select fusion algorithm, but transmission spending is very large; Local node of layered fusion system has fusion ability, it can alleviate the computing intensity of global fusion center, but local decision cannot reflect global status. In horizontal fusion system each local fusion node is parallel. The condition of other nodes could be considered while fusing, and so the local decision could reflect global status.

3 Grid System and Its Architecture

Grid system is a synthetic architecture of hardware and software, and is composed of disturbed, heterogenic, different hardware and software system which can make resources share and utilize effectively, so that user can use this resource solve all kinds of complex computational problems pellucidly, effectively and unrestricted.

Grid architecture can be looked on as a method that can decentralize essential module of system, appoint the purpose and function of system module, illuminate the mutual action among modules [3]. At present, there are two architectures: Forster's five layers sandglass architecture and Open Grid Services Architecture (OGSA).

Five layers sandglass architecture would disperse the operation and management of share resources according to the distance from each component to share resources. Different from five layers sandglass architecture that center on protocol, OGSA centers on service. In OGSA, service conception includes all kinds of compute resource, storage resource, network, program, database and so on. In short, everything is service. In order to make service thinking more tangible and more concrete, OGSA defined the conception-"Grid Service". Grid Service provides a set of interface to follow specific tradition to settle service detection, dynamic service establishment, lifecycle management and information etc. The model of OGSA which centers on grid service, can achieve grid service through providing uniform kernel interface.

4 Realizing Distributed Fusion Arithmetic and Application

In distributed information fusion system, each local fusion node made decision on the local sensor data, and transmit the decision to the global center to make decision combination and global reasoning. In the grid computing based fusion system, adopt grid node instead of local fusion node to provide function of local fusion decision, and the key point is how to combine the decision criterion from local nodes.

Considering the duality presumable H_0 normal, H_1 abnormal, the priori probabilities are P_0 and P_1. Each local fusion node make local decision, the decision criterion is, $H=\{H_0=\text{true},\ f(x_i)<\beta;\ H_1=\text{true},\ f(x_i)\ \ \beta\}$.According to the criterion, the local decision u_i is, $u_i=\{1,H_1=\text{true};\ 0,H_0=\text{true}\}$. Global fusion center make decision on the local decision, $\delta=\delta(\{u_i\}^N_{i=1})$. In them, δ is the probability of the decision result equaling to H_1, and the global fusion decision result is, $u=\{1, p=\delta; 0, p=1-\delta\}$.

The local decision is association with false alarm ratio and detection probability, detection probability P_d is the probability value of making H_1 decision when the real result is H_1, and false alarm ratio is the probability value of making H_1 decision when the real result is H_0. In the process of fusion, the usual method is to obtain the higher detection probability and lower false alarm ratio P_d, so Neyman-Pearson method is adopted.

Stability criterion is,

$$\delta=\delta(\{u_i\}_{i=1}^{N})=\begin{cases}1 & \text{if } \sum_{j=1}^{M} u_j > K\\ r & \text{if } \sum_{j=1}^{M} u_j = K\\ 0 & \text{if } \sum_{j=1}^{M} u_j < K\end{cases} \tag{1}$$

Therefore, global criterion is,

$$u=\begin{cases}1 & p=1,\ \text{if } \sum_{j=1}^{M} u_j > K\\ 1 & p=r,\ \text{if } \sum_{j=1}^{M} u_j = K\\ 0 & \text{other}\end{cases} \tag{2}$$

Applying the distributed fusion structure to Jilin Fengman hydro-electric fault diagnosis system, setting multi-sensors to gather the gas parameters dissolved in oil of the transformer equipment, and the device situation is assessed according to the range of many parameters. In order to realize the function of grid computing, Globus software package and Web service interface is adopted to form a simple grid system.

The grid system includes interfaces (Factory, Registry, GridService, Mapper), which can offer and create temporary services, search services and obtain services, the service structure of the grid system shows in figure 1. Factory is the unit of providing grid computing, and Registry is the instance of registering Factory service, Mapper is used to map the grid computing to the physical resource. Multi-sensors gather the gas parameter dissolved in the oil, and by analyzing the compo-

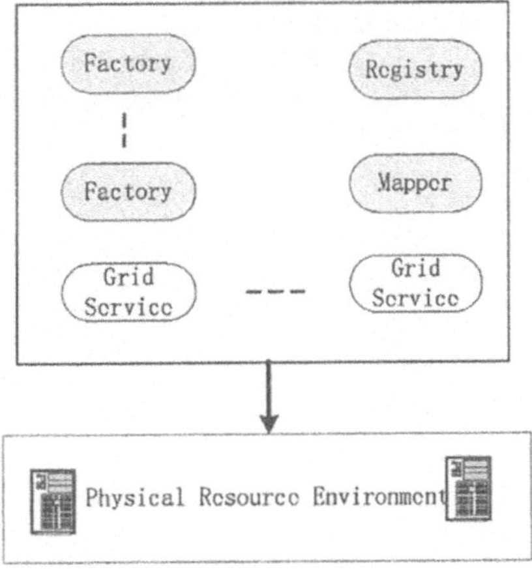

Fig. 1. Service structure of grid system

nent and the content of the gas dissolved in the oil, the serious degree of the fault can be discovered, and also can bring forward the corresponding solution. Here utilizing the grid system to realize the computing node to make local decision.

5 Conclusion

Via the research of disturbed information fusion, put forward utilizing grid computing to realize the architecture of disturbed information fusion system. And after the comparison of the architecture and performance of five layers sandglass architecture and OSGA, adopting OSGA architecture and utilizing Globus software package and Web-Service to construct grid system realizing providing grid computing function. The distributed fusion model utilizing grid computing node to realize local decision fusion function, and transform the decision to global fusion center to make global decision, and achieve more exact situation assessment and trend estimate.

Acknowledgements. This research was sponsored by the Natural Science Fund of P.R.China under Grant No. 69873007.

References

1. He Y,Wang G H: Multisensor information fusion with applications [M].Beijing: Publishing House of Electronics Industry.2000 156-160.
2. Xiao N, Ren H, Gong S L: Resource directory technology based grid system software design and application. Computer Research and Development, 2002,92(8)
3. ZHAO H: Studying of FCS Architecture and Designing/Implementing of one Model System Based on Data Fusion Theory [D]. Shenyang: Northeastern University.1994.36-45
4. Hall D: Mathematical Techniques in multisensor data fusion [M]. Artech House Inc, Boston, London, 1992. 235–238
5. Foster I, Kesselman C: The Grid: Blueprint for a New Computing Infrastructure[D] . Morgan Kauffman , 1999.
6. Xu L Y,Du X D: Application of neural fusion to accident forecast in hydropower station [A]. Proceedings of the Second International Conference on nformation Fusion[C]. 1999, 12:1166-1171

An Efficient and Self-Configurable Publish-Subscribe System

Tao Xue and Boqin Feng

School of Electronics and Information Engineering,
Xi'an Jiao Tong University,
710049 Xi'an, China
Xt73@163.com

Abstract. Efficient routing algorithms and self-configuration are two key challenges in the area of large-scale content-based publish-subscribe systems. In this paper we first propose a hierarchical system model with multicast clustering. Then a hybrid routing algorithm is presented, which can fully exploit multicast in order to reduce the used network bandwidth. We also propose multicast clustering replication protocol and content-based multicast tree protocol to make the overlay network dynamically adapt to the changing of lower network topologic raised by node or link failure, requiring no manual tuning or system administration. Simulation results show that the system has low cost, and event delivered over it experiences moderately low latency.

1 Introduction

Content-based publish/subscribe (pub/sub) middleware differs significantly from traditional subject-based pub/sub system, in that messages are routed on the basis of their content rather than pre-defined subjects or channels. The flexibility of content-based systems comes at the expense of added challenges in design and implementation. One open issue is how to efficiently route messages to subscribers through the overlay network of event-brokers. The next challenge is dynamic reconfiguration of the topology of the distributed dispatching infrastructure. Some approaches for content-based pub/sub [1], [2], [3] have been presented, but to the best of our knowledge, none of them provides any special mechanism to support the reconfiguration addressed by this paper.

2 System Framework

As illustrated in Fig. 1, our system framework consists of NEBs (normal event broker), DEBs (designated event broker), publishers, subscribers and RP (rendezvous point). A NEB lies in a multicast-enabled LAN, which can use native IP Multicast to communicate with other NEBs in the same LAN. These NEB nodes in the same LAN form a structure called multicast clustering (MC). One leader is selected as the MC's DEB. DEB nodes form a hierarchical topology

M. Li et al. (Eds.): GCC 2003, LNCS 3032, pp. 159–163, 2004.

and unicast is used between DEB nodes. RP is a dedicated server and always knows which host is the root of the tree. RP's IP address is statically configured and can be obtained off-line by brokers.

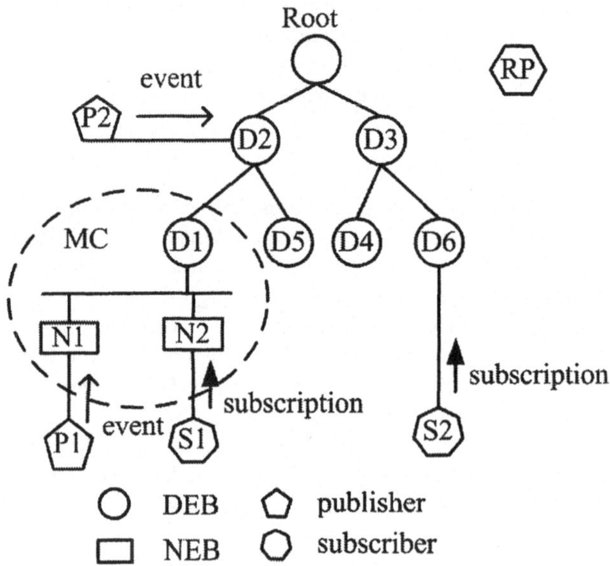

Fig. 1. A hierarchical system framework with multicast clustering

3 Hybrid Routing Algorithm

Firstly, subscribers send subscriptions to a NEB or DEB node. (1) When a NEB receives a subscription sent from a subscriber, it stores the subscription in its routing table and sends the subscription to its DEB. (2) When a DEB receives a subscription, it stores the subscription in its routing table and forwards the subscription to its parent, which, in turn repeats the procedure until the subscription arrives to the root broker.

Then,publishers send events to a NEB or DEB node. (1) When a NEB receives an event, it matches the event against all of subscriptions stored in its routing table and sends the event to those subscribers whose subscriptions matched the event. Additionally, if the event is sent from a publisher other than other event brokers, the NEB multicasts the event so that all brokers in the MC can receive it. (2) When a DEB receives an event, it also sends the event to its matched subscribers and those matched children. Moreover, the DEB forwards the event to its parent if it is not the root node.

Subscribers can also unsubscribe their subscriptions. The propagation of unsubscriptions is similar to that of subscriptions except that it removes entities of routing table other than constructs them.

4 Self-Configuration

4.1 MCRP Protocol

When a NEB bootstraps, it multicasts its IP address and id. The DEB and other NEBs in the MC will receive and store them to their member list. The DEB periodically multicasts a heartbeat message that contains the information of the DEB's neighbors (including its parent and immediate children nodes) and the member list that records NEB nodes registered. In addition, every newly created routing entity in the DEB's routing table will be multicast so that all NEB nodes construct the same routing table.

If NEB nodes detect the failure of their DEB, they elect the NEB whose id is maximal as the new DEB. If the new DEB is alive, it will multicast heartbeat messages. Otherwise, NEB nodes elect the next candidate again.

Each DEB node also periodically sends a heartbeat message that contains the DEB's member list to its neighbors. As shown in Fig.1, suppose D2 detects the failure of D1. D2 sends a probe message to the maximal NEB node in D1's MC, say N2. If N2 sends back a response message, the handshake is successful. Then D1 and N2 update their routing table respectively. N2 becomes the new DEB and the failure of D1 is healed. Otherwise, D2 sends a probe message to the next candidate. In the worst case, due to failures of all of NEB nodes in D1's MC or link failure between D1 and D2, the system cannot be recovered. So that is the issue CMTP protocol will address.

4.2 CMTP Protocol

Firstly, the immediate children of the failed non-leaf node must rejoin the tree. Our join algorithm borrowed the idea of HMTP [4] that chooses parent only the closest from a random subset of existing nodes. In Fig.1, suppose the link between D3 and D4 fails. D4 obtains the root of the tree by querying RP and sets the root as starting point of parent searching. D4 then asks the root for a list of root's children and picks the closest one, in this case D2, as a new starting point. D4 repeats this process and stops when it reaches a leaf node, or a node that is closer than all its neighbors. In the end, D4 will find an appropriate parent. Additionally, if the root fails, its immediate children nodes query RP after a random delay. The first child reaching RP becomes the new root.

Secondly, routing of the affected nodes must be reconfigured. When a link fails, the parent end-point generates un-subscriptions for each of the subscriptions the other end-point was subscribed to. It is as if the parent had received these un-subscriptions from the other end-point. The parent then processes these un-subscriptions as described in Sect. 3. Moreover, rejoined node sends all of its subscriptions to its new parent. Its new parent then constructs the new routing.

5 Evaluation

We conducted simulations to evaluate the performance of our hybrid routing algorithm against normal hierarchical routing algorithm adopted by Siena and

JEDI. The simulation hierarchical network consists of 100 DEB nodes, and 730 links. Each MC includes 10 NEB nodes. As a simplification, publishers only publish one particular kind of event, while subscribers only subscribe this class event. To judge the system's scalability and performance, we use two metrics: (1) Tree cost. It is calculated by summing the costs of all node-to-node message traffic. (2) Average event delay. It is calculated through dividing the time spent by the total number of events received.

Fig. 2 and Fig. 3 illustrate simulation results. Alias hr denotes the normal hierarchical routing algorithm adopted by Siena and JEDI, while hrm denotes our hybrid routing algorithm.

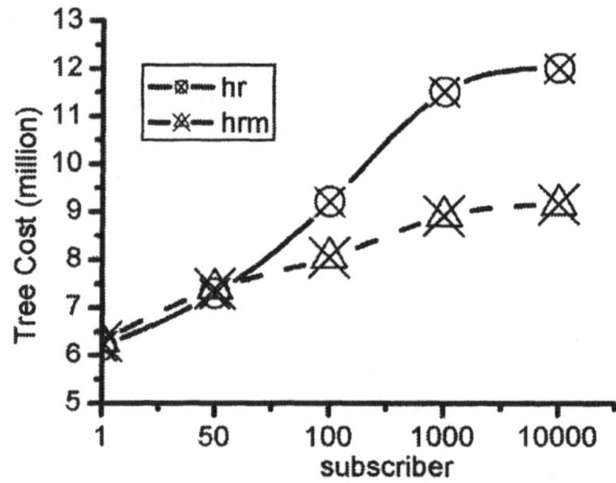

Fig. 2. Hybrid routing algorithm vs. normal hierarchical routing algorithm using tree cost metric

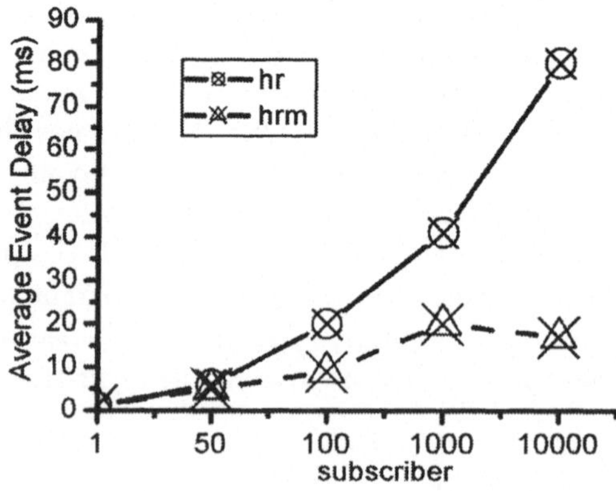

Fig. 3. Hybrid routing algorithm vs. normal hierarchical routing algorithm using average event delay metric

Tree Cost Result Analysis. In Fig. 2, there is an inflexion in the plot. Before inflexion, tree cost of the two algorithms is the same on the whole. However, tree cost of hrm algorithm is less than that of hr algorithm after inflexion. The gap between them enlarges when the number of subscriber increases. When there are fewer subscribers, they are scattered and the effect of multicast is not evident. With the number of subscriber increasing, they converge in all sites, so the advantage of multicast appears.

Average Event Delay Result Analysis. As shown in Fig. 3, there is also an inflexion. Before inflexion, event delay of the two is the same on the whole. Nevertheless, event delay of hrm algorithm is less than that of hr algorithm after inflexion. The gap between them enlarges when the number of subscriber increases. Clearly, when the number of subscriber increases, there is a great probability of using multicast in hrm algorithm. Thus, its average event delay is lower. Moreover, as the number of subscriber increases, the hr algorithm performs worse by a linear increase of event delay. In contrast, event delay of hrm algorithm descends after reaching a climax.

6 Conclusion

Scalability and fault-tolerant is essential for large-scale pub/sub systems. In this paper we present a hybrid routing algorithm. Simulation result shows that our algorithm has great scalability and performance over traditional hierarchical routing algorithm. We also propose MCRP and CMTP protocol, which bring fault-tolerant and self-configuration into the system. Our on-going work is to design and implement a prototype system that can support real-life applications.

References

1. IBM. Gryphon: Publish/subscribe over public networks. Technical report, IBM T. J. Watson Research Center, 2001.
2. A.Carzaniga, D.S.Rosenblum, and A.L.Wolf. Design and evaluation of a wide-area event notication service. ACM Transactions on Computer Systems, 19(3): 332-383, 2001.
3. G.Cugola, E.Di Nitto, and A.Fuggetta. The JEDI event-based infrastructure and its application to the development of the OPSS WFMS. IEEE Transactions on Software Engineering, 27(9), 2001.
4. B.Zhang, S.Jamin, and L.Zhang, Host Multicast: A Framework for Delivering Multicast to End Users. IEEE INFOCOM'02, New York, NY, June 2002.

The Implementation of the Genetic Optimized Algorithm of Air Craft Geometry Designing Based on Grid Computing

Xi-li Sun, Xinda Lu, and Qianni Deng

Department of Computer Science of Shanghai Jiao Tong University, 200030
xilisun@sjtu.edu.cn
{lu-xd,deng-qn}@cs.sjtu.edu.cn

Abstract. Genetic Optimized Algorithm Grid System is a network computing system based on Grid technology. It is composed by a group of Grid services, which described by WSDL. In this system, the computational resources are provided to the clients in the form of services and the computing powers are dynamically discovered and utilized across various platforms and different operating systems. By using this system, we introduce some new methods for the Air Craft Geometry designing, such as the controlling and monitoring over the designing progress and the cooperation for multi-designers around the world.

1 Introduction[1]

The Genetic Optimized Algorithm (GOA) is a widely used algorithm in designing of air craft geometry. Traditionally, we use a Parallel Virtual Machine (PVM) or a Message Passing Interface (MPI) program to finish this work. However, there are some limits of those means: the available CPUs or CPU times are limited and the number of child tasks can not be dynamically changed; during the executing time, it's hard to view the middle results and change the parameters to lead to a desired result; and the computational environment is homogeneous, so the computing ability is bound to a single computer or cluster. In order to solve those problems, we build this computing system. In this paper, we introduce the system architecture and then give the experiments results and conclusions.

2 System Architecture

The Genetic Optimized Algorithm Grid (GOAG) system is composed of services. Each service has some standard interfaces to support the registering of service, the querying of service, the building of communication and the interacting between the

[1]This project is supported by National Natural Science Fund of China (No. 60173013).

M. Li et al. (Eds.): GCC 2003, LNCS 3032, pp. 164–167, 2004.

user and the service provider. There are four services: User Service, private UDDI center, Allocate service and CFD computing service.

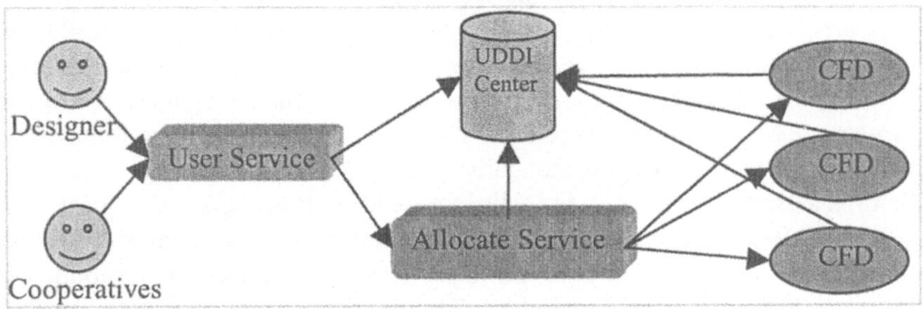

Fig. 1. System Architecture of GOAG

The system works as follow: the User service accepts the user requests and submits it to Allocate Service. The Allocate Service first query the available CFD services from the private UDDI center, then divides the task into sub tasks and distributes them to the available CFD Services to finish the computing work. After the CFD finish the computing work, Allocate Service gathers the results and then begins the next iteration. The middle results are stored in Allocate service. The User service requests those results from the Allocate service and displays them to the final user.

2.1 User Service

The user accounts management model in the User service is responsible for the account management, which identify the user's identity. After the user's identity has been identified, user may query how many CFD services are available to get a glimpse of the system computing power. Then the user may set the task's initial parameters, send the parameters and the compute task to the User Service. The User Service then looks up the Allocate Service in the UDDI center and then submits the task. After the results are come out and returned to the User service, the User Service puts that information on the user's browser, so the user can monitor the design process dynamically.

2.2 Private UDDI Center

The UDDI center acts as an information exchange center. A service uses the registry function register itself in the UDDI center before it going to provide the service. The UDDI center recodes some information of the service such as the description of the service in a WSDL document, the key words of the service and the performance related parameter of this service. Clients use the find service function to discover the appropriate services they needed. The client specifies the key words to look up the service entry in the UDDI center, and then gets a WSDL document.

2.3 Allocate Services

The Allocate Service responds to the task request, divides the task into many child tasks as the parameter indicated, and then distributes those tasks to the CFD compute services. After the results are returned, the Allocate service selects the best one from them. Using the best result and some others to generate the next generation to continue this process until the number of iterations equals the appointed iteration times or the user pauses or stops this process manually.

There is a control process in the Allocate Service. It accepts the requests from the User Service. Before each round begins, the control process will call the find services function to find the available CFD services. Then the connections are built between the Allocate Service and CFD services. The child tasks are distributed to the CFD services to finish the computing work. Because the Allocate Service will query the available services each round, the changes of the service are considered dynamically.

2.4 CFD Services

The CFD service is the working part of this system. In our system, each CFD service is a Web service and is written by Java. But the executing part of genetic algorithm is written by C and FORTRAN and called by using JNI (Java Native Interface).

3 Experiment Results

The experiment environment is composed by four computers. The UserService, UDDI center and the Allocate Service are all in the laptop which IP address is 211.80.42.7. All the other machines are the CFD service provider. The task runner can submit the task via a browser which can visit the services provided in this system, that is, it can connect to the machine through internet.

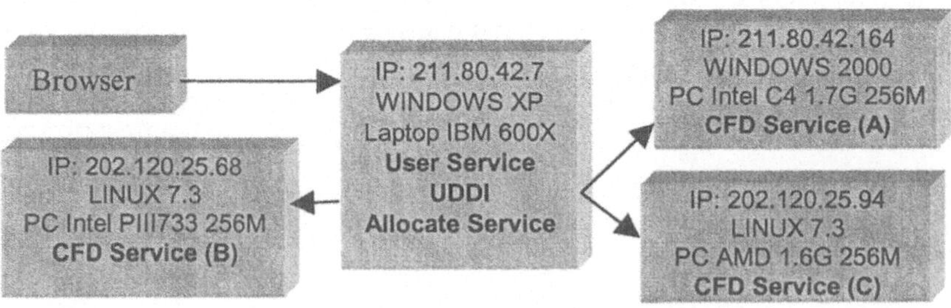

Fig. 2. Experiment Environments

In the experiment, the task iterates 8 times and each time the population of the task is 6. The data listed below is the test results.

Table 1. Experiment Data

Iteration	CFDs	Time (minu-tes)	Efficiency (%)			Speedup
			A	B	C	
1	ABC	5.86	58.19	89.53	54.38	1.63
2	A	10.23	100	-	-	1
3	B	15.74	-	100	-	1
4	C	9.56	-	-	100	1
5	AB	8.49	60.25	92.69	-	1.14
6	AC	5.63	90.85	-	85.70	1.81
7	BC	8.43	-	93.36	56.70	1.13
8	ABC	6.02	56.64	87.15	52.93	1.58

The efficiency of A in table 1 means that during the time of the first iteration how much time that A is working. The speedup of iteration 1 is calculated as fellows:

$$S = \frac{\text{Time spends by A computing alone}}{\text{Time spends by A, B and C computing together}} \tag{1}$$

From the data, we can see that because the computers are heterogeneous and we do not use powerful allocate algorithm, the over all efficiency and speedup is not good enough. However, this problem may be alleviated by the use of balanced algorithms.

4 Conclusion

We have introduced the Genetic Optimized Algorithm Grid system and outlined how the system is constructed. We also introduce the system modules and their functions. The system provides a new method for the applications like the genetic algorithm to utilize the computing power over a wide area and across different platforms and it will make significant improvement for the design method of the Air Craft Geometry.

References

1. The Physiology of the Grid: An Open Grid Services Architecture for Distributed Systems Integration. Ian Foster, Carl Kesselman, Jeffrey Nick and Steven Tuecke. 2002/2
2. Web Service Architecture W3C Working Draft 14 November 2002 http://www.w3.org/TR/2002/WD-ws-arch-20021114/
3. Parallel Programming Techniques and Applications Using Networked Workstations and Parallel Computers. Barry Wilkinson, Michael Allen
4. Open Grid Service Infrastructure Ian Foster, Carl Kesselman, Jeffrey Nick and Steven Tuecke etc. 2003/2

Distributed Information Management System for Grid Computing

Liping Niu, Xiaojie Yuan, and Wentong Cai

College of Information Technical Science, Nankai University, Tianjin, China (300071)
sunshine_nlp@eyou.com

Abstract. In this paper, a simple and dynamic information management system (IMS) is proposed for resource sharing in distributed systems. The IMS monitors computers' availability and some particular information of the resources, for such information is important for building applications that utilize the resources in the system. The IMS is constructed based on Globus and RTI, which are the most popular solutions for Grid computing. This paper discusses the IMS's architecture, and gives the implement method and a pattern of resource class hierarchy.

1 Introduction

Resource sharing is an important action in a VO (Virtual Organization [1]). We often need to use some distributed, heterogeneous and dynamic systems to realize different requests or offers of resource sharing.

Conventional methods of resource management are usually based on static information and use centralized allocators to get resource information for various requests. One simple way to implement a dynamic and scalable information services is to use "broadcast". One site broadcasts its resource information or subscription to all other sites. Certainly, this method is not an efficient one. The blind broadcast will generate a large amount of network traffic. Moreover, a consumer may only be interested in a small sub-set of all the attributes of the resource information. The useless information may also cause burden on the network and on consumer's analyzing and parsing. Considering the low performance of broadcast method, an approach based on RTI is proposed in this paper to address the problems mentioned above.

2 Information Management System's Architecture

Following basic ideas of RTI (Run Time Infrastructure [2]), in this paper, the site in a distributed system, which offers resource information, is defined as a **producer**, while the site, which requests resource information, is defined as a **consumer**.

The project is based on the peer-to-peer model, which means that producers and consumers can transfer information among each other directly. A simple centralized

M. Li et al. (Eds.): GCC 2003, LNCS 3032, pp. 168–171, 2004.

server GISDAEMON is set in IMS to discover and record all the participating producers and consumers. The GISDAEMON is like the directory service in the Grid architecture [3]. The aim is to reduce the traffic caused by blind broadcast. Figure 1 below represents actions between different roles played by producer site, consumer site and GISDAEMON.

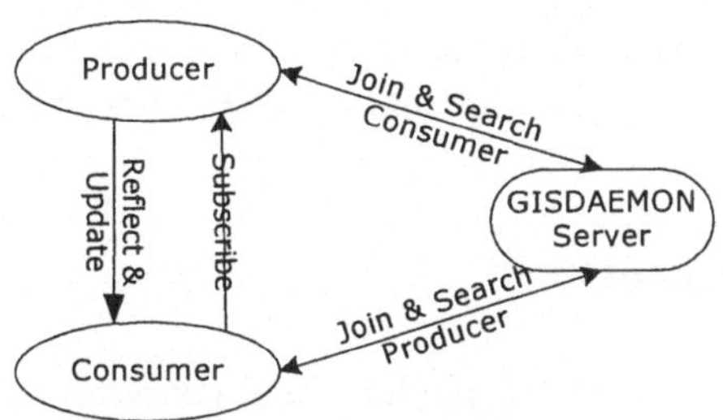

Fig. 1. The System's Description

Each consumer and producer needs to register itself to GISDAEMON first in order to get relative participants list. Each consumer broadcasts its subscription to the registered producers, while each producer periodically updates resource information to the consumer that subscribes its request.

The complex pattern not only can achieve dynamic and scalability, but also can reduce most of the traffic caused by blind broadcast and useless resource information.

3 Resource Class Hierarchy

We define a set of objects to describe the attributes of resource information in a class hierarchy. The advantages of using the hierarchy architecture are described in [4]. Figure 2 describes the resource class hierarchy defined in the IMS.

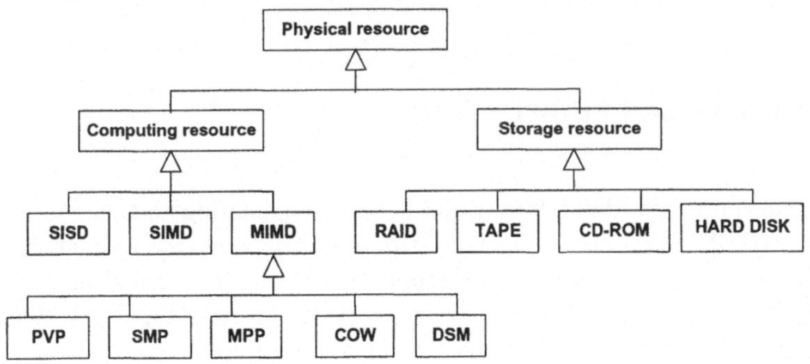

Fig. 2. The Resource Class Hierarchy

Each item represents a resource class. Super-class defines general attributes, which describe the common feature of the resource. Sub-class defines more detailed information of the resource and inherits all the attributes of its super-class. Each sub-class describes a special feature of the resource.

When a producer publishes its storage resource information, those consumers that are interested in the information class will get the information. Promotion is also permitted in the hierarchy. The producer that publishes SMP can also fulfill the consumer that subscribes physical resource. And when the detailed attributes of some information changed, the producer does not need to update them to the consumers who are only interested in the general information or other types of information.

4 System Implement

Functions of the GISDAEMON, producer and consumer, are different, and each of them is realized with a special program. In IMS a machine can act as a producer, a consumer and a server at the same time, but it cannot act as two or more same roles.

GISDAEMON program is a daemon, which maintains a producer list (record all the available producers' information) and a consumer list (record all the available consumers' information and even subscriptions). Only when a site joins and quits the system, it needs to communicate with GISDAEMON. GISDAEMON is always listening on a port and its actions are triggered by participants' messages sent here.

The program comprises of three threads. One of them is to accept provider's command, one is to listen on its well-known port receiving consumer's subscription, and one is to send (reflect or update) the information to appropriate consumers. The provider should assign the publishing information classes when the program starts.

In the three threads of the consumer program, one is to get all kinds of command from the provider, one is to listen on its well-known port receiving the information sent here, and one is to support APIs. The consumer program now can provide APIs for local applications to submit, cancel and search resource information. The consumer program can act as a local resource information provider from which other applications can benefit. Here we overleap the actions about the program communicating with local applications.

5 Conclusions and Future Work

The IMS can run in the PDP lab now and information sharing and searching functions can work well. The resource information is stored in memory so that it can easily support fast selection and matching. Exceptions are also concerned in the programs. And unexpected termination of the programs can also be caught and dealt with.

The IMS was developed on LINUX system and programs' migration to other operating systems, such as windows, should be done in the future. Now, the producer's resource information table is only an interface to the resource provider, so a function for producer program's automatic searching for attribute values that the provider wants to publish needs to be realized.

Table 1. The Site Action

GISDAEMON's Actions	
When a producer joins	Add it in the producer list and return the consumer list
When a producer quits	Delete it from the producer list
When a consumer with its subscription joins	Add or update the consumer and its subscription in the consumer list and return the producer list
When a consumer quits	Delete it from the consumer list and return the producer list
Producer's Actions	
When the producer program starts	Register to GISDAEMON, get the consumer list with the subscriptions, record the matching ones and reflect their subscribing class instances to them
When receiving a consumer's subscription from later joined consumer	Record the matching ones and reflect the class instances
When receiving a consumer's quitting information	Delete it from local matching table
When some attributes of the classes in the publish-table is changed	Update new instances of the classes to their subscribers, sleep to wait the next updating time
When the producer program ends	Notify GISDAEMON and the subscribers about quitting.
Consumer's Actions	
When a consumer program starts or subscriptions changes	Register the subscription to GISDAEMON, get the producer list and broadcast subscription to them
When receiving the producer's class instances and quitting information	Update the resource table
When the consumer program ends	Notify GISDAEMON, get the producer list and notify quitting to them

References

1. Ian Foster, Carl Kesselman, Steven Tuecke.: "*The Anatomy of the Grid*", http://www.globus.org/, (2001)
2. Dahmann, J.S.: "*The High Level Architecture and beyond: technology challenges*", in process of 13th workshop on Parallel and Distributed Simulation, 1999. (1999) 64 –70
3. T. Howes, M. Smith, and G. Good: "*Understanding and Deploying LDAP Directory Services: MacMillan Technical Publishing*", (1999)
4. http://www.informatik.uni-ostock.de/mosi/Vorlesung/Folien/SS03/PADS/DVE_up4.pdf

The Design of Adaptive Platform for Visual-Intensive Applications over the Grid

Hui Xiang, Bin Gong, Xiangxu Meng, and Xianglong Kong

School of Computer Science and Technology
Shandong University
{hxiang, mxx, gb}@sdu.edu.cn
http://vr.sdu.edu.cn/~xh.html

Abstract. In this paper, we discuss the design and implementation of an adaptive visualization platform effectively supporting Grid-enabled visual-intensive applications such as mechanical CAD, medical, virtual heritage and etc across heterogeneous network of computing resources. In our preliminary design of the visualization platform, we choose to focus on the study of the adaptive strategies and caching mechanisms for visualization applications over the Grid. The architecture of the conceptual design of the system is given and discussed.

1 Introduction

Nowadays with the help of High Performance Computing (HPC) clusters and Grid computing, we could have increasing performance at decreasing costs for visual-intensive applications including CAD, Virtual Heritage[1], Digital Human, and etc. Though many works have been done on various aspects of the visualization platform over the Grid, there are still some problems we have to address. What we emphasis on in this paper are the design and evaluation of the strategies of content adaptation, data caching and Grid-enabled distributed rendering with HPC clusters,.

The design considerations of Grid-enabled adaptive visualization platform are presented in section 2 and we review the related works in section 3. In section 4, the conceptual architecture of our design is given and we conclude this paper with discussions and future works in section 5.

2 Design Considerations

As stated above, the design of Grid-enabled visual-intensive applications effectively are not trivial and there are still many problems need to be addressed.

For example, we see an ever-increasingly complex heterogeneous networking infrastructures with all kinds of clients and servers over many different types of transportation channels with various bandwidth and other capabilities.

M. Li et al. (Eds.): GCC 2003, LNCS 3032, pp. 172–175, 2004.

To make the situation even complex, different types of users may have quite different visualization requirements even on the same data set. Different rendering techniques may also be applied on the same graphics objects for different usages.

Appropriate content adaptation techniques are necessary in above situations. We have to utilize effective adaptation techniques including on the fly Transcoding and appropriate schemes for resource monitoring and user preference collecting.

Load-balancing rendering tasks among nodes could also be regarded as a type of resource adaptation. In fact, this topic has been studied quite thoroughly in the area of distributed and parallel processing.

Another important issue about Grid-enabled visualization applications is the caching strategies. Caching is necessary to improve performance by avoiding redundant data transfers, which may be huge in visualization scenarios. Though web caching is a hot issue currently, the study of caching strategies for visualization applications is still under explored.

When adaptation and caching are both involved, the situation becomes more complex. While caching would satisfy requests from clients with previously stored data to reduce the unnecessary data transfers and improving the system performance, adaptation is meant to satisfy various kinds of requests of various types of users via a large variety of communication channels, thus making the caching much more difficult because every request may get different personalized copies even of the same object and the traditional caching strategies have to be modified to accommodate the adaptation.

3 Related Works

We do not try to work everything from scratch because we have many existing technologies as basis of our platform building efforts.

Several research works across the world have addressed one or more topics related to adaptive visualization platform building over the Grid, in which the mostly closely related works are presented below.

Sven Buchholz, et al. [2] proposed an approach to join the concepts of web caching and content adaptation in a uniform scheme. F. Cuenca-Acuna et al. try to use cooperative caching to manage the memories of cluster-based servers [3].

Greg Humphreys et al. proposed Chromium [4], a system for manipulating streams of graphics API commands on clusters of workstations, which now release as Open Source software package. Chromium's stream processing mechanism is designed to be completely general by abstracting the graphics architecture, network topology and API command processing semantics, thus making many cluster-parallel rendering applications such as Deep View System [5] to be implemented or embedded with chromium.

Dieter Kranzlmüller et al proposed Grid Visualization Kernel (GVK) [6], which is an example ongoing project to be a fully grid-enabled approach to scientific visualization, which has quite a similar goal with our project, which makes GVK an excellent reference platform.

Ioana M. Martin designed an adaptive rendering and transmission environment (ARTE) as an implementation of a general idea of adaptive graphics [7], which is very helpful in clarify what we should deal with when content adaptation of graphics objects is involved.

Vanish Talwar et al are developing mmGrid (Multimedia Grid) [8] as an extensible middleware architecture supporting multimedia applications in a grid computing environment.

4 System Architecture

To address above problems, we proposed to leverage the advantages of caching and adaptation to build the adaptive distributed visualization application framework for Grid-enabled visualization applications based on Globus Toolkit[9].

The main parts of the system are listed as following:

1. User Application: The user application initiates the visualization request to the Visualization Service Coordinator. Various adaptation specifications including computing resources, display capabilities and user preferences may be attached to the request.
2. Visualization Service Coordinator: The core of the Grid-enabled visualization platform. It accepts the visualization requests and dispatches the tasks according to resources available with information collected from Globus layer. Adaptation and Caching control module would be activated to adapt the visualization request before tasks are dispatched.
3. Globus layer: Globus middleware including the Globus Resource Allocation Manager (GRAM) [10] and Monitoring and Directory Service (MDS) [11] would process inquires about the available resources for the visualization process and perform the visualization resource allocation and initialization as requested.
4. The visualization service providers: Three types of supporting services including data service, computing service and rendering service are responsible for the fulfilling of the visualization request. In practical, the node initiating the request may also contribute to the fulfillment of the request from other nodes according to the resources and capabilities it possesses. We plan to fuse the idea of P2P into our platform.
5. Various supporting packages: Mainly distributed rendering and parallel computation packages, they act as enablers of the above services to fully utilize the powerfulness of HPC clusters and other resources.

The above design is rather conceptual and illustrative. However, it does reflect the ideas behind our design of the Grid-enabled visualization platform. We need to elaborate the design for practical implementation, hopefully with various enhancements.

5 Conclusion

What we proposed in this paper would not expect to solve all the problems and we expect to continue our work for a long-term plan and this Grid-enabled adaptive visualization platform may be further incorporated into a more general framework of Grid-enabled adaptive multimedia presentation system as the 3D visualization engine.

References

1. XIANG Hui, MENG Xiangxu, YANG Chenglei, "Design and Implementation of Digital Archaeology Museum of Shandong University", Journal of System Simulation, Vol. 15, NO.3, 2003.3
2. Buchholz, S., Schill, A., "Adaptation-Aware Web Caching: Caching in the Future Pervasive Web", Proc. of the GI/ITG Fachtagung Kommunikation in Verteilten Systemen (KiVS 2003), Leipzig, Feb 26-28, 2003
3. Francisco Matias Cuenca-Acuna, Thu D. Nguyen, "Cooperative Caching Middleware for Cluster-Based Servers", Technical Report, DCS-TR-436, Department of Computer Science, Rutgers University, 2001
4. Greg Humphreys, et al., "Chromium: A Stream Processing Framework for Interactive Rendering on Clusters of Workstations", Computer Graphics (SIGGRAPH 2002 Proceedings), 2002
5. J. T. Klosowski, P. D. Kirchner, J. Valuyeva, G. Abram, C. J. Morris, R. H. Wolfe, T. Jackman, Deep View: High-Resolution Reality, IEEE Computer Graphics & Applications, Volume 22, Number 3, PP 12-15, May/June 2002
6. Dieter Kranzlmüller, *Grid-Enabled Scientific Visualization with GVK*, SCI Seminar, Scientific Computing and Imaging Institute, University of Utah, Salt Lake City, February 28, 2003.
7. Ioana M. Boier-Martin, *Adaptive Graphics,* IEEE Computer Graphics and Applications, vol. 2, no. 1, Jan-Feb 2003, pages 6-10.
8. Basu, Sujoy; Adhikari, Sameer; Kumar, Raj; Yan, Yong; Hochmuth, Roland; Blaho, Bruce E. "mmGrid: Distributed Resource Management Infrastructure for Multimedia Applications",17th International Parallel and Distributed Processing Symposium, 22-26 April 2003, Nice, France
9. Foster and C. Kesselman. Globus: A metacomputing infrastructure, toolkit. International Journal of SuperComputing Applications, 11(2).115–128, Summer 1997. www.globus.org
10. Globus Resource Allocation Manager (GRAM), http://www-unix.globus.org/developer/resource-management.html
11. The Monitoring and Discovery Service, http://www.globus.org/mds/

Maintaining Packet Order for the Parallel Switch

Yuguo Dong[1,2], Binqiang Wang[1], Yunfei Guo[1], and Jiangxing Wu[1]

[1] NDSC, Information Engineering University
[2] Telecommunication Engineering Institute, Air force Engineering University
No. 783 P.O.Box 1001, Zhengzhou, 450002, P.R.China
Tele: 86-371-3532731; Fax: 86-371-3941700
dyg@mail.ndsc.com.cn

Abstract. In the parallel switch high-speed arrived packets (or cells) with same destination will be spread into many low-speed switching fabrics for processing. When these packets are sent to the output, however, their sequence can not be guaranteed. In this paper we propose a novel technique that includes a structure of Virtual Input Queues (VIQ) and a scheduling algorithm named Sequence keeping round-robin (SKRR), which can efficiently maintain packet order in outputs. We also evaluate throughput and average delay performance for this technique.

1 Introduction

The parallel switch is an emerging architecture for high-speed switches [1, 2]. It is critical and practical to maintain packets (cells) order in parallel switches because: if arrived packets are directly switched, packets mis-sequencing can cause problems for current versions of TCP [4]; on the other way, if packets with variable length are chipped to many cells, mis-sequencing can cause problems for recombining cells into packets [3, 5].

Though there were order-maintaining techniques for other switch architecture [5], order-keeping for parallel switches remains an open issue and we are not aware of any open literature focusing on this problem. In this paper we propose a novel technique to avoid mis-sequencing for parallel switches. This technique is composed of a structure of Virtual Input Queues (VIQ) and a scheduling algorithm named Sequence keeping round-robin (SKRR).

2 Parallel Switch Model

The work-conserving [1, 2] parallel switch model that we consider has N external output ports operating at rate R. The switching part is made up of K parallel switching fabrics, each of which is an N×N output-queued (OQ) switch with port rate r. The internal speedup S is defined by Kr/R. In this paper, speedup is 1 and arriving IP

This work was supported by the foundation of China 863 Program under Grant 2001-AA-12-4-011.

M. Li et al. (Eds.): GCC 2003, LNCS 3032, pp. 176–179, 2004.

packets with variable length are assume to be segmented into cells, which is common in high performance switches. The buffer is arranged in each port as K equal size FIFO where each FIFO holds cells destined for the specific switching element [1, 6]. Each input local scheduling part and each switching element are working independently, i.e., no information is shared among them. Some terms used throughout this paper are defined below. Timeslot: The time taken to transmit or receive a cell at the link rate of R. Layers: The center stage switches or the parallel switching fabrics.

For a parallel switch model, keeping sequence means that on any output cells from one input should maintain the same sequence as the sequence by which they arrive to the input [1, 2, 5]. For example, if cells with the same destination output j arrive to input i in a sequence Q, after parallel switching they should leave output j still by the sequence Q. However, their order will be disturbed due to the following reason.

- Cells might lose order in input buffer because of different delay among FIFOs. But cells in same FIFO can avoid mis-order.
- Cells are likely to miss order in OQ fabrics because of various delay among different OQ fabrics.

3 The Novel Technique

The basic idea for resolving the mis-sequence problem is: firstly we sort cells by their external inputs in the internal output buffer for each switching fabric; secondly we use a scheduling algorithm to reshape cells with the same input.

3.1 Virtual Input Queues

As shown in Fig. 1, cells in any output of any layer are buffered by their inputs in VIQ_1, which is composed of N FIFOs. For example, FIFO 1 stores cells from input 1. We can conclude that cells in any FIFO of VIQ_1 are same with input and output. In the following, $VIQ_1(i, k, j)$ represents FIFO i of internal output j in layer k.

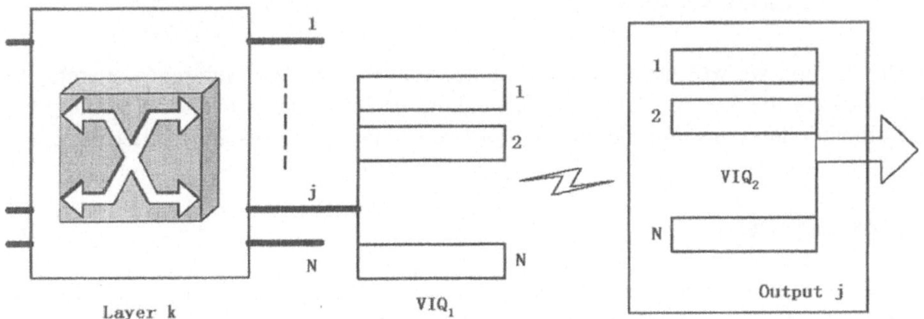

Fig. 1. VIQ_1 and VIQ_2

All cells destined for one output are buffered by their inputs in VIQ_2 composed of N FIFOs. $VIQ_2(i, j)$ represents FIFO i in output j. Each FIFO buffers cells from same input but through various layers.

3.2 Sequence Keeping Round-Robin Algorithm

As literature [6] presented, the most simple and practical load-balancing algorithm is that cells with same destination will be dispatched into layers by a round-robin way, which is accepted in this paper. For example, consider cells in input i and destined for output j, the 1st cell will be sent to layer 1 and later buffered in $VIQ_1(i, 1, j)$; the 2nd cell will be sent to layer 2 and buffered in $VIQ_1(i, 2, j)$... the Nth cell will be stored in $VIQ_1(i, N, j)$; the $(N+1)_{th}$ cell will be sent to layer 1... Without losing order, $VIQ_2(i, j)$ should collect cells like this way: firstly from $VIQ_1(i,1, j)$, secondly from $VIQ_1(i, 2, j)$... then from $VIQ_1(i, N, j)$, and again from $VIQ_1(i,1, j)$...

In SKRR (sequence keeping Round-robin) algorithm, $VIQ_2(i, j)$ uses the round-robin pointer p1(i, j) to remember which layer or $VIQ_1(i, k, j)$ the last cell came from, and output j serves VIQ_2 in round-robin order, using the pointer p2(j). p1(i, j) is used to keep the cell order while p2(j) is used to guarantee work-conserving and fairness among inputs. The major difference between these two pointers is: if p1(i, j) points to an empty $VIQ_1(i, k, j)$, it can not point to next item until this one has a cell; but if there is no cell in $VIQ_2(i, j)$ to which p2(j) points, it should skip this null one and point to next nonzero FIFO. More precisely, SKRR can be described as the following.

Each VIQ_2 performs:

Initialization: $p1(i, j) \leftarrow VIQ_1(i, 1, j)$;

$p1(i, j) \leftarrow VIQ_1(i,(k+1) \bmod K, j)$.

And each output j performs:

If $VIQ_2(i, j) \neq 0$, *then* $p2(j) \leftarrow VIQ_2(i, j)$; *else* $p2(j) \leftarrow VIQ_2((i+1) \bmod N, j)$.

SKRR is simple and straightforward to implement, but it needs N^2K VIQ_1 while N^2 buffers are needed in normal OQ, which requires more pointers and a more complicated buffer management mechanism.

4 Performance Evaluation

In this section we will use an output-queued (OQ) switch as a reference switch. We will compare the average delay and throughput performance between SKRR and OQ in following theorems. For the reason of space limitation, proofs are omitted.

4.1 Average Delay

This paper uses a similar idea of analysis as that in literature [6]: Firstly we compare SKRR with the delayed OQ which has the same arrivals as the inputs; then we will compare the delayed OQ with a regular OQ switch having the same cell arrivals as the layers.

Theorem 1: The average delay for SKRR is less than the average delay for OQ plus a constant 2NK.

Let us estimate the delay of SKRR for high-speed switches. Consider a parallel switch with 16 ports, OC768 (40Gbps line-rates) and a cell size of 64bytes. On the practical designing of such terabit switches, we use N=K and no speedup. So this switch has a delay less than the delay for an OQ plus $2NK=2\cdot16^2\cdot(13ns) = 6.7\mu s$, which can be accepted by commercial standard.

4.2 Throughput

In this paper we prove that switch A and switch B have the same throughput if total queuing size $Q^A(t)$ of A and $Q^B(t)$ of B satisfy $Q^B(t) \le Q^A(t) \le Q^B(t) + C$ where C is a constant [6].

Theorem 2: SKRR and OQ have the same throughput.

Theorem 2 is very useful since OQ switch has many important properties, e.g., SKRR switch has 100% throughput with admissible Bernoulli i.i.d. arrival traffic.

5 Conclusions

This paper solves the order-keeping problem for parallel switches. Our novel technique includes: VIQ buffer structure that can sort mis-ordered cells and SKRR scheduling algorithm that can dispatch cells to outputs for maintaining sequence and fairness. Evaluation shows that VIQ&SKRR has average delay less than OQ plus 2NK timeslots and has same throughput as OQ. The cost is that VIQ&SKRR needs too many buffers and a complicated buffer management mechanism. Possible ways to improve this technique, such as using shared buffers, will be studied in future.

References

1. Sundar Iyer and Nick McKeown, 'Analysis of the Parallel Packet Switch Architecture', IEEE/ACM Transactions on Networking, April 2003, http://klamath.stanford.edu/~sundaes/Papers/tonpps.pdf.
2. Walter Wang, Libin Dong and Wayne Wolf. 'A Distributed Switch Architecture with Dynamic Load-balancing and Parallel Input-Queued Crossbars for Terabit Switch Fabrics', INFOCOM 2002, http://www.ieee-infocom.org /2002/ papers/101.pdf .
3. ITU-T Recommendation I.363.5 "B-ISDN ATM Adaptation Layer specification: Type 5 AAL," Aug.1996.
4. E. Blanton and M. Allman, "On making TCP more robust to packet reordering," ACM Computer Communication Review, 32(1), January 2002.
5. Isaac Keslassy and Nick McKeown, 'Maintaining Packet Order in Two-Stage Switches', Proceedings of IEEE Infocom '02, New York, June 2002.
6. Yuguo Dong, Zupeng Li and Yufei Guo, 'On the Load Balancing of a Parallel Switch with Input Queues', PDCAT'03, Chengdu, China, Aug. 2003.

Grid-Based Process Simulation Technique and Support System

Hui Gao and Li Zhang

Software Engineering Institute, Beijing University of Aeronautics and Astronautics
No.37, XueYuan Road
HaiDian District, Beijing 100083
P.R.China
huigao_0611@163.com lily@buaa.edu.cn

Abstract. Grid is a new distributed computing technique, which is not only applied to large scale calculating in science domain, but also a good computing environment to integrate loose business applications in enterprises. To apply the grid technique, this document discusses the business process simulation technique and its support system.

1 Introduction of Process Simulation Technique

Based on the principle of process engineering, any enterprise can be described with its products (or providing services), the prerequisite resources (including people), and the activities that produce the products. A process is composed of activities, products, resources and the relationships among them. Process simulation plays an important role in process engineering. It is a practical approach to analyze, verify, improve and optimize a process model [1].The basic principle of process simulation is based on VPML (Visual Process Modeling Language). The full definition of VPML is in [2]. The process simulating, which is driven by event model and queue model, constitutes a discrete event system [1].

This document is structured as follows. This section introduces the basic technique of process simulation. Section 2 addresses the grid-based process simulating theory. The conceptions of activity and resource in VPML are mapping to two kinds of grid services. Section 3 discusses the architecture of the grid-based process simulating system in detail.

2 Principle of Grid-Based Process Simulation

Grid services and the relationship of services constitute the grid computing environment. Grid Service is regarded as the core conception in grid. The common computational, resources, information, data and the like, are treated as services. This service-oriented view is in favor of services' management, sharing, and reuse. Process

M. Li et al. (Eds.): GCC 2003, LNCS 3032, pp. 180–183, 2004.

model is composed of activities, products, resources and their connections. In this document, activity and resource are abstracted as two kinds of services (Activity Service and Resource Service), and product is regard as service data computed by these services. Events are responsible for exchanging information among services. The resource in process model expresses the objects that are responsible for completing the related activities. Resource Services organize Activity Services just as Virtual Organization combines services. The following is the detailed discussion in grid-based process simulating theory.

2.1 Service-Based Process Simulating Mechanism

The executing mechanism of process model is described with the producing, consuming, and queuing of events [1]. While an event is produced, the related activity checks the resource state. If the resource is available, this activity is activated. In activity's executing period, it consumes input products and produces output products. When the output products are produced, a new event is generated, and triggers another activity. So events drive the execution of a process. Because the interval of event generated time is shorter than activity executing time, an event queue is used for avoiding losing events. From the angle of Object-Oriented, the full description of every object's dynamic behaviors reflects the behaviors of whole system. Therefore, service-based process simulating mechanism is described with the dynamic behaviors of all services (Activity Service, Resource Service and other services).

The behavior of activities is described with the inner states of activities and the interaction with other external objects (resources, products ...). The inner states express the execution of activities, and interaction with objects will activate activities or produce succeeding event.

.According to the discussion above, an activity is mapped to a service. The system schedule is composed of schedules of all Activity Service instances. All of Activity Services and the other services interact on each other to complete the process simulation.

2.2 Resource in Process Model and Virtual Organization in Grid

According to VPML, resources are the executing objects of activities. In broad sense, resources in process model express organization of one enterprise or team of one project.

In grid technique, virtual organization (VO) is an important conception. From the view of VO, a complex service can be composed of some basic services without caring their implementation. When we construct the VO, we will classify the services at first, and then integrate these services. In the natural of things, it is a simple and practical way to classify services according to the organization of enterprises. The services deployment strategy in our system is that all services which belong to the same department are deployed to the same node.

2.3 The Problem of Activity Activating

If an activity arrives ready state and resources are available, this activity will be activated immediately. But in the true-life, some activities will be delayed instead of being activated at once. There is a problem that how to set the determinate starting time of these activities. The solution is to add the restricted conditions between state ready and state activate, such as evaluating the resources, and selecting a low load period to activate activities. This solution requires the system to monitor the running status, then to evaluate context by the activity starting strategies (These strategies is not the content discussed in this document), and to act by the services at last. So the services in our system are provided with intelligence. We extend the basic interface of a grid service to support intelligent characteristics.

3 Architecture of Grid-Based Process Simulation System

Figure 4.1 illustrates the architecture of Grid-based process simulation system .This architecture adopts OGSA (Open Grid Services Architecture) which is based on services. The system is composed of different services and data, and it has four layers, which is data storage layer, GT3 layer, application layer and user interface layer.

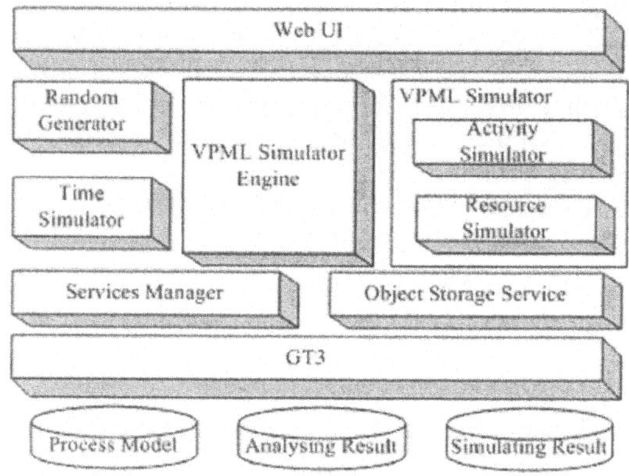

Fig. 1. Architecture of the Process simulation system

(1) Data storage layer. The data is stored in the grid, and these data is composed of Process Model, Analyzing Result and Simulating Result. The high layers can transparent access these data from the interfaces of Object Storage Services.
(2) GT3 layer provides the basic function of grid platform.
(3) Application layer is the most important part in the system design. This level is composed of a series of services described in detail below:

- ✧ VPML Simulator Engine is the core service in application layer. The engine explains VPML semantic, deploys services in grid platform in the term of process model and resource model, controls the communication among services, and at last drives the simulating of process model.

- ✧ VPML simulator group. The simulators are applied to replace all kinds of applications, which can execute the behavior of activities and resources. In addition, the simulator has another important function—generating analysis reports.
- ✧ Time Simulator. It supports time control of simulation process.
- ✧ Service Manager. It managers all services in system, including Registry Service, Query Service. There are many services dynamically created, so Service Manager facilitates dynamic discovery of these services in system, and provides the management of these services.
- ✧ Object Storage Service. Process model and analysis result are stored as XML, Object Storage Service provides basic interfaces of object access, object query and so on. The detail of this service can see [5].

(4) User Interface layer is used to display and control simulation process. It monitors simulation process by animated mechanism, and debug the process simulation step by step.

4 Conclusion

We discussed the grid-based process simulation technique and its support system in this paper. Firstly, we brought forward some techniques to solve the problems in grid-based process simulation. Secondly, this paper discussed the architecture of the grid-based process simulation system. This architecture is based on OGSA, and it is composed of some intelligent services and some normal services.

References

1. Zhang Li, Wang lei. Process Simulation Technique and its Support Environment PMSE.JOURNAL OF SOFTWARE, 1997.8 565--575
2. Zhou Bosheng, Zhang Sheing. Visual Process Modeling Language VPML. JOURNAL OF SOFTWARE, 1997.8 535--545
3. I. Foster, C. Kesselman, J.M.Nick, S.Tuecke. Grid Services for Distributed System Integration,
4. Foster, C. Kesselman, J. Nick, and S. Tuecke, 2002, "Physiology of OGSA--An Open Grid Services Architecture for Distributed System integration," Open Grid Service Infrastructure WG, Global Grid Forum, http://www.gridforum.org/ogsi-wg/drafts/ogsa_draft2.9_2002-06-22.pdf.
5. Gao Hui, Zhang Li, Sun Yi. Design and Implementation of Grid-based Object Storage Services. IDPT-2002

Some Grid Automata for Grid Computing

Hao Shen and Yongqiang Sun

Shanghai JiaoTong University, Shanghai, China

Abstract. We use 2-Dimensional language to construct 2-Dimensional computer graphics model, use MSO or other logics to specify some graph property, and use automata model checking technique to check this model whether or not satisfy this property. From above process, some grid pattern recognition problem could be transferred to Model checking problem. According to logic method, we get some grid pattern recognition problem couldn't be solved in decidable manner.

1 Introduction

Automata theory is a core theory of computer science and Automata theory has from its beginning developed in close contact to mathematical logic. A key result on this connection dating back to 1960 and due to Büchi and Elgot, states that finite automata and monadic second-order logic are equal in expressive power. Büchi, Muller, Rabin, Street and others used finite automata to solve the decision problem of logical theories, such as the monadic second-order theories S1S and S2S of one, resp. two successor functions. For this purpose, finite automata were introduced also over infinite words and infinite trees.

In computer science, another aspect is more significant. The equivalence results provide a solution to the problem of connecting the two worlds of "implementations"(given by transition systems) and "specifications"(given by logical formulas) for the case of finite-state systems. As applications, one obtains algorithms to verify finite-state programs("model checking") and algorithms for system synthesis from specifications.The essence of the transformations from logic to automata is the reduction of a global description of words or trees (using quantifiers that range over the whole set of positions) to a description which refers only to local checking of consecutive letters (plus finite memory and acceptance condition).

2 Picture and Grid Automata

This section is to generalize concepts and techniques of formal language theory to two dimensions. Informally, a two-dimensional string is called a picture and is defined as a rectangular array of symbols taken from a finite alphabet. Let Σ be a finite alphabet and $\hat{\Sigma} = \Sigma \uplus \{\#\}$. An ω-picture over Σ is a function p:$\omega^2 \rightarrow \hat{\Sigma}$ such that p(i,0)=p(0,i)=# for all i$\geq$0 and p(i,j)$\in\Sigma$ for i,j>0. We use $\#\notin\Sigma$ as a border marking of pictures. $\Sigma^{\omega,\omega}$ is the set of all ω-pictures over Σ. An ω-picture

M. Li et al. (Eds.): GCC 2003, LNCS 3032, pp. 184–187, 2004.

language L is a subset of $\Sigma^{\omega,\omega}$. We denote by S_v={((i,j),(i+1,j))|i,j∈ω} and S_h={((i,j),(i,j+1))|i,j∈ω} the vertical, respectively horizontal successor relation on ω^2. A path in a picture p is a sequence π=(v_0,v_1,v_2,...) of vertices such that (v_i,v_{i+1})∈S_v∪S_h for all i≥0. if v_0=(0,0) we call π an initial path, and if π=(v_0,...,v_n) is finite we call π a path from v_0 to v_n. A vertex v_1 is beyond a vertex v_0(v_1>v_0) if there is a path from v_0 tov_1. The origin of a picture p is the vertex (0,0), the only "corner" of p. the diagonal of a picture p is the set of vertices Di(p)={(i,i)|i∈ω}.

A two-dimensional language (or picture language) is a set of pictures. While the starting point of most studies on picture languages is based on the analogy to word automata and string languages, our model is Grid automata.

Definition 1. *$\mathcal{A}$=(Σ,Q,q_0,δ_1,δ_2,F) where each component is the same as binary tree automaton(top-down version) except that δ_i(i=1,2) are controlled by concurrent constraints, and it runs over p's.*

We introduce a kind of execution control, explaining how to compose compatible transitions (to be moves via δ_i) during the operation.

1. initial moves: For a_1,a_2,a_3,a_4∈Σ, q_1∈Q, if q_1=q_0 and there are some q_2∈δ_2(q_0,a_1) and q_3∈δ_1(q_0,a_1) such that δ_1(q_2,a_2)∩δ_2(q_3,a_3)≠∅.
2. Top moves: For b_1,b_2,b_3,b_4∈Σ, q_1,q_3∈Q with q_3∈δ_1(q_1,b_1), if there is some q_2∈δ_2(q_1,b_1) such that δ_1(q_2,b_2)∩δ_2(q_3,b_3)≠∅.
3. Left moves: For c_1,c_2,c_3,c_4∈Σ, q_1,q_2∈Q with q_2∈δ_2(q_1,c_1), if there is some q_3∈δ_1(q_1,c_1) such that δ_1(q_2,c_2)∩δ_2(q_3,c_3)≠∅.
4. Inner moves: For d_1,d_2,d_3,d_4∈Σ, q_1,q_2,q_3∈Q with q_2∈δ_2(q_1,d_1), q_3∈δ_1(q_1,d_1), such that q_4∈ δ_1(q_2,d_2)∩δ_2(q_3,c_3).
5. Boundary moves: For right side positions: δ_2(q,e)∩F≠∅. For bottom positions: δ_1(q,e)∩F≠∅. Particularly for target position, δ_1(q,e)∩F≠∅≠δ_2(q,e)∩F.

A accepts a given picture p of size m×n iff there is a successful run ρ:dom(p)→Q satisfying the following:
ρ((1,1))=q_0, ρ((i,n+1))∈F and ρ((m+1,j)), for 1≤i≤m, 1≤j≤n.

3 Tiling System

It is natural to ask for such a connection between monadic second-order logic and finite state recognizability in a more general context, in particular for classes of graphs. We use tiling system as a generalization of the transition relations in conventional finite automata.

A tiling system is a tuple $\mathcal{A}$=(Q,Σ,Δ,Acc) consisting of a finite set Q of states, a finite alphabet Σ, a finite set Δ⊆ ($\hat{\Sigma}$×Q)^4 of tiles, and an acceptance component Acc (which may be a subset of Q or of 2^Q).

We consider different acceptance conditions for tiling systems, all of them similar to the well-known ones from ω-automata over words. First consider the case where the acceptance component is a set F⊆Q of states. A tiling system $\mathcal{A}$=(Q,Σ,Δ,F)

- A-accepts p if there is a run ρ of $\mathcal{A}$ on p such that ρ(v)$\in$F for all v$\in\omega^2$.
- E-accepts p if there is a run ρ of $\mathcal{A}$ on p such that ρ(v)$\in$F for at least one v$\in\omega^2$.
- Büchi accepts p if there is a run ρ of $\mathcal{A}$ on p such that ρ(v)$\in$F for infinitely many v$\in\omega^2$.
- co-Büchi accepts p if there is a run ρ of $\mathcal{A}$ on p such that ρ(v)$\in$F for all but finitely many v$\in\omega^2$.

Similarly as for ω-words and for finite pictures, one verifies that every Büchi recognizable picture language can be defined by an existential monadic second order sentence (a Σ_1^1-formula). Here we view pictures p as relational structures over the signature $\{S_v,S_h,\leq_v,\leq_h,(P_a)_{a\in\Sigma}\}$ with universe ω^2, where S_v,S_h are interpreted as the usual vertical and horizontal successor relations, and $\leq_v$ and $\leq_h$ as the corresponding linear orderings. We write u<v if v is beyond u. P_av holds for a vertex v$\in\omega^2$ iff p(v)=a.

Proposition 2. *Let $\mathcal{A}$=(Q,Σ,Δ,Acc) be a tiling system. The ω-picture language recognized by $\mathcal{A}$ with Büchi acceptance conditions of above can be defined by an existential monadic second order sentence φ.*

$$\exists Q_1 \ldots Q_k \exists R \ \forall x \bigvee_{1\leq i\leq k} (Q_i x \wedge \bigwedge_{i\neq j} \neg Q_j x) \tag{1}$$

$$\wedge \forall x_1 \ldots x_4 (S_h x_1 x_2 \wedge S_h x_3 x_4 \wedge S_v x_1 x_3 \wedge S_v x_2 x_4 \rightarrow \bigvee_{\left(\begin{smallmatrix} a_1,q_1 & a_2,q_2 \\ a_3,q_3 & a_4,q_4 \end{smallmatrix}\right)\in\Delta} \bigwedge_{1\leq i\leq 4} P_{a_i} x_i \wedge Q_{q_i} x_i) \tag{2}$$

$$\wedge \bigvee_{i\in F} \forall x (Rx \rightarrow Q_i x) \tag{3}$$

$$\wedge \forall x \in R \exists y \in R \exists z (\neg z = x \wedge x \leq_h z \wedge z \leq_v y) \tag{4}$$

The sentence φ describes the existence of a successful run $\mathcal{A}$ on p.

4 The Complementation Problem

This method according to W.Thomas thought. Let T_1 be the set of ω-pictures over the alphabet {0,1,\$} which contain a code of an ω-tree in the first row and which are labelled 0 on the remaining positions. Let T_2 be the subset of T_1 of those pictures where the coded tree contains an infinite path.

Proposition 3. *The class of Büchi recognizable ω-picture languages is not closed under complement. In particular, $T_2\subseteq\{0,1,\$\}^{\omega,\omega}$ is Büchi recognizable, but its complement is not.*

Proof idea: We use a standard result of recursion theory, saying that the set FT of finite-path trees is $\prod_1^1$ complete. Thus it is not Σ_1^1-definable in second-order arithmetic. This implies in particular that the ω-picture language $T_1 \backslash T_2$ containing the corresponding tree codes is not definable by a monadic Σ_1^1-sentence as introduced in above Section, and hence is not Büchi recognizable.

In the next proposition we show that T_1 and T_2 are Büchi recognizable. Assuming that this class of picture languages is closed under complement, we get that $\{0,1,\$\}^{\omega,\omega} \backslash T_2$ is Büchi recognizable. Hence the set $T_1 \backslash T_2$ of pictures encoding finite-path trees, which is $(\{0,1,\$\}^{\omega,\omega} \backslash T_2) \cap T_1$, would be Büchi recognizable, too. Contradiction. □

Proposition 4. *1.the language $T_1 \subseteq \{0,1,\$\}^{\omega,\omega}$ of all ω-pictures encoding an ω-tree is Büchi recognizable.*
2.The language $T_2 \subseteq \{0,1,\$\}^{\omega,\omega}$ of all ω-pictures encoding an ω-tree with an infinite path is Büchi recognizable.

5 Conclusion

In this paper we have use labelled graph as the input of graph automata, 2-Dimensional picture language as the input of grid automata, then use tiling system unified these automata operation. For the class of Büchi recognizable picture languages we showed the nonclosure under complementaiton. We could use model checking method and other logic method to solve problem which not be solved by classic pattern recognition theory.

References

1. D.Giammarresi and A.Restivo. Two-dimensional languages. In Handbook of Formal Languages. Vol.3, pages 215-267. 1997.
2. D.Giammarresi, A.Restivo, S.Seibert, and W.Thomas. Monadic second-order logic over rectangular pictures and recognizability by tiling system. Information and Computation, 125(1):32-45, 1996.
3. M.Kaminski and S.Pinter. Finite automata on directed graphs. Computer and System Sciences, 44:425-446, 1992.
4. Shen En-shao. Grid Automata and Grid Grammars for picture Languages. Journal of Software, China. Vol.11 No.7 July 2000.
5. J. Altenbernd, W. Thomas, and S. Wöhrle. Tiling systems over infinite pictures and their acceptance conditions. In Proceedings of the 6th International Conference on Developements in Language Theory, DLT 2002,
6. H.Rogers. Theory of Recursive Functions and Effective Computability. McGraw-Hill. New York, 1967.
7. W.Thomas. Automata on infinite objects. In Handbook of Theoretical Computer Science, Vol.B, pages 133-192. Amsterdam, 1990.
8. E.M. Clarke, E.A. Emerson, A.P. Sistla, Automatic verification of finite state concurrent programs using temporal logic, ACM Transaction on Program language and Systems, Vol 8, 244-263, 1986.

The Cooperation of Virtual Enterprise Supported by the Open Agent System

Zhaolin Yin, Aijuan Zhang, Xiaobin Li , and Jinfei Sun

Department of Computer Science and Technology
Chinese University of Mining and Technology
Xuzhou Jiangsu 221008
zhlyin@cumt.edu.cn

Abstract. Virtual enterprise is a network composed of different business management domains. Developer and managers provider service through sharing resource. Every participant should provides. It's process of business disposal and resource, but form the observer outside, the virtual enterprise is a unitive enterprise. This paper introduces the sort of Virtual Enterprise, Then expatiates the structure of virtual enterprise supported by the open agent system. At last, this paper describes the virtual market structure and its realization.

1 Introduction

Virtual enterprise is a network composed of different business management domains. Developers and managers provide service through sharing resource. Every participant should provides its process of business disposal and resources. But from the observer outside, the virtual enterprise is a unitive enterprise[1].

2 The Reference of Virtual Enterprise Supported by the Open Agent System

Currently ,there are such technologies supporting virtual enterprise as Electronic Data Interchange, Distributed Component Based System, Message System, Workflow Management System, Mobile Intelligent Agent[3]. Among them, according to the perfect property of distribution, autonomy and flexibility, the technology of intelligent and mobile agent is been in favor of, the structure of virtual enterprise supported by the open agent system as Fig1.

The environment of distributed communication: It implements the communication among the systems of different internet protocols.

Open agent system: The agent system pluralizes FIPA and MASIF, supports the management, security and mobility of agent

M. Li et al. (Eds.): GCC 2003, LNCS 3032, pp. 188–191, 2004.

Agent language and message: The agents cooperate with each other using agent language (such as ACL, KQML and XML)

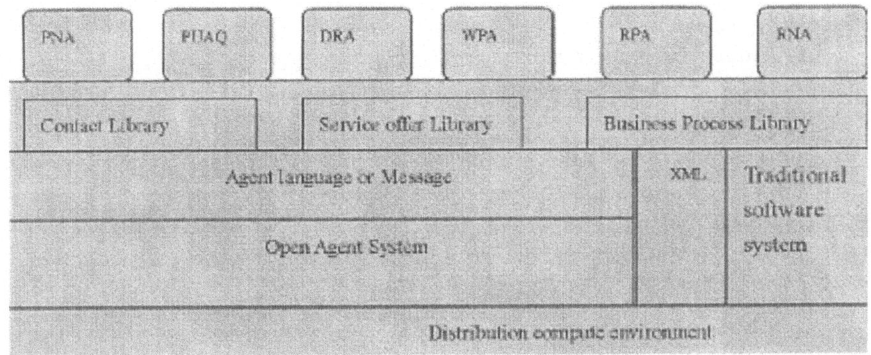

Fig. 1. The structure of virtual enterprise supported by the open agent system .

3 The Negotiation Center of Virtual Enterprise–Virtual Enterprise

Virtual market is the third party which provides medium service to the service providers [4] .The function of VE is the registration and management of the service providers of virtual enterprise. Representatives can search for the special service provider. Every business process registered in the virtual market is related to a service type[4]. Generally speaking, the service type is described by the interface of business process and the manager of virtual market manages the service type: such as creating, modifying, deleting a service type and achieving the value of a service type.

If service provider wants to register a business process in the virtual market, he should create a service provision related to the current service type, and register it in the virtual market .A service provider is an instance of a service type given value of property. Service providers are managed by every domain privately. The management of service providers include: deletion, query and modification.

In the end, the representatives of virtual enterprise who search for service providers or service providers obtain the special service providers having registered .So the fundamental service of virtual market includes: the management of service type, service providers and those who obtain the service providers. Every service can be achieved by different agents.

The communication between agents can be executed with normative FIPA ACL/XML[2] message, the format of FIPA ACL/XML is as follows:

The Cooperation of Virtual Enterprise Supported by the Open Agent System <STAMessage or SOAMessage> //the message sent to STA or SOA

```
<STARequest or SOARequest RequestId="abc"><command type>//the command
can be add,delete modify  etc   the command requested :such as
add,delete modify e.//the content of command operation ,using XML
</command type>
 </STARequest or SOARequest>
</STAMessage or SOAMessage>
</VMPMessage>):
protocol fiparequeat
//theprotocolused :
reply-with inform
//answer the message of former )
the answer to the request as follows:
(inform :senderSTAorSOA :
receiverProvider Negotiation Agent p:content (<VMPMessage>)
<STAMessage or SOAMessage >
<STAResponse or SOAResponse >
<command type>
</command type>
</STARequest or SOARequest >
</STAMessage or SOAMessage >
</VMPMessage>):protocol fi-parsponse:replywith request)
```

Generally speaking, before creating or managing providers of service type in virtual enterprise ,we need specify a certain name of service type. Then the agent having this condition will migrate to virtual market, compound the ACL/XML request, and then send this request to STA. The protocol of fundamental FIPA-Request-Response is used for the communication between agents[2]. After STA receive this request, he will parse it with ACL/XML parser ,check the request type and then decide what to do. In succession, STA execute the request through service type repertory, produce the message of ACL/XML announcement, and send this message to the request agent. Once the request agent receive this message, he also needs parse and check it, then return the domain of service offer, and in the end inform the domain putting the request forward. The inner structure of agent in virtual market are shown in Fig2.

4 Summary

This paper has analysed the dynamic virtual enterprise's business domain, role and responsibility by the thought agent oriented. Then expatiated the structure of virtual enterprise supported by the open agent system. At last, this paper describes the virtual market structure and it's realization.

In addition , The research has been partially supported by The Found of Key Laboratory for Novel Software Technology at Nanjing Unversity.

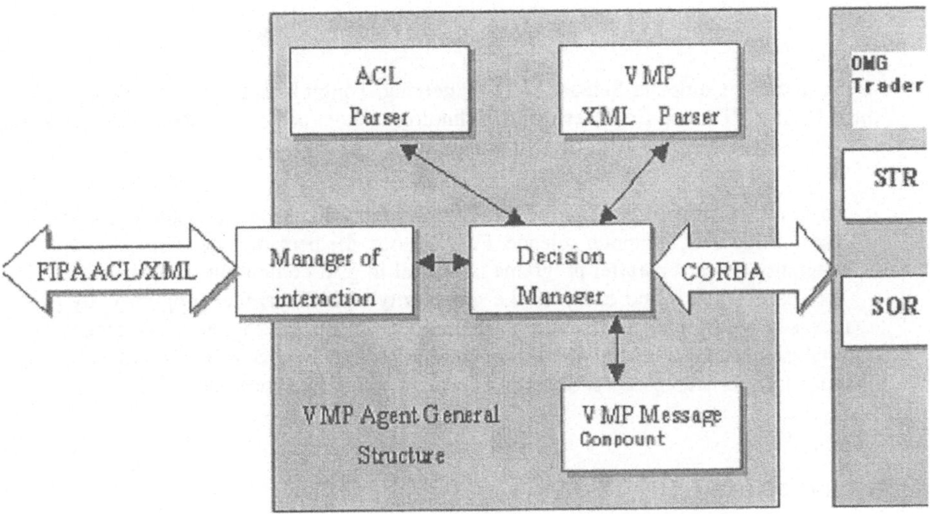

Fig. 2. The inner structure of agent in virtual market are shown

References

[1] UMAR A, MISSIE, P. A Framework for Analyzing Virtual Enterprise Infrastructure

[2] http://www.fipa.org/2000 Foundation for Intelligent Physical Agents

[3] Zhao Yanhong, Agent and Software Integration, the master thesis of the Chinese University of Mining and Technology 2002

[4] Katzy, B. Obozinski, V. (1999) "Designing the Virtual Enterprise" Proceedings of ICE 99, 5th International Conf. On Concurrent Engineering, The Hague, Netherlands, Mar 99

The Granularity Analysis of MPI Parallel Programs[1]

Wei-guang Qiao and Guosun Zeng

Department of Computer Science and Engineering, Tongji University, Shanghai 200092
Tongji Branch, National Engineering & Technology Center of High Performance Computer, Shanghai 200092, China

Abstract. Computational grid for high performance computing is the current research focus of computer science. Furthermore, the performance analysis and evaluation toward parallel programs is critical in grid computing environment. This paper studies and analyzes the granularity of MPI parallel programs. By means of basic-block and flow analysis tree, we develop a Program Basic-block Analysis System (PBAS), which is an automatic performance analysis software tool based on source codes. Some parallel algorithms have been analyzed.

1 Introduction

The granularity analysis of parallel program is one of the key technologies in high performance grid computing. Formally, for a program, granularity is defined as $g=\tau_{comp}/\tau_{comm}$, where τ_{comp} and τ_{comm} represent the computation cost and communication cost of execution, respectively[1]. In this paper, we design a software tool for automatic performance analysis for MPI source codes.

2 Performance Analysis Based on Program Source Code

MPI is an interface library for parallel programming in message-passing fashion. Its basic APIs are used as the extension of C or Fortran [2]. MPI programs, therefore, share the same syntax as hosting language.

To facilitate the computer recognition of program source code, we choose basic-block and flow analysis tree as a middle expression [1]. By lexical analysis, MPI source code can be marked as three components: sequential statements, "if" statement and "for" statement, each of them is called a basic-block and tagged with a leader, that is a key word in dominate statement. Then a flow analysis tree(FAT) is made up of basic-blocks. Figure 1 depicts the transformation from source code to flow analysis tree.

The following is a novel algorithm for basic-block recognition and performance analysis, which is the basis for designing associated software tool.

①***Initialization.*** Set a key array and a key queue to store leaders.

②***Basic-block recognition.*** Execute lexical analysis repeatedly, and store all leaders and their positions in the key array. Consecutive sequence statements between two

[1] Supported by the National Natural Science Foundation of China under grant of 60173026 and Shanghai Science Fund under grant of 025115037 and 03DZ15029.

M. Li et al. (Eds.): GCC 2003, LNCS 3032, pp. 192–195, 2004.

leaders make up a basic-block, which is used to create a child node as a leaf of FAT. The performance of child node is queried from typical code performance library built in advance.

③ ***Construction of flow analysis tree.*** Scan the whole key array, create a parent node with each gotten leader, link it with associate child nodes generated last step. Meantime, if a parent node has successive middle nodes, these leaders of middle node are inserted into the key queue.

④***Linkage of middle nodes.*** If the key queue is not empty, we can get the first element from the queue, and link corresponding node with its successive middle nodes. When finished, such element is removed from the queue. Do so till no element left in the queue.

⑤***Correction.*** During steps above, whenever the leader is "if", the matched leader "else" is treated as its child leader. Similarly, whenever the leader is "for", the number of its iteration must be calculated by a special function.

⑥***Finalization.*** If the source code has not been processed completely, jump to ①, otherwise stop.

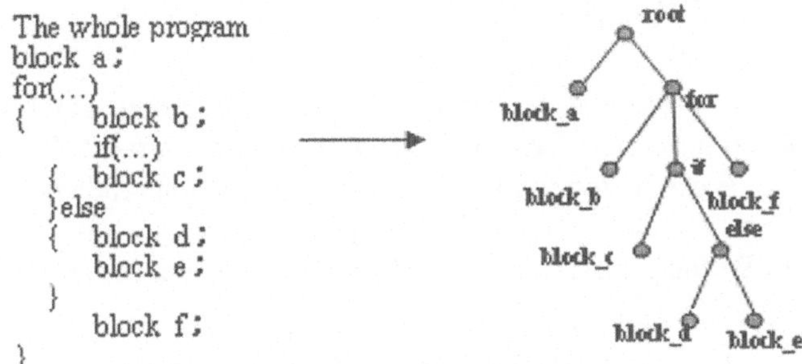

Fig. 1. The Flow Analysis Tree

3 The Implementation of Automatic Performance Analysis Tool

3.1 The Construction of Typical Code Performance Library

Typical code performance library records the execution performance of classified codes running on the target machine. It is built in advance and used by the presented algorithm above. For each classified code, we need a special benchmark to get its performance. The library file is organized in XML for portability as followings:

```
<?xml version="1.0" encoding="UTF-8"?>
<operators xmlns="x-schema:C:\pbas\src\pbas\pl1schema.xml">
            <operator>
                 <name type="1" obj="int">+</name>
                 <performance measure="us">0.014877</performance>
            </operator>
...........
</operators>
```

3.2 PBAS Design and Implementation

The architecture of PBAS is shown in figure 2. User submits parallel source code to PBAS, and then lexical analysis module invocates basic-block recognition and performance statistics to identify statement types and look up performance data automatically. In the next step, PBAS constructs FAT and traverse it to calculate the performance data of underlying node. Finally, user graphical interface is called, which demonstrates the analysis results with visual directory tree and forms.

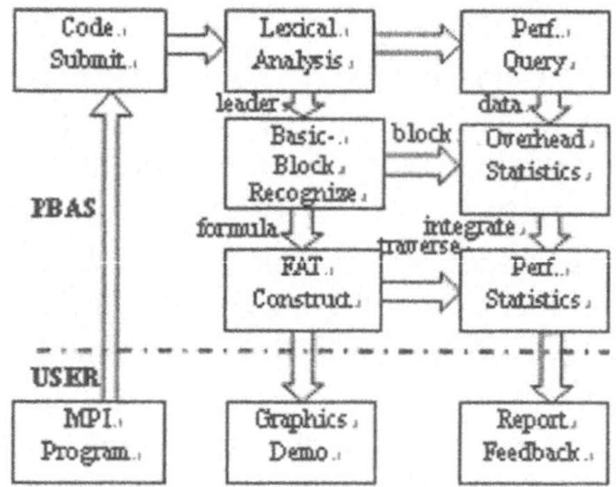

Fig. 2. PBAS Architecture

4 Experimental Results

The typical code performance library of grid computing environment in our laboratory is listed in section 3.2. Let A, B, C be a n×n matrix, MPI source code for calculating C=A×B can be found in references[3]. Execution mode is Master-slave.

For communication overhead, each slave process receives n/m rows of A and all n×n elements of B, and returns n/m rows of product C. Then, communication time is

$$t_{comm} = t_{startup}+(n^2/m + n^2)t_{data}+ t_{startup}+n^2/mt_{data} \tag{1}$$

Since the master process collects results sequentially, the total communication time is

$$t_{comm} = m(t_{startup}+(n^2/m+ n^2)t_{data}+ t_{startup}+n^2/mt_{data})=2mt_{startup}+(2n^2+mn^2)t_{data} \tag{2}$$

For computation overhead, slave processes execute most computational tasks. Once a C_{ij} element is calculated, there are n additions and n multiplications to be executed. So each slave process calculates n/m rows of C. The computation time is

$$t_{comp}= (nt_{add}+nt_{multiply}) \times n\times n/m \tag{3}$$

Figure 3 shows the predicted result by PBAS, which is close to actual execution.

Figure 4 shows the granularity distribution of an 800×800 matrix multiply program executed on 10 parallel processing nodes. Computation overhead is represented in grey and communication overhead in black. Time unit is 0.01 second. The horizontal axis follows the depth-first-traverse order of FAT. According to the granularity distribution, we may exploit the critical point between sequence execution and parallel execution [4], and design optimized parallel task scheduling strategy.

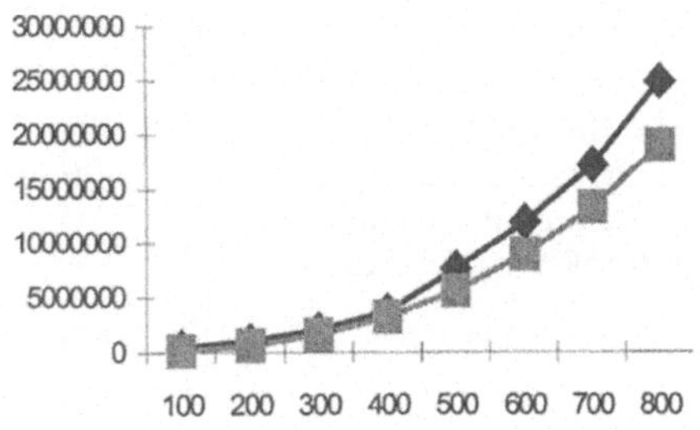

Fig. 3. Prediction vs. Actual Execution

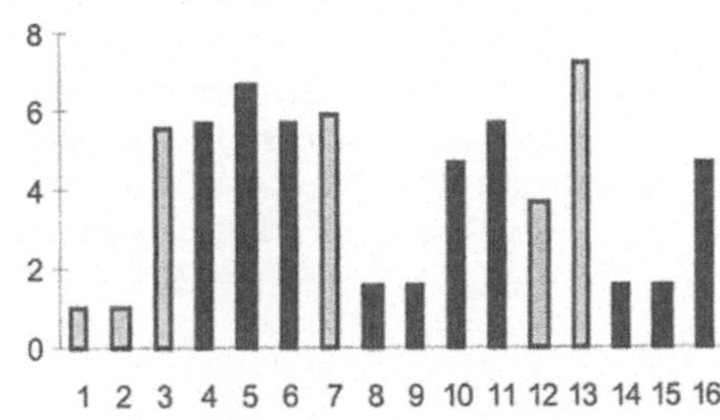

Fig. 4. Granularity Distribution

5 Conclusions

Performance analysis in grid computing is a significant branch of high performance computing research. In this paper, we have designed our automatic performance analysis tool and tested it. Our future research is to solve undetermined operations in programs, and to improve the prediction precision.

References

[1] Y.H.Zhang,The Application Research of Network Heterogeneous Computing and Its Coarse-Grain User-Directed Implementation, thesis submitted for degree of graduate of Jiaotong University,1999.1.

[2] M.Snir, S.Otto, S.Huss, and D.Walker,MPI: The Complete Reference,MIT Press, 1996.

[3] G.L.Chen,Parallel Computing,Higher Education Press, Beijing,1999.5.

[4] I. Foster, C. Kesselman, S. Tuecke. The Anatomy of the Grid: Enabling Scalable Virtual Organizations, International J. Supercomputer Applications, 15(3), 2001.

NGG: A Service-Oriented Application Grid Architecture for National Geological Survey

Yu Tang[1], Kaitao He[2], Zhen Xiang[1], Yongbo Zhang[2], and Ning Jing[1]

[1] School of Electronic Science and Engineering, National University of Defense Technology, Changsha, Hunan, P.R.China
yutang_nudt@163.com, wsmwb3200@21cn.com, ningjing@nudt.edu.cn
[2] China Geological Survey, Beijing, P.R.China
kthe@htrdc.com, yongbo@heinfo.net

Abstract. National geological survey works have characteristics of data enormousness, computing denseness, resource distribution, and applications heterogeneousness. As innovative information infrastructure and service architecture, grid can meet geological survey application requirements by implementing sharing and cooperation of distributed and heterogeneous resources. Based on grid technologies and OGSA, National Geological Grid (NGG), a novel service-oriented architecture with seven levels from information acquiring, processing to applying, is proposed. Some key technologies of NGG are discussed in detail, such as service chain, geological semantic sharing, and so on. A new service chain model (named Service/Resource net) based on Petri net and graph theory is presented. And NGG ontology is introduced to implement geological semantic sharing.

1 Introduction

National geological survey aims at collecting, processing geological data and providing information services for society, whose final products are many kinds of geological information. Geological data and information have characteristics of heterogeneity , distribution and enormousness. To meet requirements of different users, we must provide various information services, implement sharing and cooperation of different geological resources. Geological resources are all elements and components included in national geological survey works, such as computing equipments, enormous data and information, data processing systems, information services, organizations and individuals [1, 2]..

As a new technique to share distributed and heterogeneous resources, grid provides a practical way to satisfy the application demands of national geological survey works. The National High Technology Research and Development 863 Program of China support China Geological Survey to study and build National Geological Grid (NGG).

The remainder of this paper is organized as follows. In section 2, we introduce basic concepts and architecture of NGG. Some key technologies of NGG are discussed in section 3. Finally, we make a conclusion of our current research work.

M. Li et al. (Eds.): GCC 2003, LNCS 3032, pp. 196–199, 2004.

2 NGG Architecture

Based on grid technologies, OGSA and Web services [1, 3, 4], NGG is a geological information service architecture that can implement sharing, integration and cooperation of distributed and heterogeneous geological resources. NGG is a service-oriented system [1, 3] and the definition of NGG service is given as follow:

Definition 1 : NGG service is a collection of geological operations, accessible through an interface, which allows a user to evoke a behavior of value to the user.

To describe system structure of NGG, we build an open architecture of NGG with seven layers from application, integration, data sharing, to resource organizing and acquiring, which is called NGGOA (NGG Open Architecture), as Figure 1 shows.

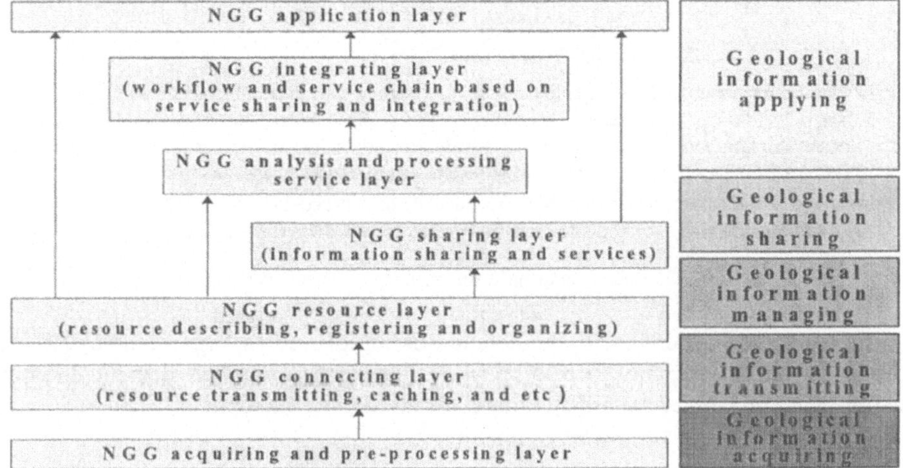

Fig. 1. Open architecture of NGG

3 Key Technologies of NGG

3.1 Service Chain Model

Service chain model can combine NGG services freely, and implement integration of NGG services to form NGG workflow. Basic Petri net is a good method to model workflow, but it can't model dynamic and conditional workflow. Then, we introduce some new elements based on graph theory to extend basic Petri net [5-7]. This extended Petri-net-based model is called Service/Resource Net(S/R-net).

Definition2: S/R-net is an extended Petri net, i.e. $\text{S/R-net} = (P,T,F,K,W,M_0)$, where

- P is a finite set of places, $P = \{P_R, P_S\}, |P| = n$, $P_R = \{P_{R1}, P_{R2}, \cdots, P_{Rn}\}$ is a set of NGG resources(data, information, and etc), $P_S = \{P_{S1}, P_{S2}, \cdots, P_{Sn}\}$ is a set of NGG services,
- T is a finite set of transitions representing the activities, $T = \{t_1, t_2, \cdots, t_m\}, m = |T|$,

- F is a set of flow relation, $F \subseteq P \times T \cup T \times P$, $P \cap T = \varnothing, P \cup T \neq \varnothing$; $dom(F) \cup cod(F) = P \cup T$, $dom(F) = \{x \mid y : (x, y) \in F\}$, $cod(F) = \{x \mid y : (y, x) \in F\}$
- K is a places capacity function, generally $K = \infty$,
- W is a weight function on F, $W(x, y) \in \{0,1,2,\cdots\}$, $(x, y) \notin F \Rightarrow W(x, y) = 0$,
- M is a marking function , $M : P \rightarrow Z, i.e., M(p)$, M_0 is the initial marking.

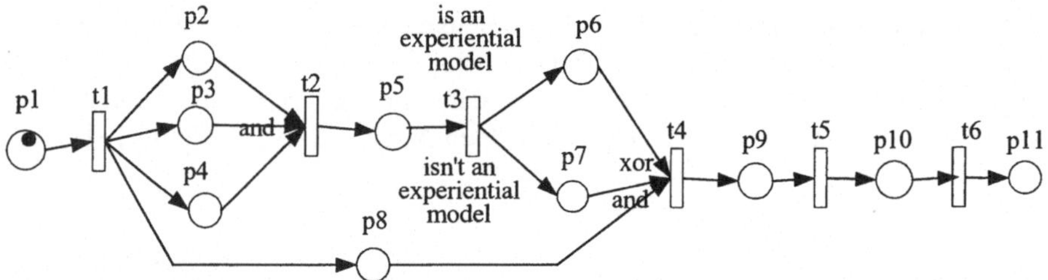

p1:request information; p2:basic geological data; p3:geophysical data; p4:geochemistry data; p5:mineral resources information extracting service; p6:experiential model analysis service; p7:non-experiential model analysis service; p8:additional data; p9:mineral area classifying service ; p10:result validating service; p11:processing result of mineral resourcesevaluating.
t1:matching data; t2:get and process data; t3:calculate the extracted injformation; t4:classify mineral area; t5:validate classified result; t6:return the result to user.

Fig. 2. S/R-net example for mineral resource evaluating

Limited by the paper length, the detailed definitions, rules, algorithms of S/R-net, such as transition structures, transition firing rules [5-7], extended elements, and etc, are presented in another paper [8]. Figure 2 is an S/R-net example.

3.2 Geological Semantic Sharing of NGG

NGG is a system of geological information services. From the view of semantic, NGG is a symbol system composed of data symbols and grammar rules. The different resources and services in NGG are classified into many different sets. To share and integrate these different sets, geological semantic sharing should be studied firstly.

As an effective model to represent concept semanteme, ontology is applied widely. Ontology is a philosophical concept originally, and becomes a framework system to describe the external concepts and their relations in knowledge sharing now [9].

In accordance with demands of semantic sharing of NGG, we introduce ontology to share NGG semanteme, define formalized concepts and knowledge models for geological survey, and describe the semanteme of geological concepts through the relations of concepts. Based on research work of other scholars [9, 10], we propose the definition of ontology of NGG (NGGonto) as below:

Definition3: NGGonto is an explicit specification of a geological conceptualization.

There are two basic factors included in NGGonto: geological concepts and their relations. And NGGonto has four basic relations between its concepts: part-of, kind-of, instance-of, and attribute-of.

4 Conclusion

NGG is a novel grid-based and service-oriented geological information infrastructure, which provides a feasible and effective way to discover, schedule, access, manage, share and integrate distributed geological resources. To date, we analyze the geological survey application requirements and study some key technologies of NGG, propose a novel seven-level open architecture, design NGG managing platform and resource information services, and present an NGGonto-based approach for geological semantic sharing. Besides these work, a new service chain model (Service/Resource Net) based on Petri net is presented to model and analyze the workflow of NGG.

The research of NGG is at the initial stage. More technologies will be introduced and studied in the future. In accordance with application demands, we will put research emphasis on NGG architecture, Service/Resource Net, NGGonto, and etc. We hope that our work will promote the development of information technology in national geological survey, environmental science and geoscience.

Acknowledgements. This work is supported in part by the National High Technology Research and Development 863 Program of China (Grant No.2002AA104220 and No.2002AA134010).

References

1. I.Foster, C.Kesselman et al. The Physiology of the Grid: An Open Grid Services Architecture for Distributed Systems Integration. June, 2002. See http://www.gridforum.org/ogsi-wg/drafts/ogsa_draft2.9_2002-06-22.pdf.
2. K.Czajkowski, S.Fitzgerald, I.Foster, and C.Kesselman. Grid Information Services for Distributed Resource Sharing. Proceedings of the Tenth IEEE International Symposium on High-Performance Distributed Computing (HPDC-10), San Francisco, IEEE Press, 2001.
3. S.Tuecke, K.Czajkowski et al. Grid Service Specification. Open Grid Service Infrastructure WG ,Global Grid Forum, Draft 2, July 2002. See http://www.globus.org.
4. World Wide Web Consortium. Web Services Architecture, Draft 14, 2002. See http://www.w3.org/TR/ws-arch/.
5. T.Murata. Petri nets: Properties, analysis and applications. Proceedings of the IEEE, 77(4), pages 541-579,1989.
6. C.Y.Yuan. Petri Net Theory(in Chinese). Publishing House of Electronics Industry, Beijing, China, 1998.
7. Y.Q.Dai, G.Z.Hu, and W.Chen. Graph Theory and Algebra Structure (in Chinese). Tsinghua University Press, Beijing, China, 1999.
8. Yu Tang et al. Grid Service Semigroup and Its Workflow Model. Proc. 2nd Int. Workshop on Grid and Cooperative Computing (GCC2003). Lecture Notes in Computer Science. Springer Verlag, 2003. To appear.
9. T.R.Gruber. A Translation Approach to Portable Ontology Specifications. Knowledge Acquisition, 5:199-220, 1993.
10. W.N.Borst. Construction of Engineering Ontologies for Knowledge Sharing and Reuse. PhD thesis, University of Twente, Enschede, 1997.

Integration of the Distributed Simulation into the OGSA Model

Chuanfu Zhang, Yunsheng Liu, Tong Zhang, and Yabing Zha

College of Mechaeronics Engineering and Automation, National University of Defense Technology, Changsha 410073
zhangchuanfu@yahoo.com.cn

Abstract. The grid technology and distributed simulation functionality were firstly introduced. We proposed two approaches to integrate actual distributed simulation application into grid environment. The first one is to take advantage of grid technology to support distributed simulation, which is independent of the development of distributed simulation. The second one consists of using specific extensions of distributed simulation based on grid technology. We mainly focused on the latter and argued about integrating HLA technology into OGSA model in detail. Under the above discussion, we defined G-RTI concept, which means the Runtime Infrastructure (RTI) based on grid technology.

1 Introduction

This paper is inspired and based on the schedule of the development of Globus Toolkit 3.0 (GT3) and OGSA technology. As distributed simulation that we discuss is based on the Globus software, it is necessary to study its evolution and distributed simulation technology. Moreover, the goals of OGSA to become a standard basis for building grid systems suggest the need of integration of distributed simulation into OGSA model. In this paper, we analyze such a possibility and its implications.

2 Grid Technology and Its Current Status

The Grid is the Future Computing Infrastructure that will provide the electronic underpinning for global society in business, government, research and just plain fun. The Grid builds on networking, communications and information technology. It integrates resources (computers, networks, data archives, instruments) together and with individuals and communities. Grids are intrinsically distributed and heterogeneous but supported in such way that the user see a relatively seamless environment.

The Globus Toolkit, developed for past few years in scientific community, addresses issues of security, information discovery, resource management, data management, communication, fault detection, and portability in grid environment. OGSA, the primary grid infrastructure, takes advantage of these researches. The toolkit com-

M. Li et al. (Eds.): GCC 2003, LNCS 3032, pp. 200–204, 2004.

ponents adopted are the Grid Resource Allocation and Management (GRAM) protocol and its "gatekeeper" service, the Meta Directory Service (MDS-2) and the Grid Security Infrastructure (GSI), and so on.

3 Overview of Distributed Simulation

Distributed Simulation defines an infrastructure for linking simulations of various types at geographically distributed locations by LAN or WAN to create realistic, complex, virtual worlds for the simulation of highly interactive activities. Distributed simulation in which application has a series of kernel protocols is Distributed Interactive Simulation (DIS). Today it has been developed into High Level Architecture (HLA).

The High Level Architecture (HLA) is an integrated architecture that has been developed to provide a common architecture for M&S. The purpose of the HLA is to facilitate interoperability among simulations and promote reuse of simulations and their components. In support of these general goals, the HLA requires the federations and individual federates can be described by an object model which identifies the data exchanged at runtime for fulfilling there tasks. The HLA Object Model Template (OMT) provides a template for documenting HLA-relevant information about classes of simulation or federation objects and their attributes and interactions.

According to the specification, the Runtime infrastructure (RTI) of HLA provides a series of services. They include: (1) Federation management, (2) Declaration management, (3) Object management, (4) Ownership management, (5) Time management, (6) Data distribution management (DDM) and so on.

4 Integration of Distributed Simulation into OGSA Model

Now the popular distributed simulation system is usually based on High Level Architecture (HLA), it provides application developers with a powerful framework, however its design was not intended to support software application that need to integrate instruments, displays, computational and information resource managed by diverse organizations. The grid was designed to address precisely those issues. So Grid Services have the potential to bring remote and decentralized Federate service discovery and invocation to HLA.

There are two ways on which distributed simulation can be integrated into grid. First one is to utilize the grid technology to support distributed simulation application. This method is independent of development of distributed simulation. By this means, current distributed simulation systems are supported in grid environment. Middleware components are provided to support to migrate current distributed simulation to grid environment. Moreover, in the process of migration current distributed simulation system have no change. The advantage of this way can maintain transplantation and compatibility. But it has many difficulties to do so. The second one may consist of using specific extensions of distributed simulation so as to be integrated into grid. In this way, we take full advantage of grid technology to modify the current distributed simulation specification and the distributed simulation architecture. As a result, actual distributed simulation system must be modified in accordance with the new simulation standard and rules of grid environment. Distributed simulation system in grid environment has become the application of grid. In this paper, we mainly discuss the second method.

Because OGSA actually has become the criterion for building grid systems, distributed simulation of grid environment will be the integration of High Level Architecture (HLA) into OGSA model. The application of HLA has three components that are RTI, OMT and application (federation and federate member), during integration various levels of granularity were considered.

4.1 Migration of RTI into OGSA

During distributed simulation, RTI provides the run-time framework and all simulation interaction of HLA application. Consequently, distributed simulation based on grid require migrate RTI to OGSA model.

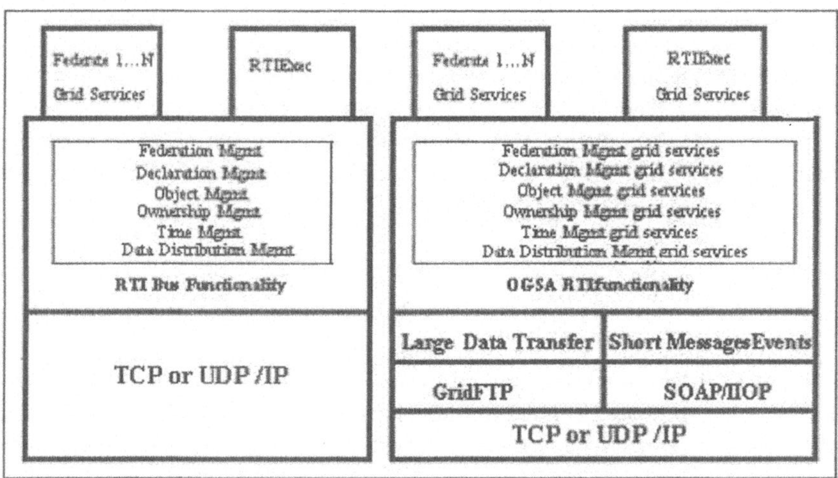

Fig. 1. Comparison of the original and the Grid-enhanced architecture

In grid, all resources are connected by highly speed network. Besides RTI, the grid application based on OGSA model can also be used to handle the network communication, data distribution management, time management and so on. Because of the difference between RTI of traditional HLA application and RTI based on OGSA model, we name the latter as Grid RTI (G-RTI), which is a core service of OGSA and the traditional RTI functionalities were encapsulated into it.

When we construct distributed simulation in grid environment, G-RTI Grid Services will be a core services to be configured with other Grid Core Services. Corresponding to RTI in traditional HLA, G-RTI Grid Services consist of six basis services.

When distributed simulation application is executed, G-RTI Grid Services will call all six cooperated basis services to achieve the functionality of RTI. The comparison between original and Grid-enhanced architecture is shown in Fig.1 which illustrates the advantages of OGSA such as support for dynamic discovery and separation of the actual protocols from the abstract RTI functionality description.

4.2 Using XML Format to Describe OMT

The HLA OMT provides a template for documenting HLA-relevant information about classes of simulation or federation objects and their attributes and interactions. This common template facilitates understanding and comparisons of different simulations and federations, and provides the format for a contract between members of a federation on the types of objects and interactions that will be supported across its multiple interoperating simulations.

In distributed simulation application based on OGSA model, we have to make a modification to the HLA OMT. In order to integrate distributed simulation into OGSA model we make use of uniform XML format to describe HLA OMT. By this means HLA OMT based XML format can provide information of grid services. The usage of XML format supports the uniform interface of grid service and provides readable and common standard mechanism of data exchanging among federate member. Therefore, the usage of XML format uniformly to describe HLA Federation Object Model (FOM) and Simulation Object Model (SOM) achieves the uniform data exchange and facilitate the interoperation of grid simulation federate. Different from RTI of traditional HLA, simulation data in G-RTI is transmitted by Service Data Element (SDE).

4.3 Distributed Simulation Application Model Based on Grid

The simulation federations based on G-RTI are implemented in different way from traditional HLA federation. In grid environment simulation front-end server submit the simulation mission to appropriate grid node by GASS, RFT and GridFTP grid services. The front-end server is responsible to monitor, collect simulation data and analyze result of simulation. On the process of simulation, front-end server submit simulation mission to each executable node. When a certain grid node fails or overload, front-end server will distribute mission again to balance the workload on each grid node.

At the beginning of this process the GASS server of the front-end server invokes the GASS server of other simulation node. When the GASS server of all executable grid nodes is successfully invoked, simulation front-end server submits simulation mission and necessary library. The process of application execution is illustrated by Fig.2.

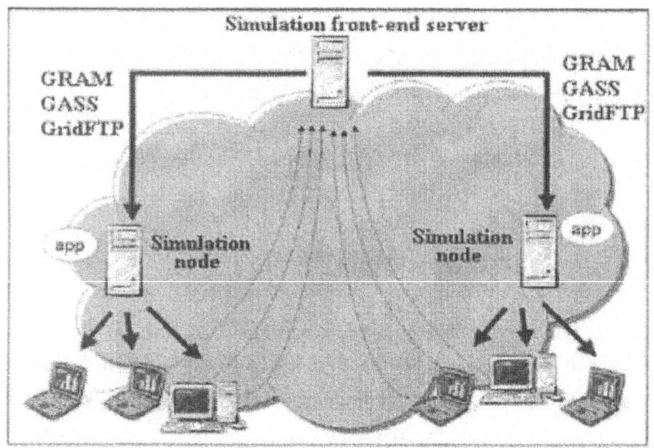

Fig. 2. Grid simulation application model

5 Conclusion

In this paper we particularly described how to integrate HLA into OGSA model to support distributed simulation application with great efficiency. After analyzing services that are developed in distributed simulation, we can conclude that they get along well with the OGSA model. Moreover, taking the advantage of GT3, many services in distributed simulation that are going to be OGSI-compliant can be provided and bond to be used.

References

1. Katarzyna Zaajac, Alfredo Tirado-Ramos, Zhiming Zhao, Peter Sloot, Marian Bubak: Grid Services for HLA-based Distributed Simulation Frameworks
2. HLA Specification http://www.dmso.mil/public/transition/hla/
3. Luis Ferreira, Bart Jacob, Sean Slevin, Michael Brown, Srikrishnan Sundararajan, Jean Lepesant, Judi Bank: Globus Toolkit 3 Early Experiences: www.ibm.com/redbooks/
4. I. Foster, C. Kesselman, J. Nick, S. Tuecke. The Physiology of the Grid: An Open Grid Services Architecture for Distributed Systems Integration [R]. Globus Project, http://www.Globus.org/research/papers/ogsa.pdf, June 2002.
5. Thomas Sandholm, Jarek Gawor. Globus Toolkit 3 Core – A Grid Service Container Framework. http://www-unix.globus.org/toolkit/3.0/ogsa/docs/gt3_core.pdf, July 2003.

An Extendable Grid Simulation Environment Based on GridSim

Efeng Lu, Zhihong Xu, and Jizhou Sun

IBM New Technology Center, Tianjin University, Tianjin 300072, P.R.China
lef23@163.com

Abstract. Simulation plays an important role in grid research. However, there is no general simulation environment for scheduling algorithms testing. In this paper we establish an extendable grid simulation environment based on GridSim by choosing and extending the appropriate modules of an open-source grid simulation environment—gridbroker. In our simulation environment, users can easily add various different scheduling policies into the task scheduler and don't need to encode for other parts of the environment repeatedly. The environment's scalability was verified by extending its task scheduler using a scheduling policy based on the ant algorithm in the last part of this paper.

Keywords: grid, GridSim, gridbroker, ant algorithm, simulation

1 Introduction

Grid enables the sharing , selection and aggregation of a wide variety of geographically distributed resources. It aims to provide users with a virtual supercomputer with high reliability and performance. Users can get access to the virtual supercomputer transparently just like using the electricity power grid[ZH1].

The resource management and scheduling of applications in grid is a complex undertaking. In order to prove the effectiveness of resource brokers and associated scheduling algorithms, their performance needs to be evaluated under different scenarios. But in an actual grid environment, it's hard and even impossible to perform scheduler performance evaluation in a repeatable and controllable manner as resources and users are distributed across multiple organizations with their own policies.

So, we have to rely on simulation. However, most grid simulation environments are algorithm-specific and not extendable. So in this paper we establish a general grid simulation environment. Users can easily add various different scheduling policies into the task scheduler and need not encode for other parts of the environment repeatedly.

2 Related Work

Our extendable grid environment is based on GridSim[RB2] and gridbroker.

GridSim: It's a grid modeling and simulation toolkit. The GridSim toolkit provides a comprehensive facility for simulation of different classes of heterogeneous resources, users, applications, resource brokers, and schedulers. It supports

M. Li et al. (Eds.): GCC 2003, LNCS 3032, pp. 205–208, 2004.

primitives for application composition, information services for resource discovery, and interfaces for assigning application tasks to resources and managing their execution.

gridbroker: It's a Nimrod-G like deadline and budget[RB1][RB3] constrained scheduling system based on GridSim. This simulated grid environment contains multiple resources and user entities with different requirements. It includes two main entities that simulate users and the brokers by extending the GridSim class. This simulated grid environment focuses on only one scheduling policy based on the economy model[RB1][RB3] and isn't extendable.

3 Implementation of the Environment Based on Gridbroker

To be extendable, we design a general structure for our grid simulation environment,as shown in Figure. 1.

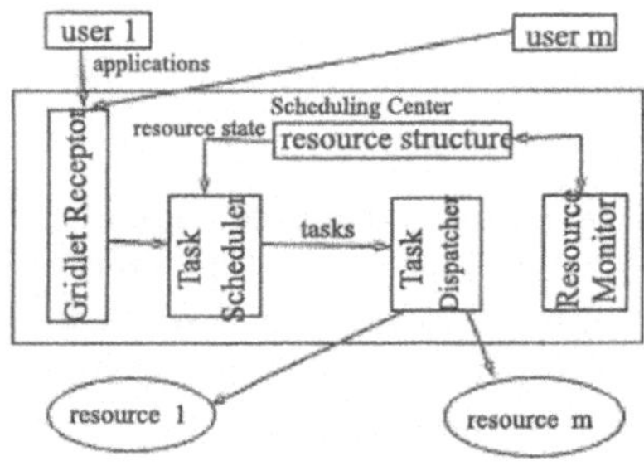

Fig. 1. The extendable structure of our grid simulation environment

In this structure, the environment consists of three main parts: the User, Scheduling Center and the Resource. And the Scheduling Center is composed of five sub-modules. Users submit application requirements to the Task Receptor, which then sends proper tasks to the Task Dispatcher based on an appropriate scheduling algorithm for mapping tasks to resources. The Task Dispatcher then dispatches the tasks to specific resources according to the selected algorithm. The Task Dispatcher also records the dispatched tasks' names,requirements and the corresponding resources. It submits the tasks to the selected resources and sends transmission delay and state to the Resource Monitor. When a task is finished, Task Dispatcher gives the result back to the User; Otherwise, when a task fails to run on a resource, the Task Dispatcher will send it back to the Task Scheduler for rescheduling.

We develop this environment by choosing and extending the appropriate modules of an open-source grid simulation environment —gridbroker, which applies only one scheduling policy based on economy model algorithm to the task scheduler and isn't extendable.

Firstly, we pick out the three main modules from gridbroker for our environment: Class UserEntity: This class simulates the User, we can use it in our environment directly. Class Broker: This class is corresponding to the Scheduling Center of our environment. As to the Resource, we directly uses the GridResource which is a basic class of GridSim.

Secondly, we develope the five sub-modules of the Scheduling Center:Task Receptor: For this module, we use a function —- ExprimentReceive() to receive tasks and requirements set of a user; Task Scheduler: In our simulated environment we have optimized gridboker's function —- ScheduleAdviser() and make it extendable to be added in more scheduling policies; Task Dispatcher: This module is used to dispatch tasks to resources actually. We use gridbroker's function —- Dispatcher() directly. As for Resource Structure and Resource Monitor, we have used the GIS entity of the GridSim.

Lastly, we implement another module to provide users with a window, which lists out all the policies that the environment supports. Users can select any one of them to tell the Scheduling Center which policy they want their tasks to be scheduled.Thus, the extendable grid simulation environment has been developed.

4 Extending the Task Scheduler

To verify that our environment is extendable, we add another scheduling policy based on ant algorithm[MD1] into the Task Scheduler.

According to the ant algorithm and task scheduling principle, we design an algorithm used for task scheduling in grid. When a new resource joins the grid, the Resource Monitor will initialize its pheromone based on formula (1).

$$\tau_j(0) = m \cdot p + \frac{c}{s_j} \tag{1}$$

In fomula (1) m is the number of CPU of resource j; p represents the MIPS of every CPU; c denotes the size of information package; And s_j represents the transmission time.

When new resources enter into the gird or some resources leave the gird, or a task runs successfully or not on it, a resource's pheromone will change depending on formula (2),

$$\tau_j^{new} = \rho \cdot \tau_j^{old} + \Delta\tau_j \tag{2}$$

In fomula (2) $\Delta\tau_j$ is the pheromone variance; ρ represents the permanence of the pheronmone (Here, it is supposed to be 0.8), and $1-\rho$ denotes the evaporation of the pheromone;When a new task was submitted to resource j, $\Delta\tau_j = -k$, Here K represents the workload for computing and transmitting the task.If a task runs successfully on resource j, $\Delta\tau_j = c_e \cdot k$, Here c_e is the encouragement argument (Here, it is supposed to be 0.8);Else if a task fails to run on it,$\Delta\tau_j = c_p \cdot k$, Here c_p represents the punishment argument (Here, it is supposed to be 1.1).

When a resource's pheromone changes, the probability for tasks to be dispatched onto it will change along according to formula (3):

$$p_j^k(t) = \begin{cases} \frac{[\tau_j(t)]^\alpha \cdot [\eta_j]^\beta}{\sum_{u=1}^{n} [\tau_u(t)]^\alpha \cdot [\eta_u]^\beta} & j, u \in \text{online resources} \\ 0 & \text{others} \end{cases} \quad (3)$$

$\tau_j(t)$ denotes the current pheromone of resource j and $\tau_u(t)$ is that of resource u. η_j represents the initial pheromone of resource j and η_u is that of resource u. α represents the importance of the current pheromone and β represents that of the initial pheromone. They are both supposed to be 0.5.

Based on these formulas and scheduling theory, we add another task scheduler implemented by function AntScheduleAdviser() into the Scheduling Center. Thus our simulated grid environment has been extended and can schedule tasks depending on two policies. By means of selecting one specific policy in the selection window, users can decide how their tasks will be scheduled.

5 Conclusion and Future Work

Our simulation environment is useful for testing and simulating different scheduling algorithms easily because of its scalability. The task scheduler of this environment can be easily added into various scheduling policies and thus we can make comparison among them so as to find the ones with higher efficiency for use in an actual grid.

For the future work, we will encapsulate more independent modules for resource management instead of using GIS of the GridSim directly. The QoS will also be taken into consideration in our environment later.

References

[ZH1] DuZhifei, ChenYu and LiuPeng : Grid Computing. TsingHua University (2002)

[RB1] Rajkumar Buyya : Economic-based Distributed Resource Management and Scheduling for Grid Computing. A thesis for the Degree of Doctor of Philosophy. Monash University, Melbourne, Australia, April (2002)

[RB2] R.Buyya and M.Murshed : GriSim: A Toolkit for the Modeling and Simulation of Distributed Resource Management and Scheduling for Grid Computing. The Journal of Concurrency and Computation: Practice and Experience(CCPE), Wiley Press, May (2002).

[RB3] Rajkumar Buyya, David Abramson, and Jonathan Giddy : Grid Resource Management, Scheduling, and Computational Economy. WGCC (2000).

[MD1] Marco Dorigo, Vittorio Maniezzo and Alberto Colorni : Ant System: Optimization by a Colony of Cooperating of Agents. IEEE TRANSACTIONS ON SYSTEMS, MAN, AND CYBERNETICS-PART B:CYBERNETICS, VOL.26, NO.1, REBRUARY (1996)

The Architecture of Traffic Information Grid[1]

Zhaohui Zhang [1,2], Qing Zhi [1], Guosun Zeng [1], and Changjun Jiang [1]

[1] Department of Computer Science and Engineering, Tongji University, Shanghai, China
Tongji Branch, National Engineering & Technology Center of High Performance Computer, Shanghai, China
[2] Department of Computer Science, AnHui Normal University, WuHu, China
ok51ok@hotmail.com

Abstract. Traffic information grid(TIG) is a grid application which uses grid technology to resolve traffic problems. TIG can utilize grid resources efficiently to resolve the city traffic problems such as uniform access to distributed heterogeneous traffic information databases, the computing of the dynamic shortest path, the showing of the dynamic traffic information. In this paper we present a scheme of TIG framework based on OGSA and implement the prototype system of TIG. The scheme of TIG is feasible by the experiments of the prototype system.

1 Introduction

At present, many counties pay more attention at grid technology. Some grid research programs such as Globus, Legion, Data Farm, Euro Data Grid[3], which are supported greatly by industry, have been launched in USA, European, Japan, India. In China, some grid programs such as NHPCE, MOE, have been launched. TIG (Traffic Information Grid) will be developed in Shanghai.

Some ITSs (Intelligent Transportation Systems)[2] have taken effect in Shanghai. In present ITSs, however, there are many drawbacks such as some bottlenecks of data storage, computing capacity and sharing traffic information.

Traffic Information Grid, which is based on grid technology, will be an effective approach to resolve traffic problems. According to present documents, it is the first attempt to build a new ITS with grid technology in China. In order to research and demonstrate TIG, we have developed a prototype system of TIG. In the system, we have primarily realized TIG's distribution, heterogeneity and cooperation.

[1] This work is support partially by projects of National 863 Plan(2002AA4Z3430, 2002AA1Z2102A); Excellent Ph.D Paper Author Foundation of China (199934); Foundation for University Key Teacher by the Ministry of Education; Shanghai Science & Technology Research Plan(03DZ15029,03JC14071); Natural Science Research of Anhui Universities(2004KJ167).

M. Li et al. (Eds.): GCC 2003, LNCS 3032, pp. 209–212, 2004.

2 OGSA and TIG

OGSA(Open Grid Services Architecture) is a key standard propose of Globus Grid Forum 4. It is a service-centered "service architecture" which emphasizes services provided by resources of VO (Virtual Organization). These services include all kinds of computing resources, storage resources, networks, application routines, databases, and so on. [1] In a word, everything is a service in OGSA.

Traffic Information Grid(TIG) is a kind of information grid based on OGSA, which utilizes grid technology to integrate traffic information, share traffic data and traffic resources, provide better traffic services to traffic participators, remove traffic bottlenecks, and resolve traffic problems. TIG is an application of information grid.

3 The Framework of TIG

A better TIG should be built on OGSA. We present a framework of TIG as Fig. 1. shows. The TIG is composed of several grid nodes. They are Broker, GRIC(Grid Resource Information Center), GSRC(Grid Service Register Center) and some GASNs(Grid Application Service Nodes). GASNs include CCNs(Cluster Computing Nodes), VDBNs(Virtual Database Nodes), DCNs(Data collection Nodes) and other grid nodes.

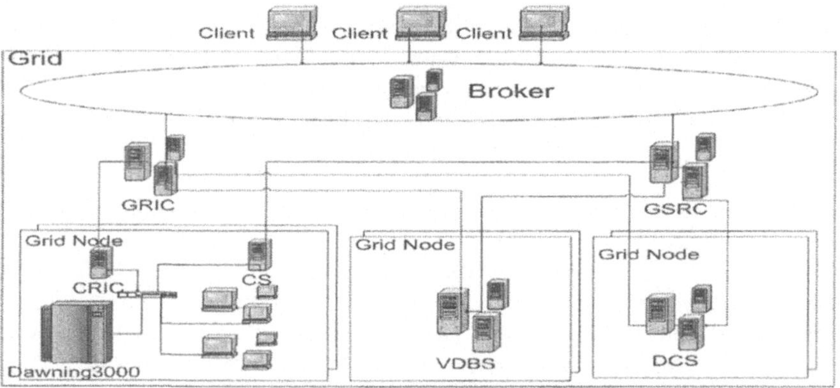

Fig. 1. Framework of traffic information grid

One of the broker's tasks is to check whether grid users are valid or not. It will receive users' service requirements if they are valid. Then the broker looks up the services in GSRC and resource information in GRIC to get the service provider. So the broker can distribute the job to corresponding grid node. When the grid node completes the task, the broker will return the result to the client.

GSRC(Grid Service Register Center) is an important grid node in grid environment that connects every node in grid environment in logic. GSRC provides *register, update, query, logout* services to other grid services.

There is a registry table in GSRC. It contains *Service Name* and *URI*. Service Name is the names of service provided by grid nodes, and URI(Uniform Resource Identifiers) is corresponding position of grid service.

GRIC(Grid Resource Information Center) is another important grid node. It provides *add*、*update*、*delete* information services to other grid services , and provides *query* service to broker.

GRIC maintains a resource information table, which contains all kinds of resource information of every grid node such as *IP, CPUs, Memory Size, Network Information, Disk Size*. Every grid node registers their resource information in the table when it joins in grid.

GASNs(Grid Application Service Nodes) provide grid application-oriented services for the users of TIG. They consist of CCNs(Cluster Computing Nodes), VDBNs(Virtual Database Nodes), DCNs(Data collection Nodes).

A CCN is not only a cluster that is composed of CS(Cluster Server), CRIC(Cluster Resource Information Center), a supercomputer (Drawing 3000) and some PCs, but also a grid node that provides cluster computing services. CS has two functions. One is deploying computing services to grid environment. The other is launching MPI routines in Linux cluster environment. CRIC registers cluster resource information and provides the information to GRIC. The other computers in cluster are used to run MPI application routines such as computing optimal dynamic path, demonstrate traffic road states, querying road or crossing information, forecasting traffic flow and so on.

Some data collection servers and devices constitute a DCN. Data collection devices collect oceans of real time traffic information that consists longitude, latitude, speed, orientation and times, and that should be stored in distributed heterogeneous databases in those servers. In the servers of this node, real database access services, which are data *query, delete, insert, update* and others, are deployed for VDBN.

A VDBN is a grid node that contains VDBSs(Virtual Database Servers). Virtual database services are deployed in these servers. They support uniform access to heterogeneous distributed database. In fact, they provide a kind of standard SQL interface with which other grid service accesses those real database. So services in VDBS should analyze and decompose SQL commands and execute them distributedly.

4 A Prototype System of TIG

According to the precious framework of TIG, we have designed a prototype system. The system includes six service modules from the point of view of grid node as Fig. 2. shows.

We describe the workflow of the prototype system by an example. Supposed that a user wants to query the least time path from Tongji University to Jiaotong University. The client uses XML to describe the services which it requires. The XML file includes grid service information and parameters. Grid service information is described by WSDL. The client sends the XML file to the broker. The broker parses the XML file, and queries GSRC to get the URI of the service. Maybe there are several grid nodes providing the same grid service. So the broker may get several URIs. Then broker queries GRIC to get the resource information of the gird nodes by the IPs. The broker selects an idle grid node from the nodes which provide LeastTimePath service. The broker converts the URI into a GSR(Grid Service Reference) which is a reference of Least Time service instance, and call the remote routine to get the shortest path.

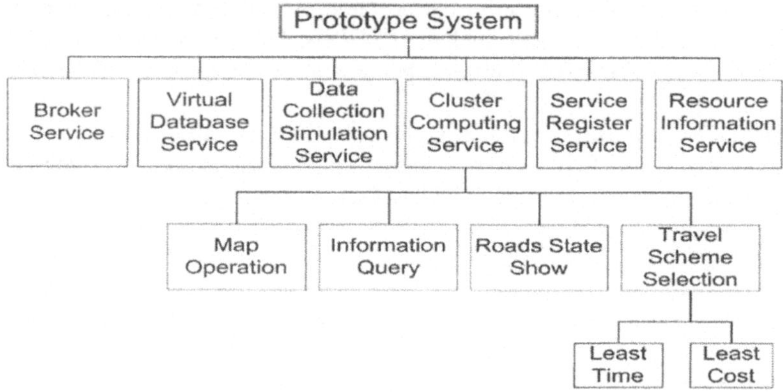

Fig. 2. Modules of the prototype system

5 Conclusions

In this paper we have proposed a scheme of TIG framework and implemented the prototype system of TIG.. The executing result of our prototype system shows that the scheme of TIG based on OGSA is feasible and that TIG can utilize grid resources efficiently to resolve the city traffic problems such as uniform access to distributed heterogeneous traffic information databases, the computing of the dynamic shortest path, the showing of the dynamic traffic information. At the same time, we can research grid technology further with research on the application of TIG .

References

1. Foster, I., Kesselman, C., Tuecke,S.: The Anatomy of the Grid: Enabling Scalable Virtual Organizations. International J. Supercomputer Applications, vol.15, 3(2001)200-222
2. Yang,Z.S.: The Theory and Model of Inducement System of City Traffic Flow. People Traffic Press, Beijing(1999)
3. Segal,B.: Grid Computing: The European Data Grid Project. In: IEEE Nuclear Science Symposium and Medical Imaging Conference, Lyon, France, October 2000

Construction Scheme of Meteorological Application Grid (MAG)

Xuesheng Yang [1], Weiming Zhang [2], and Dehui Chen[1]

[1] Zhong Guan Cun South Street 46, RCNMP, Chinese Academy of Meteorological Sciences,
Beijing 100081, P. R. China
{yangxs,chendh}@cma.gov.cn
[2] Computer Department of National University of Defense Technology
Changsha 410073, P. R. China
wmzhang104@163.net

Abstract. With respect to the existed issues in the current operational numerical NWP system and research environment, a Meteorological Application Grid (MAG) was proposed based on Grid Computing. MAG mainly includes Resource Access Portal (RAP), Product Announcement Portal (PAP) and Research Collaborative Portal (RCP). RAP provides an approach to access geographically distributed resources. PAP disseminates service to the public and professional clients. While RCP offers a universal platform for scientists to develop NWP software, to share source codes, to register modules within the grid and to perform NWP experiments. Its implementation will upgrade the current operational NWP system effectively, realize the goal of the sharing of the computer powers, meteorological data and establish a remote collaborative environment.

1 Introduction

Generally speaking, operational numerical weather prediction system is strongly dependant on computer power. Although China Meteorological Administration (CMA) installed some computers during the past few years, such as IBM SP, COMPAQ, Origin,YH -III, SW-1, DAWN etc., the current computing capability and communication resource could not satisfy the increasing service demand and the new developing NWP system especially the climate model system.

Fortunately, with the advent of the grid computing, substantial benefits can be achieved by implementing grids into the existed operational NWP system and research environment, for example, it can aggregate the geographically distributed computing resources and give end users remote access to the computing, data and storage resources they need, can establish a Virtual Research Center and a uniform platform to make good use of expertise to develop the new NWP system, can accelerate the procedure from research to operation and can help solve problems that were previously unsolvable. And some progress of grid application in meteorology has been made during the past years, especially the ECACCESS[1] system of European Center for

M. Li et al. (Eds.): GCC 2003, LNCS 3032, pp. 213–216, 2004.

Medium-range Weather Forecast, as well as NASA also planned to develop a modeling environment for atmospheric discovery [2].

In this paper, a construction scheme of Meteorological Application Grid (MAG) was proposed based on the grid computing.

2 Construction Scheme of the MAG

Grid portal is the administrative interface of MAG, where clients can get the appointed service, while grid administrators can get the status of the grid. Based on the operational consideration and research requirement, 3 portals will be constructed, which include Resource Access Portal (RAP), Product Announcement Portal (PAP) and Research Collaborative Portal (RCP).

In order to manage the resource and service in the grid, a grid administrative node will be installed which is used to manage the user, service and resource. User management includes account registration, priority and authentication. Service management includes registration of the service, authorization. Resource management consists of the registration of the computing node, meteorological data and node monitoring etc. All these application was completed by the Service Domain (SD) which is one of the IBM grid software. Generally speaking, client's service request was sent from portal to SD, and SD selects the corresponding application to satisfy user's request, such as offering the NWP products, downloading NWP source codes, uploading meteorological modules, constructing the experimental workflow.

2.1 Resource Access Portal

RAP provides an approach to access grid resources via Web browser for internal users, and reports the status of grid resource, it uses a single-sign-on to access all the grid resource distributed in Beijing, Shanghai, Guangzhou, etc. Functionally RAP includes:

- user management: application and cancellation of user account
- remote command: such as telnet, file and directory command, compilation and link command
- queue job management: submission, deletion and monitoring of the job, queue
- resource information report: configuration of resource, status of resource, queue, job, CPU, etc.
- grid bulletin: such as resource maintenance agenda, new resource introduction, etc.
- grid consulting: resource documentation and consulting.

2.2 Product Announcement Portal (PAP)

PAP disseminates its service to the public and professional users via Web browser. Clients can submit his service request via PAP, then PAP passes this request to SD, and SD returns the appropriate service according to user's priority in the format of image or data through web page, E-mail or Web service. PAP also provides the capability for remote data access, visual image browse.

2.3 Remote Collaborative Portal (RCP)

Researchers often want to aggregate not only data and computing power, but also human expertise. For example, a meteorologist who has performed a climate simulation might want colleagues around the world to visualize his results in the same way and at the same time so that the group can discuss the results in real time. RCP was designed to manage the development of NWP modules and experimental workflow. A web-oriented interface was designed to access RCP. With this interface, users can access all the resources within MAG, they can input initial data, select desired model parameters and modules to submit NWP jobs, and to browse and modify NWP modules. Workflow management and source code management are used to construct the remote collaborative environment based on the web-sphere technique. Figure 1 shows the flowchart of RCP.

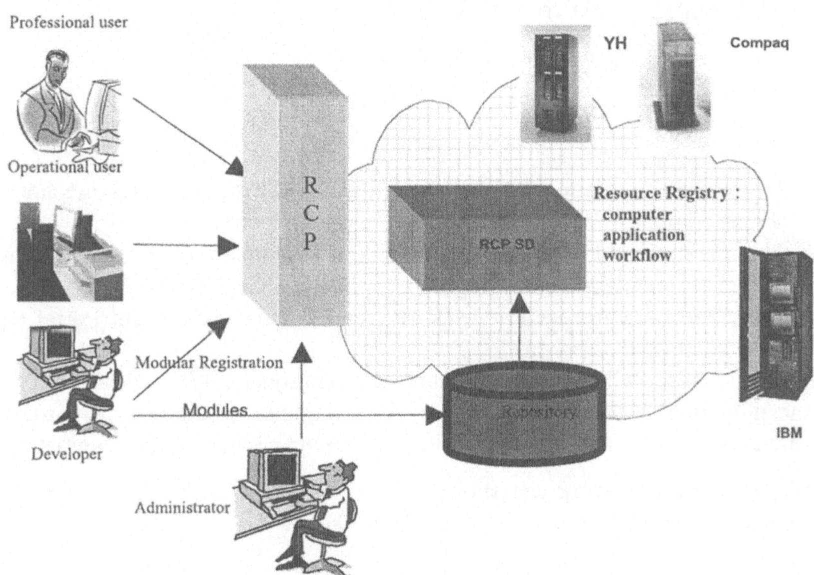

Fig. 1. Flowchart of RCP. 4 users involved. YH, Compaq, IBM SP computers connected.

Source codes were managed by CVS. For every NWP module, a corresponding web service and a query interface to describe its function should be defined. NWP workflow can be defined via web, every defined NWP flow can be considered a combination of web service, every request to the flow can be thought of a job, and through this combined web service to complete user's request. The source code manager realizes the function of CVS with WEB technology by three layers frames: portal、Web Service layer and CVS system. Users manage the source code in the manner of B/S. The web service is written in JSP. In order to response user's request, web service is performed interactively and simultaneously with command interpreter and CVS. RCP provides following functions:

· Modular register service: users can register new developed modules in the grid and module's attribute should be described.
· Module search: given search conditions, matched modules returned.
· Data search service: given search conditions, MAG returns the matched data information and its location.
· Workflow definition and edition: users can define its own workflow
· Job submission service: users can select modules and submit NWP job, jobID will be returned.
· Job status monitoring: users can check job status given job ID.
· Job notification: after job completed, grid will notify users by e-mail, etc.
· Resource registration and management: registration and management of the resource
· Source code sharing: users can upload, download, modify, maintain and search source codes.
· Visualization tools: to provide common used meteorological visualization tools, such as isoline, streamline, 2D, 3D graph making, etc.

3 Conclusions

In the current existed operational NWP system at CMA, the resources are not fully utilized, such as computing resource as well as the NWP product.

With the advent of grid computing technique, a new meteorological grid computing scheme which is called Meteorological Application Grid (MAG) was proposed. MAG includes Resource Access Portal (RAP), Product Announcement Portal (PAP) and Research Collaborative Portal (RCP).

Its implementation will upgrade the current operational NWP system effectively, realize the goal of the common sharing of the computer resources, meteorological information and establish the remote collaborative environment for the scientists.

Acknowledgement. This work was supported by National 863 Project of Department of Science and Technology under Grant 2002AA104210.

References

1. ECaccess: A portal to ECMWF, ECMWF Newsletter Number96, winter 2002/03, 28-36
2. MEAD:http://www.ucsa.uiuc.edu/expeditions/MEAD/
3. Ian Foster, et al., The Physiology of the Grid: an Open Grid Services Architecture for Distributed Systems Integration. http://www.globus.org/rearch/papers/ogsa.pdf.

OGSA Based E-learning System: An Approach to Build Next Generation of Online Education

Hui Wang [1], Xueli Yu [2], Li Wang, and Xu Liu

[1] TaiYuan University of Technology, Postcode 030024,
Shanxi, China
cherry9803@163.com
http://cs.tyut.edu.cn
[2] TaiYuan University of Technology, Postcode 030024,
Shanxi, China
xueli13287@263.net

Abstract. With the government reinforcing investment in basic network construction, with the improvement of people's livelihood and with the emergence of more and more new network technology, traditional online education system is seeing its weakness in more obvious ways. In this paper we have referred an improvement model of existing online education system: OGSA based e-Learning system, and also present the implement architecture of this e-learning system.

1 Introduction

With the government reinforcing investment in basic network construction, with the improvement of people's livelihood and with the emergence of more and more new network technology, traditional teaching and learning system is seeing its weakness in more obvious ways, take for example, failure in effective utilization of available teaching resources, excessively inflexible teaching and learning methods, great demand for accommodations in colleges and universities with their enrollment expansion, etc.. Therefore, a new way should come up to solve these problems, on the basis of which e-Learning system appears and develops. The e-Learning system makes fully use of wealthy resources and new communicating system provided by modern information technology. By means of teaching and learning through Internet, the system is in great difference with traditional CAI and ICAI in concept, system construction and fulfillment ways. However, there exist, in e-Learning system, such problems as how to achieve sharing and exchanging the ocean of network learning resources, how to store and manage the ocean of network learning resources, how to guarantee the security of online education, etc. In the background of the currently traditional network modes and technology, the above-mentioned problems are all hard to deal with. Consequently, it is imperative to find out a convenient and practicable, efficient and economical solution which promises to be well and easily applied in technology.

M. Li et al. (Eds.): GCC 2003, LNCS 3032, pp. 217–220, 2004.

2 The Share and Exchange of the Ocean of Network Learning Resources

On the basis of various programming languages and different fulfillment means, so far, the interaction among many CAIs can hardly realize. Thus the complement cannot be built among the available teaching and learning resources, and the waste of resources cannot be avoided. Web service provides a favorable solution. By taking advantage of the Web service, a standard of application program, the communication among existing systems can take no consider of operating system, component model and programming languages. In this case, the thin-client can interact with server freely with Http. Web service has three main technical fields: XML, SOAP, WSDL. XML (Extensible Markup Language) is the basic presentation of data, but more important, it is irrelevant with platform and easy to build. SOAP (Simple Object Access Protocol) provides a way to interact between a service request and a service provider. SOAP based on XML and it is independent of transport protocols such as HTTP, FTP, Java Messaging Service or something else. WSDL (Web Services Description Language) is an XML basic language; it can be used to describe the functions, parameters and returns of Web service. WSDL can be read by both computer and human because it is based on XML.

On the other hand, the feasibility of technology, Web services standards are being defined within the W3C and supported by most large cooperation. Microsoft (.NET) and Sun (Sun ONE) have embedded the mechanism of Web service in their IDEs. Therefore, most developers can decorate their systems easily to make the systems fulfill the standards of Web service. Therefore, the problem of sharing and exchanging the ocean of network learning resources can be solved ideally.

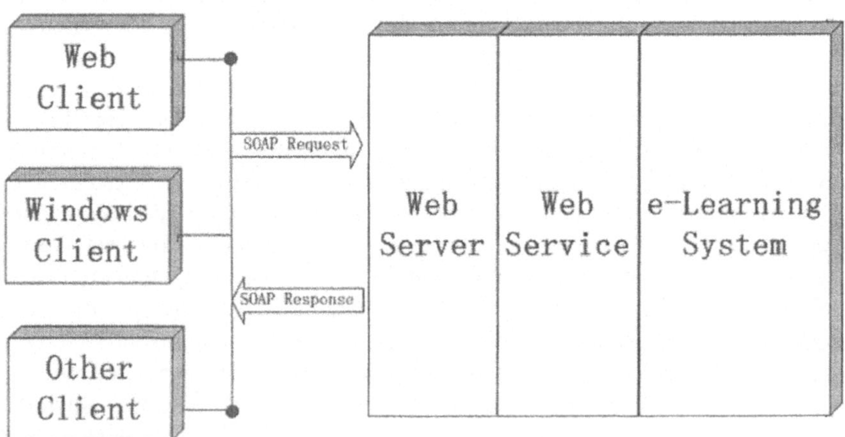

Fig. 1. Web service and e-Learning system architecture

3 The Storage of the Ocean of Network Learning Resources and Security

Web service still can not solve the problem of storing and managing the ocean of network learning resources, and it is a little bit weak in security of online education. The two problems are able to be solved in virtue of grid. With grid, the available resource need not move to a large server and what they should do is just supporting the grid service. Each computer or LAN is seemed as a VO (virtual organization), these VOs consist the grid. Therefore, the grid is coordinated resource sharing and problem solving in dynamic, multi-institutional virtual organizations. Solving the two problems with grid technology, we naturally reflect to use OGSA (Open Grid Services Architecture). In OGSA, computational resources, storage resources, networks, programs, databases, and the like are all represented as services. It is clearly that the existing storage resources, programs and databases need not change and the existing network even also can keep its original configuration because the entire existing things will be viewed as resources. The security problem is able to be resolved with OGSA by the means of GSI (Grid Security Infrastructure). GSI is based on public key architecture, and extends X.509 authentication and SSL (Secure Socket Layer) protocol; therefore the security can be promised in a high extent.

With the Globus toolkit, we can easily build our system on OGSA. It has been widely adopted as a Grid technology solution for scientific and technical computing. Web service has been included in OGSA; therefore, with Globus toolkit and other tools, we can build our system easily. At the same time; the three problems motioned above can also be resolved excellently. According that we can obtain Globus toolkit for free, and there are a lot of documents to direct us installing and configuring the environment of OGSA, so this OGSA based e-Learning system is feasible, economical and efficient.

4 An Instance of E-learning System

In the following part we will introduce a practical e-Learning system, which is based on OGSA. We are modifying and extending this traditional e-learning system in order to fill up the lack of support for flexibility and extensibility. The learning object repository has been set up and it consists of learning objects and their description data. The repository provides the index service and gets learning objects from outside with the help of LMS (Learning Management System) and OGSA.

When there are some new requests from outside the system will query the available service, if the need can not be met by existing system it will call for help from out plug-ins. Therefore the features and functions are extending dynamically and this part of operation is separated from the entire system. Clearly, the extendability and maintainability of system will be promised excellently. The available e-learning system has six modules: learning, course creating, homework, examination, and educational administration, tutoring subsystems.

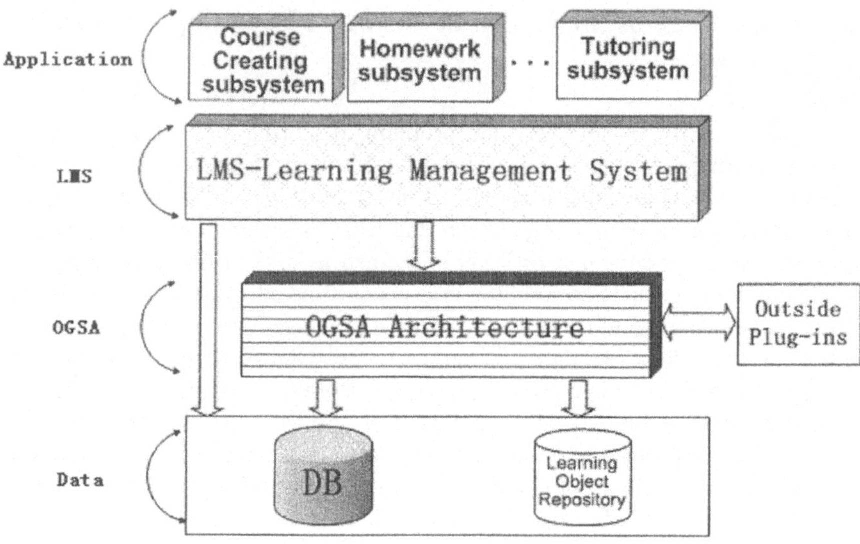

Fig. 2. OGSA Based e-Learning System Architecture

5 Conclusion

In this paper we have referred an improvement model of existing on line education system: OGSA based e-Learning system, and also present the implement architecture of e-learning system. Under this architecture, we can achieve sharing and exchanging the ocean of network learning resources, storing and managing the ocean of network learning resources, and can also guarantee the security of online education. The extendability and maintainability of system will be also promised excellently according to the change of customers.

References

1. Foster, I., Kesselman, C.: The Grid: Blueprint for a New Computing Infrastructure. Morgan Kaufmann. (1998) Chapter 3
2. Foster, I., Kesselman, C., Nick, J., Tuecke, S.: The Physiology of the Grid: An Open Grid Services Architecture for Distributed Systems Integration. http://www.globus.org/research/papers/ogsa.pdf .(2002)
3. Frank, L.: Web Services Flow Language. http://www-4.ibm.com/software/solutions/webservices/pdf/WSFL.pdf. (2003)
4. Foster, I., Cannon, D (ed.): The Open Grid Services Architecture Platform. http://www-unix.gridforum.org/mail_archive/ogsa-wg/doc00016.doc . (2003)

Multimedia Delivery Grid: A Novel Multimedia Delivery Scheme

ZhiHui Lv, Jian Yang, ShiYong Zhang, and YiPing Zhong

Department of Computer & Information Technology, Fudan University,
200433 Shanghai, China
{lzh,jianyang,szhang,ypzhong}@fudan.edu.cn

Abstract. Based on the analysis of some problems faced with traditional edge multimedia delivery technology such as CDN today, a novel grid-based multimedia delivery scheme, multimedia delivery grid, is introduced in this paper. We propose new hierarchy architecture and analyze the relationship of the elements in this architecture, and then discuss the dynamic delivery process. At last, from our research experiences and related survey, we illustrate the prospective research direction of this field.

1 Introduction

While consumption of multimedia information is steadily increasing, the usage of multimedia has not fully caught on because of the low quality of service (QoS), and the resulting poor user experience. As a developing trend, the arrival of broadband technology is solving the bandwidth limitation problem at the delivery edge of the network, but Internet backbones remain congested. To overcome this challenge of massive multimedia consuming, only installing more high-speed main pipes will not be enough; service providers need a more intelligent infrastructure layout to grow with this explosive market. Therefore, today's service providers are improving quality, bandwidth availability, profitability and service delivery levels allowing for more customers within the current infrastructure by using edge technologies, such as CDN, mirror sites, integrated caching to provide services. As a representative technique, Content Delivery Networks (CDN) is based on a large-scale distributed network of caching servers located closer to the edges of the Internet for efficient delivery of digital content including various forms of multimedia content. Moving content closer to the consumer results in greater network efficiency, improved QoS, and lower latency, while facilitating personalization of content through broadband content applications.

Although CDN is an effective means of multimedia information access and delivery, there are two main barriers to making CDN a more common service: cost and replication integrity. Deploying a CDN for publicly available content is expensive. The difficulty in maintaining replication integrity over a CDN is not because of inadequate corruption detection of single files, but the delay caused by the replication of very large files [1].

M. Li et al. (Eds.): GCC 2003, LNCS 3032, pp. 221–224, 2004.

Furthermore, in order to more effectively address the requirements to access multimedia services from everywhere at anytime, recent research has focused on the development of new scalable, efficient, and flexible "next generation" middleware platforms [5]. These middleware platforms are intended to support the deployment of mainstream broadband applications including CDN and Video on Demand. One such next-generation middleware platform is the Grid computing system. A Grid is a virtual framework that allows resources across national and international boundaries to interoperate and share capacities in a controlled fashion to form scalable systems.

The integration between the grid technology and multimedia edge technology has produced a novel technology——multimedia delivery grid. The multimedia delivery grid is an extension of the computing grid mechanism to support the deployment of multimedia services to meet the ever-increasing demand for multimedia from users engaging in a wide range of activities such as scientific research, education, commerce, and entertainment. The multimedia delivery grid will provide various new services and sustain several enabling technologies to support multimedia [3]. Some of the new services include transparent user profile location and access supporting so that adaptive applications can be developed. A user in such an environment is not tied to a specific machine but rather is a machine independent entity that exists in the grid and can transparently carry its profile across the different platforms constituting the grid. Some of the enabling technologies that will be supported include: (1) Streaming Media, (2) Multicast, (3) QoS, (4) Co-allocation of Resources, and so on.

2 The Architecture of Multimedia Delivery Grid

In order to provide a pattern for establishing a Grid for delivering multimedia content to consumers, we propose the architecture of a three-tier hierarchy of few initial media sources (original content providers), metropolitan media centers and regional media centers acting as hierarchical carriers for popular multimedia content.

As Figure1 showing, in this architecture, regional media centers are deployed in the network edge (at the inner end of the so-called "last mile"). The function of metropolitan media centers is to aggregate a number of neighbored regional media centers, for instance of a metropolitan area. Regional media centers are interconnected among each other according to their geographic neighborhoods. Consumer clients are connected to one associated regional media center from which they obtain media content. On request of a consumer, if the media content is available in the media center, the media content is directly provided from the regional media center to the consumer's home. If content is not present, the regional media center asks its neighbor or peer regional media centers for the content. If the content cannot be obtained from there, the regional media center asks its associated metropolitan media center. This procedure of asking peers before the higher-ordered element intends to avoid load at metropolitan media centers. Metropolitan media centers behave similarly as regional centers. If content cannot be obtained from peer metropolitan media centers, content is obtained from the original content provider at the top of the distribution hierarchy. Each media center has a certain capacity for storing content and maintains an index about the stored content. It is assumed that content can be uniquely identified by index data (keys), as well as that the original content provider can be derived from a content inquiry description issued by consumers [4].

At the same time, delivery grid is highly scalable, because relay mechanism is used. It means that not only the peered media centers can relay and share contents each other, but also as each additional PC client also becomes a potential microserver and software node to provide content for other future neighbored or peered requestors of the content. Therefore, in the delivery grid, some of client desktop and laptop, armed with a piece of delivery agent, can act as microserver to distribute the received content to other neighbor requesters.

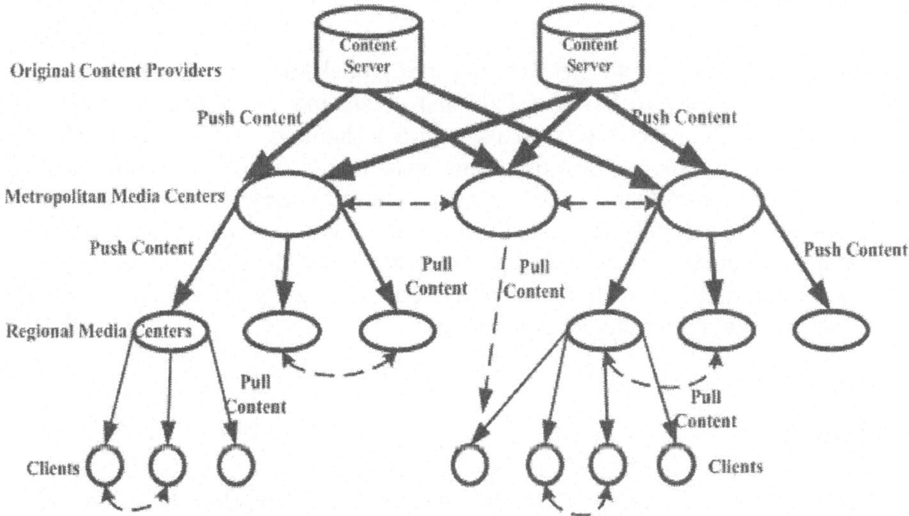

Fig. 1. Hierarchy Architecture of Multimedia Delivery Grid

3 The Delivery Process of Multimedia Delivery Grid

In our architecture, the delivery process is as following: Content owner publishes content to origin server through authorized publishing. Network Publisher applies content security settings using Network Protector and content metadata is communicated into the Directory Server. Published, secured content is propagated to Grid Servers (including metropolitan and regional media centers). When user requests the published content, he firstly logs on the Authorization Server and makes an access request. Then the authenticated user obtains the delivery ticket and requests a list of content sources to the Directory Server. Directory Server verifies requested content's validity; authenticate delivery ticket and responds with a list of optimal content sources. The requested client starts content retrieval process from optimal Grid Servers. Content downloaded successfully and verified against digital signature.

When another user on the Client Grid requests the published content from Directory Server, Directory Server recommends optimal Grid Delivery Servers and Client Grid

Nodes as content sources. The user makes requests to optimal Grid Servers and Client Grid Nodes. Requested content is Multi-Sourced from well-connected Client Grid Nodes and Grid Servers, resulting in high download performance, reliable delivery and reduction in bandwidth usage. The security protocols of the whole request and service flow comprise the typical transport layer security protocol-Security Socket Layer (SSL) and a novel XML-based Secure Distributed Delivery Protocol (SDDP). Login, authentication, authorization, and digital right management utilize SSL, while download request and content delivery employ the novel XML-based SDDP.

4 Conclusions and Future Work

Multimedia delivery grid further entering into global Internet will necessarily make grid technology closer to business field and obtain more enormous industry space. Nevertheless, the Internet use of delivery grid technology is in the research phase; researchers and developers must overcome many key technologies. Before deploying delivery grid on a worldwide scale, researchers have to carry on many experiments in grid test-bed with carefully controlled trials, continuously validating its scalability and evaluating its actual performance [2]. With the rapid development of multimedia communication and grid technology, multimedia delivery grid will necessarily have wide industrialization development prospects.

References

1. Zhihui L., Yiping Z., Shiyong Z., Jie W.: Study of Main Technology in Rich Media Grid Delivery. In the Proc. of ICCNMC'03, IEEE Computer Society Press, Oct 2003
2. Gartner Group Research Note.: Delivery grid Surfaces in Enterprise: A Tutorial, Jan 2003
3. Sujoy, B. (ed.): mmGrid: Distributed Resource Management Infrastructure for Multimedia Applications. In the Proc. of IPDPS'03, April 2003
4. Sven, G., Winfried, K., Carsten R.: Modeling and Simulation of Media-On-Demand Services -- Evaluating a Digital Media Grid Architecture. HP Laboratories Technical Report HPL-2002-192, July 2002
5. Muthucumaru M.: Main Topic- Part B: Next-Generation Middleware Platforms. Canadian Conference on Electrical & Computer Engineering2002, CCECE'02, May 2002
6. Stefan, S., Krishna P. G., Richard J. D., Steven D. G., Henry M. L.: An Analysis of Internet Content Delivery Systems. In Proc. of OSDI '02, 2002
7. Bruce M.: Global Internet Content Delivery. In the Proc of IEEE CCGRID'01, 2001
8. Foster, I., Kesselman, C., Tuecke, S.: the Anatomy of the Grid: Enable Scalable Virtual Organizations. Int J. Supercomputer Applications, 2001

The System for Computing of Molecule Structure on the Computational Grid Environment*

Yongmei Lei[1], Weimin Xu[1], and Bingqiang Wang[2]

[1] School of Computer Engineering and Science, Shanghai University, Shanghai 200072, China,
ymlei@mail.shu.edu.cn
[2] Department of Chemistry, East China University of Science and Technology, Shanghai 200237, China
wangbingqiang@hotmail.com

Abstract. The computing grid can offer users tremendous computer resources. In this paper, we proposed an application model for computing of molecule structure on the computational grid. According to the need of grid computing, a high-resolution system has been implemented; which includes middleware based OGSA, domain master-slave model, the explanation and calculation of complex molecule structure and 3D visualization in Shanghai University- East China University of Science and Technology grid environment.

1 Introduction

The term computational grids refers to infrastructures aimed at allowing users to access and/or aggregate potentially large numbers of powerful and sophisticated resources. The project was created to advance chemical scientific understanding and innovation in polymer of material research by enabling more efficient use of existing experimental facilities through more effective integration of experiment, theory, and modeling.

Users are demanding services that make more efficient use of computing facilities in a distributed environment. They are also demanding services such as interactive visualization and cooperative work environments that better support collaboration between distributed research teams. These requirements make the material simulation collaborator an interesting example of a virtual organization. To realize its goals the Collaborator aims to create and deploy collaborative software tools throughout the chemists' mole research community, which comprises over many researchers from over many institutions.

As a test bed, we have connected two super cluster computers together, one is Ziqiang 2000 in Shanghai University, and the other one is in East China University of Science and Technology .On our platform, users can put forward their calculation problems from their own computer through Internet browser, and control the

* Supported by Development Foundation of Shanghai Municipal Commission of Education

M. Li et al. (Eds.): GCC 2003, LNCS 3032, pp. 225–228, 2004.

execution of the job, then get its results and possibly along with 3D visualization effects. It is sure that this easy-to-use powerful platform will improve the cooperation of different fields and enforce their research ability.

The structure of the paper is as follows. Section 2 describes Grid technologies that we are using to create the collaborative mode of operation, and the application-specific software. Section 3 reviews the algorithm and problem solving method; we briefly summarize the visualization research carried out as part of this project, and describe how the Grid technologies will be used to address the challenges of the collaboration and Section 4 presents preliminary experimental testbed of our work, and conclude in section 5.

2 Analysis of Application Specific Requirements

More formally, Grids are defined as infrastructure allowing flexible, secure, and coordinated resource sharing among dynamic collections of individuals, institutions and resources referred to as virtual organizations. In such environments, we encounter unique authentication, authorization, resource access, and resource discovery challenges. Each new Grid application facilitates a deeper understanding of these challenges and takes the Grid technology to increasing levels of functionality, performance, and robustness. In this paper we describe a new Grid application: complex material simulation and its potential for driving the understanding and development of computational Grids.

The basic problem here is one of providing on-demand application services for large-scale data analysis and simulation. In an ideal scenario, a scientist at one of the sites (a client site) needs to remotely run code installed and maintained at another site (a service provider site) during an experiment within time bound. There are some common features in the application that can use the Grid environment effectively. Application that is satisfied with those features is called Grid Oriented Computing Application.

The stochastic computation application is satisfied with the conditions of GOCA. In this research, the system is developed as the Grid software, which can harness the feature of GOCA.

The prototype is composed of grid middleware based OGSA, implementation of the 3D Lattice MC simulation algorithm, visualization tool and portal.

It is important to consider the computing environment. This refers to the way we think about the world of files, computers, databases and programs exposed through a portal.

The portal features are as follows:

1. Access to the computational grid for execution of the compute-intensive task under deadline constrains.

2. Access to a parameter repository to store different configuration for the experiment parameter.

3. Access to uniform collaborative environment that allows the exchange sophisticated immerses visualization.

From the point of view of the research collaborator, the main capability that we demonstrate here is uniform access to remote computational capabilities. Adding these capabilities means that this interactive scenario can now leave the domain of one laboratory and instead be executed across multiple sites in a truly collaborative fashion.

3 Algorithms and Problem Solving Method

We investigate stochastic Monte Carlo simulation for morphology of block polymer separation. Monte Carlo simulations polymer are based on the time evolution of an ensemble of particles through the material in both real and momentum space. The motion of each particle in the ensemble has to be simulated in turn, for the full duration of the simulation.

3.1 Parallel 3D Lattice MC Logical Model and Implementation

These objects consist of N cells, which are chain-like connected via one of 15 bead vectors. The mixture comprises three types of beads denoted A, B and C. Within the framework of a Monte Carlo simulation it is necessary to generate a large number of statistically independent system configurations. Therefore, the algorithm lets the polymer conformations evolve via random cell displacements. In distributed parallel computations, tasks are executed by a set of intercommunicating computer systems. The MC-MPI algorithm is based on a master-slave model. The domain of particles is divided into subdomain, each of which is dedicated to a separate processor (slave). The slaves are solely responsible for simulating the particles dynamics under the influence of the internal field distribution. The master processor updates the field distribution consistently with the port conditions enforced by the external circuitry and the spatial evolution of the charge particles by solving energy equation.

The global data set is decomposed into separate sections, and each section is placed under the control of a separate process. The degree of decomposition depends on the number of processes available. The aim is to ensure that the data is distributed as evenly as possible amongst all of the processes. Each process is assigned its own section of the data – its data block.

3.2 Collaborative and Visualization Technologies

The visualization of grid computing is very different from that of local visualization. The visualization component of system is the creation of new visualization tools for both experimental and simulation data that will represent a significant increase in capability and efficiency for the research groups. Our goal is to provide users with visualizations that incorporate and compare data from experimental and simulation sources and to reflect uncertainty information to aid in data analysis and decision making.. Initial work on visualization was presented where polymer temperature data was combined with magnetic field topology computed by MC to produce multiple time-dependent 3D molecular temperature configurations.

The demand placed on visualization tools by the collaboration grid will be intense due to both the highly collaborative nature of research and the dramatic increase in data resulting from the enhanced computational capabilities. One component of this work will be the creation of a collaborative control mechanism for the experimental processes.

4 Experimental Design

Two clusters installed in Shanghai University and East China University of Science and Technology were used for experiment, and Linux is used as OS of each node. The OGSA based middleware are installed in the gateway machine.

5 Conclusions and Future Works

The large scale and characteristics of the collaborator research make computing of molecule structure of new material an important application for computational Grids. We developed a software infrastructure that is a natural fit for OGSA based grid computing applications.

Although our experiment by no means represents the extent of work that still needs to be done to satisfy all of the goals of the research, these preliminary results are very encouraging. A clear definition of challenging requirements will allow us to expand the capabilities of the OGSA based grid computing in a truly application-driven way.

References

1. Peter S. Pacheco : Parallel Programming with MPI , Morgan Kaufmann Publishers, Inc. San Francisco, California,1997
2. Ian Forster: Grid-Enabled MPI: Message Passing in Heterogeneous Distributed Computing Systems, Supercomputing 98 ., 1998
3. G. Allen, T. Dramlitsch, I. Foster, N.T. Karonis: Supporting Efficient Execution in Heterogeneous Distributed Computing Environments with Catus and Globus, Proc. SC01 (SC2001), Denver, 2001,
4. Mark Baker, Rajkumar Buyya and Domenico Laforenza: The Grid: A Survey on Global Efforts in Grid Computing, School of Computer Science, Univ. of Portsmouth, 2000

An Efficient Parallel Crawler in Grid Environment[1]

Shoubin Dong, Xiaofeng Lu, Ling Zhang, and Kejing He

Network Research Center, South China University of Technology,
510640 Guangzhou, China
{sbdong, xflv, ling, kjhe}@scut.edu.cn

Abstract. As the size of the web grows, it is imperative to run multiple crawlers to gather data for search engines. In this paper we study the parallel crawling schema in grid environment. We propose and implement an advanced parallel crawler by introducing the techniques of dynamic partition, and evaluate the crawling schema based on parallel crawlers metrics. An experimental system built on Grid middleware has been tested in the real application.

1 Introduction

It is obvious that deploying a single crawler to retrieve the whole or a significant portion of the web is very time-consuming and difficult to complete. Therefore, many search engines often run multiple crawlers in parallel to fulfill the task above, in order to achieve a maximized download rate. Competition among parallel crawling results in redundant crawling, wasted resources, and less-than-timely discovery.

In intuitive, the parallel crawler has many advantages compared to a singer-process crawler, such as scalability, network load distribution and reduction. Several researches have been conducted on parallel and distributed crawlers [1,2,3]. Different from the above work on parallel or distributed crawlers, we propose a new parallel crawling schema based on dynamic partition mechanism, where all objects of the web are partitioned based on site names, and one partition is not permanently assigned to a specific crawler. Based on the dynamic partition, we are able to extend the parallel crawler to run on grid nodes. Our aim is to construct a high performance, fault tolerant and scalable crawler in grid environment.

2 Design of KapokCrawler

Here we give a brief description of general system architecture and key techniques of a parallel crawler KapokCrawler. The design goals of KapokCrawler are: load balance, scalability, fault tolerance, high performance and politeness.

---

[1] Supported by Guangdong Key Laboratory of Computer Network under Grant 2002B60113.

M. Li et al. (Eds.): GCC 2003, LNCS 3032, pp. 229–232, 2004.

2.1 System Architecture

The parallel crawler KapokCrawler is composed of agents and coordinators. An agent is a grid node, it performs its download task by running several threads, each of which is called C-proc. Each C-proc is dedicated to the visit of a single site using a breadth-first search. A coordinator is to coordinate the behavior of the agents. As indicated in figure 1, the workflow of KapokCrawler is described as follows.

At the start of the crawling procedure, a number of seed URLs, which are grouped by site names, have to be set to “URL Queue” in the coordinator. The monitor collects the status (such as CPU usage, memory usage, disk size, network bandwidth, etc.) of every grid node (e.g. agent), and save the information in “Agent Status Info”. When the crawler gets started, the coordinator assigns the number of available C-proc’s groups of seed URLs to appropriate C-proc’s, based on agent status information and our dynamic partition algorithm, and uses “C-proc Map” to keep the information about each C-proc’s working site. Meanwhile, the “Meta-Info Extractor” collects statistics of the formerly downloaded objects in the central database and distributes them to the corresponding C-proc’s “Meta-Info”.

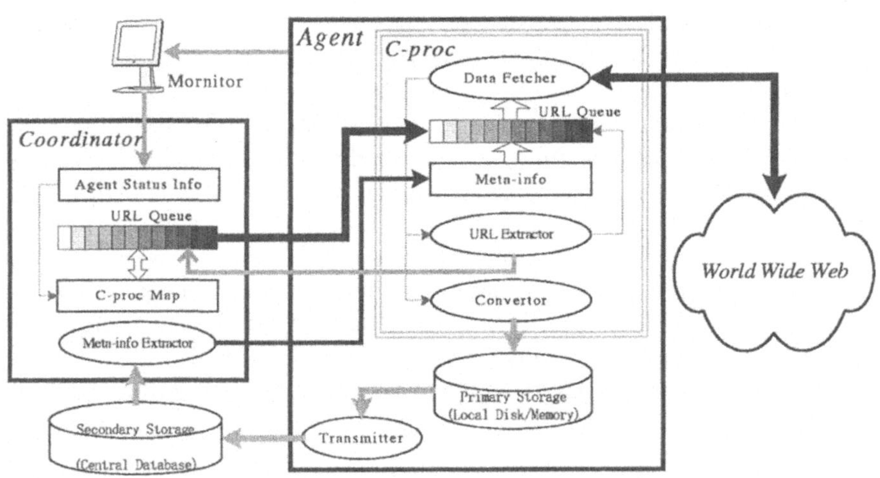

Fig. 1. The System Architecture of KapokCrawler

When the assigned seed URLs come, C-proc pushes them into its URL queue and begins to work. Objects are retrieved by “Data Fetcher” and then sent to the “Convertor”, where objects including web pages and objects of other formats are converted into XML formats and saved to the primary storage in the agent, and the “URL Extractor”. URL extractor extracts new URLs from the downloaded objects and sends those that are local to C-proc’s assigned site to the URL queue of C-proc, while sends others back to the URL queue in the coordinator. When C-proc's URL queue is empty, it asks the coordinator for new assignment. The primary storage is supervised by a "Transmitter" located in the same agent. When the number of documents in the primary storage grows to certain degree, all data in the primary storage would be packed and sent to the central database through the transmitter.

As soon as the coordinator receives the new URLs extracted by C-proc's URL extractor, it inserts those new URLs into corresponding groups in the URL queue of coordinator, based on their site names. When the request for new assignment comes, the coordinator assigns the group of URLs in the head of the URL queue to the C-proc. These steps would repeat until there is no URL in the URL-queues of both coordinator and C-proc's.

2.2 Dynamic Partition Technique

In grid environment, grid nodes are dynamic changed. Dynamic partitioning is currently done by means of partition algorithm based on two parameters: size of a site and capacity of C-proc. Size may be measured by the number of objects the site holds. Capacity of C-proc is proportional to the available resources of an agent.

It is assumed S is an ordered set of sites according to their sizes; P is an ordered set of C-proc's according to their capacities; M is the mapping list of a pair set (site, C-proc); A is the list of all agents and U is a list of global URL-queue group by sites, maintained by coordinator.

Initially assign s_0 to p_0, s_1 to p_1, …, add pair (s_0,p_0),(s_1,p_1)… to the mapping list M, and delete the assigned sites from S. While $|S| > 0$, check for the tasks of C-proc's: if the task of this C-proc p_i has been finished, delete pair (s_k, p_i) from the mapping list M, assign s_0 to p_i, delete s_0 from queue S and add pair (s_0, p_i) to the mapping list M; if the C-proc p_i found some new URLs not local to its given site s_j, then send the URLs to URL-queue of coordinator U. Check for crash agents: if the agent a_i has failed, add s_k to the head of list S, where (s_k, p_i) is a pair value in M and p_i is all C-proc running on a_i, then delete pair (s_k, p_i) from the mapping list M. Check for new agents: if the coordinator finds that some new agent is available, add new C-proc to list P and re-order P according to their capacities. Order the list of URL-queue U according to their sites. For all new URLs $u_i \in U$, suppose the site of u_i is s_k: if (s_k, p_i) exists in the lists of M, send u_i to the right C-proc; if s_k, is not belonging to S, add a new site.

If some knowledge is unavailable, for example the size of a site may not be available at first download, the result may be less than best. But dynamic partition is still better than static assignment, because it fully utilizes all available resources.

3 Implementation and Evaluation

We develop our system based on Globus Toolkit (http://www.globus.org/) and Sun Grid Engine (http://wwws.sun.com/software/gridware/). Agents and coordinator exchange URLs and control information by MPI. The GridFTP of Globus is used to transfer data from primary storage to secondary storage.
Evaluation model of parallel crawling schemes is described in details in [3]. Here we discuss the evaluation of KapokCrawler based on these four key metrics: overlap, coverage, quality and communication overlap. Even in the presence of faults, KapokCrawler achieves optimal overlap 0 and coverage 1, because of the dynamic partition features. As for the quality, KapokCrawler uses a parallel per-site breadth-first visit, without dealing with ranking and quality issues. However a breadth-first single-process visit tends to visit high-quality pages first [4]. Thus KapokCrawler tends to have a very good performance in quality. As it is stated in [2] that on the average every page contains just one link to another site, we have that n crawled pages will give rise to n URLs that must be potentially communicated to coordinator and other agents. The communication overhead is thus no more than 1.

4 Conclusion

In our work, we address the design and implementation of a parallel crawler in the context of Grid middleware. Further work will be included in the near future, such as the employment of page ranking to improve the crawling quality.

References

1. V. Shkapenyuk and T. Suel. Design and implementation of a high-performance distributed Web crawler. In Proceedings of the 18th International Conference on Data Engineering (ICDE'02), San Jose, CA Feb. 26-March 1, pages 357-368, 2002.
2. P. Boldi, B. Codenotti, M. Santini, and S. Vigna. Ubicrawler: A scalable fully distributed web crawler. In Proc. Of 8th Australian World Wide Web Conference, 2002.
3. J. Cho and H. Garcia-Molina. Parallel crawlers. In Proc. of the 11th International World–Wide Web Conference, 2002.
4. Marc Najork and Janet L. Wiener. Breadth-first search crawling yields high quality pages. In Proc. of 10th International World Wide Web Conference, Hong Kong, China, 2001.

The Development and Application of Numerical Packages Based on NetSolve

Haiying Cheng, Wu Zhang, Yunfu Shen, and Anping Song

School of Computer Engineering and Science, Shanghai University, Shanghai 200072, PRC
sunnychy@163.com, {wzhang, yfshen,apsong}@mail.shu.edu.cn

Abstract. NetSolve is a kind of grid middleware used for high performance compute. In this article, the architecture and operational principle of NetSolve are first analyzed. This paper mainly discusses the implementation of the server with several numerical packages and numerical experiment is given. At last, we point out the limitations of the Netsolve.

1 Introduction

Thanks to advance in hardware, networking infrastructure and algorithms, computing intensive problems in many areas can now be successfully attacked. Various mechanisms have been developed to perform computations across diverse platforms. The most common mechanism involves software libraries. Unfortunately, the use of such libraries presents several difficulties. This motivated the establishment of the NetSolve project.

NetSolve, underway at the University of Tennessee and at the Oak Ridge National Laboratory, is a project that makes use of distributed computational resources connected by computer networks to efficiently solve complex scientific problems. It is a remote procedure call (RPC) based on client/agent/server system that allows users to discover, access, and utilize remote software modules and the hardware needed to run these modules.

2 NetSolve

2.1 Definition

NetSolve is a client-server system that enables users to solve complex scientific problems remotely. The system searches for computational resources on the network, chooses the best one available, and solves a problem using retry for fault tolerance, and returns the answers to the user.

M. Li et al. (Eds.): GCC 2003, LNCS 3032, pp. 233–236, 2004.

2.2 Components

- **Agent:** The agent maintains a database of NetSolve servers along with their capabilities and dynamic usage statistics for use in scheduling decisions. It attempts to find the server that will service the request, balance the load amongst its servers, and keep track of failed servers
- **Server:** The NetSolve server is a daemon process that awaits client requests. It can run on single workstations, clusters of workstations, SMPs, or MPPs. One key component of the server is the ability to wrap software library routines into NetSolve services by using an Interface Definition Language (IDL).
- **Client:** The NetSolve client uses application programming interfaces (APIs) to make a request to the NetSolve system, with the specific details required with the request.

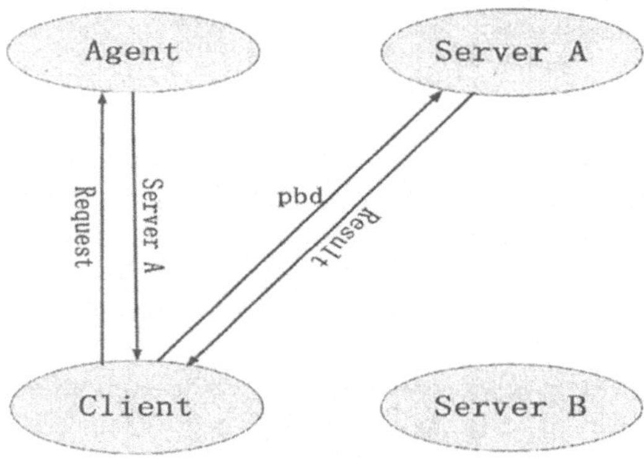

Fig.1 NetSolve Architecture

3 Problem Specification and Present Software Packages

This section describes how to configure a NetSolve problem and introduces the present numerical software.

3.1 Problems Specification

To keep NetSolve as general as possible, we need to find a formal way of describing a problem.

A problem is defined as a 3-tuple: <name, inputs, outputs>, where

- name is a character string containing the name of the problem
- inputs is a list of input objects
- outputs is a list of output objects

An object is itself described as follows: <object,data>, where object can be 'MATRIX', 'VECTOR' or 'SCALAR' and data can be any of the standard FORTRAN data types.

3.2 Scientific Packages

Many packages have been used in Netsolve, such as BLAS, LAPACK, ItPack, ScaLAPACK, PETSc, Linpack, etc.

BLAS, Basic Linear Algebra Subprograms, are high-quality building block routines for performing basic vector and matrix operations.

LAPACK is a free, portable, modern (1990) library of Fortran 77 routines for solving the most common problems in numerical linear algebra.

PETSc, the Portable, Extensible Toolkit for Scientific computation, provides sets of tools for the parallel (as well as serial), numerical solution of PDEs that require solving large-scale, sparse nonlinear systems of equations. PETSc provides several parallel sparse matrix formats, including compressed row, block compressed row, and block diagonal storage.

4 Numerical Experiment

Laplace equation:

$$u(x,y) = f(x,y) \quad \text{in} \quad \Omega = (0, NC+1) \times (0, NR+1)$$

$$u\big|_{x=0} = 0,\ u\big|_{x=NC+1} = 100,\ u\big|_{y=0,y=NR+1} = x.$$

To solve this problem, we use the finite difference method,

$$\frac{u_{i+1,j} - 2u_{ij} + u_{i-1,j}}{\delta x^2} + \frac{u_{i,j+1} - 2u_{ij} + u_{i,j-1}}{\delta y^2} = f_{ij}.$$

To avoid solve the linear system, we use the simple Jacobi iteration method

$$u_{ij}^{n+1} = (u_{i+1,j}^n + u_{i-1,j}^n + u_{i,j+1}^n + u_{i,j-1}^n - \delta x^2 f_{ij}) / 4.$$

Here we assume $\delta x = \delta y$. In our implementation, we assume $f(x,y) = 0$.

Table 1. The Results of the Two Programs

Number of Mesh Points	Runtime of S_laplace	Runtime of N_laplace	Speed Ratio
100*100	1.500 sec	1.389 sec	1.079
200*100	2.860 sec	2.688 sec	1.063
200*200	6.570 sec	4.238 sec	1.55
400*200	15.250 sec	8.534 sec	1.787
400*400	35.420 sec	20.125 sec	1.852
800*400	100.750 sec	47.789 sec	2.108

NetSolve offers a 'sparse_iterative_solve' service as a convenient interface to sparse iterative methods packages such as PETSc, Aztec, and ITPACK. We write a serial program named S_laplace, and then make use of the 'sparse_iterative_solve' service of NetSolve to solve the same question. These two programs run on the same four nodes (Double CPU PIV1.2GHz, Shared Memory 2GB).

From table1, we can see that the performance of the N_laplace is superior to the S_laplace's. And the paralleling speed ratio rises with the increase of the number of mesh points. The programs NetSolve offers have other merits, we can use N_laplace to solve the problem directly and need not programming by ourselves, and there only about 40 lines of the codes in N_laplace, otherwise there are almost 100 lines of codes in S_laplace.

But, sometimes the performance of the programs which the user writes may be better than that of NetSolve offers. We can make the excellent program as a service and integrate it into the NetSolve.

5 Limitations

Though NetSolve in itself a wonderful concept, its usage has been hampered by the arduous effort involved in setting up and using NetSolve. NetSolve has been very successful in providing easy to use interface for the users who just want to access the libraries already available within the system. However, It has not been able to attract a sizeable community to integrate their applications in the NetSolve. One of the reasons is that the user has to manually install software on all the machines and compile and start their own servers.

6 Conclusions

In this article, we have introduced the architecture and operational principle of NetSolve and discussed the implementation of server, pointed out that the program the user writes might be superior to those existed in the NetSolve, so we could integrate our own programe into NetSolve as a service. The NetSolve project is still at an early development stage, we anticipate that several promising extensions and applications of NetSolve will emerge.

References

1. Ian Foster, Carl Kesselman et al. The Grid: Blueprint for a New Computing Infrastructure, © 2001 Morgan Kaufmann Publishers.
2. J. Dongarra, J. Du Croz, I. Du_, and S. Hammarling. A Set of Level 3 Basic Linear Algebra Subprograms. ACM Transactions on Mathematical Software, 16(1):1-17, 1990.
3. R.W. Freund and N.M. Nachtigal. QMR: A quasiminimal residual method for non-Hermitian linear systems. Numer. Math., 60:315-339, 1991.
4. H. Casanova, J. Dongarra, and K. Seymour. Client User's Guide to Netsolve. Technical Report CS-96-343, Department of Computer Science, University of Tennessee, 1996.

Grid-Based Biological Computation Service Environment[1]

Jing Zhu[1], Guangwen Yang[1], Weimin Zheng[1], Tao Zhu[1], Meiming Shen[1], Li'an Qiao[2], and Xiangjun Liu[2]

[1] Department of Computer Science and Technology, Tsinghua University, Beijing, China
zhujing00@mails.tsinghua.edu.cn
[2] Bioinformatics Laboratory, Tsinghua Medical School, Beijing, China

Abstract. This paper puts forward a novel concept of "Grid-based biological computation environment". In this environment, distributed, heterogeneous computer nodes, as long as they installed biological computation software and are willing to share them for public use, can be aggregated seamlessly into a powerful computational Grid to provide on-demand computation services. Just with the widely available Web browser, biology researchers can conveniently perform highly customized computation jobs. To date, a prototype system is developed and a number of pragmatic biological applications are exploited.

1 Introduction

Biological computation mainly refers to computational management of all kinds of biological information. There have been lots of shareware and commercial software for biological computation, which are fundamental for biology researchers to utilize for further analysis and investigation. But most users may encounter problems when directly using them because of the difficulty to install, configure and maintain the software as well as to learn parameters, syntax and semantics.

As a hot research issue in recent years, one of the primary motivations of Grid computing [1] is to enable scientific researchers to better utilize distributed, heterogeneous resources to solve a set of problems. In this paper, we present the concept of "Grid-based biological computation service environment". In this environment, with the aid of grid technique, a diverse collection of computer nodes scattered around the globe, which have common biological computation software installed and are willing to share them for public use, are organized into an entire resource entity to provide computation services. Just with the Web browser which is already familiar to them, users can easily customize job request and utilize services provided by our system to

[1] This research work is supported by National Natural Science Foundation of China under Grant No. 60373004, 60373005.

M. Li et al. (Eds.): GCC 2003, LNCS 3032, pp. 237–241, 2004.

perform biological computation, even without having to be aware of the existence of individual service providers.

The rest of our paper is organized as follows: The next section gives an overview of logic architecture of our Grid-based biological computation service environment. Section 3 introduces the application model supported by our system. Several key components and issues are explained from section 4 to 6. Section 7 lists related works. Finally is the conclusion.

2 Logic Architecture Overview

A logical framework of our Grid-based biological computation environment can be represented by Fig.1.

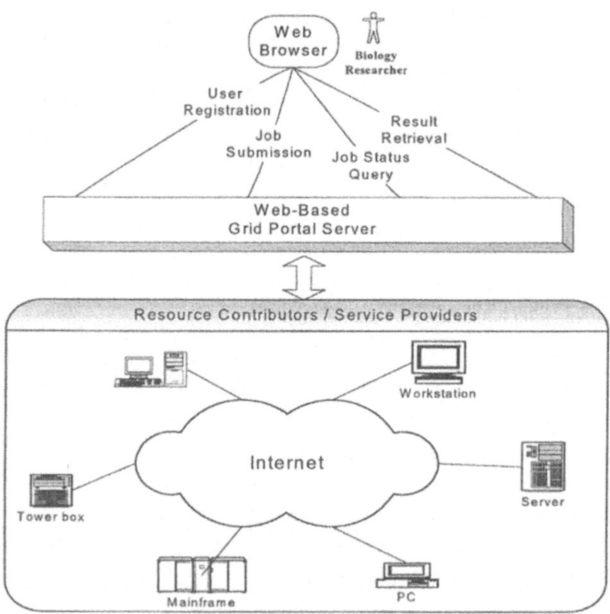

Fig. 1. Logical Architecture

Several key issues to be considered in constructing such a distributed system include how to organize widely diversified resource contributors in an efficient and scalable way, how to dynamically select appropriate resources for user's job request; how to provide a convenient interface for biology researchers. To better explain these key issues, it is helpful to first take a look at the application model supported by our system.

3 Application Model

In this paper, we call the biological computation applications user submits for execution "jobs". Generally speaking, the whole job is made up of several steps. The subsequent step cannot start until the anterior step has finished, and usually the input of the former relies on the output of the latter. Each step may also consist of several tasks, which are absolutely independent to each other.

For instance, a biology researcher wants to use three sequence alignment software (say, Blast, Faster, MUMer) to compute on the same set of two gene sequences, thus he can compare the results and make certain analysis. Then in our application model, the user's job contains only one step, which contains three independent tasks, each corresponding to a computation with program Blast, Faster and MUMer.

As stated above, a task is a computation with a specific program on input data, which usually is a file containing one or more gene sequences. It is natural to find that the task can be easily partitioned into a number of atomtasks, each referring to the computation with the program on one sequence (or two sequences in sequence alignment computation), and several atomtasks can be clustered into a subtask. If there exist more than one available computer nodes for a task, we can partition the task into a couple of subtasks to be executed in parallel in these nodes, so the makespan of the task is reduced and the whole makespan of the job may be therefore reduced.

The application model presented in this section can characterize most practical applications in biological computation. And due to the coarse grain in task partitioning, it is feasible to perform one job across multiple available computation sites in parallel.

4 Global Information Server

In our system, a global information server is responsible for providing efficient and pervasive access to information about current availability and capability of resources.

Besides hardware and software info about resources, the static information maintained in our information server also include a set of software-specific computation capacity parameters, which describe the maximum performance delivered by a computer node to execute specific software in its unloaded situation. This can be acquired by running a benchmark of the target program on a sample input in the unloaded computer node. With this information, it is possible to calculate the assumed execution time of user's task in one specific node.

The dynamic information maintained in global information server mainly refers to queue length of each computation node, which represents an estimated execution time of tasks yet to be executed in this node. Computation node periodically updates its dynamic status in the global information server. This information is of great importance to scheduling policy, which will be shown in Section 5.

5 Global Job Scheduler

There have been considerable research works in job scheduling issues. Simulation results in [2] show that the centralized policy always performs better than the distributed ones and is easier to implement and maintain. So we also take a centralized scheduling approach in a global job scheduler.

One important performance goal of our scheduling policy is to finish user' job as soon as possible. According to application model presented in section 3.2, the total execution time is the sum of execution time of each step. So it is important to reduce the execution time of each step. And due to the independency between tasks in one step, scheduling policy is made with a task as the basic unit.

Scheduling decision is made up of two phases. The first phase is to choose qualified resource nodes which provide the appointed biological software needed by the task. Next, the second phase is to further select "best" nodes from the set of qualified ones according to certain performance metrics.

The first phase can be easily accomplished by simply querying the global information server. After this, a set of qualified nodes is picked out. Then in the next phase, for each node in the set, a value representing the time to wait until the task is finished in the node is calculated as the sum of its estimated queue length and the estimated execution time of the task. The former is directly obtained from the information server, and the latter is calculated out of the maximum computation capacity of the machine running the benchmark program appointed by the task (also stored in the information server) and the amount of the task's input data.. Then a node with minimum waiting time is selected as the target node where the task will be executed.

6 Local Resource Management

In this section, we will discuss the resource management in each computation node. The request the node receives is either a task or a subtask. There is a Local Task Scheduler running in each node, which is responsible for starting the tasks/subtasks allocated by the global job scheduler. And task execution process is exclusive. Besides, a Local Resource Status Reporter component is responsible for gathering recent info about the node and updating the global information server periodically.

An important issue lies in that biological software the computation nodes provide are multiple and diversified, so it is necessary to employ a simple and unified method to invoke software programs in each node to provide computation services. With Java Runtime technique, we developed a service implementation skeleton as a template for all biological computation service. A program property file is maintained in each computation node to provide the information of all programs the node contributes for public use, such as program category, name, version, executable path and etc.

When a computation node receives a computation request, it will first extract required program information and command parameters, then check the program property file for useful information about the appointed program to generate integrated command, which is then combined with the service implementation skeleton to create a service instance to perform actual computation.

7 Related Works

Among similar works related to our paper, EBI [3] and NCBI [4] are the most famous representatives of on-line biological computation service. They maintain a number of biological software and tools in a central Web server. User can only perform computation with one software once. Complex application model as presented in our paper is not sustained yet. Moreover, with quite a lot of users competing for the limited centralized computation power, users may suffer from poor service quality.

Pise [5] is a Web interface generator for molecular biology programs in Unix. Given a description of a program and its parameters, Pise is able to generate a Web interface for this program. This work can be borrowed into our Grid-based biological computation service environment to provide more friendly Web interfaces.

8 Conclusion

In this paper, we put forward a novel concept of Grid-based biological computation service environment. The overall architecture is outlined and key components and issues are explained in detail. Up to now, a prototype written in Java has been developed and several practical biological computation applications are exploited in our system, among which is the Protein target selection for structural genomics of rice *Oryza sativa*, where several software tools are employed for analyzing proteins properties to automate the target selection process. Feedback from our copartners in bioinformatics area proves that our system can aggregate diversified distributed resources efficiently into a powerful Grid platform for biology researchers to solve their biological computation problems better than traditional approaches they adopted.

References

1. Ian Foster, Carl Kesselman, The Grid: Blueprint for a New Computing Infrastructures. Morgan Kaufmann Publishers, Inc, San Francisco, USA (1999)
2. C. Leangsuksun, J. Potter, S. Scott, Dynamic task mapping algorithms for a distributed heterogeneous computing environment. In 4th IEEE Heterogeneous Computing Workshop (HCW' 95), Santa Barbara, CA, (1995) 30-34
3. EBI Project Website: http://www.ebi.ac.uk
4. NCBI Project Website: http://www.ncbi.nlm.nih.gov/
5. Catherine Letondal, A Web interface generator for molecular biology programs in Unix, Bioinformatics, Vol. 17(1), (2001) 73-82

CIMES: A Collaborative Image Editing System for Pattern Design

Xianghua Xu, Jiajun Bu, Chun Chen, and Yong Li

College of Computer Science, Zhejiang University, Hangzhou 310027, China
{xuxh_cs, bjj, chenc, lyzju}@cs.zju.edu.cn

Abstract. In this paper, we present a Collaborative IMage Editing System (CIMES), which is developed for textile pattern design based on our previous image processing system. CIMES adopts a replicated architecture. An image operation representation approach is proposed to reduce the space cost of image operation preservation. Then a concurrent control algorithm is proposed to resolve the image editing conflicting caused by multi-user collaborative editing and maintain the consistency of shared image. An image undo/redo algorithm is also presented to support multiple undo modes in the same editing sessions, including global undo and local undo.

1 Introduction

With the evolution of Internet environment, more and more applications open collaborative working ways, such as document review and real-time online collaboration of engineering designs. In this paper, we present a Collaborative IMage Editing System (CIMES), which is developed for textile pattern design based on our previous image processing system – TOP[4]. CIMES allows a group of users to edit a large dimension image at the same time from different sites connected via high speed Internet. Image processing tools, such as painting brush, standard pen and color processing, are supported in this system.

To achieve high responsiveness and unconstrained collaboration in the Internet environment [11], a replicated architecture is adopted in CIMES. Shared images are replicated at the local storage of each collaborative site, and image editing operations are performed at local sites immediately and then propagated to remote sites. Because each user cannot instantly see changes made by other users to shared documents, so users may happen to edit the same part of the document at the same time under unconstrained collaborative editing. Therefore, the major challenge of supporting responsive and unconstrained cooperative editing is the management of multiple streams of concurrent activities so that document consistency can be maintained in the event of conflicts.

There are three consistency problems in collaborative editing systems: (1) *convergence*, (2) *causality preservation*, and (3) *intention preservation* [12]. Some algorithms[7, 10, 11] are proposed to resolve consistency problem in collaborative text/graphic editing systems, but these algorithms cannot be used directly in collabo-

M. Li et al. (Eds.): GCC 2003, LNCS 3032, pp. 242–246, 2004.

rative image editing systems. In this paper, we briefly present algorithms used to achieve consistency maintenance and group undo in CIMES.

The rest of this paper is organized as follows. In section 2, image operation representation issues is discussed and a distributed image operation algorithm is presented. Then the image operation undo/redo algorithm is given. Our work is compared with others in Section 3. A short conclusion and further works are given in Section 4.

2 Distributed Image Editing and Undo Algorithm

2.1 Image Operation Representation and Boolean Calculations

Image operations can be described as a drawing primitive: *Draw[S]*, where S is a set of pixels within the editing region. An image operation O is associated with a *Image Context*, denoted as *BC[O]*. The initial image Context is denoted as BC_0. The set of S's corresponding pixel on BC is denoted as *BS*, called background pixel set.

Definition 1. Image Operation Representation (BOR): Operation O is represented as a quadruple, denoted as <OI, SI, SV, S>, which represents Operation ID, Site ID, State vector and the set of colored pixels influenced by the operation.

Many approaches can be used to represent the S, such as run-length encoding, block encoding and quad-tree encoding. We only record the operation-image (S) for each operation but not record the previous image (BS) before executing the operation. Since the S usually contains one color, and the previous image may contain hundreds of colors, obviously space cost can be greatly reduced.

The state vector (SV) [5] is used to represent the relation among operations. The operations can be regarded as an operation sequence under state vector structure. CIMES maintains a history buffer (HB) for preserving executed operations at each site. The list of operations in HB is represented as HB = $[O_1,O_2 ,\ldots,O_n]$. All operations in HB satisfy the total ordering relationship: $O_1>O_2>\ldots>O_n$.

Given two operation O_1 and O_2 with an overlapping relation as shown in Fig. 1-a and 1-b, we define three types of Boolean calculations.

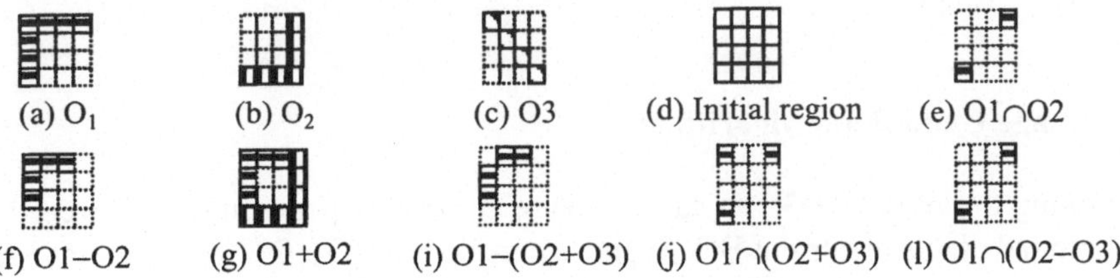

Fig. 1. Examples of join, addition and subtract calculations

Definition 2. Join Calculation "∩" (Fig. 1-e): Given two operations O_1 and O_2, $O_1 \cap O_2$ is the subset of $S[O_1]$ which is overlapping with $S[O_2]$.

Definition 3. Subtract Calculation "−" (Fig. 1-f): Given two operations O_1 and O_2, O_1-O_2 is the subset of $S[O_1]$ which is not overlapping with $S[O_2]$.

Definition 4. Add Calculation "+" (Fig. 1-g): Given two operations O_1 and O_2, O_1+O_2 is the union of $S[O_2]$ and a subset of $S[O_1]$ which is not overlapping with $S[O_2]$.

Suppose BC_0 is the result of operation O_0 and HB = $[O_1, O_2, \ldots, O_n]$. The image context of O_n, $BC[O_n]$, is the result of the orderly addition of O_0. For any operation O_i in HB, following properties depict the operation relation among operations.

Property 1. $O_i^V = O_i - O_{i+1} - \ldots - O_n$. O_i^V is the visible part of O_i in the current BC. O_i^V is equivalent to an image operation drawing the visible part of O_i in current BC. If $O_i^V = \phi$, then O_i is invisible.

Property 2. $O_i^B = BC_0 \cap O_i + O_1 \cap O_i + \ldots + O_{i-1} \cap O_i$. O_i^B is equivalent to an image operation drawing the background pixels of O_i in current BC.

Property 3. $O_i^{BV} = O_i^B \cap O_i^V$. O_i^{BV} is the part of background pixels of O_i, which is visible in current BC, as if O_i was undone. O_i^{BV} is an inversed operation of O_i and equivalent to O_i's undo operation of in current BC.

2.2 Distributed Image Editing Algorithm

As mentioned above, an HB is maintained at each site to preserve image operations executed at this site. Operations are first inserted into HB total orderly and then executed by distributed image editing algorithm.

For a local image operation (O_i), it is generated by an editing action. The editing action usually persists a duration of time. Before the editing action complete, the intermediate result is preserved as temporary operation and not written in the current BC. After the editing action is done, the image operation is generated and inserted into HB according to total order. Then the operation's visible part (O_i^V) is calculated (according to property 1): $O_i^V = O_i - O_{i+1} - \ldots - O_n$, Where O_i is an operation executed currently, $O_{i+1} - \ldots O_n$ is operations total-orderly after O_i. Finally, current BC is updated with O_i^V and then O_i is propagated to remote sites.

When a remote editing operation is received, the operation is first inserted into HB according to total order, then the operation's visible part is calculated out and then current BC is updated.

2.3 Image Undo/Redo Algorithms

According to property 1-3, we can calculate an image operation's visible part of the background pixels in current BC. Suppose current HB=$[O_1, O_2, \ldots, O_i, \ldots, O_n]$ and an undo target operation (O_i) is selected by User1. The visible background pixels are calculated by Undo algorithm: $O_i^{BV} = O_i^B \cap O_i^V = (BC_0 \cap O_i + O_1 \cap O_i + \ldots + O_{i-1} \cap O_i) \cap (O_i - O_{i+1} - \ldots - O_n)$. Then current BC is updated by O_i^{BV} and undo effect is achieved. The redo process is similar to operation execution described in section 2.2.

Above algorithm can undo/redo any operation preserved in HB. Global and local undo scopes [1] are also supported. In local undo scope, a user can undo any operation performed by himself. While in global undo scope, he can undo any operation performed by any user.

3 Compared to Related Works

Most of existing collaborative graphics editing systems are object-based, such as GRACE[11], NetDraw[8], and etc. In object-based systems, graphic objects are represented by attributes. Operations act on the objects by modifying the attributes of the objects. While in image-based systems, operations act directly on the drawing area by modifying the pixels' color in the drawing area. Therefore, algorithms in object-based collaborative editing systems, such as operation transformation [3, 5, 10] and multi-version algorithm [6, 11], cannot be used in image-based collaborative editing systems.

Wscrawl[13] and WE-MET[14] are systems similar to collaborative image editing systems. WScrawl is a multi-user sketchpad based on a centralized architecture that leverages on X-windows. There is no concurrent conflicting problem in Wscrawl. WE-MET is an image-based whiteboard tool used in local network environment. It does not consider the concurrent conflicting problem. To the best of our knowledge, there are no other systems supporting collaborative image editing on the Internet.

Some undo solutions have been proposed to resolve the undo problem in text-based and object-based collaborative editing systems [2, 9]. These solutions based on a simple operation-inversion approach, which is suitable for the text and object-based collaborative editing systems. With a simple operation-inversion approach in the image-based editing systems, such as MS Painter, the previous image of an operation should be preserved in order to achieving the inversion of the operation, while the previous image is no need to be preserved in our approach. Obviously the space costs is reduced compared to simple operation-inverse approach.

4 Conclusions

In this paper, we briefly present a collaborative image editing systems on the Internet. A transformation algorithm is proposed to achieve consistency preservation in image-based collaborative editing systems. This approach minimizes the cost for preserving, displaying and executing the image operations. A group undo approach is also proposed to realize undo/redo facility in collaborative editing environment.

The system and algorithms proposed in this paper are the beginning of our research in the collaborative image editing area, but not a complete solution. There are still some issues need to be studied further, such as optional locking and conflicting locking mechanism, how to realizing group intentions. Supporting more complicated editing operations (similar to image operations in PhotoShop) is another future work.

References

1. D. Chen and C. Sun. Undo Any Operation in Collaborative Graphics Editing Systems. In Proceedings of ACM 2001 Conference on Supporting Group Work. Boulder, Sep. 2001. Boulder, Colorado, USA. p.197-206.

2. R. Choudhary and P. Dewan. A general multi-user undo/redo model. In Proc. of European Conference on Computer Supported Work, Oct 1995. p.231-246.
3. A.H. Davis, et al. Generalizing operational transformation to the standard general markup language. Proceedings of ACM CSCW, Nov, 2002. New Orleans, USA. p.58 - 67.
4. X. Duan-Qing and C. Chun, Design and Implementation of A Digital Prepress System Based on the Unification Technology of Four-Color and Special-Color Separation. Chinese Journal of Computer Aided Design and Computer Graphics, 2000. **12**(2): p. 96-100. In Chinese.
5. C.A. Ellis and S.J. Gibbs. Concurrency control in groupware systems. In Proceedings of the ACM SIGMOD Conference on Management of Data, May 1989. Seattle, WA, USA. p.399-407.
6. T.P. Moran, et al., Some design principles of sharing in Tivoli, a whiteboard meeting support tool, In Groupware for Real-time Drawing: A Designer's guide, S. Greenberg, S. Hayne, and R. Rada, Editors. 1995, McGraw-Hill. p. 24-36.
7. E.R. Pedersen, et al. Tivoli: An electronic whiteboard for informal workgroup meetings. In Proc. of ACM INTERCHI'93 Conference on Human Factors in Computing Systems, April 1993. p.391-398.
8. D. Qian and M.D. Gross. Collaborative Design with NetDraw. In Proceedings of Computer Aided Architectural Design Futures '99, 1999.
9. M. Ressel and R. Gunzenhauser. Reducing the problems of group undo. In Proceedings of ACM Conference on Supporting Group Work, Nov. 1999. Phoenix, USA. p.131-139.
10. M. Ressel, et al. An integrating, transformation-directed approach to concurrency control and undo in group editors. In Proceedings of ACM Conference on Computer Supported Cooperative Work, Nov. 1996. New York, USA. p.288-297.
11. C. Sun and D. Chen, Consistency Maintenance in Real-Time Collaborative Graphics Editing Systems. ACM Transactions on Computer-Human Interaction, 2002. **9**(1): p. 1-41.
12. C. Sun, et al., Achieving convergence, causality-preservation, and intention-preservation in real-time cooperative editing systems. ACM Transaction on Computer-Human Interaction, 1998. **5**(1): p. 63-108.
13. B. Wilson, WSCRAWL 2.0: A Shared whiteboard based on X-Windows, In Designing Groupware for Real Time Drawing, S. Greenberg, S. Hayne, and R. Rada, Editors. 1994, McGraw Hill.
14. C. Wolf, et al. WE-MET (Window Environment-Meeting Enhancement Tools). In Proceedings of CHI'91, 1991. New Orleans, LA, USA. p.441-442.

Campus Grid and Its Application

Zhiqun Deng and Guanzhong Dai

College of Automation,
Northwestern Polytechnical University, Xi'an 710072, P.R China
zhiqundeng@tom.com

Abstract. This paper discusses the application of grid computing to the aircraft design as well as the Globus-based architecture of the test bed called campus grid. The practical scheduling policies that schedule the jobs according to different tiers are presented.

1 Introduction

Grid computing is an emerging infrastructure with a great power to solve problems in many fields. The grid provides flexible, secure, coordinated resource sharing among dynamic collections of individuals, institutions and resources (virtual organizations, VOs) [1]. It can be found that enterprise grids enable multiple departments to share computing resources in a cooperative way [2]. Enterprise grids, sometimes called campus grids, typically contain resources from multiple administrative domains, but are located in the same campus geographic location.

In the aircraft industry, most problems are time-consuming and the cost is extremely high. The coordination is therefore quite important in this field. We are building a test bed of grid computing, a campus grid, to coordinately solve the problems of the aircraft design. The campus grid is not a general grid computing environment but an infrastructure to serve for all of the faculty and students in the same research field in the university. We are establishing a prototype grid-enabled infrastructure. The test bed constructed is not a large scale one, but it can be extended to the large scale just like the development of the Internet.

The campus grid is to enable the coordinated use of distributed computing resources in all departments of the university. Many departments have high performance computers that are not to open to the outside users. For example, Aerofoil Research Center, Institute of Structural Strength and Research Center of Aerodynamics in the aircraft department have special and expensive computers. And other departments possess new high performance computers. As we know that, coordination of the aircraft design is very important. So we are building the campus grid test bed in order to integrate these computing resources to support the aircraft design.

The campus grid is to develop the necessary middleware that allows to access computing resources, run simulations on these resources based on optimized communication. Secondly, it is to set up a test bed based on Globus Toolkit, to develop campus grid application middleware, for example the scheduler. And the third it is to deliver non-trivial qualities of service, for example the aircraft design, computational fluid dynamics (CFD), etc.

M. Li et al. (Eds.): GCC 2003, LNCS 3032, pp. 247–250, 2004.

2 Campus Grid: The Application of Test Bed to the Aircraft Design

2.1 Architecture of the Campus Grid

There are four tiers in the architecture (Fig.1). The first tier is the campus grid center with high performance computers, supercomputers. The second tier is the department tier, which includes the departments' supercomputers, PC clusters, instruments, and so on. These devices belong to different departments and institutes, and are administrated by different domains. The third tier is referred to the servers belonging to different research groups. And the fourth tier is the user group.

There exists an agent in the second and the third tier. Its function is job scheduling, enhanced security checking, and so on. We call them the "department agent and research group agent".

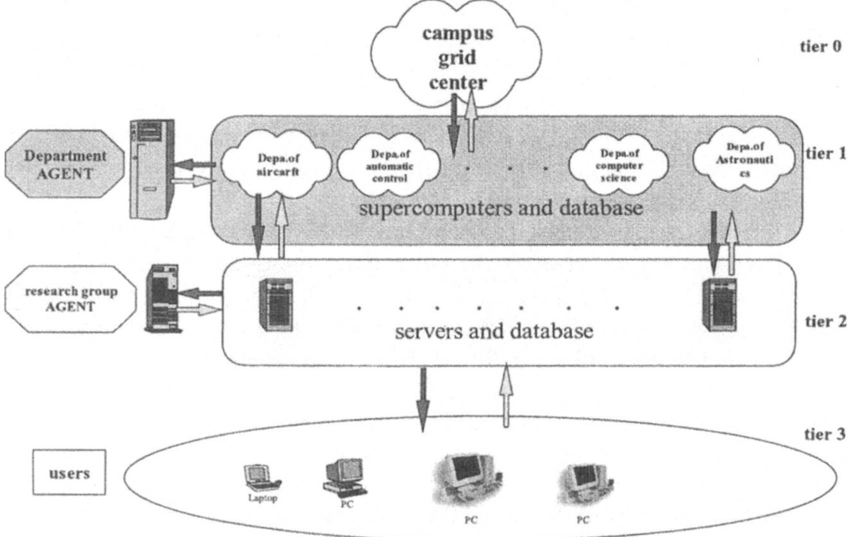

Fig. 1. The architecture of the campus grid

The campus grid adopts the Globus Toolkit [3] because it is a de facto standard of grid computing. The Globus Toolkit focuses on the following areas: resource management, data management, security, and information services.

The Globus-based architecture of campus grid is as follows (Fig.2). It is simple but practical and easy to develop.

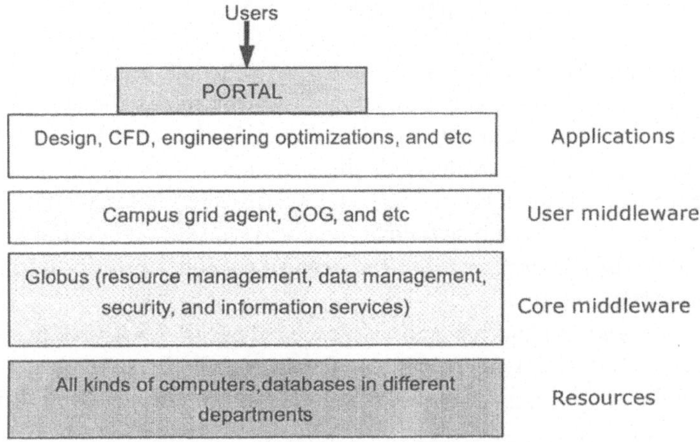

Fig. 2. Globus-based architecture of the campus grid

2.2 Coordinated Design of the Aircraft

Based on the campus grid, the coordinated aircraft design can work on the dynamic, multi-institutional virtual organizations such as departments or research groups (Fig.3).

The researchers in the aircraft design can be considered as the members of virtual organization (V.O.). Aircraft structural design, aerodynamics tests (or aerodynamics simulation) and structural strength analysis are three basic procedures. All of them need high performance computers to solve problems, and the computation is complex and the amount of data is huge. And they all need the data to be visualized.

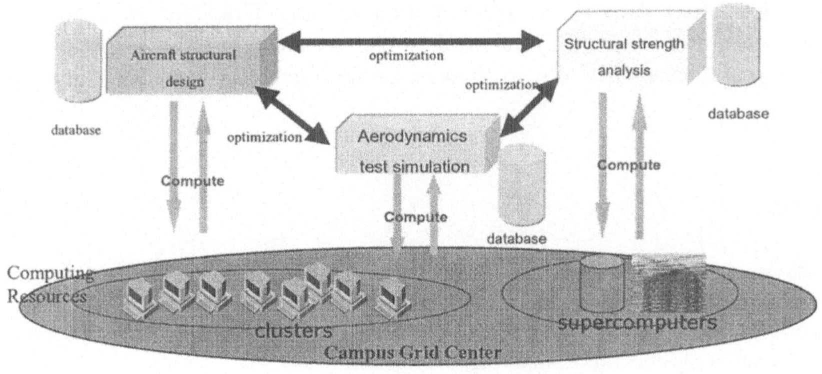

Fig. 3. Coordinated design of the aircraft

2.3 Scheduling Policies of Campus Grid

In the campus grid, in order to simplify the job scheduling and save the scheduling time, there are two levels of job scheduling. The first one is the departments' scheduler, which is mainly to schedule the departments' jobs. And the second one is the group scheduler, which is to dispatch the end-users' jobs to the group servers or higher departments' computers.

The scheduling policies are as follows:

- *Priority of the organization*: the department jobs' priority is superior to the group research jobs'.
- *The urgency*: if the job needs to be handled as quickly as possible, as it is once authorized, it can be processed superior to others.
- *The fee for the job*: if the job is not charged or charged later, it is sure to be handled later.
- *The time to be used*: if the job is time-consuming, and the computers are all busy, it should be processed later.
- *The load of computers*: according to every computer's load, the scheduler will dispatch the jobs.

3 Other Problems and the Future Work

The first problem is security. The aircraft design is different from the other fields and the security is the most important. The second problem is the scalability of the architecture. If other applications join it, they should be considered in the later development.

In the future, there are some problems to be solved in the campus grid, for example, the performance of grid, better scheduler, better user interfaces, etc.

Acknowledgements. This work is supported by the Graduate Innovation Seed Foundation of Northwestern Polytechnical University under contract Z20030051. The authors are grateful to Mr. Daowu Zhou of Cambridge University for some helpful discussions.

References

1. Ian Foster, Carl Kesselman, Steven Tuecke, The Anatomy of the Grid Enabling Scalable Virtual Organizations, www.globus.org/research/papers/anatomy.pdf.
2. Sun Microsystems Inc. Sun Cluster Grid Architecture – A technical white paper describing the foundation of Sun Grid Computing, May 2002, http://wwws.sun.com/software/grid/SunClusterGridArchitecture.pdf.
3. Globus toolkit, http://www.globus.org.

The Realization Methods of PC Cluster Experimental Platform in Linux

Jiang-ling Zhang [1], Shi-jue Zheng [1,2], and Yang Qing[2]

[1] School of Computer Science and Technology, Huazhong University of Science and Technology, Wuhan, Hubei 430074, P.R.China
Raidkick@263.net, zhengsj@ccnu.edu.cn
[2] Department of Computer Science, Central China Normal University, Wuhan, Hubei 430079, P.R.China
qingy@ccnu.edu.cn

Abstract. This paper introduces the basic concept of PC Cluster , tells user how to make the experimental platform of PC Cluster with inexpensive PC machines using Platform LSF 5, describes the method of making PC Cluster environment hardware, setting PC Cluster system, and adjusting network monitor and examination in linux.

1 Introduction

In the last decade, workstation have spread considerably as a productive, versatile and costefficient platform for the data processing needs on user's desktops. Furthermore, new concepts emerged from the integration of individual workstations through Local Area Network (LANS). Within the LAN based Client/Server computing model, clients demand the services of individual servers for particular tasks using a network. As a consequence, the computational load is distributed onto different, independent components. This model provides the possibility to adapt and scale the performance of individual system components to specific demands. We use Linux RedHat7.3 operating system, and adopt the software of Platform corporation—LSF5 (Load Sharing Facility) building a PC cluster with the combination of five inexpensive PCs and Ethernet. We develop the PC cluster of environment of imitate real in laboratory in order to many students can make up some simple PC cluster and understanding the methods of principle.

Platform is the world's leading distributed computing software provider, with desktop to Grid solutions that allow organizations to dramatically improve time to market and quality of results, while maximizing their I.T. investment. Based on a new high performance, grid-enabled architecture, Platform LSF 5 supports multiple plug-in schedulers, providing unlimited extensibility and writing customizable plug-in schedulers to meet site-specific business policies and eliminate the maintenance overhead. A new Resource Leasing Model provides a single system image across all clusters so users administrators can easily manage resource sharing policies across your Enterprise Grid. A customizable Web-based interface facilitates access to users

M. Li et al. (Eds.): GCC 2003, LNCS 3032, pp. 251–254, 2004.

distributed computing resources from any location, via the Internet. Administrators can manage clusters and resources online, and users can submit, control and monitor their workload. Dynamically manage users resources based on easy to administer workload policies. Network-centric queues support multiple policies, while new Resource Allocation Limits provide you with flexibility in defining resource utilization across the enterprise. Platform LSF 5 controls the job mix and resource usage between groups, ensuring optimal resource utilization. With its open, plug-in architecture, Platform LSF 5 seamlessly integrates with third party applications and heterogeneous technology platforms. Platform LSF 5 supports both 32-bit and 64-bit versions of all major UNIX platforms, including Sun Solaris, HP-UX, IBM AIX, Compaq Tru64 UNIX, SGI IRIX Linux for Intel and Alpha Mac OS Supports Microsoft Windows NT, and Microsoft Windows 2000 workstations Cray, Fujitsu, NEC and other supercomputers product names are the trademarks of their respective owners. According to these characteristics of LSF 5, we choose Platform LSF 5 with a working platform of PC cluster in our experiments.

2 Configuration

For our project we decide to build a cluster from scratch using 5 inexpensive PC machines(Figure1 Omitted).We use 200 MHZ processors, 64M memory per PC. Each PC has a 1.2G hard disk, 1.44 inch floppy drive, 24X CD-ROM,10M PCI network card and a STVG/1M video card, which is required for the PC to boot properly and can be used to monitor the PC if needed. The PCs are all connected using a TP-LINK 100M HUB. The facilities are assembled in a box. A keyboard ,a mouse and a 14 inch color display are shared in the PC cluster. One PC , called the front end, has a special role in the cluster: it contains the home file systems of the users , the compilers , the message-passing libraries and so on. Simulations are started and monitored from this machine. The front end is also used to log in to the nodes for maintenance purposes.

Each PC is also referred to as a node. PC cluster consists of one master node, four client nodes. The Master node is acted as the cluster's console and gateway. The master node diagnoses PCs and should boot-up by itself, so that the PC cluster will behave as a complete parallel machine. The master node assigns the tasks to the client nodes, and monitors the execution of the tasks. The four client nodes are the major platform for computation. Users can submit jobs to each client nodes separately or use parallel programming languages, such as Parallel Message Passing (MPI) and Parallel Virtual Machine (PVM), to carry out simulation tasks.

The operating system of this cluster is Linux RedHat 7.3. For master node, the installations are complete. That means every packages in RedHat 7.3 distribution are installed. For other client nodes, the installations have been minimized only a few necessary packages been installed. The IP address of each node is given in turn:202.114.39.2 ~ 202.114.39.6.The netmask, the default gateway are 255.255.255.0 and 202.114.32.1 respectively .The IP address of primary namesever is 202.114.39.2.

3 Experiments

3.1 The Experiment Simulating File Striping

In the terms of the idea of File Striping, we completed the experiment of data storage in PC cluster in Linux. The content of the experiment is as follow: set client and server, and when they build socket connection, the server choose the file to be stored based on the application, then strip the file based on the memory of the nodes, and determine the path to store the stripped file. The key practice is network communication programming to realize File Stripping.

Based on our hardware platform and the File Stripping principle, the experiment need to solve three modules.

1.In order to build log file, it is necessary to choose suitable data structure for file.

We choose Linear_List to record file, for file is linear. And it needs to move large amount of elements in Linear_List when inserting or deleting data, and the storage of large-scale data is dynamic, for example, many data are just interim and they should be modified or cleared finally, so it is suitable to select LinkList structure as file structure. The file data structure is as follow (Omitted)

2. Select the file to be stored and divide the file up, in the terms of the memory in cluster and the requirement of user.

Based on I/O, select the file in linux and open it, the first PC sends requirement to other fours, and the other send the information of their free memories. Finally divide the file into blocks in the terms of the free memories.

3.Network communication programming is to store the subfiles into several PCs and realize the simulation of File Stripping.

In order to access to data parallel, it is necessary to adopt the parallel server, in other words, to create subprocess to handle the requirement of client, in stead of the main process. It uses send (int sockfd, void *buf,int len,int flags) and recv (int sockfd, void *buf,int len,int flags) to transfer information. The part of code for transferring subfiles is as follow: (Omitted)

3.2 CPU Load Application

In the process of loading balance, it is a key step to get the resources of each node in the whole cluster and their distribution. The experiment's mainly function is to check out the type of host computer, the number of CPU, physical units and the special resources connecting with host computers. Here, we use C language to test the name of host computers, their types, their memorizes and the number of CPU as well as the special resource of each host computer. (The result of the program's execution has been Omitted)

There are 5 hosts with more than 50MB total memory. The result shows that the cluster has five nodes and five CPU. The name of each host computer is Localhost.cluster1, Localhost.cluster2, Localhost.cluster3, Localhost.cluster4, Localhost.cluster5. Their type are Intel200, their physical memory are 64M, the number of CPU in each node is one, and the resources are available. In such cluster, the use of cycling can resolve the problem of loading balance. Although the other algorithms can be used, the use of cycling is best in the terms of high performance.

3.3 Real-Time Job

In our cluster, we use client-server mode and control each node by the commands and functions of LSF. We mainly use LSF Base of LSF and NFS to allow user to access the file system of long-distance computers easily. Here, we use C language and the relative commands and functions to design the following experiments (Figure 2 Omitted)

The dispatching of real-time job The requirement of the experiment is to choose the most suitable computer host to run our proposing job. The condition is to sort the nodes in cluster by memory from large to small, and sort again by the number of users from small to large. The result is "The best host is <host D>", showing that host D have the optimal resource configuration. In the cluster, the experiment realize such function as obtaining the dynamic computing resources, sorting the computer hosts based on each kind of resource, making exact choice in the terms of the dynamic resources and jobs' condition, and sending jobs to the most reasonable computer host. Master LIM gather all nodes' loading information and loading vector, including the latest length of CPU queue, the rate of memorizers' use and the number of user, and send the information to other nodes, and then sort nodes based on the information, finally determine which node executes the job.

4 Conclusion

Our work focuses now on the implementation of PC cluster real applications. The aim was to develop a compiler that uses directly and efficiently the architecture features of inexpensive PC cluster. We have also evaluated the impact of the parallel constructs on the execution time and obtained that it is negligible when the computation part of the algorithm is more important than the communications.

References

1. Kai Hwang & Zhiwei Xu: Scalable Parallel Computing, Technology, Architecture, Programming, Mc Graw Hill Press,(1998). US
2. S.Shang and K.Hwang.: Distributed Hardwired Barrier Synchronization for Scalable Multiprocessor Cluster: IEEE Trans. Parallel and Distributed Computing System, June (1996).591-605
3. D. Juvin, J.L. Basille, H. Essafi, J.Y. Latil, Sympati2.: A 1.5D Processor array for image applications, EUSIPCO Signal processing IV: heories and applications (1988).311–314.

Coarse-Grained Distributed Parallel Programming Interface for Grid Computing*

Yongwei Wu, Qing Wang, Guangwen Yang, and Weiming Zheng

Department of Computer Science and Technology,
Tsinghua University, Beijing, 100084, China

Abstract. In this paper, a practical coarse-grained distributed parallel programming interface for grid computing (PI4GC) is introduced. It provides a group of generic and abstract function prototypes with well-specified semantics. PI4GC is an MPI-like interface plus high-level parallel tasking over grid. Following its specification, users could couple multiple computing tools distributed over grid to run complex computing problems. We first describe the motivations of PI4GC and related works. Then its specification is put forward in detail. At last, implementation of PI4GC over OGSA is also discussed simply.

1 Introduction

Grid computing has drawn so much attention within and outside the academic circles. Currently, the most popular grid middleware infrastructure, the Globus toolkit [2,3], by and large provides the basic, low-level services, such as security, authentication, job launching, directory service, etc. Although such services are an absolute necessity especially provided as a common platform and abstractions across different machines in the Grid for interoperability purposes (as such it could be said that Globus is a GridOS), there still tends to exist a large gap between the Globus services and the programming-level abstractions we are commonly used to.

We try to put forward a coarse-grained distributed parallel programming interface for grid computing (PI4GC). As a MPI-like programming model, PI4GC provides a group of generic and abstract function prototypes with well-specified semantics. It supports high-level dynamic parallel tasking over grid too. Through PI4GC, users could couple multiple different computing tools distributed over multiple heterogeneous machines to run practical complex computing applications.

In this paper, the motivations of PI4GC and related works are discussed in section 2. Then we describe the specification of PI4GC. At last in section 4, simple implementation of PI4GC over OGSA is discussed.

* This Work is supported by NSFC (60373004) and China Postdoctoral Foundation

M. Li et al. (Eds.): GCC 2003, LNCS 3032, pp. 255–258, 2004.

2 Motivations of PI4GC and Related Works

In order to reduce the number of message communication between grid nodes, we must modify the applications adjust to the relatively poor latency and bandwidth introduced by the intermachine communication over the Internet, such as SF Express [4] project based on MPICH-G2[5]. In fact, this is very difficult. So the low-level parallel computation based on frequent massage passing between the grid nodes is still a rather unrealistic, and grid enabled coarse-grained distributed parallel computing is quietly emphasized much more and more at present.

Another, Sophistication of scientific and engineering computing problems increasingly also requires complex system, relevant to several computing tools at same time. As a result, related computational procedures not only need to be run by coordinating several complementary technologies but also by integrating several extremely powerful computing platforms in a grid system. PSE[7] and Grid-RPC[6] are two typical classed in these projects. The former is designed for the computation of chemical problems and not general enough for other applications. Grid-RPC model can not confirm the load balance for the grid. And users must point out the computing nodes and computing tool before enabling individual applications.

Although PI4GC is a MPI-like programming interface, it specially supports coarse-grained grid computing. As a general computing interface over grid for various applications, PI4GC is also transparent for users greatly.

3 PI4GC Specification

PI4GC aims to be an interface general enough to work for most grid computing environments. It is specified after studying user/programming interfaces of existing computing tools and grid-enabled computing interfaces. The PI4GC is designed for programmer to access multiple compliant heterogeneous computation tools over grid at the same time, and moreover, make coordinated use of these computing tools, therefore we should supply for the programmer a mechanism to discover, secure access and flexibly use these resources. So come the following specifications. The specification of PI4GC is expressed in following Java-based format: ClassName::FunctionName.

a) Service Discovering and Selecting

Since the service information over a practical grid system is always changing dynamic, the GCluster::FindService interface is designed for getting the required service list from a famous UIID site. Another parameter for this interface is a query string which specify user required service catalogs or names.

b) GCluster and The Task Class

They are two fundamental client components of the PI4GC. GCluster class is used to manage the computing nodes over grid environment into a global cluster and the user can use these nodes with the GCluster class just like they use computing nodes in a real cluster system. The task class is a task description class file written by the PI4GC users. This is similar with the MPI program, but there are significant differences between them. The subtasks of MPI program are different running processes on remote nodes, but the subtasks of PI4GC are just different running threads in local node.

c) GCluster Initializing and Finalizing

We use the GCluster::Initialize interface to build a connection between the user client and the specific hosts, and the GCluster::Finalize interface to release the connection.

d) Task Submitting and Reporting

Just like the MPI user call *mpirun* to start an MPI program, our PI4GC client user call the GCluster::Submit interface to submit a computing task, and the GCluster::Cancel interface to cancel the task. The TaskListener::ReceiveMessage interface is used to receive reporting message from the executing task.

In following paragraphs, we will introduce the designed task interface for user to build an MPI-like computing program for practical appliance. These interfaces are only used in the task class.

e) Communication between subtasks

The communication between different subtasks is a time consuming procedure in a distributed computing system. The performance of the communications will influence the total response time of a distributed computing program. For the convenience of large-scale computing application, we design two different types of transfer interfaces, one is for the small granularity data transfer and the other is for the data file based on the gridftp protocol. The Task::SendValue and Task::ReceiveValue interfaces are used to transfer small data value and the Task::SendFile, Task::ReceiveFile and Task::BroadCast are used for large data file transfer.

f) Atom task executing

The PI4GC is designed for coarse-grained parallel programs, so the atom task of a task class means one call of the remote software. The atom task control interface provides the user a way to send the input file to remote node, start computing and get the result file from the remote node. The use can use the Task::Upload and Task::Download interface to upload the execute file and download the result file. To execute an atom task, you should call the Task::Execute interface.

g) Status Report

It is necessary for user to monitor the executing progress of a task or probe the error of a task in grid system. So the Task::ReportStatus and Task:ErrorReport interfaces are designed.

4 Implement PI4GC over OGSA

Open Grid Service Architecture (OGSA)[8] has been recognized as a uniform standard for grid computing, it encapsulates all computing resources in grid service, which is also a web service. We have implemented PI4GC over OGSA. Figure 1 shows its architecture.

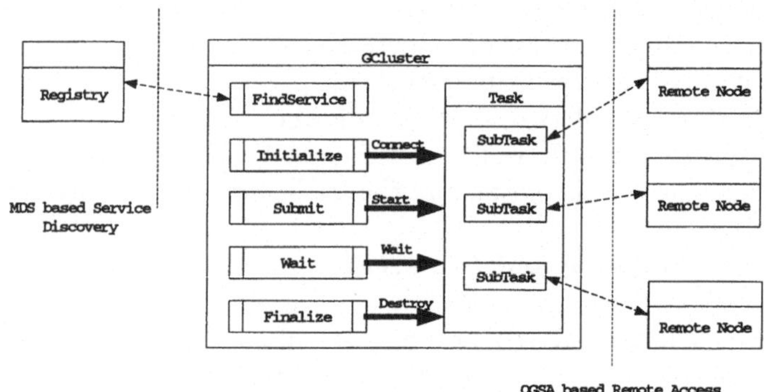

Fig. 1. PI4GC over OGSA

5 Conclusion and Future Work

In this paper, a general coarse-grained distributed parallel programming interface for grid computing, PI4GC, is introduced. One of our purposes is to present a preliminary work for the standardizing programming interface of coarse-grained computation over grid.

In the next step, we will try to refine PI4GC in order to be fit for more complex computing problems. Another, many researchers agree with the fact that frameworks incorporation CORBA service will be very influential on the design of grid environments in the future. For this, we would like to investigate on the usage of CORBA technology to enhance some features of PI4GC.

References

1. Foster, I., Kesselman, C., Tuecke, S.: The Anatomy of the Grid: Enabling Scalable Virtual Organization. International J. Supercomputer Applications **15(3)** (2001)
2. Foster, I., Kesselman, C.: The Physiology of the Grid: An Open Grid Services Architecture for Distributed Systems Integration. http://www.globus.org/ (2002)
3. Foster, I.: What is the Grid? A Three Point Checklist. Grid Today **1(6)** (2002)
4. Johnston, W., Gannon, D., Nitzberg, B.: Grids as Production Computing Environments: Theengineering aspects of nasa's information power grid. In proc. Eight IEEE International Symposium on High Performance Distributed Computing (1999)
5. Karonis, N., Toonen, B., Foster, I.: MPICH-G2: A Grid-Enabled Implementation of the Message Passing Interface. Journal of Parallel and Distributed Computing **63(5)** (2003) 551–563
6. Nakada, H., Matsuoka, S., Seymour, K.: GridRPC: A Remote Procedure Call API for Grid Computing. Lecture notes in computer science **2536** (2002) 274–278
7. Baraglia, R., Laforenza, D., Lagana, A., A Web-based Metacomputing Problem-Solving Environment for Complex Applications. Proceedings of Grid Computing 2000. (2000) 111–122
8. Tuecke, S., Czajkowski, K., Foster, I. , et.al.: Open Grid Services Infrastructure (OGSI) Version 1.0. Global Grid Forum Draft Recommendation. (2003).

User Guided Parallel Programming Platform

Yong Liu, Xinda Lu, and Qianni Deng

Computer science and engineer department of Shanghai Jiao Tong University
ly_sjtu@sjtu.edu.cn

Abstract. Parallel computing is now become a widely used solution of the complex problem in science and engineer fields. On the same time, it brings about two big challenges: I) how to simplify the sophisticate job of coding parallel program II) how to find an exact way to change the sequential code to parallel code. This article tries to face these challenges by coming out a new idea: User guided parallelized policy.

1 Introduction

The reason why the situation of the parallel program is very sorry for a long time we consider, lies in two major aspect: I) parallel programming is more complex than sequential programming by nature. As we known, parallel programming involves many paradigms and modes, each mode also involves message passing between the process or the sharing memory, and also, message passing has different modes, such as peer to peer, broad cast, etc; message passing also brings about the issue of the transformation of the different data types. II) Comparing to the sequential programming, parallel programming lacks of the software environment support, such as some libraries and an integrated IDE.

We come out a new semi-automatic way, named **user guided policy**: at first, the programmer select the parallel paradigm from the list, secondly, go through the configure wizard including several steps, by which customize the parallel paradigm, and set the parameters, then a configure file (based on xml standard) is generated. After that, submit the sequential code. The platform generate the skeleton code [1]according to the configure file and embed the sequential code into the skeleton code, hence the parallelizing process is accomplished (graph 1).

2 Philosophy of the Design

The core of the user guided policy includes: skeleton code and configure wizard.

2.1 Skeleton Code

As we known, there are several parallel paradigms mainly used in parallel programming: a) master slave b) Divide and conquer c) pipeline d) phase parallel e) work pool. We suppose that our target parallel programming includes one or many

[1] This article funded by national nature science fund NO. 60173031

M. Li et al. (Eds.): GCC 2003, LNCS 3032, pp. 259–261, 2004.

implementations of the paradigms. We divide our program into many applets, each applet has one but at most one such paradigm implementation (graph 2).

I) **Comparison** of the three method (chart 1):

Method	implementation	usability	parallel grain	effect
Full automatic	hard	easy	fine grain	medium
full automatic	hard	easy	coarse grain	good
full handed	medium	hard	coarse grain	bad

(chart 1)

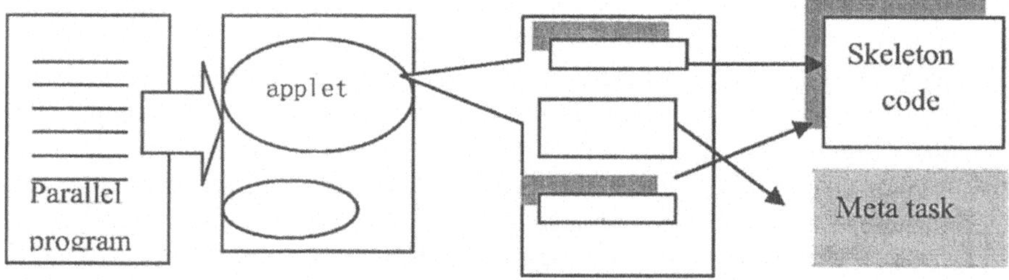

(graph 2) Skeleton code and meta-task

We analyze the applets then find out: i) each applet includes codes connected with parallel logics and codes connected with business logics ii) as to certain parallel paradigm, the location, construct, and the operation of the former always obey some rules, we can abstract these code into skeleton code, and encapsulate the code only connected with the business logic into meta-task, by this way, we decouple the parallel logic and the parallel logics and the business logics, it is probably for us to give the skeleton code template for the several widely used parallel paradigms to the

programmers, then the programmer customize the skeleton code and give the sequential code,Which will be embedded in the skeleton to form the final program?

2.2 Configure Wizard

Programmer customize the skeleton code by going through the configure wizard. We take the master slave mode as example to explain what is configure wizard. Master process divides the task into many sub tasks then dispatches them to the slaves, then merge work results. According to the paradigm we can give the skeleton code template as following:

```
if(this is master) {
//load data from data source
//data type transformation
//divide the data by process number
for(each slaves ){
send data} //send data
for(each slaves ){//collect the results receive data
from the slave }
deal with the result ; }//embeds the meta-task
```

In the real world, to entertain the application we need to adapter our skeleton code, then we need such information as below:

a) Where to get the data? From data file or from database?
b) How to cast the data type?
c) By which policy does the master divide the data: evenly, or by the power of each slaves?

The programmer should answer all these questions by going through the configure wizard, the answer will be write into a xml file (configure file)

Platform then could customize the skeleton code according to the configure file.

2.3 Meta-task

We encapsulate the code disconnected with parallel logics into meta-task. Meta-task is strongly connected with the business logics and has nothing to do with the parallel communication. In the former case, the slave's operation on the received data is a typical meta-task. Meta-task only given by the programmer, and it must be a sequential program.

3 Summary

This article introduces the user guided policy for parallelizing in detail, including the core of the policy: skeleton code, meta-task. This method can support the programmer building the parallel application rapidly, conveniently, and effectively. Until today we have implemented a parallel programming platform using the parallelizing policy. Based on the platform, we have built some parallel applications to help resolving the real word problems.

References

1. Albert Y. Zomaya, Senior Member, IEEE, and Yee-Hwei Teh, Observation on Using Genetic Algorithms for Dynamics for Dynamic Load-Balancing; IEEE; 2001.3 Theuns Verwoerd,
2. MPI : A Message-Passing Interface Standard, MPI Forum, June 12, 1995

A High-Performance Intelligent Integrated Data Services System in Data Grid[1]

Bin Huang [1], Xiaoning Peng [2], Nong Xiao [1], and Bo Liu [1]

[1] School of Computer, National University of Defense Technology,
410073 Changsha, China
hb415@163.com

[2] Department of Computer Science of Huaihua College,
418008 Huaihua, China

Abstract. It is very complex and of low efficiency for grid users to access heterogeneous diverse data resources distributed over the whole wide area network. The integrated data services can implement more wide range of transparent access to data resources in Data Grid. One of the important building blocks for any Data Grid is the server which implements data services. In this paper, we describe HPIIDS which implements integrated data services and achieves more wide range of transparencies. In order to improve its performances, we emphasis on the server called DSB which provides integrated data services. The DSB bases on cluster and agent technologies. Agent-based DSB can cleverly prefetch required data, replicate them among DSBs. Multiple DSBs are formed cluster HPIIDS. Cluster-based HPIIDS implements a single entry, provides a virtual integrated storage system for users, hides distributed heterogeneous low-level data resources, and insures load balance of each server. HPIIDS architecture supporting these various scenarios, are also described.

1 Introduction

An increasing number of applications in domains such as astrophysics, geophysics, or computational neuroscience, need to archive, retrieve, and process increasing large datasets [1]. These data-intensive applications are prime candidates for Data Grid as they involve remote access and extensive computation to many data repositories. One of the core problems that any Data Grid project has to address is the heterogeneity of storage systems where data are stored. This diversity is made explicit in terms of how data sets are named and accessed in all these different systems [2]. So data services which implement uniform access to distributed data sources are the important research part and the key technology of Data Grid. We believe that a wide range of transparencies is important for data services in Data Grid.

---

[1] This paper is supported by the National Natural Science Foundation of China under the Grant No. 60203016 and No. 69933030, and the National Hi-Tech R&D 863 Program of China under the Grant No. 2002AA131010.

M. Li et al. (Eds.): GCC 2003, LNCS 3032, pp. 262–265, 2004.

One of the important building blocks for any Data Grid is the server implementing data services [1], so in this paper, focusing on the server, we adopt some approaches to implement more wide range of transparent data services called HPIIDS, in which some strategies such as cluster-based architecture and agent technologies are used to address the purpose.

In the rest of this article, we first describe in Section 2 the architecture of HPIIDS and DSB, Then in Sections 3 describe the design of cluster-based data services. We discuss agent-based intelligent data services in Section 4. Finally, conclude in Section 5.

2 HPIIDS Architecture

Adopting three-layer architecture, we designed the architecture of HPIIDS, as illustrated in Figure 1. The first layer consists of all kinds of physical storage resources and metadata resources, including all kinds of file systems, archive systems and database systems. It accesses and operates the datasets in these systems through native protocols and methods that the physical resources support. Metadata resources include data metadata, replica metadata, user metadata, access control metadata, system metadata, configuration metadata and application metadata, etc.

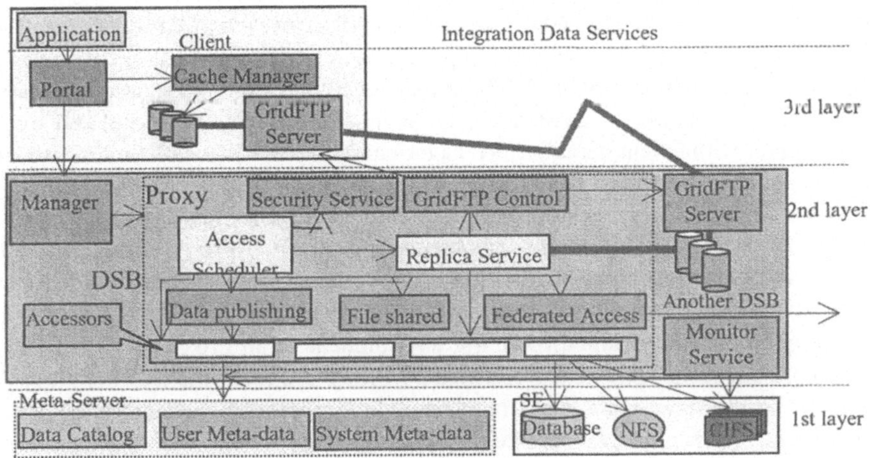

Fig. 1. The Architecture of HPIIDS

The second layer, i.e. the service layer, is the core of the system. In the layer, we abstracts the storage system distributed in Data Grid as a single virtual data object, and define common operations on the virtual data object. The major components of the layer is a server which is considered as Data Services Broker (DSB), because through it grid users can access all data services providing HPIIDS and eventually users' requests are satisfied. DSB hides from higher layers the complexities and specific mechanisms for data access which are particular to every storage system. Using the core services, DSB provide more transparencies for users and applications to manage multiple data sources and access data. DSB is designed in the light of master-slaver pattern. In DSB, slaver program called Proxy composes of *Access scheduler*, *Replica Manager*, *Data Mover*, *GridFTP Controller*, many *Accessor*, and so on.

The third layer is the interfaces called portal that our system provides for users and applications. Portal provides a single entry of all kinds of grid data resources, including uniform data access interface, uniform data and system management interface, data ordering interface, workflow and dataflow customizing interface for users. In the layer, there are also a client cache pool and its management tools, configure tools, GridFTP [3] Server.

3 Cluster-Based Data Services

In order to improve the performance of Data Services, We assume a cluster-based architecture for DSB because it uses inexpensive off-the-shelf PC components, and offers an inherently scalable aggregate I/O bandwidth, and can take advantage of existing cluster installations through double-use or upgrade of older hardware. By leveraging the high-speed communication afforded by the cluster, large files can be stored in a scalable fashion by striping the data across multiple nodes.

Each DSB is designed by adopting cluster-structure. In cluster servers, there are two types of nodes: master node and slave node. Service program also has two parts : Manager, Proxy. Manager running on master node, receive users' requests and maintain the global status of its DSB. When receiving a user's request, it creates a proxy process in a proper slave node. Other operations will be completed by that Porxy interact with Client hereafter. Manager can know the status of each slaver node and accomplishes proper load balancing and task scheduling mechanisms.

Proxy running on a slaver node achieves data replication, reading and writing according to the storage mechanism of objective data. Each Proxy is independent of manager. All communications, instructions and operations are accomplished by interaction between Proxy and clients.

Slave node not only maintain running environment of an Proxy , but also has the function of data cache. The data prefetched by Proxy and real-time data are all cached into slave node. Slave node starts high-speed transport tool to transfer the data to client's cache. Then client can operate the data object using local access mechanisms.

Multiple DSB servers can collaborate to form a federated DSB which acts like one single server and provides uniform services for data requests. A request scheduler which is placed before all DSBs implement a single entry point, and provides a virtual integrated storage system for users and hides the back DSBs' distributed property. The request scheduler also monitors DSB and its load balancing for it is the only entry of the cluster. Tasks on each DSB are dispatched by request scheduler. So it can know the status of each node inside HPIIDS and accomplishes proper load balancing mechanism to make HPIIDS has very high performance.

4 Intelligent Data Services

We adopt the agent technology to implement intelligent DSB because the data services based on agent technology has many advantages such as autonomy, responsive, proactive, objective-oriented, etc. The intelligent data services combine two aspects:

- Cleverly prefetching data

A gent-based Proxy is an intelligent program entity based on agent technologies. It can prefetch, cache data basis on some policies; redirect users' visits and other operations to other proxy in which the required data have been cached. Each Proxy in a DSB can communicate with each other, collaborate and have learning abilities, so some optimized policies can be taken to improve the data access efficiency during the information acquiring.

- Cleverly replicating data and dispatching task among DSBs

Each DSB is also intelligent and can learn from each other. By learning, more free DSBs can know the list of data which more busy DSBs often access and replicate. It can redirect users' visits and other operations to other DSB according to the distribution and frequency of data visited by users. DSBs that are busier can know the DSB whose load is the lightest by communication and then redirect client's access request to it.

5 Conclusion

In this paper, we have described HPIIDS and emphasized DSB to improve its performance. DSB utilized two technologies: cluster, agent. HPIIDS has the following many advantages such as achieving a single entry, scalable cache capacity, achieving aggregate cluster-to-cluster throughput, decreasing the data access response time for the two-layer cache is introduced, cleverly prefetch and replicate data, good failure tolerance, scalable architecture.

References

1. Keith Bell, Andrew Chien , Mario Lauria: A High-Performance Cluster Storage Server. 11 th IEEE International Symposium on High Performance Distributed Computing HPDC-11 20002 (HPDC'02).
2. Wolfgang Hoschek, Javier Jaen-Martinez, Asad Samar, Heinz Stockinger, and Kurt Stockinger: Data Management in an International Data Grid Project. In GRID, pages 77-90, 2000.
3. A. L. Chervenak, I. Foster, C. Kesselman *et al*: Data Management and Transfer in High Performance Computational Grid Environments. Parallel Computing Journal, 2002, 28 (5): 749-771.

Architecting CORBA-Based Distributed Applications[1]

Min Cao [1], Jiannong Cao [2], Geng-Feng Wu [1], and Yan-Yan Wang [3]

[1] School of Computer Engineering & Science, Shanghai University,
Shanghai 200072, China
mcao@mail.shu.edu.cn
[2] Department of Computing, Hong Kong Polytechnic University, Kowloon, Hong Kong
[3] Section of mathematics, Zhongyuan University of Technology, Zhengzhou 450002, China

Abstract. In this paper, we present a novel graph-oriented approach for architecting and modeling CORBA-based distributed applications. It provides higher-level abstractions for the architecture description of CORBA-based distributed applications. In the proposed model, the configuration of a CORBA-based distributed application is described as a logical graph separated from the programming of the constituent components of the application. It also provides more powerful support for dynamic reconfiguration and simplification of component programming.

1 Introduction

Software architecture addresses the high-level design of a software system. It plays a central role in the development and maintenance of a software system. Software architecture description defines the structure of a software system in terms of building blocks and relationship [1].

Traditional distributed software generally consists of homogeneous processing units. A component-oriented application is composed of software components that may be both heterogeneous and homogeneous. Therefore middleware technologies are adopted increasingly, and CORBA is the most widely accepted component model due to its open standard for heterogeneous computing.

Even with some existed related research work [2], [3], current CORBA specifications and implementations still have insufficient support for describing the overall software architecture and configuring the set of software components according to the operational environment. Therefore, we present a novel architectural approach named OrbGOM (ORB-based Graph-Oriented Model) for configuring, modeling and programming of CORBA-based distributed applications.

[1] This work is partially supported by Shanghai University under Shanghai Educational Committee Research Grant 01A02.

M. Li et al. (Eds.): GCC 2003, LNCS 3032, pp. 266–268, 2004.

2 The Graph-Oriented Model

Graph-Oriented Model is originally proposed to let the programmer to concentrate on the high-level application logic or to easily integrate existing building blocks into a new application [4]. The OrbGOM is based on Graph-Oriented Model. It introduces graph formalism for programming CORBA-based distributed applications. The OrbGOM consists of a directed or undirected *logical graph*, whose nodes are associated with CORBA object, and whose edges define the relationships between the CORBA objects; An *Object-to-nodes mapping* allows the user to bind CORBA objects to specific nodes; An optional *nodes-to-processors mapping* allows the user to explicitly specify the mapping of the logical graph to the underlying network of processors, with a default mapping when the mapping specification is omitted; And a library of language-level graph-oriented programming *primitives*.

Once the local context for the graph instance is set up, communication of CORBA objects can be implemented by invoking operations defined on the specified graph. The operations on a user-specified graph include several classes: *Communication and Synchronization*, *Update, Query,* and *Sub-graph generation.*

3 The Architecture of OrbGOM

From the viewpoint of the software developer, OrbGOM takes important roles in the development of software. OrbGOM not only provides an abstract graph-oriented framework for modeling and architecting composition of CORBA-based distributed applications, but also acts as the communication middleware among the CORBA objects. The architecture of OrbGOM consists of a MainFrame module including OrbGOM API and OrbGOM LIB, a Configuration Manager module, a Consistency Maintenance module and a Runtime module.

The MainFrame module helps users to develop, execute, debug, and monitor CORBA-based distributed applications. It provides the OrbGOM API with user interaction as well as providing the OrbGOM LIB with compile and execution of the user application. Based on the kernel of the OrbGOM-- the distributed representation and management of graphs, a set of graph-oriented primitives are defined in OrbGOM API and implemented in OrbGOM LIB. The Runtime module is responsible for execution of applications and communication between CORBA objects of the applications. It acts as the communication middleware among the CORBA objects. It also manipulates and really updates the graphs representing the CORBA-based distributed applications. The Configuration Manager module is used for management of configuration and reconfiguration. It is provided to ensure the consistency of the applications. The user may define a special *configuration* object, which has minimum interaction with CORBA objects through the Configuration Manager module, to monitor the configuration of applications and to trigger the reconfiguration of the applications when necessary. It can be added after the design of CORBA objects is completed. Therefore, the configuration management function can be implemented efficiently without altering the CORBA objects of the distributed applications.

4 Conclusions

A prototype of OrbGOM has been implemented on top of CORBA and the performance evaluation shows that the extra overhead introduced by OrbGOM over CORBA involves reasonable computational overheads.

OrbGOM provides developers with an intuitive abstraction of the software architecture and a set of predefined graph operations. It eases the building and execution of applications through modeling an application's structure as a user-defined logical graph and providing operations over the graph. Moreover, under this graph-oriented framework, dynamic reconfiguration of CORBA applications is supported with the help of the predefined primitives that operate over the graphs. Graph-oriented software architecture leads to the support for composition and reconfiguration at the architecture level, thus benefits the reusability of both the components and the architecture. It also makes the program simpler and more visual, as well as providing the possibility of visualization programming and debugging.

Due to the unifying graph-oriented approach for the entire process of application development and dynamic reconfiguration, OrbGOM supports the development of flexible and dynamic CORBA applications.

References

1. Nenad Medvidovic, Richard N. Taylor, "*A Classification and Comparison Framework for Software Architecture Description Languages*", IEEE Trans. on Software Engineering, Vol. 26, No. 1, pp. 70-93, January 2000.
2. G Coulson, GS. Blair, M. Clarke, N. Parlavantzas, "*The Design of a Configurable and Reconfigurable Middleware Platform*", Distributed Computing, Vol. 15, No.4, pp67-86, 2002.
3. N. Rodriguez, R. Ierusalimschy, and R. Cerqueira, *"Dynamic Configuration with CORBA Components",* in Proceedings of the Fourth International Conference on Configurable Distributed Systems, pages 27--34. IEEE Computer Society Press, May 1998.
4. J. Cao, Min Cao, Alvin S. T. Chan, Gengfeng Wu, "*Architecture Level Support for Dynamic Reconfiguration and Fault Tolerance in Component-Based Distributed Software*", to appear in Proc. 2002 International Conference on Parallel And Distributed Systems (ICPADS'02) (IEEE Computer Society Press), Dec. 2002, Taiwan.
5. Daniel Le Metayer, "*Describing Software Architecture Styles Using Graph Grammars*", IEEE Transactions on Software Engineering, vol. 24, no. 7, pp. 521-533, July 1998.
6. J.Kramer and J.Magee, "*Analyzing dynamic change in distributed software architectures*", IEEE Proceedings-Software, vol. 145, no. 5, Oct. 1998.

Appendix

CAO Min, female, current research interests include distributed computing, Grid Computing, Component Technology and Object-oriented Software Engineering. CAO Jiang-Nong, male, research interests include parallel and distributed computing, networking, mobile computing, fault tolerance, and distributed software architecture. WU Geng-Feng, male, current research interests include Data Mining, AI, Web Service. WANG Yan-Yan, female, current research interests include distributed computing, Algorithm.

Design of NGIS: The Next Generation Internet Server for Future E-society

Chong-Won Park[1], Myung-Joon Kim[1], and Jin-Won Park[2]

[1] Electronics and Telecommunications Research Institute,
161 Gajeong-dong, Yuseong-gu, Daejeon, 305-350, Korea
{cwpark,joonkim}@etri.re.kr

[2] Division of Electronics, Electrical and Computer Engineering, Hongik University,
300 Sinan-ri, Jochiwon-eup, Yeongi-gun, Chungnam, 339-701, Korea
jinon@hongik.ac.kr

Abstract. In the near future, high quality multimedia services such as Internet broadcast, remote medical services and Internet video-phones will be major information technology services. Consequently, new computer systems for providing such services are desperately called on. In this paper, we are proposing a next generation Internet server by explaining the design concept, the characteristics and the architecture for providing various e-society services. The Next Generation Internet Server(NGIS) is a computer system enforced with networking capability for providing e-society services in cyber communities.

1 Introduction

With the wide spread of computers and high speed communication networks, the Internet becomes extremely popular in recent years in our lives. The services using the Internet have expanded to high quality multimedia levels such as various web services and motion pictures. According to Berchtold et al. in McKinsey Quarterly [1] and Korea Information Strategy Development Institute(KISA) reports [2], the users who transferred from narrow band Internet service to high speed Internet, have increased the usages on the audio and video streaming contents oriented entertainment services and community services.

In the near future, high quality multimedia services such as Internet broadcast, remote medical services and Internet video-phones will be major information technology services [3] [4]. Consequently, new computer systems for providing such services are desperately called on.

In this paper, we are proposing a next generation Internet server by explaining the design concept, the characteristics and the architecture for providing various e-society services. The Next Generation Internet Server(NGIS) is a computer system enforced with networking capability for providing e-society services in cyber communities.

M. Li et al. (Eds.): GCC 2003, LNCS 3032, pp. 269–272, 2004.

2 Services and Design Issues for NGIS

The development of computer systems that are suitable for community services and multimedia services is called on for the next generation of Internet with high speed communication networks. The services in overpopulated areas in Asia such as Korea and China should be provided in wired and wireless fashions, for the area is densely populated with apartments, university campuses and high buildings.

The target services of NGIS are expected to support the cyber apartments for community services, cyber shopping, cyber learning and remote medical services, the cyber campuses for schooling, administration and groupware services and the cyber buildings for video conferencing and intranet servers.

General purpose computer systems use high level of CPU utilization for dealing with gigabit level communication overheads, which is due to the fact that complicated communication protocols are handled in host CPUs. If a dedicated processor is used for handling communication protocols, the host CPU utilization level will be decreased, which is a cheaper way of handling communication overheads. Thus, a dedicated processor for handling TCP/IP protocols in a offload fashion will be useful [5] [6].

In streaming data processing, data in a disk system are copied to the memory, duplicated many times for protocol packet handling, and are sent to the communication network. The duplication of data in the memory degrades the system performance. Thus, sending the data directly to the network without duplication will improve the overall system performance [6].

The size of the streaming data in a disk is from several hundred megabytes to gigabytes of continuous form. So, it is inefficient to handle streaming data with current file systems that normally handle only 512 bytes to several kilobytes. Handling streaming data necessitates to develop a multimedia file system which can handle the continuous form of streaming data.

Several disks are used for storing large volume of data. The disks share a disk bus, which slows the disk reading speed in a single disk's point of view. Thus, it is also called on to use striping technique such as RAID(Redundant Array of Inexpensive Disks) for preventing the degradation of disk reading speed.

3 Design of NGIS

When designing NGIS, we need to consider the target services and the design issues. The basic design concepts for NGIS are high performance, low cost, scalability and easy of maintenance. So, we adopt conventional hardware and royalty free system software for low cost. We use protocol acceleration hardware, contents distribution software and multimedia file system for new services. We decide to select a scalable architecture for easy expansion and for easy maintenance by non experts [7].

NGIS provides not only single-node server solution to achieve cost effectiveness and high price performance but also a multiple-node cluster server solution to build a scalable and high available system. Fig. 1 shows the system architecture of NGIS and Fig. 2 shows software architecture.

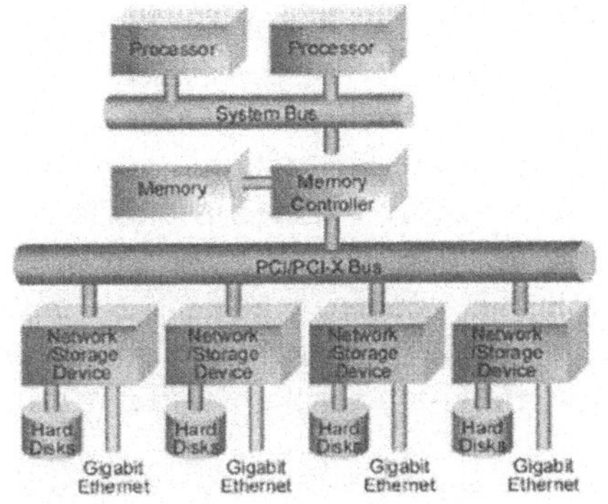

Fig. 1. System architecture of NGIS

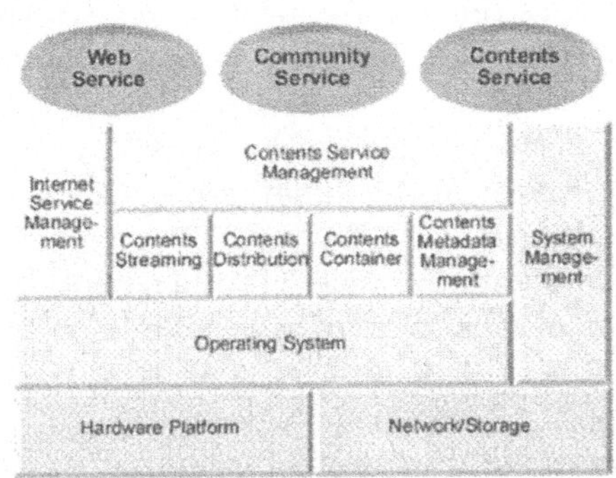

Fig. 2. Software architecture of NGIS

Hardware Platform: The Hardware Platform is consisting of one or more processing engines and a packaging unit. A processing engine includes a motherboard, one or two processors, a system memory, a memory controller hub, an I/O controller hub, several PCI/PCI-X controller hubs and slots.

Network/Storage: The Network/Storage takes the responsibility of networking and storing data in the server, and consists of a PCI bridge, a TOE (TCP/IP Offload Engine) unit, a storage controller and a memory controller. The Network/Storage transfers the stream data stored in disks to the users through the network without copy.

Operating System: As the operating system for NGIS, RedHat Linux 7.x based on Linux kernel 2.4 is adopted. The additional features for media streaming service is designed and implemented.

Contents Container: The contents container is a multimedia file system that is specially optimized to NGIS, which efficiently stores, manages and retrieves various multimedia contents.

Contents Metadata Management: The contents metadata management is a specialized database management engine to handle various kinds of metadata, and efficiently stores, manages and retrieves various metadata, such as metadata describing multimedia contents, being related with system management and with contents services.

Contents Streaming: The contents streaming plays a key role in providing streaming services. In order to provide a high-quality streaming service, the contents streaming is required to process multimedia data with the timing constraint(i.e., without delay). Contents streaming will support the delivery of MPEG-1, MPEG-2, and MPEG-4 media data.

Contents Distribution: NGIS can only store the limited quantity of contents, so it should store the right contents in the right place at the right time to satisfy client's requests. Also, when requested contents are not locally available, NGIS needs to obtain the requested contents from a remote server as fast and reliably as possible. The contents distribution is designed to solve the problems that are related with contents distribution operations.

System Management: It is for the enhancement of operating convenience as well as the improvement of the RAS(Reliability, Availability and Serviceability) properties of NGIS. In order to minimize the downtime of the system, NGIS provides the preventive maintenance by alerting abnormal symptoms to a system manager. NGIS needs three kinds of operators who should fulfill some roles of management. They are on-site supervisors, visiting engineers, and remote managers.

Contents Service Management: The contents service management is a DRM system which provides contents protection and key management transparently to users. This DRM system provides contents protection through packaging and DRM Client technologies.

Internet Service Management: The Internet service management manages web services and community services of a local community. Among various local communities, we consider a cyber apartment community as a target application domain.

4 Concluding Remarks

In this paper, we proposed a next generation Internet server by explaining the design concept, the characteristics and the architecture for providing various e-society services. The Next Generation Internet Server is a computer system enforced with networking capability for providing e-society services in cyber communities.

When designing NGIS, we needed to consider the target services and the design issues. The basic design concepts for NGIS are high performance, low cost, scalability and easy of maintenance. So, we adopted conventional hardware and royalty free system software for low cost. We used protocol acceleration hardware, contents distribution software and multimedia file system for new services. We decided to select a scalable architecture for easy expansion and for easy maintenance by non experts.

References

1. Joseph Berchtold, Veit Dengler, Bonnie M. Johnson, and Srividya Prakash: What Do Broadband Consumers Want?. The McKinsey Quarterly, Number 4 (2001)
2. C. H. Yoon, et al.: Characteristics and Trends on the high speed Internet service market. Korea Information Strategy Development Institute, December (2001)
3. 2002 Korea Internet White Paper. Korea Nation Computerization Agency (2002)
4. Nation Informatization White Paper. Korea Nation Computerization Agency (2002)
5. Advantages of a TCP/IP Offload ASIC. Adaptec, White paper, October (2001)
6. http://www.xiran.com/solutions-stream.php
7. Next Generation Internet Server Design Specification. Electronics and Telecommunications Research Institute (2002)

Video-on-Demand System Using Multicast and Web-Caching Techniques

SeokHoon Kang

Dept. of Internet Engineering, DONGSEO UNIV.
San 69-1 Churye-dong, Sasang-gu, 617-716, PUSAN, KOREA
hana@tecace.com

Abstract. VoD System is a system that transfers enormous amount of video data, its important task is to save the video and decrease the load of VoD Server that processes the client's request. When the users use VoD Service, getting the simultaneous and continuous service is important, and providing the user's interactivity such as VCR becomes one of the study area of VoD system. In this paper, MCVoD (Video-on-Demand using Multicast and Cache) System that decreases the load on network and guarantees the simultaneousness will be suggested and described. MCVoD system uses a Multicast Router and Proxy cache. MCVoD System is designed to decrease the load on server and network using Multicast Router, and it also dissolves the time delay problem by setting non-duplicated Proxy.

1 Introduction

As the internet grows bigger, the multimedia service also increases. Such multimedia service is increasing as the internet users increase, as the result the overload on network and servers became a problem. One of the most common multimedia service, Video-on-Demand Service provides enormous amount of video data to the users at the user's requested time, therefore it causes the overload on network and VoD Service servers. As users increase, it will cause more overload. In this paper, efficient ways to decrease the overload on network and VoD Server caused by Video-on-Demand Service will be suggested to provide the simultaneous service.

2 The Architecture of MCVoD System

Proxy cache is used in order to reduce a service delay caused by Multicast System, MCVoD system proposed in this paper reduces a load of VoD Server and the network with multicast method. The same video service requests of Client are tied up as one and then transmitted through Multicast Router, and the time delay caused by this can be reduced by sending the first video stream stored in Proxy cache. Also, the cache of Proxy is managed without any duplication by Interchange Agent (IA). IA searches and manages the video streams registered in each Proxy cache using the list, and

M. Li et al. (Eds.): GCC 2003, LNCS 3032, pp. 273–276, 2004.

provides the prompt video service to a request of Client. If the first stream of requested video exists in the other registered proxy, a command sending the first video stream to the proxy in which a client is registered, must be carried out to the corresponding proxy. MCVoD system is divided into 4 sections, VOD Server, Multicast Router, Interchange Agent, Proxy cache. Total system configuration is shown in Fig. 1.

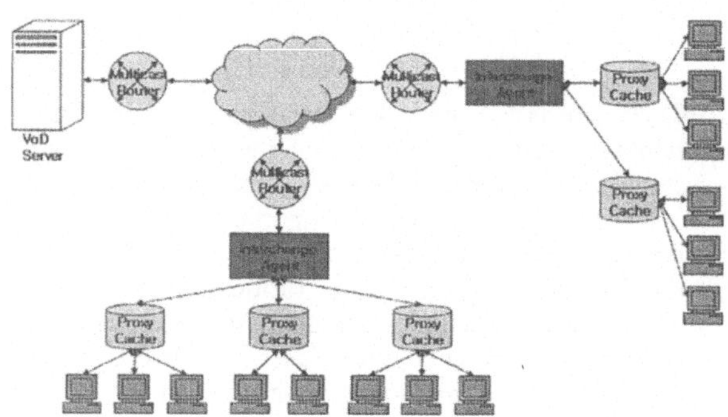

Fig. 1. Architecture of MCVoD system

Interchange Agent carries out a role to manage cache of registered Proxy. Contents of each cache are managed by a list of IA, and by using this list cache contents of each Proxy can be stored without any duplication. IA has List to manage cache of Proxy. IA searches through List in order to inspect where the first stream of a video corresponding to a request exists in the cache of registered Proxy, and it also provides the service without any delay. Also, the purpose is to manage the cache and remove the duplication of contents.

3 Operation of the MCVoD System

MCVoD system is configured with a cache of Proxy and a Multicast technique. Since the multicast technology is developed with a router, the same video service requests received from several IA are handled as one and sent to the VoD server. A load of VoD Server through this technology can be reduced depite of increasing number of VoD service requests. The multicast Router deals with the requests while Proxy data are processed so that the load on network and servers can be reduced to provide the service to the users without any time delay. The Proxy Cache part deals with the proxy before processing the multicast router. The practical operation procedures of a Multicast part are as follows. Proxy N and Proxy M are random two Proxies.

Step1. Client passes through Proxy N, and IA is asked for video service
Step2. IA searches whether there is the first stream of a video in its own list
Step3. IA confirms that there is the first stream of a video in cache of Proxy M, and Proxy2 is asked for service
Step4. IA orders relevant video stream from Multicast Router1 to service the remaining video streams. There is no additional requests if there is data in Proxy N.

Step5. Multicast Router1 transmits a request to Multicast Router3
Step6. Multicast Router2 transmits the same video service to Multicast Router3
Step7. A request of Router2 is united with Router1, and Multicast Router3 transmits them to Router4
Step8. Requests that will be processed as one are transferred to VoD Server through Multicast Router4, and it starts the corresponding VoD service as requested.
Step9. A video stream on VoD Server provides the continuous service to the Router 3 through Multicast Router4.
Step10. After Multicast Router3 transfers recieved video streams to the Router1 and Router2, Router1 provides the received streams to the client throught Proxy N.

The video service requests from a client is transferred to the IA through Proxy. IA finds the Proxy in which the first video stream of a corresponding request is stored, and it starts to provide the real-time service to the client without any time delay. The contents in the cache of Proxy should be not be fixed, since the cache of proxy is based on a popular video request. The cache of each proxy can store the n(n=10) number of video streams, and one temporary storage (temporary buffer) is provided. A counter to store the frequency of service for each video stream exists. The contents of cache can be changed using this counter. The proxy manages the Cache based on these four behaviors, Cache Initiation, Cache Hit, Cache Miss, Cache Replacement.

4 Simulation and Performance Evaluation

The simulation was proceeded based on the some assumptions. All router of MCVoD System provide a Multicast function. VoD Server stores 100 video items, and length of all video items is composed of 100 minutes. And IA can have Proxy from minimum one to three at maximum. MCVoD System in this paper is using the multi-Proxy that has a cache and this multi-Proxy keeps contents of cache without duplication by the IA which defined in this paper.

The VoD System with multi-Proxy that stores the whole video streams manages the contents in cache of multi-proxy without duplication using Switching Agnet so that a load of video service can be evenly distributed to each Proxy. VoD System manages the contents in cache without duplication using Switching Agent and stores the whole requested video streams in cache. Therefore, when 80% of the popular video streams is stored in cache based on Zipf distribution, if the service requests from clients is transmitted immediately to the client, not through VoD Server, a load of a network and servers can be reduced. However, if the first stream in proxy cache is played in the necessary time through the multicast method, it will not be necessary to store the whole video streams in the cache.

If the total popular video streams which is 80% of total requests, are stored in cache of multi-Proxy, the Multi-cache size of MCVoD System uses under 10% to have the same efficiency. This means that the efficient resources management can reduce the system costs.

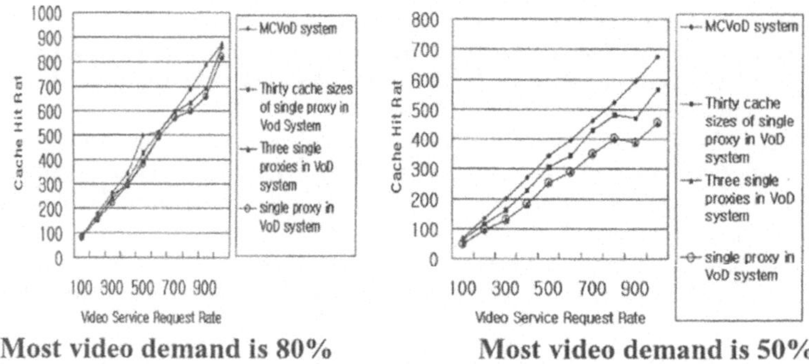

Fig. 2. Performance Evaluation at 80% and 50% of the most video demand

5 Conclusion

Video-on-Demand Service is providing convenience to the users regardless of time. As users increases, a load of VoD Server and networks becomes bigger, therefore the MCVoD System in this paper is suggested to resolve these problems. Cache of Proxy was used in order to solve a time delay problem caused by Multicast method, and MCVoD system reduces a load of a network and VoD Server using Multicast method. Each Client are connected to one Proxy, and each Proxy is registered at one Interchange Agent. A client request is transferred to IA throught the proxy, and IA detects where the requested first video stream is stored in cache of which Proxy.

Therefore, MCVoD system reduces a load of a network and VoD Server using Multicast method, manages the contents in multi-proxy cache without duplication using Interchange Agent, and reduces the costs by only storing the first video stream in cache reducing the cache size.

References

[1] Huadong Ma, Kang G. Shin "Multicast Video-on-Demand services" January 2002 ACM SIGCOMM Computer Communication Review, Volume 32 Issue 1

[2] T.D.C. Little and D. Venkatesh, "Prospects for interactive video-on-demand", IEEE Multimedia, 1(3), 1994, pp.14-24

[3] Lee, J.Y.B, Lee, C.H "Design, performance analysis, and implementation of a super-scalar video-on-demand system" IEEE

[4] Lin Huang Chang, Kuen-Chu Lai "Near video-on-demand systems with combining multicasting and unicasting batching" IEEEE, Electrical and Electronic Technology, 2001.

[5] Choi, C.Y, Hamdi, M."A scalable video-on-demand system using multi-batch buffering" IEEE, Global Telecommunications Conference, 2001.

[6] Chen-Lung Chan, Te-Chou Su, Shih-Yu Huang, Jia-Shung Wang "Cooperative proxy scheme for large-scale VoD systems", IEEE, Parallel and Distributed Systems, 2002.

[7] Ramesh, S. Injong Rhee, Guo, K. "Multicast with cache (Mcache): an adaptive zero-delay video-on-demand service" , IEEE, INFOCOM 2001.

PeerBus: A Middleware Framework towards Interoperability among P2P Data Sharing Systems [1]

Linhao Xu, Shuigeng Zhou, Keping Zhao, Weining Qian, and Aoying Zhou

Dept. of Computer Sci. and Eng., Fudan University, Shanghai, 200433, China
{xulh,sgzhou,kpzhao,wnqian,ayzhou}@fudan.edu.cn

Abstract. Current P2P application is usually built on a specific P2P platform. Different P2P applications with similar functions cannot directly share the data and services with one another. Aiming at this problem, we propose PeerBus, a P2P middleware framework, to enable interoperability among different P2P data sharing platforms. To achieve the goal, we develop a set of common operations for providing data sharing services based on extensive investigation on the services and protocols of the typical existing P2P systems. The common services mainly include a set of common APIs for routing messages and accessing routing states. A preliminary implementation shows that PeerBus can bridge P2P data sharing applications spanning over a number of existing P2P platforms effectively and efficiently.

1 Introduction

P2P is a model of applications for sharing resources available at the edge of the Internet through ad hoc overlay networks with symmetric communication. However, current P2P applications are usually built on some specific P2P platforms. Since each P2P platform has its own protocols, the applications on different P2P platforms cannot directly share data or services with one another. Suppose a P2P application of data sharing (mainly publications and experimental results), where the computers in different research groups interconnect with each other to construct a virtual research P2P community. For example, MIT research group may use Chord [12], while Microsoft uses Pastry [11] and Fudan group uses BestPeer [8]. Though intra-group data sharing is enabled by P2P model, inter-group data sharing is impossible based on state-of-the-art P2P techniques. In fact, the requirement of data sharing among P2P platforms is raised in many real-world distributed applications, especially those that have already adopted the P2P model, such as file sharing. There are two solutions to the problem. The first one is that all P2P applications employ the same P2P platform to share resources, which is apparently unrealistic. The other is to construct a P2P middleware to

[1] This work was supported by the Natural Science Foundation of China (NSFC) under grant no. 60373019, and Fudan University Innovation Foundation for Graduate Students. Shuigeng Zhou was also supported by IBM Software Research Award.

M. Li et al. (Eds.): GCC 2003, LNCS 3032, pp. 277–284, 2004.

enable interoperability among applications on different P2P platforms. Obviously, the latter is more realistic due to its ease of implementation.

In this paper, we propose PeerBus, a P2P middleware framework, to enable interoperability among P2P systems so that users of different P2P systems or platforms can share resources with one another. Through extensively investigating the services and protocols of existing P2P data sharing systems, we generalize their common operations, and define a set of common routing APIs to enable interoperability among different P2P systems. A preliminary implementation of PeerBus is built to validate the effectiveness of the proposed PeerBus framework.

The rest of this paper is organized as follows. Section 2 analyzes the services of current P2P systems, and describes the architecture of PeerBus. Section 3 defines a set of common APIs. Section 4 presents a preliminary implementation. Section 5 reviews related work, and Section 6 concludes the paper.

2 PeerBus: A P2P Middleware Framework

In this section, we first summarize the common operations of P2P data sharing systems. Then the architecture of the P2P middleware framework is presented.

2.1 The Analysis of P2P Data Sharing Systems

Current P2P data sharing systems can be divided into two categories from a point of view of overlay structure: *unstructured P2P systems* and *structured P2P systems*. Here, overlay structure refers to whether or not there exists a mapping between the data and its location.

Unstructured P2P systems include pure P2P system and hybrid P2P system. In pure P2P systems, all nodes are equal and no functionality is centralized. Each node knows only the other nodes that have directly connection with it. Breadth-first search is the basic search manner that query messages are flooded to all neighbor nodes, and so on. Recently, a lot of researches focus on how to improve the efficiency and effectiveness of BFS, such as iterative deepening, directed BFS and random walks [9]. On the other hand, in hybrid P2P systems, nodes are organized into two layers: the upper tier supernodes (or hub nodes) and the lower tier common nodes (or leaf nodes). Each leaf node connects with one or several hub nodes. The ally of hub nodes plays the role of the directory server to facilitate resource location.

Structured P2P systems, such as Chord [12], Tapestry [13], Pastry [11] and CAN [10], map the sharable data and the location of each node into the same *identifier space* by distributed hash function. Both data and node have a unique *identifier* (or *key*). The data are assigned to the live nodes with the same or nearest *key*. To deliver requests efficiently to the node contained the desired data, each node maintains a routing table, and these requests are forwarded to the nodes whose *identifier* is progressively closer to the lookup *key*.

In fact, to implement data sharing services, nodes of the P2P network need only communicate with each other by routing various messages types. During the process of routing messages, each node also need provide necessary information to forward the messages to the desired nodes by accessing local routing table. Therefore, from a perspective of semantics of the data sharing services, we can generalize different P2P data sharing services into two sets of **common operations**: *routing messages* and *accessing routing states*. The former is used to forward query or lookup messages from one node to other nodes, and exchange desired data between the online nodes. The latter is responsible for providing necessary information during the process of routing messages, and maintaining the local states of each node.

2.2 The Architecture of PeerBus

Middleware is the collection of distributed computing services that, within any given processing environment, enables clients and servers to communicate and interoperate with one another in the most expedient, flexible and correct manner possible [1]. The role of middleware is to ease the task of designing, programming and managing distributed applications by providing a simple, consistent and integrated distributed programming environment. Interoperability is the key to a middleware system.

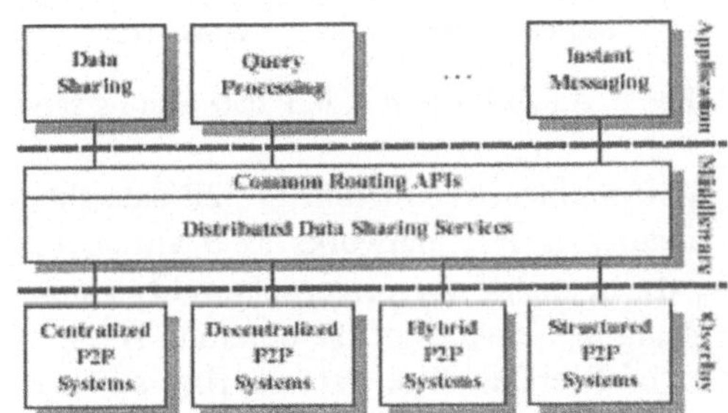

Fig. 1. The architecture of PeerBus

Specifically, we define **P2P middleware** as a distributed software layer which abstracts the complexity and heterogeneity of the underlying P2P systems with its multitude of services, protocols and applications. Currently, the most important and popular P2P applications are data sharing. Therefore, in this paper, PeerBus focuses on abstracting the common operations of data sharing services and protocols from different P2P systems. It is our first step towards the P2P middleware. As shown in Figure 1, the middleware layer of PeerBus is composed of common APIs and distributed data sharing services. Different P2P systems with specific overlay structure are at the bottom of the architecture of PeerBus. The middleware layer implements a fundamental abstraction above underlying P2P systems, and provides a common data sharing services to high-level applications through our proposed common APIs. In such a way, high-level P2P applications are independent of specific P2P systems, and can transparently access resources of different P2P systems through the middleware layer.

2.3 Abstraction of Data Sharing Services

As mentioned in Section 2.1, the common operations of current P2P data sharing systems can be generalized into two parts: *routing messages* and *accessing routing states*. All existing P2P systems provide high-level abstractions built upon the common operations, such as centralized search, BFS and DHT. Here, we adopt a hierarchical abstraction to enhance extensibility of our proposed APIs. In doing so, the changes can be limited to each tier, while not extend to other tiers.

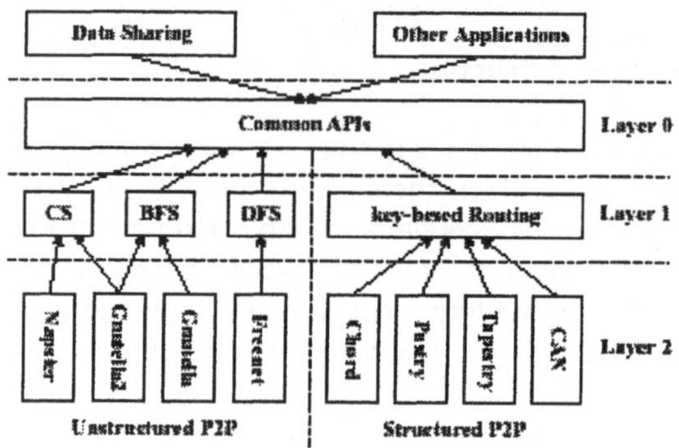

Fig. 2. An abstraction of P2P data sharing services

Figure 2 depicts a hierarchical abstraction of P2P data sharing services. P2P applications access the underlying P2P networks as a virtual P2P network through the common APIs (layer 0). In such a way, interoperability among different P2P systems can be achieved by using the services of the common APIs, which is the core part of the middleware layer of PeerBus. The data sharing services of centralized search, breadth-first search and DHT provide high-level abstractions for the underlying P2P overlays. Structured P2P overlays adopt key-based routing, while unstructured P2P systems apply heuristic-based routing. In layer 2, the concrete P2P overlays use one or several of the abstractions in layer 1 to accomplish resource location and data exchanging.

3 Common APIs

In this section, we define the common APIs to enable interoperability. We begin by defining notation and data types using language-neutral definition [7].

3.1 Data Types

A *queryID* is a *string*, which identifies a query initiated by a node. In structured P2P systems, the *queryID* is a 160-bit string to denote the lookup *key*, while in unstructured P2P systems the *queryID* is a unique string to identify the message. A *node* encapsulates the *transport address* and *nodeID* of a peer node. Messages are denoted by *msg*, which contains data, keywords, or *nodes* list. A parameter *p* will be denoted as →*p* if it is a read-only parameter, and ↔*p* if it is a read-write parameter.

3.2 Routing Message APIs

The basic operations of routing message are *route* and *send*. The former transmits messages to other nodes, while the latter updates messages by accessing local states (e.g., routing table) of each node along the query path.

route(queryID→QID, msg→M, node[]→hint) This operation delivers a message of data, query or node list to a subset of neighbor nodes by using *hint* argument, which are invoked by underlying P2P systems. The *hint* argument contains a *node* set that will be visited within the first hop during the process of routing messages. The value of the *hint* argument can be obtained by heuristic searching approaches, such as random walks. A message can be terminated by setting *hint* as NULL.

send(queryID↔QID, msg↔M, node[]↔nextHop) This operation is invoked at each node which takes part in forwarding message *M*. The upcall informs P2P applications that the message *M* is about to be forwarded to a *node* set at next hop. The applications may modify the value of arguments *M* or *nextHop*, or terminate the message by setting nextHop as NULL. Through modifying the *nextHop* parameter, an alternative routing method can be used instead of the original one.

3.3 Accessing Routing State APIs

All of the operations of accessing routing state are purely local operation and involve no communication with neighbors. Underlying P2P systems may access the routing state to identify the nodes that will be used to the *nextHop* of the *send* operation.

node[] localSearch(queryID→QID, msg→M) This operation produces a list of *nodes* that can be used at the next hop. For example, Chord may use *queryID* to identify the nodes for the next hop, while directed BFS may use keywords in *M* to select neighbors for the next hop.

node[] neighborSet(int→max) This operation returns a set of neighbor *nodes* that can be used in naive search methods, such as BFS. With respect to structured P2P systems, the operation is used to find a subset of neighbors of each node, where the default value of *max* means all neighbors.

node[] replicaSet(queryID→QID, msg→M, int→max) This operation returns a set of nodes on which replicas of the selected data will be stored, where the *max* argument specifies the maximum number of a certain replica.

boolean cache(queryID→QID, msg→M) This operation is to decide on whether the local node should cache results carried by the message *M* or not. If true, the local node will store the results locally, otherwise not.

updateNeighbor(node→n, boolean→joined) This operation is invoked to inform the applications whether the node {\it n} has joined or left the network. Also it can be used to maintain whether a neighbor is online or not.

4 Preliminary Implementation

Currently, our preliminary implementation focuses on several typical P2P systems, including OpenNap [4], Gnutella [2] and CAN [10].

4.1 Evaluation of Common APIs

Centralized search. Each node of centralized P2P systems can send query using *route(queryID, [QUERY, keywords, S], hint)*. The *queryID* argument is generated by the request node, *keywords* express a query, *S* denotes the location of the request node, and the *hint* parameter is the location of the central server. After receiving the *route* message, the central server returns results to the request node by using the *route(queryID, [RESULT, data], S)* message. The request node directly communicates with the desired nodes by using the *route(queryID, [GET, keywords, S], hint)* message, where the *hint* argument is the location of the source node. Then the source node returns the desired data to the request node with the *route(queryID, [RESULT, date], S)* message.

Breadth-first search. Each node of pure P2P systems floods a query message *route(queryID, [QUERY, keywords, TTL, S], hint)* to all neighbors, where the *hint* argument includes the location of all neighbors. Any node receiving the *route* message will use the *localSearch* operation to search local data, and relay the query to its neighbors by using *send(queryID, [QUERY, keywords, TTL, S], nextHop)* at the same time. The value of *nextHop* is generated by the *neighborSet* or *localSearch* operations. If a node has the desired data, then it returns the results by using the message *send(queryID, [RESULT, data], nextHop)* along the query path reversely. Each node along the query path can use the *cache(queryID, [RESULT, data])* operation to cache the data.

Key-based routing. Key-based routing can implement our proposed routing APIs indeed. The simplest way is to replace *queryID* argument with 160-bit value (i.e., *key*). For example, *route(queryID, [PUT, data], NULL)* can satisfy the functionality of *put(key, data)*, while *route(queryID, [GET, S], NULL)* for *get(key)*. In terms of the accessing routing state APIs, the routing APIs need only call the corresponding operations of the concrete P2P systems. Currently, the basic operations *put(key, data)* and *get(key)* are considered.

Replication and Cache. P2P applications can use replication or cache to ensure stored data survives node failure. To replicate a newly received data, the applications will call *replicaSet(queryID, [data], n)* to decide on which nodes the data should be replicated. For caching data, nodes along the query path will automatically cache data by using *cache(queryID, [data])* operation. Each node can terminate cache or replication operation by setting the *nextHop* argument of *send* or *route* messages to NULL.

4.2 Implementation Issues

OpenNap [4] is an open project of centralized P2P system, which implements all necessary protocol types of Napster. The protocol types *client search request*, *search response*, *downloading file* and *alternative download request* can implement the common APIs. For example, the *route* message can be implemented by *client search request* for locating the nodes who maintain the desired data, where all arguments can be obtained from the message type. The accessing routing state APIs, such as *localSearch* operation, can be invoked by the operations of the central server or client nodes.

Gnutella [2] is an open protocol of fully decentralized P2P systems that utilize breadth-first search manner. The basic operations, such as *Query*, *QueryHit*, *Get* and *Push*, can be used to implement the common APIs by adding *hint* or *nextHop* parameters. For example, each node can flood the network with query messages *send* to locate the desired nodes. The *send* message can be implemented by *Query* message directly, where the *nextHop* argument is generated by the *neighborSet* or *localSearch* operations. The former is used for Gnutella, while the latter for iterative deepening or directed BFS [9].

CAN is a kind of structured P2P systems. The *route* operation is supported by the existing operations and the *hint* functionality can be easily added. The *localSearch* operation is used to lookup the local routing table. The *updateNeighbor* operation is triggered every time when a node splits its *zone*, or combines the *zone* with its neighbor.

5 Related Work

Since the advent of Napster [4], P2P data sharing systems are the most popular and successful ones. However, either unstructured P2P systems (e.g., Gnutella [2] and Shareaza [5]) or structured P2P systems (e.g., CAN [10], Chord [12], Pastry [11] and Tapestry [13]) is designed for providing specific-purpose services and/or overlay structure. Recently, some researches focus on constructing general-purpose P2P platforms to support various P2P applications. JXTA [3], BestPeer [8] and IRIS [6,7] are such typical P2P systems.

PeerBus distinguishes itself from JXTA in at least two aspects: first, the motivation of PeerBus is to support interoperability among various P2P systems, including unstructured P2P systems and structured P2P overlays. On the contrary, JXTA only confines interoperability to its own platform, and cannot directly interconnect or communicate with other P2P systems; second, as a middleware, PeerBus is independent of the underlying P2P systems by abstracting common services from different P2P systems. It glues different P2P systems together to form a larger federated P2P system. Although JXTA brags of platform-independence, what it means is OS independence, instead of P2P protocols independence.

Different from unstructured P2P systems, structured P2P overlays have some limitations: first, key-based lookup support only exact-match; second, each node cannot decide what data should be stored locally; finally, each node cannot dynamically reconfigure its neighbors, which restricts the feature of self-organization. Thus, structured P2P systems are more applicable to share data and services in a relatively static environment, while unstructured P2P systems are more suitable for ad hoc environment. We argue that the next generation P2P platform should combine unstructured P2P systems with structured P2P systems. Therefore, compared with IRIS project, PeerBus is not limited to a specific P2P network, while aims at covering any ever-existing P2P network.

6 Conclusions

Current P2P applications are restricted to a specific P2P system or platform. Different P2P applications or systems cannot share the data and services with one another. To tackle this problem, in this paper, we present PeerBus, a P2P middleware framework, to enable interoperability among different P2P platforms or systems. Through an intensive analysis of the services and protocols of the existing P2P platforms, we generalize a set of common operations that are necessary for P2P data sharing applications. Our preliminary implementation shows that PeerBus can efficiently and effectively bridge P2P data sharing applications on both structured and unstructured P2P platforms.

References

1. Dsonline homepage. http://dsonline.computer.org/middleware/index.htm.
2. Gnutella homepage. http://www.gnutella.com/.
3. JXTA homepage. http://www.jxta.org/.
4. OpenNap homepage. http://opennap.sourceforge.net/.
5. Shareaza homepage. http://www.shareaza.com/.
6. IRIS homepage. http://iris.lcs.mit.edu/.
7. F. Dabek, B. Zhao, P. Druschel, J. Kubiatowicz, and I. Stoica. Towards a Common API for Structured Peer-to-Peer Overlays. In *Proc. of IPTPS'03*, 2003.
8. W. S. Ng, B. C. Ooi, and K.-L. Tan. BestPeer: A Self-Configurable Peer-to-Peer System. In *Proc. of ICDE'02*, 2002.
9. D. Tsoumakos, and N. Roussopoulos. A Comparison of Peer-to-Peer Search Methods. In *Proc. of WebDB'03*, 2003.
10. S. Ratnasamy, P. Francis, K. Handley, R. Karp, and S. Shenker. A scalable content-addressable network. In *Proc. of ACM SIGCOMM'01*, 2001.
11. A. Rowstron and P. Druschel. Pastry: Scalable, distributed object location and routing for large-scale peer-to-peer systems. In *Proc. of ACM Middleware'01*, 2001.
12. I. Stoica, R. Morris, D. Karger, M. F. Kaashoek, and H. Balakrishnan. Chord: a scalable peer-to-peer lookup service for internet applications. In *Proc. of ACM SIGCOMM'01*, 2001.
13. B. Zhao, J. Kubiatowicz, and A. Joseph. Tapestry: An infrastructure for fault-tolerant wide-area location and routing. Technical report, USB/CSD-01-1141, University of California at Berkeley, Computer Science Department, 2001.

Ptops Index Server for Advanced Search Performance of P2P System with a Simple Discovery Server

Boon-Hee Kim and Young-Chan Kim

ChungAng Univ., Dept. of Computer Science & Engineering, Seoul, 221, 156-756, Republic of Korea
{bhkim,yckim}@sslab.cse.cau.ac.kr

Abstract. As various researches with themes varying are being conducted to improve the performance of existing P2P system aimed at seeking out solutions, this paper presents the P2P index server framework designed to attach meaning to information and then improve search performance. The technique presented in this paper, in terms of the speed of search performance, showed a performance similar to that of existing systems as a result of comparison with the system initializing time considered. The technique shows a significant difference in evaluation from other systems from the viewpoint of listing of reliable resulting data against relevant peer requirements.

1 Introduction

At the time of designing a server using P2P applications, this should ensure an index listing function designed to guarantee a load-reduced server and minimum search time for each peer alike. Generally, a server has a list of peers and a list of relevant resources, and when corresponding requests come in, the server functions to transfer the whole list corresponding to names of sources, thus dubbed index server. As such, P2P applications undergo the process of searching simply file names to be searched and file names as corresponding information linked to other peers. However, the simple linking alone to huge amounts of information provided cannot search the data as desired by users. Thus, alternative methods should be presented for the existing P2P applications (only displaying information) to efficiently search information. Cited as an example of distribution applications can be the Web suggested by Tim Berners-Lee, the most widely known concept since 1989. The existing Web has been ever growing due to its simple structure, but has limitations in presenting techniques to search for desired information through huge amounts of information. This problem can be attributed to the HTML language. The Web, which is written using the HTML language designed to simply display instead of featuring contents and meaning of documents, has limitations in presenting various search techniques. Thus, a semantic Web attaches meaning to Web documents, and contributes to research in the areas of automatic extraction, expansion and sharing of information. By introducing this semantic Web concept to P2P applications, it can be determined whether such introduction contributes to improving information search function. Solutions to improve P2P-

M. Li et al. (Eds.): GCC 2003, LNCS 3032, pp. 285–291, 2004.

related performance are being sought through researches with subjects varying. This paper presents the P2P index server framework, Ptops (peer-to-peer for the semantic Web), that attaches meaning to information and improves search performance.
This paper is organized as follows: section 2 is concerning the Ptops index server, section 3 is concerning the conclusions and future works, section 4 is concerning the related works.

2 Ptops Index Server

2.1 Ptops Modules

The P2P index server framework of Ptops, which attaches meaning to information and enhances search performance, comprises the following modules.

- User Stub
- User Skeleton
- SD(Semantic Document Producer)
- SDP(Semantic Document Parser)
- Binder Modules
- Requester Modules
- SC(Server Contact)
- PC(Peer Contact)

The Ptops system peer consists of user stub and user skeleton depending on its role. The user stub is the peer to request sources, and the user skeleton is the respondent peer to supply resources in response to the request. The binder modules in the skeleton are information on IP addresses, log-in names, and sharing resources in the index server, and after log-in, they function to wait for stub's requests. Requester modules request a list of skeleton holding information desired by the index server, and receive a list of binders from the server. The requester undergoes the two steps of establishing communication such as SC(Server Contact) and PC(Peer Contact). SD(Semantic Document Producer) functions to create request and response according to user requests, and SDP (Semantic Document Parser) functions to parse created requests and responses. Ptops' core component, Index Server, upon running, links to the certificate module, thus functioning to provide support for verifying, approving and canceling binder's login requests. It likewise adds accessed binders to the binder list and manages them. The requester is not listed separately. This is because the Ptops index server has to maintain the skeleton responding to the requester request, and owned information. Index server's core module, CP (Central Process), is the key module in the index server to treat user requests delivered by the requester. It likewise indexes owning sources of skeleton peers and relevant peers, reviews meaning arrangements according to stub peer requests, and delivers to relevant SDP combination information of skeleton peers fitting stub peer requests and sources. The next chapter in the part of Ptops CP modules discusses analysis and application of semantic data in CP modules.

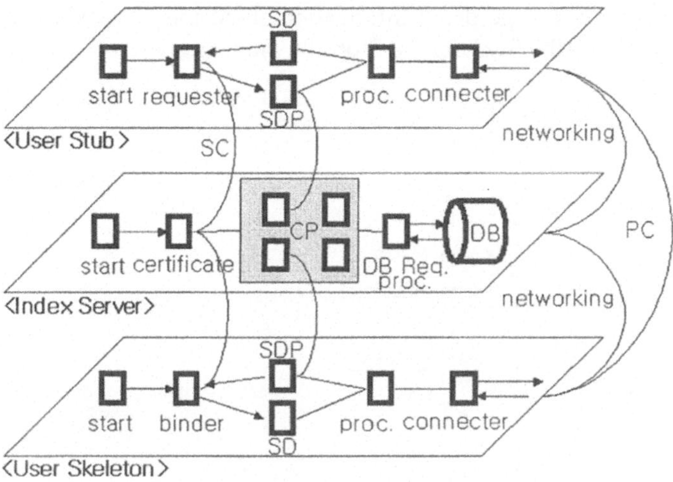

Fig. 1. Request-process of Ptops's stub

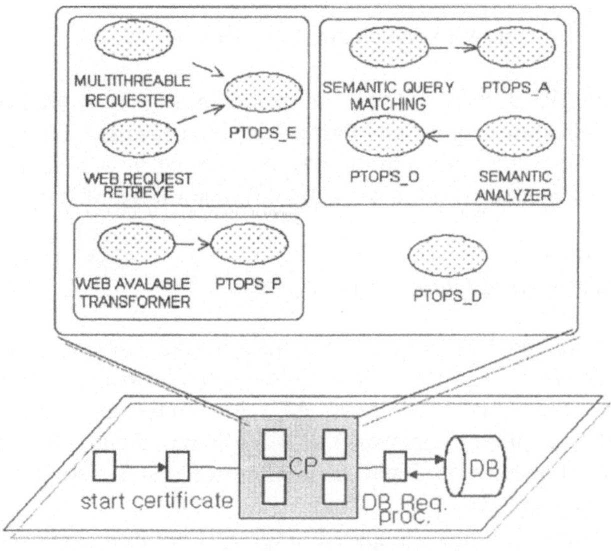

Fig. 2. CP Modules of Ptops

2.2 CP Modules of Ptops

PTOPS_E module is composed by multi-threading mechanism to process the request of many peers. Inputted semantic-information is processed and understood based on the result by PTOPS_O module. PTOPS_A is parsing adaptive semantic-peer among the peer list in the database of index server and transfer PTOPS_P, together with this. Wholly PTOPS_D arbitrate about DB-request. PTOPS_P compose the list of adaptive web and send to the encoded information to the stub. All modules of Ptops are composed adaptive web. The detail information about this is showed in implementation section. Therefore the flexibility of Ptops by implementation is guaranteed.

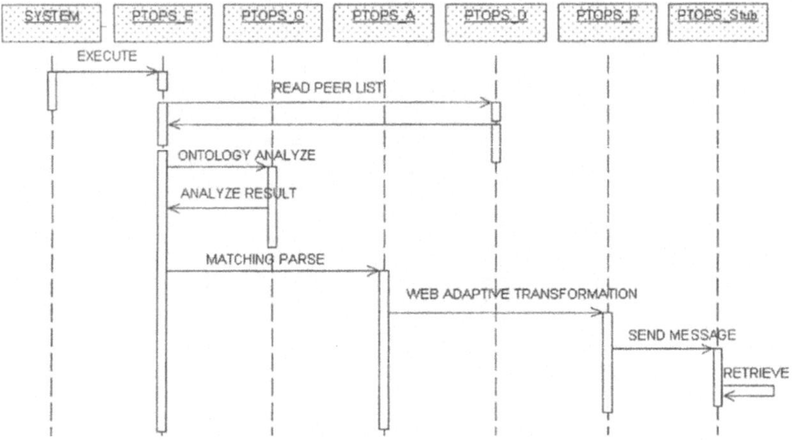

Fig. 3. Execution Process of Ptops CP Module

Firstly, running PTOPS_E at a point of execution time read the peer lists. Next, it analyzes stub's semantic-request and parses matching results. This is converting the generated information like this into the adaptive format in web-environment. Finally, this send the message composed to semantic information-list of stub.

2.3 Implementation and Comparison of Ptops

Ptops system is applied JDK(Java Development Tookit, version 1.4.1 Standard Editions) of Sun Microsystems. For the meaning IR(Information Retrieval) based on Semantic Web, Ptops is used Jena API for embedded Java application of RDF(Resource Description Framework) as W3C Standard and ARP parser for validation of RDF format documents. Database is Microsoft's SQL Server 2000. Web server is IIS 5.1 based on windows.

As shown in the table 1, Ptops, compared to the existing P2P systems, showed similar possibility in terms of expandability and mutual operability. In particular, compared to the existing systems with rudimentary function in treating semantic in-formation, Ptops presents sufficient solutions regarding relevant requests. This system gives alike ability in extensibility, interoperability and etc. compared with existing P2P system like figure. Especially this system gives efficient solution at the processing part of semantic information. This system gives advantages about the performance of client system as the embedded solution in web browser for efficient web services.

Table 1. The comparision of JXTA, OceanStore, PASTRY, and Ptops

Requirements	JXTA	Ocean Store	Pastry	Ptops
File Sharing	Only binary message	Yes		
Automatic Knowledge base creation	Not Included			Semi-automatic
Semantic Information	Not Included			Yes
Extensibility	Java allows own extensions			
Interoperability	Not integrated, small version thinkable	Needs JVM	Difficult, requires Java and RMI	Good
Scalability	Yes	Yes	Routing scales very good	Yes

3 Conclusions and Future Works

Researches with varying themes are being conducted to seek solutions to improve the performance of existing P2P systems. As such, the Ptops system presented in this paper sought to attach meaning to information and thus improve search performance. As a result of testing Ptops-implemented products, Ptops showed a performance similar to that of existing systems with system initializing time considered in terms of search performance speed, and data reliability based on evaluation through experts' feedbacks, compared to other system performance, showed a significant result. To enhance the validity of this result, this research should be furthered through other future researches by applying experimented methodologies by Duncan Watts and Steven Strogatz, and to form an environment to make this application feasible, the evaluation level should be enhanced so as to reach the average value, the starting point of experimental value.

4 Related Works

4.1 Recent P2P

Existing P2P models can be divided into the following categories generally as networking method and role between peers: Pure P2P, P2P with a simple discovery server, P2P with discovery and lookup servers, P2P with discovery, lookup and content servers. The pure P2P model completely depends on PCs, clients in the C/S model. The pure P2P model works without depending on any server as C/S model. Once the P2P application is downloaded in the memory of the machine, peers find other connected peers on the network dynamically. These communication mechanisms occur among connected peers without any support from a server on the other side. This feature of the pure P2P-based model breaks the conventional method of communication in C/S-based models in which the completely communication process between the client and server takes place based on rules the servers. The problem of this model is finding peers on the network. Because no central administration registers the entry of peers that log in to the networks, each user have to locate other peers. These things may be caused disadvantage in search time and the performance of peer itself.

P2P with a simple discovery server model do not involve a server really. To affect some administration, server boundaries have been laid down in P2P with a simple discovery server model. The server only supports each peers by providing a list of connected peers and that establishing connection and communication still remains the job of the peers. To download a resource, individually correspondent peer has to approach each connected peer and post its request, which makes the process time consuming. In the C/S-based models, any peer looking for resources needs not go around other peers as the server maintains all the required content.

In P2P with discovery and lookup servers, the server is used to offer the list of available peers along with the resources useful with each of them. P2P with discovery and lookup servers model reduces the load on peers, as there is no longer a need to visit peer personally for the required information. The establish communication between connected peers, keep it alive, and perform many activities. These activities are logging into the database the information about the connection peers, and entering an index of resources shared by them, and so on. In this model, each peer must not call at each peer to obtain information.

In P2P with discovery, lookup and content servers model, the servers are superintended as in a representative C/S-based architecture. The major disadvantage of this model is high cost because the server has to manage and store information, and carrier to all requests. Because such models are rely on the middle server, exist critically risk by failure through a single point server in the whole system.

Among well known P2P applications, Napster, which is based on the third variety of the P2P models we discussed. Napster's model focuses on sharing a particular file extension. Gnutella works more or less like a pure P2P model. Gnutella is a client-based software that has a file-sharing service and a mini-search engine. Mostly P2P applications are the functions of the tracing out other peers, the querying peers for required content, the sharing content/resources with other peers, and so on. Accordingly, this model reduces time consumption considerably as compared to the other models. We will want the base model because these features of the P2P with discovery and lookup servers model give the effectiveness at the interrelation of searching time and server overload in this paper.

4.2 Recent Semantic Web

According to the W3C, the Semantic Web is the representation of data on the World Wide Web. It is a collaborative effort led by W3C with participation from a large number of researchers and industrial partners. It is based on the Resource Description Framework (RDF), which integrates a variety of applications using XML for syntax and URIs for naming. This Semantic Web as recommendation of the Tim Berners Lee, is an extension of the current web in which information is given well-defined meaning, better enabling computers and people to work in cooperation. It is presented the Semantic Web architectual dependencies(be composed various component).

URI(Uniform Resource Identifier) is the methodology of address definition based on web protocol and the foundation of Semantic Web. In addition, the related study fields of Semantic Web are XML(Extensible Markup Language), namespace, RDF(Resource Description Foundation), RDFschema, Ontology, and so on.

Specially, XML is a simple, very flexible text format derived from SGML(Standard Generalized Markup Language). In the Semantic Web, a role of XML generate the structured documents and define the tag name freely. Hereby XML can be presented based on meaningful information. But only XML is the want of ability from the view-point of Semantic Web. For instance, many persons can be differently present documents of same contents. For interoperability among tags, here is requested new methodology. Moreover, It shows differently expression about same contents in <publish_date> tag. Therefore standard expression is demand.

To resolve these problems of XML, RDF gives roles to one meaning from same con-tents as representative meaning from a characteristic value of resource. In the matter of RDF, ontology is dictionary, contains vocabulary and relations, to get out of the overlapped tag-name and ambiguous. To offer the extensibility of this dictionary, ontology is imported inference-regulations. As these various mechanism, we will apply the linkage of resources and meaning to the P2P index server of this paper.

References

1. Brian McBrids, "Jena: A Semantic Web Toolkit", IEEE Internet Computing (2002) 55-59
2. Brian McBrids, "Jena: Implementing the RDF Model and Syntax Specification", http://www-uk.hpl.hp.com/people/bwm/papers/20001221-paper
3. Aditya Kalyanpur, and so on, "SMORE-Semantic Markup, Ontology, and RDF Editor", http://www.mindswap.org/papers/SMORE.pdf
4. Natalya Fridman Noy, and so on, "The knowledge model of Protégé-2000:combining interoperability and flexibility", http://www-smi.stanford.edu/pubs/SMI_Reports/ SMI-2000-0830.pdf
5. Ian Horrocks, "DAML+OIL: A Description logic for the Semantic Web, IEEE Bulletin of the Technical Committee on Data Engineering, vol.25, no.1, (2002) 4-9
6. David Liben-Nowell, Hari Balakrishnan, and David Karger. Analysis of the evolution of peer-to-peer systems. In Proceedings of ACM Conference on Principles of Distributed Computing (2002)
7. Stefan Saroiu, P. Krishna Gummadi, and Steven D. Gribble. A measurement study of peer-to-peer file sharing systems. In Proceedings of Multimedia Computing and Networking (2002)

Improvement of Routing Structure in P2P Overlay Networks[1]

Jinfeng Hu, Yinghui Wu, Ming Li, and Weimin Zheng

Department of Computer Science and Technology, Tsinghua University, Beijing, China.
{hujinfeng00, wuyinghui97, lim01}@mails.tsinghua.edu.cn,
zwm-dcs@tsinghua.edu.cn

Abstract. Although peer-to-peer overlays have been elaborately studied, they still have redundant overheads. Pastry and Chord use leaf sets to connect those nodes contiguous in numerical space, but these pointers have no contribution to efficient routing. In this paper we argue that if the mapping between a message key and its root node is determined in a smart way, leaf sets can be removed, largely decreasing system overheads. We present a novel overlay algorithm derived from Pastry, in which nodeIds have different lengths and form a Huffman set, routing tables have no empty items and root node exactly prefix-matching its keys. By these means, our approach abolishes the leaf sets with no ill effect on routing performance or other properties. Experimental results show that our approach saves about 22~25% messages cost for maintenance in comparison with Pastry in an overlay of 10,000 peers.

Keywords: overlay networks, peer-to-peer substrate, routing protocol

1 Introduction

Structured peer-to-peer overlays like CAN [1], Pastry[2], Chord [3] and Tapestry [4] provide a powerful collaborative substrate for large-scale decentralized applications. These algorithms let each peer maintain a small number of entries to other peers and ensure a probabilistically bounded hops number in message routing.

In this paper, we argue that there is still much unnecessary redundancy in Pastry, involving both routing entries and message cost for reliability. A Pastry node maintains both leaf set and routing table as its entries, the former for consistency and the later for routing acceleration. We believe that such overlap is a waste and leaf set can be erased if routing designed more elaborately.

We propose an improved algorithm derived from Pastry. Though our approach is similar to Pastry in nodes' routing strategy, they have three substantial differences. First, Pastry nodes have ids (noted *nodeIds*) with fixed length, 128 bits typically, while we assign nodeIds with various lengths to nodes and let all the nodeIds form a Huffman set. Secondly, Pastry routes message to the live node whose nodeId is numerically closest to the destination key. In contrast, our approach routes message to

[1] This work is granted by The National High Technology Research and Development Program of China (G2001AA111010) and Chinese National Basic Research Priority Program (G1999032702)

M. Li et al. (Eds.): GCC 2003, LNCS 3032, pp. 292–299, 2004.

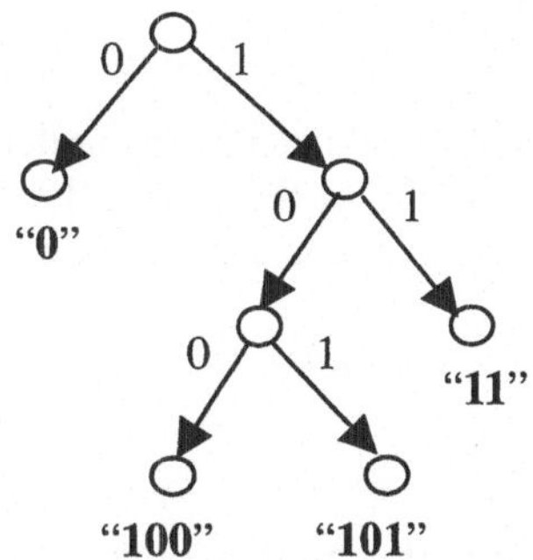

Fig. 1. Using clean binary tree to construct a Huffman set. Left branches are assigned "0" and right branches are assigned "1". Leaf nodes are encoded as the path from the root node.

NodeId: 10110010
0-110111
11-010
100-10001
1010
10111-11
101101-0100
1011000
10110011-101

Fig. 2. A sample of 2-based routing table. Note that nodeIds are not equally long and no empty entry is permitted in the table.

the only live node that prefix-matches the destination key. Thirdly, the entry list each node keeps in our approach is much tidier: leaf set is abolished and routing table has no empty items, which can be naturally kept consistent. This greatly reduces the states to be maintained and hence lightens the burden in keeping them reliable.

The rest of this paper is organized as follows. We first introduce Pastry in Section 2. Then, we detail our approach in Section 3 and analyze its cost in Section 4. Section 5 presents experimental results. Then we conclude in Section 6.

2 Pastry Overview

We first give a brief overview of Pastry protocol.

In Pastry each node has a *nodeId* with 128 bits and holds a routing table as well as a leaf set. Routing table is a matrix, in which item in row r and column c containing a point to another node whose nodeId shares the first r digits with the present nodeId and has c as its $(r+1)$th digit. Leaf set keeps pointers to the l live closest nodes in numerical space, with $l/2$ larger and $l/2$ smaller. l is commonly set to 16 or 32. To keep routing table and leaf set fresh, Pastry node sends heartbeats to related nodes.

Each message has a *key* of a 128-bit-length sequence, and is routed to the node whose nodeId is closet to the key, which is called the key's *root node*. In common cases, first several hops are via routing table and the last is via leaf set.

More Pastry details can be found in [2], [5] and [6].

In a large overlay comprised of 100,000 nodes, each node has a 16-based routing table with averagely 50 entries and a leaf set with 32 entries. The leaf set accounts for 39% entries of all, but it is not a necessity. The main usage of leaf set is to determine which node is the "closest" node in the network currently, ensuring the accurate convergence of routing. So if we leverage another relationship between keys and root nodes, perhaps leaf set is not needed. This is just the core of our design.

3 Our Approach

Our new approach makes some substantial modifications to original Pastry: nodeIds are not equally long; a key's root node's nodeId is a strict prefix of the key; and routing tables has no holes, being consistent naturally. By these changes, leaf set is of no use and removed.

For convenience of statement, we first propose 2-based algorithm.

3.1 NodeIds

We assign nodeIds with different lengths to nodes and ensure that all the nodeIds form a Huffman set. Huffman set is defined as follow:[2]

A set of 0/1 sequences is a Huffman set, if it satisfies two conditions:

a) *Prefix condition:* there is no two elements share a common prefix.
b) *Integrality condition:* given an arbitrary 0/1 sequence with infinite length, there must be an element that is its prefix. Prefix condition ensures that this element is unique.

We can obtain a Huffman set by encoding the leaf nodes for a clean binary tree, in which every node has no child or has precisely two children. As illustrated in Figure 1, we assign "0" to the left branch of each node and "1" to the right one. Then every leaf node is encoded as the path from the root to it. All of these codes form a Huffman set.

3.2 Routing Tables and Routing

Every node keeps a routing table comprising l lines and one row (based 2 here), where l is the length of its nodeId. The entry in line k points to a node whose id shares the first k bits with the current node's id and differs at the $(k+1)$th bit. We can easily deduce from prefix condition and integrality condition that for arbitrary entry there must be at lease one appropriate node in the system. Therefore the routing table will never have a hole. Figure 2 gives a sample.

Message key is a 0/1 sequence with infinite length other than 128-bit long in Pastry. A message is forwarded at each hop to the only entry in the routing table that shares longer prefix than the current node, and finally this message must arrive at the only live node whose id prefix-matches the key.

Message key can be generated in various ways. A general measure is hashing the character of message (e.g. object id of object-update message) to a real number between 0 and 1, and utilizing its binary expression as the key. To be practical, we can generate the key iteratively because only a front part of the key is desired at each hop. We can first calculate only a little fraction of the key, 20 bits perhaps, and just until it is not sufficient at some hop then calculate the next faction. Another simpler method is to use a fixed-length sequence circularly.

To achieve fault tolerance, Pastry routes a message simultaneously to a number of nodes whose nodeIds are numerically closest to the key. However, we omit the leaf sets, leaving nodes unaware of their numerical neighbors, which makes this contigu-

---

[2] Huffman set is similar to Huffman coding, but without consideration about the frequency of the elements' appearance.

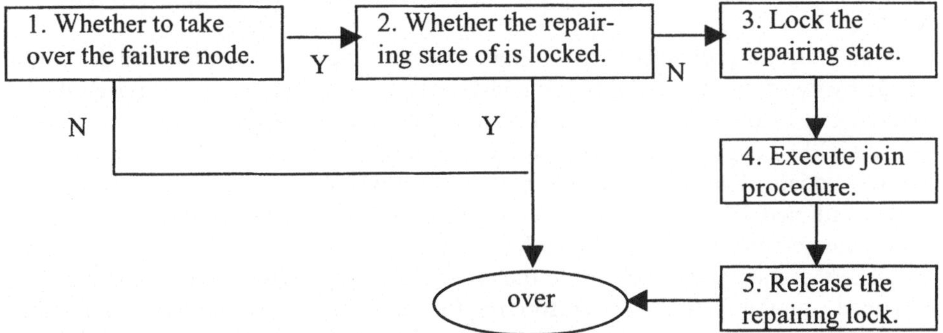

Fig. 3. Algorithm of a node to repair the Huffman set, creating a virtual node with the lost nodeId.

ous replication unfeasible. Thereby we leverage multi-keys replication strategy instead, in which a message owns diverse roots and will be forwarded to all the roots concurrently. This method is also well deployed in Tapestry and CAN.

3.3 Adaptation to Node Joining and Departure

In this section we describe how our approach realizes self-organization in dynamic peer-to-peer network, keeping the property that all nodeIds form a Huffman set and guaranteeing the availability of entries in routing tables along with node joining and departure.

Node joining. A new node first provides an infinite 0/1 sequence X, being likely hash result of its network address or randomly calculated by other means, as a seed of its nodeId to a bootstrap node, then the bootstrap node routes a joining message to X's root node, whose nodeId must be a prefix of X, noted Z. After receiving the message, the root node lengthens its nodeId by one bit with value "0", that is "Z.0", while the new node employs "Z.1" as its nodeId. It can be easily proved that prefix condition and integrality condition still hold after node joining in this manner.

Routing table is constructed by collecting corresponding items from the nodes along the way from the bootstrap to X's root, which is similar to the procedure in Pastry. Details can be seen in [6].

Node departure. Nodes leave the system silently. Node's departure will destroy the integrality condition, so we must fix the nodeIds to a Huffman set. We accomplish this in a direct way, letting another node take the place of the leaving node.

As described in section 2.1, every node sends ping messages to all entries periodically to assure their aliveness. When it finds some node no long alive, it initiates two operations. The first one is to repair the entry, by searching for another corresponding node. As is in Pastry, a node in such instance will ask another node in the same row with the failure one for a replacement. In the case that none of the nodes in this row have an appropriate entry, it then enquires the nodes in the next row.

The second necessary operation is to repair the Huffman set. After a node leaves, the left nodeIds will no longer preserve the integrality condition. So there must be another node filling in this blank in nodeId space, that is, it creates a new virtual peer with the lost nodeId on its physical server. To accomplish it, when a node detects a failure node, other than repairing the entry, it executes the algorithm in Figure 3 as well.

First it decides whether it is willing to assume the responsibility, which is influenced by two factors, capability of its physical server and id distance between the lost nodeId and its own. Id distance can be measured on the length of common prefix of two nodeIds. Longer the common prefix is, more likely the active node is to take over the lost nodeId. This is for the consideration that when a physical server contains two nodes with nodeIds only differing at the last bit, it can merge them into one node with their common prefix as its new nodeId.

Once the node determines to do the repairing work, it should check whether there is already another active node performing this task. This is by checking the repairing state residing on the root node of a consistent hash value of the lost nodeId. Who repairs the nodeId should first lock this state and releases it after repairing. To be more robust, the repairing state is soft, to be automatically unlocked after a period of time.

The process of taking over a nodeId is in a simple way, launching a joining message towards the target nodeId. Certainly the message will not reach the destination since the former root node has departed, but it helps to collect the routing table rows and to deliver the advertisement of the new entry of this nodeId.

The last problem is what to do if no active node has the passion to repair the Huffman set. We assume that the lost nodeId is "α.b", where α is a l-bit string and b is a bit of 0 or 1. For those nodes whose ids have a prefix ofα, they cannot find another node as a replacement filling the entry in the lth row of their routing table. Assuming that one of them does not take over the lost nodeId at the first time possibly for the reason of limited capability of its physical server, after *Trt* it will check this entry for a next time, which surely remains unavailable. Then it will initiate a message towards the root node of "α.b" as we aforementioned. If "α.b" has been already taken over, the message will reach the new owner, which can be employed as the entry. Otherwise, the message will vanish and the node will absolutely start the repairing procedure, i.e., execute the algorithm in Figure 3 from step 2.

3.4 2^b-Based Routing Table

To reduce routing hops, we introduce how to construct routing table based 2^b, where b>1. For a node with l-bit nodeId, its 2^b-based routing table comprises $\lceil l/b \rceil$ rows, each of which contains (2^b–1) entries, just like that in Pastry. However, two different points should be noted, one is that the last row perhaps has less than (2^b–1) entries if b does not divide l exactly, and the other is that when an entry needs a node with nodeId prefixed by α, the actual node in the entry perhaps is contrarily a prefix of α.

4 Cost Analyzing

In this section we estimate the cost for maintaining the reliability of system. We simply use the number of messages per second per node rather than bandwidth as the measurement of reliability cost because messages are all of small size.

Nodes communicate for four operations: joining of new nodes, probing the entries, recovering unavailable entries and taking over lost nodeIds. We calculate each of them on average.

Joining of new nodes. When a node arrives, it exchanges messages with $\log_2 b(N)$ nodes. Assuming that nodes arrive at rate β, message cost on this aspect is $2*\log_2 b(N)*\beta/N$.

Probing the entries. Every node probes all the entries every *Trt* seconds and these probes need response, so the cost is no more than $2*(l/b)*(2^b-1)/Trt$, where l is length of nodeld. If nodelds are generated randomly they will be almost equally long, with $\log_2(N)$ bits. Thus this message cost is $2*\log_2(N)*(2^b-1)/(Trt*b)$

Recovering unavailable entries. We assume that nodes leave the system at rate γ, then for a node keeping *M* entries, $M*\gamma*Trt/N$ of them turns unavailable every *Trt* seconds. To recover an entry, it routes a message to an appropriate node, which needs only one message at a very high probability. So this costs $2*\log_2 b(N)*(2^b-1)*\gamma*Trt/N$ messages on average.

Taking over lost nodelds. Averagely a node is known by $\log_2 b(N)*(2^b-1)$ other nodes. We assume that after its failure, half of them attempt to take over its nodeld. They all check the repairing state, generating $\log_2 b(N)$ messages each. Only one of them will finally assume the work and execute a procedure of node joining, costing 2* $\log_2 b(N)$ messages. Totally, cost for taking over lost nodelds in entire system is $(\log_2 b(N)*(2^b-1)/2+2)*\log_2 b(N)*\gamma/N$ messages per second per node.

Saroiu et al [7] measured the current peer-to-peer systems and reported an average session time of about 2 hours. This means for an overlay of 100,000 nodes there are about 14 peers joining and leaving respectively every second. When we set the parameter as N=100,000, b=4, β=γ=14 and *Trt*=30, the message cost of the above four aspects are approximately 0.0001, 4.15, 0.05 and 0.002. It can be seen that major messages are used for entry probing.

As described in [5], the cost in original Pastry for probing routing table entries can be calculated as follows:

$$Crt = \frac{2 \times \sum_{r=1}^{128/b} (2^b - 1) \times (1 - (1 - (\frac{1}{2^b})^r)^N)}{Trt} . \tag{1}$$

Given the above parameters, it results in 4.87 per node per second. Besides, a Pastry node probes its leaf set entries with a cost of *L*/*Tls* per node per second, where *L* is the length of leaf set and *Tls* is the time interval between two probes. In common configurations, *L*=32, *Tls*=30 and *L*/*Tls*=1.07. Thus the total probing cost in Pastry is about 5.94 per node per second, 41% more than that of our approach.

On the other hand, the message loss rate of our approach can be estimated by:

$$L = 1 - (1 - P(T_{rt} + 2T_{out}))^{\log_{2^b} N} . \tag{2}$$

Here P(T) is the cumulative distribution function according to which peers leave. Message loss rate of Pastry is similarly as follows:

$$L = 1 - (1 - P(T_{ls} + T_{out})) \times (1 - P(T_{rt} + 2T_{out}))^{\log_{2^b} N-1} . \tag{3}$$

We can see that when *Tls*=*Trt*, our approach and Pastry theoretically have almost equal message loss rate.

Next let us simply estimate the cost for query routing upon each node. Assuming that each peer initiates a data query every *Tq* seconds on average, the total queries initiated per second in the entire system is *N*/*Tq*. To respond these queries,

$(\log_{2}b(N)+1)*N/Tq$ totoal messages are exchanged. Consequently a node averagely forwards $(\log_{2}b(N)+1)/Tq$ messages as the contribution to routing. Conservatively letting Tq=10s, b=4 and N=100,000, the resultant value is 0.51 messages per second per node, quite fewer than self-maintenance cost. This indicates that our effort for reducing maintenance cost is of significance.

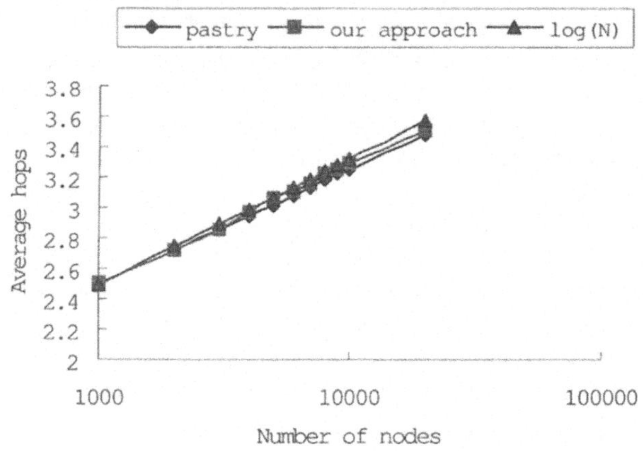

Fig. 4. Average hops versus number of peers, b=4 and Pastry leaf set containing 32 entries.

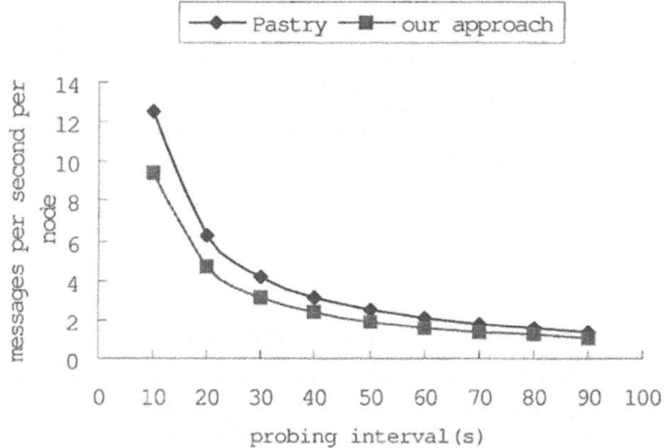

Fig. 5. Maintenance cost versus probing interval.

5 Experimental Results

In this section, we present experimental results for comparison of Pastry and our approach. We directly use FreePastry [8] as Pastry implementation and modify it to realize our approach. All the codes are written in Java and executed using standard JDK, version 1.4.1_02-b06. All experiments were performed on a Linux server with Pentium IV CPU and 2GB memory, which can at most support about 20,000 peers.

We compare our approach and Pastry mainly in two aspects: efficiency and maintenance cost. Efficiency is measured in routing hops without consideration of proximity of each hop. This is because though Pastry can improve its efficiency by proximity-aware entry selection [6], our approach can also introduce similar algorithm. To be impartial, when comparing maintenance cost of the two approaches, we measure the average messages consumed by each peer under the condition that every peer probes its neighbor at identical frequency in two approaches, which indicates almost equal availability of routing entries. Experiment results are shown in Figure 4 and Figure 5.

Figure 4 plots average hops versus number of nodes both in Pastry and our approach, with a line of $log_{16}(N)$ as reference. We can see from it that our approach and Pastry obtain almost equivalent efficiency in message routing.

Figure 5 plots message cost for maintenance versus probing interval. In this experiment, we ran 10,000 nodes and their session time is about 1 hour. Reference [5] shows that session time has little impact on maintenance cost. From the result we can see that our approach saves about 22~25% messages from Pastry. As is analyzed in previous section, it mainly attributes to the abolishment of Pastry's leaf set.

6 Conclusion and Future Work

In this paper we propose a novel overlay algorithm derived from Pastry. We assign nodeIds with diverse length to peers and let all the nodeIds form a Huffman set. In this way, routing tables no long contain empty items and a key is mapped to the only live node whose nodeId is its prefix. Leaf sets are thereupon useless and removed from system, which largely reduce the number of entries a node should maintain. Experiments show that our approach saves about 22~25% communication overheads of original Pastry. We believe that this approach also helps much in other aspects of peer-to-peer overlays and are exploiting how to use it to facilitate failure test, constructing strict routing table and resisting leaf set attacks in secure routing.

References

[1] Sylvia Ratnasamy, Paul Francis, Mark Handley, Richard Karp, Scott Shenker *A Scalable Content-Addressable Network.* SIGCOMM 2001.

[2] Antony I. T. Rowstron and Peter Druschel, *Pastry: Scalable, distributed object location and routing for large-scale peer-to-peer systems.* Middleware, 2001.

[3] I. Stoica, R. Morris, D. Karger, M. F. Kaashoek, and H. Balakrishnan. *Chord: A scalable peer-to-peer lookup service for Internet applications*. SIGCOMM 2001.

[4] Ben Zhao, John Kubiatowicz, and Anthony Joseph. *Tapestry: An infrastructure for fault-tolerant wide-area location and routing.* Technical Report UCB/CSD-01-1141, Computer Science Division, U. C. Berkeley, April 2001. 55

[5] Ratul Mahajan, Maguel Castro, Antony Rowston. *Controlling the Cost of Reliability in Peer-to-Peer Overlays.* IPTPS 2003.

[6] Miguel Castro, Peter Druschel, Y. Charlie Hu, and Antony Rowstron. *Exploiting network proximity in peer-to-peer overlay networks.* Technical Report MSR-TR-2002-82, Microsoft Research, May 2002.

[7] Stefan Saroiu, P Krishna Gummadi, Steven D Gribble. *A Measurement Study of Peer-to-Peer File Sharing Systems*. MMCN 2002.

[8] FreePastry. http://www.research.microsoft.com/~antr/Pastry/#Downloads

Overlay Topology Matching in P2P Systems*

Yunhao Liu[1], Xiao Li[1], Lionel M. Ni[2], and Yunhuai Liu[2]

[1]Department of Computer Science and Engineering
Michigan State University, East Lansing, MI 48824, USA
{liuyunha, lxiao}@cse.msu.edu

[2]Department of Computer Science
Hong Kong University of Science and Technology, Hong Kong, China
{ni, yunhuai}@cs.ust.hk

Abstract. The emerging peer-to-peer (P2P) model has gained significant attention due to its many unique features in supporting file sharing among a huge number of networked users. However, the mechanism of peers randomly choosing logical neighbors without any knowledge about underlying physical topology can cause a serious topology mismatching between the P2P overlay network and the physical underlying network. Adaptive overlay topology optimization and location-aware topology matching are two techniques aiming at alleviating the mismatching problem and reducing the unnecessary traffic and average query response time of unstructured P2P systems while still retaining the search scope. In this paper we compare the performance of these two approaches through simulation studies.

1 Introduction

The emerging peer-to-peer (P2P) model has gained significant attention due to its many unique features in supporting file sharing among a huge number of networked users, where each peer acts as both a resource provider and a consumer. There are mainly three different architectures for P2P systems: centralized, decentralized structured, and decentralized unstructured. This paper focuses on decentralized unstructured P2P systems, such as Gnutella and KaZaA. File placement is random in these systems, which has no correlation with the network topology. Unstructured P2P systems are most commonly used in today's Internet. The most popular search mechanism in use is to blindly “flood" a query to the network among peers (such as in Gnutella) or among supernodes (such as in KaZaA). A query is broadcast and rebroadcast until a certain criterion is satisfied. If a peer receiving the query can provide the requested object, a response message will be sent back to the source peer along the inverse of the query path. A query message will also be dropped if the query message has visited the peer before.

* This work was partially supported by Michigan State University IRGP Grant 41114 and by Hong Kong RGC Grant HKUST6161/03E.

M. Li et al. (Eds.): GCC 2003, LNCS 3032, pp. 300–307, 2004.

Studies in [10] has shown that P2P traffic contributes the largest portion of the Internet traffic based on their measurements on some popular P2P systems. A large portion of the heavy P2P traffic caused by inefficient overlay topology and the blind flooding is unnecessary, which makes the unstructured P2P systems being far from scalable. The mechanism of peers randomly choosing logical neighbors without any knowledge about underlying physical topology can cause a serious topology mismatching between the P2P overlay network and the physical underlying network. Aiming at alleviating the mismatch problem, reducing the unnecessary traffic, and addressing the limits of existing solutions, we had proposed two distributed approaches: adaptive overlay topology optimization (AOTO) [6] and location-aware topology matching (LTM) scheme[7]. AOTO is an algorithm of building an overlay multicast tree among each source node and its direct logical neighbors so as to alleviate the mismatch problem by choosing closer nodes as logical neighbors, while providing a larger query coverage range. LTM is another algorithm in which each peer issues a detector in a small region so that the peers receiving the detector can record relative delay information. Based on the delay information, a receiver can detect and cut most of the inefficient and redundant logical links, and add closer nodes as its direct neighbors. We compare these two approaches in terms of reduction ratio and convergent speed in dynamic P2P environments.

The rest of the paper is organized as follows. Section 2 discusses related work. Section 3 discusses unnecessary traffic cost and topology mismatch problems. Section 4 overviews the adaptive overlay topology optimization (AOTO) and location-aware topology matching (LTM) schemes. Section 5 describes our simulation methodology. Performance comparison between AOTO and LTM is presented in Section 6, and we conclude the work in Section 7.

2 Related Works

Many efforts have been made to avoid the large volume of unnecessary traffic incurred by the flooding-based search in decentralized unstructured P2P systems. In general, three types of approaches have been proposed to improve search efficiency in unstructured P2P systems: *forwarding-based, cache-based, and overlay optimization.* The three different kinds of approaches can be used together to complement each other.

The approaches based on overlay topology optimization are the most closely related to what we are presenting in this paper. There are mainly three types of solutions. End system multicast, Narada, was proposed in [4], which first constructs a rich connected graph on which to further construct shortest path spanning trees. Each tree is rooted at the corresponding source using well-known routing algorithms. This approach introduces large overhead when forming the graph and trees in a large scope, and does not consider the dynamic joining and leaving characteristics of peers. The overhead of Narada is proportional to the multicast group size. Researchers have also considered to cluster close peers based on their IP addresses (e.g., [5, 8]). Recently, researchers in [11] have proposed to measure the latency between each peer to multiple stable Internet servers called "landmarks". The measured latency is used to determine the distance between peers. This measurement is conducted in a global P2P domain. In contrast, our measurement is conducted in many small regions, significantly reducing network traffic with high accuracy.

3 Unnecessary Traffic and Topology Mismatching

In a P2P system, all participating peers form a P2P network over a physical network. A P2P network is an abstract, logical network called an *overlay network.* Maintaining and searching operations of a Gnutella peer are specifically described in [3]. When a new peer wants to join a P2P network, a bootstrapping node provides the IP addresses of a list of existing peers in the P2P network. The new peer then tries to connect with these peers. If some attempts succeed, the connected peers will be the new peer's neighbors. Once this peer connects into a P2P network, the new peer will periodically *ping* the network connections and obtain the IP addresses of some other peers in the network. These IP addresses are cached by this new peer. When a peer leaves the P2P network and then wants to join the P2P network again, the peer will try to connect to the peers whose IP addresses have already been cached. The mechanisms that a peer joins a P2P network, the fact of a peer randomly joining and leaving, and the nature of flooding search make an inefficient mismatched overlay network and cause large amount of unnecessary traffic.

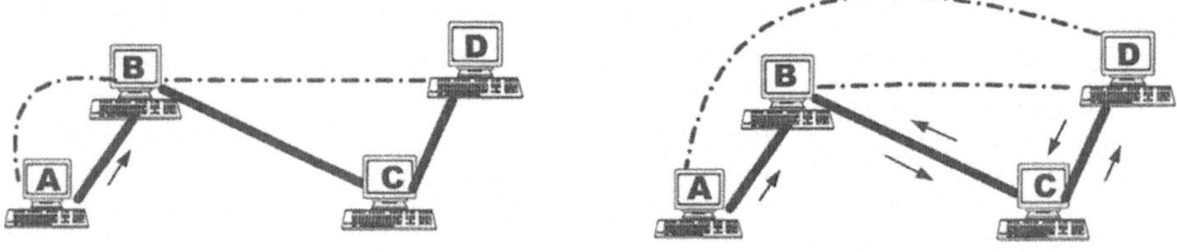

Fig. 1. Two examples of P2P overlay networks.

Figure 1 shows two examples of P2P overlay topology (A, B, and D are three participating peers) and physical topology (nodes A, B, C, and D) mappings, where solid lines denote physical connections and dashes lines denote overlay (logical) connections. Consider the case of a message delivery from peer A to peer B. In the left figure, A and B are both P2P neighbors and physical neighbors. Thus, only one communication is involved. In the right figure, since A and B are not P2P neighbors, A has to send the message to D before forwarding to B. This will involve 5 communications as indicated in Fig. 1. Clearly, such a mapping creates much unnecessary traffic and lengthens the query response time. We refer to this phenomenon as topology mismatch problem.

4 AOTO and LTM

Optimizing inefficient overlay topologies can fundamentally improve P2P search efficiency. If the system can detect and disconnect the low productive logical connections, and switch the logical connections shown in the left figure into the right figure in Fig.1, the total network traffic could be significantly reduced without shrinking the search scope of queries. This is the basic principle of AOTO and LTM. In this section, we will briefly introduce these two algorithms.

4.1 AOTO

Adaptive Overlay Topology Optimization (AOTO) includes two steps: Selective Flooding (SF) and Active Topology (AT). Instead of flooding to all neighbors, SF uses a more efficient flooding strategy to selectively flood a query on an overlay multicast tree. This tree can be formed using a minimum spanning tree algorithm among each peer and its immediate logical neighbors. In order to build the minimum spanning tree, a peer has to know the costs to all its logical neighbors and the costs between any pair of the neighbors. We use network delay between two nodes as a metric for measuring the cost between nodes. Limewire implementation of Gnutella 0.6 P2P protocol is modified by adding one routing message type. Each peer probes the costs with its immediate logical neighbors and forms a *neighbor cost table.* Two neighboring peers exchange their neighbor cost tables so that a peer can obtain the cost between any pair of its logical neighbors. Thus, a small overlay topology of a source peer and all its logical neighbors is known to the source peer. Based on obtained neighbor cost tables, a minimum spanning tree then can be built by simply using an algorithm like PRIM which has computation complexity of $O(m^2)$, where m is the number of logical neighbors of a source peer. Now the message routing strategy of a peer is to select the peers that are the direct neighbors in the multicast tree to send its queries.

The second step of AOTO, AT, reorganizes the overlay topology. Note that each peer has a neighbor list which is further divided into flooding neighbors (direct neighbors in the tree) and non-flooding neighbors in SF. Each peer also has the neighbor cost tables of all its neighbors. In this step, it tries to replace those physically far away neighbors by physically close by neighbors, thus minimizing the topology mismatching traffic. An efficient method to identify such a candidate peer to replace a far away neighbor is critical to the system performance. Many methods may be proposed. In AOTO, a non-flooding neighbor may be replaced by one of the non-flooding neighbor's neighbor.

4.2 LTM

Location-aware topology matching (LTM) consists of three operations: TTL2 detector flooding, low productive connection cutting, and source peer probing. Based on Gnutella 0.6 P2P protocol, we design a new message type called *TTL2-detector.* In addition to the Gnutella's unified 23-byte header for all message types, a TTL2-detector message has a message body in two formats. The short format is used in the source peer, which contains the source peer's IP address and the timestamp to flood the detector. The long format is used in a one-hop peer that is a direct neighbor of the source peer, which includes four fields: *Source IP Address, Source Timestamp, TTL1 IP Address, TTL1 Timestamp.* The first two fields contain the source IP address and the source timestamp obtained from the source peer. The last two fields are the IP address of the source peer's direct neighbor who forwards the detector and the timestamp to forward it. In the message header, the initial TTL value is 2. The payload type of the detector can be defined as 0x82.

Each peer floods a TTL2-detector periodically. We use d(i, S, v) to denote the TTL2-detector who has the message ID of i with TTL value of v and is initiated by S. We use N(S) to denote the set of direct logical neighbors of S, and use $N^2(S)$ to denote the set of peers being two hops away from S. A TTL2-detector can only reach peers in N(S) and $N^2(S)$. We use network delay between two nodes as a metric for measuring the cost between nodes. The clocks in all peers can be synchronized by current techniques in an acceptable accuracy[1]. By using the TTL2-detector message, a peer can compute the cost of the paths to a source peer, and optimizes the topology by conducting low production cutting and source peer probing operations.

5 Simulation Methodology

A well-designed search mechanism should seek to optimize both efficiency and Quality of Service (QoS). Efficiency focuses on better utilizing resources, such as bandwidth and processing power, while QoS focuses on user-perceived qualities, such as number of returned results and response time. In unstructured P2P systems, the QoS of a search mechanism generally depends on the number of peers being explored (queried), response time, and traffic overhead. If more peers can be queried by a certain query, it is more likely that the requested object can be found. So we use two performance metrics: average traffic cost versus search scope and query response time.

Traffic cost is one of the parameters seriously concerned by network administrators. Heavy network traffic limits the scalability of P2P networks and is also a reason why a network administrator may prohibit P2P applications. We define the traffic cost as network resource used in an information search process of P2P systems, which is a function of consumed network bandwidth and other related expenses. *Response time* of a query is one of the parameters concerned by P2P users. We define response time of a query as the time period from when the query is issued until when the source peer received a response result from the first responder.

We first generate network topologies. Based on generated networks, we simulate P2P flooding search, host joining/leaving behavior, AOTO, and LTM. Two types of topologies, physical topology and logical topology, are generated in our simulation. BRITE [1] is a topology generation tool that provides the option to generate topologies based on the AS Model. Using BRITE, we generate two physical topologies each with 20,000 nodes. The logical topologies are generated with the number of peers (nodes) ranging from 2,000 to 8,000. The average number of neighbors of each node is ranging from 4 to 10.

---

1 Current implementation of NTP version 4.1.1 in public domain can reach the synchronization accuracy down to 7.5 milliseconds [2] NTP: The Network Time Protocol, http://www.ntp.org/. Another approach is to use distance to measure the communication cost, such as the number of hops weighted by individual channel bandwidth.

6 Performance Evaluation

We present our simulation results to compare AOTO and LTM in this section.

6.1 AOTO and LTM in Static Environments

In our first simulation, we compare the effectiveness of AOTO and LTM in a static P2P environment where the peers do not join and leave frequently. This will show that without changing the overlay topology, how many optimization steps are required to reach a better topology matching. The first goal of AOTO and LTM schemes is to reduce traffic cost while retaining the same search scope. Figures 2 and 3 show the traffic cost reduction of AOTO and LTM, respectively. Note that the traffic overhead has been included. The simulation results in Figures 4 and 5 show that AOTO can shorten the query response time by about 35% after 10 steps while the LTM will reduce response time by more than 60% in only 3 steps. P2P systems with a large number of average connections offer a faster search speed while increasing traffic. One of the strengths of AOTO and LTM schemes is that they reduce both query traffic cost and response time without decreasing the query success rate.

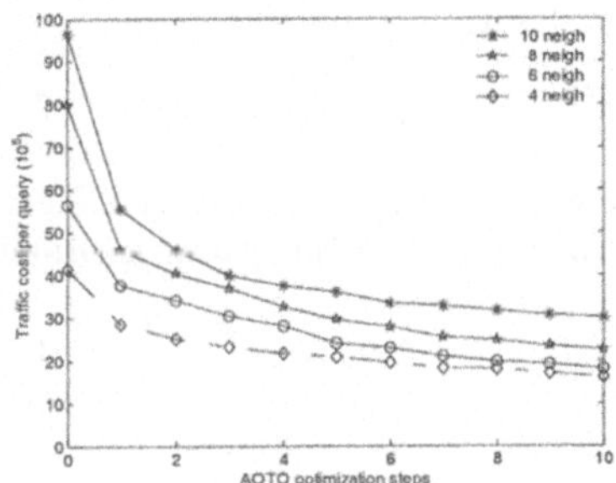

Fig. 2. Traffic reduction vs. optimization step in AOTO

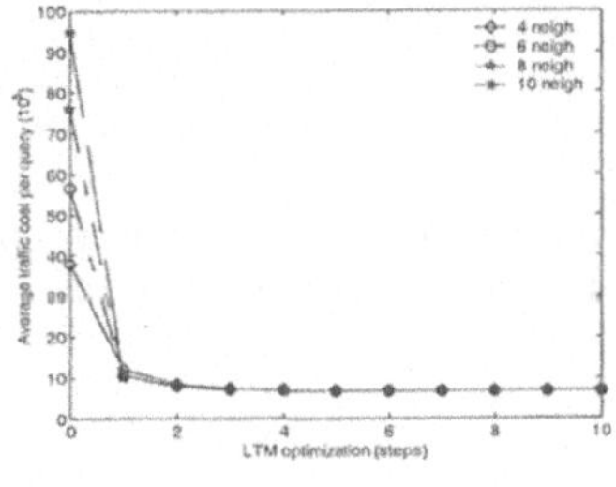

Fig. 3. Traffic reduction vs. optimization step in LTM

6.2 AOTO and LTM in Dynamic Environments

We further compare the effectiveness of AOTO and LTM in dynamic P2P environments. In this simulation, we assume that peer average lifetime in a P2P system is 10 minutes; 0.3 queries are issued by each peer per minute; and the frequency for AOTO and LTM at every peer to conduct optimization operations is twice per minute. From Figures 6 and 7 we can see that both AOTO and LTM could significantly reduce the traffic cost and average query response time when retaining the same search scope, while LTM has a better performance than AOTO.

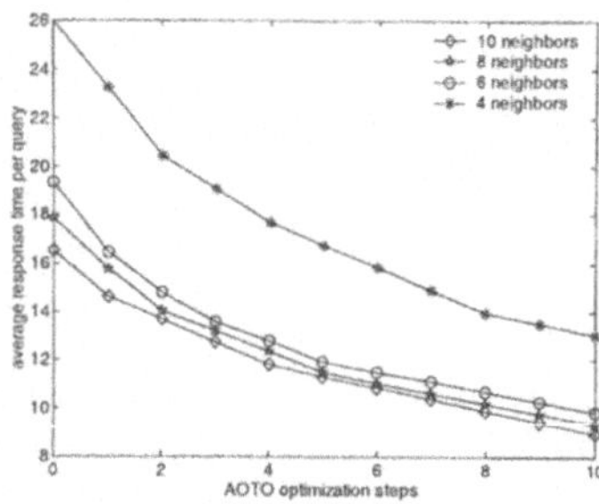

Fig. 4. Average Response time vs. opt. step in AOTO

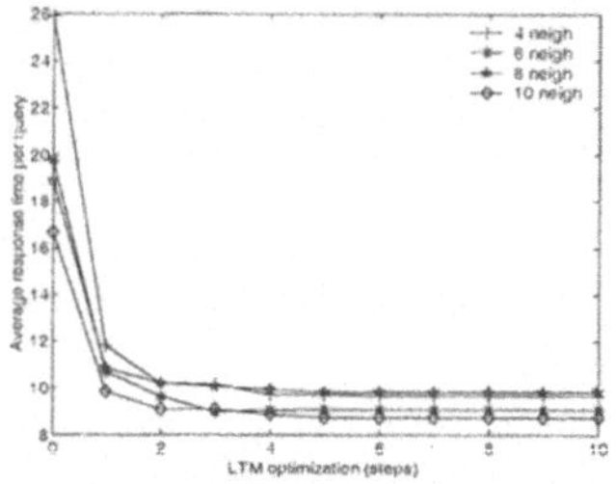

Fig. 5. Average Response time vs. opt. step in LTM

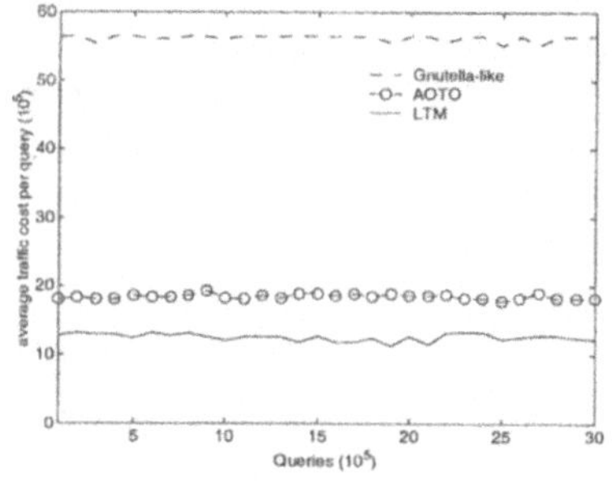

Fig. 6. Average traffic cost comparison of AOTO and LTM in dynamic environment

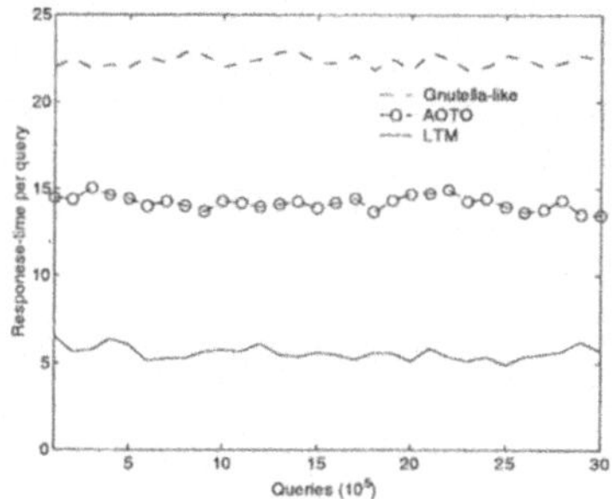

Fig. 7. Average response time comparison of AOTO and LTM in dynamic environments

7 Conclusion and Future Work

We have compared AOTO and LTM overlay topology match algorithms in both static and dynamic environments. They are both fully distributed and scalable in that they do not need any global knowledge, and each peer conducts the algorithm independently. Compared with traffic cost savings, the overhead incurred by these two algorithms is trivial. The other strength of AOTO and LTM is that they are complementary with other cache based and forwarding based approaches and can be deployed together.

LTM does show more advantages than AOTO. However, LTM creates slightly more overhead and requires that all peer clocks be synchronized, which requires additional overhead to run a clock synchronization protocol, such as NTP.

Future work will lead in two directions. One is to investigate the possibility of integrating AOTO and LTM with other existing advanced search approaches to further improve search performance. The other one is to deploy and test an AOTO and LTM prototype based on current version of Gnutella open source code in PlanetLab [9], an open, shared testbed for developing wide area network services.

References

[1] BRITE,http://www.cs.bu.edu/brite/

[2] NTP: The Network Time Protocol,http://www.ntp.org/

[3] The Gnutella protocol specification 0.6,http://rfc-gnutella.sourceforge.net

[4] Y. Chu, S. G. Rao, and H. Zhang, "A case for end system multicast," Proceedings of ACM SIGMETRICS, 2000.

[5] B. Krishnamurthy and J. Wang, "Topology modeling via cluster graphs," Proceedings of SIGCOMM Internet Measurement Workshop, 2001.

[6] Y. Liu, Z. Zhuang, L. Xiao, and L. M. Ni, "AOTO: Adaptive Overlay Topology Optimization in Unstructured P2P Systems," Proceedings of GLOBECOM, San Francisco, USA, 2003.

[7] Y. Liu, X. Liu, L. Xiao, L. M. Ni, and X. Zhang, "Location-Aware Topology Matching in Unstructured P2P Systems," to appear in Proceedings of INFOCOM 2004.

[8] V. N. Padmanabhan and L. Subrananian, "An investigation of geographic mapping techniques for Internet hosts," Proceedings of ACM SIGCOMM'01, 2001.

[9] L. Peterson, D. Culler, T. Anderson, and T. Roscoe, "A blueprint for introducing disruptive technology into the Internet," Proceedings of HOTNETS, 2002.

[10] S. Saroiu, K. P.Gummadi, R. J. Dunn, S. D. Gribble, and H. M. Levy, "An Analysis of Internet Content Delivery Systems," Proceedings of the 5th Symposium on Operating Systems Design and Implementation, 2002.

[11] Z. Xu, C. Tang, and Z. Zhang, "Building topology-aware overlays using global soft-state," Proceedings of ICDCS, 2003.

Effect of Links on DHT Routing Algorithms[1]

Futai Zou, Liang Zhang, Yin Li, and Fanyuan Ma

Department of Computer Science and Engineering
Shanghai Jiao Tong University, 200030 Shanghai, China
zoufutai@cs.sjtu.edu.cn

Abstract. Various DHT routing algorithms have been proposed in recent years. All these algorithms have tried to keep an uniform structured geometry while nodes join and leave. In this paper, we use links to capture the dynamic characteristics of the geometry and suggest there are three kinds of links in the geometry: the basic short link, the redundant short link, and the long links. Several current DHT systems have been investigated to argue these links are inherent in them and pointed out the possible improved directions of performance based on the characteristics of links. We analyze how links impact the routing performance and observe it with simulation experiments. Our experimental results show that each kind of links has its special contribution to the performance of P2P systems and it needs to take the effect of links into account as designing DHT routing algorithms.

1 Introduction

A peer-to-peer networked system is a collaborating group of Internet nodes which construct their own special-purpose network on top of the Internet. Peer-to-Peer(P2P) systems can provide the capability to organize and utilize the huge amounts of resources in the Internet. Generally, we can taxonomize these decentralized systems into two categories: structured P2P systems and unstructured P2P systems. Structured P2P system are systems where nodes organize themselves in an orderly fashion and search is routed while unstructured P2P systems are ones where nodes organize themselves random and search is blind. Structured P2P systems provide an efficient lookup mechanism by means of DHTs(Distributed Hash Tables) while unstructured P2P systems use mostly broadcast search. Systems like CAN[3], Chord[4], Tapestry[6] and Koorder[7] are examples of the former, and Gnutella[2], Freenet[5] belong to the latter.

The most important difference between structured and unstructured P2P systems is the determinate routing. A determinate routing can guarantee the location of an object and find the object in a preconcerted approach. In contrast to this, searching objects in unstructured P2P systems are indeterminate and it is often failed to find rare objects.

[1] Research described in this paper is supported by The Science & Technology Committee of Shanghai Municipality Key Technologies R&D Project Grant 03dz15027 and by The Science & Technology Committee of Shanghai Municipality Key Project Grant 025115032.

M. Li et al. (Eds.): GCC 2003, LNCS 3032, pp. 308–315, 2004.

Considering the basic topology construction, we argue that the difference between unstructured and structured systems in routing guarantee is base on the topologic geometry. Structured systems provide an efficiently uniform geometry while unstructured systems are lack of uniform geometry. These uniform geometries may be tree, ring, hypercube and DHT technique can distribute p2p nodes on to the vertex of the geometry. In this way, the edge of geometries embodies the relationship of a pair of nodes in P2P systems. A link is referred to an edge but it is very different the edge from the dynamic characteristic. The link can be dynamically adjusted according to the change of node's neighbors and it reflects how well the node senses the system. We call the original node as the owner of the links.

Though it depends on the requirements for all kinds of DHTs, in essence, each DHT geometry could provide three kinds of links: basic short links, redundant short links and long links. Basic short links are these links between the node and its adjacent nodes with only one hop. Likewise, redundant short links are these links sequentially following basic short links. That means they are these links between the node and its adjacent nodes with over one hop. The similarity of tow kinds of short links is that they maintain the connectivity of DHT geometry so that a request can be routed to any node in P2P systems. The difference is that basic short links are the commonness of all DHT geometries and must exist in the construction of DHT geometries, but redundant short links may not exist because they only enhance the connectivity of the underlying DHT geometry. Long links begin from current node to contact the remote distant nodes so as to shorten the network diameter, in that a request can be routed much faster.

We use the links to capture the dynamic characteristic of structured peer-to-peer network and in nature it is the reflection of the dynamic geometry underlying the structured peer-to-peer network. DHT systems can forward a request only using its basic short links, however, it is usually inefficient and unreliable. Therefore, to design a DHT system, one should add additional links to the "nude" DHT geometry so as to enhance the system performance. As mentioned above, redundant short links can enhance the connectivity of the geometry that improves the fault-tolerance and long links can shorten the diameter of the geometry that reduces the average path length. In this way, we have provided the linking model to anatomise DHT algorithms. In next section, we will investigate several DHT systems to argue these inherent linked constructions and the direction of the improvement of their performance.

The remainder of the paper is organized as follows. Section 2 investigates several popular P2P systems and provides the insight of links to these DHT geometries. Section 3 analyzes how the links impact on the routing performance and the construction of links and give the basic methods to establish links into DHT geometries. Experiments are discussed in Section 4 and we conclude our research and propose future work in the last section.

2 Links in DHTs

We discuss several current DHT designs in this section. We make special investigations on their inherent geometric construction and research how links impact their routing performance. We consider the following DHTs: Chord, CAN, Koorde and expect to provide the insight of links to DHT geometries through these typical designs.

2.1 Chord

Chord [4] arranges all *n* nodes into a uniform circle. It uses a single dimensional circular identifier space and forwards messages based on numerical difference with the destination address. Chord maintains two sets of neighbors. Each node has a successor list that immediately follow it in the identifier space and a finger list which includes *log(n)* contacted nodes. These contacted nodes is formed as follows: current node with identifier (say) x maintains *log(n)* contacted nodes where the ith node is the node identifier closest to $x+2^i$ on the circle. As described above, we can know that the successor list is just short links and the finger list is just the long links. So there are k short links(k is the size of the successor list) and *log(n)* long links.

The geometry of Chord is a ring. The minimal connected ring need only a link as its basic short link. That means Chord could use only one link per node to make a determinate search. However, this design is very inefficient for its very weak connectivity and a large network diameter *O(n)*. So the design needs to add redundant links to the robust connectivity and to add long links to shorten the network diameter. The successor list in Chord is just the redundant short links and the finger list is just the long links. In this design, Chord achieves *O(logn)* network diameter.

2.2 CAN

Sylvia et al [3] proposed the Content Addressable Networks as a distributed infrastructure that provides hash table like functionality on internet-like scales. CAN use a d-torus that is partitioned among nodes such that every node owns a distinct zone within the space. Each node has 2d neighbors; neighbor *i* differs from the given node on only the ith bit. Using its neighbor coordinate set, a node routes a message towards its destination by simple greedy forwarding to the neighbor with coordinates closest to the destination coordinates.

CAN embody hypercube geometry. To keep the minimal connected hypercube, it does need 2d links per node. Above described above, the design of CAN only provides *2d* the basic short links, without any other links in CAN. Therefore, CAN is deficient in robust connectivity and has a longer network diameter $(d/2)n^{(1/d)}$.

2.3 Koorde

Koorde [7] is a novel DHT that exploits de Bruijn graph [1]. It looks up a key by contacting $log_2 n$ nodes with only *2* neighbors per node. A de Bruijn graph has a node for each binary number of b bits. For the geometry of de Bruijn graph, a node has two outgoing edges: node m has an edge to node 2m mod 2^b and an edge to node $2m+1$ mode 2^b. It is easy to extend Koorde to k neighbors.

The de Bruijn graph is a compacted geometry so as to an optimal diameter. In essence, it is a minimal connected graph. So it has only the basic short links but can achieve an optimal diameter. This is a desired geometry which can keep a constant overheads with constant short links because long links would do more helps to shorten the diameter. We think it is a good choice to design the new DHT algorithm on a geometry which has inherent optimal diameter. However, the pure de Bruijn geometry is less resilience due to the lack of redundant short links. So Koorde has been designed to add k redundant short links in a similar way with Chord.

3 Link Analysis and Establishment

After surveying classic P2P geometry, we give a more comprehensive understand of links in this section. First, we analyze how the links impact on the routing performance of P2P systems. Second, we give the basic methods to establish links into DHT geometries.

3.1 Link Analysis

We use links to capture the dynamic relationship of nodes in structured P2P systems. These links form a structured geometry. We think that the well-organized and connected geometry underlying structured P2P systems is the radical difference with the free-riding unstructured P2P systems. According to the different function in the geometry, we distinguish three kinds of links, that is, the basic short link, the redundant short link, the long link. Although each kind of link has its function, the basic short link is the radical link of the geometry and is decided inherently by the geometry. Hence we emphasize on how the long links and the redundant short links impact the routing performance of P2P systems. We analyses the two metrics, average path length and resilience as follows.

3.1.1 Average Path Length

The average path length is the average hops between every pair of nodes. It identifies how quickly a request is forward to the destination. The long link is an efficient way to improve the average path length. Chord adds long links to the basic geometry to get an optimizing average path length. CAN hasn't long links in that it gets a longer average path length. The methods to add long links are diversified and have still more widely space to be explored. We point out, however, it needs the tradeoff between the number of links and the maintenance overheads of links.

3.1.2 Resilience

Resilience measures the extent to which DHTs can route around trouble even without the aid of recovery mechanisms that fix trouble. The basic short link is inner structure of the DHT geometry and redundant short links provide the chance to enhance its connectivity. The connectivity embodies the routing resilience to node failure. The lack of redundant short links would be less resilience, which will be frail for node failure or spend a long path to be rewound. Resilience is a important aspect of P2P systems. As a special geometry without redundant short links, it is suggested to add redundant short links to improve the resilience. Koorde is a example as described in section 2.3.

3.2 Link Establishment

As we have investigated in section 2, DHT systems build their routing algorithms based on a structured geometry and we can use link to capture the dynamic characteristics of the geometry and suggest there are three kinds of links in the geometry: the basic short link, the redundant short link, and the long links. We have pointed out that basic short links are the inner structure of various DHT geometries and the improved performance of DHT systems would rely on long links and additional redundant short links. Hence we discuss how to establish additional long links and redundant links into the geometries with only inner basic short links so as to improve the performance of P2P systems.

3.2.1 Long Links

Long links would shorten the average path length as mentioned above. Long links should be arranged appropriately so as to reach a good tradeoff between the number of long inks and the maintenance overheads of these links. We assume the node ID space is N. A general technique is to split the space into w non-overlapping sub intervals and establish one long link per sub-interval. That is, a node x may establish its w long links according to the formalizing description as follows:

For a node whose id is x can establish $log_2(N)$ long links to these nodes whose id is $(x+2^i)\ mod\ N, i \in (1, log_2(N))$. Chord use this method and shorten path length to $O(log_2N)$. We can extend this method from one dimension to multiple dimensions. For a d-dimensional torus, we may assume that torus is of size m^d, where $m^d = N$ and m is the width of each dimension of the torus. In each dimension, the node establishes $log_2(m)$ long links to nodes whose dimensional coordination is $(x+2^i)\ mod\ m, i \in (1, log_2(m))$. In this way, each node still maintains $O(log_2N)$ long links. This method can be applied to reconstruct CAN topology. However, we want to keep the merit of CAN with constant degree overheads. Hence we only add one long link along each dimension, that is, node x establishes one long link along each dimension to nodes whose correspondingly dimensional coordination is $(x+2/m)\ mod\ m$. This method will reduce the average path length but still keep constant degree overheads as $O(3d)$.

3.2.2 Redundant Short Links

Redundant short links will improve resilience performance because it can make routing continue to the destination even if the basic short links haven't been recovered from the failure. For one dimension such a circle, redundant short links would be established with the clockwise successors of the node. For multiple dimension, redundant short links can be established from the node to its adjacent nodes in torus with hops 2,3,4 etc.

4 Experiments

In this section, we observe how the links impact on DHT routing performance by simulation. For the better understanding the effect of links, we use CAN as the base of our simulation. More exactly, there are two reasons for selecting CAN: CAN has only 2d basic short links and it is the well-known DHT system. In section 4.1 and 4.2, we add long links and redundant short links to CAN respectively and observe the effect of links. We focus on two kinds of performance metrics: the average path length and resilience.

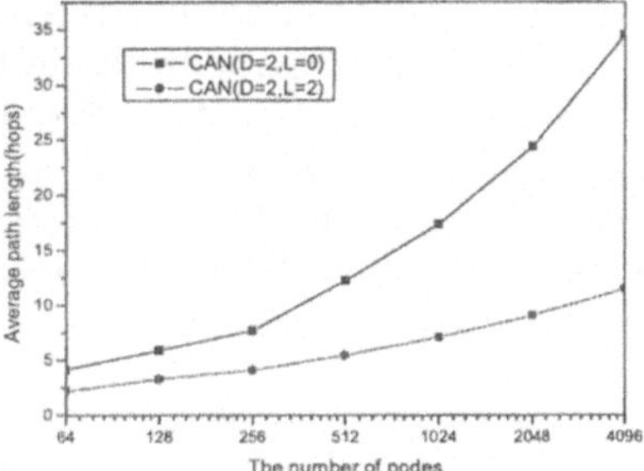

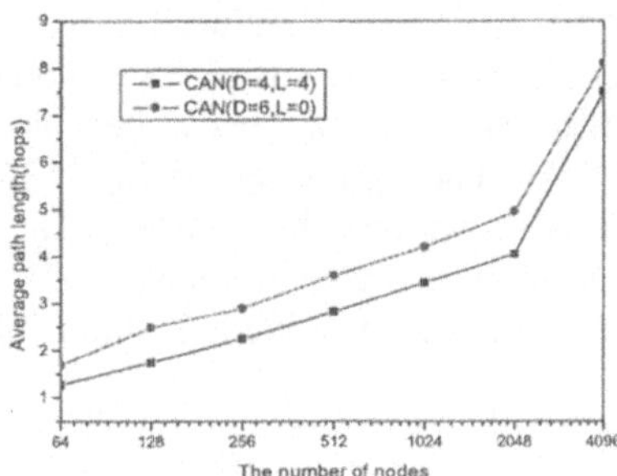

Fig. 1. Effect of long links. Left: Comparing average path length between 0 and 2 long link (L) to 2-CAN. Right: Comparing average path length between additional long links and short links in higher dimension. Note that 4-CAN with additional long links has the same number of links with 6-CAN.

4.1 Effect of Long Links

We add additional long links to CAN in according to 3.2.1. So each node in CAN has *3d* links with the additional *d* long links distributed in each dimension. We run simulation in the network with node number form 64 to 4096. First, we observe the improved performance after long links are added to 2-CAN. Second, we add 4 additional long links to 4-CAN so that 4-CAN has the same number of links with 6-CAN, then we compare their routing performance. We want to know if long links have more important than short links in higher dimension on the improvement of average path length. Fig. 1 shows the simulated results. The left graph in Fig. 1 presents the improved path length with additional long links. As it is clear to see, with the number of nodes increases, long links decrease the average path length more significantly. It can be explained that long links have more widely space to shorten the diameter of the network as the number of nodes increases. As shown in the right graph in Fig. 1, the performance with additional long links is better than short links in higher dimension. Hence, the use of long links might be the preferred option if one is focusing on the improvement of the average path length.

4.2 Effect of Redundant Short Links

We add additional redundant short link with the methods described in section 3.2.2. As mentioned earlier, short links focus on the connectivity of the network. The basic short link is inner structure of the DHT geometry and redundant short links provide the chance to enhance its connectivity. The connectivity embodies the routing resilience to node failure. To observe how redundant short links impact on the resilience, we let some fixed fraction of uniformly chosen nodes fail and disable the failure recovery mechanism. In this case, we define failed routing as any two alive nodes cannot be connected. Fig. 2 shows the simulated results. The higher failed routing is because the failure recovery mechanism has been disabled. The left graph in Fig. 2 presents the resilience would be gradually improved with the increasing redundant short links. This is because of the enhanced connectivity with redundant short links. The right graph in Fig. 2 plots the resilience in different dimension CAN. It clearly shows that the improvement in higher dimension would be less significant. This is because higher dimension CAN has more basic links than lower dimension. Hence, the effect of redundant short links would decrease accordingly.

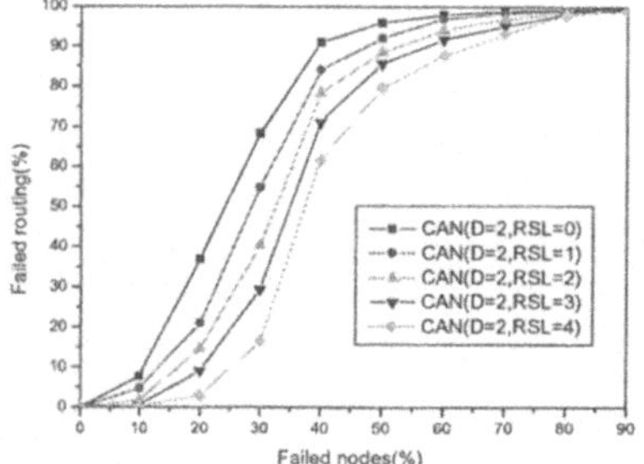

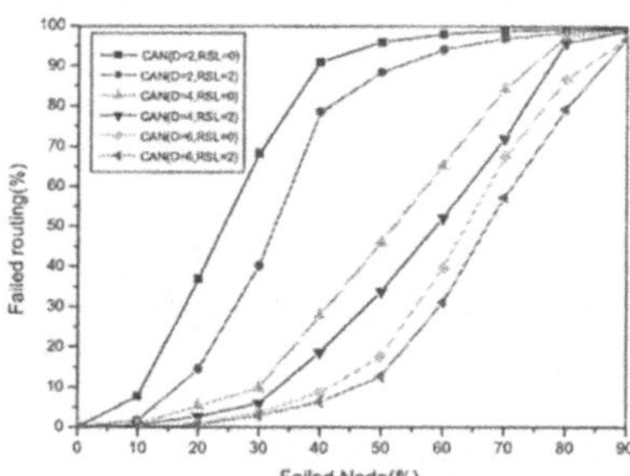

Fig. 2. Effect of redundant short links. Left: Percentage of failed routing for varying percentages of node failures considering varying numbers of redundant short links (RSL) to CAN with fixed dimension in the network of 1024 nodes. Right: Comparing failed routing between 0 and 2 redundant short links to different dimension CAN in the network of 1024 nodes.

5 Conclusions and Future Work

In this paper, we have researched the effect of links on DHT routing algorithms. Firstly, we investigate current several DHT algorithms and provide the insight of links to these algorithms and the direction of the improvement of their performance. Secondly, we analyze how links in DHT routing algorithm would impact the routing performance of peer-to-peer systems. Then we give the basic methods to establish links into DHT geometries. Our simulation results have demonstrated the great effect of links on the routing performance and have given a basic scheme to design new DHT algorithms and redesign current DHT algorithms.

Now there are several directions to extend our approach: (1) More current DHT algorithms may need to be investigated so as to provide a deep understanding how links affect routing performance and give the possible improved directions of their performance based on the effect of different kinds of links. (2) Considering the effect of links, more metrics such as load balance need to be investigated besides path length and resilience. (3) It will be an interesting and a worthwhile effort to explore how links would affect the physical delay on the underlying network.

References

[1] De Bruijn, N. 1972. Lambda-calculus notation with nameless dummies, a tool for automatic formula manipulation, with application to the Church-Rosser Theorem. Indag. Math. 34, 5, 381-392.
[2] Gnutella. http://www.gnutella.co.uk.
[3] S. Ratnaswamy, P. Francis, M. Handley, R. Karp, and S.Shenker. A scalable content-addressable network. ACM SIGCOMM, 2001.
[4] I. Stoica, R. Morris, D. Karger, F. Kaashoek, and H. Balakrishnan. Chord: A peer-to-peer lookup service for internet applications. ACM SIGCOMM, 2001.
[5] I. Clarke, O. Sandberg, B. Wiley, and T.W. Hong. Freenet: Adistributed anonymous information storage and retrieval system in designing privacy enhancing echnologies.International Workshop on Design Issues in Anonymity and Unobservability, LNCS 2009, 2001.
[6] B. Zhao, K. Kubiatowicz, and A. Joseph. Tapestry: An infrastructure for fault-resilient wide-area location and routing. Technical Report UCB//CSD-01-1141, University of California at Berkeley, April 2001.
[7] M. Frans Kaashoek, David R. Karger. Koorde: A simple degree-optimal distributed hash table. in 2st International Workshop on Peer-to-Peer Systems (IPTPS'03). 2003. Berkeley, CA, USA.

A Peer-to-Peer Approach to Task Scheduling in Computation Grid

Jiannong Cao[1], Oscar M.K. Kwong[1], Xianbing Wang[2,3], and Wentong Cai[4]

[1]Internet and Mobile Computing Lab, Department of Computing, Hong Kong Polytechnic University, Hung Hom, Kowloon, Hong Kong
csjcao@comp.polyu.edu.hk
[2]School of Computing, National University of Singapore, Singapore 117543
[3]Singapore-MIT Alliance, Singapore 117576
wangxb@comp.nus.edu.sg
[4]School of Computer Engineering, Nanyang Technological University, Singapore 639798
aswtcai@ntu.edu.sg

Abstract. Most of the existing solutions on task scheduling and resource management in grid computing are based on the traditional client/server model, enforcing a homogenous policy on making decisions and limiting the system flexibility and scalability. In this paper, we propose a peer-to-peer (P2P)-based decentralized approach, which off-loads the intermediate server by letting the peers in the grid to make the scheduling decision among themselves using their own scheduling policies. A generic architecture for metascheduler on peers, called PGS (P2P Grid Scheduler), and the task scheduling framework based on PGS have been developed. Both push and pull modes are used for distributing the tasks to peers with the support of load balancing and fault tolerance. A prototype of the proposed architecture and mechanism has been developed and simple performance tests have been conducted.

1 Introduction

Grid is a type of parallel and distributed system which supports the sharing and coordinated use of diverse resources in dynamic virtual organizations (VO) that share the same mission [6]. There are different kinds of Grid. For example, a Data Grid and [4] is mainly concerned with the collaboration of the available data resources into a unified view and a Computation Grid [5] is to offer a dependable and inexpensive access to high-end computation resources for solving computation-intensive problems.

Most of the existing solutions to resource management and task-scheduling in computation grid are based on a traditional client-server model, employing a central administrative server/manager [1, 2, 7, 13, 16, 17]. The client needs to submit to the specified job to the server, which is responsible of allocating the requested resources and scheduling the tasks of the job for execution. Since a computation grid provides a distributed, multi-domain computational resource, we argue that it should not have a single central authority for resource management and task scheduling. Also, such a centralized monotonic mechanism is not flexible, nor scalable. In this paper, we

M. Li et al. (Eds.): GCC 2003, LNCS 3032, pp. 316–323, 2004.

propose a peer-to-peer (P2P) based framework for scheduling of tasks. P2P supports direct interaction among its users [11], with the advantages of decreased dependency on the server and decentralization of control from servers. This may facilitate the autonomy of the participating users and improve system scalability and reliability. A P2P approach also eliminates the need for costly infrastructure by enabling direct communication among clients and enabling resource aggregation. A typical example of P2P system application is SETI@Home, using Internet-connected computers for conducting a scientific experiment in the search for extraterrestrial intelligence [15].

Works can be found on combining the elements of the Grid and P2P approaches. [10] presented a P2P approach to resource location in a grid environment. [14] proposed to use Agile computing to bridge the resource sharing gap between grid computing and ad-hoc P2P. In [8], Hoschek described the convergence of Grid Computing, P2P, distributed database and Web services. NaradaBrokering [12] is an event brokering system designed to run on a large network of cooperating broker nodes, providing the flexibility of both centralized and P2P interactions over the edge. But all of the above works did not address the task-scheduling problem in computational Grid.

We have developed a generic architecture for metascheduler on peer sites, called *PGS* (Peer in Grid Scheduler), and a task scheduling framework based on PGS for computation grid. PGS facilitate the integration of the P2P approach to task scheduling into the grid environment. Both push and pull methods are used for distributing the tasks to peers with the support of load balancing and fault tolerance. We will present the design of PGS, our proposed P2P based task-scheduling architecture, and describe the prototype implementation of the proposed framework.

2 The PGS Architecture

In our proposed P2P-based approach, a distributed metascheduling scheme [9] is used. There is a metascheduler at every site and jobs are submitted to the local metascheduler where the job originates. The metaschedulers interact directly with each other to collect instantaneous load information and to make scheduling decisions. Figure 1 illustrates the architecture of a local metascheduler installed on each site. It is a Napster-like architecture employing the Grid Information Service (GIS) [3] for directory services. However, the scheduling policy is user-centric and the scheduling activities are controlled and managed by each peer site. Since all jobs are submitted to and scheduled by individual metaschedulers, the distributed scheme is more scalable. It is possible for different sites to use different scheduling policies.

The Grid Peer Information Service (GPIS) is a kind of grid information service (GIS) [3]. It is the metadata infrastructure that enhances the existing GIS in grid middleware. GPIS maintains system information of peer sites and supports the resource discovery by indicating the availability of the resources and its orientations. This likes the yellow-page service in making a phone call where you can search someone and then make a direction communication. More specifically, GPIS handles the requests for peer registration, records the locations of peer sites, and processes queries of available peer services and status of dynamic utilization of registered peers. GPIS is also responsible for providing peers with communication support for requesting grid-wide services. Note, however, once the peers obtain the necessary information from GPIS, GPIS has no further direct influence on the interactions among the peers regarding their task scheduling activates. GPIS can be made scalable and reliable by using replication techniques.

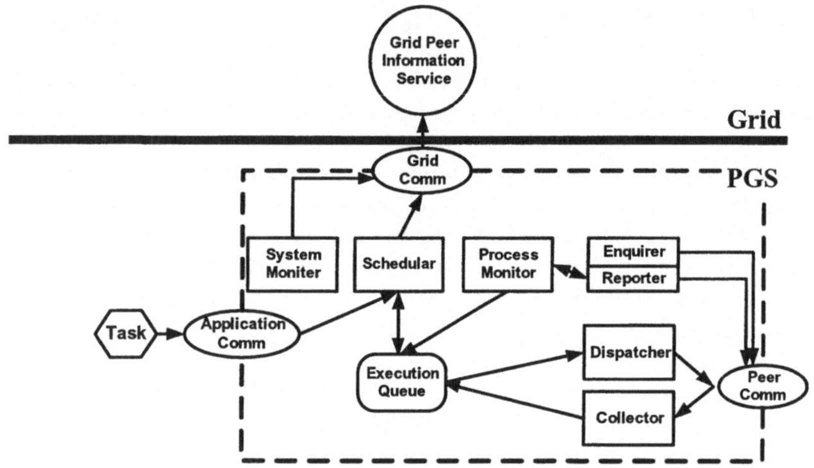

Fig. 1. PIGS system architecture

The Grid Communication (Grid Comm) module provides the GPIS messaging service through a communication interface between Grid-wide services and local components in PGS. Grid Comm is very much like a proxy service, which handles the protocol binding for specific stub in order to invoke the remote Grid services. Through Grid Comm, the client application is insulated from the details of the Web service invocation. Grid Comm also provides local authentication, authorization and mapping of grid credentials.

The Application Communication (Application Comm) module is the front end exposed to the application layer. It is responsible for providing an interface for user to provide resource details, edit the service dataset for GPIS, and specify the policies under which the resources are used.

In a grid environment, the system information becomes outdated very quickly, mainly because that membership in a VO is dynamic as participants may join or leave at any time, changes to administration policy, and possible system failures. In order to support the stateful nature of the information in GPIS, we provide a quality matrix to describe the states of resources in the environment. The gathering of the quality matrix parameter is the responsibility of the System Monitor module. It collects information such as the CPU load, current memories available etc. The information is either captured in the peer's operating system periodically or on demand, and can be converted to a readable format conforming to the standard for selection of resources.

The Scheduler module is responsible to schedule the tasks of the submitted jobs. It first forms a group of peer sites by requesting the peer information from the GPIS and analyze and filter the returned peer list based on the strategy used for dispatching or capturing tasks. Then according to the scheduling policy specified by the user and the information obtained from the System Monitor, it determines whether the tasks should be done locally or in some remote sites. The scheduler model can be equipped with enhanced capabilities, such as extended scheduling policies, advanced reservation, and local accounting.

In relation with the Scheduler are the Dispatcher and the Collector modules. The Dispatcher module is in charge of dispatching tasks of jobs to other peer sites. The Collector module is in charge of capturing tasks from the other peers. Usually the dispatch operation is triggered when the local site is busy so that the overall utilization level can be relieved, and the collection operation is triggered when the local site is free so that the unused computing powers can be utilized.

Finally, there are three modules used to collect and querying the status of dispatched tasks. The Process Monitor module is responsible for monitoring the status of the tasks in the local execution list and providing this information on demand. . The Reporter module is responsible for gathering the related task information from the Process Monitor when enquired by other peers. The Enquirer module is responsible for enquiring the status of the tasks on remote sites.

3 Task Scheduling Framework in PGS

In this section, we describe the task scheduling framework in PGS and the mechanisms designed for peer registration, task scheduling, and task execution.

Peer Registration. A peer site with the PGS installed will first initiate a registration request to GPIS, providing necessary information including its address. GPIS will verify the peer and record its capability, indicating what types of operations the peer can perform. Upon receiving the capability message from GPIS, the peer uploads its Service Data Set (SDD), which contains the information about resources to be shared. Then, GPIS verifies the SDD and acknowledges the peer.

Task Scheduling. PGS defines the resource utilization function which is used to make the task scheduling decision. Based on the result of evaluating the utilization function, either the push or the pull mode will be adopted. For simplicity, we consider only CPU and memory as computing resources. For more complicated definition, it may also include I/O consumption, roundtrip time (RTT), failure factor, etc. The following equation defines the utilization of resources in a site:

$$U = 100 \times ((X)\, C + (1-X)\, M) / (C+M)$$

where C is CPU normalized (1-100), M is memory normalized (1-100), and X is normalizing factor (0-1). Peer can decide the normalizing factor X which ranges from 0 to 1. Each peer can also define their own utilization threshold value. The system is regard as free if the U value is below the lower threshold set.. The system is regard as busy means the U value generated is higher than the upper threshold set.

The push mode is used when the local site is judged to be busy and needs to be off-loaded by dispatching tasks to some other peers. The task scheduling process works as follows. The local PGS sends request to GPIS to find 1 to N peers who can help performing the specified job. According to the capability of the requesting peer, GPIS acknowledges with the peer service data sets and their status. Depending on the local policy used (e.g. best peer scheme, random select scheme etc), local PGS chooses a target peer for help. Local PGS Sends a dispatch task request to the target peer. Upon receiving the acknowledgment from the target peer, local PGS dispatch the task to the remote peer. Local PGS receives the acknowledgment of completion and notes down the interaction details on local database.

The pull mode is used when the local site is judged to be free and needs to share its resource by catching tasks from some other peers. The task scheduling process works as follows. The local PGS sends request to GPIS for status of peer in friendly-peer list. Upon received the peer-list report from GPIS, local GPS queries the selected peer according to the policy set, asking whether it needs help by sending the Capture Request message. If the answer is "no", the local GPS tries another peer in the list. If the answer is "yes", the local GPS downloads the job information in the peer's queue. The local GPS captures the tasks of the job and executes them.

Both modes will be implemented by the task dispatch mechanism and the task capturing mechanism respectively, which will be described later in this section.

Task Execution. All tasks of jobs submitted locally or captured from remote peers are stored in an execution queue of the PGS. For every task that is in the queue, a task definition object is created indicating what the program command is being invoked, the command argument sets, location to output the result set, and the expected deadline etc.

A local Job is broken into a number of small tasks and being imported in the queue noted as "LO" (Local) status. There are five task statuses in the PIGS system.

Task Status	Priority	Description
LO	High	**Local**. The task is a local job (since creation)
DA	Low	**Dispatch Active.** The task is dispatched to the other peers
DP	High	**Dispatch Passive.** The task is dispatched here by other peers
CA	High	**Capture Active.** The task is captured from other peers
CP	Low	**Capture Passive**. The task is captured by other peers

The priorities of the tasks are simply classified into high or low. Tasks with status LO, DP, CA have higher priority then the DA and CP. The priority is set based on which party is expected to take the responsibility to execute the task.

For execution queue that only has LO, DP, and CA tasks, the order of executing the tasks is the same as the order the tasks enter the queue. For execution job queue that have DA and CP tasks, however, the order of execution is not always the same as the tasks enter the queue.

Task Dispatching. In PGS design, each peer site sets up an upper and lower threshold value for resource utilization, which is ranged from 0 to 100. When the utilization value returned by the utilization function is higher than the upper threshold value, the peer will query the GPIS to find suitable peers for dispatching tasks to them. According to common heuristics in distributed computing, 65-70% of utilization is regarded as a critical turning point for the exponential growth that can make the system to boom, and therefore can be used to define the upper threshold.

How to determine which peers to select for dispatching tasks is an interesting problem. Intuitively, the best peer should be chosen. However, if all peer sites always use this selection policy, the best peer will soon become overloaded and can no longer be able to serve incoming requests. The requesting peer will then need to find another peer for help, which incurs extra communication overhead. Therefore, in PGS, we chose to use the random selection scheme. After the requesting peer has generated a filtered peer list, it will randomly choose one of the peers in the list and send the probing message. The random selection scheme is proven to have better hit-ratio on the successful communication target compared with the best selection scheme.

The dispatch mechanism chooses the task to dispatch in a Last-In-First-Serve (LCFS) manner. It clones the task object of the task at the end of the execution queue, and sends it to the remote peer which has acknowledged the acceptance of the request. It then changes the status of the task object from LO to DA, indicating that the task have been dispatch actively to the other peer, and put the task at the back of the queue. On the remote side, the received task is assigned the DP status, meaning that the task is dispatched here by another peer site and the local site is the passive party. The DP-task will be put at the back of the queue. In cases where there are tasks with other status in the execution queue, the one to be dispatched will be the last local task (LO).

PGS supports fault tolerance in scheduling and executing a job. The reason of cloning the task object rather than truly moving the task is the concern of the uncertainty factors in a grid environment, including broken network links and shutdown of peer sites. They make it impossible to guarantee that the dispatched tasks can be safely completed according to the user's expectation level on the quality of service. In PGS, as described earlier, the requesting peer will also keep a copy of the dispatched task with a status of DA and put it at the back of the location execution queues. If the dispatched task can not be successfully executed in the remote peer, after the detection of the failure of the remote site or upon the expiration of timeout, the requesting peer can reschedule the task for execution.

Task Capturing. Following the P2P philosophy, peers not only ask others for help by also make contributions to their communities. Just implementing the push mode is not adequate to make full utilization of all the available resource, as the idle hosts are passive. In PGS, in addition to the push mode, a pull-mode is also implemented for task scheduling.

When the resource utilization of a site is below the specified lower threshold value, the local PGS will actively contact a friendly peer to offer help. The friendly peers can be obtained from the GPIS or by the user's preference. The helping peer sends the task-capturing request to the target peer selected using the pre-defined selection policy, such as the best-peer-scheme and the random selection scheme. Upon receiving the request, the remote peer will select a task for cloning and let the task to be captured by the helping peer. It will also change the status if the task status LO to CP and then put the task at the end of the execution queue. For the helping peer, the captured task will be put at the end of the execution queue and labeled as "CA", meaning that the task is actively captured from another peer.

4 Prototype Implementation and Experiments

A prototype of the proposed PGS architecture and the task scheduling framework has been implemented using the Java programming language. Figure 2 shows the system structure of the prototype. Due to limit in space, Implementation issues are not discussed here.

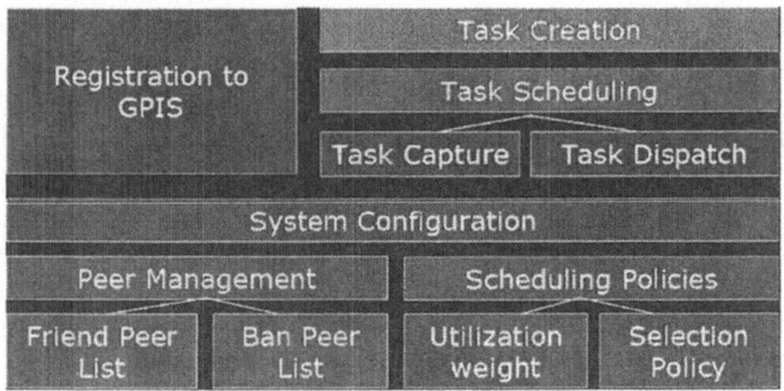

Fig. 2. Implementation system structure of PGS

Preliminary experiments have been performed using the prototype. We have implemented a simple prime number generator program which are parallelized and distributed to hosts for execution. The prime generator program tasks an upper bound and a lower bound as the parameters and generates the prime numbers within the range. Experiments have been carried out to find all prime numbers within the range from 1 to 100000000. The experiments are conducted using PCs with Intel Pentium 1.6 MHz CPUs, 512 DDR333 memory, and Window XP as the operating system. A job is divided into 1000 subtasks.

Preliminary performance data were collected. Figure 3 shows the speedup obtained by using different task scheduling schemes.

Speedup for	Push Only		Push & Pull	
	2Peer	4Peer	2Peer	4Peer
1 - 5x10^7:	1.10	2.43	1.24	2.81
1 - 1x10^8:	1.18	2.52	1.24	2.98
1 - 5x10^8:	1.19	2.75	1.30	2.94
1 - 1x10^9:	1.30	2.77	1.42	2.98
Avg. Speedup	**1.19**	**2.62**	**1.30**	**2.90**

Fig. 3. Speedup obtained by using different schemes

The experimental result shows that the combination of pull and push techniques achieved a faster convergence in speedup than using the push strategy alone.

5 Conclusion and Future Works

In this paper we have proposed an approach to integrating P2P-based decentralized task scheduling into a computational grid. The advantages over the existing solutions include offloading/reducing the costs incurred by the central scheduler architecture, user-centric and user-manageable scheduling policy, and heterogeneous queuing system. It advocates the design of modified grid architecture equipped with P2P technologies for enhancing the services for resource allocation in the hybrid environment with the improvement of flexibility, scalability and reliability. We have described the design of the PGS architecture and the associated task scheduling framework and mechanisms. We have also addressed the implementation issues and described the prototype implementation of the proposed approach.

Our future work includes improving the current implementation with more effective resource utilization model and conducting more experiments to evaluate how the proposed approach enhances the system scalability and performance.

Acknowledgement. This work is partially supported by the Hong Kong Polytechnic University, under HK PolyU research grant G-YY41.

References

1. F. F. Berman, and R. Wolski, *The AppLeS Project: A Status Report*, Proceedings of the 8th NEC Research Symposium, Germany, May 1997.
2. H. Casanova, and J. Dongarra, *NetSolve: A Network Server for Solving Computational Science Problems*, Int'l. Jour. of Supercomputing Appl. and HPC, Vol. 11, No 3, 1997.
3. K. Czajkowski, S. Fitzgerald, I. Foster, C. Kesselman. *Grid Information Services for Distributed Resource Sharing*. Proc. HPDC-10, August 2001.
4. The European DataGrid Project Team. http://www.eu-datagrid.org
5. I. Foster and C. Kesselman, The Grid: Blueprint for a New Computing Infrastructure. Morgan Kaufmann Publishers, Inc., San Francisco, USA, 1999.
6. I. Foster, and C. Kesselman, and S. Tuecke, The Anatomy of the Grid: Enabling Scalable Virtual Organizations. *Inte'l Jour. High Performance Computing Applications, 15* (3). 200-222. 2001.
7. Globus Grid Project. http://www.globus.org
8. W. Hoschek, Peer-to-Peer Grid databases for web service discovery, Concurrency: Pract. Exper. 2002; 00:1-7
9. V. Hamscher, U. Schwiegelshohn, A. Streit, and R. Yahyapour. Evaluation of Job-Scheduling Strategies for Grid Computing. In *Proc. Grid '00*, pages 191–202, 2000.
10. A. Iamnitchi, I. Foster, D.C. Nurmi, A peer-to-peer approach to resource location in grid environments, Proc. of 11th IEEE Inte'l Symp. High Performance Distributed Computing, 23-26 July 2002, Page(s): 419
11. D.S. Milojicic, *et al. Peer-to-Peer Computing*. HP Lab. HPL-2002-57 March, 2002.
12. NaradaBrokering project. http://www.naradabrokering.org
13. R. Buyya, D. Abramson, and J. Giddy: Nimrod/G: An Architecture for a Resource Management and Scheduling System in a Global Computational Grid. In *Proc. HPC ASIA'2000, Beijing, China, 2000.* 05 September 2002
14. N. Suri, *et al*, Agile computing: bridging the gap between grid computing and ad-hoc peer-to-peer resource sharing, Proc. 3rd Inte'l Symp. on Cluster Computing and the Grid, 12-15 May 2003, Page(s): 618 -625
15. SETI@HOME. http://setiathome.sslberkeley.edu
16. J. Commer, Solution Technology Group, UK Charu Chaubal, Grid Computing Sun BluePrints Online *Introduction to the Cluster Grid – Part1 & 2*
17. K. Hawick, H. James, etc., *DISCWorld: An Environment for Service-Based Metacomputing*, Future Generation Computing Systems (FGCS), Vol. 15, 1999.

Efficient Search in Gnutella-Like "Small-World" Peer-to-Peer Systems*

Dongsheng Li, Xicheng Lu, Yijie Wang, and Nong Xiao

School of Computer, National University of Defense Technology,
410073 Changsha, China
leedongsh@hotmail.com

Abstract. Gnutella-like peer-to-peer file-sharing systems have been widely deployed on the Internet. However, current search techniques used in existing Gnutella-like peer-to-peer systems are often inefficient. We demonstrated the strong "small-world" property of Gnutella systems and proposed an efficient search approach CSTM to utilize the property. In CSTM, each peer maintains a local state table, which contains keyword information of data on all neighbors within T hops to guide query. A new data structure based on Bloom Filter is introduced to represent the state table compactly to reduce storage and bandwidth cost. Query cache is also adopted to utilize query locality and build shortcut connections to lately accessed peers. Simulations show that CSTM can reduce message cost remarkably while maintaining short search path length compared with flooding or random forwarding algorithm.

1 Introduction and Related Work

In recent years, peer-to-peer (P2P) computing has emerged as a novel and popular model of computation and gained significant attentions from both industry field and academic field [1,2,3]. Gnutella-like P2P systems, such as Gnutella, Freenet [4], Morpheous and Nuerogrid [5], are widely deployed and predominant on the Internet in real life because of their simplicity and usability.

However, flooding in Gnutella systems costs too much bandwidth and limits the scalability. Recently much work has been done to improve the performance and scalability of Gnutella-like P2P system. Markatos [6] studied the characteristic of Gnutella traffic and proposed some caching strategies to improve its performance; but they still used flooding for search. Lv [7] suggested random walks instead of flooding, Cohen [8] proposed and analyzed three replication strategies, and proved that the square-root strategy is optimal. Yang [9] suggested iterative deepening and Directed BFS technique to reduce messages cost. Joseph [5], Yang [9], Adamic [10], and Crespo [11] suggested that each node maintain some kind of metadata that can

* This work was supported by the National Natural Science Foundation of China under the grant No. 69933030 and 60203016, the National 863 High Technology Plan of China under the grant No. 2002AA131010 and 2003AA1Z2060, and the Excellent PHD Dissertation Foundation of China under the grant No. 200141.

M. Li et al. (Eds.): GCC 2003, LNCS 3032, pp. 324–331, 2004.

provide "hints" to guide search. Yang [9] used local indices where nodes index of neighbors in the system, however flooding was still used for query. Adamic[10] utilized local information such as connectedness of a node's neighbors and forwarded query to neighbors with high degree. Crespo [11] built summaries of content that is reachable via each neighbor of the node in different topics.

In this paper we demonstrated the "small-world" property of Gnutella network and proposed a new search approach—CSTM, to utilize the property to improve the performance and scalability of Gnutella-like P2P systems. In CSTM, each peer in the system maintains a local state table, which contains indices of keywords on all neighbors within a few hops to guide query. For the reason of "small-world" property, the desired data could be found within only a few hops. *Extended Bloom Filter* (EBF), which is based on Bloom Filter [12] technique, is introduced to represent the state table with little storage and bandwidth overhead. Meanwhile the query cache is adopted to utilize the locality of query and build shortcut connections to remote peers. Simulations show that CSTM can achieve much better performance compared with flooding and random forwarding algorithm in Gnutella-like P2P systems.

Bloom Filter [12] technique has been widely used as a summary technique. Summary Cache [13] uses bloom filters as compact representations for the local set of cached files. Sean C. [14] uses Bloom Filters to find nearby replicas quickly in OceanStore systems. CSTM uses Bloom Filter in some similar way to [14], but they are for different purposes and achieve different tradeoff. To our knowledge, CSTM is the first to use Bloom Filter technique to improve search in Gnutella-like P2P systems.

The rest of this paper is organized as follows. Section 2 demonstrates the "small-world" property with data traces crawled from Gnutella networks. Section 3 presents CSTM in detail. Section 4 analyzes the performance of CSTM. Conclusions are made in Section 5.

2 "Small-World" Property of Gnutella

The "small-world" phenomenon was first discovered by Stanley Milgram in the late 1960s. "Small-world" networks [15] exhibit a highly clustering; yet have typically short path lengths between arbitrary nodes, i.e., short diameter. In this paper, we model Gnutella network as an undirected graph and use the concepts of clustering coefficient and characteristic path length proposed by Watts and Strogatz [15] to analyze the characteristic of Gnutella-like peer-to-peer networks.

We determined the properties on the actual Gnutella topology data crawled by Clip2 Company [16] in the summer of 2000. We perform the experiments on many different snapshots of Gnutella networks, which are selected randomly from the data traces. We calculate the characteristic path length and clustering coefficient for Gnutella networks, compared to corresponding random networks with the same number of nodes and average degree per node. Table 1 shows five samples.

As Table 1 shows, all the Gnutella topology snapshots exhibit strong "small-world" property: characteristic path length is close to that of corresponding random network, but the clustering coefficient is much higher (i.e., $L_{Gnutella}$ L_{random} and $C_{Gnutella}$.>> C_{random}).

Table 1. "Small-world" property of Gnutella

	$L_{Gnutella}$	L_{random}	$C_{Gnutella}$	C_{random}
1	3.8643	3.1876	0.04513	0.006789
2	4.2884	3.6546	0.05403	0.004254
3	4.4368	4.1794	0.02311	0.003201
4	3.3728	3.0545	0.01887	0.002456
5	4.6510	3.7397	0.06033	0.008512

The "small-world" property of Gnutella networks can help to guide the design of search mechanisms in such systems. For examples, the small diameter property means that if a peer in the system has the knowledge of the data on its neighbors within several hops, it can forward query for desired data to appropriate neighbors directly and doesn't need flooding any more. The property is utilized in CSTM.

3 Approach Description

In Gnutella-like P2P systems, peers submit some keywords of desired data for search and acquire results from the systems. In CSTM, each peer has a local state table that contains keywords information of data files on all neighbors within T hops (T is a system-wide constant). We use keywords rather than full name of files in the state table because keywords can support flexible query.

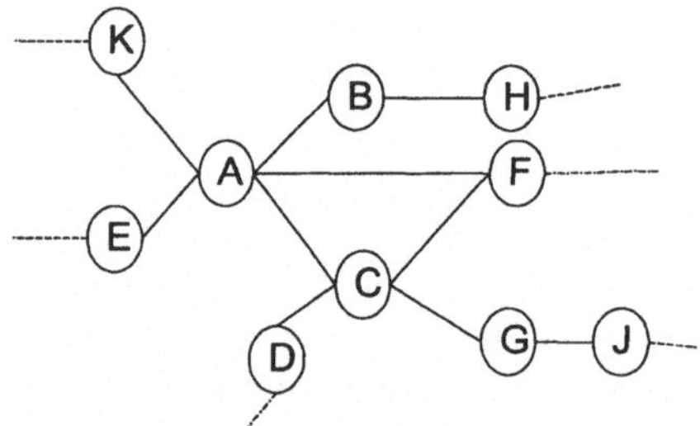

Fig. 1. Neighbor graph of peers

There are three columns in the state table. For example, Table 2 shows the state table of peer A in Figure 1.The first row of Table 2 shows that the keyword "car" is two hops away from peer A through neighbor B, and the fourth row show that the keyword "red" is one hop away from peer A through neighbor C. Each keyword may be stored on multiple peers which are either different hops away from peer A or through different neighbors of peer A, so the same keyword can take up multiple rows in the state table.

Hop information can be used to determine which neighbor queries are forwarded to. For example, a query for "car" will be forwarded to not neighbor B but neighbor C first because "car" is one hop away through neighbor C while two hop away through neighbor B. Hop information in the state table can also be used to support query for multiple keywords. Take peer A as an example, if peer A receives a query for "red car", peer A knows keywords "red" and "car" are both one hop away through peer C, thus peer A can forward query to peer C. If peer A receives a query for "black car", peer A knows that though both keyword "black" and "car" are on some peers through peer C, but they are different hops away, thus peer A knows that the two keywords are not on the same peer through neighbor C and doesn't forward the query to C. The state table only maintains information within T hops, i.e., the value in "hop" column of the state table is no more than T.

Table 2. State table on peer A

Keywords	Hop	Neighbor
"car"	2	B
"car"	3	B
"car"	1	C
"red"	1	C
"black"	3	C
...	...	...

Assuming each neighbor has M neighbors, the state table stores keyword information of M^T neighbor peers. To reduce the storage and update cost of the state table, a data structure, *Extended Bloom Filter* (EBF), which is based on Bloom Filter technique, is used to represent state table.

Generally speaking, if peer A accesses some date on peer B, then peer A and peer B may have some common interests and peer A is more likely to access data on peer B later. To utilize the query locality, each peer maintains a query cache, which contains the mapping information between keywords lately accessed and their location. Query cache uses a timeout mechanism and discards the content that hasn't been accessed for certain time. The replacement of query cache is performed based on LRU policy.

The state table provides nearby information around the peer and query cache provides shortcut connections to some remote peers. The combination of the two mechanisms could accelerate the process of search.

3.1 Extended Bloom Filter

Bloom Filter (BF) [12] is a compact data structures for probabilistic representation of a set. Consider a set $A=\{a_1, a_2, \ldots, a_n\}$ of n elements. BF describes membership information of set A using a bit vector V of length m with all bits initially set to 0. BF chooses k independent hash functions $hash_1, \ldots, hash_k$, each with range $\{1,\ldots,m\}$.

For each element $a \in A$, the bits at positions $hash_1(a)$, $hash_2(a)$, ... , $hash_k(a)$ in V are all set to 1. A particular bit might be set to 1 multiple times by various elements. Given a query for b BF check the k bits at positions $hash_1(b)$, $hash_2(b)$, ..., $hash_k(b)$ in V. If any of them is 0, then certainly b is not in the set A. Otherwise BF conjectures that b is in the set although there is a certain probability that it is wrong (because all the k bits have been previously set by other elements).

We use BF (k=4) to represent the keywords on each peer. But state tables need to store hop information thus can't be represented by BF directly. We propose a new data structure *Extended Bloom Filter (EBF)* based on BF technique to represent state tables in a compact way. The main idea of EBF is that the bit vector V of Bloom Filter is replaced with an array VV of T-bit binary numbers. We associate each neighbor of a peer with one EBF to represent the keywords that can be accessed through the neighbor. Each entry of the array VV is a T-bit binary number and each bit of the number represents keywords corresponding hops away through the neighbor: The highest bit of the number represents the keywords one hop away from the neighbor and the second highest bit represent the keywords two hops away from the neighbor, and so on. The lowest bit represents the keywords T hop away through the neighbor. Each EBF of the peer corresponds to one neighbor, and we use term *EBF(A,B)* to represent the EBF of peer A about its neighbor B. So each peer has multiple EBFs and the number of EBFs is the same as the number of its neighbors.

The values of four hash functions of keyword *key* are acquired as below: first calculate the MD5 signature of the *key*, which produces 128 bits; then divide the 128 bits into four 32-bit numbers, and finally module each 32-bit number by m and get the four values. MD5 is selected because of its well-known random properties and relatively fast implementation. The detail of EBF is referred to [17].

3.2 Query and Update

In Gnutella-like P2P system, users submit queries to any node with a stop condition (e.g., the number of results desired). When a peer receives a query for the keyword "key", it first evaluates keywords on itself. If it could satisfy the query itself, it returns the results and the query is over. Otherwise it first gets the k hash values h1,..., hk by calculating k hash functions hash1(key), hash2(key), ..., hashk(key). For each neighbor of the peer, it gets the k T-bit binary numbers, i.e., the value of h1,..., hk entries of the corresponding EBF. It uses operator "AND" to operate all the k T-bit binary numbers and acquire the result f. The result f is also a T-bit binary number, and the position of '1' (from left to right) in value f indicates how many hops it needs to access key through the neighbor. Thus the larger value f is, the less hops it needs to pass through to access the keyword. We rank all the neighbors by the corresponding result f, then the peer sends the query to each neighbor in sequence, checking if the stop condition is reached whenever each query returns.

When a data object is added to or deleted from a peer, there is a possibility that the BF of the peer might change as well. If such changes occur, the peer should propagate the changes of its BF to its neighbors. The neighbors receive the update messages and update their EBFs accordingly. If needed, the neighbors will send update messages to their neighbors as well. When update messages pass through one peer, the position of the value updated in the corresponding EBF is shifted one to right. Update messages are propagated at most T hops from the sources. When peers join in or depart from the system, the update process is also needed.

There may be some cycles in P2P networks. Cycles in P2P networks may cause the same query or update message to reach the same node multiple times. To avoid that, the identifier of source peer and sequence number is added into the messages. Duplicate messages are discarded by the peers. The detail of the query and update algorithm is referred to [17].

4 Performance Evaluations

We implement CSTM in the open source NeuroGrid simulator [5] and use a Gnutella snapshot topology in which there are 1005 peers as the underlying topology of simulated Gnutella-like P2P systems. The simulations are conducted over 1005 peers with four files per peer and three keys per file. Files and keywords in the system are selected from a pool with 10000 files and 5000 keywords.

In the experiments we simulate four algorithms: Gnutella flooding, two-way random forwarding (peers forward queries to two random neighbors each time), CSTM without query cache and CSTM with query cache (the cache size is 30). The TTL in flooding and random forwarding algorithm is 7 and 13 respectively. We run 20,000 searches in the simulation, with each search being started at a randomly selected node. Each search was for a randomly selected file – the search terms would be the keywords of desired file. After each 2000 searches we probe the system to acquire average search length and messages cost at that time. Simulation results are shown in Figure 2.

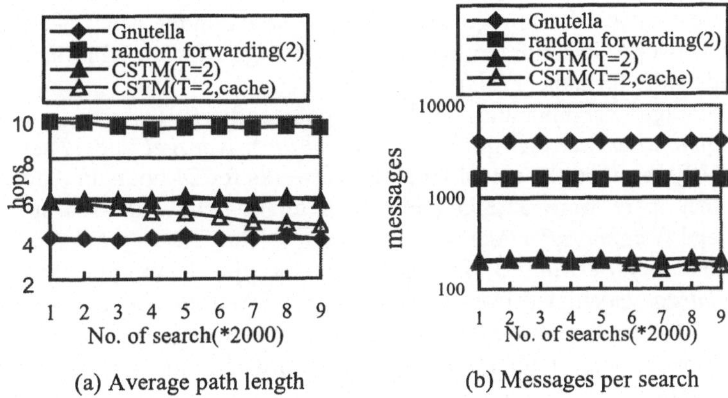

(a) Average path length (b) Messages per search

Fig. 2. Average path length and Messages per search with the four algorithms

Figure 2(a) shows that the average search length of CSTM is a little more than that of flooding, but it is much less than that of two-way random forwarding algorithm. Figure 2(b) shows that flooding in Gnutella produces too many messages (about 4000 messages per search) and two-way random forwarding also causes about 1500 messages per search, while CSTM causes no more than 250 messages, one order of magnitude less. Figure 2 also shows that the query cache has some self-learning ability and contains more effective shortcut connections after a large number of searches. This ability can lead to the descending of the average search length and the message cost.

Then we evaluate CSTM with different values of parameter T. Figure 3 presents the simulation results when T is 1,2,3 respectively. The results show that when the value of T is increased, the search length and messages cost decreases dramatically. When T=3, the search length is almost the same as that of Gnutella while the messages produced is only about 100. The query cache is again validated to be very effective.

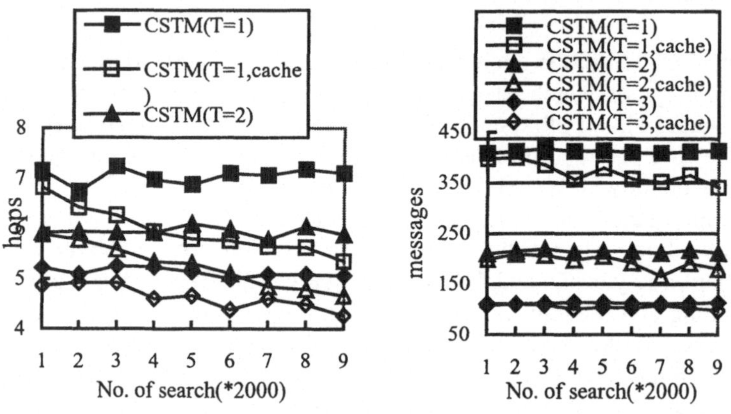

Fig. 3. Average path length and message cost with different T

Now we evaluate the storage cost of CSTM based on the data traces crawled from Gnutella network. The storage cost *AverageStorage* of state table in CSTM can be computed by the formula (1) showed below:

AverageStorage=NeighborsPerPeer * AverageSizeofPerEBF

= *NeighborsPerPeer* * *T** *(m/n)* * *KeysPerFile* * *AverageFilePerPeer* (bit) (1)

Adar [18] observed the actual Gnutella networks for 24 hours in August, 2000 and learned that there were 31,395 peers with totally 3,019,405 sharing files in the systems and *NeighborsPerPeer* was less than 4. Thus *AverageFilePerPeer* is about 96. We take *KeysPerFile* =3, T=7, m/n=32 as a typical example, then the value of *AverageStorage* calculated from formula (1) is 258048 bit, i.e. about 32KB. Even if the value of *AverageFilePerPeer* is increased ten times, the storage cost is only 320KB. What's more, duplicate files and keywords are not eliminated from formula (1), so the actual storage cost is much less than the value provide by formula (1). Thus we can conclude that the storage cost of CSTM is very little.

5 Conclusions

Experiments show that Gnutella networks exhibit strong "small-world" property, which brings about important effect on search performance in such systems. A new search approach CSTM is proposed to utilize the "small-world" property of Gnutella-like P2P systems. Compared with flooding and random forwarding algorithm, the approach can reduce message cost remarkably while maintaining short search path length, thus it can improve much the performance and scalability of Gnutella-like P2P systems.

References

1. Clark, D.: Face-to-face with peer-to-peer networking. IEEE Computer, Vol. 34, No.1, IEEE press (2001) 18-21
2. Schoder, D., Fischbach, K.: peer-to-peer prospects. Communications of the ACM, Vol.46, No.2, (2003) 27-29
3. Li Dongsheng, Fang xinxin, Wang Yijie, Lu Xicheng, *et al.*: A scalable peer-to-peer network with constant degree. Lecture Notes in Computer Science, Vol. 2834, Springer-Verlag, Berlin Heidelberg, New York (2003) 414-424
4. Clark, I., Sandberg, O., Wiley, B., and Hong, T.: Freenet: a distributed anonymous information storage and retrieval system. Proc. of the Workshop on Design Issues in Anonymity and Unobservability, Berkeley, CA (2000) 311–320
5. Joseph, S.R.H: NeuroGrid: semantically routing queries in peer-to-peer networks. Proc. of International Workshop on Peer-to-Peer Computing, Pisa, Italy (2002)
6. Evangelos, P. Markatos: Tracing a large-scale peer-to-peer system: an hour in the life of Gnutella. Proc. of CCGrid2002, Berlin, Germany (2002)
7. Lv, Q., Cao, P., Cohen, E., Li K, and Shenker, S.: Search and replication in unstructured peer-to-peer networks. Proc. of the 16th annual ACM International Conference on Supercomputing (ICS), New Work (2002)
8. Cohen Edith, Shenker Scott: Replication strategies in unstructured peer-to-peer networks. Proc. of ACM Sigcomm'2002, ACM Press, Pittsburgh (2002)
9. Yang, B. and Garcia-Molina, H.: Efficient search in peer-to-peer networks. Proc of the 22nd IEEE ICDCS, Vienna, Austria (2002)
10. Adamic L. A., Humberman B., Lukose R., and Puniyani A.: Search in power law networks. Phys. Rev. E, Vol. 64, No.4 (2001) 46135–46143
11. Crespo A. and Garcia-Molina H.: Routing indices for peer-to-peer systems. Proc of the 22nd IEEE ICDCS, Vienna, Austria (2002)
12. Bloom B.: Space/time trade-offs in hash coding with allowable errors. Communications of the ACM, Vol. 13, No.7 (1970) 422–426
13. Fan, L., Cao, P., Almeida, J., and Broder, A.: Summary cache: a scalable wide-area web cache sharing protocol. Proc. of ACM SIGCOMM'1998, ACM Press, (1998) 254–265
14. Sean, C. R. and Kubiatowicz J.: Probabilistic location and routing. Proc. Of IEEE Infocom'2002, IEEE Computer Soc press, New Work (2002)
15. Watts, D. J. and Strogatz, S. H.: Collective dynamics of small-world networks. Nature, Vol.393 (1998) 440-442
16. Clip2 Company. http://www.clip2.com/
17. Li Dongsheng *et al.*: Efficient Search in Gnutella-like "Small-World" Peer-to-Peer Systems. Tech Rept. PDL-2002-11-2, National University of Defense Technology, Changsha City, China (2002)
18. Adar, Eytan and Huberman, Bernardo A.: Free riding on Gnutella. First Monday, Vol.5, No. 10 (2000)

Dominating-Set-Based Searching in Peer-to-Peer Networks*

Chunlin Yang[1] and Jie Wu[2]

[1] Siemens Network Convergence LLC, Boca Raton, FL 33487
[2] Dept. of Comp. Science & Eng., Florida Atlantic University, Boca Raton, FL 33431

Abstract. The peer-to-peer network for sharing information and data through direct exchange has emerged rapidly in recent years. The searching problem is a basic issue that addresses the question "Where is X". Breadth-first search, the basic searching mechanism used in Gnutella networks [4], floods the networks to maximize the return results. Depth-first search used in Freenet [3] retrieves popular files faster than other files but on average the return results are not maximized. Other searching algorithms used in peer-to-peer networks, such as iterative deepening [9], local indices [9], routing indices [2] and NEVRLATE [1] provide different improved searching mechanisms. In this paper, we propose a dominating-set-based peer-to-peer searching algorithm to maximize the return of searching results while keeping a low cost for both searching and creating/maintaining the connected-dominating-set (CDS) of the peer-to-peer network. This approach is based on random walk. However, the searching space is restricted to dominating nodes. Simulation has been done and results are compared with the one using regular random walk.

1 Introduction

Peer-to-peer network models such as Gnutella [4], Freenet [3], and Napster [5] are becoming popular for sharing information and data through direct exchange. These models offer the important advantages of decentralization by distributing the storage capacity and load across a network of peers and scalability by enabling direct and real-time communication. In fully decentralized peer-to-peer networks, there is no need for a central coordinator. Communication is individually handled by each peer. This has the added benefit of eliminating a possible bottleneck in terms of scalability or reliability. The peer-to-peer approach offers an alternative to traditional client-server systems for some application domains. It circumvents many problems of client-server systems but results in considerably more complex searching, node organization and reorganization, security, and so on [7].

The searching problem is a basic issue that addresses the question "Where is X". Breadth-first search (BFS), the basic searching mechanism used in Gnutella

* This work was supported in part by NSF grants CCR 0329741, ANI 0073736, and EIA 0130806. Contact person: jie@cse.fau.edu.

M. Li et al. (Eds.): GCC 2003, LNCS 3032, pp. 332–339, 2004.

networks [4], floods the networks to maximize the return results. Depth-first search (DFS) used in Freenet [3] retrieves popular files faster than other files but on average the return results are not maximized. Other searching algorithms used in peer-to-peer networks, such as iterative deepening [9], local indices [9], routing indices [2] and NEVRLATE [1] provide different improved searching mechanisms. In this paper, we propose a dominating-set-based peer-to-peer searching algorithm to maximize the return of searching results while keeping a low cost for both searching and creating/maintaining the connected-dominating-set (CDS) of the peer-to-peer network. A connected-dominating-set (CDS) [8] of a peer-to-peer network is a connected subset of nodes of the network from which all nodes in the network can be reached in one-hop. Finding a minimum CDS is NP-complete for most graphs. Wu and Li [8]'s marking process gives a simple and distributed algorithm for calculating CDS. In this paper, we propose a peer-to-peer network searching algorithm using CDS generated by the marking process with some modification of the reduction rules 1 and 2 to maximize the searching results while keeping the cost of searching and maintaining the CDS low. This approach is based on random walk. However, the searching space is restricted to dominating nodes. Simulation results have been presented and discussed.

2 Related Work

Gnutella [4] is the foremost large-scale, fully decentralized directory and distribution system running on the Internet. It uses a BFS with predefined depth D, where D is the system-wide maximum time-to-live (TTL) of a message in hops. Upon receiving a request, a node sends a query to all its neighbors and each neighbor searches its own resources and forwards the message to all of its own neighbors. If a query is satisfied, a response will be sent back to the original requester using the reverse path. Queries are assigned unique IDs to avoid repetition. Gnutella uses a TTL of 7 (about 10000 nodes) to avoid network congestion [6]. BFS can still be cyclical, and can cause excessive traffic and waste resources.

In Freenet [3], information is stored on hosts under searchable keys. It uses a DFS with depth limit D. Each node forwards the query to a single neighbor, and waits for a definite response from that neighbor. If the query was not satisfied, the neighbor forwards the query to another neighbor. If the query was satisfied, the response will be sent back to the query source using the reverse path. Each node along the path copies data to its own database as well. In this approach, more popular information becomes easier to access. However, DFS suffers from poor response time.

Iterative Deepening [9] searching method initiates multiple DFSs with successively larger depth limits, until the query is satisfied or the maximum depth has been reached. Searching in Local Indices [9] needs to store information of all nodes within a defined number of hops. Each node maintains an index of the data of all nodes within r hops, where r is a system-wide variable known as the radius of the index. When receiving a query, a node can process it on behalf of every node within r hops, data can be searched on fewer nodes to reduce the cost while keeping the query satisfaction.

In NEVRLATE [1] (Network-Efficient Vast Resource Lookup At The Edge), directory servers are organized into a logical 2-dimensional grid, or a set of servers enabling registration (publish) in one "horizontal" dimension and lookup in the other "vertical" dimension. Each node is a directory server. Each set of servers, the vertical cloud, can reach each other member of the set. The set of sets of servers is the entire NEVRLATE network. Each host registers its resource and location to one node of each set. When a query comes, only one set needs to be searched to get all locations containing the satisfied query information.

Routing Indices [2] uses only single DFS but allows a node to select the "best" neighbor to send a query to. Routing Indices is a data structure and associated algorithms that, given a query, returns a list of neighbors ranked according to their *goodness* for the query. The goodness is measured by k-hop ranking which is a weighted total number of documentations within k hops. In general, the larger the k the smaller the weight assigned to the number of documentations at k hops. The 0-hop ranking reflects the number of documentations associated with the node. However, if u has a higher k-hop ranking than v, it does not imply that u has a higher 0-hop ranking than v.

3 Extended Marking Process

The dominating-set-based searching algorithm defined below tries to maximize the return results while minimizing the searching and maintenance costs. No global information is needed to construct and reduce the CDS using the marking process and reduction rule 1 and rule 2 [8].

Specifically, the marking process is a localized algorithm described in [8] in which hosts interact only with others in a restricted vicinity. Each host performs exceedingly simple tasks such as maintaining and propagating information markers. Collectively, these hosts achieve a desired global objective of finding a small CDS. The marking process marks every vertex in a given connected and simple graph $G = (V, E)$. $m(v)$ is a marker for vertex $v \subset V$, which is either T (marked) or F (unmarked). The marking process consists of: (1) Initially, assign marker F to each v in V. (2) Each v exchanges its open neighbor set $N(v)$ with all its neighbors. (3) Each v assigns its marker $m(v)$ to T if there exist two unconnected neighbors. It is shown that given a graph $G = (V, E)$ that is connected but not completely connected, the vertex subset V', derived from the marking process, forms a connected dominating set of G.

Two localized reduction rules 1 and 2 [8] are provided to reduce the size of the CDS: if the neighbor set of node u in the CDS is covered by that of another node v or those of two connected nodes v and w in the CDS, then node u can be removed from the CDS. In this case, u is said to be covered by v (or by v and w). To avoid simultaneous removal of two nodes covering each other, each node

u is assigned a distinct id. A node is removed from the CDS when it is covered by node(s) with higher id(s).

In this paper, we modify rules 1 and 2 [8] to use the a special 1-hop ranking, denoted as *docs*, of each node as the priority to break a tie. 1-hop ranking, *docs*, is defined as *the total documentation number of node v plus the highest documentation number of a v's neighbor.* We treat all types of documentation the same and will classify them in the future research. To get a unique total number of documentations, we can easily assign a unique node id. In case of a tie in the 1-hop ranking, node id is used to break a tie. Here are the modified rules 1 and 2:

Rule 1: Consider two vertices v and u in V'. If $N(v) \subset N(u)$ in G and $docs(v) < docs(u)$, change the marker of v to F if node v is marked, i.e., G' is changed to $V' - v$.

Rule 2: Assume that u and w are two marked neighbors of marked vertex v in V'. If $N(v) \subset N(u) \cup N(w)$ in G and $docs(v) = min(docs(v), docs(u), docs(w))$, then change the marker of v to F.

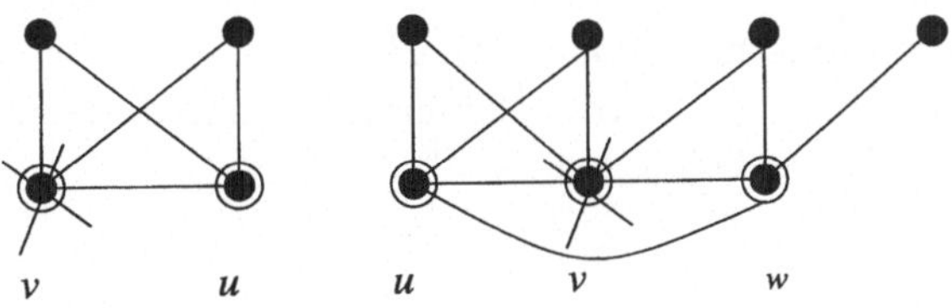

Fig. 1. Examples of rule 1 (left) and rule 2 (right).

In the example shown in Figure 1 (left), using the marking process and above modified reduction rule 1, node u will be the only dominating node in the graph if node u has a higher 1-hop ranking than node v. If node u has a lower 1-hop ranking than node v, node v will be the only dominating node in the graph. In the example shown in Figure 1 (right), node v can be eliminated from the dominating set based on rule 2 if node v has the minimum *docs* within these three nodes u, v, and w.

4 Dominating-Set-Based Peer-to-Peer Searching Algorithm

For a peer-to-peer network, we can use the above marking process with the modified rules 1 and 2 to get a CDS and use this subset of nodes for the searching in the network. The searching process resembles a random walk with an assigned TTL (depth). The searching process stops when TTL expires or a visited node is reached again. Unlike regular random walk, the searching process is restricted to dominating nodes only. In addition, we allow "one-hop branches" along the walk when certain conditions are met. Each one-hop branch connects to a non-dominating neighbor with the maximum 0-hop ranking in the neighborhood of the corresponding dominating neighbor.

1. First calculate 0-hop ranking and 1-hop ranking (*docs*) of each node.
2. Use the above defined marking process and modified reduction rules 1 and 2 to get a CDS.
3. When a node S receives a request, S searches from its own database and returns the results to the requester if there is any documentation.
4. If node S is the original request node and is not a dominating node (marked as F), it forwards the request to the dominating neighbor (marked as T) which has the highest 1-hop ranking among all of its dominating neighbors. If node S is not the original requestor nor a dominating node, it will not send a query to any of its neighbors.
5. If node S is a dominating node, it sends the request to the dominating neighbor with the highest 1-hop ranking among all of its dominating neighbors. Node S also sends the request to the non-dominating neighbor which has the highest 0-hop ranking among all of its neighbors (dominating neighbors and non-dominating neighbors) if there is one.
6. Repeat steps 3 to 5 until either the maximum number of hops is reached or a visited node is reached again.

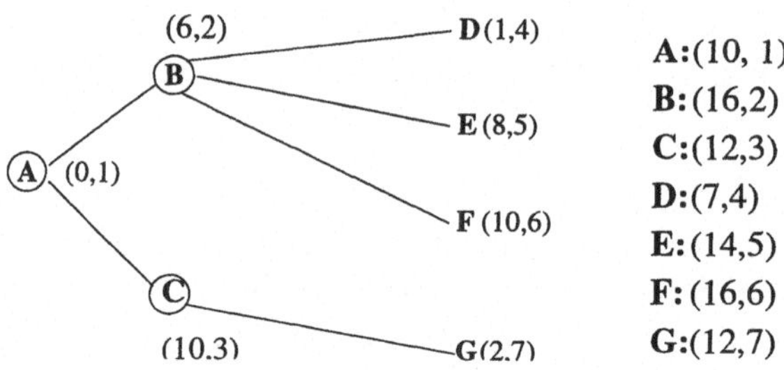

Fig. 2. A sample network with three dominating nodes.

For example, in Figure 2, each node has two numbers: the first number is the 0-hop ranking of that node and the second number is the unique node id. In Figure 2, the right column lists *docs* (i.e. 1-hop ranking) of each node. When node A gets a request, it first searches its own database. Then node A sends the request to node B which is the dominating neighbor with a higher *docs* than node C. Node B sends the request to node F, which has the highest priority (0-hop ranking and node id) of all neighbors of node B, and gets additional 10 documentations. Overall, this searching process gets a total of 16 documentations. If node F is a requester, it will send a message to node B and then to A

and C to get a total of 26 documentations. Note that in this case G will not be searched, since it has a smaller 0-hop ranking than the dominating node C.

Notice if in the same example we use random walk by treating all nodes the same and by sending a message to the "best" ranking neighbor, node A will send the request to node B, which has a higher 1-hop ranking than the other neighbor C, node B will send the request to node F. If node F is the requester, after sending the message to node B, node B will choose node E for the next searching because E has the next highest 0-hop ranking in all non-dominating neighbors of B. The process will stops because E has no more unvisited neighbor. The the searching process initiated from F will get 18 documentations instead of 26 as in the dominating-set-based approach. The searching stops before the defined maximum TTL (we use 20 in our simulation) has been reached.

The above proposed dominating-set-based searching algorithm in peer-to-peer networks needs only local information to get the CDS. Wu [8] has proven that the process calculates CDS in $O(\Delta^2)$ time with distance-2 neighborhood information, where Δ is the maximum node degree in the network. The above modified reduction rules 1 and 2 will not change the complexity of the calculation of the CDS and reduction. The proposed algorithm also uses constant (2) rounds of message exchange.

In general, a ranking just gives a "direction" towards the document, rather than its actual location. To create and maintain an "accurate" routing ranking, global information is needed or we can use *hop count ranking* [2] which also needs information from nodes within a certain number of hops. More cost will be added to create and maintain ranking of all affected nodes of the network if there are loops in the network.

In the CDS approach, when a node is added or dropped from the network, only its neighbors will be notified whereas the routing indices will update almost all nodes within k-hops to keep k-hop ranking up-to-date. In our simulation, we will see that the average ranking of all dominating nodes will be higher than the non-dominating nodes. That means by restricting the searching space to dominating nodes more documentations can be found.

5 Simulation

A C++ program has been implemented to simulate a peer-to-peer network searching using random walk and CDS described above. The network is randomly generated with a maximum degree of *max_degree*, each node is randomly assigned a number from 0 to *max_docs* documentations. To generate the network, 1 or 2 nodes with a degree less than *max_degree* are randomly selected from the connected set, which was initially assigned with one node, to connect to a new selected node from the unconnected set. This procedure repeats until all nodes in the unconnected set get connected to the connected set. This will guarantee that the result network is connected and can have loops. After all nodes get connected and assigned a number of documentations, both 0-hop ranking and 1-hop ranking are calculated for each node. The above defined marking pro-

Table 1. Average 1-hop ranking in a network with 50,000 nodes.

Max degree	All nodes	DS nodes	Non-DS nodes
2	2.5230	2.6735	1.9856
5	6.1677	6.4964	4.9937
10	12.1713	12.7712	10.0288

cess with modified rules 1 and 2 will mark/unmark a node to a T (a dominating node) or F (a non-dominating node) to get a CDS for the network.

Table 1 shows the average 1-hop ranking for all nodes, dominating nodes and non-dominating nodes in a network with 50,000 nodes. It is clear that dominating nodes have a higher average 1-hop ranking than non-dominating nodes. This is due to the fact that the dominating nodes have higher connectivity than non-dominating nodes. Based on the modified rules 1 and 2, the dominating nodes have more $docs'$ than non-dominating nodes.

Two searching methods are simulated. First, in regular random walk, a request will only be sent to the "best" neighbor with the highest 1-hop ranking. The second searching method is dominating-set-based, which sends a request to the "best" dominating neighbor which has the highest 1-hop ranking of all of its dominating neighbors and to the non-dominating neighbor which has the highest 0-hop ranking if there is one. We used 20 hops as the maximum number for both searching methods.

In Table 2, *search_no* is the number of trials. *RW_docs* (*RW_cost*) is average documentation returned from (average number of hops using) random walk searching. *DS_docs* (*DS_cost*) is average documentation returned from (average number of hops using) dominating-set-based searching. We can see that the number of documentations retrieved from dominating-set-based searching is much higher than the number returned from random walk searching. In *DS_cost*, two costs are recorded, $c_1(c_2)$, where c_1 is the number of steps in depth and c_2 is the number of one-hop branches. *RW_avg* (*DS_avg*) measures the average number of documentations returned for each step (in depth) in random walk searching (dominating-set-based searching). In general, *DS_avg* is higher than *RW_avg*. The reason for this is that dominating-set-based searching sends requests to the "best" dominating neighbor which has higher connectivity and higher *docs* and to the non-dominating neighbor which has the maximum number of documentations. As mentioned before, the cost of maintaining CDS in dominating-set-based searching is minimum since only local information is required.

Based on the results of Tables 1 and 2, we have the following conclusions: (a) Dominating-set-based searching terminates later than random walk searching. As a result, the average number of documentations returned from dominating-set-based search is more than random walk searching. (b) The number of "one-hop branches" is relatively insignificant. This is because such branches are generated only when it has a higher 0-hop ranking than its dominating node. (c) In dominating-set-based searching, the average number of documentations returned per step (in depth) is higher than random walk searching.

Table 2. Searching results.

nodes_no	5,000	5,000	5,000	50,000	50,000	50,000
max_docs	2	5	10	2	5	10
max_degree	6	6	6	6	6	6
search_no	100	100	100	100	100	
RW_docs	19.88	40.02	102.78	15.35	42.86	92.83
RW_cost	13.00	10.74	14.25	10.04	11.21	12.53
RW_avg	1.5292	3.7262	7.2126	1.5288	3.8233	7.4086
DS_docs	30.63	75.71	148.66	33.01	80.11	161.47
DS_cost	17.92 (2.37)	18.03 (2.92)	18.62 (2.64)	18.60 (3.27)	18.29 (3.59)	19.31 (2.54)
DS_avg	1.7103	4.1991	7.9838	1.7747	4.3799	8.3619

6 Conclusion

In this paper we have proposed a peer-to-peer searching algorithm using CDS. The CDS is constructed using the marking process [8] with the modified rules 1 and 2 for reduction. Simulation shows that dominating-set-based searching returned more documentations than random walk searching and kept the searching cost low. The cost of creating and maintaining the CDS is lower than that of the cost to create and maintain the routing indices ranking or hop count ranking as in [9]. Our future research will focus more on in depth simulation of dominating-set-based approach using different searching algorithms, such as DFS. Other ways of defining k-hop ranking ($k > 1$) will also be explored.

References

1. A. Chander, S. Dawson, P. Lincoln, and D. Stringer-Calvert. Nevrlate: scalable resource discovery. *Proc. 2nd IEEE/ACM Int'l Symposium on Cluster Computing and the Grid*, pages 382–388, 2002.
2. A. Crespo and H. Garcia-Molina. Routing indices for peer-to-peer systems. *Proc. 22nd Int'l Conference on Distributed Computing Systems*, pages 23–32, 2002.
3. http://freenet.sourceforge.net (Freenet website).
4. http://www.gnutella.com (Gnutella website).
5. http://www.napster.com (Napater website).
6. M. Portmann and A. Seneviratne. The cost of application-level broadcast in a fully decentralized peer-to-peer network. *Proc. 7th Int'l Symposium on Computers and Communications*, pages 941–946, 2002.
7. M. Krishna Ramanathan, V. Kalogeraki, and J. Pruyne. Finding good peers in peer-to-peer networks. *Proc. Int'l Symposium on Parallel and Distributed Processing*, pages 232–239, 2002.
8. J. Wu and H Li. On calculating connected dominating sets for efficient routing in ad hoc wireless networks. *Proc. 3rd Int'l Workshop on Discrete Algorithm and Methods for Mobile Computing and Communications*, pages 7–14, 1999.
9. B. Yang and H. Garcia-Molina. Improving search in peer-to-peer networks. *Proc. 22nd Int'l Conference on Distributed Computing Systems*, pages 5–14, 2002.

GFS-Btree: A Scalable Peer-to-Peer Overlay Network for Lookup Service

Qinghu Li[1], Jianmin Wang[2], and Jiaguang Sun[2]

[1] Department of Computer Science & Technology, Tsinghua University, Beijing, China
liqinghu99@mails.tsinghua.edu.cn
[2] School of Software, Tsinghua University, Beijing, China
{jimwang,sunjg}@tsinghua.edu.cn

Abstract. A fundamental problem that confronts peer-to-peer applications is to efficiently locate the node that stores a particular data item. We propose a new scalable Peer-to-Peer overlay network, GFS-Btree, which is resembling a Btree network. By adding additional linkages to Btree, GFS-Btree can relieve the congestion at the root and the other branch nodes. The events of a node joining and leaving the GFS-Btree system require no global coordination and require maximally $O(logn)$ nodes to change their state. Lookup routing is achievable on GFS-Btree network in $O(logn)$ hops with $O(1)$ connection cost.

1 Introduction

GridFS is an extension to Data Grid[1], constructed with peer-to-peer concepts over the web, for the sharing of educational resource files geographically distributed all over China as well as their consumers[2]. The same as other recent peer-to-peer applications, GridFS should be scalable, dynamic and serverless. All the machines from personal computers to high-end clusters of different educational institutions should be able to join or leave GridFS freely at any time. In order to share resources and access services over such a large, dynamic wide-area network, the means to locate them in an efficient manner is required.

The discovery and location of data and resources in a dynamic and scalable network is the fundamental problem of peer-to-peer systems. Recently, a number of groups have proposed structured peer-to-peer design. These proposals[3,4,5,6] all offer a distributed hash table (DHT) functionality. While there are significant implementation difference between these DHT systems, these systems all employ consistent hashing[7] and support (either directly or indirectly) a hash-table interface of *put(key, value)* and *get(key)* to manage the distribution of data among a changing set of nodes, and allowing one node to contact any node in the network directly or through routing to find any stored resource by name.

All of the existing DHTs have path lengths of $O(logn)$ hops with $O(logn)$ neighbors except that CAN[4] has longer paths of $O(dn^{1/d})$ and requires $O(d)$ neighbors. Here, n is the network size and d is the constant number of dimensions in CAN.

M. Li et al. (Eds.): GCC 2003, LNCS 3032, pp. 340–347, 2004.

Viceroy[6] achieves short path lengths with $O(1)$ neighbors. But Viceroy can not achieve $O(logn)$ path lengths with 100% probability. The contribution of this paper is to present the GFS-Btree, a variant of Btree to ensure that a lookup can be routed through a sequence of $O(logn)$ nodes toward the target with 100% probability. However, GFS-Btree maintains the properties of having $O(1)$ neighbors.

The rest of this paper is structured as follows. Section 2 describes the background, our motivation and objectives. Section 3 presents the topology of GFS-Btree. Section 4 presents the LOOKUP algorithm and section 5 describes the LEAVE operation and JOIN operation of one node. Finally, we summarize our contribution in Section 6.

2 Background and Objectives

This work is one part of the GridFS project[2] which is for sharing of educational resource files geographically distributed all over China as well as their consumers. GridFS is an extension to Data Grid[?] constructed with peer-to-peer concepts over the web. There are two key services each node should provide: file access service and metadata service.

We are interested in GFS-Btree's behavior in networks of extreme scale, dynamism and traffic. First, the forwarding path of a lookup for a key should involve as few machines as possible to achieve short latency and to produce few messages. It is difficult, even impossible, to exceed the achievement of $O(logn)$ hops in most existing peer-to-peer systems. Since it is enough for a lookup operation to reach the target node after $O(logn)$ hops, we take Btree as the basis to modify.

Second, since huge amounts of consumers are to access GridFS, GFS-Btree should be able to cope with large volumes of client lookups, so it is wished to guarantee that no server should be a bottleneck on the performance of the lookup service. The load incurred by lookup routings through the system should be evenly distributed among participating lookup nodes. As we know, Btree suffers from the congestion problems at the root. Our remedy is to add additional linkages to Btree.

Third, the joining or leaving of a single node should not impair the availability of the lookup service. Such changes are required to have only a small and mostly local impact on the network. Ideally, the number of neighbor nodes of each node should not vary as the network size varies. We want that GFS-Btree has constant degree, which is subjectively adjustable and which yields a constant expected linkage cost, and want that the larger the GFS-Btree's degree is, the more reliability GFS-Btree achieves as well as the less congestion GFS-Btree encounters. We emphasize constant linkage cost for that the practical cost of updating linkages far exceeds normal lookup costs because it involves coordination and sometimes huge metadata exchange between multiple nodes especially when a node notifies its joining or leaving to its neighbors.

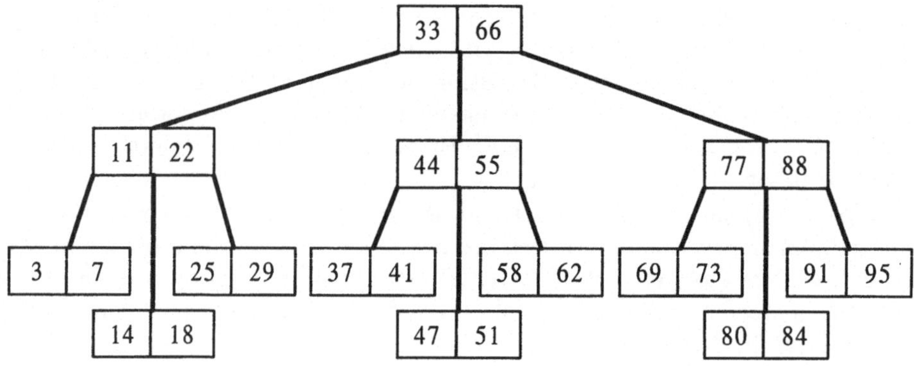

Fig. 1. A sample of Btree with order 2.

3 The GFS-Btree Network

The beauty of Btree[8] lies in the methods for inserting and deleting stored keys that always leave the tree balanced. This leads to large potential savings on the key search since the longest path in a Btree contains at most about $O(log_d n)$ nodes. This is the main reason that we select Btree as the basis of our GFS-Btree.

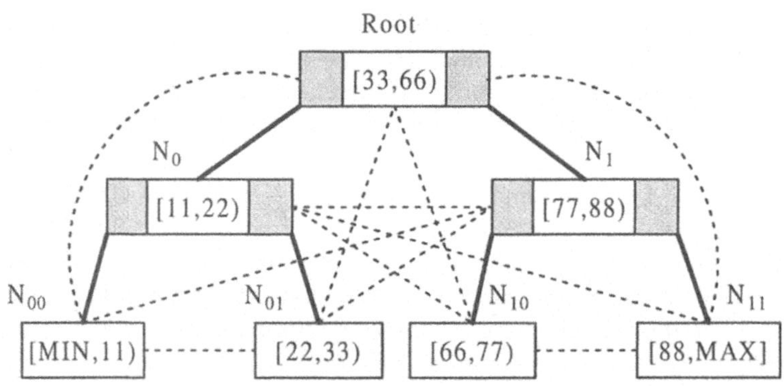

Fig. 2. A sample of GFS-Btree (corresponding to Fig. 1)

In Btree, each node retains between d and $2d$ keys (d is called the Btree's order) and the total number of nodes should vary as the total number of keys stored in them varies. But the dynamism of GFS-Btree means that it is free for each node to leave or join. It is required that despite how many nodes in GFS-Btree, all the keys should be retained. The only difference between more nodes and less nodes is the load on one node. So, we let each node in GFS-Btree retain ranges. That is, the keys retained by a node in Btree are transformed into, in GFS-Btree, the ranges. For example, the GFS-Btree illustrated in Fig. 2 is one corresponding to the Btree in Fig. 1. The root retains [33, 66), and its two children, N_0 and N_1 retain [11, 22) and [77, 88) respectively. All the newcome keys included by [33, 66) will be stored in the root, the newcome keys included by [11, 22) will be stored in node N_0 and so on. It is obvious that the ranges retained by the root and all of its descendants are adjacent one by one and they can combine to make the whole continuous range, [MIN, MAX].

The same as the other different kinds of trees, Btree may suffer from congestion problems at the root in key search. We tackle this problem by adding additional connections between two nodes, the ranges retained by which are adjacent to each other, and making them two to exchange routing information. Moreover, children of the same parent node are connected to one another, and each node is connected to its grandparent and uncles if they exist. Besides decreasing the congestion, all of these additional connections increase the reliability of GFS-Btree.

The detailed definition of GFS-Btree is as follows:

1). It can be a null tree.
2). Each node, denoted by N, maintains a tuple, $(m, A_0, R_1, A_1, R_2, A_2, \cdots, R_m, A_m)$. m is the number of ranges($R_i, 1 \leq i \leq m$) retained by N. m of N must be larger than 0 except that N is the root. Let M denotes N's capacity, $m \leq M$ and $M \geq 3$ should also be satisfied. $A_i(0 \leq i \leq m)$ is a reference to one of N's children. For any u, v, w that satisfy $0 \leq u < v \leq w \leq m$, any range $r_{up}(1 \leq p \leq A_u.m)$ retained by A_u and any range $r_{wq}(1 \leq q \leq A_w.m)$ retained by A_w, $r_{up} < R_v < r_{wq}$ is satisfied. (Here, for any two ranges, $[a, b] < [c, d]$ means that $a < c$ and $b < d$).
3). For each node, the union of its m ranges is called its *local-range* and the union of all the ranges of both itself and its descendants is called its *overlay-range*. Commonly, the *local-range* is discontinuous. But the *overlay-range* must be continuous.
4). The leaves are all at the same level.
5). Each node is connected to not only its parent and its children but also its siblings, uncles and grandparent if they exist.
6). Each branch node, include the root, is also connected to its *successor* and *predecessor* and exchanges routing information with them. The *successor* of a node indicates the leftmost leaf of its rightmost sub-tree. The *predecessor* of a node indicates the rightmost leaf of its leftmost sub-tree.

4 Lookup Algorithm

In a Btree, searches for keys all begin at the root and then are directed to the target node step by step by each node on the path. This leads to the abysmal congestion at the root. In a GFS-Btree, which is designed mainly for decreasing the congestions at the root and the other branch nodes, searches can start at any node and then be directed to the target by routing. Table 1 illustrates the routing table at N_1 in the GFS-Btree illustrated in Fig. 2.

Table 1. The routing table at N_1 in Fig. 2

Neighbor	Overlay-Range	Local-Range
N_{10}	[66,77)	[66,77)
N_{11}	[88, MAX]	[88, MAX]
N_{00}	[MIN, 11)	[MIN, 11)
N_{01}	[22, 33)	[22, 33)
N_0	[MIN, 33)	[11,22)
Root	[MIN,MAX)	[33,66)

Routing occurs in three distinct phases at one node, denoted by N. In the first phase, N checks whether the key searched for is included in its *local-range*, if yes, the target is no other than the current node. In the second phase, N searches in its routing table for a neighbor whose *overlay-range* includes the key, if such a neighbor exists, N transfers the query to it. In the third phase, N searches for the neighbor whose *overlay-range* is the nearest to the key and then transfers the query to it. The following is the detailed procedure.

LOOKUP(Key, N):

```
if (N.local-range includes Key) return VALUE(Key);
j = 0;
for (int i=0; i<N.neighbors_count; i++)
{
  if (N.overlay-range[i] includes Key)
  return LOOKUP(Key, N.neighbors[i]) ;
  if (N.neighbors[i]is nearer than N.neighbors[j] to Key)
  j = i;
}
return LOOKUP(Key, N.neighbors[j]);
```

Obviously, in GFS-Btree, the additional connections of each node to its grandparent, uncles, siblings,predecessor, successor and nephews make the lookup faster than that in Btree. But theoretically, it still requires $O(logn)$ steps for the lookup to reach the target.

5 GFS-Btree Construction and Maintenance

In this section, we describe how a GFS-Btree lookup network is constructed and maintained dynamically in a completely decentralized manner. We describe two main operations: JOIN and LEAVE.

5.1 JOIN Operation

The main operation we describe first is how a node joins the network. To allow the GFS-Btree to grow incrementally, a newcome node, denoted by NN in the following, must be allocated its own *local-range*. This is done by an existing node making NN its child and handling a range to it. In some case, one of NN's siblings may handle its two sub-trees to NN. The process takes several steps as follows:

1). NN must discover a node currently in the system. We assume that a GFS-Btree has one or more associated bootstrap nodes which are public. A bootstrap node maintains a partial list of GFS-Btree nodes which are believed currently in the system.
To join a GFS-Btree, NN contacts a bootstrap node. Then the bootstrap node supplies a randomly chosen node currently in the system. Of course, NN can select, by itself, an existing node that it believes is currently in the system.
2). NN is directed to a leaf's parent, denoted by PN, randomly but along the connections from top to down. If such PN does not exist (That is, there is only a root in the GFS-Btree), let PN denote the root. This step is simple and its path length is less than $O(logn)$ hops.
3). PN checks whether $PN.m < PN.M$ or not. If yes, PN makes NN its child, splits one of its ranges into 3 parts and handles the middle one to NN, and goto step 6). If no, goto step 4).
4). If PN is the root, goto step 5). Let PPN denote the parent of PN.
If $PPN.m < PPN.M$, NN is made PPN's new child. PN divides its ranges, by handling the $\lceil PN.m/2 \rceil$'th range to PPN, into two groups. One group of ranges along with the corresponding sub-trees are handled to NN. Then goto step 6).
Or else, if PPN is not the root, let $PN \leftarrow PPN$ and repeat step 4); if PPN is the root, goto step 5).
5). Make NN the parent of the root with no ranges is splitted or reallocated. That is, make NN's *local-range* equal null and make NN's *overlay-range* equal that of the root. Thus, NN becomes the new root.
6). Redress connections of those nodes correlative with this JOIN process.

Since it takes less than $O(logn)$ hops in step 2) and so does it in step 4) , the JOIN operation takes at most $O(logn)$ hops totally. The number of affected existing nodes depends only on the number of PPN's neighbors which is $O(1)$ and is independent of the network size, n.

5.2 LEAVE Operation

When a node, denoted by LN, leaves, we need to ensure that the ranges it retains are taken over by the remaining nodes and that the remaining nodes still compose a GFS-Btree. There are two actions LN should do before it leaves. One is that LN must transfer its *local-range* and the associated (*key, value*) database to its neighbors; the other is to notify all of the nodes connected to it that they must change their states. After LN leaves, LN's ex-parent should CHECK to see if it still satisfies the definition of GFS-Btree. If not, some adjustment should be done. The LEAVE algorithm and the CHECK algorithm are as follows.

LEAVE(LN):

```
if (LN is a leaf){
  LN handles its range to its parent;
  LN notify its neighbors its leaving;  CHECK(LN.parent);
}else{
   PRE=LN.predecessor; PN=PRE.parent;
   PRE handles its range to PN;
   PRE notify its neighbors its leaving;
   Replace LN with PRE;  CHECK(PN);
}
```

CHECK(PN):

```
if ((PN.children_num>1)||(PN is the root)) return;
//children_num denotes the number of the children of a node.
CPN=PN's only child; PPN=PN's parent; SPN=PN's nearest sibling;
if (such SPN does not exist)  //PPN must be the root with 1 child
{
  Let CPN become PPN's child;
  Reallocate correlative ranges;
}else
if (SPN.children_num>2)
{
  CSPN=SPN's child(the nearest to PN);
  Let CSPN become PN's child;
  Reallocate correlative ranges;
}else
{
  Let both PN and CPN become SPN's children;
  Let CPN's two children(the nearest to SPN) become PN's children;
  Reallocate correlative ranges;  CHECK(PPN);
}
```

The CHECK procedure may be executed $O(logn)$ times in one LEAVE operation at the worst case, but with very low probability. And each adjustment requires $O(1)$ nodes to change their state.

6 Conclusion

In this paper, we present a new scalable peer-to-peer overlay network called GFS-Btree. GFS-Btree is a variation of Btree by changing the retained objects from keys to ranges and by adding additional connections. Besides the parent-to-child connection, there are also uncle-to-nephew, grandparent-to-grandchild, sibling-to-sibling, branch-to-predecessor and branch-to-successor connections in

GFS-Btree. These additional connections increase the reliability of the system and decrease the congestion at the root and the other branch nodes. GFS-Btree achieves $O(logn)$ hops in lookup operation and the JOIN operation of a node takes at most $O(logn)$ steps to find an appropriate position. Since each node has constant ($O(1)$) neighbors, only $O(1)$ nodes are required to change their states when a node joins. For LEAVE operation, readjustment of $O(logn)$ times to the GFS-Btree are required at the worst case which emerges rarely. Each readjustment requires $O(1)$ nodes to change their state.

Acknowledgement. This work is supported by the Ministry of Education P.R.C under contract 2001BA101A12-02 and the National Key Basic Research and Development Program of China (973 Program) under Grant No.2002CB312006.

References

1. A. Chervenak, I. Foster, C. Kesselman, C. Salisbury, and S. Tuecke. The Data Grid: Towards an architecture for the distributed management and analysis of large scientific datasets. Journal of Network and Computer Applications, 23:187-200, 2001.
2. L. Qinghu, W. Jianmin, K. Yanlam, S. Jiaguang. GridFS: A Web-based Data Grid for the Distributed Sharing of Educational Resource Files. The 2nd International Conference on Web-based Learning, 2003. Published by LNCS.
3. B. Y. Zhao, J. Kubiatowicz, and A. Joseph. Tapestry: An infrastructure for fault-tolerant wide-area location and routing. Tech. Rep. UCB/CSD-01-1141, University of California at Berkeley, Computer Science Department, 2001.
4. S. Ratnasamy, P. Francis, M. Handley, R. Karp, and S. Shenker. A scalable content-addressable network. In Proc. ACM SIGCOMM (San Diego, CA, August 2001), pp. 161-172.
5. I. Stoica, R. Morris, D. Karger, M. F. Kaashoek and H. Balakrishnan. Chord: A scalable peer-to-peer lookup service for internet applications. In Proceedings of the ACM SIGCOMM '01 Conference (SanDiego, California, August 2001).
6. D. Malkhi, M. Naor and D. Ratajczak. Viceroy: A Scalable and Dynamic Emulation of the Butterfly. In Proceedings of the 21st ACM Symposium on Principles of Distributed Computing (PODC '02), 2002.
7. D. Karger, E. Lehman, F. T. Leighton, M. Levine, D. Lewin, and R. Panigrahy. "Consistent hashing and random trees: Distributed caching protocols for relieving hot spots on the World Wide Web". Proceedings of the 29th Annual ACM Symposium on Theory of Computing (STOC), pp. 654-663, May 1997.
8. D. Comer. "The Ubiquitous B-Tree". ACM Computing Surveys, 11(2):121–128, June 1979.

An Approach to Content-Based Approximate Query Processing in Peer-to-Peer Data Systems

Chaokun Wang, Jianzhong Li, and Shengfei Shi

P.O.Box 318, Department of Computer Science & Engineering
Harbin Institute of Technology, 150001, Harbin, Heilongjiang, China
{chaokun,shengfei}@hit.edu.cn lijz@mail.banner.com.cn

Abstract. In recent years there has been a significant interest in peer-to-peer (P2P) environments in the community of data management. However, almost all works, as far, focused on exact query processing in current P2P data systems. The autonomy of peers also doesn't be considered enough. In addition, the system cost is very high because the information publishing method of shared data is based on each document instead of document set.

In this paper, abstract indices are presented to implement content-based approximate queries in P2P data systems. It can be used to search as few peers as possible but get as many returns satisfying users' queries as possible on the guarantee of high autonomy of peers. Also, abstract indices have low system cost, can improve the query processing speed, and support very frequent updates.

In order to verify the effectiveness of abstract indices, a simulator of 10,000 peers, over 3 million documents is made. The experimental results show that abstract indices work well in P2P data systems.

1 Motivation

Peer-to-peer (P2P) systems have been greatly successful in facilitating storage and exchange of very large volumes of data since their scalability, fault-tolerance, and self-organizing nature. It calls for index techniques that provide users the abilities to retrieve data efficiently. In this paper, peer-to-peer data systems mean peer-to-peer systems in which peers share data instead of storage space each other.

Imagine that you are sitting before your computer connecting to a P2P music file sharing system. You suddenly hear a song. It's the best song you have heard for a long time, but you missed the announcement and don't recognize the artist. Wouldn't it be nice if you could hum a melody you remembered or push a few keys on your keyboard, and a few seconds later the P2P system would tell you the name of the artist and the title of the music you're listening to? Perhaps the system even sends this piece of music to your computer. This example shows that the content-based query is a kind of important query in P2P environments.

Supposing that there are a lot of documents satisfying the user's query, the P2P system only needs to return some of them instead of all of them. This kind

M. Li et al. (Eds.): GCC 2003, LNCS 3032, pp. 348–355, 2004.

of query is called the approximate query. Approximate query processing is very important in P2P environments because that the user just wants some delegates randomly selected from the document set, that is, the top k nearest neighbors similar to the query are not always the user's needs.

Current running P2P systems only support queries based on meta-data, such as file names, and lack the abilities of content-based queries. Moreover these systems always focus on exact queries without paying adequate attention to approximate queries.

In this paper, an approach called abstract indices is proposed to process content-based approximate queries in P2P environments on the premise of high autonomy of peers. Abstract indices can be used to search as few peers as possible but get as many returns, i.e. documents similar to users' queries, as possible. The main contributions of the paper are as following. (1). The abstract of a set of documents and the abstract of a peer are proposed. (2). Based on abstracts of peers, the abstract indices are designed to process content-based approximate queries in centralized and distributed P2P data systems.

For the limitation of space, a lot of material, such as abstract indices in structured P2P data systems, can not be included in the paper. More details can be found in [1].

The rest of this paper is organized as follows. In the next section related work is reviewed. In Section 3, abstract indices in centralized and distributed P2P data systems are described. In Section 4, the results of simulated experiments in centralized and distributed P2P data systems are presented. Conclusions and future work are given in Section 5.

2 Related Work

There are several kinds of P2P data systems in applications and theory research, such as centralized systems (Napster, Kazaa, [2]), distributed systems (Gnutella) and structured systems ([3, 4]). No matter which mode is based, there is not enough attention is paid to content-based approximate query processing in current running P2P systems, especially for multimedia documents. The query processing technology used in existing P2P data systems can be classified as follows.

The first kind of method is meta-data based query processing. It means that these systems work on meta-data of documents, such as file names, rather than the content of documents [5,6]. It is used in Napster, Gnutella, Kazza, and so on. The second kind of method is document digital identifier based query processing, i.e. key based query processing. It means that these systems run on document digital identifiers that are computed from meta-data of documents [4, 7, 3, 8]. The third kind of method is content-based querying processing. It means that the query processing is based on keywords or features that are extracted from shared documents of peers [9, 10, 11, 12]. The fourth kind of method is query processing on relational data [13, 14].

3 Abstract Indices

The abstract of a set of documents is some statistics of all documents in the set. Let X be a document set, $X = \{(x_1, x_2, \ldots, x_m)\}$, and f_a be a mapping defined on $\{X\}$, where $f_a : \{X\} \rightarrow \{(y^1, y^2, \ldots, y^n)\}$. $(y^1, y^2, \ldots, y^n)$ is called an abstract of X and f_a is called an abstract mapping, if $f_a(X) = (y^1, y^2, \ldots, y^n)$, where $y^k(k = 1, ..., n)$ is normalized into a range between y^k_{min} and y^k_{max}, such as 0 and 1, $m, n \geq 1$.

An abstract of a peer is an abstract of the shared document set in the peer. Let D be the set of shared documents in a peer. An abstract of D, $f_a(D) = (y^1, y^2, \ldots, y^n)$, is called an abstract of the peer. In a P2P data system, the set of abstracts of all peers in the system, $\{(y^1, y^2, \ldots, y^n)\}$, is called an abstract space S. S can be normalized as $[0, 1]^n$.

An abstract index of a P2P data system is an effective organization of all abstracts of peers in the system, i.e. an effective organization of the abstract space S. The abstract of a query is the abstract of the document set just consisting of the query.

Besides the function of content-based approximate queries, abstract indices have low system cost, can improve the query processing speed, support high autonomy of peers and very frequent updates, and support the information publishing method based on document set.

3.1 Central Abstract Indices in Centralized P2P Data Systems

Coordinators exist in centralized P2P data systems. For convenience to talk about the abstract indices, only one coordinator is considered in the following discussion. The abstract space $S = \{(y^1, y^2, \cdots, y^n)\}$ is saved in the coordinator.

In order to organize S better, the abstract space is partitioned under the following rules above all.

Given $0 \leq y^1_{r_1}, y^2_{r_2}, \ldots, y^n_{r_n} \leq 1$ $(r_1, r_2, \ldots, r_n = 0, \ldots, v)$, $y^k_0 = 0 < y^k_1 < y^k_2 < \cdots < y^k_{v-1} < y^k_v = 1$ $(k = 1, \ldots, n)$, S is partitioned by these points into v^n subspaces marked as $S_{p_1 p_2 \cdots p_n}(p_1, p_2, \ldots, p_n = 1, \ldots, v)$, where

(1). $S_{p_1 p_2 \cdots p_n} = \{(y^1, y^2, \ldots, y^n) |$ if $p_k = v$ then $y^k_{v-1} \leq y^k \leq y^k_v$ else $y^k_{p_k - 1} \leq y^k < y^k_{p_k}, k = 1, ..., n\}$;

(2). $S_{p_1 p_2 \cdots p_n} \cap S_{p'_1 p'_2 \cdots p'_n} = \Phi$, where $p_1 \neq p'_1$ or $p_2 \neq p'_2$ or $\cdots$ or $p_n \neq p'_n$;

(3). $\bigcup\limits_{p_1, p_2, \cdots, p_n = 1}^{v} S_{p_1 p_2 \cdots p_n} = S$.

$\{S_{p_1 p_2 \cdots p_n} | p_1, p_2, \ldots, p_n = 1, \ldots, v\}$ is called **a partition of** S, denoted as Ω, and $(y^k_0, \ldots, y^k_v)$ is called **the partitioning sequence** on the k_{th} component of abstract.

For establishing the relation between peers and abstract subspaces, the concepts of peer mapping and subspace mapping are introduced.

Let $\{id\}$ be the set of network identifiers of all peers. $\Omega = \{S_{p_1 p_2 \cdots p_n} | p_1, p_2, \ldots, p_n = 1, \ldots, v\}$ is a partition of S. The mapping $f_p : \{id\} \rightarrow \Omega$ is called a **peer mapping**, if $f_p(id) = S_{p_1 p_2 \cdots p_n}$, that is, the abstract of a peer whose identifier is id belongs to the abstract subspace $S_{p_1p_2\cdots p_n}$. Then one abstract subspace corresponds to a set of peers, which is denoted as $f_s(S_{p_1p_2\cdots p_n}) = \{id \,|\, f_p(id) = S_{p_1p_2\cdots p_n}\}$. The mapping $f_s : \Omega \to 2^S$ is called a **subspace mapping**. Obviously in a P2P system, $f_s(S_{p_1p_2\cdots p_n})$ may be a null set.

Given an element of S, a subset of S can be determined as follows.

$\forall y_* = (y_*^1, y_*^2, \cdots, y_*^n) \in S$, S_{y_*} is called the **expanding set** of y_* if $S_{y_*} = \{(y^1, y^2, \ldots, y^n) \,|\, y^1 \in [max(y_*^1 - \alpha_1, 0), min(y_*^1 + \alpha_1, 1)], y^2 \in [max(y_*^2 - \alpha_2, 0), min(y_*^2 + \alpha_2, 1)], \ldots, y^n \in [max(y_*^n - \alpha_n, 0), min(y_*^n + \alpha_n, 1)]\} \subseteq S$, where $0 \leq \alpha_1, \alpha_2, \cdots \alpha_n \leq 1$. α_i is called the expanding factor on the i_{th} component of abstract.

In order to normalize a subset of S, the concept of minimal overlay is introduced as following.

Let $E \subseteq S$, Ω be a partition of S, $G \subseteq \Omega$. G is called the **minimal overlay** of E if

(1). $E \subseteq \bigcup_{S' \in G} S'$;

(2). $G' \subseteq G$, $E \subseteq \bigcup_{S' \in G'} S' \Leftrightarrow G' = G$.

Thus S_{y_*} can be normalized to the union of several subspaces of S.

The abstract space S, partitioning sequences, expanding factors, mappings f_a, f_p and f_s make up of abstract indices in a centralized P2P data system, which are called central abstract indices.

when a user submits a query, the abstract of the query is extracted and sent to the coordinator. Based on central abstract indices, the expanding set of the abstract of the query and the minimal overlay of the expanding set can be computed. On the basis of f_s, the set of candidate peers can be gotten. In a P2P data system, a peer is called a **candidate peer** of a query if there are perhaps a lot of documents similar to the query on the peer. The documents that satisfy the user's query on the candidate peers will be returned.

3.2 Plain Abstract Indices in Distributed P2P Data Systems

In a distributed P2P data system, the creation and maintenance of the abstract of each peer is same as that in a centralized P2P data system. However there are still some differences between the two kinds of P2P systems. For example, no coordinator exists in a distributed P2P data system. Therefore abstract indices in such a system are dispersed over all peers.

The abstracts of all peers in a distributed P2P system comprise an abstract index, called a plain abstract index, of the system. Each peer only holds its own abstract.

In a distributed peer-to-peer data system without index mechanisms, a peer that receives a query sends the query to its neighbors and compares the query with its local shared documents. In order to decrease the computation of the whole system, during a query processing in a distributed P2P data system, peers can be classified as reached peers or searched peers according to plain abstract indices.

In a distributed P2P data system with a plain abstract index, peers involved in a query processing are classified to reached peers and searched peers. **A reached peer** is a peer that receives the abstract of the query. **A searched peer** is a peer that receives the abstract of the query and whose abstract belongs to the expanding set of the abstract of the query. Searched peers must be reached peers, but reached peers perhaps are not searched peers. Only the searched peers compare the feature of the query with their shared documents.

There is an area for a query processing in distributed P2P data systems. When a user submits a query on a peer of a distributed P2P data system, the abstract of the query is extracted. Then the querying peer is marked as a reached peer, and compares the abstract of the query with its abstract to judge whether it is a searched peer. If it is a searched peer, it compares features of its shared documents with the feature of the query to get the local result. Simultaneously it sends the abstract of the query to several peers randomly selected from its neighbors. If it is not a searched peer, the querying peer only sends the abstract of the query to the selected neighbors. Each peer receiving the abstract of the query in the area repeats the same steps.

The querying peer gathers all the local results and sorts them according to the matching values. After the user selects his favorites from the final result, the querying peer connects to the peers that have the selected documents. If the connections between the querying peer and the appropriate peers are established, the querying peer downloads the documents.

Several abstract indices can be established in a P2P data system. Abstract indices can also be combined with other indices or meta-data of document. The filtering of duplicates in the results can be found in [11].

In addition, abstract indices can be used to grid systems, deep webs, digital libraries, federated database systems, and so on. In a data grid, abstract information of a node can be gotten from data of the node, and all abstracts of nodes can be organized as an abstract index of the grid system. In a deep web, abstract information can be gotten from each database, and abstracts of all databases make up of an abstract index of the deep web.

4 Experiments

In this section, experiments are made to verify the effectiveness of abstract indices in centralized and distributed P2P data systems. For the limitation of space, the results on other metrics, such as recalls, the first accelerating factors and the second accelerating factors, can not be included in the paper. More material can be found in [1]. Above all, a simulator is made.

4.1 Experimental Setup

The simulated P2P data system is comprised of 10,000 peers. The number of documents in the system is 3,854,400. The minimum of documents in a peer is 70, and the maximum is 1,000. The number of documents in each peer is determined randomly. Documents in each peer are also generated randomly. Each document is represented as a 3-dimension vector (x_1, x_2, x_3), where the range of x_i is [0,1].

The abstract of a document set is defined as (y^1, y^2, y^3, y^4), where y^i is the mathematical expectation of X_i $(i = 1, 2, 3)$ and y^4 is the average of standard deviations of X_1, X_2 and X_3. X_i is a random variable used to represent x_i.

Suppose that documents in the system are all shared. Two documents are called similar if the Euclidean distance between them is not more than a given constant $offset$. The values of $offset$ used in the experiments are 0.05, 0.1, 0.15, 0.2, 0.25 and 0.3.

In order to test the effectiveness of abstract indices, 512 different queries are generated under the uniform distribution. Each query is a triple.

4.2 Experimental Results of Central Abstract Indices

In the simulated centralized P2P data system, the partition sequence $(y_0^k, \cdots, y_5^k)$ is determined by the experimental data. In detail, y_0^k is little smaller than the minimum of $\{y^k\}$; y_5^k is little bigger than the maximum of $\{y^k\}$; y_1^k, y_2^k, y_3^k and y_4^k are evenly distributed between y_0^k and y_5^k, where $k = 1, \cdots, 4$.

Table 1. Returns in a centralized p2p data system

offset	(0.18, 0.18, 0.18, 0.15)	(0.09, 0.18, 0.18, 0.15)	(0.18, 0.09, 0.18, 0.15)	(0.18, 0.18, 0.09, 0.15)	(0.18, 0.18, 0.18, 0.07)	(0.09, 0.09, 0.09, 0.07)
0.05	1,186.79	1,036.30	1,037.73	1,035.89	515.30	456.61
0.1	9,279.78	8,025.27	8,034.13	8,026.40	4,055.80	3,431.60
0.15	29,401.44	24,985.72	25,012.50	24,990.32	12,949.06	10,060.88
0.2	64,040.30	53,085.41	53,137.39	53,103.21	28,336.56	19,468.27
0.25	111,388.02	89,513.98	89,609.74	89,535.82	49,248.62	29,094.50
0.3	166,357.05	129,307.82	129,442.22	129,331.43	72,755.53	36,732.98

In the following experiments, the expanding factors are respectively set to (0.18, 0.18, 0.18, 0.15), (0.09, 0.18, 0.18, 0.15), (0.18, 0.09, 0.18, 0.15), (0.18, 0.18, 0.09, 0.15), (0.18, 0.18, 0.18, 0.07) and (0.09, 0.09, 0.09, 0.07). Under different expanding factors, the numbers of returns, i.e. the numbers of the satisfying documents in all candidate peers, under various offsets are listed in Table 1. Numbers in the table are all decimal fractions because they are all averages. Each number is the mean of 512 results corresponding to the 512 queries.

At given expanding factors, the returns increase with the increase of the offset because the similarity demands are loosed. At a given offset, the returns decrease with the decease of an expanding factor because the candidate peers become less. Because y^1, y^2 and y^3 have the same attributes, they almost have the same reflection when the same change happens on the expanding factor on the first, second and third component of abstract.

It can be found from Table 1 that there are mostly more than 1,000 satisfied documents returned in given expanding factors and offset. Therefore the effects of abstract indices are very well in centralized systems.

4.3 Experimental Results of Plain Abstract Indices

The simulator can be modified to simulate a distributed P2P data system if its topology structure is altered. In order to define the querying area, it is assumed that a query can be sent by a peer to at most 5 neighbors, and a query can be sent to at most 7 peers along a path. Of course the parameters can be altered to other values. Please note that in the distributed P2P data system, "candidate peers" are "searched peers".

In the simulated distributed P2P data system, the numbers of returns under various expanding factors and offsets are listed in Table 2. The querying peer is randomly selected in each test.

Table 2. Returns in a decentralized p2p data system

offset	(0.18, 0.18, 0.18, 0.15)	(0.09, 0.18, 0.18, 0.15)	(0.18, 0.09, 0.18, 0.15)	(0.18, 0.18, 0.09, 0.15)	(0.18, 0.18, 0.18, 0.07)	(0.09, 0.09, 0.09, 0.07)
0.05	717.52	435.13	433.66	434.27	277.08	78.06
0.1	5,329.97	3,045.63	3,048.76	3,043.24	2,072.75	464.96
0.15	15,204.06	8,064.55	8,072.34	8,067.79	5,801.74	944.04
0.2	28,119.06	13,967.63	13,988.40	13,975.86	10,286.93	1,235.34
0.25	39,729.11	18,878.75	18,913.58	18,887.56	13,497.04	1,321.93
0.3	47,833.02	22,208.64	22,267.36	22,227.11	14,777.24	1,331.68

It can be found from Table 2 that there are still many satisfied documents returned at certain expanding factors and offset. Then the effects of plain abstract indices are still very well. The returns under expanding factors (0.09, 0.09, 0.09, 0.07) are relatively small because the expanding factors are too strict. In detail, 121 out of 512 queries don't have any candidate peer when the offset and expanding factors are respectively set to the given values.

If the expanding factors are set to (0.09,0.09,0.09,0.15), the returns will be (160.42, 992.67, 2248.41, 3449.74, 4356.34, 4956.93). If the 121 queries are deleted from this experiment, the better results (102.21, 608.84, 1236.19, 1617.63, 1731.02, 1743.79) can also be gotten. So it can be concluded that 1) the effectiveness of plain abstract indices is still good; and 2) the expanding factors may be refined to get more returns if the current return seems not enough.

5 Conclusions and Future Work

In this paper, abstract indices are proposed for content-based approximate queries in peer-to-peer data systems. Experimental results show that abstract indices work well in the simulated environments. There are still many problems on abstract indices. For example, what are the proper query features for various media documents? We will study them in the future.

Acknowledgements. This work was supported by the National Grand Fundamental Research 973 Program of China under Grant No. G1999032704 and the National Doctor Foundation of Chinese Education Committee under Grant No. 2000021303.

References

1. Wang, C., Li, J., Shi, S.: AbIx: An Approach to Content-Based Approximate Queries in Peer-to-Peer Data Systems. Tech. Report HIT/DCSE-DB-03-0710, Database Lab. of Harbin Institute of Technology, Harbin, China (2003)
2. Yang, B., Garcia-Molina, H.: Comparing Hybrid Peer-to-Peer Systems. In: Proceedings of the 27th International Conference on Very Large Data Bases, Roma, Italy (2001) 561–570
3. Stoica, I., Morris, R., Liben-Nowell, D., Karger, D.R., Kaashoek, M.F., Dabek, F., Balakrishnan, H.: Chord: A Scalable Peer-to-Peer Lookup Protocol for Internet Applications. IEEE/ACM Transactions on Networking **11** (2003) 17–32
4. Ratnasamy, S., Francis, P., Handley, M., Karp, R., Schenker, S.: A Scalable Content-Addressable Network. In: Proceedings of ACM SIGCOMM. (2001) 161–172
5. Yang, B., Garcia-Molina, H.: Efficient Search in Peer-to-Peer Networks. In: Proceedings of the 22nd International Conference on Distributed Computing Systems. (2002) 5–14
6. Crespo, A., Garcia-Molina, H.: Routing Indices for Peer-to-Peer Systems. In: Proceedings of the 22nd International Conference on Distributed Computing Systems. (2002) 23–34
7. Rowstron, A., Druschel, P.: Pastry: Scalable, Distributed Object Location and Routing for Large-Scale Peer-to-Peer Systems. In: IFIP/ACM International Conference on Distributed Systems Platforms (Middleware). (2001) 329–350
8. Zhao, B.Y., Kubiatowicz, J., Joseph, A.D.: Tapestry: An Infrastructure for Fault-tolerant Wide-area Location and Routing. Tech. Report UCB/CSD-01-1141, University of California, Berkeley, California 94720 (2001)
9. Cuenca-Acuna, F.M., Nguyen, T.D.: Text-Based Content Search and Retrieval in *ad hoc* P2P Communities. In: Proceedings of the International Workshop on Peer-to-Peer Computing. (2002)
10. Tang, C., Xu, Z., Mahalingam, M.: pSearch: Information Retrieval in Structured Overlays. In: Proceedings of the 1st HotNets-I, Princeton, New Jersey, USA, ACM Press (2002)
11. Wang, C., Li, J., Shi, S.: A Kind of Content-Based Music Information Retrieval Method in a Peer-to-Peer Environment. In: Proceedings of the 3rd International Symposium on Music Information Retrieval, Paris, France (2002) 178–186
12. Gao, J., Tzanetakis, G., Steenkiste, P.: Content-Based Retrieval of Music in Scalable Peer-to-Peer Networks. In: The 2003 IEEE International Conference on Multimedia & Expo(ICME'03), Baltimore, MD, USA, IEEE CS Press (2003)
13. Gribble, S., Halevy, A., Ives, Z., Rodrig, M., Suciu, D.: What Can Database Do for Peer-to-Peer ? In: Proceedings of the 4th International Workshop on the Web and Databases. (2001) 31–36
14. Halevy, A.Y., Ives, Z.G., Suciu, D., Tatarinov, I.: Schema Mediation in Peer Data Management Systems. In: Proceedings of the 19th International Conference on Data Engineering. (2003)

A Hint-Based Locating and Routing Mechanism in Peer-to-Peer File Sharing Systems[1]

Hairong Jin, Shanping Li, Tianchi Ma, and Liang Qian

College of Computer Science, Zhejiang University,Hangzhou, P.R.China 310027
zjujhr@163.com, shan@cs.zju.edu.cn, mtc@cad.zju.edu.cn, qianliang@zju.edu.cn

Abstract. A hint-based file locating & routing mechanism was proposed to improve the performance of peer-to-peer file sharing systems. The framework was based on the Freenet document routing model with file location hints to enhance the performance of file searching and downloading. Experiment shows that the proposed mechanism improves the system performance by saving disk space, as well as reduces file transfer latency and alleviates network load.

1 Introduction

Statistical data shows that P2P file sharing systems are very popular nowadays. Internet2 administrators report that about 11.6% of the traffic carried by the network is produced by P2P file sharing system [1] (August 2003). The KaZaA Media Desktop (KMD) has become the world most downloaded software [2]. Another two popular P2P software packages, iMesh and Morpheus [3], are at the downloading rate 400,000 per week and 200,000 per week respectively. These three are all in the top 10 most popular downloads [4]. Survey on several large ISPs shows that about 15%~30% of residential clients use KaZaA or Gnutella [5].

New challenges are imported in guaranteeing or improving large system performance. Three main approaches are adopted in previous work to solve this issue, namely replication, caching and intelligent locating & routing [19]. The intelligent locating & routing will be the main focus of this paper.

There are three general P2P locating & routing models: centralized directory model, flooded requests model, and document routing model. The former two had been the most popular P2P locating & routing models used in famous systems such as Napster [6] and Gnutella [7]. However, they are comparatively simple and inefficient in a current point of view.

The document routing model is an advanced model, which is first used in Freenet [10]. In this scheme, the file request is transmitted on a path that is dynamically chosen according to routing table searching, which continues until the file is found or the request step reaches a maximum number. The found file is also transferred back along

[1] The Project Supported by Zhejiang Provincial Natural Science Foundation of China (No.602032)

M. Li et al. (Eds.): GCC 2003, LNCS 3032, pp. 356–362, 2004.

the path and cached on all the peers it passes. The cached copies can be used for later requests, but occupy too much space. Furthermore, the system logical architecture probably doesn't match the physical network well, and a peer probably will retrieve file from a physically distant peer.

In this paper, a reformed scheme is proposed based on the document routing model used in Freenet, which is called "Hint-based Locating & Routing (HBLR)". Comparing to the mechanism used in Freenet, HBLR has several advantages:

1. Saving disk space on peers;
2. Reducing the file transfer time by retrieving file from a best peer;
3. Achieving lower network load because of the shortened file transfer path.

The rest of this paper is organized as follows: Section 2 describes HBLR. Section 3 gives simulation and discussion. Section 4 surveys related work. At last the author's work was summarized at Section 5.

2 HBLR Mechanism

HBLR is used to save space, and to minimize the adverse influence produced by the mismatch between logical and physical layers. HBLR provides file location hints for the peer that requests the file to select download location.

2.1 Architecture

Each peer or file in HBLR has a random ID, which is a string of numbers. A peer maintains two structures: routing table and hint table. The routing table is used as request transmission basis. The hint table provides all probable locations of the file.

Each entry in routing table consists of two fields: file ID, peer ID. Thus an entry associates a file with a peer, which is the file's "owner". Owner here means a file's publisher, which originally produced the file and usually holds a copy excepting the file has been evicted out of local store. Fig. 1 shows a routing table instance, which indicates that file 001200's owner is peer 01500.

File ID	Peer ID
001200	01500
013398	24081
112780	03345
000127	12007
⋮	⋮

Fig. 1. A routing table instance.

An entry in hint table contains two parts: file ID and location hint list. The location hint list implies which peers have copy of the corresponding file. But how many location items can be kept in an entry? There are two solutions. The first is to keep all the possible locations, attaching a time stamp to each location item, which is called a "full hint" solution. The time stamp points out the item's building time, newer item is more credible. All the location items are linked into a chain indexed by the timestamps. Either the entry's holder or the requester can respectively decide to use how many location items for selection according to system workload. Fig.2 shows a full hint solution instance.

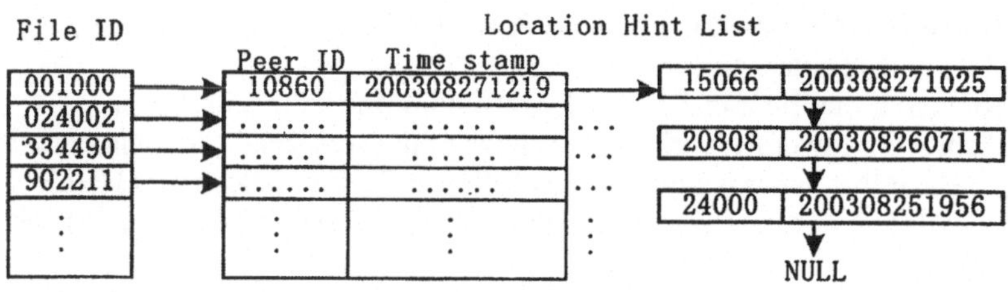

Fig. 2. An instance of hint table which uses full hint solution. According to this table, file 001000 at least exists on peers 10860, 15066, 20808 and 24000.

The second solution is a "finite hint" solution in which each entry contains location items in a finite number. The holder and requester use all the items for decision. Items are managed with a LRU replacement policy.

The full hint solution provides comparatively overall locations but requires more space, while the finite hint solution provides incomplete but the most credible hints and consumes less space. The latter is more suitable for mobile device, which has limited storage space. Hint tables update their contents during the request process, which will be explained later.

2.2 Requesting File

To request a file, a peer designates a hops-to-live value, which specifies the number of peers the request can be passed. The initiator first checks its own local store for the file. If not found, the initiator looks up the routing table to find out an entry, which has the most similar file ID to the requested ID. It then forwards the request to the peer in the selected entry. When a peer receives a request, it checks its hint table for the file's hint entry. If not found, it looks up the nearest file ID in its routing table to the ID requested, and forwards the request to the corresponding peer. If a hint entry, whose file ID matches the requested ID, is found, then location items in this entry will be transferred back through the upstream requesting path to the initiator. Each peer on the path will update its hint table using the items.

If no matched hint entry is found before the hops-to-live value is reached, then the request is failed and a failure message will be transferred back to the initiator. To avoid looping every request is assigned a unique identifier for looping check.

The initiator uses network operational instruction such as "ping" to detect peers' reachability and their response latency. It can furthermore obtain peers' workload with the help of operating system. Based on all these information, the peer can select a best peer from whom to download the file. While downloaded, the initiator and file provider add the initiator as the file's newest location item in hint table.

In summary, a request course can be divided into four steps: 1. Find a hint entry according to the requested file. 2. Using the location hint items to select a best download peer. 3. Retrieve the file from the selected peer. 4.Update hint table.

2.3 Storing File

When a new file is produced, the peer that produces it must publish the file to the system. The producer, also the publisher, keeps the file in its own local store and initiates a request with the new file's ID for ID collision detection. The request is similar to a normal file request excepting the result judgment. Failure case in normal file request here is a good result, which shows there is no ID collision. On the contrary, successful result in normal request here implies ID collision. Thus the publisher must create a new ID for another detection. If no collision exists, the peers on the detection path will add an entry in their hint table about the new file, including a location item pointing to the publisher. These peers also add a routing table entry about the new file associating with its publisher.

2.4 Brief Comparison to Freenet

Freenet distributes files to peers while HBLR distributes files' location hints to peers. The latter requires less storage space, hence less disk replacement. Freenet downloads file wherever the file is while HBLR use hints to select a best peer with the lowest latency and downloads file from it. So HBLR uses a more reasonable download model which can reduce file transfer time and network load.

3 Simulation and Discussion

A simulation experiment is taken to check HBLR's effectiveness. For comparison, locating & routing mechanism in Freenet is also simulated. Performance parameters such as average request latency and number of disk replacement are concerned.

In simulations two systems run on the same network topology with a set of peers and files. 100 peers and 4000 files are used and the files are even distributed over peers. Each peer's disk space contributed to P2P system is 300MB. The files' size can be adjusted as a parameter. The simulations are processed under mature environment, which means systems have run for enough time, so useful information and files have been distributed over the systems. Each simulation course contains 1000 file requests.

As Fig.3 shows, disk replacement in HBLR is rare because only requester stores file in its own local store, and has the probability to take disk replacement. Since Freenet caches file on every peer along the request path, it takes much more disk replacement than HBLR in simulation, especially when the average file size is bigger. Overall, HBLR saves disk space and takes less disk replacement.

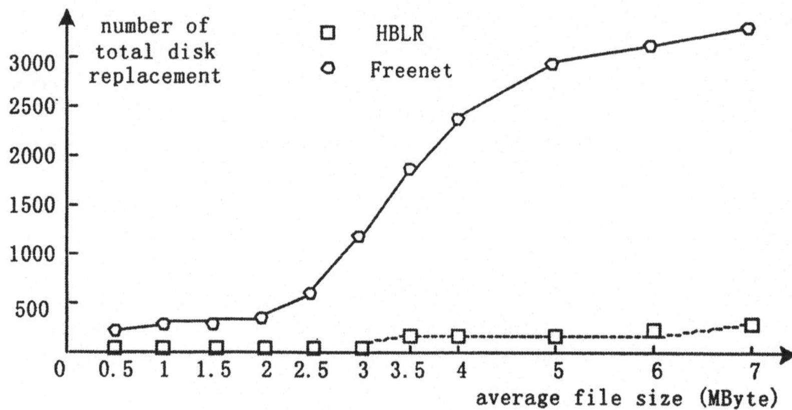

Fig. 3. Number of disk replacement. The data is achieved by 1000 times of requests.

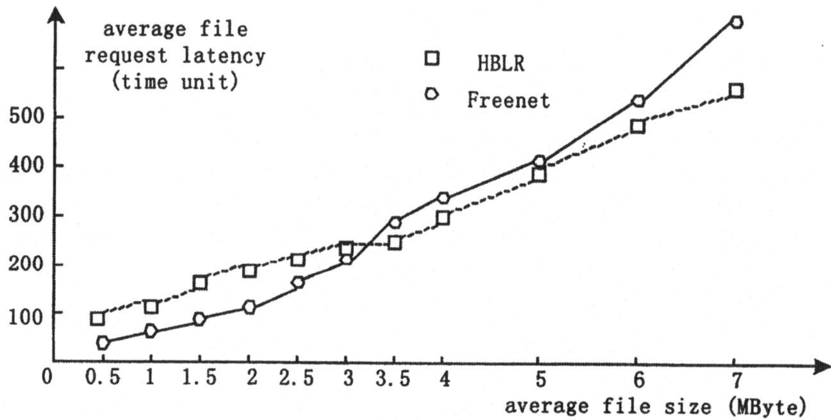

Fig. 4. Average file request latency. The value is the average of 1000 times of requests.

In Fig.4, the simulation shows two mechanisms' average request latency. In Freenet, when file size is small, a peer can keep a large number of files, and so a file can be kept on many peers. A request in Freenet will find a file soon because of the small file's broad distribution. While file size increases, it can't be widely distributed, and then some requests need to take a longer path to find and to download it. And big file takes more time to be downloaded. So the latency increases quickly. In HBLR, a best position will be selected to download the file from, so the latency increases only due to the file size and the climbing curve is relatively flatter.

According to the simulation, HBLR takes less disk space than Freenet. And it provides good request latency dealing with relatively big files. If peer's disk space is set smaller than 300MB, HBLR will have more advantage over Freenet in the latency.

4 Related Work

Locating & routing mechanism is a core component in P2P file sharing system, and much research work have been done about it and many algorithms are proposed.

There are several algorithms about document routing model: CAN [11], Chord [12], Tapestry [13] and Pastry [14]. They all are efficient, but they all take no account of the mismatch between underlying network topology and the logical architecture.

The Ohaha system uses Freenet-style query routing [15]. As a result, it shares some of the weaknesses of Freenet.

Ripeanu et al. [16] studied the topology of the Gnutella network and found that the Gnutella network topology does not match well the underlying Internet topology, leading to the inefficient use of the network bandwidth.

K. Sripanidkulchai [17] and Evangelos P. Markatos [9] studied Gnutella traffic and proposed the use of caching to improve locating & routing performance.

Arturo Crespo and Hector Garcia-Molina [18] achieved greater efficiency by placing Routing Indices in each peer.

5 Conclusions and Future Work

HBLR is an effective locating & routing mechanism for P2P file sharing system. Comparing to the mechanism used in Freenet, HBLR can save much space and reduce request latency along with lower network load.

But some improvements to HBLR are needed. First, the hint entries on different peers about the same file may be not consistent. A newest requester retrieves the file and has the newest hint items. A synchronization mechanism should be introduced. Second, HBLR is designed in a general form, not especially optimized for desktop system or mobile device. Special customization must be done before application. At last, the simulations process in a small environment, large-scale experiment is needed.

References

1. Internet2 NetFlow Reports, http://netflow.internet2.edu/weekly/20030825/, August 2003.
2. The KaZaA home page, http://www.kazaa.com, August 2003.
3. The Morpheus home page, http://www.morpheus.com, August 2003.
4. Download.Com Site, http://download.com.com, August 2003.
5. InformaticsOnlineWebSite, http://www.infomaticsonline.co.uk/News/1134977.
6. The Napster home page, http://www.napster.com.
7. Fernando R. A. Bordignon et al. Gnutella: Distributed System for Information Storage and Searching Model Description. Journal of Internet Technology, Taipei (Taiwan), Vol.2, No.5.
8. Jordan Ritter. Why Gnutella Can't Scale. No, Really. 2001.
9. E. P. Markatos. Tracing a large-scale Peer to Peer System: an hour in the life of Gnutella. 2nd IEEE/ACM International Symposium on Cluster Computing and the Grid. 2002.
10. Ian Clarke et al. Freenet: A Distributed Anonymous Information Storage and Retrieval System. Lecture Notes in Computer Science. 2000.

11. Sylvia Ratnasamy et al. A Scalable Content-Addressable Network. In Proceedings of the ACM SIGCOMM, 2001.
12. Ion Stoicay et al. Chord: A Scalable Peer-to-peer Lookup Protocol for Internet Applications. Proceedings of the 2001 conference on applications, technologies, architectures, and protocols for computer communications. 2001.
13. Ben Y. Zhao et al. Tapestry: An Infrastructure for Fault-tolerant Wide-area Location and Routing. U.C.Berkeley Technical Report, UCB//CSD-01-1141. April 2000.
14. A. Rowstron et al. Pastry: Scalable, distributed object location and routing for large-scale peer-to-peer systems. IFIP/ACM International Conference on Distributed Systems Platforms (Middleware), Heidelberg, Germany, pages 329-350, November 2001.
15. Ohaha, Smart decentralized peer-to-peer sharing. http://www.ohaha.com/design.html.
16. M. Ripeanu et al. Mapping the gnutella network: Properties of large-scale peer-to-peer systems and implications for system design. IEEE Internet Computing Journal, 6(1), 2002.
17. K. Sripanidkulchai. The popularity of gnutella queries and its implications on scaling, 2001.
18. Arturo Crespo et al. Routing Indices For Peer-to-Peer Systems. International Cofenrence on Distributed Computer Systems. July 2002.
19. D. S. Milojicic et al. Peer-to-Peer Computing. Hewlett-Packard Internal Document. March 2002.

Content Location Using Interest-Based Subnet in Peer-to-Peer System*

Guangtao Xue, Jinyuan You, and Xiaojian He

Department of Computer Science and Engineering, Shanghai Jiao Tong University, Shanghai 200030, China
{xue-gt, you-jy, he-xj}@cs.sjtu.edu.cn

Abstract. Intuitively, the peers who share similar interests tend to have a high probability of connecting to each other and sharing the resources. In this paper, we use ontology model represent user's interests instead of using the conventional *Vector Space Model*. Each interest concept hierarchy is then interpreted within the Information Theory framework as a probabilistic decision tree. The interest-matching algorithm uses the *KL* (*Kullback-Leiber*) distance as a measure of deviation between two probabilistic decision trees. Then we use an interest-based group model to organize the peers with similar interests into a subnet. Our content location solution is on top of the existing Gnutella network. When using our algorithm, called interest-based subnet, a significant amount of flooding can be avoided, making Gnutella a more competitive solution. The extensive simulation results show the efficiency of the proposed model in peer-to-peer system.

1 Introduction

There are many challenges in providing peer-to-peer content distribution systems. There are two classes of solutions currently proposed for decentralized peer-to-peer content location. Structured content location is based on the Distributed Hash Table (DHT) abstraction [1, 2] has been proposed to address scalability. In this context, peers organize into a well-defined structure that is used for routing queries. Although DHTs are elegant and scalable, their performance under the dynamic conditions common for peer-to-peer systems is unknown [3]. Another class of solutions is used by Gnutella, relies on flooding queries to all peers. Peers organize into an overlay. In this solution, a peer sends a query to its neighbors on the overlay. In turn, the neighbors forward the query on to all of their neighbors until the query has traveled a certain radius or the content is located successfully. While this solution is simple and robust even when peers join and leave the system, it does not scale.

* This paper is supported by the Shanghai Science and Technology Development Foundation under Grant No. 03DZ15027

M. Li et al. (Eds.): GCC 2003, LNCS 3032, pp. 363–370, 2004.

The traditional peer-to-peer systems have ignored those following facts [4]:

-Group locality. Users with the same interest tend to work in the same group. An interest-based group of users, although not always located in geographical proximity, tends to use the same set of resources (files). File location mechanisms such as those proposed in CAN, Chord, or Tapestry do not attempt to exploit this behavior: each member of the group will hence pay the cost of locating a file of common interest.

-Time locality. The same user may request the same file multiple times within short time intervals. For example, in scientific collaborations p2p network peers often access newly produced data to perform analyses or simulations. File location mechanisms such as Gnutella do not attempt to exploit this behavior: each member in the system will hence pay the cost of locating same file time after time.

We discovered that the peers who share similar interests tend to have a high probability of connecting to each other and sharing the resources [5, 6]. If we can find the peers who share similar interests and organizes them in a same set of subnet to locate content. When subnet fails, peers resort to using the underlying Gnutella overlay. Interest-based subnet provides a loose structure on top of Gnutella's unstructured overlay. Then we can retain the simple, robust, and fully decentralized nature of Gnutella, while improving scalability, its major weakness.

2 Ontology

User's interest is conventionally represented by the Vector Space Model. Each component of the vector represents the importance of a keyword of the user's interest. For example: $\vec{v}_d = (k_1,w_1 \,;\, k_2,w_2 \,;\, \ldots \,;\, k_i,w_i)$. k_i represents one keyword of the user's interest, and w_i represents the weight of the importance of the keyword k_i. VSM has the advantage of simplicity and speed. However, representing a user with a simple set of keywords is insufficient; it lacks the proper semantics to describe the complex nature of a user. Feature vectors ignore conceptual relations between keywords.

Ontology can be defined as "a specification of a conceptualization" [7]. The semantics of the tree representation of ontology is defined as follows:

- Hierarchically structured, and not just a list of keywords,
- Each node represents a distinct concept,
- Each directed edge represents a sub-concept relationship between the parent (the outgoing node) and the child node (the ingoing node)

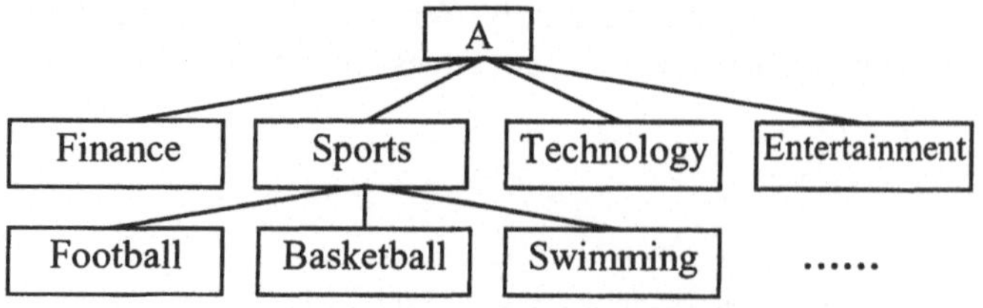

Fig. 1. User A's interest ontology

In Figure 1, the root node can be regarded as the simplest classification of the user's interests. The nodes in the next level of the tree then represent the first broad categorization of the user's interests. Subsequent levels of the tree describe increasingly finer categorization of the interests, right down to the leaf nodes of the tree.

2.1 Probability Tree

It is difficult to profile users because every user's interests change over time and are dynamic. Along with the previous treatment of the tree representation of the ontology, the probability tree paradigm offers a way to personalize the standard ontology. A probability tree is a useful mathematical construct that imposes a hierarchical structure on the outcomes of a random variable. Figure 2 shows a graphical representation of a random variable in terms of a shallow tree.

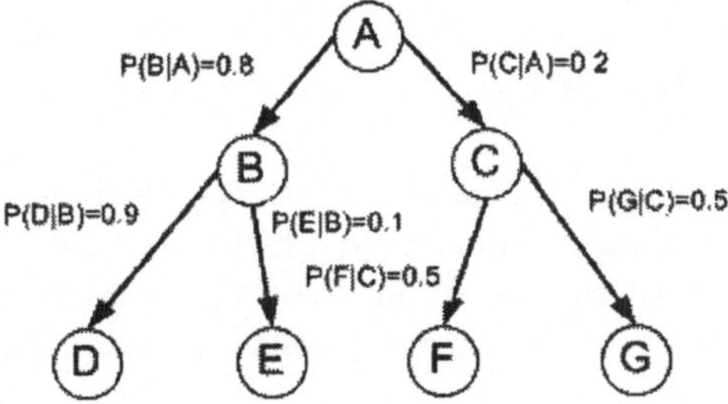

Fig. 2. An Interest Probability Tree

The root node represents the Interests random variable. The outcomes of the random variable are the leaf nodes of the tree. Each parent-child node relationship in the ontology can be quantified by assigning probabilities to each parent-child edge. The probability associated with each outcome is the product of all the probabilities along a single path leading from the root node to the leaf node.

2.2 KL Distance

In the previous section, since each user is represented by a probabilistic distribution over a standard ontology, information theory can be used to derive ensemble properties of each user. KL is a measure of the deviation between two probability distributions [8].

$$D(p\|q) = \sum_{i=1}^{N} p_{xi} \log \frac{p_{xi}}{q_{xi}} \qquad (1)$$

Or $$D(p\|q) = -\left(\sum_{i-1}^{N} p_{Xi} \log(q_{Xi})\right) - \left(\sum_{i=1}^{N} p_{Xi} \log(p_{Xi})\right) \qquad (2)$$

In KL distance, $D(p||q)$ measures the error in predicting the uncertainty of a random variable X when its probability distribution is assumed to be q while the true distribution of X is p. As such, KL distance is usually used as a measure of the probabilistic deviation of $q(x)$ from $p(x)$. The probability associated with each edge can be regarded as a measure of the relative importance of the concept represented by each child node.

The advantage of using KL distance comparing to keyword overlap become clearer in general problems that involves multi-level probability trees. In such problems, the semantics of the keyword overlaps becomes unclear in feature vectors because it does not consider the relations between concepts. In contrast, KL distance remains obvious; it is simply the measure of the deviation between the probability distributions. I believe that tree-representations of the ontology are richer and more accurate descriptions of a user's interest. KL distance is therefore more general than keyword overlaps as a similarity measure.

3 Interest-Based Subnet

In this section, we study how to organize the peers with similar interests into a subnet. We propose a content location solution in which peers loosely organize themselves into interest-based subnet on top of the existing Gnutella network. A significant amount of flooding can be avoided, making Gnutella a more competitive solution.

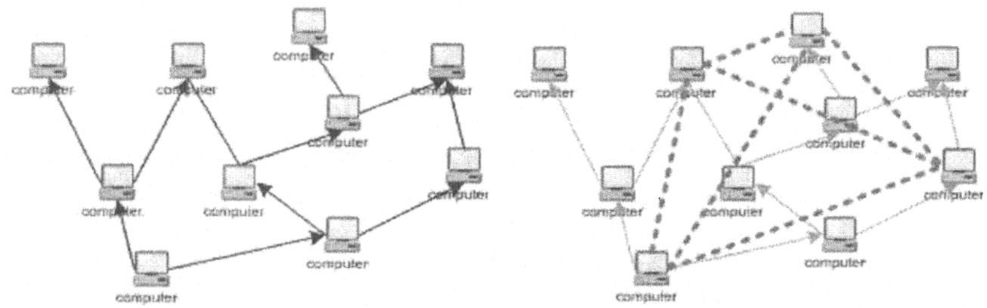

Fig. 3. (a) Gnutella (b) Interest-based Subnet

Figure 3(a) illustrates how content is located in Gnutella. A query initiated by the peer at the bottom is flooded to all peers in the system. Figure 3(b) depicts an interest-based subnet with 4 peer links on top of the existing Gnutella network. To improve performance, content is located first through subnet. A query is flooded to the entire system only when the subnet hasn't the content.

To construct subnet based on interests for content location in Gnutella, we propose an interest group model. In this work, we assume that the peers only have access to its local states, which include its KL distance to all its connecting peers.

3.1 Interest Group Model

In this paper, we assume that all peers have a same standard ontology O_s. Interest probability tree of user is learnt from the user's behavior in the system. And the interest probability tree of user will change over the time. Interest discovery is piggy-backed on Gnutella. When a peer joins the system, it may not have any information about other peers' interests. Its first attempt to locate content is executed through flooding. The lookup returns a set of peers that store the content, and their ontologies of their interests are piggy-backed. These peers are potential candidates to be in the same interest group.

r is the maximal deviation value between the similar interests. The peers A and B share similar interests if the KL distance $D(A\|B) \leq r$. $D(A\|B)$ varies since each user's interest may change over time. However, if A and B are in the same interest group, $D(A\|B)$ is less variable and relatively steady. The following definitions are adopted from [9, 10]. In this paper, we extend the definitions to satisfy our system needs.

Definition 1: Peers A and B form an Adjacent Interest Group Pair (*AIGP*), denoted by $A \overset{0}{\sim} B$, if $D(A\|B)$ obeys a normal distribution with a mean $\mu < r$, and a standard deviation $\sigma < \sigma_{\max}$.

Definition 2: Peers A and B form a k-related Adjacent Interest Group Pair (*k-AIGP*), denoted by $A \overset{k}{\sim} B$, $k \geq 1$, if there exist k intermediate peers $C_1, C_2, \ldots, C_k$, such that $A \overset{0}{\sim} C_1$, $C_1 \overset{0}{\sim} C_2$, ..., $C_i \overset{0}{\sim} C_{i+1}$, ..., $C_k \overset{0}{\sim} B$.

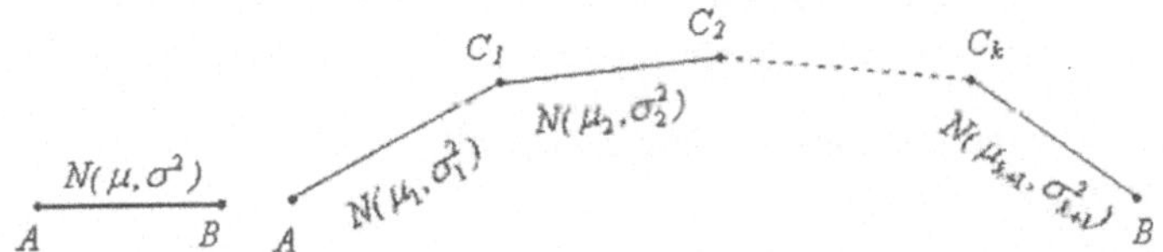

Fig. 4. (a) Adjacent Interest Group Pair, (b) *k*-related *AIGP*

Fig.4 (a) shows such a pair of peers. Intuitively, definition 1 captures the fact that if two peers are in the same interest group over a period of time, the KL distance between them stabilizes around a mean value μ with small variations. Although it is possible that their interests may change out of range from each other ($\|AB\| > r$) intermittently, the probability is low based on the density function of normal distribution. In addition, σ represents the degree of variations. Definition 2 extends the stable interest relation to non-connecting peers. Fig.4 (b) gives an example of *AIGP* and *k*-related *AIGP*.

Definition 3: Peers $A_1, A_2, \ldots, A_n$ are in one interest group G, denoted by $A \in G$, if $\forall i, j, 1 \leq i, j \leq n$, $Ai \sim Aj$.

Definition 3 denotes that group memberships are determined by similarity of interest patterns (or relative stability of KL distances) discovered over time.

3.2 Distributed Interest Grouping Algorithm

We use a fully distributed grouping algorithm [10] for a peer to identify its stable interest group — the group of peers it has reliable similar interests— at run-time, using only local observations.

On each peer *Ai*, the following local states are maintained for running the distributed grouping based on interest algorithm:

1. $T(A_i)$**:** the table of the KL distances of connecting peers: the table record the KL distance between peer A_i and each connecting obtained from one round of measurements. After l measurements, l samples of KL distances are obtained from A_i to each neighbor.
2. The set of *AIGP* peers [$AIGP(A_i)$]**:** the set of connecting peers that has been identified to have *AIGP* property, using table $T(A_i)$.
3. The set of peers in the same stable interest group [$G_S(A_i)$]**:** updated regularly by exchanging information with *AIGP* connecting peers. During boot-strapping, G_S in a peer *Ai* is initialized to $\{A_i, AIGP(A_i)\}$.

The distributed grouping based on interest algorithm allows the peers to find their *AIGP* neighbors and construct their stable interest group G_S in a fully distributed fashion. Peer A_i exchanges its $G_S(A_i)$ with the peers which are in $AIGP(A_i)$. Upon receiving information from other peers, it constructs its local copy of G_S the algorithm shown in Table 1:

Table 1. FORMATION OF $G_S(A_i)$ ON PEER *Ai*

```
GS(Ai) initialized to {Ai , AIGP(Ai)};
Let GP(Aj) be the previously received GS(Aj) from Aj;
On receiving GS(Aj) from Aj ;
foreach Ak in GS(Aj)
  if Ak ∉ GP(Aj) then
     GS(Ai) = GS(Ai) + Ak
End
foreach Ak in GP(Aj)
  if Ak ∈ GS(Ai) and Ak ∉ GS(Aj) then
     GS(Ai) = GS(Ai) - Ak
End
```

Such exchange of G_S between the *AIGP* peers ensures that the local copy of G_S on all peers of the same stable interest group eventually converge to an accurate group snapshot that includes all current members. This holds when new peers are discovered and added to the stable interest group, or when existing members change interests and are subject to removal.

4 Performance Evaluation

In this section, we discuss the design of experiments to expose interest-based subnet and evaluate the effectiveness of our proposed subnet scheme. We discuss the performance indices we use for our evaluation, and describe our methodology and experimental setup.

We simulated the search algorithm on a crawl of the actual Gnutella network of approximately 1000 nodes. We use a standard ontology with 100 categories to represent each user's interest. Each user's probability tree is created random, but it will not change over time. Assuming that every file is stored on only one node, 50% of the files can be found in eight steps or less. Furthermore, if the file one is seeking is present on multiple nodes, the search will be even faster.

In this section, we present evaluation results comparing the performance of Gnutella against Gnutella with interest-based subnet.

Success Rate: Success rate is defined as the number of lookups that were successfully resolved through interest-based subnet over the total number of lookups. If the success rate is high, then subnet is useful for locating content. Note that peers who have just joined the system do not have any subnet, and have no choice but to flood to locate the first piece of content. We start counting the success rate after the first flood (i.e., when peers have its subnet).

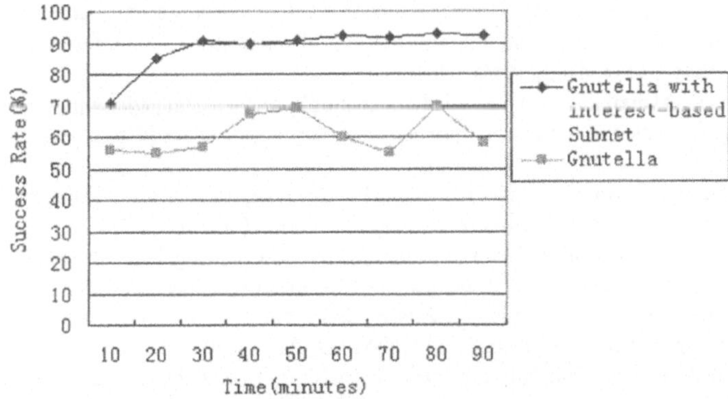

Fig. 5. Success rate using Gnutella and Gnutella with interest-based subnet

Fig. 5 depicts the average success rate for interest-based subnet. The vertical axis is the success rate, and the horizontal axis is the time after the start of the simulation when the observation was made. The average success rate at the end of 1 hour is as high as 90% for the content location. The individual success rate observed at each peer increases with longer simulation times as peers learn more about other peers and have more time to refine their interest group.

Path Length: Path length is the number of overlay hops a request traverses until the first copy of content is found. For Gnutella, path length is the minimum number of hops a query travels before it reaches a peer that has the content. Peers can directly observe an improvement in performance if content can be found in fewer hops. The simulation result depicts the average path length in number of overlay hops. On average, content is 4.6 hops away on Gnutella. Interest-based subnet reduces the path length by more than half to only 2.2 hops.

5 Conclusion and Discussion

In this paper, we propose an interest-based group model in content location overlays. Content is located first through subnet. A query is flooded to the entire system only when the subnet hasn't the content. Interest-based subnet is designed to exploit user's interest, they can significantly improve performance. Furthermore, layering enables higher performance without degrading the scalability or the correctness of the underlying overlay construction algorithm.

As a part of the future work, we will evaluate how to classify interest to reflect user's detailed psychological profile. In addition, we are evaluating the effects of the size of the interest-based subnet on the performance of our system.

References

1. A. Rowstron and P. Druschel, Pastry: Scalable, distributed object location and routing for large-scale peer-to-peer systems, in IFIP/ACM International Conference on Distributed Systems Platforms (Middleware), 2001.
2. I. Stoica, R. Morris, D. Karger, M. F. Kaashoek, and H. Balakrishnan, Chord: A scalable peer-to-peer lookup service for Internet applications, in Proceedings of ACM SIGCOMM, 2001.
3. S. Ratnasamy, S. Shenker, and I. Stoica, Routing algorithms for DHTs: Some open questions, in Proceedings of International Peer-To-Peer Workshop, 2002.
4. Adriana Iamnitchi, Matei Ripeanu and Ian Foster, Locating Data in (Small-World?) P2P Scientific Collaborations, in Proceedings of International Peer-To-Peer Workshop, 2002.
5. K. Sripanidkulchai, B. Maggs, H. Zhang, Efficient content location using interest-based locality in peer to peer systems, INFOCOM'03, April 2003.
6. Guangtao Xue, Hua Shi, Jinyuan You, Wensheng Yao, Distributed Stable-Group Differentiated Admission Control Algorithm in Mobile Peer-to-Peer Media Streaming System, China Journal of Electronics, Vol.40, 2003.
7. T. Gruber, A translation approach to portable ontology specifications, Knowledge Acquisition, 1993.
8. T. M. Cover and J. A. Thomas, Elements of Information Theory, Jon Wiley & Sons, Inc, 1993.
9. Baochun Li. QoS-aware Adaptive Services in Mobile Ad-hoc Networks, in Proceedings of the Ninth IEEE International Workshop on Quality of Service (IWQoS 01), also Lecture Notes in Computer Science, ACM Springer-Verlag, Vol. 2092, pp. 251-268, Karlsruhe, Germany, June 6-8, 2001.
10. K.Wang and B. Li. Efficient and guaranteed service coverage in partitionable mobile adhoc networks, In Proceedings of IEEE INFOCOM 2002, June 2002.

Trust and Cooperation in Peer-to-Peer Systems

Junjie Jiang, Haihuan Bai, and Weinong Wang

Department of Computer Science and Engineering
Shanghai Jiaotong University, Shanghai 200030, P.R.China
{jjj, baihh, wnwang}@sjtu.edu.cn

Abstract. Most of the past studies on peer-to-peer systems have emphasized routing and lookup. The selfishness of users, which brings on the free riding problem, has not attracted sufficient attention from researchers. In this paper, we introduce a decentralized reputation-based trust model first, in which trust relationships could be built based on the reputation of peers. Subsequently, we use the iterated prisoner's dilemma to model the interactions in peer-to-peer systems and propose a simple incentive mechanism. By simulations, it's shown that the stable cooperation can emerge after limited rounds of interaction between peers by using the incentive mechanism.

1 Introduction

During the recent few years, peer-to-peer computing has caught much attention. Informally, a peer-to-peer system is comprised of many peer nodes, which have equal roles and responsibilities. They differ from traditional distributed computing systems in that no central authority controls or manages the various components; instead, all the peer nodes form a dynamically changing and self-organizing network.

Much of the past work in peer-to-peer systems assumes that all these peers will follow prescribed protocol without any deviation and they will cooperate voluntarily in order to perform some task or share their resources by direct exchanges. However, it's not always true in real case. This assumption is based on user's voluntary altruism and ignores the user's ability to modify the behavior of an algorithm for self-interested reasons. In fact, the free riding problem has become a severe obstacle of the deployed peer-to-peer applications. A recent study of Gnutella has found that an overwhelming proportion of its users take advantage of the network without contributing anything to it [1]. As a growing number of users become free riders, the system starts to lose its peer-to-peer spirit, and begins to retrogress to a traditional client-server system. Therefore, an appropriate incentive mechanism is necessary, which motivates peers to contribute their resources to the system.

The rest of this paper is organized as follows. In section 2, a decentralized reputation-based trust model is introduced. Incentive patterns are also discussed in this section. Section 3 uses the iterated prisoner's dilemma to model the interactions in peer-to-peer systems and proposes a simple incentive mechanism. In section 4, results from simulation experiments are provided. Section 5 shortly discusses related work and section 6 concludes this paper.

M. Li et al. (Eds.): GCC 2003, LNCS 3032, pp. 371–378, 2004.

2 Trust Model and Incentives Patterns

There is no central authority in a pure peer-to-peer system. Obviously a centralized trust model is not suitable for peer-to-peer systems. The usual decentralized alternate to central CA is the web-of-trust model. But web-of-trust is susceptible to the treachery of even one trusted peer and it has primarily been used for privacy purposes. In this section, we will introduce a decentralized reputation-based trust model.

2.1 A Reputation-Based Trust Model

Trust is an essential element in peer-to-peer systems. In a peer-to-peer system, each peer faces complicated trust relationships with others. It's necessary to help peers build such trust relationships. This should appeal to an appropriate trust model.

Trust is a basic feature of social situations that require cooperation and interdependence. However, there's still lack of consensus on the definition of trust in the literature. In this paper, we use the following definition for trust:

- Trust is the belief that the counterpart will behave as the expectations. It is a variable value associated with the peer but yet it is subject to the peer's behavior and applies only within a specific context at a given time.

According to the definition above, trust is subjective, mutable and non-quantifiable. But in order to characterize different trust levels, we can represent the trust as a real number within a specific range. Abdul-Rahman and Hailes [2] have proposed that the trust concept can be divided into direct and recommender trust. We divide the trust into direct and indirect trust. Direct trust can be derived from the experiences of direct interactions between peers while indirect trust can be derived from others' recommendations. Moreover there is a special type of direct trust called as recommender trust, which is the trust that one peer has in its recommenders (who provide recommendations to it). We subject recommender trust to direct trust and specifically here, the direct interaction is request and recommendation. But for the clarity of notions, we still distinguish the recommender trust from direct trust. As shown in Figure 1, there are three types of trust relationships distinguished.

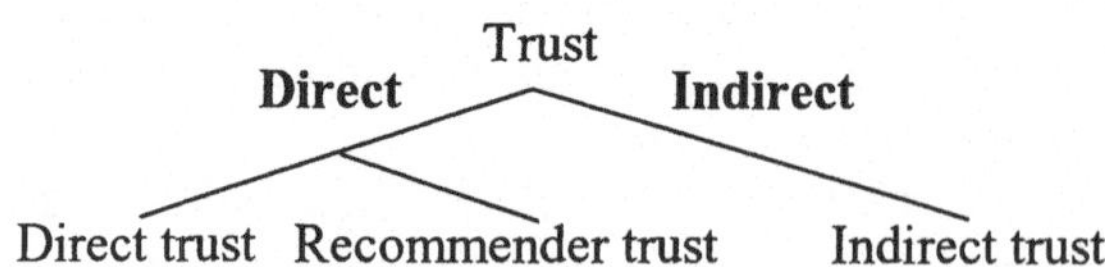

Fig. 1. Three types of trust relationships

Since a peer-to-peer system always involves a large number of peers (up to millions of peers), there is little chance of direct interaction between any pair of peers. As to most of the peers, especially a newcomer, there are too many strange peers. They cannot derive the direct trust towards these strangers based on their direct interaction experiences. So they have to appeal to the recommendations from their familiar peers, namely the recommenders of them. By requesting these recommenders, the peer can gather recommendations about a specified peer and infer the indirect trust value. Generally, the recommendations about a peer are based on its reputation. The definition of reputation is shown as follow:

- The reputation of a peer is an expectation of its behavior based on other peers' observations or the collective information about the peer's past behavior within a specific context at a given time.

In fact, each peer is involved in a trust net. A trust net encodes how peers estimate the quality of other peers they have not interacted with before. Trust net is a logical network that interconnects the requestor peer and the objective peer, where the intermediate nodes are those recommenders. All the recommenders of a peer constitute the recommenders' group of the peer. The trust net, as well as the recommenders' group, is dynamic and context-specific. An example of trust net is shown in Figure 2.

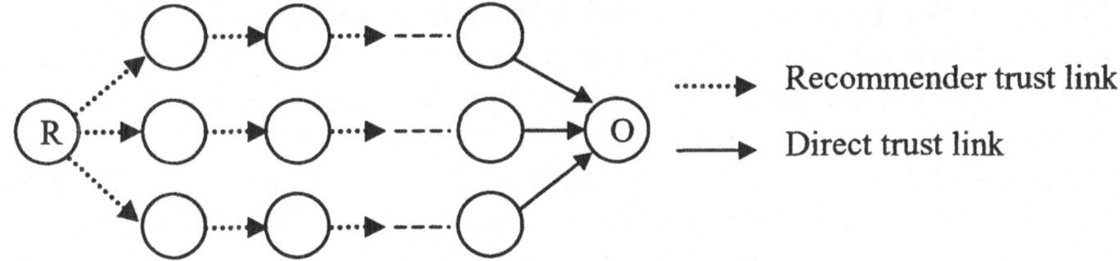

Fig. 2. An example of trust net

When a requestor peer wants to evaluate the trustworthiness of a objective peer, it may request the members of its recommenders' group. These recommenders will return their direct trust value in the objective peer if they have, otherwise request their own recommenders on the trustworthiness of the objective peer. The rest may be deduced by analogy. Finally, all these recommendations will be passed to the requestor peer. Many computational models [3] [4] have been proposed for translation from recommendations to trust value.

In the trust net, a path from requestor peer to objective peer is referred as a recommendation chain. A recommendation chain is always composed of two types of links, i.e. direct trust links and recommender trust links. The procedure of recommendation is just the propagation of the objective peer's reputation along the recommendation chain. The inference of trust values may recur to the theory of Dempster-Shafer [5]. There are two basic operations for the inference in this theory. The first is trust decay operation along a recommendation chain. The second is independent similar trust reinforcement among multiple recommendation chains. We can also choose other approaches for the inference of trust value such as the cross product and dot product operations [6].

Actually, the accuracy of the acquired reputation information relies upon not only the honesty of recommenders, but also the similarity of the preference between the requestor peer and recommender peers. After each recommendation evaluation, the peer will update its recommender trust according to the variance between the recommendations from these recommenders and the final trustworthiness of the objective peer. If the recommender trust in a certain recommender is under a threshold value, the recommender will be eliminated from the recommenders' group. Also there some peers may be added into the recommenders' group at any moment. Through a period of in and out, most members in recommenders' group will have somewhat similar preference with the peer.

Perhaps some peers can derive neither direct nor indirect trust value towards a given peer. They may use the default trust value, which reveals their default attitude (e.g. altruistic, rational or free riding) to the society of peers.

2.2 Incentive Patterns

Peers can benefit from free riding on the resources contributed by others. Thus, incentives for sharing resources are indispensable to combatting free riding on peer-to-peer systems.

There are two forms of incentives that have been considered in the past [7]: (1) Trust based patterns, in which peer will be rewarded good appraisement (good reputation) if it cooperates, otherwise, it will be criticized. Good reputation will help the peer obtain better services in the future. (2) Trade based patterns, in which rewards are explicit, and before each interaction, the resource consumer should pay for the service in advance. Alternatively, the pay may occur after the service by the negotiation with the resource provider. There are also different labels for incentives [8]: (1) monetary payments (one pays to consume resources and is paid to contribute resources), and (2) differential service (peers that contribute more will get better quality of service). They correspond to the trade based and trust based incentive patterns respectively. The two forms of incentives may be applied in different application situations. Particularly, three incentive schemes (token-exchange, peer-approved and service-quality) are referred in [9].

3 Strategy for Cooperation

We can outline the interrelationship among peer's reputation, and trust and cooperation between peers (See Figure 3). Improvement in reputation will make peers more trustworthy. Mutual trust between peers and appropriate incentives will bring out cooperation. Also more cooperation will get more rewards in reputation.

The iterated prisoner's dilemma is an elegant model for the emergence of cooperation in a multi-agent system. This section uses the iterated prisoner's dilemma to model the interactions between peers.

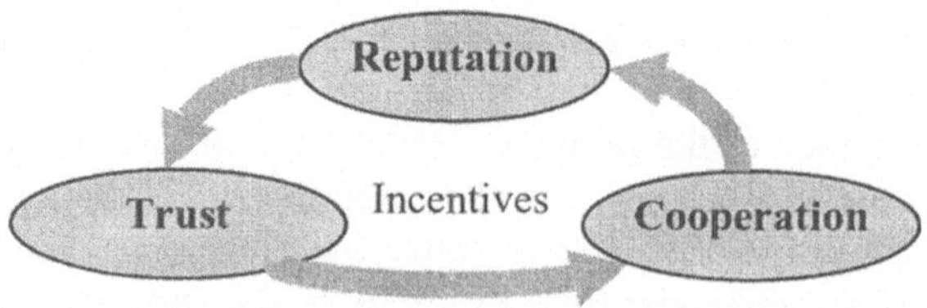

Fig. 3. Interrelationship among reputation, trust and cooperation

3.1 Iterated Prisoner's Dilemma

The prisoner's dilemma is a classic problem of conflict and cooperation. The dilemma stands on the fact that individual interests differ from collective ones. The prisoner's dilemma is a two-person non-zero-sum, non-cooperative and simultaneous game. In the simplest form, two players are both faced with a decision – either cooperate (C) or defect (D). The payoff depends on the decisions made by the two players and each receives payoff according to a payoff matrix. Table 1 shows the scores of each player in each combination of strategies.

Table 1. Payoff matrix in the prisoner's dilemma

Player A \ Player B	**Cooperate**	**Defect**
Cooperate	R / R	S / T
Defect	T / S	P / P

R = 3
T = 5
P = 1
S = 0

If both the players cooperate, they receive a reward ***R***. If both defect, they receive a punishment ***P***. However, there is a temptation ***T*** to defect for a player because the temptation is more beneficial than reward when the other player cooperates. Simultaneously, the sucker receives a more severe punishment ***S***. The following inequality should be respected:

$$S < P < R < T$$

The one-shot prisoner's dilemma is not very interesting since rational players will always select defection. A variation of the prisoner's dilemma is known as the iterated prisoner's dilemma, in which more complex strategies become possible. The iterated prisoner's dilemma is about how the members of a social group either win or lose through repeated interactions with other members of the group and each player's payoff is the sum of the score in each past round. In the iterated prisoner's dilemma, a history of prior behavior and the opportunity for payback in the future may influence the decision that each player makes. It has been shown that cooperation can emerge in the iterated prisoner's dilemma. In addition, the payoff matrix in the iterated prisoner's dilemma should meet the following inequality:

$$T + S < 2R$$

3.2 Incentives and Strategies

We use the iterated prisoner's dilemma to model the interactions in peer-to-peer systems. Each peer is a player and an individual interaction is modeled as a single round in the iterated prisoner's dilemma.

The iterated prisoner's dilemma format tends to offer a long-term incentive for cooperation, even though there is a short-term incentive for defection. The reputation of one player will influence the strategy choice of its opponent and thus its payoff. So each player must care the effect on its reputation at each move.

There are many well-known strategies, such as tit-for-tat, studied in the iterated prisoner's dilemma. ***Credit Score*** is a strategy in the iterated prisoner's dilemma, in which a player cooperates on the first move, and thereafter plays opponent's most used strategy (if equal then cooperates).

Incentive schemes for peer-to-peer systems may be derived from these strategies. For a trust based incentive scheme, a reputation system is always used to maintain the reputation information of peers [9]. Here we assume the existence of such a reputation system. Such reputation just records the history of prior behaviors of peers. Based on such information of opponents, peers make decisions according to their own strategy.

Here, we propose a trust based incentive scheme named as ***Credit Score***. In ***Credit Score***, a peer cooperates at its first interaction. Hereafter it will evaluate its counterpart before each interaction. The peer, if it cooperated no less than defected before, is taken as a popular peer, otherwise an annoying peer. A ***Credit Score*** peer will cooperate while facing such a popular peer, otherwise defect. We present this incentive scheme just to illustrate that we can derive some effective incentive schemes from strategies in the iterated prisoner's dilemma.

4 Simulations and Results

The purpose of this section is to investigate the effectiveness of the ***Credit Score*** incentive scheme under simulations. Our simulator implements the interaction model described in Section 3, and each peer is implemented as an agent. The experiments emulate the natural selection process. At the end of each generation, the total score for the population is tallied. Strategies that have relatively higher payoff become more widespread in the population, and those that have relatively lower payoff become less common. The evolution continues until there are no changes in population between two generations.

Figure 4 depicts the evolution of peers to higher score strategies over time. The original population consists of 1000 unconditional cooperators, 1000 unconditional defectors and 1000 peers who use ***Credit Score*** scheme. After several generations, the population eventually stabilizes. By the end of the simulation, the number of unconditional defectors decreases to zero since the unconditional defectors can only achieve a very low fitness in the society and are naturally eliminated from the population generation by generation. The result shows that the ***Credit Score*** scheme is effective. We also conduct another simulation experiment, in which the original population consists of only 1500 unconditional cooperators and 1500 unconditional defectors. It's shown that all the peers become unconditional defectors by the end of the simulation. This indicates that the peer-to-peer system collapses.

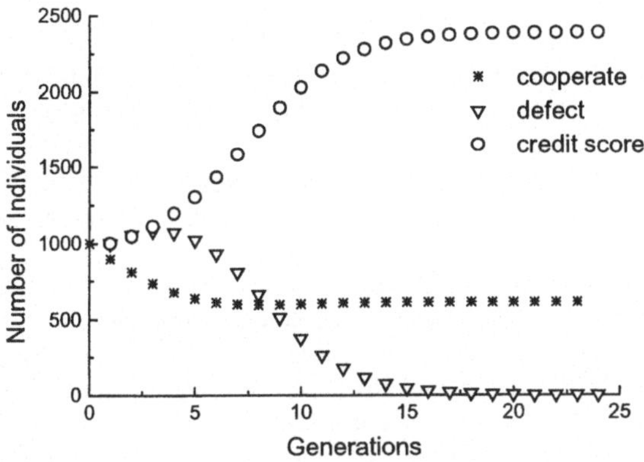

Fig. 4. An example of the evolution of strategy populations over time

5 Related Work

The incentive problem is indispensable for wide deployment of peer-to-peer systems. Some work has involved in this problem. Buragohain et al [10] study the interaction of strategic and rational peers and propose a differential service-based incentive scheme to improve the system's performance. They also use the Cournot duoploy like model to analyze the utility model. Golle et al [8] construct a formal game theoretic model of peer-to-peer file sharing system and analyze equilibria of user strategies under micro-payment mechanisms. Wang et al [11] model the peer-to-peer system as a Cournot Oligopoly game with dynamic payoff function and propose a control-theoretic solution to the problem. Kevin Lai et al [12] use evolutionary prisoner's dilemma to model the cooperation in peer-to-peer systems and they outline the design space of incentive strategies. We use iterated prisoner's dilemma to model the interactions in peer-to-peer systems and emphasize that the reputation of peers will influence their future payoff.

6 Conclusion

This paper has introduced a reputation based trust model for evaluating the trustworthiness of a peer. In the model, the reputation of peers is derived based on the history of their behaviors. We use the iterated prisoner's dilemma to model the interactions in peer-to-peer systems and propose a trust based incentive scheme named as ***Credit Score***. By simulations, we found that we can derive some effective incentive schemes from strategies in the iterated prisoner's dilemma.

References

1. Stefan Saroiu, P. Krishna Gummadi, and Steven D. Gribble. A Measurement Study of Peer-to-Peer File Sharing Systems. In Proceedings of Multimedia Computing and Networking (MMCN'02), 2002.
2. Alfarez Abdul-Rahman, Stephen Hailes. Supporting Trust in Virtual Communities. In Proceedings of 33rd Hawaii International Conference on System Sciences, Maui, Hawaii, 4-7 January 2000.
3. L. Mui, M. Mohtashemi, and A. Halberstadt. A computational model of trust and reputation. In Proceedings of 35th Hawaii International Conference on System Science, 2002.
4. Abdul-Rahman and S. Hailes. Using Recommendations for Managing Trust in Distributed Systems. In Proceedings of IEEE Malaysia International Conference on Communication '97 (MICC'97), Kuala Lumpur, Malaysia, 1997.
5. G. Shafer. A Mathematical Theory of Evidence. Princeton University Press, 1976.
6. T. Beth, M. Borcherding, and B. Klein. Valuation of Trust in Open Network. In Proceedings of the European Symposium on Research in Computer Security (ESORICS), Brighton, UK. LNCS 875, 1994.
7. Obreiter, P., Nimis, J. A Taxonomy of Incentive Patterns: the Design Space of Incentives for Cooperation. In Proceedings of the Second International Workshop on Agents and Peer-to-Peer Computing (AP2PC'03), LNCS, Melbourne, Australia, 2003.
8. P. Golle, K. Leyton-Brown, I. Mironov, and M. Lillibridge. Incentives for Sharing in Peer-to-Peer Networks. In Proceedings of the 2001 ACM Conference on Electronic Commerce, LNCS 2232, 2001.
9. D. Dutta, A. Goel, R. Govindan, and H. Zhang, The Design of A Distributed Rating Scheme for Peer-to-peer Systems. In Proceedings of the Workshop on the Economics of Peer-to-Peer Systems, 2003.
10. Chiranjeeb Buragohain, Divyakant Agrawal, and Subhash Suri. A Game Theoretic Framework for Incentives in P2P Systems. In Proceedings of the 3rd IEEE International Conference on Peer-to-Peer Computing, 2003.
11. Weihong Wang, Baochun Li. To Play or to Control: a Game-based Control-theoretic Approach to Peer-to-Peer Incentive Engineering. In Proceedings of the 7th International Workshop on Quality of Service, LNCS 2707, 2003.
12. Kevin Lai, Michal Feldman, Ion Stoica, and John Chuang. Incentives for Cooperation in Peer-to-Peer Networks. In Proceedings of the Workshop on the Economics of Peer-to-Peer Systems, 2003.

A Scalable Peer-to-Peer Lookup Model*

Haitao Chen, Chuanfu Xu, Zunguo Huang, Huaping Hu, and Zhenghu Gong

School of Computer Science, National University of Defense Technology
Changsha, Hunan, China
nchrist@163.com

Abstract. One of the core problems of P2P computing is resource locating. The main research results of determined resource locating algorithms are four distributed hash table algorithms, i.e: CAN, Chord, Pastry and Tapestry. Based on these algorithms , this paper presents a hierarchical and manageable resource locating model (HMRLM) which can provide P2P networks with scalability and manageability.

1 Introduction

The objective of P2P (peer-to-peer) computing is to make full use of potential computing resources of the Internet. P2P means that every node of a distributed system is logically equivalent. P2P computing model does not discriminate servers from clients, and data communication can be directly carried out among every node in the system without the help of an intermediate server [1].With the popularity of the P2P information sharing application like Napster [2], P2P computing technologies attract more and more attention.

One of the core problems of P2P computing is the resource locating algorithms. This paper presents a hierarchical and manageable resource locating model (HMRLM). The model can be compatible with distributed hash table (DHT) and introduces the hierarchical and manageable features into it, thus it effectively solves some problems of current DHT algorithms.

2 Related Work

DHT has been implemented in four recent P2P systems (CAN [3], Chord [4], Pastry [5] and Tapestry [6]), in which any object can be located within a bounded number of routing hops, using a small per-node routing table. DHT provides minimal interfaces and shared infrastructure for a variety of distributed applications, including archival stores and application-level multicasts. Applications can inherit some good properties from DHT such as security, robustness, scalability, load balance, etc.

---

* This project is supported by 863 Foundation of China , grant no.2003AA142080

M. Li et al. (Eds.): GCC 2003, LNCS 3032, pp. 379–387, 2004.

The node Id of Chord, Pastry and Tapestry constitutes a logical circle among identifier space. While being looked up, Chord makes a spanning approach in the circle, while Pastry and Tapestry make approaches on the basis of identifier prefix. CAN is different from the other three. It approaches its destination gradually with Euclid distance in a d-dimension virtual coordinate space. The routing table maintained by it is small, but its path length is longer. The primary benefit of Pastry and Tapestry over CAN and Chord is that they actively try to exploit network proximity to reduce the latency of each P2P hop and the number of hops during lookup , but CAN and Chord are simpler.

The P2P network constructed by classical DHT algorithms has the following problems:

- The network has no hierarchy, and can not self-adapt the scope of the network node very well, and the scalability of the network is limited.
- The long network latency of Internet leads to the long responding time of application.
- The manageability of the network is poor, and basically speaking, it's uncontrollable.
- It cannot provide the support for QoS.
- It doesn't take into account of the difference in capacity between each node, which leads to the low running efficiency of the network.

HMRLM presented in this paper not only optimizes the performance, but also helps to solve these problems, Furthermore, it inherits the advantages of DHT.

Hierarchy is a famous model to solve scalable and manageable problem in computer science. There are two-layers hierarchical systems like KaZaa[7] which is an unstructured p2p system and brocade[8] which is a structured p2p system. Brocade is a two-layers landmark routing algorithm over tapestry, but it is just routing aggregation and not a full hierarchical system. HMRLM is a general model for hierarchical peer-to-peer systems.

3 HMRLM

3.1 Model Description

The nodes of HMRLM constitute an N-layer network according to a certain policy, which you can refer to Figure 1. Each layer of the model includes some sub-nets which are constructed by the revised classical DHT algorithms, and different DHT algorithms can be adopted according to different layers and different sub-nets. Every node of upper-net is related to a sub-net, and at the same time it is an entrance node which relates the sub-net with the upper-net. Every sub-net has one or more nodes which serve as the entrance nodes of its upper-layer. These P2P sub-nets aggregate into a multi-layer P2P network layer by layer.

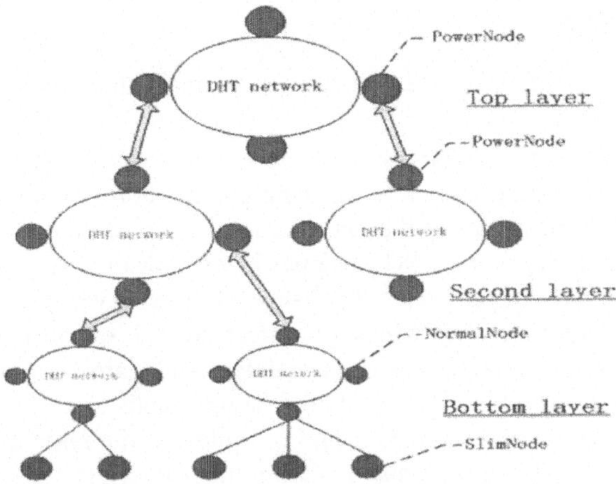

Fig. 1. Logic topology of HMRLM

In order to improve the efficiency and reliability of the system, this algorithm classifies nodes into four kinds according to their different capacity: SlimNode, NormalNode, PowerNode, MotherNode.

The measuring factors of the node capacity include connective bandwidth, stability of nodes, computing ability of CPUs, storage capacity, etc. We take the measurement of node capacity as a selective implementing policy, and users can make different choices according to the characteristics of different P2P applications.

3.2 Basic Operation

We will take the algorithms of a two-layer HMRLM system as an example to illustrate the basic algorithms of this model.

- Resource publishing: Firstly, node can publish its resources in local subnet, and then publish it in remote subnet through PowerNode.
- Resource locating: Firstly, node tries to locate resources in local subnet. If it fails to find the resources, then the node will locate resources in remote subnet through PowerNode.

4 Performance Analysis

In this section, we will analyze path length, network latency, neighbor state, load to join or exit and load balancing of HMRLM, etc.

4.1 Assumptions

For the convinces of quantitative analysis, we make the following assumptions on HMRLM :

1. To make it simpler, we suppose there are only two layers in HMRLM, and DHT of both layers are Chord. The relevant data about Chord mentioned in the following passage are all the results of theoretical analysis and simulating tests from [4].
2. The dynamic change of HMRLM upper-layer nodes has a great influence on performance, so we will only take the change of upper-layer nodes into account. Suppose the network has two kinds of states: state 1 denotes upper-layer network neighbor state information has been updated; and state 2 means that the neighbor state information of upper-layer network is inaccurate.
3. The influence of the dynamic change of nodes on the node quantity of the whole network is ignored. Suppose that no matter the network is under the first state or the second state, the node number of upper-layer sub-net is about N_1; and that of the sub-layer sub-nets is almost the same, N_2; thus the whole network node number is $N = N_1 N_2$, let $c = \frac{N_1}{N_2}$; suppose the average latency of each hop in the upper-layer, sub-layer and Chord are respectively t_1, t_2 and t_3 ms; suppose the probability of the local sub-net successful look-up is p; then the probability of the remote look-up in other sub-network is $(1-p)$ .we suppose $0.1 =< c <= 1$ and $0.5 =< p <= 0.9$.

4.2 Path Length and Network Latency

Initially we will take into account the path length and network latency of one lookup in network.

Theorem 1: when the network is under state 1, HMRLM optimizes the search performance, compared with DHT. Its path length is

$$\frac{1}{2}\log N_1^{(1-p)} N_2 \text{ (hop)},$$

and its network latency is

$$\frac{1}{2}[t_2 \log N_2 + (1-p) t_1 \log N_1] \text{ (ms)}.$$

Proof: the simulating result of [4] shows that the path length of a lookup in a N nodes network is $\frac{1}{2}\log N$,then the path length of HMRLM under state 1 should be $m_1 = \frac{1}{2}[p \log N_2 + (1-p)(\log N_1 + \log N_2)] = \frac{1}{2}\log N_1^{(1-p)} N_2$,and the corresponding path length of Chord is $m_2 = \frac{1}{2}\log N_1 N_2$; suppose that $l_1 = \frac{m_1}{m_2}$ is the optimized ratio of path length,, then $l_1 = 1 - \frac{p}{2} - \frac{p}{2}\frac{\log c}{\log N}$.when N is great and c is a determined value, l_1 is approximately $(1-\frac{p}{2})$.Figure 2 is given below, in which N is supposed to be fixed to be 10000, and l_1 changes with the change of c and p. From Figure 2 we know that l_1 decreases with the increase of c and p,and can be reduced to 55% of former DHT at most.

For the same reason, the network latency of HMRLM should be $r_1 = \frac{1}{2}[pt_2 \log N_2 + (1-p)(t_1 \log N_1 + t_2 \log N_2)]$, while the corresponding network latency of Chord should be $r_2 = \frac{1}{2}t_3 \log N_1 N_2$. Suppose that $l_2 = \frac{r_1}{r_2}$ is the optimized ratio of network latency and $\frac{t_1}{t_2} = 50, \frac{t_3}{t_2} = 20$, then $l_2 = \frac{51-50p}{40} - \frac{(49-50p)\log c}{40 \log N}$. When N is large and c is a determined value, l_2 is approximately $\frac{51-50p}{40}$.Figure 3 is given below, in which N is supposed to be fixed to be 10000, and l_2 changes with the change of c and p.from Figure 3 we know that l_2 increases slightly with the increase of c , and we know that the upper-layer path length will increase with the increase of c, the upper-layer network latency is much more great than the network latency of sub-nets, so the whole latency will increase; l_2 decreases rapidly and can be reduced to 10%-20% of the former DHT at most.

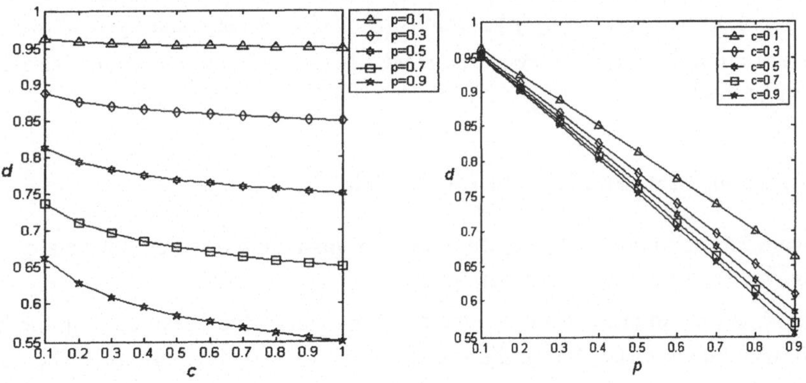

Fig. 2. (a) The optimized ratio of path length changes with c. (b) The optimized ratio of path length changes with p

Theorem 2: when the network is under state 2, with high probability the path length and network latency of HMRLM are still

$$\frac{1}{2}\log N_1^{(1-p)} N_2 \text{ (hop)},$$

and

$$\frac{1}{2}[t_2 \log N_2 + (1-p)t_1 \log N_1] \text{ (ms)}.$$

Proof: from [4] we can know that with high probability Chord can still maintain its original lookup performance when the network nodes are under dynamic changes. In the following passage, we will only analyze the influence of the dynamic changes of upper-layer network on lookup. First we analyze the correctness of lookup. At this time part of the routing information in upper-layer network has not been updated, and there will be three kinds of situations: (1) some of the lookup regions are not influenced by the change of nodes, which means the routing information we need are still current and the lookup can maintain its original efficiency and can ensure its correctness. (2) although the whole routing information lacks correctness, the routing information which can ensure correctness is still updated. Under this condition, the lookup can still ensure its correctness, but with low efficiency. (3) the routing information which can ensure correctness is also incorrect, thus some of the network data can not be found, and the application software should retry after proper pause.

Now we will talk about the influence on performance. Under situation (1), the performance is not influenced at all, while under situation (2) and (3), the whole network latency of the lookup will be prolonged because of the longer average latency of upper-layer network. However, the upper-layer nodes of HMRLM are comparatively stable, and as we can know from [4], with proper revision, the probability of influence on performance of situation of (2) and (3) will be very small, and the probability of remote lookup will just be $(1-p)$, which will lead to a very small probability for the whole searching latency to increase, so HMRLN can maintain its original performance with high possibility.

4.3 Neighbor State and Load to Join or Exit

Theorem 1: each node of HMRLM averagely maintains less neighbor state, and the average load to join or exit will also be less.

Proof: as we can know from [4], the neighbor state which each node in the N-node Chord maintains is $O(\log N)$, and the load to join or exit is $O(\log^2 N)$. The neighbor state which each upper-layer node of HMRL upper-layer maintains is $O(\log N_1) + O(\log N_2)$, and that of the sub-layer node is $O(\log N_2)$. the average number is $n_1 = \frac{O(\log N_1) + N_2 O(\log N_2)}{N_2}$,while the neighbor state of each node in corresponding Chord is $n_2 = O(\log N_1) + O(\log N_2) > n_1$ .when $N_1 \approx N_2$, $\frac{n_1}{n_2} \approx \frac{1}{2}$,thus each node of HMRLM averagely maintains less neighbor state.

The load to join or exit of HMRLM upper-layer node is $O(\log^2 N_1) + O(\log^2 N_2)$, that of the sub-layer is $O(\log^2 N_2)$,and that of the corresponding Chord is $O(\log^2 N_1 N_2)$ .Similar to the above discussion, the average load to join or exit of HMRLM node is smaller.

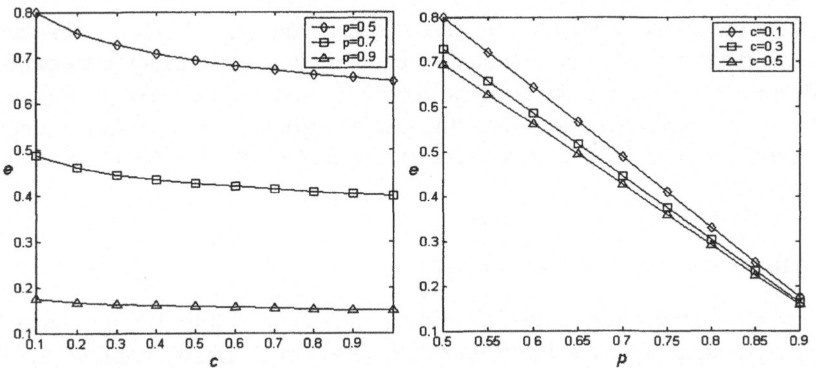

Fig. 3. (a) The optimized ratio of network latency changes with c. (b) The optimized ratio of network latency changes with p

4.4 Load Balance

DHT itself has quite good load balancing features. For instance, there are the following theorems [9] about the consistent hashing of Chord: For any set of N nodes and K keys, with high probability each node is responsible for at most $(1+\varepsilon)K/N$ keys, where $\varepsilon = O(\log N)$, [12] as well proves that mapping key to several virtual nodes can reduce ε to arbitrary small.

Theorem 1: HMRLM can ensure that every sub-net in the same layer and every node in the same layer sub-net share the inherent load balancing feature of DHT.

Proof: there are two kinds of keys which can be mapped to the sub-net nodes: local publishing key and global publishing key. Suppose the i th sub-net totally publishes $K_i (i = 1,2.....N_1)$ keys, $K = \sum_{i=1}^{N_1} K_i$ refers to all the keys in the whole network. We will first analyze the load of every sub-net. On the basis of the load balancing features of upper-layer DHT, with high possibility the number of keys which are published to every sub-net may be $\frac{(1+\varepsilon)}{N_1} K$, where $\varepsilon = O(\log N_1)$ corresponds to upper-layer network; while the key number published by each sub-net is K_i, so with high possibility the i th sub-net is responsible for $(K_i + \frac{(1+\varepsilon)}{N_1} K)$ keys. In the following section, the load of each node of sub-nets will be discussed. On the basis of the load balancing features of sub-layer DHT, with high possibility each node of the i th sub-net is responsible for $\frac{(1+\varepsilon_i)}{N_2}(K_i + \frac{(1+\varepsilon)}{N_1}K) = \frac{(1+\varepsilon_i)}{N_2}K_i + \frac{(1+\varepsilon_i)(1+\varepsilon)}{N_2 N_1}K$ keys , where $\varepsilon_i = O(\log N_2)$ $(i = 1,2,.....N_1)$ corresponds to each sub-net. As we can see from the above, HMRLM can ensure that all the same-layer sub-nets and all the nodes in the same-layer sub-nets share the inherited load balancing features of DHT.

Besides, by providing the policies like ID sharing to make several sub-layer nodes share one upper-layer ID and share the task of mapping sub-layer key to upper-layer, it ensures the load balancing of the entrance nodes of sub-net and upper-layer network.

5 Manageability of P2P Network

Mature applications must solve the problem of manageability. We introduce the hierarchy with innate manageability into P2P networks to greatly improve the manageability of P2P network, and make a sound foundation for P2P to become more mature.

The manageability of HMRLM algorithm can be represented in the following points:

- Control the function and behavior of nodes in networks through the measure of node capacity.
- Control the joining of upper-layer node through MotherNode.
- Supervise P2P network through hierarchy and PowerNode.
- Take every sub-layer DHT network as sub-net; thus the entrance node of this sub-net can serve as the managing node to supervise this sub-net.
- SlimNode takes NormalNode as proxy. NormalNode can serve as its supervisor to some extent.

6 Advantages of HMRLM

- The manageability of P2P network is improved by using of hierarchical structure. It will help P2P to be applied in more important fields.
- High scalability: HMRLM revises the traditional single-hierarchical model into multi-hierarchical model. As a result, it decreases the scale of each sub-net, and improves the scalability of traditional DHT algorithms.
- It makes full use of network proximity and network accessing localization. The ID distances of the nodes are related to physical distances, and this model relieves the latency by aggregating physically local nodes.

- It is compatible with the current DHT algorithms, and inherits their advantages.
- This model provides the load balancing of inter-layer and upper-layer entrance nodes, as well as the load balancing property of classical DHT.

7 Conclusion

P2P computing has become a hot topic in large-scale distributed computing. The four great challenges P2P faces as it approaches to mature applications are: the scalability of the Internet scale, the long responding time caused by the Internet latency, the manageability of large-scale application networks, and the controlling problem of service quality. HMRLM presented by this paper solves partly the four problems: further improves the scalability of the traditional DHT algorithms by hierarchical DHT; relieves the latency problem by the aggregation of physical neighbor nodes; implements network management by managing advantages of hierarchical structures; and provides QoS support to some extent by hierarchical managing policy and classification of node capacity.

We believe that HMRLM is promising in P2P application. At present we are studying the application of HMRLM in network security cooperation.

References

1. Dejan S. Milojicic, Vana Kalogeraki, Rajan Lukose,Kiran Nagarajal, Jim Pruyne, Bruno Richard,Sami Rollins, Zhichen Xu: .Peer-to-Peer Computing. HP Laboratories Palo Alto HPL-2002-57
2. Napster. http://www.napster.com/
3. Ratnasamy, S, Francis, P., Handley, M., Karp, R., and Shenker, S: A scalable content-addressable network. In Proc. ACM SIGCOMM (San Diego,CA, August 2001)161–172
4. I. Stoica, R. Morris, D. Karger, M. F. Kaashoek, and H. Balakrishnan: Chord: A scalable peer-to-peer lookup service for internet applications. In Proceedings of the ACM SIGCOMM '01 Conference, San Diego, California,August 2001
5. A. Rowstron and P. Druschel: Pastry:Scalable, distributed object location and routing for large-scale peer-to-peer systems. In International Conference on Distributed Systems Platforms (Middleware), Nov. 2001
6. B. Y. Zhao, J. D. Kubiatowicz, and A. D. Joseph.Tapestry: An infrastructure for fault-resilient wide-area location and routing. Technical Report UCB//CSD-01-1141, U. C. Berkeley, April 2001
7. Kazaa. http://www.kazaa.com/
8. Ben Y. Zhao, Yitao Duan, Ling Huang, Anthony D. Joseph, and John D. Kubiatowicz: Brocade:Landmark Routing on Overlay Networks. Lecture Notes in Computer Science, Vol. 2429. Springer-Verlag, Berlin Heidelberg New York (2002)34-44
9. David Karger, Eric Lehman, Tom Leighton, Matthew Levine, Daniel Lewin, Rina Panigrahy: Consistent hashing and random trees: Distributed caching protocols for relieving hot spots on the World Wide Web. In Proceedings of the 29th Annual ACM Symposium on Theory of Computing (El Paso, TX, May 1997) 654–663

Characterizing Peer-to-Peer Traffic across Internet[1]

Yunfei Zhang, Lianhong Lei, and Changjia Chen

School of Electronics and Information Engineering
Beijing Jiaotong University, Beijing, China, 100044
hishigh@sohu.com, leiei8852@163.com, changjiachen@sina.com

Abstract. In this paper we, to the best of our knowledge, for the first time, launch a peer-to-peer network traffic measurement across the Internet backbone in China. Different from the existing studies, our data are derived from core routers on the Internet. Our study focuses on the three periodic peak value groups in the aggregation flow traffic, the heavy-tailed property in the distribution of traffic by different hosts and the long range dependence (LRD) in p2p traffic. Moreover we propose a novel data mining approach, *ADTE* to differentiate signaling and data traffic. Our study also shows that Napster dominates p2p traffic. In addition, we observe that the aggregation of p2p traffic is less than 1% of the total Internet traffic, much different from the observations in other studies. We analyze the possible reasons and wish that our conclusion could be a good guideline for the software developers.

1 Introduction

In order to develop workload model and network traffic engineering with considerations of the impact of p2p traffic, several measurement studies[1][2][3][5] have been done recently. [2][3][5]all employed active measurements by setting up p2p crawlers on the Internet focusing on protocol analysis. Different from these studies, our work and [1] employed passive measurements using Cisco's Netflow[7] to record the sampling traffic. Our work and [1] are similar in some aspects, but our focus and the result are quite different from [1]. So we compare these difference in related places. Our work differs from [1] greatly as follows. First, the two studies are different in network scale and measurement points. In [1] measurement was launched within an ISP and accordingly it recorded p2p traffic on edge routers within this ISP while ours was launched in Internet backbone and therefore it records p2p traffic on core routers on the Internet. As far as we know, this is the first measurement made in such a scale. Second, the two studies target on different measurement objectives. Our work focuses on the three periodic peak value groups traffic characteristic in the aggregation traffic, the heavy-tailed property in the distribution of traffic and the LRD property in p2p traffic. All these are not studied in the existing studies in p2p traffic. Although LRD of the aggregation traffic on the Internet have been well studied, few studies and agreement have been achieved for specific applications. Vern Paxson et al. pointed out the applications with more degree of participation of human behaviors were more likely to exhibit long range dependent property [6]. We will discuss it at

1 This research is supported by China National Science Foundation under grant 60132030.

M. Li et al. (Eds.): GCC 2003, LNCS 3032, pp. 388–395, 2004.

length in Section 4. Third, we examine much more existing measurable p2p systems (Napster, KazaA, FastTrack, Gnutella, DirectConnect, Rendezvous and p2p media steaming) than [1]where only 3 kinds of p2p systems(Gnutella, FastTrack and DirectConnect) were studied.

The reminder of the paper is organized as follows. Section 2 introduces the communication mechanism in p2p networks. In section 3, we depict our methodology in the measurement and the advantages over [1]. Section 4 reveals p2p traffic characteristics. We summarize the paper in section 5.

2 Communication Mechanism in P2p

A p2p network communication mechanism is as follows. When a node searches some data, it sends Query to its neighbors. Nodes mismatched forward this Query to their neighbors continuously until a qualified peer is found. Any peer satisfying this request returns Response and a connection is set up between the source and one or more of these peers to finish the file sharing procedure. In [1], the two stages were called signaling and data transfer respectively. There is a Time-To-Live (TTL) in the Query which is decremented on each hop. When TTL decreases to 0, this Query is ignored.

3 Measurement Techniques of P2p Traffic

3.1 Methodology

Network measurements include active measurement and passive measurement. Active measurement introduces probe packets to test the network conditions such as network topology, average packet loss rate, latency, etc. But it cannot provide information of specific nodes on the Internet while augments the overall Internet traffic. On the contrary, passive measurement sets up some probe equipments in several links and records traffic information on these links such as flow number, packet number and other useful information. It will not add or change Internet traffic.

In this paper we recorded data in the core routers interfaces in the backbone of a Network Service Provider in China during Apr. 15th to Apr. 21st, 2002. Obviously active measurement was unsuitable in such a large-scale network. We used Netflow[7] to record our data with the sampling rate 1000:1 and aggregated once every 10 minutes with DetailASMetrics aggregation scheme[7]. Thus we got 1008 record files all together. Every entry includes *source IP, destination IP, source AS, destination AS, input port of the router, output port of the router, source port, destination port, protocol, packet number, octet count, and flow number*. Then we separated p2p data according to their ports including Napster class (Napster, KazaA, and FastTrack with 1214/8875/6699), Gnutella (6346/6347), DirectConnect (411/412), Rendezvous (5289) and p2p media steaming (8311). Some other applications (eg., GRID, SETI@HOME) on distributed computing are beyond the discussion of this paper for their relative unpopularity compared with the file sharing systems mentioned above.

3.2 Advantages over Approach in[1]

In [1] the authors pointed out two limitations of their approach. We settle both limitations as follows.

First, we solve the problem of incomplete flow of traffic in [1] by gathering data in core routers in the Internet backbone. In [1] the author gathered netflow data in the backbone of a tier-1 ISP and collected data sets periodically trying to alleviate the incomplete flows. Our measurement scale solves this problem essentially.

Second, lacking of application-level details of traffic in [1] made it hard to understand the actual communications in peers. Rather we make good use of the flow information and the sampling rate to estimate the proportion of request and download. We will explain this novel data mining approach, *ADTE* to differentiate signaling and data traffic in Section 4.

4 Traffic Characteristics of P2p Systems

Because our goal is similar to that in [1] and [3], which characterizes p2p systems behavior to understand how these systems impact the underlying network, we will compare our results with those of [1] and [3]in the overlapping aspects.

We catalog p2p traffic characteristics into 8 aspects: (1) p2p traffic proportion on the Internet; (2) dynamics of traffic transmitted over time; (3) flow statistics in the aggregation traffic; (4) proportion of signaling and data traffic; (5) distribution of traffic in different p2p systems; (6) distribution of traffic in different hosts; (7) long range dependent property; (8) reexamining property 7 in different p2p systems respectively.

As far as we know, item 1,3,4,7 and 8 are all studied in detail for the first time.

4.1 P2p Traffic Proportion on the Internet

All the traffic we have obtained in the core routers is totally 60.438Gbytes and p2p traffic is about 456Mbytes accounting 0.76% of the overall traffic. It is quite different from the results in the papers[3][4]. [3] points out that p2p traffic has surpassed web traffic and become the mainstream on the Internet traffic. We explain this difference for two reasons. First, the network scale of our measurement is different from that in [3]. This is pointed out in Section 3. Our result reflects that p2p applications are not as popular on the current Internet as we have expected. In addition the difference shows that p2p applications have a strong locality. So p2p traffic prevails web traffic in LAN scale while exhibit converse result in our measurement. Second, according to our statistics, 89% packets are transferred from and to China. Considering the proportion of p2p traffic, our result implies that p2p applications in China are much less popular than overseas. We hope it will provide some hints to the software developers and policy makers.

4.2 Dynamics of Traffic Transmitted over Time

We have found that the dynamics of traffic transmitted over a week and over a day is similar to any other applications over Internet. The reason has been studied well showing human's activities in a day affect the dynamics of traffic transmitted in the backbone of Internet over a day and the traffic in a week is roughly fluctuated in a period of 24 hours. Figures can be found in an extension version of this paper [14].

4.3 Flow Statistics in the Aggregation Traffic

Fig1 shows the flow statistics where X-axis represents flow length and Y-axis represents the proportion in the aggregation traffic. Records with the same flow length are cumulated. Note there are 3 periodic peak value groups. The first group includes 40-bytes-flows and their harmonic flows. The second group includes 576-bytes-flows and their harmonic flows and the last group is constituted by 1500-bytes-flows and their harmonic flows. It seems that the first and the second group are TCP requests and TCP responses. Theoretically the ratio between the number of two groups should be 2:1. But our research reveals that the ratio is 13:2. It shows that there are many other non-TCP-connections with a packet of 40 bytes in p2p systems. All of them are signaling traffic. The third group reveals that non-TCP-connections (1500bytes) accounts most of the traffic. The linear increase in the figure bottom indicates that the flow numbers are identical for each certain flow length. Meanwhile note that the sampling rate is 1000:1 and most records include only one flow(details are discussed in the next subsection). Therefore the flow number of each flow length is 1. This is the unique result in such a sampling rate.

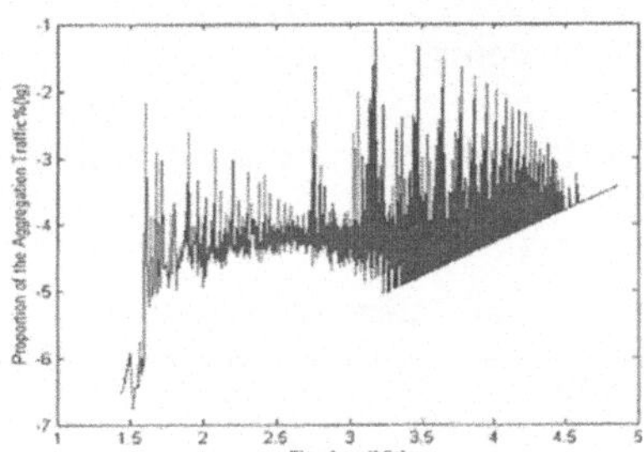

Fig. 1. Flow Statistics

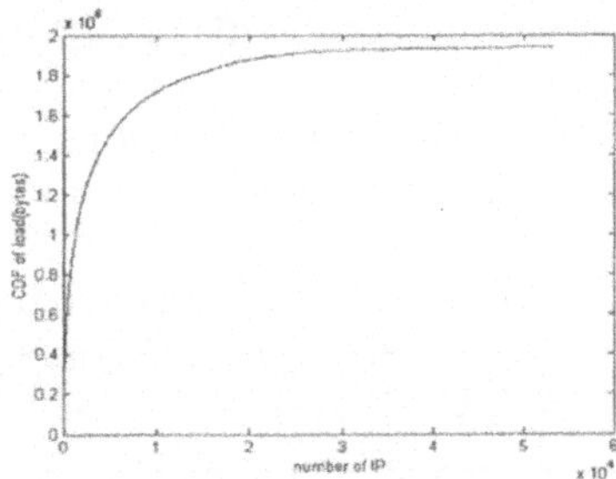

Fig. 2. CDF of IP number vs. Traffic

4.4 Proportion of Signaling and Data Traffic

In[1] the authors cataloged p2p traffic as signaling and data traffic but they did not measure the proportion of signaling and data traffic because the coarse grain limitation of flow-based data. We put forward a novel data mining approach, *ADTE* (Average Packet Length differentiating traffic estimation) to differentiate signaling and data traffic. We observe that in the sampling rate of 1000:1, more than 61.2%

records include only one flow and more than 88% records have the same number of flows and packets and more than 96.6% records have at most 1 difference in the number between flows and packets. We future observe that the average number of packets in our records is approximately 2. The rational to use Average Packet Length (APL for short, APL=octet count/packet number) as a metric to differentiate signaling and data traffic based on the observations above is omitted for the page limit. Detail explanations can be obtained in [14]. To sum up, ADTE is reasonable to estimate this proportion between signaling and data traffic in such a sampling rate. We set the lower and the upper APL bound threshold 100 and 500. This setting is fit for the past measurements [2].

Table 1 summarizes the estimation of proportion of the overall Records (POR) and proportion of the overall traffic (POT) under different thresholds. Because packets with APL less than 100 and more than 500 account for 83% of the total packets, we think that most flows are well differentiated.

Table 1. Results of *ATDE*

APL	50	100	500	1000
POR	33.34%	42.36%	40.63%	25.06%
POT	1.80%	2.62%	87.34%	68.73%

We conclude the results that (1) the proportion of the records between signaling and data transfer is between 1:1 to 2:1. (2) the proportion of the traffic between signaling and data transfer is about than 1:20 to 1:10.

4.5 Distribution of Traffic in Different P2p Systems

We list the traffic transmitted or received in different p2p systems according to their ports in the following table.

Table 2. Distribution of Traffic Transmitted in Different P2P Systems

Port	1214	6346/6347	6699	411/412	5289	8311	8875
Traffic %	66.54	25.48	7.46	0.38	0.06	0.05	0.03

It shows that Napster class applications aggregate 74.03% of all p2p traffic; Gnutella accounts 25.48% of all p2p traffic while other applications account less than 0.5% of all p2p traffic. The domination of Napster shows some potential advantages of super-nodes and hierarchical topology over complete p2p structure[11][12]. This argument is also verified by the fact that Chord, CAN and etc are not practically used. We attribute this to two reasons. First, the specific topologies in these applications limit nodes' arbitrary join. Second, node discovery mechanism in complete p2p systems relies on unified naming. It is difficult to realize in practical networks.

4.6 Distribution of Traffic in Different Hosts

Although in theory nodes in p2p systems are equal, their contributions in p2p traffic are quite different. In our measurement there are 16582 different hosts (different IP) with an average traffic of 0.56Mbyptes in a day, 1/3 of the result observed in [1]. This also supports the conclusion we have drawn in Section 4.1. Note that the traffic distribution is far from even. Fig2 is a cumulated distribution figure of IP number vs. traffic distribution. We observe that 20.7% of IP addresses transmit 90% p2p traffic; 2.3% of IP addresses transmit 50% p2p traffic. It shows an obvious heavy-tailed distribution in traffic contribution in different hosts. This indicates super nodes do exist in p2p systems. Note that this is a *lighter* heavy-tailed distribution compared with [1]. We owe it to the sampling rate. The sampling rate 1000:1 we used tends to break long flows into short flows[13] and the sampling rate in Netflow discriminates against short flows. We are developing a model to evaluate the impact of the sampling rate on this heavy-tailed distribution.

4.7 Long Range Dependent Property

Long Range Dependent Property and Hurst Parameter[8]. Recent studies in network traffic measurement analysis in different networks have shown that packet traffic exhibits LRD property. It is generally viewed that monopolization of TCP traffic on the Internet causes long range dependent in network traffic [10]. In this hypothesis, a specific application traffic is generally modeled to be a short range dependent (eg., Poisson process) and the aggregation traffic long range dependent. Vern Paxson et al. studied this problem in another viewpoint [6]. They cataloged Internet traffic according to the applications and studied the LRD of different applications. They concluded that the more human behaviors involved in the applications, the more possibility the application exhibits LRD. It is necessary to study the dependence property in p2p system to validate Paxson's conclusion and learn the contributing factors in p2p traffic simulation.

Using Hurst parameter to check LRD is a good idea. Some experiments show that for the real traffic, Hurst parameter is relatively constant. When Hurst parameter is between 0.5 to 1, the traffic exhibits LRD. The bigger Hurst parameter is, the greater the degree of LRD is. In this test we use Variant Time Plot[9]to calculate Hurst parameter[8][9].

Let $X=(X_t:t=0,1,2,\ldots)$ be packets arrival process at the router, X_t be the bytes of arrival packets at the tth time slot(time slot=10 minutes). For each $m=1,2,3\ldots.$, let $X(m)=(X_k^{(m)}: k=1,2,3\ldots)$ denote the new covariance stationary time series obtained by averaging the series X non-overlapping blocks of size m. That is, for each $m=1,2,3\ldots.$

$$X_k^{(m)}=(X_{km-m+1}+\ldots+X_{km})/m, \quad k>=1 \tag{1}$$

where $X^{(m)}$ $m=1,2,\ldots$is the same covariance stationary stochastic process as the time series X. For each $X^{(m)}$ we calculate its variance and plot a curve with m and the corresponding variance as X-axis and Y-axis respectively. Let the slope of the curve be β, define Hurst parameter $H=1-\beta/2$. When H is between 0.5 and 1, X is long range dependent.

Long Range Dependence of P2p Traffic. Let m be 1,2,...,9,10, 20,...,90,100, 200,500 respectively. We calculate the time series $X(m)=(X_k^{(m)}: k=1,2,3...)$. The slope β of the curve X(m) is shown in Fig3.

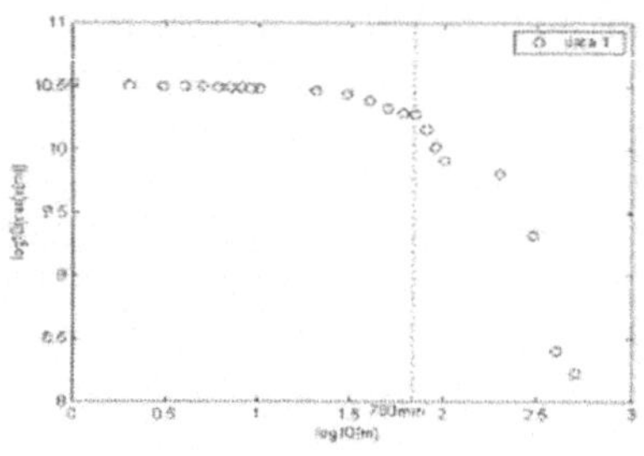

Fig. 3. Hurst Parameter of P2P Traffic

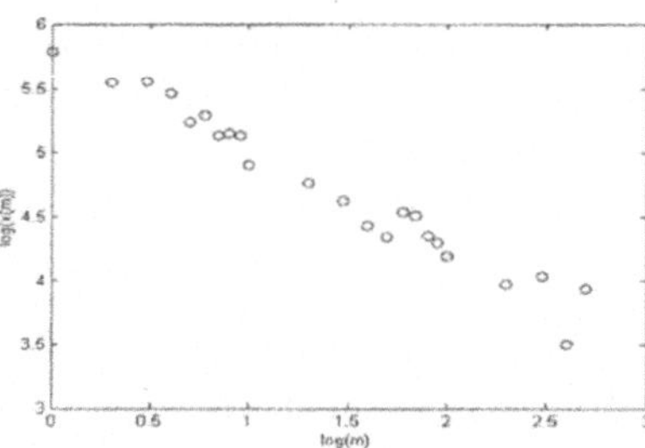

Fig. 4. Hurst Parameter of Gnutella

It is easy to observe that p2p, as a kind of application, still follows long range dependence in traffic in Fig3. Note that the minimum unit of time slot is 10 minutes, so the dependence of p2p traffic in the time intervals of less than 10 minutes can not be shown in this figure. But because long range dependence focuses on the dependence of p2p traffic in the ever-increasing time intervals, it will not affect Hurst parameter much. In Fig3, we can observe obvious long range dependence within the time intervals of between 10 minutes to 700 minutes where β=0.1295, H=0.935. The Long range dependence of p2p traffic should be paid attention in p2p simulation.

4.8 Reexamining Long Range Dependence Property in Different P2p Systems

It is essential to reexamine this property because different p2p systems have different traffic characteristic which results in difference in long range dependence. We have found that β and H in Napster are close to those in Fig3 while β and H in other less popular p2p systems are quite different from those of the aggregation traffic. For the page limit, we only show the curve of Gnutlella in Fig4 to show their difference. The difference shows that the long range dependence property of the aggregation traffic follows that of the dominating applications. This is the foundation of our future work.

5 Conclusion

In this paper we examine p2p traffic across large networks. Different from [1] and [3], we launch the network measurement in a much larger scale and overcome the limitations in the past studies. Our study reveals three periodic peak value groups traffic characteristic in the aggregation traffic, the heavy-tailed contribution in the traffic for different hosts and the long range dependence in p2p traffic. We use *ADTE* to differentiate signaling and data traffic in p2p systems. We also analyze the possible reasons of Napster's dominance in p2p traffic and unexpected unpopularity of p2p traffic over Internet and wish it a good guideline for the software developers.

References

1. S. Sen and J. Wang, "Analyzing peer-to-peer traffic across large network", in Proceedings of ACM Sigcomm Internet Measurement Workshop, Marseille, France, Nov. 2002.
2. S. Saroiu, P. K. Gummadi, S. D. Gribble, "A Measurement Study of Peer-to-Peer File Sharing Systems" , in Proceedings of Multimedia Computing and Networking, Jan. 2002.
3. N. Leibowitz et al, "Are File Swapping Networks Cacheable? Characterizing P2P Traffic", in Proceedings of 7th International Workshop on Web Content Caching and Distribution, Aug. 2002.
4. Gwendolyn Mariano, "Schools Declare File-Swapping Truce" , CNET News.com, Mar.14 2002, http://news.com.com/2100-1023-859705.html
5. B. Krishnamurthy et al, "Early Measurements of a Clusterbased Architecture for P2P Systems," in Proceedings of ACM Sigcomm Internet Measurement Workshop, Nov. 2001.
6. Vern Paxson, Sally Floyd, Wide-Area Traffic: The Failure of Poisson Modeling, IEEE/ACM Transactions on Networking,3(3), June 1995.
7. White paper-netflow services and applications, http://www.cisco.com/warp/public/cc/pd/iosw/ioft/neflct/tech/napps wp.htm.
8. T.Hagiwara et al, "High-Speed Calculation Method of Hurst Parameter Based On Real Traffic" in proc.IEEE Conference on Local Computer Networks (LCN 2000), Tampa Florida, U.S.A., Nov 2000.
9. H.F.Zhang et al, "Estimation of Hurst Parameter by Varariance-Time Plots" in Proceedings. IEEE Pacrim 97,pp.883-886.
10. Junwen Zhang, "A Study on the Characteristics and Causes of Internet Traffic," Ph.D thesis, June 2000.
11. Ion Stoica et al, Chord: A Scalable Peer-to-peer Lookup Service for Internet Applications, In Proc. ACM,SIGCOMM,San Diego, CA, August 2001.
12. Sylvia Ratnasamy et al, A Scalable Content-Addressable Network, In Proc. ACM,SIGCOMM ,San Diego, CA, August 2001.
13. N. Duffield et al, Properties and Prediction of Flow Statistics from Sampled Packet Streams, In Proceedings of ACM Sigcomm Internet Measurement Workshop, Marseille, France, Nov. 2002.
14. Yunfei Zhang et al, Characterizing Peer-to-Peer Traffic across Internet, Tech Report, Jan. 2003.

Improving the Objects Set Availability in the P2P Environment by Multiple Groups

Kang Chen, Shuming Shi, Guangwen Yang, Meiming Shen, and Weimin Zheng

Department of Computer Science and Technology
Tsinghua University, Beijing, 100084, PR China
ck99@mails.tsinghua.edu.cn

Abstract. The availability is often used to measure how well a system can provide the service continuously. The measures of availability for a single computer and for multiple computers are very different. In this paper, we discuss the objects set availability in the distributed environment especially in the case of P2P environment. The objects set availability is defined and formalized. In the P2P environment, the hosts are divided into groups by their availability values. Objects are evenly distributed among groups. The experiments show that such simple but practical method has good efficiency in achieving high objects set availability.

1 Introduction

The availability can be considered as how well the computer system can provide its services. With the development of Internet based applications, the availability becomes more crucial because the users always want those applications to work properly. For a single computer, the availability can be defined as the probability of its working properly. In the distributed environment, the availability of a single host can be measured automatically by its surrounding hosts by using the heartbeat messages. However, the availability for a computer cluster is very different. In such case, the failure of a single node will not cause the total crash of the system. The system might provide services normally i.e. the user can be serviced very well. The availability here should be defined from the out-side of the system.

In the recent years, researches in the fields of P2P system become more and more popular. There are no centralized infrastructures exist in a P2P system while the peers can join and leave the system freely. Some of the P2P discussions emphasize on the cooperative global storage [7] [8] [9]. Although the hosts are often treated equally in the P2P environment, the capabilities of the hosts in the P2P system are very different in fact. In [6], the authors found out that bandwidth, latency and availability etc. vary three and five orders of magnitude across the nodes in Gnutella and Napster. The P2P storage systems provide some mechanisms to improve the availability. PAST [7] stores each file on the k nodes. The nodeIds of those nodes are numerically closest to the 128 most significant bits of fileId for that file. CFS[8] replicate each block on k nodes in a similar

M. Li et al. (Eds.): GCC 2003, LNCS 3032, pp. 396–403, 2004.

way. The OceanStore[9] stores objects in two forms: active and archival. Erasure codes are used to encode the archival versions. However, all these systems only use redundancy to achieve high availability. In this paper, peer-grouping and redundancy are combined together to improve availability more efficiently.

There are two basic means of redundancies to store an object in a system: replication and erasure code. Replication is easier to implement that it just construct many copies of the same object in the system. The erasure coding such as [2](Reed-Solomon codes) and [3](Tornado codes) treat the object to be n parts and transform them into $m(m > n)$ pieces. Any n pieces will reconstruct the original object. None of them can improve the availability efficiently [4]. The reason is that the availabilities of some of the hosts in the P2P environment relatively poor and the effective of redundancy. In this paper, we only consider the replication availabilities.

The paper is organized as following. In section 2, the availabilities for different systems are defined and discussed. In section 3, the availability problem in the distributed environment is formalized. In section 4, the multiple groups algorithm for improving the availability in the P2P environment is designed. The experiments and results are discussed in the section 5. Finally, in section 6, we give the short conclusions.

2 Objects Replica Availability

2.1 Single Host Availability

As discussed in the introduction, the host availability can be defined as the probability of the host working properly. To get this value, the time of the user which use the host or the time of the host when it is providing services will be divided into two different parts. The *uptime* is the time which the host can provide the accurate services while the *downtime* is the part that the host can not be used or considered to be crashed. It is obvious to see that the *Host Availability* H_a can be defined as in the equation 1.

$$H_a = \frac{uptime}{uptime + downtime} \tag{1}$$

It can be seen that the availability for a single host is considered to be the average available value over a given time interval.It is reasonable to assign the availability for an object stored in the specific host to be the same value of the availability for that host. The availabilities for replicas of a same object are different because they will be stored in different hosts.

2.2 Availability for a Single Object in the Distributed Environment

The availability defined for the single host can not be used directly to compose the availability definition of a distributed systems (e.g. peer-to-peer systems or grid computing systems). For the user of a specific object in the system, the object can be considered to be available unless all those hosts which store the object replicas crashed. So for an object in the distributed environment, its availability o_a can be calculated from all its replicas availabilities as in the equation 2.

$$o_a = 1 - \prod_{\text{host } j \text{ contains object } o} (1 - H_{aj}) \tag{2}$$

That is only if all the hosts containing object o are failed, the objects is considered to be unavailable. Host j (h_j) is the host to store a copy of the object o and H_{aj} is the host availability for host j.

2.3 Objects Set Availability

Based on the single object availability as mentioned above, the availability for the multiple objects can be defined. Suppose that there exist N distinct objects in the distributed environment, the overall availability can be defined as the function of the availabilities of those objects. Here O is the set containing N objects $o_1, o_2, \cdots, o_N$.

$$O_a = f(o_{a1}, o_{a2}, \cdots, o_{aN}) \tag{3}$$

The function f must fulfill the property that it will increase monotonously with the increasing of each o_{ai}. The easiest way to define the function f is to calculate the average value of the availability of those objects.

$$O_a = \sum_{i=1}^{N} o_{ai}/N \tag{4}$$

Also we can assign different weights for each object i.e. important objects will have higher weights. The availability for such objects set can be defined as the weighted average for those availabilities values as in the equation 5.

$$O_a = \frac{\sum_{i=1}^{N}(o_{ai} \times w_i)}{\sum_{i=1}^{N} w_i} \tag{5}$$

The goal is now clear that we should try our best to improve the object set availability O_a.

3 Resource Restriction in the Distributed Environment

Suppose there are M hosts $h_1, h_2, \cdots, h_M$ in the distributed environment together with N distinct objects. Each object has a number of replicas. We denote the capability for the host to be V_j. To store a copy of object o_i in the host h_j will consume the resource $res_j(o_i)$. Each object has r_i copies distributed in different hosts. The problem is to maximize the objects set availability subject to the redundance parameter and the system resources. If an object o_i is stored in the host h_j, the value x_{ij} will be set to 1, otherwise, it will be 0. Each object o_i have r_i copies, this can be described as $\sum_{j=0}^{M} x_{ij} \leq r_i$. Meanwhile, the resource consumed by the objects for each host can not get beyond the capability of that host i.e. $\sum_{i=1}^{N} res_j(o_i) \times x_{ij} \leq V_j$. The programming problem can be gotten in the equation 6.

$$\begin{array}{ll} Maximize & O_a = f(o_{a1}, o_{a2}, \cdots, o_{aN}) \\ & o_{ai} = 1 - \prod_{j=1}^{M} (1 - h_{aj} \times x_{ij}) \\ s.t. & \\ \sum_{j=1}^{M} x_{ij} \leq r_i & \forall\, 1 \leq i \leq N \\ \sum_{i=1}^{N} res_j(o_i) \times x_{ij} \leq V_j & \forall\, 1 \leq j \leq M \\ x_{ij} \in \{0,1\} & \forall\, 1 \leq i \leq N,\ 1 \leq j \leq M \end{array} \tag{6}$$

In general, it's hard to solve the programming above even we have all those parameters in hand i.e to get the best objects distribution is not easy. One way is to use the greedy algorithm i.e. put the most valuable objects to the most reliable hosts. The greedy algorithm does not guarantee to get the best distribution of the objects. In some special cases, we should put more small but less important objects in the hight available hosts instead of putting one big and important object in those hosts. But it is still reasonable to put some important objects in high available hosts. In some cases, the objects are considered to be in equal size i.e. each object will consume the same amount of system resources. An object in a P2P system is often considered as one atom. We can define the capacity of a host to be the number of objects that are permitted to stored in that host. For further simplifying the problem we suppose that each object will consume the same resource of each host and has same number of replicas. Each host is able to contain the same number of objects. If the objects are equal important, the simpler problem can be re-written as in the equation 7.

$$\begin{array}{l} Maximize \\ \qquad O_a = \sum_{i=1}^{N} o_{ai}/N \\ \qquad o_{ai} = 1 - \prod_{j=1}^{M} (1 - h_{aj} \times x_{ij}) \\ s.t. \\ \sum_{j=1}^{M} x_{ij} \leq r \ \forall\, 1 \leq i \leq N \\ \sum_{i=1}^{N} x_{ij} \leq V \ \forall\, 1 \leq j \leq M \\ x_{ij} \in \{0,1\} \quad \forall\, 1 \leq i \leq N,\ 1 \leq j \leq M \end{array} \tag{7}$$

As discussed above, host availability values h_{aj} can be collected via heartbeat messages exchanging in the nearby hosts. It is still not easy to get the best distribution in such a simple case. Think about the object availability calculation $o_a = 1 - \prod_{o \in h_j} (1 - H_{aj})$, the replicas of the same object can not be put in the high available hosts too many times. If not, replicas of some objects will have to be all put in the low available hosts. This will hurt the overall availability O_a. It is reasonable that each object should put some of its replicas in high available hosts while others in low available hosts. The following rules lead to the design of the multiple groups algorithm in the P2P environment.

- **Greedy** Make good use of high available hosts.
- **Even** Distribute the replicas of an object to the system evenly, put its replicas in both high and low available hosts.

4 Multiple Groups in the P2P Environment

In the P2P environment, given the object identification, the routing algorithm must find the object correctly. This can be solved by using DHTs[10]. Under such limitation, the object might not be put into the most high available host firstly. However, according to the rules discussed above, we can divide the hosts into groups. Each group has the hosts with similar availability. Now the replicas of an object can be distributed *evenly* to the groups.

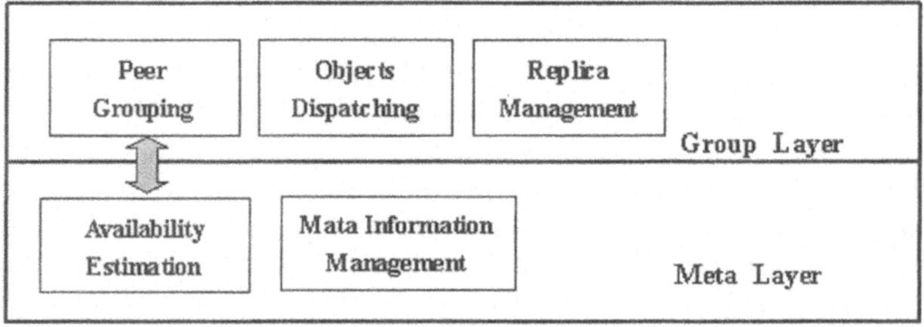

Fig. 1. Two Layers DHTs for Supporting Multiple Groups

For implementation of such multiple groups schema, each host has two layers of DHTs as shown in figure 1. The meta layer is used to construct the whole system and manage the meta information. The availability values is managed in this layer. Here is the two things the meta layer has to do.

Estimate the Hosts Availabilities. Hosts in the P2P environment are highly dynamic. The heartbeat messages are maintained between every pair of neighbors. The neighbors of a host know when a host is "up" or "down". So, the history data is one way to estimate the host availability.

Split the Hosts by their Availabilities into Groups. SOMO [5] is a highly scalable, efficient and robust infrastructure build on any DHT to perform resource management in the P2P system. The availability information of a host is collected by its neighbor and transferred by SOMO nodes to the root of the SOMO tree. The hosts then are split into groups. The hosts with similar availabilities will join the same group using the peer grouping module in the group layer.

Different from the meta layer, the group layer is different among hosts i.e. each host will join different groups and have different data in the group layer. The group layer has the duty to do the following jobs.

Dynamic Reconfiguring the Groups. Because the dynamic property of the P2P system, it is necessary to reconfiguring the groups i.e. moving some hosts from one group to another. Still, we use SOMO to reconfiguring the group layer. Each host will be re-estimated of its availability and put to the appropriate group. Each group has approximately the same number of hosts. Such information can also be collected by using the SOMO trees.

Objects Dispatching. As SOMO is used to perform the resource management, some other statistical information can also be collected such as disk spaces, group size etc. As a result, total objects number and free disk spaces in each group can be computed. All these information is needed for the distribution of the objects. The DHT in the group layer is used to locate the host which is used to store the object. And also the same DHT is used to retrieve the objects.

Replica Management. A modified version of DHT in the group layer is used to store the replicas of an object in the same group.

5 Experiments and Results

In order to test the efficiency of the algorithms discussed above, we performed some experiments. Here we use two different host availabilities distributions (HAD). The first one (in table 1) is extracted approximately from the statistic information for application level uptime of Napster [6]. The other one (in table 2) is the availability measurement of the Overnet(http://www.overnet.com) file sharing network [1].

Table 1. Host Availabilities Distribution 1 (HAD1)

Percent of Hosts	20%	20%	20%	20%	10%	10%
Availability(%)	0.1-4.0	4.0-15.0	15.0-35.0	35.0-80.0	80.0-95.0	95.0-99.9

Table 2. Host Availabilities Distribution 2 (HAD2)

Percent of Hosts	10%	10%	10%	10%	10%
Availability(%)	0.1-15.0	15.0-22.0	22.0-30.0	30.0-40.0	40.0-50.0
Percent of Hosts	10%	10%	10%	10%	10%
Availability(%)	50.0-62.0	62.0-75.0	75.0-85.0	85.0-95.0	95.0-99.0

For each distribution, we build a P2P objects storing system containing M hosts(M is from 256 to 8192). The number of objects N is set to be ($N = 1000 \times M$). And also we vary the redundance value r ($r = 4, 8$) and the groups number g ($g = 1$ *to* 8). Here we suppose that each host can contain 10000 objects i.e. each host is large enough to contain "some" objects while not large enough to contains all objects. The whole system can contain total number objects replicas. For each of the objects, we use the multiple groups algorithm to locate its own host. After all the objects have been distributed, the formula 2 is used to calculate the availability for each object and the average availability (equation 4) is used to estimate the final objects set availability O_a.

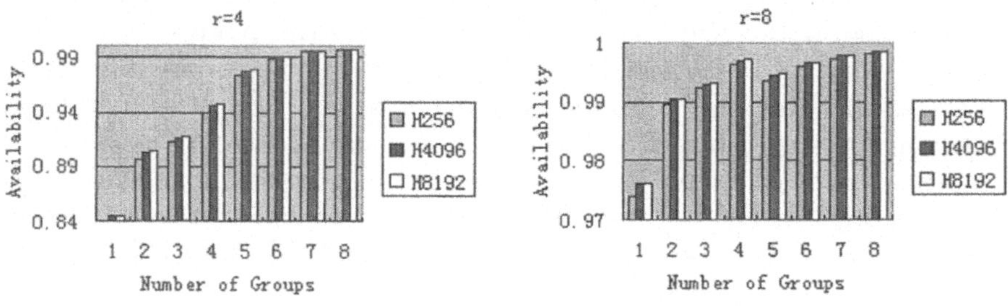

Fig. 2. Objects Set Availability in Host Availability Distribution 1 (HAD1)

Figure 2 is the experimental results using the hosts availability distribution 1(HAD1). We can see that the multiple groups algorithm does improve the availability of the object set. In all cases ($M = 256, 4096, 8192$ hosts respectively), the multiple groups algorithm ($g > 1$) works better than the plain DHT schema ($g = 1$). The improving of the multiple groups algorithms is significant. In the case of $r = 4$ the objects set availability O_a increase monotonously when increasing the number of groups because when $g > 4$, the objects (only 4 replicas for each) will only distributed to the high available 4 groups. In the case of $r = 8$, the O_a decreases a little while grouping number increases. This is because the number 8 can not be divided exactly by some numbers, and at that point, some objects will choose to locate in lower available groups for the load balance purpose. Same results can be observed from the experiments using hosts availability distribution 2(HAD2) as shown in figure 3.

6 Conclusions

In this paper, we define the availability for a single host and for an object located in the distributed environment. The objects set availability O_a is then defined as the optimization goal. In the distributed environment, there are many limitations. The optimization problem is further formalized as an programming problem subject to the resources limitation as in the equation 6.

In the case of P2P system, the object must be found using DHTs. We designed the multiple groups algorithm to improve the availability while still satisfying this limitation. The experiment shows that such simple method can improve the

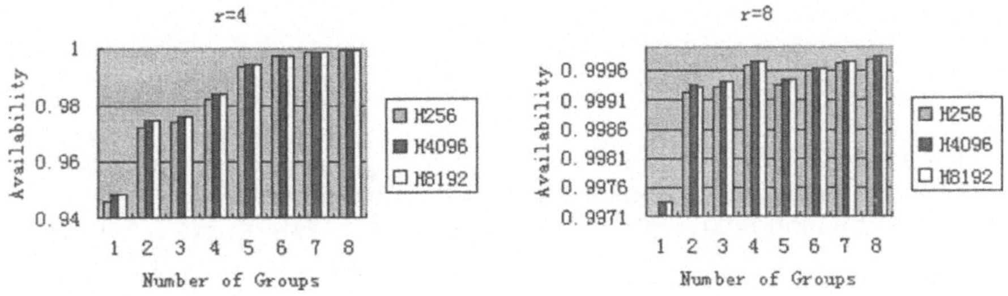

Fig. 3. Objects Set Availability in Host Availability Distribution 2 (HAD2)

availability and is quite practical. For the complexity issue, the experimental results figures suggest that 4 groups is enough to use in practice.

Acknowledgement. This work is sponsored by two research grants from National Natural Science Foundation of China (NSFC60131160743 and NSFC60373005).

References

1. R. Bhagwan, S. Savage and G.M. Voelker. Understanding Availability. In Proc. of the 2nd International Workshop on Peer-to-Peer Systems, 2003
2. J. Plank. A tutorial on reed-solomon coding for fault tolerance in RAID-like systems. Software Practice and Experience, 27(9):995 C1012, Sept. 1997.
3. M. Luby, M. Mitzenmacher, M. Shokrollahi, etc. Analysis of low density codes and improved designs using irregular graphs. In Proc. of ACM STOC, May 1998.
4. S.Shi,G.Yang,J.Yu,Y.Wu,D.Wang. Improving Availability of P2P Storage Systems. In proc. of APPT'03,Xiamen,September,2003
5. Z. Zhang, S. Shi and J. Zhu. SOMO: self-organized metadata overlay for resource management in P2P DHT. In Proc. of the 2nd International Workshop on Peer-to-Peer Systems, 2003.
6. S. Saroiu, P. K. Gummadi and S.D. Gribble. A Measurement Study of Peer-to-Peer File Sharing Systems. In Proc. of the Multimedia Computing and Networking (MMCN), San Jose, January, 2002
7. A. Rowstron and P. Druschel. Storage management and caching in PAST, a large-scale, persistent peer-to-peer storage utility. In Proc. of ACM SOSP'01, 2001.
8. F. Dabek, M.F. Kaashoek, D. Karger, etc. Wide-area cooperative storage with CFS. In Proc. ACM SOSP'01, Banff, Canada, Oct. 2001
9. J. Kubiatowicz, D. Bindel, and Y. Chen, etc. OceanStore: An Architecture for Global-Scale Persistent Storage. In Proc. of the 9th international Conference on Architectural Support for Programming Languages and Operating Systems, 2000
10. Kager D., Lehman E., Leighton F.,Levine M., Lewin D., Andpanigrahy R. Consistent hashing and random trees: Distributed caching protocols for relieving hot spots on the world wide web. In Proc. of the 29th Annual ACM Symposium on Theory of Computing, pp.654-663,May 1997

PBiz: An E-business Model Based on Peer-to-Peer Network

Shudong Chen [1], Zengde Wu, Wei Zhang, and Fanyuan Ma

The Department of Computer Science and Engineering, Shanghai Jiaotong University, No. 1954 Huashan Rd., Shanghai, China, 200030
{Chenshudong, Wu-zd, Zhangwei, Ma-fy}@cs.sjtu.edu.cn

Abstract. The resource of e-Business is distributed, but the existing e-Business resource management is processed in a centralized approach, which has the limitations of single point failure and performance bottleneck. We propose PBiz, an e-Business model based on peer-to-peer to overcome these limitations. In PBiz, resource is managed in a totally decentralized approach. Moreover, we extend the routing algorithm Chord with XML to enable PBiz could support SQL-like query. Experimental results show that PBiz has good robustness and extensibility.

1 Introduction

In the last few years, there have been many successful specifications and cases [1], [3], [4] in e-Business but some weaknesses have also appeared at the same time. Firstly, the existing e-Business resource is managed in centralized approaches such as ebXML [3] and UDDI [4], which leads to single point failure and performance bottleneck. Secondly, e-Business couldn't provide real-time information for users because the information index updating speed of centralized database servers is too slow. So the necessity of using a kind of new approach to manage the e-Business resource increases. Peer-to-Peer (P2P) [2], [5], [6] as a completely distributed computing model, could supply good scheme for e-Business.

We designed a distributed e-Business model based on P2P named PBiz (P2P based e-Business). In PBiz, e-Business resource is managed by a decentralized approach named PARM (P2P Approach for Resource Management). Since the usual P2P routing algorithm cannot be applied in e-Business processes, we extended the P2P routing algorithm Chord [7]. And the new algorithm XChord has made PBiz support SQL-like (fuzzy) search. A prototype system realized e-Business processes on P2P and could supply real-time information navigation service for users has been worked out in order

[1] This paper has been supported by the Science & Technology Committee of Shanghai Municipality Key Technologies R&D Project Grand (No. 03dz15027) and the Grid Research Program of Shanghai (No.025115032)

M. Li et al. (Eds.): GCC 2003, LNCS 3032, pp. 404–411, 2004.

to test the correctness of PBiz. Experimental results have showed that PBiz has good robustness and extensibility.

The rest of the paper is organized as follows. In section 2,we explain the architecture of PBiz. Section 3 presents the key technologies used in PBiz, including the working principle of PARM and XChord. The prototype system is described in section 4. Section 5 presents the emulation and experimental results. Conclusions are given in the section 6.

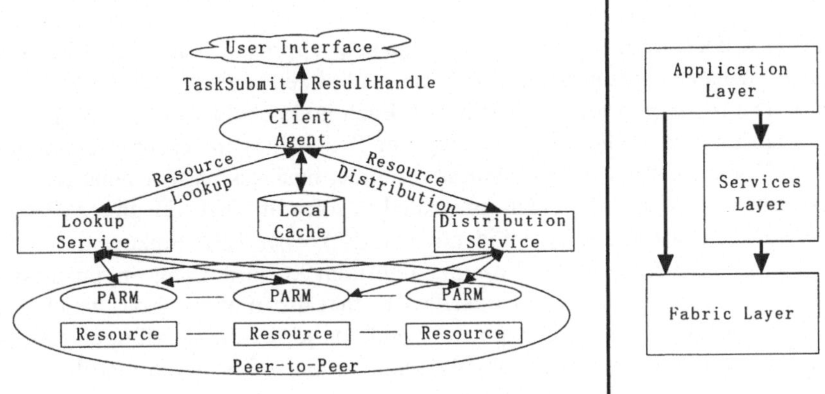

Fig. 1. Layered structure of PBiz

2 Architecture of PBiz

PBiz has a three-layer structure. The layered structure of PBiz is shown in Fig. 1.

In fabric layer, PARM is used to manage the decentralized e-Business resource. It supplies physical e-Business resource access interfaces for upper layers.

Through two web services: resource distribution and resource lookup, services layer enables PBiz to process users' requests and coordinates functions of each layer.

Application layer supplies access interfaces for users to distribute and lookup e-Business resource. There are two processes in this layer: TaskSubmit and ResultHandle.

Because the principle of resource distribution and lookup are almost the same, we select the lookup service to describe the working principle of PBiz. At first, TaskSubmit process submits user's lookup request to client agent with an SQL-like query message. Client agent verifies whether there is a satisfying result in local cache firstly. If there is, returns it to ResultHandle process. Otherwise, resource lookup service will search exact result. At last, ResultHandle process deals with the returned result. Then, user could use the offered hyperlinks to contact e-Business partners.

3 Key Technologies of PBiz

In this section, we present the key technologies used in PBiz including decentralized resource management approach PARM and extended routing algorithm XChord.

3.1 P2P Approach for Resource Management

In PBiz, a decentralized resource management approach named PARM is used to manage e-Business resource. There is no centralized registry in PARM like that of UDDI. The registry is totally distributed. Each node could have a registry to keep a local registry index. The key technology of PARM lies in resource distribution and lookup. Before distributing e-Business resource, business partner generates metadata of e-Business resource. Metadata presented in form of XML document. PBiz hashes the key of metadata to get a hash identifier (HID). Then PBiz lookups the distribution node by means of extended P2P routing algorithm XChord. Later on, business partner presents the XML document of metadata to that distribution node, which saves the distribution resource to router repository and completes the distribution process. The process of resource lookup is roughly same as that of resource distribution. Fig. 2 shows an example of resource lookup.

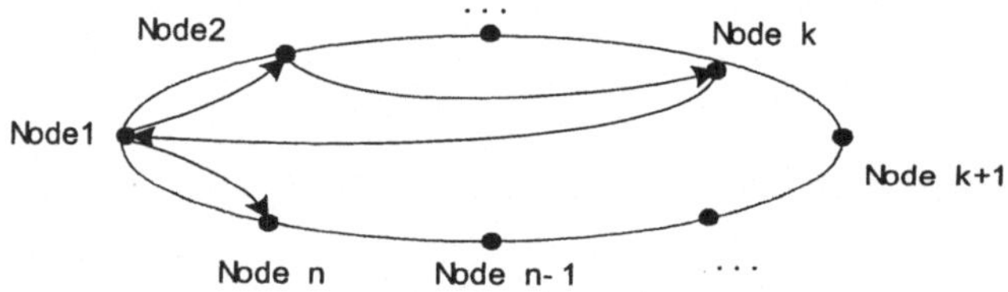

Fig. 2. Example of resource lookup in PBiz

Suppose Node1 is an automobile agent, who wants to lookup automobile manufactories in China. Node1 hashes the key 'Car' and gets an HID. Node1 lookups local routing table and finds that identifier Node2 is closest to that HID among all identifiers in local tables. Then the request is routed to Node2, which operates the same lookup process as Node1 and routes the query to next node. The process continues until the node (Node k for example) with identifier closest to the HID is found. Node k searches in its local router repository for metadata that satisfies the query condition 'Region is China, BusinessType is manufactory', and return the result to Node1. The following XML document shows the result If Node1 wanted to get more detailed business information, it could communicate with business partners through hyperlinks, such as http://www.dfmc.com.cn.

```
<?xml version="1.0"?>
<Business_list>
  <HID>
    <Value>" B28AD5C3E516F6D63AC5"</Value>
```

```
      <BusinessType>Manufactory</BusinessType>
      <Region>China</Region>
      <Details>
        <URL="http://www.dfmc.com.cn"/>
        <Description>DongFeng</Description>
      </Details>
    </HID>
    <HID>
      <Value>"B28AD5C3E516F6D63AC5"</Value>
      <BusinessType>Manufactory</BusinessType>
      <Region>China</Region>
      <Details>
        <URL="http://202.98.11.132/faw/index.asp"/>
        <Description>YiQi</Description>
      </Details>
    </HID>
  </Business_list>
```

3.2 Extended Routing Algorithm

Usual structured routing algorithms only support exact-match lookup. For e-Business applications, conditional lookup is of great importance. Chord has the features of simplicity and provable performance, so we extended Chord protocol to enable PBiz support SQL-like lookup. The Extended routing algorithm called as XChord.

Fig. 3 shows the structure of PBiz router, which consists routing table and repository. Structure of PBiz routing table is the same as that of Chord, maintaining no more than 160 items. Each is consisted of 160bit ID and 32bit IP address. Router repository maintains maps between hashing ID and the corresponding business resource lists. Lists appear in form of XML document.

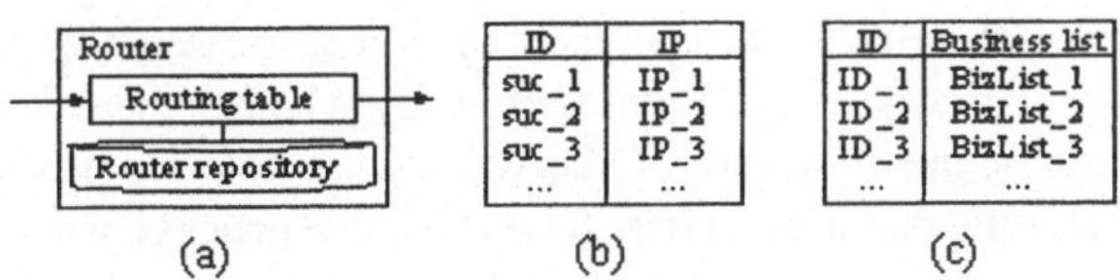

Fig. 3. (a) Structure of router (b) Items of routing table (c) Repository map of router repository

Before presenting PBiz lookup algorithm XChord, we first introduce a definition. Let И be identifier set, and Ω be the node set. Then the definition of node is given as follow:

node: И$\rightarrow\Omega$, И is HID set, and Ω is the node set. node maps HID to corresponding node. This mapping is achieved by Chord algorithm.

The pseudocode of XChord is given as follow. FindNode completes the lookup process. Firstly, node n hashes *key* and gets HID *id*. Then function Route finds the successor of *id*, which is the closest to *id* from the local routing table. If node that satisfies the condition is found, then result is returned. Otherwise, node *id* calls the remote process Route (*id*, *Msg_query*) to continue lookup process.

```
n.FindNode(key, Msg_query){
id = Hash (key);
n.Route(id, Msg_query);
}
Route(id, Msg_query){
if (id<=id`) and
  (∀id``∈И, id<=id``∧id``<=id` → id`=id``)
  Find results from repository to generate Msg_result;
  Returns Msg_result to the source node;
Else
  node(id`).Route(id, Msg_query);
}
```

4 Prototype System

In order to verify the performance of PBiz, a prototype system is presented in this section. This prototype system realized e-Business process of PBiz, providing two web services: resource distribution and lookup.

4.1 Definition of Resource Distribution Style

In Sect. 3.1, the style of resource distribution document has been presented. Firstly, HID of node is given, then the BusinessType, Region business partner belongs to and the partner's details followed. Details include partner's URL and other description.

4.2 The Design and Implement of Prototype System

The working flow that PBiz looks up resource is just the same as the description in Sect. 2 of this paper. Firstly, client agent will verify whether there is an exact result in local cache. If there is, use it directly. Otherwise, QueryService process will be called to search the satisfying resource. Then ResultHandle process will deal with the returned result.

According to the style of resource distribution document, QueryService is realized with the following program code.

```
<?xml version="1.0"?>
<QueryService>
  <ServiceName>
    QueryService
  </ServiceName>
  <Request>
    Where <Business_list>
      <BusinessType>Manufactory</BusinessType>
      <Region>China</Region>
      </Business_list >
```

```
    IN "<XChord > Car</XChord >"
  </Request>
</QueryService>
```

Using simple link technology of XLink, ResultHandle realizes to display the result in form of layered menu to users. ClassSet is a XML document to store the result.

```
<?xml version="1.0"?>
<ResultHandle xmlns="http:// ClassSet"
  xmlns:xlink=http://www.w3.org/1999/xlink
  xlink:type="simple"
  xlink:href=" http://ClassSet "
  xlink:actuate="onload"
  xlink:show="embed">
  current list of Business_list in ClassSet
</ResultHandle>
```

5 Evaluation and Experimental Results

In this section, we evaluate PBiz by simulation. In order to compare with centralized resource management approach such as UDDI, we also evaluated UDDI approach (for simplicity). We compared space overhead, load, and robustness of PBiz with UDDI.

5.1 Experiment Setup

We use the Georgia Tech Internetwork Topological Models (GT-ITM) [8] to generate the network topologies used in our simulations. We use the "transit-stub" model to obtain topologies that more closely resemble the Internet hierarchy than pure random graph. An Internetwork with 600 routers and 28800 business partners are used in our experiment. The latency of physical hops between nodes in the same stub domain, nodes in stub domain and transit domain, nodes in same transit domain, and nodes in different transit domains are 1, 3, 5 and 7, respectively. The routing process obeys the following rules. The path connecting two nodes in the same domain stays entirely within that domain. The path connecting node u in stub domain U to node v in another stub domain V goes form U through one or more transit domains to V, and does not pass through any other stub domains. In case two stub domains are connected directly via a stub-stub edge, the path between two nodes on the two domains may go along that edge and avoid any transit domains.

5.2 Space Overhead

The space overhead is consisted of two parts: routing table overhead and router repository overhead. The memory size of routing ID and corresponding IP is called memory unit, size of which is σ. It is assumed that Node ID and file business information ID is distributed uniformly in ID space, and there are n business partners in e-Business system, each partner distributes m business information in average. Also, we assume that the average overhead of each business information item is $k \times \sigma$.

Since there are $\log(n)$ items in PBiz routing table, and overhead of every item is σ, thus the overhead of routing table is $\log(n) \times \sigma$. Each router repository have m items, overhead of router repository is $m \times k \times \sigma$. Overhead of PBiz is: $\log(n) \times \sigma + m \times k \times \sigma$. Since UDDI maintains all information in central repository, overhead of UDDI is: $n \times m \times k \times \sigma$. Set $m = 80$ and $k = 2$, experimental results in Fig. 4 show that the space overhead of PBiz is between $171 \times \sigma$ and $175 \times \sigma$, and that of UDDI is between $10^6 \times \sigma$ and $6 \times 10^6 \times \sigma$. When there are 20000 nodes in GT-ITM, space overhead of PBiz is 18285 times lower than that of UDDI. Thus, space overhead of PBiz is much better than that of UDDI.

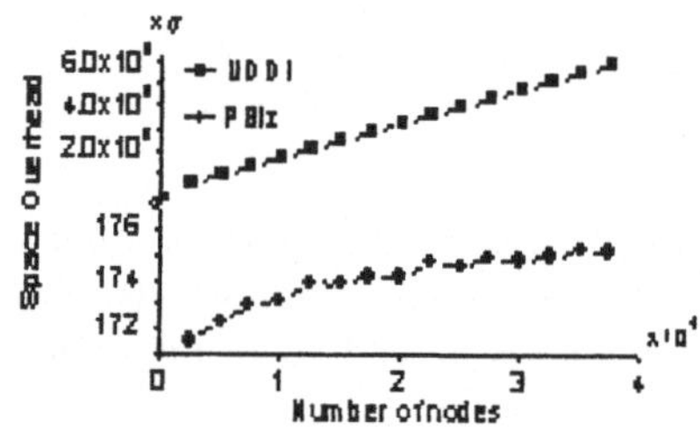

Fig. 4. Effect of number of nodes on Space overhead

5.3 Load Evaluation

We use the number of messages in and out of node as evaluation metric to load. Fig. 5 shows the comparisons in loads between PBiz and UDDI. The load of UDDI increases with number of nodes linearly, but the load of PBiz and number of nodes is in logarithmic relation. The reason is, for each resource lookup request, there is an in message and an out message. Thus, if each business partner sends one request, the load of UDDI registry is $2 \times N$. While in PBiz, each resource lookup needs $\log(N)/2$ logical hops in average, thus, total logical hops of N resource lookup request are $N \times \log(N)/2$.

5.4 Robustness Evaluation

In this experiment, we evaluated the ability of PBiz to regain consistency after a large percentage of node fail simultaneously. We consider 28800 nodes with each node distribute 10 pieces of business information, and randomly select a fraction of the nodes that fail. After the failures occur, we wait for the network to stabilizing, and measure the fraction of keys that could not be looked up correctly. Fig. 6 plots the effect of node failure on resource lookup. The lookup failure rate is almost equal to node fail rate. This is just the fraction of keys expected to be lost due to the failure of the responsible nodes. That is to say, there is no significant lookup failure in PBiz resource lookup. We conclude that PBiz is robust in face of node failure.

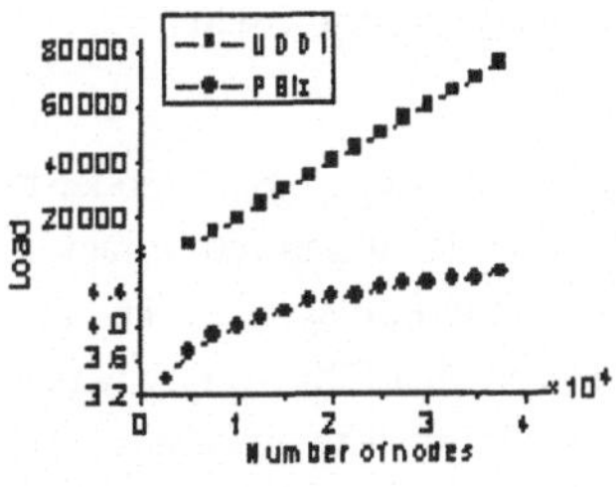

Fig. 5. Load of PBiz and UDDI

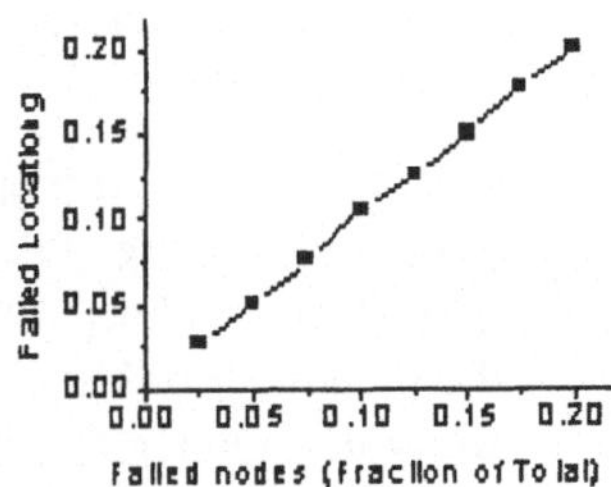

Fig. 6. The effect of node failure on resource lookup

6 Conclusion

PBiz, distributed e-Business model based on P2P, uses a distributed approach PARM to manage e-Business resource. The new routing algorithm, XChord makes PBiz could support SQL-like search and supply real-time information explore service for users. Compared with centralized resource management in existing e-Business specifications, P2P approach has the following advantages: lower load, better space overhead and better robustness. We conclude that P2P approach for e-Business is practical and promising.

References

1. WU Zeng-De, Liu Yan, MA Fan-Yuan: Research on service-based e-business application integration framework. Journal of Shanghai Jiaotong University, 2002.09.1341-1345
2. WU Zeng-De, RAO Wei-Xiong, MA Fan-Yuan: Efficient topology-aware routing in peer-to-peer network. International workshop on grid and cooperative computing, China (2002)
3. Cole J, Milosevic Z: Extending support for contracts in ebXML. Proceedings 2001 Information Technology for Virtual Enterprises, Queensland, AUSTRALIA: ITVE (2001) 119 – 127
4. Http://www.uddi.org/, UDDI Version 3.0, Published Specification
5. Peer-to-Peer Working Group committees. http://peer-to-peerwg.org/
6. David Clark: Face-to-Face with peer-to-peer networking. IEEE Computer, January 2001
7. Ion Stoica, Robert Morris, David Karger, M. Frans Kaashoek, and Hari Balakrishnan: Chord: a scalable peer-to-peer lookup service for Internet applications. Proceedings of ACM SIGCOMM`01, San Diego (2001)
8. Zegura, E. w., Calvert. k., and Bhattacharjee, S: How to model an Internetwork. Proceedings of IEEE INFOCOM (1996).

P2P Overlay Networks of Constant Degree

Guihai Chen[1,2], Chengzhong Xu[2], Haiying Shen[2], and Daoxu Chen[1]

[1] State Key Lab of Novel Software Technology, Nanjing University, China
[2] Department of Electrical and Computer Engineering, Wayne State University, USA
{gchen, czxu, shy}@ece.eng.wayne.edu

Abstract. This paper proposes an abstract and generic topological model that captures the essence of P2P architecture. Such model should in return facilitate the exploitation of the new design space for more novel P2P systems. The paper also proposes a variant of the cube-connected cycles as a P2P overlay network that achieves O(log N) path length with O(1) neighbors. The simulation result has shown that our system is no worse than other systems of the same complexity such as Viceroy and Koorde.

1 Introduction

Several research groups have independently proposed a second generation of P2P systems that support scalable routing and location schemes. Examples include Chord[10], CAN[6], Pastry[8], Tapestry[12], Koorde[2] and Viceroy[4]. We find that all such new generation of P2P systems share a common feature that peers are connected at application-level as a regular network such as a ring, a mesh, or a hypercube that are often called overlay network. As the P2P architecture is becoming popular and more systems are introduced, we think an abstract and generic topological model that captures the essence of P2P architecture is needed. Such model should in turn facilitate the exploitation of the new design space for more novel P2P systems.

Based on the above investigation, we propose a generic topological model in Section 2 to abstract the new generation of P2P systems. We also address the fundamental metrics to evaluate the performance of P2P systems and the parameters that affect the metrics. While the typical P2P overlay networks have O(log N) path length and O(log N) routing table space, we propose yet another new topology for P2P overlay network in Section 3 that achieves O(log N) path length with O(1) neighbors. Section 4 concludes the paper by compareing our system with other systems[2,4] that have the same complexity and pointing out the possible direction for future research. We expect more novel P2P overlay networks to be found in the near future. We also expect the well-established technologies for interconnection networks could be borrowed for the study of P2P overlay networks.

2 Topological Model

In developing our abstract model, we made two observations. First, in any P2P system, we can see that there are multiple nodes spreading across the entire Internet and

M. Li et al. (Eds.): GCC 2003, LNCS 3032, pp. 412–419, 2004.

contributing their local resource (*e.g,*. storage and data) to the global P2P system. The Internet can be modeled as a general interconnection network that connects these nodes. Second, we note that the main functions of peer node in a P2P system are message routing and data locating besides data storing and caching. The routing function routes a given request/reply message from the source to the destination node. The data locating function attempts to find out the location or *home node* of a data item, with the help of routing table. All peer nodes are connected as an overlay network in somewhat regular way so that both the routing table size and the routing path are dramatically reduced. In such systems, entries of routing table (*e.g,*. IP address of neighbors) serves as logical links to other neighboring nodes and thus are regarded as edges of the overlay networks.

The complexity of an overlay network often determines the size of a P2P system that can be constructed. Likewise, the attainable performance of a P2P system is ultimately limited by the characteristics of the overlay network. Apparently, the selection of the overlay network is the first and also the most crucial step for the design of the new generation of P2P systems. Fig 1 displays our simple model. Each component will be clear after we define and descript the following terms

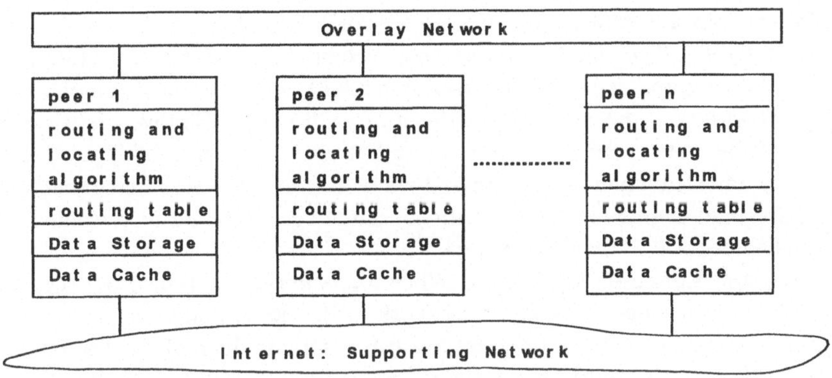

Fig. 1. A Generic Topological Model of P2P Systems

Data ID and Node ID: Each data (*e.g,*. a file) is assigned a globally unique identifier or a key that corresponds to the cryptographic hash of the file's textual name, the owner's public key, and/or a random salt. All keys are ordered linearly or circularly in 1-dimensional or d-dimensional key space. *Note that the ordered key space is the first necessary requirement for an overlay network.* Each node(*i.e.*, a peer) is also mapped into the same key space as data. It can be computed as a cryptographic hash of the node's IP address or public key.

Data Placement: Data ID and Node ID belong to the same space, but the number of nodes is often much less than the number of Data. Each node is responsible for storing a certain range of keys in the key space. Data is stored on the node that has the same or the closest ID as data ID, as implemented in Pastry and Viceroy. Different implementation might have a slightly changed policy. In Chord, data is stored in its successor node; this simplicity can bring about the convenience in self-organization. In CAN, all data of one zone is stored on the representative node of that zone.

Hash function: All data or nodes are mapped by hashing into a point in the same key space. The functionality of Hash should guarantee a uniform and random distribution of data or nodes within the key space. Consistent hashing[3] was proposed to guarantee the uniformity no matter how the input keys are intentionally chosen. SHA-1 function is used in practice as a good substitute for consistent hash function since producing a set of keys that collide under SHA-1 can be seen as inverting or decrypting the SHA-1 function that is believed to be hard to do[10].

Overlay Network: All live nodes are connected logically as an overlay network at application level with the help of routing table. Each entry of the routing table serves as a logical edge, usually containing the IP address of one neighbor. Recent P2P systems have adopted structured topologies such as ring, mesh and hypercube and showed advantages in scalability and lookup efficiency. Interestingly and importantly, none of them is a simple application of a traditional interconnection network. Each one embodies an insightful anatomy of an existing interconnection network and provides a resilient connection pattern for fault tolerance and self-organization. Seeking for better topologies for overlay network is becoming a new search topic. Recent work focus on the constant-degree overlay networks[1, 2, 4].

Routing Table: The size (or the number of entries) of the routing table is determined by the outgoing degree of the overlay network. It is the space complexity of an overlay network, *i.e.*, the memory overhead of each node. Moreover, it is not just a measure of the state required to do routing but also a measure of how much state needs to be adjusted when nodes join and leave. For this reason, interconnection networks with small degree (especially with constant degree) should be restudied as possible candidates for P2P overlay network.

Routing and Locating Algorithm: When a *lookup(key)* is issued or received, the *lookup* is routed through the overlay network to the home node responsible for that *key*. Each hop makes the most progress towards resolving the lookup. The notation of progress differs from algorithm to algorithm, but any routing algorithm should be convergent in the sense that each hop makes the distance between the current node ID and the home node ID becomes smaller and smaller. *Note that the convergent routing algorithm is the second necessary requirement for an overlay network.* The real distance performance is determined not only by the path length in key space but also by the communication delay of each hop in the Internet. Proximity in key space does not mean proximity in geological space. If the supporting network is represented as a graph in some regular way, the proximity problem can be studied in the form of embedding the overlay network into the supporting network with the smallest possible dilation and congestion. An adjustable Hash function might also be helpful if such a function could map nearby IP addresses into close values in key space. Other possbile solutions include the neighborhood set[8] and the landmark vector[11].

Self-organizing: To make P2P systems completely distributed, the routing table should be automatically reconfigured when a node joins or departs from the system. A node might leave abruptly due to crash or gracefully by informing its neighbors and submitting its keys. Systems are supposed to be small enough at beginning so that nodes could just exchange information directly to build the initial routing table. After that, nodes should have an automatic way to detect the node join or node leave to reconfigure their routing table state in such cases. Since not all nodes are alive in the key space and they often join and depart dynamically, the resilient topological connection pattern must ensure the routing table has full or enough number of neighbors. When one node fails, another node can substitute. *Note that self-organizing is the third necessary requirement for overlay network.*

Now we give the following thumb rule to judge if a network can be manipulated as an overlay network for P2P systems. This rule is empirical since we cannot give a mathematical proof.

A network can be manipulated as an overlay network if and only if the network meets the above-mentioned 3 requirements, *i.e.*, an ordered key space which is used to measure the distance between any two nodes, a convergent routing algorithm that sends a message closer to the destination at each step, and self-organizing ability that reconfigure the network topology when nodes join or depart.

3 Cubical Cycles: A Novel Overlay Network

We were first motivated by the open question in [7], *i.e.,* Can one achieve O(logN) path length or better with O(1) neighbors? If it were possible, how are some aspects of routing affected? Our recent investigation into CCC (cube-connected cycles) has shown that a modified CCC works well as an overlay network with O(1) neighbors and O(log N) path length. In addition to Koorde[2] and Viceroy[4], this is yet another new overlap network that has ever been found to meet the super-scalable requirement.

3.1 Resilient Connection Pattern

In a one-dimensional circular key space with $N = n \times 2^n$ nodes, each node is represented as $(k, a_n a_{n-1} \cdots\cdots a_1)$, where $1 \le k \le n$ and $a_i = 0$ or 1. $a_n a_{n-1} \cdots\cdots a_1$ is the cubical index and k is the cyclic index. Nodes are ordered according to the value of $a_n a_{n-1} \cdots\cdots a_1$. Nodes with the same $a_n a_{n-1} \cdots\cdots a_1$ are ordered again as a circular cycle but they are of equal valence to the outside. So, data with key $(k, a_n a_{n-1} \cdots\cdots a_1)$ will be put on the node that is first numerically closest to $a_n a_{n-1} \cdots\cdots a_1$ and then numerically closest to k. In the routing table, for example in Fig. 2, each node $(k, a_n \cdots a_k a_{k-1} \cdots a_1)$ has a cubical neighbor $(k-1, a_n \cdots a_k x \cdots x)$, where x denotes an arbitrary bit value, and two cyclic neighbors, $(k-1, a_n \cdots a_k b_{k-1} \cdots b_1)$ and $(k-1, a_n \cdots a_k c_{k-1} \cdots c_1)$, where

$$(k-1, a_n \cdots a_k b_{k-1} \cdots b_1) = Min\{\forall(k-1, a_n \cdots a_k y_{k-1} \cdots y_1) \mid y_{k-1} \cdots y_1 \ge a_{k-1} \cdots a_1\}$$

$$(k-1, a_n \cdots a_k c_{k-1} \cdots c_1) = Max\{\forall(k-1, a_n \cdots a_k y_{k-1} \cdots y_1) \mid y_{k-1} \cdots y_1 \le a_{k-1} \cdots a_1\}.$$

The cubical and cyclic neighbors allow us to change cubical index from left to right. It is easy to see that the network will be the traditional cube-connected cycles if all nodes are alive. We refer authors to [5] for topological properties of CCC. However, our connection pattern is resilient in the sense that even if many nodes are absent, the remaining nodes are still capable of being connected.

Node ID (5,101-1-1010)	
Routing table	
cubical neighbor: (4,101-0-xxxx)	
cyclic neighbor: (4,101-1-1100)	
cyclic neighbor: (4,101-1-0011)	
2 Leaf Sets(half smaller, half larger)	
Inside Leaf Set	
(3,101-1-1010)	(6,101-1-1010)
Outside Leaf Set	
(7,101-1-1001)	(6,101-1-1011)

Fig. 2. Routing table state of a hypothetical CCC node (5,101-1-1010). x indicates an arbitrary value, 0 or 1. Inside leaf set maintains the closest neighbors in the same cycle. Outside leaf set maintains the links to the previous and the next cycles.

We borrow the idea of the leaf set from Pastry[8]. But differently, each node $(k, a_n a_{n-1} \cdots\cdots a_1)$ maintains two leaf sets in addition to the routing table. The routing algorithm is greatly assisted by the leaf sets for the purpose of effectiveness and fault tolerance. The inside leaf set points to the predecessor and the successor in the same cycle. That is, nodes with the same cubical index are connected as a doubly linked cycle. The outside leaf set point to nodes with the highest cyclic index in the preceding cycle and the succeeding cycle. The outside leaf sets is important for self-organization such as node join, node departure and stabilization, as discussed in Section 3.3.

3.2 Routing Algorithm

The routing algorithm is used not only for looking up a data with data ID=$(l, b_n \cdots\cdots b_1)$, but also for joining a new node with node ID=$(l, b_n \cdots\cdots b_1)$. We suppose MSB is the most significant bit where $a_n \cdots\cdots a_1$ and $b_n \cdots\cdots b_1$ differs. The following routing algorithm of Cubic Cycles emulates the routing algorithm of CCC[5] from current node A=$(k, a_n \cdots\cdots a_1)$ to destination node B=$(l, b_n \cdots\cdots b_1)$, incorporating the resilient connection pattern of Cubic Cycles.

Routing Algorithm

1. (Termination Condition) If D is within the leaf sets, inside leaf set or outside leaf set, forward to the nearest node in the leaf sets. In particular, if D is within or closer to the local cycle than to the 2 neighboring cycles, forward to the predecessor or the successor in the same cycle, otherwise forward to one of the 2 neighboring cycle which is numerically closer to D.
2. (Ascending) If $k <$ MSB, change k until $k \geq$ MSB by using inside leaf and outside leaf set. In particular, the local cycle is first searched in index-increasing order for the first node with cyclic index ≥ MSB. If such a node is not found locally, the neighboring cycle is searched continuously until a node is found to have cyclic index ≥ MSB. Among 2 neighboring cycles, preceding cycle and succeeding cycle, the one that is numerically closer to D is always chosen.

3. (Descending) If $k \geq$ MSB, change $(a_n \cdots\cdots a_1)$ so that it shares a longer common prefix as $b_n \cdots\cdots b_1$ by using cubical links and cyclic links. In particular, if $a_k \neq b_k$, the cubical link is followed. If $a_k = b_k$, the cyclical link is followed. Between the 2 cyclical links, the one that is numerically closer to D is chosen. In the cases when the appropriate entry in the routing table is empty or the associated node is not reachable, the neighboring cycle closer to D is chosen.

The algorithm has the following features:

1. It is convergent and thus correct, because each step sends the message to a node that either shares a longer prefix with the destination than the current node, or shares as long a prefix with, but is numerically closer to the destination than the current node.
2. It is deadlock free. This feature derives directly from the convergence of the algorithm.
3. It can be easily augmented to increase the fault tolerance. When the cubical link or the cyclic link is empty or faulty, the message can be forward to neighbors in the leaf sets. Our simulation experiment has shown that 4-element leaf sets can greatly reduce the number of lookup failures. Discussion in this paper is based on the 2-element leaf sets.
4. It is executed in O(log N) hops since each of 3 steps is bounded by O(log N) hops. The detailed analysis of probability is omitted due to the space limitation. Interested authors may write to get the full version of this paper.

3.3 Self-Organization

P2P systems are notoriously dynamic in the sense that nodes are frequently joining in and departing from the network. Accordingly the overlay network should be capable of self-organization without using a centralized database like Napster or a flooding-based multicast like Gnutella. When a node joins and departs, only local or a small part of nodes are disrupted.

Node join: When a new node joins, it needs to initialize its routing state tables and then inform other related nodes of its presence. Like other systems, we assume the new node knows initially about a live node A. Let us assume the first contact node is A=$(k, a_n \cdots\cdots a_1)$ and the new node is X=$(l, b_n \cdots\cdots b_1)$. By the routing algorithm discussed in section 3.2, the contact node A routes the join message to the existing node Z whose ID is numerically closest to the ID of X. Moreover, Z's leaf sets are the basis for X's leaf sets. In particular, the following two cases are considered:

1. If X and Z are in the same cycle, Z's outside leaf set directly becomes X's outside leaf set. Z's inside leaf set needs a slight modification to become X's inside leaf set, considering that Z should be among X's inside leaf set. Note that the inside leaf set points to one immediate predecessor and one immediate successor in the same the cycle. For fault tolerance, multiple predecessors and multiple successors might be pointed by the inside leaf set.
2. If X and Z are not in the same cycle, this is because that X is the first node in its cycle. Z's outside leaf set need a slight modification to become X's outside leaf

set, considering that Z should be among X's outside leaf set. Note that the outside leaf set points to one immediate preceding cycle and one immediate succeeding cycle. For fault tolerance, multiple preceding cycles and multiple succeeding cycles might be pointed by the outside leaf set. Z's inside leaf set is of no use for X's inside leaf set and instead all entries of X's inside leaf set refers to X itself since X is the only member in the cycle.

Now we consider the initialization of 3 neighbors in routing table. If we can find a node with ID= $(l, b_n \cdots b_l x \cdots x)$ where x represents any bit value, 0 or 1, we can borrow the cubical neighbor from this node to X. We start from one member of X's outside leaf set since X's outside leaf set members share the longest prefix with X and thus are close to such a required node $(l, b_n \cdots b_l x \cdots x)$. The possibility of such an existing required node depends on the value of l or the length of string $x \cdots x$. If there is no such node at all, it is usually because l is very small. In this case we just leave the cubical neighbor entry blank, as we have seen in the routing algorithm that it doesn't affect the routing too much. A more sophisticated scheme is to find such a required node during the routing path when inserting node X, and a close investigation shows that such a node exists with a high probability although such a node can not always be find in any case. Similarly for the 2 cyclic neighbors, we first search for $(l-1, b_n \cdots\cdots b_1)$ in the same cycle. If it doesn't exist, we continue to search in the next neighboring cycle that is reachable from the outside leaf set until we find such required cyclic neighbor on either side of node X.

Node departure: Nodes might leave the network abruptly or break down suddenly. Routing tables should be dynamically updated to reflect the newest network situation. Both lazy algorithm and greedy algorithm can be used. The lazy algorithm updates the routing table only when the entry is found to be obsolete. The greedy algorithm sends the hello message to all neighbors periodically and thus incurs some unnecessary messages. The initializing algorithm discussed above for node join can also be used for node departure. In particular, if a neighbor is found to be obsolete, the initializing algorithm is started to find a new neighbor to replace the obsolete one.

4 Conclusion

Our system bears the most resemblance with Viceroy[4]. Table 1 lists the difference between two systems. Our recent simulation[9] has shown the obvious performance advantage of cubic cycles over Viceroy.

Table 1. Comparison of Cubical Cycles and Viceroy

	Viceroy	Cubic Cycles
Topology	Butterfly	CCC
Node number	2^n	$n \times 2^n$
Fault tolerance	Difficult to be augmented	Easy by using larger leaf set
Climbing of levels	To the top level	Not to the top level

Hundreds of networks have been proposed in the past decade or so. Only few of them are proposed and modified as the overlay networks for P2P systems. We believe that more interconnection networks will be studied as promising candidates for P2P systems. Meanwhile, the new generation of topology-aware P2P systems will ignite a new chance for the study of Interconnection network.

As should be clear by our discussion, this paper is not about a finished works. We hope that presenting such a discussion will promote synergy between research groups in this area and help clarify some of the underlying issues. We expect in the near future to answer such a question: which kinds of networks topologies, after being modified, can be used for the overlay network and which cannot.

Acknowledgement. The work is partly supported by China NSF grant (No. 60073029), China 973 project (No. 2002CB312002), TRAPOYT award of China Ministry of Education, and US NSF grant (No. ACI-0203592).

References

1. G. Chen and C.Z. Xu, Topological Analysis of P2P Systems, Proc. of 1st Int. Workshop on Grid and Cooperative Computing, Hainan, China, December 2002.
2. M.F. Kaashoek and D.R. Karger, Koorde: A simple degree-optimal distributed hash table, Proc. of 2nd Int. Workshop on Peer-to-Peer Systems, March 2003.
3. D. Karger, *et al*,. Consistent hashing and random trees: distributed cashing protocols for relieving hot spots on the World Wide. In Proc. ACM STOC'97, El Paso, TX, May 1997.
4. D. Malkhi, M. Naor and D. Ratajczak, Viceroy: A scalable and dynamic emulation of the butterfly, PODC2002.
5. F.P. Preparata and J. Vuillemin, The cube-connected cycles: A versatile network for parallel computation. CACM, 24(5):300--309, 1981.
6. S. Ratnasamy, P. Francis, M. Handley, R. Karp, and S. Shenker, A scalable content-addressable network, Proc. ACM SIGCOMM'01, San Diego, CA, Aug. 2001.
7. S. Ratnasamy, S. Shenker, and I. Stoica, Routing algorithms for DHTs: Some open questions, Proc. of 1st Int. Workshop on Peer-to-Peer Systems, March 2002.
8. Rowstron and P. Druschel, Pastry: Scalable, decentralized object location and routing for large-scale peer-to-peer systems, Proc. of 18th IFIP/ACM CDSP'01, Nov. 2001.
9. H.Y. Shen, C.Z. Xu and G. Chen, Cycloid: A consistent-degree and Location efficient P2P overlay network, technical report ECE-03-08, Wayne State University, 2003.
10. Stoica, *et al*, Chord: A scalable peer-to-peer lookup service for Internet applications. In *Proc. ACM SIGCOMM'01*, San Diego, CA, Aug. 2001.
11. Zhichen Xu, Chunqiang Tang and Zheng Zhang, Building Topology-Aware Overlays Using Global Soft-State, ICDCS03.
12. B.Y. Zhao, *et al*, Tapestry: An infrastructure for fault-resilient wide-area location and routing. Technical Report UCB//CSD-01-1141, U. C. Berkeley, April 2001.

An Efficient Contents Discovery Mechanism in Pure P2P Environments*

In-suk Kim, Yong-hyeog Kang, and Young Ik Eom

School of Information and Communication Engineering, Sungkyunkwan University
300 Chunchun-dong, Jangan-gu, Suwon, Kyounggi-do, 440-746, Korea
{easy, yhkang1, yieom}@ece.skku.ac.kr

Abstract. Recently, the rapid growth of Internet technology and the deployment of high speed networks make many kinds of multimedia services possible. Preexisting multimedia services are designed based on the client-server model which has the problems such as the server failure and the low speed communication due to the high load on the central server. To solve these problems, P2P (peer-to-peer) networks have been introduced and they have also been expanded through Internet environments. In this paper, we propose a pure P2P network based contents discovery mechanism for multimedia services. In the proposed scheme, each host maintains the location information not only on the contents which are recently requested by other hosts but also on the replicas of its local contents. In pure P2P network environments, our proposed scheme has faster response time and incurs smaller traffic than the pre-existing discovery schemes. By decentralizing the location information and differentiating the reply path, our proposed scheme can also solve the search results loss problem that occurs when the network is unsettled.

1 Introduction

Recently, the rapid growth of Internet and the deployment of high speed networks make many kinds of multimedia services possible. These multimedia service environments can be designed by client-server model which is made up of several high capacity servers. However, this model is apt to degrade the performance of the network and decrease the download speed due to the high load on the central server. In order to solve these problems and to provide easy accessibility for users, P2P networks are introduced and expanded through Internet with high performance PCs and high speed networks [1-2].

The research on the P2P network environments is actively ongoing these days. P2P network environments are based on collaboration concept, and so, we can expect the network effect that the value of the network to an individual increases as the network increases in size [1-3]. Representative P2P applications are Napster [4], Gnutella [5], Freenet [6], etc.

---

* This work was supported by the Korea Research Foundation Grant (KRF-2002-041-D00420)

M. Li et al. (Eds.): GCC 2003, LNCS 3032, pp. 420–427, 2004.

In this paper, we propose a contents discovery mechanism in pure P2P network environments. In our proposed scheme the distributed location information is maintained in each host instead of central index servers. In detail, each host maintains the location information on the contents which are recently requested by other hosts and on the replicas of the local contents. By decentralizing the location information and differentiating the reply path from request path, our proposed scheme can solve the search results loss problem that occurs when the network is unsettled. In our proposed scheme, each host checks whether the received request message is duplicated or not. So we can reduce unnecessary traffic generated by repeated request messages in the P2P network.

The rest of the paper is organized as follows. Section 2 outlines the P2P network and describes the pre-existing discovery schemes in pure P2P network environments. In section 3, we propose a new discovery scheme. Section 4 discusses and analyzes the performance of our proposed scheme. Finally, Section 5 concludes this paper.

2 Backgrounds

2.1 P2P Network

P2P network is a distributed network whose participants share a part of their own resources such as processing power, storage capacity, softwares, and files/contents. The participants in the P2P network can act as a server and a client at the same time [8].

The P2P network is classified into two types: hybrid P2P network and pure P2P network. The hybrid P2P network allows the existence of central entities in its network and the central entities have an important role in the discovery process. On the other hand, in the pure P2P network, there are no central entities and each peer actively participates in the discovery process [8].

2.2 Discovery Algorithms in the Pure P2P Networks

The discovery mechanisms in pure p2P networks can be classified into two types, flooded requests model and document routing model. In this section, each type of discovery mechanism is described briefly.

(1) FRM(Flooded Requests Model)

FRM is the discovery model in which each peer does not maintain any central directory and each peer publishes information about the shared contents in the P2P network. When a peer wants to find some contents, it floods the request message through its adjacent peers. The request message is flooded to other peers repeatedly until the content is found or the maximum number of flooding steps is tried. This model is used by Gnutella [9-11].

But this model requires a lot of network bandwidth and is not scalable due to the flooded messages [9]. In Gnutella, the reply messages are routed back along the path that they came through until they reach the clients that originally issued them. The problem with this type of routing in Gnutella is that the message loss can be occurred when the reverse path is broken. To solve this problem, KaZaA [7] is introduced but the problem is not settled completely [12].

(2) DRM(Document Routing Model)
DRM is the discovery model in which contents discovery is based on document ID shared in the P2P network. Each peer routes a document to the peer whose ID is most close to the document ID. When a peer wants to find a document, it sends the request message to the most close peer to the document ID. This process is repeated until the document is found. This mechanism, however, has the problem that the document IDs must be known before posting a request for a given document. Network partitioning can also lead to an islanding problem. This model has been used by Freenet [6,9,10].

3 The Proposed Discovery Mechanism

3.1 System Architecture

We assume a P2P network environment whose members are multimedia hosts. Our proposed scheme uses three types of messages: QM, RM, and DM. Each message caused by a user request has the same Message ID.

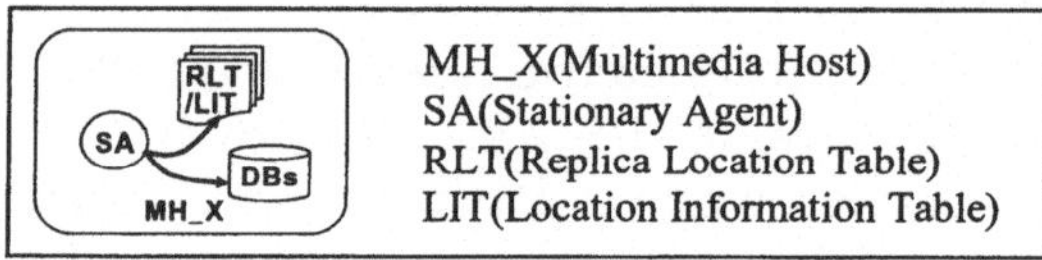

Fig. 1. The architecture of multimedia host

Figure 1 shows the components of each MH in our model. As shown in Figure 1, MH has some DBs that contain the information on its multimedia contents. MH also has SA which is an agent for contents discovery and managements of DBs and content tables such as RLT and LIT. RLT maintains the information on the contents which are locally owned including the location information on the replicas of the contents in other hosts. LIT maintains the location information on the contents that are recently requested by other hosts but are not locally owned. SA sends a QM(Query Message) to request a content, and another SA that received the QM replies to original requestor with RM(Reply Message) including the search result. SA sends DM(Delete Message) to notify the deletion of a content.

3.2 Data Structures

Figure 2 shows the structure of the content tables. Each content is described by its C_Id(Content Identifier), C_Type(Content Type), and C_Attr(Content Attribute). The mixture of these attributes is assigned as a keyword to identify the content. C_Loc(Content Location) field in RLT means the physical address of the content. The

Valid field in RLT contains the information on the validity of the content. The CH_List(Content Host List) field in RLT/LIT contains the location information of the replicas. The More field in LIT is used to decide whether MHs were added to CH_List or not.

C_Id	C_Type	C_Attr	C_Loc	C_Size	Valid	CH_List

(a) RLT : Replica Location Table

C_Id	C_Type	C_Attr	More	CH_List

(b) LIT : Location Information Table

Fig. 2. Data structures of the content tables

Figure 3 shows the structure of the messages for our discovery mechanism. In Figure 3, the O_Id(Original requestor Identifier) field in QM is set to original requestor identifier, that may be used for returning the search result. The M_Id(Message Identifier) fields in QM and DM mean the message identifier. The TTL(Time To Live) field in QM and the M_Path(Message Path) field in DM are used for preventing the message from being repeated in the P2P network. The CH_Id field in RM is set to the identifier of the MH where the content is discovered.

C_Id	C_Type	C_Attr	O_Id	M_Id	TTL	M_Path

(a) QM : Query Message

C_Id	C_Type	C_Attr	C_Loc	C_Size	CH_Id	O_Id

(b) RM : Reply Message

C_Id	C_Type	C_Attr	O_Id	M_Id	M_Path

(c) DM : Delete Message

Fig. 3. Data structures of the messages

3.3 Discovery Algorithms

Contents discovery procedure is initiated by the request of a user. The algorithm in Figure 4 shows the contents discovery procedure of SA at the original requestor. It shows the procedure from receiving a user request to updating its RLT with the search results. If the content exists in the MH, the corresponding SA sends the QM to the MHs specified in CH_List of RLT. On the other hand, if the content doesn't exist in current MH but there exist some location information in LIT, the SA sends the QM to the MHs specified in CH_List of LIT. If there is no location information for the content, the SA sends the QM to the neighbor MHs. After sending the QM, the SA waits for RM to fill the CH_List in RLT. Although the user terminates the request, SA does not stop waiting for RM because the record of CH_List helps next user to search the content faster.

The algorithm in Figure 4 is also used to maintain the location information of the contents. SA updates the location information of the contents in content table when a user adds or deletes a content to/from the MH. When a content is inserted, the SA sends the QM to search replicas of the content. As a result, the SA receives the RM and updates CH_List in RLT with the information in the RM. When a content is deleted, the SA sends the DM to the MHs in CH_List of the RLT to notify the deletion of the content. After sending the DM, the SA deletes the information associated with the content from RLT. Afterwards, each MH that receives the DM deletes the MH information from CH_List in its RLT.

```
when a SA receives a request from a user
  find an entry E in RLT with the specified keywords;
  if (there exists E) {
    send E to the user;
    send QM to each MH in CH_List;
  }
  else {
    create and insert a new entry E'into RLT with the specified keywords;
    find an entry E in LIT with the specified keywords;
    if (there exist E) {
      send QM to each MH in CH_List;
      E' in RLT = E in LIT;
    }
    else
      send QM to the neighbor peers;
  }
when the SA receives RM from another SA
  update the CH_List information in RLT;
```

Fig. 4. Contents discovery procedure of SA at original requestor

```
when SA receives a QM from another SA
  if (M_Id of the QM has already been registered in current MH)
    discard the QM;
  else {
    find an entry E in RLT with the specified keywords;
    if (there exist E) {
      send RM to the original requestor;
      send QM to each MH in CH_List;
      if (CH_List is not fully occupied)
        insert O_Id into CH_List;
    }
    else {
      find an entry E in LIT with the specified keywords;
      if (there exist E) {
        send QM to each MH in CH_List;
        if (CH_List is not fully occupied)
          insert O_Id into CH_List;
      }
      else {
        send QM to the neighbor peers;
        create a new entry E' in LIT with the specified keywords;
        insert O_Id into E'.CH_List;
        E'.More in LIT = 1;
      }
    }
  }
```

Fig. 5. Contents discovery procedure of SA in other MHs

The algorithm in Figure 5 shows the contents discovery procedure of SA in other MHs except the original requestor. When the SA in a MH receives a QM, it checks whether a QM with the same M_ID has visited the MH or not. If the QM has visited the MH before, the SA discards the QM. Otherwise, the SA checks whether there is location information on the requested content in its content tables or not. If the information exists, the SA sends the QM to each MH in CH_List of the corresponding entry. It also sends RM to the original requestor. If there is no location information on the content, the SA sends the QM to the neighbor MHs and it records O_Id to CH_List in LIT in advance because, in the future, the original requestor will have both the contents and the location information of the contents. Whenever a QM arrives at any MH, the SA records its host ID to the M_Path in QM, which will be used to reduce unnecessary traffic.

4 Performance Evaluation

We used Simlib [13] to simulate our proposed scheme and compared the performance of our scheme with that of flooded requests scheme with no cache. We ran each simulation five times with different random seeds. Our results are shown with the average values of the five runs. The parameters used in the simulation are given in Table 1.

Table 1. Simulation parameters

	No. of MHs	Size of CH_List in RLT	Size of LIT	No. of requests	No. of kind of contents
Sim-1	30~430	25	35	1000	200
Sim-2	30~430	25	35	1000	200
Sim-3	300	4~28	35	1000	200
Sim-4	300	25	5~105	1000	200

Figure 6 (Sim-1) shows the average response time according to the number of MHs. In Figure 6, we can observe that both schemes have the longer average response time, as the number of MHs increases in the system. But the average response time of our proposed scheme is better than that of flooded requests scheme, because the record of RLT and LIT made during the discovery process improves the contents discovery speed of the proposed scheme.

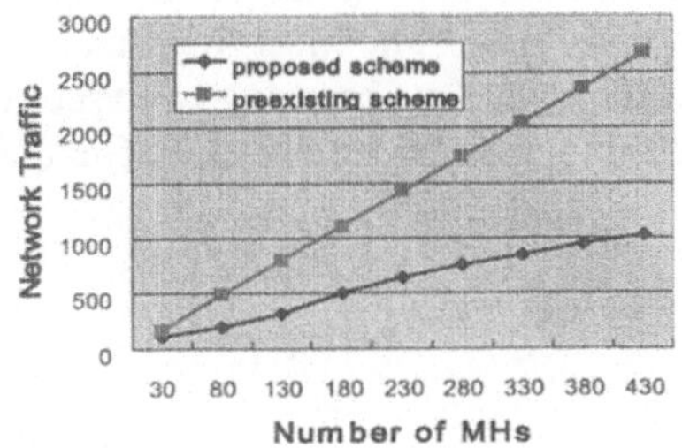

Fig. 6. Response time according to the number of MHs

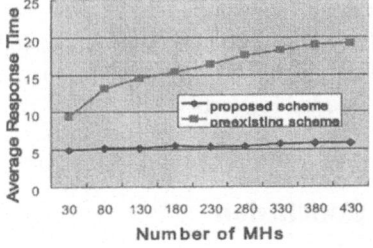

Fig. 7. Network traffic according to the number of MHs

Figure 7 (Sim-2) shows the network traffic according to the number of MHs. In Figure 7, we can observe that the more MHs incur the more network traffic in both schemes. But the amount of traffic of the proposed scheme is less than that of flooded requests scheme, because the record of RLT and LIT made during the discovery process reduces the number of QMs sent to the neighbor MHs and the duplication check of the QM at each MH also reduces unnecessary network traffic of the proposed scheme.

Figure 8 (Sim-3) shows the average response time according to the size of CH_List in RLT. In Figure 8, we can observe that the average response time of the proposed scheme is better than that of flooded requests scheme. In our proposed scheme, the larger the size of CH_List, the shorter the average response time, because the larger size of CH_List in RLT helps to store more location information on the replicas.

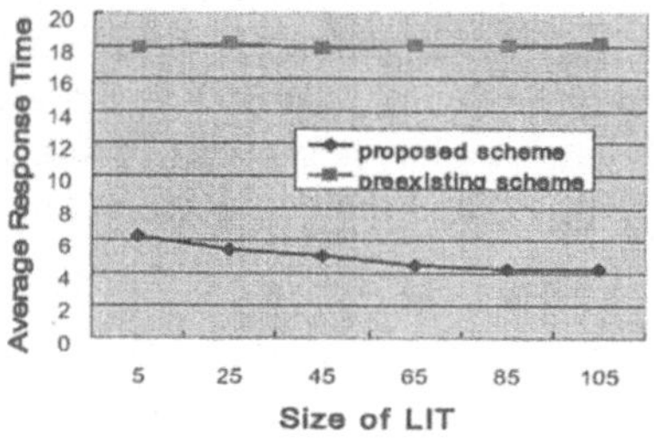

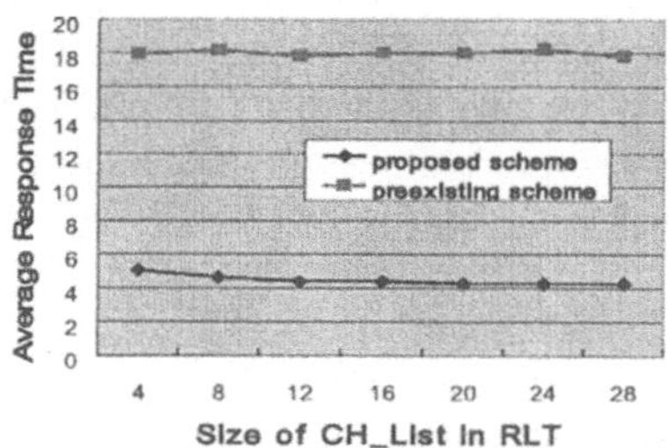

Fig. 8. Response time according to the size of CH_List in RLT

Fig. 9. Response time according to the size of LIT

Finally, Figure 9 (Sim-4) shows the average response time according to the size of LIT. In Figure 9, we can observe that the average response time of the proposed scheme is better than that of flooded requests scheme. In our proposed scheme, the larger the size of LIT, the shorter the average response time, because the larger size of LIT helps to store more location information on the contents that are recently requested by other MHs.

In this Section, we can observe that the proposed scheme has better performance in average response time and network traffic than that of flooded requests scheme, especially when the number of nodes is large. We can also see that the larger size of content tables contributes for the shorter average response time. The most important fact is that our proposed scheme can speed up average response time by using two types of content tables. Also, the scheme is more scalable and incurs less network traffic than the flooded requests scheme.

5 Conclusion

Currently, most of the multimedia service environments incur high load on central server. To solve this problem, many solutions that use P2P concepts are proposed. In P2P computing environments, contents discovery scheme is very important for efficient content services. The two typical contents discovery mechanism in pure P2P network environments are flooded requests model and document routing model. But, flooded requests model has a drawback in that the scheme requires a lot of network bandwidth, and document routing model also has some drawbacks in that the scheme requires some knowledge about the document ID and the network partition can cause the islanding problem.

In this paper, we proposed an efficient contents discovery scheme for multimedia services in pure P2P network environments. In our proposed scheme the distributed location information is maintained in each host to reduce the amount of traffic and to shorten the discovery time. The information that should be maintained in each host is the location information of the contents which are recently requested by other hosts and the location information of the replicas of the local contents. We differentiate the reply path from the request path to minimize the loss of search results occurred when the network is unsettled. We also control the traffic generated by repeated request messages in P2P networks by maintaining the list of nodes that the message went through with the message ID.

References

1. Oram, A. (ed.): Peer-to-Peer: Harnessing the Benefits of a Disruptive Technology. O'Reilly (2001)
2. IBM.: Peer to Peer Networking: Addressing Scaling Issues in Peer to Peer Architecture. http://www.research.ibm.com/smartnetwork/peer.html
3. Espinoza, F., Hamfors, O.: ServiceDesigner: A Tool to Help End-Users Become Individual Service Providers. In Proc. of the Hawaii International Conference on System Sciences (2003) 296–305
4. Napster.: http://www.napster.com
5. Clip2.: The Gnutella Protocol Specification v.0.4. (2001) http://www.ovmj.org/GNUnet/pa-pers/gnutella_protocol.pdf
6. Clarke, I., Sangberg, O., Wiley, B., and Hong, T.: Freenet: A distributed anonymous information storage and retrieval system. In Proc. of the ICSI Workshop on Design Issues in Anonymity and Unobservability (2000)
7. KaZaa.: http://www.kazaa.com
8. Schollmeier, R.: A Definition of Peer-to-Peer Networking for the Classification of Peer-to-Peer Architectures and Applications. In Proceedings of the IEEE 2001 International Conference on Peer-to-Peer Computing (2001)
9. Milojicic, D., et al.: Peer-to-Peer Computing. HP Labs Technical Report HPL-2002-57 (2002)
10. Yang, B. and Garcia-Molina, H.: Improving Search in Peer-to-Peer Networks. In Proc. 22nd International Conference on Distributed Computing Systems (2002) 5-14
11. Jovanovic, M., et al.: Scalability Issues in Large Peer-to-Peer Networks - A Case Study of Gnutella. University of Cincinnati Technical Report (2001)
12. Aitken, D., et al.: Peer-to-Peer Technologies and Protocols. http://matrix.netsoc.tcd.ie/~neo/4ba2/p2p/
13. Law, A. and Kelton, W.: Simulation Modeling and Analysis. 3rd ed. Mc Graw Hill (2001)

Distributed Computation for Diffusion Problem in a P2P-Enhanced Computing System

Jun Ni[1,2,4], Lili Huang[1,2], Tao He[1,2], Yongxiang Zhang[1,2], Shaowen Wang[1,3], Boyd M. Knosp[1], and Chinglong Lin[4]

[1]Academic Technologies-Research Services of Information Technology Services,
[2]Department of Computer Science,
[3]Department of Geography,
[4]Department of Mechanical Engineering, The University of Iowa, Iowa City, IA 52242, USA
{jun-ni, tao-he, lili-huang, shaowen-wang, boyd-knosp, ching-long-lin}@uiowa.edu

Abstract. Basic exploration of diffusion equation solvers in distributed computing systems has been a very important issue for computational fluid dynamics (CFD). This paper presents a fundamental study of a distributed computing solution for diffusive phenomena in a P2P enhanced Grid system. We propose a simple distributed system with the architecture of multi-clients and multi-servers (MCMS). Multithreading is implemented on both the client and server nodes, enabling them to communicate. This paper focuses on architecture, model implementation, multithreading, network communication, domain decomposition/composition, problem convergence, fault-tolerance, and dynamic load balancing. A discussion of the results from conducted numerical experiments is useful for performing future intensive CFD computations on Grids.

1 Introduction

Emerging technologies of Grid computing enable researchers to submit intensive computational jobs to shared computer resources [1]. With the improvements in networking, Grid systems can aggregate globally scaled resources for the next generation of CDF computations [2]. Although parallel algorithms for diffusion problems are mature in both shared and centralized distributed memory systems, conducting intensive CFD computations on P2P-enhenced Grid systems still presents challenges [4]. Pioneer studies in the deployment of CFD algorithms for large-scale computation demonstrate that a main source of parallel inefficiency is latency due to network communications [3]. Appropriate "breakup" schemes (decomposition) of the loads are crucial to avoiding greater latency. Finding new CDF algorithms for Grid computing requires extensive research and development. This study seeks primarily to develop a generalized algorithm for CFD simulations on computational Grids. We focus on a parallel solution for diffusion problems in a lightweight P2P-enhanced multi-client/multi-server system (MCMS) that simulates a Grid environment.

M. Li et al. (Eds.): GCC 2003, LNCS 3032, pp. 428–435, 2004.

This paper serves as a fundamental study of distributed computing for diffusion problems, emphasizing diffusion simulations that use multithreading client/server architecture in a Grid system. The study considers multi-thread creation, job control and termination, physical domain-decomposition, load-balance, fault tolerance, node communication, problem convergence, and memory. It depicts several important issues that impact CFD applications performed on computational Grids. The study has yielded many experiences and ideas for future research, which will help solve challenging CFD problems using Grid computing technologies. This study provides fundamental insights into CFD simulations on Grids.

2 Related Work

There are many parallel algorithms for diffusion problems. The most popular algorithm is the finite difference method (FDM) [5]. Although many alternatives have been developed [6], [7], [8], FDM is still a popular solution, which leads to a generalized solution for transport equations in thermo-fluid sciences.

Researchers have begun to deploy parallel algorithms to distributed environments. Weissman recently presented a method that utilizes adapting data techniques (ADT) in distributed PC clusters [9]. According to Weissman, evaluating his parallel computing was a complex process. The difficulties were due to complicated physical problems, dynamic networking, serious data communications, heterogeneous resources, tedious distributing algorithms, load balance, and fault-tolerance. Recently, Garbey and co-workers developed the Aitken-Schwarz algorithm (ASA), which modifies the traditional Schwarz algorithm by imposing an artificial inner interface. This interface serves as a "virtual boundary" for each sub-domain submitted to a distributed computational node [10], [11]. The ASA approach is highly tolerant to low bandwidth and high latency. It therefore decreases large data transferring and is suitable to parallel computing over distributed computational nodes. Along with the advantages of this algorithm come relative complexity and inefficiency, hence, low performance.

3 System Design and Node Communication

3.1 Experimental System Using MCSM Model

We designed a simple MCMS-enhanced system [13] to simulate a distributed environment. The system architecture provides efficient communications among customer/service (client/server) nodes. The client serves as a job manager and distributor, handling domain decomposition, load balance, and convergence. Intensive computations are performed on server (computational) nodes. The system assumes full authorization to use all participating nodes in order to eliminate security implementations so we may focus on algorithms development and multithreading. The MCM architecture has been successfully implemented in testing software named

H3S (Fig. 1). It has several functional components that allow users to quickly and easily develop a system for deploying applications.

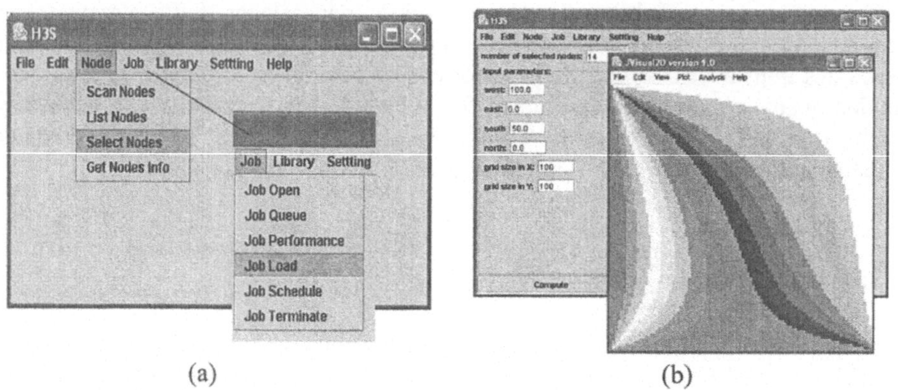

(a) (b)

Fig. 1. (a) H3S for scanning and selecting available nodes, opening, queuing, and scheduling jobs, and measuring performance; (b) H3S GUI for testing system feasibility of diffusion simulation in Grids and JVisual2D (a tool for visualizing and analyzing data results).

3.2 System Hardware and Software Development

The system hardware components, imitating a heterogeneous environment, are fourteen legacy G3-Macs with MacOSX (350MHz, 128/265MB RAM) and four legacy Pentium III-PCs with WindwoXP (700MHz and 128MB RAM); these aggregate through a 3Com switch (SuperstackII 3300-24ports). The system is developed in Java to preserve platform independency. Each node has its own TCP/IP address, allowing it be used as either a client or a server.

3.3 Multithreading in the P2P Communications

Each computational node has a server socket with a specified port number. Through the socket, multiple connection sockets for data I/O can be established. The server socket is always available so it can keep receiving jobs from, and returning data to, clients. Each server contains at least one thread for performing a computation; and each thread handles specific data I/O, performs a "local" computation, checks local convergence, and controls job status.

At the client node, two multithreading models are tested.

The first model basically creates multi-threads within the main iterative procedure with a "global convergence" check-point. Each thread submits one sub-task at a time to its own corresponding computational node. Each must wait for all threads to return their computations before initiating the next task. The model's implementation is simple, but performance is low.

The second model keeps each thread continuously performing sub-tasks until "global convergence" is achieved. In this approach, the domain decomposition/ composition algorithm is built within the run() method implemented in the thread class. Each thread becomes more productive in generating, distributing, and completing jobs, thereby significantly enhancing performance. Following is a sample segment:

```
public void run(){
  while(DiffusionMTClient.allThreadsOn){
    ...
  osToServer.writeInt(DiffusionMTClient.iterLocalMax);
   osToServer.writeDouble
     (DiffusionMTClient.localTolerence);
   osToServer.flush();
   ...
   oosToServer.writeObject(subObj);
   oosToServer.flush();
   subObj = (HPC2DArray) oisFromServer.readObject();
   updateGloalObject();
   if(DiffusionMTClient.checkConverge())
     DiffusionMTClient.controlThread[subObj.getID()]
       =false;
   else
     DiffusionMTClient.controlThread[subObj.getID()]
       =true;
    decompositionLoalObject();
    DiffusionMTClient.copyArray();
    DiffusionMTClient.iterGlobal++;
    ...
  }  ///end of while
  ...
}
```

3.4 Object Streaming in Multithread Communication

The authors use Java's `DataObjectStream` to exchange sub-domain packed data as an object of the `HPC2DArray` class passing between a client and multiple server nodes. `HPC2DArray` encloses 2D CFD data. After the data is computed on the server side, it returns to the client for global variable updating. Java's object streaming is easier to implement and more flexible for various CFD data formats.

Such object passing has some disadvantages: (1) a large amount of data is being transferred; (2) the data is not in XML format; (3) continual type casting causes memory leaks in Java garbage collections.

4 Mathematical Modeling and Domain Decomposition

The diffusion problem can be mathematically governed by a diffusive equation, namely the Laplace equation: $\nabla^2\Psi = 0$. The physical domain is decomposed into 1-D slab sub-domains [14]. Each sub-domain is submitted to an individual node for intensive computation, using an explicit Jacobi's iterative scheme: $\psi_{(i,j)} = 0.25(\psi_{(i+1,j)} + \psi_{(i-1,j)} + \psi_{(i,j+1)} + \psi_{(i,j-1)})$, where i and j are the x and y indices of uniform geometrical grid points. The neighboring sub-domains are shared, with overlapping regions of width, or δ, through which the physical quantity can be passed from a sub-region handled by one node to an adjoining sub region handled by another node.

Two decomposition algorithms are tested. The first algorithm employs a static method. Each computational node statically works on the pre-selected sub region during the entire computational procedure (Fig. 2). With the second algorithm, we introduced a dynamic scenario in which each computational node works different sub-domains on a rotating basis. That is, the i+1th sub-domain is assigned to the ith computation node, while the last sub-domain is assigned to the first computational node. Although this approach causes fluctuation during the converged iterative process, it balances the loading of distributed jobs performed heterogeneously, thereby increasing fault tolerance and performance.

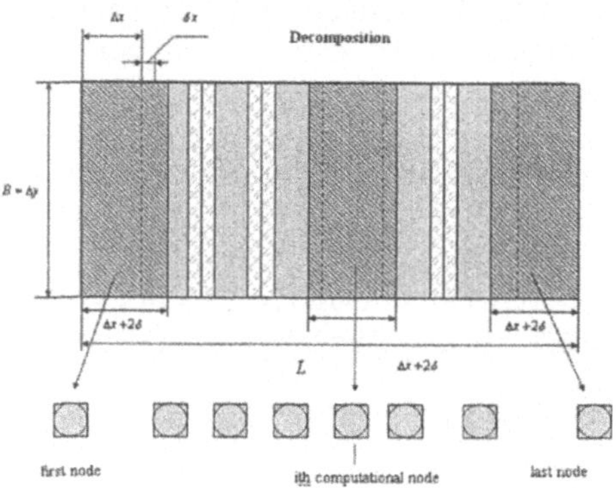

Fig. 2. 1-D slab-decomposition. L and B are "global" domain sizes in horizontal and vertical directions. The size of each sub-domain is $\Delta x + 2\delta$ and *B*. Each thread statically or dynamically selects one sub-domain during the computational process.

5 Experiments

Several diffusion simulations are conducted on a 100x100 square domain. The first task is to test static domain-decomposition. Fig. 3 shows the residual report during the converged iterative procedure.

In static decomposition, convergence is smooth and stable, yet it is also relatively slow. Each thread has to wait for all the other threads to finish their subtasks before going on to the next step. The accumulated global time strongly depends on the performance of all servers, which decreases fault tolerance and overall performance. By contrast, in dynamic domain-decomposition, each thread continues submitting sub-tasks until the convergence of the global domain is completed. This approach avoids delays, thereby increasing performance rate.

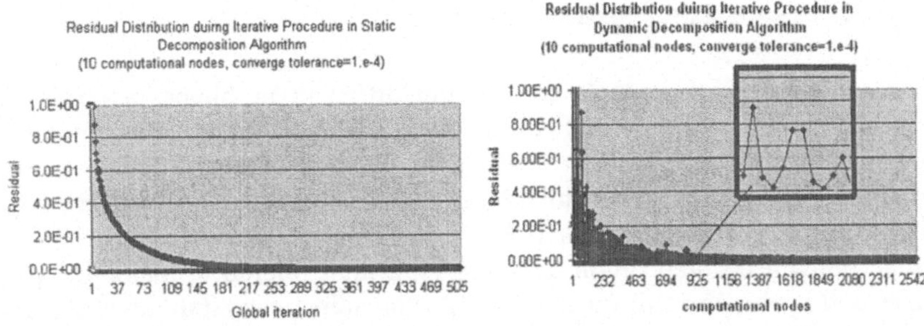

Fig. 3. The convergence in iterative processes in static and dynamic decomposition.

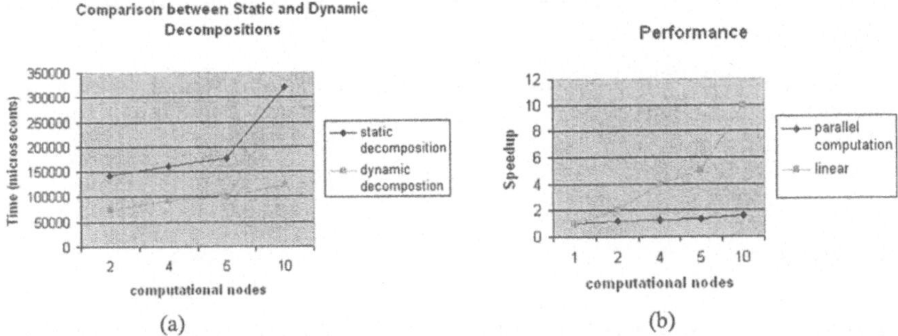

Fig. 4. (a) Performance benchmarks between static and dynamic decompositions; (b) speedup measurement of computations with a domain size 200x200.

A shortcoming of dynamic decomposition is that the converging process fluctuates, as shown in Fig 4(b). The disturbance is caused by the data synchronization in multi-threading and latency delays in communications. This area will require intensive study. Our current approach to reducing the degree of fluctuation is to impose a relaxation factor: $\psi^{g}_{(i,j)} = (1-\varpi)\psi^{g}_{(i,j)} + \varpi\psi^{l}_{(i,j)}$ This moderates the rate of dating of the global variable, where the superscripts g and 1 stand for global variable sub-domain variable, respectively. If ϖ is small, the updating is less aggressive. We suggest using a low relaxation value in dynamic decomposition. The performance comparison between static and dynamic domain-decomposition algorithms can be seen in Fig. 5(a). Fig. 5(b) illustrates that if we increase the domain size, the computation has a moderate speedup, since the loading of computational nodes are heavier. The more independent and intensive are computations on server nodes, the higher the performance will be. However, increasing the domain size results in an out-of-memory error message due to the slow memory flushing of Java's garbage collection.

6 Conclusion and Future Work

Traditional iterative procedures for solving diffusion problems in Grids may not achieve desirable results due to network latency and slow multithreading communications between client and server nodes. Domain decomposition, job distribution, load-balance, fault tolerance, and convergence checking are all heavily loaded to the client node, which reduces performance and efficiency. By contrast, dynamic domain decomposition achieves high fault tolerance, maintains good load balance, and increases performance. In multi-threading, each individual thread should intelligently check the global status of convergence before submitting new jobs. Future studies will focus on (1) how the client node intelligently selects efficient computational nodes, (2) how to effectively discard class-casting memory; (3) how to reduce the size of data transferred by integrating the ASA algorithm. This fundamental study provides insights into CFD applications in Grid computing environments.

Acknowledgements. The project is financially supported by the Internal Funding Program/Mathematical and Physical Sciences (MPSFP) program at The University of Iowa.

References

1. Foster, I. : The Gird: A New Infrastructure for 21st Century Science. Physics Today, **55** (2): 42. (2002)
2. Foster, I., Kesselman, C., Tuecke, S.: The Anatomy of the Grid: Enabling Scalable Virtual Organizations. Int. J. of Supercomputer Applications. **15** (2001)
3. Barnard S., Biswas R., Saini S., Wijngaart R. Van der, Yarrow M., Zechter L., Foster I., Larsson O.: Large-Scale Distributed Computational Fluid Dynamics on the Information Power Grid using Globus. In: Proc. of Frontiers '99. (1999)
4. Casanova, H.: Distributed Computing Research Issues in Grid Computing. Quarterly Newsletter for the ACM Special Interest Group on Algorithms and Computation Theory (SIGACT News). **33** (2002)
5. Smith G.D: Numerical Solution of Partial Differential Equations. Oxford University Press, New York (1978)
6. Davies A.J. Mushtaq J. Radford L.E. and Crann D.: The Numerical Laplace Transform Solution Method on as a Distributed Memory Architecture. In: Power H. and Cesares L. (eds): Application of High Performance Computing V. CMP (1997). 245-254
7. Zeng H, and Zhu J.: An Efficient Parallel ADI Algorithm for Solving 3-D Convection Diffusion Equations with Neumann Boundary Conditions. In: 2002 International Conference on Parallel Processing Workshops (ICPPW'02). August 18 - 21 , Vancouver, B.C., Canada (2002)
8. Oritigosa E.M., Romero L.F., and Ramos, J.I.: Three-dimensional Simulation of Spiral Wave in Reacting and Diffusing Media on DSM Computers. In: Ingber, M., Power H., Brebbia (eds): Application of High-performance Computing in Engineering VI, WIT Press (2000)
9. Weissman J.B: Prediction the Cost and Benefit of Adapting Data Parallel Applications in Clusters, J. of Parallel and Distributed Computing, **62** (2002) 1248-1271

10. Barberou N., Garbey, M., Hess, M., Resch, M., Rossi, T., Toivvanen J., and Tromeur-Dervout D: An Aitken-Schwarz Method for Efficient Metacomputing of Elliptic Equations. In: Fourteenth International Conference on Domain Decomposition Methods (2002)
11. Barberou N., Garbey, M., Hess, M., Resch, M., Rossi, T., Toivvanen J., and Tromeur-Dervout D: Efficient Metacomputing of Elliptic Linear and Non-linear Problems. J. Parallel and Distributed Computing, **63** (2003) 564-577
12. Lee H., Carpenter B., Fox, G., Lim, S.: HPJava: Towards Programming Support for High-Performance Grid-Enabled Applications. In: Proceedings of the International Conference on Parallel and Distributed Processing Techniques and Applications. (PDPTA'03) Las Vegas June (2003)
13. Loo A., Choi Y.K., and Bloor C.: Free Upgrade of Computer Power with Java, Web-based Technology and Parallel Computing. In: Ingber, M., Power H., Brebbia (eds): Application of High-performance Computing in Engineering VI, WIT Press (2000)
14. Newhouse, S., Mayer, A., Darlington J.: A Software Architecture for HPC Grid Applications (Research Note). Euro-Par (2000) 686-689

Applications of Peer to Peer Technology in CERNET

Chang-ji Wang and Jian-Ping Wu

Network Research Center, Tsinghua University, Beijing, China 100084
wangcj@cernet.edu.cn

Abstract. Public Key Infrastructure (PKI) is well recognized as the only possible complete solution for network security problem nowadays, and Peer-to-Peer (P2P) has also been viewed as one of the most potential network technology today. The design of CERNET (China Education and Research Network) PKI, which make the best of P2P technology to implement certification revocation information distribution, was presented in this paper. P2P based content distribution in CCERT (China Education and Research Network Computer Emergency Response Team) was also discussed.

1 Introduction

Public key cryptography is widely recognized as the technology to develop and deploy authentication, integrity, confidentiality, and non-repudiation services. The services typical of public key cryptography require a PKI in charge of securely managing keys/certificates for complex and large-scale organizations.

Despite widely recognized importance of PKI, PKI deployment and use has not met its expectations. Some significant issues in the development of PKI are still to be solved. Certificate revocation is one of the many challenges faced by PKI. Although many schemes have been proposed for certificate revocation, almost every scheme suffers from efficient distribution of certificate revocation information.

P2P technology has risen to prominence due to the success of free file-sharing networks like Napster and Gnutella. In P2P networks, each peer host contributes its local resources to serve the common good, and may benefit from resources contributed by other peers in return. P2P applications have emerged as a popular way to share huge amounts of data, compute cycles, knowledge/expertise, and other resources.

As an emerging technology, P2P presents serious security challenges. In order address the need for confidentiality, integrity, and availability, a robust method of authentication, encryption, and non-repudiation must be built in. Integration with PKI is the most obvious solution. In this paper, we present the design of a hierarchical PKI model for CERNET, which make the best of P2P technology to implement certificate revocation information distribution. P2P based content distribution in CCERT was also discussed.

M. Li et al. (Eds.): GCC 2003, LNCS 3032, pp. 436-439, 2004.

2 CERNET PKI with P2P CRL Distribution

The CERNET PKI adopted hierarchy PKI model. The CERNET Root CA is located in Tsinghua University, which is responsible for operation and management of campus CA nationwide. And every university sets up its own campus CA. Campus CA takes charge of issuing and managing end-entity certificate in his domain.

Efficient and timely distribution of certificate revocation information is one of the biggest challenges currently faced by PKI. Many schemes have been proposed to deal with disseminating the certificate revocation information. CRL (certification revocation list) and OCSP (On Line Certificate Status Protocol) were two standard certificate revocation schemes adopted by IETF, and CRL was the well deployed certification revocation scheme in current PKI.

Under the CRL scheme, a list of revoked certificate, known as CRL, which is within its validity period is periodically generated by CA for its domain. All the revoked certificates by the certificate issuer must be made available to all the end-entities, which need to verify a certificate. Scheme that uses CRL do not need to have trusted directory because the CRL is digitally signed by CA.

The revocation scheme that use CRL to distribute certificate status information can be divided into three steps. Firstly, CA periodically generates CRL for all its revoked certificates. Each CRL has two dates field named thisUpdate and nextUpdate. A CRL is said to be valid if the current date is greater or equal to thisUpdate and smaller than nextUpdate date. Secondly, CA will send the generated CRL to a LDAP directory server where all the end-entities have access. Finally, the end-entities query the LDAP server for a CRL.

The existing CRL schemes place a considerable processing, communication, and storage overhead on CA and LDAP server, as well as the relying parties. Because the big file size for CRL will increase the network delay and hence causing the end-entities to wait for longer time. At the same time, when the number of relying end-entities is big, the query that has to be served by LDAP server will be very high.

CERNET PKI makes the best of P2P technology to implement CRL distribution. The CERNET Root CA and all campus CAs construct a *hybrid P2P network*, and Campus CA and all the end-entities in his domain construct a *pure P2P network*. In the following discussion, we assume there is no pre-caching of CRL (i.e., the end-entities will only query the CRL to LDAP server when it needed to validate a certificate), and once the CRL is obtained from a LDAP server, it is being cache in local directory. Further validation will refer to this cache until it expired before query CRL to the LDAP server again.

Algorithm for GetCurrentCRL describes the procedure for getting current CRL in certificate validation by an end-entity in our proposed model. The procedure is different from existing CRL in that there is extra query to the direct peer for current CRL. As seen in the *GetCurrentCRL* procedure, every hit of valid CRL on local cache and direct peers will reduce the access make to LDAP server and therefore reduced the processing over at LDAP server.

```
Algorithm for GetCurrentCRL

1. Check local cache for current CRL

2. If (no CRL or not CRL valid) then

  3. Check for current CRL in direct end-entity peers

    4. If (no valid CRL in end-entity peers) then

      5. Check for current CRL from Campus LDAP server

        6. If (no valid CRL in Campus LDAP server)

           7. Get a link to current CRL from CERNET CA's
LDAP server

           8. Get current CRL from the link

        9. Else Get current CRL from Campus LDAP server

    10. Else use CRL from end-entity peers

11. Else use CRL in local cache
```

3 P2P Based Content Distribution in CERNET

CCERT (China Education and Research Network Computer Emergency Response Team) is the first CSIRT (Computer Security Incident Response Team) in China who provides computer security related incident response service for people and organizations all over China. It is imperative for CCERT to efficiently and securely distribute content (such as patches for operation system and updates for virus-detection software, tools and so on.) with security incidents increase.

There are two kind of service architectures employed to provide content distribution services on the Internet: traditional centralized client-server and distributed Peer-to-Peer. In the client-server model, manager distributes content via web by uploading the resource file on to a web server. But the bandwidth limitations lead to poor performance and scalability of the delivery process in client-server model. In P2P based content distribution, apart from the original server, the peers requesting the content will also start distributing it. P2P based content distribution provides more resilience and higher availability, but security is the major problems that hinder the P2P deployment, peers must trust the confidentiality, integrity, authenticity, non-repudiation of all content they will receive over the network.

CCERT intend to adopt P2P based content distribution with CERNET PKI to provide security. The CCERT content distribution system is two-layer structure approximately. CCERT and campus CERTs (Computer Emergency Response Team) constitute a *hybrid P2P* as Napster network. Campus CERT and all the end-entities in the domain construct a *pure P2P*. Instead of making millions of individuals contact with the CCERT Web site, campus CERT contact the CCERT Web site, and then campus CCERT pass on the content to end-entities in his domain.

Our P2P based content distribution system is not only more efficient than routine Web downloads, but more secure. Each participant owns a digital certificate which can provide confidentiality, integrity, authenticity, non-repudiation, and users of each campus have to go outside their campus network only a few times to get the content. Most of the networking takes place inside the campus network, presumably protected by a firewall and the general LAN architecture.

The CCERT server holds an indexed list of all contents together with information about the peers (campus CERT nodes) hosting these files as Napster network. It is a very efficient way to search and distribute files and other resources. The CCERT server checks its indexes and responds to every request with a list of matching filenames together with campus CERT node addresses of the hosting machines. The requesting campus CERT node will then be able to select a target campus CERT node from the list and send a download request directly to the target campus CERT node. The campus P2P network environment will be formed automatically when peers log into the system and establish connections to other peers as *Gnutella network*.

4 Discussions and Future Works

In this paper, we presented the design of CERNET PKI, which make the best of P2P technology to implement certification revocation information distribution. And P2P based content distribution in CCERT was also discussed. We will focus our researches on P2P based anti-spam handling and reporting system.

References

1. Housley R. etc al.: Internet X.509 Public Key Infrastructure Certificate and Certificate Revocation List (CRL) Profile. RFC 3280, Internet Engineering Task Force, April 2002.
2. Roman K.: An Overview of Peer-to-Peer Topologies. Distributed Systems Group, Technical University of Vienna, 2003. http://www.infosys.tuwien.ac.at/.
3. Lee H., Jim K.: An Adaptive Authentication Protocol based on Reputation for Peer-to-Peer System. Symposium on Cryptography and Information Security, 2003.
4. Gnutella. www.gnutelliums.com.
5. Freenet. http://freenetproject.org/lang/en/.

PSMI: A JXTA 2.0-Based Infrastructure for P2P Service Management Using Web Service Registries

Feng Yang [1], Shouyi Zhan [1], and Fuxiang Shen [2]

[1] Department of Computer Science and Engineering, Beijing Institute of Technology, Beijing, 100081, P.R. China
{mryangfeng, Zhan_shouyi}@263.net
[2] Communication and Software lab, Institute of Command Automation of Navy, Beijing, 100036, P.R. China

Abstract. Peer-to-peer (P2P) computing has been becoming popular due to direct interaction and self-organization. However, the ability of managing peer resource based on service content and type has been observed to be poor in current systems. We proposed a new infrastructure called PSMI in this paper for peer service management and Web based development. It provides a type based classification of index mechanism in JXTA architecture. We also represent some attributes of service to achieve better knowledge of content and service type of peers distributed in a P2P network. In addition, we construct a Web Service based registry as the portal to help any peer with only a web browser access to service. At last, the data of an emulating program shows the performance of peer service management is improved in the JXTA architecture.

1 Introduction

Unlike client-server or Web-based computing, which is today's traditional distributed computing model, peer-to-peer (P2P) computing offered a intuitive approach that all members share a part of their own resource (service and content) and play roles as resource providers as well as resource consumers [1]. It has potential to overcome several limitation of client (browser)-server computing such as scalability, single point of failure and bottleneck at the server, because peers can directly find and access other peers often without requiring a central server.

At present, various new systems in different application domains have been built based on P2P computing. However, these popular applications development based on P2P network is inefficient as developers solving the same problems and duplicating similar infrastructure implementation. In addition, most applications often address a single function, run primarily on a specific platform, use their own protocol or specification and are unable to communicate and share resource with other applications.

These drawbacks to P2P solutions have been recently recognized by Sun Microsystems, which announced the Project JXTA to provide a platform with the basic functions necessary for a P2P application. JXTA technology seeks to overcome these shortcomings with defining common protocols that allow for shared infrastructure and

M. Li et al. (Eds.): GCC 2003, LNCS 3032, pp. 440–445, 2004.

interoperability [2]. But it would be another potential problem that is a global distributed resource management in a whole P2P network. Compared to P2P computing, Web Service is a more scalable and robust solution to manage global distributed resource, lookup and invocate remote services. With Web Service standards such as UDDI, WSDL and SOAP maturing so quickly, some attempts are being made to apply them to organize and manage shared resource in a P2P network [3] [4].

This paper proposes a P2P resource management infrastructure, Peer Service Management Infrastructure (PSMI), which is based on JXTA 2.0 platform and Web Service registries. The primary goal of PSMI is to provide an efficient global publication subscribing and discovery service in a JXTA network based on publish-subscribe model. Moreover, PSMI provides a web-based interface using Web Service Registry (WSR) that is a special rendezvous with Web Service function. We also compared PSMI with a share resource distributed index of JXTA, and evaluated the performance of this infrastructure.

2 The JXTA 2.0 Architecture

In order to provide the common functions necessary for P2P applications, JXTA is developing an open P2P computing platform with basic building blocks and service, which provides a common set of open protocols for higher-level functions. JXTA architecture is divided into three layers [2]: core layer, services layer and applications layer.

The JXTA core encapsulates minimal and essential primitives that are common to P2P networking, in which the functions of peer groups, peer pipes, peer advertisements, and peer IDs are provided. It also provides peer monitoring and security mechanisms, which allows one peer to monitor other members of the same peer group and can be used to implement P2P network management such as peer metering, load balance, network connection and bandwidth [5].

The main facilities provided in services layer include two levels of network services: peer service and peer group service. Examples of network services are searching and indexing, directory, resource aggregation and renting, protocol translation, authentication, and PKI (Public Key Infrastructure) services [6].

In this layer, the main function of peer service management within JXTA network has been primarily accomplished with peer group and rendezvous, which maintain an index of advertisements published by peers to provide an efficient mechanism for propagating discovery requests by using a shared resource distributed index (SRDI) [6]. Peer group and rendezvous provide service management such as peer publishing new advertisement, deleting non-response peer, and discovery of other peer service.

The applications layer includes implementation of integrated applications, such as instant messaging, document and resource sharing, enterprise collaborative application, P2P Email systems, distributed auction systems, and many others.

3 The PSMI Architecture

Although JXTA has provided fundamental functions necessary to enable to build and deploy interoperable P2P services and applications, it still lacks an effective approach for a large number of peer services management and web based service development. Attempting to solve such problems, we present a new infrastructure called PSMI to manage peer service in JXTA. We have structured the PSMI as three layers: Web Service Registry (WSR), three kinds of services and the Service Type based Classification of Index (SCI), as shown in Figure 1.

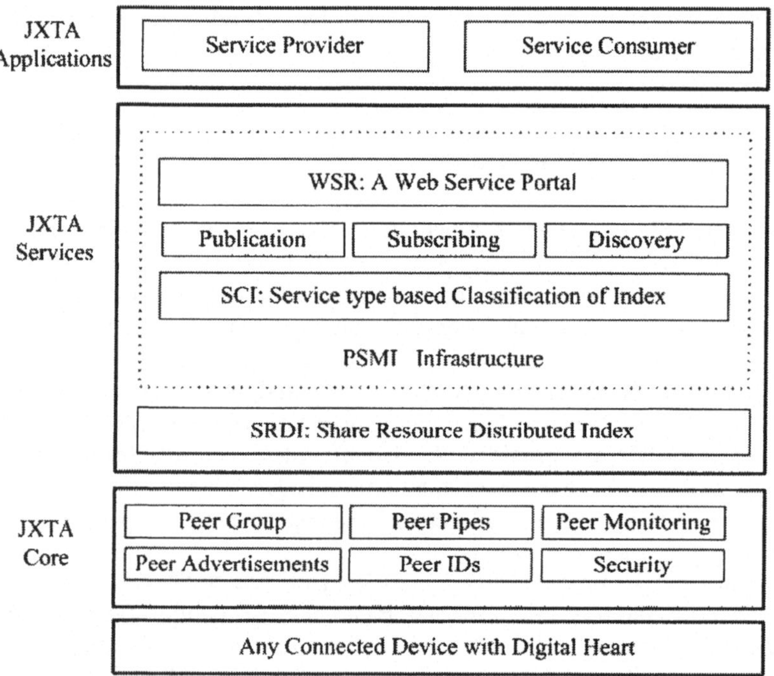

Fig. 1. PSMI and its position in JXTA architecture

In SRDI, rendezvous just maintain a single index of service advertisements published by their edge peers [7]. Compared to SRDI, SCI uses multiple indices of service advertisements distinguished by service type. When a peer consumer initiates a request to discover a type of service, the corresponding index of this type is selected from all indices and then SRDI is used to look for peers or other rendezvous. Rather than searching all services registered in a single index, SCI rejects many irrelevant peers included in other indices. As a result, bandwidth of the uninvolved peers is saved, especially some slow peers that are excluded from the searching domain.

Furthermore, in order to address the problem of "lookback" caused by excessive propagation of requests [8], a Time To Live (TTL) attribute (hop count) is made to specify the maximum number of times the request can be forwarded. And we have also defined other attributes for describing the services that are tabulated in Table 1.

Table 1. Attributes of service provide by peer provider

Service Type	Expiration	QoS	Security	TTL
Music sharing	10	B	Yes	4
Instant messaging	1000	C	No	7
...	...	...	...	...

Except for TTL has been described above, the Expiration attribute defines the expiration days of a peer service, which means this service is considered valid if expiration is not equal to zero. An expiration of "zero" means that advertisement of this service will be refreshed or be eliminated in the index. The next attribute for the service is the QoS. As an example, we have considered three levels: A, B, and C, corresponding to delay-sensitiveness, throughput-sensitiveness, and loss-sensitiveness, respectively. As shown in Table1, music sharing would be throughput-sensitiveness, and instant messaging would be loss-sensitiveness. The third attribute refers to the security of a peer service because some services may require the use of a secure protocol and authentication. By combining these attributes, large number of peer services that do not correspond with consumer's request and old dead peers (according to expiration) may be excluded from the selected index.

As an Interface between PSMI and applications, Web Service Registry (WSR) is a special rendezvous that supports Web Service function. When a service provider wants to issue one's own service advertisement, it defines its service with corresponding parameters in Table1 and then registers it on the WSR through a web browser (called Publication Service). Any peer that needs service can access the WSR to get such index of service advertisements.

In three kinds of service that PSMI offers, discovery service may be used popularly. This is followed by description of the algorithm for discovery service.

When an service query is issued from Peer A, the query is sent to Peer A's WSR and this algorithm will be run as follow:

1. WSR checks at first whether there is an index of this service type. If it has, it searches the index with attribute provided by query and forwards the query to matching edge peers. These edge peers will directly send their detailed advertisements to Peer A.
2. WSR revises some attributes of query, such as TTL. The Zero of TTL means the end of query.
3. If TTL is more than Zero, WSR chooses its neighbors that include the index of this type according to the algorithm of SRDI.
4. And it propagates the query to these WSR.

When the query reaches the next WSR, this algorithm will be retrieved from 1 to 4.

4 Evaluation

To demonstrate the feasibility and validation of PSMI, we implemented the algorithm for discovery service of SRDI and PSMI by developing a Java program based on JXTA 2.0 and JDK 1.4.0. We assumed a P2P network setting in program that has 1000 peers including 900 edge peers, which published their services on 100 rendezvous. Within them, 200 edge peers published same type of services that would be discovered by this test. Then, the test was performed by sending a request at different values of TTL and recording the numbers of involved peers.

From the left side of Figure 2, it is noticeable that numbers of involved peers using SRDI are greatly higher than that using PSMI. This is the main reason that it puts all service advertisements edge peers published in one index rather than multiple indices divided by service type. It is another indication that the process of discovering all peers in PSMI (at TTL = 5) is faster than in SRDI.

We define success rate of SRDI is the number of matching peers divided by the one of involved peers. As involved peers in PSMI include edge peers and rendezvous joined in discovery process, its success rate is the number of edge peers divided by that of involved peers. Comparing the data for success rate as show in the right side of Figure 2, we see that the success rate of PSMI is significantly higher than SRDI.

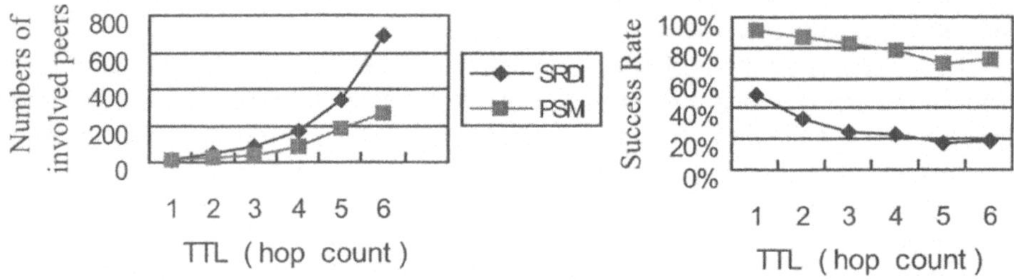

Fig. 2. Evaluation result

This Figure also shows a problem that the success rate of PSMI is decreased when it has also retrieved all peers at TTL equals to 5. We find the reason is that quite a number of rendezvous participated in this process and caused "lookback" discussed above along with the value of TTL increased. The number of these rendezvous to send query circulating was accounted repeatedly. We will solve it in future.

5 Conclusions

A new infrastructure called PSMI has been proposed in this paper for peer service management in the P2P application and Web based service registration. The infrastructure provides a service type-based classification of index mechanism for efficiently building publication subscribing and discovery services in JXTA architecture. We also represent some attributes of service to achieve better knowledge of content and type of peer service distributed in a P2P network. In addition, we construct a Web Service based registry as the portal to help any peer with only a web browser access to service. It provides a very flexible and efficient environment to manage peer services in the P2P architecture.

References

1. R. Scholl Meier, "A Definition of Peer-to-Peer Networking for the Classification of Peer-to-Peer Architectures and Applications", Proceedings of the First International Conference on Peer-to-Peer Computing (P2P'01), IEEE, 2002, PP 101-102
2. Sun Microsystems, Inc. "Project JXTA v2.0: Java Programmer's Guide", May 2003
3. C. Yau, "Creating Peer-To-Peer Middleware From Web Services", Intel Developer Update Magazine, September 2001
4. Available at http://www.jxtra.org
5. Sun Microsystems, Inc. "JXTA metering and Monitoring Project version 1.0", by Project JXTA http://www.jxta.org 2003
6. Sun Microsystems, Inc. "JXTA v2.0 Protocols Specification", by Project JXTA http://www.jxta.org 2003
7. Bernard Traversat, Mohamed Abdelaziz, Eric Pouyoul "Project JXTA: A Loosely-Consistent DHT Rendezvous Walker algorithm " by Project JXTA http://www.jxta.org 2003
8. Brendon J. Wilson "JXTA" Published by New Riders 2002 PP 24-28

CIPS-P2P: A Stable Coordinates-Based Integrated-Paid-Service Peer-to-Peer Infrastructure

Yunfei Zhang[1], Shaolong Li[1], Changjia Chen[1], and Shu Zhang[2]

[1]Beijing Jiaotong University, Beijing, 100044, P.R. China
hishigh@sohu.com, lovelyboyleee@etang.com
[2] Southeast University, Nanjing, 210096, P.R. China zhang_shu417@sohu.com

Abstract. We propose CIPS-P2P, a stable coordinates-based integrated-paid-service peer-to-peer infrastructure and its implementation. We are trying to integrate the characteristics of Grid computing and p2p technologies. We develop a novel Internet economy model. This model is for certain appealing for end users and makes contents and services on the Internet much richer. Network coordinates are adopted to improve the performance of distance-sensitive applications. Credit and bonus point are used not only to ensure PC-earning realization, but to keep the network more stable. User programmable mechanism is employed to facilitate the end users to launch new services in their own nodes. We illustrate medium/small scale Internet computing under this infrastructure.

1 Introduction

Consider an urgent small scale task that needs only several or some tens of collaborative nodes. Grid[3] and p2p networks are not fit for such computation. The reasons are as follows. First, the admission control and special configurations in Grid are too complex for users who need quick entries and quick feedbacks. Next, although Open Grid Services Architecture (OGSA) has been proposed to ease the users to join, efforts in OGSA standardization are still on the fly. Similarly current p2p systems cannot solve this problem efficiently mainly because nodes join and leave the network arbitrarily. It brings much instability to the network and therefore does not fit for computation either.

In this paper we propose CIPS-P2P, a stable coordinates-based integrated-paid-service peer-to-peer infrastructure to meet such demands. Our infrastructure aims at creating a new Internet commerce model, i.e., nodes make profits using their on-the-shelf resources to provide services for other nodes. This infrastructure has strengths as follows. Firstly, it integrates services of Grid and p2p computing to form an integrated-service p2p platform. So far, both Grid and p2p systems having been deployed are single-serviced. Our infrastructure provides COM interfaces[2] to supports integrated-services and ease the developers for further developing novel applications. Secondly, every node is provided with network coordinates by base node cluster to facilitate peer choice especially for distance-sensitive applications.

M. Li et al. (Eds.): GCC 2003, LNCS 3032, pp. 446–451, 2004.

Finally, this infrastructure provides paying and credit mechanism for realizing the new Internet economy model. It ensures the served nodes to pay and the serving node to gain. Therefore the value chain in the Internet exists not only between the ICP and its subscribers, but between these peers. The user programmable mechanism also enforces this model by impulsing end users not only to share their resources but also to initiate services. The paying and credit mechanism has also an effect to make the system more stable. As far as we know, this paying and credit mechanism is proposed in p2p networks and adopted in the network scalability first.

2 CIPS-P2P: Entities and Their Operations

CIPS-P2P is illustrated in Figure1. It is essentially a p2p network. Besides peers existing in every p2p network, there are two more parts in CIPS-P2P, including base node cluster and bank server. Note that although base nodes are shown close between one anther, they are not necessary to be in a local place physically.

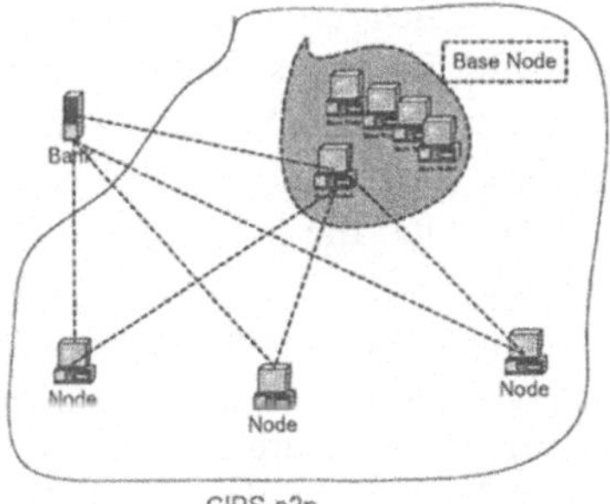

Fig. 1. CIPS-P2P Infrastructure

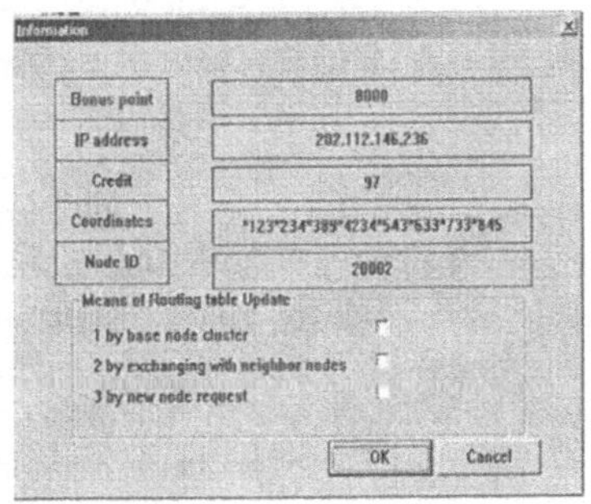

Fig. 2. Node Information Snapshot

2.1 Base Node Cluster

Base node cluster allocates nodeID for each new joined node, measures its network coordinates and notifies bank server of creating a new record for this node. In addition, base node cluster maintains available task list and node list. The available task list follows FIFO and the available node list is ranked by a hybrid FIFO and high credit priority mechanism. Note that even for the new nodes, when base node cluster is temporarily unavailable, they can still join in CIPS-P2P just like other p2p networks to finish the basic operations without network coordinates.

Network Coordinates Generation and Deployment. Our system uses a predicting Internet network distance with coordinates-based approach developed by T. S. Eugene Ng et al[1]. [1] studied the sensitivity of landmark nodes number to the measurement accuracy to find that more than 7 landmark nodes can assure the accuracy of 90% regardless of their locations[1].

In this infrastructure we use 8 nodes to form the base node cluster. The base nodes first compute their own coordinates in a chosen geometric space. More details can be found in [1]. When a new node joins, it connects with the well-known base nodes to get its coordinates in the form of ($x_ib_1,x_ib_2,\ldots,x_ib_8$) by sending ICMP ping messages to each base node respectively. When node x_1 exchanges information with node x_2, x_1 calculates its distances to x_2 with their network coordinates using the formula

$$D(x_1, x_2)=\min (x_1b_i+x_2b_i) , i=1,2,...8 \quad (1)$$

The accuracy of formula (1) has been verified in [1] showing a better performance than other formulae.

List Maintenance. Base node cluster also keep two partial global lists, available task list and available node list, with constant size. The term "partial" means only part available resources are in the lists and the term "global" means the available resources are from the overall network in the node's viewpoint and will not be replaced by local reference. Each entry in both lists includes *nodeID, network coordinates, credit, bonus point and service type*. Service type is an identification to differentiate services generated by nodes. We would not keep large-sized lists. It is neither necessary nor useful to improve the node selection and task hunting much. Medium size, say, 200 records, is enough. There is an additional benefit to have multiple base nodes in list maintenance. An old node can visit any base node to get the lists. This disperses the requests for one base node to avoid the crowed flush.
Available Node List. Available nodes list recodes current live nodes in the system. As mentioned above, it uses a hybrid FIFO and credit value ranking mechanism. The reason to use such a hybrid refresh mechanism is to ensure serving nodes well enough; meanwhile to prevent high credit nodes from occupying the list too long. This will cause unfairness to the newly joined nodes.
Available Task List. Available tasks list enables requesters to publish their tasks attracting more peers to bid for the tasks. It will surely receive more replies than merely submitting requests to its neighbor nodes. Better serving nodes and lower bids are expected to achieve. This list is ranked by FIFO.

2.2 Bank Server

Bank server is associated with the real bank. The scalability of bank server is beyond the scope of this paper.
Once a new node joins this system, base node cluster notifies bank server of creating a node record for this node with default credit value. Nodes inform the bank server of their credit evaluation marking on the other side and bonus point transfer to the other side in each transaction and bank server updates their corresponding records after validating reports from both sides. Because there are bonus point flows between both sides, compromise is hard to get to send bank server a pseudo report, i.e., neither node is willing to report a node with better behavior than it really has. Also malicious reporting will not take great effects by averaging the credit in each transaction using the following formula:

$$\text{Credit}=\text{OldCredit} * a + \text{NewCredit} * (1\text{-}a),\ 0<a<1 \tag{2}$$

Some may argue that there are some security problems when the node colludes with majority of the participating nodes to screen the minority. We have shown that such majority compromise is impossible in [6].

Credit. Credit is an attribute of a node to represent its reputation and appreciation in executing past tasks. Each node will check the candidates' credit in the selection. The node with a low credit will not be selected. So every node is expected to abide by its agreements such as not exceeding the time bound in submitting the task results and avoiding abandoning an accepted tasks on the way lest its credit be marked low. This leads to the stability of the system.

Bonus Point. Bonus Point is another attribute of a node to represent its wealth and ability to afford its requesting tasks. The bonus point can be exchanged for corresponding cash and vice versa with some out-of-band means to realize PC-earning. In order to get paid, nodes must provide qualified services. Besides accepting other's tasks, a node may initiate appealing services for money earning. In a word bonus point is the impulsion for nodes to provide and enrich the services. Together with credit, bonus point regulates the nodes join and leave less frequently.

To prevent some "knavish" nodes from bilking their bills and some "undisciplined" nodes from fleeing before finishing the tasks, bonus points of both sides will be temporarily decreased before the tasks are finished.

2.3 Participating Nodes

As described in the last two subsections, a new node connects with base node cluster, to get a nodeID, a password and its network coordinates. If base node cluster is temporarily unavailable, new nodes execute p2p nodes join procedure as in other p2p networks.

Every node maintains a neighbor table, including the nodeID, network coordinates, credit, bonus point items. The entries are ranked and refreshed by a combination of the value of network distance and credit. Details of nodes activity such as updating the neighbor table, peer hunting being a requester or service providing being a requested peer can be found in [6]. Such tasks can be finished by either connecting with the base nodes or exchanging information locally.

After selecting nodes, the transaction begins and one side (it may include more than one node) marks the other side and sends it to the bank server before and after the transaction.

3 An Service Modules Example: Medium /Small Scale Internet Computing

For the page limit, user programmable module and the developed file sharing application are omitted. Readers can find details in [6]. Recall the problem we raised in the beginning, we introduce the following service module to settle it under CIPS-P2P infrastructure.

Different from large scale Internet computing projects like Grid[3], our project aims to provide a medium/small scale internet computing, say, with several or some tens of nodes participating in the computation. It's appealing for some ad-hoc tasks which will waste too much time by a single PC and also much time in learning how to become a Grid user. The easily used p2p interface in our project bridges this gap.

It's rather difficult to decompose the computing tasks. It needs identifying the independent computing subtasks and avoiding frequent communicating among those subtasks. We are not intended to address this problem in our implementation since many researches focus on the optimization in this problem [4]. Instead, we use a well-studied FFT distributed algorithm [5] to show how the computing functional module works under our proposed infrastructure. Any optimization algorithm in decomposing the tasks can be added to this module.

We then introduce our computing module. Figure2 is a snapshot of node information. Network coordinates, credit, bonus point, IP address and nodeID are listed in each node. The three means of updating neighbor tables are optional.

After setting the refresh means in the neighbor table, nodes either request others for doing their FFT tasks or wait for the FFT tasks.

In the requesting part, nodes are asked to set the task input, the would-be paid bonus points, the requirements of credit and time consuming on the serving nodes. It is shown in Figure3.

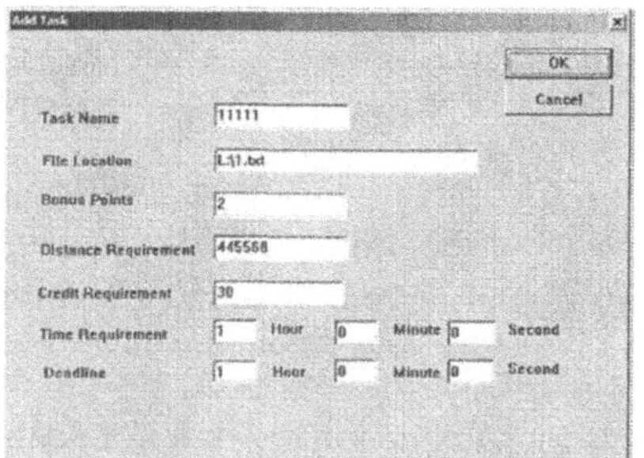

Fig. 3. Task Customization before Requesting

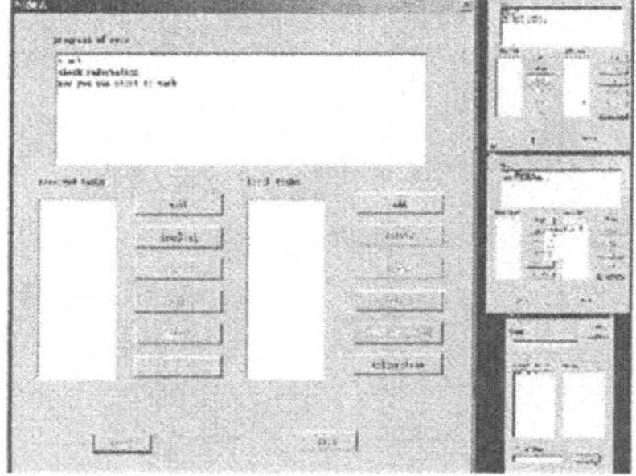

Fig. 4. Base Node Cluster, Requesting Node and Replying Nodes Interfaces

In the replying part, whether nodes that meet the requirements accept the task or not rely on their own condition. Nodes that accept the task execute their FFT procedure to finish the computation assigned to them and return their results to the requester. The requester then combines all the results from different nodes to form the output. As expected, the credits and bonus points in both sides are changed correspondingly after the computation. For the page limit in Figure4 we show the interfaces of base node cluster, one requesting node and two replying nodes collectively.

4 Conclusion and Future Work

In this paper we propose CIPS-P2P, a stable coordinates-based integrated-paid-service peer-to-peer infrastructure and its implementation. As one instance, medium/small scale Internet computing is exhibited. We address a novel Internet economy model where value chain exists among nodes in this system. This model is for certain appealing for most end users and makes contents and services on the Internet much richer than what only ICPs provide. We use network coordinates to alleviate the effect of physical distance to the performance in distance-sensitive applications. Credit and bonus point are used not only to ensure PC-earning realization, but also to control the nodes' join and leave. It is less tedious than that of Grid and more rigid than that of current p2p systems. Therefore it permits ordinary nodes to join and knocks out the ill-behaved nodes from the network. We open some APIs to facilitate the end users to launch new services in their own nodes. Together with bonus points, it enforces the nodes to update their contents and improve their services.

As for future works, we are interested in expanding the platform to be independent of operation systems. Currently it works in Windows only. We also study how to realize the bank server functions inside the system. It is a challenge to realize the security and billing function in distributed environment. Some novel mechanisms such as gossiping 'bad egg' and keeping constancy of the node information all over the network are being explored. Another thing to be discussed is the lists in the base node cluster. Whether keeping the lists all the same in every node or independent of each other is an open question. Lastly, the dynamics of this infrastructure is to be explored.

References

1. T. S. Eugene Ng et al, Predicting Internet Network Distance With Coordinates-Based Approach, in Proceedings of INFOCOM02, NY, June 2002.
2. D.J. Kruglinski et al, Inside Visual C++(the fifth version), Hope Press,1999.
3. I.Foster et al, The Anatomy of the Grid: Enabling Scalable Virtual Organizations. Supercomputer Applications, 15(3), 2001.
4. P. Liu et al, Computing Pool: a Practical and Necessary Evolutionary Step towards Practical Computational Grid, http://grid.cs.tsinghua.edu.cn/grid/liupeng.htm.
5. R.C. Agarwal et al., A high performance parallel algorithm for 1-D FFT, In Proceedings of the Conference on Supercomputing,1994.
6. Y. F. Zhang et al, CIPS-P2P: A Stable Coordinates-Based Integrated-Paid-Service Peer-to-Peer Infrastructure, Tech Report, 2003.

A Multicast Routing Algorithm for P2P Networks

Tingyao Jiang and Aling Zhong

College of Electrical Engineering & Information Technology
China Three Gorges University, Yichang 443000 China
tingyao_jiang@263.net

Abstract. Multicast communication is one of particular important services in peer-to-peer networking context. The problem of finding a minimum cost multicast routing is NP-completeness. We present a novel solution to improve the MPH algorithm. The cost of multicast tree generated by the proposed algorithm with the same time as MPH is not larger than that of MPH in the worst case.

1 Introduction

In the world of Internet technologies, peer-to-peer(p2p) solutions are currently receiving considerable interest. Communication cost considerations are critical in p2p networks because of dynamic, sometimes rapidly changing, random topologies. Multicast is an important communication primitive. It involves sending messages to an arbitrary subset of nodes, also termed peers, where peers can be either mobile or stationary and may exist in anywhere and at anytime. Multicast is very useful in a large number of application in a p2p distributed systems, where a set of nodes need be informed of a specific event.

The multicast routing is to find a routing tree rooted from the source node s and containing all destination nodes Z. The problem of finding a minimum cost multicast tree can be formulated as a minimum Steiner tree problem in networks(SPN), which attempts to minimize the total cost of the multicast tree. The cost is usually measured as the bandwidth assumed by the tree. Due to NP-completeness of the optimal solution of SPN, practical multicast routing algorithms are based on heuristic.

Multicast routing problems have received much attention from many researchers. For detailed description and more information on both exact and heuristic methods, one can refer to three survey papers, Winter[1], Hwang[2] and Salama[3]. MPH(Minimum Path Cost Heuristic) algorithm is a famous heuristic approach[4]. It was discussed in Ref.[1~9], in particular S.Ramanathan[8] regarded it as a standard algorithm compared with the other algorithms. MPH works in $O(pn^2)$ time, where p is number of destination nodes and n is number of network nodes. Based on MPH, LSMPH[9] whose multicast tree's cost is larger than that of MPH and FMPH[10] whose multicast tree's cost is the same as that of MPH were introduced on the premise of known shortest paths that is impossible in p2p netwoks. In this paper, a novel solution to constructing the multicast tree is presented. The cost of multicast tree generated by the proposed algorithm with the same time as MPH is not larger than that of MPH in the worst case.

M. Li et al. (Eds.): GCC 2003, LNCS 3032, pp. 452–455, 2004.

2 System Model

We assume that no node leaves the system and no new node joins in the system. Thus, the network graph has always the same node set but different edge sets. The communication network is modeled as an undirected graph G= (V , E , c) , where V is the set of nodes which represent communication nodes, E is the set of edges which represent communication links. The total number of nodes is n. The nodes is denoted by v_i (i=1,2, …, n). $< v_i, v_j >$, (1≤i<j≤n), represents the edge between node i and j. Let $\cos t(< v_i, v_j >)$ be the cost of edge $< v_i, v_j >$. The cost of graph G is defined as $c = \sum_{<v_i,v_j>\in E} \cos t(< v_i, v_j >)$.

Definition 1. The shortest path between a pair of nodes, e.g., v_i and v_j. It is a path between v_i and v_j, whose total cost of edges along the path is minimum of all paths connecting v_i and v_j.

Definition 2. The shortest path between a node, e.g., v_i, and a tree. It is a shortest path between a pair of nodes, whose cost is minimum of all shortest paths between v_i and each node in the tree.

Definition 3. The minimum cost Steiner tree problem in networks(SPN). It can be formulated as follows.

Given: An undirected network G= (V , E , c) , a set $Z \subseteq V$ of destination nodes with p nodes(without special indication in this paper, the source node belongs to Z).

Find: A subgraph, i.e., a multicast tree, T=(V_t , E_t , c_t) such that there is a path between every pair of source node and destination node, $T \subseteq G, V_t \subseteq V, E_t \subseteq E, Z \subseteq V_t$. If the cost of tree T, i.e., $c_t = \sum_{<v_i,v_j>\in E_t} \cos t(< v_i, v_j >)$, is minimum, then tree T is so-called minimum cost multicast tree.

Lemma 1. A minimum cost multicast tree T=(V_t , E_t , c_t) must be a minimum spanning tree(MST) of G',where G' is a pruning subgraph of G in such a way that the edge in G is pruned as long as one node of the edge is not contained in V_t and the node in G is pruned if the node is not contained in V_t.

3 TPMPH Algorithm

Definition 4. The worst case error ratio f. The f is the ratio of the cost of multicast tree constructed by the heuristic algorithm to the cost of the minimum cost multicast tree.

Takahashi and Matsuyama[4] suggested a heuristic for the SPN.The error ratio of MPH is bounded by 2-2/p, i.e., $f_{mph} \leq 2-2/p$ [1]. An excellent heuristic algorithm strives to decrease the error ratio in time as short as possible.

MPH seeks a destination node from remaining destination nodes in such a way that the cost of the shortest path between the destination node and the part multicast tree is minimum. Then nodes and edges along the selected shortest path are joined in part multicast tree. After all the destination nodes are joined in part multicast tree, multicast tree is ready.

The pruning subgraph is the result of pruning the edge having at least a node not belonging to V_t and pruning the node not belonging to V_t. Lemma 1 indicates that the minimum cost multicast tree should be a MST of pruning subgraph. But we found that the multicast tree generated by MPH may not be a MST. Then we prove a MST of the pruning subgraph is a multicast tree.

Theorem 1. Given a network graph G= (V , E , c) , a destination node set Z. Let T_{mph}= (V_t , E_t , c_{mph}) be a multicast tree generated by MPH. G' is G's pruning subgraph through pruning the edge as long as a node of the edge is not contained in V_t and pruning the node not belonging to V_t. If T_{tpmph}=(V_t' , E_t' , c_{tpmph}) is a MST of G', then T_{tpmph} is a multicast tree for Z.

Theorem 2. the cost of multicast tree T_{tpmph} is not larger than that of T_{mph} in the worst case.

A two phase MPH algorithm, called as TPMPH, is presented to generate the multicast tree T_{tpmph}.

Step 1: Determine the shortest path between each destination node and each other node in network graph by Dijkstra[12] algorithm.

Step 2: Part multicast tree T_{tpmph} firstly consists of only a source node, $V_t'=\{s\}$.

Step 3: Seek a minimum shortest path between each destination not belonging to V_t' and part multicast tree T_{tpmph}. All nodes along the selected shortest path are joined in V_t'.

Step 4: Repeat Step 3,4 until all destination nodes are contained in V_t'.

Step 5: Prune graph G by pruning the edge having at least a node not belonging to V_t' and pruning the node not belonging to V_t'. The remaining graph is denoted by G'.

Step 6: Determine a MST of G' by Prim[13] algorithm. All edges of MST are joined in E_t'. The heuristic minimum cost multicast tree T_{tpmph} is finished.

In TPMPH algorithm, Step 1 requires at most $O(pn^2)$ time. Step 2,3 takes $O(p^2n)$ time. Step 5 and Step 6 works in $O(n^2)$ time respectively. Thus the TPMPH's time complexity is $O(pn^2)$, which is the same as MPH. But the error ratio is not larger than that of MPH by theorem 2, i.e., $f_{tpmph} \leq f_{mph} \leq 2-2/p$.

4 Conclusion

This paper presented a heuristic multicast routing algorithm TPMPH. The cost of multicast tree generated by the proposed algorithm in the same time as MPH is in no case larger than that of MPH. This is a substantial improvement on previous improved works.

References

1. Pawel Winter, Steiner problem in networks: a survey, Networks, 1987, 17(2):129~167
2. F.K.Hwang, Steiner tree problems, Networks, 1992, 22(1):55~89
3. H.F.Salama, D.S.Reeves, Evaluation of multicast routing algorithms for real-time communication on high speed networks, IEEE Journal on selected areas in communication, 1997,15(3):332~349
4. H.Takahasi and A.Matsuyama, An approximate solution for the Steiner problem in graphs, Math. Japonica, 1980, (24):573~577
5. R.Novak, A note on distributed multicast routing in point-to-point networks, Computers and Operations Research, 2001,28(12):1149~1164
6. M.I.Smirnov, Efficient multicast routing in high speed networks, Computer communications,1996,19(1):59~75
7. Chu-Fu Wang et al., Heuristic algorithms for packing of multiple-group multicasting, Computers and Operations Research, 2002,29(7):905~924
8. S.Ramanathan, Multicast tree generation in networks with asymmetric links, IEEE ACM Trans. On Networking, 1996, 4(4):558~568
9. LiHan-bing,YuJian-ping,XieWei-xin, Locally Searching Minimum Path Cost Heuristic, ACTAELECTRONICA SINSCA, 2000, 28(5) : 92~95
10. HuGuang-ming, LiLe-ming, A fast heuristic algorithm of minimum cost tree, ACTAELECTRONICA SINSCA, 2002, 30(6) : 880~882
11. M.waxman, Routing of multipoint connections, IEEE Journal on Selected Areas in communication, 1988,6(9):1617~1621
12. E.N. Dijkstra, A note on two problems in connection with graphs, Numerische Mathematik, 1959,1(2):269~271
13. R.C.Prim, Shortest connection networks and some generalizations, Bell Systems Tech., 1957,(36):1389~1401

Leveraging Duplicates to Improve File Availability of P2P Storage Systems[1]

Min Qu, Yafei Dai, and Mingzhong Xiao

CNDS Lab, Peking University, Beijing, China
{qm, dyf, mzxiao}@net.cs.pku.edu.cn
http://net.cs.pku.edu.cn

Abstract. This paper proposes a strategy of improving file availability of peer-to-peer file storage systems, which provides the ability of identifying duplicate files and leveraging the duplicates. Our mechanism includes 1) strategy of building indexes for files to be stored in the system, 2) method to automatically identify identical files and policy to merge the indexes, and 3) comparison to former work and evaluations of this mechanism.

1 Introduction

File storage applications generate many files having identical content. Files with identical content are logically independent to each other since they have different owners, file names etc., occupy different portion of disk space etc. In this paper, we propose a mechanism of identifying files with identical content. We manage those files uniformly and leverage them to improve file availability. For clarity, we refer to the file copies system generates as *replicas*, and we refer to logically distinct files with identical content as *duplicates*. The number of replicas of a file is referred as *replication factor*, and the number of duplicates is referred as *duplication factor*. Our goal is to guarantee a certain level of availability for all files in a P2P system. System automatically detects duplicates content and leverages them as replicas.

2 Indexing and Mapping

Build Index. We build indexes for all the files in the system, which provides the probability of identifying files with the same content. The indexes are established based on SHA-1 hashing algorithm which is responsible for mapping a given key to a value defined as *content identifier (CID)*. CID is calculated by running hashing function on a fixed portion of the file's content. Hashing part of the file means that any differences in the portion of the file not hashed will not be detected by comparing the signature. However, the possibility of hash collisions will still exist even if the

[1] This work is supported by National Advanced Technology Project Fund #2001AA111013

M. Li et al. (Eds.): GCC 2003, LNCS 3032, pp. 456–459, 2004.

whole file is hashed, and this tremendously increases the amount of work especially for a large file.

Upon a storage request, system doesn't immediately search duplicates of that file, which would otherwise be a long latency. The machine to store the index is located by routing algorithm, according to CID. As hashing algorithm has the property that the same inputs generate the same outputs, and each peer symmetrically runs the same software, indexes of the same content files are stored on the same machine. After the machine is located, the index of the uploaded file is established. The index includes CID, file length, file name, owner, file access list etc.


```
<?xml version="1.0" encoding="UTF-8" ?>
- <root>
 - <index fileLength="17035203" CID="68a0d86e" storedAmount="1" virtualAmount="1" amountLimit="3">
  - <item fID="e56a98eb" fileName="braveHeart.rm" owner="hankson" pwd="23071f0352ba" acl="111" flag="1">
     <store nodeID="38f9da37" />
    </item>
  </index>
</root>
```


Fig. 1. An example of index

In this index, the fields of *storedAmount* and *virtualAmount* represent duplicate amount of already stored in system and duplicate amount users already required to store separately. *AmountLimit* field describes the maximum amount of duplicates to be stored in system. *FID* is the identifier of the uploading file assigned by the machine that stores the index. FID consists of two parts: one is the identifier of the machine stores the file (*nodeID*), and the other is a unique value on the machine that represents the file that the index describes, which may be set to the value of current system clock. System also maintains a mapping between FID and file index. After storing the file into the system, FID is returned to user. Upon a download request, FID is used to locate the node and the according index. Access control list is described in the *acl* field. And the flag field represents whether the file described by the corresponding item is stored in system or not. Value 1 means the file is stored and 0 means not. *Pwd* filed is the login key of the file owner. NodeID is the node identifier of the machine that stores the physical file.

File Placement Policy. In our research, we assume host failures are independent and identically distributed, allowing replicas to be assigned to any hosts.

System first runs hash function on the connection of several attribute values. The connection of values, referred as *logical position*, consists of the following parts: file owner, password, and file name, which are recorded in the index. The hash value of logic position, named *physical position*, is then recorded in the index. User node sends file content to physical position located by the underlying routing algorithm. FID is also stored together with file content so as to locate the corresponding index from the content and thus update operation can be done.

3 Identify Duplicates

As have described above, the indexing and mapping mechanism guarantees that indexes of same part of files are located on the same peer, which is the precondition of detecting duplicates.

On each machines, system runs a low important background task to identify the duplicates. System also maintains a log to record operation information, through which we know the information about the new-stored files. System compares new-stored files' length, FID, and file content consequently with that of existing files. If they are all equal, duplicates are found. What system does is coalesce of indexes of those duplicates and change the mapping relationship. FIDs are mapped to new index while their values remain unchanged.

4 Evaluations

In this section, we give the evaluation of our research. [1] provides an analytic model for reasoning about the efficiency of replication and then extends this framework to model the availability of groups of files or file systems. We compare analytic results of our work with those of their model.

We assume that the probability of Y hosts out of h randomly picked hosts are available is P. Any host chosen at random from h hosts has an expected availability of μ_H, Replica factor for conventional replication is represented as c and the duplication factor is represented as d. We use the following formula to calculate the replication factor for a desired degree of file availability A.

$$A = P(Y \geq 1) = 1 - (1 - \mu_H)^{c*d}$$

$$c = \frac{\log(1 - A)}{\log(1 - \mu_H) * d}$$

We choose a mean host availability of 0.5 based upon the measurements in [2]. We have also analyzed a distributed storage system providing storage service in Peking University, whose duplicate factor is 1.43. Another measurement [3] of 550 file systems shows that removing duplicates from the whole population of 550 file systems reclaims 47% used file space. We assume files in those systems are identically distributed and the duplicates are evenly distributed. We give value 1.43 and 1.89 separately to the variable d. Table 1 gives the comparison results of the value of c for a range of required file availabilities.

Table 1. Replica number needed for said file availability for mean host availability 0.5

Required Availability	Replication factor		
	In [1]	d=1.43	d=1.89
0.800	3	2	2
0.900	4	3	2
0.950	5	4	3
0.990	7	5	4
0.995	8	6	4
0.999	10	7	6

Different values of mean reapplication factor may result in different file availability in different systems. Study of [3, 4] shows that typical replication factors are three or four replicas per file. We calculate the file availability for given replication factor shown in Table 2. It is observed obviously that our mechanism of detecting duplicates improves file availability tremendously.

Table 2. File availability for said replication factor for mean host availability 0.5

Replication factor	Achieved availability		
	In [1]	d=1.43	d=1.89
1	0.500	0.629	0.730
2	0.750	0.863	0.927
3	0.875	0.948	0.980
4	0.938	0.981	0.995
5	0.965	0.993	0.999

5 Conclusions

In this paper, we have described the architecture and performance of the strategy of leveraging duplicates to improve availability. The method of indexing and detecting duplicates is described in detail. An evaluation is also given to demonstrate this policy is effective in improving file availability of distributed file storage systems.

Further research is called for. Since all the duplicates are available, it is possible to realize parallel access to replicated content [5] to improve download performance, which means end users access multiple servers at the same time, fetching different portions of that file from different servers and reassembling them locally.

As all the information about the duplicates that belong to different users is recorded in the indexes and the attribute values may be greatly different, we can leverage those values to provide suggestions on file classification and organization to achieve flexibility and diversity. Multiple views can also be provided to achieve personality.

References

1. R. Bhagwan, D. Moore, S. Savage, and G. M. Voelker: Replication Strategies for Highly Available Peer-to-peer Storage Systems. In proc. of FuDiCo: Future directions in Distributed Computing, June 2002.
2. S. Saroiu, P. K. Gummadi, and S. D. Gribble: A Measurement Study of Peer-to-peer File Sharing Systems. In Proc. of Multimedia Computing and Networking (MMCN), 2002.
3. W. J. Bolosky, J. R. Douceur, D. Ely, and M. Theimer: Feasibility of a Serverless Distributed File System Deployed on an Existing Set of Desktop PCs. SIGMETRICS 2000, ACM, Jun 2000.
4. J. R. Douceur and. P. R. Wattenhofer: Optimizing File Availability in a Secure Serverless Distributed File System. 20th SRDS, IEEE, Oct 2001.
5. P. Rodriguez and E. W. Biersack: Dynamic Parallel-Access to Replicated Content in the Internet. IEEE/ACM Transactions on Networking, Aug 2002.

Distributing the Keys into P2P Network

Shijie Zhou, Zhiguang Qin, and Jinde Liu

College of Computer Science and Engineering
University of Electronic Science and Technology of China
Sichuan, Chengdu 610054, P.R.China
{sjzhou,qinzg,ibmcenter}@uestc.edu.cn

Abstract. This paper concentrates on analyzing and discussing the basic secure service: key management (PKey). By adding a security service layer, PKey is carefully built on the base of a routing and location layer to simple the application development. According as the layered architecture of PKey, some key protocols of PKey, which include key producing, retrieving and transferring, are designed and analyzed in detail. Other important aspects of this new kind of distributed key management system are also addressed and analyzed.

1 Introduction

Peer-to-Peer (P2P) computing is a popular approach used to remedy the Internet hotspots problem resulting from a sudden unpredicted increase in an on-line object's popularity. P2P systems offer an alternative to the traditional client/server computing model and present a new distributed computing infrastructure suited for companies and enterprises with resources aggregating, information sharing, collaborative computing and any other applications. In academia, there are a number of projects in progress at universities, such as Chord [1], PAST/Pastry [2] [3], CAN [4], Tapestry [5] and Gnutella [6] .

2 The Architecture of PKey

Fig.1 shows the layered structure of our P2P based distributed key management system (*PKey*). A security service layer (*SSL*) is added to address the problems caused by the floating characteristics of P2P.

Public key cryptograph is adopted in PKey to encrypt information. In order to avoid single failure point, no key distribution center exists. Each peer generates a pair of keys: public key and private key. It keeps both the public key and private key. At the same time, the public key is distributed in some peers of PKey. When other peers want to get the public key of a specific peer, it uses the key searching protocol to retrieve it from the PKey community.

M. Li et al. (Eds.): GCC 2003, LNCS 3032, pp. 460–463, 2004.

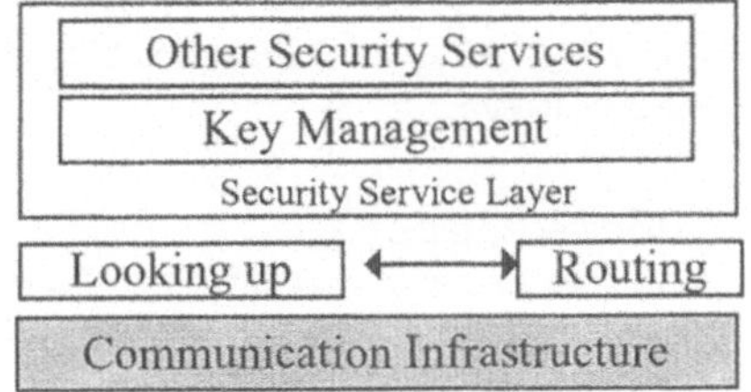

Fig.1. The layered structure of PKey

3 Base Key Management Protocol in PKey

Public key cryptograph is adopted in PKey to encrypt information. In order to avoid single failure point, no key distribution center exists. The key generation algorithm is showed in below.

```
//Node Generates Public Key And Private Key
Peer.Generate_Key(Peer)
  Peer.Key(Pulic_Key, Private_Key);
  Peer.Store_Key(Peer.ID,Private_Key, Peer.KeyFile);
  Peer.Store_key(Peer.ID,Public_key, Peer.KeyFile);
  If(!Peer.Lookup_Peers(N, Peers[]))
    Return Error;
  Else
    Ret=Peer.SendKey(Peers[N], Public_Key, Peer.ID);
    If(Ret==False)//Fail to Send the key
     Peer.Cancel_Sendkey(tPeers[N],Peer.ID);
     Return Error;
    End If
  End If
//End of The Peer.Generate_Key Function
```

When other peers want to get the public key of a specific peer, it uses the key searching protocol to retrieve it from the PKey community. This algorithm is showed as follows.

```
//Node gets the Public Key From SPeer in PKey
Peer.Retrieve_Key(SPeer)
Ret=Peer.Ping_Peer(SPeer.ID);//Contact the Owner
If(Ret==True) //Owner Is Alive
  Return SPeer.Key;
  Peer.Store_key(SPeer.ID,Public_key,Peer.KeyFile);
Else
  Peer.Lookup_Peers(N,Peers[]);
  While(Peers[] Is Not Empty)
    tPeer=Peer.Select_Peer(Peers[]);
    If(Peer.Lookup_Key(tPeer,SPeer.ID)<>NULL)
```

```
        Peer.Store_key(SPeer.ID,Public_key,Peer.KeyFile);
        Return tPeer.key;
      Else
        Peers[]-tPeer→Peers[]
      End If
    End While
  End If
//End of The Peer.Retrieve_Key Function
```

4 Experimental Results

The factors impact the performance of PKey include the number of pees (*N*), the number of replica of key (*R*), and the availability of peers (*D*). In order to simulate PKey, this paper assumes that the number of peers is a constant (where *N*=100). The value of *R* will be changed in our test to show how this factor will have impacts on the performance of PKey. As for *D*, the peers' offline probability will be taken to simulate it. That is, the Bernoulli distribution (the peer's offline probability is *p*) model is adopted to simulate the PKey. Hence, the traffic in PKey is considered to be

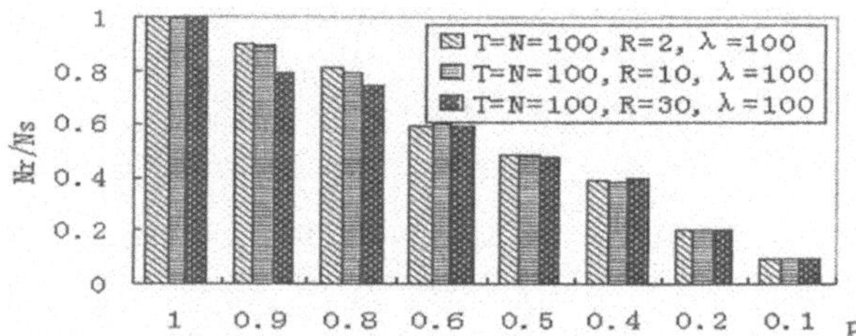

Fig. 2. The relationship among the offline probability *P*, the routing items *R* and the ρ

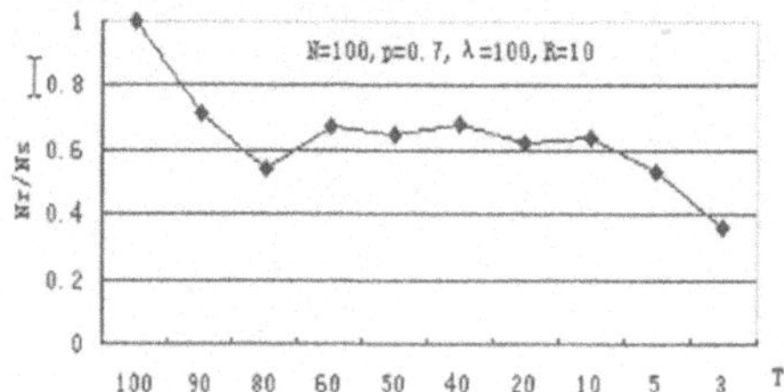

Fig.3. The relationship between the size of local routing table(*T*) and the value of ρ

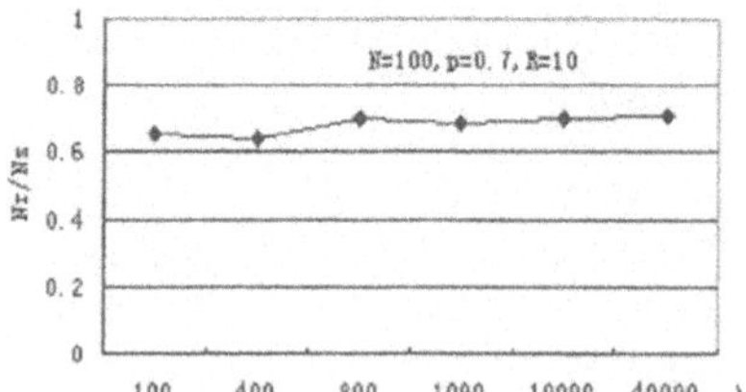

Fig.4. The relationship between λ and value of ρ

the Poisson distribution(λ). Each peer in PKey must have a local routing table which maintains T routing items. Finally, the performance of PKey is defined as the probability of successful operation: $\rho = \frac{N_r}{N_s}$, where N_s is the number of operations peers sending out , and N_r is the number of operations be meet by the PKey.

In Fig.2, the traffic is considered to be a constant (λ). And the flooding routing method is adopted to relay the peer's requests. The result shows that the p has a heavy impact on the performance of system. Fig.3 shows the simulating results in various size of routing table. It's obvious that while the size of local routing table is decreased, the performance of PKey will also be decreased. In Fig.3, the value of ρ is relatively stable if the ratio of N and T is between 0.6 to 0.1. The result in Fig.4 show that while increasing the value of λ, there is no clearly fluctuation in the value of ρ .

5 Conclusion

This paper gives a detail discussing about the P2P based key management system. With the special fully distributed infrastructure, P2P based key management system can provide common key management services without CA and KDC, and thus avoid the single failure point in traditional client/server computing model. The test results show the PKey needs to be improved to make it suitable for other requirements.

References

[1] I. Stoica, R. Morris, D. Karger, M. F. Kaashoek, and H. Balakrishnan. Chord: A scalable peer-to-peer lookup service for internet applications. In Proceedings of ACM SIGCOMM, San Diego, California, 2001: 149–160.

[2] A. Rowstron, and P. Druschel. Pastry: Scalable, distributed object location and routing for large-scale peer-to-peer systems. Proceedings of the 18th IFIP/ACM International Conference on Distributed Systems Platforms (Middleware 2001) Heidelberg, Germany, 2001.

[3] D. Peter, and R. Antony, PAST: A large-scale, persistent peer-to-peer storage utility, in Proc. of HOTOS Conf., Lake Louise, Alberta, Canada, 2001.

[4] S. Ratnasamy, P. Francis, M. Handley, R. Karp, and S. Shenker. A scalable content-addressable network. In Proceedings of ACM SIGCOMM, San Diego, California, Aug. 2001: 161–172.

[5] B. Zhao, J. Kubiatowicz, and A. Joseph. Tapestry: An infrastructure for fault-tolerant wide-area location and routing. Tech. Rep. UCB/CSD-01-1141, Computer Science Division, UC Berkeley, 2001.

[6] M. Ripeanu, I. Foster. Mapping the Gnutella network: macroscopic properties of large-Scale Peer-to-Peer systems. 1st International Workshop on Peer-to-Peer Systems, Cambridge, MA, USA , 2002

SemanticPeer: An Ontology-Based P2P Lookup Service*

Jing Tian, Yafei Dai, and Xiaoming Li

CNDS Lab, Peking University, Beijing, China
tianjing@net.pku.edu.cn
{dyf, lxm}@pku.edu.cn
http://net.pku.edu.cn

Abstract. Locating content efficiently and conveniently is the key issue in P2P systems. In this paper we present SemanticPeer, an Ontology-Based P2P lookup service, to address this problem, which is an extension of Chord protocol. In SemanticPeer, one can easily locate desired data items using the domain knowledge, beyond the keywords scheme. By the separate of share knowledge and private knowledge, SemanticPeer provides a high degree of node autonomy. SemanticPeer clusters the documents according to the domain knowledge, so we can answer a query with a specified characteristic efficiently.

1 Introduction

Locating a content is the core operation in a P2P system, and there are two classes of solutions for P2P content location, flooding queries as Gnutella[1] and direct locating based on Distributed Hash Table(DHT) as Chord[2]. Based on DHT, Chord has been proved to be efficient. But unfortunately none of these two methods support semantic lookup, and we can only use some keywords to locate the content. But Human brains remember objects based on their features, namely the concept of "role" in AI technology. Fortunately now more and more data gives out its metadata, and ontology description language, like RDF[3], has been developed. However, how to deploy knowledge in a completely distributed manner is challenging, because of the management of knowledge. In this paper, we present SemanticPeer, an Ontology-Based P2P lookup service, to address this problem.

SemanticPeer is a semantic extension of Chord protocol (refer to [2] for details), and it places its indices and routes queries according to the combination of ontology and DHT. SemanticPeer is built upon Chord, so a node in SemanticPeer also has the unique ID and the finger table same as in Chord, and it can use the operations defined in Chord. And SemanticPeer uses RDF to describe its knowledge. RDF is the W3C metadata standard, which is based on description logic, and it can define concepts and individuals, as while as properties.

* This work is supported by National Advanced Technology Project Fund #2001AA111013 and National Grand Fundamental Research of China G1999032706

M. Li et al. (Eds.): GCC 2003, LNCS 3032, pp. 464–467, 2004.

2 The SemanticPeer Protocol

SemanticPeer protocol specifies how to distribute domain knowledge, how to distribute the indices according to the knowledge and how to find the results of a given query based on ontology. In the following, we will introduce how to distribute the indices and how to deal with queries in this section.

Knowledge Distribution. SemanticPeer uses a layered knowledge management, which includes *share knowledge* and *private knowledge*. Share knowledge is composed of domain concepts and the instances upon which most users agree, so each peer will get a copy when it joins SemanticPeer. Private knowledge is close to the concrete data items. Therefore, node *n*, who stores data file *f*, is responsible to establish private knowledge file f_{pk} with *f*. Fig. 1 gives out example ontology. Some resources in f_{pk} may have relationship with resources in share knowledge, therefore, f_{pk} and share knowledge will act as a whole KB *k*, and it should be consistent within *k*.

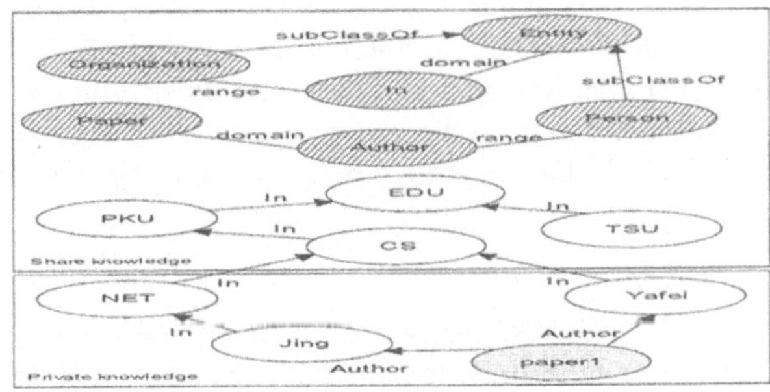

Fig. 1. Structure of knowledge in SemanticPeer. The upper part is share knowledge, including concepts (denoted by the shading ellipses) and the acknowledged instances (e.g. EDU) in publication field. The private knowledge at the bottom attaches to concrete data closely, and is easy to change with data items

Here, we introduce two data structure in SemanticPeer, *express table* and *index table*. For each resource *r* in share knowledge, there is a corresponding express table of *r* on node n_r = *successor(r)* (*successor* is defined in [2]). And express table of *r* records information of <*r*, *p*, *r'*, null, *n'*> if resource *r'*, in share knowledge, has immediate relationship *p* with *r*, and express table of *r'* resides on *n'*, as well as the information of <*r*, *p'*, #FILE, *fname*, *n''*> if resource *r''* has immediate relationship *p'* with *r*, and *r''* is in a private knowledge file *fname* stored on node *n''*. There is one express table for every resource in share knowledge, while index table is for every node. Node *n*'s index table includes the information of <*k*, *h*, *fname*, *n'*>, *k* is the key of some resource in private knowledge file *fname* stored on node *n'*, *h* is hash value of *k* and *successor(h)* = n_r. Fig. 2 illustrate the express table and index table in a SemanticPeer network with 3 nodes. The node, who establishes a private knowledge, is responsible to register the corresponding tables, and when node joining and leaving these tables may shift in Chord protocol, due to the space limit we do not discuss in detail in this paper.

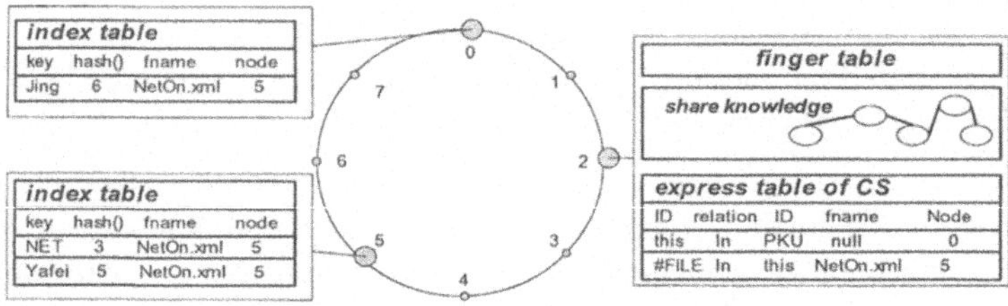

Fig. 2. A SemanticPeer network with 3 nodes. The ontology here is defined in Fig. 1. The private knowledge is stored in file "NetOn.xml" on node 5. 2's index table and other express tables are ignored here

Deal With Query. In order to locate a concrete data file *f*, our main task will focus on how to navigate the query *q* to node *n* holding f_{pk}, for *q* can be resolved at *n* in the combination KB of share knowledge and f_{pk}. SemanticPeer protocol supports query in the form of RQL[4], for instance, to the knowledge illustrated in Fig. 1, we can write our needs "Return me all the papers written by a person in organization 'NET'" as

```
Select X, Y                                    (Q1)
from Paper{X}.Author{Y}.In{'NET'}
```

There are two different classes of queries in SemanticPeer network, *local query* and *data query*. Local query is mainly to get what resources are in share ontology. Therefore, local query is just a query to local share knowledge, and we can resolve it as in a traditional knowledge base. Data query is to locate concrete data files in SemanticPeer, and this process is divided into three phases as follows, (a) *Consistency checking*, to check whether the properties applied to the resources in this query are appropriate according to the schema defined in share ontology. (b) *Ontology-based private knowledge locating*, to forward this query to all nodes that may hold the private knowledge file of desired data file, let *N* denote this nodes set. (c) *Query resolving*, to resolve this query on every node in *N* using combination knowledge of share knowledge and corresponding private knowledge, and return the results. Here, (a) and (c) are only operations on one node; therefore the key issue is how to forward the query to every node in *N*. To do the locating in (b), we study two different situations. One is to query with some resources in private knowledge like (Q1), then we can simply use the index table to locate the desired nodes (to access index table, we should fall back on Chord's function). Consider (Q1) in SemanticPeer network of Fig. 2 for example, we first compute the hash value of 'NET', and get node 5 as *successor(*'NET'*)*, then use Chord protocol to access index table of node 5, finally we get 'NetOn.xml' on node 5. The other situation is to query with only resources in share knowledge, then we can not use index table to locate private knowledge directly, so we should navigate to private knowledge by express table. First, we contact node *n* = *successor(r)*, *r* is the known resource in query, and then we can bind the variant *r'* neighbor to *r* in query by express table of *r*. If *r'* is bound to a share knowledge resource, we will access the express table of *r'* recursively (we can get the address of the node holding the express table of *r'* directly from express table of *r*); otherwise if *r'* is in a private knowledge file, then we get its file name and the node's address from express table.

3 Related Works

In SON[5], nodes with semantically similar content are "clustered" together in one SON, thus one query can be directed to the SONs that are better suited to answer it. To cluster the peers and queries, SON relies on a fixed classification hierarchy, what makes it less flexibility than SemanticPeer.

HyperCup[6] presents a hypercube topology of P2P network. HyperCup clusters its nodes based on a set of global ontologies. Similar to SON, this limits the flexibility of knowledge management. HyperCup relies on the super-peer to direct a query to subset of nodes that may answer it, so the super-peer will be the bottleneck.

4 Conclusions and Future Works

In this paper, we advocate the layered knowledge management in P2P system to make the management simpler and more flexible. Based on the consistent knowledge bases, SemanticPeer provides a convenient semantic lookup service. In contrast to clustering peers in other P2P systems, SemanticPeer reflects the properties in share knowledge to neighbor relationship in identifier ring, and thus makes clusters of documents according to their characteristic, so that we can find the similar documents within one cluster.

In fact, there are some problems remaining in SemanticPeer protocol for further research. For example, how to get a pretty good availability in the face of failure, and what strategy to take to enhance performance when there are more than one known resources in query. And also, we should focus on the performance analysis and simulation in our research.

References

1. "Gnutella" http://gnutella.wego.com.
2. I. Stoica, R. Morris, D. Karger, F. Kaashoek, H. Balakrishnan: Chord: A Scalable Peer-To-Peer Lookup Service for Internet Applications. In Proceedings of the ACM SIGCOMM, 2001. 13.
3. O. Lassila and R. R. Swick: W3C Resource Description framework (RDF) Model and Syntax Specification. http://www.w3.org/TR/1999/REC-rdf-syntax-19990222/
4. G. Karvounarakis, S. Alexaki, V. Christophides, D. Plexousakis, M. Scholl: RQL: A Declarative Query Language for RDF. In Proceedings of the World Wide Web Conference (WWW2002), Honolulu, Hawaii, USA, May 7-11 2002.
5. A. Crespo and H. Garcia-Molina: Semantic Overlay Networks for P2P Systems http://www-db.stanford.edu/~crespo/publications/op2p.pdf
6. M. Schlosser, M. Sintek, S. Decker, W. Nejdl: HyperCup - Hypercubes, Ontologies and Efficient Search on Peer-to-peer Networks. In Proceedings of the AP2PC, July 2002.

Authentication and Access Control in P2P Network*

Yuqing Zhang [1] and Dehua Zhang [1,2]

[1]National Computer Network Intrusion Protection Center, GSCAS, 100039, Beijing, China
[2] College of Electronics and Engineering, National University of Defense Technology, 410073, Changsha, Hunan,China
{zhangyq,zhangdh}@nipc.org.cn

Abstract. Peer-to-Peer (P2P) networks are the latest addition to the universe of distributed systems. The security issues become more important then ever. Authentication and access control are the two main fields of the security issues. Different applications have different security requirements. In this paper, we analyze the settlements of the P2P Network security issues and the difficulty of the technology. And this provides the reference of the latter research.

Keywords: P2P Network , network security ,authentication , access control

1 Introduction

P2P Network and its application is the hotspot of research of network applications since [1]. Like other network applications, security issues have become the core issues which should been settled. Authentication and access control are the two main fields of the security issues. Different applications have different requirements of authentication and access control. Because of the characteristics of the P2P Network itself[2], the security issues of the P2P Network are of particularity and complexity. So the authentication and access control methods chosen in different applications must adapted to the characteristics of P2P Network. This is the issue to be solved when a security settlement is designed.

This paper briefly introduces the concept, characteristics and the security requirements and settlements of P2P Network. we sum up the security settlement of current P2P system. We analyze the security issues and existing security hidden trouble of current settlements.

2 Basic Concept

2.1 Security Requirements

P2P applications may have different security requirements. Here we analyze the security requirements of main type of P2P applications from the point of view of authentication and access control.

* This work is supported by National Natural Science Foundation of China under Grant 60373040 and National “863” Program Grant 2003AA142150.

M. Li et al. (Eds.): GCC 2003, LNCS 3032, pp. 468–470, 2004.

2.1.1 Requirements of Authentication

Authentication is the basic security requirement of P2P applications. Here we list the security requirements of authentication of different applications.

RA1. weak authentication: RA2.Strong authentication
RA3.accountability: RA4. Cost effectiveness :
RA5.authentication based on attribute. RA6. Scalability:
RA7. Community authentication:

These authentication methods mentioned above have several implementations. This issue will be described in following subsection.

2.1.2 Access Control

Access control is another security issue which should been solved of P2P applications. Here we list the security requirements of different P2P applications in access control.

RB1. Providing Discretionary Access Control.
RB2. Providing Mandatory Access Control.
RB3. Providing access control based on attribute.
RB4. Access control is of diversity. In P2P Network, different nodes choose the most efficient access control methods according to different requirements.

2.2 Implementation of Authentication and Access Control

Here we list the some authentication methods in common use .

MA1.Using nickname: MA2.PGP:
MA3.PKI: .MA4.Self assigned.

The last three methods are based on asymmetric algorithms.

Access control is the mechanisms and policies that restrict access to computer resources only by correct users. Many models have been extended and modified in some applications. These model are including

MB1.Bell-LaPadula model. MB2.Role Based Access Control.
MB3.Flowing Control Model. MB4.Access Control List (ACL).
MB5.SandBox model. MB6.Token model.
MB7.Trust Management System. MB8.Field-Type model.

3 Classification and Comparison

We divide the P2P applications into four types according to the different functions of these applications. Here we list the security requirements and implementations of several types of P2P applications .

Auth: Authentication. AC: Access Control

We can see that the security settlements of P2P applications are of diversity. Different applications have different security requirements. To satisfy these requirements, implementations are chosen accordingly.

Table 1. Security requirements and implementations of typical P2P applications

Type of P2P	P2P System	Security Requirements		Implementations	
		Auth	AC	Auth	AC
P2P Computing	Avaki[3]	RA2,RA3,RA4,RA6	RB1,RB2,RB4	MA4	MB2,MB4
	SETI@home[4]	RA1	x	MA1	x
Cooperation Computing	Groove[5]	RA2,RA3,RA6,RA7	RB1,RB4	MA2,MA3	MB2,MB4,MB8
	Magi[6]	RA2,RA3,RA4,RA6	RB1,RB2,RB3,RB4	MA2,MA3	MB4
File Sharing	Gnutella[7]	RA1	RB1	MA1	MB8
	Freenet[8]	RA1	RB1	MA1	MB8
P2P Platform	JXTA	RA1-RA7	RB1,RB3,RB4	MA1-MA4	MB2,MB4,MB5,MB8
	PtPtl[9]	RA2	RB1	MA2,MA3	MB4

4 Open Questions

At present the researches on security issues of P2P Network mainly concentrate on authentication and access control. Here we analyze the difficult problem in these researches, including: the ID of users and resources , establishing initial trust relation, description of security strategy, mandatory access control in P2P Network. These Questions is proposed in the P2P Network circumstance, and this questions are the elements of P2P applications. If these questions can not be solved correctly, the P2P application can not been secure in deed.

Some traditional security settlements play important role in P2P Network. But they also face now security problem. To solve these problems, we should start with cryptology, artificial intelligence, computer semantics and agent technology.

References

1 Napster. http://www.napster.com/.
2. Dejan S.Milojicic, Vana Kalogeraki, Rajan Lukose, Kiran Nagaraja, Jim Pruyne, Bruno Richard, Sami Rollins, Zhichen Xu, HP Laboratories Palo Alto. Peer-to-Peer Computing.HPL-2002-57, March 8th, 2002.
3. Avaki. http://www.avaki.com .
4. SETI@home. http://setiathome.ssl.berkeley.edu.
5. Groove. http://www.groove.com.
6. Peer-to-Peer Architectures and the Magi Open-Source Infrastructure http://www.endtech.com/pdfs/ETIP2Pwhitepaper.pdf, January 2002.
7. Gnutella. http://www.gnutella.com.
8. I.Clarke, O.Sandberg, B.Wiley, T. W. Tong. Freenet: Adistributed anonymous information storage and retrieval system.
9. PtPtl. http://sourceforge.net/projects/ptptl.

Methodology Discussion of Grid Peer-Peer Computing

Weifen Qu[1,2], Qingchun Meng[1], and Chengbing Wei[2]

[1]Computer Science Department, Ocean University of China, 266071
qwf02@mail.china.com
[2]Electronics Engineering Department ,Qingdao University, 266071
wei_20002000@yahoo.com

Abstract. With Peer-to-Peer computing on the increase, we take a look at how Web Services can get involved. This article discusses the convergence between Web Services and P2P computing. We engage in a discussion of how Web Services and P2P technologies alleviate each other's core complexities, the applications of the two. At the same time, we discuss the issues of trust and security appear on the P2Pand some of resolutions to it.

1 Introduction

The Gartner Group defines P2P computing as: "characterized by direct connections using virtual namespaces, it describes a set of computing nodes that treat each other as equals (peers) and supply processing power, content or applications to other nodes in a distributed manner, with no presumptions about a hierarchy of control".

Peer-to-peer computing based architecture allows for decentralized application design, moving from centralized server models to a distributed model where each peer, independent of software and hardware platforms, can benefit and profit from being connected to millions of other peers. In such architectures, clients and servers have a lateral relationship rather than the traditional vertical relationship, giving the whole peer group tremendous processing power and storage space.

2 Features of a P2P Application

In this section, we briefly review some of the core features of a P2P application:

A P2P application should be able to locate other peers in the network.

Once an application is able to locate other peers, it should be able to communicate with them using messages.

Once the communication is established with other peers, the application should be able to receive and provide information, such as content.

This research is supported by National Science Foundation project 60374031

M. Li et al. (Eds.): GCC 2003, LNCS 3032, pp. 471–474, 2004.

3 Convergence of P2P and Web Services

There are quite a few common features of P2P and Web Services technologies, as they both aim to become a common stack for publishing and discovery across networks. P2P computing is based on a decentralized model and primarily focused on supplying processing power, content, or applications to peers in a distributed manner, and less focused on the semantics of messaging formats and communication protocols. Web Services, on the other hand, is based on a centralized model and primarily focused on standardizing messaging formats and communication protocols.

It is reasonable to state that Web Services are a boon to the world of P2P computing, as XML-based standards hold the key for the success of P2P applications and the widespread adoption of this technology by companies of all sizes. Web Services provide a very elegant way to handle registration, discovery, and content lookup for P2P applications. Web Services standards for security, as they mature, would also ensure the integrity of data and services accessed by P2P software.

4 Based on Open Standards

Since B2Bi using P2P computing would still require integration of processes across corporate boundaries, the communication between different peer systems should be based on open standards, like Web Services. This would allow companies to have different architectures and platforms for their P2P systems.

Since Web Services run through industry standard protocols, companies could in the future be able to eliminate the need for proprietary hardware and software.

5 Directory Services

As far as directory services are concerned, P2P technology has a lot to offer to Web Services technology as well. Using P2P, the Web Services implementation of using a single central UDDI registry, which contains the service description of Web Services, can be transformed into a decentralized mode. The decentralization of UDDI is especially important in the B2B world, as the size of the UDDI registry for any vertical industry would grow exponentially.

The realistic projection at least for the foreseeable future, however, is that the peer systems would continue using the decentralized discovery model, while Web Services systems continue using the centralized discovery model of UDDI.

Easy integration with applications

XML-based Web Services are an ideal technology for orchestrating business processes in P2P systems as they allow applications to communicate across the Internet in a platform- and language-independent fashion.

6 Challenges of P2P and Web Services Working in Conjunction

P2P technology is indeed alluring, but the road to designing, developing, and executing P2P-type applications based on Web Services is not a straight one. There are several major challenges that may hamper its early adoption for both EAI and B2B applications.

Following are some of the potential problems with P2P-based architectures in the light of its usage with Web Services.

7 Network Bandwidth

If companies use P2P and Web Services based applications for EAI and B2Bi, it may severely slow down their network connections and hamper the core business activities. By definition, P2P applications eliminate central servers and create a loose, dynamic network of peers. For any content retrieval operation, such as a search for a specific item in a catalog, all the peers in the network are searched, using a lot of network bandwidth. As this network size increases and becomes more distributed, it may be affected by poor and slow connections.

8 Security

The most important feature of the P2P-based application - decentralized, distributed architecture - is also its weakest link. This holds true even if these applications are implemented using Web Services, as security standards for Web Services are themselves not yet defined and matured.

It can be safely stated that P2P systems typically have very strong security if they are run as a closed system, as in enterprise application integration (EAI). If, however, they run as open systems, say for business-to-business integration (B2Bi) the security risks are much higher. As of now, though, the security issue remains one of the primary roadblocks to both P2P systems and Web Services adoption going beyond use with previously known and trusted partners.

9 Complex Architectures and Difficult Maintenance

Trust is an issue in every non-trivial distributed application -- peer-to-peer applications included. In a distributed application, the level of trust is the metric that measures how confident we are that we are communicating with whom we think we are, and that we are accessing the resources we think we are.

It's easy to establish trust in small networks where every entity knows every other entity. In small networks entities are on a first-name basis, and trust can be maintained by the same social forces that operate in the real world. The difficulty establishing trust arises when a network application grows big enough that conventional social forces no longer fit the bill. The exact size of the network obviously depends on the application, but growing pains typically begin at the point at which any entity on the network no longer expects to interact only with known entities.

At this point we immediately encounter two problems: peer authentication and authorization. First, entities can no longer assume that other entities are who they say they are. This is the authentication problem. Second, entities can no longer simply allow other entities indiscriminate access to the functionality they provide and the resources they manage. This is the authorization problem.

Even before trust becomes an issue, we encounter the issue of privacy. Whether an interaction is between two entities that have never before met or between two long-standing acquaintances, the entities concerned must have a guarantee that their interaction is secure.

There is one final aspect of trust that is not given the attention it deserves in many P2P applications. While peer authentication is clearly important, it is often just as important to authenticate shared resources -- content in particular. Without a guarantee on the integrity and identity of shared content, a P2P application runs the risk of introducing so many security holes.

10 Conclusion

P2P computing represents the next revolution in the computing age, as it will alter dramatically the way businesses communicate, collaborate, and exchange data over the Internet. P2P, however, is still in its infancy and much work needs to be done, as well as establishing industry standards and specifications.

Web Services standardization will provide the means for P2P architecture to be broadly adopted by companies for enterprise and business-to-business application integration. Finally, the convergence projection will materialize only after both Web Services and P2P technologies mature individually. At the same time, we must solve some security issues such as Authorization, Authentication , which still exist in the P2P computing.

References

1. Participate in the discussion forum on this article by clicking Discuss at the top or bottom of the article.
2. Read about the http://www.wired.com/news/technology/0,1282,41838,00.html.
3. Read this Introduction to SSL from Netscape.
4. developer Works hosts an entire topic area devoted to the practice of security.

PipeSeeU: A Scalable Peer-to-Peer Multipoint Video Conference System

Bo Xie [1], Yin Liu [2,3], Ruimin Shen [1], Wenyin Liu [2], and Changjun Jiang [3]

[1] Department of Computer Science, Shanghai Jiaotong Univ., Shanghai, China
{bxie,rmshen@sjtu.edu.cn}
[2] Department of Computer Science,City Univ. of Hong Kong, Hong Kong SAR, China
{liuyin,csliuwy}@cityu.edu.hk
[3] Department of Computer Science, Tongji Univ.ersity, Shanghai, China
cjjang@online.sh.cn

Abstract. Peer-to-peer computing and multipoint video conference are both gaining popularity with the explosive development of Internet. Although there are many existing video conference systems in the world, these solutions are all centralized and none of them can run without MCU (Multipoint Control Unit). The centralized nature usually causes single-point failure and does not make efficient use of network resources. Moreover, many IM (Instant Messenger) applications begin to support point-to-point video conference. However, to the best of our knowledge, none of them can support multipoint video conference. In this paper, a peer-to-peer multipoint video conference system "PipeSeeU", which is based on existing IM applications, is proposed to solve the problem mentioned above.

1 Introduction

In recent years, more and more multipoint video conference systems are deployed on the Internet. However, traditional large-scale multipoint video conference systems are usually centralized and require a lot of MCUs. The centralized nature usually causes single-point failure and does not make efficient use of network resources. Nielsen/NetRating data shows that nearly 40 percent of active Internet users at home communicate via IM applications. However, to the best of our knowledge, there are no IM applications that can support multipoint video conference.

The problem mentioned above is the motivation of our peer-to-peer multipoint video conference system "PipeSeeU". "PipeSeeU" has some key features, which make it different from existing solutions. (1) "PipeSeeU" is a peer-to-peer system. It is not like traditional multipoint video conference systems that are centralized and depend on a lot of MCUs. The primary tasks of video conference, how to manage a conference and how to transfer audio/video streams, are done among peers without a central server; (2) "PipeSeeU" is based on existing IM system. PipeSeeU version 1.0 is implemented as an MSN Messenger Add-In instead of a stand-alone peer-to-peer application for easy deployment and sharing the existing large population of IM users; (3) "Pipe

M. Li et al. (Eds.): GCC 2003, LNCS 3032, pp. 475–479, 2004.

SeeU" focuses on audio/video features. It is not like popular peer-to-peer file sharing systems, which are only interested in bandwidth. In addition to bandwidth, it is also interested in latency, which is another important factor that affects QoS (Quality of Service) in video conference.

2 The PipeSeeU Approach

There are two problems to solve in peer-to-peer video conference system. The first is how to manage a conference. The second is how to transfer audio/video streams among peers. We will demonstrate our approaches to these two problems in the following sections.

2.1 Coordinator Election Algorithm

In order to manage the conference in a peer-to-peer environment, our approach requires one peer to act as coordinator, which is the logical owner of this conference. In PipeSeeU version 1.0, we use "Bully Algorithm" [1] to elect a coordinator. We assume that each peer has a unique number, for example, its MSN Messenger username. When a peer finds that the coordinator is no longer responding to requests, it will hold an election as follows:

1. *P* sends an *ELECTION* message to all peers with its own numbers.
2. If no one responds, *P* wins the election and becomes coordinator.
3. If one peer with higher number answers, it will take over and *P*'s job is done.

The voted coordinator will only solve the first problem. In order to solve the second problem, we propose following routing algorithms.

2.2 Routing Algorithms

Because of network situations and limited resources of peers, in order to alleviate stress on the peers and network, it is necessary for us to find some peers, which act as application level routers, to distribute audio/video streams to other peers. We will present two router (we call it "reflector peer" here) selection algorithms in this section. In section 2.3, we will describe how to organize the selected routers to construct application-level multicast tree, through which audio/video streams are distributed to all participants in a conference.

• **DHT and Area Based Reflector Peer Selection**

Several research groups have proposed a new generation of scalable peer-to-peer systems that support *distributed hash table* (DHT) functionality, such as CAN[2] and Chord[3]. In Chord[3], each peer keeps track information of *logN* other peers (*N* is the total number of peers in the community). When a peer joins and leaves the overlay network, this highly optimized version of DHT algorithm will only require notifying *logN* peers about that change. However, DHTs have poor locality. In most of the DTH algorithms, the node identifiers are chosen randomly (e.g. hash functions of the IP address, etc.) and the neighbor relations are established solely based on these node identifiers. This will result in poor QoS (high delay and low bandwidth) so that we cannot distribute real-time audio/video streams on traditional DHT overlay networks. In PipeSeeU, we propose a novel algorithm which benefits from DHT's scalable, wide-area lookup services, and uses area information to cover the gap between DHT overlay network and the underlying IP topology.

A key feature of our approach is to use DHT overlay network to lookup neighbors according to underlying IP topology and transfer audio/video streams on another application-level multicast tree constructed by the selected peers instead of the DHT overlay network. The algorithm is illustrated in Fig. 1(a). We first use the DHT's *put(key,ip)* function to divide all peers into several area groups. The connections among peers in the same area are usually of low delay and high bandwidth. When we start to create a conference, the DHT's *lookup(key)* function will be used to find the peer list in the corresponding area group.

```
peerlist dht_neighbor_list(IPAddress ip)
{
  string areacode = find_area_code(ip);
  string key = dht(areacode);
  if( peer is not behind NAT/Firewall)
      put(key,ip);
  peerlist l = lookup(key);
  while( the count of l < N)
  {
    string neighbor_areacode=find_neighbor_area_code(areacode);
    if( neighbor_areacode is null)
          return l;
    string neighbor_key = dht(neighbor_areacode);
    peerlist neighbor_list = lookup(neighbor_key);
      append neighbor_list to l;
  }
  return l;
}
```

(a) DHT and Area Based Reflector Peer Selection

```
list participant_list,buddy_list;

construct_buddylist()
{
  foreach(participant p)
        add p to participant_list;
  buddy_list = buddylist(participant_list);
}

buddylist(list buddy_list)
{
  foreach( element e of buddy_list)
    foreach( buddy b with public IP address of e)
     if(b is not in buddy_list)
     {
      add b to buddy_list;
      if( the count of buddy_list < K*N)
        buddylist(buddy_list);
      else
        return;
     }
}
```

(b) Buddy List Based Peer Selection

Fig. 1. Two Reflector Peer Selection Algorithms

- **Buddy List Based Reflector Peer Selection**

Looking for appropriate reflect peers in a wide range of peers in the overlay network is a time consuming job, even with DHT algorithm. In order to improve the efficiency of the *lookup(key)* function, we propose a heuristic approach for it in Fig. 1(b). This heuristic approach uses some existing information of IM application for the neighbor peer selection problem. People usually use IM application to communicate with friends, colleagues and classmates, and store information of them in the IM application's buddy list. It is really possible that someone in the buddy list of a user is geographically near to him. Hence, the delay between that buddy and him is usually low, and the bandwidth is high. Based on this assumption, we collect all participants' buddy lists in a conference and try to find some peers from them to act as application level routers and distribute audio/video streams to other peers. In most cases, this heuristic approach can greatly improve the efficiency of the DHT's *lookup(key)* function.

2.3 Centralized Diverse Tree Management for MDC Distribution

In a single application-level multicast tree, participating peers are either interior nodes or leaf nodes. The interior nodes carry all the burden of forwarding multicast streams. In a k-level balanced tree with arity f, the number of interior nodes is $(f^{k+1}-1)/(f-1)$ and the number of leaf nodes is f^k. If all nodes in this tree have equal inbound bandwidth, the internal nodes of a balanced tree with arity 16 have an outbound bandwidth requirement of 16 times the inbound bandwidth.
PipeSeeU is designed to overcome the inherently unbalanced forwarding load and strives to distribute the forwarding load over all participating nodes. It will also respect different capacity limits of individual participating nodes. PipeSeeU achieves this by splitting source audio/video stream into MDC (Multiple Description Coding) streams, and using separate multicast trees to distribute each stream. Fig. 2(a) illustrates the basic idea of two diverse application-level multicast trees.

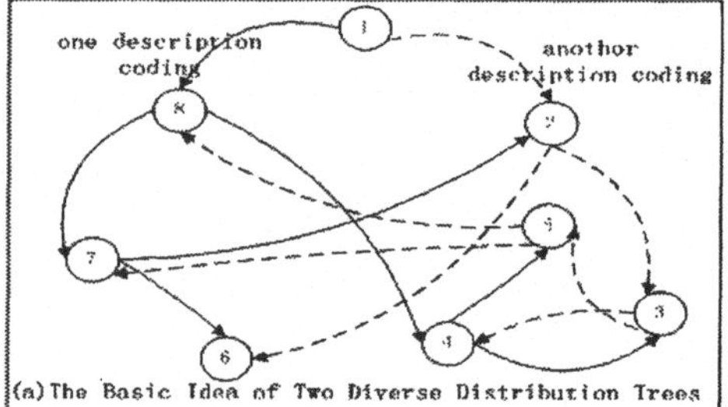

(a) The Basic Idea of Two Diverse Distribution Trees

	Bandwidth	Lost Rate
UDP	1 Mbps	0%
UDP	5 Mbps	0.51%
Traditional TCP	142kbps	0%
10-Parallel TCP	1.2Mbps	0%
50-Parallel TCP	4.2Mbps	0%

(b) UDP vs. TCP vs. Parallel TCP

Fig. 2. Two Diverse Distribution Trees using N-Parallel TCP through NAT/Firewall

In the above sections, coordinator is elected to manage a conference and reflect peers are selected to build several multicast tree to distribute audio/video streams to other peers. Based on these approaches, it is possible for us to hold a multipoint video conference in a peer-to-peer environment. However, there are still some small factors which will affect the QoS of our peer-to-peer video conference system. It is impossible to ignore them in a real network environment. How to traverse NAT/Firewall is one of them. We will discuss it in the following section.

2.4 NAT/Firewall Traversal

Most Firewalls are configured to block communication initiated by outside machines to computers inside the network in order to protect inside systems from intruders. PipeSeeU is designed to enable communication between two peers that cannot ordinarily establish connection with each other because of NAT/Firewall. The key issue is to find a public reflector peer to forward audio/video streams between two peers that are both behind different NAT/Firewall. In addition, PipeSeeU supports the placement of standard RTP/RTCP data in HTTP requests and replies. As a result, peers behind firewalls can access audio/video streams through HTTP proxy servers. In order to improve end-to-end network throughput, PipeSeeU opens parallel TCP network connections to "stripe" the data across a parallel set of sockets. Our experiments show that this approach can greatly increase aggregate network throughput, and consequently increase the video frame rates, which is illustrated in Fig. 2(b).

3 Experiments

We have developed PipeSeeU version 1.0 as an MSN Messenger Add-In to evaluate our peer-to-peer multipoint video conference model. This experimental evaluation mainly focuses on the DHT and area based reflector peer selection. As illustrated in Table 1, we have constructed a local network area database which consists of 10,484 tuples of 32 bit IP address. For more experimental data or full technical report about PipeSeeU, please visit

http://sourceforge.net/projects/PipeSeeU.

Table 1. Network Area IP Map Database

IP-From	IP-To	ISP	Network Area Code
202.120.0.0	202.120.63.255	CERNET	Shanghai Jiaotong University Network
202.120.64.0	202.120.79.0	CERNET	Shanghai Medical University Network

4 Conclusions

In this paper, a peer-to-peer multipoint video conference system "PipeSeeU", which is based on existing IM applications, is proposed. For alleviating stress on the peers and network, it uses "DHT and area based" and "buddy list based" peer selection algorithms find some peers, which act as application level routers, to distribute real-time audio/video streams to other peers. In addition, PipeSeeU uses multiple, diverse distribution trees to provide redundancy in network paths and MDC to provide redundancy in data.

References

1. Garcia Molina, H. "Elections in a Distributed Computing System", IEEE Trans. on Coputers,vol.31,pp.48-59,Jan.1982
2. S. Ratnasamy, P. Francis, M. Handley, R. Karp, and S. Shenker. A scalable content-addressable network. In SIGCOMM, Aug. 2001
3. Stocal I et al. Chord:A scalable peer-to-peer lookup service for Internet applications. In ACM SIGCOMM, San Diego,CA,USA,2001,pp.149-160

Vega Grid: A Computer Systems Approach to Grid Research

Zhiwei Xu and Wei Li

Institute of Computing Technology, Chinese Academy of Sciences, Beijing 100080, China
{zxu, liwei}@ict.ac.cn

Abstract. This paper presents a computer systems approach used in the Vega Grid project at Institute of Computing Technology, Chinese Academy of Sciences. The main feature is to view a grid as a computer system at the hardware and operating system level, and utilize the knowledge and methodologies accumulated in the past 40 years in computer systems design. Following this method, the Vega Grid team identified several core problems, developed a Vega Grid systems architecture, and proposed several systems technologies, such as grid-enabling servers, grid routers, grid switches, grid address spaces, grid process (grip), grid community (agora), and GSML software. Taking advantage of web services and OSGA/Globus grid services, these techniques have potentials in developing a dynamic, open society of people and computers.

1 Introduction

Grids must accommodate a dynamic, open society of people and computers in a world of network computing. Grids need to provide single system image and nontrivial quality of services through resource sharing, collaboration, and integration over the Internet, based on general-purpose open standards. At the same time, users and resources in a grid are not necessarily subject to centralized control.

Of the questions raised by users to the grid research community, a frequently asked question is this: Why is grid different? After all, there exist many systems that already provide nontrivial quality of services through resource sharing, collaboration, and integration. Some of them are even based on open standards. The utility computing concept is not new either. People have been trying to provide information utility since the 1960's. So why all the buzz?

We believe one answer to this question lies in the approach used, which directly affect how people build, use, operate, and maintain grids. Several approaches have been used in grid research. In the solution-oriented approach, the emphasis is on the total solution for a specific grid application that achieves resource sharing, collaboration, and integration. The middleware approach focuses on realizing grid capability through a general-purpose middleware platform. Its methodology is similar to systems such as CORBA and the previous IBM San Francisco project.

In the new wave of grid research started from the 1990's, the computer systems approach is revived. For instance, the Globus project [4] tries to provide a grid operating

M. Li et al. (Eds.): GCC 2003, LNCS 3032, pp. 480–486, 2004.

system kernel, while the Legion project [7] aims to build a worldwide computer. IBM is consolidating its grid-related activities into a massive On Demand Computing initiative, and is using WebSphere as IBM's brand of an Internet operating system. Microsoft also describes its .Net as an Internet operating system.

This paper presents a computer systems approach used in the Vega Grid [12] project at Institute of Computing Technology, Chinese Academy of Sciences. The main feature is to view a grid as a computer system platform at the hardware and operating system level, and utilize the knowledge and methodologies accumulated in the past 40 years in computer systems design. This approach helps clarify applications and resources requirements, reveal computer science problems, and provide a reference framework to organize our research activities. Following this method, the Vega Grid team identified several core problems, which are integrated into the problem of *man-computer society*. We also developed a Vega Grid systems architecture, and proposed several systems technologies, such as grid-enabling servers, grid routers, grid switches, grid address spaces, grid process (grip), grid community (agora), and GSML software [13]. Taking advantage of web services and OSGA/Globus grid services, these techniques have potentials in developing a dynamic, open society of people and computers.

2 Computer Science Problems

In his Turing award lecture of 1999, Jim Gray pointed out three lasting visions of computer science research, symbolized as Charles Babbage's computers, Vannevar Bush's Memex, and the Turing Test [6]. Bush's vision mainly deals with the problem of how to design/use computers to help humans, or human-computer relationship. Since Bush published his article "As We May Think" in 1945, the 1960 has witnessed another surge in human-computer relationship research: J.C.R. Licklider published his influential article "Man-Computer Symbiosis", the Mutlics team proposed time-sharing, and John MaCarthy developed Lisp. These studies produced significant innovations that have been used to this date, such as process, virtual address space, time-shared operating system, and dynamic scoping.

As we enter the 21st century, network computing is becoming a mainstream paradigm, with grid a driving technology. The landscape of human-computer relationship has changed from man-computer symbiosis to *man-computer society*, as characterized by the following six distinct features of a grid:

- *People and Computers*. Although the idea of a networked world is touched upon, Licklider's man-computer symbiosis [9] is mainly concerned with a 1-person-1-computer system. However, a grid, by definition, is an m-person-n-computer system, where both m and n could be large. This raises several challenging issues. We must consider scalability, load balancing, availability, while at the same time maintain single-system image. Human-computer relationship is not limited to man-computer interaction any more, but also includes man-man interaction and computer-computer interaction.

- *Open Society*. A grid is a dynamic, open society of heterogeneous users and computing resources. We cannot assume a closed-world with predetermined user requirements and resource space. User requirements are always changing. A user or a resource can join or leave a grid at any time. A grid program may reference a resource that the programmer does not even known its existence. Users and resources are often autonomous, not subject to the control of a centralized entity such as the case of the kernel in Unix.
- *Standards-Based Interactions*. The grid program itself is not a pre-specified algorithm any more, but changes through sophisticated, standards-based interactions. Unlike the World Wide Web, which mainly allows users to read the contents of a Web page through the HTTP protocol, a grid calls for a small set of more sophisticated, standards-based interaction operations for write, operate, and inter-creation. Furthermore, it is desirable that the user interface for interaction is as user-friendly as the Web interface (e.g., HTML). Users should not be forced to learn or perform procedural programming in order to create or use an interface page. Our goal is an interface such that a secretary should be able to program, and an executive should be able to use.
- *4A Patterns*. The grid computing paradigm inherits the utility concept from the electricity grid. We should be able to obtain and use computing resources the same way as we obtain electric resource, at *any time*, *any place*, on *any device*, by *any user*. This calls for, among other things, characteristics of persistence and context.
- *Full Lifecycle*. Past computing models such as the Turing machine focus on only the usage phase of the lifecycle [1]. With grid computing, we must consider the full lifecycle, including development, deployment, usage, and maintenance. The time complexity of a grid should not be just the algorithmic time complexity of an application run, but new measurements such as *time to production*.
- *High-Productivity Service*. Although algorithmic time/space complexities are still important, performance evaluation in grid computing is more user-centric, emphasizing user visible productivity and service-level agreements.

If we follow the computer systems approach, if we view a grid as a distributed computer, several computer science questions must be asked, such as the following:

- What should be the underlying theoretical model?
- What should be this grid computer's basic encoding?
- What should be this grid computer's system architecture?
- What should be this grid computer's address space?
- What should be this grid computer's process?
- What should be this grid computer's programming language?

For the encoding question, we already have a consensus, which is XML. The remaining questions are still active research topics [10]. The grid community has made significant progress in answering the architecture question. The Global Grid Forum has proposed the OGSA architecture [3], and the OGSI standard is becoming stable, with several implementations available. However, much remains to be done at the OGSA Platform layer [5]. Furthermore, the OGSA/OGSI standards may be considered as offering a grid system software architecture, and there is no standard yet for grid system hardware.

Following the OGSA standards work, the Vega Grid project is researching these problems. In the rest of the paper, we present some progress on the problems of grid theoretical model, grid architecture, grid address space, grid process, and grid programming language. Some of these techniques have been deployed and used in the China National Grid.

3 CAM: A Theoretical Model for Grid Computing

The CAM model (Computer with Active Memory) is a theoretical model for grid computing developed by the Vega Grid research team. The CAM model is derived from the traditional RAM and PRAM models [2] [8] [11]. It has been used to guide the design of the GSML grid interface language and the Vega GOS grid software.

Similar to the PRAM model, a CAM model consists of *m* processors and an infinitely long memory space, where each memory cell can hold a word of length *r*. However, the behavior of a CAM is quite different from that of a RAM/PRAM:

- In a RAM/PRAM, each memory cell is a passive entity, holding a word that can be read or written by a processor. In the CAM model, each memory cell can also serve as an active entity. A processor can execute a memory cell to run an algorithmic computation.
- In a RAM/PRAM, a program (parallel program) is stored in the processor(s), the execution of which represents a run of an algorithmic computation. In the CAM model, each processor represents a user or a user-side client device, and each memory cell represents a grid node (or grid resource). Algorithmic computations are performed in the memory cells. The program executed by a CAM processor mainly deals with interaction between a user and a grid.
- In a PRAM, the number of processors, m, is usually predetermined, and all processors are implicitly assumed to know how the other processors are using the resources. In a grid environment, we cannot make such an assumption. A processor as well as a resource can join or leave the grid at any time. Explicit operations must be executed to make a resource "known" to the processors.

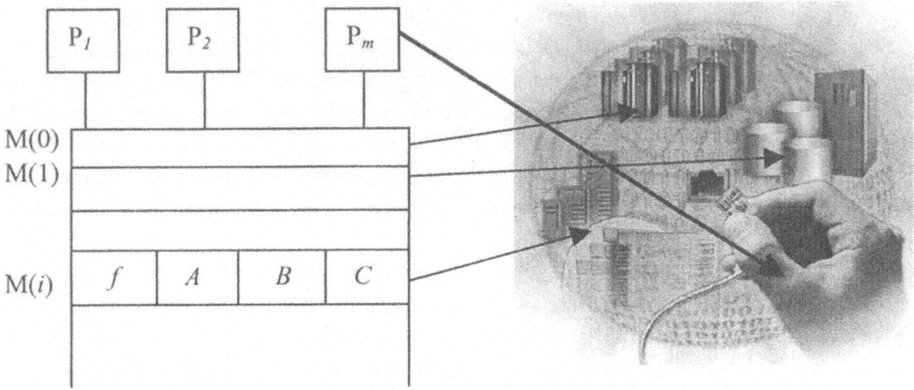

Fig. 1. The CAM model for grid computer (The picture on the right is courtesy of Irving Wladawsky-Berger of IBM)

Five types of instructions are available in the CAM model: deploy, execute, internalize, persist, and glue. The **deploy** instruction explicitly deploys a grid service to a memory cell (grid node) and makes it known to all the other processors and services. This instruction may also be used to destroy a deployed service with a NULL operand. The **execute** instruction initiates the execution of a service at the specified node. For instance, **execute** M(i) means service *f* is executed, with parameters stored in *A*, *B* and *C* (see Fig. 1). Once the service is started, the processor can go on to execute the next instruction. A service is executable only if it is deployed; otherwise an error (null) will be returned. The **persist** instruction helps to make a resource or service persistent, which could help with sharing, collaboration, and 4A usage. The **internalize** instruction helps the client side to compose individual services and resources into one entity, and makes it known to the grid. The glue instructions include several simple instructions in the RAM model, such as halt and if-then-else.

4 The Vega Grid Systems Techniques

Figure 2 illustrates the Vega Grid system architecture for a grid computer system, including both software and hardware. The hardware architecture consists of multiple grid nodes that could span wide-area locations. Within each node, there are one or more computers (servers) that host computing, storage, data, and program resources. All resources are encapsulated as services. Currently, the Vega Grid architecture mainly supports web services and OGSI-compliant grid services (such as GT3 services). Two new architectural components are the grid resource router and switch. They differ from a network router/switch in that they do not just route messages, but provide a link to other grid nodes and to the users. The main function of the grid router/switch is to connect grid resources together at the applications level. A grid switch connects resources within a grid node, which is often managed by one institute. A grid router connects resources among multiple grid nodes, which could be owned by multiple institutes. These hardware features are being implemented by Dawning 4000A, a grid-enabling superserver under development at National Research Center for Intelligent Computing Systems (NCIC) of China.

Learning from the experience in computer architecture and operating systems design, we developed an address space model for grid, call the EVP grid resource space model. Native resources and services located in individual grid nodes are called *physical resources* (P), such as “real” Web services and GT3 grid services. These resources and services are abstracted into location-independent *virtual resources* at the grid operating system layer (the OGSA Platform layer). The grid users see *effective resources*.

A runtime construct called grip is proposed to solve the grid process problem. A grip is a handle for users to access grid resources and services. Agora is a persistent construct realizing the virtual organization concept, which is frequently used in the grid community but rarely precisely defined. In the Vega Grid architecture, an agora consists of grid subjects (e.g., grid users), grid objects (e.g., resources and services), policies, and context. The grip and the agora constructs are helpful for achieving open society and 4A usage.

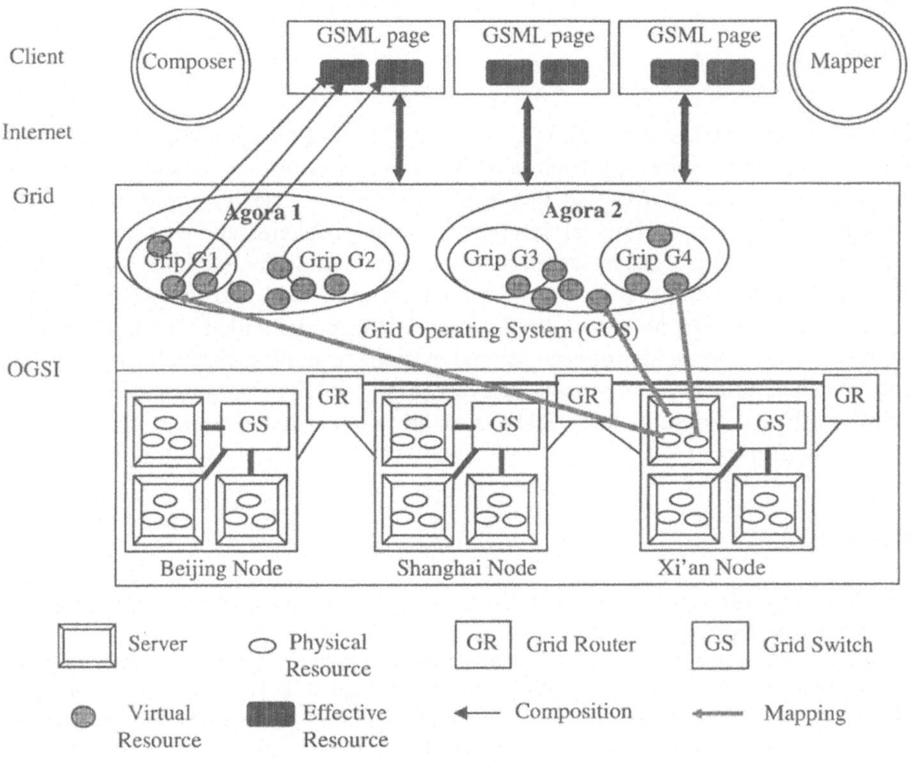

Fig. 2. The Vega Grid System Architecture

For the grid programming question, we are developing a suite of software, called the GSML suite, which includes a GSML language and a set of tools that enable end users to use grid resources conveniently. The GSML (Grid Service Markup Language) is an XML-based markup language for users to program a grid and to access grid services. The language design focuses on ease of use by limiting expressive power. Our goal is an interface such that a secretary should be able to program, and an executive should be able to use the grid.

A grid application is eventually presented to the user as a GSML page. A tool called GSML browser is provided at the client side, which renders GSML pages and provides an interface for users to access a grid. This grid browser is different from a Web browser in that it allows the users not only to read contents from a grid, but also to write to and to operate a grid, by sending service requests to the grid side. A GSML server receives service requests from the client side, processes the requests, and sends results back to the client side. A protocol called Grid Service Request Protocol (GSRP) is used between the GSML server and the GSML browser. A software tool called grid resource Mapper converts native grid resources into virtual resources. Another tool called grid resource Composer allows a user to browse/select virtual resources and integrate them into a GSML page.

5 Concluding Remarks

The computer systems approach is a viable one in developing grids. This paper presents a computer systems approach used in the Vega Grid project. Our experience in the past three years shows that this approach helps us clarify applications and resources requirements and reveal computer science problems, and provide a reference framework to organize our research activities. Following this method, the Vega Grid team identified several core problems, which are integrated into the problem of man-computer society. We also developed a theoretical model called CAM, a Vega Grid systems architecture, and proposed several systems technologies, such as grid routers, grid switches, grid address spaces, grid process (grip), grid community (agora), and GSML software. Some of these techniques are already being used in the China National Grid project.

References

[1] A.V. Aho, J.E. Hopcroft, and J.D. Ullman, The Design and Analysis of Computer Algorithms, Addison-Wesley, 1974.

[2] S.A. Cook and R.A. Reckhow, "Time Bounded Random Access Machines", *Journal of Computer and System Science*, Vol. 7, No. 4, 1973, pp. 354-375.

[3] I. Foster, C. Kesselman, J. Nick, S. Tuecke, "Grid Services for Distributed Systems Integration", *IEEE Computer*, 35 (6), 2002, pp. 37-46.

[4] I. Foster et al., "The Globus Project: A Status Report", *Proc. IPPS/SPDP '98 Heterogeneous Computing Workshop*, pp. 4-18, 1998.

[5] I. Foster, D. Gannon, Open Grid Services Architecture Platform, http://www.ggf.org/ogsa-wg, July 31, 2003.

[6] Jim Gray, "What next?: A dozen information-technology research goals", *Journal of the ACM*, Vol. 50, Issue 1, 2003, pp. 41 – 57.

[7] A. Grimshaw et al., "Legion: The Next Logical Step toward a Nationwide Virtual Computer", *Tech. Rep. CS-94-21, Department of Computer Science*, University of Virginia, 1994.

[8] K. Hwang, Z. Xu, *Scalable Parallel Computers: Technology, Architecture, Programming*, McGraw-Hill, New York, 1998.

[9] J.C.R. Licklider, "Man-Computer Symbiosis", *IRE Transactions on Human Factors in Electronics*, HFE-1, pp. 4-11, 1960.

[10] Zsolt Németh, Vaidy Sunderam, "Characterizing Grids: Attributes, Definitions, and Formalisms", *Journal of Grid Computing*, Vol. 1, Issue 1, 2003, pp. 9-23.

[11] P. van Emde Boas, "Machine Models and Simulations", *Handbook of Theoretical Computer Science*, J. van Leeuwen (Ed.), Elsevier, 1990.

[12] Z. Xu, W. Li, H. Fu and Z. Zeng, "Mathematic Education on Vega Grid", *Journal of Distance Education Technologies*, Vol. 1, No. 3, July-September, 2003, pp. 1-12.

[13] Z. Xu, W. Li, D. Liu, H. Yu, B. Li, "The GSML Tool Suite: A Supporting Environment for User-level Programming in Grids", *Proceedings of PDCAT 2003,* pp. 629-633, 2003.

RB-GACA: A RBAC Based Grid Access Control Architecture*

Weizhong Qiang, Hai Jin, Xuanhua Shi, Deqing Zou, and Hao Zhang

Cluster and Grid Computing Lab
Huazhong University of Science and Technology, Wuhan, 430074, China
{wzqiang, hjin}@hust.edu.cn

Abstract. Because the distribution of services and resources in wide-area networks are heterogeneous, dynamic, and multi-domain, security is a critical concern in grid computing. This paper proposes a general authorization and access control architecture, RB-GACA, for grid computing. It is based on classical access control mechanism in distributed applications, *Role Based Access Control* (RBAC). We also use a kind of standard policy language as the presentation of access control policies to provide a general and standard support for different services and resources.

1 Introduction

Due to the characteristics of heterogeneity, dynamic and organization self-governed, there are many challenges to be solved for grid technology, such as authentication, authorization, and resource discovery [1]. *Authentication, authorization and audit* (AAA) [2] are general issues for grid environment. Most of the research interest presently is on authentication, and little is on authorization and access control.

Authentication is the first problem. The Globus project proposed and developed the *Grid Security Infrastructure* (GSI) [3] that is authentication architecture for grid computing. This mechanism provides single-sign-on approach, cross-domain protocol and some convenient security API for grid applications.

Authorization is a challenge mission. The authorization mechanism of Globus is very inflexible and coarse-grain, which uses a mapping table in every grid node that only maps the global name (a ticket or certificate) [4] into a local name (login name or user ID). A flexible, fine-grained, and general authorization and access system is significant for grid computing.

In this paper, we present a *role based grid access control architecture* (RB-GACA). We provide a flexible framework for policy management that treats the whole grid as a series of independent, dynamic domains. The policy evaluating and decision making is based on *role-based access control* (RBAC). XACML [5] is used as the presentation policy language.

---

* This paper is supported by National Science Foundation under grant 60125208 and 60273076.

M. Li et al. (Eds.): GCC 2003, LNCS 3032, pp. 487–494, 2004.

The paper is organized as follows. First, we present some related works about RBAC and some classical access control approaches. Then we describe our access control model. Our system architecture and access control policy expression are presented later. Then we give the performance analysis. Finally, we conclude our paper and present some future considerations.

2 Related Works

Role Based Access Control model (RBAC) [6][7] is an alternative approach to traditional access control model *discretionary access control* (DAC) and *mandatory access control* (MAC). In MAC and DAC access control models, subjects and objects have direct relationships, which cause oppressive burden of security management.

In RBAC, there are three layers, users, roles and permissions. Users are assigned roles, and permissions are assigned to roles. Because users and access permissions are separated, the management of access control is more expediently and costs less [8]. In RBAC, the user-role relationship is more dynamic than the role-permission relationship.

Permis [9] is a policy driven RBAC *Privilege Management Infrastructure* (PMI). The policy is written in XML and stored in X.509 *attribute certificates* (AC) in the local LDAP directory. The credentials may be widely distributed. The core model of Permis is *Access Control Decision Function* (ADF).

Akenti [10] is an access control architecture that addresses issues that all the resources are controlled by multiple authorities. The Akenti policy engine gathers user-conditions certificate and attribute certificates, and grants access to a resource by verifying these two types of certificates. In *Community Authorization Service* (CAS) [11], the owners of resources grant access to a community account as a whole. The CAS server is responsible for managing the policies that govern access to a community's resources. It maintains fine-grained access control information and grants restricted GSI proxy certificates to the users of community. K. Keahey et al [12] propose a fine grain authorization system in grid by modifying GRAM of Globus. But it has the limitation of management and scalability. L. Ramakrishnan et al [13] also present an authorization infrastructure by providing authorization at the component interface. But their special objects are component-based grid applications.

3 Model of RB-GACA

The access control model of our system is based on the RBAC model presented in NIST [5]. As the NIST model is a complete proposal and is too complex for our system, we make some simplification to adapt it to our system. In RB-GACA access control model, all the access control domain of the grid is naturally divided into a series of domains, each of which is an autonomous region.

RB-GACA access control model consists of following components:

1) U, R, OP, OB are sets of users, roles, options and objects in an access control domain, respectively

2) $P = 2^{(OP \times OB)}$ is a set of permission in the domain
3) $PA \subseteq P \times R$ is a relationship set that defines permission to role assignment in the domain, a role in R can have the operating permission defined in PA
4) $UA \subseteq U \times R$ is a relationship set that defines role to user assignment, a user in U can enable the roles defined in UA

We also used some administrative operation definitions in RB-GACA, which includes add/delete user, add/delete role, assign/de-assign user-to-role assignment, and grant/revoke permission-to-role assignment. Definition 1 is one of the definitions.

Definition 1. A domain manager may execute the $AddUser(user : NAME)$ operation if it is a new $user : NAME$ ($user \notin U$) to the domain and the user is authenticated by the domain, $authenticated(user) = true$. The result is that the $user : NAME$ is added to the set U, $U' = U \cup \{user\}$.

4 System Architecture

For an authorization and access control infrastructure, two factors must be predefined: the repositories location of the access policies, the relative location of the *policy decision point* (PDP) and the *policy enforcement point* (PEP). For the first factor, there are two choices: the policies may be stored in one repository centrally or stored in several repositories distributed. To the first choice, the management is convenient but it lacks scalability and reliability. The later choice has the contrary characteristics. As to the second factor, arranging PDPs locally with the distributed PEPs have the benefit of scalability and reliability, but it is harder to manage. However, arranging PDP centrally has the benefit of management and the limitation of scalability.

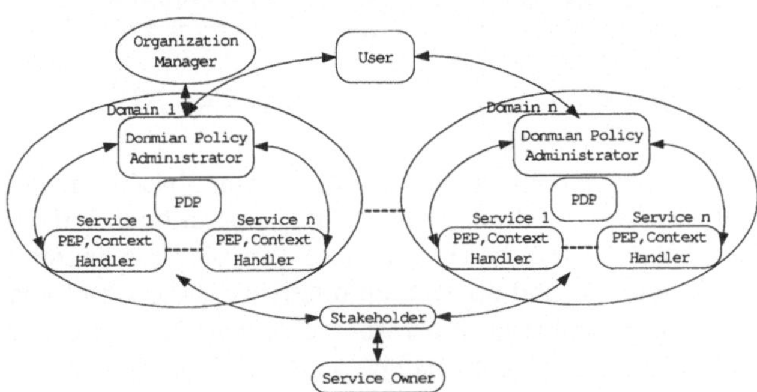

Fig. 1. RB-GACA System Architecture

Figure 1 shows the overall RB-GACA system architecture. The grid is divided into a series of logical domains each of which is an independent access control region. Our system architecture predefines the two factors mentioned above. Repositories location of the access policies is in every domain separately. PDP is domain based, and PEP is service or resource based. If a manager of an organization wants to put some access control polices on the resources, he may initially construct an access control domain to apply the RB-GACA system to these services and resources.

This arrangement is a tradeoff between central and distributed approaches. The advantages are convenient and scalable. If a domain is too huge to be managed, the domain may be divided into two or more domains by the domain policy administrator.

4.1 System Components

As shown in Figure 2, RB-GACA access control architecture is composed of four components: Policy management modules, policy decision modules, policy enforcement modules, and context handler module. For policy management module, there are two sub-modules according to the functions requirement from core RBAC in NIS, Element Sets management agent and Relationship maintenance agent.

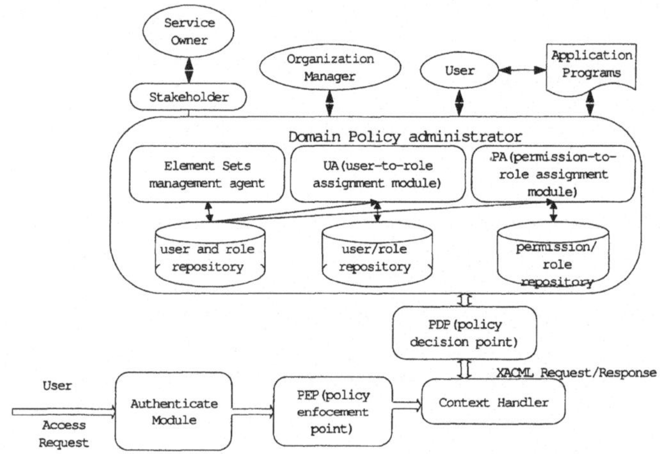

Fig. 2. Access Control System Components

Element Sets management agent is a domain based module for element management. In NIST definition, users, roles, operations, and objects are basic element. These elements may be divided into two classes: operations and objects, users and roles. Operations and objects are relatively static which may be predefined when RBAC system is deployed to a resource or service. For example, in a virtual instruments grid system, the objects may be predefined as some instruments, such as a telescope. The operations may be predefined as steer object, view object, and some other basic operations. However, users set and roles set are relatively dynamic which may be managed by the domain policy administrator.

From Fig.1, the functions of creation and deletion of roles or users are provided by *AddUser* and *DeleteUser* operations for users and *AddRole* and *DeleteRole* operations for roles. The elements set is stored in the user and role repository.

Relationship maintenance agent module accomplishes two policy assignment operations: user-to-role assignment (UA) and permission-to-role assignment (PA). For scalable and dynamic benefit, it is also domain-based. It includes *AssignUser* and *DeassignUser* operations for UA and *GrantPermission* and *RevokePermission* operations for PA.

PEP and authenticate module are both service based, which means that we must separately enforce each type of service. In our preliminary research, we have modified the Globus gatekeeper authorization call-out interface to add the policy enhancement point for job submission service, the GridFtp module for ftp service and Information search module for information search service.

Context Handler is an entity that converts access requests in native request format to XACML canonical form and converts authorization decision in XACML canonical form back to native response format. In our prototype implementation, we convert the native request expression such as Globus RSL request into XACML presentation.

PDP gets the XACML request from Context Handlers and responses according to the set of polices from domain policy administrator. Polices are embedded in X.509 attribute certificates [14] which assure secure binding of polices with the domain policy administrator. Sun XACML implementation [15] is used in our initial implementation.

4.2 Scenarios of RB-GACA

4.2.1 Scenarios of Management Roles

There are two different types of management roles, Organization Manager and Service Owner. Organization Manager is domain based which is responsible for policy administration of the whole domain. Service Owner is service based which is responsible for services or resources. If an organization or a research group wants to grant access control mechanism to the services or resources, the Organization Manager may construct an authorization and access control domain.

Organization Manager must predefine some basic users set, roles set, operations, and the objects through the domain policy administrator, which is a GUI daemon process. The domain policy administrator daemon utilizes Element Set management agent to store these users and roles elements into the user and role repository.

Organization Manager must also predefine some basic policies through the domain policy administrator, which utilizes Relationship Maintenance agent to store the UA policies into user/role repository and the PA policies into permission/role repository.

The Service Owner uses the stakeholder, which is also a GUI daemon process, to interface with the domain policy administrator and get the view of the user set and role set from the user and role repository. The Service Owner references the above view from stakeholder and makes decision of the access control policies for the objects it owns, and stores polices into the user/role repository and permission/role repository through the stakeholder. A Service Owner has the permission to add, revoke or modify his own policies. He also has the permission to consult with the domain policy administrator, which notifies the Organization Manager to add some new roles or users into the user and role repository.

4.2.2 Scenarios of User

Fig.1 shows the scenario for a user to get the authorization to access the resource. He submits the request, which contains the identity certificate and some native description, such as RSL to the domain. The request is first evaluated by the authenticate module and forwarded to the PEP if valid. The PEP forwards the request to the context handler module, which translates the native request into XACML canonical form. After that, the context handler forwards the XACML request to PDP. The PDP calls the function of the domain policy administrator module to get the access control policies. The PDP evaluates request based on the XACML attributes and polices, and makes access decision.

5 System Access Control Policy Expression

RB-GACA access control architecture is based on the XACML standard from OASIS [3]. XACML provides platform-independent expression for access control policies. XACML policies contain three levels of components: 1) Policy and PolicySet, 2) Targets and Rules, 3) Attributes, Attribute value, and Function.

Table 1 illustrates a simple example of user-to-role assignment relationship in a domain named "ICCC laboratory" for grid services.

Table 1. An Example of User-to-Role Assignment Realtionship

Users	Roles
Users inside ICCC lab (DN contains the "ICCC" label)	Advanced user
Users that collaborate with ICCC lab (DN contains some specific label specified by policies)	Basic user
Users inside ChinaGrid	Guest

The pseudo code on next page shows Role-to-User assignment policies for *Advanced user*. It indicates that users within the organization *ICCC laboratory* are allowed to have the *Advanced user* role enabled.

6 Performance Evaluation

The following is performance evaluation of RB-GACA access control architecture. Evaluation framework is illustrated in Figure 3. The reference model using coarse-grain access control approach from Globus toolkit and the system using RB-GACA access control modules are compared.

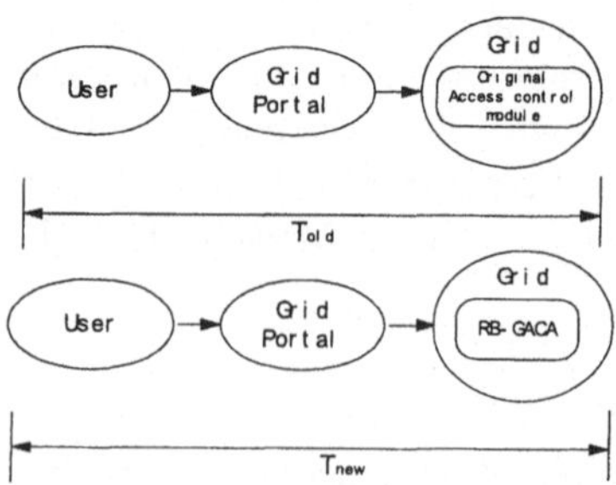

Fig. 3. Performance Evaluation Framework

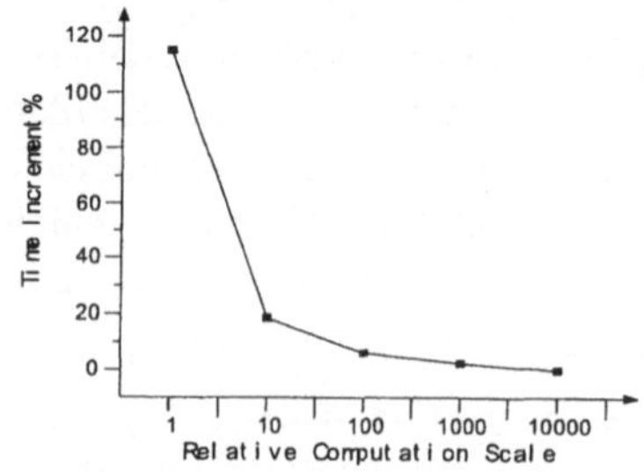

Fig. 4. Time increment vs. Relative Computation Scale

```
<Policy PolicyId="Role Assignment Policy"
  RuleCombiningAlgId="permit-overrides">
<Target>
  <Subjects><AnySubject/></Subjects>
  <Resources><AnyResource/></Resources>
  <Actions><AnyAction/></Actions>
</Target>
<Rule RuleId="Advanced user role"
Effect="Permit">
  <Target>
   <Subjects>
    <Subject>
     <SubjectMatch MatchId="string-equal">
      <AttributeValue>ICCC</AttributeValue>
      <SubjectAttributeDesignator
AttributeId="subject-id"/>
     </SubjectMatch>
    </Subject>
   </Subjects>
<Resources>
    <Resource>
     <ResourceMatch MatchId="string-
equal">
      <AttributeValue>Advaced
User</AttributeValue>
       <ResourceAttributeDesignator
AttributeId="Role"/>
    </Resource>
   </Resources>
  <Actions>
    <Action>
     <ActionMatch MatchId="string-equal">
<AttributeValue>enable</AttributeValue>
      <ActionAttributeDesignator
AttributeId="action-id"/>
    </Action>
   </Actions>
  </Target>
 </Rule>
 </Policy>
```

We use the job submission services in Globus and count the interval between job submitting and ending. The time in the reference model and in experiment system are described as T_{old} and T_{new}. We calculate the percentage of time increment.

A kind of parameter sweeping tasks is used. Figure 4 illustrates experiment result. The Relative Computation Scale is the relative parameter space. From the result, we conclude that the overhead of access control from RB-GACA is reasonable.

7 Conclusion and Future Works

In this paper, we illustrate our role based grid access control models and the system architecture. Our architecture provides convenient policy evaluating and decision making approach. By dividing the grid into independent and dynamic domains, our system provides scalability. We provide the interface for users, Service Owner or Organization Manager with the domain policy administrator module, and also provide the interface for PDP to get valid access policies from domain policy administrator to make decision. The policy language is based on XACML, which ensures generality for variant type of services or resources.

In our preliminary prototype of RB-GACA, we will consider the hierarchy relationship of roles and the cross authorization among domains. Also we will consider the organization of policies to improve the efficiency of policy querying.

References

1. I. Foster, C. Kesselman, and S. Tuecke, "The Anatomy of the Grid: Enabling Scalable Virtual Organizations", *International Journal of Supercomputer Applications*, 15(3): pp.200-222, 2001.
2. Global Grid Form, http://www.ggf.org/.

3. Overview of the Grid Security Infrastructure, http://www.globus.org/security/ overview.html
4. I. Foster, C. Kesselman, G. Tsudik, and S. Tuecke, "A Security Architecture for Computational Grids", *Proceedings of the 5th ACM Conference on Computer and Communications Security*, pp.83-92, San Francisco, CA, USA, 1998.
5. Organization for the Advancement of Structured Information Standards (OASIS), *eXtensible Access Control Markup Language (XACML) Specification Set v1.0*, Oasis XACML TC, February 2003.
6. R. Sandhu, E. Coyne, H. Feinstein, and C. Youman, "Role-based access control models", *IEEE Computer*, Vol.29, No.2, February 1996.
7. D. F. Ferraiolo, R. Sandhu, et al., "Proposed NIST Standard for Role-Based Access Control", *ACM Transactions on Information and System Security*, 4(3): pp.224-274, 2001.
8. D. F. Ferraiolo, J. F. Barkley, and D. R. Kuhn, "A Role Based Access Control Model and Reference Implementation within a Corporate Intranet", *ACM Transactions on Information and System Security*, 2(1): pp.34-64, 1999.
9. D. Chadwick and A. Otenko, "The Permis X.509 Role Based Privilege Management Infrastructure", *Proceedings of SACMAT 2002 Conference*, ACM Press, pp.135-140.
10. M. Thompson, W. Johnston, S. Mudumbai, G. Hoo, K. Jackson, and A. Essiari, "Certificate-based Access Control for Widely Distributed Resources", *Proceedings of the Eighth Usenix Security Symposium*, Aug. 1999.
11. L. Pearlman, V. Welch, I. Foster, C. Kesselman, and S. Tuecke, "A Community Authorization Service for Group Collaboration", *Proceedings of the IEEE 3rd International Workshop on Policies for Distributed Systems and Networks*, 2002.
12. K. Keahey, V. Welch, S. Lang, B. Liu, and S. Meder, "Fine-Grain Authorization Policies in the GRID: Design and Implementation", *Proceedings of the 1st International Workshop on Middleware for Grid Computing*, 2003.
13. L. Ramakrishnan, et al., "An Authorization Framework for a Grid Based Component Architecture", *Proc. of the 3rd International Workshop on Grid Computing*, 2002.
14. S. Farrell and R. Housley, "An Internet Attribute Certificate Profile for Authorization", *IETF RFC*, April 2002.
15. Sun's XACML implementation, http://sunxacml.sourceforge.net/

GriDE: A Grid-Enabled Development Environment

Simon See[1,2], Jie Song[1,2], Liang Peng[1,2], Appie Stoelwinder[1,2], and Hoon Kang Neo[2]

[1] Asia Pacific Science and Technology Center, Sun Microsystems Inc.
[2] Nanyang Center for Supercomputing and Visualization,
Nanyang Technological University, 50 Nanyang Avenue, Singapore 639798

Abstract. Computational grids have become an important emerging platform for high-performance and resource consuming scientific computing. However, there are still obstacles for potential grid users to be involved into the trend and the grid application development is far from mature. Few applications have been designed for and hence benefit from the grids. This is largely due to the immature enabling grid computing environment/tools.
While the traditional established programming tools can possibly be used to build grid applications, they are not particularly suitable for the nature of the grid environment. Our GriDE project aims to provide the fundamentally required features for grid application development and hence narrow the gap between applications and grid computing facilities. We present an overview architecture of GriDE, an application development oriented environment and the integrated basic functionalities such as grid job submission, grid resource discovery/browsing, job status monitoring, and preliminary grid workflow editing. Our experience of GriDE environment shows the feasibility of creating a easy-to-use computing environment for development and execution of grid applications.

1 Introduction

In the past few years grid computing as a technology has been developed rapidly as a next generation computing model in scientific and even commercial world. Although grid computing technology shows increasingly potential advantages in many fields of sciences, currently there are still some obstacles for easy grid application development. There are still few grid-enabled real applications. Even though in some fields the application developers have shown their interests in developing grid-oriented applications, there are few user level enabling tools available, let alone a relatively complete developing environment integrating multiple tools together as a whole to ease the grid application development and execution.

It is therefore necessary for the grid community to endeavor to enable end users to do grid programming. Some testbeds based on Globus Toolkit have been set up for prototyping and experimenting with various application scenarios, but they are far from mature for grid programming.

M. Li et al. (Eds.): GCC 2003, LNCS 3032, pp. 495–502, 2004.

Our grid IDE project, in short the GriDE, is motivated by this gap and its primary goal is to provide end users and application developers an easy to use integrated environment to develop, debug, run, and monitor their applications by exploiting the power of grids. The GriDE environment is based on NetBeans [6] and is intended to include grid schedulers like Sun Grid Engine [10], grid resource management tools like Globus [3], programming libraries like MPICH-G2 [5, 16], and some other grid services. So far the basic functionalities like grid job submission, grid resource browsing, job monitoring are realized based on Globus and Java Cog Kit. Some preliminary functions of grid workflow editing, which is an essential part of grid programming, are also supported by our prototype.

The remainder of this paper is organized as follows: The overall architecture of GriDE is described in Section 2. The basic grid workflow editing functions are also introduced in Section 3. Section 4 introduces the grid job submission module, Section 5 introduces the grid resource discovery and display in GriDE, and job status monitoring and result fetching is explained in Section 6. Some related works are mentioned in Section 7, and finally we end this paper with a conclusion in Section 8.

2 GriDE: Architecture and Overview

The GriDE project is proposed to provide a grid computing environment to cater the requirements of grid applications and promote the usage of grid computing in various scientific research areas. This section describes more details of the overall architecture of GriDE.

Figure 1 shows the layered GriDE architecture, from top user application level to the underlying computing resources.

The grid programming environment is built based on NetBeans IDE, which already has provided basic functions such as editing and compiling, etc. GriDE extends the these functionalities and creates some new features to simplify the development procedure for grid applications:

- Flow Editor: The flow editor provides an easy, fast way to create grid applications without much knowledge about the grid. A number of grid components such as resource node and jobs are to be designed. A few grid application templates are also to be implemented to illustrate the workflow.
- Cross Compiler: GriDE is designed to support multiple programming languages and various platforms. There is a unique application programming interface enabling the usage of various grid facilities/tools.
- Grid Debugger: The debugger is designed to not only debug the applications in a grid simulation environment, but also submit jobs and track the execution status in the real grid resources.
- Performance tuning: This is to estimate the performance in terms of execution time and resource cost. It also provides tools to, if necessary, migrate the jobs somewhere to obtain more powerful resources or improve the resource utility.

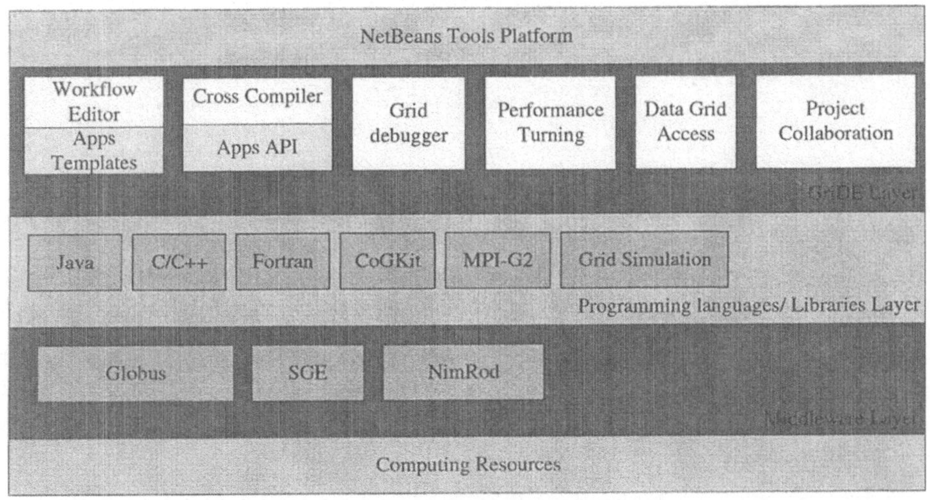

Fig. 1. The Architecture of Grid IDE

- Data grid access: It is a tool to manage the information saved in data grid in forms of files or databases.
- Project collaboration: It is a collaboration working environment for distributed developers including grid based version control tools and project management tools.

Under the GriDE layer, there is a layer of libraries or tools for different programming languages communicating with underlying grid middleware. For example, Java CoGKit [4]is an open source commodity grid kit acting as an interface to Globus. SimGrid [9] is one of the grid simulation tools. Some third party Grid services include OGSI/OGSA [8,15] as well as the tools for parallel computing, like MPICH-G2. Alternatively, JXTA [11] could also be embedded.

At the middleware level, we utilize Globus as a global resource manager. Meanwhile other modules will be embedded, like Sun Grid Engine and NimRod/G [7].

It is obvious that GriDE is a big picture shown in the Figure 1. The GriDE project is still in progress. At present we have finished the integration of the basic features (i.e. grid job submission, grid resource discovery/browsing, and grid job status monitoring) as a grid computing workspace in the NetBeans IDE, as Figure 2 shows. These features are built on Globus middleware. Some other advanced functions like multi-job flow editor are being added.

3 Grid Workflow Editor

Workflow is critical to grid computing for its ability of connecting different grid jobs together to create a more complex computation. From the perspective of

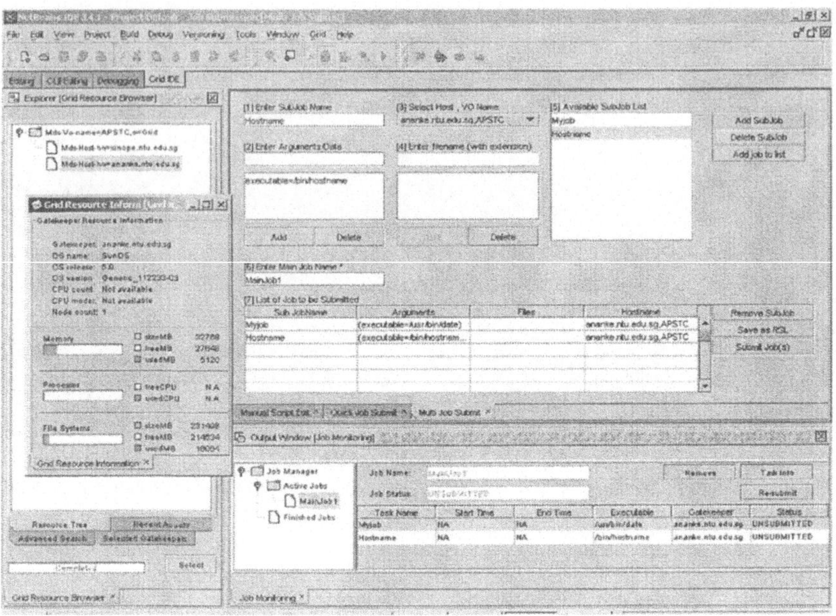

Fig. 2. Grid computing workspace of GriDE.

grid programming, a grid workflow is a well defined set of objects with a well defined of data or control dependencies. The objects can be lower level grid jobs. Workflow is an important part of grid programming in that many grid computing tasks can be composed from of applications and data sets in some particular manners.

Because of its inherent features, workflow makes itself readily to a graph-based representation in a grid developing environment, where the nodes of the graph represent the computation/activities of a particular job, and the directed edges of the graph represent either control flow or data flow. In GriDE this can be accomplished by using the flow editor.

Based on the predefined templates and grid components, developers can easily define the workflow of their grid applications. The script or source code can be automatically generated for deployment over grid resources. Figure 3 shows the approach to develop a grid application using the flow editor.

Developers are not required to know much about the grid. They can select the suitable template, for example, batch job template, and define the workflow with the parameters of each grid components. Then the flow editor will generate the script which can be submitted to grid.

Developers can also implement each job component separately, and finally conduct a more complex workflow to integrate all the jobs.

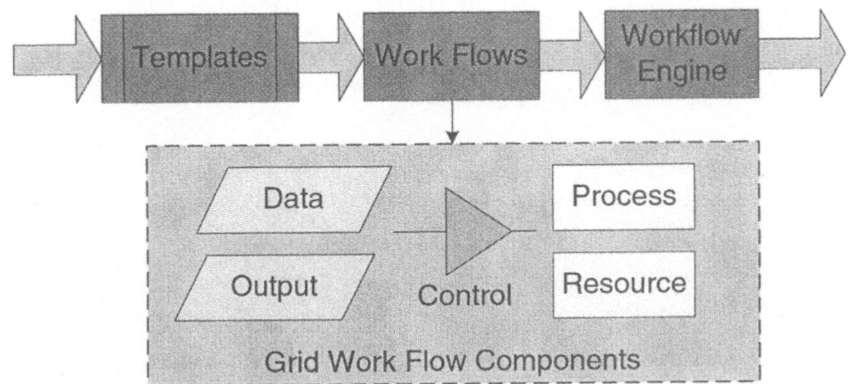

Fig. 3. Approach of using flow editor to create grid applications

4 Grid Job Submission

Job submission is an entry point for the end users to work on grids. Within the GriDE, the user is able to submit GRAM job to remote Globus gatekeeper. Meanwhile, the Globus Resource Specification Language (RSL) provides a common interchange language to describe resources. RSL provides the skeletal syntax used to compose complex resource descriptions, and the various resource management components introduce specific $< attribute, value >$ pairs into this common structure. Each attribute in a resource description serves as a parameter to control the behavior of one or more components in the resource management system.

Besides the backend Globus GRAM job management and RSL description language, GriDE environment also provides a GUI for the ease of job submission, as demonstrated in Figure 4. In GriDE, the job submission procedure can be described as follows:

1. The user inputs the appropriate parameters within the GUI. Consequently, the GriDE will generate RSL description for the current submitted job.
2. After the RSL description is built, it must be submitted to the server. In order to do that, it must be ensured that the gatekeeper is alive on remote machines.
3. Next, a GramJob object is instantiated.
4. Feedback from the remote server is provided in order to interact with the job. A listener can be used to receive notifications about job status from the server.
5. The job is now ready for submission. The actual submission is done through the request method, which takes two arguments, namely the remote server and whether job is submitted through batch or interactive mode.

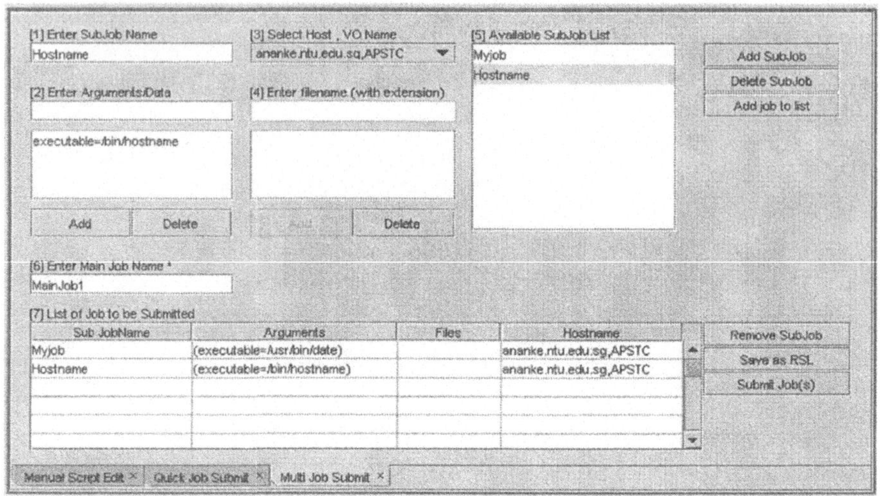

Fig. 4. Multiple Job Submission Screen

5 Grid Resource Discovery/Browsing

Besides providing the functionality of submitting jobs, grid resource discovery and display is also a major concern. In GriDE, users are able to search the resource information and select the resources that can satisfy their requirements.

GriDE provides a function to retrieve the information from the GIIS/GRIS on the MDS or LDAP servers. The resource information is displayed in a tree-view structure and the user is able to refine the search by putting some detailed resource requirements such as memory, CPU, OS, etc (see left part of Figure 2).

6 Job Status Monitoring

After submitting a job, watching the execution status and fetching the execution results become the user's major concern. So job monitoring and result fetching is another important feature provided by GriDE. So far the brief status (like stage in, running, stage out, waiting, etc) information can be displayed in the displaying window. Fetching the execution results is accomplished by accessing Globus Access Secondary Storage (GASS) services via Java Cog Kit.

Java CoG Kit provides GASS to access distributed data using secure HTTP protocol. It provides standard file I/O interfaces such as open, read, write, and close to access remote files. Thus, GASS can be used to transfer data files needed for computational job, from/to any other host on the grid. The method, called file staging, frees grid application developers from transferring the data files manually. File staging requires a GASS server, which is basically an HTTPS server running on the machine submitting the job. When the GASS server is started, it generates a GASS Uniform Resource Locators (URL). This GASS

URL must be passed to the GRAM server through the Globus RSL description of the job. To redirect the output to the client machine, the GASS URL must be passed to the server through the stdout and stderr parameters in the job RSL. This will stream the job output and error streams to the local GASS server.

7 Related Work

In the Global Grid Forum [2], there are several research groups like Advanced Collaborative Environments Research Group (ACE-RG) and Grid Computing Environments Research Group (GCE-RG) are working in the area of applications, programming models and environments. Their working are still on the way and the related information can be found from their websites.

Cactus [1] is a framework and toolkit for parallel and distributed computing over the Internet. It has been used successfully by some scientific computing applications in many areas. So far it is still not a complete IDE enabling grid programming, but it provides a Web-based portal for grid users. In the meantime, the Cactus people are also working for GridLab [12], a coming grid computing environment enabling grid applications.

EGrid [13] is a testbed based on Globus Toolkit for prototyping and experimenting with various application scenarios. It was established by the Applications Research Group (ARG) of the Global Grid Forum (GGF). GridLab [12] is yet another application oriented project funded by the European Commission. Its architecture consists of two levels: user space and service space. The user space includes the application layer and Grid Application Toolkit API layer. The service space includes a GridLab service layer and a core service layer. The applications should be programmed using the GAT API, and the GAT itself uses adapters for all kinds of services it can make available through the GAT API. It is also work in progress and only the architecture overview is provided.

GrADS [14] is yet another on going project aiming at providing a complete grid computing environment for grid users, including high level application support, middleware architecture, execution environment, etc. Its GrADSoft architecture replaces the discrete steps of application creation, compilation, execution, and post-mortem analysis with a continuous process of adapting applications to both a changing grid and a specific problem instance.

8 Conclusion

In this paper we described the GriDE, a grid computing environment which was proposed to provide the required features for grid application execution. Our grid programing environment is built on Globus, plus our provided grid application interface for easily utilizing the underlying grid facilities. This enabling environment is designed for both grid programing and execution. So far only Java applications are supported, and one of the future work should be extending the GriDE to support other programming languages such as C/C++ and Fortran.

With such an environment, we expect more new applications to be developed to exploit the power of the grids.

GriDE is an ongoing project and a lot of work need to be done in the future. Grid service concepts are to be integrated, more sophisticated job monitoring and performance tuning mechanisms are required. In the mean time some other grid middleware can be introduced and cooperate with the existing environment.

References

1. Cactus Computational Toolkit. http://www.cactuscode.org/.
2. Globle Grid Forum. http://www.ggf.org/.
3. Globus Project. http://www.globus.org/.
4. Java CoGKit. http://www.globus.org/cogkit/java.
5. MPI Standard. http://www3.niu.edu/mpi/.
6. NetBeans IDE. http://www.netbeans.org/.
7. NimRod/G. http://www.csse.monash.edu.au/ davida /nimrod.html/.
8. Open Grid Services Infrastructure (OGSI). http://www.ggf.org/ogsi-wg.
9. SimGrid. http://juggler.ucsd.edu/simgrid/.
10. Sun Grid Engine. http://wwws.sun.com/software/gridware/.
11. JXTA project. http://wwws.sun.com/software/jxta.
12. G. Allen, D. Angulo, T. Goodale, T. Kielmann, A. Merzky, J. Nabrzysky, J. Pukacki, M. Russel, T. Radke, E. Seidel, J. Shalf, and I. Taylor. GridLab: Enabling Applications on the Grid. In International Workshop Grid Computing (GRID2002).
13. G. Allen, T. Dramlitsh, T. Goodale, G. Lanfermann, T. Radke, E. Seidel, T. Kielmann, K. Verstoep, Z. Balaton, P. Kacsuk, F. Szalai, J. Gehring, A. Keller, A. Streit, L. Matyska, M. Ruda, A. Krenek, H. Frese, H. Knipp, A. Merzky, A. Reinefeld, F. Schintke, B. Ludwiczak, J. Nabrzyski, J. Pukacki, H. Kersken, and M. Russel. Early experiences with the EGrid testbed. In 1st International Symposium on Cluster Computing and the Grid (CCGRID'01), 2001.
14. F. Berman, A. Chien, K. Cooper, J. Dongarra, I. Foster, D. Gannon, L. Johnsson, K. Kennedy, C. Kesselman, J. Mellor-Crummey, D. Reed, L. Torczon, and R. Wolski. The GrADS Project: Software Support for High-Level Grid Application Development. 15(4):327-344, 2001.
15. I. Foster, C. Kesselman, J. M. Nick, and S. Tuecke. The Physiology of the Grid. http://www.globus.org/research/papers/ogsa.pdf.
16. N. Karonis, B. Toonen, and I. Foster. Mpich-g2: A grid-enabled implementation of the message passing interface. Journal of Parallel and Distributed Computing, 2003.

Information Grid Toolkit: Infrastructure of Shanghai Information Grid[1]

Xinhua Lin, Qianni Deng, and Xinda Lu

Department of Computer Science and Engineering, Shanghai Jiao Tong University
200030 Shanghai, China
lin-xh@sjtu.edu.cn
{deng-qn, lu-xd}@cs.sjtu.edu.cn

Abstract. A fundamental problem that confronts Shanghai Information Grid is to adopt a good Grid toolkit, since the "de facto" standard Globus Toolkit does not support Information Grid well enough. We have developed an OGSA-compatible Grid Middleware, Shanghai Information Grid Toolkit (IGT), which is optimized for Information Grid. Some important new features are provided in IGT: a small and fast core supported by self-developed standalone lightweight server program as hosting environment; extended Grid security infrastructure with additional security rules for Information Grid; information resource services used to manage and control remote information resources; lightweight monitoring and discovery service and enhanced index services employed in information services.

1 Introduction

In July 2003, Shanghai began building a Grid, with IBM's help, to integrate information resources spread across the city's municipal government, as well as to handle citywide emergency, to forecast city weather and to manage remote medical services. Information Grid aims to eliminate isolated island of information, uses the Grid technologies to sharing and managing information resources, therefore it plays a key role in ShanghaiGrid.

Nowadays lots of Grid Projects in the world focus computing resources (such as NASA Information Power Grid) and data resources (such as European Data Grid), however, Shanghai Information Grid focuses on information resource. Furthermore, Globus Toolkit 3 (GT3) is wildly used in Computational Grid and Data Grid, but is seldom used Information Grid. Part of the reason is GT3 does not support well on information resources. Therefore, we develop an OGSA-compatible Grid Toolkit called Information Grid Toolkit (IGT) as the infrastructure of Shanghai Information Grid. It mainly includes core components, security services, information resource services, data services, information infrastructure and packaging.

---

[1] This work is supported by the Shanghai Science and Technology Development Foundation under Grant No. 03DZ15027, National Natural Science Fund of China No. 60173031.

M. Li et al. (Eds.): GCC 2003, LNCS 3032, pp. 503–510, 2004.

2 Related Work

The Globus Toolkit is the fundamental enabling technology for Computational Grid developed by Globus Alliance [1], letting people share computing resources, databases and other tools securely online across corporate, institutional and geographic boundaries without sacrificing local autonomy. The latest version Globus Toolkit 3.0 (GT3) is based on Open Grid Service Architecture (OGSA) mechanisms

Condor [2] is the product of the Condor Research Project at the University of Wisconsin-Madison (UW-Madison). The goal of the Condor Project is to develop, implement, deploy and evaluate mechanisms and policies that support High Throughput Computing (HTC) on large collections of distributively owned computing resources.

The IBM Grid Toolbox [3] is a set of installable packages that includes the Globus Toolkit 2.2 with additional documentation and custom installation scripts written for IBM eServer hardware running AIX and Linux.

3 IGT Architecture and Components

IGT adopts a four-layer architecture some similar to GT3, as illustrated in Fig. 1. The first layer is the core of IGT, which is based on the Open Grid Services Infrastructure (OGSI) primitives and protocols. The second layer is security services, which uses Extended Grid Security Infrastructure (X-GSI) for enabling secure authentication and communication over an open network. The third layer is base services layer, including three services: Information Resource Services (IRS) focuses on the management of information resources; Data Services involves the ability to access and manage data in an Information Grid; Information Services provide information about Grid resources. The fourth layer is Packaging, using Grid Packaging Toolkit GPT to package IGT installation packages and providing easy-to-install package formats.

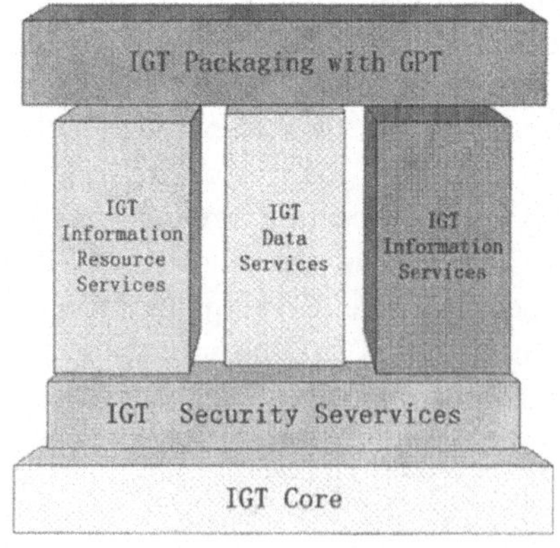

Fig. 1. The Four-layer Architecture of IGT

We mainly discuss the Core, Security Services and IRS, because these they are fundamental to IGT.

3.1 Core

The core of IGT only contains the basic infrastructure needed for Grid services, much smaller than GT3's [4]. The two subcomponents are presented in Fig. 2.

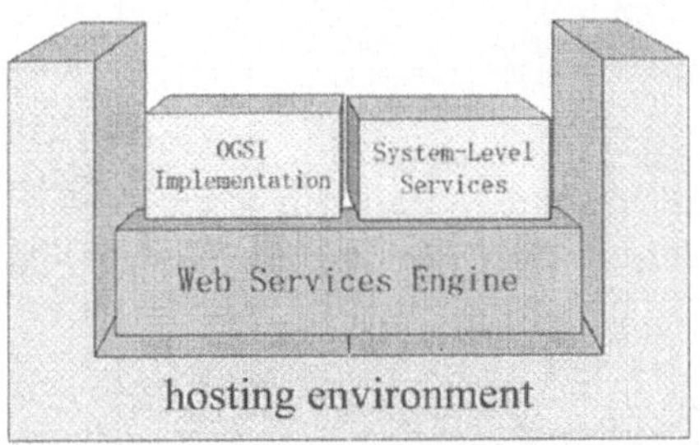

Fig. 2. The Components of IGT Core

OGSI implementation means giving all OGSI specified interfaces. System level services are OGSI compliant Grid services that are generic enough to be used by all other Grid services, including three different services. The first one is Administration Service that is used to interface a hosting environment and to shut down a Grid Service container. The second one is Logging Management Service which allows users to modify log filters and to group existing log producers into more easily manageable units at run time. The Third one is Management Service that provides an interface for monitoring the current status and load of a Grid service container. It also allows users to activate and deactivate service instances.

The core depends on two components: A web service engine responsible for implementing XML Messaging. Like other Grid toolkits, IGT uses Apache Axis as its engine; a hosting environment that provides traditional web server functionality. IGT uses self-developed standalone lightweight server program as a hosting environment to support the core. In ShanghaiGrid some emergency information should be transferred in time across the different departments of government, while the current existing hosting environments (such as Servlet and EJB) are very big and run very slowly. To satisfy those requirements from ShanghaiGrid, IGT adopts a small but fast hosting environment to support the core.

3.2 Security Services

IGT uses the Extended Grid Security Infrastructure (X-GSI) for enabling secure authentication and communication over an open network. X-GSI extends the components of Grid Security Infrastructure (GSI) to support information Security effectively. It has three-layer architecture, as illustrated in Fig. 3. The first layer includes public key encryption, X.509 certificates and Secure Sockets Layer (SSL) communication protocol. Proxy certificates for single sign-on and delegation, delegation protocol for remote delegation and DNSsec and IPsec enhanced for SSL security are in the middle layer. The top layer is Extended Information Security Mechanism for specific security requirements in Information Grid.

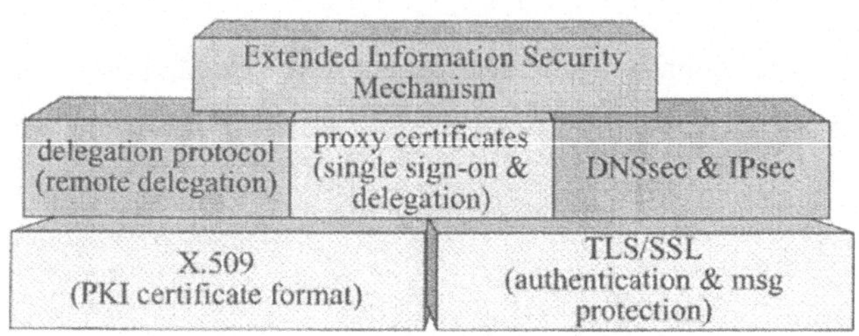

Fig. 3. The Three-layer Architecture of X-GSI

Project Certification Authority

The central concept in X-GSI authentication is the certificate. Every user and service on the Grid is identified via a certificate, which contains information vital to identifying and authenticating the user or service.

The X-GSI certification includes four primary pieces of information: 1) A subject name identifying the person or object that the certificate represents. 2) The public key belonging to the subject. 3) The identity of a Certificate Authority (CA) that has signed the certificate to certify that the public key and the identity both belong to the subject. 4) The digital signature of the named CA.

CA is the heart of X-GSI authentication system. Some Gird projects have their own project CA, e.g. NASA Information Power Grid (IPG) [5]. In ShanghaiGrid, We setup Shanghai Information Grid Project CA (SIGPCA) for authentication all users and services on the Grid. SIGPCA includes both basic features provided by SimpleCA [6]package and advanced features for extended information security mechanism.

Mutual Authentication

Mutual authentication means if two parties have certificates, and if both parties trust the CAs that signed each other's certificates, then the two parties can prove to each other that they are who they say they are. X-GSI uses SSL for its mutual authentication protocol. In practice, the parties involved must first trust the CAs that signed each other's certificates , that means they must have copies of the CAs' certificates and they must trust these certificates really belong to the CAs.

Once mutual authentication is performed, X-GSI does not establish confidential communication between parties for getting out of the overhead of constant encryption and decryption. However in some cases we need keeping some information securely. Therefore X-GSI provides two methods to satisfy the requirements: a shared key for encryption and communication integrity. Communication integrity means that an eavesdropper may be able to read communication between two parties but is not able to modify the communication in any way. It introduces some overhead in communication, but not as large an overhead as encryption.

Delegation and Single Sign-On

X-GSI provides a delegation capability: an extension of the standard SSL protocol that reduces the number of times the user must enter his pass phrase. The need to re-enter the user's pass phrase can be avoided by creating a proxy that consists of a new certificate (with a new public key in it) and a new private key. The new certificate that is signed by owner contains the owner's identity, modified slightly to indicate that it is a proxy. The proxy's private key can be stored in a local storage system without being encrypted because proxy isn't valid for long time. The user can use the proxy certificate and private key for mutual authentication without entering a password.

DNSsec and IPsec

SSL are mainly focused on protection of data in flight and are not focused on truly identifying end-points. Some dsniff toolkit makes it easier to thwart the security of connections with these protocols by impersonating endpoints. X-GSI prevents these attacks by using DNSsec and IPsec [7]. DNSsec helps make the key management harder to subvert and makes DNS spoofing harder. IPsec makes man in the middle attacks harder by denying IP spoofing.

Extended Information Security Mechanism

There are some special security requirements from ShanghaiGrid. Firstly to handle with citywide emergency, some important information should be transferred quickly and reliably across the government, even the city. So in this condition information should not be encrypted for reducing overheads as much as possible. Secondly, in other cases, when municipal government delivers some secret documents on ShanghaiGrid, the documents should be encrypted (even double encrypted) before transfer. Thirdly, some typical applications on ShanghaiGrid, such as Traffic Information System (TIS) need some special security rules. In TIS, taxi drivers who want to provide some traffic information on Grid should certificated by their real names and ID numbers. The different conditions need different security rules. We adopt extended information security mechanism as a container. When having concluded new security rules from some specific conditions, we put them into the container, which means security mechanism.

3.3 Information Resource Services

Computational power is the resource of Computational Grid, and databases are resource of Data Grid. In consequence, information is the resource of Information Grid. Information Resource Services (IRS) is used by IGT to manage information resource effectively and it is totally different from Globus Resource Allocation Manager (GRAM).

IRS adopts three-layer architecture as illustrated in Fig. 4. The first layer is information fault tolerance that is managed by a coordinated set of Grid container handlers and background sweeper tasks in both the Mater Hosting Environment (MHE) and User Hosting Environment (UHE). The second layer includes three components: information Receiver, information Sender and information notification.

These components manage information transferring and mapping. The third one is Classifying and Indexing, which classify the information, then send them to Data service and provide some specific information index services.

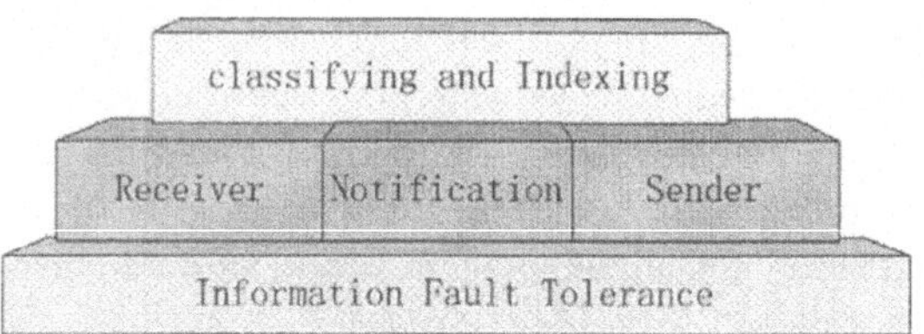

Fig. 4. The Three-layer Architecture of IRS

IRS simplifies the use of information in remote systems by providing a single standard interface for requesting and using remote system information resources. In ShanghaiGrid, we use IRS to manage and control remote information resources on Grid.

IRS provides a single common protocol and APIs for indexing and sharing remote information resources. It is based on a simple authorization mechanism provided by X-GSI identities and a mechanism to map X-GSI identities to local user accounts.

3.4 Data Services

Data Services of IGT are mainly based on data management components of GT3, including GridFTP, RFT, and RLS [8]. However, data management components of GT3 are originally designed for data on Computational Grid and Data Grid. Hence, we have made some optimizations in IGT data services to support Information Grid effectively.

GridFTP is a high-performance, secure, reliable data transfer protocol optimized for high-bandwidth wide-area networks. Its protocol is based on FTP, which is the highly popular Internet file transfer protocol. In ShanghaiGrid, GridFTP is mainly used to transfer some large video files, so we have added a set of protocol features and extensions those already defined in IETF RFCs to GridFTP.

The Reliable File Transfer Service (RFT) is an OGSA based service that provides interfaces for controlling and monitoring third party file transfers using GridFTP servers. The client controlling the transfer is hosted inside of a Grid service so it can be managed using the soft state model and queried using the Small Service Data (SSD) interfaces available to all Grid services. RFT of IGT is optimized to transfer important information securely and reliably for meeting requirements in ShanghaiGrid.

The Replica Location Service (RLS) maintains and provides access to mapping information from logical names for data items to target names.

3.5 Information Services

IGT adopts Lightweight Monitoring and Discovery Services (LMDS) to collect the critical information about Grid resources for using in resource discovery, selection and optimization; it also uses an Enhanced Index Services (EIS) to provide an information aggregation service.

Lightweight Monitoring and Discovery Service

LMDS is built on some basic features of Monitoring and Discovery Service (MDS3) of GT3. When LMDS is used in conjunction with standard Open Grid Services Infrastructure (OGSI) mechanisms, it provides a consistent way of querying any Grid service about its configuration and status information within an OGSA-compliant environment.

In ShanghaiGrid, most of Grid services are transient services, and they have at lest one instances. Thus these instances have limited lifetime. Small Service Data (SSD) is used to describe the state of each Grid service and is optimized to describe large quantity Grid services those with short lifetime. Therefore, the elements of SSD are much smaller than Service Data Element (SDE). Some important features about SSD are provided, such as SSD can be collected, aggregated and queried; data feeds can be monitored; SSD can be created dynamically on demand.

Enhanced Index Services

ELS provide information aggregation services. According to OGSI, ELS add an important function: a consistent mechanism for notifying services of changes in Service Data Elements, allowing data to be pushed or pulled into indexes. For facilitating querying and indexing large quantity information about Gird services in Information Grid, we have optimized querying and indexing of ELS.

3.6 Packaging with GPT

Grid middleware always means different things to different people, so the packaging system of IGT includes different features for supporting different requirements from Grid builders and application developers, as illustrate in Table 1. IGT adopts Grid Packaging Tools (GPT) [9] to provide both client/services installation packages and development installation packages.

Table 1. Different things to Grid Buliders and Application Developers

	Grid builders	Application developers
Focus on	Building infrastructure	Developing new software
Files they use	Executables and configure files on servers	Libraries and header files on developer systems
Installation package	Services and client installation	Development installation

GPT is a multi-platform packaging system used to deploy Grid middleware, and it provides a collection of packaging tools built around an XML based packaging data format. This format provides a straightforward way to define complex dependency and compatibility relationships between packages. The packages generated by GPT are compatible with other packages and can be easily converted.

By using GPT, IGT provides these four tools for installation 1) IGT-install, installs IGT components from a package into a standard directory structure; 2) IGT-build, converts source packages into binary packages; 3) IGT-verify, verifies that all prerequisite software is available to installed components; 4) IGT_LOCATION, points to the active IGT directory structure.

Currently GT3 has great improvements in most aspects, but its installation is still painful to users, especially beginners. IGT will provide much easier and friendlier installation package formats, such as RPM.

4 Summary

The architecture of IGT is some similar to GT3. They are both OSGA-compatible and adopt GSI, GridFTP, GPT and etc. But the goal of IGT is to build an Information Grid, we have made some improvements from GT3 in several aspects: 1) IGT utilizes standalone lightweight server program as hosting environment to support the core. 2) IGT uses Extended Grid Security Infrastructure (X-GSI) to enhance the security of Information Grid. 3) IGT adopts Information Resource Services (IRS) to manage information resource. 4) Lightweight Monitoring and Discovery Service (LMDS) and Enhanced Index Services (ELS) are used in information services. 5) IGT provides easy-to-install package formats.

References

1. The Globus Alliance, http://www.globus.org, 2003.
2. The Condor Project, http://www.cs.wisc.edu/condor/, 2003.
3. Shawn Mullen, "Install and configure the IBM Grid Toolbox v2.2", http://www.alphaworks.ibm.com/tech/Gridtoolbox, 2003.
4. Thomas Sandholm and Jarek Gawor, "Globus Toolkit 3 Core – A Grid Service Container Framework ", http://www-unix.globus.org/toolkit/3.0/ogsa/docs/gt3_core.pdf, July 2003.
5. NASA Information Power Grid (IPG) Certificate http://www.ipg.nasa.gov/ipgusers/gettingstarted/cert_top.html
6. Sam Lang, "Setup Instructions of Globus Simple CA Package ", http://www.globus.org/security/simple-ca.html, July 2003.
7. DNSsec and IPsec, http://securityportal.com, 2000.
8. Data Management Services, http://www-unix.globus.org/developer/data-management.html, June 2003.
9. Eric Blau and Michael Bletzinger et al, Grid Packaging Tools, http://www.ncsa.uiuc.edu/Divisions/ACES/GPT/, December 2002.

On-Demand Services Composition and Infrastructure Management

Jun Peng and Jie Wang

Department of Civil and Environmental Engineering, Stanford University,
Stanford, CA 94305, USA
{junpeng, jiewang}@stanford.edu

Abstract. This paper presents several engineering applications that involve distributed software services. Due to the complexity of these applications, an efficient and flexible service composition framework is needed. A reference service composition framework is introduced to address two issues prevailing in current service composition: interface incompatibility and performance. The reference framework applies active mediation to enhance efficient execution of applications employing composed services. As the number of services becomes large, the composed application imposes challenge on the service infrastructure management. A reliability model is introduced for building an automatic infrastructure management paradigm.

1 Introduction

The service composition has been utilized in many fields to improve the flexibility of software development, and to reuse existing software components. One such significant field is engineering, where services are composed to perform simulations, data integration, real-time monitoring and other on-demand applications. However, there are many issues associated with the current prevailing service composition frameworks, and two noticeable ones are interface incompatibility and performance. Web services are typically heterogeneous and adhere to a variety of conventions for control and data. Even when standards are promulgated, such as SQL, the precise meaning and scope of the output will not necessarily match the expectations of another service. In a typical composed application, all results from one service now have to be shipped back to the application site, handled there, and then shipped to the next service. We argue that this centralized data-flow approach is inefficient for integrating large-scale software services.

While great advances have been made to simply the development of distributed and on-demand service infrastructures, managing these infrastructures still remains a daunting task. Currently, most large-scale data centers that host service infrastructure experience severe problems in managing the large N-tier, networked environments. Most of these problems arise from the complexity of the infrastructure itself rather than building the applications. Maintainability of the infrastructure system for long-term efficient operation is largely missing.

M. Li et al. (Eds.): GCC 2003, LNCS 3032, pp. 511–518, 2004.

2 Example Engineering Applications

2.1 Engineering Simulation

The first example is a web service framework that facilitates engineering simulations [11]. In this framework, the users can remotely access the core simulation program through a web-based user interface or other application programs, such as MATLAB. The users can specify desirable features and methods that have been developed, tested, and contributed to the framework by other participants. A standard interface/wrapper is defined to help developers to build/wrap engineering components as web services. Many components of the simulation program, such as linear solver, design tools, visualization tools, and etc., can be wrapped as web services and run on distributed computers to participate in engineering simulation.

Engineering simulations normally require a great deal of computation effort. To improve the performance of engineering simulations, parallel and distributed computing environment can be employed. The simulations are performed on dedicated parallel computers, cluster of local workstations, or even distributed network workstations by utilizing Gird-enabled MPI [4]. Database systems served as web services are linked with the central server to provide persistent storage of simulation results [12].

2.2 Data Integration

The second example is a web services framework for integrating a variety of engineering applications, which involves large volume of data communication. In this example, the web services are linked together through an integration framework to provide project scheduling [8]. Proprietary software applications, such as Microsoft Project, Excel, Primavera Project Planner, and 4D Viewer are wrapped as web services that export their functionalities. Although the applications run on heterogeneous platforms and utilize different interfaces, they can be accessed homogeneously through standard web services interfaces. The prototype also incorporates a variety of devices ranging from PDA, web browsers, desktop computers, to server computers. Using the infrastructure, field personnel can conduct project management with the latest project information on the construction site, in a truly ubiquitous fashion [8]. In short, by using the web services model to develop the integration framework, engineering applications can collaborate regardless of location and platform.

2.3 Real-Time Monitoring

The third example is a distributed wireless structural monitoring system [9]. The transfer of measurement data is carried out by wireless communications. In addition, computational power is integrated with each sensing node of the system. By providing each sensor the means to process its own data, computational burden is removed from the centralized server in addition to many benefits associated with parallel data processing. The wireless structural monitoring system is applied to perform real-time monitoring of a district or even a city, where a hierarchical system is used. Sensor units are deployed on numerous buildings. The sensor units within a building or a small region send their collected measurement data to a data server. All the data servers then send their data to a data processing center. In the monitoring system, the infrastructure management is a key factor to the successful deployment of the system. An automatic mechanism is needed to detect mal-functional sensor units, to adapt to varying circumstances, and to operate robustly under severe conditions.

3 Software Service Composition

FICAS, an experimental Flow-based Infrastructure for Composing Autonomous Services, supports a service composition paradigm that integrates software using a loose parallelism [7]. Since there is an overhead for each remote invocation of a service, this framework focuses on the composition of large and distributed services.

3.1 Service Composition Framework

Fig. 4 illustrates the main components of the FICAS framework. The buildtime components are responsible for specifying composed application and compiling application specifications into control sequences. For FICAS, we have defined the CLAS (Compositional Language for Autonomous Services) to provide application programmers the necessary abstractions to describe the behaviors of their composed applications. The CLAS language focuses on functional composition of web services. The runtime environment of FICAS is responsible for executing control sequences. The service directory keeps track of available web services within the infrastructure.

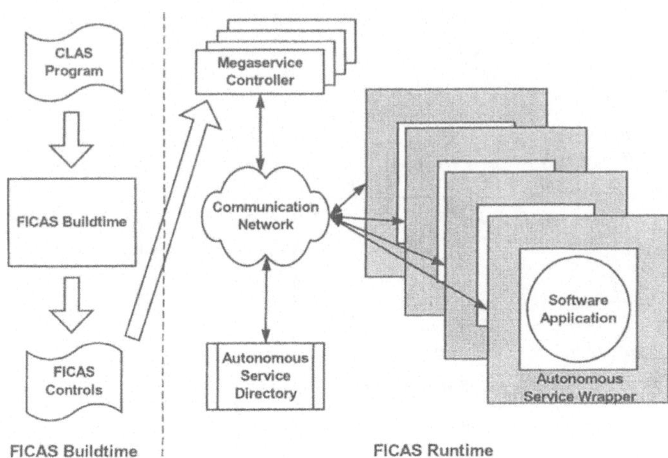

Fig. 1. Service Composition Architecture

Web services are formed by wrapping legacy or new software applications. A metamodel is defined to allow the construction of homogeneous web services in a heterogeneous computing environment. The metamodel defines a service core, which encapsulates the computational software and provides the data processing functionalities. While each component operates asynchronously, the service core ties the components into a coordinated entity.

3.2 Separation of Control and Data Flows

Traditionally, both control flows and data flows are centrally coordinated. There are performance and scalability issues associated with this model. When large amounts of data are exchanged among the services, the controlling node becomes a communication bottleneck. It is especially problematic in an Internet environment, where the communication links between controlling node and the services likely suffer limited bandwidth.

The issues associated with the centralized data and control flows motivate us to distribute the data-flows among the services. Instead of using the controlling node as the intermediate data relay, the composed application can inform the services to exchange data directly. A sample application of this model is shown in Fig. 2. The decision to retain a centralized control-flow hinges upon ease of implementation and management. The distributed data-flow model utilizes the communication network among web services, and thus alleviates communication loads on the controlling node. Moreover, the computation is distributed efficiently to where data resides, so that the data can be processed without incurring communication traffic.

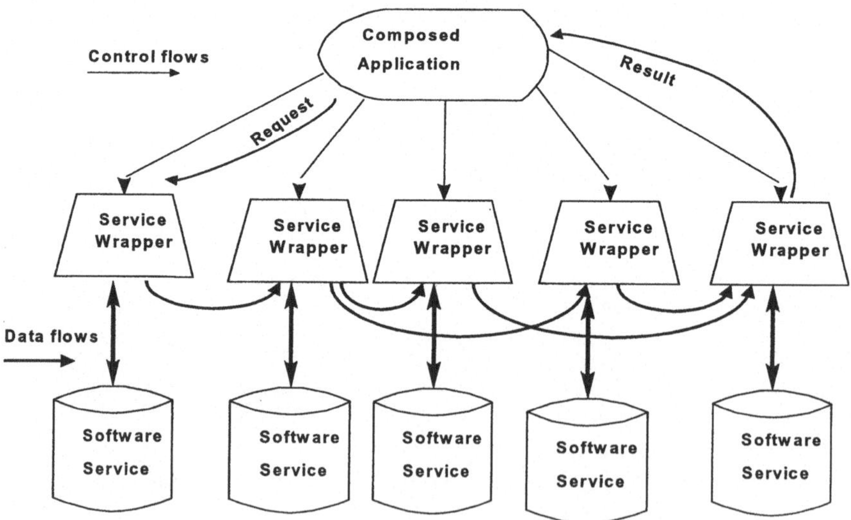

Fig. 2. Sample Centralized Control-Flows and Distributed Data-Flows

3.3 Active Mediation

In the semantic web setting [1], where we expect a large collection of autonomous and diverse service providers, we cannot expect that each service will deliver results that are fully compatible and useful to further services that the composed application will need to invoke. Active mediation is introduced to provide client-specific functionalities so that services can be viewed as if they were intended for the specific needs of the client. Active mediation is enabled by mobile class, which is an information-processing module that can be dynamically loaded and executed. The mobile class is similar to the mobile agent technology [14] in that they both utilize executable program that can migrate during execution. However, the mobile agents are self-governing, whereas the mobile class is an integral part of the service composition framework. The management and deployment of mobile classes are controlled by the composed application.

Mobile classes can be used to support data processing, such as relational data operations. A mobile class can be constructed for each relational operator. Mobile classes are also used in place of type brokers to handle data conversion. In a large-scale service composition framework, data exit in various types and will continue to appear in different types. Rather than forwarding data among the type brokers, the composed application loads the mobile classes on the services to provide the type mediation function. The type mediation supported by mobile classes eliminates intermediate data traffic. Services can produce a wide variety of data suitable for extraction and reporting [13]. Mobile classes are loaded onto the upstream service to mediate the output data for the downstream service.

4 Automatic Infrastructure Management

The lack of management tools in distributed applications, coupled with the increasing dependence on the availability of these systems, is causing significant resources to be put into managing these infrastructures. There is also a pressing need to address Quality of Service (QoS) and Service Level Agreements (SLA) for infrastructure management. Consequently, new IT technologies aiming at automating the deployment and maintenance of IT infrastructure are emerging. One promising technology is autonomic computing where the IT infrastructure and its components are self-configuring, self-healing, self-optimizing and self-protecting.

The IBM autonomic computing manifesto presents challenges to develop and deploy systems and software that can run themselves [3], can adapt to varying circumstances, and can operate robustly under the damaged conditions. This vision is an amalgam of analogies from biology [2, 5, 6, 10], where the self-regulating control systems can maintain steady state. While research for these analogies begins to draw more attentions, building software that is aware of its own behavior, its surrounding context, and the control and interaction among components is extremely difficult [10].

4.1 Topology-Based Modeling for IT Infrastructure

One of the most urgent needs for managing IT infrastructure is to know the infrastructure system itself. Based on this information, we can then discuss the possibility of a more automatic management paradigm. Once we establish a proper model to describe the system, we can use it for

- monitoring the real-time system,
- better trouble shooting the system,
- estimating the reliability of the system, and
- calculating the QoS and SLA based on the reliability.

The starting point for self-managing a complex infrastructure is to determine the topology of the underlying applications. For this purpose, we define topology as the combination of the static description of the application's components and the relationships that exist among these components. All applications have two parts to them: (1) infrastructure, and (2) application entities. The model for IT infrastructure needs to include entities for the above two parts and their relations.

More specifically, a model for infrastructure can be considered to consist of three tiers as follows: (1) Network Tier, which consists of devices such as switches, routers, load balancers, firewalls, and etc.; (2) Systems Tier, which provides the computing infrastructure and consists of computer servers and operating system; (3) Applications Infrastructure Tier, which provides the software *containers* in which application components execute.

4.2 Estimating Reliability

The reliability of an IT infrastructure can be estimated based on the underlying infrastructure model. As the first step, we should establish a reliability model for the IT infrastructure. The model reflects the following intuitive system feature:

- In general, the reliability of a system decreases as the complexity of the system increase.
- If there is a single point of failure in the system, the system cannot be more stable than that component.
- Redundancy enhances reliability.
- However, redundant components may be prone to fail at the same time because the failure may have the same cause.

The reliability estimation method includes the following four steps, which can be summarized as:

- Mapping the system as a graph.
- Determining the critical graph for outage.
- Assessing the reliability of basic modules.
- Computing the system reliability.

4.3 Using Reliability Model for QoS and SLA

Due to high reliability and availability requirements for on-demand distributed service, we need to employ an industrial standard for assuring the quality of such service. We propose using QoS (Quality of Service) and SLA (Service Level Agreements) to help on-demand service providers cope with the unprecedented demands on management of their service infrastructures.

There are basically two approaches to deliver QoS. One is to create business service that requires very high infrastructure reliability. For this approach, we calculate the current reliability of the infrastructure. If it cannot support the business requirements, predication is needed for an acceptable IT infrastructure to fulfill the requirements. The precdication is based on simulations of reliability model for planned infrastructures. The second approach is to dispense with the current IT infrastructure to prioritize the business requirements and maximize the business service offering. The dispensation is based on the calculation of the best capability and usage of the infrastructure using the reliability model. Both approaches need the information of the reliability model for the IT infrastructure.

After we understand the available QoS for the infrastructure, we can establish SLA for the IT service. SLA monitoring and enforcement become increasingly important in an IT service environment. By using the predications obtained from a reliability model and the estimated QoS, we can set up the foundation for supporting SLA. By using SLA, distributed services may be subscribed dynamically and on-demand based on the requirements and priorities. As a result, for economic and practical reasons, we should use the model-based infrastructure management paradigm to reach an automated process for both the service itself as well as the SLA management system that measures and monitors the QoS parameters, to check the agreed-upon service levels, and to report violations to the authorized parties involved in the SLA management process.

5 Summary

In this paper, we discuss several distributed services in engineering applications domain. A composition framework for such services is proposed to deal with the efficiency and flexibility for integrating complex applications. More specifically, a reference service composition framework is introduced to address the two issues prevailing in current service composition: interface incompatibility and performance. The reference framework applies active mediation to enhance efficient execution of applications employing composed services.

As the number of services becomes large, the composed application imposes challenge on the service infrastructure management. To tackle this ever-increasing complexity in the deployment and management of the infrastructure for services, we introduce a topology based infrastructure model and the reliability for an automatic infrastructure management paradigm. Finally, we propose a procedure for establishing QoS and SLA for managing on-demand and distributed services.

References

1. Berners-Lee, T., Hendler, J. and Lassila, O.: The Semantic Web. Scientific American. 284(5) (2001) 34-43
2. Blair, G.S., Coulson, G., Blair, L., Duran-Limon, H., Grace, P., Moreira, R. and Parlavantzas, N.: Reflection, Self-Awareness and Self-Healing in OpenORB. Proceedings of the First ACM Workshop on Self-Healing Systems. Charleston, SC (2002) 9-14
3. Dashofy, E.M., van-der-Hoek, A. and Taylor, R.N.: Towards Architecture-based Self-Healing Systems. Proceedings of the First ACM Workshop on Self-Healing Systems. Charleston, SC (2002) 21-26
4. Foster, I., Geisler, J., Gropp, W., Karonis, N., Lusk, E., Thiruvathukal, G. and Tuecke., S.: Wide-Area Implementation of the Message Passing Interface. Parallel Computing. 24(12) (1998) 1735-1749
5. Garlan, D. and Schmerl, B.: Model-based Adaptation for Self-Healing Systems. Proceedings of the First ACM Workshop on Self-Healing Systems. Charleston, SC (2002) 27-32
6. George, S., Evans, D. and Davidson, L.: A Biologically Inspired Programming Model for Self-Healing Systems. Proceedings of the First ACM Workshop on Self-healing Systems. Charleston, SC (2002) 102-104
7. Liu, D.: A Distributed Data Flow Model for Composing Software Services. Ph.D. Thesis. Department of Electrical Engineering, Stanford University, Stanford, CA (2003)
8. Liu, D., Cheng, J., Law, K.H., Wiederhold, G. and Sriram, R.D.: Engineering Information Service Infrastructure for Ubiquitous Computing. Journal of Computing in Civil Engineering. 17(4) (2003) 219-229
9. Lynch, J.P., Law, K.H., Kiremidjian, A.S., Carryer, E., Kenny, T.W., Partridge, A. and Sundararajan, A.: Validation of a Wireless Modular Monitoring System for Structures. Proceedings of Smart Structures and Materials, SPIE. San Diego, CA (2002)
10. Mikic-Rakic, M., Mehta, N. and Medvidovic, N.: Architectural Style Requirements for Self-Healing Systems. Proceedings of the First ACM Workshop on Self-Healing Systems. Charleston, SC (2002) 49-54
11. Peng, J. and Law, K.H.: A Prototype Software Framework for Internet-Enabled Collaborative Development of a Structural Analysis Program. Engineering with Computers. 18(1) (2002) 38-49
12. Peng, J., Liu, D. and Law, K.H.: An Engineering Data Access System for a Finite Element Program. Journal of Advances in Engineering Software. 34(3) (2003) 163-181
13. Sample, N., Beringer, D. and Wiederhold, G.: A Comprehensive Model for Arbitrary Result Extraction. Proceedings of ACM Symposium on Applied Computing. Madrid, Spain (2002)
14. White, J.E.: Mobile Agents. In: Bradshaw, J.M. (eds.): Software Agent, MIT Press, (1997) 437-472

GridDaen: A Data Grid Engine[1]

Nong Xiao, Dongsheng Li, Wei Fu, Bin Huang, and Xicheng Lu

School of Computer, National University of Defense Technology,
410073 Changsha, China
xiao-n@vip.sina.com

Abstract. The volume of datasets in scientific computing domain is increasing explosively and data is becoming the center of scientific computing. Data Grid is an emerging technology to provide uniform access and management of the large scale distributed scientific datasets. In this paper, the GridDaen system, a new Data Grid middleware, which provides uniform APIs and GUI to access and manage resources, is presented in detail. GridDaen utilizes a three-level naming scheme that shields users from low-level resource discovery and provide global uniform view for users. Coordinated DRB servers and multiple-layer distributed metadata servers are adopted in GridDaen to provide uniform secure access and management of heterogeneous distributed resources across multiple administrative domains. Role-based multi-level access control policy is used in the system and caching and replication mechanisms are utilized to improve the performance of the system. The virtual dataset functions are also supported in GridDaen. GridDaen can achieve good scalability, reliability and can be flexibly deployed and configured according to the application demands.

1 Introduction

In recent years, the volume of datasets in modern large-scale scientific researches, information services and digital media applications is growing explosively. Large data collections have become very important community resources in many application domains; such as global climate simulation, high-energy physics research, etc. The volume of datasets in these applications has already reached tens of terabyte to petabytes and is still growing. Meanwhile, the users who need to access and analyze these large volumes of distributed datasets are often geographically distributed and their tasks performed on the data are sophisticated and computationally expensive. Such applications, which combine large dataset, geographic distribution of users and resources and computation-intensive analysis, bring about urgent demands for high-performance and large-capacity storage and processing capability that can't be satisfied by any existing data management infrastructure or technologies. The effective storage, distribution, management, processing, analyzing and mine of mass datasets

[1] This paper is supported by the National Natural Science Foundation of China under the Grant No. 60203016 and No. 69933030, and the National Hi-Tech R&D 863 Program of China under the Grant No. 2002AA131010.

M. Li et al. (Eds.): GCC 2003, LNCS 3032, pp. 519–528, 2004.

with high performance have become the main problems that many applications faced. The Data Grid [1, 10] technologies are emerging efforts to solve this problem. Data Grid can constitute a single virtual environment for data access, management and processing by integrating all kind of datasets distributed on the network. It can shield the heterogeneity of underlying physical resource and build an infrastructure to provide uniform access, storage, transfer, management and service capability for large-scale distributed datasets.

GridDaen(Grid Data Engine) system is a part of our efforts to provide Data Grid middleware in GridOppen Grid system which is designed and implemented by us. GridDaen integrates many kinds of file systems and provides uniform seamless access to distributed datasets. It supports virtual file sets and virtual datasets and provides replication and caching mechanism to improve data access performance. Distributed multi-domain federated servers and high-available technology are also adopted in GridDaen system.

The rest of the paper is organized as below. Section 2 introduces the related work. Section 3 presents the architecture of the GridDaen system. Section 4 discusses the design and implementation of GridDaen. Section 5 gives the summary and the future work.

2 Related Work

Data Grid is a hot topic that develops rapidly these days. The famous European Data Grid project [2] is for the large datasets in CERN which is measured in Terabytes to Petabytes. The project is constructing a grid environment including software and hardware by utilizing all kinds of technologies and tools, such as Globus, object-oriented database, grid database service and so on. SpitFire [3] is its sub-project to implement the database interface ODBC with Grid Service and OGSA-DAI is its another sub-project to integrate database technology, especially federate database technology in data grids.

The GriPhyN [4] project proposes the concept of "virtual data" and provides a language to describe how to acquire and use derived data and information. It helps to make decision on whether acquiring data by accessing remote data or acquiring data by local computing and provides a relatively integrated method for automatic generation and regeneration of the data.

The SRB [5] provides a middleware for uniform data access in distributed heterogeneous storage environments. The SRB can integrate file systems, databases and archive systems and provide transparent data services for higher-level applications and users. SRB uses centralized metadata catalog MCAT for data access and management over wide-area network. Initially it wasn't fit for the grid environment but it has been improved to support the characteristics of Data Grids. Now it is designed and implemented in a decentralized structure and is planning to support environments with multi-domain management (mainly for file access).

The Punch Virtual File System (PVFS) [6] uses proxy mechanism to accept NFS client's requests and access the data in server side of NFS system after analyzing and processing clients' requests. It has achieved uniform data access to multiple NFS systems.

The Globus [7] system uses standard protocols for data movement and remote access (GASS [7]) and provides a basic mechanism for high-speed data transfer (GridFtp) [8]. Based on that, it implements data replica management, metadata catalog management and replica selection services and thus provides a good underlying development platform for Data Grids.

The Avaki [9] Data Grid system has achieved data access to multi-domain NFS file systems by object-oriented methods. It also provides uniform security authentication and supports data replica management.

The goal of GridDaen is some similar to SRB and Avaki Data Grid system. They all have achieved system's global naming, uniform data access, single sign-on, etc. But GridDaen is much different from them in several aspects. Firstly, GridDaen utilizes a three-level naming scheme that shields users from low-level resource discovery and provide global uniform view for users. Secondly, the metadata in GridDaen is organized in a multi-layer distributed structure, thus it is scalable and reliable and can be configured flexibly. Thirdly, GridDaen adopts the multi-domain federated server technology and request optimizing technology to achieve good scalability and availability. Fourthly, role-based multi-level access control policy is used to implement the access control of the system. Replication and caching mechanism is also used in GridDaen to improve the performance.

3 GridDaen Data Grid Architecture

GridDaen is a general data grid middleware to support uniform secure access and management of various types of heterogeneous distributed storage and data resources. GridDaen can integrate many kinds of wide heterogeneous storage resources, such as file systems (e.g., Linux ext2, Windows NTFS, etc.), network file systems (e.g. NFS) and database systems, etc. It can organize them uniformly and shields the heterogeneity and different administrative domains of underlying storage resources. Also it provides visual global views and convenient, standard access and management APIs and Interfaces for users and application.

GridDaen adopts a three-layer Data Grid architecture, as illustrated in Figure 1. The first layer includes various kinds of access interfaces to physical storage resources and metadata resources, including various kinds of file systems, archive systems and database systems. It accesses and operates the datasets in these systems through native protocols and methods that the physical resources support.

The second layer, i.e. the service layer, is the core of the system. The GridDaen system uses the core services to manage multiple data sources and provide uniform data access and management for users and applications. The second layer is consisted of five core services, including *resource aggregator*, *data service*, *metadata service*, *security service* and *system management service*. The *resource aggregator* is mainly for the connecting, monitoring and scheduling of computational and instrumental resources and supports the functions that the computational grid needs. The *data service* mainly provides data access and management as well as request dispatching, scheduling, and optimizing services. It uniformly manages the heterogeneous distributed storage and data resources, provides uniform data access, enables high-speed data transfer and replica management, and provides the management for virtual datasets. The *metadata service* provides information services of global resources in the system. It provides query and maintenance for system resources information, access and management of user metadata, security and authorization information, replica location, management and selection information. It provides data registry and publishment services and also provides a common metadata access protocol and interface for the other services. The *security service* mainly supports single sign-on authentication, multi-level access control and authorization mechanism. The *system management service* mainly includes the creation and deletion of grid system's users, system configuration and deployment and status monitoring for the whole grid system.

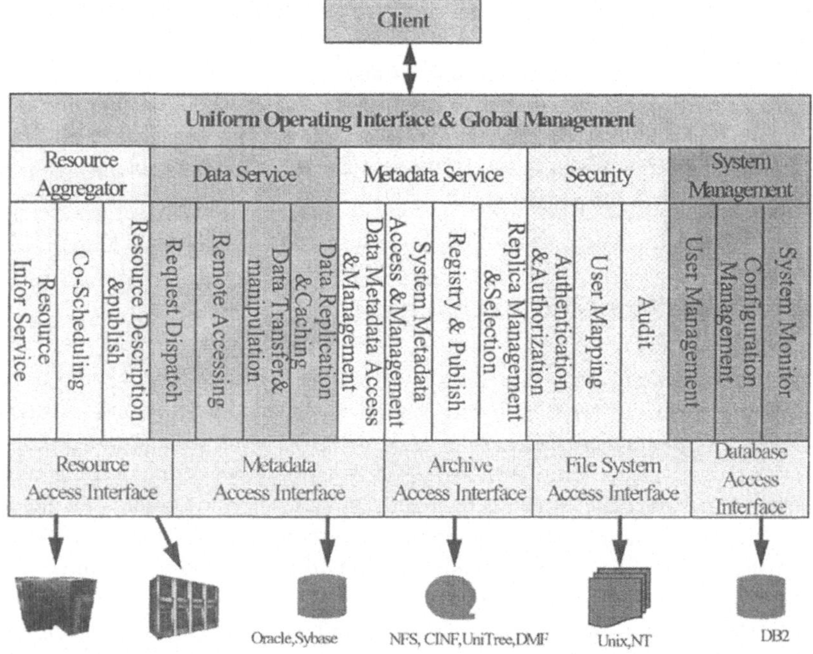

Fig. 1. The Architecture of GridDaen

The third layer is the interfaces that GridDaen provides for users and applications. Applications can easily access and manage data stored in multiple distributed storage systems by the interfaces that GridDaen provides.

The GridDaen Data Grid architecture presents the major logical functions the GridDaen provides. The detail design and implement will be shown in the next section.

4 GridDaen Design and Implementation

The main components of the GridDaen system include Client tools, DRB (Data Request Broker) servers and metadata information servers (MDIS), as illustrated in Figure 2. The GridDaen system is implemented in Java.

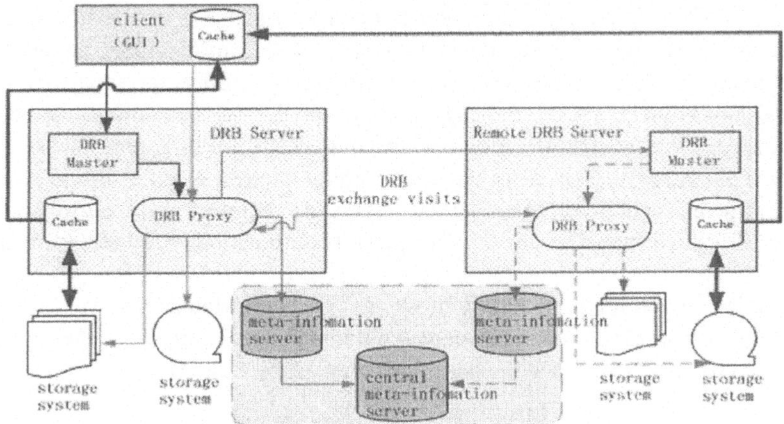

Fig. 2. The Components of GridDaen

The Client tools of GridDaen provide a set of APIs and user interfaces for users and applications. The user interfaces that it provides include command line tools (for Windows and Linux) and portable client GUI, which can show the global view of the system. The Client tools receive the requests from users or applications and submit them to DRB servers. Meanwhile it accepts the processing results from DRB server and displays it to users. The Client tools maintain a local cache to store temporary information, such as the files opened and so on.

The DRB servers receive the requests from the clients or other DRBs and provide all kind of data access and management functions of the system. In every administrative domain there is a DRB server that independently acts to perform data operations on local storage and data resources. To improve the performance, the DRB Server is composed of two components: DRB Master and DRB proxy. DRB Master is a daemon thread which acts as the entry of DRB and maintains the global information of the DRB (e.g., the online users). When a request from clients or other DRB server arrives, the DRB master receives the request and validates the security characteristic of the request, and then it adds the request to the waiting queue. Then DRB master schedules the requests in the waiting queue and assigns a DRB proxy to serve the request scheduled. The schedule policy can be configured in the system and now the default policy is FIFO. The DRB proxy is under the control of DRB Master and performs the actual data operation according to the request, such as data access, transfer and replication and so on. DRB proxy operates data in local storage system by native access protocol and methods, and performs operation on data in remote storage systems by sending requests to the corresponding remote DRB server and collaborating with the DRB server.

Multiple DRB servers can collaborate to form a federated DRB which acts like one single server and provides uniform services for data requests. User's request can be sent to any DRB server. The DRB server analyzes users' request, then sends it to the corresponding DRB server that is responsible for the resources the request requires. Once the DRB has acquired data, it directly transfers data to client by high-speed data transfer protocol.

The MDIS (Metadata Information Server) is organized in a distributed structure which is composed of local metadata servers and central global metadata servers. Each local metadata server provides the metadata service for local resources. The central global metadata server only builds the indices and maintains caches for local metadata servers to achieve global view and location-transparent access. Users can query replica information from any local replica metadata server in the system rather than from the central metadata server. When the required information isn't found in the local replica metadata server, the query is automatically redirected to the central server.

The design and implementation of DRB server and Metadata server are completely independent and the relationship between them can be configured when the system is deployed.Now we introduce the detail mechanisms in GridDaen.

4.1 Naming

In order to achieve the global view of datasets which are distributed over multiple administrative domains, a global naming space is needed to uniformly name the datasets in the system. The GridDaen system adopts three namespaces for datasets: site file name (SFN), internal persistent filename (IPFN) and user file name (UFN).

(1)SFN (Site File Name). It's the physical name which can uniquely identify the dataset in the actual storage system. In some file systems (e.g., NTFS, ext2, etc.), it's the complete path of the data file. In some network file systems (e.g., NFS, HPSS, etc.), it's the URL through which the dataset can be accessed.

(2)IPFN (Internal Persistent File Name). It's the 128-bit name that is only used in the interior of GridDaen system. IPFN is globally unique and unchanged during the entire lifetime of the dataset. Each IPFN can be uniquely mapped to one SFN. The internal operations in the system are performed by the IPFN names of the datasets.

(3)UFN(User File Name). UFN is the user logic name for the datasets. It is a user-oriented name and only used in user's logic view. The name in client GUI is UFN.

The relationships among them are illustrated in Figure 3. Multiple UFNs may be mapped to one IPFN when one or more soft links are built for the same dataset. One IPFN can only be mapped to one SFN and vice versa. The relationships are stored in the MDISs.

The advantage of this naming scheme is that the logic view is separately from the physical characteristics of datasets, thus changes in physical layers won't affect the logical layers and vice versa. For example, when a dataset is moved, its SFN is changed but its IPFN is unchanged. Such a naming scheme can facilitate the global uniform view for users with the support of MDIS.

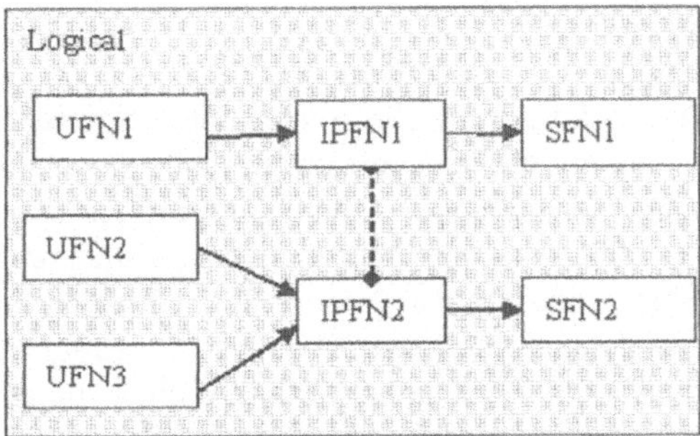

Fig. 3. The relationships among the namespaces

GridDaen provides the capability to allow users assemble many datasets into a *Virtual Dataset* (or *Collection*). The datasets in one virtual dataset have the same or similar attributes but may be distributed in multiple heterogeneous storage systems. The naming scheme of virtual dataset is the same as that of the ordinary dataset. In GridDaen, a virtual dataset is implemented with the set of IPFNs. Thus whatever changes have taken place in user file names and physical file names, the actual composition of the virtual dataset doesn't change.

At the same time, in order to achieve uniform naming in the whole system, similar naming mechanisms can be applied to resources and users. We omit them here due to the space limit.

4.2 Data Access and Management

The GridDaen system provides a set of uniform APIs and software packages for data access and management, such as read, write, copy, movement, link and so on. Virtual dataset and data directory operations, such as creation, deletion, adding or deleting an element and so on, are also supported. Users and applications can use uniform interfaces that are similar to NFS file system to access and manage geographically distributed data and storage resources.

After a data access (or management) request is sent, GridDaen will perform a series of operations to accomplish the request. The main process of "read" operation is shown as below (the other operations is similar):

(1) Users send access requests (e.g., open, read, write, move, etc.) to a DRB server using the uniform API or GUI

(2) The DRB master listens and accepts the request, validates its security property. DRB master assigns an idle DRB proxy in DRB server to server the request

(3) The DRB proxy checks the cache to get to know if the data requested exists. If true, it directly transfer the data from the cache to clients; else turn to (4)

(4) The DRB proxy thread queries MDIS to acquire the corresponding metadata, such as the access method, storage systems information and so on.

(5) If the metadata shows the data requested is managed by another DRB server, the proxy sends the request to the corresponding remote DRB server and the remote DRB server will handle it; else the DRB proxy reads the data with native data access protocol to the cache and then transfers the data from the cache to the client.

4.3 Replica Management

The replicas of the same dataset may be created for performance, availability and load balance. The users and high-level applications only know the original dataset, and GridDaen can manage the replicas for them. The replica management framework in GridDaen includes the following three components, as illustrated below:

(1) Replica Location: Finding one or more desired replicas of a dataset for the applications or users. A dynamic self-adaptive replica location method (DSRL) [11] is proposed to support efficient locating of multiple replicas of a data element.

(2) Replica Selection: Selecting the fittest replica for a certain user to improve performance and provide location transparency and enhanced time transparency.

(3) Replica Maintenance & Management: Maintain the consistency among different replicas of the datasets and provides some mechanism (such as automatic replication mechanism) to manage the replicas to improve the performance and load balance. In GridDaen, the replica itself is an important data resource. The changed replica is published as a new version of the dataset or invalidates other replicas.

4.4 Cache Management

In order to improve performance, GridDaen uses cache mechanism in client tools and DRB Servers, as illustrated in Figure 1. Remote datasets can be replicated to the local cache on the principle of locality to improve the efficiency of continuous operation on the certain dataset. Noteworthy, cache is much different from the replica. The data in the cache isn't registered in replica information tables and isn't managed by the replica management mechanism. Generally, the replica is a complete copy of the dataset, but the cache may be only a part of one dataset. GridDaen provides some cache replacement policies, such as Least Frequently Used (LFU), Least Recently Used (LRU), LRU-K, Greedy Dual Size (GDS), etc. The applications and users can configure it as needed and the default replacement policy is LRU.

4.5 Security

Generally, the resources in data grids belong to different institutions or organizations which may use different security mechanisms and policies. Thus multiple institutions or organizations need to coordinate to solve the problem of multi-domain security management.

The GridDaen system uses existing grid security standard GSI and security software packages of Globus. GridDaen builds a global unique CA center and use delegation and credential for authentication, authorization and single sign-on in the system.

In GridDaen, the security policies are as below:

(1)When a user logins to the system, identity authentication is needed and a time limited proxy credential is created for the valid user

(2)When a physical resource is published into the system, an identity and a resource proxy credential representing its identity will be assigned to it

(3)When a user uses a certain physical resource, it needs to exchange credentials with the resources to perform bidirectional authentication. The communication between them must be encrypted to ensure security.

(4)A global user of the system will ultimately be mapped to multiple local users of the physical resources. The local user's privileges for using the physical resource are determined by the local security policies.

Ticket is a random identifier with privileges and limited timestamp generated by the valid user. Tickets can be transferred between users. For example, a valid user A can transfer its ticket to another user B, then user B can own user A's privileges during the time limited in the ticket. Ticket mechanism is mainly used to solve the security and authentication problems of temporary access.

4.6 Role-Based Multi-level Access Control

The GridDaen system uses role-based multi-level access control mechanism (RBAC).

A role is a set of actions and privileges related to specific operations. The system administrator creates roles according to application characteristics and security policy. For a specific user, the system administrator assigned one or many roles and enables the user to perform the operations in the roles. This mechanism has a moderate independence and is convenient for privileges' granting and reclaiming.

The access control procedure includes two steps. Before mapping the global grid users to local users, the system needs to validate the global users' authorization. Only the valid global users can be mapped to the local users in the local system in which the data resources locate. The local system still needs to validate local users' authorization using its local access control mechanism. Only the users that have passed the two-step validation can access data.

5 Summary and Future Work

The GridDaen system utilizes three-level namespaces, coordinated DRB servers and distributed MDIS to integrate underlying heterogeneous resources and provide uniform global view and uniform access and management. GridDaen allows applications and users to access and operate various heterogeneous data and storage resources through standard APIs and interfaces, thus it shields the geographical locations, different naming, discovery and access mechanisms of the underlying physical resources. The GridDaen system is designed to be in a distributed structure can achieve good scalability, reliability and flexibility.

The GridDaen system is a part of the GridOppen grid system which is designed and implemented in School of Computer, National University of Defense Technology. Now a prototype system of GridDaen has been implemented, which can support uniform operation and access of files and storage systems, such as NFS, CINF, Http, etc. GridDaen has been tested in local area network and now we are performing the tests in wide-area environments with the other members of China National Grid(CNGrid). Many efforts are being made to provide data consistency, integrate more kind of storage systems, and support OGSI in GridDaen.

References

1. Chervenak, A., Foster, I., Kesselman, C., Salisbury, C., Tuecke, S.: The Data Grid: Towards an Architecture for the Distributed Management and Analysis of Large Scientific Data Sets. Journal of Network and Computer Applications, Vol. 23 (2001) 187-200
2. Wolfgang Hoschek, Javier Jaen-Martinez, Asad Samar, Heinz Stockinger, and Kurt Stockinger: Data Management in an International Data Grid Project. Proc. of 1st IEEE/ACM International Workshop on Grid Computing (Grid'2000), Bangalore, India (2000)
3. William, H. Bell, Diana Bosio: Project Spitfire - Towards Grid Web Service Databases. Global Grid Forum 5, Edinburgh, Scotland (2002)
4. Vöckler, Jens-S., Wilde, M., Foster, I.: The GriPhyN Virtual Data System. Technical Report GriPhyN-2002-02 (2002)
5. Baru C., Moore, R, Rajasekar, A, Wan, M,: The SDSC Storage Resource Broker. Proc. Of CASCON'98 Conference, Toronto, Canada (1998)
6. Figueiredo, R. J., Kapadia, N. H., and Fortes, J. A. B.: The punch virtual file system: Seamless access to decentralized storage services in a computational grid. Proc. of the 10th IEEE International Symposium on High Performance Distributed Computing, IEEE Computer Society Press (2001)
7. Bester, J., Foster, I., Kesselman, C., Tedesco, J., and Tuecke, S.: GASS: A data movement and access service for wide area computing systems. Proc. of the Sixth Workshop on Input/Output in Parallel and Distributed Systems, ACM Press, Atlanta (1999) 78–88
8. Chervenak, A. L., Foster, I., Kesselman, C. *et al.*: Data Management and Transfer in High Performance Computational Grid Environments. Parallel Computing Journal, Vol. 28 No.5 (2002) 749-771
9. The Avaki Data grid: Easy Access, Less Administration,More Science. At http://www.avaki.com
10. Foster, I., Kesselman, C., Tuecke, S.: The Anatomy of the Grid: Enabling Scalable Virtual Organizations. International Journal of High Performance Computing Applications, Vol. 15, No.3 (2001) 200-222
11. LI Dongsheng, Xiao Nong, LU Xicheng, *et al.* Dynamic Self-Adaptive Replica Location Method in Data Grids. Proc. of IEEE Cluster'2003, IEEE Computer Society Press, Hong Kong (2003)

Research on Security Architecture and Protocols of Grid Computing System[1]

Xiangming Fang, Shoubao Yang, Leitao Guo, and Lei Zhang

Computer Science Department, University of Science and Technology of China, Hefei 230026, P.R.China
{xmfang,ltguo,leizh}@mail.ustc.edu.cn,
syang@ustc.edu.cn

Abstract. This paper analyzes security problems existing in Grid Computing System and describes the security mechanism in Grid Computing System. After briefly introducing the security abstract of grid computing system at Grid Security Basic Layer, several protocols are defined at Grid Security Protocol Layer based on security architecture model. Broker protocols are then thoroughly discussed.

Keywords: Grid Computing System, Security Abstract, Grid Security Protocols, Broker

1 Introduction

With the development of application requirements for high-performance computing, it is impossible to solve super large-scale issues using a single high performance computer or a single computer cluster. Therefore, it is needed to connect distributed heterogeneous high-performance computer, computer cluster, large-scale database server and large-scale file server with high-speed interconnection network and integrate them into a transparent virtual high-performance computing environment. This environment is named Grid Computing System[1-3].

2 Security in Grid Computing System

Essentially, security assurance of the Internet provides two kinds of security services: access control service, which protects various resources from being used by violate user and prevents resources abused from authorized user; Secure communication service, which provides mutual authentication, and message protection as well, such

[1] This paper is supported by the National Natural Science Foundation of China under Grant No.60273041 and the National '863' High-Tech Program of China under Grant No. 2002AA104560.

M. Li et al. (Eds.): GCC 2003, LNCS 3032, pp. 529–535, 2004.

as message integrity and confidentiality. But these services cannot solve all the security problems in Grid Computing System.

Security of Grid Computing System should solve the following problems: user masquerade, server masquerade, data wiretapping and sophisticating, remote attack, resource abusing, malicious program, and system integrity. Grid Computing System is a complicated, dynamic and wide-area system, adding restricted authorization on user cannot be solved by the current technologies. So developing new security architecture is necessary. By now, GSI (Globus Security Infrastructure) [4-6] is one of the most famous schemas.

Based on the analysis of GSI, we present five-layered security architecture[7] on considering the designation and accomplishment of Grid security project. The security architecture that we have already briefly depicted at GCC2002 is shown as Fig. 1.

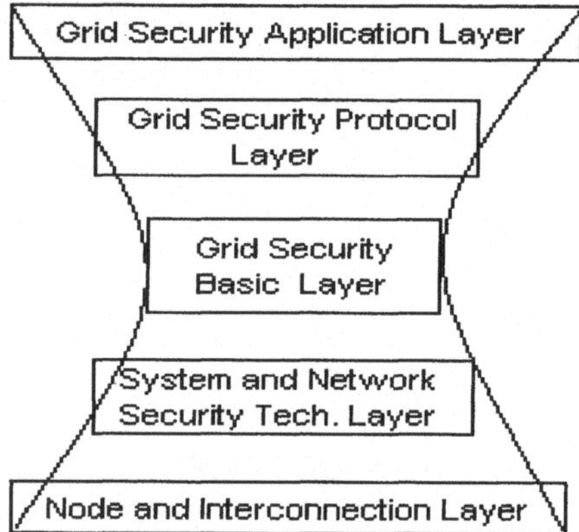

Fig. 1. Security architecture of the Grid computing system

Our security architecture is a good schema for Grid research because of its good scalability and its ability of adapting to the dynamic system environment. In succession, we place our emphases on the Grid Security Basic Layer and Grid Security Protocol Layer, which are of great importance in grid security architecture.

3 Grid Security Basic Layer

Grid Security Basic Layer provides user and resource mapping policy, including general mapping rules. In this layer, the Grid Computing System is abstracted to the elements as Objects, Subjects, Security Policies, Trust Domains, Operations, Authorization, etc. The security of Grid Computing System can be regarded as the relationships among the basic elements, which gives an effective way to realize user's restrictive authorization.

- **Definitions of Basic Elements**

  First of all, some definitions are given in the following.

  Object is resource or process of Grid Computing System. Object is protected by security policy. Resource may be file, memory, CPU, equipment, etc. Process may be process running on behalf of user, process running on behalf of resource, etc. "O" denotes Object.

Subject is user, resource or process of Grid Computing System. Subject may destroy Object. Resource may be file, memory, CPU, equipment, etc. Process may be process running on behalf of user, process running on behalf of resource, etc. "S" denotes Subject.

Security Policy is a set of policies of Grid Computing System. Security Policy protects Object against Subject. "P" denotes Security Policy.

Trust Domain is a logical, administrative region of Grid Computing System. Trust Domain has clear border. "D" denotes Trust Domain.

Operation is a set of instructions by which Subject access or use Object. "O_P" denotes Operation.

Authorization is the process by which Security Policy is acted on Subject. There are two kinds of results of Authorization. One is Subject passed Security Policy and the other is not. "A" denotes Authorization.

- **Representation of Basic Elements**

Representation of Object: There are two kinds of Object in Grid Computing System, which are Global Object O_G and Local Object O_L. A Global Object is the abstraction of one or many Local Objects. Global Objects and Local Objects exist in Grid Computing System at the same time.

Representation of Subject: There are two kinds of Subject in Grid Computing System, which are Global Subject S_G and Local Subject S_L. A Global Subject is the abstraction of one or many Local Subjects. Global Subjects and Local Subjects exist in Grid Computing System at the same time.

Representation of Security Policy: There are two kinds of Security Policy in Grid Computing System, which are Global Security Policy P_G and Local Security Policy P_L. Global Security Policy is the abstraction of all Local Security Policy. Global Security Policy and Local Security Policy exist in Grid Computing System at the same time.

Representation of Trust Domain: There are two kinds of Trust Domain in Grid Computing System, which are Global Trust Domain D_G and Local Trust Damian D_L. Global Trust Domain is the abstraction of all Local Trust Domains. Global Trust Domain and Local Trust Domain exist in Grid Computing System at the same time.Trust Domain of Grid Computing System consists of three elements: Objects existing in this Trust Domain, Subjects existing in this Trust Domain and Security Policy which protect Objects against Subjects. Trust Domain can be denoted by $D=(\{O\},\{S\},P)$, D denotes Trust Domain, $\{O\}$ denotes the set of all Objects existing in this Trust Domain, $\{S\}$denotes the set of all Subjects existing in this Trust Domain, and P denotes Security Policy of this Trust Domain. Global Trust Domain can be denoted by $D_G=(\{O_G\},\{S_G\},P_G)$, and Local Trust Domain can be denoted by $D_{Li}=(\{O_{Li}\},\{S_{Li}\},P_{Li})$ I=1,2,3...

Representation of Operation: Operation of Grid Computing System may be executed in many Local Trust Domains. Operation cannot be executed until Subjects passed Security Policy (Authorization) of corresponding Trust Domain.

- **Security Abstract of Grid Computing System**

The Grid Computing System is abstracted to the elements such as Objects, Subjects, Security Policies, Trust Domains, Operations, Authorization, etc. Grid Computing System is composed of four parts: Global Trust Domain, Local Trust Domain, Operations and Authorizations. It can be denoted by

$$G=(D_G,\{D_{li}\},\{O_{Pj}\},\{A_K\})\ i=1,2,3\ldots\ j=1,2,3\ldots\ k=1,2,3\ldots$$

G denotes Grid Computing System, D_G denotes Global Trust Domain, $\{D_{Li}\}$denotes the set of all Local Domain, $\{O_{Pj}\}$ denotes the set of all Operations, $\{A_K\}$ denotes the set of all Authorizations.

The security of Grid Computing System can be regarded as the relationship among the basic elements. That is to say, "user access and use resources" can be abstracted as "Subject operate Object", this can be denoted by $S\text{—}^{OP}\text{—}>O$. Checking the relationship of Subject, Object and Security Policy, we can examine whether Subject can operate Object, and also can tell whether user can access resource.

4 Grid Security Protocol Layer

We define seven protocols[8] at Grid Security Protocol Layer on considering the course of grid computing especially the course of resource management. These protocols are listed in table 1. Then we will thoroughly discuss broker protocols that of great importance.

Table 1. Protocol at Grid Security Protocol Layer

Name	Representation
User Proxy Creation Protocol	User how to create user proxy
Resource Proxy Creation Protocol	System how to create resource proxy
User Proxy's Resource Application Protocol	User proxy how to apply for resources
Process's Resource Application Protocol	Process how to apply for resources
Process's Signature Application Protocol	How to sign the process's certificate
Broker Creation Protocol	System how to create broker
Broker Service Protocol	Broker how to allot resources coordinately

- **Broker Creation Protocol**

Grid computing system sets up a process, and then grants the broker certificate for this process. The process that gets the certificate can offer broker service. Broker sends broker service notification to resource proxy. Resource proxy gives broker message of resources and informs broker modification. Broker tidies up the information.

Broker Creation Protocol is shown below.

(1) Grid computing system set up a broker certificate, and then sends the certificate that hasn't been signed to the CA.

(2) CA sign the broker certificate by using its own certificate then send it to the grid computing system.

(3) After receiving the certificate, grid computing system creates a process that hold this new signed certificate. The process then becomes a broker.

- **Broker Service Protocol**

All resource proxies send information of resources in charge to broker. So the broker can see the whole resources of grid computing system while the proxy can only see parts of resources. When user requires a large quantity of resources, the broker must offer its information in contrast to the locality of the resource proxy.

The workflow of Broker Service Protocol is shown as Fig. 2.

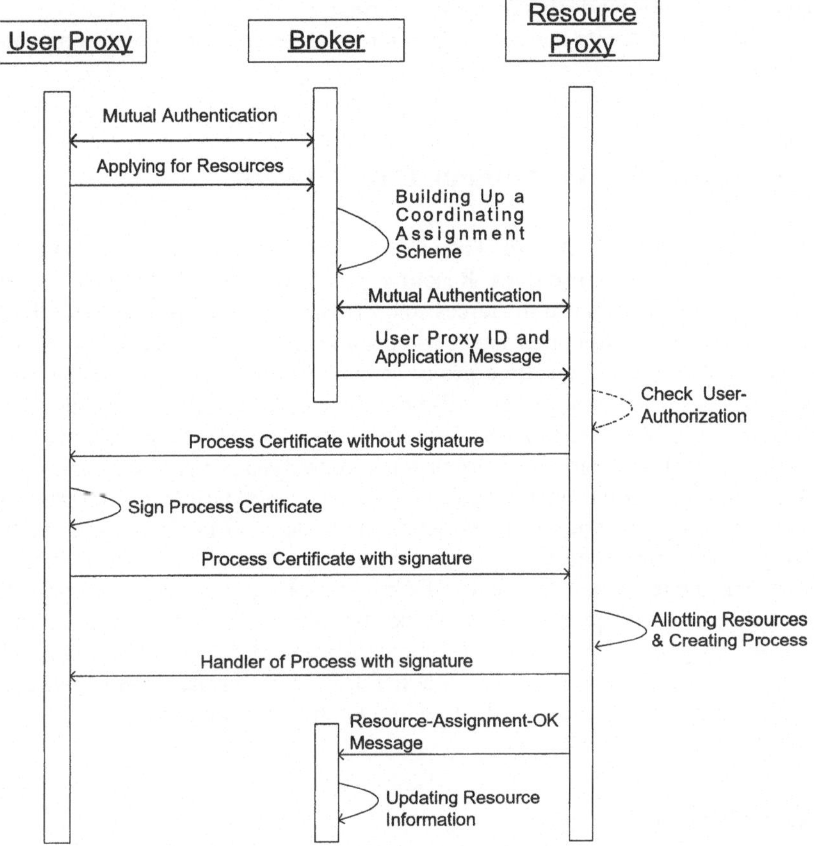

Fig. 2. Workflow of Broker Service Protocol

Broker Service Protocol is illustrated below:

(1) User proxy and broker carry out mutual authentication. As a part of mutual authentication, broker should check the expiration of the certificate.

(2) After mutual authentication, user proxy uses its proxy certificate add its signature to the message of applying for a lot of resources. Then user proxy sends this application to broker.

(3) Having received the application, broker builds up a coordinating assignment scheme by analyzing current resources available.

(4) In accordance with the assignment scheme, broker separates the full application to small pieces, which can easily be found.

(5) Broker and resource proxy need mutual authentication if they are not in the same trusted domain.

(6) When resources are available, broker sends resource proxy the user proxy ID and application message that have already signed by broker with its own certificate.

(7) On receiving the user ID and application message, resource proxy allots the corresponding resources to the user proxy.

(8) Resource proxy creates a resource-assignment-ok message signed with its own certificate and then sends this message to broker.

(9) Broker updates its resource information while the resource-assignment-ok message arrives.

5 More Adaptive to Dynamic Environment

When some resources join in the Grid Computing System, the system will create a resource proxy for these resources. Resource proxy manages these resources and sends the information about these resources to a broker. Then the broker can allocate these resources to user. On the other hand, when some resources are failed or leave the Grid Computing System, the resource proxy sends an update message to the broker. The broker receives this message and will not allocate these failed or leaved resources to user. Mapping file is used to map users to resources. Mapping files are created dynamically. So this mapping measure is adaptive to dynamic environment.

When the scale of Grid Computing System is not large, one resource proxy is enough to manage all the resources; when the scale of Grid Computing System is increasing, two or more resource proxies are needed; Secondary user proxy and multi-brokers are needed when the scale of Grid increases to a certain degree. Resource proxies directly manage the resources, so they can gather resources' information in time. Brokers gain information of resources from resource proxies, and co-allocation these resources. Resource proxies cooperating with brokers, this make the five-layered security architecture is adaptive to dynamic environment.

6 Conclusion

This paper analyzes security problems existing in Grid Computing System and describes the security mechanism of Grid Computing System. Several protocols are defined at Grid Security Protocol Layer based on our security architecture model. Broker protocols in the schema are more adaptive to dynamic environments.

References

[1] Ian Foster and Carl Kesselman. The Grid: Blueprint for a New Computing Infrastructure. Morgan Kaufmann Publishers, Inc., San Francisco, California, 1999.

[2] Ian Foster, Carl Kesselman, and Steven Tuecke. The Anatomy of the Grid: Enabling Scalable Virtual Organizations. International Journal of Supercomputer Applications, 2001.

[3] Ian Foster. Internet Computing and the Emerging Grid. Available from http://www.nature.com/nature/webmatters/grid/grid.html.

[4] The Globus Project. Available from http://www.globus.org/

[5] Ian Foster and Carl Kesselman. Globus: A Meta-computing Infrastructure Toolkit. International Journal of Supercomputer Applications, 1996.

[6] Ian Foster and Carl Kesselman. The Globus Project: A Status Report. In Proc. Heterogeneous Computing Workshop. IEEE Computer Society Press, 1998.

[7] Ian Foster, Carl Kesselman, Gene Tsudik, and Steven Tuecke. A Security Architecture for Computational Grids. Proc. 5th ACM Conference on Computer and Communications Security Conference, 1998.

[8] Randy Butler Von Welch, Douglas Engert, Ian Foster, Steven Tuecke, John Volmer, Carl Kesselman. A National-Scale Authentication Infrastructure, IEEE Computer, 33(12), 2000.

A Multi-agent System Architecture for End-User Level Grid Monitoring Using Geographic Information Systems (MAGGIS): Architecture and Implementation

Shaowen Wang[1], Anand Padmanabhan[1], Yan Liu[1], Ransom Briggs[1], Jun Ni[1], Tao He[1], Boyd M. Knosp[1], and Yasar Onel[2]

[1]Academic Technologies-Research Services of Information Technology Services, The University of Iowa, Iowa City, IA 52242, USA
{shaowen-wang, anand-padmanabhan-1, yan-liu-1, ransom-briggs, jun-ni, tao-he, boyd-knosp}@uiowa.edu
[2]Department of Physics and Astronomy, The University of Iowa, Iowa City, IA 52242, USA
yonel@newton.physics.uiowa.edu

Abstract. This paper illustrates a Multi-Agent system architecture for end-user level Grid monitoring using Geographical Information Systems (MAGGIS). The purpose of this research is to investigate MAGGIS architecture and implementation issues, and to verify the following two hypotheses: 1.) multi-agent systems provide an effective and scalable architecture to synthesize various Grid information providers for monitoring Grid resources; and 2.) geographic information systems (GIS) provide an ideal solution to organizing and managing the geographic aspect of Grid resource information as well as to providing an effective user interface for monitoring Grid status. The MAGGIS framework is implemented in a Grid portal environment based on the open Grid service architecture. It is observed that the MAGGIS not only helps end-users monitor the status of Grid resources, but also provides quick and comprehensive information for resource scheduling and management on behalf of user applications.

1 Introduction

Grid technologies enable large-scale coordinated sharing of distributed computing resources within Virtual Organizations (VO) [1, 2]. Grid monitoring solutions are required to provide information to determine the source of performance problems, tune Grids and their applications to optimal performance, detect faults and execute recovery mechanisms, and predict performance and schedule computational tasks [3].

Recent active research in Grid monitoring has covered a broad scope of research topics [4]. These topics mainly include Grid monitoring architectures [3], monitoring information modeling [5], query methods for Grid information services [6], and performance study of monitoring and information services for distributed systems [7].

Grid monitoring can be classified as two types based on its purposes: end-user level monitoring and system level monitoring. Although some researchers, e.g.,

M. Li et al. (Eds.): GCC 2003, LNCS 3032, pp. 536–543, 2004.

Laszewski et al., have conducted research on the end-user level Grid monitoring in a service-oriented way [8], most current research has been focusing on system level monitoring. However, end-user level monitoring must be designed to meet the needs of user applications as opposed to the emphasis of the system level monitoring has on helping manage Grid resources.

This paper demonstrates a Multi-Agent system architecture for end-user level Grid monitoring using Geographical Information Systems (MAGGIS) and its prototype implementation. Agents can be defined to be autonomous, problem-solving computational entities capable of effective operation in dynamic and open environments [9]. Agents are often deployed in a multi-agent system in which they interact, and maybe cooperate, with other agents that have possibly conflicting aims [10]. Agent-based approach has been applied to address issues in Grid computing such as load balancing [11] and system level monitoring [12]. However, it is advantageous to apply the multi-agent system approach to end-user level monitoring for the following two reasons: 1.) knowledge about Grid resource information can be transferred from Grid information services to user applications in a consistent way through agent communication mechanisms such as the Knowledge Query and Manipulation Language (KQML) [13]; 2.) agents, on behalf of users and user applications, can represent the preferences and goals of monitoring resources, which potentially leads to high efficiency and optimal performance of the MAGGIS.

In MAGGIS, geographical information systems (GIS) are used to handle the geographical aspect of Grid information. GIS is defined as an information system that is used to input, store, retrieve, manipulate, analyze, and output geographically referenced data or geospatial data [14]. Map-based geographic referencing [15] has been used to monitor Grid resources in several large European Grid projects. However, this type of research effort needs to be extended to fully address the needs of monitoring the Grids that span across multi-scale and dynamic VOs.

In rest of this paper, section 2 articulates the MAGGIS multi-agent architecture. Section 3 explains how GIS is used to handle the geographic aspect of Grid information based on a spatial-temporal data model. Section 4 provides a prototype implementation for MAGGIS in a Grid portal [16] context based on the Open Grid Service Architecture (OGSA) [17]. Finally, section 5 draws several conclusions, based on which some future research directions are pointed out.

2 Architecture

In principle, the MAGGIS multi-agent system adopts the classical multi-agent architecture used in distributed artificial intelligence [18].

2.1 Functions

The MAGGIS multi-agent system architecture includes two logic layers: a data collection layer and a knowledge layer. The data collection layer is comprised of monitoring and synthesizing components while the knowledge layer incorporates data representation, modeling, communication, and analysis components. This two-layer architecture can be translated into a functional view (Fig. 1) in which the data collection layer is equivalent to monitoring agents while the knowledge layer is equivalent to user agents. Consequently, the monitoring agents have capabilities for monitoring and synthesizing information as well as for modeling data. The user agents are primarily responsible for analyzing Grid information from monitoring agents and presenting the aggregated information to a user client.

In addition, the user agents handle user requests and maintain user profiles through the use of the services provided by the monitoring agents. The communication between user agents and monitoring agents is implemented using the KQML [13]. The monitoring agents store information that is based on a spatial-temporal data model described in section 3.

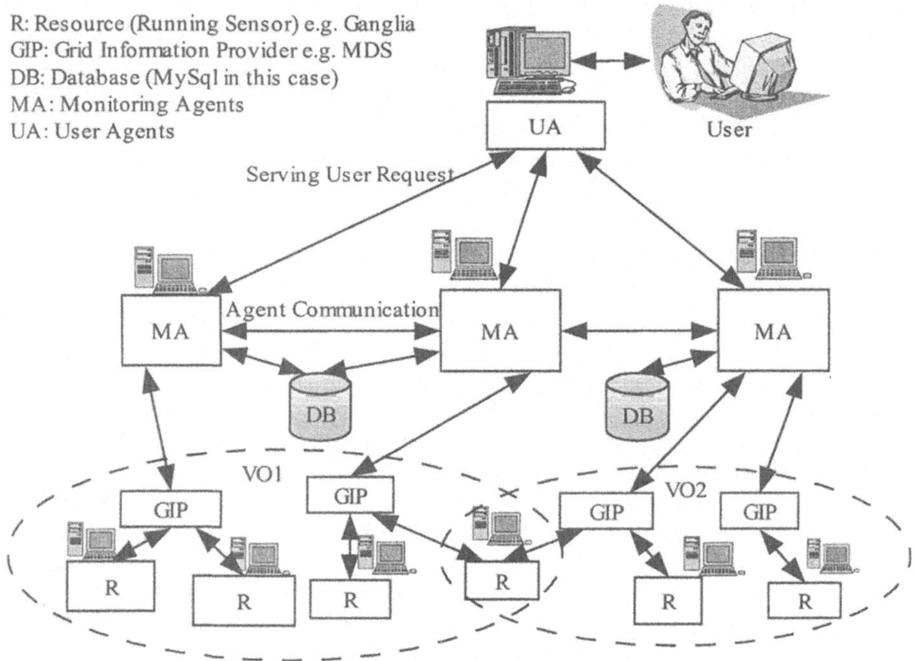

Fig. 1. Multi-agent system architecture of MAGGIS

2.2 Scalability

The main advantage of using this multi-agent system approach to Grid monitoring is that the multi-agent system architecture by its inherent nature is scalable and capable of aggregating information from disparate monitoring data sources (e.g., MDS [1], Ganglia [19], NWS [20], and local job managers). In the present architecture, databases are associated with VOs. The number of databases per VO can be determined based on the VO size. There is a monitoring agent process at the database level that manages the registration information of Grid resources. This process will also be employed to dynamically balance monitoring loads among available monitoring agents.

2.3 Methods

The methods used to implement the multi-agent system architecture are mainly reflected in the following two tasks agents perform autonomously.

1. Collecting monitoring information: When a monitoring agent is instantiated, it acquires the information about particular Grid resources it is supposed to monitor. The monitoring agent implements a multi-threaded model that allows the agent to independently monitor various Grid resources throughout its lifetime. The resource information can be collected from different information providers and stored in databases.
2. Servicing user agents: A non-blocking multi-threaded mechanism was implemented to handle requests from multiple users. The communication between user and monitoring agents is realized through the use of KQML.

The format of a KQML message sent from a user agent to a monitoring agent along with an illustrative example is provided as follows:

- *Performative: Sender: Receiver: Message Content*
- Example: "Ask-All: UserAgent1: MonitoirngAgent1: Provide information about CPU utilization of machine *XYZ* for the past hour"

The monitoring agent responds to the user agent using "*tell*" or "*sorry*" performative. A "*sorry*" performative is used when the monitoring agent is unable to comply with the user requests. A "*tell*" performative is used to send the requested information to the user agent. Moreover, all agents are autonomous and a failure of one agent or failure of one thread within an agent does not affect the other agents.

3 Geographic Information Integration

The integration of geographic information has been addressed in the past research of Grid monitoring to emphasize the needs of visualizing the geographic distribution of computing resources [21]. However, no existing data model for monitoring information has specifically taken geographic information into account. It is necessary to develop a generic spatial-temporal data model to handle the monitoring data that includes geographic attributes.

3.1 Spatial-Temporal Data Model

Our spatial-temporal data model adopts the conceptual pyramid model [22]. At the knowledge level, it is integrated with the MAGGIS multi-agent system architecture that is independent from the implementation of a particular Grid information service. Consequently, the model can be developed independently from the implementation aspect of data models in Grid information services such as the relational data model [5], the directory service based on the Lightweight Directory Access Protocol (LDAP)

[1], or XML. In addition, our spatial-temporal data model is able to be incorporated in the agent communication through an event-based mechanism [23].

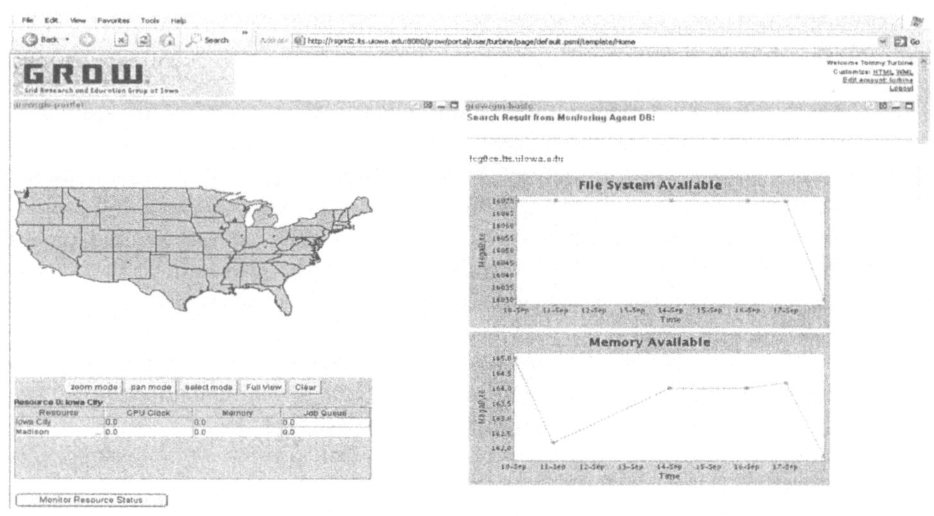

Fig. 2. A MAGGIS user interface

3.2 Data Model Implementation

An implementation of our spatial-temporal data model is based on an extended relational data model implemented in a popular GIS software solution – ArcGIS [24]. In this data model, the attribute information that may or may not be location-sensitive is stored and managed using a relational database. The association between geographic information and attribute information is established through the use of an indexing method for geometric objects. GeoTools [25] is used to handle the geographic knowledge aspect of the spatial-temporal data model in an object-oriented way, which meets the needs of translating the spatial-temporal data to specific knowledge in the multi-agent system architecture. For example, the left part of Fig. 2 shows an applet-based interface that provides map-based resource visualization, browsing, selection, and spatial information query functions.

4 MAGGIS Implementation

MAGGIS was prototyped as a Grid service in a Grid portal that is called Grid Research & educatiOn group @ IoWa (GROW) portal. The GROW Grid portal was developed using Jetspeed [26] as a Grid portal server and development toolkit. The relationship between Jetspeed and other technologies used is illustrated in Fig. 3.

4.1 MAGGIS Grid Service

MAGGIS Grid service was implemented based on Globus Toolkit 3.0 [17]. It includes three major portlets: GeoTools portlet, user-agent portlet, and visualization portlet. GeoTools portlet was developed using GeoTools and it directly interacts with user-agent portlet to manage geographic aspect of monitoring information. User-agent portlet provides the capability for aggregating information based on user preferences through the communication with monitoring agents. Visualization portlet displays the aggregated information collected from user-agent portlet. These three portlets are integrated together as a Grid service that is portable to other Grid-service-based portal environment.

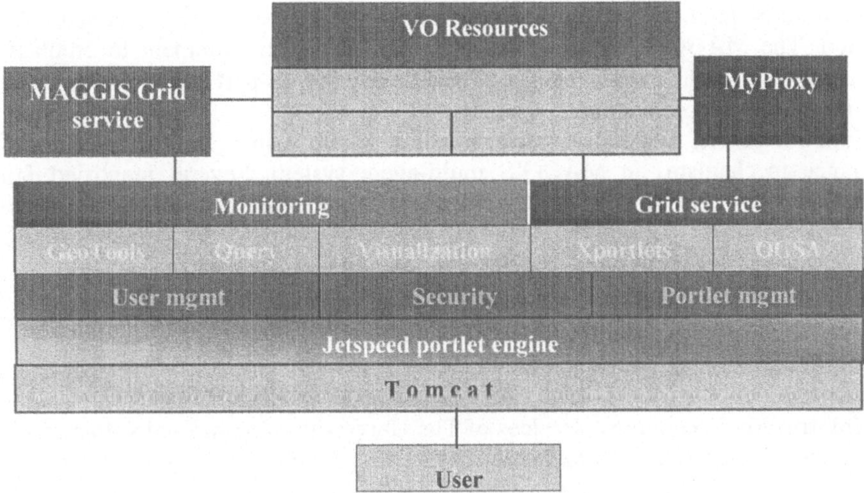

Fig. 3. Grid portal technologies employed

4.2 Case Study

MAGGIS Grid service is coupled with the GROW portal that uses Java CoG Kit [27] and Sun's Java XML for developing OGSA-compliant Grid services. MyProxy [28] is integrated with Jetspeed to provide a Web-based Grid security solution. The MAGGIS service in the context of GROW portal is deployed to a prototype campus Grid at the University of Iowa, several resources of which are belong to a few national Grid testbeds.

Fig. 2 shows an end-user level Grid monitoring scenario in which the MAGGIS Grid service in the GROW portal was used. This scenario took place after a user selected a VO from a VO list. All the resources of this selected VO are displayed on a map. Also, the user can select particular resources in the VO, examine their dynamic performance, and visualize aggregated and summary information. Our case study has demonstrated that MAGGIS Grid service provides a user-friendly environment in which monitoring information is presented in an effective way.

5 Concluding Discussions

End-user level Grid monitoring is critical to ensure that Grid resources are useful for user applications. The MAGGIS multi-agent system is designed to achieve scalable monitoring for multiple VOs of Grid resources from the perspective of user applications. The system interacts with heterogeneous Grid information providers through the "drivers" of monitoring agents. User agents are characterized to work on behalf of user clients to pull preferred information out of MAGGIS.

The information in the MAGGIS multi-agent system is represented using a spatial-temporal data model and communicated using KQML. The data model is implemented using GIS software to manage geographic aspect of Grid information. It is found that GIS provides an effective solution to releasing the cognitive load for users to understand and manage the information of Grid resources organized in a VO fashion. The MAGGIS is prototyped in a Grid portal environment to emulate the situation in which user-level Grid monitoring is a part of problem solving environments for applications.

Future research will focus on evaluating performance and developing fault tolerance mechanisms in MAGGIS multi-agent system. Several identified failure scenarios will be addressed. These failures mainly include monitoring agent failure (e.g., fail to collect monitoring data, or fail to respond to user agents), database failure, and user agent failure (e.g., not responding to user requests).

Acknowledgements. A subcontract with National Science Foundation and Department of Energy of U.S.A., The University of Iowa Informatics Initiative, and the Information Technology Services of The University of Iowa funded this research. The authors would like to thank Frederick M. Noth for his helpful suggestions.

References

1. Czajkowski, K., Fitzgerald, S., Foster, I., Kesselman, C.: Grid Information Services for Distributed Resource Sharing. Proceedings of the Tenth IEEE International Symposium on High-Performance Distributed Computing (HPDC-10), IEEE Press (2001)
2. Foster, I., Kesselman, C., Tuecke, S.: The Anatomy of the Grid: Enabling Scalable Virtual Organizations. International Journal of Supercomputer Applications, **15** (2001)
3. Tierney, B., Aydt, R., Gunter, D., Smith, W., Taylor, V., Wolski, R., Swany, M.: A Grid Monitoring Architecture. The Global Grid Forum GWD-GP-16-2, January (2002)
4. Casanova, H.: Distributed Computing Research Issues in Grid Computing. Quarterly Newsletter for the ACM Special Interest Group on Algorithms and Computation Theory (SIGACT News), **33** (2002)
5. Fisher, S.: Relational Model for Information and Monitoring. Technical Report GWD-Perf-7-1, GGF (2001)
6. Plale, B., Schwan, K.: Dynamic Querying of Streaming Data with the dQUOB System, IEEE Transactions on Parallel and Distributed Systems, **14** (2003)

7. Zhang, X., Freschl, J. L., Schopf, J. M.: A performance Study of Monitoring and Information Services for Distributed Systems. Proceedings of HPDC-12 (2003)
8. Laszewski, G., Gawor, J., Pe na, C. J., Foster, I.: InfoGram: A Peer-to-Peer Information and Job Submission Service. Proceedings of the 11th Symposium on High Performance Distributed Computing (2002)
9. Luck, M., McBurney, P., Preist, C.: Agent Technology: Enabling Next Generation Computing A Roadmap for Agent-based Computing Version 1.0. Available at: http://www.agentlink.org/roadmap/distribution.html (2003)
10. Jennings, N., Sycara, K., Wooldridge. M.: A roadmap for agent research and development. **1** (1):7 - 38 (1998)
11. Shen, W., Li, Y., Ghenniwa, H., Wang, C.: Adaptive Negotiation for Agent-Based Grid Computing. Proceedings of AAMAS2002 Workshop on Agentcities: Challenges in Open Agent Environments, Bologna, Italy, pp. 32-36 (2002)
12. Newman, H. B., Legrand, I. C., Bunn, J. J.: A Distributed Agent-based Architecture for Dynamic Services. CHEP, Beijing, China (2001)
13. Finin, T., Labrou, Y., Mayfield, J.: KQML as an Agent Communication Language. Software Agents, AAAI/MIT Press (1994)
14. Goodchild, M. F.: Geographical information science. *International Journal of Geographical Information Systems,* **6**, 31-45 (2003)
15. Map Center Project. Available at: http://ccwp7.in2p3.fr/mapcenter/ (2003)
16. Fox, G., Pierce, M., Gannon, D., Thomas, M.: Overview of Grid Computing Environments. Technical Report GGF-GCE-OVERVIEW2, GGF (2003)
17. Foster, I., Kesselman, C., Nick, J., Tuecke. S.: Grid Services for Distributed System Integration. Computer, **35** (6) (2002)
18. Hartvigsen, G., Johansen, D.: Co-operation in a Distributed Artificial Intelligence Environment – the StormCast Application. *Pergamon Press,* Oxford, England (1990)
19. Ganglia, a Distributed Monitoring and Execution system. Available at: http://ganglia.sourceforge.net/ (2003)
20. Network Weather Service (NWS). Available at: http://nws.cs.ucsb.edu/ (2003)
21. Baker, M. A., Smith, G.: A Prototype Grid-site Monitoring System, Version 1, DSG Technical Report, January (2002)
22. Mennis, J. L., Peuquet, D. J., Qian, L.: A Conceptual Framework for Incorporating Cognitive Principles into Geographical Database Representation. International Journal of Geographical Information Science, **14** (6), 501-520 (2000)
23. Peuquet, D. J., Duan, N.: An Event-based Spatialtemporal Data Model (ESTDM) for Temporal Analysis of Geographical Data. International Journal of Geographical Information Science, **9** (1), 7-24 (1996)
24. ArcGIS Software. Available at: http://www.esri.com/software/arcgis/ (2003)
25. GeoTools Open Source Project. Available at: http://www.geotools.org (2003)
26. Jetspeed Open Source Project. Available at: http://jakarta.apache.org/jetspeed/site/index.html (2003)
27. Java Cog Kit Open Source Project. Available at: http://www-unix.globus.org/toolkit/cog.html (2003)
28. Novotny, J., Tuecke, S., S. Welch. V.: An Online Credential Repository for the Grid: MyProxy. Proceedings of the Tenth International Symposium on High Performance Distributed Computing (HPDC-10), IEEE Press (2001)

An Architecture of Game Grid Based on Resource Router

Yu Wang, Enhua Tan, Wei Li, and Zhiwei Xu

Institute of Computing Technology of CAS
Beijing China, 100080
{wangyu, tanenhua}@software.ict.ac.cn, {liwei, zxu}@ict.ac.cn

Abstract. Current MOGs (Multiplayer Online Games) have many drawbacks for their conventional architecture, such as bottlenecks, poor scalability and redundant data. And since each game is developed solely by a company or team, sharing resources among different games is extremely difficult. The aim of grid computing is to fulfill the fully sharing of distributed resources, and we borrow the idea of grid to solve the above problems of MOGs. In this paper, we analyze traditional architecture's characteristic and propose an architecture of Game Grid based on the technology of Resource Router [1]; other key issues such as the scalability and load-balancing are also presented; a prototype called VEGA [2] Game Grid is introduced and evaluated.

1 Introduction

With the development of Internet and game industry, MOGs become more and more popular with Internet users. There have been many online games that support hundreds or thousands players at the same time. As a typical network application, MOGs have many problems in their function and capability for their architecture.

Conventional online game's design usually uses one of the two models: Client/Server or Peer-to-Peer model. In the former model, each client sends the game state update information to a server he has connected and then receives corresponding message from the server. Then the server becomes a critical medium between game players, it will unavoidably be a bottleneck which affects all players' game performance, even worse it may result in the collapse of the whole game world. In the Peer-to-Peer model [3], each player sends updates to the other players directly, which provides optimal response time to the players. But a pure Peer-to-Peer model is difficult to scale and has no authoritative control to game resources.

There is a mirrored-server model [5, 6] which is wildly used in current MOGs, it is a compromise between Client/Server and Peer-to-Peer model, in this model, every player connects to a server closed to him, and a lot of servers perform the same functions as one single server [4]. In fact, in this model the problem mentioned in the forepart still exists. Furthermore, current MOGs have a same problem that they are always developed by a given company or team and have not provided an entry for other developers. This kind of enclosed game maintenance will inevitably restrain the development of the whole online game industry.

M. Li et al. (Eds.): GCC 2003, LNCS 3032, pp. 544–551, 2004.

The architecture of Game Grid based on Resource Router presented in this paper retains many merits of both models, and resolves some problems which traditional models have. The paper is organized as follows: in section 2, we will discuss some related work, including the other games' architecture and implementation. Then in section 3, our architecture's design will be shown in detail, section 4 will explains how this architecture is implemented in a grid environment, and in section 5 we will analysis the benefits of our architecture. Finally, we will talk about some future work of this architecture's application and give conclusions.

2 Related Work

Our work is mainly motivated and influenced by two aspects: one is current MOGs architecture's characteristics [7, 8], the other is the advantages of using Resource Router. These two aspects are also our work's foundation.

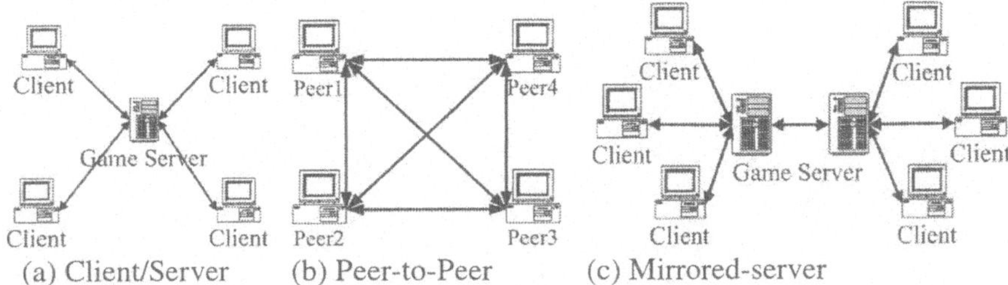

Fig. 1. Traditional models

To some extent, the architecture this paper presents is a mixture of Client/Server and Peer-to-Peer architecture. In pure Client/Server architecture, players send message only to a centralized server; the server computes game state and then issues updates. As shown in Figure 1 (a), we can learn that the server is an authoritative control of the whole game world, and is also a single point of failure in rush hour. The real game companies often have several servers deployed in different place, but still cannot avoid bottleneck, and the players are constrained to playing with players on the same server because every server is independent of the others. Figure 1 (b) shows us a Peer-to-Peer model, differ from Client/Server model, players send their message directly to other players. The most attractive advantage of this model is reduced latency, but it has poor scalability which makes it unfeasible to construct a massive multiplayer online game world using pure Peer-to-Peer model. In the mirrored-server model currently using, as shown in Figure 1 (c), we know that game server mirrors are topologically distributed across the Internet and clients connect to the closest mirror, we can also know that this model must deal with multiple copies of the game states. Considering latency, scalability, consistency, and authoritative control, each of these three models has its own advantages and disadvantages.

The other related work is the Resource Router; it is an important component in VEGA grid, its primary function is maintaining resource routing table, receiving resource request, transferring resource request by special routing algorithm, handling the register/unregister/update action of resources. We only concern how to use Resource Router here. In the following part of this paper, we will show the design of our architecture and will explain the role of Resource Router in detail.

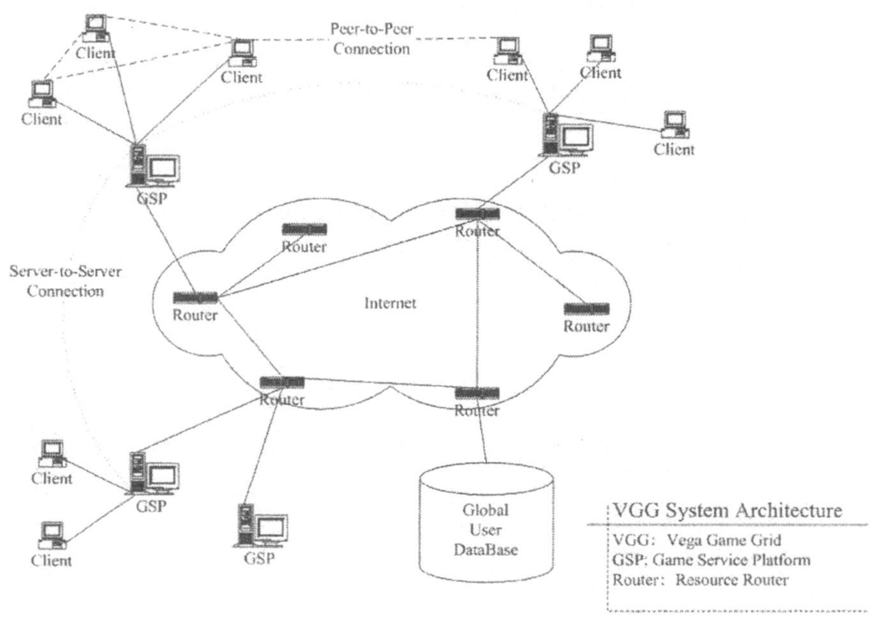

Fig. 2. VGG System Architecture

3 Design

Our Game Grid architecture is a three-layer structure including Resource Router, Game Service Platform (GSP), and Client. The Figure 2 exhibits the organization of the three layers, and the following paragraphs will explain each layer's role and function; the motivation of our design will also be explained.

3.1 Resource Router

To satisfy the need of resource sharing and coordination in wide area, in this architecture we use Resource Router to fulfill the work of resource locating, for that the idea of Routing-Transferring method which Resource Router adopts is effective [1]. The Resource Router works as follows: the resource provider periodically updates its resource information to a router. The routers receive the provider's resource information and maintain them in routing tables. When a router receives a resource request from a requestor, it checks routing tables to choose a route for this request and transfer it to another router or send back search result to the requestor. In our architecture, the GSP is both the resource provider and requestor. When a GSP registers to a Resource Router, it becomes a resource provider: it will update the information of its online game players to the Resource Router periodically. When a player wants to find some other players to play with, he can submit his search request to the GSP, the GSP will search its local database first, if there are no satisfied records, the GSP will send search request to the Resource Router as a resource requestor, then the Resource Routers works, at last, the requestor will be told which GSP is suitable to search available players next. In our design, we only take advantage of the Resource Router's characteristics; its detailed mechanism is not concerned in this paper.

3.2 Game Service Platform

Game Service Platform is a platform whose function is managing local game resource including game and player's information, and handling various requests from clients and other GSPs. The request of players includes register, login, logout, select game, update player information, and search other players and so on. As shown in the Figure 2, every client has a connection with a GSP, and every GSP has a connection with Resource Router, and besides, each GSP can connect to the other GSPs directly when needed. When a player wants to play with other players, he connects to a GSP close to him to get other players' state and address information through the connection with GSP. And then he can directly connects to other players to play game if the game's start condition is satisfied, the message in a real game is transferred between players, which is a Peer-to-Peer interaction having no relevance with GSP, we will explain its design in detail in the client part. Moreover, through analyzing the game player's common demands, we sum up some behavior which is necessary to user management and game control, and make GSP provide a set of APIs (Application Program Interfaces) for developers. This set of APIs is designed to the life cycle of an online game; it is a minimum set but adequately to support developing different type of games; so a game developer or team can use these APIs to develop his own game deployed on Game Grid. Table 1 shows a simple introduction about these APIs. Traditional game programs based on the Client/Server or Peer-to-Peer architecture can be deployed on Game Grid with a small quantity of modifications, it makes game sharing on the Internet easier than ever before.

Table 1. VGG interface brief description

API Name	Function Description
reg_newuser	Register to GSP
Login	User login game world
Choosegame	Select a game to play
refresh_userlist	Get the newest online user list
Search	Search other players in the whole game world
Invite	Invite other players to play with
Update	Update a user's game information
Logout	Logout the game world

3.3 Game Client

In the client layer, the primary issue is how the clients communicate with each other in the real game procedure. We adopt Peer-to-Peer communication in this layer's design. Each client sends its game state updates to the other clients who are playing with him in a round of game and receives the other clients' messages at the same time; we can regard the players in a round of game as a group, and their communication is a kind of group communication. Through analyzing the demands of client's network transmission and characteristics of the Peer-to-Peer communication, we have designed a set of APIs called group communication APIs which makes programming easier and concision.

4 Implementations

We implement this architecture through a simple MOG called VGG (Vega Game Grid). The GSP and Resource Router are deployed together; on the client, we use the API offered by GSP to develop an online game GUI (Graphical User Interface). When a player runs the client program, he should first register a new id if he hasn't one, and then he can login to an available GSP, select a game he wants to play, and then find other players to play game. In this procedure the client only interacts with one GSP, and we choose a TCP-based connection between client and GSP to ensure the message is reliable. Next is the real game procedure, we choose the Peer-to-Peer model to implement the game's interaction. As shown in the Figure 3, when player A has got B's address, he firstly sends invite message to B; when receiving B's confirm message, A and B will start the game to play; when game is over, both clients will send game result to GSP to record the players' scores. Whether to use TCP or UDP protocol in game message transmission is decided by real game: for a chess game, TCP will be better for its reliability and in-order-delivery; and for a real-time strategy game UDP-based interaction will be more appropriate for its lower latency.

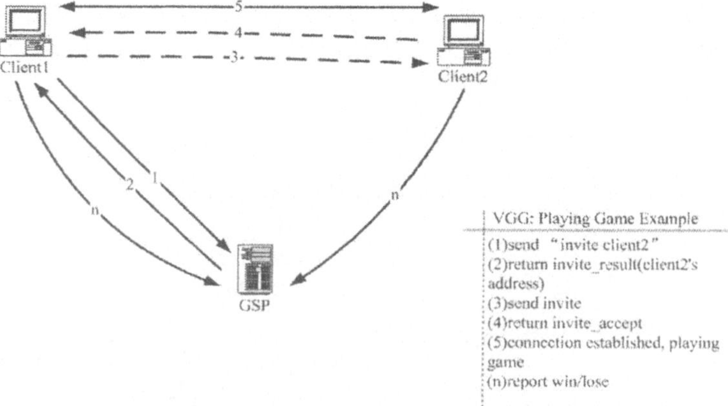

Fig. 3. A Scene of inviting other players before playing game

5 Evaluations

In this section, we will give our analysis to show the architecture's benefits. Our key issues considered in this part are GSP, scalability, and load balancing related.

5.1 Benefits of GSP

Current game server or platform based on traditional model are always designed and implemented for one game or one same type of games and divide game resources by fixed server. Compared to them, our GSP can support global game resource sharing for the various games running on this platform according to our architecture design. We know that GSP handles client resource requests, when the network topology and resource distribution is definite, the Resource Router using SD-RT algorithm can find a resource finally [1]. To the game players, this architecture is single sign-on: once he logs in a GSP, the other game resources including games and other players are visible to him. The test result of our implementation can verify this advantage. In the test, three Resource Router which have several GSPs registered on them are deployed on our lab's LAN, then we run some client programs on different PCs, here, each client represents a player, they login different GSP, each of them are visible to others and they can play with any online players freely. Furthermore, the GSP offers a set of APIs supporting different game developed by different programmers openly.

5.2 Scalability of the Architecture

Scalability is an essential performance for MOG architecture. Traditional Client/Server architecture is a star topology; it has badly scalability for the server's limitation in performance. As to the mirrored-server architecture, a lot of severs were deployed to do the same thing, but global data was copied to every server, when a new server node is added, the augmentation of the data's quantity is too massive, which greatly affect the scalability of the whole system. Pure Peer-to-Peer architecture is not good in scalability for the reason that when quantity of clients increases the augmentation of connection between clients will mount up egregiously.

The whole topology of our architecture is a mesh topology which is an easy-scale architecture inwardly, as shown in Figure 2, we can deploy a new GSP or a Resource Router optionally, it has no effects to others, client's request is transferred to different GSP to handle, there has no a single point of failure.

5.3 Load-Balancing

To the question of load-balancing, we know it is unpractical to eliminate bottleneck absolutely for the limitation of the Internet environment, we can only try our best to reduce the possibility which makes a net node to be a bottleneck. In the traditional Client/Server model, all clients send their messages to the server, their messages include not only requests of finding other players but also game state updates in playing, therefore, the server must handles huge quantities of data from different clients in rush hour and becomes a bottleneck unavoidably for the limitation of the server's capability and network bandwidth. Even though the mirrored-server model has many servers to handle clients' messages, there is no difference to the bandwidth's total consumption. So, we should consider that whether we can make the node which acts as a server handle fewer messages. Just as shown in anterior description of this paper, the architecture we present is better in resolving this problem. The GSP in the architecture acts as a server to a extent, the clients send only a part of messages to the GSP such as login, search user and so on, and when players are in game, the game state updates are sent directly to other players, the GSP is not responsible for computing and transmitting these game state updates which is a majority of data in client's message set. So for the GSP, bandwidth is saved and load is reduced, the whole system will run more smoothly and can support more players online at the same time.

Moreover, we take a mechanism to decrease burden of GSP: when there are too many clients to login the same GSP in the same time, the GSP can transfer a part of login request to another GSP. This mechanism can balance the load of GSP to a great extent.

6 Conclusions and Future Work

We have designed and implemented an architecture based on Resource Router for multiplayer game which can be deployed on both local and wide networks, and the simulate running of our program has verified the benefits over traditional architecture in platform, scalability and load-balancing aspects. This architecture is not restricted to the game only, and we believe that a great variety of other applications will be benefited by adopting this architecture.

There are several aspects in which this architecture could be advanced. Despite we have reduced a majority of data handled by the GSP and taken a mechanism to balance load of GSP, the mechanism we take is somewhat too simple.We can do some research on how to detect the status about the whole system's load and how to balance the load more efficiently. The security issue has not been concerned in this paper, we need to concern the problems such as user identity authentication, preventing cheating in the game progress and etc. We will do some research in these issues in the future.

References

1. Wei Li, Zhiwei Xu, Fangpeng Dong, Jun Zhang, "Grid Resource Discovery Based on a Routing-Transferring Method", Proceedings of the 3rd International Workshop on Grid Computing, Baltimore, MD, 2002, pp. 145-156.
2. Zhiwei Xu, Wei Li, "The Research on VEGA grid Architecture", Journal of Computer Research and Development, August, 2002, 39(8), pp.923-929 (in Chinese).

3. Benjamin H. Brinckerhoff. "Peer to Peer Multiplayer Games", http://students.cec.wustl.edu/~cs333/calendar/peer2peer.ppt.
4. V. Ramakrishna, M. Robinson, K. Eustice and Peter Reiher, "An Active Self-Optimizing Multiplayer Gaming Architecture", proceedings of the Fifth Annual International Workshop on Active Middleware Services (AMS 2003).
5. Eric Cronin, Burton Filstrup, Anthony Kurc, "A Distributed Multiplayer Game Server System", UM EECS589 Course Project Report, http://www.eecs.umich.edu/~bfilsrtu/quakefinal.pdf, May 2001.
6. Eric Cronin, Burton Filstrup, "An Efficient Synchronization Mechanism for Mirrored game Architecture", Proc. Of the first Workshop on Network and System Support for Games, pp. 67-73, 2002.
7. Jouni Smed, Timo Kaukoranta, Harri Hakonen, "A Review on Networking and Multiplayer Computer Games". Turku Centre for Computer Science, TUCS Technical Report No 454, April 2002.
8. Jouni Smed, Timo Kaukoranta, Harri Hakonen, "Aspects Of Networking in Multiplayer Computer Games", Proceedings of International Conference on Application and Development of Computer Games in the 21st Century, pp. 74-81, Hong Kong SAR, China, Nov. 2001.
9. "Butterfly.net: Powering Next-Generation Gaming with Computing On-Demand --An IDC e-business Case study", http://www.butterfly.net/platform/technology/idc.pdf.

Scalable Resource Management and Load Assignment for Grid and Peer-to-Peer Services [1]

Xuezheng Liu, Ming Chen, Guangwen Yang, and Dingxing Wang

Department of Computer Science, Tsinghua University, Beijing 100084, P.R.China
{liuxuezheng00, cm01}@mails.tsinghua.edu.cn,
{ygw,dxwang}@tsinghua.edu.cn

Abstract. In this paper we propose DRMI, a fully decentralized, highly scalable and efficient resource management infrastructure, which is built on top of prefix-based DHT. DRMI provides large-scale resource monitoring and management for arbitrary metadata in variational Grid and peer-to-peer environment. DRMI monitors resources with their natural organizations and can trace them in a wide scope from large aggregations to a single resource. Based on DRMI we also propose "gradual-decision" principle and algorithm, which is consistent with requirement of self-organizing or autonomy in distributed system management. Using gradual-decision we can accomplish variety of and programmable resource management, e.g. the balanced load assignment.

1 Introduction

Grids [1] and peer-to-peer (P2P) overlay networks [4,5,6,7] provide environments that allow software applications to integrate computational, data and storing resources belonging to diverse organizations and individuals in widespread locations. To fully exploit resources and facilitate services in Grid or P2P environments, there must be a distributed infrastructure for resource management and monitoring that can gather system information, monitor resource states and utilizations, and assign user loads.

Traditional approaches to resource management and load assignment in parallel computing and Grid environment mainly use centralized controls [2, 3, 9, 20]. They make use of one or several specific resources monitors to take charge of collecting all needed information from computers or clusters, and also answer for assignment of all tasks. They may work well in small-scale parallel applications, but due to non-scalable they cannot be utilized in large-scale resource management, e.g. Grid resource management. In a large-scale system containing tens of thousands of nodes and, centralized monitor tends to become a bottleneck of system. In P2P applications, Unstructured P2P designs [4, 5] make no efforts on resource management, while query dissemination is performed in a random manner. Structured P2P designs [6, 7] utilize distributed hash tables (DHT) to implement uniform task assignment. This

[1] Supported by National Natural Science Foundation of China (60373004,60373005)

M. Li et al. (Eds.): GCC 2003, LNCS 3032, pp. 552–559, 2004.

simple assignment cannot fully exploit heterogeneous resources, where powerful peers are not enough utilized while weak peers tend to overload.

In this paper we propose a scalable and fully decentralized infrastructure for large-scale resource management and load assignment. We make use of prefix-based DHT as underlying organization of all nodes or resources in Grid and P2P networks, and build our *decentralized resource management infrastructure* (*DRMI*) on top of DHT. DRMI is very efficient with low costs, in which each node only needs to gather a handful of resource metadata from O(log*N*) neighbor nodes (*N* is the total number of nodes), while every system variation (e.g. node failures, workload and capacity variations, etc) can be detected and notified to entire system within O(log*N*) time. Based on DRMI, it is very easy to implement various kinds of resource controls and management as we want, e.g. a balanced load assignment in which each resource entity (i.e. node) is assigned with a workload proportional to its capability, so that we can make full utilization of all resources. We use simulations to inspect our design, and our experimental results illustrate both efficiency and robustness of our approach.

The rest of paper is organized as follows. Section 2 gives a brief outline of prefix-based DHT and explains the resource groups. Section 3 presents the DRMI. Section 4 proposes DRMI-based resource management and load assignment, i.e. gradual-decision algorithm. Section 5 presents performance evaluation and Section 6 concludes paper.

2 Prefix-Based DHT and Hierarchical Resource Groups

We first present background on prefix-based DHT and routing, using Pastry [7] as example. A Pastry node is assigned with a unique digital number as identifier named "*nodeId*", an *l*-digit long number with radix *k* (*k* is usually equal to 2^b), i.e. each digit of nodeId varies from 0 to *k*-1, and all potential nodeIds form a nodeId space $[0, k^l-1)$. Each node maintains a routing table with *l* rows and *k* columns, which is organized by prefix-based matching of nodeIds. In a node *P*'s routing table, each entry in row *n* (n=0,1,...*l*-1, in this paper we call the first row of table as row 0) contains a pointer to node (i.e nodes' IP addresses) whose nodeId shares the first *n* digits with *P*'s nodeId and the $(n+1)^{th}$ nodeId digit equals to the column number of that entry. A routing table entry is empty if the node with appropriate nodeId is inexistent. Note that in each row *n* of a node's routing table, there is one entry that contains pointer to the node itself, in the column that equals $(n+1)^{th}$ digit of its nodeId. We call these entries the "self-pointing" entries. For details of prefix-based DHT, please see [7].

Now we assign a unique nodeId to each individual resource entity which we want to manage and utilize in Grid or P2P services. A resource entity may be a single computer, a cluster, a supercomputer in Lab, or even the monitor and entrance of all inner resources of an organization. Indeed, we regard resource entity as an indivisible unit in Grid or P2P system which can provide services. So if an organization joined in Grid uses single entrance for answering queries, with its inner resources invisible to Grid, then the organization is regarded as one resource entity with the capability equal to the summation of its inner resources. In rest of paper we interchangeably use the word "node", "resource", "resource entity" and "entity" for the same meaning.

The nodes with prefix-based DHT organization can be regarded to form a hierarchical structure. Nodes are organized as nested "groups" in l levels, where all nodes with the same n-digit-long prefix in their nodeIds form an "n-level group". We use the n-digit common prefix as the "groupId" of an n-level group, e.g. group "G-121" denotes a 3-level group which consists of all nodes with prefix "121" in their nodeIds. All nodes in the system form a 0-level group G-ϕ, and each node is also an l-level group. Groups are organized in hierarchical structure, since each n-level group G_n is made up of k (n+1)-level groups whose groupIds share G_n's groupId as a common prefix in the first n-digits and traverse from 0 to (k-1) in the $(n+1)^{th}$ digit. For example, a 3-level group G-121 is composed of k 4-level group, namely G-1210, G-1211,..., G-121(k-1).

3 Decentralized Resource Management Infrastructure

3.1 Metadata of Resource Entities and Resource Groups

In order to manage resources and facilitate applications, the resource monitoring and management infrastructure need to collect concerned information of resources. This information may be soft-states, current status or other metadata, e.g. the current free resource capability in computation, throughput, bandwidth or storage. We use MD(R) to denote the metadata of resource entity R. These metadata are obtained or measured locally, and DRMI provides a common infrastructure for collecting and monitoring arbitrary metadata as needed.

Based on metadata of individual resource, we define the *metadata of resource group*, namely MD(G) where G is a group defined in Section II.B. Metadata of a resource group is the status, soft-states of the entire group corresponding to resource metadata, which can be calculated from all metadata of resource entities in the group. For example, if our resource metadata is the free capability (e.g. free computational power), then metadata of resource group G is defined as the summation of free capabilities of all resource entities contained by G, i.e. $\mathrm{MD}(G) = \sum_{R \in G} \mathrm{MD}(R)$. Since groups form hierarchical structure where a high level group is made up of some low level subgroups, the metadata of higher group can be calculated from that of its lower subgroups, e.g. MD(G-12)=$\sum_{i=0..(k-1)}$MD(G-12i) for metadata of free capabilities.

3.2 Resource Metadata Tables

In DRMI, each resource entity maintains a *resource metadata table* (*RMT*) with l rows and k columns, which is based on the routing table in the resource entity.

A resource entity's RMT records current or recent collected metadata of some (i.e. lxk) specific resource groups. Each entry at row n of the RMT records the metadata of the (n+1)-level group whose groupId shares the n-digit-long prefix of the resource entity's nodeId, and has the $(n+1)^{th}$ digit equal to the entry's column. That is, in a RMT of resource entity with nodeId id_R, the entry in row n and column m contains MD(G) where G is an (n+1)-level group with groupId id_G, where id_G = Prefix(id_R,

$n) \oplus m$. (We use Prefix(id_R, n) to indicate id_R's n-digit-long prefix, and $\oplus$ for numeric connection).

Table.1 shows an example of resource metadata table. In table.1 the resource entity R's $nodeId_R$ is 12203 and resource metadata is defined as free resource capability (denoted by an integer). The GroupId column shows corresponding groupIds of entries in each row, and the numbers in cells are the values of MD(group), e.g. value "236" in row 2 column 1 is the MD(G-121), etc. There is one shaded entry in each row, which is situated at the "self-pointing" entry in that row. We call these shaded entries as "self-group" entries, since they record the metadata of resource groups that contain the resource entity R itself, in each level. From Section III.*A* we know the values in self-group entries should be able to calculated from values in the next row (for free capacity information, we use "summation" operation, e.g. value 807 in row 1 is equal to 153+236+203+215). In general, in RMT we can calculate each self-group entry from the row just below that entry. We use this property to maintain our RMTs.

Table 1. Example of resource metadata table in resource entity with nodeId 12203 (k=4).

GroupId	0	1	2	3
0~3	3235	4350	3002	2310
10~13	1023	1335	807	1185
120~123	153	236	203	215
1220~1223	56	27	73	47
12200~12203	21	0	0	35

3.3 Maintaining RMTs

To maintain underlying node organization for variation, DHT approaches employ neighbor-probing, where each node periodically communicates with all its neighbors to detect neighbor failures [7, 8]. We build DRMI on top of DHT, so we have an elegant and efficient maintaining approach for metadata in RMTs, which is carried out along with DHT's maintenance and only needs to piggy-back a few bytes in each communication of DHT's neighbor-probing.

When a resource entity R is to update an entry in its RMT, i.e. seeks for new value of a resource group G's metadata, R asks its neighbor for MD(G) who is more "aware" of MD(G) than R. Therefore, If R does not belong to G, we let R ask its neighbor entity N which belongs to G for MD(G), since N is closer to G's resources than R in the routing distance, and can be sooner aware of G's variation. Since we use expressive nodeIds whose prefix indicates resource affiliation, N should be more familiar to G since they are physically closer. In other cases if R belongs to G, then MD(G) is locally measured or calculated from G's subgroups in R's RMT. In more details, For entries that are not self-group entry, the resource entity periodically updates them by querying its neighbor along with DHT's neighbor-probing in every T_{probe} of time, and piggy-back the new value of group metadata from the neighbor. Since in DHT a node communicates with all its neighbors every T_{probe} [7,8], each entry of RMT is updated in T_{probe}. For self-group entries, we needn't any communication but only to measure or calculate them locally from metadata of subgroups.

4 Gradual-Decision-Based Resource Management and Balanced Load Assignment with DRMI

4.1 Monitoring Arbitrary Resource Group and Resource Entity

With DRMI, we can easily monitor needed information in arbitrary group. We define the MD(R) and MD(G) as what we want to monitor for resource entity and resource group. For any group G with groupId Id_G, each resource entity belonging to G records MD(G) in its RMT. So, when need MD(G) we can ask any resource entity in G, by either routing to group G via routing tables or direct ask some node in G if we know it. Since the routing trip is a tree-like approaching from higher groups to lower groups (Section II), for a j-level group we can reach it and obtain its metadata within j hops from any place in the Grid or P2P networks. When reach l-level group, we thus obtain metadata of a resource entity.

In addition, since each resource entity in G has the probability to answer the query of MD(G), in our decentralized infrastructure both cost for collecting resource metadata and cost for answering user queries for MD() are completely disseminated throughout the system. This avoids the overhead and potential overload in centralized monitor. Comparing with centralized management approaches, if we want to monitor arbitrary resource group in arbitrary level, the only way is to record metadata of all individual resource entity in the monitor. Thus, the heavy burden in maintaining the data and answering queries would be a serious problem for centralize monitors, esp. in large-scale Grid or P2P systems.

4.2 Balanced Load Assignment

In most distributed systems, load-balancing is a crucial factor, i.e. user loads and tasks should be balanced assigned to distributed computers so as to avoid hot-spot and overload. In heterogeneous environments, we need a *balanced load assignment* in which each resource entity is assigned with a workload in proportion to its capability, so that both powerful and weak resources are fairly utilized, and the system can achieve its largest utilization without single resource overload.

Now we illustrate how to use DRMI to perform resource management, using balanced load assignment as an example. Based on DRMI, a group is divided into k subgroups whose status or metadata (e.g. capability) is known in RMT. For a user load assigned to the resource group, we can make a decision that which subgroup is selected to carry the load. The decision is made according to current status of each subgroup, in order to achieve a certain purpose of management (e.g. load-balancing between subgroups). After that, we do the same thing with the selected subgroup, level by level, and at last we arrive at a resource entity to finish the current management mission (e.g. assign the load to that entity), as well as achieve our management purpose (e.g. load balance between all groups in each level). We call this procedure as "*gradual-decision*".

In more details, let us investigate the gradual-decision-based load assignment for load-balancing, as mentioned above. In gradual-decision we make step-by-step decisions of the final destination resource to carry out the load, rather than traditional direct decision. When there's a user task to be assigned in Grid, say, a task T is submitted to entity with nodeId N_0, we need to determine the resource entity's nodeId D ($D=(d_0d_1...d_{l-1})$) for carrying out T. We first choose a 1-level group for T. From the 0th row in N_0's RMT, N_0 can find the total capability of each 1-level group (we record resource capability in metadata MD). From this information N_0 is able to make the best decision of which 1-level group is selected to carry out T, i.e. make a decision of D's first digit d_0, under the requirement that balancing these 1-level groups.

Now, N_0 inspects row 0 in its RMT to make decision of d_0. If our MD(R) and MD(G) in DRMI is defined as "inherent capability" of resource entity and group, then N_0 can make a *probability-based random choice* for d_0 from $\{0,1,...k\text{-}1\}$, where d_0's probability distribution is in proportion to the distribution of inherent capabilities of these groups. Thus, each 1-level resource group has the probability of receiving workload in proportion to its capability (balanced assignment). If MD(R) and MD(G) is defined as "current free capability", then N_0 chooses the 1-level group with the largest current free capability for d_0 in order to balance the their workloads. If the metadata is "percentage of consumed capability" (i.e. rate of assigned workload to total capability), then we choose the smallest one in order to assign T to resources with slightest burden. After generates the first digit d_0 for D, N_0 routes query demand of T to the selected group $G\text{-}d_0$ (i.e. to one resource entity in $G\text{-}d_0$) by hopping to its neighbor in row 0 and column d_0 of the routing table. We call this new resource entity in $G\text{-}d_0$ as N_1. N_1 has digit d_0 as prefix. In N_1 the similar decision is made, that is, N_1 selects the best 1-level group in $G\text{-}d_0$ to carry out T (i.e. generate digit d_1 of D) according to its own RMT.

In general, at i-th step of gradual-decision algorithm, the first i-digit prefix of D $(d_0d_1...d_{i-1})$ has been decided. The demand of task T is routed to resource entity N_i with prefix $(d_0d_1...d_{i-1})$, which belongs to i-level resource group $G\text{-}d_0d_1...d_{i-1}$. Row i of N_i's RMT records MD($G\text{-}d_0d_1...d_{i-1}0$), MD($G\text{-}d_0d_1...d_{i-1}1$), ..., MD($G\text{-}d_0d_1...d_{i-1}(k\text{-}1)$), i.e. status of the k subgroup of $G\text{-}d_0d_1...d_{i-1}$. Now N_i needs to choose d_i from $\{0...k\text{-}1\}$ according to the above row i, meaning that to choose the best $(i+1)$-level subgroup for task T. Similarly, N_i makes a probability-based random choice for d_i in accordance with the distribution of capabilities in row i, if the MD(R) is defined as "inherent capability"; and for "current free capability" or "percentage of consumed capability", N_i can also make the decision accordingly. After that, N_i forwards the demand of T to its neighbor N_{i+1} in the selected $(i+1)$-level group.

When d_{l-1} is finally decided, we achieve to assign user task T to a resource entity and simultaneously keep load-balancing between groups in each level. Then, T is uploaded from N_0 to D directly to be carried out. Generally, our gradual-decision algorithm can assign a user task in l hops with very little communication, and also distribute the heavy burden of task scheduling in centralized resource manager. If all user loads are assigned with above algorithm, we can guarantee load-balancing everywhere, from organization level to the finest resource entity level.

5 Performance Evaluation

We use simulation to examine DRMI design. We run our simulation on a workstation with Pentium IV CPU and 1GByte memory, and simulate an environment with more than 10,000 individual resource entities. Each resource entity has a certain resource capability to provide services, and we use the capability as collected resource metadata (i.e. MD(*R*) and MD(*G*)). We first evaluate the efficiency of DRMI by examine its maintenance costs. For comparison, we implement traditional centralized resource management with multiple resource monitors. We use 100 centralized monitors in simulation, which is a very large number in practical cases. Fig.1 shows the number of resources that are traced and managed in each centralized monitor (the straight and steep line), and the number in each resource entity of DRMI (the gentle curve). Fig.1 illustrates remarkable scalability in DRMI that when the resource number grows from 1,000 to 10,000, the number of maintained metadata (and neighbors) in each resource entity has only a very slight increase, while in centralized management the maintained resources per monitor increase at 10 times. More resources to maintain means heavier burden and more communication cost, so centralized strategy can hard afford large-scale management even with numerous monitors, because maintenance cost grows linear to system scale. In contrast, DRMI has a O(log*N*) cost growth with scale *N* and is inherently scalable.

Second, we evaluate the validity of DRMI-based monitoring. Practical resources may keep varying due to customers' utilization or failures, and we model this situation by varying capability value of resources in simulation. The variation of capability follows a Normal distribution with variance σ^2, and the occurring time of variations follows an exponential distribution with parameter λ. We periodically inspect current capabilities of each resource group or entity and their values in all RMTs, in order to make a comparison. Due to capability variation and delay of synchronization, there must be a bit difference between the "real" capabilities and recorded capabilities, and we use mean square error to measure this difference.

Fig.2 shows the correlation between probing time T_{probe}, message number per second per resource, and the accuracy of values in RMTs (i.e. validity of DRMI-based monitoring). We simulate three environments with different resource variation frequency, in which variations take place in each resource entity averagely every 5 minutes, 1 hour and 2 hours, respectively (corresponding to the three curves in Fig.2). Each environment contains 10,000 resources. The accuracy in vertical axis equals to 1-*err* where *err* is the mean square error between capability values in RMT and their real values. Fig.2 shows that more frequent maintenance (small T_{probe}) has better accuracy, and that the environment with more frequent variations needs more bandwidth in messaging to achieve same accuracy level. In DRMI we can achieve more than 96% accuracy by using 2 messages per second per entity, even under the most variational situation where metadata of resources vary in less than 5 minutes. This is much rigorous than most Grid and P2P service environments, because computation Grid usually deals with long running-period tasks and has stable resource states, while P2P hosts also have averagely more than 1 hour on-line time.

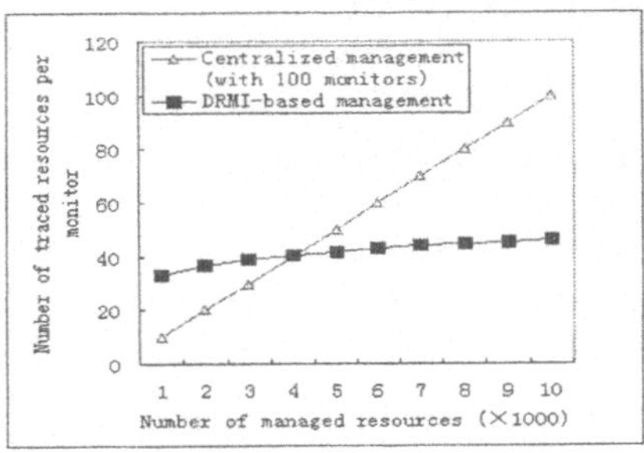

Fig. 1. Number of maintained re-sources per monitor

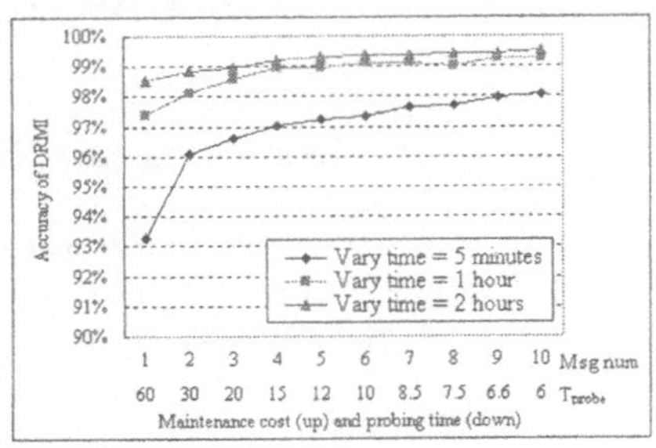

Fig. 2. Probing time, Message number v.s. Accuracy

6 Conclusions

We present a fully decentralized, scalable and very efficient resource management infrastructure named DRMI, which is built on top of prefix-based DHT. DRMI provides large-scale resource monitoring and management for arbitrary metadata in variational Grid and P2P environment. DRMI has an efficient synchronization strategy, by which resources variations can be updated to entire system within only small communication. We also propose "gradual-decision" principle and algorithm for load assignment, which is consistent with requirement of self-organizing and autonomy in distributed system management. Gradual-decision supports variety of and programmable resource management, including the balanced load assignment.

References

[1.] Forster I, Kesselman C, Tueche S. The anatomy of the grid: Enabling scalable virtual organizations. Int. J. Supercomputer Applications. 2001

[2.] Buyya R, Abramson D, Giddy J. Nimrod/G: An architecture of a resource management and scheduling system in a global computational Grid. In High Performance Computing Asia 2000.

[3.] Maheswaan M, Ali S, Siegel J. Dynamic mapping of a class of independent tasks onto heterogeneous computing systems. In HCW'99

[4.] Gnutella protocol specification, http://dss.clip2.com/GnutellaProtocol04.pdf

[5.] Clarke I, Sandberg O, Wiley B, Hong T W. Freenet: A distributed anonymous information storage and retrieval system. In Proc. Workshop on Design Issues in Anonymity and Unobservability, 2000

[6.] Stoica I, et al. Chord: A scalable peer-to-peer lookup service for Internet applications. In ACM SIGCOMM, San Diego, CA, USA, 2001.

[7.] Rowstron A, Druschel P. Pastry: Scalable, distributed object location and routing for large scale peer-to-peer system. In IFIP/ACM Middleware, Heidelberg, Germany, 2001

[8.] Mahajan R, Castro M, Rowstron A. Controlling the cost of reliability in peer-to-peer overlays. In Proc. IPTPS'03, Berkeley, 2003.

[9.] Braun D, et al. A taxonomy for describing matching and scheduling heuristics for mixed-machine heterogeneous computing systems. In IEEE Workshop on Advances in Parallel and Distributed Systems. 1998.

Research on the Application of Multi-agent Technology to Spatial Information Grid[1]

Yan Ren, Cheng Fang, Honghui Chen, and Xueshan Luo

Department of Management Science and Engineering,
National University of Defense Technology, Changsha 410073, China
yanzi916@sina.com, jackeyphoenix@china.com

Abstract. Spatial Information Grid (SIG) is an infrastructure that integrates and shares distributed, heterogeneous and large amounts of spatial information resources, organizes and processes them systematically, and provides capabilities of serve-on-demand for users. Aiming at the challenges and requirements in spatial information application area, the idea of applying multi-agent technology to SIG research is proposed in consideration of the characteristics of SIG. First, the necessity and feasibility are analyzed. On the basis of the research work at home and abroad, SIG Multi-Agent Environment (SIGMAE) is proposed, including the architecture and the agent structure. Then, the detailed application functionality of SIG multi-agent environment in SIG is studied. At last, the benefits and challenges are concluded.

1 Introduction

Spatial Information Grid (SIG) connects the widespread, heterogeneous and large amounts of spatial information resources such as spatial data resources, computational resources, storage resources, processing resources and users, organizes and integrates them cooperatively, and analyses and processes them uniformly. It can form certain capabilities of serve-on-demand and realize certain spatial information services and applications.

SIG is an innovative system of concepts and technologies used to resolve problems in spatial information application area and to meet the various needs of spatial information application. These problems and needs are mainly focused on:

- Integrative organization of spatial information resources;
- Sharing of large amounts of spatial information resources;
- High performance collaboration in analyzing and processing spatial information;
- And integration of geographically distributed spatial information services.

We believe multi-agent technology has distinct advantages in dealing with the above issues. Due to the universality and complexity of spatial information, SIG becomes a large-scale, distributed, open and complicated information environment. Agent-based information technology provides effective methods in conceptualizing and realizing such information systems. It is suitable for the design and implementa-

[1] This paper is supported by National ‘863’ Program (2002AA131010 and 2002AA134010).

M. Li et al. (Eds.): GCC 2003, LNCS 3032, pp. 560–567, 2004.

tion of three types of large-scale and reactive information systems: open information systems, complicated information systems and human-machine coexistence information systems [2]. SIG conception framework presents exactly these characteristics at the system level. Therefore, it can be an effective way to accomplish SIG objects that applying multi-agent technology to SIG research, design and implementation.

2 Related Work

Along with the focus of grid development is turning from computational grid and data grid to information grid and knowledge grid, the importance of intelligent agents in grid research is being more and more evident. According to Shi et al. [1], there is a strong sense of automation in the new grid generation. Agent-based information technology that puts emphasis on negotiation and collaboration can be particularly well suited to those requirements.

Then, an important issue is how to successfully make use of multi-agent technology to solve the problems in SIG. We can view SIG as a multi-agent environment filled with a number of interacting agents. Thus, we can use the theories and methods of multi-agent technology to address the complicated issues in SIG such as resource management, information integration, collaboration in analysis and processing, information sharing and interoperability, and personalized services. Multi-AGent Environment (MAGE) described in [1] is an agent-oriented environment for software designing, integrating and running. It has facilities to support agent mental state representation, reasoning, negotiation, planning, cooperation and communication, and provides system designing support, description and assembling of knowledge and capability, etc. Another multi-agent infrastructure called AgentScape presented in [4] is a scalable middleware layer that supports large-scale agent systems. The following multi-agent environment proposed by us is based on above and other work.

3 SIG Multi-agent Environment (SIGMAE)

3.1 SIGMAE Architecture

According to the application demands and characteristics of spatial information grid, we present a multi-agent environment for SIG, called SIG Multi-Agent Environment (SIGMAE). An overview of SIGMAE architecture is shown in Fig.1.

SIGMAE is composed of the following components:

(1) Agent Management System (AMS): This is the core of SIGMAE, which controls access to agents and manages their states. It consists of the following modules: Directory Services module provides services for agents such as registration, search, and update; Communication Management module supports multiple communication protocols and languages used by agents with different qualities-of-service; Life Cycle Management module is responsible for state management of agents such as creation, deletion, activation, suspension and so on; Location Services module associates an agent identifier with an address (or contact-point), and provides location services for

objects as well; Security Management module is responsible for authentication and authorization of agents and objects to prevent malicious intrusion.

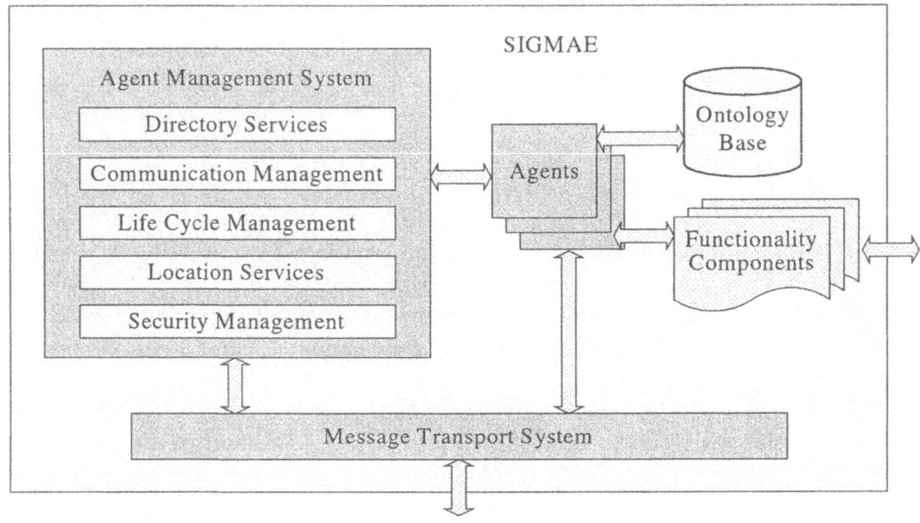

Fig. 1. Architecture of SIGMAE

(2) Message Transport System (MTS): It supports messages passing, information exchange and services invocation between SIGMAE and SIG environment.

(3) Agents: Each agent has a specific capability set so that it can implement certain functions and be assigned to accomplish certain tasks. Agents can interact autonomously and cooperate in executing complex tasks to achieve their common goals.

(4) Ontology Base: Ontology base is indispensable for such a large-scale and complicated application environment as SIG. Ontology is the expression of sharing comprehension within some domain including definitions of concepts, relationships between concepts and axioms that the relationships satisfy. The ontology base stores not only ontologies within spatial information area and SIG scope, but also ontologies shared by the agents in SIGMAE.

(5) Functionality Components: The functions provided by agents can be encapsulated and stored in form of components that provide services for SIG through APIs.

3.2 SIGMAE Agent Structure

The agents are classified into multiple types by their functionalities, and agents of same types cooperate in performing their tasks. Though the functions implemented by agents are different, every agent has uniform basic structure as below (Fig.2).

Every agent in SIGMAE consists of six parts: Belief and Knowledge Base, Intention Base, Basic Capabilities, Local Sensor, Communicator and Function Module Interface. Belief and Knowledge Base and Intention Base compose the inner state of agents. [2] Belief Base includes facts and state information about outer environments. Knowledge Base stores the knowledge needed for collaborative problem solving. The belief and knowledge may be given beforehand, or be gained by local sensor or communication with other agents. Intention Base contains the goals that agents intend to achieve and part of action plans that agents promise to carry out in order to achieve those goals. The formation of intention base relies on the organization roles of agents and the relationships between agents. Basic Capabilities of agents involve Learning Capability, Reasoning Capability, Negotiation Capability, Coordination Capability and Planning Capability. [1][2][3]

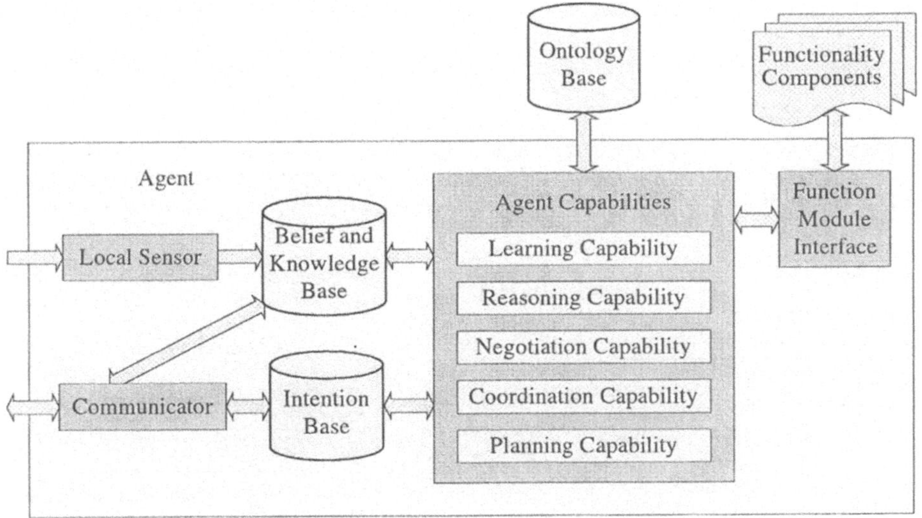

Fig. 2. Basic structure of agents in SIGMAE

4 SIGMAE Application Architecture

SIGMAE is a platform for multi-agent technology application in SIG, which provides an environment that agents rely on for living and working. SIGMAE supports basic capabilities and mental state expression of agents, provides management and communication services for agents, and supports interaction between agents and SIG environment or other platforms. It can extend functions independent of SIG in spite of the detailed implementation at bottom layer. Through function interfaces and message transport system, multi-agent environment can be combined with SIG environment as an organic whole. Hence, the theories and methods of multi-agent system technology can be used to deal with the issues that SIG is faced with.

SIG is a multi-layer system of spatial information services. The SIG Open Architecture Framework contains Acquisition Layer, Connection Layer, Resource Layer, Sharing Layer, Service/Analysis/Processing Layer, Integration Layer and Application Layer from bottom to top [7]. From Resource Layer to Application Layer, SIGMAE can be applied well to SIG in such aspects as integration of spatial information resources on demand, cooperation on spatial information analysis and processing, and integration of spatial information services. And SIGMAE application in these layers is mainly realized by the functionalities provided by each kind of agents. The application architecture of SIGMAE in SIG is shown in Fig.3.

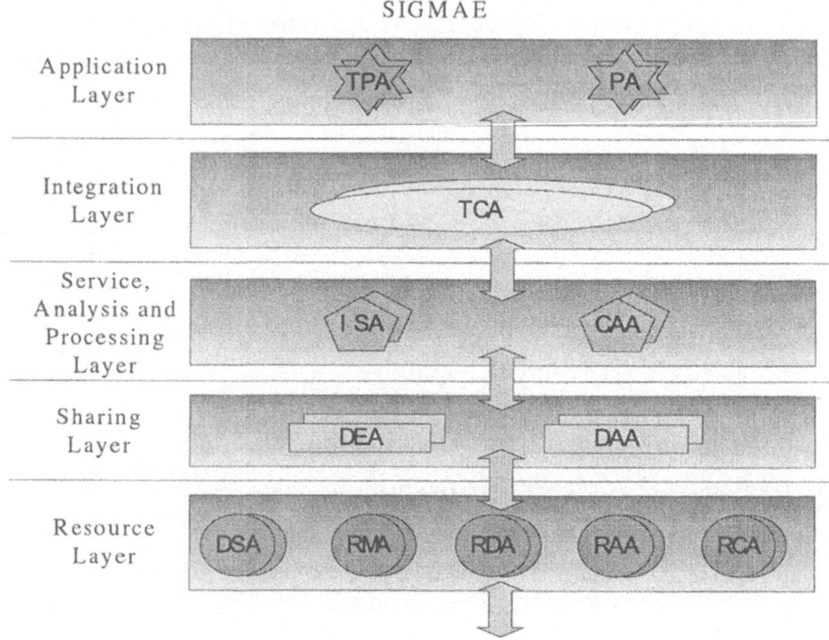

Fig. 3. SIGMAE Application Architecture

Now we will discuss the detailed functions of every kind of agents in SIGMAE and what problems they can resolve in SIG. [3][1][5][6][8]

(1) Resource Layer Agents

There are large amounts of heterogeneous resources in SIG environment, including all kinds of spatial data, computing resources, storage resources, software and tools, GIS, databases, etc. These resources are not only vast in amount, but also distributed and changing dynamically. The management and usage of these resources are very complex, including state monitoring and maintenance, discovering of new resources, registration and search, allocation and deployment, organization and integration, and so on. Hence, the agents in resource layer consist of the following types:

● Directory Service Agents (DSA): These agents maintain the directory of resources automatically. They can provide the services of resource registration and resource search, and maintain the information of resource state and availability. They can also find the needed resources and their state information according to query requests.

● Resource Monitoring Agents (RMA): These agents monitor the usage condition of resources such as load balancing and maintenance of QoS. They also monitor the working state and availability of resources, deal with entering and leaving of resources, and notify the change of resource state, availability and capabilities to Directory Service Agents. The ideal RMAs are able to cooperate with Resource Allocation Agents to optimize the usage of resources.

● Resource Discovering Agents (RDA): When Directory Service Agents have found the needed resources and need to use them, RDAs begin to discover and locate these resources. When new resources enter SIG environment, RDAs can discover them and register with DSAs.

● Resource Allocation Agents (RAA): These agents negotiate and coordinate with each other, and make proper resources match with relevant requests on the basis of their learning capability and reasoning capability. The ideal RAAs can select the best ones from available resources according to specific scheduling strategy, and schedule the resources by their planning capability and reasoning capability in order to allocate the most suitable resources to the most proper location.

● Resource Combination Agents (RCA): The accomplishment of most tasks in SIG needs multiple resources to combine together. In the cases of single resource being unable to meet the requests, RCAs group and combine the resources as a whole on the basis of interaction and cooperation in order to match the requests. When the requests have been fulfilled and these resources are no longer needed, RCAs should be able to decompose them in order that they can be combined next time.

(2) Sharing Layer Agents

The sharing layer of SIG mainly focuses on sharing and interoperability of spatial information and systems. It is responsible for format conversion and mergence of heterogeneous spatial data, direct access to multi-format data, storage and management of spatial data in distributed computing environment, and interoperability of spatial information at semantic level. The agents in this layer involve:

● Data Exchange Agents (DEA): There are several kinds of DEAs. Some DEAs serve as software agents. They cooperate in format conversion, data replication and mergence of data from multiple sources. Some DEAs serve as data engines and middleware. They can access multi-format data directly. Some other DEAs can help understanding data automatically and accessing data transparently according to spatial information sharing protocols such as OpenGIS.

● Data Access Agents (DAA): Distributed spatial information applications often need to use large amounts of data from many places, or need to store large amounts of data in many places. DAAs mainly focus on remote data access and storage and on management of distributed data.

(3) Service, Analysis and Processing Layer Agents

On the one hand, this layer deals with online analysis and processing of spatial information; on the other hand, it focuses on encapsulating the spatial information, the functions of analysis and processing of spatial information, and the application programs into user-oriented services. The agents in this layer include:

● Information Service Agents (ISA): These agents can maintain static and dynamic information of services automatically and provide directory services about service information. And they are able to search service information according to query requests.

● Cooperative Analysis Agents (CAA): Not only spatial information is distributed, but also analysis and processing tasks are done in distributed conditions. Then, cooperation of distributed programs is needed. CAAs negotiate with each other according to their own sub-tasks, reach uniform goals and rules, and communicate with each other continuously to fulfill specific tasks. This process includes not only synchronized cooperation but also asynchronous cooperation. Hence, CAAs are also required to maintain synchronization mechanism and asynchronism mechanism.

(4) Integration Layer Agents

The integration layer realizes interaction, integration, schedule and allocation of services. It can form specific workflow according to user requirements, realize system interoperability according to standards and protocols, and form an environment of spatial information service integration.

● Task Composition Agents (TCA): In spatial information applications, single service often cannot meet the needs of users. So composition and integration of services are needed to form specific workflow in order to accomplish complicated services. After TPAs in the application layer have parsed the user requests into sub-tasks, TCAs can create service workflow according to SIG Service Task Language (SSTL) and task processing model, and cooperate to complete the composition.

(5) Application Layer Agents

The application layer is responsible for designing friendly task-oriented user interfaces based on Web application pattern, and for providing personalized, customized, convenient and clear services for users.

● Task Parsing Agents (TPA): These agents comprehend and analyze user requests. The complicated requests are parsed to form the tasks and sub-tasks, which will be processed in lower layers.

● Personalization Agents (PA): The work of these agents mainly includes recording personal behavior information and usage history of users, representing users to interact with services and customize services, removing unsuitable services according to user tastes, and customizing user interfaces according to user tastes.

5 Conclusions and Future Work

Applying multi-agent technology to the study, design and implementation of SIG has many advantages, such as:

● Multi-agent technology provides a new idea for SIG study and design;

● It provides a clear and comprehensible high-level model for SIG architecture;

● It provides an effective design and implementation method for SIG applications;

● The application of mature agent technology is helpful for breaking through the key technologies of SIG.

How to concretely direct the research of SIG by multi-agent technology is a new issue. There are many challenges such as communication, interoperability, security, performance, robustness, etc. The potential and perspective of multi-agent technology application need to be mined and explored. There are much more development and innovation space in this area, which will also promote the development of grid technology greatly.

References

1. Z.Shi, M.Dong, H.Zhang, Q.Sheng, Agent-based Grid Computing, International Symposium on Distributed Computing and Applications to Business, Engineering and Science, 2002.
2. L.Yao, W.Zhang, Information Technology on Intelligent Collaboration (in Chinese), Beijing: Electron Industry Press, 2002.
3. F.Manola, C.Thompson, Characterizing the Agent Grid, http://www.objs.com/agility/tech-reports/990623-characterizing-the-agent-grid.html, 1999.
4. B.J.Overeinder, N.J.E.Wijngaards, M.van Steen, F.M.T.Brazier, Multi-Agent Support for Internet-Scale Grid Management, In Proceedings of the AISB'02 Symposium on AI and Grid Computing, 2002.
5. W.Shen, Y.Li, H.H.Ghenniwa, C.Wang, Adaptive Negotiation for Agent-Based Grid Computing, http://www.agentcities.org/Challenge02/Proc/Papers/ch02_25_shen.pdf, 2002.
6. Z.Du, Y.Chen, P.Liu, Grid Computing (in Chinese), Beijing: Tsinghua University Press, 2002.
7. I.Foster, C.Kesselman, S.Tuecke, The Anatomy of the Grid: Enabling Scalable Virtual Organizations, International Journal on High Performance Computing Applications, 2001.
8. Y.Zhang, W.Zhang, W.Xiao, J.Sha, Z.Xu, Agent-Based Information Resource Management in the Information Grid, In Proceedings of the International Workshop on Grid and Cooperative Computing, 2002.

An Optimal Method of Diffusion Algorithm for Computational Grid

Rong Chen[1], Yadong Gui[2] , and Ji Gao[1]

[1] Zhejiang University Computer College, Hangzhou China, 310027
[2] Shanghai Supercomputer Center, Shanghai China, 201203

Abstract. Computational grid nowadays has become a hotspot in high performance computing environments because it can solve larger scale computing problems. The present load balance strategy in computing grid such as the Globus tools is static. This paper mainly focuses on dynamic load balance in the computational grid. We put forward a new model that solves the dynamic load balance problems on computational grid.

1 Introduction

Computational grid is an important direction in the massively scale parallel computing. Many middleware have emerged to support the implementations of computational grid, such as Legion, Globus, Gridbus, and so on. Many methods and mechanism have been used on the middleware. The resource finds, resource bind, resource registry, resource share and so on. We can use the Globus toolkit to build the computational grid. We also can use the OGSA to building service grid.

In the computational grid, the dynamic load balance is an important aspect that must be taken into account. In the computational grid environments, the various resources are dynamically added and left in the WAN environments. The load balance is a very difficult problem in the dynamic environment and heterogeneous system.

Many papers have contributed on this aspect. Literature [1] Willebeek-LeMair has put forward dynamic load balancing on highly parallel computer. Literature [2] put forward interactive dynamic balancing in multi-computer. Literature [3] put forward a diffusion method for the load balance. Literature [4] put forward dimension exchange method. Literature [5] considers that can use the diffusion algorithm for heterogeneous system. Literature [6] put forward that hydrodynamic load balance to the heterogeneous system. We can see that the connected utensils reach to same level after flowing. Different levels will reach the same level because the potential energy.

In this paper, we present a modified hydrodynamic theory to the computational grid for load balance.

Section 2 gives a brief introduction of computational grid. In section 3, we introduce the dynamic load balance method in heterogeneous system. Section 4, we introduce the computational grid environment. Section 5 we introduce the algorithm.

M. Li et al. (Eds.): GCC 2003, LNCS 3032, pp. 568–575, 2004.

2 The Dynamic Load Balance Method on Computational Grid

2.1 Computational Grid

Computational grid is used to solve the vast scale application computing. To an application, computing resource must be problem. The present resources including the cluster, MPP can't support the vast scale application computing. So if we have an application-computing problem that needs the computing power larger than present computer power, we needs the computational grid. If we have different compute in an application such as the vector computing, visualization and so on, we must need the resource that outside a enterprise. We can organize these resources in a virtual organization to finish a compute. We call it computational grid.

Computational grid has many characters. At first, we know the resource is dynamic added into the computing environments. The computing resources are dynamic. Second, these resources we know are inter-enterprises, and the inter-enterprises organize as one big virtual enterprise. Third the virtual organization is dynamic. These are main characters of the computational grid. So we know the computational grid has several key difficult different from the common cluster or MPP.

The dynamic resource management is a serious problem. We must solve the problem that includes resource discovery, resource description, resource binding, and resource use. In Globus project, we know the module GRAM that is used to manage the resources and use the resource. The MDS is used to monitor and discover the resources. In the computational grid, this is a key problem to solve the computational resources, but not a difficult problem. Second important theme that we must solve is the dynamic load balance for vast parallel computing has the dynamic load balance. In Globus project, we know that the DUROC has some of the function of dynamic load balance. An intelligent co-allocator has two functions: deal with resource description and decide how a task distributed to the resources, deal with the bottom layers resource description and do the resource allot. This is simple task allot not a really dynamic load balance. We must solve the dynamic load balance in computational grid. We also need to have the solution that implement the computing on the heterogeneous system. This is a basis of the grid computing and difficult to solve. If we can't implement this we can't do the computing automatically. The last problem is that we must improve the bandwidth and latency of the network. This is a bottleneck to implement the grid computing.

2.2 Dynamic Load Balance

We can use the directed graph to express the structure of computing grid. As we know, the computational grid has not only dynamic resources, but also span domain and may be the heterogeneous system. The compute power of each system may be unbalance and the problems are computed in fact through Internet. The topology structure can be express as the directed graph.

We can express distributed graph of computational grid as $G(V,E).V$ is computing node. A computing node is a node that has the processing capacity. E is the brim of computing node. So we can interconnect the computing nodes as a directed graph.

Here we mark nodes as $P_1 \ldots P_n$. We mark all the nodes not only the inter-domain. *Presume: In computational grid environment, the nodes don't layer,and nodes inter-domain are same only the transfer costs are different.*

In the domain the computing node can be computed as $P_1, P_2, P_3, \ldots, P_n$, which we use the sequence number to replace the present number e_i . We use the e_{ij} express the number.

The computing speed of ith node is s_i ,the workload is w_i, the computing time is $w_i / s_i = l_i$ The average time is

$$\bar{l} = \frac{\sum_{i=1}^{n} w_i}{\sum_{i=1}^{n} s_i} \tag{1}$$

The average computing time is under the condition that all the workloads are distributed on the computational nodes without considering the transfer costs.

The load balance can be concluded as the follows:

Computing the w_i, and make the time be $\bar{l}$. This system can be load balance on the view of the theory. The computing time variation is

$$B = (\bar{l}-l_1, \bar{l}-l_2, \ldots\ldots, \bar{l}-l_p)^T \tag{2}$$

There is the time difference in the computational grid. Also we know that is a load difference. So we must modify the load distribution. From the view of theory we know the load always can get relative balance.

From the theory we know the load balance problem like the node of single machine. So the formula[7] is

$$\frac{\sum_{j<->i} \theta_{ij}}{s_i} = \bar{l} - l_i, i = 1, \ldots., P \tag{3}$$

We can write it as the matrix[7]:

$$S^{-1} Ax = b \tag{4}$$

The S is diagonal matrix, S=diag$(s_1, s_2, \ldots s_n)$,A this near connect matrix. And its dimension number is $|V| \mathrm{x} |E|$, and its elements

$$\alpha_{ij} = \begin{cases} 1, i \leftrightarrow j \\ -1, i \leftrightarrow j \\ 0, other \end{cases} \tag{5}$$

3 Hydrodynamic Model on Computational Grid

Literature [5] put forward the hydrodynamic method to solve the load balance problem. We can use the graph to express our idea about the dynamic load balance. From the figure we can see the distinctions between the inner domain and inter-domain. As we know, the latency and bandwidth of the network are the key problem that limits the grid computing efficiency. So on one side we must lessen the communication quantity, on other side lessen the latency.

In one domain, the node has the different water level. The water will reach the same level for the potential energy. And so this water level has the same energy. In the inter-domain the energy transferring has a bigger cost, and the containers have different water level. If the water flows among the containers, then the result of different potential energy will bigger than the connected channel's height.

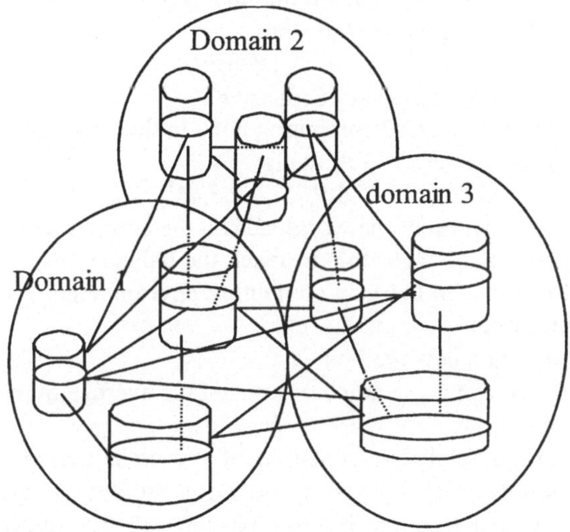

Fig. 1. The hydrodynamic model on Computational grid

If the height of the difference levels lessens than the connected channel, then we know the water won't flow. In the system, the bulk of the water corresponds to the computing number. Water levels correspond to the compute time of nodes. The cross-section of the container corresponds to the speed of the processors.

We can express the diffusion algorithm. For *i,j* is near number, at the step we know the diffusion algorithm

$$l_i^{(t+1)} = l_i^{(t)} + \frac{1}{S_i} \sum_{j<->i} \beta (l_j^{(t)} - l_i^{(t)}) \tag{6}$$

β -------a constant variable

S_i-----Compute speed

4 Algorithm of Hydrodynamic Model on Computational Grid

4.1 Theory Method

In the dynamic computing environment, the hydrodynamic system can reach the stable status after some time. Reaching stable status in diffusion algorithm, the cost is very expensive.

Here we suppose that:

1.The task can be divided infinitely in this model, and the subtask is the water molecule.

2.tasks can be migrated freely, and needn't any cost.

According to the presumption, we find that the complexity of reaching stable status is $n!$ through the diffusion algorithm. .

$$O(t)=n!,$$

Computing complexity is very expensive.

For example, we select 10 computing node in the grid computing system.

We express these nodes as following:

$$G(E, V)=(5,6,9,1,3,4,2,3,4,1)^T$$

These numbers represent the workloads on the computing nodes.

We use the diffusion algorithm to reach the balance after 3628800 steps. This is time-consumed method. In the grid computing environments, we must try our best to reduce the balance time.

Next, we present a new method.

At first, we average these numbers and get the average number.

$$\underline{h}=3.8$$

Then we can get global information of resources including the computing resource information, network resource information, storage resource information. In the Globus project, we get resource information through the information service of this system. The next step, we array workload sequence according to potential energy.

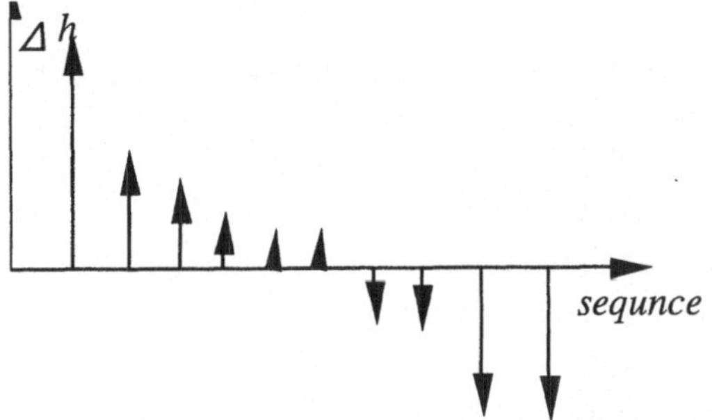

Fig. 2. Sequence Graph

TheΔh is the result of workloads subtracting the average workload. We get the positive value and negative value.

In the second step, we compute the complexity and the result is $n\,(n-1)/2$ steps.

$$O(s)= n\,(n-1)/2$$

In the third step, we use the best-fit algorithm and put the positive value into the negative value. The complexity is

$$O\,(t)=n\,(n+1)/2$$

We can see that use this method; we can easily reach balance. We can also use this algorithm to computing the time

$$O\,(t)=55 \text{ steps.}$$

Here, we can see that the computing result is very simple and this complexity of algorithm is polynomial. From figure 4,we find that the brim is less but the time is longer that the optimal methods.

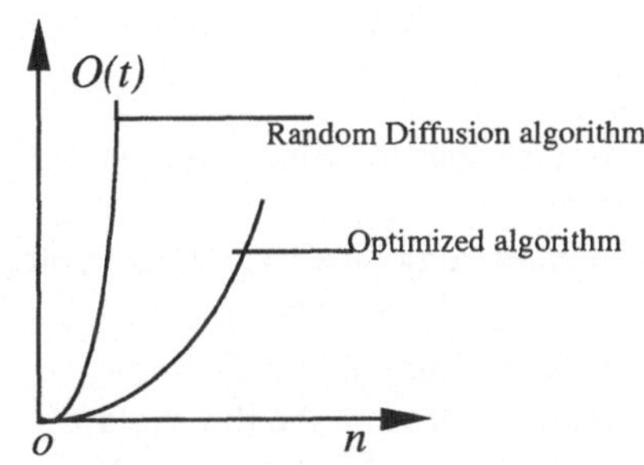

Fig. 3. Time complexity

4.2 Real Situation

In the real situation, we have to cast off the supposed conditions.

We know that the migration of process needs cost. In the theory model, we presume that the migration of process has no cost. And the hydrodynamic flow flows freely. But in fact we know that not only migration of process has cost but also the costs are different. So we know that the migration has different resistances.

4.2.1 Migration Cost

The task can't be divided infinitely, that is each task has task entity.

We define the cost C_t as the total cost.

$$C_t = C_{nb} + C_{nl} + C_{sd} + C_{oc}$$

C_{nb}—network bandwidth

C_{nl}—network latency

C_{sd}—scheduler decision cost

C_{oc}—other costs

These costs we call migration cost.

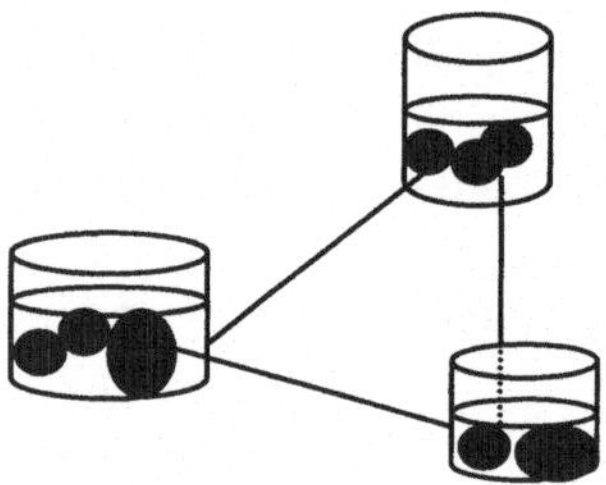

Fig. 4. Hydrodynamic Graph

Here we see that the costs are different. So we use the height of the connection to express the cost. The grains of tasks are also different. In the figure 5, we can see that the black ball represent the task and the balls are different in sizes.

We look at the potential energy as the network flow and the migration costs are thought as the resistance of the flow.

We can estimate the costs C_t. We call the costs as the threshold in the hydrodynamic model.

4.2.2 Algorithm

In this system, we hope that the time reaching the balance is shorter. Here we use the multi-flow algorithm.

Step1: The scheduler computes the average potential energy.

$$\underline{h}=(h_1+h_2+\ldots+h_n)/n$$

Step2: The scheduler compute the $\Delta h' = h_i - \underline{h}$

Step3: The scheduler compute the threshold C_{ti}

Step4: The scheduler searches the result that match positive potential energy and negative potential energy. The result will be a multi-flow equation.

$$\Delta h'^{+}(a)+\ldots+\Delta h'^{+}(i) \approx \Delta h'^{-}(b)+\ldots+\Delta h'^{-}(j) - C_{cu}$$

$$\Delta h'^{+}(p)+\ldots+\Delta h'^{+}(s) \approx \Delta h'^{-}(q)+\ldots+\Delta h'^{-}(t) - C_{cv}$$

....

$$\Delta h'^{+}(l)+\ldots+\Delta h'^{+}(m) \approx \Delta h'^{-}(n)+\ldots+\Delta h'^{-}(o) - C_{cw}$$

Step5: The scheduler sends the notification to the nodes.

Step6: Multi-flow flows and reach the balance

Step7: Report the result to scheduler.

5 Conclusion

This algorithm can be used in the computational grid. It can be used easily to solve the dynamic load balance. Different with the hydrodynamic model, this method will discuss the hydrodynamic cost on WAN with costs. We also put forward a simple optimized method to solve the fast algorithm.

The dynamic load balance on computational grid environment is a difficult problem. The cost isn't the only problem, and we must consider the process migration to resist the virus and other conditions. This is the future theme that we must research.

References

1 Willebeek-LeMair MH,Reeves AP, Strategies for dynamic load balance on highly parallel computer. IEEE Transactions on Parallel and Distributed system,1993,4(9):979-993.

2 Xu CZ,Lau FCM. Iterative dynamic load balancing in multicomputers. Journal of Operational Research Society,1994,45(7):786-796

3 Cybenko G. Dynamic load balancing for distributed memory multiprocessors. Journal of Parallel and Distributed Computing,1989,7(2):279-301

4 Hosseine SH,Litow B Dynamic load balancing for distributed memory memory multiprocessors. Journal of parallel and distributed computing,1989,7(2):279~301

5 Lin CH,Keller RM. The gradient model load distribution mothods.IEEE transactions on software engineering,1987,13,(1):32~38

6 Hui CC,Chanson ST.Hydrodynamic load balancing.IEEE transactions on the parallel and distributed system,1999,10(11)

7 金之雁，王鼎兴，异构系统中负载平衡扩散算法的加速方法.软件学报.Vol 14.No5

8 I. Foster, C. Kesselman. The Physiology of the Grid: An Open Grid Services Architecture for Distributed Systems Integration. Open Grid Service Infrastructure WG, Global Grid Forum

9 I. Foster, C. Kesselman. The Anatomy of the Grid: Enabling Scalable Virtual Organizations. International J. Supercomputer Applications,15(3), 2001.

10 I. Foster, C. Kesselman. Computational Grids. Chapter 2 of "The Grid: Blueprint for a New Computing Infrastructure",Morgan-Kaufman, 1999

11 I. Foster, C. Kesselman. Globus: A Metacomputing Infrastructure Toolkit. Intl J. Supercomputer Applications, 11(2):115-128, 1997.

12 W. Smith, I. Foster, V. Taylor. Scheduling with Advanced Reservations. Proceedings of the IPDPS Conference, May 2000

13 K. Czajkowski, I. Foster, and C. Kesselman. Resource Co-Allocation in Computational Grids. Proceedings of the Eighth IEEE International Symposium on High Performance Distributed Computing (HPDC-8), pp. 219-228, 1999.

14 I. Foster, C. Kesselman, A Distributed Resource Management Architecture that Supports Advance Reservations and Co-Allocation.Intl Workshop on Quality of Service, 1999.

A Reconfigurable High Availability Infrastructure in Cluster for Grid

Wen Gao [1, 2], Xinyu Liu [1], Lei Wang [1], and Takashi Nanya [2]

[1] Institute of Computing Technology, Chinese Academy of Sciences
P.O.Box 2704, Beijing 100080, China

[2] Research Center for Advanced Science and Technology, The University of Tokyo
4-6-1 Komaba, Meguro-ku, Tokyo 153-8904 Japan
gaowen@hal.rcast.u-tokyo.ac.jp

Abstract. The paper presents the implementation and analysis of a service-based reconfigurable High Availability infrastructure of cluster system for Grid. Based on service notion, the High Availability infrastructure is constructed for mission critical applications on Grid. The application high availability service is responsible for registered applications' high availability. The Service Manager is in charge of monitoring all services via heartbeat and automatically recovering from failure to assure service high availability. To improve flexibility and dependability, a dynamic reconfiguration mechanism is designed so that the configurations can be changed without interrupting application's running. A dependability modeling and simulation tool is deployed in the reconfiguration procedure. Dependability parameters can be inputted into the simulation tool. With the objects and sub-model library in the tool, corresponding global model will be constructed and statistic result for different recovery strategies is given. The configuration of application can be adjusted based on these statistic results.

1 Introduction[1]

A Grid is a hardware and software infrastructure that provides resource sharing and coordinated problem solving in dynamic, multi-institutional virtual organizations. In contemporary cluster systems for Grid, a broad range of scientific and commercial applications coexist and require flexibility and dependability. Grid based cluster management software is expected to support a variety of heterogeneous architecture or platforms. Meanwhile it must be capable to guarantee the high availability of crucial applications. It should be able to detect system failures and recover the involved applications. To provide persistent services, Grid based cluster management software itself must be reliable, have no single point of failure, and be able to recover from possible failure.

While common middleware, such as CORBA [1] and SOAP [2], and other middleware for Grid, exhibits attractive features (i.e. portability, interoperability), from an

[1] This research is supported by the Japan Society for the Promotion of Science and Institute of Computing Technology's foundation of initial research for young scientist.

M. Li et al. (Eds.): GCC 2003, LNCS 3032, pp. 576–583, 2004.

application development perspective, they are still lack in reliability and availability. Research projects, such as UIUC's Chameleon[4][9], UCLA's FTCT[3] and Berkeley's ROC[5], are more general-purpose and recovery-oriented. Our approach of service-based reconfigurable High Availability infrastructure differentiates itself from this previous work in two ways. First, both flexibility and dependability are considered for Grid based cluster in our work. Second, a dynamic reconfiguration mechanism is designed so that configurations of applications can be adjusted based on the statistic results of a dependability modeling and simulation tool.

The paper is organized as follows: In section 2, the High Availability infrastructure for mission critical applications is demonstrated in detail. In the following section 3, the design of a dynamic reconfiguration mechanism is presented. In section 4, the experimental analysis is given. Finally, the conclusion of this paper and the future work for this service-based reconfigurable High Availability infrastructure are described in section 5.

2 High Availability Infrastructure

2.1 Service-Based Design

For the interoperability, portability and reusability of the function modules in the cluster system software for Grid, the idea of service-based design is used. A service is a packed component that implements certain functions. The service-based system architecture does everything possible to isolate the high-level system services from low-level cluster node operation systems. It can mask the details of low-level platform and underlying communication details among cluster nodes. With multi-layer encapsulations, the service-based interfaces enable clients, whether remote or local, to use the uniform methods to access the services, without knowing the specific implementation details and location information of the services. A service-based framework, which includes service management and service encapsulation, is implemented to fulfill the notion of service. The service management, called Service Manager, provides interoperations such as service registration, service locating, service binding and service invoking operations, between service provider and service requestor.

Upon such service-based framework, the High Availability Infrastructure is constructed for mission critical applications in three layers, which are middleware layer, service layer and system interface layer. In middleware layer, Service Manager is responsible for service's high availability. In service layer, the application high availability service, incorporated with other services including loader, detector, and database service, is responsible for registered applications' high availability. In system interface layer, applications can be registered, monitored or controlled through a Graphical User Interface.

2.2 Application High Availability Service

The relationships among the application high availability service and other components, including Loader, Detector, and Database service, are illustrated in Figure 1. The Loader provides the basic services of process loading. Each host node or server node is deployed together with a Loader. The Detectors implement the basic services of status detecting. It can collect the system load and application status information efficiently. The basic principle of Detector is based on event notification mechanism. Detector allows service requestors to define the detection events including the owner, object, period, event and the notification method. Detector monitors the registered object periodically. Once the event occurs, Detector notifies the owner of the event by calling the predefined method immediately. Database service is responsible for searching, adding, deleting, updating the configuration of system, applications or users.

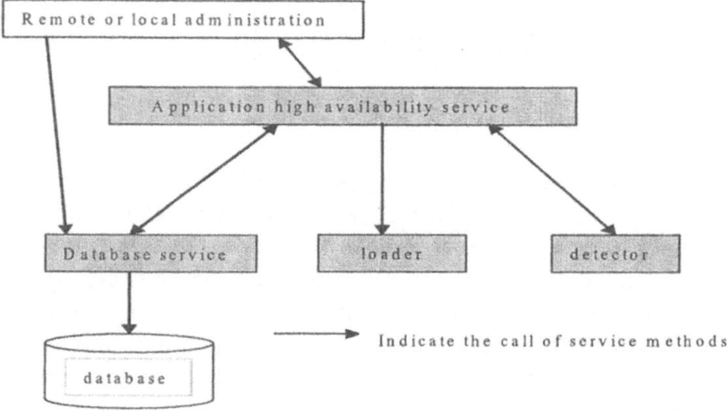

Fig. 1. Application high availability infrastructure

In normal situations, the typical workflow of application high availability service is described as follows: After receiving a submitted request from the user interface, the application high availability service analyses it based on its configuration and informs the loader on related nodes to execute the user processes. Then it registers application-related events to the detector for detecting the status of application processes and application-related failure. Once receiving the notification of application-related failure from the detector, it informs the involved Loader to process the failure predefined in the application configuration, such as restart or takeover of the application instance.

2.3 Service High Availability Management

Service Manager, which is responsible for service's high availability, is designed as master and backup architecture, which is illustrated in Fig.2, to avoid single failure point. In normal situations, Master Service Manager(SM) is in charge of management of services, exchanging the heartbeat message with Backup Service Manager(SM), and sending service registration list to Backup Service Manager. When failure occurs in Master Service Manager, the Backup Service Manager will be upgraded as Master Service Manager. At the same time, it will select one node to run as the Backup Service Manager. On the other side, when Backup Service Manager fails, the Master Service Manager will select a node to run as Backup Service Manager.

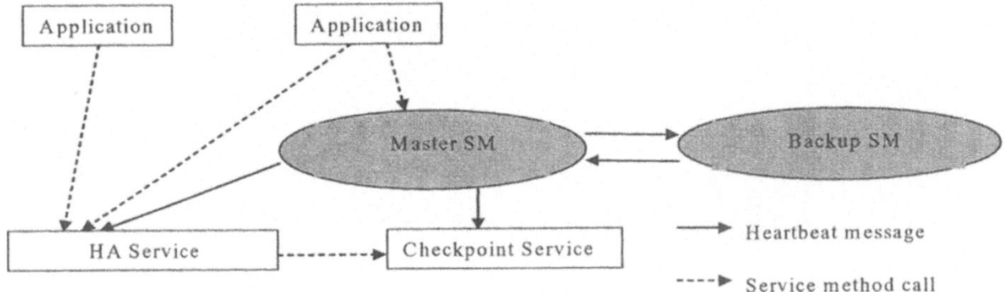

Fig. 2. Service high availability management

Service Manager also sends heartbeat message to each service in the registration list to detect the status of the service. If it finds out service failure, it will select a proper node to restart the service based on system and application configuration. To recover the service and roll back status before failure, a checkpoint service is deployed on each node. It can make checkpoint in a shared memory in local node and other backup nodes. The restarted service will read the backup date from the shared memory.

3 Dynamic Reconfiguration

3.1 Reconfiguration Procedure

To improve scalability, flexibility and dependability of cluster, the configurations of system and applications are tending to change all the times. For example, the number of nodes in cluster can be increased. Failure detection strategies and failure processing methods can also be adjusted according to dependability improvement.

In order to change configuration without interrupting application's running, a dynamic reconfiguration mechanism is designed as Fig.3. Current Configurations of applications and system are stored in database. Based on current configuration, parameters of system and application can be inputted into a Modeling and Simulation Tool to experiment dependability of the cluster. Based on statistic result as feedback, administrator can adjust current configurations through the GUI using database service to improve dependability. An invocation method of database service is supported to inform Application High Availability Service to reload the new configuration. The new configuration can take affect afterwards without interrupting the running of application.

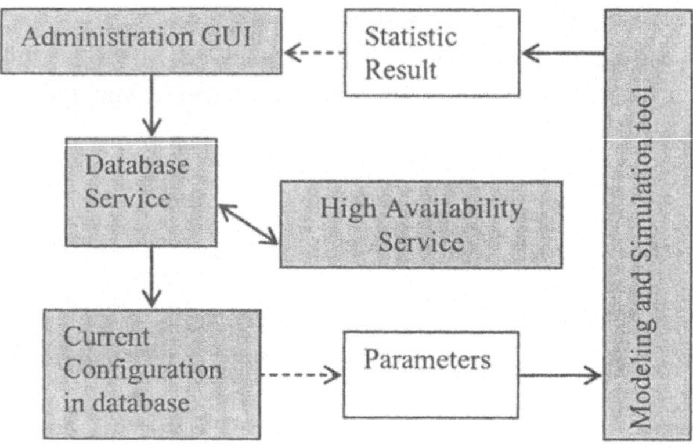

Fig. 3. Reconfiguration Procedure

3.2 Application Reconfigurable Parameters

Applications can have different failure detection strategy and flexible failure processing method. Therefore, these application parameters must be reconfigurable. Different applications concern different system component's status, such as CPU average load, memory usage, network interface, I/O devise and so on. One system component error may affect some applications running, but some applications may not be affected. Therefore, different failure detection policy for different applications must be adopted and some user defined failure detection interfaces may be added in failure detection configurations.

Flexible failure processing method includes recovery strategies and scheduler algorithm. There are three recovery strategies in configuration: restart, take-over and take-over after failure of restarting maximum times. Scheduler algorithms are designed to choose the highest priority node when the application instance takes over. There are three policies of scheduler algorithms: static balance, dynamic balance and custom balance. By static balance, administrator should assign a priority level to the nodes which will run an application instance. The highest priority node is the first to be selected to start a new instance. By dynamic balance, system load parameters and their relevant weights are used to compute priority dynamically. By custom balance an application must provide a callback program to compute the priority by its own rules and give out the expected application instances distribution.

3.3 Dependability Modeling and Simulation Tool

A convenient and efficient dependability evaluation tool with build-in facilities for High Availability cluster is deployed in the reconfiguration procedure stated above. It is developed to characterize different components and structures of High Availability clusters, and to facilitate the dynamical modeling and evaluation of the dependability. It can be applied to study behaviors of applications with various configurations, and reveal the dependability at the application layer.

Components in cluster, such as Node, Application and High Availability Infrastructure, are regarded as objects. Four functionality modules, which are fault module, failure detection module, failure recovery module and High Availability management module, are regarded as sub-model library. Fault module depicts permanent, transient and intermittent faults. Failure detection module characterizes the behavior of detector and heartbeat mechanism. Failure recovery module describes rebooting of node, restarting of high availability infrastructure, or failure processing of applications. With the objects and sub-model library in the tool, a corresponding global model can be seamlessly integrated based on cluster and application parameters. An event-driven simulator for Coloured Petri Nets [6] is used in the tool to give dependability statistic result.

4 Experimental Analysis

Experiments are taken to analyze dependability of this service-based reconfigurable high availability system. The parameters used in the experiment are listed in table 1. Most parameters are obtained from fault injection experiments in DAWNING 4000L cluster [7]. 16 nodes in a cluster share the same parameters and have the same failure distributions. More precise evaluation is possible by substituting with practical parameters or trace files.

An application with three different failure processing configurations is simulated for running one year with 1000 times respectively. Statistic result of the application availability is listed in table 2. The availability of the application with only restart method, named App1, is less than that of the application with take-over methods, named App2 and App3 respectively.

To evaluate the effects of different recovery strategies, the availability improvement factor (AIF) [8] is used, which is denoted as

$$AIF = \frac{Availability_{new} - Availability_{old}}{1 - Availability_{old}}. \tag{1}$$

AIF of the application with different recovery strategies is shown in table 3. A considerable AIF is achieved in App 3, which tries to restart before taking over. Note that due to the communication time and resource reallocation, time of take-over strategy is more than that of restart. Compared with permanent failures, transient failures are much more frequent to occur in this application. The recovery strategy of App 3 combines the advantages of restart and take-over, and gives the best availability of this application. Thus, the application configuration of recovery strategy can be tuned to take-over after restart. Other tests, such as which scheduler algorithm is most suitable for the application, can be experimented to improve the availability of the application running on this service-based reconfigurable high availability system.

Table 1. High Availability cluster parameters

Parameters of	Description	Value / Distribution (hours)
Node	Failure distribution	weibull(720,2,0)
	Reboot Time	Normal(0.0333,0.0056)
	Repair Time	normal(0.5,0.17)
Application	Failure distribution	exp(0.006)
	Restart Time	normal(0.0167,0.0028)
	Take-over Time	normal (0.025,0.0028)
High Availability Infrastructure	Failure distribution	exp(0.00083)
	Restart Time	normal(0.0002,0.00007)
	Failure Detection Time	uniform(0.0083,0.1667)
	Failure Coverage Rate	0. 99

Table 2. Availability of the Application with different recovery strategies

Application with different recovery strategy	Availability
App1: restart	0.999778
App2:take-over	0.999784
App3: take-over after failure of restart	0.999810

Table 3. AIF of the application with different recovery strategies

Availability Improvement between	AIF(%)
App3 to App2	12.04
App3 to App1	14.41

5 Conclusion

The paper presents the implementation and analysis of a service-based reconfigurable High Availability infrastructure of cluster system for Grid. Based on the notion and framework of service, the High Availability infrastructure, which includes the application high availability service and Service Manager, is constructed to assure application and service high availability respectively. To improve flexibility and dependability, a dynamic reconfiguration mechanism is designed so that the configurations of nodes or applications, such as failure detection strategies and failure processing methods, can be changed without interrupting application's running.

A dependability modeling and simulation tool for High Availability cluster is deployed in the reconfiguration procedure. Dependability parameters of nodes, high availability infrastructure and applications can be inputted into the simulation tool. With the objects and sub-model library in the tool, corresponding global model will be constructed and statistic result of experimenting different recovery strategies is given. The configuration of application in the high availability infrastructure can be adjusted based on these statistic results.

To improve the availability of the application running on this service-based reconfigurable high availability system, other experiments, such as which scheduler algorithm is most suitable for the application, can be considered in the future. Failure correlation and failure latency can also be considered in the dependability simulation tool and reconfiguration procedure in the future.

References

1. J. Siegel, An Overview of CORBA 3, Proc. 2nd IFIP int'l Working Conf. Distributed Applications and Interoperable Systems (DAIS 99), Kluwer, Boston, 1999.
2. SOAP, http://www.w3.org/TR/SOAP/
3. Ming Li, Wenchao Tao, Daniel Goldberg, Israel Hsu, Yuval Tamir. Design and Validation of Portable Communication Infrastructure for Fault-Tolerant Cluster Middleware. Proc. of the IEEE int'l conf. on Cluster Computing (CLUSTER'02), Chicago.,USA, September 2002.
4. Zbigniew T. Kalbarczyk, Ravishanker K. Iyer, Saurabh Bagchi, Keith Whisnant, Chameleon: A Software Infrastructure for Adaptive Fault Tolerance, IEEE Trans. Parallel and Distributed System, vol. 10. No.6. June 1999
5. David Patterson et al. Recovery Oriented Computing (ROC): Motivation, Definition, Techniques, and Case Studies. Technical Report CSD-02-1175, UC Berkeley Computer Science, 2002.
6. L. Xinyu, G. Wen, S. Ninghui. NCPN: A Simulation Tool for Coloured Petri Nets. Proc. of 14th IASTED Int'l conf. on Parallel and Distributed Computing and Systems, Cambridge, Nov 2002.
7. SUN Ning-Hui MENG Dan, Key Design Issues of Dawning3000 Superserver, Chinese Journal of Computers, Vol.25 No.11, 2002. 11
8. S. Hariri, H. Mutlu. Hierarchical Modeling of Availability in Distributed Systems. IEEE Trans. Software Engineering, vol. 21, no. 1, Jan. 1995.
9. K.Whisnant, R.K.Iyer, P.Jones, R.Some, D.Rennels. An Experimental Evauation of the REE SIFT Environment for Spaceborne Applications. Proc. of the 2002 int'l conf. on Dependable System & Networks(DSN2002), Washington, D.C.,USA, June 2002.

An Adaptive Information Grid Architecture for Recommendation System

M. Lan and W. Zhou

School of Information Technology, Deakin University
221 Burwood Hwy, Burwood, Vic 3125, Australia
{mlan, wanlei}@deakin.edu.au

Abstract. This paper presents an adaptive information grid architecture for recommendation systems, which consists of the features of the recommendation rule and a co-citation algorithm. The algorithm addresses some challenges that are essential for further searching and recommendation algorithms. It does not require users to provide a lot of interactive communication. Furthermore, it supports other queries, such as keyword, URL and document investigations. When the structure is compared to other algorithms, the scalability is noticeably better. The high online performance can be obtained as well as the repository computation, which can achieve a high group-forming accuracy using only a fraction of web pages from a cluster.

1 Introduction

A key goal of the Semantic Grid is to provide the e-customers with the right information at the right time, i.e. personalization and a degree of context-awareness. This requirement is amplified by the huge scale of information that will be generated by e-Technology [1].

This is particularly problematic for the web linking technology. The basic problem is that once a document is published, anybody on the planet can embed a link to it within their own documents. That link is then hardwired, and it is also vulnerable to decay as the original document might be renamed or moved. An alternative architecture maintains the link information separately from the document. This facilitates dynamic generation of the hyper-structures and maintenance of link integrity. Web standards have evolved to accommodate this mode of working, supporting 'out of line' links.

To illustrate the creation of user models, consider the following two techniques. Firstly, the user might specify their interests, perhaps on a form or by providing a representative set of documents (perhaps from bookmarks). Secondly, the model might be obtained by incidental capture of information based on browsing habits. A popular mechanism to realize adaptive systems in the web context is the use of proxies, using them to perform other functions as the requests pass through and documents pass back. There are many examples:

Caching Proxies. It includes hierarchical caching in which caches are arranged as parents and siblings.

M. Li et al. (Eds.): GCC 2003, LNCS 3032, pp. 584–591, 2004.

Proxies Producing Logs. This enables logging local to part of a network, rather than using server logs. Logs can be used for management purposes but also to capture user browsing behaviors as part of an adaptive information system.

Proxies Modifying Document Content. Simple modifications include rewriting URLs, introducing links, prepending or appending content. With a full parser, the proxy can do more sophisticated transformations (but may take more time to do it).

Proxies Modifying Requests. The proxy can rewrite a request, or respond to a request by redirecting the client.

In our model, we take advantage of approaches of Caching proxies and Proxies modifying requests to build an adaptive information grid model. Through this model e-customers can realize empty searching and context searching. The rest of paper is organized as follows, section 2 introduces general architecture for an information grid. Section 3 then provides algorithms in proxy data collection. Section 4 describes evaluations and analysis and the related works of this topic are presented in section 5. The final section will then provide some concluding remarks and future work under consideration.

2 General Architecture for an Information Grid

We have identified the following four types of architectures for an information grid:

Distributed Architecture. In this architecture, a receiver sends a query to all sources of events of interest. Later, whenever an event occurs, the source delivers the event directly to all subscribers.

Single proxy Architecture. In the single-proxy architecture, the proxy acts like a central directory and maps all events to sources and receivers. Every receiver subscribes at the proxy, which records the subscription in its database. When a source generates an event, it sends the event to the proxy, which looks up the subscribers and forwards the event to them. With events going through the proxy, sources do not need to maintain states about their subscribers. The single proxy architecture is shown in Fig 1 (a). Using clustering techniques, the proxy can be scalable enough to handle the amount of state and traffic, and robust enough to provide uninterrupted service. However, some scalability and failure handling problems still exist [2] .

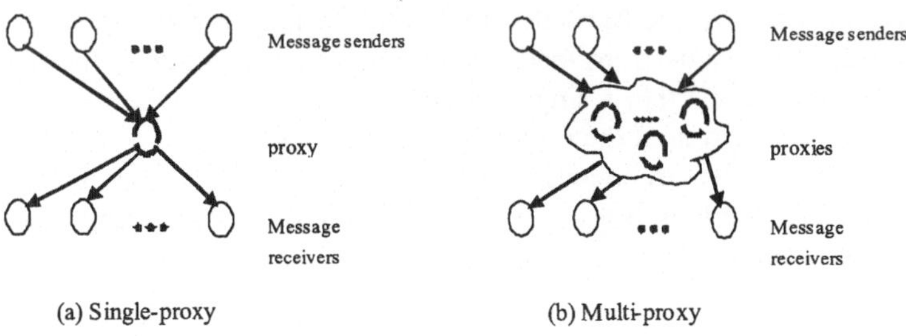

Fig. 1. Architecture of *single-proxy* and *multi-proxy*.

Multi-proxy Architecture. A natural solution to the above problems is to use multiple proxies. In this scheme, each receiver sends event subscriptions to its nearest proxy. Similarly, each source sends events to its nearest proxy. The proxies collectively implement an event dissemination mechanism that "routes", at the application level, events towards the subscribers. Sources and receivers only send heartbeats to their local proxies, and proxies exchange heartbeats among themselves. This architecture is not susceptible to a single point of failure—a source may be able to reach some receivers even if some proxies fail or are disconnected from other proxies. Fig1 (b) shows multi-proxy architecture.

Hierarchy Proxy. Proxy hierarchy is glued together by multicast groups. Each group is "owned" by one proxy, which is called the parent proxy; all other proxies in the group are called child proxies. Every source (and receiver) attaches to the hierarchy via a proxy, which is called its primary proxy. Every proxy joins the group owned by its parent, and its own group if it is not a leaf. We do not address the issue of creation and maintenance of the hierarchy; protocols in previous work can be readily applied here[3].

3 An Adaptive Architecture for Information Grid

From above, we know those architecture might be used as a framework of information grid. But they have their own problems. In order to adapt to the environment of an enormous Web, we present an adaptive architecture as follows.

There are two aspects in our architecture. One is from cached proxies. We scan the cache contents and obtain history contents. Then we take advantages of effective clustering algorithms to classify cache contents into different classes. When an e-customer sends a query, this part retrieves recommended results for him. The other part comes from history records. For instance, if an e-customer looks for a new concept or query, we can re-rank the searching result according the past log. This re-organization is different from metasearch engine. In a typical session of using a metasearch engine, a user submits a query to the metasearch engine through a user-friendly interface. The metasearch engine then sends the user query to a number of underlying search engines (which will be called component search engines here) Different component search engines may accept queries in different formats. The user query may thus need to be translated to an appropriate format for each local system. After the retrieval results from local search engines are received, the metasearch engine merges the results into a single ranked list and presents the merged result, possibly only the top portion of the merged result, to the user [4].

Here we use proxy architecture as the framework. The work is done asynchronously. This method avoids a lot of workload and shortens waiting time. The architecture is shown in Fig 2.

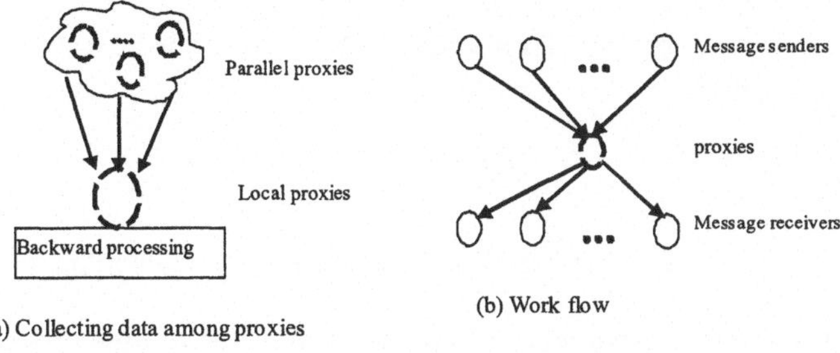

Fig. 2. Architecture of adaptive information grid using *multi-proxy*.

4 Co-recommendation Algorithms

In our architecture, we create an co-recommendation algorithms. Using the method described in [5], and using index term weighting, a correlation-based similarity computation is applied in this research to determine the similarity, $s_{i,j}$, between web pages. This approach changes the cocitation+ algorithm in that it now has to adapt to a term-based cluster for a user. Preceded by some assumptions, the basic steps of the co-recommandation algorithm are as follows.

Firstly, assume that an indexer module exists in a server, thus providing an index term weighting for the new algorithm. This algorithm can then be binded to an existing searching engine. Or, an agent can be created using the Tf-idf scheme on a proxy server (e.g. a university proxy server) to calculate index terms and their weighting for a users link, by scanning the cache. This method is feasible since most proxy servers incorporate a temporal algorithm.

Secondly, a threshold, *P*, for clustering web pages is located, using a Metric Clusters algorithm to organize groups in the user-based web page link collection. The metric clusters algorithm can be found in [6].

List 1 shows an initial data collection of the new proposed algorithm.

```
Initial data collection(){
  while (TRUE){
    receive(user uk);
    assign user set U={u1, u2,..., uk}, web page number N;
    assign index term set T={t1,t2,..tm};
    assign weighting set WT=(w1, w2, ..wl};
    webpageSimilarity.calculate(T, WT){
    return S={sij};
    N++;
    }
    similarityDecision(sij){
      assign threshold P;
      int x=0;
      do {
        if(sij>P){
```

```
            create a group of webpage gi;
            store web page di and dj in gi;
            Get group index term Tsup and their weights Wsup;
            x++;
        }
      while(x<N)
      }
}
```

List 1. Initial data collection of the new algorithm.

After a users initial group clustering, list 2 shows the routine process of the new algorithm.

```
routineProcess(){
  assign another threshold Pp;
  webpageGroupSimilarity.calculate()
  {return sg(i,j);}
  similarityDecision();
  store some users who provide high correlation with sg(i,j) ;
}
```

List 2. Routine Process of the new algorithm

This algorithm can support queries such as keyword, link and document. It can deliver the high recommendation links and survey users with a similar preference. If the client provides two different links in one query, the algorithm can process them separately and provide the user with two preferences, which can even be further increased to present the users with even more suitable preferences. Suggesting that G is the parent of links for the cocitation+ algorithm, G_{sup} refers to the results, which introduce related contents from the cocitation algorithm.

A set of web page groups helped alleviate coverage and improved quality in the integration of users with different preferences. The repository can own a lot of attributes (item ID, item title, frequency, URL, rated terms, and top amount of groups detail etc.) for further analysis. These analyses can then provide other useful recommendations for different fields. The biggest advantage is that this algorithm does not only support keyword searching, but it also supports URL and preferences searching. When users use keywords, it searches weighted index terms in total groups. When a user clicks a URL, this recommendation algorithm can provide top frequency links from a similar group, or the group that owns that particular URL. As a result, a much faster recommendation procedure can be produced.

5 Evaluations and Analysis

5.1 Document Clustering Evaluation

The testing data used for evaluating the proposed document. Clustering method are formed by mixing documents from multiple topics arbitrarily selected from our evaluation database. At each run of the test, documents from a selected number k of topics are mixed, and the mixed document set, along with the cluster number k, is provided to the clustering process. The result is evaluated by comparing the cluster label of each document with its label provided by original corpus.

5.2 Analysis

Normally, most recommendation algorithms require a lot of interaction in order to determine the user's preferences. The experiment mentioned in [7] shows that the more a user interacts with the system, the better its recommendations will be. The new algorithm differs in that it obtains a message from the user's web page. When one value web page is accessed, the system automatically proposes some value links based on the other usage. The content-based data group then encompasses other related interests. If another user's link is involved in the group, recommendations can be considered to enhance the correlation. This feature solves the underlying problem that the recommendation is related to the users interests.

A very important observation from [5] is that the high group-forming accuracy can be achieved using only a fraction of web pages. The following case demonstrates this study. Consider set $D=\{d_1, d_2, \ldots d_n\}$, $d_i, d_j, d_k, d_m \in D$. If *sim (i,j)*, *sim(i,k)* and *sim(i,m)* is high, then *sim (j,k)*, *sim(j,m)* and *sim(k,m)* can be considered high too. A higher accuracy is achieved when using the same proportional web pages with bigger dimensions. This is an important advantage for the new algorithm. We can use this observation to decrease the computation coverage.

The results in [7]also show that *item-item* scheme provides better recommendations than the *user-user* (k-nearest neighbour) scheme. Here, *item* is changed to *term* and *user* is changed to *web pages*. It is worthy to note that the results from the *term-term* scheme are better than the other *link-link* collaborative filtering recommendation scheme.

On the other hand, good recommendations have been identified from experiments of the cocitation+ algorithm [8]. The cocitation+ algorithm is described in Section 3.3. The parents of a URL can be changed to related groups. For *B-part* algorithms, the number of common parents is used to determine the most relevant page. However, a lot of factors will affect the sibling relevant pages. Whereas some links may be just friendly links, the situation is different in the new scheme. Since a user visited a clustered link on the basis of its contents, the relevant probability should be higher than that of the cocitation+ algorithm. The *A-part* algorithm will find the people who have similar preferences. The results do not exceed the guessing for the cocitation+ algorithm, where people tend to focus on the similar topic by combining the number of web pages between a supergroup and a user's related group. Certainly, this supergroup is similar to the active user's query web pages. Since this algorithm supports a query with two or more different preferences, it can solve the problem when a user changes his interests from one subject to another.

There are two conflictive challenges for the user-based scheme; the scalability of collaborative filtering algorithms and the quality of the recommendation for the users. The less time the algorithm spends on searching for neighbours, the more scalable it will be, but the quality will appear inferior. The off-line computation and the observation of [5] do not require this algorithm to address the issue.

6 Related Work

The *Netscape-Alexa* algorithm is based on links from web sites and its contents. Successful URL 'hits' and annotations of web pages are used to rank the sites. This algorithm also examines the 'surfing' paths to determine the relationship between the different sites that have been visited. Moreover, it utilizes the users usage of query results to improve its own performance for the future. This scheme can be applied in the broad Internet community. A disadvantage of the *Netscape-Alexa* algorithm is that it only focuses on the website URLs, but does not consider the specific interests of those sites[5, 9]. In the *Sinergis* project, useful knowledge is aggregated so that users with common preferences can find relevant material whilst doing similar search queries. It can present users with a customized list of pages related to their current pages[10]. HITS [11] relies on the query and examines the set of pages that point to, or are pointed by the pages in the result [6]. PageRank [12, 13] is a global ranking scheme deriving from citation ranking which is concerned with hyperlink structure. It takes the importance of a directed page into considerations. In this scheme, recursive-importance of a page does not only depend on, but indeed influences the importance of other pages. The Cocitation+ algorithm focuses on a different approach for information retrieval from the Web [8]. It uses a URL to find other URLs of related pages. Related pages are defined as pages on the same topic as the query page. The experiments show that the technique performs extremely well for finding related web pages but its performance is disappointing for finding people with similar interests.

In [5], the authors propose item-based algorithms, which integrate a collaborative filtering approach. The bottleneck in conventional collaborative filtering algorithms is the searching for potentially related neighbours among a large user population. Item-based algorithms eliminate this bottleneck by exploring the relationships among items rather than the relationships among users. *Surflen* is an information recommendation system, which recommends interesting web pages to users [7]. It captures a users navigation history and applies "association rule" of data mining to discover hidden knowledge contained in this history. Its experiments show that the more a user interacts with the system, the better its recommendations will be. It also indicates that the users browsing history becomes more indicative of their interests if the number of successful recommendations increases.

7 Conclusions and Remarks

This paper presents an adaptive information grid architecture. It takes advantage of the Co-Recommendation and the clustering Algorithm, and consists of the features of the recommendation rule and the co-citation algorithm. Visited history links from a user are considered as recommended links for other users.

The algorithm focuses on challenges that are fundamental for other searching and recommendation algorithms. It does not require users to heavily participate in an interactive communication environment. Furthermore, it supports different queries, such as keyword, URL, and document. This algorithm also supports a query with two or more different preferences thus allowing the user to change his interests from one subject to another. If a user has several preferences, this algorithm can still find similar users for him. Compared to other algorithms, its structure affords scalability. With most of the computation being done off-line, the high online performance can be obtained. In the repository computation, it can achieve a high group-forming accuracy using only a fraction of web pages of a group.

References

1. D. De Roure, N. Jennings, and N. Shadbolt, "A Future e-Science Infrastructure," *EPSRC/DTI Core e-Science Programme*, 2001.
2. H. Yu, D. Estrin, and R. Govindan, "A Hierarchical Proxy Architecture for Internet-scale Event Services," *Proc. of the WETICE Workshop*, 1999.
3. A. Rosenstein, J. Li, and S. Y. Tong, " MASH: The multicasting archie server hierarchy," *SIGCOMM Computer Communication*, vol. Review, 27(3), 1997.
4. W. Meng, C. Yu, and K.-L. Liu, "Building efficient and effective metasearch engines," *ACM Computing Surveys (CSUR)*\, vol. 34\, pp. 48--89\, 2002.
5. B. Sarwar, G. Karypis, and e. al, "item-based collaborative filtering recommendation algorithms," *The tenth international World Wide Web conference on World Wide Web*, 2001.
6. B.-Y. Ricardo and R.-N. Berthier, "Modern information retrieval," *ACM Press*, vol. ISBN 0-201-39829-X, 1999.
7. X. Fu, J. Budzik, and K. J. Hammond, "Mining navigation history for recommendation," *In Proc. 2000 International Conference on Intelligent User Interfaces*, pp. 106-112, 2000.
8. A. Barabasi, R. Albert, H. Jeong, and G. Bianconi, "Response: power-law distribution of the World Wide Web,," *science 287 2115a 9in technical comments*, 2000.
9. A. Inc., " http://www.alexa.com."
10. J. N. Sanchez and R. Singh, "Sinergia: Improving Browsing By Exploiting Community Knowledge," *http://www.stanford.edu/~javiers/cs241/writeup.pdf, Stanford University*, 2002.
11. J. Kleinberg, "Authoritative sources in a hyperlinked environment.," *ACM 46,6(Nov.)*, 1999.
12. L. Page, S. Brin, R. Motwani, and T. Winograd, "The pagerank citation ranking:Bringing order to the web," *Tech. Rep.. Computer Systems Laboratory,Stanford University, Stanford, CA*, 1998.
13. J. C. Arvind Arasu, Hector Garcia-Molina, Andreas Paepcke, and Sriram Raghavan,, "Searching the web," *ACM Transactions on Internet Technology*, vol. Vol.1, No.1,August 2001, Pages 2-43, 2001.

Research on Construction of EAI-Oriented Web Service Architecture[1]

Xin Peng, Wenyun Zhao, and En Ye

Software Engineering Lab, Fudan University, Shanghai, 200433, China
cspengxin@163.com, wyzhao@fudan.edu.cn, yeen@vip.sina.com

Abstract. Web service based data exchange has been the trend of EAI. We can create Proxies to expose existing systems as web services. There have been some tools that can help users to construct web services on the basis of existing systems. However, authority control and dynamic service configuration are not taken into account in the process of construction. In this paper we present an EAI-Oriented unified authentication model, and then put forward the service-items-based authority control and dynamic service configuration management in the construction of EAI-oriented web service architecture. Tool support in the process of construction is also discussed.

1 Introduction

One trend of EAI is the data exchange service based on web service. It supports the data interaction not only between systems in the same kinds of platforms but also between the cross-platform systems. A usual method of adopting web service is to add a layer of web service proxy on the basis of the original systems and then convert the systems into web services [1].

XML-based web service can be seen as a representation layer which is from program to program [2]. The business service provided as web service is aimed at external applications and hence should be able to deal with the various and changing service requests. At the same time, web service is also required to construct the authority system of the service requesters, which can guarantee the security of data exchange.

In the environment of EAI, each service publisher can integrate and publish local services on the basis of local business services and external services. The integrated elements are much more complicated. Therefore, it is important to make interdependent web services in the EAI system evolve controllably and keep dependable.

We introduce service configuration management in EAI-Oriented Web Service Architecture. All the local business components and external web services needed will be put under configuration management. Each service item is published through the unified service interface, which acts as a proxy to expose inner services.

---

[1] Supported by the National High Technology Research and Development Program of China (863 Program) under Grant Nos. 2002AA114010; 2001AA113070. It is also Supported by Shanghai Technology Development Foundation (No.025115014).

M. Li et al. (Eds.): GCC 2003, LNCS 3032, pp. 592–600, 2004.

Some recent tools can help to perform the construction of web service based on existing systems automatically. For instance, the WebSphere platform can help users to create service proxies for CICS middleware, Java class and EJB automatically [1]. The paper [2] designs a tool to help publish web service by constructing service packages acting as different roles. The constructions of web service discussed above do not deal with the needs of authority control and dynamic service configuration.

This paper is organized as follows. Section 2 presents a unified authentication mechanism in EAI. Section 3 describes the unified data service interface. Section 4 discusses an EAI-oriented web service architecture of authority control and service publication based on the diverse granularity configuration items.

2 EAI-Oriented Web Service Unified Authentication

It is thought in [3] that the web service model supports not only the reuse of software but also the reuse of the operating environment. And it proposes that authentication should be abstracted as a component and act as a web service of the third party.

The systems operating independently have their own system of authentication. Therefore, the most important task for EAI is to build a unified authentication system in the enterprise. The unified authentication system must provide unified user authentication and role management at the enterprise level.

We bring forward an EAI-oriented unified authentication model of web service (Figure 1). The authentication server deals with the requests of authentication and the role management unifiedly.

In the unified authentication system the role is managed unifiedly. Each service provider has its own authority control system, which determines the corresponding authority of different roles in local service. The security of the whole transfer channel and data transfer itself can be solved by adopting techniques such as SSL and PKI, which are discussed in [3],[4].

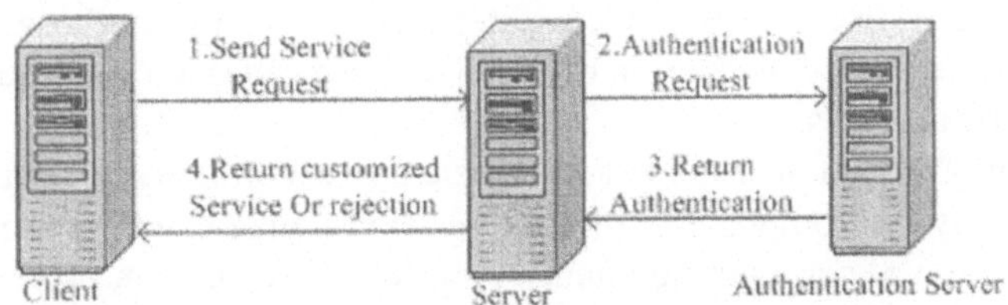

Fig. 1. EAI-Oriented Web Service unified Authentication

3 Unified Data Service Interface

The paper [2] thinks that what the web service should do is to provide information to the invoker and transfer the received information to the underlying system. When a web service is introduced into a system, the web service should simply form another layer, and play a role analogous to and parallel with the user interface layer [2]. Therefore, a proxy layer should be deployed on the basis of the original application, which is responsible for the sending and receiving of data. Meanwhile, authority control and service customization should be carried out.

The paper [2] designs two data service interfaces (.Net interface), which aim at a single method invocation and method sequence invocation separately (Figure 2). In the interfaces, the Get and Post method are used to receive and set the data. The unified service interface serves as the web service proxy, which receives the service request of the client, drives the local services to execute according to the sequence and sends the return data as a unified interface.

```
public interface IDataService
{
  object GetData(string method,object[] values);
  bool PostData(string method,object[] values);
}

public interface ISequenceDataService
{
  object[] GetSequencedData(string[] methods,object[][] values);
  bool[] PostSequencedData(string[] methods,object[][] values);
}
```

Fig. 2. Data Service Interfaces

The advantage of this design is to improve the abstraction level of service interface. Moreover, the method sequence reduces the amount of messages between the client and the server and thus decreases the occupation of bandwidth [2].

4 Management of Diverse Granularity Service Items

4.1 Web Service Items Management and Configuration Management

In the web service based on data exchange, the core is the data items that service requestors concern. In our web service system, service items are those provided public methods. And a service invocation of the client is composed of a sequence of invocations of public methods.

In the configuration management, the basic unit is configuration item. And software configuration is the composition of configuration items. Configuration is the significant composition of configuration items. After the development, products can be managed by version-publishing, which is the composition of baselines.

4.2 Authority Control Based on Public Service Items and Their Interfaces

In our web service system, the service interface published publicly is the smallest unit invoked by the client. It is also the basic unit of authority control. On the basis of it, the method parameters should be controlled further. It is because that the selection of parameters determines the data returned or the inner executing mechanism.

We should first set up the authority distribution records. The authority control divides into two levels: method level and parameter one, which should be both maintained by every service provider. The control at the method level only needs to check whether the authority list of the method includes the role of the client. Contrarily, the control at the parameter level is complicated because the format of parameters is different and the authentication principles are various.

As illustrated in Figure 3, the process of authentication is that the component of authority control returns the results to the unified interface component after the authority authentication at the method level and parameter level. Only the information of roles accepted by every method is required to be registered in the authority list at the method level. At the parameter level, however, the authority information in every method should be registered. These methods take the parameters required when the client invoke them as their own parameters and return the result of authentication.

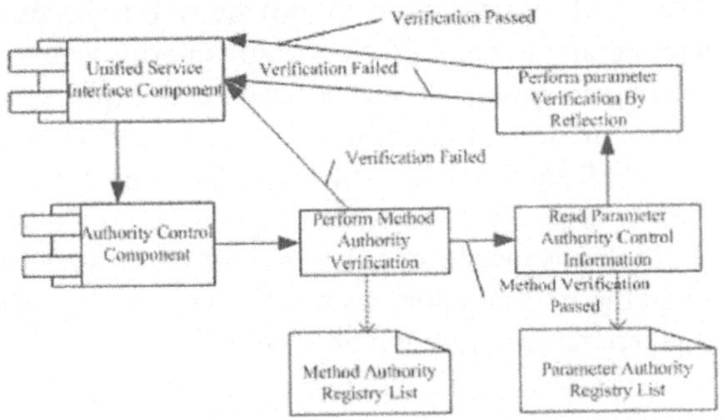

Fig. 3. The Process of Authority Verification

We define two java interfaces for authority verification (Figure 4). The class performing authority verification should implement the interface IServiceCheck, which defines three methods. The checkInvokeMthod method and the checkInvokeParams method perform authority verification at the method level and the parameter level separately. And the checkInvokeSequence method verifies sequencing of methods. The sequencing verification will return false as long as any method verification in the sequence fails. Considering that a user can own several roles, the parameter role is an array.

```
public interface IServiceCheck
{
 public static boolean checkInvokeSequence(String[] methods, object[][] values, String[] role);
 public static boolean checkInvokeMethod(String method, String[] role);
 public static boolean checkInvokeParmas(String method, String[] role, Object[] values);
}

public interface IMethodParamsCheck
{
 public static boolean checkInvoke(String role, Object[] values);
}
```

Fig. 4. Authority verification interfaces

IMethodParamsCheck is an interface that each class defining the rules of verification at the parameter level should implement. In a concrete implementation each method to be published should define a corresponding class implementing the IMethodParmasCheck interface to perform parameter authority verification and register the class in the service publishing information.

4.3 Web Services Publishing of Diverse Granularity

WINGCM [5][6] proposed the concept of software configuration management of Diverse Granularity. The issue of granularity also exists in web services. Web services of coarse granularity can make the services more efficient and the corresponding invocation will be simple. However, web services of fine granularity can present more flexibility, since the client can assemble the service sequence flexibly.

We create proxies of various levels to provide web services of diverse granularity. Figure 5 presents the architecture of diverse-granularity web services publishing system. The Service objects represent web service items exposing existing application to the clients. They are proxies of the business services and invoked through the unified service interface by reflection mechanism. The Class objects are class components encapsulating business logic. In the situation described in figure 5 Class 1 represents business logic of high abstract level and is published through Service C. At the same time Class 2, 3 and the EJB components which compose the bottom service of Class 1 can be exposed independently through Service A, B and D to provide services of finer granularity. These business components can also invoke web services provided by other server to compose local service.

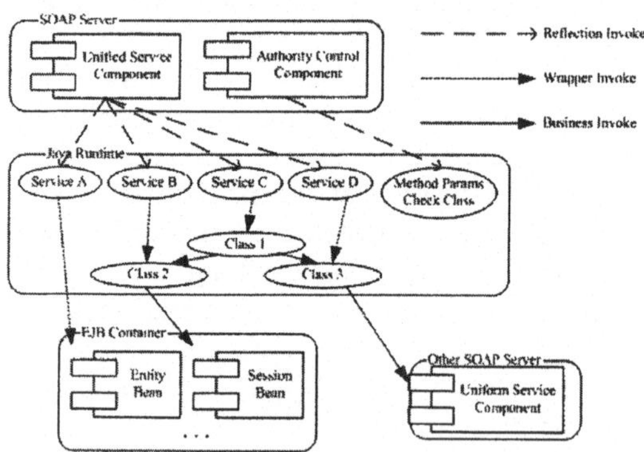

Fig. 5. Diverse-granularity web services publishing

4.4 Dynamic Service Configuration Management

Each service item invoked through the unified service interface is composed of correlative bottom components directly or indirectly. A concrete invoking process concerns certain versions of bottom components. So the evolvement of any component involved in the entire service system will lead to the evolvement of versions of some services. In our web service system the configuration item and the service item are defined as follow:

Configuration item: java classes, EJBs, or components of other types at various abstract levels, which compose the entire service system. The web services provided by other servers can also become configuration items.

Service item: The public methods exposed through the unified service interface. They will be invoked by reflection mechanism.

A configuration item is the basic unit of service configuration management. Atomic configuration items can be an EJB, or a java class or a class package which acts as a single component entirely. Especially, web services invoked from other servers will be treated as local atomic configuration items. A configuration item is also a unit of maintenance and version evolvement, which means an atomic configuration item should be modified or replaced as a whole. Each configuration item has a unique and unalterable identity including external services. Configuration items are stored in the repository according to the identities and can be gotten by certain way. External services are special configuration items since they can only be maintained on other servers. Information about the external services will be recorded locally. The evolvements of external services can only be informed by external entities, such as the private UDDI registry.

A service item is a public method that acts as the proxy of certain bottom components. It is the basic unit of authority control. The wrapping components providing these methods are configuration items of the highest abstract level. Correlative information about service items of each web server in the EAI system, including the description of service classes, methods and the parameters, should be published to the private UDDI registry of the enterprise.

A service configuration management layer should be added into our web service system (Figure 6). The aim of that management layer is to guarantee that the service items under dynamic configuration evolve correctly and keep traceable. The repository in software configuration management maintains resources in the project development, while the repository in our service configuration management takes runtime components as resources. Various versions of the components are stored in the repository according to the version number. The version of certain component is determined by not only the component entity itself but also the versions of bottom components concerned. So the evolvement of a component will result in the evolvement of components at higher abstract level, which depend on the component directly or indirectly.

The objects that web service configuration management aims at are runtime components, such as java classes or EJBs. There exist two kinds of configuration items. One of them is service components developed and maintained locally. The management of these components should integrate SCM tool, which manages the development resources such as document, source code etc entirely. While the service publishing will be managed by the service configuration tool. In addition to delivery of source code the "check in" operation of components will contain compiling of the code to get runtime components. Sometimes deployment will be involved too. There still exists another kind of components. They are entirely runtime components. The service administrator can perform management directly by the service configuration management tool.

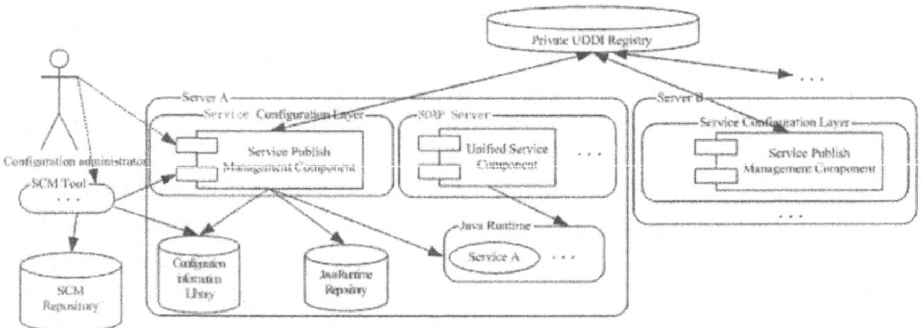

Fig. 6. Web Service Configuration Management Model

The relations between configuration items also need systemic management, most of them are dependencies of various kinds. The version evolvement of certain component will make the components invoking its services directly or indirectly evolve in turn. The whole historical information in the dynamic configuration process is stored in the configuration information library (Figure 6). A service item of certain version is composed of components of certain versions from the bottom up. Therefore according to the history of version evolvement, the dynamic configuration information of service items can be traced and service items can smoothly evolve or roll back.

Consistency control of the evolvement of configuration items should be performed. For example, the tool can use reflection to check the downward compatibility of new versions of components. This can guarantee that the interfaces referred by other components are still available in the new version. On the other hand the service items, which are configuration items of the highest abstract level, determine the versions of all the components involved directly or indirectly in the service. So it is possible that version conflicts exist between several service items. For example, two service items may have different version demands for the same component, then this is a configuration containing conflicts. The solution can be that a service item adopts another version or imports new component to replace the conflicting component. It should be illuminated that the version of a service item is determined directly by the wrapping class which the method belongs to. It is the wrapping component that is the object of configuration management.

4.5 Dynamic Service Configuration and UDDI Registry

Web services provided by other servers are difficult to be involved in the service management, because the versions of external services can hardly be managed under local control. The enterprise private UDDI registry can then act as a coordinator of the servers. When publishing services each server should register information about the services on the UDDI registry, such as involved classes, methods, parameters and the versions. The function of the UDDI registry should be extended to provide additional coordinating service. When a server needs to invoke services of others, the configuration administrator should register this inter-server service requirement on the UDDI registry by using service configuration management tool. In this way when a server registers a service version evolvement the registry can inform those servers invoking this changed service. Thus the scope of service configuration management is extended and the entire EAI system can highly cooperate with each other.

5 Summary and Conclusions

In this paper, we introduce some concepts in SCM, and present the service item based authority control and the dynamic service configuration management architecture. In such EAI system each integration unit represents more coordination and EAI is implemented by services exchanges between various servers. The unified authentication is performed on authentication server, and each web server constructs its own integrated authority control system under the unified role definition. Then the authority control can be performed at the method level and parameter level. At the same time, the publishing of web services will be maintained under systemic configuration management. Certain versions of components involved in exposed services compose the various service items of corresponding versions, which can be invoked through the unified service interface.

Such web service architecture makes a high request for the interaction of integration units and meets the needs of the EAI within enterprises better.

The construction of the entire web service system needs the support of tools, including the SCM tool, the web services configuration management tool and the service construction tool. [2] presents a web exposer tool which can generate web services on existing business objects. In our future work we will research on these support tools. One of our research teams has developed a diverse granularity SCM tool [6]. We will extend support interfaces on the basis of the work and make the SCM tool integrate seamlessly with the future web service configuration management tool. Integration with the enterprise component library is also a significant orientation. If enterprise component library, SCM tool and web service management can be integrated seamlessly, it is out of question that the resource management of the enterprise can be promoted greatly and the software reuse can exert greater effect.

References

1. Litoiu, M.. Migrating to Web services - latency and scalability, Web Site Evolution, 2002.Proceedings. Fourth International Workshop on , 2 Oct. 2002
2. Nicoloudis, N., Mingins, C.. XML Web services automation: a software engineering a proach, Software Engineering Conference, 2002. Ninth Asia-Pacific , 4-6 Dec. 2002
3. Baldwin, A., Shiu, S., Mont, M.C.. Trust services: a framework for service-based solutions,Computer Software and Applications Conference, 2002. Proceedings. 26th Annual International , 26-29 Aug. 2002

4. Song Zhiqiang, Chen Huaichu, Shen Xichen. An Uniform Authentication Architecture in Campus Network and an Implementation of Application Roaming Based on the Architecture, COMPUTER ENGINEERING AND APPLICATIONS, 2002Vol.38No.20
5. Software Engineering Lab, Fudan University. WINGCM technology report
6. Ke Liping, Zhao Wenyun, Zhang Zhi. R&D on Process-Based Software Configuration Management, COMPUTER ENGINEERING, 2003 Vol.29 No.5

GridBR: The Challenge of Grid Computing

S.R.R. Costa[1], L.G. Neves[1], F. Ayres[1], C.E. Mendonça[1], R.S.N. de Bragança[1], F. Gandour[2], L.V. Ferreira[3], M.C.A. Costa[3], and N.F.F. Ebecken[3]

[1] PETROBRAS Research and Development Center,
Av. Hum, Quadra 7, Cidade Universitária, Ilha do Fundão,
21949-900 Rio de Janeiro, RJ, Brazil
{scosta,luisgustavo,fabricio.FPLF,cem,braganca}@petrobras.com.br

[2] IBM Brazil,
Av. Pasteur, 138/146, 22296-900 Rio de Janeiro, RJ, Brazil
fgandour@br.ibm.com

[3] COPPE, Federal University of Rio de Janeiro,
P.O.Box 68516, 21945-970 Rio de Janeiro, RJ, Brazil
lvalente@coep.ufrj.br, myrian@nacad.ufrj.br, nelson@ntt.ufrj.br

Abstract. The use of grid computing technology is being boosted in last years by the growing demand of low cost computing resources and idle computing capacity in collaborative research and development environments. GridBR is a PETROBRAS project done with the collaboration of COPPE/UFRJ and IBM Brazil partnership. This project aims at grid computing technology in the information technology strategy of PETROBRAS Research and Development Center (CENPES). The present environment comprises a heterogeneous mix of architectures and operating systems with AIX IBM and Linux workstations providing the required support for collaborative execution of applications. The results of a genetic algorithm optimization application are presented as an example of how to take advantage of the existing grid computing infrastructure at PETROBRAS.

1 Introduction

Nowadays, high performance computing faces the growing need of computational and storage resources. The performance growth of different architecture machines compared with network bandwidth growth shows an uneven scenario that directly affects efficient use of data center resources [1]. The increasing complexity of scientific computing problems leads to an explosive demand for computational resources, sometimes rendering isolated projects planning unfeasible. Grid computing technology allows a more rational use and conscious planning of available resources. Integration of geographically dispersed systems and heterogeneous platforms becomes another great benefit. The resources offering in a transparent way to users releases them from the overhead of having to know specific features of execution environments.

The GridBR pilot project was proposed to fulfill an increasing demand at PETROBRAS for low cost computing resources for scientific purposes. The most

M. Li et al. (Eds.): GCC 2003, LNCS 3032, pp. 601–607, 2004.

cost effective solution is to take advantage of the company working schedule, which provides a huge amount of idle computing resources, since most of the computers tends to be idle every day from 5:00pm to 6:00am, and on the weekends. The primary goal of GridBR is to take advantage of this idle computing capacity and the grid computing technology is the natural solution to this problem.

CENPES has various high performance computing environments: an IBM pSeries 690 (Regatta), an IBM RS/6000 SP, several workstations (RISC and Intel), some high performance Intel clusters with Linux operating system, and a high capacity centralized storage system, with SAN and NAS solutions. These resources are dispersed across many departments and have different administration policies. We believe that GridBR environment implementation will make possible rational integration and use of these resources, preserving their peculiarities and administration policies.

In order to demonstrate the potential of this technology a grid demonstrating environment was placed and some tests were implemented.

There are many applications at PETROBRAS which are suitable for execution in a grid environment, like seismic modeling and imaging, basin modeling, seismic interpretation, engineering design optimization and scientific visualization. Some of them cannot be presented because of company security policies. One application, with encouraging results, is a parallel genetic algorithm optimization program. This paper is divided as follows: the grid demonstration environment is presented in section 2; section 3 describes an application adapted for execution and some results; conclusions are discussed in section 4.

2 The GridBR Environment

A grid is a collection of shared computing resources that work in a collaborative environment, where some resources may be available to all users on the grid and have access restrictions to other users. In this context, the word resource has a quite general meaning. It can designate, for example, a computer program, a service or a hardware device. The GridBR project is being carried out since April 2003 by PETROBRAS inside its Research and Development Center with collaboration of COPPE/UFRJ and IBM partnership. A workshop has been organized in order to demonstrate the results obtained in its initial phase. Fortunately, some users not formerly engaged to the project showed interest in adding resources to the grid and porting their applications to the environment. The project aims at implementing a fully functional grid environment within the current year.

The project uses the Globus Toolkit available at Globus Project site [2,3, 4]. The grid demonstration environment available so far consists of two IBM RS6000 RISC workstations running IBM AIX 5.1, two workstations running Red Hat Linux 7.3 and 8.0 and a virtual machine, running Red Hat Linux 7.3 built in the Linux workstation named SPIDER, providing a heterogeneous grid environment for GridBR. The scheme of this environment is depicted in Figure 1.

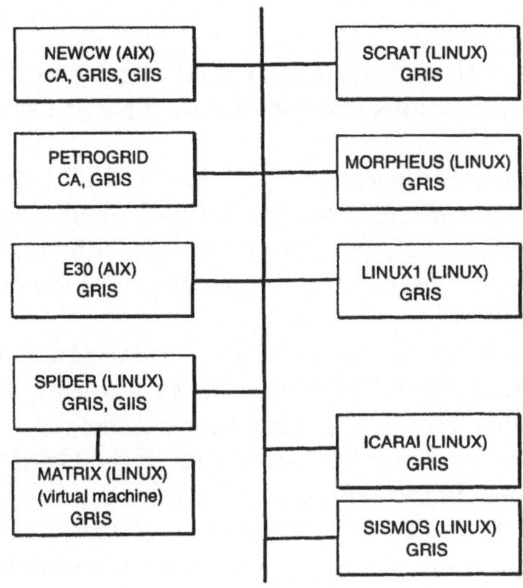

Fig. 1. Grid demonstration environment available at CENPES.

2.1 Certificate Authority

The IBM workstation NEWCW is the certificate authority (CA) of the grid. It is an IBM RS6000 F80 workstation with two processors running IBM AIX 5.1 and is located at CENPES data center, which comprises the security requirements that a CA demands. The CA software used in this present phase is the Simple CA, provided by Globus, and it is being used only for the purposes of test and demonstration.

2.2 IBM Grid Toolbox

The grid software used is the IBM Grid Toolbox [5]. The grid toolbox provided by IBM consists of the Globus Toolkit 2.2.4, with installation scripts that automate installation and configuration for IBM AIX 5.1 and RPM packages for Red Hat Linux.

The environment so far described does not comprise with the demands of a grid production environment, but is capable of getting information of all the grid resources and computing tasks are submitted and executed successfully on the grid. Data management is straightforward through the grid using the GASS API, which allows retrieving through the grid the output of applications running on remote resources.

We are now beginning the phase of adding functionality as well as resources to the existing grid environment; the MDS services have just been configured, MPI support will also be implemented soon and by November a fully functional grid environment will be available at CENPES.

2.3 Grid Portal

The GridBR counts with a utility widely used in grids worldwide and in systems that need easy submission jobs from anywhere. This utility is known as GridPort [6].

The GridPort is a set of packages developed to build and customize a portal, making grid technology usage more attractive to end users. It will provide an easy way to use the Globus Software features for job submission, data and file manipulation, as well as monitoring the performance status in a lot of sites. All of this is done via "WEB".

The GridPort relies on a client/server infrastructure. On server side, data pages are created with Perl language and its libraries. On client side a web browser with JavaScript support is used to view the pages.

Some of the most important characteristics of the GridPort are: it is based on Globus security infrastructure and on the advanced public key (PKI) structure; it is a flexible and customizable environment written in PERL/CGI language; supports "single-login" among many portals; uses the interactive Globus software environment.

3 Genetic Algorithm Application

The outstanding potential of the GridBR environment can be demonstrated using the GAlua software. GAlua is a prototype of genetic algorithm optimization multipurpose library. It includes several facilities for multiobjective optimization and supports scientific and business applications. Program code was written in Lua 5.0 [7] and implements a simple GA code based in a real chromosome. Lua is an interpreted programming language developed by Tecgraf, PUC-Rio.

A genetic algorithm (GA) [8] is a search procedure that optimizes some objective function by maintaining a population of candidate solutions (individuals) and employing operations (crossover and mutation) inspired by genetics to generate a new population from the previous one.

The genetic operators available are: blend crossover, uniform crossover, creep mutation and random mutation. The program implements both roulette and tournament selection.

The ranking schemas available are linear scaling, linear ranking and exponential ranking. Different sizes among the first population and the others are possible. GAlua implementation has three possible termination criteria:

- Minimum diversity value reached;
- Desired objective value reached;
- Maximum number of generations reached.

The problem we are interested to solve is the maximization of the function,

$$F(x,y) = (1-y^2)(2-x^2-x^4)\cos(3\pi x)\cos(2\pi y), \tag{1}$$

subject to the following constraints:

$$-1 \leq x \leq 1$$
$$-1 \leq y \leq 1.$$

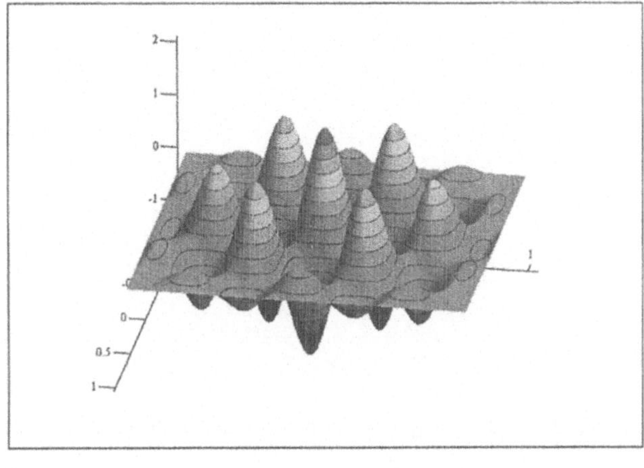

Fig. 2. Graphic of the objective function (1).

Figure 2 shows the graphic of the function (1). The expected solution of this problem is $x = 0$, $y = 0$ and the corresponding value of the objective function is $F(x, y) = 2$.

This example used five machines on the grid with one process per machine. There is a master process that controls the genetic algorithm process and the individuals distribution for objective function evaluation in the other processes.

The initial population has 30 individuals and the others have only 10. The execution stopped at generation 178 when the specified objective value of 2 was reached. Figures 3 to 5a) show a sequence of populations over the objective function contour plot to show the program behavior. Figure 5b) shows a graph with the objective values evolution through generations.

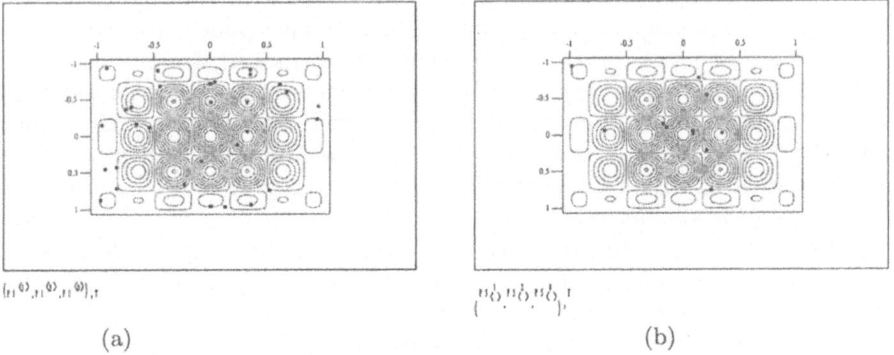

(a) (b)

Fig. 3. a) Initial population; b) Fifth generation.

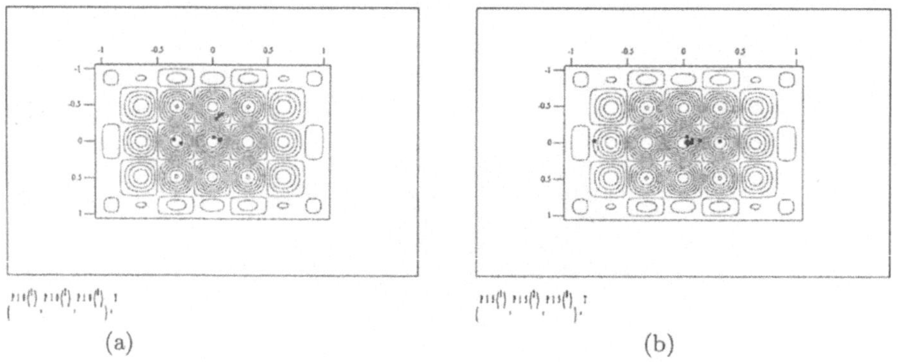

(a) (b)

Fig. 4. a) Tenth generation; b) Fifteenth generation.

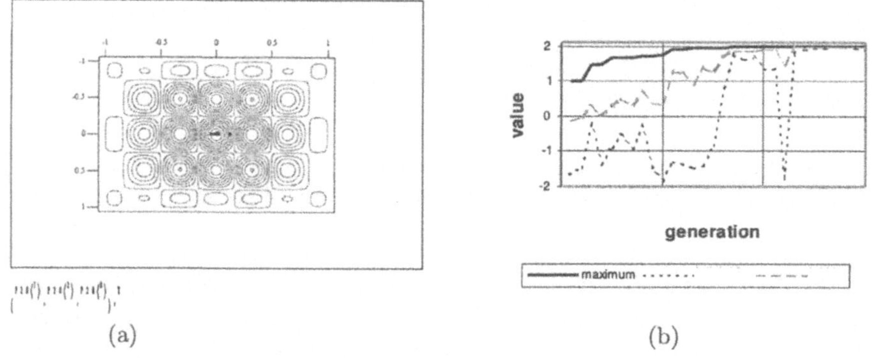

(a) (b)

Fig. 5. a) Twentieth generation; b) Objective value evolution.

4 Concluding Remarks

The GridBR pilot project intends to raise issues about implementation and use of the grid computing technology for CENPES. This paper covered the main topics for construction of an environment that demonstrates the potential of this technology. The results obtained so far have encouraged us to extend the scope of the environment beyond CENPES to other departments of the company and to try to implement a Data Grid based on the availability of the centralized storage system of CENPES. Now, the words are integration, collaboration and rational use of available resources.

Essentially, we can say that the grid model came to stay. At least for one reason: the concept allows a better return on the IT investments. However, it is fair to suppose that good and bad experiences will come up. As usual in the IT environment, the grid model became a very fashionable solution and there may be attempts to build a grid without checking the basic premises to support this endeavor. Those are the cases where bad results may emerge. By the other hand, we are convinced that if the set of rules and recommendations proposed by the creators of the grid concept are followed, the benefits of adopting the model are evident and tangible, even for the low-end user at the remotest workstation in any net. After a period of internal stabilization in each experience, we envision also the perspective of having grids connected between them, making the dream of the theoretical ExtraGrid come true. Again, we will try it with the same care and attention we have done so far.

References

1. I. Foster and C. Kesselman. The Grid: Blueprint for a New Computing Infrastructure. Morgan Kaufmann Publishers, Inc. San Francisco, CA, 1999.
2. The Globus Project. Globus Toolkit. http://www-unix.globus.org/toolkit
3. L. Ferreira et al.. Introduction to Grid Computing with Globus. IBM Redbooks, IBM Corp., 2002.
4. I. Foster, C. Kesselman, S. Tuecke. The Anatomy of the Grid: Enabling Scalable Virtual Organizations. International J. Supercomputer Applications, 15(3), 2001. http://www.globus.org/research/papers.html
5. IBM Grid Toolbox. Grid Toolbox Administration Guide. IBM Corp., 2003. http://www.alphaworks.ibm.com/tech/gridtoolbox
6. GridPort. GridPort Toolkit. http://gridport.npaci.edu.
7. The Programming Language Lua. Lua 5.0 Reference Manual. http://www.lua.org
8. D. E. Goldberg. Genetic Algorithm in Search, Optimization and Machine Learning. Addison-Wesley Publishing Company, Inc., 1989.

Autonomous Distributed Service System: Basic Concepts and Evaluation

H. Farooq Ahmad[1], Kashif Iqbal[2], Hiroki Suguri[1], and Arshad Ali[2]

[1]Communication Technologies
2-15-28 Omachi, Aoba-ku, Sendai, 980-0804 Japan
{farooq, suguri}@comtec.co.jp
[2]National University of Sciences and Technology
NUST Institute of Information Technology
Chaklala Scheme III, Rawalpindi, Pakistan
{kashif.iqbal, arshad.ali}@niit.edu.pk

Abstract. In both e-business and e-science, we often need to integrate services across distributed, heterogeneous, dynamic "virtual organizations" formed from the disparate resources within a single enterprise and/or from external resource sharing and service provider relationships. This integration is technically challenging because of the need to achieve various levels of quality of service (QoS) when running on top of different native platforms and under dynamic workload conditions. We present an *Autonomous Distributed Service System Architecture* that addresses these challenges. Building on concepts and technologies from the Semantic Web, Multi-Agent Systems, Grid and Web services communities, this architecture put together a proposition made to cope with heterogeneous and continuously changing needs of information processing, service provision and utilization in dynamically evolving environment to meet these requirements. Autonomous Distributed Services Architecture also define agents' capabilities in terms of Web services Description Language (WSDL), so that agents can describe and advertise themselves in UDDI (Universal Description Discovery & Integration) as and when required.

1 Introduction

Computers are fulfilling an increasingly diversified set of tasks in our society. The convergence of computers and telecommunication has enhanced the processing and transmission of information from one location to other on the globe. Many researchers agree that information age is rapidly replacing industrial era.

Distributed system is the backbone of information services on the Internet [4]. However, rapidly evolving and highly diversified world of information services requires huge information processing capacity and service provision on the Internet time scale. But the state of the art of distributed systems is human dominated administered, which cannot meet Internet time scale and quality of service for e-commerce. A critical prerequisite for distributed system technology to comply with the new challenge is that it must be completely self-tuning with autonomous adaptation to evolving work

M. Li et al. (Eds.): GCC 2003, LNCS 3032, pp. 608–615, 2004.

load with "zero" human administration. Clearly applications, executing on behalf of providers and users, in such an environment have the following requirements [6]:

- Components that coordinate through negotiation in highly complex and dynamic environment
- Resource availability on supply demand basis
- Visibility of services on large and public scale

As we know that the Internet was originally designed to share the information between a small numbers of users, with no quality of service requirements. However, due to the emergence of e-commerce, there is urgent need to change fundamental philosophy of the underlying system. Information services have become mission critical as heavy loss may result if the system does not provide required functionality and resources to achieve QoS under changing conditions, such as changing workload. The system needs to provide guaranteed quality of services at application levels, not at low level like guaranteed packet delivery [4]. There are different concerns in quality of service, such as timeliness, reliability, and fault tolerance for information service utilization and provision. A system is called a high-assurance system, when heterogeneous and changing requirement levels of QoS are satisfied [9]. In addition to quality of service, we identify that users have two more basic views of customization and situation regarding information services utilization but these do not exist on the current information service systems as well. Consequently, using information services on the Internet is frustrating experience for most of the users. Many information services on the Internet return poor results- inconsistent, arbitrarily inaccurate or completely irrelevant data or the performance is so poor that the whole service becomes useless [5]. We conclude that current information service systems on the Internet do not provide guaranteed quality of services, customization and situation based information services. There is urgent need for new models for information services for e-commerce in the Internet. If the research community fails to provide necessary technology and framework, the success of e-commerce may be delayed or even may become questionable.

This fosters an urgent need to design an information service system with high-assurance that provides information services to meet the above-mentioned requirements. Autonomous distributed service system is a proposition made to cope with heterogeneous and continuously changing needs of information processing, service provision and utilization in dynamically evolving environment to meet these requirements. The proposed distributed system architecture is based on synergy of software agents integrated with Web services and Grid computing to bring high-assurance of services through supply-demand basis. When demand of services change due to change in users' requirement, the system dynamically adapts to achieve the same QoS for all users.

The remainder of the paper is organized as follows. The next section presents the concept of autonomous distributed service system and introduces architecture we have developed for it. This section also includes existing technologies used in the proposed system. Description of the prototype implementation and evaluation of the proposed system is detailed in section 3. The last section draws conclusions.

2 Autonomous Distributed Services System

2.1 Concept

The main concern of the information service system in the past has been to efficiently retrieve from enormous repositories the relevant information for a particular request [7][8]. Due to the emergence of mission critical applications, such as e-commerce, the main focus of our research on information service system is to provide high-assurance in information services to satisfy users' and providers' requirements as outlined in the previous section. We abstract the system based on the following two concepts:

- Resources: The system can be viewed as a collection of resources. Resources may be physical, such as hardware, networks, and logical resources such as software, a piece of document and so on.
- Services: Resources either individually or in combination of more than one resources offer services.

In the system, we identify two co-existing active entities:

- Service Provider (SP) is the provider of services as well as resources as resources are consumed as a service.
- User is the consumer of services and resources.

Service provider and user may be human, an organization or a software component, which may posses negotiating capabilities.

In order to provide high-assurance of services in dynamically changing environment, the system needs to assure functional as well as non-functional requirements i.e. QoS in continuously evolving environment of the system. The abstraction of the system based on resources and services, and conceptualizing providers and users as actors provides the foundation to meet the requirements of autonomous distributed service system as will be made clear in the next section on the system architecture.

2.2 System Architecture

The system architecture approach attempts to identify key principles and layers of abstractions for interactions between actors and resources to provide services on supply demand basis to meet requirements. The system realization strategy builds on and reuses as much of the architectural foundations in related standards and emerging technologies as possible.

Resource virtualization is the fundamental tenet that leads toward sharing of resources on supply demand basis. Providers willing to share resources use mechanisms to publish them along with the terms of usage, and users discover the required resources using some mechanism. Resources can be aggregated dynamically to complete a task to provide a service. Alternatively the task may be executed in distributed way on some resources, and then integrated into a single service, if required. Based on this philosophy, the architecture of the proposed system is shown in figure 1.

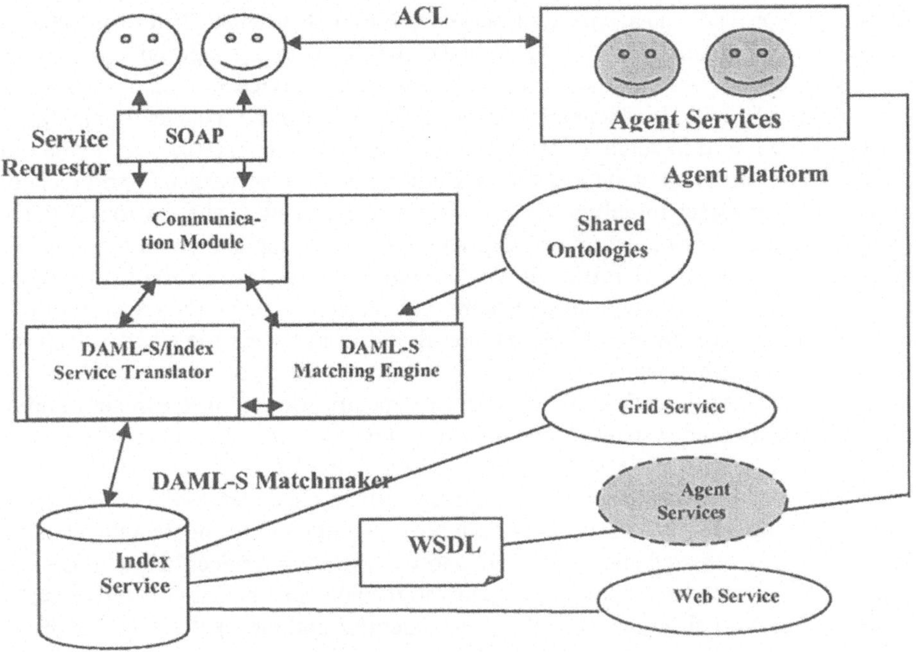

Fig. 1. Autonomous Distributed Service System Architecture

We have sought related areas that could provide concepts, technology, and standards to reuse or adapt to autonomous distributed service systems' realization. Web services, Grid computing, and software agents provides useful basis for it.

2.2.1 Web Services

Web services are emerging as a standard for Web-based technology for exchanging information [6]. Web services are modular, self-describing, self-contained applications that are accessible over the Internet. Based on open standards, Web services enable to build Web-based applications using any platform, object model, and programming language that is required for the application. Web services are loosely coupled software components that use Internet protocols to describe, publish, discover, and invoke each other. They can dynamically locate and interact with other Web services on the Internet to build complex machine-to-machine programmatic services. These services can be inspected using Web Services Inspection Language. Web Services Description Language (WSDL) is used to describe the services in the well-structured manner. The Simple Object Access Protocol (SOAP) defines communitions protocol between the components. The semantic meaning issues of the services may be addressed by the Semantic Web initiative.

2.2.2 Grid

The Open Grid Services Architecture (OGSA), an enhanced form of GRID [10], has been proposed as an enabling infrastructure for systems and applications that require the integration and management of services within distributed, heterogeneous, dynamic "virtual organizations" [11]. Whether confined to a single enterprise or extending to encompass external resource sharing and service provider relationships, service integration and management in these contexts can be technically challenging because of the need to achieve various end-to-end quality of service (QoS) when running on top of different native platforms. Building on Web services and grid technologies, OGSA proposes to define a core Grid service semantics and, on top of this, an integrated set of service definitions that address critical application and system management concerns. The purposes of this definition process are twofold: first to simplify the creation of secure, robust systems and second to enable the creation of interoperable, portable, and reusable components and systems via the standardization of key interfaces and behaviors.

It is important to mention that grid service specification defines essential building blocks for distributed systems; it certainly does not define all elements that arise when creating large-scale interoperable systems. There is need to address a wide variety of other issues, both fundamental and domain-specific to create large-scale open services and applications. For example, how to establish identity and negotiate authentication? How is policy expressed and negotiated? How to discover services? How to negotiate and monitor service level agreements? How to manage membership of, and communication within, virtual organizations? How to monitor and manage collections of services, and other related issues [11]. Without appropriate technology and standardization in these areas, it is hard to build large-scale interoperable systems.

2.2.3 Software Agents

Agents have come a long way from research to industrial applications, but still it is one of the most difficult tasks to have a concrete definition of agent. However, from the viewpoint of clarification we define agent as a computer system, situated in an environment that acts on behalf of its user, in an autonomous way, to achieve its objectives. Agent architecture analyzes agents as independent reactive/proactive entities. Agent architecture conceptualizes agents as being made of perception, action, and reasoning components. The perception component feeds the reasoning component, which governs the agents' actions, including what to perceive next. Agent system architecture analyzes agents as interacting service provider/consumer entities. System architectures facilitate agent operations and interactions under environmental constraints, and allow them to take advantage of available services and facilities. Agent infrastructure provides regulations that agents follow to communicate and to understand each other, thereby enabling knowledge sharing. Agent infrastructures mostly deal with the communication among agents based on a communication language using common ontological system.

Now we consider multi-agent system. As seen from DAI, a multi-agent system is a loosely coupled network of problem-solver entities that work together to find answers to problems that are beyond the individual capabilities or knowledge of each entity [14]. In broader sense, the term multi-agent system has been given a more general meaning, and it is now used for all types of systems composed of multiple autonomous components showing the following characteristics [13]:

- Each component has partial capabilities to perform a task
- No global system control; subsystems are autonomous
- Actors, resources and services are decentralized

2.2.4 Synergy of the Technologies

The World Wide Web is evolving toward machine-readable infrastructure for sharing knowledge among human as well as machines. Application designers that are building systems that harness web services are facing many of the same issues that designers of agent systems have been tackling since last 10 years. We believe that agents have much to offer in overcoming some of the inherent difficulties when dealing with complex and dynamic environment. As pointed out in the introduction that such environment requires autonomous and negotiating components, and agents can offer these capabilities. Agents are able to play at run-time where each component can become commodity. Agents will be able to make decision at run to which resources and/or service to use for particular task.

An open system is one in which the structure of the system itself is capable of dynamically changing. The characteristics of such a system are that its components and resources are not known in advance, can change over time, and may be highly heterogeneous. The best-known example of a highly open software environment is the Internet, and the Grid will be much more an open system than the Internet. The functionality is almost certain to require techniques based on negotiation or cooperation, which lie very firmly in the domain of agent system. Interaction between computer and user must become an equal partnership. The machine should not just act as a dumb receptor of task descriptions, but should cooperate with the user to achieve their goal. These considerations give rise to the idea of an agent acting as an expert assistant or delegate with respect to some application, knowledgeable about both the application itself and the user, and capable of acting with the user in order to achieve the user's goals.

The above discussion relates agents to web services and grid computing environment. Similarly, we can argue that Grid need web services to publish resources and service for users. Our vision of the integration of agents with web service and Grid computing is to lay foundation for self-regulating system, namely autonomous distributed service system for e-business realization.

3 Prototype Implementation

Initially the objective of the research work was integration of Web service with agent but there exists an inherent gap between the two (i.e. web services use SOAP as a communication protocol while agents send ACL messages for communication). Two alternatives can be used to bridge this gap. Firstly, SOAP based Web services calls can be implemented in the client agent in order to invoke a Web service (see figure 1). But this approach is static, as it restricts the use of a particular client agent to a certain

Web service only. Secondly, a wrapper in the form of Web service proxy agent can be created for each Web service [9].

The next plan was to integrate Grid service to an agent: Grid services built on Web services standards (SOAP, GWSDL based on WSDL etc.) show many improvements over Web services. In order to integrate agents with a Grid service, a proxy agent approach has been implemented, that serves as a wrapper to mask the heterogeneity between the two, as was done with Web services.

In carrying out above experiments, we observe that using a wrapper for each Web service to make it visible in agent world is neither scalable nor efficient and is static as well. So, there arises a need of incorporating the use of ontologies for services in both Web and Grid environments, such as DAML-S to automate service usage (Discovery, Invocation, Monitoring etc.) with the help of agents. We are now in the phase of incorporating this concept in our system.

The results based on the prototype implementation of the system are given below:

1. WSDL (and GWSDL) are better than interface languages (such as Java or IDL) as they are semantically rich and offer more control.
2. WSDL is not rich enough to specify the semantics of the composition or of the interaction protocol needed for composition. In contrast to WSDL, DAML-S, rather than describing Web services in terms of their ports or the messages that they receive, it describes the capabilities of Web services in terms of the abstract function that they provide, their Process Model and the Grounding, which describes how services interact. So, WSDL and DAML-S are complementary to each other: DAML-S provides the abstract information about composition of operations and information exchange, while WSDL describes how such abstract information is mapped into actual messages.
3. Service Data is a structured collection of information that can be associated to a Grid Service or a Web Service; it facilitates the process of service discovery by providing query support over it by the client. But while automating the process of service discovery by entities like software agents, this service data cannot be mapped and shared between two negotiating agents to provide context matching. So, ontologies should be used to define service characteristics like that of DAML-S profile which provides both provenance and non-functional information about a service.

4 Conclusions

This paper has discussed the requirements for the emerging applications such as e-commerce. In order to meet the challenges of the new applications, the thesis outlines that these applications requires huge information processing capacity and service provision on the Internet time scale. The manuscript emphasizes the concept of high-assurance, which is achieved when heterogeneous and changing requirement levels of QoS are satisfied. Autonomous distributed service system is a proposition made to cope with heterogeneous and continuously changing needs of information processing, service provision and utilization in dynamically evolving environment to meet these requirements. Prototype implementation has been carried out as a proof of the effectiveness of the proposed architecture. Currently, we are working on the application in the domain of bioinformatics to show the effectiveness of the proposed system.

References

1. Lotfi Maherzi, "World Communication Report: The media and the challenge of new technologies", UNESCO Publishing (1997).
2. Richard T. Watson, "Data Management: An organizational perspective", John Wiley & Sons, Inc. (1996).
3. Mahesh S. Raisinghani, "Electronic Commerce at the Dawn of Third Millenium", Idea Group Publishing, (2000).
4. Gerhard Weikum, "The Web in 2010: Challenges and Opportunities for Database research", Informatics 10 Years Back, 10 Years Ahead, Springer LNCS2000.
5. Gerhard Weikum, "Towards Guaranteed Quality and Dependability of Information Services(invited keynote)", 8th German Conference on Databases in Office, Engineering, and Scientific Applications, (1999)
6. M. Milenkovic, Scot H. Robinson, Rob C. Knauerhase, D. Barkai, S. Garg, V. Tewari, Todd A. Aderson, M. Bowman, "Toward Internet Distributed Computing", IEEE Computer, vol.36, no.5, pp.38-46, (2003).
7. Venkat N. Gudivada et al, "Information retrieval on the World Wide Web", IEEE Internet Computing, vol.1, no.5, pp. 58-68, 1997.
8. Wolfgang Theilmann and Kurt Rothermel, "Domain Experts for information retrieval in the world wide web", Lecture Notes in Artificial Intelligence 1435, Springer-Verlag, pp.216-227, (1998).
9. I-Ling et al , "Toward Integrated Methods for High-Assurance Systems", IEEE Computer, vol. 31, no. 4, pp.32-34, 1998.
10. Global Grid Forum http://www.gridforum.org/
11. Foster, I., Kesselman, C., Nick, J. and Tueske, S., "The Physiology of the Grid: An Open Grid Services Architecture for Distributed Systems Integration", Globus, Project, www.globus.org/research/papers/ogsa.pdf (2002).
12. Paton, N.W., Atkinson, M.P., Dialani, V. Pearson, D. Storey, T. and Watson, P. "Database Access and Integration of Services on the Grid", UK National eScince Center, www.nesc.ac.uk , (2002).
13. Nicholas R. Jennings, Katia Sycra, Michael Wooldbridge, "A Roadmap of Agent Research and Development", Autonomous Agents and Multi-Agent Systems, pp.275-306, Kluwer Academic Publisher, Boston, (1998).
14. Durfee, E.H., Lesser, V.R. and Corkill, D.D. "Trends in Cooperative Distributed Problem Solving", IEEE Transactions on Knowledge and Data Engineering, pp. 63-83, (1989).
15. K. Mori, "Autonomous Decentralized Systems: Concept, Data Field Architecture and Future Trends", Proc. of the first International Symposium on ADS (ISADS93), IEEE, Kawasaki, Japan, pp.28-34, 1993.

ShanghaiGrid in Action: The First Stage Projects towards Digital City and City Grid[1]

Minglu Li, Hui Liu, Changjun Jiang, Weiqin Tong, Aoying Zhou, Yadong Gui, Hao Zhu, Shui Jiang, Ruonan Rao, Jian Cao, Qianni Deng, Qi Qian, and Wei Jin

Department of Computer Science and Engineering,
Shanghai Jiaotong University, 200030 Shanghai, China
{li-ml, liuhui@cs.sjtu.edu.cn}

Abstract. The nearest goal of ShanghaiGrid is to going to connect all supercomputers in this metropolis together to form a sharing environment for massive storage and grid computing. The first stage projects of ShanghaiGrid comprise four sub-projects, including 1) research on environment, protocols and standards of information gird infrastructure; 2) development of system software for information grid and establishment of four major grid nodes; 3) development of peer-to-peer based virtual research platform; 4) research on the application of grid based traffic-jam control and guidance. This paper introduces the background of ShanghaiGrid, provides a glimpse at features and challenges of its sub-projects, and summarizes the general goal of them.

1 Introduction

Grids offer us a new vision, infrastructure and trend for the coordinated resources sharing, problem solving and services orchestration in dynamic, multi-institutional virtual organizations [1]. It is a natural evolution of distributed computing and Internet computing for the large-scale science and engineering problems. Both academia and computer industry are regarding the development of grids as another chance to shuffle the current paradigm of Internet.

As a quick response to this worldwide technical tide, several grand fundamental research projects had been launched by Chinese government to face the challenges and capture the opportunities, such as, NHPCE (1999-2001), CNGrid (2002-2006), ChinaGrid (2002-2005), E-Science Grid (2002-2005), Spatial Information Grid (2001-2005), etc [2]. In parallel with these national grids, a city gird project to enhance the digitalizing of city, going by the name of ShanghaiGrid, is kicked off at the end of this year by the science and technology commission of Shanghai municipality.

[1] Supported by the National Grand Fundamental Research 973 Program of China (No.2002CB312002), the Grand Project (No.03dz15027) and Key Project (No.025115033) of the Science and Technology Commission of Shanghai Municipality.

M. Li et al. (Eds.): GCC 2003, LNCS 3032, pp. 616–623, 2004.

The rest of this paper is organized as follows. Section 2 presents the background of ShanghaiGrid. The general goal, fundamental features and main challenges of four sub-projects are discussed respectively in section 3. Section 4 concludes this paper.

2 Backgrounds on ShanghaiGrid

Shanghai is a municipality of eastern China at the mouth of the Yangtze River. Today, it has become the largest economic center and important port city in China, with a land area covering 6,340 square kilometers and a population of 16 million people. It is the entrepreneur city of 2010 Shanghai World Expo. The municipal government is working towards building Shanghai into a modern metropolis and into a world economic, financial, trading and shipping center by 2020. They have been always paying attention to the development and establishment of information industry and society. For example, the general secretary of the CPC Shanghai Committee, Mr. Cheng Liangyu had indicated: connecting all supercomputers in the municipality area to form a sharing environment for massive storage and grid computing. This indication could be regarded as activators for ShanghaiGrid.

The primary goal of ShanghaiGrid is to develop a set of system software for the information grid and establish an infrastructure for the grid-based applications. By means of flexible, secure, open standards sharing and coordinating of computational resources, data information and dedicated services among virtual organizations, this project will build an information grid tailored for the characteristics of Shanghai and support the typical application of grid based traffic-jam control and guidance. In order to achieve such a goal within two years, this project must act in accordance with OGSA and other de facto industry standards, and adopt the up-to-date research results of some related grant fundamental research projects, such as, NHPCE, CNGrid, ChinaGrid, etc.

The innovation of ShanghaiGrid could be expressed mainly in three aspects. In the perspective of technique, it is going to implement an information grid across the connectivity layer, resource layer, collective layer and application layer [1]. In the perspective of resource management, it is going to integrate current supercomputing power, dispersive information data and isolated applications together, and manage them as uniform services. This is a further and necessary step towards digital city and city grid. In the perspective of society functionality, it is going to leverage traditional service industry with effectiveness and inject immense add-value to all related custom-supplier chains.

The first stage projects of ShanghaiGrid have drawn the investment of ¥28 million. Participants are Shanghai Jiaotong University, Tongji University, Fudang University, Shanghai University, Shanghai Supercomputer Center, Shanghai Transportation Information Center, East China Institute of Computer Technology, IBM, Intel, etc.

3 Sub-Projects of ShanghaiGrid

The first stage projects of ShanghaiGrid comprises four sub-projects, including 1) research on environment, protocols and standards of information gird infrastructure (Sub-Project-I); 2) development of system software for information grid and establishment of four major grid nodes (Sub-Project-II); 3) development of peer-to-peer based virtual research platform (Sub-Project-III); 4) research on the application of grid based traffic-jam control and guidance (Sub-Project-IV). The detail information of them is discussed as follows.

3.1 Sub-Project-I

The goal of Sub-Project-I is to encapsulate available hardware, software and other resources of each organization into different Intra-Grid. Intra-Grid could be defined as connecting resources throughout whole campus or enterprise by campus network or intranet, and managing them as virtual services. For example, campus grid could be regarded as a concrete Intra-Grid [3].

The middleware to support Intra-Grid must possess two fundamental features. Firstly, it manages different resources without destroying their current autonomy and communicates with them with different 'dialects', i.e., protocols, API, primitives, etc. Secondly, it acts as the role of both services provider and services consumers in the information grid and speaks one common 'official language', i.e. SOAP.

Challenges of Sub-Project-I are:

- How to encapsulate different supercomputers, devices, data and software packages into virtual services?
- How to implement services management according to the OGSA at the Intra-Grid level?
- How to provide services and APIs tailored for the calling from system software for information gird? This point will be further explained in next section.
- How to propose certain protocols, standards and solutions for the standardization of building Intra-Grid?

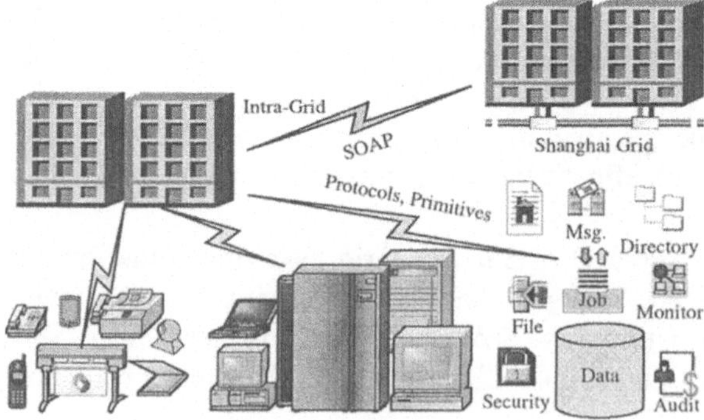

Fig. 1. Sub-Project-I is going to form several Intra-Grids. Each Intra-Grid comprises different supercomputers (e.g., SW-I, SUHPCS, IBM P690, IBM E1350, SGI Origin 3800, etc.), devices (e.g., GPS sensors, traffic surveillant, mobile phones, etc.), software packages (e.g., PBS, LFS, etc.) and other resources. Intra-Grid abstract different resources as virtual services

This project will form four major Intra-Grids, including Shanghai Jiaotong University, Tongji University, Shanghai University and Shanghai Supercomputer Center.

3.2 Sub-Project-II

The goal of Sub-Project-II is to provide a set of system software for the information grid and connect several major Intra-Grids as ShanghaiGrid. ShanghaiGrid is going to be a sophisticated container or component based hosting environment relied on different Intra-Grids within the metropolitan area. It must define not only programming model, programming language, developing tools, debugging tools, deploying tools, but also how an implementation of a grid service meets its obligations with respect to grid service semantics [4].

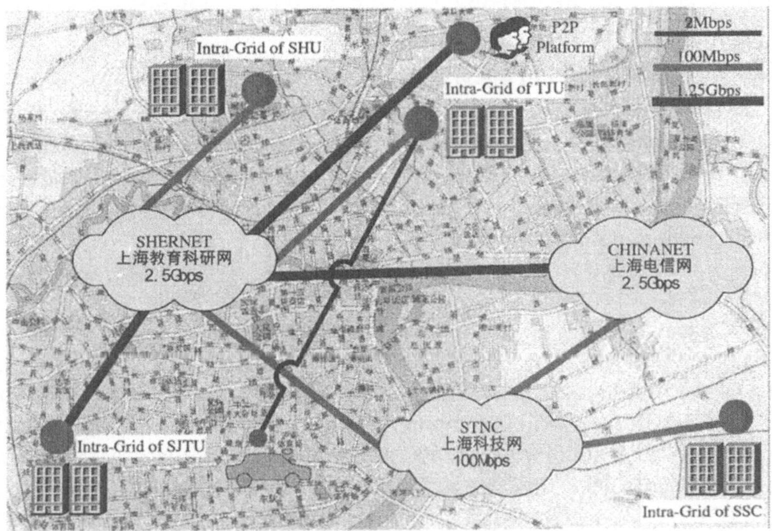

Fig. 2. ShanghaiGrid must connect several major Intra-Girds together to form a sophisticated hosting environment, which includes Shanghai Jiaotong University, Tongji University, Shanghai University and Shanghai Supercomputer Center. Other sites could be connected to some of the major nodes

As shown in Fig.2, in order to bring ShanghaiGrid into reality, we must connect major Intra-Grids located at Shanghai Jiaotong University, Tongji University, Shanghai University and Shanghai Supercomputer Center together to form a platform of information gird. Comparing with Intra-Grid, information grid could be regarded as Extra-Grid, whose direct building blocks are not resources but virtual services. If the clients want to explore the underlying resources warped in services directly, calling to operations, services, APIs of Intra-Grid must be performed transparently.

The middleware to support information grid must possess three fundamental features. Firstly, it connects some kinds of Intra-Grids. Secondly, it manages various kinds of virtual services directly. Thirdly, it communicates with various resources through the middleware of Intra-Grid transparently and hierarchically.

Modules or functionalities of system for gird must meet following challenges.

- How to manage services and resources in a feasible console?
- How to access and transfer different data with some uniform protocols?
- How to register, discover and locate different services and resources?
- How to monitor and diagnose the runtime status of services and resources?
- How to abstract and build a set of J2EE based components that could be easily reused?
- How to coordinate short and long term transactions within the grid environment?
- How to reserve services and resources in advance?
- How to negotiate a contract between the resources providers and consumers?
- How to implement accounting and payment services for the grid community?
- How to construct workflow level collaboration frameworks by integrating different services?
- How to keep the security in the grid environment?
- How to deploy and deliver the middleware for grid in a feasible solution?

These problems must be settled at both information grid level and Intra-Grid level. Therefore, the middleware for information grid and Intra-Grid must have compatible APIs, primitives and interface definitions, which could be bound together smoothly to provide certain complete functionality.

3.3 Sub-Project-III

The goal of Sub-Project-III is to development a peer-to-peer based virtual research platform, which will offer grid community a uniform cooperation, communication and research environment. It comprises some more effective alternatives to several client-server applications, such as P2P based file system, instant messaging, etc.

Such a P2P based virtual research platform must possess one fundamental feature. That is, the functionalities of each application remain the same except that the end users do not interact with TCP/IP.

Challenges of the P2P based virtual platform are:

- How to manage small granularity data in the P2P network, such as fields or data items in database?
- How to search different information with P2P techniques?
- How to transfer messages instantly and securely?
- How to share information with P2P techniques?
- How to collect and publish information of certain subjects automatically in the P2P network?

Because P2P techniques promise to improve the effectiveness of network performance and reinforce the techniques of gird, this sub-project is going to keep an eye on the application and advancing in this field.

3.4 Sub-Project-IV

The goal of Sub-Project-IV is to provide a typical application of traffic-jam control and guidance that could be run on ShanghaiGrid. Such an application is driven by the real demands from citizens of Shanghai. Obviously, the information of traffic status is distributed, dynamic, local autonomy and holistic mutuality, which could be naturally mapped onto information grid. By means of this kind of application, traffics status could be monitored, forecasted, displayed, subscribed, simulated and stored. Of course, they could be used to choose optimal routing in future.

The application of grid based traffic-jam guidance and control must possess three fundamental features. Firstly, the information data gathered are distributed, real-time and massive. Secondly, the computation of the city traffic mathematical model is complicated. Thirdly, the demand on traffic information may be quite different and must be customized.

Challenges of the application of grid based traffic-jam guidance and control are:

- How to propose and implement an OGSA based specification for traffic-jam guidance and control?
- How to collect, transfer, store, syncretise traffic information data in the grid environment?
- How to model the traffic status and traffic-jam accurately, dynamically, adaptively and in time?
- How to analyze and forecast traffic status from the massive information data?
- How to simulate traffic status accurately for the decision-making of government?
- How to provide traffic information on demand services and publish traffic status to community, vehicles and passenger?

Typical GUIs of the application of traffic-jam guidance and control are shown in Fig.3 and Fig.4. The former is a simulation picture and the latter shows current traffic-jam status.

Most importantly, the hosting environment of this application is information grid.

4 Summary

The nearest goal of ShanghaiGrid is going to connect supercomputers in this metropolis together to form a sharing environment for massive storage and grid computing. Its first stage projects have the duration of two years, which started at November 2003 and will end at October 2005.

The first stage projects of ShanghaiGrid comprise four sub-projects. Nowadays, four research groups are working cooperatively to sweep all technical obstacles in the way towards digital city and city grid. We hope the hardworking of these research groups and the intelligence of whole grid communities would bring ShanghaiGrid into reality as quickly as possible.

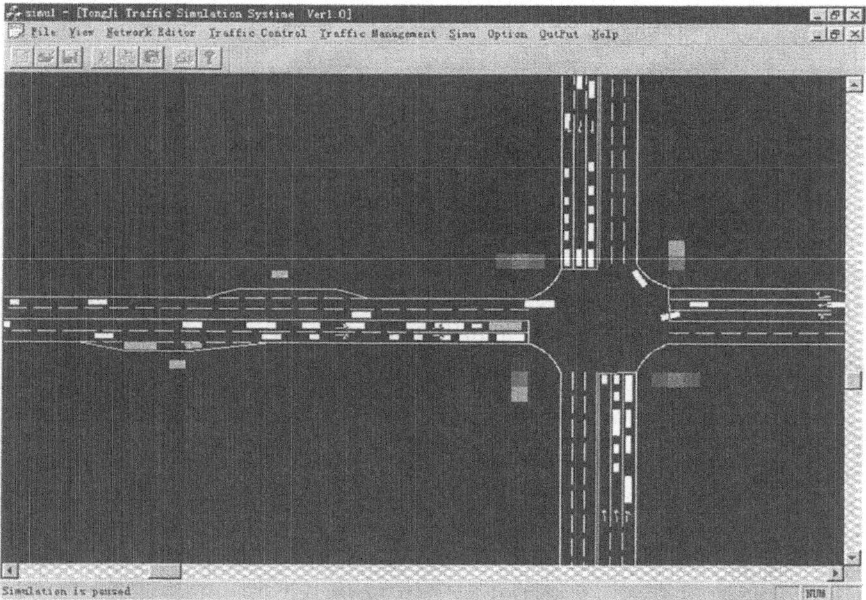

Fig. 3. This GUI simulates the traffic status in the crossroad. Road surface, traffic lights, and vehicles flows are shown in the scene

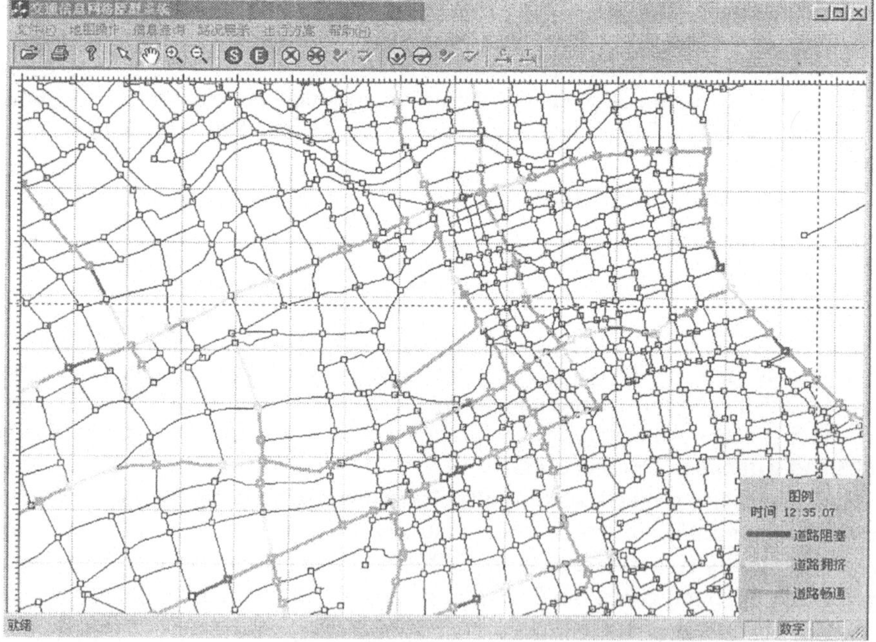

Fig. 4. This GUI simulates the traffic status in the crossroad. Road surface, traffic lights, and vehicles flows are shown in the scene

Acknowledgements. We would like to thank colleagues who have contributed to providing material for ShanghaiGrid, including Changjun Jiang, Aoyin Zhou, Weiqin Tong, Hai Jin, etc. Our projects are supported by the national grand fundamental research 973 program of China (No.2002CB312002), the grand project (No.03dz15027) and key project (No.025115033) of the science and technology commission of Shanghai Municipality. Thanks go for their supports.

References

1. Foster, I., Kesselman, C., Tuecke, S.: The Anatomy of the Grid: Enable Scalable Virtual Organizations. Int. J. of H. Performance Computing Applications. 15 (2001) 200–222
2. Hai, J.: Development and Current Status of China Grids Technology. In: Minglu, L. (ed.): Int. Forum on Digital City and City Grid --- IBM Grid Techno. Workshop. Shanghai, China (2003) 57–100
3. Gentzsch, W.: Grid Computing, A Vendor's Vision: In: (eds.): Proc. of 2nd IEEE/ACM Int. Symposium on Cluster Computing and the Grid. IEEE Press, Berlin, Germany (2002) 272–277
4. Foster, I., Kesselman, C., Nick, J., Tuecke, S.: The Physiology of the Grid An Open Grid Services Architecture for Distributed Systems Integration. http://www.globus.org/research/papers/ogsa.pdf.
5. Foster, I., Kesselman, C.: The Grid: Blueprint for a New Computing Infrastructure. Morgan Kaufmann. (1999)

Spatial Information Grid – An Agent Framework

Yingwei Luo, Xiaolin Wang, and Zhuoqun Xu

Dept. of Computer Science and Technology, Peking University, Beijing, P.R.China, 100871
lyw@pku.edu.cn

Abstract. Spatial information grid (SIG) is a spatial information infrastructure that has the capability of providing services on-demand. In this paper, agent technology is adopted to construct a SIG framework, which contains three layers: users/applications layer, agent services layer and information layer. Different applications can get their spatial information via agent services, and agent services make the procedure of navigating and accessing spatial information transparent to users. Also, the implementation issues of the framework are discussed.

1 Spatial Information Grid (SIG)

SIG (Spatial Information Grid) is a spatial information infrastructure that has the capability of providing services on-demand. SIG integrates and shares massive distributed heterogeneous spatial information resources, and provides uniform management and process. SIG is a distributed network environment, which links spatial data resources, computing resources, storage resources, software, tools and users. SIG can coordinate different spatial information resources to complete different spatial tasks and applications. In such an environment, users can present all kinds of requests for spatial data and its process, and SIG can joint distributed data, computing, network and software resources to cooperate and accomplish different users' requests. SIG adopts a new architecture, method and technology to manage, access, analyze and integrate distributed spatial data, take full advantage of services from existing spatial information systems, so as to realize effective spatial information share and interoperation, and provides spatial information on-line analyzing processes and services. The functions that SIG should provide are:

(1) The capability of processing massive spatial data. Storing, accessing and managing massive spatial data from TB to PB; efficiently analyzing and processing spatial data to produce model, information and knowledge; and providing 3D and multimedia visualization services.

(2) The capability of high performance computing and processing on spatial information. Solving spatial problems with high precision, high quality, and on a large scale; and process spatial information in real time or on time, with high-speed and high efficiency.

(3) The capability of sharing spatial resources. Sharing distributed heterogeneous spatial information resources and realizing interlink and interoperation at application level, so as to make best use of spatial information resources, such as computing

M. Li et al. (Eds.): GCC 2003, LNCS 3032, pp. 624–628, 2004.

resources, storage devices, spatial data (integrating from GIS, RS and GPS), spatial applications and services, GIS platforms (such as ESRI ArcInfo, MapInfo, …), …

(4) The capability of integrating legacy GIS system. A SIG can not only be used to construct new advanced spatial application systems, but also integrate legacy GIS system, so as to keep extensibility and inheritance and guarantee investment of users.

(5) The capability of collaboration. Large-scale spatial information applications and services always involve different departments in different geographic places, so remote and uniform services are needed.

(6) The capability of supporting integration of heterogeneous systems. Large-scale spatial information systems are always synthetical applications, so SIG should provide interoperation and consistency through adopting open and applied technology standards.

(7) The capability of adapting dynamic changes. Business requirements, application patterns, management strategies, and IT products always change endlessly for any departments, so SIG should be self-adaptive.

2 Agent-Based SIG Framework

Agent is an autonomous, interactive, initiative and reactive computing entity in a distributed environment. Agent encapsulates some computing resources and can reach its designed goals initiatively. An agent is not only able to work on itself, but also impact environment, receive feedback information from environment and readjust its own behavior. At the same time, an agent can cooperate with other agents. Agent system reduces the restrictions of concentricity, non-openness and sequential control, provides distributed controlling, dynamic emergency processing and parallel processing services [1][2].

Agent technology will provide a new thought and method for processing massive distributed heterogeneous spatial information efficiently [3]. An agent-based SIG framework can be illustrated as figure 1. This framework contains three layers: Users/applications layer, agent services layer and information layer. Different applications can get their spatial information via agent services, and agent services make the procedure of navigating, accessing and processing spatial information transparent to users. The exchange format of spatial information between applications and agent services is XMLized (such as GML2.0)[4]. Agent services layer plays a most important role in the framework.

Interface Agent presents personalized UI (user interface) for different users in different applications. Get users' requests, communicate with the facilitator, then deal with these requests and return results to users. By the facilitator's help, different interface agents can negotiate with each other to combine or re-plan these requests so that these requests can be replied more rationally and effectively.

Facilitator administrates agents in the system, including register and message of agents. Facilitator also prompts cooperation between agents, including initializing negotiation among interface agents; acting as a bridge lying between interface agents and search agents, provider agents and process agents; scheduling search agents to navigate users' requests; helping search agents find proper provider agent to access to spatial database, and assigning process agents to filter spatial information.

Search Agent is interested in finding and locating spatial information by the users' requests. XML repositories of spatial semantic information network that describe different heterogeneous spatial Databases support the whole searching procedure of search agents. By the facilitator's scheduling, search agents can parallel to carry one request. As the result, search agents can acquire the constitution of spatial information and the unique locators of them.

Instructed by the result of search agent, **Provider Agent** accesses spatial information from a right spatial database. Because the spatial databases are heterogeneous, provider agents are constructed based on different GIS product. Provider agent also translates spatial information to XMLized spatial information (such asGML2.0).

Process Agent filters or queries XMLized spatial information according to the users' requests.

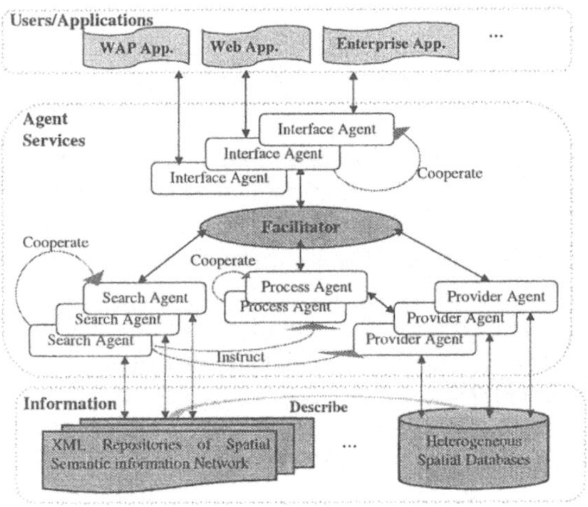

Fig. 1. SIG - An Agent Framework

3 Geo-agents: An Agent Implementation

Aiming to above SIG framework, an agent-based distributed GIS Geo-Agents is designed and implemented (see figure 2)[5][6]. Geo-Agents consists of four types of GIS agent: Facilitator, Interface agent, GIS function agent and GuServer, where Facilitator and interface agent are same with those in above SIG framework, and GIS function agent is mapping to "Search Agent" and "Process Agent", GuServer is mapping to "Process Agent" in SIG framework.

Facilitator is the manager of Geo-Agents. The functions of Facilitator include registering available GIS agents, searching for practicable GIS agents, managing all active agent instances, coordinating communication and coordinating cooperation.

GIS function agent encapsulates spatial querying, spatial processing or spatial analyzing services. The encapsulated services in GIS function agent may come from different existing GIS platforms. Each GIS function agent can complete a same type of problem. According to the features of GIS, GIS function agent is classified into another two types: basic function agent and domain-oriented function agent. Basic function agent completes basic GIS services, such as spatial data search, spatial data access, network analysis, overlay analysis, buffer analysis and so on. Domain-oriented function agent is responsible for application tasks in various domains, and can be constructed by domain-oriented model and used generally in one domain.

Interface agent provides interfaces for users or applications to hand task. Geo-Agents provides GeoScript, an agent manipulating language to describe GIS tasks [6]. When solving a practicable problem, users or applications can simply use GeoScript statements to describe the task, and then hand the statements to interface agent. Interface agent has a GeoScript interpreter and can disassemble the task to subtasks autonomously, recruit GIS function agents to complete the task concurrently.

GuServer is in charge of spatial information accessing services, which manages spatial information and spatial metadata in spatial databases.

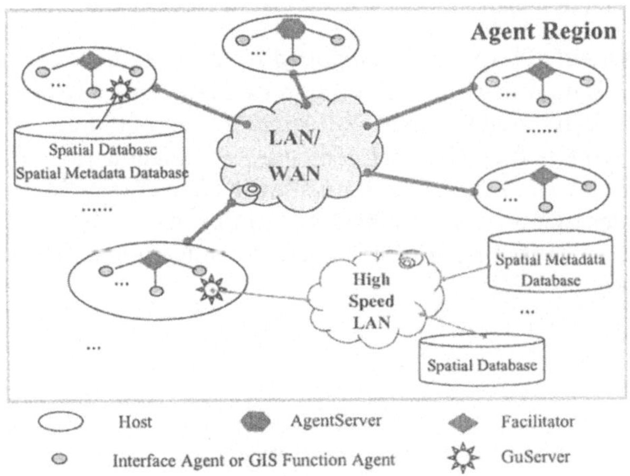

Fig. 2. Geo-Agents System

"Agent Region" mode is adopted to control the distributed scenario for Geo-Agents. An "Agent Region" consists of one or more hosts, which must be installed with a Facilitator (and or other GIS agents). There are many Facilitators in an "Agent Region". Different Facilitators can cooperate to control and coordinate every GIS agent to run correctly, and hold the distributed controls of the whole system.

In an "Agent Region", there is one and only one Facilitator that will be configured as AgentServer. Facilitator is used to manage and coordinate agents inside one "Agent Region". Besides the functions of Facilitator, AgentServer serves as a bridge among different "Agent Regions". That is to say, an agent in one "Agent Region" can only communicate with agents in other "Agent Regions" through AgentServer. Of course, an authorization is required. AgentServer manages a table to register other "Agent Regions" that are authorized with itself each other. Between two directly authorized

"Agent Regions", agents between them can communicate via the coordination of their AgentServers. The authorization relation in Geo-Agents can be passed one by on: If a directly authorized AgentServer chain can be found for two "Agent Regions" that have no direct authorization, agents between the two "Agent Regions" can communicate via the coordination of the AgentServer chain.

4 Conclusion

Agent technology is adopted to construct a SIG framework, which contains three layers: Users/applications layer, agent services layer and information layer. Different applications can get their spatial information via agent services, and agent services make the procedure of navigating and accessing spatial information transparent to users. The construction of SIG will give a powerful technology support for users to share, access, analyze and process spatial information, and provide a powerful management infrastructure for spatial applications, so as to guarantee that, spatial information came from any resources can be sent to any authorized users in anywhere at anytime in suitable way.

Acknowledgement. This work is supported by the National Research Foundation for the Doctoral Program of Higher Education of China under Grant No. 20020001015; the National Grand Fundamental Research 973 Program of China under Grant No.2002CB312000; the National Science Foundation of China under Grant No.60073016 and No.60203002; the National High Technology Development 863 Program under Grant No. 2002AA135330, No. 2002AA134030 and No. 2001AA113151; the Beijing Science Foundation under Grant No.4012007.

References

1. Hyacinth S. Nwana: Software Agent: An Overview, Knowledge Engineering Review, 11(3): 205-244(1996).
2. M. Wooldridge, N. R. Jennings and D. Kinny: Methodology for Agent-Oriented Analysis and Design, Proceedings of the3rd International Conference on Autonomous Agents, P69-76, Seattle, WA, USA(1999).
3. Tang C, Xu LD and Feng S: An Agent-based Geographical Information System, KNOWLEDGE BASED SYSTEMS, 14 (5-6): 233-242(2001).
4. Open GIS Consortium: Geography Markup Language (GML), http://www.opengis.org/.
5. Luo Yingwei, *et al*: The Model of Distributed GIS-oriented Multi-agent System (in Chinese), Acta Scientiarum Naturalium Universitatis Pekinensis,38(3): 375-383(2002).
6. Luo Yingwei: The Study on Agent-based Distributed GIS (in Chinese), [Ph.D. Dissertation], Peking University, Beijing(1999).

Agent-Based Framework for Grid Computing*

Zhihuan Zhang [1] and Shuqing Wang [2]

[1] Information science and engineering college, Ningbo University, 315211, China
[2] National lab. of industrial control technology, Zhejiang University, 310027
zhzhang6486@163.com

Abstract. one of the key reasons for developing Grid Computing is to enable an engineer to use a high performance 'super-computer' with Internet network resources, resolve complexity problem. How to integrate these disparate systems resources, together under a unified framework, can be easily shared with other systems is very important. An Agent Framework for the Grid Computing is presented. Agent-based approaches are becoming increasingly important because of their generality, flexibility, modularity, and ability to take advantage of distributed resources.

Keywords: grid computing, framework, network agents, Agent

1 Introduction

The word 'Grid' is chosen by analogy with the electric power grid, which provides pervasive access to power and, like the computer and a small number of other advances, has had a dramatic impact on human capabilities and society. We believe that by providing pervasive, dependable, consistent and inexpensive access to advanced computational capabilities, databases, sensors and people, computational grids will have a similar transforming effect, allowing new classes of applications to emerge.

The principle benefits that the Grid will bring are:

- Enabling more effective and seamless collaboration of dispersed communities, both scientific and commercial.
- Enable large-scale applications comprising of 10,000 computers, large-scale pipelines etc.
- Transparent access to "high-end" resources from your desktop
- Provide a uniform "look & feel" to a wide range of resources
- Location independence of computational resources as well as data.

The Grid supports complete process initiation and execution including any necessary data location and retrieval. You will ask questions and not know what computer was used to process the data, or where the data came from. This allows it to carry out significantly large tasks and opens up new capabilities for knowledge generation.

Currently Grid tools provide a relatively low level of operational control, but higher level tools will be developed to automate low level processes and agent technology will eventually support real time dynamic process optimization.

* Foundation item: supported by the National Science Foundation of China (No:60174035)

M. Li et al. (Eds.): GCC 2003, LNCS 3032, pp. 629–632, 2004.

2 Grid Architecture Description [2]

The establishment, management, and exploitation of dynamic, cross- organizational sharing relationships requires new technology. This technology is a Grid architecture and supporting software protocols and middleware.

This section identifies and introduces these fundamental system components, describes their purpose and function, and indicates how these components interact with one another. Foster, Kesselman and Tuecke, in their definition of a Grid architecture, start from the perspective that effective operation requires that we be able to establish sharing relationships among any potential participants. Interoperability is thus the central issue to be addressed. In a networked environment, interoperability means common protocols. Hence, their Grid architecture is first and foremost a protocol architecture, with protocols defining the basic mechanisms by which users and resources negotiate, establish, manage, and exploit sharing relationships.

This description of Grid architecture identifies requirements for general classes of component. The result is an extensible, open architectural structure within which can be placed solutions to key user requirements. The architecture is organized into component layers, as shown below. Components within each layer share common characteristics but can build on capabilities and behaviors provided by any lower layer.

The architectural description is high level and places few constraints on design and implementation.

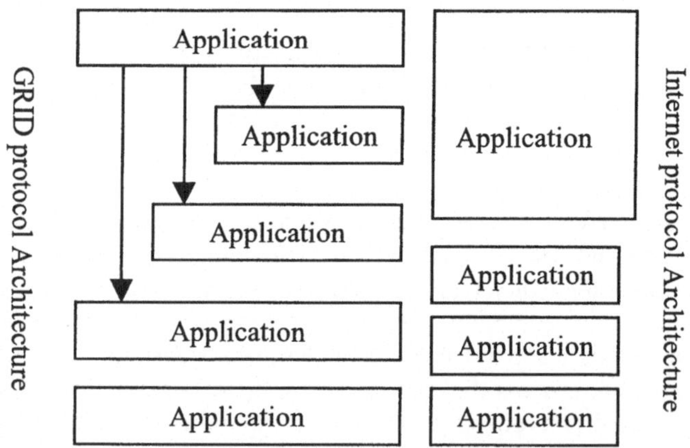

Fig. 1. GRID protocol architecture

The layered Grid architecture and its relationship to the Internet protocol architecture is shown above. (1) Fabric: Interfaces to Local Control (2) Connectivity: Communicating Easily and Securely (3) Resource: Sharing Single Resources (4) Collective: Coordinating Multiple Resources (5) Applications

3 Agent-Based Framework with Grid Protocol

An agent framework with Grid protocol is shown in Fig. 2, the salient features of agent framework with Grid protocol are:(1)Grid Protocol Communication(2)Support for creating and modifying the multi-plane state machine(3)Support for development of behaviours (called strategies or rules) for multi-plane state machine(4)Database & Knowledge Base replication services(5)Support for the Belief, Desire, Intension (BDI) model.
Graphical User Interface for monitoring state machine's current status.

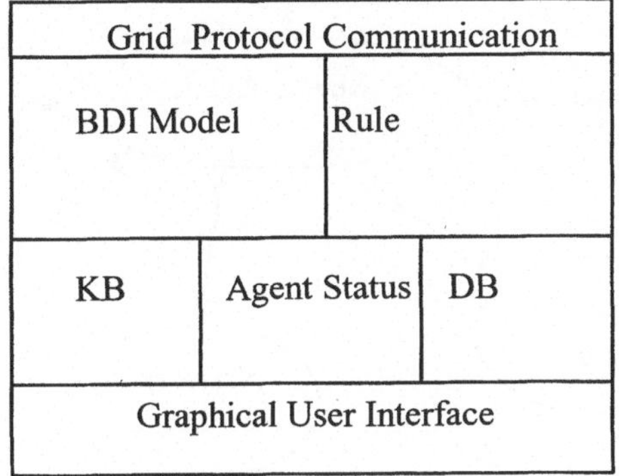

Fig. 2. An agent framework with Grid protocol

4 Agent Grid: Coordinating Multiple Agent

Grid technology takes this concept one stage further by allowing seamless access and use of computing resources as well as information. An enquiry to a Grid search engine will not only find the data you need but also the data processing techniques and the computing power to carry them out before sending you the results.
A collection of Network Resource contains:

- Hardware Resource - computer, instrument, parallel machine and so on.
- Software system - Grid operation system, communication agent software, security management, database, knowledge database and so on.

A unified framework for Grid computing is shown in Fig.3, it provides management of system resources using master agent and subagent protocol, such as Desktop Program, Interface which the master agent responds to management requests. Allows coordinating communication between master agent and multiple agents on multiple network nodes. Provides meta-computing toolkits, application-level scheduling mechanisms. This view covers resource description, management, load balancing, data management, leading eventually to the aggregation of computational resources.
An agent can contain behaviour rules, and interacts with other agents using specialized communication language. Each agent provides a particular service to other agents, an agent provides: (1) A collection of resource (2) Behavioural rules which

can change with time and interactions(3) An interaction language (4) A strategy or long term goal that the agent intends to pursue
Grid computing environments can vary with problem complexity and size. Therefore, Service Integration for multi-agent is needed. The coordinating multiple resources includes:(1)Application development tools that enable an end user to construct new applications (2)Development tools that enable the execution of the application on a set of resources(3)Resources management agent

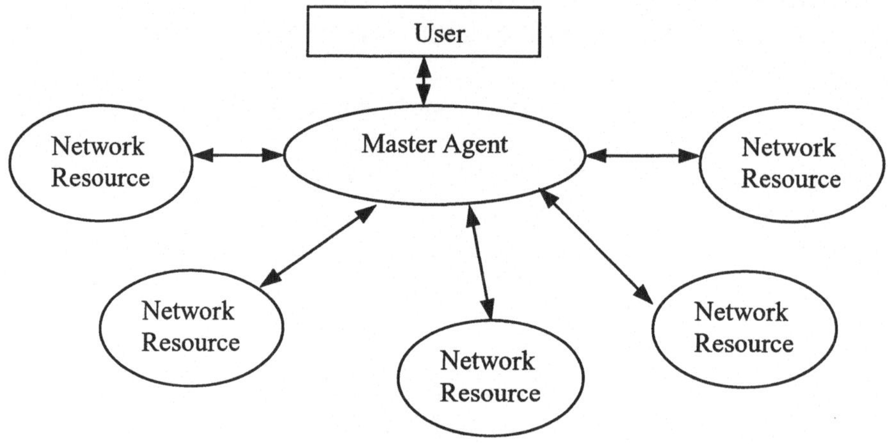

Fig. 3. A unified framework for Grid computing

5 Technical Challenges

Grid technology is developing at a rapid pace but there are many technical challenges that remain, including:(1)Predictability and robustness of accuracy and performance (2)Run time resource management(3)Support for multiplicity of resource environments(4)Security, access policies and payment mechanisms(5)Hidden complexities

References

1. Ian Foster, Carl Kesselman, and Steve Tuecke. The Anatomy of the Grid: Enabling Scalable Virtual Organizations. International Journal of Supercomputer Applications, Vol.15 (2001)
2. http://www.escience-grid.org.uk/docs/links.htm
3. T. Drashanasky, E. N. Houstis, N. Ramakrishnan, and J. R. Rice. Networked Agents for Scientific Computing, Communications of the ACM, Vol.42 (1999) 48-54

A Hierarchical Grid Architecture Based on Computation/Application Metadata[1]

Wan-Chun Dou, Juan Sun, Da-Gang Yang, and Shi-Jie Cai

State Key Laboratory for Novel Software Technology
Department of Computer Science and Technology, Nanjing University, Post Code 210093
wanchun_dou@sina.com

Abstract. Grid technology is the collection of tools and services that integration widely distributed, heterogeneous, and multi-organizational resource. For better understanding grid's structure, an object-oriented framework of C/A component is explored. Then, a hierarchical grid architecture combining data Grid, information Grid, and knowledge Grid is explored based on a general hierarchical grid architecture. The conclusions are presented at last.

1 Introduction

In recent years, it's becoming more and more prevalent that geographically distributed groups can collaborate by taking advantage of computer and communication technologies. To eliminate resource islands, scalable, secure, and high-performance mechanisms for accessing and sharing remote resources (information and computation) are indispensable for supporting the cooperative fashion efficiently. This technology is commonly referred to the *Grid* that is initially explicated in the Grid computing technology [1]. Grid computing promises users the ability to harness the power of large numbers of heterogeneous, distributed resources such as computing resources, data storage systems, instruments, etc. Nowadays, the notation of Grid has been extended and the content of resources is enriched with data, computation, software, agent, and even people [2]. Many Grid research projects are, now, funded in various scientific researches such as TeraGrid sponsored by the National Science Foundation of U.S.A, European Data Grid sponsored by European Union, China National Grid sponsored by Ministry of Science and Technology, etc. Taking into account the recently initiated research activity of semantic Web, a hierarchical Grid architecture is explored in this paper based on the C/A (Computation/Application, C/A) metadata. The remainder of this paper is constructed as follows. In section 2, general hierarchical gird architecture is presented. In section 3, a framework of object-oriented C/A component is discussed. In section 4, the interoperability is explored among C/A component. Finally, the conclusions are presented in section 5.

[1] This research is supported by the National Natural Science Foundation of China (NO.60303025)

M. Li et al. (Eds.): GCC 2003, LNCS 3032, pp. 633–636, 2004.

2 A General Hierarchical Grid Architecture

Theoretically, Grid technologies form the underpinning and enabling middleware for pursuing e-Science. Unfortunately, in contrast to the rapid growth of Information on the web, we still lack effective means to store or manage the knowledge distributed on the Internet up to now; in despite of that knowledge is becoming an important resource for enhancing the cooperative processes. According to [1], the Grid can be characterized, as demonstrated in Fig.1, by (i) a computation/data Grid, (ii) an information Grid, and (iii) a knowledge Grid. Whilst considerable advances have been made on the computation/data Grid such as Globus and Condor, collaborative engineering design optimization requires further developments at all levels, especially when the knowledge sharing is leaded into collaborative engineering.

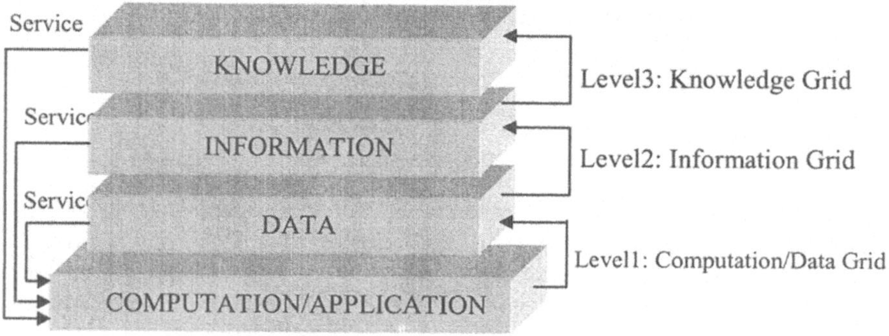

Fig. 1. Hierarchical relations among Grid resource

In Fig.1, knowledge/information Grid is the sophisticated part of the Grid and provides a computational framework based on definitions of computation or application metadata and syntactic interoperability. Data Grid is the infrastructure of the Grid that provides basic Grid services such as communication, authentication, information and resource management.

3 Framework of C/A Component

In this section, an object-oriented framework of C/A component is put forward in conformance with local C/A fragments as illustrated in Fig.2. Here, the resource geographically distributed on Internet is indexed by taking advantage of the concept of file that could take the form of HTML or XHTML linking certain web page or dataset in telnet://..., ftp://..., http://..., etc. Additionally, Graphical User Interface along with some on-line analytical processing tools is needed for capturing the information or knowledge, efficiently, through Grid based on those files.

In Fig.2, the data resources could be classified into static, demand and output resource. File1 stands for the static resource, File2 the demand resource and the File3 the output resource. Static resource is the basic resource achieved independent of the Grid, such as local database or self-reliant computation. Demand resource is the computation or datasets that must be captured on Grid. While output resource is the regenerated data or information by the execution of C/A component.

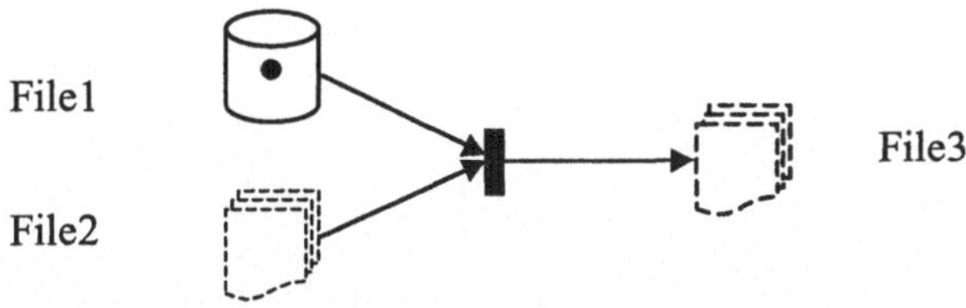

Fig. 2. Framework of C/A component

Fig.2 is initially a local information model accompanied by data operational method. The interactive space of data Grid can be formalized as below:

(C/A-component-*i*-File2, C/A-component-*j*-File1/File3)

Note that (C/A-component-*i*-File2, C/A-component-*j*-File1) describes the static property of the data Grid and (C/A-component-*i*-File2, C/A-component-*j*-File3) presents the dynamic invocation inhered in data Grid among C/A component. If we treat the knowledge as one kind of resource, the data Grid mentioned above is refined into knowledge Grid. Furthermore, the meta-data of those files is indispensable in a knowledge Grid. The C/A metadata accentuate mainly on the prescription of problem property and problem-solving method. Some markup languages like RDF and formal semantic expressing some semantic knowledge make up of the metadata. Some AI-inspired knowledge representation such as DAML+OIL, OWL, ontology-based reasoning and other XML-inspired case mark language can also be introduced to perfect meta-data [3].

4 Interoperability among C/A Components

According to Fig.2, the interactive mode between two C/A can be illustrated as Fig.3. The logical operation can be described as follows. (1) Read the C/A metadata; (2) If the problem type is similar to encountered problem, to consult the related problem-solving method; if the related problem-solving method is applicable, to locate the data resource according to metadata and refer to the related C/A.

Accordingly, the metadata is indispensable to assist the user in decision-making. The operational logic based on meta-learning underlies the semantic web oriented knowledge sharing. Moreover, persistent data Grid middleware plays important in enactment of step 3, which offers basic Grid toolkit and services such as high-performance, secure, robust data transfer mechanism or mechanism for maintaining a catalog of dataset replicas [2]. User authentication is often granted in step 3 with permission to access dataset of other C/A resources. Role-based access control mechanism is in common use to initialize the trust domains. Besides, the step 3 demonstrated in Fig.3 is optional and could be omitted in practice if user finds that the problem type is not similar or the related problem-solving method is not inapplicable to his/her encountered problem [4-5].

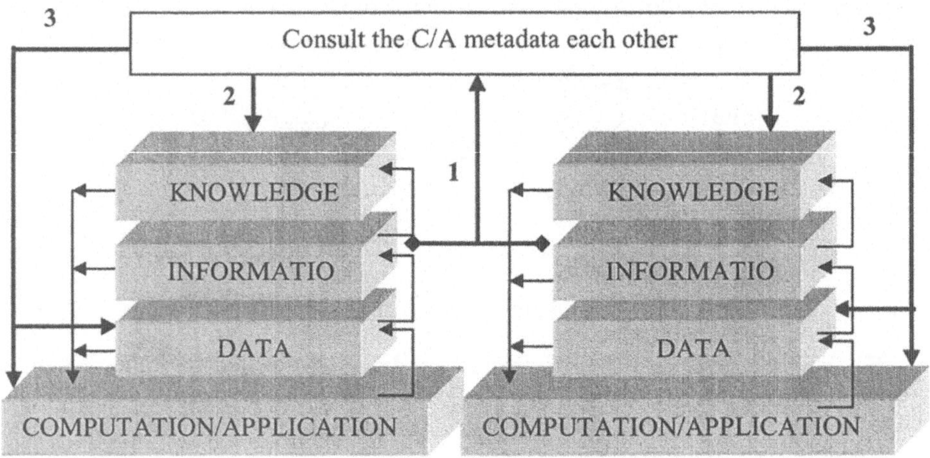

Fig. 3. Interoperability between C/A components on Grid

5 Conclusions

Grid can be characterized from different view of points, in which knowledge Grid can be treated as a sophisticated application. Knowledge Grid, along with the data Grid, will enhance the collaborative computation by extracting the knowledge from large amount of online data collections taking advantage of certain intelligent technologies, although the integration of the data, computing, networking hardware, the development of the software, and the coordination of a large and distributed human infrastructure will promote difficult challenges.

References

1. Cannataro, M. and Talia, D.: Towards the Next-Generation Grid: A Pervasive Environment for knowledge-based Computing. Proceeding of the International Conference on Information Technology: Computers and Communications (ITCC'03). 30-34
2. H.Zhuge: A knowledge Grid model and platform for global knowledge sharing. Expert System with Application, Vol.22. 4(2002)313-320
3. L.McGuiness, D., Fikes, R., et al: DAML+OILL: An Ontology Language for the Semantic Web. IEEE Intelligent System. 5(2002)72-28
4. Deelman, E., et al.Mapping Abstract Complex Workflwos onto Grid Environment. Journal of Grid Computing, Vol.1.1(2003)25-39
5. Cannatrao, M., et al.: Distributed Data Mining on the Gridm, Future Generation Computer Systems, Vol18. 8(2002)1101-1112

A Transparent-to-Outside Resource Management Framework for Computational Grid[1]

Ye Zhu and Junzhou Luo

Department of Computer Science and Engineering, Southeast University,
Nanjing, 210096, P.R.China
tonyzhuye@263.net, jluo@seu.edu.cn

Abstract. In this paper, we make some improvements on the domain-based resource discovery architecture and present a transparent-to-outside resource management framework (TRMF). Its uppermost characteristics are the different discovery modes for inside and outside resources, the interdomain transfer of aggregated resource information and the corresponding scheduling policy. These key mechanisms and main operation processes have been described here.

1 Introduction

In the analysis of the Information Service performed by MDS in Globus project, some ideas have drawn our attentions: 1. Both global and distributed strategies of information image have their limitations. Therefore, some researchers have proposed the domain-based resource discovery model [1], in fact a compromise of the two schemes above. It maintains locally the overall image of the intradomain resources but obtain the outside resource information when necessary by request-transfer among domains. 2. In current domain-based models, the search request can get the detailed information of all qualified resources. But in fact, the requester may only need a certain amount of resources. Besides, it would be more efficient to let the domain schedule the inside tasks itself. As a result the outer requester needn't know detailed information in this domain but simply regard it as a container of resources. 3. Besides the simple gathering of information in directory service there is another technology: aggregation of information, which makes it possible to simplify the data transferred among domains--transfer the profile information. 4. The workload of information service comes mainly from two aspects: the inquiry and dynamic update, the latter can not be ignored especially in computational grid. So we need to make a compromise between totally real-time updating and estimating of the information.

After considering the above problems synthetically, we make some improvements on the domain-based framework, and combining with task scheduling, propose a Transparent-to-outside Resource Management Framework (TRMF).

[1] This work is supported by National 973 Fundamental Research Program of China (G1998030402) and National Natural Science Foundation of China (90204009).

M. Li et al. (Eds.): GCC 2003, LNCS 3032, pp. 637–640, 2004.

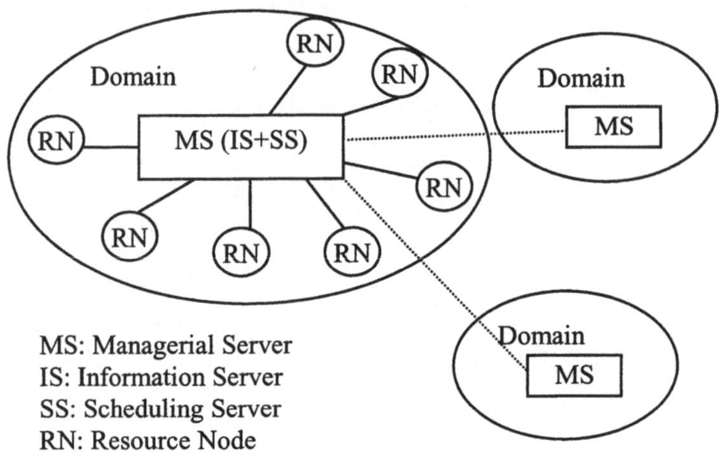

Fig. 1. The architecture of TRMF

2 TRMF Architecture

TRMF architecture consists of several managerial domains. Each domain contains:

- All the resource nodes registered in this domain: These resources have been described in some resource description language (maybe RSL or improvement of WSDL, also for description of resource request) and through deploying the fundamental grid service, it provides the interface for access to the resource information and resource invoking.
- A Managerial Server (MS): It can be divided into two function entities: Information Server (IS) and Scheduling Server (SS). We put them together because their relation is so close in TRMF. IS gathers the resource information inside domain, interchanges them between different domains and provides the inquiry service. SS is responsible for intradomain task scheduling and task-transfer among domains.
- Several Spare Servers: It's for backup of MS. The operation should be switched to Spare Servers in time if MS breaks down.

Every domain has its independent managerial policy and cost model. However, a series of standard mutual agreements must be implemented to assure various types of communications among domains. Built up on a unified architecture, all domains form the whole computational grid. Such structure can be extended to more hierarchies, combining several domains to a larger one by higher level administrative center.

3 Key Mechanisms

The key mechanisms of TRMF mainly focus on the following operation processes: information aggregation and interdomain transfer, resource discovery and also task scheduling.

3.1 Information Aggregation and Interdomain Transfer

Inside the domain, every node sends its resource information to the IS periodically or when changes happen. Since the status of resource is the main fluctuation factor, we can divide the changes into several grades based on some thresholds under a certain measure, the change below a threshold should not trigger an update operation to IS. A directory service possessing the detailed intradomain resource information shall be maintained on IS to timely respond to the search and update requests. However for outside nodes, they can only know the profile information of this domain.

Information aggregation is the key component of TRMF, which refers to aggregating many resource items of the same or similar types to fewer ones. For resources that can be aggregated a unified measure must be found. Fortunately, computational resource is such a kind to be aggregated in some extent. In TRMF, IS aggregates local resource information by various measures to obtain a profile list, which means ignore or omit some detailed attributes such as the positions, real-time states or invoke parameters of certain resources. Also, some new control parameters may be added in, for example the original granularity of an aggregated item. The aggregating process is not required to be very accurate, allowing a little less than the actual total amount. The aggregated information will not be sent out directly, but be disposed by the local policies first, such as keeping resources of a certain amount as the backup space for task scheduling, or limiting the publishing of those resources of lower performance.

IS sends the profile information of local-domain to its neighbors in other domains. By such transfer, finally the aggregated information will spread to the whole gird environment in the way similar to the transfer mechanism in BGP (Border Gateway Protocol). To reduce the transmission load, the total amount of intradomain resources can also be divided into several grades under certain measures, so that the profile needn't to be transmitted again if the change is within a certain range.

3.2 Resource Discovery

By interdomain transfer mechanism, every IS obtains detailed information of local-domain resources and the profile of outer domains. When a local client submits a search request, IS searches the local information directory first. If enough qualified resources are found, IS returns the corresponding information in detail. If the suited local resources are not enough, then IS will refer to the profile information of other domains from the closest one. Once it finds a certain domain possessing qualified resources, IS will return the corresponding part of the profile and the information about that domain. If such still can not satisfy the client's request, search will be continued to further domains until enough qualified resources are found. Otherwise IS will return error message if there's no proper result when search ends. All these are performed locally, not by request-transfer. The profile information may only tell us which domain has qualified resources, unable to exploit directly. However, the client still can send the task request to that domain's MS, which will be responsible for task scheduling inside. In requester's view the domain is just like a unitary resource.

3.3 Task Scheduling

After getting the required resource information, if only need local resources, the client may choose itself, or local SS, or even a third party to schedule the task, which can be determined by combining the domain's and the node's policies. If the task surely needs outer resources, the request should be submitted to the SS of the objective domain. Because the profile information which the client has obtained from its local IS may be different from the real-time status of this domain, SS has to inquire IS and local policies here to determine whether local resources can support the task at that time. As a result, (1). if the task is local-executable, it will directly be scheduled by SS; (2). if it's partly executable, then SS begins to allocate the executable part to qualified resources; the other part will either wait or be transferred to other domains according to the requester's policy, also the client should be informed; (3). otherwise an error message will be returned.

All above components form the implementary architecture of TRMF. In fact, most of the technologies have already been provided; just need some further improvements under the framework and to operate along the above-mentioned process.

4 Conclusions

We combine the resource discovery and allocation into an integrated framework in TRMF. Its uppermost characteristics are the different discovery modes of inside and outside resources, the interdomain transfer of aggregated information and the corresponding scheduling policy. This paper just describes an improved architecture and key mechanisms, many technical problems haven't been thoroughly discussed such as: the description method of resource and request, the technology to measure and aggregate information, the design of communicating protocols and the security architecture in grid environment, etc. Only if these problems get satisfying solutions, can a relatively stable, low-cost resource management platform be constructed.

References

1. Y. Gong, F. Dong, W. Li and Z. Xu: A Dynamic Resource Discovery Framework in Distributed Environments. In Proceedings of the 1st International Workshop on Grid and Cooperative Computing, Hainan, P.R.China, 2002
2. W. Li, Z. Xu, F. Dong, and J. Zhang: Grid resource discovery based on a routing-transferring model. In Proceedings of the 3rd International Workshop on Grid Computing, Baltimore, MD, 2002
3. Z. Xu, W. Li: The Research on Vega Grid Architecture. Journal of Computer Research and Development, 2002 (Chinese)
4. K. Czajkowski, S. Fitzgerald, I. Foster, C. Kesselman: Grid Information Services for Distributed Resource Sharing. Proc. 10th IEEE International Symposium on High-Performance Distributed Computing (HPDC-10), IEEE Press, 2001

A Service-Based Hierarchical Architecture for Parallel Computing in Grid Environment

Weiqin Tong[1], Jingbo Ding[1], Jianquan Tang[1], Bo Wang[1], and Lizhi Cai[2]

[1] School of Computer Engineering and Science,
Shanghai University, Shanghai 200072, P. R. China
[2] Shanghai Software Test Laboratory, Shanghai 200235, P. R. China
wqtong@mail.shu.edu.cn

Abstract. Grid computing technologies enable widespread sharing and coordinated us of networked resources, including computing resources. Open Grid Service Architecture (OGSA) marries Web services to grid protocols, thereby making progress in defining interfaces for grid services. We put forward here a hierarchical architecture, which is based on grid service, for parallel computing in grid environment. Several grid services are proposed in this paper for building our architecture, including cooperation service, resource information service, computing service, communication service, and other atomic services such as MOM service. The technology of building high layer grid service is also introduced in this paper.

1 Introduction

The traditional parallel computing models, such as PRAM, LogP model, C3 model, are based on non-hierarchical parallel computers. In grid environment, both the physical and logical characters of grid model are hierarchical. On one hand, the physical character of grid model is hierarchical as Figure 1 shows. All the resources are connected in grid environment. But the direct connection is the one between grid nodes. All other resources, including computing resources, depository resources, high performance apparatus, etc., are indirected connected through grid nodes. On the other hand, the logical character of grid model is also hierarchical as Figure 2 shows. In grid environment, computing resources are connected with grid middleware such as Globus Toolkit. But the grid middle is too sophisticated to be installed in all computing nodes. So an advisable method is to install grid middleware in one node of a computing block (such as parallel computer, cluster), and all the computing nodes of the same block are built to a service to be invoked by remote client. The result of this method is to build Virtual Organizations (VO) in grid environment.

Because of the hierarchical characters of grid model that are described above, we should build hierarchical computing model to adapt itself to the hierarchical characters of grid model.

M. Li et al. (Eds.): GCC 2003, LNCS 3032, pp. 641–644, 2004.

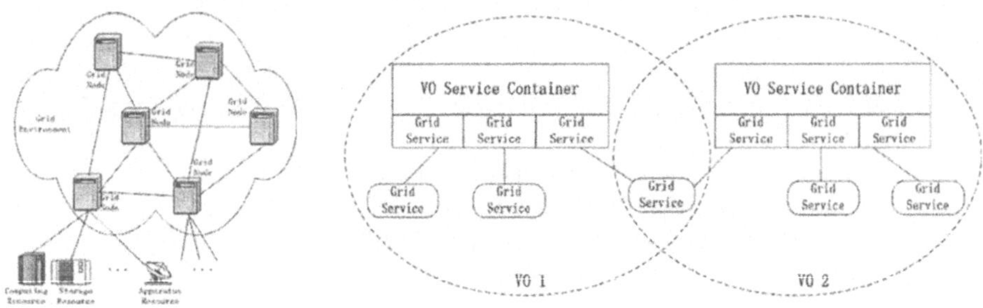

Fig. 1. Physical hierarchical character of grid

Fig. 2. Logical hierarchical character of grid

2 Service-Based Hierarchical Architecture

Our architecture is based on grid services which is kernel of OGSA frame. To make parallel application be able to run in grid environment, some grid services as following are required in our architecture.

- Cooperation service. This is the highest layer in our architecture. The major function of cooperation service is to accept computing tasks, utilize its lower services, manage them, and monitor status of tasks.
- Resource information service. It collects the resource information of all grid nodes. The service is based on index service which is a part of OGSA. One of the aims of constructing this service is to collect host information such as CPU occupied rate, memory available, network bandwidth. The host information can be utilized by cooperation service to realize load balance of grid nodes.
- Computing service. It is an important service in our architecture. The task of this service is to execute programs in local computational nodes. It is based on MMJFS (Master Managed Job Factory Service)
- Communication service. This service takes charge of the communication between grid nodes. It is based on notification service, which is one of grid services in OGSA, and our new implementation of MOM (Message-Oriented Middleware).
- Some atomic services. There are some atom services which are abstract of local resources of grid hosts. They include index service, MMJFS, notification service, MOM service, GASS (Global Access to Secondary Storage) service.

These services introduced above are constructed as a hierarchical architecture, which is showed in Figure 3. All the services are divided into three layers. The highest service, cooperation service, not only administrates services in lower layers, but also takes charge of the interaction with users or applications. The services in the middle layer have a common character – they provide some useful functions such as computing, communication, or collecting and providing information. In the lowest layer there are some atomic services that implement some basic operations. So, the three layers can be called administration layer, function layer, and implementation layer.

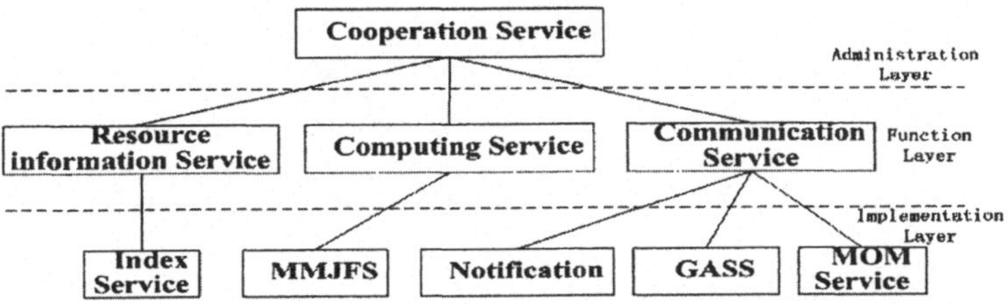

Fig. 3. Hierarchical services in our architecture

OGSA convention provides some technologies to build grid services. But it do not include something about hierarchical services. We should use some existing technologies to implement higher grid services without violating the OGSA convention. The detail of the technology for building higher grid services is described in detail in Section 3.

There are two communication mechanisms in our architecture – Notification and MOM. In the lowest layer, both the two mechanisms are implemented as atomic services.

The notification is an essential part in Grid Services. They are two portTypes of Grid Services: notificationSource and notificationSink, which allow services to carry out asynchronous delivery of messages between each other. In our architecture, notification communication service implements an interface of notification, which have portTypes both notificationSource and notificationSink. So, any notification communication service is both source and sink of any other notification communication service. For example, service A is source and service B is sink when service A sends data to service B. And service B is the source of service A when B sends data to A.

But notification mechanism has low efficiency because it uses JAX-RPC (Java APIs for XML based Remote Procedure Call) convention, which is redundant for data transmission. So we implement a new mechanism – MOM in our architecture. Figure 4 shows the architecture of MOM. We add three key components into the OGSA framework: Sender component, message processor and receiver component.

3 Technology of Constructing Higher Grid Services

As introduced above, our architecture is based on some hierarchical grid services, which accord with the convention of OGSA. But unfortunately, the OGSA convention does not define the construction of hierarchical services, though it defines the specification of grid service so sophisticated. So, we should study the technology of constructing higher grid services based on basic grid services. Figure 5 shows an example of high-level grid services in OGSI (Open Grid Service Infrastructure).

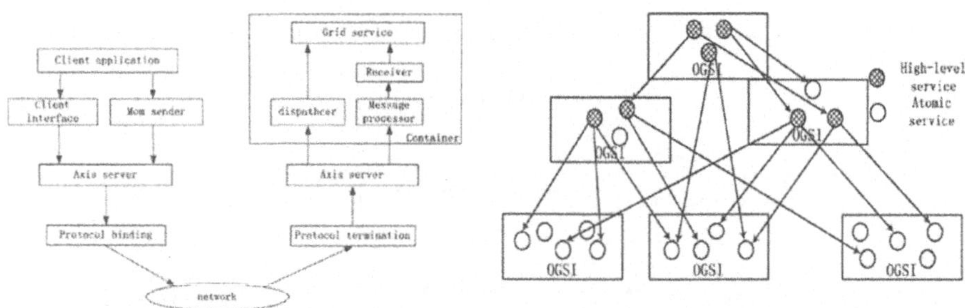

Fig. 4. Mechanism of MOM communication

Fig. 5. An example of high-level gird services

We can organize the workflow of grid services by writing the appropriate GSFL language. For example, the cooperation service starts up computing service when RIS (Resource Information Service) is done. RIS return the result to cooperation service through interface Q to P. Cooperation service invokes computing service through interface R. For this situation, we can get the knowledge that the activity P has two control links P->Q, P->R, and one data link Q->P.

For the construction of high-level services, the information about the required services and their relationships must be available. XML document can be used to describe it. Note that every grid service has its description which is represented by WSDL document, we can extend the WSDL document to add the information about the required services and their relationships.

4 Summary

In this paper, we introduce a hierarchical architecture for parallel computing in grid environment. It is based on some grid services which conform to the OGSA convention. The grid environment could be regarded as a virtual parallel machine because every implementation details are concealed by our architecture and the grid resources are transparent for users. The layered services, which are delegate of grid resources, constitute our architecture.

References

1. I. Foster, C. Kesselman, S.tuecke, The Anatomy of the Grid: Enabling Scalable Virtual Organizations, International J. Supercomputer Applications, 15(3), 2001.
2. Weiqin Tong, Jingbo Ding, Lizhi Cai, A Parallel Programming Environment on Grid, Proc. of International Conference on Computational Science, 2003, pp. 225-234.
3. Lizhi Cai, Weiqin Tong, BSP-G: Grid-Enabled Bulk Synchronous Parallel, Proc. of the International Workshop on Grid and Cooperative Computing, 2003, pp.323-335.
4. Cole-Gomolski, Barb, Messaging Middleware Initiative Takes a Hit, Computerworld, 31(39), 1997.

A Grid Computing Framework for Large Scale Molecular Dynamics Simulations*

WenRui Wang, GuoLiang Chen, HuaPing Chen, and Shoubao Yang

National High Performance Computing Center, University of Science and Technology of China, Hefei, Anhui 230027 wangwr@mail.ustc.edu.cn

Abstract. Molecular Dynamics(MD) is computational study through simulating in detail the interatomic interactions in protein. Currently, there is no better simulating algorithm due to the demand on accuracy. However, a ensemble/distributed dynamics method is developed to run the simulation in parallel on many distributed computers on the internet. The objective of this research is to design and code a reliable framework to run molecular dynamics computing in a distributed environment ,to make use of the contributed CPU time better and to fasten the computing process of computing. We have sucessfully implemented the framework with Web Service and Java, and have extended this framework transparent to applications for further use on our grid computing environment. The experiments demonstrated that the MD simulation will successfully run on this framework.

1 Introduction

Proteins have a stable, unique, 3D structure which is responsible for a biological function[1]. There is relationship between the amino acid sequence and the 3D structure, which is a major goal of theoretical molecular biology. The process and dynamics from sequence to 3D structure is helpful and important in understanding the diseases, protein design and nanotechnology. With the improvements in software and hardware providing a powerful computational platform, the atomistic protein folding simulations are heavily used by biologists in their studies[2].

However, due to the great complexity of atomistic interactions, simulating how proteins fold is unresolved. The current techniques to perform molecular dynamics computing is limited by the long time scales needed for biologists to gather the useful information. Current single processor can only do the simulation on the scale of femtoseconds(10^{-15} seconds) in order to keep the precision, while the fastest protein fold in tens of microseconds(10^{-6} seconds).This means a complete simulation will take at least 10^9 steps. The computing process will take at least more that one day even if 1000 steps can be done in one second. In fact,

* Supported by the National High-Technology Research and Development Program (2002AA104560), the National Natural Science Foundation of China(60273041) and the Scientific Research Foundation for the Returned Overseas Chinese Scholars, State Education Ministry

M. Li et al. (Eds.): GCC 2003, LNCS 3032, pp. 645–648, 2004.

due to the large number atoms in proteins and the electronic force computing time on pairs of atoms, the each step's comutation requires more time when proteins are bigger. Various parallel computing technique has been studied[3][4][5][6] to fasten each steps. Duan and Kollman have proved that parallel molecular dynamics simulations can break the microsecond barrier[7]. However, this method has fundamental drawbacks. Fast communication bandwidth is needed between processors. And scalibility is limited when the size of molecular and the number of processors grows.

Recently, a new method[8] is developed to extend the computing to the distributed environment. Large amount of contributed CPU time is gathered to perform the computing, which cannot even be accomplished on today's supercomputers. Some projects based on this diagram have been set up and succeeded. Such as SETI@HOME, Folding@HOME, Distributed.net. For example, SETI@HOME has gathered hundreads of thousands years of CPU time in about three years.

This kind of problems have their congenital advantage to be solved in a distributed computing environment. First, the solution space is too large to explore and we have few knowledge to design effective algorithm against it. Second, instances of the problem can be splitted into small units which will be assigned to computing nodes in the distributed environment.

Motivated by the success of this projects and the demanding of computing resources from biologists, we start our project following this method to provide a integrated computing resource based on a distributed environment. Computing resources contributed(contributor) by individuals will be gathered by a central server. When a job is submitted by biologists, it is splitted into small units(workunits), which will be allocated to contributors. The result of computing workunits will be returned from contributors to central server. A scheduler resides on the central server is responsible to allocate the workunits to contributors, to create new workunits according to jobs and results. On the other hand, our central server provides a grid service for jobs or workunits came from outside. This interface hides the details dealing with the distributed environments, and provides grid users uniform means to access it.

2 Model and Design

In order to support various applications, we design and implement a application independent framework. There are two major parts in our framework: contributors and a central server. Contributors are the desktop PCs that contributes their idling CPU time and returns the result. The central server is responsible for splitting submitted jobs into workunits, managing workunits ,contributors and results. The contributors talk to the central server via web service.

The central server provides two major interfaces: "Central" and "Control". The Central interface's operations is called only by the contributors. The registerClient operation is called when contributor program installed and run for the first time. The getWorkunit operation is called by contributor asking for a new workunit. The reportResult operation is called when the contributor ends its computation and give a result back to the central server. The Control interface's operations is called only by the framework user to operate their jobs. The submitJob operation is used to submit a new job. It returns a jobID to the user for operating this job in the future. The cancelJob operation is called by the user to cancel a job submitted earlier. The queryJob operation is called to get the status of a certain job. The contributor runs as a background process on the computing node. The contributor is constructed by two major components: the client program and one or more application package. At first run, the contributor registers itself to the central server, then holds the returned ID locally. The client program should be kept running. It will call getWorkunit regularlly. Once a workunit is received, the executable code in the corresponding application package is launched as a sub-process doing the computation. After the sub-process ends, the result in the output file will be returned to the central server.

We have implemented the framework by the Java and Web service technology. The central server is based on Apache AXIS, the open source SOAP implementation.

3 Experiments

We have deployed our framework onto 3 existing LANs which have 54 contributed nodes totally. Each of them have one Intel P4 class CPU. We perform a simulation with the molecular of A S-peptide as our experiment, whose data is taken from our partener biologists. We submited the job data file to our central server, which then start scheduling computation on its 54 contributors. After the simulation, various biological and physical properties are extracted from the simulation's record data: Figure 1 shows the deviation of the current phase to the starting phase, while Figure 2 shows the deviation to the objective. It can been seen from the deviation that the simulation successfully steps from the original phase to the objective phase.

4 Conclusion and Acknowledgements

We have designed and implemented a general distributed computing framework which is basically application independent. We have ported GROMOS, a classic molecular dynamics simulating software to our framework. We plan to integerate our framework into a GRID environment and investigate its performance in near future. A computing application from our partner chemists are also porting to our framework.

This work is supported by the National High-Technology Research and Development Program (2002AA104560), the National Natural Science Foundation of China(60273041) and the Scientific Research Foundation for the Returned Overseas Chinese Scholars, State Education Ministry. Thanks to our partener biologists from the Key Laboratory of Structural Biology, and School of Life

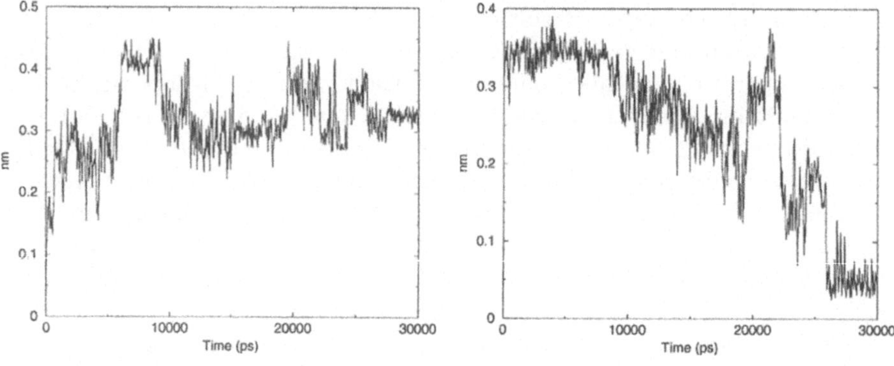

Fig. 1. RMS Deviation to the begin

Fig. 2. RMS Deviation to the end

Science, the University of Science and Technology of China: Liu HaiYan, Zhang ZhiYong and Chen ShanMei.

References

1. R. Callender et al. Protein physics. *Physics World*, pages 41–45, 1994.
2. Christopher D. Snow, Houbi Ngyen, Vijay S. Pande, and Martin Gruebele. Absolute comparison of simulated and experimental protein-folding dynamics. *Nature*, 2002.
3. Witold Dzwinel, Witold Alda, Jacek Kitowski, Jacek Moscinski, Marek Pogoda, and David A. Yuen. Large-scale molecular dynamics experiments on cray t3e system. *HPCN Europe*, pages 881–883, 1998.
4. Greg Eisenhauer and Karsten Schwan. Design and analysis of a parallel molecular dynamics application. *Journal of Parallel and Distributed Computing*, 35(1):76–90, 1996.
5. Ravi Murty and Daniel Okunbor. Efficient parallel algorithms for molecular dynamics simulations. *Parallel Computing*, 25(3):217–230, 1999.
6. George S. Almasi, Calin Cascaval, Jos G. Castaos, Monty Denneau, Wilm Donath, Maria Eleftheriou, Mark Giampapa, Howard Ho, Derek Lieber, Jos E. Moreira, Dennis M. Newns, Marc Snir, and Henry S. Warren Jr. Demonstrating the scalability of a molecular dynamics application on a petaflops computer. *International Journal of Parallel Programming*, 30(4):317–351, 2002.
7. Duan Y. and Kollman. Pathways to a protein folding intermediate observed in a 1-microsecond simulation in aqueous solution. *Science*, 282:740–44, 1998.
8. Stefan M. Larson, Christopher D. Snow, Michael Shirts, and Vijay S. Pande. Folding@home and genome@home: Using distributed computing to tackle previously intractable problems in computational biology. In Richard Grant, editor, *Computational Genomics*. Horizon Press, to appear.

Principle and Framework of Information Grid Evaluation*

Hui Li, Xiaolin Li, Zhiwei Xu, and Ning Yang

National Research Center for Intelligent Computing Systems,
Institute of Computing Technology, Chinese Academy of Sciences, Beijing, 100080
{lihui, lxl}@ncic.ac.cn, {zxu, yangning}@ict.ac.cn

Abstract. Information grid researches on enabling technologies for sharing information and application effectively and expediently in a wide-area enterprise environment. The Grid-Key/Grid architecture of Vega Information Grid aims to enable user to use grid application at anytime, anywhere by any device, and to achieve a high productivity services. Accordingly, the evaluation of information grid needs to measure those functionalities and performance that can embody these features. This paper presents how to use the full life cycle principle to evaluate and analyze information grid, and provides an evaluation framework based on Service Level Agreement.

1 Introduction

Grid Computing has its promise of universal connectivity and reach, and making it work far better by bringing the qualities of service that people are used to in enterprise computing, and the qualities of service that we all have gotten used to in utilities like electricity [1]. Information grid (IG) is one of the branches in the research of grid technologies [2,3]. It has the same promise and qualities of service. But it is obvious that with the traditional evaluation metrics we can't evaluate whether grid systems and services go farther or nearer from these goals. There is no metric to evaluate the electricity quality of the grid ideal service.

In this paper, section 2 presents utilization mode of information grid. Section 3 gives evaluation principle based on full life cycles of subject and object. Section 4 mentions a framework of the evaluation. Lastly, section 5 gives a conclusion.

2 Utilization Mode of Information Grid

In view of users, the utilization mode of information grid has such characters [4,6,7,8,9] as users and resources built dynamically, various and autonomous-controlled applications, transparent utilization mode, high productivity services etc.

* This work is supported in part by the National Natural Science Foundation of China (Grant No. 69925205), the China Ministry of Science and Technology 863 Program (Grant No. 2002AA104310), and the Chinese Academy of Sciences Oversea Distinguished Scholars Fund (Grant No. 20014010).

M. Li et al. (Eds.): GCC 2003, LNCS 3032, pp. 649–652, 2004.

We conclude all the characters above into two requirements that are 3A(any where, any time and any device to use grid) and HPS (high productivity service). Many efforts are made to reach these two goals. K/G [4] architecture of Vega Information Grid under our research is a case in point. In the K/G mode, if a user wants to get a grid service wherever he is and whenever it is, what he should do is just to plug his grid key into a grid terminal [4], the grid key provides user identity, role and session etc. Afterward, grid server dynamically deploys service interface, user context, and service runtime environment to the user's terminal. When the user terminates the service, grid reclaims all the recourses, and stores the user's data and logs to grid community user space [4].

3 Principle of the Information Grid Evaluation

Two of key features [5] of grid are its dynamic and openness. The user subjects and resource objects of a grid system are decoupled, as well as dynamically change in time and space. Their behavior and state are composed of a series of life cycles. A user subject's life cycles may consist of registration, login, usage, suspending, maintenance, logout, and exit. A resource object's life cycles may include creation, integration, deployment, usage, offline, maintenance, and exit. For grid subject or object, what is different from that of traditional system is that its full life cycles must be considered in the process of design, usage, and evaluation of grid, which is called the full life cycle principle for grid.

A Subject is a user identity [10]. From the utilization mode of section 2, the full life cycle of subject and their relationship is displayed in figure 1.Some processes of the life cycle should draw our attention. The first two steps are from start to register and from Sign-in to use. During these two courses, does the user terminal need any deployment? If the answer is "no", user can use IG service anywhere by any device. The next important step is from sign-out to sign-in. May user go on with the service not completed after sign-out? If the answer is "yes", user can use IG service at anytime.

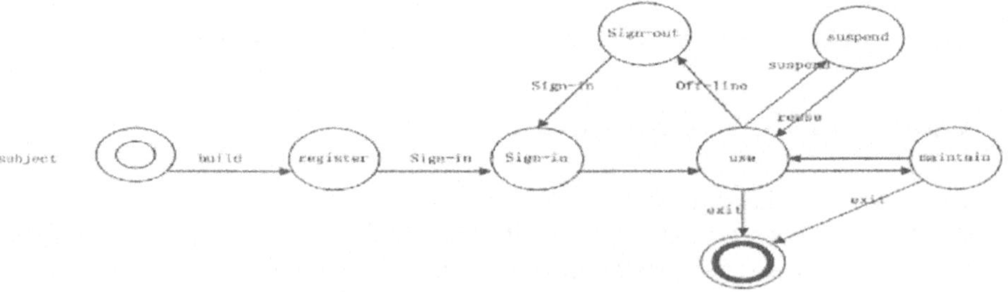

Fig. 1. The subject full-life cycle

During all the periods of the life cycle, users' motivation is to use the IG. Therefore the less time the other periods spend, the better the IG service is. The ideal instance is that the periods except the use period spend no time, here we define the HPS in this case is 100%. It means 100% time of the system is in use. And then we give object HPS definition in the actual running.

Object HPS [5]= Time in use/ (Time in use+ start time +register time+ sign-in time+ suspend time+ maintain time+ sign-out time+ exit time).

The higher the HPS is, the more efficiently the users are served.

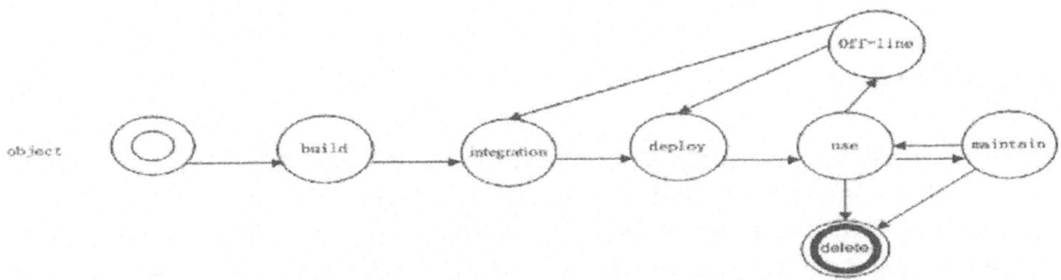

Fig. 2. The object full-life cycle

Showed by figure 2, object full life cycle is the same as that of subject.

4 SLA Framework of the Evaluation

Our evaluation principle is implemented in the framework of Web Service Level Agreement (WSLA [11]) proposed by IBM. Service level agreement (SLA) is made in order to make sure users being well served. Our evaluation system signs service level agreement with users (developers, administrators and end-users) firstly. Giving all these metrics: response time, availability, reusability, deploy time, maintenance time, develop time, subject HPS, object HPS etc., uses can choose some even all of these metrics given by the evaluation system and prescribe every value range of the metrics. As to the system, it will display every value of the metric chosen and warn while exceeding the range or even make some management to make sure the value is in the range.

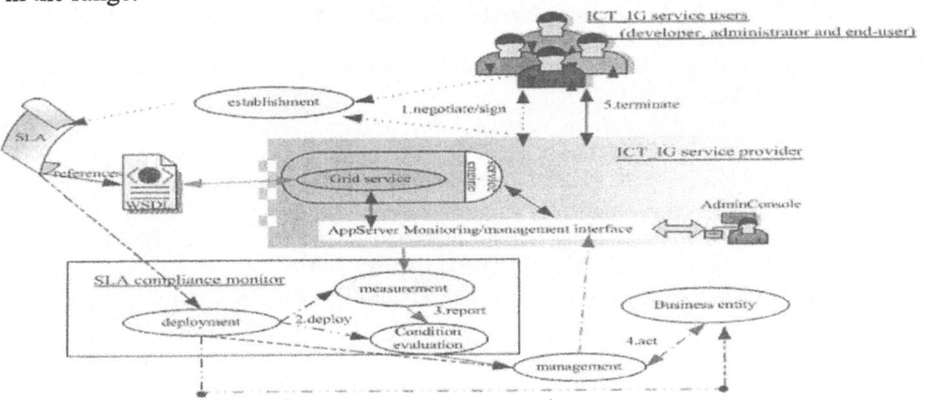

Our evaluation Framework is deployed on the project of Institute of Computing Technology Information Grid (ICT_IG). The evaluation system in the software structure of ICT_IG is displayed in figure3.

5 Conclusion

Vega Information Grid aims to enable user to use grid application at anytime, anywhere by any device, and to achieve a high productivity services. We put forward the Grid-Key/Grid architecture of information grid in our other paper. In this paper, we describe how to use the full life cycle principle and Service Level Agreement to evaluate information grid. A concept framework is presented to measure the life cycle productivity of users and resources.

Continuing works include how to define each life cycle metrics and design Service Level Agreement for diverse users.

References

1. Ephraim Schwartz Exec makes grid computing sound simple. CTO Forum: IBM's Wladawsky-Berger talks grids. 2002.
2. I Foster, C Kesselman, S Tuecke, The anatomy of the grid: Enabling scalable virtual organizations, International Journal of Supercomputer Applications.2001, 15 (3): 200~222
3. X. Li, N. Sun, Z. Xu. Three Essential Issue of Enterprise Information Grid. Grid and Cooperative Computing, 2002
4. N. Yang, X. Li, Z. Xu. K/G: A Kind of Grid use architecture and application. Journal of Computer Research and Development, 40 (11), 2003.
5. X. Li, N. Yang, H. Li, Y. Lu. Full life cycle principle for grid and its application. Journal of Computer Research and Development, 40 (11), 2003.
6. G You, Z, Xu, X. Li. A Behavior-Oriented Model for Information Grid. Grid and Cooperative Computing, 2002
7. Z. Xu. Architecture of VEGA. Institute of Computing Technology, Chinese Academy of Science, Tech Rep: VGD-1, 2001.
8. Z. Xu, W. Li, "The Research on Vega Grid Architecture", Journal of Computer Research and Development, 39 (8), 2002, pp. 923-929.
9. K. Hwang, Z. Xu, Scalable Parallel Computers: Technology, Architecture, Programming, McGraw-Hill, New York, 1998.
10. X. Li, Z. Xu, X. Liu. Community-Based Model and Access Control for Information Grid. Proceedings of IEEE/WI conference, Halifax, Canada, 2003
11. Alexander Keller, Heiko Ludwig. The WSLA Framework, IBM Research Report, May 22, 2002

Manufacturing Grid: Needs, Concept, and Architecture

Yushun Fan[1], Dazhe Zhao[2], Liqin Zhang[1], Shuangxi Huang[1], and Bo Liu[1]

[1] Department of Automation, Tsinghua University, Beijing 100084, China
{fan, zhangliqing98, huangsx, liubo03}@cims.tsinghua.edu.cn
http://www.simflow.net

[2] Faculty of Information Science and Engineering, Northeastern University, Shenyang 110179, China
zhaodz@neusoft.com

Abstract. As a new approach, grid technology is rapidly used in scientific computing, large-scale data management, and collaborative work. But in the field of manufacturing, the application of grid is just at the beginning. The paper proposes the concept of manufacturing. The needs, definition and architecture of manufacturing gird are discussed, which explains why needs manufacturing grid, what is manufacturing grid and how to construct a manufacturing grid system.

1 Introduction

Today the design and manufacturing of product are becoming more and more complex. The enterprise should utilize all the resources within or outside it to satisfy the business objective. Up to now, there is no network computing platform which can provide a single portal for users to access the enterprise resources (databases, files, devices and etc.) and there are no unified protocols for the use of manufacturing resources. Grid technology can be competent for this situation. It inherits the dominance of existing network technologies, and upgrades the performance in facets of resource sharing, cooperation, network security and access transparency. In a word, Grid technology can establish a sound fundament for building manufacturing network systems [1].

2 The Needs of the Field of Network Manufacturing

The services needed by network manufacturing are very different from the information services supplied by the Internet. The main needs or characteristics, which differentiate manufacturing services from information services provided by the Internet, are as follows:

- Interaction: Manufacturing services need to supply the interaction between users and services.

M. Li et al. (Eds.): GCC 2003, LNCS 3032, pp. 653–656, 2004.

- Real time: manufacturing services must reflect the state of actual equipment and design unit and response the request of customer in real time.
- Multi-cooperation: The customer should be able to integrate various different manufacturing services. The customer's demand should be satisfied by cooperating work between different manufacturing services.
- Long lifecycle: Compared with information services, some manufacturing services may have a long lifecycle.
- Data-intensive: Manufacturing services need to transfer a large quantity data comparing to the information of webpage provided by the Internet.
- Complex function and structure: The structure of the system that provides manufacturing services is often relatively complex.
- High-degreed specialization: Manufacturing services show high-degreed specialization.
- Knowledge-based: Manufacturing services usually are based on special knowledge.

3 The Concept of Manufacturing Grid

The aim of Manufacturing Grid (MG) is to effectively organize all kinds of resources separated in different regions, enterprises, organizations, and individuals. Through the services provided by MG, users can obtain various manufacturing services as conveniently as obtain information from the Internet nowadays. Under the support of MG, the specialized application system faced special manufacturing demand of the enterprises can be established, and the cooperation of design, manufacturing, business of the enterprises can be achieved. The definition of MG is as follows:

MG is an integrated supporting environment both for the share and integration of resources in enterprise and social and for the cooperating operation and management of the enterprises. Based on the grid and relative advanced computer and information technologies, MG shields the heterogeneousness and the regional distribution of resources by the way of encapsulating and integrating of the design, manufacture, management, information, technology, intelligence and software resources separated in different enterprises and social groups. It not only provides various manufacturing services for the customers in a transparent way, but also makes enterprises or individuals conveniently obtain all the services related to manufacturing in the way of requesting services, and use all the resources encapsulated in manufacturing grid as conveniently as using the local ones. It achieves the integration and optimal operation of all kind of resources and provides a cooperative work environment for the construction of the manufacturing grid application system faced the special requirement of network manufacturing.

Based on MG, future enterprises, even individuals could obtain various manufacturing services from the Internet as conveniently as obtaining water, electricity, and gas in daily.

4 The Architecture of Manufacturing Grid System

MG is a manufacturing-oriented virtual network on the basis of Internet, Grid, and other related technologies. Internet is the physical network of MG. The construction and operation mode of MG is some similar to that of Internet today. MG provides manufacturing enterprises and individuals with manufacturing services in the similar way that Internet provides information services. Furthermore, MG supports the cooperation between services and therefore it enables the cooperation of enterprises. Based on the basic network connection provided by Internet, Intranet and Extranet, and supported by manufacturing Grid Resources Lib, Platform Infrastructure System and Manufacturing Grid Operating Management System, all kinds of resources can be shared and integrated in MG system. A regional MG system in special region can be built. And by combining different regional MGs, a whole MG system can be constructed to support network manufacturing.

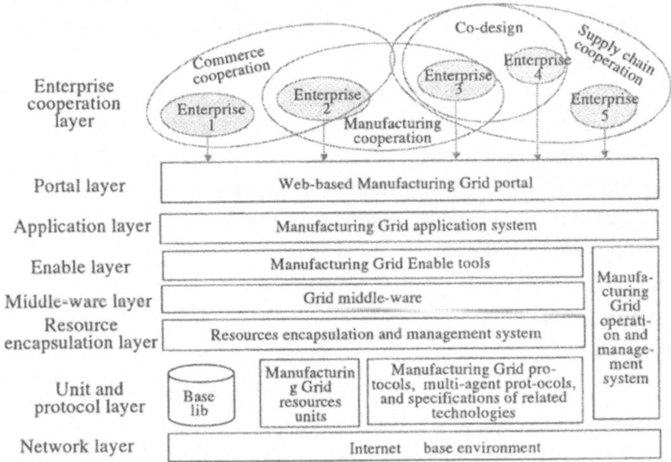

Fig. 1. The Architecture of Manufacturing Grid system

Similar to Internet, the architecture of MG system is a hierarchical structure shown in Fig. 1. The functions of each layer are described as follows [2]:

1. Network layer : Network layer provides the base communication environment to all the resources and organizations in MG system.

2. Unit and protocol layer : Unit and protocol layer provides common and basic technology supports to the construction and operation of MG, including base lib, manufacturing resource units and fundamental protocols.

3. Resource encapsulation layer : Resource encapsulation layer encapsulates all types of resources with special Grid technologies, which converts local resources into global resources through the grid. The management system has the responsibility for control and management of the resources encapsulated.

4. Grid middleware layer : Grid middleware layer provides the basic functions for manufacturing services and service cooperation, such as, remote process

management, resource co-allocation, storage access, information security, QoS, and etc. It also provides languages/compilers, class libs, APIs and integral developing environment to users who want to develop manufacturing Grid applications.

5. Enabling layer : Enable layer provides some enabling tools which are necessary to develop or operate the MG application system, such as tools for registration management, service management, resource scheduling, project management, visualization of user interface and etc..

6. Application layer : Application layer primarily develops special manufacturing grid application systems according to the specific demand of enterprise cooperation, such as MG-based PDM system, collaborative design system, cooperative commerce system, supply chain system, remote device control and diagnoses system and etc..

7. Portal layer : Portal layer provides a web-based, consistent and secure interface for users, through which users can access all the manufacturing services in MG system.

8. Enterprise cooperation layer : Supported by the MG, different kinds of cooperation can be realized, including commerce cooperation, manufacturing cooperation, collaborative design, and etc..

9. Manufacturing Grid operation and management system : This layer crosses four layers of the MG, and it takes charge of managing, monitoring and adjusting the users and resources running in the MG system. The functions of Manufacturing Grid operation and management system include user management, interface management, security management, operation inspection, service agent management, policy adjustment management and etc.

5 Conclusion

This paper presents the concept of Manufacturing Grid based on Grid technology for network manufacturing, and discuss its needs, definition, and architecture. The developer of manufacturing Grid should refer to some standards of existing platforms (for example, Globus, Condor and NIIIP), combining with agent, Web Service and other technologies, and finally develop a set of theories, technologies, protocols and methods of Manufacturing Grid with its own characteristics [3].

References

1. Ian Foster, Carl Kesselman. The Grid : Blueprint for a Future Computing Infrastructure. USA: Morgan Kaufmann, 1999
2. Fan Yushun, Liu Fei, Qi Guoning. Network manufacturing system and its application. Beijing. China Machine Press.2003
3. Zhang Liqing, Fan Yushun. Grid Technologies and its Application in Manufacturing. Aeronautical manufacturing Technology. 2003(2): 32 ~ 37

Developing a Framework to Implement Security in Web Services

Fawaz Amin Alvi[1], Shakeel A. Khoja[2], and Zohra Jabeen[1]

[1] Sir Syed University of Engineering and Technology, Karachi, Pakistan.
alvi@iodomain.com, zjabeen@ssuet.edu.pk,
[2] Karachi Institute of Information Technology, Karachi, Pakistan.
shakeel@kiit.edu.pk,

Abstract. Recent advancement in XML and increasing use of World Wide Web allow users to use internet as a document sharing and hosting system, with certain security features. Currently no guidelines are available for developers to enforce security policies for XML and Web Services. It is crucial in order to facilitate a secure dissemination of XML documents, containing information of different sensitivity levels, among (possibly large) user communities. The paper concentrates on developing a framework and proposing design considerations to implement the PKI enables security in XML documents and web services, by defining a component model and processing rules that can be shared across applications using common tools, avoiding the need for extensive customisation of applications to add security. This allows interoperability with a wide range of existing infrastructures and across deployments.

1 Introduction

Older security models, such as public/private key encryption model, do provide a set of core security algorithms and technologies that can be used as a wrapper over XML document, but don't allow working within the document itself and managing the contents. SSL/IPSEC is very popular way for patching the security lack in XML but is useable only if communication is between two fixed points which is not always applicable for web services. Additionally SSL can only ensure security while information is in transit where as XML and web services are equally popular in transmission and storage technologies. Another possible technique widely used is IP Blocking or Filtering. These techniques can be use intelligently to fill the missing security gaps in webservices but a list of IP to be blocked or filtered is maintained in this technique which can get very huge and un manageable with time specially keeping in view the IPV6 enhancements this technique will be very difficult to be implemented. Two standards, proposed by W3C, XML encryption and signature, tackles security issues in XML documents like authentication, message integrity, and non-repudiation. With the help of XML signature, only desired parts of an XML document can be signed and verified. Next is SOAP SEC proposed by which is there to overbuild some of the security problems in SOAP by enabling message signing using added header to

M. Li et al. (Eds.): GCC 2003, LNCS 3032, pp. 657–660, 2004.

SOAP. Another extension in the row is WS Security worked out by the collaborated efforts of IBM, Microsoft and VeriSign. WS-Security was formed to provide a standard for secure message exchange, signing etc. The extensions provide authentication, message integrity confidentiality and signature to messages.

2 Consideration during Development of Framework

There should be a two way flow of XML data inside the model. One way the XML data will move to get secure and as it moves towards the end the relevant security assertions are inserted over it and when it gets out, the resultant XML will be a perfect secure XML following all the standard XML security standards. The other way in, will be the secure XML document and its output will be the XML that would be extracted as the result of applying the various XML security assertions or access control policies.Developers should define the security system in forms of components. It can consist of various independent components. These components should be independent and will be providing atomic operations that are needed while implementing a secure a web service. Each component should be designed with respect to the level they are categorized into. For example level 2 components will be using the functionalities of level 1 components so cannot be designed before level 1 components.

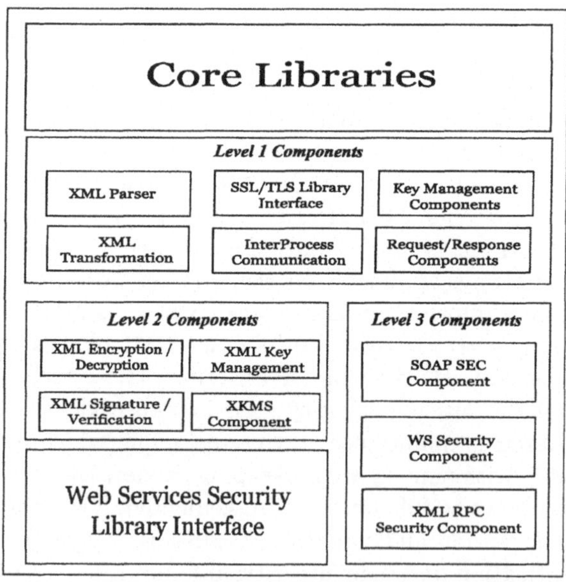

Fig. 1. A Basic Web Services Security Model is shown in this figure showing various component levels and elaborating possible components that are fitted at various levels.

2.1 Level 1 Components

The level 1 Components constitutes the first layer of the model. It consist of the all the basic level functionality needed. The level 1 component will give an interface to the next level components to use the traditionally available methods for security and also provide XML parsing capabilities to the other level components. Some of the first level components can be XML Parser Components, Traditional Security Components, Request/Response management Component, Inter-Components Communication Component, Key Management Components and XML Transformations Component.

Transformation Components: Transform is basically any operation performed on the XML data: reading data from an URI, XML parsing, XML transformation, calculation digest, encrypting or decrypting. Each transform provides at least one of the following call-backs: "`push binary`", "`push XML`", "`pop binary`" or "`pop XML`". In order to simplify transforms development, additional "`execute`" call-back can be added. This call-back updates internal transform buffers and is used by default. XML/binary push and pop call-backs. When necessary, a transforms chain can be constructed as specified in the template or document and processes data by "`pushing`" or "`popping`" through the chain.

Key Management Component: Processing of some of the key data objects require additional information which is global across the application (or in the particular area of the application). For example, `X509`certificates processing require a common list of trusted certificates to be available. All the common information for key data processing can be kept in a collection of key data stores called keys manager. Keys manager can have a special keys store which lists the keys known to the application. This keys store can be used to lookup keys by name, type and crypto algorithm (for example, during `<dsig: KeyName/>` processing).

2.2 Level 2 Components

The level 2 components are basically the core of the security model. These components will be providing the methods and their implementations that are defined or outlined in the various XML/Web Services Security related specifications provided by the W3C. There is one very important consideration of these components that is they will be talking XML as input and after successful operation the output will also be an XML document. Thus a true XML developer will be enjoying the fun of using XML and also making the web services conforming to one of property of XML documents i.e. XML in and XML out. All the information is in XML format. Possible level 2 components can be XML Key Management Component, XML Encryption/Decryption Component, XML Signature/Validation Component and XML Access Control Component.

XML Signature/Encryption Component: There can be a possible need of counter signature, or partial encryption, in the Encryption and Signing. It is therefore better to perform these operations by processing input XML along with a stencil/template that specifies a signature or encryption skeleton, the way to use transformation component, the usage methods for traditional cryptographic/algorithms components, and the way to interface with XML key management component for key selection process.The key for signature/encryption can be obtained from the key managers in the key management component using the information from the stencil document, does necessary computations and puts the results in empty nodes of the given stencil. Signature or encryption component controls the whole process and stores the required temporary data. Since the Stencil information is also a XML file, it might be created in advance and saved in a file and can be given to the application as an input.

2.3 Level 3 Components

The level 3 components are basically the components designed for web services layer. They will be making use of level 2 components for processing raw XML but in the output giving implementation dependent output for particular web services. These components will be use acting as a web services security library. These components can be SOAP Security Components, XML RPC Security Components and WS Security Components.

3 Summary

These are the considerations that can be helpful for developers while implementing security into web services. But a lot of issues will come during the exact implementation. These considerations were found during the implementation of security for a web service. There is still a lot that can be done on this area. The features that are lacking to be discussed in this paper are: Access Control Component and Digital Rights Protection Component. These modules are not used in most of the XML applications but are part of security of any system. In-fact these components are not rated as very necessary. This paper is not the exact solution to the problems of XML/Web Services security, but it is basically to show the way of how all the various available methods of implementing security can fit together to provide what is actually needed.

References

1. E. Bertino & E. Ferrari (2002), "Secure and Selective Dissemination of XML Documents": ACM Transaction on Information and System Security, Vol 5
2. Blake Dournee (2002): "XML Security" McGraw Hill Inc USA, 2002
3. Jake Sturm (2002): "Developing XML Solutions", Microsoft Press Inc, USA 2002
4. R Allen Wyke, Sultan Rehman & John Brad (2001): "XML Programming", Microsoft Press Inc, USA, 2001
5. Deutsch, A., Fernandez, M., Florescu, D., Levy, A., And Suciu, D. (1999), "Securing XML documents" Proceedings of the International Conference on World Wide Web.

Computing Pool: A Simplified and Practical Computational Grid Model

Peng Liu, Yao Shi, and San-li Li

Institute of High Performance Computing,
Department of Computer Science and Technology,
Tsinghua University, Beijing, 100084, China
Pengliu@ieee.org

Abstract. Even though grid research is prosperous in an extensive context, few grid platforms for high performance computing are practical and in operation so far. Since most applications are moderate ones, trying to decompose these applications among distributed supercomputers will results in complexity in programming and optimizing, and heavy cost of communications. In this paper we advocate computing pool which shares distributed supercomputers but does not decompose applications. Analysis proves that it is a practicable computing platform, which can greatly improve quality of service and utilization of resources.

1 Introduction

The ultimate goal of grid [1] is to build an information processing infrastructure on the base of the rapidly improving information transporting infrastructure (e.g. information highway), by connecting enormous computers, instruments, databases and people in the world together and make them be an organic macrocosm, providing nontrivial quality of services [2], for example, immense computing power, enormous storage capacity, smart instrument accessing capability and intensive information processing/retrieving competence. Presently, dozens of grid research projects have being carried out, which include Globus [3], Legion [4], Condor [5], IPG [6], DOE Science Grid [7], GriPhyN [8] and TeraGrid [9] in America, DataGrid [10], UNICORE [11] and DAS-2 [12] in Europe, Nimrod/G [13] and EcoGrid [14] in Australia, and Ninf [15] in Japan, etc.

Traditionally, people hope a grid can accumulate computing power of many supercomputers, to form an unprecedented virtual supercomputer (which we call it full-fledged grid). In fact, many efforts have being seen towards this goal, for example, SF Express project [16] that had achieved a record setting level of performance running military simulations, and Cactus project [17] that had got remarkable achievements in numerical relativity research [18] which won the 2001 Gordon Bell Prize in Supercomputing 2001 meeting [19] . So far as we know, however, most of the grid applications are still in their tentative stages: they are for specific applications, and few of them can meet the requirement of a long-term service for general applica-

M. Li et al. (Eds.): GCC 2003, LNCS 3032, pp. 661–668, 2004.

tions. For instance, the SF Express project hasn't reported any obvious progresses after it had simulated 100,298 battle units on 13 computers among 9 sites in 1998, although it is said that it will "*continue to incorporate emerging computational grid tools and techniques into the distributed interactive simulation environment*" [20]. As to the numerical relativity applications on Cactus, some obvious drawbacks can also be found out, according to its representative paper [17]: (1) although four supercomputers had been used, it is not a complicated heterogeneous computing platform, since three of the supercomputers are of the same type and at the same site; (2) there is a conflicting situation that higher performance was got from smaller system: a performance of 249 GFlop/s had been achieved from the four supercomputers (the efficiency was 63.3%), yet a 14.7% better performance of 285.5 GFlop/s had been achieved from two of the four supercomputers (this figure can be calculated from its remarkable efficiency of 88% as it was reported); (3) its scale cannot prove the advantages of grid, since there are only 1500 processors used by the application, while ASCI White, a giant computer made by IBM, has 8192 processor in the same year; and (4) part of the success of the work should be owed to the characteristics of the application, which can be optimized to keep the communications exist only between adjacent processors, making the long distance link between NCSA and SDSC does not seem to be a problem.

In the rest of this paper, we will first analyze what have been limiting the practicability of full-fledged grids. We then bring forth computing pool, which stays between full-fledged grid and traditional supercomputer centers. Further analysis will show how it shuns the disadvantages of full-fledged grid, and how it greatly improves quality of service for users and efficiency of supercomputers in the pool.

2 The Latency and Bandwidth Problem

Why is full-fledged grid not practical at present? We think the major reason is that only a few applications can be divided into independent smaller parts which need zero or little communications between one another. Though there does exist this type of applications, they may be more suitable to be run in a much more powerful, looser and cheaper platform, the P2P computing environment, which can aggregate power of millions of personal computers. For instance, SETI@home (the Search for Extraterrestrial Intelligence at home) project [21] has aroused more than 4 millions contributors since July 1999, and has consumed more than one million years of CPU time for free. Compared to the amount of thousands of processors integrated by grid currently, P2P computing seems to be a better solution for applications that can be partitioned into independent parts.

When an application is run on a full-fledged grid, the main problems come from latency and bandwidth. Latency is really a tough problem, since it is limited by the speed of light, which is 300,000 km/s, and it will take 10ms for light to cover 3000 km. In addition, as there are many gateways, switches and routers lies between the sender and receiver, and TCP/IP protocol is inevitable and inefficient, the real latency will be even more. Compared to a delay of several microseconds in SAN (System

Area Network) in a cluster or MPP, the latency in grid is at least 3 orders of magnitude higher than that within a supercomputer. Relatively, bandwidth problem is easier to overcome, as backbones ordinarily have Gbps bandwidth and can easily reach Tbps in the near future thanks to DWDM technology [22]. Currently, however, bandwidth is still a problem, since backbones are always shared by many services, and the cost of renting lines must be taken in account when grid platform will be applied for daily operations. Compared to latency of several microseconds and bandwidth of 2Gbps of Myrinet [23] and 10Gbps of Infiniband [24], the System Area Networks (SAN) often used in clusters, the communication efficiency in WAN cannot beat LAN or SAN.

It is true that we have many methods to relieve the influence of communication problems, by using adaptive algorithms to hide part of the latency or cut down data transmission, so as to relieve the dependency on communication. For example [17], we can overlap computation and communication; we can increase granularity of computation or use redundant computation to commute communication; we can reduce times of transmission by increasing size of each transmission; we can compress data before transmitting it and decompress it after receiving; we can find a balance between accuracy of computation and cost of communication; or we can adjust some protocol parameters (e.g. parameters of TCP/IP protocol) to optimize transmission, etc. Nevertheless, all the above optimizations should be based on an intensive study on properties of applications and grids, and there does not have any universal solutions so far. In short, there are still a lot of works on algorithms, protocols, and middleware to do, before an efficient communication platform for general grid applications may emerge and eliminate the need of additional optimization works for each application.

3 Computing Pool

As a generic full-fledged grid may not be realistic presently, how can we build a practical computing infrastructure for general applications? Fortunately, most of our high performance applications are relatively moderate ones, which can be solved on only one supercomputer in a tolerable time limit. In this condition, it is more practical to run an application on a sole supercomputer instead of many different supercomputers, since the former will save a lot of communication time of the application and a lot of programming, debugging and optimizing time of the programmers. That is why supercomputer centers are still towers of strength for today's high performance computing applications, though grid seems to be getting popular.

However, we can see drawbacks of traditional supercomputer centers too. First, they are not sharing their computing resources among distributed sites. Each supercomputer center has its own users. The users of site A often do not visit site B to run their applications due to geographical and policy limits. Thus a condition may often happen: supercomputer A is underloaded while supercomputer B is overloaded. Second, it is not convenient for users that they may need reservation, traveling, pending and more cost to use a supercomputer. Third, although this does not always happen, the user's application may be too big to be run on the supercomputer he can access.

Here we put forward an idea of Computing Pool, which may ease the disadvantages of both full-fledged grids and supercomputer centers. Computing pool is an elementary grid which follows three rules: (1) dynamically shares resources among supercomputers in distributed sites; (2) never divide one application into smaller parts to run on different supercomputers. Instead, it will find a suitable supercomputer in the pool for the application; and (3) it will provide a web portal for users to access the computing resources.

As may be proved in the following context, rule (1) will greatly improve utilization of the supercomputers in the pool, and provides a much better quality of service by sharply reducing user's pending time. Also, it is possible for users to solve bigger problems that cannot be settled at local supercomputer center since there will averagely be 50% supercomputers in the pool have more power than the local one. In addition, rule (2) will shun the complexity problem of decomposing applications among distributed sites, and what is more, it will cut most of the communication cost by restricting all communications happen locally. This makes general applications can be easily and cheaply run on the platform. Finally, rule (3) provides a convenient interface to users. They need not travel to and stay in a supercomputer center. Instead, they can hand in their applications at home in 24 hours. Generally speaking, the communication cost of task submission, controlling, and result retrieving is much lesser than the communication cost among subtasks.

4 Performance Analysis

Theoretically, the behavior of computing pool can be described as followings.

Suppose computing pool S has N supercomputers, whose computing power are P_1, P_2, …, and P_N. When a user put forward a task A that requires computing resource of M_A, the computing pool will assign a proper supercomputer i (instead of several supercomputers) to A, to meet the requirement of P_i*T M_A. Here T is an acceptable duration time to the user.

The dominant advantages of computing pool are (1) it can serve users more quickly than independent supercomputers, and (2) evidently improves the throughput of supercomputers in the pool. This can be proved as followings.

To simplify the problem, suppose each supercomputer has the same computing power, i.e. $P_1=P_2=\ldots=P_N$.

If there is no computing pool, each supercomputer works independently for specific users. Suppose both arrival rate of users' applications and service time of supercomputers are negative exponentially distributed (i.e. Poisson process). λ_1 is average arrival rate, and μ_1 is average service rate. In short, it is a M/M/1 queuing system. So, the average waiting time W_{q1} for an application on the supercomputer will be:

$$w_{q_1} = \frac{\lambda_1}{\mu_1(\mu_1 - \lambda_1)} \tag{1}$$

If we have a computing pool of c supercomputers, then it will be a M/M/c queuing system that has c parallel servers. In this system, the average waiting time for an application Wq_c will be:

$$W_{q_c} = \frac{C(c,a)}{\mu_c(c-a)} \qquad (2)$$

in which a is loaded ratio,

$$a = \frac{\lambda_c}{\mu_c} = \frac{c\lambda_1}{\mu_1} \qquad (3)$$

and C(c,a) is the probability of all the supercomputers are busy when an application arrives and must wait.

$$C(c,a) = \frac{\dfrac{a^c}{c!(1-a/c)}}{\sum_{n=0}^{c-1}\dfrac{a^n}{n!} + \dfrac{a^c}{c!(1-a/c)}} \qquad (4)$$

(0□a<c)

Using different values of c, λ_1 and μ_1 for formula (2), we can get a set of curves shown as Fig. 1.

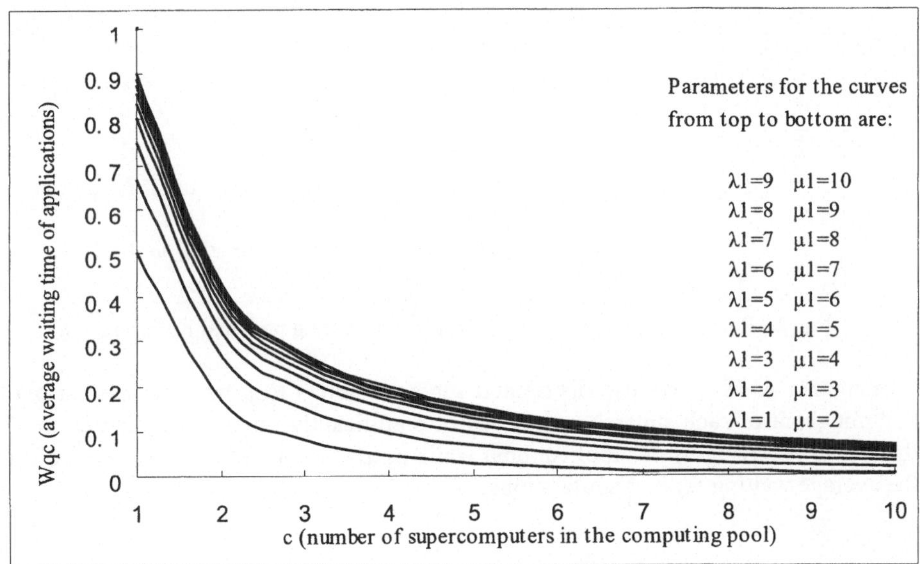

Fig. 1. Relationship between volume of computing pool and average waiting time

From the figure, we can see distinct differences between c independent supercomputers (c=1 for each supercomputer) and a computing pool of c supercomputers (c>1). For example, suppose λ_1=9 and μ_1= 10, i.e. a supercomputer can averagely see 9 arriving applications while it can carry out 10 applications every hour. If c=1, arriving applications should wait 0.9 hour in average when the supercomputer is 90% ($=\lambda_1/\mu_1$) busy; if c=4, however, applications only need 0.2 hour of waiting time in average. All the curves in Fig. 1 show that as the number of supercomputers in the pool increases, the waiting time of the arriving applications gets shorter and shorter, i.e. quality of service is improved.

Now we will examine how computing pool improves throughput of supercomputers. When μ_1 is fixed ($\mu_1>\lambda_1$), a M/M/c queuing system will have the following properties: If c does not change, Wq_c will increase with the growth of λ_1, i.e. Wq_c is a monotonic increasing function of λ_1; on the other hand, if λ_1 does not change, Wq_c will decrease with the growth of c, i.e. Wq_c is a monotonic decreasing function of c. Then we can imagine there will be a balanced condition: Wq_c can be kept unchanged, while λ_1 can be increased with the growth of c. This condition will be illustrated in Fig. 2, in which $\mu_1=10$ and $Wq_c=0.1$. If the supercomputers are independent ones, λ_1 can only be 5, which means 50% of the computing power can be utilized; but if it is a computing pool of 4 supercomputers, λ_1 can be as high as 8.3, which means 83% of the computing power can be utilized. The values of λ_1 in Fig. 2 are figured out by using formula (2) in a reversed manner in MATLAB.

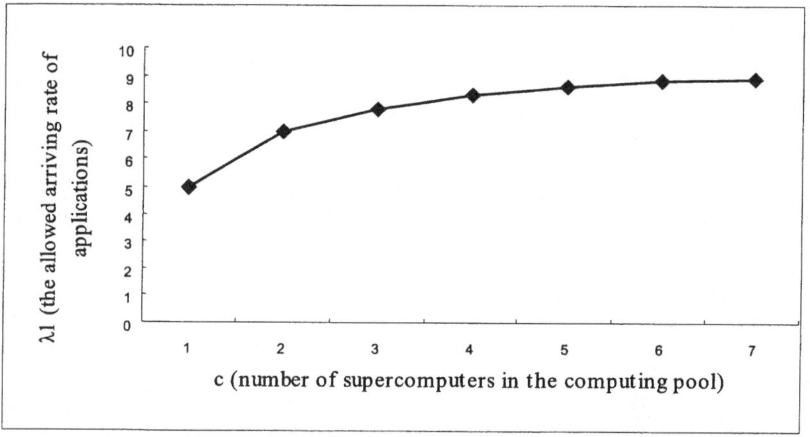

Fig. 2. Relationship between the volume of computing pool and its throughput

In another word, if we use distributed supercomputers to form a computing pool, the throughput of each supercomputer can be significantly improved by increasing λ_1 (the rate of receiving users' applications) while keeps the same quality of service Wq_c (the average waiting time of applications).

5 Conclusions

Decomposing applications to distributed computers is one of the core ideas of grid to solve grand challenges problems [25]. Nevertheless, most live applications are relative moderate ones which can be settled easily on one of the supercomputers. Neglecting this fact and dividing application any way, will result in severe communication cost and many redundant programming and optimizing work.

On the other hand, many supercomputer centers are still operated in traditional ways. They are not convenient to users, and their QoS and efficiency cannot compete with computing pool. Analysis shows that if a computing pool has four identical supercomputers and each one can handle ten applications in average, the waiting time for applications can be reduced from 0.9 hour to 0.2 hour, or utilization of each supercomputer can be increased from 50% to 83% without prolonging waiting time.

Although computing pool is a simple idea, it is worth emphasizing its advantages (as shown in Table 1) and importance here. There are some grid applications have been developed, tried, and then abandoned, since they are designed for the future. But now it is time to deploy the practicable, inexpensive, general-purpose computing pool, to enhance QoS and performance of traditional supercomputer centers.

Table 1. A comparison of the three high performance computing platforms

	Computing Pool	*Full-fledged Grid*	*Computing Center*
Good for tasks that have this size	Medium to large	Huge	Medium
Utilization of resources	High	High	Low
Quality of service	High	High	Low
Complexity of programming and optimizing	Medium	High	Low
Communication Cost	Medium	High	Low

References

1. Foster, I., Kesselman, C., Tuecke, S.: The Anatomy of the Grid: Enabling Scalable Virtual Organizations. International J. Supercomputer Applications, 15(3), 2001.
2. Foster, I.: What is the Grid? A Three Point Checklist, Grid Today, July 22, , 2002: Vol. 1 No. 6, http://www.gridtoday.com/02/0722/100136.html
3. Foster, I., Kesselman, C.: Globus: A Metacomputing Infrastructure Toolkit. Intl J. Supercomputer Applications. 1997, 11(2):115-128
4. Grimshaw, A. S., Wulf, W. A.: the Legion team. The Legion Vision of a Worldwide Virtual Computer. Communications of the ACM, 1997, 40(1): 39-45
5. Litzkow, M. J., Livny, M., Mutka, M. W.: Condor - A hunter of idle workstations. 8th International Conference on Distributed Computing Systems, 1988, 104-111
6. Johnston, W., Gannon, D., Nitzberg, B.: Grids as production computing environments: The engineering aspects of nasa's information power grid. In Proc. Eighth IEEE International Symposium on High Performance Distributed Computing, 1999.
7. DOE Science Grid, http://doesciencegrid.org/
8. GriPhyN – Grid Physics Network, http://www.griphyn.org/index.php
9. TeraGrid, http://www.teragrid.org/

10. Segal, B.: Grid Computing: The European Data Project, IEEE Nuclear Science Symposium and Medical Imaging Conference, Lyon, 15-20 October 2000.
11. Almond, J., Snelling, D.: UNICORE: uniform access to supercomputing as an element of electronic commerce, Future Generation Computer Systems 15(1999) 539-548, NH-Elsevier.
12. The Distributed ASCI Supercomputer 2 (DAS-2), http://www.cs.vu.nl/das2/
13. Buyya, R., Abramson, D., Giddy, J.: Nimrod/G: An Architecture for a Resource Management and Scheduling System in a Global Computational Grid. In: Proc. of 4th Int'l Conf. on High Performance Computing in Asia-Pacific Region, Beijing, 2000, 283-289
14. Buyya, R., Abramson, D., Giddy, J.: Economic Models for Resource Trading in a Service Oriented Grid Computing Environments , Monash University, http://www.csse.monash.edu.au/~rajkumar/ecogrid/, Oct 2000 (in publication).
15. Sato, M., Nakada, H., Sekiguchi, S., et al.: Ninf: A Network based Information Library for a Global World-Wide Computing Infrastructure. In: Proceedings of HPCN'97 (LNCS-1225), 1997, 491-502
16. Brunett, S., Davis, D., Gottschalk, T., Messina, P., Kesselman, C.: Implementing distributed synthetic forces simulations in metacomputing environments. In Proceedings of the Heterogeneous Computing Workshop, pages 29-42. IEEE Computer Society Press, 1998.
17. Allen, G., Dramlitsch, T., Foster, I., Karonis, N., Ripeanu, M., Seidel, E., Toonen, B.: Supporting Efficient Execution in Heterogeneous Distributed Computing Environments with Cactus and Globus, Supercomputing 2001.
18. Benger, W., Foster, I., Novotny, J., Seidel, E., Shalf, J., Smith, W., Walker, P.: Numerical relativity in a distributed environment. In Proceedings of the Ninth SIAM Conference on Parallel Processing for Scientic Computing, Apr. 1999. http://citeseer.nj.nec.com/benger99numerical.html
19. Awards Cap SC2001 HPC and Networking Conference, NPACI & DSC Online, Volume 5, Issue 24 - November 28, 2001 , http://www.npaci.edu/online/v5.24/sc2001.awards.html
20. Synthetic Forces Express, http://www.cacr.caltech.edu/SFExpress/
21. SETI@home: Search for Extraterrestrial Intelligence at home, http://setiathome.ssl.berkeley.edu/
22. Elmir, J. M. H., Muftah. H. T.: All-optical wavelength conversion: technologies and applications in DWDM networks. IEEE Communication Magazine, 2000, 38(3): 86~92
23. Myricom Home Page, http://www.myri.com/
24. InfiniBand Trade Association Home Page, http://www.infinibandta.org/home
25. Committee on Physical, Mathematical and Engineering Sciences, Grand Challenges: High Performance Computing and Communications, Office of Science and Technology Policy, Washington, D.C. 1991.

Formalizing Service Publication and Discovery in Grid Computing Systems

Chuliang Weng, Xinda Lu, and Qianni Deng

Department of Computer Science and Engineering, Shanghai Jiao Tong University, Shanghai, 200030, People's Republic of China
{weng-cl, lu-xd, deng-qn}@cs.sjtu.edu.cn

Abstract. Considering the autonomy of resources in the grid environment and based on the service-oriented thought, a resource management system for grid computing can be abstracted to a multi-agent system that consists of service requestor agents, service provider agents and service broker agents. For looking into the interaction characteristics of agents, the formal method is adopted. Firstly, we present an abstract model of agent-based service publication and discovery for resource management in grid computing systems, and specify agent actions with π-calculus in the grid context. Secondly, we define the interaction protocol among agents as processes. Finally, The consistency between agent actions and the interaction protocol is discussed.

1 Introduction

Grid computing is concerned with "coordinated resource sharing and problem solving in dynamic, multi-institutional virtual organizations"[1]. According to Ian Foster, in the grid architecture, five levels of management can be distinguished: fabric, connectivity, single resource, collective multiple resources, and application. The fabric layer typically constitutes computational resources, network resources, etc. The connectivity layer is concerned with easy and secure communication by providing single sign on, delegation, etc. The resource layer cares individual resources, and the two primary classes of resource layer protocols are management protocols and information protocols. The collective multiple resources layer is not associated with anyone specific resource but rather is global in nature and captures interactions across collections of resources, it can implement a wide variety of sharing behaviors without placing new requirements on the resources being shared. The final layer in the grid architecture comprises the user applications that operate within a virtual organization environment.

In this paper, the resource management is discussed from the point of view of the collective multiple resources layer. Coordinating collective resources is a very complex high-level task that integrates the multiple resources into a wide-area distributed system. Brokering services, scheduling, workload management and collaboration frameworks, and collaborative services are processes that require intelligence, autonomy, and social capabilities, which are characteristics of intelligent agents [3,4,9,10].

M. Li et al. (Eds.): GCC 2003, LNCS 3032, pp. 669–676, 2004.

Motivation for this study comes from previous works [3,5,7,8,10] on agent-based resource management for grid computing and works [6,12,13] on modeling MAS (multi-agent systems) with formal method. In this paper, we extend previous works by integrating two aspects of works together, and study agent actions and interaction protocols with formal method in the model of agent-based service publication and discovery for resource management in grid context.

2 Related Works

Attempts to apply intelligent agents in realizing the grid vision have been made by academic researchers during the past few years. AgentSpace [3] is a scalable agent-based distributed system, which supports large-scale systems such Internet environments. Agent grid concept is proposed under the DARPA ISO's Control of Agent-Based Systems (CoABS) program [5]. The CoABS grid provides a unified, heterogeneous distributed computing environment in which computing resources are seamlessly linked based on a number of application level and functional requirements. Another good example of an agent grid is described in [7]. It integrates services and resources for establishing multi-disciplinary problem solving environments. Heterogeneous agents contain behavioral rules, which can be modified based on their interaction with the environment where they operate. In contrast, another example ARMS [8]: an agent-based resource management system for grid computing, it uses a hierarchy of homogenous agents for both service advertisement and discovery.

3 System Model and Agent Actions

Considering the autonomy of resources in grid environment and based on service-oriented thought [2], an agent-based resource management system can be abstracted to a system that consists of service requestor agents, service provider agents and service broker agents, where agents are identified by *handle*, and services are identified by *service port* (which is different from the term *port* in the π-calculus).

3.1 Hierarchical Model

For requesting the service, a service requestor agent should firstly query the information service that is provided by a service broker agent. After receiving the request for locating the special service, the service broker agent queries the information database in itself to fetch the handle and the service port of the service. Finally, with the handle and the service port returned by the service broker agent, the service requestor agent directly asks for the service provider agent to fulfill the special service. That is the primary system model.

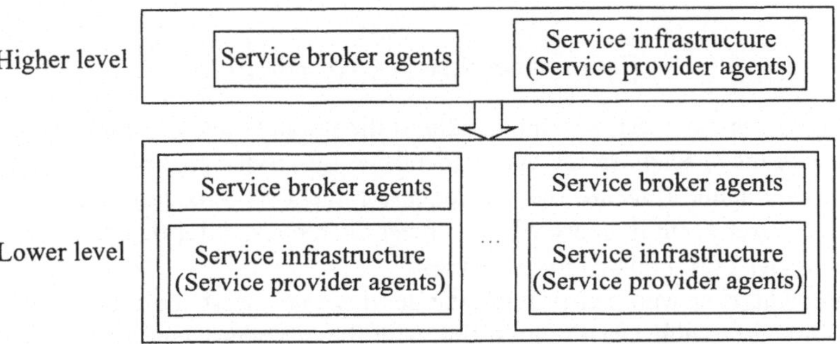

Fig. 1. The hierarchical model

The agent-based resource management hierarchical model (see Fig.1.) can be build based on the primary model. Higher-level service provider agents can delegate the requests to lower-level service provider agents, so a higher-level service can be implemented by collaboration of lower-level service provider agents. In this case, higher-level service provider agents evolve into service requestor agents from the point of view of lower-level service provider agents.

Similarly, higher-level service broker agents can be created that keep the information of the corresponding higher-level service provider agents. When a higher-level service provider agent creates a new service that is implemented by composing the behaviors of those multiple lower-level service provider agents, it should register the new service to a corresponding higher-level service broker agent so that service requestor agents can locate it and request the service.

Since the behavior of agents is concurrent and dynamic, process algebra is adopted to specify actions and interactions of agents in the grid context. In the paper, the polyadic π-calculus [11] is chosen as the formalizing method, this is because [6]: π-calculus is a model of concurrent computation based upon the notion of naming, and it is a way of describing and analyzing systems consisting of agents which interact among each other, and whose configuration or neighborhood is continually changing.

3.2 Requestor Agents

Service requestor agents (hereafter, referred as to requestor agents) aim at grid users and grid applications, and they deliver requests of grid users or grid applications. When a service request is put forward, a corresponding requestor agent should query the information service of a service broker agent (hereafter, referred as to broker agent) to locate the service provider agent (hereafter, referred as to provider agent). After obtaining the location of the provider agent, the requestor agent will represent the grid users or grid applications to ask for the service of the provider agent.

Firstly, according to the request, a requestor agent queries a broker agent to locate the provider agent.

$$DiscoveryService(r) \overset{def}{=} \overline{d}(r).r(h,p) \tag{1}$$

Where, *r* is a request, *h* is the handle of the provider agent, which can meet the request with the special service that is identified by service port *p*. *h* and *p* are returned by a broker agent. It means that the requestor agent send request name *r* through port *d* to the broker agent to query who can meet the request, after that waits for the handle *h* and service port *p* related to the request.

After knowing who can provide the service that meets the request, the requestor agent directly establishes a request link with the provider agent, and waits the service on name *x* at the location *w*.

$$Req(w,h,p) \overset{def}{=} \overline{h}(w,p).w(x) \tag{2}$$

3.3 Provider Agents

We integrate the information service into the function of the broker agent. When a provider agent is registered, a broker agent will assign a global unique handle to it, and the provider agent is observable to the outside. Each provider agent can provide more than one service to the outside, which is identified by service port after it is registered to a broker agent.

The provider agent registering process is defined as follows:

$$RegService(sa) \overset{def}{=} \overline{reg}(sa).reg(h) \tag{3}$$

It will return a handle to the provider agent exported by a broker agent. And the service registering process is defined as follows:

$$RegServicePort(h,r) \overset{def}{=} \overline{regr}(h,r).regp(p) \tag{4}$$

It will obtain a service port *p* of the service that meets the request *r*, which is provided by the provider agent which handle is *h*.

After a provider agent receives a request for a special service provided by it, it would export the service corresponding to the request. The request can be classified into two classes. One is that can be satisfied independently with a single service exported by the special provider agent. In this case, the sub-request is *nil*. The other is that should be fulfilled by composing the services provided by multiple lower-level provider agents, consequently the request will be divided into multiple sub-requests *r'*. In this case, it is the higher-level provider agent that integrates multiple lower-level services into a single service of itself, and only after all sub-requests *r'* are fulfilled, the provider agent notifies the requestor agent that the request is fulfilled. The service providing process can be defined as follows:

$$ProvideService(h, p_s, s) \stackrel{def}{=} !(h(w,x).[x = p_s]((\upsilon x')Subreq(x').$$
$$([x' = nil]0 + (\upsilon h, p)DiscoverService(x').Req(w', h, p)).\overline{w}(s))) \tag{5}$$

Where, h is the handle of a provider agent, s is the service the agent will provide, p_s is the service port number of s, w is the place that the service will be transmitted to, w' is the place of the provider agent itself, x is the request from outside which has been transformed to a service port number, and x' represents the sub-request of x.

When a provider agent destroys a service, it should unregister the service to the broker agent. And when a provider agent leaves the system, it should unregister itself to the broker agent.

$$UnregServicePort(h, p) \stackrel{def}{=} \overline{unregp}(h, p) \tag{6}$$

$$UnregService(h) \stackrel{def}{=} \overline{unreg}(h) \tag{7}$$

3.4 Broker Agents

Broker agents are abstracted to manage the available information of all kinds of resources in the presented model. When a new provider agent joins the system, it is a broker agent that designates a global unique handle to it. Broker agents also designate a service port number to a new service created by a provider agent. After that when a request arrives for the registered service, the broker agent responds to the request, and returns the handle of the provider agent and the service port of its service. Broker agents will unregister provider agents and their services when they leave the system.

The process corresponding to the provider agent registration and unregistration is defined as follows:

$$RegedService \stackrel{def}{=} !((\upsilon h)reg(sa).Allocate(sa,h).\overline{reg}(h) + unreg(h).Unallocate(h)) \tag{8}$$

The service registering process is defined as follows:

$$RegedServicePort \stackrel{def}{=} !((\upsilon p)regr(h,r).AllocatePort(r,h,p).\overline{regp}(p)$$
$$+ unregp(h,p).UnallocatePort(h,p)) \tag{9}$$

Broker agents have a table which item is <r, h, p>, where r is a request, h is the handle of a provider agent, and p is the service port of a service provided by provider agent h to meet request r, by which broker agents can keep the information about provider agents and services provided by provider agents.

The service finding process is defined as follows for responding to the request of querying service:

$$FindService \stackrel{def}{=} !((\upsilon p,h)d(r).Find(r,p).Map(p,h).\overline{r}(h,p)) \tag{10}$$

4 Interaction Protocols and Consistency Discussion

Interaction protocols provide rules for interactions between agents, and guarantee that interactions occur with correct sequence and consistence. Interaction protocols for service publication and discovery in the grid context include the register protocol, the query protocol, and the request protocol. Register protocol defines how to register service and service port for the registering side and how to response to request for registering service and service port for the register service side, through which service publication is accomplished. It also includes correspondingly unregister process.

Register service protocol is defined as follows:

$$RegServiceIP = (\upsilon a, h)(\overline{reg}(a).reg(h) \mid \overline{unreg}(h) \mid \\ !(reg(a).Allocate(a,h).\overline{reg}(h) + unreg(h).Unallocate(h))) \quad (11)$$

Register service port protocol is defined as follows:

$$RegServicePortIP = (\upsilon r, h, p)(\overline{regr}(h,r).regp(p) \mid \overline{unregp}(h,p) \mid \\ !(regr(h,r).AllocatePort(r,h,p).\overline{regp}(p) + unregp(h,p).UnallocatePort(h,p)) \quad (12)$$

Therefore, the register protocol can be defined:

$$RegisterIP = RegServiceIP/RegServicePortIP \quad (13)$$

For requesting services in the grid context, which agent can provide the services should be determined at first. That is, the second kinds of interactions occur between the sides of querying services and the sides of providing information services.

$$QueryIP = (\upsilon r, h, p)(\overline{d}(r).r(h,p) \mid !(d(r).Find(r,p).Map(p,h).\overline{r}(h,p))) \quad (14)$$

The third kind of interactions in the system is that requestor agents ask for services according to the information obtained during the querying phase and provider agents answer the requests.

$$RequestIP = (\upsilon h, w, p)(\overline{h}(w,p).w(x) \mid !(h(w,x).[x = p_s]((\upsilon x')Subreq(x'). \\ ([x' = nil]0 + (\upsilon h, p)DiscoverService(x').Req(w', h, p)).\overline{w}(s)))) \quad (15)$$

Finally, we can define the interaction protocol as a combination of the three interaction protocols above:

$$InteractionProtocol = RegisterIP \mid QueryIP \mid RequestIP \quad (16)$$

In the system, agents perform themselves' actions according to respective demands. It is necessary that the consistency between agents' actions and the interaction protocol should hold. This consistency guarantees that the agent can implement the individual goal and interactions among agents go on wheels. This consistency means that the actions of agents conform to the interaction protocol and agents interact with each other in accordance with the interaction protocol.

As the counterpart of interactions among agents, each agent's actions also include internal communication actions. From an external point of view, only interactions among different agents are observable while internal actions are unobservable. Therefore, actions of agents are considered to be consistent with the interaction protocol if observable actions coincide with the interaction protocol. Comparing agent actions with the interaction protocol, which are defined by π-calculus above, it can be easy to see that agent actions and the interaction protocol satisfy the relation of consistency, i.e., agent actions conform to the interaction protocol.

5 Conclusions

In this paper, an abstract model of agent-based service publication and discovery for resource management in grid context is presented, which is the basis for analyzing service publication and discovery. And we specify actions and interactions of agents in the model with the formal method to look into the mechanism of interactions across the collective resources layer. The major contributions of this research work include an abstract model of agent-based service publication and discovery for resource management in grid computing systems, and formalizing actions and the interaction protocol of agents in the model as well as analyzing the relation of consistency between agent actions and the interaction protocol.

Acknowledgements. This research was supported by the National Natural Science Foundation of China, No. 60173031.

References

1. Foster, I., Kesselman, C., Tuecke, S.: The Anatomy of the Grid: Enabling Scalable Virtual Organizations. The International Journal of Supercomputer Applications, Vol.15, No.3 (2001) 200-222
2. Foster, I., Kesselman, C., Nick, J.M., Tuecke, S.: The Physiology of the Grid: An Open Grid Services Architecture for Distributed Systems Integration. Open Grid Service Infrastructure WG, Global Grid Forum (2002)
3. Wijngaards, N.J., Oereinder, B.J., Van Steen, M., Brazier, F.M.: Supporting Internet-scale Multi-agent Systems. Data and Knowledge Engineering, Vol.41, No.2 (2002) 229-245
4. Wooldridge, M., Jennings, N.R.: Intelligent Agents: Theory and Practice. The Knowledge Engineering Review, Vol.10, No.2 (1995) 115–152
5. Manola, F., Thompson, C.: Characterizing the Agent Grid, Technical Report. Object Services and Consulting Inc. (1999)
6. Jiao, W., Shi. Z.: Formalizing Interactions and Interaction Protocols in Multi-agent Systems. Journal of software (Chinese), Vol.12, No.8 (2001) 1177-1182
7. Rana, O.F., Walker, D.W.: The Agent Grid: Agent-based Resource Integration in PSEs. In: Proceedings of the 16th IMACS World Congress on Scientific Computation, Applied Mathematics and Simulation. Proceedings on CD-ROM, Lausanne, Switzerland (2000)

8. Cao, J., Jarvis, S.A., Saini, S., Kerbyson, D.J., Nudd, G.R.: ARMS: An Agent-based Resource Management System for Grid Computing. Scientific Programming, Vol.10, No.2 (2002) 135-148
9. Wooldridge, M., Ciancarini, P.: Agent-Oriented Software Engineering: The State of the Art. In: Ciancarini, P., Wooldridge, M. (eds.): Agent-Oriented Software Engineering. Lecture Notes in Artificial Intelligence, Vol.1957. Springer-Verlag, Berlin Heidelberg New York (2001) 1-28
10. Rana, O.F., Moreau, L.: Issues in Building Agent-based Computational Grids. In: Proceedings of the 3rd Workshop of the UK Special Interest Group on Multi-Agent Systems (UKMAS'2000), Oxford, UK (2000)
11. Milner, R.: The Polyadic π-Calculus: A Tutorial. In: Bauer, F.L., Brauer, W., Schwichtenberg, H. (eds.): Logic and Algebra of Specification. Springer-Verlag, Berlin Heidelberg New York (1993) 203-246
12. Brazier, F.M., Dunin Keplicz, B.M., Jennings, N.R., Treur, J.: DESIRE: Modeling Multi-Agent Systems in a Compositional Formal Framework. The International Journal of Cooperative Information Systems, Vol.6, No.1 (1997) 67-94
13. D'Inverno, M., Fisher, M., Lomuscio, A., Luck, M., De Rijke, M., Ryan, M., Wooldridge, M.: Formalisms for Multi-Agent Systems. The Knowledge Engineering Review, Vol.12, No.3 (1997) 315-321

An Improved Solution to I/O Support Problems in Wide Area Grid Computing Environments*

Bin Wang [1], Ping Chen [1,2], and Zhuoqun Xu [1]

[1] Department of Computer Science & Technology, Peking University, 100871, Beijing, P.R.China.
{wangbin, zqxu}@ailab.pku.edu.cn
[2] Computer Centre, Peking University, 100871 Beijing, P.R.China
pchen@pku.edu.cn

Abstract. In wide area Grid computing environments, computation is often performed at a site distant from data needed and from the user console. Therefore, it necessitates I/O support to run computation jobs at remote sites. Major Grid software providers have implemented their own I/O solutions. However, in existing solutions, two important user requirements for I/O support are not satisfied, namely, run-time standard input from user console and run-time stage-out of scratched files during computation. Regarding these deficiencies, the paper puts forward an improved I/O support solution. In addition, the paper presents a reference implementations and describes application experience of our implementation in PCG(PACT Computational Grid) project.

Keywords: I/O, Grid computing, standard input, scratched files, Globus

1 Introduction

In wide area computational grids, it is often the case that computation is often performed at a site distant from data needed and from the user console. As a result, it inevitably involves providing I/O support to start and run remote computations.

This paper is focused on I/O support problems (I/O mechanisms for submission and running of remote computation jobs) in wide area Grid computing environments.

Based on careful investigations of user requirements, we found the following I/O requirements occurring in Grid computing environment:

a. Input data files needed by a computation job, located at user-specified sites, need to be staged in to the computation site prior to start of the computation job;
b. Output result data files produced by a computation job need to be staged out to user-specified sites as soon as the computation job ends;
c. Parameter files needed by a computation job need to be staged in to the computation site prior to start of the computation job;

* The work is supported by National Natural Science Foundation of China under contract #60173004 and #60073016.

M. Li et al. (Eds.): GCC 2003, LNCS 3032, pp. 677–684, 2004.

d. When a computation job is in progress, the run-time standard output and error of computation processes need to be real-time transferred from computation site to the user console and meanwhile, if requested by users, the run-time standard output and error may also be stored into disk files at user-specified location;
e. During the course of a computation job, the run-time standard input can be real-time transferred from the user console to the remote computation site in order to intervene or to direct the course of the computation job;
f. If requested by users, run-time scratched result files produced by a computation job in progress need to be transferred from the computation site to user-specified sites in order to keep close track of progress of the computation job or to make simulated real-time visualized output.

With these requirements in mind, we studied major known software systems for wide area computing. These systems meet most of the requirements, but, regarding requirement e. and f., not enough support is given yet. Regarding the deficiencies, we advance an improved solution to address requirement e. and f.

This paper makes the following contributions:

1) For the first time, puts forward the addition, design scheme and reference implementation of run-time standard input support to I/O support mechanisms in wide area Grid computing environments;
2) For the first time, puts forward the addition, design scheme and reference implementation of run-time scratched results transfer support to I/O support mechanism in wide area Grid computing environments.

The rest of the paper is structured as follows. Sect. 2 introduces the background of I/O requirements and conventional solutions. Sect. 3 reviews existing I/O support solutions in wide area computing, and illuminates their deficiencies. In Sect. 4, we propose an improved I/O support solution. Sect. 5 presents a reference implementation of our design scheme, and briefly describes application of the improved I/O solution in PCG project. Sect. 6 concludes the whole paper and expects future work.

2 Background

As a rule, I/O involved in application processes at least consists of:

1) regular file I/O: one or more input disk data files, one or more output disk data files;
2) special file I/O: standard I/O, namely, standard input(shortened as "stdin"), standard output(shortened as "stdout"), standard error(shortened as "stderr").

Here we omit PIPE, FIFO or Sockets, because they are not necessarily required in application processes.

I/O involved in an application process of wide area computing is almost the same. Due to the specialty of wide area Grid computing environments, it is quite different and difficult to implement necessary I/O support.

In wide area computational grids, computational resource cannot be determined till the moment when a computation job is submitted. It is often the case that computation is often performed at a site distant from data needed and from the user console. So in this case, how shall we implement required I/O support for computation jobs running in the environments?

As to the issue of regular file I/O, there are usually two approaches [6]:

1) Move job/application to the data;
2) Move data to the job/application

In practice, 1) is less common. Because computational power may be insufficient on storage sites and it is inefficient for a storage resource to handle data maintenance and computation simultaneously. Besides, 1) doesn't scale well. So usually, we stage data needed to computation sites, execute computation jobs there and stage result data back to storage sites after the computation is done.

As to the issue of standard I/O, there are also two alternatives:

1) Store the standard output and error as files on a disk, then send the whole file back by FTP or a similar protocol after the computation is done.
2) Connect the standard output and error directly to a TCP stream back to the home machine

Both of the solutions are problematic in a sense.

1) does not satisfy the user who needs to see progressively updated output. Many users rely on log-like output to determine if their applications are running correctly. In addition, the remote computation site may not have enough disk space to store all of the output. Both of the objections are magnified for a program that is designed to run for a quite long time. 2) makes the application dependent upon the whims of the network. We expect users will be making use of hundreds of machines spread around the globe, and at any given time, some of them will be disconnected from the home machine. We want the user's to make forward progress when they are disconnected from home. Although the user prefers to have continuous output, a partitioned network should not bring all work to a screeching halt.

So, in practice, there need to be a tradeoff between these two alternatives.

3 Existing Solutions and Deficiencies

Major known software systems for wide area computing, like Globus, Condor, Legion, have implemented their own I/O solutions in their released packages. These I/O solutions meet most requirements(a.,b.,c.,d.) for I/O support mechanisms put forward in Sect. 1 of this paper, but none of them meet requirement e. and f..

Condor's strategy for regular file I/O can be summarized as follows: use shared file system if available; use Condor to transfer files instead, if unavailable. Condor system can automatically send back changed files and atomically transfer multiple files. Condor utilizes remote procedure call to achieve transparent migration across different administrative domains.

To resolve regular file I/O, Legion introduces its own special I/O calls. In the Legion system, global access to data is supported via specialized I/O methods [8]. Global access is provided via shell commands such as "legion_cp" (the Legion version of the Unix copy command). First, Legion copies binaries and input data files needed to computation sites selected. Then the computation starts under the monitor of Legion. As soon as the computation is done, Legion copies the output data files to user-specified location.

I/O support mechanism in the Globus Toolkit can be summarized as "GRAM+GASS" solution. GRAM(Globus Resource Allocation Management) is used to process resource request, to allocate computational resources requested, and to initiate and manage jobs started at remote computation sites [1]. GASS(Global Access to Secondary Storage) is a data access and movement service provided in Globus Toolkit. This service defines a global name space via Uniform Resource Locators(URLs) and allows applications to access remote files via standard I/O interfaces [2]. GRAM can be integrated with GASS services to provide I/O support for computations executing at remote sites. GRAM is extended such that it allows parameter to be named by URLs with GASS mechanisms used to fetch URL-named files, e.g. input data files, executables, standard input, into the cache and to redirect standard output and error.

As to standard output and error, solutions are offered in Condor, Legion and Globus. In Condor's job submit description file, parameters "**Output**" and "**Error**" are used to indicate standard output and error respectively [5]. The standard I/O files are mapped to regular files set by the parameters. In Legion, a TTY object is employed to redirect standard output and error to one or more consoles, or(and) to files if requested [9]. In Globus, standard output and error are temporarily stored in GASS cache, and then transferred to user-specified consoles or(and) files. But in the case of Condor, users cannot expect to watch the real-time standard output or error from their consoles and can only get log-like disk files after the remotely running computation is over.

When it comes to the standard input, none of the existing solutions do a good job. So far, we fail to find any mention of standard input support in Legion papers. Both in Condor and in Globus, standard input of the computation job at remote sites is viewed as a fixed regular file determined before computation starts, rather than an input device.

In fact, standard input is quite different from regular input data files, in that users' inputs(captured by reading standard input) vary with the progress of the computation job and cannot be determined prior to the start of computation. If standard input is treated as a regular input data file, flexibility of programs is sacrificed. Consider the following C program segment,

```
...
fprintf(stdout, "Time consumed in parallel comput-
ing: %f seconds, %d iterations, tolerence is %f in
Processor %d\n", timeused, num, tolerence,me);
fprintf(stdout, "Please input your directions:(yes
or no, yes to continue,no to quit");
if(fgets(buf,sizeof(buf),stdin)!=NULL){
   if(strcmp(buf,"no\n")==0) exit(0);
}
...
```

The program, after a certain period of time or a certain number of iterations, sends information about the progress of program(time consumed, number of iterations, tolerance, etc.) to user's screen by writing to standard output. Then the program pauses, waiting for directions by reading standard input from the user. The user analyzes information received from standard output of the program, and decides whether to continue the computation job. If the user is satisfied with the job's progress, he types "yes" to continue the job process; if not, he types "no" to halt the job process.

In this example, the standard input of the job cannot be determined prior to the start of computation. So, in Condor or Globus, programs like the above cannot get enough support, nor can they run properly.

In addition, I/O support system without run-time standard input support is unidirectional and "half-interactive". The direction of I/O stream is from computation jobs to users, but not the other way around.

Requirement f. originates from the demand for run-time scratched results. In wide area Grid computing environments, many computations take a long time(sometimes for days, even for months or years) to run their courses. Users want to keep real-time track of computation progress, rather than in the dark about what's going on. So it necessitates storage and stage-out of run-time scratched files produced by computation jobs. With these scratched files in hand, users can make simulated real-time visual output or perform computation retrieval and analysis afterwards [4]. However, pitifully it is not addressed in any existing I/O support solutions.

4 An Improved I/O Support Solution

Regarding the deficiencies of existing I/O support mechanisms, we advance an improved I/O support solution for wide area Grid computing environments. It consists of two additions, run-time standard input support and run-time scratched results stage-out support.

4.1 Addition of Run-Time Standard Input Support

Let's consider two possible ways to add support for run-time standard input:

1) Prior to the start of computation, establish a stable TCP socket connection from user console to the remote computation site. The connection is alive throughout the whole computation process, responsible for connecting run-time user input directly to the standard input of the computation job at the remote site.
2) Add standard input to transfer in channels used for transferring standard output and error in existing I/O solutions.

1) is unsuitable for wide area Grid computing environment. 1) has been successfully applied in parallel programming environments, like MPI. A stable TCP connection is established between MPIRUN process at the user console and the process manager at Node 0 to forward user's input as standard input of the computation job [7]. However, considering the environment of wide area Grid computing, method 1) doesn't work. In wide area computing, users cannot expect the network connection between user console and remote computation site to be stable and reliable throughout the whole computation course. It is a commonplace for some part of the network chain to break down sometime. 2) is not feasible in that it overlooks the difference between

standard input and standard output or error. In a connection transferring standard output or error between the user console and remote computation site, it is the side at the remote computation site that initiates data transfers through the connection. While in the connection transferring standard input, it is the side at the user console that is expected to initiate data transfers.

After ruling out the above two solutions, we propose the following one:

Use short connections to transfer standard input; user console side is responsible to initiate the connection upon receiving users' input.

Adoption of short connections shuns the dependence on the whims of the unreliable network in wide area computing environment. User console as the initial side of connection ensures prompt staging of standard input information.

The above solution we proposed has both advantages and disadvantages in itself:

Advantages: it implements complete, bidirectional interaction between user console and computation jobs running at remote sites. Users can exert run-time intervention on the remote computation jobs according actual progress of the jobs.

Disadvantages: it increases management and communication burden.

We can adopt the way of setting the staging as optional to overcome disadvantages. Set staging of standard input as an optional item in the user-specified job submit description file(e.g. condor_submit input file in Condor, or RSL file in Globus). Not all the computation jobs need run-time standard input. If users don't specify this item, it is defaulted as no need for startup of staging standard input mechanism. We only run the mechanism for computation jobs needing run-time standard input. Thus, it avoids unnecessary management and communication spending.

4.2 Addition of Run-Time Scratched Files Stage-out Support

To add run-time scratched files stage-out support, we take almost the same method as proposed in Sect. 4.1, that is

Use short connections to transfer run-time scratched files; remote computation site is responsible to initiate the connection upon a new run-time scratched file is found.

Add an item of "**Middle_Result_Files**" to the job submit description file. Under that item in the job submit description file, names and destinations(URLs) of scratched files are specified. Upon finding this item in the parsed job submit files, stage mechanism for run-time scratched file is activated. Of course, it is optional, not compulsory. If unnecessary for scratched files transfer, users may choose not to start up the service and save system's cost.

5 Implementation and Application

5.1 Implementation

We chose "GRAM+GASS", I/O support solution in the open source Globus Toolkit, as a basis to implement improved I/O support mechanism advanced in Sect. 4.1 and 4.2.

In order to support run-time standard input, the following work is done: add interfaces for standard input; in user's job submit RSL file, add support to identification of standard input by setting parameter "**stdin**" to a special device file name of "url/dev/stdin"; within GRAM Job Manager, add mechanisms to redirects the standard input to a file in the GASS cache; within GRAM Client, add mechanisms to periodically check standard input data from user, and if any, to initiate a short connection to transfer the data.

In order to support stage-out of run-time scratched files, the following work is done: in job submit RSL file, add an item of "**Middle_Result_Files**" to specify whether and where to stage run-time scratched files; within GRAM Job Manager, add mechanisms to transfer scratched files.

5.2 Application

We have applied the improved I/O support mechanism to the development work of PCG(PACT Computational Grid) project and received satisfactory results.

After the addition of run-time standard input support, users can interact with and intervene their remotely running computation jobs. For example, in Laplace calculations, users can halt the computing process or alter the value of tolerance to adapt to practical computation situation through the run-time standard input channel, when a Laplace computing job is in progress.

In addition, after implementation of run-time scratched files stage-out support, users can get valuable scratched data of the computation job in progress. With the data in hand, users can perform real-time visualized output of the computation jobs to show the computation progress. It is very meaningful for run-time remote diagnosis and afterwards retrieval. Fig. 1 is a real-time two-dimensional visual output of a Laplace calculation job in progress. The four bitmaps within Fig. 4 are drawn by a VC++ application according to scratched data gathered through our scratched files stage-out mechanism.

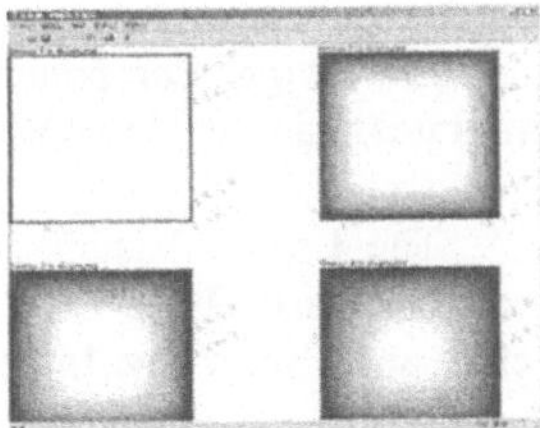

Fig. 1. Two-Dimensional Visual Output of a Laplace Calculation Job in Progress

6 Conclusions and Future Work

Improved I/O support mechanisms can better serve the requirements of remotely running computation jobs in wide area Grid computing environments. Users can collect sufficient information as to the progress of computation processes, then make accurate decisions based on them, and run-time intervene the remote computation course. In addition, with the run-time scratched result data in hand, users have a better knowledge of what's going on inside the computation. Application experiences show its feasibility and practical utility.

In the future, more experiments are expected to test run-time I/O performance under our improved I/O support mechanisms. In addition, we need expand usage of run-time standard input and scratched result data of remotely running computation jobs in order to make the most of the improved I/O solution.

References

1. K. Czajkowski et al. A Resource Management Architecture for Metacomputing Systems. Proc. IPPS/SPDP '98 Workshop on Job Scheduling Strategies for Parallel Processing, 1998, pp 62-82
2. J. Bester, I. Foster, C. Kesselman, J. Tedesco, S. Tuecke. GASS: A Data Movement and Access Service for Wide Area Computing Systems. Sixth Workshop on I/O in Parallel and Distributed Systems, May 5, 1999.
3. I. Foster, D. Kohr, R. Krishnaiyer, J. Mogill. Remote I/O: Fast Access to Distant Storage. Proc. Workshop on I/O in Parallel and Distributed Systems (IOPADS), pp 14-25, 1997.
4. Wang Bin et al. A Grid-computing-based Solution to Science&Engineering Computing and its Implemenation. ISTM/2003: 5th International Symposium on Test and Measurement, June 2003, Vol.1, pp 581-586
5. Peter Couvares, Todd Tannenbaum. Condor Tutorial. In 1st EuroGlobus Workshop, June 2001.(Powerpoint)
6. Tevfik Kosar, Managing and Scheduling Data Placement (DaP) Requests. In Talk-Condor Week, March, 2002. (Powerpoint)
7. Butler, Ralph, Gropp, William, Lusk, Ewing. Components and interfaces of a process management system for parallel programs. Parallel Computing Volume: 27, Issue: 11, October, 2001, pp 1417-1429
8. Grimshaw, A. S., Wulf, W. A. The Legion Vision of a Worldwide Virtual Computer. Comm. of the ACM, vol. 40, no. 1, January 1997.
9. Legion: The Grid OS Architecture and User View. In 2nd International Global Grid Forum Meeting, July 15-18, 2001. (Powerpoint)

Agora: Grid Community in Vega Grid

Hao Wang, Zhiwei Xu, Yili Gong, and Wei Li

Institute of Computing Technology, Chinese Academy of Sciences
Beijing 100080, P.R. China
wanghao@software.ict.ac.cn, {zxu,gongyili,liwei}@ict.ac.cn

Abstract. In grid environment, how to organize, discover and use grid resources is one of the basic research problems. In this paper, we introduce a new concept called agora, which refers grid community in our Vega grid project. We propose a principle on agora as one of the basic design principles of Vega grid, which is the community principle. We give a detailed definition of the agora as a 4-tuple (S, O, C, P), representing the set of Subject, Object, Context, and Policy respectively. Our research methodology is comparative studies, drawing an analog between the grid and other platform systems such as OS, CPU, and MPI. We also study some properties about the agora, for example, grid law of inertia. This agora approach could be used to unify the grid invariability and dynamic variability effectively, develop the appropriate technology to support the dynamic and open properties of the grid, and deal with the complexity in the grid more efficiently.

1 Introduction

The research work in this paper is a part of *Vega Grid* (one research project of the Institute of Computing Technology, Chinese Academy of Sciences). Vega is an acronym, which represents ***V***ersatile Services, ***E***nabling Intelligence, ***G***lobal Uniformity, and ***A***utonomous Control. In Vega, three properties of the grid system we summarized are diversity, variability, and heterogeneity.

Diversity: The grid system is a multi-person-multi-computer society, including various kinds of subjects and objects. *Variability*: The society is not stable or close, but dynamic and open. *Heterogeneity*: The heterogeneity in the grid represents various kinds of subjects, objects, software platform, hardware platform, use mode, administration mode, context, policies, protection mode, exception handling mode, safe mode, etc. The architecture of the grid is changing. Grid doesn't appear the clear architecture and no widely known theory model like RAM and Von Neumann Model.

Hence, we have to face the challenges of the complexity brought by these three properties. Further more; one of the core aims of Vega Grid is to enhance the usability by Enabling Intelligence. We hope the grid is easy to use like Web so to enlarge the quantity of the users and the developers. In [7], we propose EVP model of grid resource space with three layers. The EVP model is helpful to implement the grid community.

M. Li et al. (Eds.): GCC 2003, LNCS 3032, pp. 685–691, 2004.

This paper will focus on discussing the community principle, especially the concepts and technology to implement the community. In section 2 of this paper, we will discuss the community principle in the Vega Grid. From section 3 to section 5, we will define the agora and discuss it in detail. The agora correlates with GSML [5], the grip [6], and EVP resource space [7]. In section 3, we will propose some assumptions and give a detailed definition of the agora. In section 4, we will discuss the implementation of the agora and give an example. In section 5, we will conclude and prospect the further research.

2 Review the Community Principle in Vega Grid

The community principle in Vega Grid is: "The community being composed of the user and the resource, makes the user describe the requirement more abstractly, reduces the requirement of the degree of the knowledge structure, reduces un-boundedness to boundedness, reduces inordinance to orderliness, and implements the enlarging effect by the context, then empowers user."

The community principle is a method to solve the open and out-of-order problem in the grid. The principle is based on the following two assumptions. (1) The finite assumption: Although the requirements of all users can be infinite and open in whole time, the requirement of one user is finite and close in a given moment or period of time. (2) The iceberg assumption: The orderly, bounded, and persistent group hides great energy, then can bring the enlarging effect which can't be brought by a simple set of individuals.

In a nutshell, the community is a 4-tuple (S, O, C, P). "*S*" represents the set of "Subject"; "*O*" represents the set of "Object"; "*C*" and "*P*" represent context and policy respectively. The context and policy in one community shouldn't have different meanings or be paradoxical. The policy is chosen intentionally and explicitly, but the context is formed naturally and implicitly. If we regard the community as the iceberg, the context is the part hiding under the water, which is the reason providing the enlarging effect. The community is somewhat like the group in Distributed Operating System, the VO (Virtual Organization), and the file system in Operating System. But the group and VO are usually the sets of the same kind of things, such as the subjects or the objects, and the community is usually the set of the two different kinds of things, such as the subjects and the objects. But because the VO has not been defined in detail by now, to avoid arguments, we may define the community as the detailed definition or the detailed implementation of VO.

The community makes the users describe the requirement more abstractly. In Vega Grid, the resources that can be used directly by users are those in the GSML pages, being called the effective resources; the resources in the community are the virtual resources; and the actually local resources in each grid node are the physical resources. In addition, as the address space technology and virtual address technology in the computer architecture, the abstraction is basic and essential to reduce the degree of the complexity.

The community reduces the degree to the requirement of the knowledge structure. If we distinguish the users as the managers, the secretaries, and the engineers, the community and the GSML SDK can reduce the requirement degree of the end users' knowledge structure. The managers can use the GSML pages directly, and the secretaries can compose the GSML pages. Only when the physical resources in the grid node must be converted to the virtual resources in the community, the engineers are necessary.

The community reduces inordinace to orderliness. To a single end user, Internet, Web, and Grid are usually unbounded and out-of-order. With the community technology, what the user can see is a bounded and orderly sub grid which is far smaller. It reduces the complexity, enhances the usability, and then improves the efficiency.

The community implements the enlarging effect. The community can use the information, the knowledge, and the processes which are implicit in the context and the policy, to complete the detailed work and keep the consistence. So the community implements the enlarging effect that is the work can be completed when the user only gives a little information.

3 Assumptions and Properties about the Grid and the Definition of the Agora

In this section, we list some assumptions and some properties. From now on, we use "agora" represent the community in Vega Grid.

3.1 Grid Assumptions and the Properties about Agora

Assumption 1. There is only one grid. In this paper only one grid is considered.

Property 1. (Grid Law of Inertia). Subjects, objects, and communities in the grid keep stable until some exterior factor (usually subject) changes them by certain means. This property says that there are no spontaneous and casual behaviors in the grid. Any change results from some exterior event, and the occurrence of the event is due to the action of some subject in a certain way. In the one-person-one-computer world, it is easy to understand this. When we use application software, such as the word processor, the law of inertia is assumed potentially: a text will not be changed spontaneously. But in the multi-person-multi-computer open society, this does not go without saying. For example, when a user is browsing a database, he may find the data changed, though he does nothing, because the change is caused by another user. So the law of inertia should be stated explicitly.

3.2 Exterior Characteristics of Agora

Assumption 2. Except possibly in the lowest level (physical layer), the agora is an indispensable and user-visible basic concept. In virtual layer and effective layer, the agora is visible to users, but it is not necessary for the users to use the agora explicitly. For example, the user only need mention the agora in the head part of a GSML page; the other possibility is that there is a default (so implicit) agora in the whole grid. This assumption is very strict. The agora is indispensable, which is like the communicator in MPI.

Assumption 3. The agora is a persistent entity. This means that the agora must be kept in a persistent storage. In this point, the agora is similar to the file system, rather than the communicator in MPI.

Assumption 4. The grid has a unique agora set. This means that every agora has a unique identity in the whole grid.

Assumption 5. (Specific agora law of inertia). An agora has stability and dynamic. This is like a configuration file. The agora keeps stable (invariable) until some subject changes it by certain means. What is changed involves the interior characteristics of the agora (see to later), including changing our elements of the agora (subject, object, context and policy), or add/delete agora members, etc.

Assumption 6. (Grid agora law of inertia). The agora of grid has stability and dynamic. This is similar to a file system. The agora set keeps stable (invariable) until some subject (or grip) change it by certain means. The change includes creating, converging and splitting communities.

3.3 Interior Characteristics of the Agora

Definition 1. A agora A is a 4-tuple $A = (S, O, C, P)$, where S is the set of subjects, O is the set of objects, C and P are the sets of context and policy shared by the agora. We define the agora as the community in Vega Grid.

Property 2. Every element of (S, O, C, P) is a abstract data type. The operations includes: add a new element (add), delete an element (delete), and update an element (update). Every operation is atomic. Every operation keeps the consistency of the agora . The idea of property 2 is that operations on an agora should be simple, interleaved semantics and every operation makes the agora transfer from a good state to another good one. The operations in property 2 are the exterior actions in the law of inertia.

4 Implementation Consideration on Agora

The main data structures of the agora implementation (visible to the exterior) are the context set C and the policy set P. And the main active component is the agora engine E. In the effective layer, subjects uses object $o_e = <Q_e, Z_e, D_e>$. The agora automatically searches the corresponding object in the physical layer $o_p = <Q_p, Z_p, D_p>$, and the context set C and the policy set P are the parameters to the searching procedure.

The searching procedure is carried out by the agora engine. At present, the agora engine in the resource locating of the Vega Grid adopts two technologies: dynamic deploying and routing addressing. In the Vega Grid the searching procedure is fully distributed, which is similar to distributed Google.

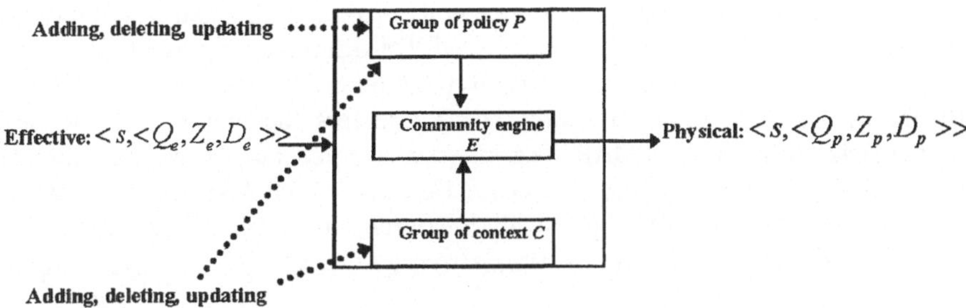

Fig. 1. The implementation of the agora

Besides the searching procedure, the grid agora should provide some functions, such as agora maintenance, automatic update and exceptional handling. We can refer to figure 1.

Now we give an example that implement a grid service by the agora and appropriate technology. A user asks the grid for the matrix multiply services, which is $matrixC = matrixA \times matrixB$. The resource is denoted as a 3-tuple $<Q, Z, D>$, where Q is the identification, Z is the parameters, and D is the specification.

The user gives the information: (1) scientific computing; (2) matrix multiply; (3) the source is the matrix A, and the matrix B; (4) the destination is the matrix C; (5) the specification is the least time. In this example, the user even doesn't know $A = \begin{pmatrix} 1 & 7 \\ 8 & 9 \end{pmatrix}$, $B = \begin{pmatrix} 2 & 4 \\ 5 & 6 \end{pmatrix}$, $C = \begin{pmatrix} 0 & 0 \\ 0 & 0 \end{pmatrix}$.

In the effective resource space, the resource is denoted as a 3-tuple $<Q_e, Z_e, D_e>$, which is < {Scientific Computing, Matrix Multiply}, {Matrix A, Matrix B, Matrix C}, {the least time} >. The user can choose the information through the buttons in the GSML page, which is described as following:

```
<Agora>
  <AgoraName>Scientific Computing</AgoraName>
  <ServiceName>MatrixMultiply </ServiceName>
</Agora>
<Parameter>Matrix A, Matrix B, Matrix C</Parameter>
<PolicyDescription>
      <PolicyName>The Least Time</PolicyName>
</PolicyDescription>
```

By the Mapper between effective resource space and virtual resource space, the resource is mapped into < {100, 1000}, {10.0.2.58/working/MA.dat, 10.0.2.60/working/MB.dat, 10.0.2.68/working/MC.dat}, {99} >. In this 3-tuple, "100" represents the agora code of the scientific computing agora. “1000” represents the matrix multiply service code in the scientific computing agora. “100:1000” represents the exclusive service in the whole grid. “99” represents the policy code of the least time.

By the Mapper between virtual resource space and physical resource space, we can get the physical resource. The grid service node providing the matrix multiply service is found. It is 10.0.2.65. The service is MPIMMService, representing the matrix multiply service. The directory is http://10.0.2.65:8080/ogsa/ services/sample/mpi/ MPIMMService. The virtual resource space transfers the matrixes to the physical resource space through the SOAP. The matrixes are put into the working directories. The matrixes are 10.0.2.65/now/MA.dat, 10.0.2.65/now/MB.dat, and 10.0.2.65/now/MC.dat. The physical resource is also denoted as a 3-tuple $< Q_p, Z_p, D_p >$, which is < {http://10.0.2.65:8080/ogsa/services/ sample/mpi/ MPIMMService}, {10.0.2.65/now/MA.dat, 10.0.2.65/now/MB.dat, 10.0.2.65/now/ MC.dat}, {99} >.

The grid service provides the interface MPIMM. The description about the interface is:

```
<wsdl:portType name="MPIMMPortType">
   <wsdl:operation name="mpi_multiply">
    <wsdl:input message="impl:mpi_multiplyRequest"
name="mpi_multiplyRequest"/>
<wsdl:outputmessage="impl:mpi_multiplyResponse"
name="mpi_multiplyResponse"/>
    </wsdl:operation>
</wsdl:portType>
```

The method mpi_multiply implements the matrix multiply service. It has three parameters (three matrixes). The process of transferring the matrixes is described as:

```
POST /ogsa/services/sample/mpi/MPIServiceHTTP/1.0
Content-Type: text/xml; charset=utf-8
Accept: application/soap+xml,...
User-Agent: Axis/1.1 Host: 10.0.2.65
<? xml version="1.0" encoding="UTF-8"?>...
<soapenv:Body>
<mpi_multiply
xmlns="http://mpi.gos.cngrid.ict.org/MPIMM">
<in0 xmlns="">1 7 8 9</in0> <in1 xmlns="">2 4 5 6</in1>
<in2 xmlns="">0 0 0 0</in2>
</mpi_multiply>
</soapenv:Body>...
```

The string “in0”, “in1” and “in2” represent the matrix A, B, C respectively. The code of the method mpi_multiply is:

```
public class MPIMMImpl extends
PersistentGridServiceImpl{
 public void mpi_multiply(String a, String b, String
c){
        String cmdarray[]={"mpirun -np 2 cmm",a,b,c};
        try {
              Runtime.getRuntime().exec(cmdarray);
        }
        catch (IOException ex) {
        }
    }
}
```

cmm is the C program of the matrix multiply. The running environment is mpi-1.2.5.

5 Conclusions and Future Works

As early as in 1979, Licklider proposed the idea of Multinet, and he indicated that the human society might come into a non-centralized controlled electronic commons, whose mode of operations would be one featuring cooperation, sharing, meeting of minds across space and time in a context of responsive programs and readily available information.

The grid agora is the development and embodiment of this idea. As the developing of the research, we would find that the grid agora technology is indispensable, and the benefits it brings are as follows: Reducing cost, especially the cost of using and developing; increasing online scalability; increasing capability of deep interactivity; decreasing the requirement on users, and accordingly extending the range of application.

References

1. I. Foster, C. Kesselman, J. Nick, S. Tuecke, "Grid Services for Distributed Systems Integration", IEEE Computer, 35 (6), 2002, pp. 37-46.
2. K. Hwang, Z. Xu, Scalable Parallel Computers: Technology, Architecture, Programming, McGraw-Hill, New York, 1998.
3. J.C.R. Licklider, "Computers and Government", in The Computer Age: A Twenty-Year View, M.L. Dertouros and Joel Moses (Eds.), MIT Press, Cambridge, Mass., 1979, pp. 88-129.
4. Z. Xu, W. Li, "Research on Vega Grid Architecture", Journal of Computer Research and Development, 2002, 39 (8) 923-929.
5. Z. Xu, W. Li, D. Liu, H. Yu, B. Li, "The GSML Tool Suite: A Supporting Environment for User-level Programming in Grids", Proceedings of PDCAT 2003.
6. T. Liu, X. Li, W. Li, N. Sun, Z. Xu, "Notes on a Runtime Construct for Grid", Journal of Computer Research and Development, 2003, 40 (12).
7. W. Li, Z. Xu, "A Model of Grid Address Space with Applications", Journal of Computer Research and Development, 2003, 40 (12).

Sophisticated Interaction – A Paradigm on the Grid[1]

Xingwu Liu and Zhiwei Xu

Institute of Computing Technology, Chinese Academy of Sciences
xlw@software.ict.ac.cn, zxu@ncic.ac.cn

Abstract. Though how a grid and its users interact is an important topic, it's almost ignored in the grid community as far as we know. This problem is quite challenging because of the openness and dynamics of grids. To meet this need , sophisticated interaction is developed, which is an extension of the traditional interaction. A model of sophisticated interaction, PRASP, is also presented and a theorem that PRASP is as powerful as PerRAM is proved. The concepts and views in this paper are the basis of our further work.

1 Introduction

The grid as a promising computing architecture has been increasingly focused on. Many individuals and groups have contributed to this field. However, they are mainly concerned with the server end, ignoring the client end, which involves how to use the grid. Thus our VEGA group has proposed sophisticated interaction (SoI), a computer with active memory (CAM) [1], and the grid service markup language (GSML) to meet this demand. Interaction is the theme of our work.

This paper is devoted to SoI. In section 2, related work on interaction is sketched, followed by our understanding of interaction. In section 3, we define SoI and show its importance in grids. In section 4 a model of SoI and a related theorem are presented. Section 5 is the conclusion.

2 Interaction

2.1 Related Work

As early as 1930', Turing recognized that computation is more than functional transformation and suggested a model called c-machine [2] which interacts with the operator while computing. And the later models, o-machine [3] and u-machine [4], are also based on interaction. In the 1960', Licklider [5] declared that through interaction

[1] This work is supported in part by the National Natural Science Foundation of China (Grant No. 69925205), the China Ministry of Science and Technology 863 Program (Grant No. 2002AA104310), and the Chinese Academy of Sciences Oversea Distinguished Scholars Fund (Grant No. 20014010).

M. Li et al. (Eds.): GCC 2003, LNCS 3032, pp. 692–699, 2004.

computers shift from human's tools to partners. Then with the personal computers and networks widely spread, interactive computation prevails over algorithm as the dominant mode. This trend has great impact on both application and theoretical research. People have developed graphic user interface to facilitate interaction, and object-orientation to model, analyze, and program interactive system. Besides, more profound questions have emerged: what's the semantics of interaction, what's the abstract model of interactive computing, and how powerful interaction is. The answers are partially achieved, though without complete consensus. The representatives are π-calculus [6][11], site machines [7], interaction machines, interactive extensions of Church-Turing thesis [8], and the expressiveness of PTM [10].

2.2 Definition of Interaction

Interaction is the communication of a computing system with its external world during the computation. The points are as follows. (1) Bi-lateral. Interaction is between a computing system and its environment, with the latter possibly including human operators and other systems. It affects not only the system but also the environment. (2) Communication. Interaction is embodied as information flow. The participants act and respond in a dialogue following some protocol. (3) Dynamical binding. Not all the information a system needs must be provided before the computation starts. It can be bound according to the specific situation during computation. For example, an interactive controller may adjust its parameters in order to adapt to the controlled system. (4) Input non-determinism. Inputs are dynamically provided, unlike algorithms that operate in a closed-box fashion. Even after the computation begins the system still has no complete knowledge on what the operator wants it to do. The computation is thus based on stream processing but not on string or number processing.

2.3 Impact of Interaction

Interaction, above all, is a computing paradigm which provides services over time rather than a functional transformation of input to output. It allows a computing device to process ongoing arrival of new inputs and continuously generate new outputs. Importantly, the impact of the shift from algorithm to interaction is profound enough. (1) Human-computer partnership. In the algorithmic style, computers only work as tools, just like a dictionary or an abacus. However, if interaction is permitted, computers dialog and cooperate with the operator for problem solving. Philosophically, it may be claimed that through interaction, human becomes part of the program and the program is an extension of human. (2) More powerful problem-solving ability. Turing [3] showed that o-machine is more expressive than Turing Machine (TM) because it can ask the "God" for help. And D. Goldin and P. Wegner [10] proved that TM becomes stronger if extended with the ability to dialog, even without the access to God. The power comes from history-dependence, which we believe is foundational to interaction. (3) Intentionality. For an input stream, the later input token may be related to the previous output tokens, and vice versa. Moreover, even if a later input is the same as a previous one, their corresponding output may be different because the current states are possibly different. As a result, the computation seems intentional, something like the adaptation of the system to the environment.

3 Sophisticated Interaction

3.1 Definition of Sophisticated Interaction

From the above, it's safe to say that the essence of interaction is to enable the environment (especially the operator) to be part of the computing system itself. Then what can the operator do? (1) To transit the machine from one state to another, with both belonging to a predetermined state set. (2) To modify the machine. Take PTM (persistent TM) as an example. A PTM is a multi-tape TM with a persistent tape preserved between successive interactions. After each output, the PTM waits for a new input to continue. For the operator, this is a question-answer process, and his decision only changes the contents on the persistent tape. It's easy to see that site machine and interaction machine are all in state-transition style. This state-transition interaction is called simple interaction (SiI). Consider a little further: can the operator change the finite control of the PTM through interaction? In this case, we say that the machine is online modifiable.

Sophisticated interaction (SoI) is a kind of interaction through which a computing system can be online modified. In contrast to SiI, which permits a computer to take advantage of the environment to solve problems but leave itself not augmented, a SoI machine augment itself while serving the others. Altogether, bi-lateral intellect augmentation is achieved through SoI.

SoI has the following desirable properties. (1) High productivity. A system can be improved or modified during its operation, resulting in the overlapping of the design, operation, and maintenance period of its lifecycle. (2) Human-guided computation. A user not only uses a prepared machine for problem solving, but also adjusts the system so that it becomes more clever and fit for his demand. Thus any consumer of a system is at the same time its producer.

3.2 Some Scenarios Where SoI Is Highlighted

Service modification. A client wants a travel reservation service to book plane tickets for one of recent days if it's fine in the destination city. Unfortunately, the service isn't designed to consider weather and the client isn't professional enough to program such a service. If SoI is permitted, the client may easily modify the service so that the reservation service can interact with a weather-forecast service to meet his demand. More importantly, his purpose is achieved through a sequence of interaction with the reservation service, so he needn't know its interior structure.

Remote cooperation. Two programmers want to cooperatively develop a software system. Currently, they have to work respectively and communicate sometimes about their progress. This may brings about repeated work and low productivity. In the SoI style, the system under construction runs somewhere and interacts with the two programmers. Either of them may make any modification to the system. Their modification immediately goes into operation through their interaction with the system being developed. See figure 1 as an illustration. For the programmers, it seems as if they are discussing and working together on a desktop.

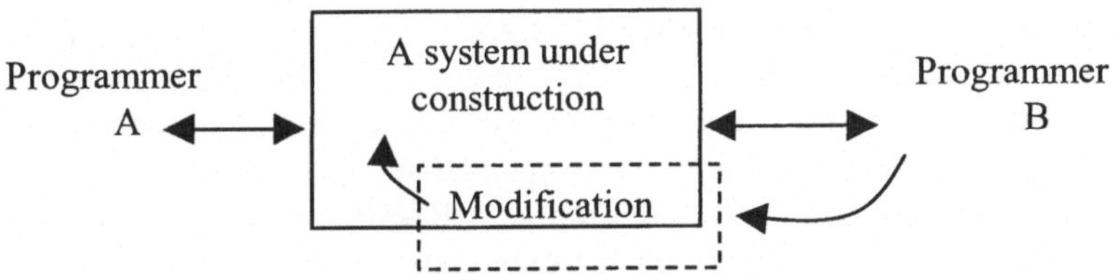

Fig. 1. Remote cooperative programming.

Interactive programming. Today, programming is tough work for a non-well-trained person, because the whole process only involves the creativity of the programmer, with the target program totally passive. However, SoI enables the program to interact with the programmer even when it's being created. For the programmer, he is directed actively and cooperatively by his target, so he needn't know much technical detail and only has to "guide" the evolution of the program. This paradigm makes programming more easy and productive than ever.

3.3 SoI in Grid Computing

Grid is an infrastructure for widespread resource sharing and coordination. From the viewpoint of OGSA, everything on the grid is a service that is specified with a set of interfaces and behaviors. A user may invoke a service to achieve his purpose, which is the main paradigm of using the grid. However, this usage mode is challenged by two particular properties of the grid, which calls for SoI. (1) Openness. The demand openness, which is emphasized on here, means that at any time, a grid can't meet the demand of all potential users. When a satisfactory service doesn't exist, a user should be facilitated to adapt an approximate one as needed. The adaptation should be as easy as possible, so that even a layman of programming and the domain can achieve his goal. As a result, the grid gets improved in the course of serving its users, and the users are active and creative when they use the grid. SoI provides such facilities, since it permits interactive programming. (2) Dynamics. Resources and their states on the grid vary over time, because any one is possible to use, deploy, modify, or destroy a service. An application may run down unpredictably at any time because a needed resource malfunctions or is non-existent now. Measures should be taken to deal with such runtime exceptions. The factory mechanism in OGSA can be regarded as such an approach, but it's too rigid to allow the user to make expedient decisions. Through SoI, the user may tell the application to use another kind of resource or a temporarily provided one.

4 A Model of SoI

4.1 PRASP

Here is a model of SoI, called PRASP (persistent RASP), which is an extension of RASP [9]. RASP differs from RAM [9] only in the fact that its program, stored in its memory, is modifiable by itself during its operation. Before the computation begins, the input is completely provided, the memory cells are initially all zero except those storing the program (this configuration is denoted as ε), and the location counter (LC) is set to the first instruction. A configuration of RASP memory is illustrated in figure 2. Suppose the memory is persistent between consecutive computations, then we get PRASP. Here the persistence means that PRASP processes the inputs one after another and that every time the computation for a new input starts, only the LC is set back to the first instruction (stored in the cell next to the accumulator), with the whole memory preserved. See figure 3. PRASP is history-dependent: previous computations modify not only the memory, but also the program itself; the latter is more essential than the former and justifies PRASP as an appropriate model for SoI. This model shows that modifying a program through interaction with it is quite feasible with the existing mechanisms.

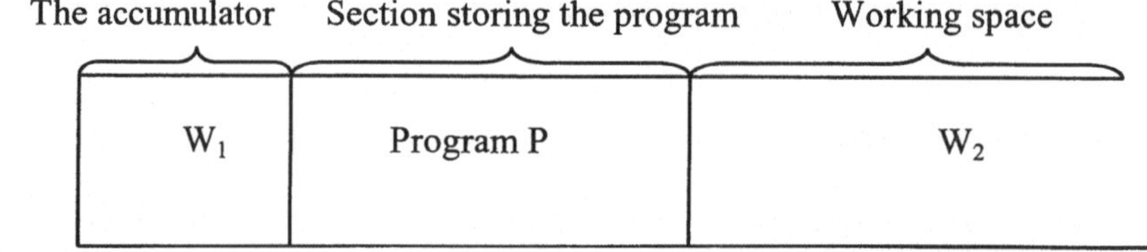

Fig. 2. A configuration of RASP memory. The first instruction of the program is in register 1.

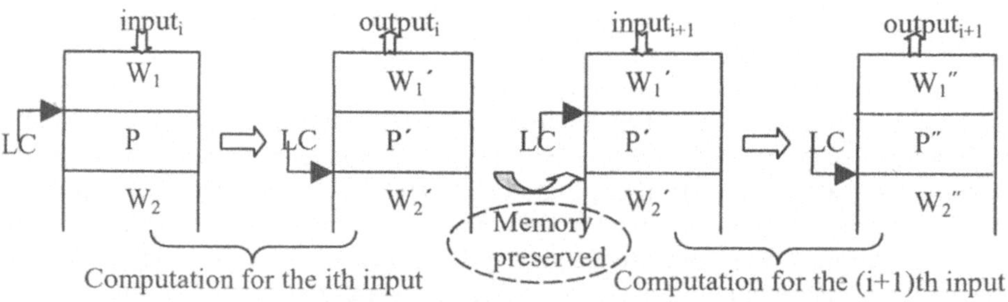

Fig. 3. The memory configuration in two consecutive computations of PRASP.

4.2 Expressiveness of PRASP

To show how powerful a PRASP is, we likewise define an interactive machine called PerRAM (persistent RAM), an extension of RAM whose memory is persistent be-cannot be modified; through interaction one can only affect the configuration of the memory.

Like the language of a PTM [10], the language L of a PerRAM or PRASP is defined as the set of its streams of input-output pairs. For two configurations C_1 and C_2 of a machine M (PerRAM or PRASP), the expression $(C_1, I) \vdash_M (C_2, O)$ means that M computes input I with C_1 as the initial configuration, outputs O, and halts with C_2 as the final configuration. Let ε_M be the all-zero configuration if M is a PerRAM or the ε defined above if M is a PRASP. The language of M:

$L_M=\{s=(I_1, O_1)(I_2, O_2)\ldots(I_n, O_n)\ldots|$s is a finite or infinite sequence such that there are configurations $C_1, C_2, \ldots, C_n, \ldots$ satisfying $(\varepsilon_M, I_1) \vdash_M (C_1, O_1)$ and $(C_{n-1}, I_n) \vdash_M (C_n, O_n)$ for any index n 2}.

M_1 is as expressive as M_2 if and only if $L_{M_1}=L_{M_2}$.

Theorem 1: for any PRASP M there is a PerRAM M′ that is as expressive as it, and vice versa.

Idea of the proof: Let R be the RASP whose interactive extension is M. In [9] a RAM, which functions the same as R, is constructed. We adapt the RAM to another RAM R′ such that the extension of R′(M′) with persistent memory also behaves in the same way as that of R. Then the first part of the theorem holds. We omit the proof of the other part since it can be done likewise.

Now, we define R′ at first, then some properties of R′ and R are presented, and the theorem follows.

Remark: in this paper the instruction sets of RAM and RASP and their semantics are from [9].

Certain registers of R′ will have special purposes: register 1-used for indirect addressing, register 2-the location counter of R, register 3-computation tag, and register 4-storage for the accumulator of R. Register 3 is a facility for interactively extending R′. Register i of R will be stored in register i+4 of R′ for i 1.

The program of R′ is in figure 4. In this program, P_1 is an instruction sequence which loads the finite-length program of R in the memory of R′ starting at register 5, and continue: P_2 is a simulation loop which begins by reading an instruction of R (with a LOAD *2 RAM instruction which is labeled 'continue'), decoding it and branching to one of 18 sets of instructions, each designed to handle one type of RASP instruction. On an invalid operation code R′, like R, will halt.

The decoding and branching operations are straightforward; figure 5 is an example of the instructions of R′ to simulate the instruction SUB i of R. This sequence is invoked when the location counter of R points to a register holding 6, the code for SUB.

The further detail of the program of R′ is omitted.

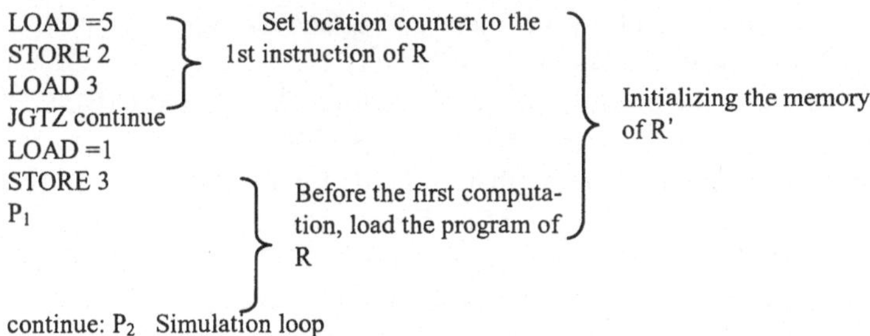
LOAD =5
STORE 2
LOAD 3
JGTZ continue
LOAD =1
STORE 3
P_1
Set location counter to the 1st instruction of R
Initializing the memory of R'
Before the first computation, load the program of R
continue: P_2 Simulation loop

Fig. 4. The program of R′, where P_1 and P_2 are instruction sequences.

Instructions	Comment
LOAD 2 ADD =1 STORE 2	Increment the location counter by 1, so it points to the register holding the operand i of the SUB i instruction.
LOAD *2 ADD =4 STORE 1	Bring i to the accumulator, add 4, and store the result in register 1.
LOAD 4 SUB *1 STORE 4	Fetch the contents of the accumulator of R from register 4. Subtract the contents of register i+1 and place the result back in register 4.
LOAD 2 ADD =1 STORE 2	Increment the location counter by 1 again so it now points to the next RASP instruction.
JUMP continue	Return to the beginning of the simulation loop.

Fig. 5. Simulation of SUB i by R´ in the loop continue: P_2.

Lemma 1: for any input I, R outputs O and halts at a configuration C if and only if R´ outputs O and halts at a configuration C´.

Proof: Starting from $\varepsilon_{R'}$, whose registers are all zero, R´ will execute "LOAD =1; STORE 3; P_1" in the initialization. The configuration after the initialization is denoted as c_1'. Let $c_1=\varepsilon_R$. Then $Q(c_1, c_1')$ holds, where

Q(c, c´): (1) Register j of c is equal to register j+4 of c´ for j 0
(2) Register 3 of c´ is 1.

Since register 2 of c_1' is 5, R´ first simulates the first instruction of R and shifts to configuration c_2'. If R executes the first instruction, shifts to configuration c_2, and sets its location counter to h_2, it's obvious that condition* holds for n=2, where

Condition*: (1) R halts if and only if R´ does
(2) R output some integer O if and only if R´ output O
(3) $Q(c_n, c_n')$ holds
(4) Register 2 of c_n' stores h_n+4.

Repeat this process, and condition* holds for each step of the simulation of R by R´. As a result, R halts in some configuration C if and only if R´ does in some configuration C´, and Q(C, C´) holds. The proof ends.

For an input sequence $I_1, I_2, \ldots, I_N$, let F_n, 1 n N, be the proposition that there are C_j and O_j such that $(C_{j-1}, I_j) \vdash_M (C_j, O_j)$ for j n if and only if there are C_j' and O_j' such that $(C_{j-1}', I_j) \vdash_{M'} (C_j', O_j')$ for j n, where $C_0=\varepsilon_R$ and $C_0'=\varepsilon_{R'}$.

Lemma 2: F_N is true and $O_j=O_j'$ for j N.

Proof: Let G_n be the proposition that F_n is true, $O_j=O_j'$, and $Q(C_j, C_j')$ holds for all j n. Obviously, we only have to prove the truth of G_N.

By lemma 1, G_1 holds. Assume that G_n holds for all n k, where k<N. Because register 3 of C_k' is 1, the initialization of R´ for computing I_{k+1} only stores 5 in its register 2 and transits R´ from C_k' to a new configuration C_k'' which is the same with C_k' except that its register 2 is 5. Since $Q(C_k, C_k')$ holds, so does $Q(C_k, C_k'')$. Following the proof of lemma 1 but replacing the c_1 and c_1' with C_k and C_k'' respectively, we can prove that G_{k+1} holds. By induction, G_N holds. The proof ends.

Proof of theorem 1: by lemma 2, for any stream $s=(I_1,O_1)(I_2,O_2)\dots(I_n,O_n)\dots$, $s\in L_M$ if and only if $s\in L_{M'}$. Thus $L_M= L_{M'}$. It follows that for any PRASP M there is a PerRAM M′ that is as expressive as M. The proof of the other part of the theorem is omitted here. The proof ends.

Theorem 1 indicates that this seemingly weaker interaction (SiI) is actually as powerful as SoI. Furthermore, since the power of a PerRAM is restricted by the fixed program, what program can be obtained by modifying a specific one through SoI is also pre-determined.

Corollary 1: PRASP is as powerful as PTM.

Proof: it's justified by theorem 1 and the obvious fact that PerRAM is as powerful as PTM. The proof ends.

5 Conclusion

We propose sophisticated interaction as a key to the problems brought about by the openness and dynamics of grids. A model of SoI, PRASP, is developed and a theorem of its expressiveness is proved. We hope that our effort will be helpful in the research on how to use a grid.

References

1. Xu, Z.: *A model of Computer with Active Memory*. Journal of Computer Research and Development 39(2002) 898-901
2. http://www.abelard.org/turpap2/tp2-ie.asp
3. Turing, A.: *Systems of Logic Based on Ordinals*. Proceedings of the London Math Society 45(1939)161-228
4. Turing, A.: *Intelligent Machinery*. In: D.C. Ince (editor), Mechanical Intelligence, North Holland (1992) 107-127
5. Licklider, J.C.R.: *Man-computer symbiosis*. IEEE Transaction on Human Factors in Electronics, HFE-1(7), (March 1960) 4--11
6. Sangiorgi, D., Walker, D.: *The π-calculus : a Theory of Mobile Processes*. Cambridge University Press, Cambridge, England ; New York, 2001.
7. Van Leeuwen, J., Wiedermann, J.: *The Turing machine paradigm in contemporary computing*. In: B. Enquist and W. Schmidt (Eds.), Mathematics unlimited (2001).
8. Wegner, P., Goldin, D.: *Interaction, Computability, and Church's Thesis*. Technical Report, CS Dept., Brown University. www.cs.brown.edu/people/pw
9. Aho, A.V., Hopcroft, J.E., Ullman, J.D.: *The Design and Analysis of Computer Algorithms*. Addison-Wesley (1974)
10. Goldin, D., Wegner P.: *Behavior and Expressiveness of Persistent Turing Machines*. www.cs.brown.edu/people/pw
11. Milner, R.: *Elements of Interaction*. Communications of the ACM, 36(1):78--89, 1993. Turing Award Lecture

A Composite-Event-Based Message-Oriented Middleware

Pingpeng Yuan and Hai Jin

Huazhong University of Science and Technology, Wuhan 430074, China
yuanpingpeng@163.net, hjin@hust.edu.cn

Abstract. There is an increasing interest in tying together software systems to interoperate and cooperate over the Internet. One common glue technology for distributed, loosely coupled, heterogeneous software systems is *Message Oriented Middleware* (MOM). In this paper we present a framework for composite-event-based MOM (cMOM) and its implementation. The cMOM can also be considered as a grid event service, which is a basic component needed by many grid services. cMOM allows distributed applications registered their interests in composite-events. When composite-events occur, cMOM notifies responding applications and those applications performed action. Our framework comprises an execution model – the event-service interacting model. The paper discusses some aspects of the event-service interacting model. The novel aspect of our cMOM lies in supporting composite event and its detection and enabling the integration of services within and across organizations without requiring changes in other applications.

1 Introduction

Advances in networking and the pervasive deployment of the Internet have created new opportunities of using distributed computers as a single, unified computing resource, leading to grid computing [1]. Early research on grid computing mainly concentrates on computational grid and data grid. With the development of e-Business, the requirement of using applications available on Internet as a single, unified application, namely business grid, is also impending.

The key problem in business grid is how to glue applications distributed over Internet. The basic observation about applications is that widely disseminated events (or messages) are becoming ubiquitously available through the Internet, mobile devices. These public events, as well as internal events can form the *glue* to link applications within and across organizations. As this technology is based on messages, thus, *message oriented middleware* (MOM) naturally becomes one of the most prospective gluing technologies. Using MOM environment to glue together a large number of stand-alone applications, each application may evolve independently from others in this environment. The MOM environment will allow new applications to *tap into* information generated by existing applications without disturbing them.

The remainder of this paper is organized as follows: First, we review some related works and evaluate some common MOMs found in the literature. Then, we present a new approach to MOM: composite-event-based MOM and its implementation. Finally, we end this paper with conclusion.

M. Li et al. (Eds.): GCC 2003, LNCS 3032, pp. 700–707, 2004.

2 Related Work

Message oriented middleware (MOM) is a commonly used to glue distributed applications. Many attempts have been made to gain more and more expressive power and flexibility in MOM. In the following, we introduce some research briefly.

The CORBA Event Service [2] and Notification Service [3] components are defined in the *CORBA Object Services* (COS) layer. The most important feature introduced by the two services is to enable each client to subscribe to the precise set of events it is interested in receiving.

Examples of MOM products include MQSeries [4], MSMQ, Active Web, Message Q, TIB/Rendez-vous, Open MOM, Pipes, etc. More detail comparison of those products can be found in [5]. Here we only introduce the representative product - MQSeries briefly. MQSeries allows applications to communicate using messages and queues. However, MQSeries treats events as uninterpreted data and cannot perform content-based publish/subscribe. Moreover, it can not deal with composite events or complex messages.

In contrast to MQSeries and CORBA Notification Service, the Gryphon project [6] is an advanced technology of MOM and extending its range of application. Gryphon introduced the following extensions: content-based publish/subscribe, stateless event transformations, and event stream interpretations. Gryphon's approach to event distribution middleware is based on the concept of *information flow graphs* [7, 8].

Although those research mentioned above are carried on MOM, current MOM reveals that these systems or specifications have two main limitations:

1) Provide no methods to express composite events. In many legacy applications, a set of predefined events has been provided. Although it is possible to glue applications together using primitive-event-based MOM according to those predefined events, supporting only a small number of predefined events severely limits the ability of MOM to link complex applications where temporal and external events need to be combined with internal events.

2) Lose trace of execution of the application and cannot rollback tasks at any level. The execution models those MOMs based on are too simple; therefore, it cannot record the execution of applications and maintain the states of all executing tasks. When exceptions occur or users want to abort tasks, those MOMs cannot correctly rollback all or specified tasks.

3 Composite-Event-Based Message-Oriented Middleware

The above observations lead us to explore *Composite-event-based Message-Oriented Middleware* (*cMOM*). The behavior of cMOM is modeled through the concept of event-service interacting model. The model for cMOM specifies how events are handled, how reactions are triggered and executed - with respect to the applications that produce the events and that may be concerned by the execution of the reactions. The model consists of several parts: event specification language, *Event-Service-*

Event rule (ESE-rule) and its graphic representation, Event-Service-Chain, event detection, event retrieval and delivery. In the following, we introduce those aspects respectively.

3.1 Event Specification Language

In general MOMs, only primitive event is supported, it is not easy to tie together applications that have predefined events. Event composition obviously provides a flexible way to define various complex events. cMOM provides a means for specifying composite events in. For the definition of events in cMOM, an event specification language [9] is proposed. Different with other languages [10][11][12][13], this language incorporates a small number of event operators and allows users to add new composite events to cMOM. With the help of the event specification language, cMOM provides a richer set of event expression and a set of useful constructs for building composite events.

In this language, an event consists of two parts, the event descriptor and the event body. The event descriptor tells event mediator what to do with the message. It contains information such as the target and source of the event, the global identification of event, event name, timestamp, the identity of interaction group and the priority of the event. The event body is completely user customizable and contains the data to be sent between applications.

3.2 Event-Service-Event (ESE) and Event-Service-Chain (ESC)

The use of the reactive paradigm requires different execution models in a variety of contexts and applications. The behavior of cMOM is modeled through the concept of event-service interacting model. The main parts of model are *Event-Service-Event* rule (ESE-rule) and its graphic representation, Event-Service-Chain. ESE-rule is used to describe the relationship between events and services. The rules of Event-Service-Event are derived from *Event-Condition-Action-Alternative Action* (ECAA) [14]. The syntax of ESE-rules is given as follows:

< ESE-rule>::=on <Event> do <Service> produce <Event>
<Composite_Event>::=<Event>{{AND|XOR|OR}<Event>}*
<Event>::=<Composite_Event>|< Primitive_Event>
<Atomic_Service>::=<Operation>
<Complex_Service>::=<Service>{{AND|XOR|OR}<Service>}*
<Service>::=<Complex_Service>|< Atomic_Service>

According to ESE rules, each reaction is associated with an event type and produces another event type. When the reaction is triggered by an occurrence of an event which application registers interest in, the reaction outputs a new event occurrence, and the new event occurrence fires a new reaction. Therefore an event occurrence can lead to chains of reaction.

ESE-rule is employed to describe how applications interact. However, since ESE-rules are isolated, it is not straightforward. Thus, we adopt a graphic style to describe static interactions among distributed applications. The graphical representation is named as *Event-Service Graph* (ESG). ESG is a directed graph and is constructed from ESE-rules. If the input event of ESE rule is output event of another ESE rule, two rules are connected in ESG. Figure 1 gives an example of an ESG. In the figure, diamond, circle and rounded rectangle indicate event, logical connector, service or action respectively.

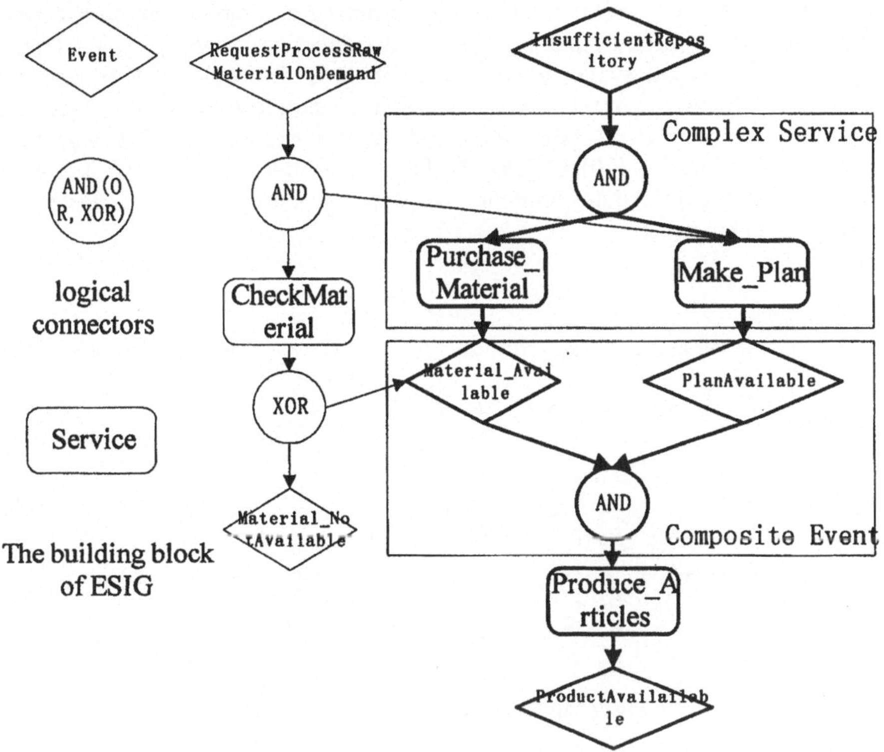

Fig. 1. A Simple ESG Example

Because ESG only represents possible interaction among services, the interactions occurring in reality are subset of ESG. Thus, *Event-Service-Chain* (ESC), constructed from ESG, is used to model dynamic interaction of applications. When one interaction is invoked, a corresponding ESC is created. When one invoking ends, it produces new event occurrences and those new event occurrences trigger other execution. With progress of the interaction among applications or services, the ESC is extending. Thus ESC keeps track of interaction. An example of ESC is shown in block line in Fig. 1. When event *InsufficientRepository* in Fig.1 occurs, the ESC indicated in block line is created.

ESC is not only used to track the execution of applications, but also detect event occurrence. Events occurring in an ESC may not combine with other ESCs, thus, it assures the correction of event semantics (The method to detect event occurrences will be discussed in section 3.3). Moreover, since events are transmitted through cMOM, cMOM keeps track of the sequence of executing tasks and events by the execution model. Once exception has been detected, recovery invoked and recovery manager performs compensation services or tasks. If any compensation services or tasks exist, traces back the method execution log for semantic recovery.

3.3 Event Detection

Since an event may have multiple instances during a computation, composite event detection is more difficult than primitive event detection. Snoop [10] and TriGS [15] use syntax trees and syntax graphs. SAMOS [16] uses colored Petri nets for the detection of composite events. Ode [17] uses finite state automata, which are based on the equivalence of event expressions and regular expressions. The way of event detection mentioned in [10][15][16][17] did not consider event context, it often incurs semantic ambiguity, thus limiting the expressiveness of those general event specification languages.

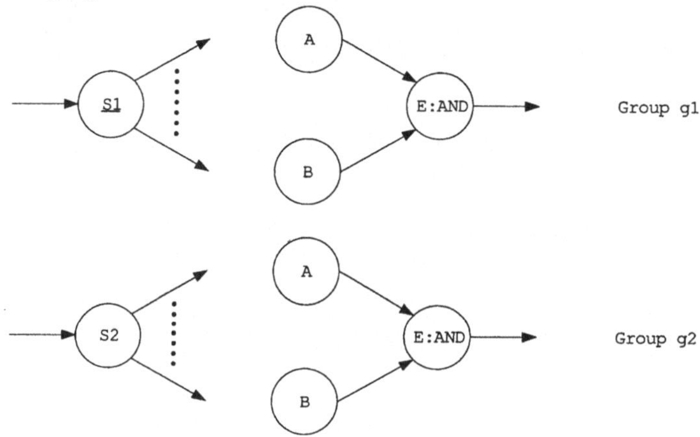

Fig. 2. An Example of Two Interacting Groups

cMOM implements an efficient composite event detection method. In cMOM, the ESC is the context of all events occurrences. The ESC is named as interacting group and assigned a group identifier - *GroupId* by cMOM. When an interaction is fired, an interacting group is created, and a group identifier is assigned. During the interaction, every event occurrence is assigned the group identifier. Events with different group identifiers do not form new composite events. An example shown in Figure 2 will help to understand the method. Fig.2 illustrates two interacting groups g_1, g_2, where events A and B are generated and a composite event E is also generated. A composite event E defined with AND operator and its component events are event A and B. When interaction reaches the nodes A and B of groups g_1, g_2, there will be four event instance occurrences a_1, a_2, b_1, b_2 of A and B (we use a small letter with a subscript index as the event identifier), where $a_1.GroupId=b_2.GroupId$ and $a_2.GroupId= b_1.GroupId$. So event occurrences a_1 and b_2, a_2 and b_1 form two occurrences of event E. Other potential triggering combinations of events, such as a_1 and b_1, a_2 and b_2 are not tested, because the occurrence of E caused by (a_1, b_1) or (a_2, b_2) is not possible.

3.4 Event Retrieval and Delivery

In most MOMs, timely detection and delivery of various events are usually implicitly required but seldom explicitly defined; let alone any effort to guarantee it. Simply queuing events and dispatching them in a best-effort approach at the MOM does not guarantee the timely delivery of these events. Formalism for specifying various event-timing requirements and corresponding dispatch algorithms are needed.

When event occurrences are received by cMOM, cMOM inserts those event occurrences into *Handling Event Queue* (HEQ). Event processor retrieves event occurrences in HEQ. There are several ways in which an event can be retrieved from a queue. If an event is more important, it can be manipulated in several ways rapidly. For example, an application can use message priority levels for cMOM to deliver urgent messages first. The priority level of event occurrence ranges from 0 (lowest) to 9 (highest). If application does not specify a priority level, the default level is 4. cMOM tries to process higher-priority messages before lower-priority ones. If the event occurrences have the same priority level, event occurrences are processed according to expiration time. cMOM tries to process event occurrences before event occurrences expire.

4 Framework Implementation

cMOM requires four basic types of event service: delivery, receive, storage and process. The delivery service distributes events as they are processed. The storage service stores events for later retrieval. In addition, cMOM provides applications with service to register and un-register their ESE-rules. cMOM needs to be augmented for composite event specification and detection, as well as timely delivery semantics which are necessary in many real world applications. We first describe the requirements for these services.

- Transparency. Brokers should not learn about which brokers produce the events they consume, or which brokers consume the events they produce.
- Specificity. A broker should be passed only the set of events it currently expresses an interest in. cMOM must match announced events to those brokers that have expressed interest in them.
- Dynamic. Brokers can register and un-register ESE-rules dynamically.
- Support for *quality of service* (QoS). In addition to end-to-end latencies and persistence, applications often have particular requirements for delivery ordering semantics during synchronous working.
- Event storage and retrieval. Users often need to go back in time selectively to review, replay and reconcile object histories.

We implement a framework of cMOM, which is composed of ES (Event Sender), ER (Event Receiver), EA (Event Analyzer), ET (Event synthesizer), EM (Event Matcher), ESE Register, and Interaction History Management. Figure 3 shows the overall architecture of cMOM designed to meet these requirements. As their names indicate, ES and ER send and receive events, respectively. Event producers and consumers transfer events over an interaction group, which manages event scoping as well as storage. Events pertaining to a cluster of objects are propagated with a default scope that is equal to the collection of sites where those objects reside. Fig.4 also shows an import-export service, which is used for federating sessions, and an event store, which is used for temporary and permanent storage of events.

cMOM supports applications by providing event management, storage, and notification functionality. The middleware performs the function of collecting messages from producers, filtering and transforming them as necessary, and routing them to the appropriate consumers.

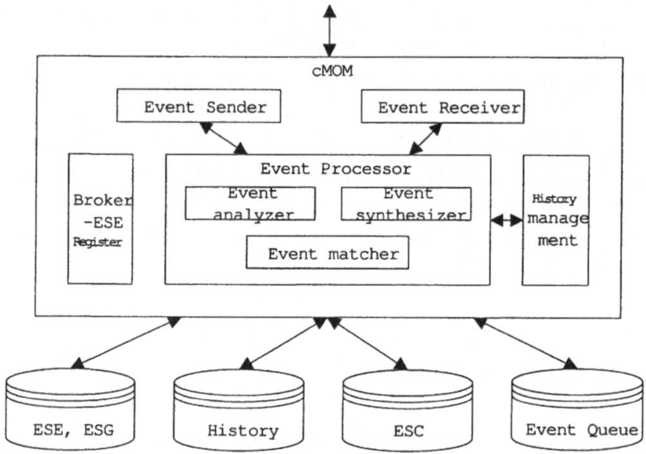

Fig. 3. The Architecture of cMOM

The principle of using cMOM is as follows: applications' ESE-rules are translated to rules stored and executed in cMOM. cMOM then performs event detection and determines applications that have registered a notification interest for such event occurrences. These applications are then appropriately informed and react as defined by their ESE-rules. The whole procedure of interaction is recorded by ESC. When a broker generates an event, it notifies the ER about the occurrence. The ER inserts the event into HEQ. ET retrieve event from HEQ, checks whether new composite events can be detected. EM determines brokers that have registered a notification interest for such event occurrences, and then adds the pair of action and event into SEQ (Sending Event Queue). The EA decomposes composite events into primitive events. The ES posts events to respective brokers.

5 Conclusion

In this paper, a composite-event-based Message-Oriented Middleware is developed. cMOM enables the integration of services and resources within and across enterprises or other organizations. We emphasize that the semantics is a key to capture the actual meaning of events in real life. Same composite event patterns may imply totally different semantic meanings in different context. We study an event and service interacting model. Based on this model, a graph-ESG, constructed according to ESE-

Rules, and a graph-ESC, which keep track of applications' interaction, are adopted to detect event. The ESG and ESC greatly enhanced the expressive power to detect event correctly, which matches situations in reality. The composite event detection method solves the problems that multiple event occurrences incur semantic ambiguity.

References

[1] I. Foster and C. Kesselman, *The Grid: Blueprint for a Future Computing Infrastructure*, Morgan Kaufmann Publishers, USA, 1999.

[2] OMG, Event Service Specification, http://www.omg.org/technology/documents/corbaservices_spec_catalog.htm.

[3] OMG, Notification Service Specification, http://www.omg.org/technology/documents/corbaservices_spec_ catalog.htm.

[4] IBM, MQSeries for Windows NT and Windows 2000 Version 5 Release 2.1, http://www-3.ibm.com/software/integration/wmq/v521/MQNT20002Q01521.pdf.

[5] M. Korhonen, Message Oriented Middleware (MOM), http://www.tml.hut.fi/Opinnot/Tik-110.551/1997/mqs.htm.

[6] G. Banavar, T. Chandra, B. Mukherjee, J. Nagarajarao, R. Strom, and D. Sturman, "An Efficient Multicast Protocol for Content-based Publish-Subscribe Systems", *Proceedings of IEEE International Conference on Distributed Computing Systems*, Austin, TX, 1999.

[7] G. Banavar, M. Kaplan, K. Shaw, R. E. Strom, D. C. Sturman, and W. Tao, "Information Flow Based Event Distribution Middleware", *Proceedings Middleware Workshop at the International Conference on Distributed Computing Systems*, 1999.

[8] M. Aguilera, R. Strom, D. Sturman, M. Astley, and T. Chandra, "Matching Events in a Content-based Subscription System", *Proceedings of ACM Symposium on Principles of Distributed Computing*, Atlanta, GA, 1999.

[9] P. Yuan, G. Chen, J. Dong, and W. Han, "Research on an Event Specification for Event-Based Collaboration Support Software Architecture", *Proceedings of the Seventh International Conference on CSCW in Design*, Sep. 2002, pp.99-104.

[10] S. Chakravarthy and D. Mishra, "Snoop: An Expressive Event Specification Language for Active Databases", *Data and Knowledge Engineering*, 14(10), 1994, pp.1-26.

[11] N. Gehani, H. V. Jagadish, and O. Shmueli, "COMPOSE: A System for Composite Event Specification and Detection", *Advanced Database Concepts and Research Issues* (N. R. Adam and B. Bhargava, eds.), Lecture Notes in Computer Science, Springer Verlag, 1994.

[12] G. Liu, A. K. Mok, and P. Konana, "A Unified Approach for Specifying Timing Constraints and Composite Events in Active Real-Time Database Systems", *Proceedings of Real-Time Technology and Applications Symposium*, June 1998.

[13] S. Gatziu, K. R. Dittrich, "Detecting Composite Events in Active Database Systems Using Petri Nets", *Proc. of 4th Intl. Workshop on Research Issues in Data Engineering*, Houston, USA, 1994, pp.2-9.

[14] D. McCarthy and U. Dayal, "The architecture of an active database management system", *Proceedings of the 1989 ACM SIGMOD international conference on Management of Data*, Portland, Oregon, May-June 1989, Vol.18, No.2, 1989, pp.215-224.

[15] W. Retschitzegger, "Composite Event Management in TriGS Concepts and Implementation", *DEXA'98*, pp.1-15.

[16] S. Gatziu and A. Vaduva, "SAMOS: an Active Object-Oriented Database System: Manual", *Technical Report 96.02*, Computer Science Department, Univ. of Zurich, 1996.

[17] N. Gehani and H. V. Jagadish, "Ode as an Active Database System: constraints and Triggers", *Proc. of the International Conference on VLDB*, September 1991, pp.327-336.

An Integration Architecture for Grid Resources

Minglu Li, Feilong Tang, and Jian Cao

Department of Computer Science and Engineering
Shanghai Jiao Tong University, Shanghai 200030, P.R. China
{li-ml,tang-fl,cao-jian}@cs.sjtu.edu.cn

Abstract. The growing demand of e-business and development of Grid technologies increasingly drive to integrate heterogeneous Grid resources in uniform way. However, this can not be satisfied by existing integration schemes. And at the time of writing, little efforts have been done. This paper[1] proposes a Grid service integration architecture, which is based on the Open Grid Services Architecture (OGSA), for addressing how various Gird resources are integrated into a virtual Grid application in the service-oriented approach. The architecture can integrate extremely heterogeneous Grid resources in "Plug and Play" way and provides abilities to handle transaction, workflow and accounting. The agent simplifies use of Grid resources because it shields user from complex process. Moreover, the paper discusses implementation of the architecture.

1 Introduction

Grid computing is becoming a mainstream technology for sharing large-scale resources, accomplishing collaborative tasks and integrating distributed systems [3]. As a result of the growing demand of commerce and the rapid development of Grid technologies, however, its application field will increasingly extend from scientific computing to commercial application, where it is of crucial significance to integrate heterogeneous hardware and software resources in convenient and standard way [4].

In this paper, based on the OGSA, we present an integration architecture that may be used to integrate seamlessly various heterogeneous Grid resources, including compute, data and application resources, and can support for transaction management, service composition and accounting.

2 Related Work

The OGSA presents the conception of Grid service, defines standard mechanisms for discovery, dynamical creation, name and notification of transient Gird service

[1] This paper is supported by 973 project (No.2002CB312002), 863 project (No.2001AA415310) of China, grand project (No.03dz15027) and key project (No.025115033) of the Science and Technology Commission of Shanghai Municipality.

M. Li et al. (Eds.): GCC 2003, LNCS 3032, pp. 708–715, 2004.

instances so that it supports integration with underlying native platform facilities [1]. It describes standard interfaces for discovery, execution, communication, notification and a variety of other services needed in the Grid environment. [2] further provides the technical details, presents a full specification of the behaviors and Web Service Definition Language (WSDL) interfaces to define a Grid service.

Grid Database Service (GDS) [5] is a Grid service that can integrate multiple databases located in different sites into a virtual database. [6] proposes a service-based architecture which wraps database within a Grid-enabled service interface.

Our motivation is to provide a model, which will be developed into an integration middleware very soon, for integration of various Grid resources. By means of this middleware, organizations and individual can encapsulate their resources into Grid services and integrate them together in "Plug and Play" way. As a result, some organizations can provide common computing capabilities while others may look up and use them to save investments.

3 Integration Architecture for Grid Resources

Our architecture, as shown in Fig. 1, is based on Grid technologies and Web Services standards. Here, any Grid resource has to be encapsulated into a service by defining a set of standard interfaces, describing them in an extended WSDL document and publishing it for being discovered later.

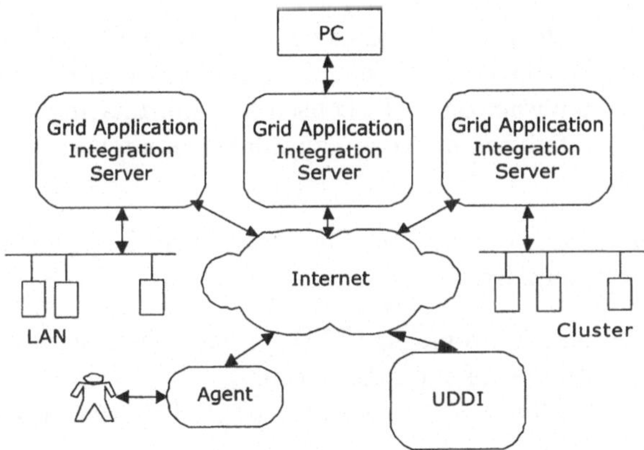

Fig. 1. The architecture of integration of Grid resources. The Grid Application Integration Server connects Internet with Grid resource such a LAN, a Cluster or a PC.

We adopt following key technologies of the Web Services:

- The Simple Object Access Protocol (SOAP) [7] provides a mechanism of messaging between a service provider and a service requestor.

- The Web Services Description Language (WSDL) [8] is an XML document to describe what capabilities a service provides, where it is and how messages can be sent, what parameter and data type a requestor must pass.
- The Universal Description, Discovery, and Integration (UDDI) [9] refers to the repository used to store description information of Grid services.

This architecture typically works like this:

- Publish. Service providers publish Grid services description and URLs of their Grid Application Integration Server (GAIS) in UDDI to advertise which capabilities the services provide and where they can be contacted.
- Look up. A service requestor discovers the GSH and GSR of desired Grid service by means of UDDI, Registry and HandleMapper in turn.
- Invoke. The service requestor binds the Grid service instance according to the GSR and finally obtains the execution results.

4 Implementation of GAIS

4.1 Transaction Service

In Grid environment, transaction management must have the abilities to coordinate both short-lived operations and long-lived business activities. We employ two types of transaction mechanisms to satisfy different application demands [12,13]:

- Atomic transaction (AT) is used to coordinate short-lived operations. It has "all or nothing" property. All participants must commit synchronously.
- Compensatory transaction (CT) is used for coordinating long-lived business activities. Here, failures of some candidates don't result in ceasing of the entire transaction.

Atomic transaction coordination. The agent in client-side responds the transaction request from user by:

- Creating a TransactionManager (TM) service, which serves as the coordinator and lives until end of the transaction.
- Sending CoordinationContext messages to all Transaction services of participants.

Transaction service of the GAIS returns a Response message to TM service.After receiving the Response messages from all participants, TM service coordinates the Atomic transaction as follows:

Phase1: It sends Prepare message to all participants for them to prepare for the transaction.

All participants reserve necessary resources and return Prepared or NotPrepared, depending on whether the reservation is successful or not.

TM service gathers all returned messages from participants within T1.

Phase2: If TM service receives Prepared messages from all participants, it commits the transaction by sending Commit messages to them and records the commit in log. Otherwise, TM sends Abort messages to all participants.

Having received Commit message, all participant's Transaction services perform the following tasks:

- Request for allocating the reserved resources;
- Record the Commit information in log;
- Monitor the execution of corresponding task and report result to TM.

Within T2,if any participant reports Failed message or the number of returned messages is less than N, the TM service reports failure to user and sends Rollback messages to all participants for them to recover to the previous states. Each participant must acknowledge this message after execution by using Rollbacked message. Otherwise, TM judges the transaction is correctly completed and then reports final result to user.

Compensatory transaction coordination. In CT, instead of reservation of resources, candidates immediately commit the transaction. The process to join in a CT is similar to the AT.

Having received the Response messages, Coordinator TM service sends Enroll messages, which contain timestamp T, to all candidates.

Candidates that have successfully reserved and allocated necessary resources record operations in log and then directly commit the transaction. Next, they return Committed messages to the TM.The Candidates which failed to reserve resources return Aborted messages and are removed from the transaction.

According to returned results, user may do the following through the TM:

- For candidates committed successfully, he selects some and cancels the others by sending Confirm and Cancel messages to them respectively within T.
- For candidates failed, he needn't reply them and may renew to send Enroll requests to locate new candidates until success or attempting N times.

As such, within T, the candidate that has committed successfully may perform either the following:

- In case of receiving Confirm message, it responds a Confirmed message.
- In the event of receiving Cancel message or nothing, it automatically rollbacks the operations taken according to its log record and returns a Cancelled message or nothing respectively.

4.2 Service Discovery

Service discovery includes two steps: find GSH and then GSR. Typically, the GSH is the URL of a service instance while the format of the GSR is specific to the binding mechanism used by the client to communicate with the Grid service instance.

In this architecture, each Factory and Grid service instance must register its GSH with Registry. Mapping relationship between GSH to GSR is registered in HandleMapper. The service discovery is described in Fig. 2:

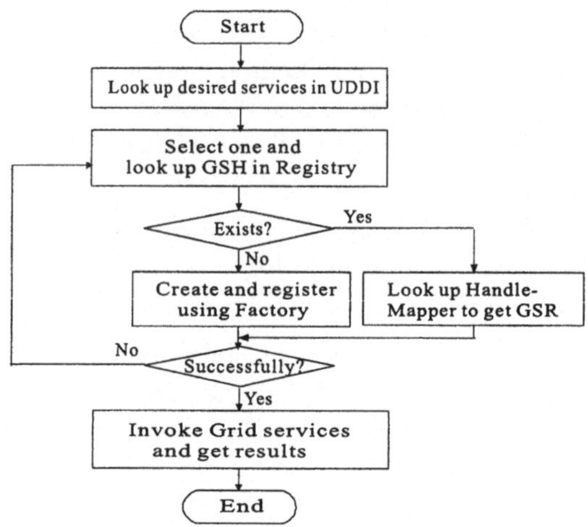

Fig. 2. The procedure of service discovery

- Look up UDDI. A client finds desired services from UDDI according to service discriptions. Generally, the client will get a set of services and their GAIS' URLs. Based on some policies, the client may select one of them.
- Discover GSR. Using the selected URL, the client can contact GAIS and discover the GSR of a Grid service instance:(1) The Grid service instance has been created and is still valid. In this situation, its GSH and mapping relationship between GSH and GSR(s) have existed in Registry and HandleMapper of local GAIS respectively. What the client needs to do is to look up the GSH of the service instance in Registry and then resolves it into GSR by querying HandleMapper. (2) It has not been created.The client finds the GSH of Factory in Registry, creates a Grid service instance using Factory interface and holds this service instance's GSH and initial GSR.

After getting the GSR of the Grid service instance, the client has enough information to bind it and then receives the execution results.

4.3 Workflow Management

Workflow service supports execution of multiple coördinated applications on different distributed Grid resources. It resolves workflow information, invokes dynamically other services, mediates the interaction between sub-services and handles the exceptions and faults that may occur in the workflow execution [10].

We use the Grid Services Flow Language (GSFL)[11] to implement workflow management. The wrokflow service consists of three parts:

- GSFL Parser. It reads a GSFL instance document, which is an XML document describing how a business process invokes a set of services, generates binding information and provides methods to transfer date format.

- WSDL generator. It is used for creation, representation, and manipulation of extended WSDL documents which contain enough information to bind sub-services.
- GSFL coordinator. After receipt of the GSFL document, it dynamically generates a WSDL document with all of the newly exported operations, by calling GSFL Parser and WSDL generator in turn. Then it invokes new sub-services on behalf of user according to the WSDL document newly created.

4.4 Accounting Service

Accounting service is used to record information that a user consumes resources and decide how much the user has to pay for resource usage. It works through the following function units:

- Record module. It records the raw usage data for user to use the Grid resources, such as how much time CPU is employed.
- Billing module. It gathers, analyses all records of correlating services and forms an entire one for a service request.Because these correlating services may locate in different sites,an approach is to look up the service list to find all called services, and then query these services recursively.
- Accounting module. It calculates the total that the user should pay for a service request in terms of the entire record and accounting policies. The policies must be stored in database and cached in memory to improve performance.

4.5 Management and Monitoring

Management service performs the management of the service integration and fulfills the dynamic configuration of enterprise application policies, including workflow, transaction, accounting, application resource management service and universal interface service.

Monitoring service manages and monitors the processing of services, including accounting rules,workflow execution,service status and security policies.

5 Case Study

We show how to integrate Grid resources and how for a client to use these integrated services by means of an e-business example. Here, a client orders several cars and hire a garage to store the cars. This process involves four services: car manufacture service, credit evaluation service, part manufacture service and garage hire service. According to client's demand, car manufacture and garage hire services should be handled as a compensatory transaction. In addition, to facilitate the client, the agent in client-side is implemented in a web site. What the client need do is to submit request and make appropriate selection through a browser.

The four service providers respectively integrate their services into the Grid in term of the following steps:

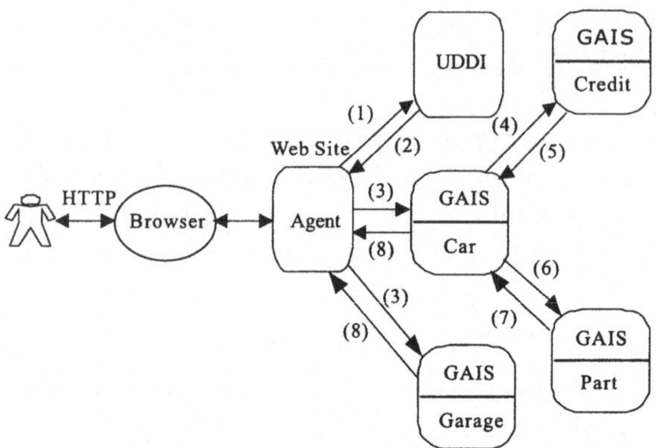

Fig. 3. An example of e-business,where Car,Credit,Part,Garage stand for car manufacture, credit evaluation , part manufacture and garage hire service respectively.

1. Generate the extended WSDL document, which is stored in corresponding GAIS.
2. Apply for an account in UDDI and get a pair of user ID and password for publishing.
3. Publish the description of services they can provide and their GAIS' URL in UDDI.

The trade process is shown in Fig. 3:

1. Using a browser, the client queries the UDDI to look for car manufacture and garage hire services.
2. The client gets some GAIS' URLs corresponding to desired car manufacture and garage hire service.
3. The client simultaneously issues requests to providers of car manufacture and garage hire services. Each request includes the same timestamp T, which stands for the expiration of this transaction.
4. Through workflow service, the GAIS belonging to the car manufacture service requests the credit evaluation service to examine the client's credit rank.
5. Credit evaluation service returns the client's credit rank.
6. If the client is eligible,the car manufacture service then sends part order request to part manufacture service.
7. The part manufacture service returns part order.
8. Within T, the car manufacture service returns car order result to the client. As such, the garage hire service also reports garage hire result to the client.

Within T, if both car manufacture and garage hire services execute successfully, the client may acknowledge them in Confirm messages and the entire transaction completes. Alternatively, if the client does not give acknowledgement to one service because he is not interested in it any longer, this service will autonomously cancel the order result after T. On the other hand, if any of above two services fails, the client may renew to select other candidate to repeat above process until he succeeds in trading.

6 Conclusions and Future Work

Combining Grid computing and Web Services technologies, we have presented an integration architecture for Grid services. The architecture can integrate extremely heterogeneous Grid resources in "Plug and Play" way. It provides abilities to manage transaction, workflow, accounting and security. Especially, it can handle both short-lived operations and long-lived business activities and ensure data consistency in face of most failures. Agent shields user from complex process.

The architecture is extensible because it is built on a series of standard protocols and technologies. Next, we will develop it into an integration middleware for e-business based on Grid.

References

1. I. Foster, C. Kesselman, J. M. Nick and S. Tuecke. The Physiology of the Grid-An Open Grid Services Architecture for Distributed Systems Integration. June, 2002.
2. S. Tuecke, K. Czajkowski, I. Foster, J. Frey, S.Graham and C. Kesselman. "Grid Service Specification (Draft 3)". July, 2002.
3. I.Foster, C.kesselman, and S.Tuecke. The anatomy of the grid: enabling scalable virtual organizations. Int'l J. High-Performance computing Applications. March 2001.
4. F. L. Tang, M. L. Li, J. Cao et al. Technology of Enterprise Application Integration Based on Web Services. Proceeding of International Workshop on Grid and Cooperative Computing (GCC 2002). December, 2002.
5. N. W. Paton, M. P. Atkinson, V. Dialani, D. Pearson, T. Storey and P. Watson. Database Access and Integration Services on the Grid. Technical Report UkeS-2002-3, National e-Science Centre. http://www.nesc.ac.uk. 2002.
6. P. Watson. Database and the Grid. Technical Report CS-TR-755, University of Newcastle, 2001.
7. D.Box, D.Ehnebuske, G.Kakivaya, A.Layman, N.Mendelsohn, H.F.Nielsen, S.Thatte, D.Winer. "Simple Object Access Protocol (SOAP) 1.1". W3C.May 2000.
8. E.Christensen, F. Curbera, G..Meredith, S.Weerawarana. "Web Services Description Language (WSDL) 1.1". W3C.Note 15 March 2001.
9. UDDI: Universal Description, Discovery, and Integration. http://www.uddi.org/.
10. OGSA-WG. Open Grid Services Architecture: A Roadmap, Draft v2. 2002.
11. S. Krishnan, P. Wagstrom, and G. V. Laszewski. GSFL: A Workflow Framework for Grid Services. Argonne National Laboratory. Aug 2002.
12. F. L. Tang, M. L. Li, and J. Cao, A Transaction Model for Grid Computing. In LNCS 2834, Springer Verlag (2003).
13. F. L. Tang, M. L. Li, and J. Cao. A Transaction Coordination Mechanism and Compensation Technology in Grid Environment. To appear in Journal of Computer Research and Development, December, 2003 (In Chinese).

Component-Based Middleware Platform for Grid Computing

Jianmin Zhu[1], Rong Chen [2], Guangnan Ni [1], and Yuan Liu [3]

[1] Institute of Computing Technology, Chinese Academy of Sciences, Beijing, 100080
kevinzjm@hotmail.com
ngn@public.bta.net.cn
[2] Beijing Koretide Corporation, Beijing, 100080
chenrong@koretide.com.cn
[3] College of Machinery and Engineering, Jilin University, ChangChun 130000
wangyuing@sina.com

Abstract. In the Grid environment, user can manage and make use of web services, such as uploading or downloading web services. But when user wants to download one web services to run it in a local machine, one problem may occur: The web service can only be run on a special operating system, which is not the operating system that the user operates. To solve this problem, we need construct one middleware to emulate the running environment of the web service in the operating system that user operates. Middleware is the component created by the Operation System according to its metadata, and it is also the center from which the Internet technology extended. Component-based middleware has emerged as an important architectural component in modern distributed systems, such as XPCOM, UNO and the CORBA Component Model. Java Virtual Machine (JVM) is a middleware, aimed at making application cross platform to run. The goal of our research is to extend this work in order to exploit one component-based middleware platform that can make web services to run on different operating system platforms, such as Elastos, Windows and Linux operating system. In this paper, a new and efficient component model based on COM (ezCOM) is proposed. More specifically, this paper describes in detail how ezCOM can be used to construct a full component-based crossing Operating system middleware platform and also puts forward one new measure model to compare the performance of ezCOM, Wine-COM, XPCOM and UNO.

1 Introduction

In the distributed network environment, user can manage and make use of web services, which were placed in Grid. The web services can run in a local machine or a remote machine, which is in distributed network environment. Many of web services can only run on a special operating system. For example, a user, who is working on Linux, wants to download a web service to perform some complex operations in his local machine. However, the web service, which is based on Microsoft.net, can only run on Windows operating system and cannot run on Linux. In this case, the problem

M. Li et al. (Eds.): GCC 2003, LNCS 3032, pp. 716–723, 2004.

may occur. To solve this problem, the best way is to construct the crossing platform middleware to emulate the running environment of web services based Microsoft. Net.

Middleware is the component created by the Operation System according to its metadata, and it is also the center from which the Internet technology extended. The role of middleware is to provide underlying support for the third party development, composition and subsequent deployment of components, and also typically ease the task of the management of non-functional properties of applications (e.g. security). Examples of key component-based middleware platforms include XPCOM [8], UNO [9] and the CORBA Component Model.

ezCOM is an efficient, lightweight and reflective component model, which is compatible with Microsoft COM (Component Object Model) binary standard. It supports many programming language, including C, C++, VB, etc. ezCOM component-based middleware can run executable files in ELF or PE-COFF format. ezCOM supports applications that can run on many operating systems, such as, Elastos, Windows and Linux, as long as the applications are written in the ezCOM standard.. The specific goals of this paper are [1].

- To provide a detailed introduction to ezCOM
- To illustrate how ezCOM can be used to construct a full component-based crossing Operating system middleware platform, which can make web services run on different operating systems.
- To put forward one measure model to investigate the performance of ezCOM.

This paper is organized as follows. Section 2 reports on the design of ezCOM, Section 3 reports on the principle that ezCOM can make applications cross operating systems to run. Section 4 then reports on the associated ezCOM implementation on Linux. Following this, section 5 puts forward one measure model to compare the performance of ezCOM, Wine-COM [3], XPCOM and UNO, while Section 6 contains some discussions of related work, and section 7 contains some concluding remarks. Because web services are the special applications, we will consider them as normal applications in this article.

2 Background

The ezCOM technique created by Beijing Koretide Century Technology Ltd. is an original idea of the software platform towards the three-ties programming architecture. It makes efficient use of hardware resources to support dynamical component loading on the kernel of independent copyrighted operating system-Elastos, so as to achieve higher efficiency by running Native Code [2].

From the technical point, ezCOM adopts the fundamental idea of COM and implements the platform compatible to Microsoft COM. To mask the heavy and complicated details of COM component, ezCOM developing environment provides CDL-component descriptive language-to implement component encapsulation automatically. Compared to Microsoft COM, software engineers need not to notice the complex disciplines of COM but just put their attention on what they want to do.

3 The Principle

ezCOM Component middleware can make Web services or applications to run on different operating systems. The principle of crossing platform of ezCOM is similar with JVM, but there is a litter different between JVM and ezCOM. The most important thing is that the compatibility of applications is different between ezCOM and JVM. The applications have binary compatibility on ezCOM, but source code compatibility on JVM. Why ezCOM component platform can make applications cross platforms to run? Because it does these aspects:

- ezCOM provides uniform interface on different operating system.
- For application, whatever operating system it runs, I can call uniform API function.
- ezCOM provides corresponding executable program loader on different OS.
- ezCOM provides different system call switching on different operating system.

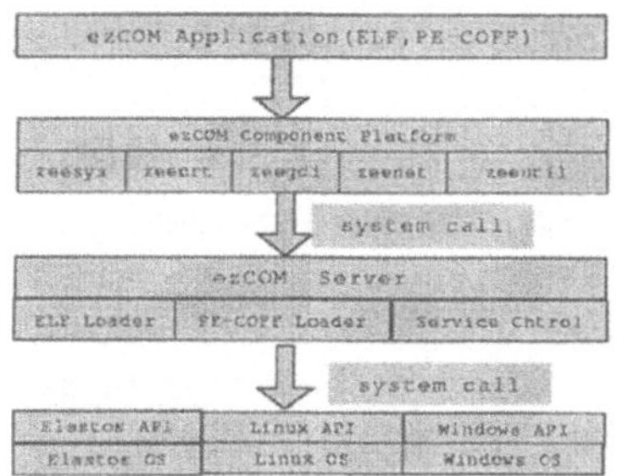

Fig. 1. Principle of ezCOM on different OS.

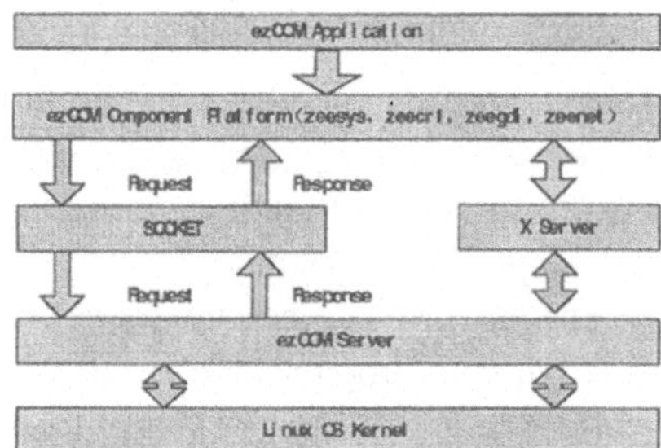

Fig. 2. ezCOM on Linux

From figure 1, we know, ezCOM component middleware platform includes two modules: ezCOM API module and ezCOM server module. ezCOM API module provides the uniform interfaces to applications on different platforms. This module provides many API functions to developer. It has many sub modules, such as, zeesys, zeecrt, zeegdi, zeenet and zeeuil. ezCOM server module provides application loader, system call switching and service request controlling.

Because ezCOM is the subset of Microsoft COM, so it is easy to implement ezCOM on Windows. If only we develop one layer to encapsulate the API of Windows and switch those system calls to system calls of Windows. In ezCOM component middleware platform, this layer is zeesys module. Zeesys is an indispensable module. It provides APIs to applications and switches some API calls to system calls on Windows.

On different operating systems, there are different environments to run COM. The aim of implementing of ezCOM on Linux is in order to provide a complete COM solution for Linux operating system. Figure 2 represents the principle of implementing ezCOM on Linux. In the figure 2, the application runs on Linux by these steps:

- System creates socket connection between ezCOM platform and ezCOM server.
- Application calls API of ezCOM component platform.

- ezCOM platform fills request buffer and sends request to ezCOM through socket.
- Judging the type of request, ezCOM server switches the API call to system call On Linux; if there isn't the corresponding system call on Linux, we will call the function that is implemented in ezCOM server module.

4 Implementing ezCOM on Linux

During implementing ezCOM component middleware platform on Linux, in order to maintain that the application is independent on operating system, we will face a lot of difficult technologies to resolve. Such as switching the format of executable program and switching system calls.

4.1 Switching the Format of Executable Program

For Elastos, Windows and Linux, not only they have different file formats of executable programs, but also do they have different file formats of function libraries. The file format of executable programs on Linux is ELF, and it is PE-COFF on Windows.

To all executable programs, they have one header structure. Header structure describes all relative information with executable program. There are different header structure in PE-COFF and ELF. Because of the different header structure, the loader model is different to PE-COFF and ELF.

Though the ezCOM component can be easily loaded on Elastos and Windows, but it will be not same as Linux. Because Linux OS only can recognize ELF format executable program, if we want to let the ezCOM-based program run on Linux, we must switch the PE-COFF format executable program to ELF format executable program. In the ezCOM server module, there is a loader module. The function of loader module:

- Switching the file format of executable program from PE-COFF to ELF
- Loading the ELF format executable program to OS memory space.

After the program is loaded into memory, operating system will initialize the program, such as: creating process space, creating image map, creating module, etc. During initialization, some data will be gotten from the file of program. In first, the Loader module will read the initializing data. For PE-COFF and ELF, the different file format leads the different loading method.

For every executable program, to run it on operating system, OS must create one date structure for it. Because the file format of PE-COFF is different with ELF, Loader must create different date structure for PE-COFF and ELF.

4.2 Switching System Calls

For the ezCOM-based application, it doesn't need know the detail of operating system. Because the application calls the API of ezCOM and it doesn't need call system calls, which are provided by operating system. After the application calls the APIs of ezCOM, ezCOM component middleware will switch those APIs calls to system calls. How switch system calls, which are provided by ezCOM, to system calls, which are provided by operating system?

4.2.1 Elastos and Windows

On Elastos and Windows, we have implemented switching system calls. Figure 3 describes the principle:

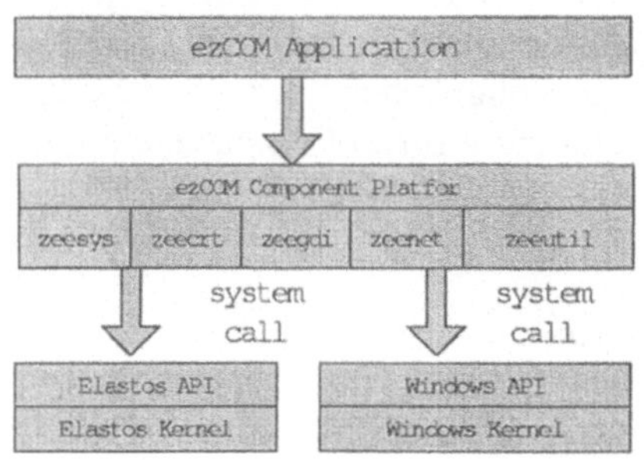

Fig. 3. ezCOM on Elastos and Windows

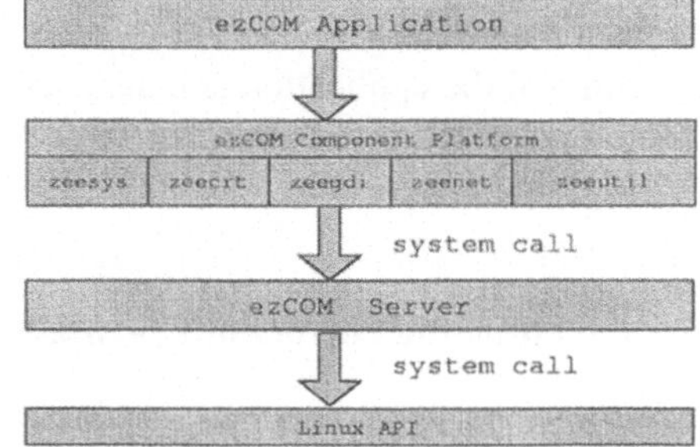

Fig. 4. ezCOM on Linux

From the figure 3, we know the ezCOM Application implements the system calls switching through those steps:

- ezCOM application calls APIs, which are provided by ezCOM
- ezCOM component middleware searching corresponding API from “Elastos API” and “Windows API” module. If there is the corresponding API function, the system will call it; if not, we will implement this API function in “zeesys” module
- After find the API function in APIs, which are provided by operating system, the ezCOM component middleware will make system calls switching.

4.2.2 Linux

On Linux, we also implement system calls switching. Figure4 describes the principle that ezCOM component middleware implements the system calls switching on Linux. Although the APIs, which are provided by ezCOM component middleware on different operating system, are the same, the implements of APIs are different. For example: Zeesys is the kernel module in ezCOM component middleware platform. It includes some important interfaces, such as, Isystem, Iprocess, Ithread. In Iprocess, there is an API function: CreateProcess. Its implement is different on Elastos, Windows and Linux. When an application calls CreateProcess, ezCOM will switch it into different system call, which is provided by OS kernel:

- On Elastos: System will call CreateProcess
- On Windows: System will call CreateProcess
- On Linux: Because there is not the function CreateProcess, system will call Fork, which is provided by Linux kernel.

From figure 4, we know that ezCOM server module will manage the service requests from ezCOM component middleware platform. If the application wants to make system call, as usual, it need finish those steps:

- The application calls the API than is provided by ezCOM
- ezCOM fills in the service request buffer.
- ezCOM platform sends this service request to ezCOM server through socket.
- ezCOM server manages the service request from socket
- ezCOM server switches service request to system call of Linux kernel
- Linux kernel returns result to ezCOM server
- ezCOM server returns result to ezCOM middleware platform
- ezCOM middleware platform returns result to application

In the solution of implementing ezCOM on Linux, the system call is mainly implemented through service request and service response. We define the service request structure in ezCOM component definition. As soon as creating client process for application, system will create a service request structure for application. After client process sends service request to ezCOM, ezCOM will fill in request buffer, then sends the service request to ezCOM server. At the end, ezCOM server will switch the request to system call of Linux kernel.

The function, which deals with service request, maybe exists or doesn't exist in Linux kernel. If the function doesn't exist, we will implement it in ezCOM server module.

5 Performance

When application calls component, it has system time spending in two aspects: Creating component and function calling, which is provided by the component. To different component solution, the system time spending is different. We bring forward one performance measure model to compare component performance of XPCOM, UNO, Wine-COM and ezCOM. The method is:

$T = Ts + K*Tc$

T: Total time, **Ts**: The time to Create component, **Tc**: The time to make one function calling, which is provided by component, **K**: The amount that application has make function calling

In this testing, we call function, which do anything but make calculation: "1+1" and return result. Using this method, we make 0, 0.5 Million, 1Million, 1.5Million, 2 Million function callings and calculate the time spending, the result is (M =Million, S=second, MS= microsecond):

According the test data, we can draw the figure 5 to describe the performance of four component models:

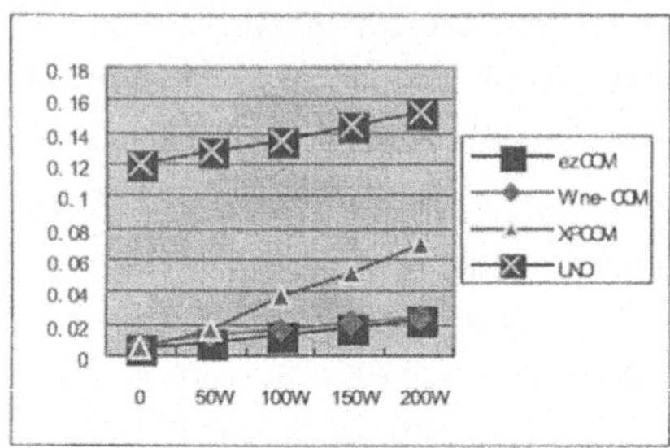

Fig. 5. Performance comparison

Table 1. The values of Ts and Tc

Component mode	Ts(S)	Tc(MS)
ezCOM	0.0045	0.0092
Wine-COM	0.0076	0.0088
XPCOM	0.0002	0.0350
UNO	0.1196	0.0163

From figure5 and table 1, we will know the performance of ezCOM is the best, and then Wine-COM, XPCOM, the performance of UNO is the worst.

6 Related Work

XPCOM, UNO, Wine-COM and ezCOM are the component models. All of XPCOM, Wine-COM and ezCOM are subset of COM. But the performance of those component models is different. ezCOM is the best.

Wine-COM is subset of MSCOM on Linux, but it doesn't implement all functions, which have been implemented in MSCOM. Wine-COM emulates the environment to run MSCOM-based application on Linux.

XPCOM is a lightweight component model that, similarly to ezCOM, is built on top of the core subset of COM. However, it does not provide any special support for dynamic reconfiguration.

UNO (Universal Network Objects) is the interface based component model of OpenOffice.org. UNO offers interoperability between different programming languages, different objects models, different machine architectures and different processes either in LAN or via the Internet..

7 Conclusions

This paper has considered the design and implementation of ezCOM, a lightweight and efficient reflective component model designed specifically for the development of middleware platforms.

ezCOM component platform can make web services to run on different operating system platform, such as Elastos, Windows and Linux operating system

We also demonstrated in detail how ezCOM can be used to construct a full component-based crossing Operating system middleware platform and also put forward one new measure model to compare the performance of ezCOM, Wine-COM, XPCOM and UNO. Recently, More and more software companies attach importance to Linux in this world. If we can implement the ezCOM on Elastos, Windows and Linux operating system, we can provide another choice about crossing platform middleware besides JVM. This is the main overall contribution of this paper.

Acknowledgements. We would like to acknowledge the contributions of my partners on the ezCOM project.

References

[1] Chen Rong. Evolution of operating system in Internet age [J].Computer World.No.42. October 2001
[2] Beijing Koretide Corporation. Elastos Handbook [EB/OL]. October 2002
[3] Wine Group. Wine Developer's Guide [EB/OL]. March.2002
[4] Box, Don. Essential COM. 3rd Edition [M]. Addison-Wesley. January 1998. PP: 10-37
[5] Jianmin Zhu, Rong Chen, Guangnan Ni. Elastos browser model design [J]. Computer engineering and applications. Vol.39 No.13, May.2003
[6] Ian. Foster, C. Kesselman, and S. Tuecke. The Anatomy of the Grid - Enabling Scalable Virtual Organizations [J]. Supercomputer Applications, 2001
[7] Balen,Henry. Distributed Object Architectures with CORBA.Cambridge University [M]. February 2000.pp: 50-70
[8] The Mozilla Organization. The Mozilla Handbook [EB/OL]. March.2001
[9] The OpenOfffice Organization. http://udk.openoffice.org. [EB/OL].Jul.2002

Grid Gateway: Message-Passing between Separated Cluster Interconnects *

Wei Cui, Jie Ma, and Zhigang Huo

Institute of Computing Technology, Chinese Academy of Sciences
P.O. Box 2704, Beijing 100080, P.R. China
Graduate School of the Chinese Academy of Sciences, Beijing 100039
{cw, majie, zghuo}@ncic.ac.cn

Abstract. Geographically distributed computing requires high-performance clusters to be integrated to solve problems in computational Grid. Because cluster interconnect is isolated, its low-level communication protocol doesn't exchange messages with others directly. This paper presents a plug-in, Grid Gateway, which enables separated low-level communication protocols to communicate with each other. Grid Gateway can be used in many topologies of inter-cluster network. It has some dynamic features, such as support for multi-gateway mechanism to enhance communication performance. Grid Gateway allows low-level communication protocol to involve in the high-performance Grid computing. Thus it is expected to support the implementation of Grid-enabled tools over it, such as Grid-enabled MPI. This paper describes its architecture and implementation, and presents some design issues.

1 Introduction

Computational Grid provides more computational power than present machines, which meets the needs of many fields in science and commerce [1]. Clusters with lots of applications and deployed plentifully play an important role in the Grid environment. Currently, cooperative computing among clusters is discussed widely.

Because cluster interconnect is isolated, low-level communication protocol can't exchange messages with each other directly. Grid Gateway (GGW) is introduced to enable separated low-level communication protocols to communicate with each other. There is a gateway process each on the nodes, namely gateway nodes, in each cluster. When a node attempts to send messages to the node in a remote cluster, messages are transferred to one gateway node of local cluster at first. Then gateway process sends them to the remote gateway node, which forwards the messages to the destination at last. This data movement is transparent to users, thus user has a single image to the involved clusters. GGW extends the functionality of low-level communication protocol. Grid-enabled tools such as Gird-enabled MPI[3] can be implemented over it.

* This work is supported by the National '863' High-Tech Program of China (No. 2002AA104410, 2002AA1Z2102)

M. Li et al. (Eds.): GCC 2003, LNCS 3032, pp. 724–731, 2004.

Grid Gateway introduces four key design issues as follows, which are described in the paper.

- Global ID. Communication between cluster low-level communication protocols requires that sender and receiver could identify each other uniquely. Designing a hostname and address space is the first consideration.
- Communication semantic. Extension of communication path and data buffering at Gateway nodes result in some semantic issues of protocol, such as how to notify sender the send success, what sender does when the receiving buffers of gateways are unavailable.
- Multi-routing mechanism. To send a message out of local cluster, sender chooses a gateway node to transfer the message. The gateway node also needs to choose a route to the target gateway node. In GGW a multi-routing mechanism is used to deal with the things.
- Flow control. Gateway stores messages of all the nodes before sending successfully, but the number of buffers is limited. Therefore a flow control mechanism is designed to avoid buffer overflow.

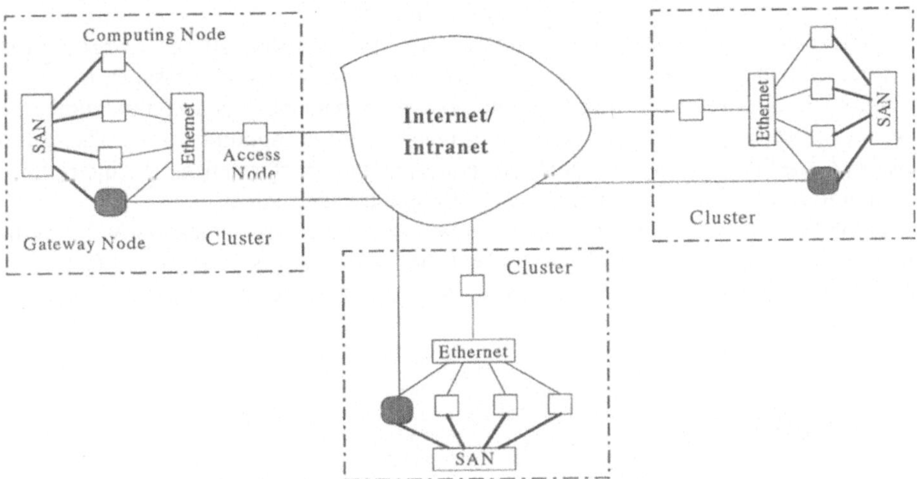

Fig. 1. Grid Gateway Background Topology

This paper is organized as follows. Section 2 presents the architecture of GGW. Section 3 describes some design issues. Then the design and implementation of GGW is described in section 4. In the final section the paper is summarized briefly.

2 Architecture of Grid Gateway

As shown in figure 1, several clusters are interconnected through Internet or Intranet (also called inter-cluster network) and compose of a computational Grid. Data moving between clusters reaches computing nodes through Grid Gateway node, which is in the cluster system area network (SAN). On the gateway node, there is a Grid Gateway process responsible for forwarding data the inter-cluster network. When a computing node sends messages to a node in the remote cluster, messages are sent to the local gateway node through SAN at first. Then the gateway node transfers the messages to the remote gateway node through inter-cluster network, which forwards the messages to the destination through SAN at last.

Gateway node connects directly with inter-cluster network. If not, it still can communicate with remote clusters through access node via Ethernet. Access nodes actually act as Ethernet gateways to forward IP packets. The flexibility makes Grid Gateway independent of inter-cluster network, which means that we can connect clusters through an Intranet in a building or the Internet.

Every node can act as a gateway node as well as a computing node. A computing node requires that its tasks be assigned enough CPU time. Gateway process has blocking-receiving function and supports intra-node communication. It sleeps when it is idle, so doesn't affect the task running on the node.

There can be more than one gateway nodes in a cluster. At the extreme every computing node is a gateway node, which only transfer itself messages to remote clusters. Static strategy is used in the system to balance loads if the number of gateway nodes is more than one but less than that of computing nodes. This multi-gateway mechanism is expected to enhance the performance of inter-cluster communication when lay grid-enabled MPI implementation over it.

In the Grid, it is possible that the clusters become unavailable suddenly during the time of executing tasks. In order to prevent the local gateway process and tasks from their affect, GGW allows every cluster to join or leave the computational Grid dynamically.

3 Design Issues

Grid Gateway enables low-level communication protocol to pass messages between each other directly. The domain of the protocol is extent to include several clusters. Gateway process has complex buffer management and flow control mechanisms because of the performance gap between cluster interconnect and inter-cluster network. These factors result in several design issues in the Grid Gateway. For instance, how to design the hostname and address space that identify communication end-points for all nodes of clusters; how to cope with unavoidable semantic change caused by the external communication of low-level communication protocol, and so on.

3.1 Global ID

In a low-level communication protocol every end-point needs a unique node ID in a cluster. To identify the sender or receiver when communicating between clusters, the node ID should be unique or global in all the involved clusters. That means all the end-points of the clusters will share a hostname and address space.

In GGW, net adapter is the communication end-point. Every net adapter is assigned a global ID to identify itself. The global ID is derived from the net adapter's MAC address that can identify the net adapter globally. Gateway process knows all the node's global IDs that are gotten from the remote clusters during initialization. Every computing node has a name table containing all the nodes' global ID, which is filled by the data gotten from gateway process if it's empty when opening a port.

3.2 Communication Semantic

In the low-level communication protocol, after sending a message sender will receive a send event to notify the result of the send. A send-completed event suggests that the message get to the receiver. In Grid Gateway, the communication path is extended to include local and remote gateway nodes. If the operation of sending messages to a remote cluster conforms to the semantic of the low-level communication protocol, high latency will result in a great number of return events blocking in the event queue to waiting for ACK/NACK from receiver. At last the blocking-event number will reach the capacity of low-level communication protocol so that the node will be unable to send and receive. GGW changes the semantic of the send operation. After sending a message to a gateway successfully, sender will receive a send event notifying that the message arrives at the gateway other than the remote cluster node.

In addition, the performance gap between SAN and Ethernet makes the buffer of Grid Gateway process often full of data. In order to avoid buffer overflow, Gateway process returns send-failed event. Therefore sender probably encounters more failures when sending messages to a remote cluster than to a local cluster. But for some low-level communication protocols this effect is slight. For instance, in GM2.0 if target node has no receiving buffers available, messages stay in the send queue for about one minute until the buffers is provided. This waiting time is long enough to allow gateway process to release a few buffers and provide them for receiving messages.

3.3 Multi-routing Mechanism

Since communication involves the nodes at remote clusters, every computing node has a multi-routing mechanism. When a computing node sends a message, it judges whether the destination is in local the cluster or a remote cluster at first, then chooses a route to the nodes in local cluster, or to the local gateway if the destination is at a remote cluster. To forward the message, the local gateway also needs to choose a route to the remote gateway node for the message.

Grid Gateway uses global ID as the parameter of send and receive operations. Hostname and global ID of all the nodes are stored in a name table on every host.

Routing operation on the computing node and gateway just is to retrieve the table. But the retrieving operation may be inefficient when name table is very large. We assign each cluster an ID. The name table catalogs global IDs according to the cluster IDs. The first byte of a global ID word is set as a cluster ID, and local cluster ID is zero. It is very fast to locate a node by its cluster ID.

3.4 Flow Control

For the sack of the performance gap between cluster interconnect and inter-cluster network, it's possible that the Gateway buffers are full of data and cannot receive messages. In case that buffer overflow results in data loss and out-of-order of messages, an efficient flow control mechanism is needed between computing node and gateway node.

Grid Gateway use tokens to regulate sends between computing node and gateway node. A computing node port may send a message to gateway node only if when it possesses a token for that port, and so does gateway. Receiver returns tokens after it deals with the messages.

Each send token imply these is a corresponding receiving buffer on the gateway. In fact the number of send tokens is so large that the number of buffers is far less than it. As a solution, in GGW only if it is confirmed that a send is successful, the next message can be sent.

4 Design and Implementation

Grid Gateway implementation is based on the DAWNING 4000A[4] high-performance Grid-enabling computer, which will consist of 512 SMP nodes based on the AMD 64-bit processor and connected with the 1024-port Myrinet. In current version of Grid Gateway we choose GM2.0[2] as low-level communication protocol.

4.1 Communication Path

Communication end-point is identified by global ID. All global IDs and hostnames are store in the global ID table. If it is empty gm_open() will get it from gateway. To interact with gateway node, some control messages is transferred by the single-side operation (or called RMA operation). The base address of RMA buffers is exchanged in gm_open(). When a port is closed, gm_close() must notify the gateway the state change of the port in order to stop the gateway passing any message to the port..

When a computing send a message to a remote cluster's node through gateway, gateway process should know the destination's information, such as global ID, port ID, and size etc. To tell the gateway the destination's information, we may contain it in the message body, or send an additional control message. GGW uses the latter method, because by the former method excessive data may causes receiver's buffer overflow. The additional control message is sent by a RMA operation, gm_put(), shown as dotted line in the figure 2. Since the order of the transfer of gm_put() is preserved relative to messages of the same priority sent by gm_send(), it is easy to keep the mapping between the additional control message and data message. Every opened port of each node in the local cluster has two RMA areas both on the gateway and local node.

Gm_put() writes data into a target node's buffer specified by the parameter of virtual memory address. The first message can't by sent by this means in gm_open() because local node haven't that address. Fortunately the gateway can recognize it for it's the first message that the gateway receives from that node's port.

As shown in figure 2, we implement gm_send() and gm_put() functions mainly used at first. In gm_put() we use gm_send() to pass data to the gateway. If we use gm_put() to do so, to notify the gateway process the data's arrive will complicate the gateway process. The type of messages is implied by the additional RMA control message. When receiving a message from GM, Gateway process deals with it according to its type. The message is packed with gateway protocol form and then sent to other gateway. When receiving a message from other gateway, the message will be sent to target node by gm_send() or gm_put() according its type. For messages from the gateway gm_receive() fills the additional message's information into the receive event.

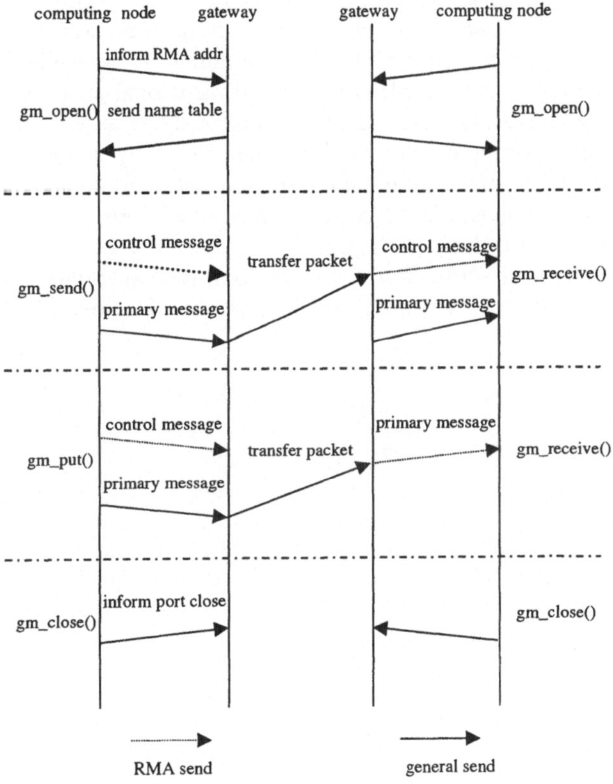

Fig. 2. Message Sequence in the Functions

4.2 Gateway Process

Gateway process maintains connections with other gateway, and receives messages into local cluster's nodes or sends out to remote clusters. We use two threads to deal with the receive-in and send-out operation respectively. Gateway process has to be able to sleep to wait for messages from GM and sockets simultaneously; otherwise busy waiting will waste much of CPU time so that gateway node can't run as computing node. So only one single process isn't suitable. Multi-process is capable of realizing gateway's functions, but to share complicated buffers and data queues between processes is challenging. Based on the above analysis multi-thread structure is an ideal choice. Gm_blocking_receive() and socket select() calls enable gateway process to sleeping receiving in different threads; and careful dividing data structure to diminish shared data and locks may make program very simple but effective.

So gateway process consists of three parts: main procedure and receive-in thread and send-out thread. Main procedure collects information of local cluster and remote, initiate those two threads, and bock itself to accept new clusters' connection requests. Receive-in thread is in charge of the responsibility shown at the upper part of Figure 3. It repeatedly receives data from TCP/IP, enqueue it into receiving FIFO, and send it to its destination through GM. Send-out thread is responsible for Figure 3's lower part, and do at the same steps with receive-in thread but in the contrary direction.

The two threads don't share buffers so that it is not necessary to consider mutex locks. Both threads have message FIFO organized under the consideration for picking out packets efficiently. Sending FIFO is a two-dimensional array, with item divided by its target gateway. Receive-in thread's FIFO is a list, because target port number is very huge that array structure may be inefficient. Sending a message to a specific gateway or nodes' GM ports may be not permitted when the socket's buffer is full or GM port's buffer is unavailable. To pick out another item to send can speed up proceeding instead of to block at the point. Logically GM2.0 can transfer 2^{31} bytes one time maximally, but MPICH-GM divides long messages into several fragments with 1M bytes length each at most. So a buffer block about 1M bytes length is enough.

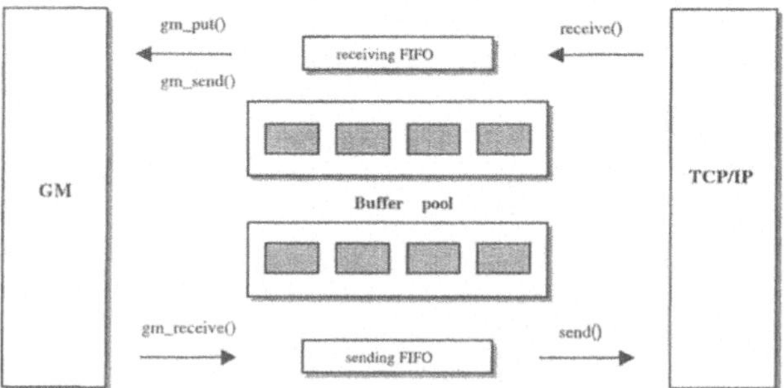

Fig. 3. Gateway Process Structure

5 Summary

Grid Gateway connects separated low-level communication protocols, and enables messages to move between distributed cluster interconnects. This paper describes its architecture and implementation. Several design issues are presented, including global ID, message passing semantic, multi-layer routing mechanism, and flow control. Now the project is under way. We expect to present its performance evaluation later.

GGW can be applied to different structures of inter-cluster networks flexibly. It allows clusters to be inter-connected through the Intranet or the Internet. A node can be a computing node as well as a gateway node, which suggests that the number of gateway node can be as many as that of the computing nodes. GGW extends the functionality of low-level communication protocol so that it might facilitate the implementation of Grid-enabled tools.

References

[1] I. Foster, C. Kesselman, S. Tuecke: The Anatomy of the Gird: Enabling Scalable Virtual Organizations. International Journal of Supercomputer Applications, 2001, 15(3): 200-222.

[2] Myricom, Inc: GM Reference Manual 2.0.3, http://www.myri.com.

[3] I. Foster, N. Karonis: A Grid-enabled MPI: Message Passing in Heterogeneous Distributed Computing System, Proc. 1998 SC Conference.

[4] Zhiwei Xu, Ninghui Sun, Dan Meng, etc: Cluster and Grid Superservers: The Dawning Experience in China, Proc of the 3rd IEEE Int'l Conf on Cluster Computing, 2003.

[5] R. A Bhoedjang: User-level Network Interface Protocols, IEEE Computer, November 1998.

[6] N. Karonis, B. Toonen, I. Foster: MPICH-G2: A Grid-enabled Implementation of the Message Passing Interface, Journal of Parallel and Distributed Computing, 2003, 63(5): 551-563.

[7] T. Imamura, Y. Tsujita, H. Koide, H. Takemiya: An Architecture of Stampi: MPI Library on a Cluster of Parallel Computers, LNCS Vol. 1908, 200-207, Springer, 2000.

[8] M. Muller, M. Hess, E. Gabriel: Grid enabled MPI solutions for Clusters, The 3rd IEEE/ACM International Symposium on Cluster Computing and the Grid, 2003.

[9] E. Gabriel, M.Resch, T. Beisel, R. Keller: Distributed computing in a Heterogeneous Computing Environment, LNCS Vol. 1497, 180-187, Springer, 1998

[10] I foster, C Kesselman: The Grid: Blueprint for a New Computing Infrastructure, Morgan Kaufmann Publishers, 1998

[11] Zhiwei Xu, Wei Li: Research on VEGA Grid Architecture, Journal of Computer Research and Development, 2002, 39(8)

[12] V. G. Cerf, R .E. Kahn: A Protocol for Packet Network Intercommunicaiton, IEEE Trans on Comms, Vol Com-22, No5, 1974

[13] D. E. Comer, D. L. Stevens: Internetworking With TCP/IP Vol I: Principles, Protocols, and Architecture, 3rd edition, Prentice-Hall, 1995

A Model for User Management in Grid Computing Environments

Bo Chen[1,2], Xuebin Chi[1], and Hong Wu[1]

[1]Computer Network Information Center, Chinese Academy of Sciences, Beijing, 100080, P.R.China
{chb, chi, wh}@jupiter.cnc.ac.cn
[2]Institute of Software, Chinese Academy of Sciences, Beijing, 100080, P.R.China

Abstract. Grid user management aims to effectively manage grid user accounts. The traditional model to manage grid user accounts has several disadvantages. With the enlargement of the scale of the grid computing environment, these disadvantages will become more obvious. In contrast to the traditional model of grid user management, we propose a model that is based on the concept of account mapping. This allows us to facilitate user management and improve the scalability, security and accounting, and make uniform management possible.

1 Introduction

Grid computing aims to couple geographically distributed heterogeneous resources to offer consistent and inexpensive access to computational resources and cooperative computing, similar to the electric power grid. In existing grid computing environments, each user must register individually with each computing facility to access the computational resources. The scale of grid computing environments is becoming increasengly large, with potentially tens of thousands of users using grid resources available to them. Managing so many user accounts is a heavy burden because of the overhead associated with creating, maintaining and deleting user accounts[2]. Therefore, the question of how to manage user accounts in a feasible and effective way in grid computing environments is a realistic problem that needs to be addressed.

The Supercomputing Center of Chinese Academy of Sciences (SCCAS) is setting up a computing grid environment named "ScGrid", which will be established as a main body of Project SEA(Supercomputing Environment and its Application) of the CAS E-Science program. The "ScGrid" consists of basic infrastructure based on the Globus toolkit, web-based portals and grid user and resource management. The computers involved in our ScGrid are four kinds of parallel computers for scientific computation and data processing. The first one, SGI Power Challenge with 16 processors, was installed in 1996. The second one, Hitachi SR2201, was installed in 1998 and has 32 processors. The third, Dawning 2000-II with 164 processors, is made by National Center for Intelligent Computing System, and was installed in 2000[6]. In the near future, a new supercomputer will be installed in our center. All these parallel

M. Li et al. (Eds.): GCC 2003, LNCS 3032, pp. 732–737, 2004.

computers are provided for the scientific computing research in China. With the development of ScGrid, more and more members will join the ScGrid to access these parallel computing resources, therefore, a feasible and effective method to manage the increasing user accounts is needed.

2 Grid User Management

Grid user management aims to effectively manage grid user accounts. It supports at least the following different functions: authentication, authorization, accounting and uniform management.

2.1 Traditional Model and Analysis

The traditional model to manage grid user accounts is based on the fact that each user must have its own real account on each host to access computational resources. This model has several disadvantages.

1. No support for uniform management
Because grid computing aims to couple geographically distributed heterogeneous resources, it not only goes across domains but also covers different platforms. However, according to the traditional model, the administrator is restricted because of different platforms. How the administrator adds or deletes a real user account depends on the user's platform. Therefore, the administrator cannot manage grid user in the same uniform way he manages local users.

2. Unscalability
With the increasing scale of the grid computing environments, it would overwhelm systems because of the overhead of creating, deleting and maintaining a user account [2]. With a new host added into a grid, we have to create all the existing accounts on that host with a lot of work like signing the certificate and initiate the proxy. This will be an obstacle for new hosts to participate in the Grid.

3. Insecurity
The method adopted in the traditional model has some potential security problems because when we create or delete a user account, we need broadcast the user account with the corresponding password to the whole grid environment. This broadcast across domains is likely to create some potential security problems for the hosts.

To address the above problems, a method of 2-layer portal user account to real user account mapping on each host is proposed. We will classify the users into inner-domain users and across-domain users to simplify the problems.

4. Accounting difficulties

Although, at present, access to computational resources in SCCAS is not economy-based, there is still a need for an accounting infrastructure that would allow unambiguous recording of user identities against resource usage to share computational services across administrative domains.

Because in the traditional model there is no accounting of a grid user who is distributed on so many host machines will have difficulty to implement.

2.2 A New Model of Grid User Management

In order to simplify grid user management, we classify web portal user accounts into two types: inner-domain user accounts and cross-domain user accounts. Inner-domain user accounts can only be used to access the resources within one domain, while cross-domain user accounts can access resources in the whole grid.

Inner-domain user accounts and cross-domain user accounts are not real user accounts on each host in the grid computing environment. We first create the same real user accounts on each host within a domain, then create a logical user account is created which maps to the real user account created earlier. When we need to add a new web portal user, all we need to do is to associate the web portal user account to the logical user account on each domain.

Therefore we introduce two new concepts: Logical User Account (LUA) and Real User Account (RUA). The logical user account (LUA) is a logical account used throughout a domain. Each domain must have at least one logical user account for mapping. The real user account (RUA) is the real account on each host within the domain. The relationship among them is shown in Fig .1.

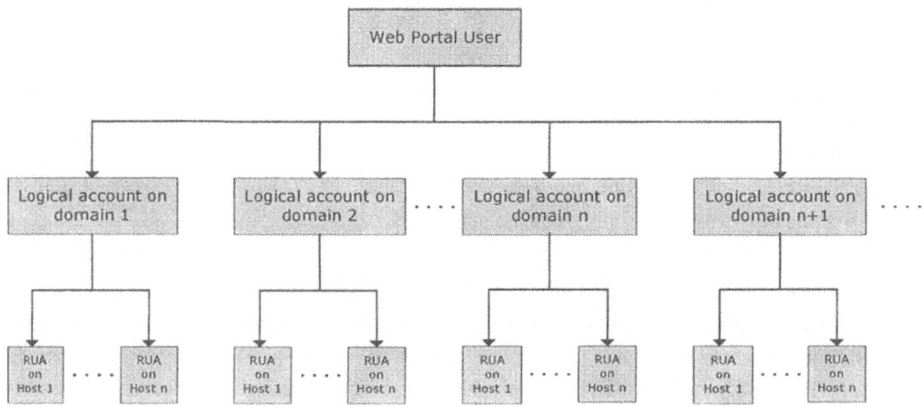

Fig. 1. The relationship between the web portal user account, the LUA and RUA.

3 Method and Function

3.1 User Management Flow

First of all, we assume that a grid user has access to the grid resources through the web-based portal. So we will begin our grid user management from user's login through web-based portals.

In order to identify the inner-domain user account and the cross-domain user account, an additional markup field will be defined to help us distinguish between the inner-domain user accounts and cross-domain user accounts. If the user is an inner-domain user, we will search the domain for the user's information, if we verify that it is the right user in that domain, the user can access the resources in that domain through the logic user account which is bound to that inner-domain user account. A similar procedure is used for cross-domain user

So to create a web portal user account, we should do the followings:

1. Decide whether it is an inner-domain user account or not, and if it is an inner-domain user account, determine which domain it belongs to.
2. If it is an inner-domain user account, map the inner-domain user account to a logical user account of the domain. If it is a cross-domain user account, first broadcast it to each domain, and then map it to a logical account on each domain.

3.2 User Discrimination

If a user submits a job with its real account, he or she has to apply for a certificate for this account. Using this certificate, a proxy from which the job can be submitted to run is created. For the portal, a web portal proxy is also needed.

If multiple jobs are submitted to the same host by different web portal users and all of the web portal users are mapped to the same logical user in that domain, it is difficult for the host to distinguish those web portal users since they all share the same logical account (i.e. disk space or process information). To solve this problem, we must map different web portal users to different logical accounts within that domain. We also need get more information about their distinct identities from the web portal users when they login from web-based portal (i.e. IP and time, inner domain or across domain) . This is done as follows.

First, when a user wants to register a web portal user account, the user must provide username, password, inner-domain or cross-domain and the right domain name. We then map the user to the logical account on each or one domain and allocate disk space. We will use the system facilities to encrypt the password and save and also encrypt the password for transfers on the network.

Second, when a registered user logs in from a web portal, the user must provide not only username and password, but also domain information. In addition, the login IP address will be logged for later use.

Third, when the administrator wants to see the status of online users, he or she will use the globus toolkit function and system calls using the information obtained during the login.

Finally, if the administrator wants to delete a user, he only needs to delete the disk space and cancel the association between the logical account and the web portal user account.

3.3 Authentication and Authorization

Authentication and authorization are two basic concepts in security systems. In grid computing environment, authentication and authorization are more important because the cooperative computing which grids aim to offer is based on security.

In our grid computing environment, authentication is the process verifying that the user is who he claims to be and authorization is how the system decides what this user can and can not do. Authentication requires evidence, known as credentials (e.g. A password is a kind of credential). If the user presents the correct credentials, he is assumed to be who it claims to be. Once a user's identity is authenticated, authorization decisions can be made.

3.4 Accounting

Accounting is an important part to support resource sharing. Usually we get several chargeable items such as: higher job queue priority within a job class, charge for memory, charge for network bandwidth usage, special application charges, charge for CPU utilization, and so on. In a grid computing environment, a domain does not necessarily charge for all the items listed above but can decide what it will charge for. Thus when an inner-domain user submits a job to run, the accounting may be limited in the domain, if on the other hand, a cross-domain user submits a job, accounting information consists of all accounting information of all the domains.

3.5 Uniform Management

Grid computing environments are often heterogeneous environments, therefore it could be useful to provide uniform management to effectively administrate user accounts as to facilitate the use of the grid. By mapping web portal users to logical accounts, we can support a uniform user management. Since the objects we manage are not the real accounts, that differ on different platforms but logical accounts, we can design uniform methods and tools to effectively manage those user accounts. For instance, if the administrator wants to delete the user, he or she need not execute different commands on different platforms but only delete the associations between the logical accounts and the web portal users.

4 Conclusion and Future Work

In this paper, a model for user management in Grid computing environments is presented that addresses problems with uniform management, scalability and security. User management is a very critical issue in grid computing environments. It is associated with the success of management of Grid. The traditional model to manage users is an undesirable and unfeasible method. In contrast to the traditional model of user management, our model supports grid administrators with a uniform way to manage users, and improves the scalability and security. It separates web portal users and real users and provides a mapping system to relate them.

The Project for supercomputing environment, one of the CAS projects for formation infrastructure construction during the 10th Five-Year Plan Period (2001–2005), aims to offer consistent, seamless and inexpensive access to resources. For future work, we will implement this method and make it perfect with solving some problems like the problem between user management and resource management.

References

1. Foster, C. Kesselman, J. Nick, S. Tuecke, "The Physiology of the Grid: An Open Grid Services Architecture for Distributed Systems Integration", the 4th Global Grid Forum, Toronto, Canada, (2002)
2. Thomas J. Hacker, Brian D. Athey, "A Methodology for Account Management in Grid Computing Environments", Proceedings of the 2nd International Workshop on Grid Computing, November 2001, Denver Colorado, Lecture Notes in Computer Science, Springer-Verlag Press.
3. Warren Smith, NASA Ames Research Center, "A System for Monitoring and Management of Computational Grids", IEEE 2002 International Conference on Parallel Processing (ICPP'02) August 18 - 21, 2002 Vancouver, B.C., Canada
4. Thigpen, B., Hacker, T., McGinnis, L., Athey, "Distributed Accounting on the Grid", Proceedings of the 6th Joint Conference on Information Sciences (JCIS), 2002
5. Laura F. McGinnis, William Thigpen, Thomas J. Hacker, "Accounting and Accountability for Distributed and Grid Systems", Proceedings of the 2nd IEEE/ACM International Symposium on Cluster Computing and the Grid
6. Hong Wu, Xue-bin Chi, Hai-li Xiao, Sun-gen Deng, "Creating of Computational Grid Using Globus Toolkit and GPDK", 11th International Conference on Parallel Architectures and Compilation Techniques (PACT-02), Sep, 2002

GSPD: A Middleware That Supports Publication and Discovery of Grid Services

Feilong Tang, Minglu Li, Jian Cao, Qianni Deng, Jiadi Yu, and Zhengwei Qi

Department of Computer Science and Engineering,
Shanghai Jiao Tong University, Shanghai 200030, P.R. China
{tang-fl,li-ml}@cs.sjtu.edu.cn

Abstract. Grid applications are increasingly extending from scientific computing to commercial field, where the service discovery is a key and challenging issue. Unfortunately, it can not directly be supported by technologies of Web services and so far, no existing schemes can effectively solve this issue in scope of the Internet. In this paper[1], we propose a general service discovery middleware GSPD that provides abilities both for service providers to publish services and for consumers to discover the expected Grid service that meets specified requirements on the Internet, without knowing of the complex process. The paper presents the implementation and software design of GSPD. GSPD consists of two-level registry, which enables it to adapt to persistent and transient Grid services. Moreover, we set up a prototype and test the feasibility of GSPD.

1 Introduction

Grid service is becoming the next-generation mainstream technology for large-scale resource sharing and commercial application cooperation, in which the infrastructure that supports the publication and discovery of Grid services is necessary. However, how to locate Grid services that satisfy users' requirements effectively and optimally in dynamic and heterogeneous Grid environment is a key and challenging issue because:

- Services can join and leave Grid dynamically and autonomously.
- Grid services may be persistent or transient. The two types of services need different discovery technologies.
- The status of a Grid service instance may change over its lifetime.

In this paper, based on the Open Grid Services Architecture (OGSA), we present a middleware that provides abilities both for service providers to publish services and for consumers to discover and invoke expected remote Grid service that meets specified requirements. The middleware consists of two-level registry and integrates the advantages of both centralized technology, which facilitates consumers to discover services , and distributed technology, which is useful to avoid the bottleneck.

[1] This paper is supported by 973 project (No.2002CB312002), 863 project (No.2001AA415310) of China, grand project (No.03dz15027 and 03dz15026) and key project (No.025115033) of the Science and Technology Commission of Shanghai Municipality.

M. Li et al. (Eds.): GCC 2003, LNCS 3032, pp. 738–745, 2004.

2 Related Work

The conception of Grid service is firstly presented by OGSA [1,5]. [2] further provides the technical details, and presents a full specification of the behaviors and Web Service Definition Language (WSDL) interfaces that define a Grid service.

UDDI defines how to publish and discover Web services [6,7]. However, it can not directly support for discovery of Grid services because Web services all are persistent but Grid services may be either persistent or transient.

Gridbus project proposes a Grid Market Directory (GMD)[3], which serves as a registry for high-level service publication and discovery in Virtual organizations. InfoGram service [4] provides the ability to serve as information service.

Our work focuses on a complete solution to publication and discovery of Grid services on the Internet, which can not be found in other works so far.

3 The Architecture for Publication and Discovery of Grid Services

In our model, the transient Grid service refers to the service whose instance is created only when it is invoked and lives for a request while the persistent Grid service means that its instance is activated when the container starts up and may exist all the time. Its key components include(see Fig. 1):

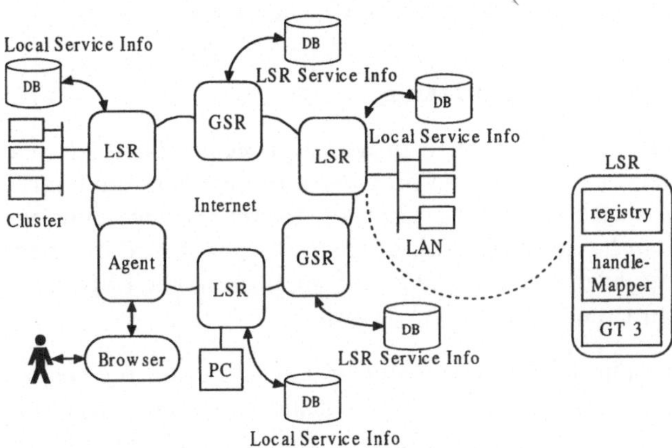

Fig. 1. The architecture of service publication and discovery. The service provider registers services in the LSR, which publishes or updates periodically service information to the GSR.

- LSR (Local Service Registry). It serves as (a)publishing or updating local Grid service information to the GSR for service providers, and

(b)maintaining and querying the handles and references of local service instances or factory instances for service consumers.
- GSR (Global Service Registry). It records all Grid service information and the handles of their home LSRs, which connect them with Internet.
- Agent. It discovers and invokes the qualified services according to the requirements specified by a consumer.

Our GSPD can meet the features and requirements of highly dynamic Grid environment because it provides:

- Abilities to discover both persistent and transient Grid services.
- Adaptability to Grid. The GSR maintains simple information of all services and the details (handles and references of factory or service instances) are only placed in the corresponding LSR and updated in time.
- Functionality to express and meet the consumer's requirements.

4 Implementation

4.1 Representation and Storage

We represent Grid services as a 3-tuple S=(T_n, S_n, SP). The T_n and S_n are the sets of service types and names respectively. The SP expresses the set of service specification (see Fig. 2), which describes the attributes of services.

In GSR, we organize and store services in terms of service type to speed up service discovery. Instead, the LSR only considers the service name because there are small amount of services in a local network.

4.2 Publication and Updating

Register in LSR. The service provider publishes Grid services to the home LSR. For a transient service, the provider only registers the handle of the service factory instance with the registry. For a persistent service, however, the provider registers the handle and reference of the service instance itself with the registry and handleMapper respectively. The information in the LSR is accurate because it is updated in time by either two ways:

- Pull mode. The LSR periodically broadcasts updating request in local network to notify service or factory instances of reporting their current information. If a service instance fails to reply to the request, its status field is set to 0.
- Push mode. The service instance reports up-to-date information to its home LSR periodically or when the important thing happens. For example, the service is invocated or free again.

The data structure of registry in the LSR is described as follows:

```
Class localServiceRegistry
{ String: serviceFactoryName;
  String: serviceName;
```

```
String: gsh;        //handle of Grid service or service factory instance
boolean: persistent;
int: status; }
```

The field persistent denotes whether a service is persistent or transient. If the service is persistent the field gsh is the handle of service itself. Otherwise, the gsh refers to the handle of the service factory. The status indicates whether a service is available: 1 and 0 mean that it is available and unavailable respectively.

The handleMapper simply maintains the mapping between handle and reference in order to resolve a handle into corresponding reference(s).

Register in GSR. The LSR publishes the Grid services, which are provided by its local network or a PC, to the GSR and updates the information in a longer period, such as an hour.

The GSR organizes service information in following structure:

```
Class globalServiceRegistry
{ String: serviceType;
  String: serviceName;
  String: gsh;        //handle of LSR having published this service
  String: attribute;
  int: mlt  }
```

The gsh refers to the handle of the service's home LSR, which has published this service. The attribute expresses the properties of a service. In particular, the mlt is used to specify the maximal lifetime of the service information and its value continuously decreases. When the value of mlt becomes zero the entry of the service is deleted from the GSR, which provides the model with fault-tolerance ability. For example, after a LSR crashes the GSR at most keeps the service information published by this LSR for the length of mlt.

```
request:= (type_name [cop service_name]) [?<specification>] | service_name
type_name:= string
service_name:= string
specification:= attribute_value | (specification cop specification)
attribute_value:= attribute bop value
attribute:= string
value:= string | request
string:= +([a..Z][0..9][_])
bop:= > | = | < | >= | != | <= | include | exclude | satisfy
cop:= and | or
```

Fig. 2. The syntax of service request in BNF, where the operator + specifies combination of string value, and the | expresses disjunction of parameter specifications.

4.3 Discovery

The service discovery relies on above register mechanism. Fig. 2 shows the BNF representation of service request. The discovery process includes:

1. Querying qualified services in the GSR, by (type_name [cop service_name]) [?<specification>]. The GSR checks its database according to the type and name of service, then returns qualified services and handles of their home LSRs.
2. Selecting the desirable service, based on some policies.
3. Discovering the reference of the selected service's instance in the LSR, by service_name. The agent encapsulates the query request into a SOAP message on behalf of the consumer and sends it to the home LSR of the service. Then, LSR returns the reference of service instance. If the service is unavailable, the consumer may reselect another service to renew the query process.

4.4 Invocation

After the service reference is discovered, invocation of the service is a relatively simple work because the reference contains enough information about how to bind the service. To shield the invocation process from the consumer, the agent automatically constructs the SOAP message about service invocation by means of the returned reference. How to coordinate [9,10] services is out of the scope of this paper.

Currently, we use the ant tool to statically (at compile time) generate the proxies both for the service instance and for the service consumer. Future work includes generating dynamically (at run time) all the proxies to improve flexibility of the model.

5 Design

Fig. 3 illustrates the modules that make up of GSPD.

5.1 GSR

LSRs periodically publish or update service information to GSR, and consumers query services from it. GSR functions by the following modules.

- Data Transformer & Scheduler. It provides abilities to: (1) transform data format between XML (SOAP message) and data structure of the GSR, and (2) schedule different modules according to request type.
- Account Management. It is responsible for LSR registration, modification and removal.
- Service Registration. Each LSR publishes or updates periodically services provided by its local network.
- Identity Authentication. It prevents illegal clients from modification of service and account information, which is implemented by the mapping between a login name and a password.
- Filter. It matches services according to the constraint specified by the consumer to reduce the number of returned services.

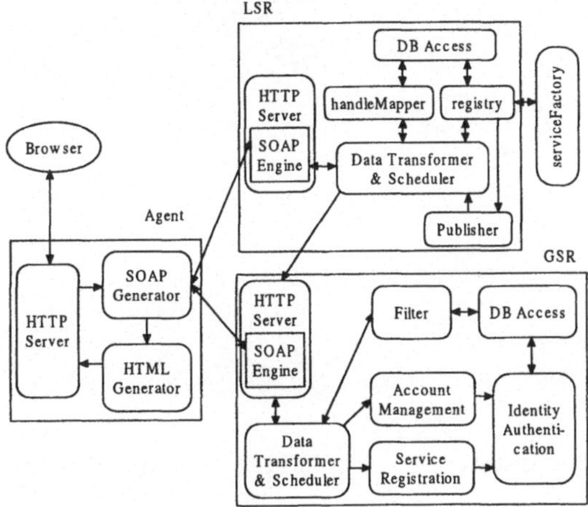

Fig. 3. The software structure of the model

5.2 LSR

The LSR provides a set of modules for publication of service information, discovery of service reference and/or creation of service instance.

- Data Transformer & Scheduler is used to: (1) transform data format between XML and data structure of the LSR, (2) schedule corresponding module to get service reference, and (3) publish periodically local service information to the GSR.
- The registry holds (a)the service handles of persistent services, and (b)the factory handles of transient services. For the request discovering a transient service, it calls the serviceFactory to create a service instance in the local machine of the service, using discovered factory handle, and obtains the initial service reference.
- The handleMapper maintains the mapping between handles and references for persistent services.
- Publisher. Consulting with the registry service, Publisher periodically registers local service information to the GSR, through Data Transformer & Scheduler module.
- The serviceFactory resides in the same machine with the discovered service and serves for creating a service instance.

5.3 Agent

The agent serves as the interface for consumers to contact the GSR and LSR.

- SOAP Generator. It provides the abilities to: (1) encapsulate the request into SOAP message to query expected service in GSR, discover reference in LSR, and invoke the service instance; (2) send the SOAP message to the GSR and LSR; and (3) call the HTML Generator to construct html files that contain the qualified service information or execution result.

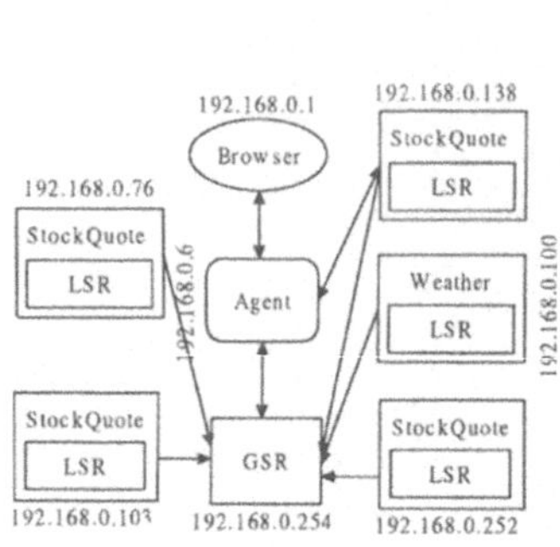

Fig. 4. The prototype

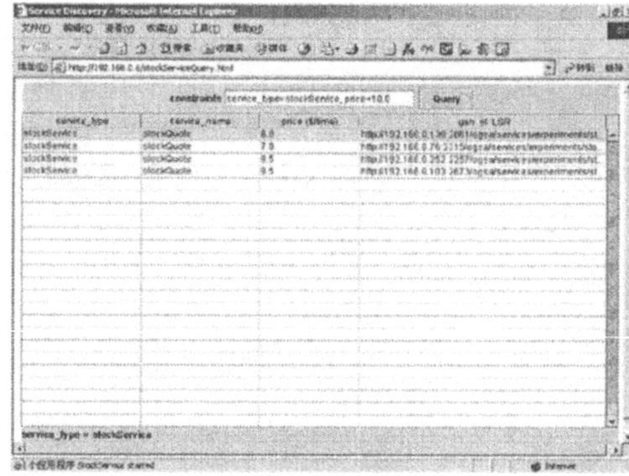

Fig. 5. The qualified stockQuote services

- HTML Generator. After receiving call from the SOAP Generator, it generates html file containing specified data and passes the file to the HTTP Server.

6 Experiment Results

To test the feasibility of GSPD, we construct a prototype in our LAN, including eight PC machines running Windows 2000, as shown in Fig. 4. The prototype consists of a web browser, an agent, a GSR and five LSRs and Grid services: a Weather and four stockQuote services. We build all services on the Globus Toolkit 3 [8], and use SQL Server as database server and Java as development language. For convenience, we only use price as the constraint condition.

We implemented an information service application: a service consumer queries current stock information. All stockQuote service providers require consumers to pay for their services at different prices. The process is as follows:

1. Five service providers register services with respective LSRs, which then publish service information to the GSR in the form of globalServiceRegistry.
2. By a browser, the consumer fills in a service query request for stockService. The agent encapsulates and issues the request to the GSR in a SOAP message.
3. According the type stockService, the GSR returns qualified stockQuote services, whose prices are less than 10.0, and the handles of their home LSRs, as shown in Fig. 5.
4. The consumer selects the cheapest stockQuote service, whose machine IP is 192.168.0. 138. Here, this stockQuote service and its home LSR reside in the same machine.
5. Agent queries the LSR, whose handle has been obtained in last step, and gets the reference of stockQuote service instance created in the machine 192.168.0.138.
6. Agent invokes the stockQuote service instance then returns up-to-date stock information to the consumer.

7 Conclusions and Future Works

We propose a Grid service publication and discovery middleware GSPD, which can allow not only service providers to publish services but also consumers to discover expected services conveniently. Agent shields consumers from complex process.

We also present the implementation and software design of GSPD, set up a prototype. GSPD consists of two-level registry, which enables it to adapt to the dynamic Grid environment. By means of a stock query experiment, we test its feasibility. GSPD is extensible because it is built on a series of standard and open technologies and infrastructures. Next, we will incorporate security into GSPD to satisfy requirements of commercial applications.

References

1. I. Foster, C. Kesselman, J. M. Nick and S. Tuecke. The Physiology of the Grid-An Open Grid Services Architecture for Distributed Systems Integration. June, 2002.
2. S. Tuecke, K. Czajkowski, I. Foster, J. Frey, S.Graham and C. Kesselman. "Grid Service Specification (Draft 3)". July, 2002.
3. J. Yu, S. Venugopal and R.Buyya. Grid Market Directory: A Web Services based Grid Service Publication Directory.
4. G. V. Laszewski, J. Gawor et al. InfoGram: A Grid Service that Supports Both Information Queries and Job Execution. In Proceeding of HPDC-11, 2002.
5. D. Talia. The Open Grid Services Architecture: Where the Grid Meets the Web. IEEE Internet Computing. November.December 2002.
6. F. L. Tang, M. L. Li, J. Cao et al. Technology of Enterprise Application Integration Based on Web Services. Proceeding of International Workshop on Grid and Cooperative Computing (GCC 2002). December, 2002.
7. UDDI: Universal Description, Discovery, and Integration. http://www.uddi.org/.
8. T. Sandholm, R. Seed and J. Gawor. Globus Toolkit 3 Core - A Grid Service Container Framework (Draft). June, 2003.
9. F. L. Tang, M. L. Li, and J. Cao, A Transaction Model for Grid Computing. In LNCS 2834, Springer Verlag (2003).
10. F. L. Tang, M. L. Li, and J. Cao. A Transaction Coordination Mechanism and Compensation Technology in Grid Environment. To appear in Journal of Computer Research and Development, December, 2003 (In Chinese).

Partially Evaluating Grid Services by DJmix

Hongyan Mao, Linpeng Huang, and Yongqiang Sun

Department of Computer Science and Engineering,
Shanghai Jiaotong University, Shanghai 200030, P.R. China
{mhy, lphuang, sun-yg}@sjtu.edu.cn

Abstract. Conventionally, middleware and modularity technologies are adopted to comply with the changing characteristics of distributed computing environments, however, which gives rise to some inefficiency for generic design. In this paper, we propose a new approach based on partial evaluation to partially evaluate Grid services. Partial evaluation is a program transformation technique used to specialize generic programs by known parameters. Our method adopts a distributed partial evaluator DJmix, which is built on the Byte Code Specialization and Web services to optimize Grid services for known usage context. We present the speedup by a distributed ray tracing application with DJmix running in the Grid environments. The results show that partial evaluation can be used to improve the performance and flexibility of Grid services and can be used to specialize legacy applications for Grid computing.

1 Introduction

In Grid computing environments, a notable feature is the changing nature such as heterogeneous machines, migrating tasks, and varying services. In order to adapt to the various characteristics of the distributed and heterogeneous environments, traditionally Grid services adopt modularity and hierarchy structure at the design level. However, the generic design always causes efficiency problems for an ad hoc implementation such as execution time and program size, in particular to applications involved with massively repeated computations. Therefore, by optimizing Grid services for a given context, specialization allows the elimination of some of the inefficiency due to a generic design.

Partial evaluation, as a form of program transformation or program specialization, is widely applied to optimize programs in a variety of fields such as scientific computation, computer graphics, and compiler generation [3], [4]. More researchers are interested in partial evaluation on functional and logic languages because of their well algebraic basis. There is a little study about partial evaluation building on object-oriented languages and heterogeneous environments. Hence, we propose and implement a partial evaluator, named Jmix, building on the specialization of Java Byte Code. In addition, we present the architecture of DJmix, a distributed partial evaluator, along with the mechanism of DJmix based on the infrastructure and services offered by the Globus Toolkit and Web service such as SOAP and WSDL [1], [2]. To check the performance of the application service via DJmix, a distributed ray tracing

M. Li et al. (Eds.): GCC 2003, LNCS 3032, pp. 746–753, 2004.

service involved with a great deal of repeated computations and massive memory demands, is running on Shanghai Supercomputer Center (SSC) situated in Zhangjiang High-Tec Park. The performance speedup obtained shows DJmix is effective to enhance the performance of application services.

The remainder of this paper is organized as follows. Section 2 describes Jmix and DJmix. Section 3 presents the architecture of DJmix in Grid environments, together with the mechanism of DJmix. Section 4 shows how DJmix serves a Grid application by a case study of the ray tracing, and illustrates the experiment results done on SSC. Finally, Section 5 discusses the related work and presents the future work.

2 Partial Evaluation

2.1 Partial Evaluation

Partial evaluation is a source-to-source program transformation technique, which improves efficiency of a program by performing as much computations as possible before all the inputs become available [3]. Using partial evaluation technique, we can construct a partial evaluator that produces the specialized version of a given program for the available context information. The residual program generated only with dynamic parameters is equivalent to the original program.

In terms of [7], we give the formal description of partial evaluation. Program p takes static and dynamic inputs, i.e., s and d, respectively. The partial evaluator (PE) specializes p and generates the residual program p_s, such that

$$(p<s,d>) = (p_s<d>) . \tag{1}$$

In addition, p_s runs faster than p. Particularly, when p is called n times, we have a expression that

$$\text{Times } (PE<p,s>) + n^* \text{Times}(p_s<d>) << n^* \text{ Times } (p<s,d>) . \tag{2}$$

The following example explains the usage of partial evaluation. Fig. 1 gives the general implementation code of a dot product algorithm. If the parameter x is bound to {10, 4}, y to {3, 8}, we get the residual code shown in Fig. 2 that eliminates the constant propagation and redundant computations.

```
double dotproduct(double[] x, double[] y, double[] z)
{
double result = x[0] * x[1] + y[0] * y[1] + z[0] * z[1];
return result;
}
```

Fig. 1. A dot product program

```
double dotproduct_z(double[] z)
{
   double result= 64 + z[0] * z[1];
   return result;
}
```

Fig. 2. Specialized dot product program

Many of Grid services are involved with the complicated operations of Matrix and Vector similar to the dot product algorithm of Vector. The application program with static values is evaluated in advance, thus enhancing the execution efficiency.

When constructing a partial evaluator, the principles of partial evaluation must be considered. (1) How the specialized code is produced? Partial evaluation has manual and automatic forms. (2) When the specialized code is generated? Partial evaluation can be implemented at compile time or at run time. (3) Contemporary partial evaluators are divided into two classes: online and offline. More detailed description about partial evaluation is found in [3], [4].

2.2 The Partial Evaluator–Jmix

The platform neutrality of Java language is convenient for running on heterogeneous hosts, and that programs based on Java are simple and portable. However, Java programs also give rise to performance problems due to the interpreted feature of Java. Accordingly, we combine partial evaluation into Java Virtual Machine (JVM) to enhance the execution efficiency of Java programs. Partial evaluation for object-oriented languages is more complex than that for functional or logic language, because object-oriented mechanisms must be seriously taken into account such as encapsulation, inheritance and virtual dispatch. We propose a partial evaluator called Jmix based on the Byte Code Specialization (BCS). The BCS may generate better code than the traditional run-time specialization technique by exploiting Just-In-Time (JIT) compilers [6].

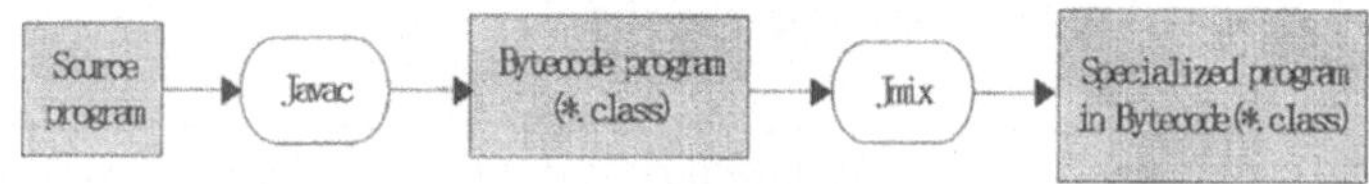

Fig. 3. The model of Jmix

Fig. 3 gives the specialization process of Jmix. In Jmix, online specialization approach is adopted that records the states of any variable, instruction and stack. The byte code program is treated as an evaluated object during the evaluation. By parsing the structure of Java class, Jmix gets the constant pools and keeps in the Vector object. Finally, the specialized instruction sequence is obtained. Moreover, we describe the syntax of expressions and statements, and give their evaluation rules formally.

Comparing with other partial evaluators for functional and logic languages, Jmix has some observable features. (1) Jmix can evaluate virtual function calls, stack accesses, inclined methods, and array bounds. (2) Jmix solves the control-shift instructions via the static semantic of the byte code in the undetermined conditions. (3) Jmix not only handles the specialization of the methods and the single object, but also deals with the specialization of multi-objects. (4) In terms of the byte code, it's easy to prove the correctness of the evaluation using λ calculus.

2.3 The Distributed Partial Evaluator–DJmix

To cope with the modern computing environments, the partial evaluation technique is extended to geographically dispersed environments to enhance the efficiency of the distributed applications. We construct a distributed partial evaluator named DJmix building on Jmix.

Jmix only performs the specialization in a single host. DJmix not only possesses the capability of Jmix, but also handles the specialization of the remote objects and the communication of the distributed environments. DJmix specializes the generic program into the specialized version with respect to the specific context. By means of the specialized class and the parallel execution, the performing efficiency increases as compared to running in the single host.

Our DJmix is aimed at the distributed computing environments according to the requirements of Web services and Grid technologies. Firstly, DJmix distributed in various sites collaborates to evaluate Grid services. Secondly, the security of DJmix is dependent on the security mechanism of HTTP and the security model of OGSA. Thirdly, DJmix adopts the standard interface and facility provided by Web services, OGSA and the Globus Toolkits. Finally, DJmix has well adaptation that it's installed in each host such as PC, Workstation and Server of Grid environments.

3 The Architecture of DJmix Working in Grid

3.1 The Architecture of DJmix Working in Grid

Web services and Grid technologies provide the large-scale aggregation and resource sharing in geographically distributed environments. A Grid service is a Web service that conforms to a set of conventions such as interfaces and behaviors [1]. The conventional way utilizes the middleware technologies like J2EE and CORBA to match the requirements of commercial and scientific applications in distributed computing environments. But it results in performance problems and increases complexity for an ad hoc implementation. Therefore, we integrate a general distributed partial evaluation technique adapted to Grid services. By means of the partial evaluator, the Grid service generates the specialized program for the specific context. Based on the Grid services and the partial evaluation technique, we present the architecture of DJmix in a network (see Fig. 4).

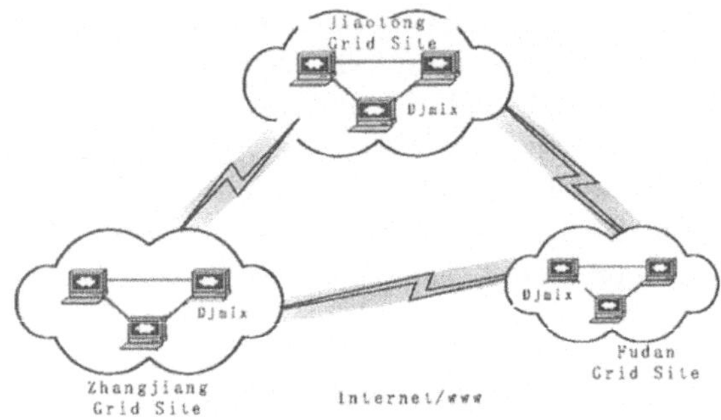

Fig. 4. The architecture of DJmix

The interaction of DJmix uses XML-based SOAP message, in that SOAP does not take into account the heterogeneous characteristics. DJmix is registered with Universal Description, Discovery and Integration (UDDI) in the registry. The Web Services Description Language (WSDL) is used to describe the interface of DJmix to Grid services, through which services can invoke DJmix.

3.2 The Mechanism of DJmix

DJmix is composed of a name server, a client and many of servers as shown in Fig. 5. DJmix built on Jmix is platform-independent, hence DJmix can be hosted on any operating system like Windows, Unix and Linux with JVM.

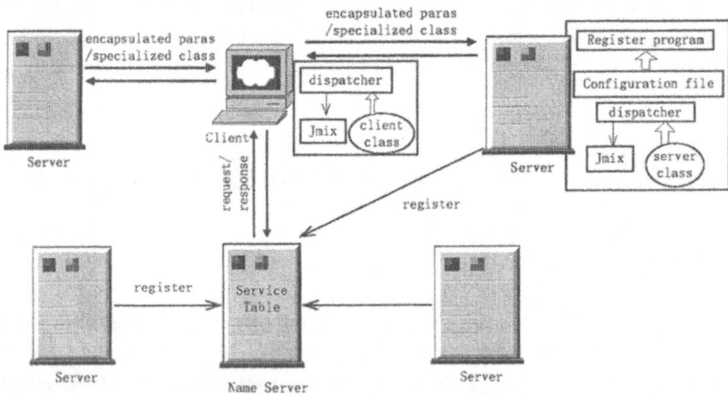

Fig. 5. The mechanism of DJmix

- The name server keeps a table that comprises all the configuration information of each server. The client and server contain a dispatcher and a Jmix, in addition each server has a register program and a configuration file.
- The dispatcher, the key core of DJmix, is responsible for the communications of the client, the name server and other servers. The dispatcher of the client constructs a request message, including the specialized service and the context parameters, and sends

to the name server, and that the name server returns the correlevant service description. If the specialized service is in the local, the dispatcher allocates the local Jmix, otherwise the dispatcher calls the service from other servers. Then the remote Jmix specializes the service class, and the remote dispatcher delivers the specialized service to the requested dispatcher.

• The configuration file describes the information relevant with class files by XML-built WSDL. The register program registers this information in the service table of the name server.

In DJmix, we adopt EJB technologies under Weblogic by parsing Java Byte Code instruction sequences. We utilize Apache SOAP2.2 API to process the request and response of the dispatchers. UDDI is used to publish services available for the client and look up the service table of the name server.

4 A Case Study

4.1 Ray Tracing

In Grid computing environments, many of Grid services are involved with considerable computations and massive memory demands such as advertising, fashion design, virtual reality and other computer graphics. In order to investigate the performance of DJmix in Grid services, we use the ray tracing application running in SSC.

Ray tracing is an object space rendering technique for image synthesis, which produces life-like images by calculating each pixel on the screen. The main rays are sent from the eye to each pixel on an imaginary scene and are traced when they are reflected and transmitted by objects. The more detailed information about the ray tracing will be found in [8], [9]. Many researchers present corresponding algorithms to reduce the intersection times, scale up researching the nearest intersection point and accelerate execution efficiency. The ray tracing is suitable for optimizing with partial evaluation in distributed environments. The reasons are presented as follows. (1) The viewpoint determining how scenes display is variable, but the objects of a scene are fixed; (2) The computation of each pixel is independent of the other pixels; (3) The image-based approach is to parallel the ray tracing that all the workstations cooperate to process one or a few rays; (4) Moreover, once the objects are determined, the algorithms of objects are the same and called repeatedly.

4.2 Performance Results

According to the architecture in Fig. 4, each host contains a DJmix, and the ray tracing runs on top of DJmix. The ray tracing looks up the required service in the UDDI registry, and the registry sends back the service description information of DJmix, with which the ray tracing contacts with DJmix. Accordingly, every subtask of the ray racing program distributed among hosts is specialized before running via DJmix.

As discussed above, the experiment is carried out on Shanghai Supercomputer Center located in Zhangjiang High-Tec Park. In the experiment, DJmix and the ray tracing are performed on Shen Wei-I (384 CPUs, 48G Memory, 1.28Tbytres Disk Storage). We list three generated images: Golf, Snowgoon, and Chess (see Fig. 6). And every program separately runs in three conditions: ① the single host (S), ② the distributed hosts without DJmix(D), and ③ the distributed hosts with DJmix (DD). The results of the experiment are given in Fig. 7.

$$Speedup = \frac{Original\ \ program\ \ execution\ \ time}{Specialize\ d\ \ program\ \ execution\ \ time} \quad . \tag{3}$$

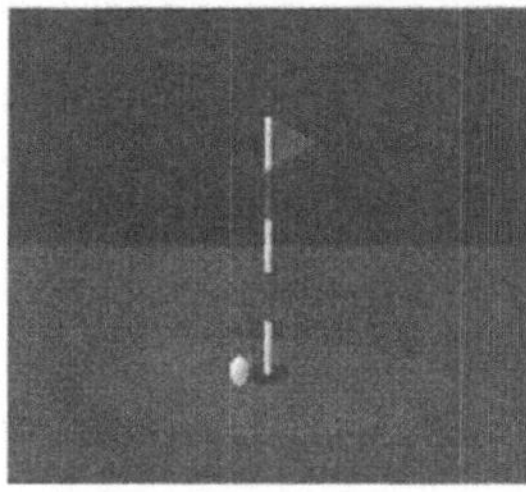

Fig. 6. Ray tracing images

The golf consists of 4096 circles and 1024 triangles. The snowgoon contains 12288 spheres and 8192 cylinders. The chess is composed of 20480 cylinders and spheres. Three images are illuminated by two light sources, and that the image size is 640*480 pixels. In our experiment, the network overheads can be ignorable in contrast with the executing time. In some cases, the communication overheads have to be considered, especially there are many ray tracing services and these services are very complex.

Execution time (ms)	Size (Pixels)	Single Host	Distributed hosts without DJmix	Ratio	Distributed hosts with DJmix	Ratio
Golf	640*480	73.2	44.14	1.66	31.23	2.14
Snowgoon	640*480	98.32	50.37	1.95	29.30	3.36
Chess	640*480	294.38	79.67	3.69	56.31	5.23

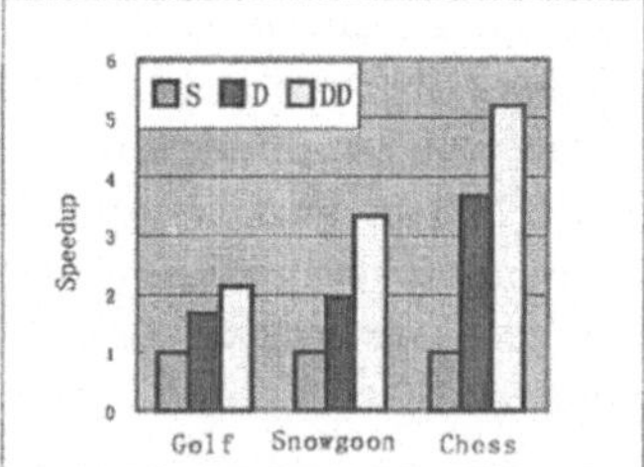

Fig. 7. Performance results

As illustrated in Fig. 7, thanks to the integration of the ray tracing with DJmix, the maximum speedup achieved is 5.23. Moreover, it's observed that the execution time of programs with DJmix decreases obviously, and the more complex image, the higher speedup is achieved.

5 Related Work and Conclusions

Tempo is a partial evaluator for C developed by Consel et al. [4]. JSpec is a specializer for Java using Tempo and Harissa, a Java-to-C compiler [5], but the specialized programs are no longer applied to other application programs. Masuhara and Yonezawa [6] give the Byte Code Specialization. Currently, there is only little work on partial evaluation with respect to the pure object-oriented languages and distributed environments. Jmix is a Java-oriented partial evaluator based on BCS, and DJmix is the first distributed partial evaluator adapted to the Grid environments.

In this paper, we introduce a new approach to partially evaluate Grid services via the partial evaluation technique. We propose the architecture of DJmix in Grid environments, together with the mechanism of DJmix. Further, we show the results of the experiment done on SCC by the integration of the distributed ray tracing with DJmix. In addition, the specialization of other applications is on research.

The partial evaluator for the specialization of application services has been implemented with DJmix. It's interesting to specialize system-level services to improve the performance of all Grid services. In the near future, we are striving to expand DJmix to specialize OGSA platform services such as registry, monitoring, data access, SOAP-RMI, and so on.

References

1. Global Grid Forum, http://www.gridforum.org/.
2. International Symposium in High Performance and Distributed Computing. High Performance and Grid Programming in Java and Python, San Francisco, CA, 6 August 2001. http://www.cogkits.org.
3. C. Consel and O. Danvy "Tutorial notes on partial evaluation", in ACM Symposium on Principles of Programming Languages, Pages 493-501,1993.
4. C. Consel, L. Hornof, R. Marlet, G. Muller and S. Thibault, "Tempo: Specializing Systems Applications and Beyond", ACM Computing Survey, Vol. 30, Issue 3es(September 1998).
5. U.P. Schultz, J.L. Lawall, C. Consel, and G. Muller, "Towards Automatic Specialization of Java Programs", Compose Project, IRISA/INRIA, France.
6. H. Masuhara and A. Yonezawa, "Generating optimized residual code in run-time specialization", in Proceedings of International Colloquium on Partial Evaluation and Program Transformation, 1999, pp. 215-225.
7. M. Sperber, H. K laeren and P. Thiemann "Distributed Partial Evaluation".
8. A.S. Glassner (Ed.), "An Introduction to Raytracing", Academic Press, 1989.
9. R.L. Cook, T. Porter, and L. Carpenter, "Distributed ray tracing", Computer Graphics, 165-174 (1984).
10. Y. Hou, "the Design and Implementation of Jmix-a Java Partial Evaluator", graduate thesis, SJTU, China, September 2002.
11. K. Asai, "Can partial evaluation improve the performance of ray tracing", Natural Science Report, Vol.53, No.1 (2002).
12. P. H. Andersen, "Partial Evaluation Applied to Ray Tracing", Software Engineering in Scientific Computing, pp. 78-85, (1996).

Integrated Binding Service Model for Supporting Both Naming/Trading and Location Services in Inter/Intra-net Environments

Chang-Won Jeong, Su-Chong Joo, and Sung-Kook Han

School of Electrical, Electronic and Information Engineering,
Wonkwang University, Korea
{mediblue,scjoo,skhan}@wonkwang.ac.kr

Abstract. In this paper, we propose the Integrated Binding Service model for supporting the location and replication transparencies of distributed service objects in Inter/Intra-net environments. We focus on the model based on the integrated naming/trading service, the replicated object supporting service and the load balancing service. This model can logically reconfigure and viewed by clients as a single view system can support the binding service of the replicated objects with the same types. These types can be categorizes by names or properties of objects. So far, existing naming and trading services have been separately served and also have not supported with the binding service for replicated service objects with the same service type due to deficiency of location-independent service on the current Internet environments. For this reason, we designed and implemented a new integrated binding service model that can not only support both naming and trading services at the same time, but also provide an appropriate service object selection mechanism and efficient resource sharing from the replicated objects by using the load balancing information extracted through each system with replicated service objects in Inter/Intra-net environments. Finally, we showed the prototype implementation environment on our model, and a series of the binding procedures and the executed results of this model suggested.

1 Introduction and Related Works

In recent years, distributed systems based on Inter/Intra-net environments have been radically changing toward the various typed logical and physical structures, like mobile, heterogeneous and federal Grid systems for general or specific developing purposes of distributed applications. Under these environments, lots of researchers and developers have been propelling the studies in point of view of distributed transparency[1]. These studies are suggesting the transparent mechanisms for providing distributed service objects management and the various retrieval services, like directory[2,3], domain naming[4] and trading services[5] for supporting distributed services in a viewpoint of a single view system logically. For instance, the naming service traditionally used to provide the name-to-address mapping[6]. That is, the one-to-one mapping cardinality with a name and an IP address per a service object. So far, existing naming and trading services have been separately served and

M. Li et al. (Eds.): GCC 2003, LNCS 3032, pp. 754–761, 2004.

also have not supported with the binding service for replicated service object with the same service type due to deficiency of independent location service on given Internet environments. For this reason, we focused on the model that can provide the integrated naming/trading service, the replicated object supporting service and the load balancing service. Firstly, we combined the naming service and the trading service to the integrated service for retrieving the desiring objects using both names and properties[7]. Secondly, for support of replicated objects, we introduced the object handle as a mediator for mapping between naming/trading service and location service. Our model can support the location-independent transparency and replication transparency by using this object handle. And lastly, our model executes all of services defined under the load balancing strategy. The framework of our model consisted of the CORBA–based distributed systems connected by Inter/Intra-net environments. This paper is organized as follows; Section 2 presents the architecture of the model. In details, we give a Name/Property and a Location servicing requirements and procedures in the model, respectively. In Section 3, our prototype implementation is described, and we showed the binding procedures and executed results of components of Naming/Trading Service and Location Service in the Integrated Binding Service model. Finally, in Section 4, we discuss the conclusions and future works.

2 Architecture of Integrated Binding Service Model

2.1 Requirements and Procedures of Integrated Binding Service Model

The distributed system connected by Inter/Intra-network may contains a large set of service objects, as server systems or client systems, For the sake of access of one of these objects, we define a structured way, like optimal object selection algorithms for the minimal response time, to refer to a unique service object. As a structured way, the binding phase for accessing a distributed object is, in details, divided into mapping a path name or properties of an object to the object handle and mapping the object handle to one or more contact addresses, and then an instance of the selected object is initialized and created for ready to provide some services.

This model for a new solution has the following requirements for functionalities of components and interfaces among them;

- The physical Inter/Intra-net environments serving this model can be logically reconfigured a single view system for purposing the resource sharing according to how to set the physical service domain.
- The service objects may be replicated on a system or several systems.
- This model for integrating binding service consists of 2 components; Naming/Trading service, and Location service including additional Destination selection service of replicated objects. In Naming/Trading service, this service is similar to existing naming service or trading service. We do not obtain the network addresses from this service, but object handles, as unique location-independent identifiers of the service objects, given object's names or properties.
- Assume that a client requests to an arbitrary service object locating in somewhere.
- In Location service, this component will support to map the object handle to one or more contact addresses. i.e. if service objects are replicated, these objects has

only an object handle and in location service phase, this object handle may have at least one or more contact addresses describing the physical locations in which the service objects locate.

- In Destination selection service, this component will select an appropriate service object of replicated objects. For selecting an object, this service must to be implemented to an optimal selection algorithm for selecting one of replicated objects. This algorithm uses the load information of each system connected by Inter/Intra-network as input parameters. The performance of this algorithm will be depended on how to minimize the load deviation of systems uniformly and the response time of servers from clients' requests.

In accordance with the requirements of our model described above, we explain the detailed procedures of Naming/Trading Service, Location Service and interacting service among clients and servers. The procedures are divided into 4 steps: a Name/Property lookup, a Location lookup, Destination selection and Implementation object Selection, as shown in Figure 1 below.

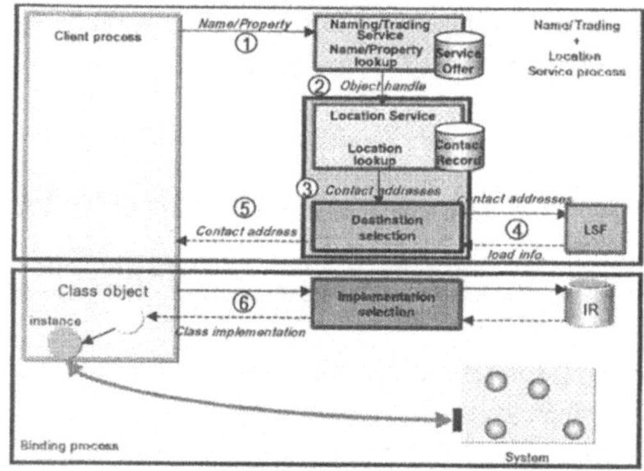

Fig. 1. Architecture of Integrated Binding Service Model

In the integrated binding service, The Step 1(①) and the Step 2(②) perform the Name/Property lookup and the Location lookup operations, respectively. In the former step, when the path names or properties, as arguments to the lookup method invocation, of objects requested come in this model, this operation resolves to an object handle corresponding by using information of the Service Offer that stores the service objects. The latter step executes that the object handle can be resolved to one or more contact addresses according to either the service object may replicated or not. These contact addresses are stored to the Contact Record Repository. The Step 3(③-⑤) is being executed under load balancing strategy using load information loading in systems connected by Inter/Intra-network. Given object handles obtained from the Step 2, this step selects a contact address describing of a location of a system with the minimum load and communication cost via mapping the object handle. We used the software package, Load Sharing Facility(LSF) for extracting load information from distributed systems. In Step 4(⑥→), Implementations of object selection is stored to an Implementation Repository(IR). Also, the names of the class that can implement the relating protocols in the selected contact address have to be passed to the IR. The IR returns a class implementation, which is returned to the class process. This class object creates a new instance, like a client Stub program for accessing the service object selected from Step 3. And then using this instance, a client will be bound and mutually interacted with the server object obtained through the procedures described above.

2.2 Naming/Trading Service

In the previous paragraph, we briefly explained the Lookup procedures of a Naming/Trading Service and a Location Service. A Naming/Trading Service in our model maps given names or properties to object handles. In this time, a Naming/Trading Service generates object handles to refer to the service objects qualified from client's requests. The object handle(OH) is for the unique location-independent identifier. Figure 2 and Table 1 show the Naming/Trading service component and its detailed operations using a given Service Offer Repository, respectively. The structure of the Service Offer Repository consists of ObjectName, ObjectHandle, ObjectServiceTypeName and PropertySequence.

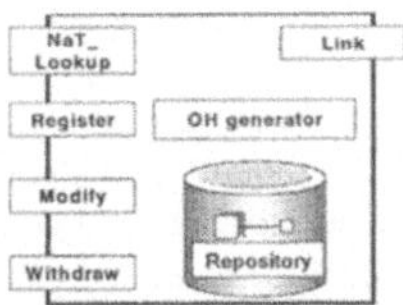

Fig. 2. Naming/Trading Service component

The component of Naming/Trading service has five operations for interfacing the Service Offer Repository, called Service Offer: NaT_lookup, Register, Modify, and Withdraw operations for managing service objects and Link operation for relationships with other Naming/Trading services. Also, the OH generator creates object handles by referring the Service Offer. The operations of Naming/Trading Service are shortly described in Table 1.

Table 1. The operations of Naming/Trading Service

Operation	Description
NaT_Lookup	Name/property lookup object handles from Service Offer
Register	Register new service objects to Service Offer
Modify	Modify object's description in Service Offer
Withdraw	Withdraw objects from Service Offer
Link	Supports for linking with other Naming/Trading services
OH generation	Creating object handles, on registering new objects

2.3 Location Service

The component of Location Service provides for mapping object handles to a set of the relating contact addresses. Here, the contact addresses mean the locations of systems with service objects in point of view of location-dependent system. If a service object is replicated on one or server systems, an object handle of replicated object will be mapped to two or more contact addresses in this Location service phase. In this time, the contact addresses are stored in the Contact Record Repository. Given object handles in Location Service component, they will be mapped to the contact addresses stored in this Repository. The structure of the Contact Record Repository consists of ObjectHandle and ContactAddress. The component of Location Service has four operations for interfacing with the Contact Record Repository, as showed in Figure 3: Location_Lookup, Insert and Delete operations for managing and changing the information of the Repository, and Load_info operation for obtaining load information of each server system connected by Inter/Intra-net environments. Each operation and its description are listed in Table 2.

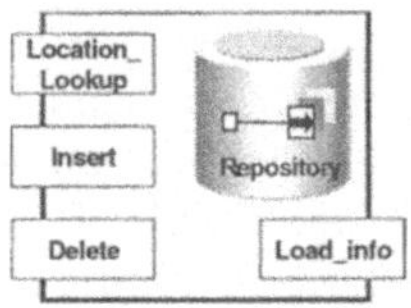

Fig. 3. Location Service Component

Table 2. The operation of Location Service

Operation	Description
Location_Lookup	Lookup contact addresses mapping given object handles
Insert	Insert contact addresses for object handles to the Repository
Delete	Delete contact addresses for object handles from the Repository
Load_info	Obtain load information loading on each system using LSFs

2.4 Destination Selection of Replicated Objects

Load information is obtained from each system by Load-Info operation. The arguments of its operation is a series of the contact addresses. For obtaining the load information, we installed LSF program on each system. Load information of each system consists of loads extracted from Load Information Managers(LIMs) in LSFs.
The contact addresses and these loads of the corresponding systems with these addresses are constructed to Load information. The load information is dynamically updated by using loads generated by LIM. The structure of load information consists of a set of a system record with 3 fields per a contact address; the available memory capacity, the CPU's load, and communication traffics. Destination selection service of replicated objects chooses an appropriate object among the replicated objects with the same object handle. In Destination selection service, this service is implemented to an optimal selection algorithm for selecting an appropriate one of replicated objects. Our one is focused on the selection of system with minimizing the load deviation of systems uniformly considering loads and communication cost in the point of view of load balancing. For improving high performance, we can adopt the better ones instead of our strategy. But in this paper, we are interested in the service model rather than system performance. The Figure 4 below depicts the Load information structures and the relating software for showing the destination selection of replicated objects in Location service.

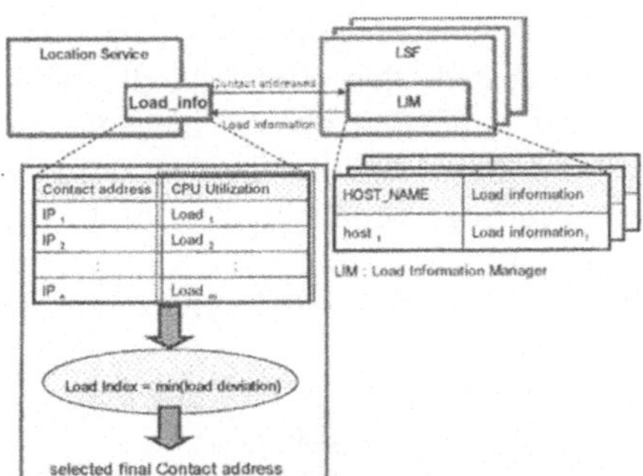

Fig. 4. Destination selection of replicated objects

3 Prototype Implementation of Integrated Binding Service Model

In this section, we explain a prototype implementation of the Integrated Binding Service Model. The physical system configuration for implementation is showing in Figure 5.

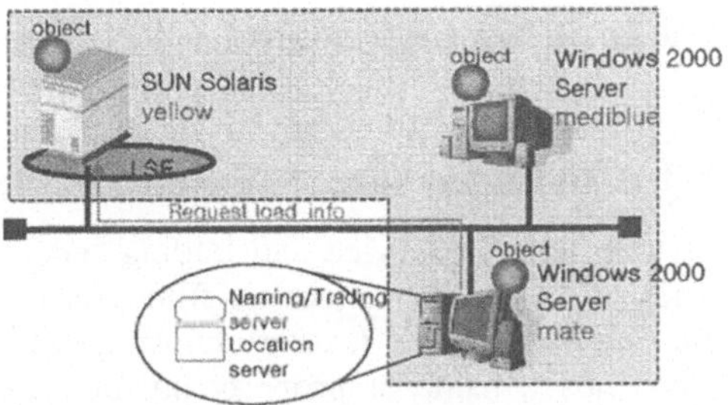

Fig. 5. Physical System Configuration for Implementing Our Model

From this prototype implementation, we showed the executed results of the Naming/Trading service and the Location service in the model. For only step-by-step showing the executing procedure and the executed result of each service from the model, we implemented the GUI-window screening panel without something to do with this model. This panel consists of five-tabbed display with for Lookup, Register & Insert, Modify, Withdraw and Link operations for the Naming/Trading Service and the Location service. As examples, we will show the Register and some operations as preparing phases for binding service objects that clients will be requested in the Naming/Trading service, and the Lookup for obtaining the object handles in the Naming/Trading service and selecting the contract addresses extracted using the object handle in the Location service.

3.1 Registering Distributed Service Objects

Figure 6 is showing the initial executing screen for registering a new service object, and inserting the object handle and contact addresses in a Naming/Trading Service. After registering some information on upper level part, we insert the generated object handle and the contact address of the service object corresponding to the given object handle, like registering(called, exporting) domain names and IPs on Domain Name Server. If the object is replicated, this object handle will be mapped to multiple contact addresses. Here, the replicated objects have the same object handle. This relating information will be stored in the Service Offer and the Contact Record Repositories, respectively. Through Modify button on the upper horizontal tabs, we can modify the partial information registered before. Withdraw and Delete operations can completely erase all information filled by Register and Insert at a time.

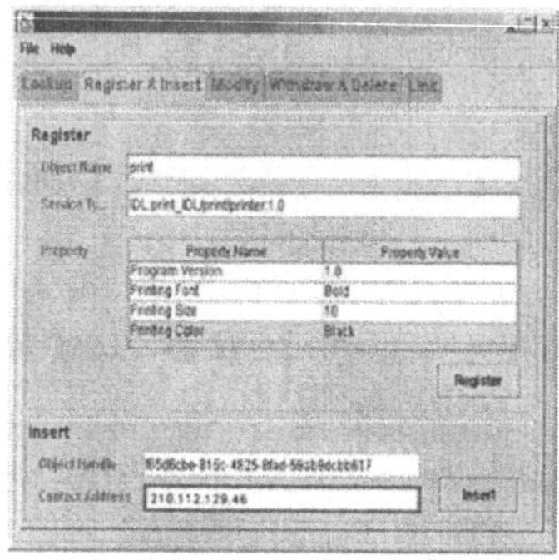

Fig. 6. GUI-Window Screening Panel for Registering A New Distributed Service Object

3.2 Lookups for Selecting Destinations of Distributed Service Objects

This model supports both naming service and trading service at the same time. The name and its properties of the service object are filled out in the registering phase. In Input box of Lookup phase of Figure 7, after choosing either name or property that you want, you fill the chosen name or property out in blank space, and then click NaT_Lookup button.

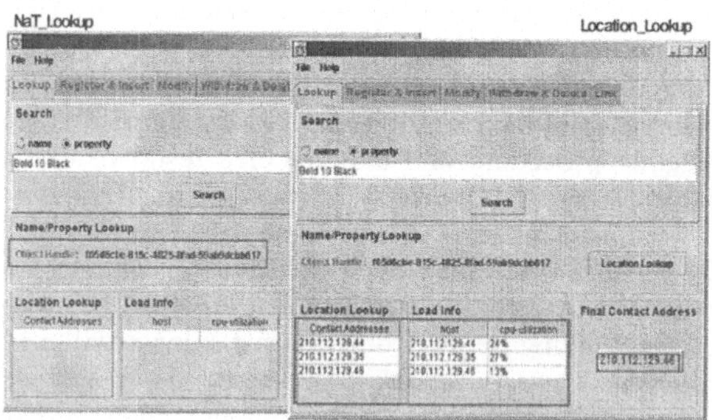

Fig. 7. GUI-Window Screening Panel for Lookuping Contact-Addresses of Given Service Objects

You can see the object handle corresponding to a given service object. Via Location Lookup operation, the screening panel is showed whether the service object is replicated or not, and how many it is replicated. Finally, assume that the service object is replicated, as 3 replicas, like the bottoming part of the below Figure 8. For selecting one of them for an optimal binding service, for this purpose, load information of system load and communication cost among sources and destinations is extract from LIMs. We calculate the load index of system with minimizing the load deviation in the point of view of load balancing. By this load-index as showed in Figure 4, the service object locating on the system with the contract address(210.112.129.46) is selected. This selected service object will be interacted with client object requested on distributed computing systems connected by Inter/Intra-net environments.

4 Conclusions

In distributed systems connected by Inter/Intra-net environments, the logical service domain depends on the physical domain due to the deficiency of independent location service. And existing naming and trading services have been separately served and also have not been supported with the binding service for replicated service objects with the same service type. Hence, the goal of this research is to develop the model that can be supported the location and replication transparencies in distributed environments. For this reason, we proposed a new integrated binding service model that can not only support both naming and trading services at the same time, but also provide an appropriate service object selection mechanism and the efficient resource sharing by using the load balancing information extracted through each system with replicated service objects in Inter/Intra-net environments.
Our future works of our model will be considered the performance evaluation in the Grid environment, extended to the model with adaptability for improving performance and reusability of components. Based on our future works, we will research and develop the federated framework that consists of multiple integrated binding service models in Wide-Area Internet Environments.

Acknowledgements. This paper was supported by KOSEF under ContractR05-2000-000-00285-0(2000~2002), and partially by Wonkwang University in 2001.

References

1. M. Van Steen, G. Ballintijn : Achieving Scalability in Hierarchical Location Services. Proc. 26th International Computer Software and Applications Conference(CompSac), Oxford UK, August (2002)
2. K. Obraczka, P. Danzing, and S. – H.Li. : Internet Resource Discovery Service. Computer, Vol. 26, No9, (1993) 8-22
3. S.Radicati. X.500 Directory Services : Technology and Deployment. International Thomson Computer Press, London (1994)
4. P.Mockapetris : Domain Names -Concepts and Facilities. RFC 1034 (1987)
5. Neukirchen, H. : Optimizing the Set of Set of Selected Service in a CORBA Trader by Integrating Dynamic Load Balancing. Diploma thesis at the Department of Computer Science, Infomatik IV, Aachen University of Technology(1999)
6. G. Ballintijn, M. van Steen, A.S. Tanenbaum : Exploiting Location Awareness for Scalable Location-Independent Object IDs. Proc. Fifth Annual ASCI Conf., Heijen, The Netherlands (1999) 321-328
7. B.T. Jun, C.W. Jeong, S.C. Joo : A Federated Naming/Trading Model for Binding Global distributed Objects. Proc. of the 28th KISS Spring Conf. Vol 28, No 1(2001) 427-429

Personal Grid Running at the Edge of Internet*

Bingchen Li, Wei Li, and Zhiwei Xu

Institute of Computing Technology, Chinese Academy of Sciences, Beijing, 100080, China
{libingchen, liwei, zxu}@ict.ac.cn
http://www.ict.ac.cn

Abstract. The common Grid systems are running on the backbone of Internet. These high performance computing environment provide a high scalable, high reconstructive Grid services in a C/S mode, while more and more Grid applications require a P2P liked infrastructure for personal intercommunication, resources sharing and collaborative work. Personal Grid, we proposed in VEGA Grid project of ICT, would establish such kind of platform to facilitate the messages transmitting and resources sharing for the end Grid users who are using Grid at the edge of the Internet. The core protocol of Personal Grid gives attentions to security, network bandwidth usage and real time requirements. The Personal Grid running environment is very similar to P2P system; it inherits some advantages of P2P system and enhances some parts for Grid usage such as security protection of mandatory access control.

1 Introduction

The Grid system deployed in the backbone of Internet provides a high performance, high scalability and high manageable computing environment, while the users of Grid are at the edge of network. The successful experiments of Peer-to-Peer systems indicate that combining the desktop PCs can also establish a spectacular super computer, whose performance is even much higher than any super computer of the top 500 supercomputers. When we mention the word of Grid, the direct ideal in our mind is a C/S structured system; we also do research on the behavior of servers cooperation in a S/S mode, while care less about the C/C or P2P usage of Grid although a great deal of applications occur pervasively around us. The Personal Grid proposed by us aims at establish a Peer-to-Peer platform for Grid end users who are at the edge of network. Such platform facilitates the communication applications of grid participators and shares the desktop resources at the edge of network. In this article we will not only discuss some interesting topics on our research of personal grid, but also illustrate and evaluate the communication platform we implemented firstly in our test-bed.

* This work is supported in part by the National Natural Science Foundation of China (Grant No. 69925205), the China Ministry of Science and Technology 863 Program (Grant No. 2002AA104310), and the Chinese Academy of Sciences Oversea Distinguished Scholars Fund (Grant No. 20014010).

M. Li et al. (Eds.): GCC 2003, LNCS 3032, pp. 762–769, 2004.

2 Requirements

We list the requirements of Personal Grid in the following two sections.

2.1 Personal Intercommunication Requirement

Mobile phone is substituting the status of fixed phone and being treated as common communication equipment in this century. The booming industry brings considerable society benefit. It presents strong needs for intercommunication in daily society actions. The same phenomena take place in computer world. Prevalence of computer network enables Grid System to be born and widely used. The Grid system connects resources and applications not only in physical layer but also in semantic layer. These connections still rest on the traditional network service pattern client-to-server or server-to-server. The research result of collaborative work indicates that more and more Grid applications require personal intercommunication. Commercial communication software have existed for a long time since the born of computer network such as ICQ and NetMeeting. These systems are not standard-opened and machine-independent, and not satisfied with the OGSA request. The Access Grid establishes a collaborative work environment for group-to-group requirement but not for individual requirement. The Personal Grid of VEGA Grid project will fill the blank of Grid users' intercommunication in a peer-to-peer way. The difference between Personal Grid and common Grid is that it is not a server-centric system but a user-centric system and the object of Personal Grid is not resource but human.

2.2 Desktop Resources Sharing Requirement

From the surprising result of SETI@Home project and some P2P file sharing system such as Kazaa and BearShare, we found that the desktop resources located at the edge of the Internet is a huge mine for Grid application, while interesting research field of Grid system is still in large-scale storage sharing such as Data Grid. The desktop resource sharing is ignored by public eyes in Grid. In the view of Personal Grid, it is a challenge to integrate distributed, heterogeneous, less available desktop resources into Global Grid system. The key issue of desktop resources sharing is availability. The services such as file sharing service and CPU circles sharing service are not in 24*7 mode. Fault tolerance and redundancy are widely used in this area.

3 Relation Work

From the previous discuss about the aims of Personal Grid, We find that the running environment and the key issues of Personal Grid are quite similar to P2P system. The Personal Grid inherits some advantages of P2P system and enhances some components for Grid usage. We list some features that we inherited from P2P system and some special requirement of Grid usage.

- Scalability
- Self-Organization
- Cost of ownership
- Fault Resilience
- Ad-Hoc Connectivity
- Interoperability

Special requirement of Grid system:

1. **Authentication**
   The organizer of Personal Grid is Grid Community. It provides authentication service for community members.
2. **Delegation**
   To establish intercommunication between different Grid Communities, the communities act the role of service delegation.
3. **Enhanced Security**
   P2P system has security protection mechanism for every communication channel, but it is not satisfied for Grid usage, because the real-name user is the main part while anonymous user is only allowed in a limited field controlled by mandatory access control of Grid Community.

Comparing Personal Grid with P2P system we find these differences between them: firstly, Personal Grid depends on the services provided by Grid Community and also be controlled by it while the main aim of P2P system is to minimize the role of server; secondly, the anonymity is the main characteristic of P2P system while Grid system requires real-name authentication for security consideration; thirdly, Personal Grid provides a platform for Grid usage and supports developing work based on this architecture. But the word of P2P means a connection mode only, they are not based on a standard protocol or same architecture.

4 The Architecture of Personal Grid

4.1 The Platform of Personal Grid

The Personal Grid platform includes two main parts: intercommunication and sharing. It is based on the Grid Community Service. The architecture is as following figure:

This platform considers three factors of data stream.

Security requirement. For some kinds of Personal Grid application such as talk and Grid mail, message contents need to be protected. In Personal Grid system, we use public key authentication system to protect the communication channel. Every client keeps the public key of Grid Community, and the Community Server also keeps the client's public key. Comparing to P2P system, no listen port is needed in Personal Grid client side. Every session between two clients uses a random and temporary port.

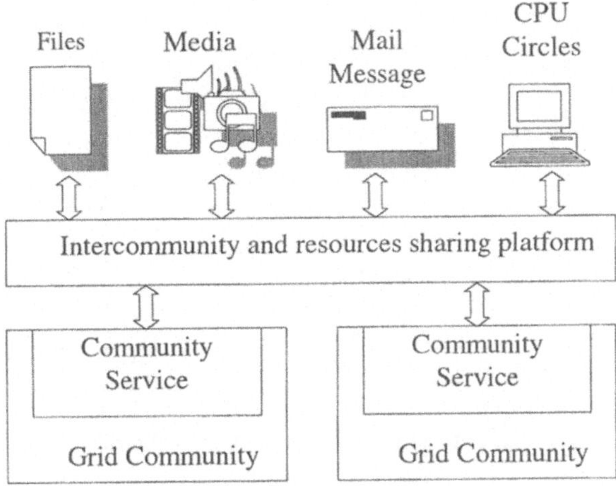

Fig. 1. The architecture of Personal Grid

Real-time requirement. Real-time media stream is a main part of inter-communication. Its network bandwidth occupation rate is higher than that of any other protocol. For home and office usage, RTP protocol based on UDP is used in unicast and multicast mode. In Internet environment, another RTP protocol adaptor, which is based on TCP protocol, has been used because of proxy service of Grid Communication.

Response-time requirement. Large quantity data transmission through Grid Community server is unreasonable, but the content sharing is dominated by the mandatory access control deployed on the server side. To balance these two requirements, in our implementation, the server controls the control stream instead of data stream, which runs in a P2P mode.

4.2 The Protocol Stack of Personal Grid

As we mentioned above, the platform of Personal Grid includes intercommunication and resources sharing.

In the resources sharing platform, the protocol works in an order-preserving mode. The two recognizable ends keep the session semantic. The resources sharing mechanism of Personal Grid is a three-dimension resources space. The first dimension is resource type, the second is the items of this type and the last dimension is reserved for special usage of individual resources such as access control. The following picture illustrates a desktop resources sharing hierarchy under Personal Grid platform.

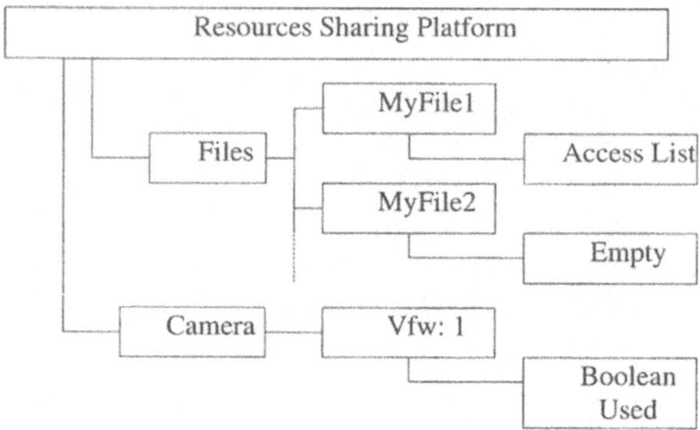

Fig. 2. Resources sharing in Personal Grid

In the intercommunication platform, the input and output data are in an out-of-order mode because of the indetermination messages incoming sequence. The following figure illustrates the protocol stack of input and output stream:

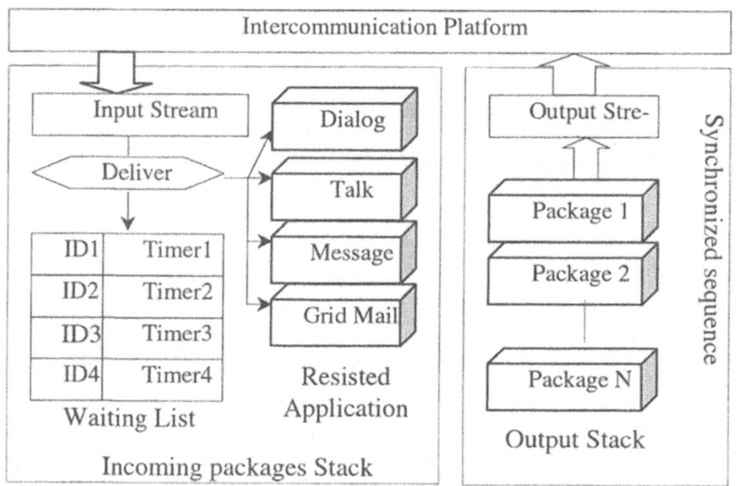

Fig. 3. The protocol stack

The output sequence is a synchronized array. The sending process of every package is atomic. The server side processes data control package only because of the requirement of response time.

The input stream has a more complex structure than that of the output stream. It works in a group of threads and a wait list. Each registered application launches up a thread, each thread contains a vector of running items. There are two kinds of incoming packages delivered by this stream; the incoming messages and responses from the server. If the package type is incoming message, the stream distributes it to the registered application thread; otherwise, it wakes up the wait object in the wait list by its unique ID. For example, when UserA send a dialog request to UserB, he builds an invite form, sends it to the output stream and gets a message ID from system time call. A wait object is inserted into input stream wait list and the timer is set to 30 seconds for waiting. The community server receives this package and distributes the content to UserB. Community server will return processing result (success or failure) to the sender.

5 Implementation of Personal Grid

5.1 Grid Community and Its Service

Grid Community is the basic Personal Grid organization unit in VEGA Grid project. It likes hub for each client. The control stream and messages are dominated by the 'hub', but the data streams such as media stream and file data block are transmitted in P2P mode. The subjects of Personal Grid are community users. We define the user identity as following format:

user@community, for example Darwin@ict.ac.cn. The resources locations such as files are defined as following format:

Pgfile://user@community/dir/dirs/filename.

The Community resolves the real location of a user. The file owner resolves the sub-directories.

The basic community services includes:

1. **Authorization.** Personal Grid is a real-name world. The services of community provides to assured users, although some public information such as advertisement is opened for anonymous user.
2. **Delegation.** Messages and data transmitting cross communities require delegation service. The intercommunication between Grid Communities comprises two layers of trust relationship: first, the user is authorized by his community; second, his community is trusted by the target community. If these two conditions are satisfied, the target community can accept the messages coming from the user.
3. **Proxy.** The following picture illustrates why the proxy services are so important in the Personal Grid environment.

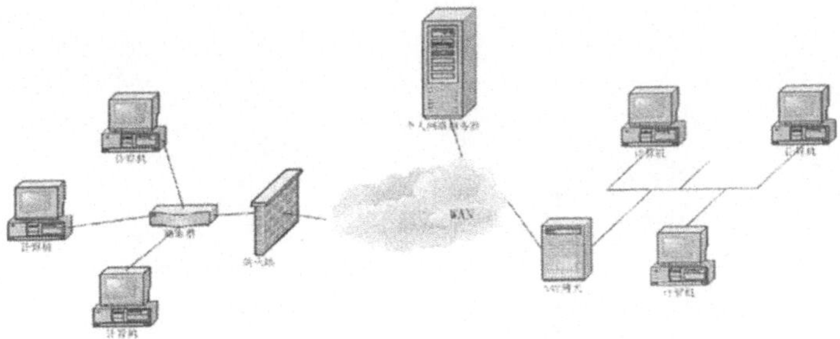

Fig. 4. Various nodes reside at the edge of Internet

At the edge of Internet, so many computers reside behind a firewall or NAT gateway server. An important work in P2P world is to establish available connection through some relay nodes. The Grid Community performs the 'relay' work in Personal Grid. Another issue is that the server would be the bottleneck of the whole system. To decrease the data communication load, two orient-opposite connection attempts are performed at the beginning. The extreme instance is that all nodes are behind different NAT gateways or firewalls.

4. **Grid mail and message.** When some broadcast messages and mails, the receiver may not be online, this service storages the content for receiver. This is the only offline service in Personal Grid.

5.2 Applications

In the test-bed of Personal Grid, we implemented 'talk', 'message', 'visual dialog', and 'media presenter' based on the communication platform. File sharing is the main application in our resources sharing platform.

Compare to commercial software of instant message, videoconference and Video-on-Demand, our intercommunication platform realized all applications working under an opened standard protocol. It has no compatible problem, Personal Grid user can select his or her favorite applications even develop a new application on our platform. The following pictures illustrates our intercommunication tools of our test-bed:

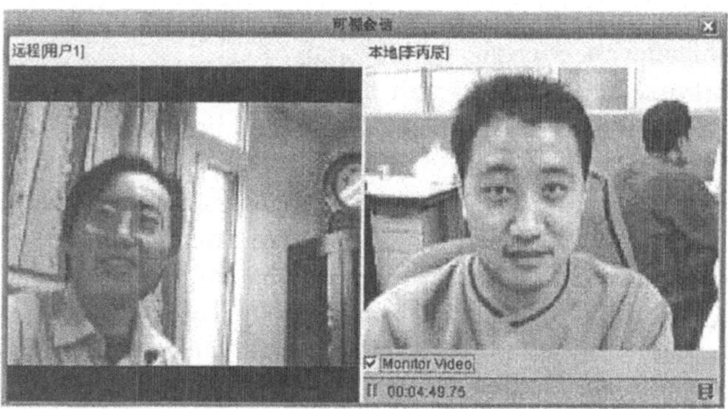

Picture 1. The Visual dialog of Personal Grid

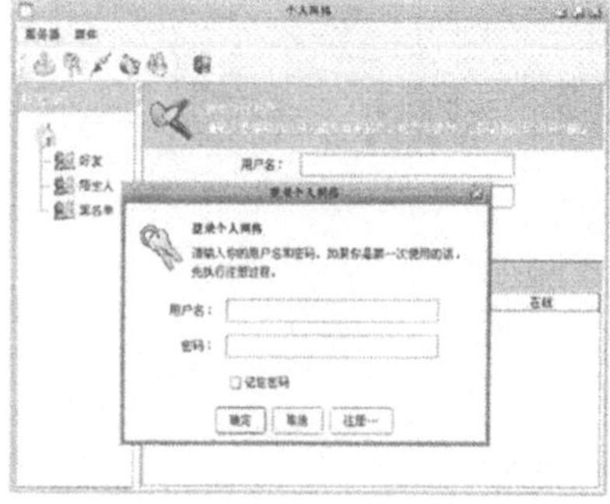

Picture 2. The Personal Grid client app

Picture 3. Chat of Personal Grid

6 Conclusion and Future Work

Personal Grid as a part of our VEGA Grid project introduces some P2P advantages into Grid system for the first time, and solved intercommunication and resources sharing among Grid end users who resided at the edge of Internet successfully. These two platforms of Personal Grid not only realized the common requirement of communication requirement, but also enabled developing work. More applications will be developed and deployed on demand of intercommunication and resources sharing. In the future we will improve the file and device sharing mechanism for other Grid applications of VEGA Grid project. The stream media tools will be import to GSML tool suit.

References

1. Z. Xu and W. Li "Research on Vega Grid Architecture", Journal of Computer Research and Development Vol 39, No 8, pp. 923 – 929
2. A. Reinefeld, F. Schintke "Concepts and Technologies for a Worldwide Grid Infrastructure", Euro-Par 2002 Parallel Processing, Springer LNCS 2400, pp 62-71.
3. D. S. Milojicic, V. Kalogeraki, R. Lukose "Peer-to-Peer Computing", HP Laboratories Palo Alto HPL-2002-57 March 8 th , 2002
4. I. Foster, C. Kesselman, S. Tuecke "The Anatomy of the Grid Enabling Scalable Virtual Organizations", International of High Performance Computing Applications, 2001, 15(3): pp. 200-222.
5. I. Foster, C. Kesselman, J. M. Nick, S. Tuecke, The Physiology of the Grid An Open Grid Services Architecture for Distributed Systems Integration. Grid Service Infrastructure WG, Global Grid Forum, June 22, 2002.
6. J. Apgar, A. Grimshaw, S. Harris, M. Humphrey, A. Nguyen-Tuong, Secure Grid Naming Protocol (SGNP): Draft Specification for Review and Comment, Global Grid Forum, 5 February 2002.
7. L. Childers, T. Disz, R. Olson, "Access Grid: Immersive Group-to-Group Collaborative Visualization" Computer Science Department University of Chicago
8. SETI@Home current total statistics, http://setiathome.ssl.berkeley.edu/totals.html

Grid Workflow Based on Performance Evaluation[1]

Shao-hua Zhang, Yu-jin Wu, Ning Gu, and Wei Wang

Department of Computing and Information Technology, Fudan University, Shanghai 200433, P.R. China
{shaohuazhang,022021183,ninggu,weiwang1}@fudan.edu.cn

Abstract. As the complexity of Grid applications increase, it becomes more important and urgent to provide grid workflow to construct and manage the applications. The grid workflow based on dynamic scheduling and performance evaluation is presented in this paper according to the standards of GCC and WFMC, which consists of user portal, resource management component, grid services management, performance management, grid workflow engine featured by dynamic scheduling. Then the prototype implemented on the Globus is introduced. Finally the experiment of genome sequencing based on shotgun algorithm is analyzed and the result is promising.

1 Introduction

Grid[1,2] provides users the ability to utilize the power of a large variety of heterogeneous, distributed resources, computing resources, data storage systems, instruments etc, which is becoming a new computing infrastructure for scientific and cooperation and a mainstream technology for large-scale resources sharing and distributed systems integration. Up to now much of the focus of Grid computing has been on developing middleware, which provides basic functionality such as the ability to query information about grid resources and the ability to schedule tasks onto the resources. As the complexity of Grid applications increase, it becomes ever more important and urgent to provide grid workflow to construct and manage the applications. Some projects and systems such as GridPhyN[3], McrunJob[4] and GridAnt[5], adopt the workflow or planning with the characteristics of workflow to automate the complex Grid applications. At the same time some international organizations and researches propose some standards and specifications such as Grid Service Flow Language[6] and Grid Workflow[7] from Global Grid Forum, Grid Workflow Services[2] in Open Grid Service Architecture. The researches of Grid workflow gradually interest the grid and workflow communities.

Though Grid workflow is similar with traditional workflow, which covers fundamental components: workflow model, workflow running mechanism, user and application, there are some distinctions between each other. Virtual Organization (VO): The process of a grid workflow involves in the virtual organization that encompasses multiple administrative domains (organizations) defined by some

[1] Project 60173028 Supported by National Natural Science Foundation of China

M. Li et al. (Eds.): GCC 2003, LNCS 3032, pp. 770–777, 2004.

sharing rules. Dynamism: Since grid resources are not entirely dedicated to the environment, computational and networking capabilities can vary significantly over time. Application based on grid services: OGSA defines mechanisms for creating, managing, and exchanging information among grid services. A grid service is a Web service that conforms to a set of conventions (interfaces and behaviors) that define how a client interacts with a Grid service. Computing and data intensive tasks: the most of grid applications are high performance computing and large-scale data processing that harness fully the Grid computing and storage ability, the key factors are efficiency and performance. Resource allocation is a critical and delicate aspect of the grid-based workflow enactment.

A grid workflow based on dynamic scheduling policy and performance evaluation is presented in the paper according to the standards of GCC and WFMC, which consists of user portal, resource management, grid services management, performance management, grid workflow engine featured dynamic scheduling. Then, the prototype implemented on the Globs is introduced. Finally the experiment of fragment assemble of genome sequencing is analyzed and the result is promising. We focus on the friendly user interface and high performance scheduling.

The remainder of the paper is organized as follows: the next section introduces the related works. Section 3 presents the workflow architecture and details the components. The prototype and experiments is described and result is analyzed in section 4. The last section is the conclusion and future work.

2 Related Works

There is a limited amount of works related to grid workflow comparing with other grid technologies in the grid computing community. The researches can be classified two types: draft standards or specification, practical projects or systems. Firstly we introduce the former. Global Grid Forum proposes a standard for the sequencing of complex high-performance computational tasks within a Grid [7]. The standard is an XML vocabulary that provides a single grid programming interface. OGSA defines grid workflow service[6]. Grid Computing Environments (GCE) and the Grid Service Management Frameworks (GSM) Research Groups present a grid workflow management architecture[8]. The lifetime of Grid workflow covers creation of the Workflow Process Description (WPD), verification of the WPD, creation of a Workflow Case Description (WCD), enactment of a case. GSFL [6] analyzes existing technologies that address workflow for Web services, and tries to leverage them for Grid services, which have different needs from standard Web services, and addresses them for Grid services within the OGSA framework.

Then we analyze the latter. The workflow management system for grid computing, called GridFlow[9], is presented, including services of both global grid workflow management and local grid sub-workflow scheduling. Simulation, execution and monitoring functionalities are provided at the global grid level. McRunjob[4] is a grid workflow manager used to manage the generation of large numbers of production processing jobs in High Energy Physics. It converts core metadata into jobs submitted in a variety of environments. GALE[10] is an HPC workflow vocabulary that uses key grid services to provide a "run code X anywhere, then post process results, then ..." grid-level scripting language for users and problem solving environments. The project in [11,12,13] is part of PhyGridN, mainly includes Chimera and Pegasus which are used to create and manage the grid computational workflow that must be present to deal with the challenging application requirements.

3 Grid Workflow Architecture

As mentioned before, grid workflow elements and grid workflow architecture have new features consistent with the grid computing environment and OGSA. The run-time environment is different with that of traditional environment, so the concepts have more grid service characteristics. Activity: According to OGSA, an activity can be encapsulated a grid service which finishes the logical step within a process or sends a message to a participant to execute something. So we can view the activity as grid service, which is convenient to model workflow. Process: Actually the process can be treated as composition of grid services conformance to some relationship and constraints in the virtual organization. Instance: The representation of a single enactment of a process, or activity within a process. Each instance represents a separate thread of execution of the process or activity, which may be controlled independently. Instance is a single execution of the grid services according to the process. Resource: The gird resources are configured in the virtual organization.

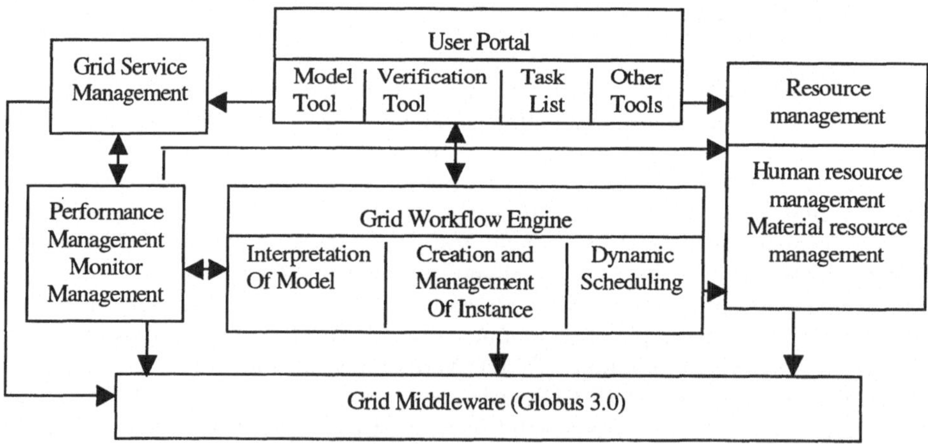

Fig. 1. The Grid Workflow Architecture

The grid workflow architecture consists of five major components(Fig.1). Grid User Portal is an integrated GUI that mainly covers grid workflow model and verification tool, grid task list and other GUI tools for users to manage workflow such as monitoring tool. It provides friendly interfaces and facilitates user to construct and management the workflow using the grid service management and resource management. Grid Workflow Engine provides operational functions to support the execution of (instances of) business processes, based on the process definitions. These functions include Interpretation of the process definition. Creation of process instances and management of their execution, Navigation between activities and the creation of appropriate work items for their processing, Supervisory and management functions. Performance management evaluates the grid service according to execution condition of the grid service and facilitates the dynamic scheduling of workflow engine for optimal performance. Monitoring management collects the execution information of the instances and resources to provide the portal GUI tools. Though the Globus provides the basic grid services management, which is lack of supporting of easily constructing, retrieving and management of grid service for grid workflow model, dynamic scheduling and execution that are solved by Grid services management component. Resource management component is responsible for management and maintenance of the human and material resource, especially it provide the classified and the real-time information for process model tools and workflow engine. The workflow engine can dynamically schedule the workflow using the performance and resource information.

3.1 Modeling and Verification

The above mentioned grid workflows lack formal and precise workflow description language which normally adopt DAG(directed acyclic graph) as modeling language. We select Petri net as the modeling language because it has the accepted advantages of formal semantics, graphical nature, abundance of analysis techniques, rich expressiveness and the Petri Net Markup Language(PNML) [14] based on standard XML. To avoid enactment errors the process description is need to be verified and desirable properties such as safety and liveness are checked.

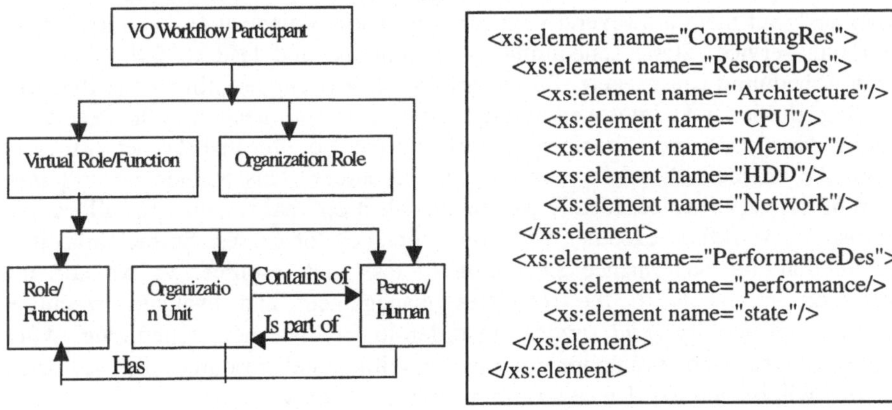


```
<xs:element name="ComputingRes">
  <xs:element name="ResorceDes">
    <xs:element name="Architecture"/>
    <xs:element name="CPU"/>
    <xs:element name="Memory"/>
    <xs:element name="HDD"/>
    <xs:element name="Network"/>
  </xs:element>
  <xs:element name="PerformanceDes">
    <xs:element name="performance/>
    <xs:element name="state"/>
  </xs:element>
</xs:element>
```

Fig. 2. VO Model

Fig. 3. Argument of Resource

The workflow model covers three sub-models: organization model, resource model and process model which is the most important. The grid workflow is in the dynamic environment of virtual organization. The VO model can be analyzed on a strategic level and an operational level. The strategic level is concerned with the co-operation between all the partners of the VO. The operational level is concerned with the way the individual partners carry out their own processes. It not only covers the whole VO structure and relationships of participant organizations, but also deals with some internal participant of partners and the relationships between VO and partners. The new two elements that are Virtual Role/Function and Organization Class are introduced to solve the problems. The organization model of VO is as follows (Fig.2). The detail is in the paper[15].

A Petri net can fully model a workflow process definition defined in WFMC, whose verification can be implemented by existed tools and technique. The grid process modeling is based on our previous work [16] with the support of grid service (The sample is Figure 4 in the following section).

The resources are organized into a hierarchy according to the resources types and arguments. The component uses the Globus MDS for storing grid resource information and retrieving available grid resources. The model tools and grid workflow engine access the resources information. The performance component sends the result to update the corresponding performance arguments. The resource arguments are listed in figure 3 expressed by XML(Figure 3 has omitted some expression for paper space).

3.2 Performance and Dynamic Scheduling

The scheduling of workflow engine has two types: static scheduling which engine allocates the needed resources according to the process description statically binding the resources, dynamic scheduling which engine allocates dynamically the resources consistent with the process description according the current condition of grid resources. Due to unforeseen circumstances at the process definition and execution time, for example, an activity in a process description involves a service that has been discontinued, but there are several new services whose composition is equivalent to the missing service. Static scheduling can't continue and lead to fail, while the dynamic scheduling can execute. So the grid workflow engine utilizes the dynamic scheduling. But it can be improved by the performance optimization in the execution. Normally when there are suitable resources that can be allocated the activity (grid service), the engine will select randomly the resources. This method doesn't take account of the performance. Ideally we should select optimal resource for allocation. Otherwise the workflow executes with low efficiency, or ceases, further fails. It is important that the performance evaluation of task and resource. So we add the performance arguments to the resources management and evaluate execution performance of activity (grid service) in order to facilitate next scheduling. After multiple analysis and evaluation of the activities and resource, the dynamic scheduling will be optimal. The algorithm is described below.

A grid workflow can be defined as s set of activities (grid service) A_i(i=1,…,n),n is sum number of activities. Resources can be expressed as a list of resource class R_k(k=1,…,m),m is sum of resource class, and each class R_k containing same type resources Rk_j(k=1,…,j), each grid services requires a resource or more resources. When the engine schedules, it not only selects the required type resources, but also matches performance arguments between the resources and grid service.

```
// initialization: set the performance arguments  null,
the scheduling select randomly the satisfied resources
For m=1 to n do
   Arg=get the currentacivityarg(Am);
   If  arg=null then
      Schedule randomly the resource Rkj from the
      satisfied resources class Rk;
   Else
      Match the performance arguments;
      Schedule optimal resource Rkj from the satisfied
      resources class Rk;
   End if
   Update the performance arguments according the
   condition of execution;
End for.
```

There are some notices about the scheduling algorithm. Firstly the engine is multi-thread. So maybe many instances are scheduled. Secondly the workflow model can be added QoS. So the engine schedules the resource according the QoS and performance. The algorithm focuses on the performance issues and omits the detail of QoS.

4 Prototype and Experiment

The prototype is implemented based on the Globus toolkit 3.0 and previous virtual organization workflow system. The Globus provides the basic GSI, GRAM, MDS services. We have designed other parts in the architecture.

The prototype has been tested by the example of sequencing genome [17], which involves many organizations. The figure 4 outlines workflow model of the process expressed in Petri Net that comprises of three main phase and organizations. We focus on the second phase that handles the Genome Shotgun assembly and is computational intensive. The first phase is simple denoted A which creates the genome database in the biology organization responsible for genome fragment randomly of DNA and other disposing in order for database. From B to I is the second phase named Genome Shotgun assembly in computational organization. The last phase is the result evaluation and analysis in the biology community. The process model only is sequential in the figure. In fact the subprocess from C to G in the dashed line can be multiple and parallel because it iteratively computes the data. The testing environment is IBM 670(memory 8GB) and some PC Server(2CPU+2G memory), and the testing sequence DNA is 15Kbp with each sequence data is 500bp, all data is about 10Mbyte.Three type of experiments are implemented. Firstly the common sequential shotgun algorithm is run on the IBM 670. The second is the parallel scheduling in the IBM 670 and 4 PC Server. The last is parallel scheduling with performance evaluation. The different number of parallel sub-process instance is taken account in the experiment. The results are described in figure 5.

The dynamism is simulated by adding the workload of the nodes in the grid. The late two type experiments are re run. The workloads added in the environment are equal. The result is shown in figure 6. From the result of figure 5 and 6, some conclusion can be derived. Firstly there is an optimal sub-process instance number in which the running time is least. Because the resource in the experiments is limited, when the number exceeds the optimal point, the waiting time of scheduling and joining activity node F is more. Secondly when the workload is added into the grid, the running time increases, but the dynamic scheduling with performance evaluation is more efficient than the common dynamic scheduling, which is suitable for dynamic grid environment.

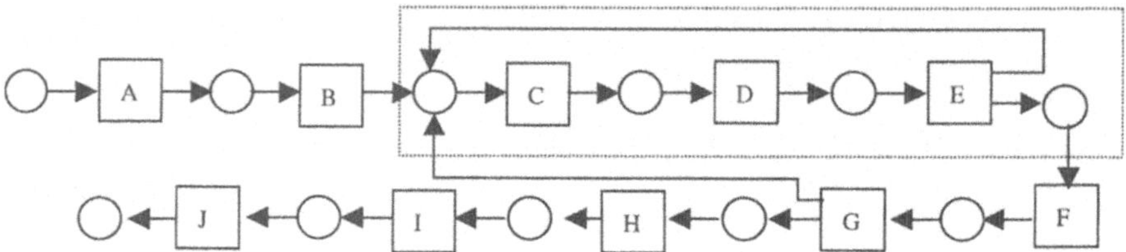

Fig. 4. Process Model of Genome SequencingA: Fragment. B: Process Raw Data. C: Blast. D: Phrap. E: Evaluate. F: Round Evaluate. G: Reset Raw Data. H: Scaffold. I: Consensus. J: Annotate

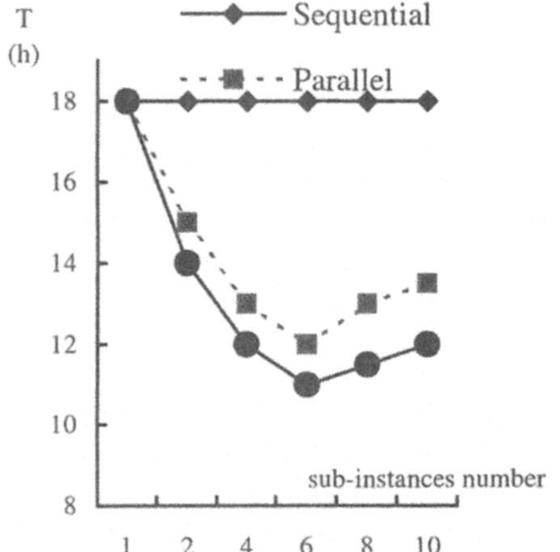

Fig. 5. Experiment Result

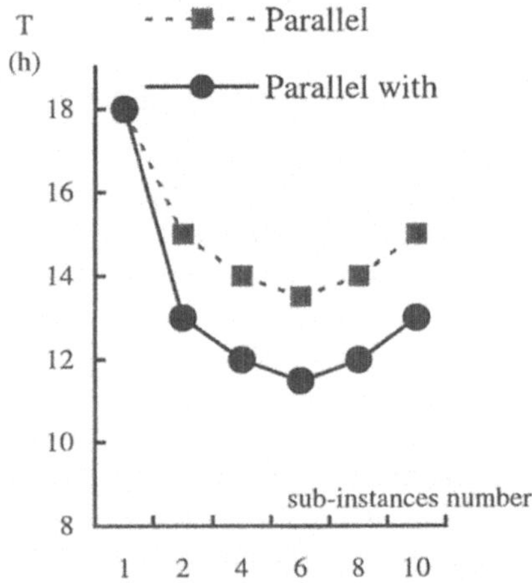

Fig. 6. Experiment Result with workload

5 Conclusion and Future Work

Grid computing is becoming a new computing infrastructure for scientific and cooperation. The Grid workflow which constructs, automate, manages and monitoring complex grid applications facilitate the large-scale resource sharing and distributed system integration in the grid environment. The grid workflow based on dynamic scheduling and performance evaluation is presented in this paper according to the standards of GCC and WFMC, which consists of user portal, resource management component, grid services management, performance management, grid workflow engine featured dynamic scheduling. The work is in progress. Now the data management in the grid workflow is simple, which adopt the central database and files. We will strengthen the data management in the future.

References

1. I. Foster, C. Kesselman, et al: The Anatomy of the Grid: Enabling Scalable Virtual Organizations. Int. J. High Performance Computing Applications. vol 15(2001)200-222
2. I. Foster, C. Kesselman, J. Nick, et al: The Physiology of the Grid: An Open Grid Services Architecture for Distributed Systems Integration.(2002)
3. E. Deelman, J. Blythe, Y. Gil, Carl Kesselman: Workflow Management in GriPhyN. Chapter in The Grid Resource Management: State of the Art and Future Trends. Kluwer Publishing (2003)
4. G.E. Graham,D. Evans and I. Bertram: McRunjob :A High Energy Physics Workflow Planner for Grid. Computing in High Energy and Nuclear Physics. La Jolla, California 3(2003)
5. G. von Laszewski, N. Zaluzec, M. Hategan, et al: GridAnt: Client Side Workflow Management in Grids with application onto Position Resolved Diffraction. Midwest Software Engineering Conference. Chicago. DePaul University, 6 (2003)
6. S. Krishnan, P. Wagstrom, and G. von Laszewski: GSFL: A Workflow Framework for Grid Services. in ANL/MCS-P980-0802, Argonne National Laboratory, 9700 S. Cass Avenue, Argonne, IL 60439, U.S.A.(2002)
7. Hugh P. Bivens: Grid Workflow. Grid Computing Environments Working Group, Global Grid Forum,(2001)
8. D.C. Marinescu. A Grid workflow Management Architecture. GGF white paper.
9. J. Cao, S. A. Jarvis, S. Saini, G. R. Nudd. GridFlow: Workflow Management for Grid Computing. In Proceedings of the 3rd IEEE/ACM International Symposium on Cluster Computing and the Grid (CCGRID'03) (2003)198-205,
10. Hugh P. Bivens and Judy I. Beiriger: GALE: Grid Access Language for HPC Environments. Available at sass3186.sandia.gov/ hpbiven.
11. Blythe, J., E. Deelman, et al :The Role of Planning in Grid Computing. in Proc. International Conferenceon Automated Planning and Scheduling (ICAPS), (2003) 154-163.
12. Blythe, J., E. Deelman, Y. Gil: Planning for workflow construction and maintenance on the grid in ICAPS 03 Workshop on Web Services Composition, (2003)8 – 14,.
13. E. Deelman, J. Blythe, et al: Mapping Abstract Complex Workflows onto Grid Environments. Journal of Grid Computing, vol 1, (2003) 25-29,.
14. J. Billington, et al: The Petri Net Markup Language Concepts, Technology, and Tools. In Proc. 24th Int. Conf. Application and Theory of Petri Nets (ICATPN'2003), Eindhoven, The Netherlands, volume 2679 of Lecture Notes in Computer Science, 6(2003)483-505.
15. Shao-hua Zhang, Ning Gu: Research on Workflow of Virtual Organization, The Eighth International Conference on Computer Supported Cooperative Work in Design, Xiamen, China, 10(2003)
16. Shao-hua Zhang, Ning Gu: Workflow Process Mining Based on Machine Learning. The Second International Conference on Machine Learning and Cybernetics,Xi'an, China,11(2003)
17. Gene Myers: Whole-Genome DNA Sequencing. IEEE Computational Engineering and Science 3, 1 (1999) 33-43

Research on User Programming Environment in Grid

Ge He, Donghua Liu, Zhiwei Xu, Lin Li, and Shengliang Xu

Software Division, Institute of Computing Technology, CAS, Beijing 100080
hege@ict.ac.cn

Abstract. Principal among the technical obstacles when using the grid environment is usability. Owing to the inherently complex, programs in grid will reflect some of the complexity. To make grid resources useful and accessible effectively to the users, as we think, it requires new software or environment to build and program applications. The goal of the user programming environment of Vega Grid is to simplify the programming of the grid in the same way that the Web simplified information sharing over the Internet. To the end, it is easier for ordinary users to develop, execute, and tune applications on the grid. In this paper, we firstly analyse the properties and capabilities grid programming tools should possess; and then describe our research on end-user programming environment when developing Vega Grid. We are now going to further develop our Grid End-user Programming Environment prototype.

1 Introduction

The aim of the grid is to connect the distributed computers, databases, instruments, and people in a seamless web of computing and distributed intelligence, which can be used in an on-demand fashion as a problem-solving resource. As a platform, it has been implemented in many application domains, and innovate many new application paradigms, including on-demand applications[1], ubiquitous applications[2], robust, portable applications[3].

Although there still many other research groups focus on the grid technology, however, existing efforts are not addressing one fundamental problem: the programming of the Grid system, which is highly complex and dynamic. Although they're still many tools used for developing the grid applications, but these are only by teams of specialists, and it is too difficult for grid to achieve widespread acceptance. As we think, entirely new approaches to software development and programming are required for grid to become broadly accessible.

In research of Vega Grid, which is the name of our grid research project, we intend to develop programming paradigms that can execute ubiquitously and easily in large-scale grid environments. We have begun to develop the language and systems required to support application execution in this new computing infrastructures of the OGSA environment, along with application development strategies to make grid resources accessible to ordinary users. To do this, we are pursuing research in 3 major areas: (1) end-user oriented programming language to access grid resources; (2) design and implementation of programming and execution systems and environments that support

M. Li et al. (Eds.): GCC 2003, LNCS 3032, pp. 778–785, 2004.

the development of grid applications by end-users in high-level languages; and (3) the software tools to help the users' development their grid applications.

We anticipate that the successful completion of this research program will lead to a new programming and executing ways of utilizing the global computing and information resources.

2 Background and Motive

2.1 Properties for Grid Programming Models

Except the general properties that are desirable for traditional parallel programming modes, the grid environment will emphasis on some new properties dramatically.

1. Usability. Grid programming tools and environment should support a wide range of programming concepts and paradigms, and to the users, there should be a low barrier to acceptance the tools and environment.

2. Dynamic adaptability. A grid programmer should be able to adapt to the dynamic of the architecture or configurations of the grid.

3. Portability. Grid programming models and language should allow grid codes greater software portability.

4. Interoperability. Having the open and extensible architecture, grid may support many different kinds of protocols, services, applications programming interface, and software development kits, and they should be interoperable when appropriate.

5. Reliability. Grid user should be able to check, recover or react to the faults of the system helped by programming environment.

2.2 Issues When Designing a Grid Programming Environment

When designing and implementing a grid programming environment, many issues should be think about.

1. Execution Models. Owing to the hierarchy of bandwidths and latencies of the wide-area grid, we need an execution models to hide latency. Hence, what kind of execution models should be used? In the execution models, can asynchronous models or styles of programming be developed?

2. Grid QoS. In grid, it will be difficult for applications to provide reliable performance. So grid QoS is clearly desirable. In grid environment, we can broadly apply the meaning of the QoS for example capacity reservations, the Service Model as temporal reservations etc.

3. Global Name Space. A global namespace is useful when the program locates, names, refers, and interact to the grid resources.

4. Structure. What is the most appropriate software architecture that supports the flexibility and effectively grid programming?

5. Language, compiler and run-time system. When designing programming environment, we must consider the basic programming elements. How to co-design and co-implement the language, compiler and run-time system is an important problem.

2.3 Related Works

There have many related research works focused on grid programming environment. In GGF[4], there has a research area, named Applications, Programming Models and Environments Area (APME), to collect and coordinate the related works, which are centralized in the grid portal, application development middleware, and problem solving environments. Currently, the main works in APME are partial to computing process and data processing, and did not focus on service processing to end-user.

Now, the most popular grid infrastructure, the Globus toolkit, by and large provides the basic, low-level services for interoperability purposes, there still tends to exist a large gap between the Globus services and the programming-level abstractions we are commonly used to.

There have many programming methodologies, including tools, languages, and environments developed in order to solve the programming problem of the grid. CoG Kit Project[5] and Legion[6] provide the object-oriented tools for grid applications development. CoG Kit enable "Commodity Grids" through an interface layer that maps Globus services to a CORBA API. Legion provides objects with a globally unique and opaque identifier to make an object, and its members can be referenced from anywhere. GridRPC[7] system, such as Netsolve, and Ninf offers a simple yet powerful programming paradigm. It provided new features and capabilities that make it easy to program medium- to coarse-grained, task parallel applications spread over a wide-area network. Still, it supported other grid features as dynamic resource discovery, dynamic load balancing, fault tolerance etc. Cactus[8], and DataCutter[9] are designed as the grid application development frameworks for special application domain. Cactus is developed to provide a flexible, modular, portable and importantly easy-to-use, programming environment for large-scale simulations. DataCutter supports for developing data-intensive applications which make use of scientific datasets in remote storage systems across a wide-area network.

2.4 Evolution of Programming Language

The basic trend for the evolution of the programming languages, as we think, is the programming language is becoming more and more abstract, more and more closer to end-user. So, the programming is becoming more easily for end-user to learn and use and this make the programming work simpler.

As showed in Fig.1, we analysis the evolution of the programming languages through 4 stages featured by the evolution of the computer architecture.

1. Used in Lab. In this stage, computer can be used only by a little specialist, as in the mainframe stage. The assembly languages can be seen as the featured language of this stage. In assembly languages, programmers must deal with low-level details, so it is difficult to write and maintain large programs.

2. Early adopters. At the client-server stage, more specialists and ordinary users begin to use computers. The feature language of this stage is system programming languages, which are less efficient than assembly languages but they allow applications to

be developed much more quickly. So, they have almost completely replaced assembly languages for the development of large applications.

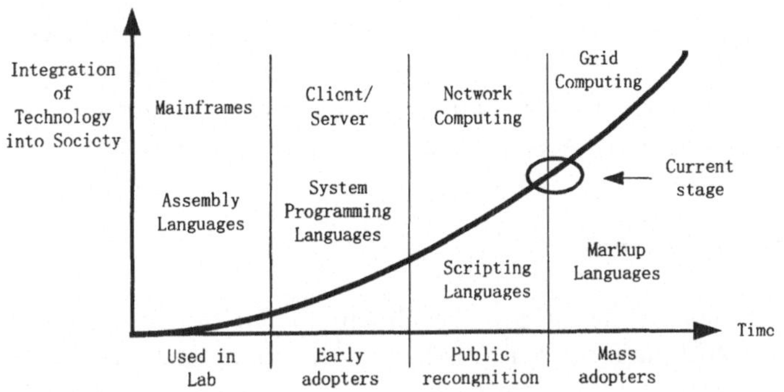

Fig. 1. Evolution of Technology

3. Public recognition. At the Internet stage, much more ordinary users benefit from the computer technology. The growth of the Internet has popularized scripting languages which is designed for "gluing" applications, and is not a replacement for system programming language; they use typeless approaches to achieve a higher level programming and more rapid application development than system programming languages. So it sacrifices execution speed to improve development speed.

4. Mass adoption. At this stage, every ordinary user can easily and deeply benefit form the computer technology, even though he do not know where the computer is and which computer served her. This just is the aim of the grid technology. We think the featured language of this stage should be Markup Languages. In this stage, more and more people's job relied on computer and Internet, and with the personal computer, they joined the programmer community, which we called casual programmers. For them, programming is not their main job function; it is a tool they use occasionally to help with their main job. Examples of this kind of casual programming are simply to express queries to a database, or reassemble a spreadsheet. They are not willing to spend months learning a programming language, but only hope to express basic demand in a few hours by an easy way, just as they can program a web page easily by the FrontPage or Dreamweaver. HTML is easier to learn because they have simpler syntax and omit complex features like function and objects.

Being seen as the universal programming language for delivering web content in the next generation, XML adapts the development of the Web. It is easy to learn and use for the end-users. Markup Language is higher-level than but not replaces the system programming or scripting languages. And based on them, XML is closer to the end-users. In our view, raising the level of programming should be the single most important goal for language designers, since it has the greatest effect on programmer productivity. For the end-user, programming with markup languages owns a higher-level programming paradigm than using scripting languages. So we design the Markup Language as the end-user programming language in grid, named Grid Service Markup Language (GSML), which will be introduced in the next section.

3 End-User Programming Environment of Vega Grid

The main research content of the Vega Grid includes grid address space, grid operating system, grid end-user programming environment, etc. In this paper, we will introduce the end-user programming environment of Vega Grid. In our vision, the end-user should be able to specify applications in high-level programming languages and expect he could seamlessly access the grid to find required resources when needed.

3.1 Software Structure

Currently, based on the OGSA, the Globus toolkit provides the basal software for construction grid platform. But it is lack of favorable interfaces for development and execution applications. To access grid service, the user must program complex application. Then, it is difficult to fast develop the lightweight applications. That is to say, it missed the virtues of the web, which is suppleness, fit for fast development.

In Vega Grid, we resolved the problem of the end-user programming at different level, including language level, toolkit level, protocol level etc.

Fig.2 shows the software structure of the end-user's application executing and programming environment in Vega Grid.

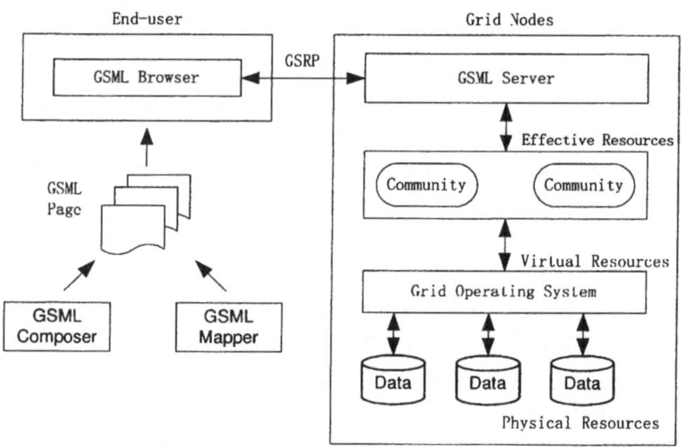

Fig. 2. Structure of End-user Programming Environment in Vega Grid

GSML Browser is designed as the interface for the end-user to access the grid resources, including browsing, programming, and executing. GSML Server is the proxy to access the grid resources. Using GSML language, the end-user creates the ".gsml" files to express his access requirement to the grid resources and through the GSML Browser and GSML Server's interpreting and referring to the grid resources, the end-user get the grid resources he needed. We aimed at satisfied most grid user's accessing requirement by this simple mode.

The research of Community and Grid Operating Systems is belong to the research of grid address space, which provide the function of grid address transform and virtual grid resource management, to provide a domain-specific resources vision to the end-user. In this way, we think it can depress the special knowledge level needed when end-user accessing and programming the grid resource. Physics resources is the real local resources distributed in the grid nodes, including grid services, web services, files, and database etc.. After organized by the Grid Operating System and Community, the resources presented in the Community are the virtual application domain-specific resources. And the resources used directly by the end-user is referenced is the GSML page, which we called effective resources.

GSRP is the message transfer protocol we developed to adopt the application model of the GSML language, which will be introduce in other paper.

GSML Composer is the tools we developed for the user to edit the ".gsml" files. It adopts the characteristic of the GSML language, to provide a familiar interface to edit, revise, and maintain the ".gsml" files to the users.

We use GSML Mapper to achieve the encapsulation, registration, lookup, and reference to the grid resources. It provides end-user the grid resources as the visible manner to access and program, which, as we think, can increase the usability and decrease the special knowledge-level needed to the end-user. In this way, the end-user would be free to concentrate on how to solve a problem rather than on how to map a solution onto the available grid resources.

A total procedure for the end user to program and execution his application includes: firstly, the end-user edit the ".gsml" files helped by the Composer and Mapper using GSML language at the grid client; after finished, the user submits the .gsml files to the GSML Server, which will interpret the .gsml files; at last, the .gsml file will be executed and the result will be shown on the GSML Browser. GSML browser will communicate with GSML server by GSRP protocol, and the user finally accesses the physical resource through the Community and GOS.

We aimed through this end-user programming environment toolkit, the user can browser, program, and instantly dynamic modify the grid resources.

3.2 End-User Programming Language

Grid Service Markup Language (GSML) is designed specially for the grid environment as the end-user programming language in Vega Grid. As we talked about above, using the markup language to realize the end-user level programming language makes the developing and programming more easily, the user's program prone to read and revise. So it satisfied the knowledge level of the ordinary users, and the requirement for fast development applications.

Based on the XML, GSML's main body is the structured data description, and gives attention to data representation. It does not contain all elements of a system programming language, but only provide the basic data representation and the join mechanism between the user, data, and service, because it does not express the detail of the computation. From the function, GSML provide an easy to use, flexible, robust approach to access, operate and integrate the all kinds of distributed grid resources.

To implement the interworking between the user and the grid resource, GSML provide the user not only read and browser, but also interactively write and operate the grid resource.

Currently, the elements of GSML can be divided into several classes.

1. File structure elements, which mark the different parts of the gsml file, include file head, file body, and file tail.

2. Data elements. In GSML, owing to the source of the data, the data processed can be divided direct data and indirect data. The direct data is the structured data contained by the file itself, such as Instant Data. The indirect data is the Reference to the outer grid resource, including file and service, which were divided by the accessing mode to the resource. The file is the readable, static grid resource. The service is the operable grid resource, which is provided as a service, includes the grid service defined by the OGSA and the web service.

3. Display elements, which control the display of the data and executing result.

4. User input elements, which process the data input interface, to get the user's input data.

5. Data processing elements, which used to represent the processing to the data, including the processing manner and processing procedure. Currently, the data processing elements include Block and Control Transition. The Block describe the processing procedure, including the concurrently processing tag: Description and the sequence processing tag: Sequence. The Control Transition represents the conditional jump routine and event driver.

Unlike HTML, which is designed for format the displayed data based on XML, GSML is mainly designed for operate the grid resource, and dynamic interactive between user and grid resource. It supports the read, write and operate the grid resource at the grid client-side.

Compared to the Server-side Script languages, such as JSP, ASP, or PHP, which is mainly interpret and execute by the server, and return the HTML formed executing result to the client-side, GSML support not only the sever-side interpret and execution, but also the client-side interprets and execution for the application program executing efficiency.

4 Conclusion

Our project aims to established technologies that will be need for ordinary users to develop applications for the Grid. We have constructed the infrastructure of the GSML runtime system, which will provide generic mechanisms for programming and execution of applications on the grid. In addition, the project has developed and defined the concept and basic elements of a Grid Service Markup language, named GSML, which is an end-user oriented programming language in grid.

We are now going to further develop our prototype. It inherits the virtue of the Web, such as easy-to-use, expansibility, etc. and redesigned to apply to the features of grid environment. In this way, it satisfied the user to access the grid resource by a simple and familiar fashion, and then support the light-weigh, fast development manner of the ordinary user. Still, we hoped that helped by our software toolkits, the user can simple and effectively finished the developing, maintaining, revising, and executing work to get the aim of improving the application productivity at whole life-cycle.

References

1. Alfredo Gutierrez, E-business on demand: A developer's roadmap. http://www-900.ibm.com/developerWorks/cn/ebod/i-ebodov/index_eng.shtml
2. Search for Extraterrestrial Intelligence. http://setiathome.ssl.berkeley.edu
3. NASA Information Power Grid. http://www.nas.nasa.gov/About/IPG/ipg.html
4. Global Grid Forum. http://www.gridforum.org
5. S. Verma, J. Gawor, etc. A CORBA commodity grid kit. In Grid 2001, November 2001
6. M. Lewis, A. Grimshaw. The Core Legion Object Model. Technical report, University of Virginia, 1995. TR CS-95-35
7. H. Nakada, S. Matsuoka, K. Seymour, etc. GridRPC: A Remote Procedure Call API for Grid Computing. http://www.eece.unm.edu/~apm/docs/APM_GridRPC_0702.pdf. 2002.7
8. Cactus Webmeister. http:// www.CactusCode.org
9. M. D. Beynon, R. Ferreira, T. Kurc, A.Sussman, etc. DataCutter: Middleware for filtering very large scientific datasets on archival storage systems. In Mass2000
10. Irving Wladawsky-Berger. Advancing e-business into the Future: The Grid. http://www.ibm.com/services/events/gridcomputing.pdf
11. Francine Berman, Andrew Chien, etc. The GrADS Project: Software Support for High-Level Grid Application Development. The International Journal of High Performance Computing Applications. 2001.9
12. C. Lee, S. Matsuoka, etc. A Grid Programming Primer. http://www.eece.unm.edu/~apm/docs/APM_Primer.0801.pdf
13. J. Ousterhout. Scripting: Higher level programming for the 21th century. IEEE Computer. March 1999

The Delivery and Accounting Middleware in the ShanghaiGrid*

Ruonan Rao, Baiyan Li, Minglu Li, and Jinyuan You

Department of Computer Science and Engineering, Shanghai Jiao Tong University, Shanghai 200030, China
{rao-ruonan,li-by,li-ml,you-jy}@cs.sjtu.edu.cn

Abstract. The ShanghaiGrid is a Grid Computing Environment (GCE) being under construction based on the Grid Service standards and technologies in Open Grid Services Architecture (OGSA). The primary motivation of the grid is to build a general, shared Information Grid Platform and to terminate the history of the case-by-case designing pattern in the development of grids. In this paper, we give a brief introduction to the concept, infrastructure, and key technologies of the ShanghaiGrid. Particularly, we focus on the introduction of the Grid Services Delivery Toolkit and the Grid Accounting Toolkit, which play an important role in the ShanghaiGrid as Grid middleware.

1 Introduction

Grid computing has been widely accepted as a promising paradigm for large-scale distributed systems in recent years [1, 2]. Although no a widely accepted agreement has been reached on the classifying of the grids, the concepts of Computational Grid, Data Grid, and Information Grid are increasingly recognized and accepted. The Computational Grid and Data Grid have received much attention in the past few years. A lot of well-known projects for Computational Grid and Data Grid, such as, TeraGrid, GIG, EUROGRID, DataGrid, and UICORE have been initiated worldwide [3, 4, 5, 6]. Quite a few open source Grid development toolkits, such as Globus Toolkit [7], and Legion [8], are developed and available over the Internet. However, the research on the Information Grid has achieved less progress although it seems to be more closed to our daily life than the Computational Grid. Furthermore, there are few development toolkits available for the Information Grid by this time.

Now, the emergence of Web Services technologies and the Open Grid Services Architecture (OGSA) [9], provide us a solid foundation and pragmatic approach to develop the Information Grid. In this approach, the information data is abstracted as accessible Grid services over the Internet. The customers of the information need not to acquire the rude data. Instead, they can access the information through standard interfaces. The standard interfaces are the

* This paper is supported by the Shanghai Science and Technology Development Foundation under Grant No. 03DZ15027.

M. Li et al. (Eds.): GCC 2003, LNCS 3032, pp. 786–793, 2004.

so-called the Grid services, which have been defined as a kind of specific Web services in the OGSA. Using the Grid services, we could build the Information Grids that can be applied in many areas such as E-government, E-education, Digital Library, etc.

In this paper, we introduce a Grid Computing Environment (GCE), the ShanghaiGrid, which is under construction using the technologies discussed above. In our context, the GCE is a set of tools and technologies that allow user "easy" access to Grid resources and applications [12]. In the past years, almost all grids were designed in a *case-by-case* pattern. This situation is due to the lacking of available tools and standards to support the design of these grids. However, in the research of the ShanghaiGrid, we are intended to adopt an original and flexible approach. In the approach, the research work is led by driving applications. We use the driving applications to evaluate the grid in the whole lifetime of the project. We will focus on the general mechanisms rather than specific techniques. So it is expected that the ShanghaiGrid would become a shared platform for various Information Grids.

As in any grid, the middleware plays an important role in shielding the heterogeneity of the components in the ShanghaiGrid. More important, the middleware provides a series of useful tools to facilitate the use of the grid. In this paper, we will introduce two distinguished middleware implemented in the ShanghaiGrid: the Grid Services Delivery Toolkit (GSDT) and the Grid Accounting Toolkit (GAT).

The rest of this paper is organized as follows. In Section 2, we give an overview of the ShanghaiGrid. In Section 3, we describe the functionalities and infrastructure of the GSDT. In Section 4, we introduce the architecture and key technologies of the GAT. Finally, we give the conclusion of this paper and the future work in Section 5.

2 An Overview of the ShanghaiGrid

The ShanghaiGrid, led by Shanghai Jiao Tong University and other partners, is a significant, Grid-related project funded by the Shanghai Science and Technology Development Foundation. The subjects to be researched in the project cover a wide range, including infrastructure, standard protocol, software, and collaboration platform. Now we give a brief introduction to some important issues of the grid.

2.1 Software Architecture

The software architecture of the ShanghaiGrid is illustrated in Fig. 1. The layers of the software are organized according to the requirements of the OGSA. The software consists of the following components:

- Resource Management
- Data Access and Transfer

- Resource Discovery and Grid Monitoring
- Data Sharing and Integration
- Grid Service Middleware
- Security Service

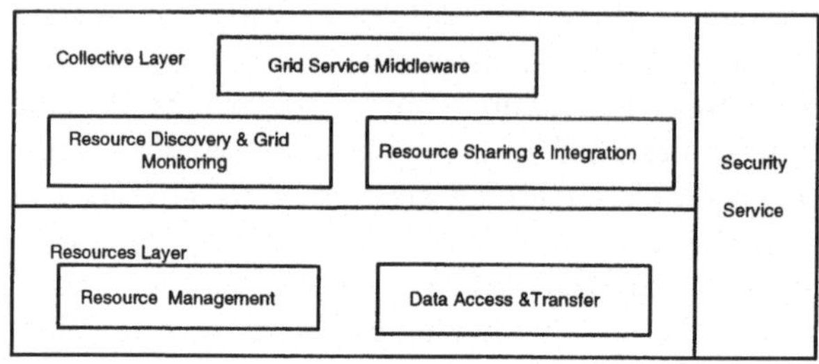

Fig. 1. The software architecture of the ShanghaiGrid

2.2 Facilities and a Driving Application

In the primary phrase, the ShanghaiGrid has 4 nodes, including a supercomputing center and 3 universities equipped with supercomputers. The nodes are connected by the China Education and Research Network (CERNET) with a transfer speed at least 100M bps.

We use a driving application, the Traffic Information System (TIS), to evaluate and test our works in the underway project. The TIS will run on the constructing grid. It collects the real-time information for traffic jam from the taxis scattered around the Shanghai city. The TIS will process the huge traffic information in real-time and give the on-demand suggestions to the drivers who are seeking their best routes to their destinations.

3 Grid Services Delivery Toolkit

The GSDT is located at the middleware layer in the software architecture of the ShanghaiGrid. It is an important tool to glue the distributed parts of a Grid-enabled application together in the GCE. It is also designed to support the major exiting Service Discovery facilities and mechanisms such as GIIS/GRIS [7], UDDI, as well as the Java Network Launching Protocol (JNLP).

3.1 Functions and Architecture

The GSDT is a tool that provides basic and additional services for the Grid-enabled applications in the ShanghaiGrid. Its principal functions are listed as following:

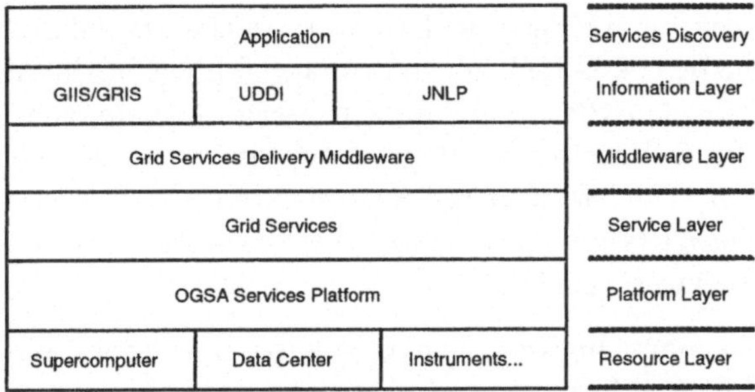

Fig. 2. The Architecture of Grid Services Discovery in the ShanghaiGrid

- Support various Service Publishing mechanisms, including the UDDI, GIIS/GRIS and the JNLP approach.
- Provide the support for the "push" as well as "pull" models for Grid Services delivery. In the "push" model, the GSDT is responsible for publishing the Grid services on a Registration Center (UDDI), a LDAP Server (GIIS/GRIS), or a Web Server (JNLP). In the "pull" model, The GSDT client could download a java program (Applet or Java application) and access Grid services via it.
- Provide APIs that facilitate the Grid services accesses. The GSDT client provides a suit of useful APIs for the cached java applications that are intended to access Grid services. For example, an API is needed to convert a Java invocation to a SOAP message.
- Provide a general mechanism supporting Grid accounting protocols. Although the GSDT has not straightforward relationship with the Grid accounting protocols, it indeed offers a suitable framework in which the later can run.
- Support various computing devices as Grid client, from the simple PDA to the complex desktop computer. Because GSDT is implemented in the Java programming language, any Java-enabled devices can act as GSDT client to access Grid services.
- Support software distribution. The GSDT fully implements the JNLP protocol that can be used to distribute the software written in Java.

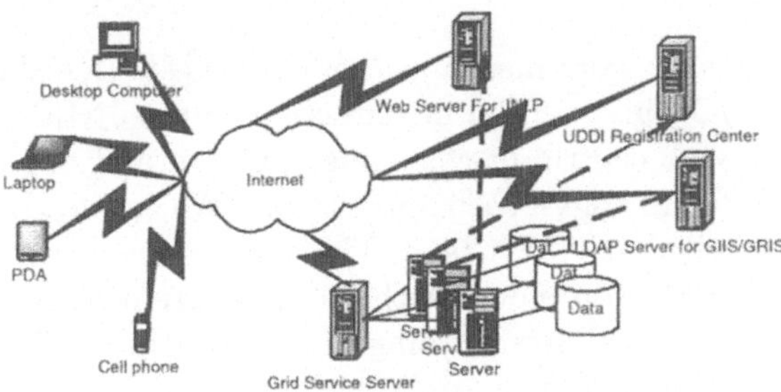

Fig. 3. The infrastructure of the GSDT

The architecture of the Services Discovery in the ShanghaiGrid is illustrated in Fig. 2. Obviously, the GSDT is the primary subject of the Middleware Layer in the architecture. On the other hand, the Fig. 3 shows the infrastructure of the GSDT. The dash lines in the diagram represent the service publishing. The client-end tools of GSDI form a full-implemented JNLP runtime environment, in addition to the APIs for Grid services. We now describe functions of GSDT through the following scenario.

1. Charles owns many high-performance supercomputers and databases that store the address information of all the firms in the city where he lives. In order to share those resources with others, he creates a telephone number query service using those resources. The service is implemented as a Grid Service, denoted TelephoneNumberQueryService. Charles then publishes the service by registration using UDDI or GIIS/GRIS mechanism implemented in GSDT.
2. Having known Charles' service available, Bob writes a JNLP-enabled application using Java to access the service. Bob's software provides user a friendly interface for telephone number querying. Then Bob publishes the application on his homepage using GSDT.
3. Alice, who wants to acquire the telephone number of some company, found Bob's application when she was browsing Bob's web using her PDA. After she clicked the icon that represents the application, her JNLP-enabled PDA automatically starts to download and launch the application.
4. After the application is launched, Alice inputs the company name and pushes the submit button.
5. Bob's application access the Charles' service with the support of GSDT, and return the result of the query to Alice's PDA.
6. After a while, Alice found her desired telephone number emerging on the screen of her PDA.

In the scenario, the Grid service is transparent for Alice. She needn't care where the service is deployed. She just submits her task, and waits for her desired results. So our scenario demonstrates the important concept of "Virtual Organization" in the GCE.

3.2 JNLP Protocol

The JNLP protocol is the core mechanism of the GSDT. In order to understand the GSDT well, we now give a brief introduction to the JNLP protocol.

The JNLP is a Web-centric provisioning protocol and application environment for the Java 2 Technology-based applications. An application implementing this specification is called a JNLP Client. The main concepts in this specification are a Web-centric application model with no installation phase, which provides transparent and incremental downloading of an application. The JNLP specification describes how to package an application and deliver it across the Internet.

The key component in the protocol is the JNLP file, which describes how to download and launch an application in a XML document. The execution environment of JNLP application includes a safe environment and a restricted environment. The restricted environment is similar to the well-known Applet sandbox, but extended with additional APIs.

4 Grid Accounting Toolkit

The accounting system is the basic component for any practical Grids [11]. Because of the heterogeneous nature of the Grid, we have to build a specific accounting middleware for the ShanghaiGrid to provide uniform accounting services, which shied the heterogeneity of various local environments.

4.1 Architecture

A Grid accounting system consists of three functionality parts: the usage information collecting system, the records processing system, and the charging system.

The Fig. 4 illustrates the architecture of the accounting system in the ShanghaiGrid. It can be noted that an accounting node has a Grid Resource Meter(GRM) and a Usage Recording Module (URM). The GRM is responsible for sensing the resource access, and creating the original usage records. The acquired usage information of various heterogeneous resources is then translated into usage records with a uniform format by the GRM. After that, the formatted records are passed to the URM where further processes will be carried on.

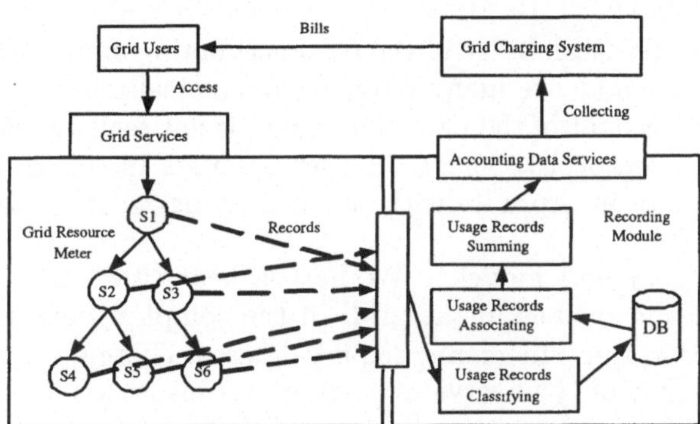

Fig. 4. The architecture of accounting system in the ShanghaiGrid

The processes of usage information consist of three sequential steps. First, the URM classifies those collected records of usage information by their types, and stores them in a database. Second, some usage records need to be associated with each other. The association of records is processed using a recursive algorithm that traces the relationships among those Grid resources. Finally, all the usage records of an access are combined into several independent records.

There are two approaches to exchange information between the URMs and the Grid Charging Subsystem (GCS). If the GCS has subscribed the Accounting

Data Service (ADS) in advance, the ADS would directly forward it to the GCS, where a sink is waiting for the information. In the other approach, the GCS simply queries the ADSs periodically. However, in both case, the usage records should be conveyed securely using XML. Using such ways, the (GCS) collects all the necessary usage records from the related nodes to charge grid users. After the charging, bills may be created and delivered to corresponding grid users.

In general, the GAT provides the accounting services in two levels. In the low level, the accounting services are presented to local systems as a suit of APIs. The local environment can invoke those APIs to process their usage records, and thereby prepare data for the high level services. The Accounting Data Services are the so-called high level services. It should be pointed that the high level accounting services are supported by the security system in the grid while the low level accounting services are not.

4.2 Key Technologies for GAT

The accounting system of the ShanghaiGrid is developed using Grid Service technologies under the OGSA framework. Unlike the traditional accounting systems, the Grid accounting systems are operated in a large-scale, open, distributed environment. Some new technologies must be adopted or developed to deal with the challenges.

- Information format. A unified format for accounting information exchange in the Grid must be specified. As a natural choice, we use the standard Extensible Markup Language (XML) as media to convey the accounting information in the grid.
- Scalability. The scalability of the Grid accounting system is a challenge for us. A grid user may use many resources dynamically in a single access. The idea to keep account of the user in all nodes is not realistic. So it is necessary to develop a protocol to share the user accounts in the grid. Furthermore, the GAT has to incorporate with the underlying security mechanism of the grid [13].
- Charging policy and model. We have a heavy task to study the charging policies and models in the grid. In the complex environment of Grids, different services providers may require different charging policies or models.
- QoS. The QoS of Grid services is an important issue in the ShanghaiGrid

5 Conclusion

In this paper, we describe the concept, framework and design of the ShanghaiGrid. As the major content of the whole paper, we present two impressive tools that play an important role in the ShanghaiGrid. Both of them can be located at the middleware layer in the software architecture of the grid. They provide the functions ranging from the Grid services delivery to the unified accounting services for the grid. Under the support of the tools and other components, the ShanghaiGrid will became a general, shared Information Grid Platform for various Grid-enabled applications.

References

1. Foster, I., Kesselman, C.(eds.).: The Grid: Blueprint for a New Computing Infrastructure. Morgan Kaufmann (1999)
2. Foster, I., Kesselman, C., Tuecke S.: The Anatomy of the Grid: Enabling Scalable Virtual Organizations. International Journal of High Performance Computing Application, **15(3)** (2001) 200–222
3. Mark, B., Rajkumar, B., Domenico, L.: Grids and Grid Technologies for Wide-Area Distrib-uted Computing. Journal of Software: Practice and Experience (to appear)
4. Leinberger, W., Kumar, V.: Information Power Grid: The new frontier in parallel comput-ing? IEEE Concurrency (1999)
5. Almond, J., Snelling, D.: UNICORE: uniform access to supercomputing as an element of electronic commerce. Future Generation Computer Systems **15** (1999) 539–548
6. Matsuoka, S.: Grid RPC meets Data Grid: Network Enabled Services for Data Farming on the Grid. First IEEE/ACM International Conference on Cluster Computing and the Grid (2001)
7. Foster, I., kesselman, C.: Globus: A Metacomputing Infrastructure Toolkit. International Journal of Supercomputer Applications, **11(2)** (1997) 115–128
8. Grimshaw, A., Wulf, W.: The Legion Vision of a Worldwide Virtual Computer. Communi-cations of the ACM **40(1)** (1999)
9. Tuecke, S., Czajkowski, K.,Foster, I., Frey, J. Graham, S., Kesselman, C., Vanderbilt, P.: Grid Service Specification. Global Grid Forum (2003)
10. Foster, I., Kesselman, C., Nick, J., Tuecke, S.: Grid Services for Distributed Systems Inte-gration. IEEE Computer **35(6)** (2002) 37–46
11. Alexander B., Rajkumar, B.: GridBank: A Grid Accounting Services Architecture (GASA) for distributed systems sharing and integration. Technical white paper of University of Melbourne (2002)
12. Fox, G., Pierce, M., Gannon, D., Thomas, M.: Overview of Grid Computing Environments. Global Grid Forum (2003)
13. Foster, I., Kesselman, C., Tsudik, G., Tuecke S.: A Security Architecture for Computational Grids. Proc. 5th ACM Conference on Computer and Communications Security Conference (1998) 83–92

Applying Agent into Web Testing and Evolution*

Baowen Xu[1,2,3], Lei Xu[1,2], and Jixiang Jiang[1,2]

[1] Department of Computer Sci. & Eng., Southeast University, Nanjing 210096, China
[2] Jiangsu Institute of Software Quality, Nanjing 210096, China
[3] Computer School, National University of Defense Technology, Changsha 410073, China
bwxu@seu.edu.cn

Abstract. Automatic Web testing and evolution is an effective method to ensure the quality of Web applications. In this paper, we apply Agent into this area, i.e. firstly, we explain the necessity and feasibility, and also give the general description of our method; then, we apply Agent into the Web performance testing, Web regression testing and Web usability evolution; conclusion remarks are given at last.

1 Introduction

With the prevalence of the Internet and the WWW, Web quality assurance becomes increasingly important [1,2,3]. This makes the testing and evolution especially important. Automatic and intelligent testing is needed so as to improve the testing efficiency.

Intelligent Agent [4,5,6] is a self-contained, autonomous software module in the distributed systems that could perform certain tasks on behalf of its users. These characters make Agent rather fit for the Internet and WWW platform, and Agent has made effective progress in Information Retrieval (IR), user personalize services, and etc [7].

Based on the previous work [3,8], the rest of this paper is organized as follows: Section 2 analyzes the necessity and the feasibility, and gives the general description of our method; in Section 3, we apply Agent into the Web performance testing, Web regression testing and Web usability evolution; conclusion remarks and future work are given in Section 4.

2 General Description

Since there are numerous of contents to be tested in the Web application, it is hard to finish these tasks without the assistant tools. Furthermore, testers are also needed in

* This work was supported in part by the National Natural Science Foundation of China (NSFC) (60073012), National Grand Fundamental Research 973 Program of China (2002CB312000), National Research Foundation for the Doctoral Program of Higher Education of China, the Opening Foundation of State Key Laboratory of Software Engineering in Wuhan University, Opening Foundation of Jiangsu Key Laboratory of Computer Information Processing Technology in Soochow University, and SEU–NARI Foundation.

M. Li et al. (Eds.): GCC 2003, LNCS 3032, pp. 794–798, 2004.

the whole process because the tools have no intelligent and cannot deal with the abnormity. If there are a certain of intelligent entities to assist the test case generation, selection, and execution, the testing efficiency will be greatly improved.

Agent has such primary behavioral attributes as autonomy, cooperation and learning. Thus we find it is possible to apply Agent into Web testing so as to improve the degree of automatization and intelligence of testing. For example, we need to obtain the accurate and effective user visiting scenes in Web performance testing and regression testing, and the main aspect of Agent application is information retrieval, so it is natural to obtain users' visiting actions through Agent and determine virtual users' actions and testing steps by multi-Agents' associations. In addition, Agents have the learning ability, and they can adjust and improve their functions due to users' feedback, so we can obtain objective and exact results in Web usability evolution.

As far as we know, we haven't seen people applying Agent into Web application testing and evolution. In order to implement the automatic retrieval of users' visiting actions and feedback information, we add the testing Agent and user Agent on the base of the general Web application architecture. We set the user Agent in every client-side and let the testing Agent do the detailed testing work. And the user Agent consists of three portions: recorder, analyzer and repository.

The information obtaining process can be described as follows: (1) While the users browse the pages, the user Agent recorder "learns" the actions taken [9]: which links were clicked, what was typed in a form, which scrollbar was dragged, and so on. Thus the Agent can distinctly record the total actions. (2) After a period of time, the Analyzer in the Agent disposes the contents of the recorder, classifies users' actions according to the different page characters. (3) After obtain the different visiting situations of different users in certain types of pages, save them in the repository in a certain sequence. This information can be used as important guidance to users' visiting scenes. (4) Update this information due to the changes of the users' visiting. So we can ensure the contents in the repository consist with the facts of user visiting.

3 Detailed Application Scenes

Now we apply Agent into the Web testing and evolution in three scenes, i.e. obtain users' visiting actions through Agent automatically so as to provide the authentic and accurate user's visiting scenes; implement the capture-replay based on Agent so as to test the often-changed Web functions; adjust the layout and information of the page based on users' feedbacks in time so as to improve the usability of Web applications.

3.1 Web Performance Testing Based on Agents

The most widely used method in Web performance testing is simulation, i.e. firstly record the real users' visiting actions, and then automatically replay these actions to the system under testing with a certain control. So the virtual users with high quality are the preconditions to ensure the effect of performance testing, and we must try our best to guarantee that the visiting effect of virtual users is consistent with the reality.

In order to gain the user visiting scenes, traditional method is using the Web mining technology to analyze the Log files, but when only the preparation for mining [10] is considered, we must do lots of work. Thus we need a more effective method.

Before we begin a performance testing to a new Web application, we should determine the virtual users' actions. The detailed method is described as follows:

(1) The testing Agent integrates and cooperates the information in the several related client-side Agents' repositories, thus we can obtain the user visiting actions in the general situations, which are adapt to most of the common users.

(2) Based on this knowledge, we determine the virtual users' visiting actions, classified by the different pages, which are distinguished by their characters.

(3) The testing Agent monitors the execution of the virtual users, making the effect of the visiting be consistent with the realities.

(4) We gain the authentic and accurate testing results of the Web performance.

3.2 Web Regression Testing Based on Agents

Users often change their requirements to the Web applications. Once the changes take place, we must retest all the existing functions to ensure the changes reach the prospective aims and not damage the previous normal functions; at the same time, new test cases are needed to test the new or modified functions. As we know, the regression testing is hard and tedious, so the assistant tools are needed.

We adapt the object-oriented recording technology to capture the testing actions for the system's functions, denoted as the testing Scripts; and when we enter the next repeated cycle, we can automatically validate the software functions by replaying these Scripts. With the help of Agents, we can carry out the regression testing more efficiently and intelligently. The detailed method is described as follows:

(1) Obtain users' visiting actions automatically in every client-side by the Agent, and the method is shown in Section 2. This step is the "capture" process.

(2) Combine the information in the repository of each user Agent, and generate the test Scripts by the testing Agent, denoted as:

$\{<t, u, d, a, dt>|\ t\in\{\text{Time}\}, u\in\{\text{URL}\}, d\in\{\text{Mouse, Keyboard, etc}\}, a\in\{\text{Click, Move, Press, etc}\}, dt\in\{\text{During Time}\}\}$

(3) Set parameters in the Scripts based on the detailed demands, and each testing case has each value. Thus we can cover all the possible situations.

(4) Under the supervision of its monitor, the testing Agent executes the test cases automatically by its executor. This is corresponding to the "replay" process.

3.3 Web Usability Evolution Based on Agents

The criterion of page's usability is not very explicit because it is a subjective concept. Paper [9] presented the usability testing method and steps. However, this method not only need testers do numerous and tedious work but also reach the usability in a general way, which cannot satisfy users' personalizing requirements.

So we consider adjusting the layout and information of the page based on users' feedback information. And the detailed process is shown in the below:

(1) Set the Agents in the relevant client-sides. These Agents are used to obtain these users' visiting actions and their usage feedback information so as to improve the Web application's usability more conveniently.
(2) Obtain the users' visiting actions by the recorder in the Agent. This step is the same with the step (1) of the method shown in Section 2.
(3) Compare and analyze the users' real actions with their general habits through the analyzer, and the main method is determining the user's fancy degree with the page due to the visiting counts and staying time.
(4) Obtain the influences to the usages due to the page changes by the Agent.
(5) Store the feedback information and consider it as the judging criterion.

Since the client-side Agent collects and analyzes the usage information of users automatically, we can determine the page's usability in the view of users and adjust the pages' contents in time based on the feedback information in the repository, thus we can provide the personalizing services to the users and improve the usability.

4 Conclusion Remarks

In order to carry through Web testing intelligently and effectively, this paper applies Agent into the Web testing and evolution. Firstly, we give the general description of the Web application testing and evolution based on Agent, which focuses on the capture-replay technology combined with Agent; then, we apply Agent into the Web performance testing, regression testing and Web usability evolution so as to improve the automatic and intelligent degree of Web testing and obtain better testing effect.

We have presented the architecture of the Web application testing and evolution based on Agent and the relevant application situations. Next, we will research on the detailed methods and steps for the Web testing and realize the system of the Web application testing and evolution based on Agent. Finally, we can put the automatic and intelligent Web testing and evolution into practice and gain ideal results.

References

1 Ricca, F. and Tonella, P.: Web Site Analysis: Structure and Evolution. Proc. of Int. Conf. on Software Maintenance (ICSM) (2000): 76-86.
2 Warren, P., Boldyreff, C., and Munro, M.: The Evolution of Websites. Proc. of the Int. Workshop on Program Comprehension (1999): 178-185.
3 Xu, L., Xu, B.W., Chen, Z.Q., and Chen, H.W.: Website Evolution Based on Statistic Data. Proc. of the 9th IEEE Int. Workshop on Future Trends of Distributed Computing Systems (FTDCS) (2003): 301-306.
4 Zhang, W.F., Xu, B.W., Xu, L., Chen, Z.Q., and Zhao, K.H.: Personalizing Search Result Using Agent. Mini-Micro System (in Chinese), 2001, 22(6): 724-727.
5 Murugesan, S.: Intelligent Agents on the Internet and Web. IEEE Region 10 Int. Conf. on Global Connectivity in Energy, Computer, Communication and Control, 1998, 1(1): 97-102.
6 Green, S., Hurst, L., Nangle, B., Cunningham, P., Somers, F., and Evans, R.: Software Agents: A Review. Technical report. Trinity Collega, Dublin, Ireland, May 1997.

7 Gao, X., and Sterling, L.: Knowledge-Based Information Agents, In the Proc. of the Pacific Rim Conf. on Intelligent Information Agents (PRIIA) (2000): 48-58.
8 Xu, L., Xu, B.W., Chen, H.W., Chu, W., Lin, J.M., and Yang, H.J.: Test Web applications based on Agent. Journal of Software, 2003,14(Suppl.): 9-16.
9 Krulwich, B.: Automating the Internet: Agents as User Surrogates. IEEE Internet Computing, 1997, 1(4): 34-38.
10 Cooley, R., Mobasher, B., and Srivastava J.: Data Preparation for Mining World Wide Web Browsing Patterns. Knowledge and Information Systems, 1999, 1(1): 5-32.

Experiences on Computational Program Reuse with Service Mechanism

Ping Chen [1,2], Bin Wang [2], Guoshi Xu [2], and Zhuoqun Xu [2]

[1] Computer Center, Peking University, Beijing, 100871
[2] Network and Information Institute, School of Information Science & Technology, Peking University, Beijing, 100871
{pchen, wangbin, xuguoshi, zqxu}@pku.edu.cn

Abstract. Grid technology changes the scientific computing mode. In our computational program reuse framework, scientists only need to specify which computational service to use and provide the location of raw data and computing results. All the other works are done automatically. "A computational service" is the key concept that is an abstract of multiple programs that realize the same function. This paper introduces the technical problems and solutions in this area which consist of program reuse mechanism, detailed information getting, computing resource decision, running environment preparation and restoration, remote program starting up and management. The information service tool and the resource management tool of Globus Toolkit provide supports to some problems. The last part of the paper discusses our understanding to grid scientific computation and the predicted works.

1 Introduction

Grid technology is changing the scientific computing mode. Scientists only need to specify which computational service to use and provide the location of raw data and computing results. All the other works are completed automatically. Suppose data is provided by scientists, the key technical problem for automatic running is to execute a user-satisfied computational program at a user-satisfied computer in a user-visible progress. This process includes reusing computational program, getting information of data and running environment, computing resource decision, running environment preparation and restoration, remote program starting up and running management.

This paper reports our experiences on this. Here, the precondition is one computational program is only deployed and to run on one computing resource without considering resource co-allocation. Next section, related researches and projects are introduced. In section 3, we discuss the key technical problems and solutions to computational program reuse. The fourth part introduces our understanding to Globus Toolkit. Finally it will be given our opinion to support computation on grid environments.

M. Li et al. (Eds.): GCC 2003, LNCS 3032, pp. 799–802, 2004.

2 Related Researches and Projects

To our knowledge, currently, the researches concerned with computing on grid environment mainly concentrate on grid programming and a program running over multiple wide-area computing resources. Based on Configurable Object Program and Performance Contract, GrADS[4] project focuses on grid program coding, debugging and running. Program's adaptability to unreliable, heterogeneous, dynamically changing grid environment is emphasized here. MPICH-G2[5] is a wide area network MPI implementation. It is well adopted by many grid computation supporting projects one of which is Cactus-G. The Cactus-G[7] project supports legacy computational codes to run across wide area network without any modification. Application developers use the same APIs, *thorns* in his words. Transparent to them, the running environment supports the thorns to run over wide area network. The communication among different parts of the program is supported by MPICH-G2. The research goal of the Albatross[6] project is to support parallel computation to run over multiple clusters. The communication interface among different clusters is MagPIe[8] which is an optimizing version of MPI and is more efficient than MPICH-G2.
Our research is also to support computing on grid. But instead of helping a program to run across wide area network, our interests focus on how to run currently available and mature computations on separated grid resource and how to relieve scientists from works other than scientific research.

3 Technical Problems and Solutions to Computational Program Reuse

In computational program reuse, a computational service is an important concept that is a standard abstract to multiple computational programs that fulfill the same function. It hides hosting computers, running environments, and program implementations from computational users. A service provider writes, debugs, and tests programs on specified computers with one computer deployed one program, configures the running environments, and publishes the service interface through the running support platform. The deployed program can be executed at any time. Users interact with a service interface to do computation. After receiving a service request, the running support selects a suitable computer and starts up the deployed program. The information service[2] and resource management[3] of Globus Toolkit provide basic support .
In running support of computational program reuse, key technical problems consist of getting detailed descriptive information of data and resource requirements, computing resource decision, running environment preparation and restoration, and remote program starting up and management. This section introduces our experiences in detail.

3.1 Getting Detailed Information of Data and Resource Requirements

Computing resource decision requires grid-recognizable requirements. This information comes from two sources: users and the running support. User-provided information is got from a service request. The compulsory part for every service interface includes, data information (scale, type, etc.), the raw data and result data files' URI(s) and program running arguments. The optional information includes running progress feedback demand, special requirements to running environment, resource decision criteria (such as , CPU first, memory first, I/O first, etc). The running support analyzes, calculates this information and complements insufficient ones. One example is to get memory and disk requirements on user-provided data scale and type. Another example is to complement grid-concerned information such as CPU busy rate.

3.2 Computing Resource Decision

The goal of information analyses and complement in the previous section is grid middleware-useable. The simplest solution for computing resource decision is to match this information with the resource information and deployed computational program information sustained by Globus information service. The latter is an extension to MDS[2]'s basic information. Decision criterion provided by users can instruct the process to some extent. More complex solution includes referring to resource allocation history, to get more accurate resource performance and others.

3.3 Running Environment Preparation and Restoration

In the simplified working mode, the hosting computer of a program is determined dynamically. To ensure computational services serve well and have no side effects to other users of the sharing resource, it is indispensable to prepare the running environment before a program running and restore after it. Preparation is to load raw data to site, create temporary working space, and others. The restoring process is to move the result data to the specified location, release space and restore the environment.

3.4 Remote Program Starting Up and Management

GRAM[3] supports to start up a resource-deployed program. The running management of a remote program is to know the running situation and control when necessary. It can be realized at different levels. GRAM provides job scheduling state monitoring and controlling. But users prefer running progress feedback that is measured by the running percentage and the left time. This function needs supports from inside program codes to output relating information to its stdout. The running support transfers program's stdout to user's console transparently. If a user wants to control the running program, user's input has to be transferred to the program's stdin. GASS[1] supports stdout redirection. We complemented the runtime stdin to the kernel of GRAM that originally only supports stdin pre-stage.

4 Conclusion

The grid environment computational program reuse is one of the on-going researches of Net. & Info. Tech. Inst., School of Info. Sci. & Tech., Peking Univ. Our opinion is on current stage, it is feasible and practical to support a mature computational program to run on a grid resource instead of over multiple ones. This paper introduces a solution to it. It separates program debugging and using. One program needs only to be written and test run once. After deployed, everyone else can use it directly without knowing each other. Scientists will not be bothered by where to run their computation and how to make it run any more. Just use it. Done. Another on-going research is to support complex computations that are composed of multiple independent computing tasks with data dependency or concurrent relationships among them to run on grid. A task acts as a computational service user introduced in this paper. The performance and robustness of the complex computation running support is our major goal.

References

[1] J. Bester, I. Foster, C. Kesselman, J. Tedesco, S. Tuecke. GASS: A Data Movement and Access Service for Wide Area Computing Systems. Sixth Workshop on I/O in Parallel and Distributed Systems, May 5, 1999.

[2] K. Czajkowski, S. Fitzgerald, I. Foster, C. Kesselman.Grid Information Services for Distributed Resource Sharing. Proceedings of the Tenth IEEE International Symposium on High-Performance Distributed Computing (HPDC-10), IEEE Press, August 2001.

[3] K. Czajkowski, I. Foster, N. Karonis, C. Kesselman, S. Martin, W. Smith, S. Tuecke. A Resource Management Architecture for Metacomputing Systems, Proc. IPPS/SPDP '98 Workshop on Job Scheduling Strategies for Parallel Processing, pg. 62-82, 1998.

[4] F. Berman, A. Chien, K. Cooper, J. Dongarra, I. Foster, D. Gannon, L. Johnsson, K. Kennedy, C. Kesselman, J. M. Crummey, D. Reed, L. Torczon, R. Wolski, The GrADS Project: Software Support for High-Level Grid Application Development.

[5] I. Foster, N. Karonis. A Grid-Enabled MPI: Message Passing in Heterogeneous Distributed Computing Systems. Proc. 1998 SC Conference, November, 1998.

[6] Thilo Kielmann, Henri E. Bal, Jason Maassen, Rob van Nieuwpoort, Ronald Veldema, Rutger Hofman, Ceriel Jacobs, Kees Verstoep, The Albatross Project: Parallel Application Support for Computational Grids.

[7] Gabrielle Allen, Thomas Dramlitsch, Ian Foster, Tom Goodale, Nick Karonis, Matei Ripeanu, Ed Seidel, Brian Toonen, Cactus-G: Enabling High-Performance Simulation in Heterogeneous Distributed Computing Environments.

[8] Thilo Kielmann, Rutger F.H. Hofman, Henri E. Bal, Aske Plaat, and Raoul A.F. Bhoedjang: MagPIe: MPI's Collective Communication Operations for Clustered Wide Area Systems, Proc. Seventh ACM SIGPLAN Symposium on Principles and Practice of Parallel Programming (PPoPP'99), pp. 131-140, Atlanta, GA, May 4-6, 1999.

Research and Implementation of the Real-Time Middleware in Open System*

Jian Peng [1,2], Jinde Liu [2], and Tao Yang [2]

[1] School of Computer, Sichuan University, Chengdu, 610065, P.R.China
penguest@163.com

[2] School of Computer, University of Electronic Science and Technology of China, Chengdu
jdliu@uestc.edu.cn

Abstract. In the paper, a technical discussion and the implementation of real-time middleware are presented. After introduction of characteristics of open system and current researches on real-time open system, the real-time middleware is proposed to build an open system with real-time attribute. Based on real-time CORBA specification, the key technology of the real-time middleware is discussed in detail. It includes the technology of the real-time POA, the real-time ORB, thread pools, multiplexing and demultiplexing and presentation layer optimizations etc. And then the real-time performance experiments show that the implementation (rtORB) is capable of supporting real-time application. According to the analysis, a conclusion that real-time middleware provides a feasible method to build real-time open system is made.

1 Introduction

The open system is very popular in today's IT world, though the definitions of open system are not consistent or precise, it has some recognized characteristics, that is, (1) Portability; (2) Interoperability; (3) Scalability; (4) Availability.[3] we notice there are much more efforts made on interoperability attribute than on the real-time attribute. With the increasing expansion of real-time applications' arena, it is necessary to conduct research on how to build an open system with real-time attribute. In this paper, the authors explore the fusion of being open and real-time at the same time; conduct research on the key technology of real-time middleware in open system.

2 The Real-Time Policy in the Open System

Real-Time attribute is the new attribute for open system. The directions in the research can be divided into three schemes as the follows:

(1) Middleware solution

The solution has been proposed by those people dealing with open system for a long time. Basing their research on the open system solution, they adopt real-time

* Supported by Nation Defense Fund (41315010103) and The youth Fund of SCU

M. Li et al. (Eds.): GCC 2003, LNCS 3032, pp. 803–808, 2004.

extension to support the requirement. The earliest research is the ANSAware/RT carried out by APM.[2]

(2) Real-time scheduling solution

The solution is proposed by those people who deal with real-time scheduling mechanism. They want to construct real-time open system on the basis of new scheduling mechanism. One famous and representative research is described in reference [5] in which one open environment to deal with real-time application is implemented by two-level schedule in Windows NT core.

(3) Real-time QoS solution

The solution is raised by DAPA[7] . The solution incorporates the QoS mechanism into middleware and provides necessary resources to real-time applications by the flexible mechanism.

All the solutions mentioned above discuss the real-time attributes in open system from different perspectives, but all solutions are not complete because they do not investigate real-time in relation to open system. We can conclude that the right way to solve real-time problem in open system is to use real-time middleware supported by real-time scheduling and real-time QoS.

3 Research on the Key Technology of Real-Time Middleware in Open System

CORBA middleware takes the lead in the middleware field. The Fixed Priority Real-time CORBA Model shown in Figure 1. To guarantee the global real-time features, each component in Figure 1 should support real-time.

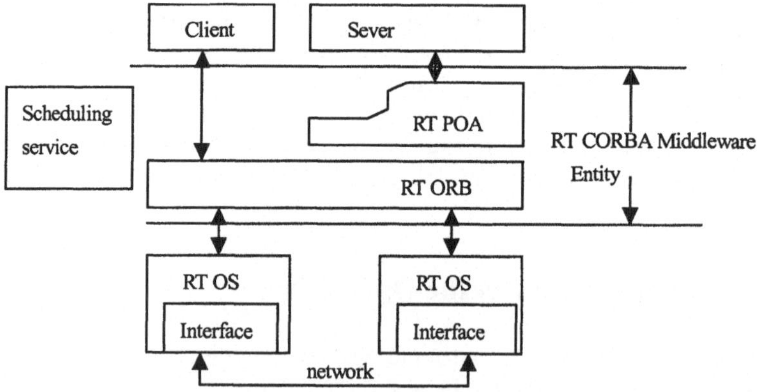

Fig. 1. RT CORBA Model

3.1 Design of the Application Interface for Real-Time ORB Endsystem

The real-time ORB endsystem is the base on which to offer an overall end-to-end guarantee of performance for the activity in the real-time application. It needs to provide appropriate application interface by which the application can specify the timing constraints such as deadline, periods, executing time, importance etc. It also provides a mechanism to bind the client and server explicitly and to permit user to specify the network protocol. Explicit binding is the mechanism by which user can set up the connection in advance before the operation [4]

3.2 Configure of Thread Pools for the Real-Time Application in the ORB

Compared to the ORB in existing CORBA, the special component in the ORB of real-time CORBA is thread pools, which serve as a flexible multi-thread service provider. When there are few applications (or activities), the prepared threads can deal with them one to one; when there are some applications, the thread pools can use the standby threads to provide service; when there are a lot of applications, the pools can borrow threads to supplement service; when there are overload applications, the threads have to wait in the buffer queues because the pools can not provide enough threads for applications.

3.3 Selection of the Connection of C/S in the ORB

A non-real-time CORBA system emphasizes efficiency rather than the timing constraints, so it usually uses the multiplexing connection technology, which uses one connection for several requests by multiplexing and demutiplexing. But if we use the multiplexing connection technology in real-time CORBA system, many requests of different levels of priorities may be transferred in one connection, so priority reversions easily take place. To solve the problem, a high-level measure needs to be constructed so that the client can select the appropriate C/S connection.

3.4 The POA for Real-Time Application

Although not mandated in the standard, most real-time CORBA implementations will keep persistent servers so that servers are always active; A CORBA server use one or more POAs to manage the CORBA objects. The server uses information in the request to find the appropriate POA to dispatch the servant to handle the request. The POA policies listing below can allow the POA to make specific dispatching decisions. [1] (a) Thread configuration RT CORBA POA policy; (b) Server Priority RT CORBA POA Policy; (c) Communication Protocols RT CORBA POA Policy.

3.5 The Scheduling Service for the Real-Time CORBA System

The end-to-end real-time applications in RT CORBA have the timing restraints, so they need the support of the real-time scheduling mechanism by which the activities or applications can be controlled. It is known that the algorithm or the scheduling policy decides the performance of real-time application. Currently, there are static and dynamic scheduling mechanisms, and there is a lot of algorithm such as EDF.

3.6 The Optimization for the Presentation Layer

In CORBA system, the requests from clients are translated into operation with parameters by stub. The operations and the parameters are marshaled by stub, and are transferred to server through the network. When the packages come to the server, they need to be demarshaled to up-call object implementation. After the task execution, the results need to return to the client, and then the results will be marshaled and demarshaled again, so the process costs much time. To solve the problem, the presentation layer including the dynamic memory and data coping optimizations needs to be optimized. [6]

3.7 Real-Time Operation System Support for the Real-Time CORBA

To real-time application, the activities of the underlying operation system are shielded by ORB, but in fact, the execution of the real-time application must need the operation system support. For example, the priority of real-time CORBA application must be mapped to the priority of local operation system. Therefore, we need to select the appropriate real-time operation system, which should have the ability of multi thread management and the ability to specify the priority and the scheduling policy.

4 The Implementation and the Real-Time Performance Test

According to the above analysis, our implementation of real-time CORBA is the rtORB. We simplify the rtORB without the real-time DII (dynamic invocation interface) and DSI (dynamic skeleton interface).

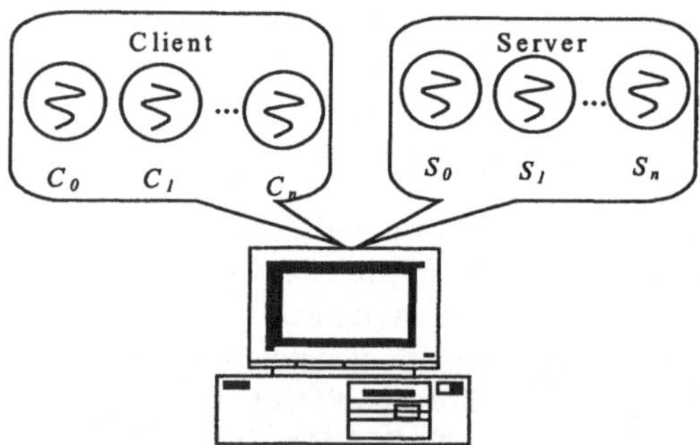

Fig. 2. Real-time performance test system

To evaluate the real-time performance of rtORB, we construct the real-time test system shown in Figure 2 according to the methods described in reference [8,9]. And the client and the server are located in the same host to minimize the chance of priority inversion, which may be caused by TCP protocol. The server process includes a servant, whose priority (P_h) is the highest one, and several(n) low priority servants(S_1, S_2,..., S_n), whose priority (P_l) is same. Each servant corresponds to a thread. The client process includes threads such as C_0, C_1, C_2,..., C_n. The priority of C_0, *is* P_h, *other threads* C_1~C_n priority is P_l. The request of C_i is dealt with by S_i. The frequency of C_0 request is 20HZ, that is, there are 20 bi-directional requests every second. The frequency of other clients (C_1~C_n) request is 10HZ, that is, there are 10 bi-directional requests every second. Every process sends a float to the corresponding servant thread, after the servant receives the float, cube calculation will be done 1000 times, and then the results return.

TAO has a good real-time performance, so we test rtORB in comparison to the TAO. Our testes run on Solaris system. As in the reference [8,9], The test focus on the delay and delay jitter, the test results are shown in Figure 3 and Figure 4 respectively.

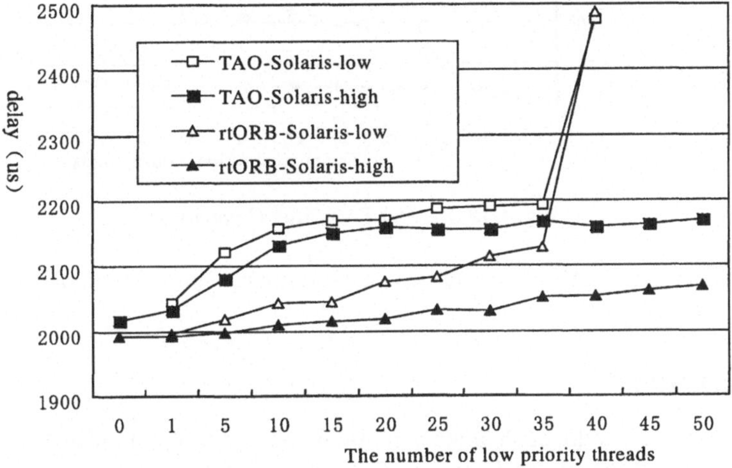

Fig. 3. rtORB and TAO Delay Comparison

The delay change of the high priority client in TAO and rtORB are both small, it shows the high priority client in rtORB and TAO has good real-time performance. Compared to each other, the delay change of TAO is better than that of rtORB especially when the low priority client number exceeds 50.

The delay of low priority client of TAO and rtORB increases with the number of the clients. Especially when the low priority client exceeds 40, the increase of the delay is obvious. We conclude that in the system the memory (64M) is too small to provide enough space for a lot of threads, so a part of threads in the memory need to be replaced to virtue memory. Most of the replaced threads are the low priority threads, so the delay of low priority clients increases quickly.

The change of the delay jitter is shown in Figure 4. We can conclude that the high priority client delay jitter changes little (<500us) with the number of the low priority client. It shows that the TAO and rtORB have good predictability. But the delay jitter of low priority clients changes obviously, especially when the number of low priority clients exceeds 45, we conclude the reason is that a part of threads need to be replaced out of memory.

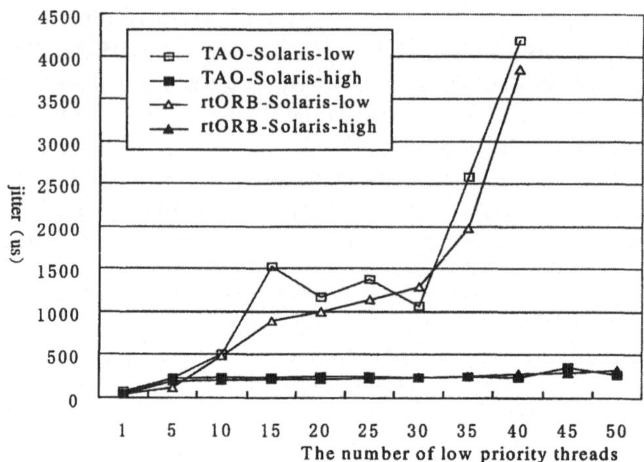

Fig. 4. rtORB and TAO Jitter Comparison

In summary, the real-time performance experiments show that rtORB is capable of supporting real-time application.

5 Conclusion

In this paper, we conduct a detailed and systematical discussion of real-time CORBA specification and the key technology of real-time CORBA, which provides a viable method and research for open system real-time extension.

References

1. Victor Fay-Wolfe, et al., Real -Time CORBA, IEEE Trans. on Parallel and Distributed Systems Vol.11 No. 10, 2000
2. Guangxing Li. "An Overview of Real-Time ANSAware 1.0". ANSA Phase 3 Project Report APM.1285.01 ,March 1995.
3. LIU Jinde, Clarification for the connotation of open system, Computer Application, 1997.6
4. D.C. Schmidt, An Overview of the Real-time CORBA Specification, IEEE Computer special issue on Object-Orient Real-Time Distributed Computing, Vol. 33 No.6, 2000
5. Zhong Deng, et al., An Open Environment for Real-Time Applications, Real-Time Systems Journal, 1998
6. Irfan Pyarali, et al., Applying Optimization Principle Patterns to Real-Time ORBs, the 5th USENIX COOTS'99, 1999.5
7. DARPA. "The Quorum Program". http://www.darpa.mil/ito/research/quorum/ index.html. 1999
8. David Levine, Douglas C. Schmidt, and Sergio Flores-Gaitan. An Empirical Evaluation of OS Support for Real-time CORBA Object Request Brokers[C]. Proceedings of the Multimedia Computing and Networking 2000 (MMCN00) Conference, ACM, San Jose, CA, Jan. 2000
9. Douglas C. Schmidt, Sumedh Mungee. Software Architectures for Reducing Priority Inversion and Non-determinism in Real-time Object Request Brokers[J]. Journal of Real-time Systems, 2001, 21(1-2)

An Object-Oriented Petri Nets Based Integrated Development Environment for Grid-Based Applications

Hongyi Shi and Aihua Ren

School of Computer Science and Engineering, BeiHang University
No. 37, Xueyuan Road, Haidian, Beijing, 100083, China
shi_hongyi@sina.com, renah@buaa.edu.cn

Abstract. The Object-Oriented Petri Nets (OOPN) based integrated solution to a grid-based application system modeling and enacting is proposed in this paper for simplifying designs and developments of the grid-based applications. An Integrated Development Environment is also provided to support the methodology proposed. Visual modeling to the system can be made by using OOPN to give a reliable system structure. Computing resources can be dispatched reasonably in terms of basic services of a grid-computing platform. Since the user requirement described in OOPN is an operational system requirement, as soon as the user creates the requirement model in OOPN, the grid-based application program can be generated automatically and executed actually on a grid system. The safe and reliable system structure can be obtained after getting through the deadlock detection.

1 Introduction

Grid computing[1] enables the virtualization of distributed computing and data resources such as processing, network bandwidth and storage capacity to create a single system image, granting users and applications seamless access to vast IT capabilities.

However, recent projects and researches on grid computing focus on grid infrastructure, which providing the most essential functions. As grid computing is a kind of distributed computing pattern[2], the reliability of system, consistency and indeterminacy of resource accessing need be solved effectually. But it needs very special programming skill to solve these problems in a traditional describing way. The general users need spend much effort on mastering concurrent programming technology. Executing a grid-based application software is another difficulty because executing a grid-based application software always needs too many configure operations. It will prevent a great deal of general users from joining in grid computing if executing a grid-based application only through the interface of command line. If there is a visual Integrated Development Environment to help them develop and run grid-based applications, it will attract more and more people to use grid resources.

In order to overcome the difficulties mentioned above, we propose the Object-Oriented Petri Nets (OOPN) based Integrated Development Environment to support grid-based application system development. OOPN is a high-level Petri net which

M. Li et al. (Eds.): GCC 2003, LNCS 3032, pp. 809–812, 2004.

combines the Object-Oriented idea with traditional Petri net, and is suitable for complicated concurrent and distributed system description. The visual OOPN is not only the base of system modeling, but also an effective system enacting solution[3].

There are many projects on researching grid computing around the world right now. Some of most influential projects are Globus[4] , Condor[5] , Legion[6]. The Globus project gains more and more attention, and becomes a leading grid platform and developing tool. The Globus Toolkit is used as test-bed in our research.

This paper is organized as follows. Section 2 introduces the basic concept of OOPN and the grid computing infrastructure——Globus Toolkit. Section 3 introduces the two-level programming pattern and the implement scheme of compiling and running tools. Section 4 is conclusions of the paper.

2 Basic Concept

2.1 OOPN

Object-Oriented Petri Net(OOPN) is a high-level Petri net which combines the Object-Oriented idea and traditional Petri net. It divides up a Petri net into some simple subnets and composite subnets. The composite subnet comprises several simple subnets and composite subnets, and can describe concurrent status. The subnets of a composite subnet are connected by gate, which is a special transition. In addition, the message queue, a special place, is the communicative window of subnets. The transition in a simple subnet can embed java code to explain its activation condition and firing process.

We have much experience on concurrent and distributed software developing based on OOPN. We have developed OOPN based Integrated Development Environment (OOPN-IDE) for concurrent software and mobile agent system[7][8].

2.2 Globus Toolkit

The Globus Project is one of the most important projects related to grid computing around the world right now. Globus Toolkit, the globus project's open source software, includes software services and libraries for resource monitoring, discovery, and management, plus security and file management. The Globus Toolkit makes it easier to build computational grids.

At the same time, the Globus Project focuses on providing the most essential functions. So users need to master the software architecture and almost all the APIs of the Globus Toolkit to develop a grid-based application software, which is very difficult for the general users. If we model a system with OOPN, the detail of the Globus Toolkit is encapsulated. Then users need not master the complicated architecture and the numerous APIs and need not care of reliability of system. All the users need to do is modeling with OOPN and entered Java code into transitions.

3 The Design and Implement of IDE

3.1 The Two-Level Programming Pattern

The two-level programming pattern describes a grid-based application in two levels. At the high level (job level), OOPN is used as modeling language to model a grid-based application. OOPN acts as the designing method and run-time controlling scheme. At the low level (task level), users can enter code into the transitions of the simple subnets to describe a concrete job. Every subnet will be compiled and submitted as a Grid computing job to a grid node to execute.

3.2 The Compiling Tool

The compiling tool is developed to convert an OOPN model to a grid-based application system.

The compiling process: The grid-compiling tool reads the OOPN model and creates a configure file and several java source files. The configure file is an XML file which includes information of the environment requirement and resource assigning status. The java source files are java class files which are created according to the subnets of OOPN model. Every java source file describes the structure and behavior of a subnet.

3.3 The Simulating Tool

In the simulating tool, every subnet of OOPN is not submitted to a remote grid node, but running as a java thread. During the simulating process, we can detect dead-lock dynamically: dead-lock exists if no transition is fired in a given interval.

With the simulating tool, users can find out defects before a system runs truly and try their best to assign resources rationally. This avoids reassigning resources after a system runs truly and wasting time, material and other resources.

3.4 The Running Tool

In order to support configuring and running the grid-based applications automatically, the running tool is developed to reduce users' environment configuring tasks. The running tool read and parse the configure file, and submit the subnets to the correct grid nodes according to the configure file.

Here we make use of the Index Service, Reliable File Transfer Service, Managed Job Factory Service and Notification mechanism of the Globus Toolkit. The running tool can query resources according to environment requirement through the Index service, transfer the executable programs to the correct grid node through the Reliable File Transfer service, submit jobs to the correct grid node through the GRAM service, and obtain the status of the job through the Notification mechanism. The running tool will reassign resource and submit the job according to the configure file when the running tool is notified that a job is failed.

4 Conclusion

Grid computing is one of the best solutions for resource sharing in dynamical, multi-institutional virtual organizations. But Grid computing brings up some programming difficulties to grid-based application developers. This paper proposes one solution: the Object-Oriented Petri Nets based Grid-based Application Integrated Development Environment. In this solution, two-level programming pattern is adopted to convert the OOPN model to executable programs. A running tool is developed to support configuring and running the grid-based applications automatically and reduce users' environment configuring tasks. All these will attract more and more people to use grid resources.

References

1. I. Foster, C. Kesselman, S. Tuecke: The Anatomy of the Grid: Enabling Scalable Virtual Organization. International J. Supercomputer Applications (2001) 15(3). Also in: Cluster Computing and the Grid (2001). Proceedings. First IEEE/ACM International Symposium on (2001) 6-7
2. Zhihui Du, Yu Chen, Peng Liu. Grid Computing. Tsinghua University Press (2002)
3. Aihua Ren: Research of An Object-Oriented Petri Nets Based Developing Method for Concurrent Software. PhD Thesis, BeiHang University (2001)
4. Globus Project. http://www.globus.org
5. Condor Project. http://www.cs.wisc.edu/condor/
6. Legion Project. http://legion.virginia.edu
7. Jinzhong Niu: Research and Implementation of An OO Petri Nets Based Integrated Development Environment for Concurrent Software, Master Thesis, BeiHang University (1999)
8. Aihua Ren, Hui Jiao, Yunfeng Sun: Modeling Mobile Agent with Object-Oriented Petri Net. ACTA AERONAUTICA ET ASTRONAUTICA SINICA. Vol.24 No.1 (Sum No.182) (2003) 57-61.

Some Views on Building Computational Grids Infrastructure

Bo Dai [1, 2], Guiran Chang [1], Wandan Zeng [1], Jiyue Wen [1], and Qiang Guo [1]

[1] College of Information Science & Engineering, Northeastern University, post code 110004, Shenyang, Liaoning, PR, China
Daibo33511@163.com, change@neu.edu.cn, zengdd@neusoft.com
[2] College of Computer Science & Engineering, Liaoning Institute of Technology, post code 121001, Jinzhou, Liaoning, PR, China

Abstract. This paper gives some opinions about grid bottleneck problem, and makes some suggestions about grid structure. It also introduces how to construct the global grid with sub grids, and to make use of the advantages of administrative hierarchy. The paper presents the conceptions of static resources, dynamic resources and the ways of scheduling resources. Also, the functions of resource marketplace are discussed. Finally, we describe the relationship, function and structural the principle of virtual organizations.

1 Some Views on the Improvement of Grid Structure

There are bottleneck problems [10] not only in five-layer hourglass architecture but also in OGSA (Open Grid Services Architecture) [8]. It cannot be settled only by middleware. Some changes are needed in grid structure [4].

Because of the heterogeneity and scalability of grid structure, it makes us have to use Internet administration mode to build grid organizations. We could change local networks into local grids, namely sub-grids, and then link these sub grids together.

Each sub grid can be looked as a node. They can be connected to form a global grid [7]. A grid management server should be set in the sub grid. It is good to make use of local network servers. The globus is run on it. The users access sub grids through web pages.

Administrative hierarchy is used in them. Firstly, schedule of tasks and resources are carried on in a sub grid. If there are not enough resources, the task can be scheduled between other sub grids. It can be handed up global grid and apply for new resources.

In order to translate protocols between sub grids, "half gateway" should be set on each node. We can use XML to do it.

Taking administrative hierarchy could reduce the remote communication, which can decrease remote access, remote replica catalog and error in communication. It can avoid restriction of network bandwidth, and resolve the bottleneck problem with the integrated schedule management system. It is convenient to change and expand grid structure.

M. Li et al. (Eds.): GCC 2003, LNCS 3032, pp. 813–816, 2004.

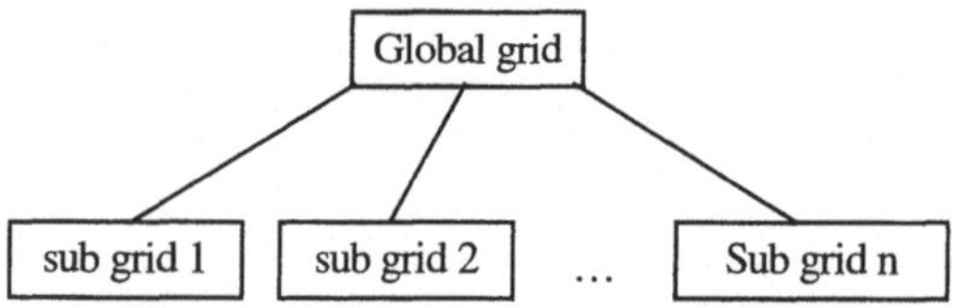

Fig. 1. Global organization structure

Grid should be built on Internet based on TCP/IP and take advantage of benefits of Internet in communication and security mechanism[5].

Because of using present Internet structure, they need not to make any change in topology of networks. Users are willing to accept and join grid virtual organizations.

Currently, grids are only found in several famous universities, national key laboratories and computing centers [1]. Thousands of common PC users are ignored. Now, the speed and capacity of PCs can compare with those of small type computers before. These vast amounts of resources should not be ignored. It is the great demanded by the great number of common PC users for computing resources that will open up a wonderful prospect for computational grids in the future. So did Internet. It is necessary to change local networks into sub-grids and to treat them as the bottom layer of global grids.

2 Some Views on the Improvement of Resource Management

It is possible for us to classify resources into two kinds: static resources and dynamic resources. Static resources include data, documents, programs etc. dynamic resources include CPU time, entities, processes, variable parameters etc.

Static resources can be managed by catalogue mode. Dynamic resources management adopts broadcast query mode, because they are random. Scheduling resource takes "nearby "principle. It can decrease communication largely and increase the access speed.

The integrated task management system is adopted within a sub grid. A server on the node schedules the tasks.

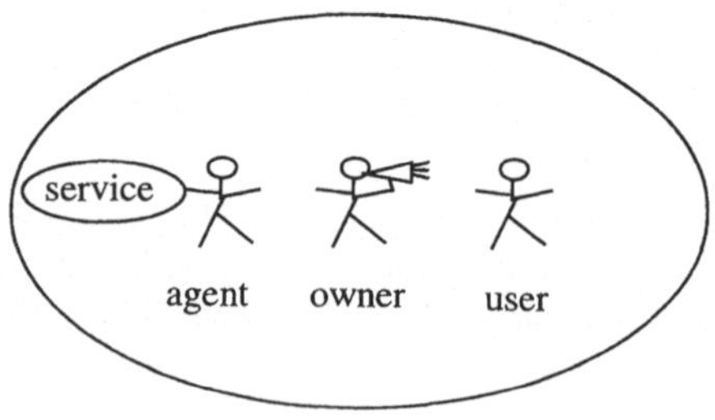

Fig. 2. Resource marketplace

Distributed task management system is adopted among sub grids. Through brokers of marketplaces, connections between users and resources can be realized [2].

The relationship between service owner and service consumer is codified through a service contract. This contract specifies the terms and conditions under which the owner agrees to provide the services to the consumers. The precise structure of a contract will depend upon the nature of the service and the relationship between the owner and the provider. However examples of relevant attributes include the price for invoking the service, the information the consumer has to provide to the provider, the expected output from the service, an indication about when this output can be expected, and the penalty for failing to deliver according to the contract [9].

The service owners and service producers interact with one another in a particular environmental context. The particular environment will be called a marketplace. Each owner-consumer interaction takes place in a given marketplace whose rules are set by the market owner [3].

Marketplaces should be able to be established by any agent in the system. The entity, which establishes the marketplace, is here termed the market owner. The owner is responsible for setting up, advertising, controlling and disbanding the marketplaces. In order to establish a marketplace, the owner needs a representation scheme for describing the various entities that are allowed to participate in the marketplace, a means of describing how the various allowable entitled are allowed to interact with one another in the context of the marketplace, and what monitoring mechanisms are to be put in place to ensure the marketplaces rules are adhered to [9].

3 Some Views on the Relationship of Virtual Organizations

In grids, a lot of users, resources and entities need to be managed by virtual organizations. Also, all kinds of agents and many resource marketplaces need to be managed by virtual organizations [8]. A user can take part in different virtual organizations. And a resource can be managed by different virtual organizations.
Every virtual organization has its rules and regulations that should be obeyed by all participants. There should be registry in every virtual organization. A participant can apply for joining or exiting from an organization at anytime he wants. For example, an entity will exit automatically from its virtual organization when it finishes its task. In virtual organization, an agent can be designated as the monitor and responsible for registering and monitoring.

Every virtual organization should have the functions of advertising and security authenticating. At the same time there should be communication and interaction ability among different virtual organizations. And they need a common communication language.

Virtual organizations (VO) are different both from classification and level. The superior VO can call the functions of the lower VO unconditionally. The lower VO can inherit some attributes of the superior VO. Different functions can also be scheduled among VOs. They can be conjugated as an alliance grid [6] to finish a large scale task. The processes of task scheduling and resource assignment in VOs are transparent for users.

A virtual organization can be established or revoked, which should be confirmed and registered by superior VOs. And a virtual organization that has no member for a long time would be cancelled.

In fact, computational grid itself is a large virtual organization. When it works efficiently, users could make use of the vast computing resources transparently as they use electric power.

4 Conclusion

In the paper, we have presented a grid structure that use sub grids to connect a global grid. And it describes mode of scheduling resources and management. Moreover, we have discussed the functions of marketplaces. It is important to connect service providers with service consumers by agents for service-oriented architectures. Finally, some opinions are given on relationship, functions and structural principles of virtual organizations.

References

1. William E. Johnston: Computational and data grids in large-scale science and engineering. Journal of Future Generation Computer Systems, 18(2002) 1085-1100
2. David Abramson, et al: A computational economy for grid computing and its implementation in the Nimrod-G resource broker, Journal of Future Generation Computer Systems, 18(2002) 1061-1074
3. Li Chunlin, Li layuan: Integrate software agents and CORBA in computational grid, Journal of Computer Standards & Interfaces, 25(2003) 357-371
4. Brian E. Carpenter: Future applications and middleware, and their impact on the infrastructure, Journal of Future Generation Computer Systems, 19(2003) 191-197
5. Du Z H, et al: Research on grid computing and Prototype grid implementation, Journal of Computer Science, Vol. 29(2002) 1-5, Beijing
6. James W. Ferguson: John Towns, The alliance grid, Journal of Advances in Engineering Software, 32(2001) 417-422
7. Xu Zhi Wei, et al: Research on vega grid architecture, Journal of Computer Research and Development,39(2002) 923-929. Beijing
8. I.Foster et al: The Physiology of the Grid: An Open Grid Services Architecture for Distributed Systems Integration, Argonne National Laboratory, Argonne, Ill.(2002) 1-21
9. David De Roure, et al: The Semantic Grid: A Future e-Science Infrastructure, International Journal of Concurrency and Computation: Practice and Experience, 5.(2003)
10. Du Zhihui, et al: Grid Computing, Tsinghua University Press, Beijing (2002)17-43

Research on Computing Grid Software Architecture

Changyun Li [1,2], Gansheng Li [1], and Yin Li [1]

[1] Department of Computer Science & Technology, Zhejiang University, Hangzhou 310027
[2] Department of Computers, Zhuzhou Institute of Technology, Zhuzhou 412008
lichangy@sina.com

Abstract. The paper designs a new distributed software architecture: CGSA according to the theory that integrates computing resources on computing grid into a composite computation with application logic. CGSA expresses the fabricative logic of composite computation with XML document and deals with the difficulty due to the heterogeneity among the computing sources. Based on CGSA structure, it can make good use of network ability, construct a new application fast, and offer a new method for the integration of enterprise legacy business system.

Keyword: computing grid, computing source, SA

1 Preface

At the view of computation, computing grid is an integrated computation and resource environment, or a computing resource pool. If we regard each service offered by the grid as atom computing, the same atom computing sets may form complex composite computing with application logic through the different assembled-logic. "Hourglass" model[1] and OGSA[2] offer the support of protocol and realization for integrated grid atom computing but they don't define the assembled-logic of composite-computing explicitly. The assembled-logic is realized by specific application implicitly so that it is still complex and difficult to integrate grid computing effectively. It shows as the following 2 aspects: (1) The assembled atom computing logic is realized in the application implicitly. Once this kind of assembled-logic changes to form a new application, we need redesign and realize application software, therefore, the changeability and extensibility of software will be restricted; (2) The computing resources under the environment of grid are distributed vastly, different in structure, dynamic and different on access-mode, so it is very complicated to manage and schedule resources.

This paper puts forward a kind of CGSA (Computing-Grid Software Architecture) model. Its basic idea is to divide the whole grid into numerable autonomous sub-grids; each of them manages its internal computing resource ; they connect with each other through the grid-core among the sub-grids; each executable object to offer services outwards is considered to be computing source, single service is taken as atom computing; atom computing forming a composite computing and its assembled logic expresses explicitly with XML document; CGSA deals with the heterogeneity among computing sources and integrates each atom computing into loose, extensible and reliable application.

M. Li et al. (Eds.): GCC 2003, LNCS 3032, pp. 817–820, 2004.

2 The Design of CGSA

2.1 Top Frame

Computing grid environment wants not to affect native management or autonomy of each node, permits nodes have choices to enter or retreat from the system. An ideal computing grid should be established on all the current hard platforms and software platforms, and offer absolutely computing transparent for the user. To ender user, it changes quite few under different resource on a same virtual computing condition.

The top frame of computing grid as figure 1, the whole grid is divided into some autonomous federal child grids; each of them manages some computing sources with the help of management node. There is atom-computing infor-mation offered by internal comput-ing source in the child grid. Computing source is dynamic and may be inserted or drawn from the child grid and the information on the management node is dynamic, too.

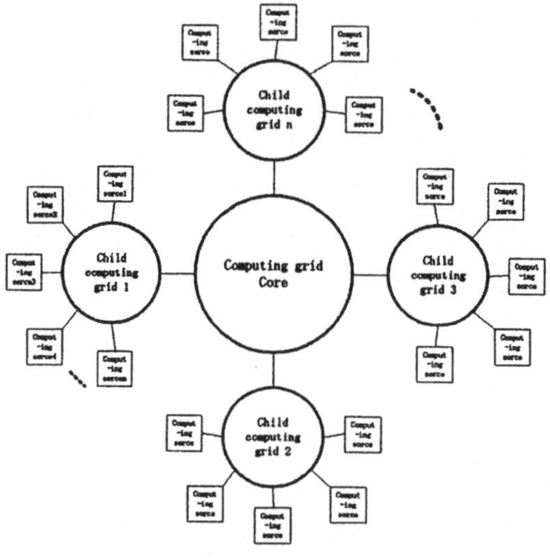

Fig. 1.

The atom-computing in the child grid relate with each other closely and offer field-upright-establishment service, the basic computing ability may be combined to construct the application in the specific field. Computing grid core offers basic service to establish public equipments for the whole grid.

The assembled logic of composite computing with application logic is expressed explicitly and is stored in the management node of its child computing grid. The assembled logic of composite computing only emphasizes how to converge atom-computings into the related basic activities. The key of assembled logic lies in atom-computing collocation and combination in programming field. Composite computing is oriented towards specific application system and the management node implements its basic activities through transferring and combing domain-upright atom-computing. The management node interprets the assembled logic formula of composite Computing, deals with the cooperation with computing source of its child computing grid, implements the transfer of result of composite computing and accomplishes its link with computing grid core. The child-grid offers all or most of atom-computing of a composite computing. Few atom-computing asks for other child computing grids through computing grid core. Schema of child computing grid is the key of CGSA, details in 2.2 chapter . The design of computing grid core accord as OGSA.

2.2 The Design of Software Architecture of Child Computing Grid

The design of child computing grid software architecture as figure 2.

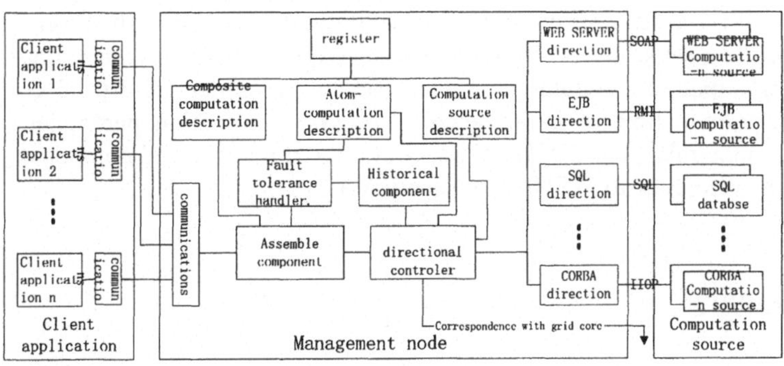

Fig. 2.

The work process of system as the following:

The application client asks for composite computing to the management node, then the assembled component in the management node asks for combination express formula to composite computation description component, then invokes directional controller to get atom-computing result. The directional controller chooses a direction component to invoke according as the information of atom computation description component and computation source description component. A direction component corresponding with the computing atom deals with the difference among computing source and asks for atom-computing with the different-format information protocol and returns the computing results with the uniform format. If this child computing grid doesn't offer atom-computing of some field, the directional controller will ask for help of other child computing grids through grid core. The result of every atom-computing return through the directional controller with the uniform format, at the same time, the latest results of atom-computing and its relative information will be stored into the historical component. If the atom-computing results stored in historical component still is effective, the directional controller can directly draw out and sent them to assembled component but not to invoke a direction to ask for computing source, in order to lessen network transfer and higher its efficiency. The assembled component converges atom-computing results and then gets the results of composite computing according to assembled logic and returns these results to the application client. If some atom-computings joining composite computing can't return the result for some reasons, the assembled component turn round to fault-tolerance component and it will do some fault-tolerance management. The register component will initially register, correct and collate the description of composite computing, atom-computing and computing source.

We express computing source, atom-computing and composite computing with XML document. The description of atom-computing is similar to WSDL of web services, The parameter type uses XML schema Specification of W3C as the default type. The difference from WSDL is that our atom-computing doesn't need binding segment and information transfer protocol explains with the description of computing source; The location of computing source is defined in the computing source description, only need binding computing source ID; Each supplier to each atom-computing has the features of superiority, dependability, response time and so on, which are used for to come to a decision by the directional controller, simultaneously, the value of these features are dynamic according to the actual situation. The express of composite computing is similar to the description of atom-computing but besides describing input and output parameter, data type, dependability of computing, it describes combination rules, simple computing in combination, parameter passing and fault-tolerance rules, etc. XML Schema of atom-computing and composite computing omits here, reference to WSDL specification[3].

3 Summary

This paper designs a kind of software architecture of computing grid: CGSA on the basis of idea that integrates combines computing grid ability into a new application. Through defining the assembled logic of composite computing explicitly and describing with XML document, CGSA solves the dynamic integration of computing-grid, deals with the heterogeneity among computing sources , has these characteristics such as transparency, maturity, dependability, dynamic collocated, expansibility, load balance of computing source. Based on CGSA structure , it can make good use of network ability, construct a new application fast, and offer a new method for the integration of enterprise legacy business system.

References

[1] I Foster,C Kesselman,S Tuecke. The anatomy of the grid: Enabling scalable virtual organizations. International Journal of Supercomputer Applications,2001 ,15(3)

[2] OGSA Specification . http://www.gridforum.org/ogsi-wg/drafts/GS_Spec_draft03_2002-07-17.pdf

[3] Org Inc. WSDL Version 1.2 . http://www.w3.org/tr/wsdl2

[4] Dongwon Lee , Murali Mani , Makoto Murate . Reasoning About XML Schema Languages Using Formal Language Theory . Technical Report,IBM Almaden Research Center, Rj # 10197,Log # 95071 , November 16,2000

[5] I Foster,C Kesselman. The Grid:Blueprint for a New Computing Infrastructure. San Francisco,CA:Morgan Kaufmann Publishers,1 998

Research on Integrating Service in Grid Portal[1]

Zheng Feng, Shoubao Yang, Shanjiu Long, Dongfeng Chen, and Leitao Guo

Computer Science Dept, University of Science and Technology of China,
230026 Anhui, China
{fzheng,jlshan,dfchen,ltguo}@mail.ustc.edu.cn
syang@ustc.edu.cn

Abstract. With the complexity of applications, researchers need more resources to resolve their computation. It is very important to provide the general interface to access the distributed resources. Grid environment is distributed, heterogeneous and dynamics, so integration of different native platform is a challenge. We present a service-oriented Grid Portal building on concepts and technologies from OGSA. An approach to efficient grid resources and customize grid applications is in our framework.

1 Introduction

Portals are commonly used to provide people with access to information and applications in a condensed form.

Grid Portals are necessary for two reasons. On one hand, the Grid environment is very complex including scheduling, co-allocation, security, quality of service, data transfer, network protocol, Grid programming model, etc. On the other hand, computational science environment is also complex. It's cumbersome for users to access a variety of grid resources in single application and follow the changes of interface, operation system and Grid tools. As a result, users may get overwhelmed in one single scientific application! Thus, a Grid Portal is defined to be a web based application server enhanced with the necessary software to communicate with Grid services and resources.

Most of the existing science portals are application-centric portals, and they actually share a similarity in some services such as login service, user profile management, etc. Unfortunately, these common characters have been neglected, which results in the redundancy in portal implementation. Since developing a professional portal is not an easy job, why not stop doing repeat jobs and provide a universal service for public use? What's more, goal of Grid, by its initiator, is to provide user ubiquitous access to the Great Global Grid.

Our Portal enables Web Service based universal access to Grid resources.

[1] Supported by the National Natural Science Foundation of China under Grant No.60273041

M. Li et al. (Eds.): GCC 2003, LNCS 3032, pp. 821–824, 2004.

2 Grid Portal

In our Portal design, we pack every Portal function, from Login function to Create Application Instance function, into a service. Therefore, we can develop a uniform platform for users and administrator to use these services. This idea facilitates the complexity of development, as well as the complexity of integrating new services. The base architecture shows in Fig. 1, so we can get a general idea of our grid portal.

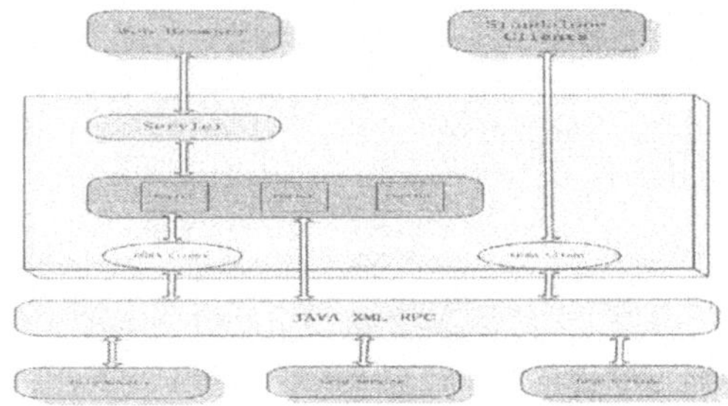

Fig. 1. Architecture of Grid Portal

End user can use web browser or other standalone client to access our grid portal. When browser sends a HTTP Request to Portal, it will decide which Portlets to complete the request and diver to them. Portlets use the standard interface to interactive the Grid Service which described with WSDL. Some standard protocol such as SOAP, HTTP, and JAVA RPC will be used in communications between OGSA Client and Grid Service. Portal also provides an interface of Web Service to standalone client which can use standard SOAP protocol to access the OGSA Client.

3 Integration with Grid Service

3.1 Service Orientation and Virtualization

A Web service is a software system identified by a URI, whose public interfaces and bindings are defined and described using XML. Its definition can be discovered by other software systems. These systems may then interact with the Web service in a manner prescribed by its definition, using XML-based messages conveyed by Internet protocols.

OGSA defines what we call a Grid service: a Web service that provides a set of well-defined interfaces and that follows specific conventions. The interfaces address discovery, dynamic service creation, lifetime management, notification, and manageability; the conventions address naming and upgradeability.

OGSA put heavy emphasis on the concept of “services”: computation resources, storages resources, networks, programs, databases, and the like are all presented as services. Everything is service [1].

Virtualization allows the composition of services to form more sophisticated services—without regard for how the services being composed are implemented. Virtualization of Grid services also underpins the ability of mapping common service semantic behavior seamlessly onto native platform facilities.

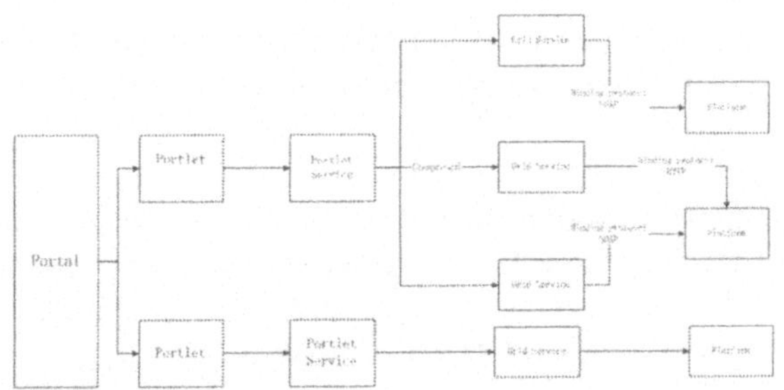

Fig. 2. Relationships of Portal and Grid Services

In our Grid Portal, we integrated grid service in the portlets [6]. Every portlet service is compounded by one or more grid service. Portal has a few portlets which can provide service to users.

3.2 Standard Interface of Grid Service

Dynamic service creation. The ability to dynamically create and manage new service instances is a basic tenet of the OGSA model and necessitates the existence of service creation services [1]. The OGSA model defines a standard interface (Factory) and semantics that any service creation service must provide.
Lifetime management. Any distributed system must be able to deal with inevitable failures. In a system that incorporates transient, stateful service instances, mechanisms must be provided for reclaiming services and state associated with failed operations.
Notification. A collection of dynamic, distributed services must be able to notify each other asynchronously of interesting changes to their state. OGSA defines common abstractions and service interfaces for subscription to (NotificationSource) and delivery of (NotificationSink) such notifications, so that services constructed by the composition of simpler services can deal with notifications (e.g., for errors) in standard ways [1]. The NotificationSource interface is integrated with service data, so that a notification request is expressed as a request for subsequent "push" mode delivery of service data.

3.3 Class Design

So all classes of grid service inherit from AbstractGridService and implement ServiceInterface. [4][5] To write a grid service follows 4 steps:

1. Provide a Service Interface
The first step of writing a Grid service is to provide a WSDL definition for the service interface. We can write service interface definition in WSDL ourselves, or use tools such as java2wsdl to generate the definition.
2. Generate Service Stubs
The JAX-RPC compliant interfaces are generated to be used both on the client and on the server side. Client side stub implementations of these interfaces will also be generated.
3. Implement the Service
All remotely available operations must be public and throw java.rmi.RemoteException as defined in the PortType interface. The ServiceSkeleton class that must be inherited from is provided by our framework and implements the GridServicePortType interface, along with other core Grid service behavior [4][7].
4. Deploy the Service

4 Summary

We design and implement a Grid Portal based on concepts and technologies from OGSA. And with integrating Grid Service in Portal, we provide users a more easy access to grid resources. Users can also customize their own style of Portal to get more abundant services.

5 Future Work

We will extend role of Grid Portal. It can take the role of auction , balance...That is, we can extend our Portal to be a Grid resource agency center. There exists some research on economic marked base Grid resource management. We think Portal will be particular sense to those economic market based Grid applications.

References

1. I Foster, C Kesselman, J Nick, S Tuecke. Physiology of the Grid: An Open Grid Services Architecture for Distributed Systems Integration. January, 2002.
2. I Foster, C Kesselman, S Tuecke. The Anatomy of the Grid: Enabling Scalable Virtual Organizations. International J. Super Computer Application, 15(3), 2001.
3. D Gannon, R Ananthakrishnan, S Krishnan, M Govindaraju. Grid Web Services and Application Factories.
4. Globus Toolkit. See http://www.globus.org
5. The Global Grid Forum. See http://www.gridforum.org
6. J Novotny, M Russell, O Wehrens. Jetspeed Evaluation. GridLab and Application Portlets Design.
7. V Welch, F Siebenlist. GT3 Grid Security Infrastructure Overview.

GSRP: An Application-Level Protocol for Grid Environments

Zhiqiang Hou, Donghua Liu, Zhiwei Xu, and Wei Li

Institute of Computing Technology, Chinese Academy of Sciences, Beijing, 100080, China
houzhiqiang@software.ict.ac.cn
{dliu, zxu, liwei}@ict.ac.cn

Abstract. The Grid Service Request Protocol (GSRP), a multi-pattern application-level protocol supporting session management and asynchronous communication, is designed to meet application requirements of Web service and Grid service. The GSRP consists of two layers: Message Transporting Layer (MTL) and Application Session Layer (ASL). The MTL controls the transmission procedure of packets on network channels, named as GSRP Dialog. The ASL manages GSRP Session, a cluster of related Dialogs to fulfill a task with certain pattern. Soft connection mechanism enables Session to maintain a persistent state, independent on physical connections. In a simple GSRP implementation, an extensible set of APIs and a transmission intermediate is developed, showing the power of GSRP.

1 Introduction

Web service describes a service-oriented architecture that defines interactions between software agents as exchanges of messages [1]. The Open Grid Service Architecture [2] characterizes the Grid service concept, aligning the Grid computing technologies with Web service mechanisms.

GSML [3] is a markup language and toolkit facilitating end users' programming and resource accessing in a service environment, which is important for the usage of Grid technologies. But the widely-applied standard protocols presently cannot meet the points of the user-centric service architecture, because of the reasons below:

- Hard to implement asynchronous communications such as subscription or notification. In HTTP [4] and Browser/Server Model, the asynchronous service call is difficult to implement.
- User session contexts can not be effectively recorded by protocols. HTTP manages session state by cookies [5]. But this extension to the protocol is considered as leading to confusion on both sides of communication [6].
- Lack of lightweight distributed communication mechanism. CORBA and RMI do not suit for pervasive clients of the Grid. Numerous protocol stacks and protocol extensions about web service and grid service will damage the interoperability.

The Grid service request protocol (GSRP) is designed to be suitable for user-centric service applications. GSRP supports session management with persistent status, and provides solutions for both synchronous and asynchronous communication mechanisms. With it continuous sessions in unreliable networks are enabled.

M. Li et al. (Eds.): GCC 2003, LNCS 3032, pp. 825–828, 2004.

There are several related protocols. BEEP [7] permits simultaneous and independent exchanges of messages between peers. The VNC protocol [8] is a "thin client" protocol and makes clients stateless. When a client disconnects from a given server and reconnects to that same server, the state is preserved. HTTPR [9] supports the reliable transport of messages layered on top of HTTP, with it's a persistent storage capability providing reliable synchronous and asynchronous mechanisms.

2 GSRP Structure

GSRP consists of two protocol layers: Application Session Layer (ASL) and Message Transporting Layer (MTL).The MTL is on the top of TCP level and below ASL. The ASL describes the sessions of user application environments. In GSRP, a session is bind to a complete user application. It may contain several different interactions. The MTL manages the message transmission. The concept of dialog, a full-duplex channel between the two ends of an interaction, is defined in this layer.

2.1 Message Transporting Layer

Concepts

A GSRP packet is the basic transport unit which contains a complete request or response. The packets may be transported in the form of pipeline. A GSRP dialog is an interaction process of related packet sequences. Request and response packets can be sent in different direction independently. So a GSRP dialog can implement a full-duplex communication.

Communication Primitives

This layer defines three basic communication primitives: Request, Response and Emergency, which also represent different packet types. Any communication patterns can be separately denoted by request and response. The order of responses must be in the same order of requests, though a request needn't wait the response of the prior request (pipelining). GSRP also transfers emergent packets containing system state information and control information. Emergency is a primitive that can be inserted into dialog packet queues anytime and transmitted as early as possible.

Protocol Packet Format

GSRP Packet is composed of a fixed length segment and a variable length segment (see Figure 1). Version NO field defines protocol version to support extensions. The Primitive Type field represents three packet types of request, response and emergency. Address Type and User ID Type can accommodate various categories of address and User ID in Web service and OGSA. Session ID and Dialog ID respectively record the relative session and dialog of user application. Serials Number field counts sequential packets in a dialog sequence. The length of user ID, request address, origin address and payload is variable. Extended head length field records the length of next extended packet. GSRP Message is a self-description document contained in the Payload field.

Chaining of Protocol Packet Heads

The extended heads length field is designed to define the length of next extended packet. Extended packet heads are appended to the previous head segment. They will be used for capability negotiation, user authentication or other extensions.

Version NO *8bit*	Primitive Type, *8bit*	Address Type, *8bit*	User ID Type, *8bit*	Fixed length
Session ID, *16bit*		Dialog ID, *16bit*		
Serials Number, *32bit*				
Origin Address Length, *16bit*		Request Address Length, *16bit*		
User ID Length, *16bit*		Extended heads Length, *16bit*		
Payload Length, *32bit*				Variable length
Origin address				
Request Address				
User ID				
Packet Payload				

Fig. 1. Protocol Packet format

2.2 Application Session Layer

GSRP Session

A GSRP session is the whole semantic related interaction process defined by application. Session may have multiple dialogs. The lifetime of session is decided by applications. If they do not finish a session explicitly, the session would last all along.

Session States

A session has four states. The state transition diagram is displayed in Figure 2.

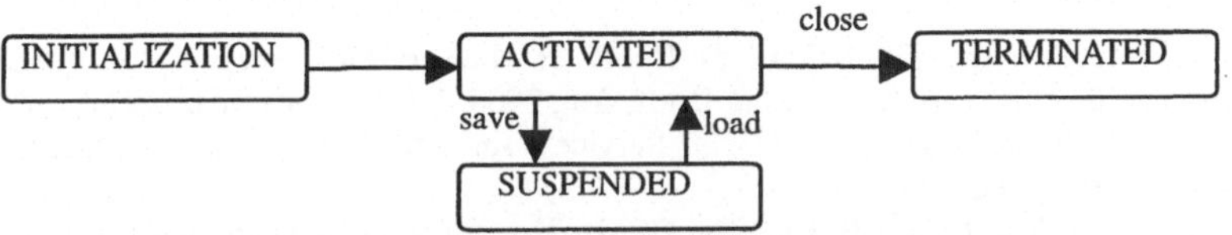

Fig. 2. Sessions State Transition Diagram

The INITIALIZATION state is the beginning of sessions. The ACTIVATED state is reached after successful initialization. The ACTIVATED state can be preserved by *save* action or be *closed* to The TERMINATED state. The SUSPENDED state holds the state information of session and waits *load* action to resume it.

Session ID and Dialog ID

In GSRP, an ID is used to identify sessions uniquely, which can be assigned by the application or GSRP system. As a global identifier, Session ID can be used and re-used by multiple processes on different hosts. Dialogs are distinguished by unique dialog IDs in a session. A Dialog ID represents a logical persistent connection. We name this logical connection as *soft connection*, which means connections are virtual and can be suspended, resumed and transferred. The GSRP Session is a container for persistent handles of soft connections.

3 Java API Implementations and Evaluation

There are three parts in GSRP APIs which are respectively responsible for user applications, service providers and transmission intermediates. API packages were implemented in high level and programmers do not know the mechanism of sockets. The intermediates keep the dialog packets and forward the messages to the other end (see figure 3).

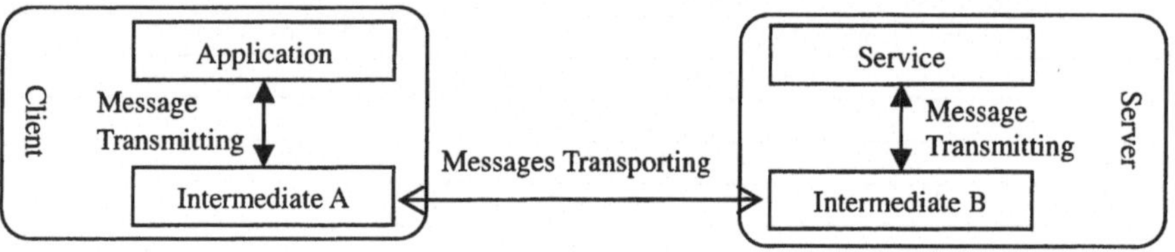

Fig. 3. GSRP Implementation

The protocol supports extensible various application communication patterns including request/response, subscription and notification. The intermediates can help the implementation of 3A (Any time, any where, any device) access. With the session and dialog management mechanism a session can be reused among different applications and can be migrated among different sites. The soft connections are kept along the life cycle of an application session. We apply GSRP to the communication of GSML [3] applications and gain prospective results.

References

1. M. Champion, C. Ferris, D. Orchard, D. Booth, H. Haas, F. McCabe, E. Newcomer, "Web Services Architecture", W3C Working Draft, Aug 2003, *http://www.w3c.org/TR/ws-arch/.*
2. I. Foster, C. Kesselman, etc., "Grid Services for Distributed System Integration", *Computer*, 35(6), 2002.
3. Z. Xu, W. Li, D. Liu, H. Yu, B. Li, "The GSML Tool Suite: A Supporting Environment for User-level Programming in Grids", *PDCAT'03*, 2003, pp.629-633.
4. R. Fielding, J. Gettys, J. Mogul, "Hypertext Transfer Protocol", RFC 2616, Jun 1999.
5. D. Kristol, L. Montulli, "HTTP State Management Mechanism", RFC2109, Feb 1997.
6. R. T. Fielding, R. N. Taylor, "Principled Design of the Modern Web Architecture", *ACM Transactions on Internet Technology*, Vol. 2, No. 2, May 2002, pp.115-150.
7. M. Rose, "The Blocks Extensible Exchange Protocol Core", RFC 3080, March 2001.
8. T. Richardson, Q. Stafford-Fraser, K. R. Wood ,A. Hopper, "Virtual Network Computing", *IEEE Internet Computing*, Vol.2 No.1, Jan/Feb 1998, pp.33-38.
9. A. Banks, J. Challenger, P., "HTTPR Specification", IBM, Dec 2001, http://www.ibm.com/developerworks/library/ws-httprspec/.

Towards a Mobile Service Mechanism in a Grid Environment

Weiqin Tong[1], Jianquan Tang [1], Liang Jin [1], Bo Wang [1], and Yuwei Zong [2]

[1] School of Computer Engineering and Science, Shanghai University, Shanghai 200072, P. R. China
wqtong@mail.shu.edu.cn
[2] Shanghai Software Test Laboratory, Shanghai 200235, P. R. China

Abstract. With the rapid development of Internet, Grid becomes more and more popular. In this paper, mobile service is introduced to solve some key problems in Grid environment, such as load balance and fault tolerance etc. A mobile service is the combination of Grid service and mobile agent and has migration ability that can make it migrate between grids and ability to detect surroundings to decide when and where to migrate.

1 Introduction

For satisfaction of various needs such as coordinated resource sharing and problem solving in dynamic, multi-institutional virtual organizations, the Grid technologies come into being. The Grid technologies provide discovering resource, data management, scheduling of online resources, security management, etc. in distributed and heterogeneous environment. Integrated with Web Services technology, the grid has evolved into OGSA (open Grid Service Architecture), which is based on the Grid Service. Grid service integrates the resources including software with the Web Services and conforms to a well-defined set of basic interfaces.

OGSA provides a plain grid framework for grid developers, a convenient way for the grid user so that energy is focused on how to implement the logic of Grid Service instead of how to interact with the implementation of the OGSA. But it does not leave nothing to be desired, the deficiency of OGSA exists in latest version. The first factor is the efficiency. Considering the characteristics of Java—write once, run everywhere at anytime, OGSA is implemented in Java. Thus, besides improving the efficiency of Grid service, we must invent a method that can obtain low consumption and good performance. Another is about the load balance. While some Grid Service is commonly used or has burdensome task, it will overtask the workstation or the cluster that loads this Grid Service and impairs the QoS. Thus, we must deal with this subtle and challenging problem as how to divert some part of the task to a comparably free one in an appropriate point.

So we provide the mobile service to resolve these problems. The rest of this paper is structured as follows: in the next section, the mechanism and framework of the Mobile

M. Li et al. (Eds.): GCC 2003, LNCS 3032, pp. 829–832, 2004.

Service is discussed in detail. In the section.3, we propose the effective application of the Mobile Service. The conclusion and future work about our research is included in the last section.

2 Anatomy of a Mobile Service

With the assistance of the Mobile Agent technology, a Grid Service can be freely migrated from one node to another and be automatically deployed to the container of this node to enable this node have the similar function as the former one. And if the kind of Grid Services is equipped with the capability of autonomy, migration, feedback and interaction, we conclude it as Mobile Service. In this section, we will introduce the mechanism and principle of the Mobile Service

2.1 Migration of Grid Service

To enable the mobile capability of the Grid Service, the necessary step is to locate a method to migrate a service between the grid nodes. The Mobile Agent is more suitable for this task. One Mobile Agent is a software entity running under the Context environment that is in charge of initiating, migration, security, callback and eradication of the agent entity. However the creation of a Grid Service, which conforms to both OGSA framework and the convention of Mobile Agent, is difficult.

Fig.1 shows us a lifecycle of the Aglet—the Mobile Agent System of Corp. IBM. A Mobile Agent initialization is completed with the instantiation of a series of static classes. After that, the Context is responsible for maintaining the agent and offers it a running environment.

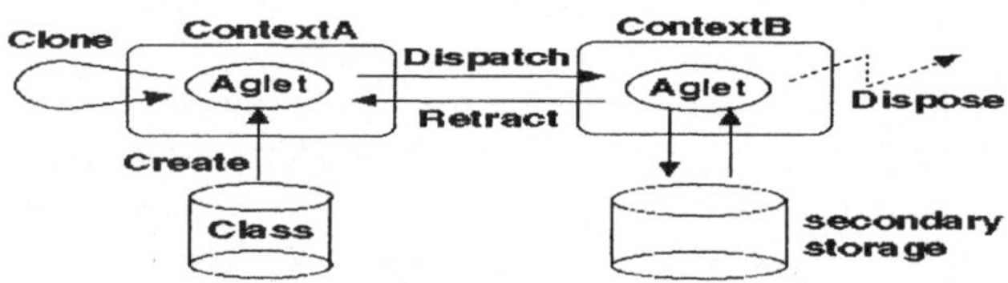

Fig. 1. The lifecycle of Mobile Agent

If we take the Agent as the carrier of the Gird Service package and the Agent environment on this node can interact with the Grid environment to deploy the sent file to the container, the Grid Service has the capability of motion. Firstly when a Grid Service decides to migrate, it firstly sends a initiation request After receiving the request, Context will extract the essential class and activate the proxy. This instance will take charge of transmitting the Grid Service to appropriate nodes and guarantee the intact transmission. After the initiation, the agent will interact with the target Context based on the provided Grid Service target address and transmit the packed package to the target using ATP protocol. The security problem of the transmissions is considered by the Context. When the agent reaches the target, the first thing should be done is to invoke the local API interface of the Globus Toolkit to deploy the Grid Service to the container. This step mainly includes adding service items to the Service Node and service description to the WSDD file.

After the three steps, a local Grid Service will be redeployed onto a remote host.

2.2 Mobile Service

There are two important characteristics of Mobile Service. The first is autonomy. A Mobile Service should run without the personal intervene and be accustomed to its environment to control the running. It can determine when to migrate and destination of the migration or whether replication should be proceeding on itself. For the replication, a Mobile Agent only knows when to duplicate and the destination of the duplication. The rest of this replication should be completed with technology that we show in above section. But when a Grid Service wants to migrate itself, the stuff that should be considered is the capture of the Grid Service context. In the next section, when we introduce the fault-tolerance, the detail discussion will be demonstrated.

Another characteristic is Interaction between Grid Services. In local environment, since the communication between Grid Services is implemented with the notification mechanism, the interaction between Grid Services is focused on the communication between the remote hosts. In this process, because the Mobile Agent is the carrier, the communication between them should use the technology of the Mobile Agent. When the Grid Service is migrated to a remote host, for the sake of the remote interaction, the appropriate adjustment to the GT3's communication should be done. Here we give an integrate definition of the Mobile Service. A Grid Service that has the capability of spanning hosts and network bridge, the autonomy and interaction is a Mobile Service.

3 Function of a Mobile Service

Utilizing the characteristic of the Mobile Service, we may construct a new fault tolerance mechanism for the Grid. To enable the fault tolerance, the Grid Service firstly should have the capability of periodical capture the state of itself in case that the system will establish the Grid Service according to the latest state that is stored by the capture. We integrate the Java thread capture technology with the Mobile Service. The Java thread capture will take a snapshot of the running thread and store it in a file or other medias. We should adjust the Java Virtual Machine (JVM) to provide the API (Application Program Interface) to peek the internal memory of the running program. Fig. 2 depicts the architecture of the revised JVM

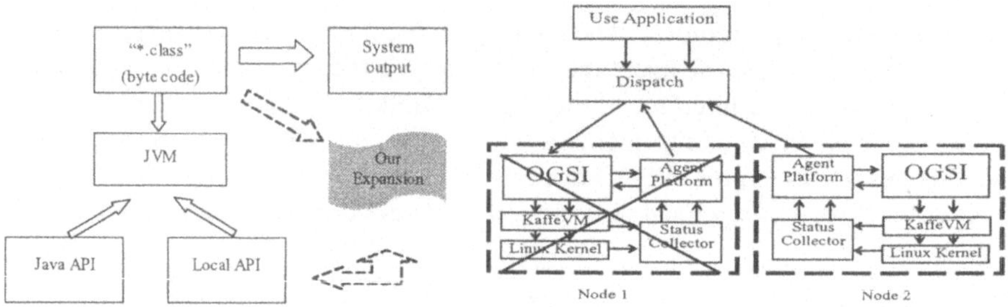

Fig. 2. Architecture of the revised JVM

Fig. 3. Architecture of fault-tolerant mechanism

The standard JVM is expanded to extract the java key data structures including the stack, the program counter and all heap memory into some media and reestablishing the running state from the stored information. Fig.3 shows the architecture of our fault-tolerance that utilizes the above introspection of the java thread. The fact that Grid users couldn't get the results of submitted tasks owes to three reasons: instance failure, Grid node crash, and agent crash. Mobile service can easily solve these failure and crashes especially node crash. When the running mobile service detects a local grid platform fail, it will save statues information, migrate to another grid site and deploy it to run again without any user's interaction.

4 Conclusion and Future Works

We mainly introduce the construction of the Mobile Service with the integration of the Mobile Agent and the Grid technology in detail, the application of it in the Grid and what characteristics and functions a Grid Service should possess. Meanwhile, the security is a key problem of the Mobile Service. Our future work will be focused on these subjects.

References

1. I. Foster, C. Kesselman, and S. Tuecke, The Anatomy of the Grid: Enabling Scalable Virtual Organizations, International Journal of SupercomputerApplications, vol.15, no.3, 2001.
2. Li Chunlin, Li Layuan, "An Agent-oriented and Service-oriented Environment for Deploying Dynamic Distributed Systems", *Journal Computer Standard and Interface*, Elsevier, Vol 24/4, pp. 321-334, Sept, 2002
3. S.Bouchenak. "Making Java Applications Mobile or Persistent", 6th UNENIX Conference on Object-Oriented Technologies and Systems (COOTS'01), 29th January-2nd February 2001.
4. R.Buyya, S.Chapin, D.DiNucci, "Architectural Models for Resource Management in the Grid", *First IEEE/ACM International Workshop on Grid Computing (GRID 2000)*, Germany, Dec. 17, 2000,

Mobile Middleware Based on Distributed Object

Song Chen, Shan Wang, and Ming-Tian Zhou

College of Computer Science and Engineering, UESTC of China Chengdu 610054
chensong233@sina.com

Abstract. Some limitations exist in the mobile middleware based on the Java RMI Technology. On the background of middleware, distributed object computing and mobile computing, the paper proposes an architecture of mobile middleware based on distributed object (MMDO), which is consist of the dynamically customizable base core, the general mobile agent platform, asynchronous message service, the distributed resource discovery service. MMDO can resolve the efficiency of Java in the mobile middleware, and extend the service of mobile middleware, which could provide the best support environment for mobile application. Lastly the paper gives the result of simulation test and proves the validity of the MMDO.

1 Introduction

In recent years, the technology of wireless communication and mobile computing have developed rapidly, mobile users can implement the application from simple mobile device to advanced mobile device. The application running on the mobile device brings some challenge problem to software designer [1, 2]. So we need a supporting environment of mobile application, shield the difference of the operation system and network, which could give higher layer of abstract interface to application designer, and simplify the development of the mobile application. Mobile middleware is such a software platform, which use the technology of the middleware to mobile network environment. This article provide mobile middleware based on distributed object technology, which shields the difference of operate system, language, and network, resolves the problem of the lower efficiency of Java, and aim at characteristic of mobile network, offers different mobile service.

2 Relative Works

Currently, research about mobile middleware was mainly based on mobile Agent, which provides a mobile application supporting environment. Reference[3-4] implement the technology that integrate mobile Agent into middleware, provide suitable protocol, administration function and application program interface. It can track mobile user and permit communication and negotiation between entities. Reference[5] implements a mobile transaction service named GoldRush by using Java

M. Li et al. (Eds.): GCC 2003, LNCS 3032, pp. 833–838, 2004.

object replication technology and it can support mobile device to access the database. Reference[6] implements a mobile middleware MASE(mobile application supporting environment) based on universal mobile telecom system(UMTS).
Above research about mobile middleware is based on the Java RMI technology. Java technology resolves the problem of crossing-platform, but Java runs very slowly, especially when it run on the server or mobile gateway and it becomes the bottle-neck of system performance. RMI can implement the access to the remote object, but it only limit in the Java application and can't resolve the problem of crossing-language. So middleware based on Java RMI inevitably exist some limitation.

3 System Design and Implementation

3.1 System Framework

Fig. 1. shows the architecture of mobile application support platform MMDO based on distributed object technology CORBA/IIOP. The platform shields the differences of operation system, network, and computer languages, provides a uniform API for the mobile application, and it simplifies complexity of mobile application development. To resolve the efficiency of Java, MMDO client provides Java ORB API to support different mobile terminal. MMDO server provides C++ ORB API which can dispose the request message more efficiently, and crossing-languages feature of IIOP to ensure the right communication and negotiation between client and server.

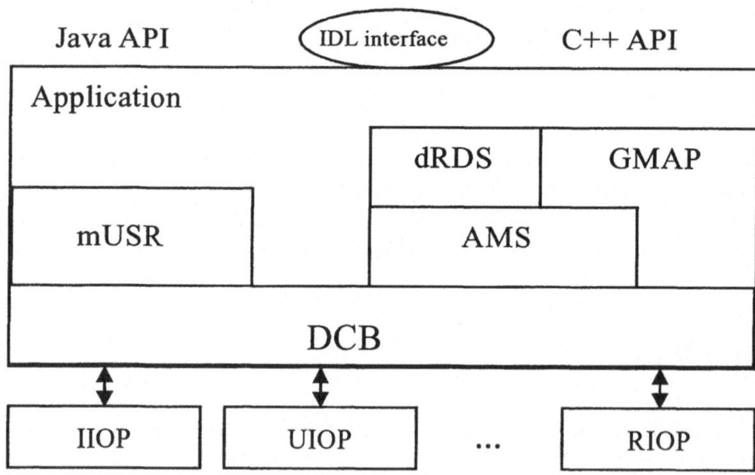

Fig. 1. MMDO system structure

We implement a general distributed mobile middleware system structure based on the open source of CORBA platform named ORBacus which supports both c++ and java. The system comprises basic core, extended platform, facilities and services, and it can also support the following applications: (1) application according with some specification of distributed object, such as CORBA、RMI; (2) distributed object application which supporting the mobile equipment; (3) mobile agent application; (4) mobile application supporting the dynamic resource deployment; (5) dynamically querying the above application by using the DRDS.

3.2 Implementation of the System Components

3.2.1 DCB (Dynamic Customized Base Core)

As the high layer communication facilities, DCB is the basic platform for distributed object communication. It can be mapped to ORB or RMI on function. But DCB is different from general ORB: DCB has reflective core, it's critical implementation, such as communication protocol、message encode/decode, can be customized and even can be adjusted dynamically. so it can adapt well to mobile environment comparing with general distributed object platform.

For the multiplicity of the mobile environment, the system ensures the flexibility and dynamic adjustability in the communication layer by the method of reflection. From the aspect of implement structure, the communication layer can be divided into two child layers: message layer and transmission layer.

3.2.2 Asynchronous Message Service

Mobile communication exist two important features: intermittent non-connection status, communication bandwidth is relatively narrow. In the mobile application system, distributed interactive should be in loose couple model.

Two typical distributed interactive models (message transmission, client-server) are shown in Fig.2. The first model is message driving and there is no apparent interactive processing, so it belongs to loose couple and is suitable for mobile application environment. But in the second model, data and server resource are accessed by client and are not available for the client in non-connection status. The cost of interaction must be great in the weak connection network.

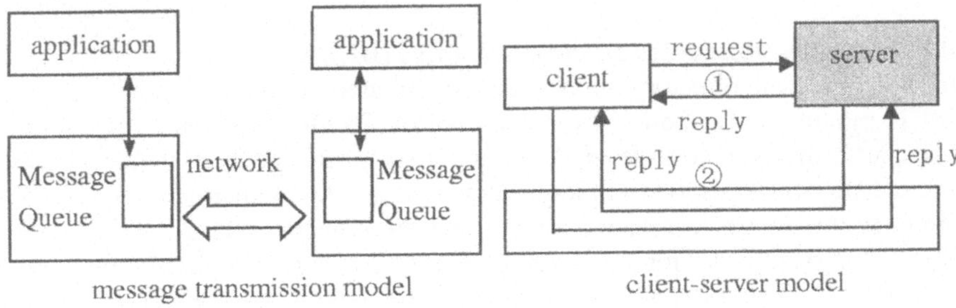

Fig. 2. Comparison of the two distributed interaction model

Implementation of MMDO asynchronous message service is mainly divided into three parts: changing the synchronous interaction model into asynchronous message service model; using buffer to store data or server resource at client to ensure resource usability at non-connection status; reduce the degree of couple in application related or non-related method. MMDO asynchronous message service defines two asynchronous request models: poll and call-back. It provides call service which is time non-related and supports message "store and forward".

3.2.3 General Mobile Agent Platform (GMAP)

GMAP is a general and abstract mobile agent platform. It provides the framework of agent design and development, and it supports many basic function of mobile agent such as create/destroy, active/inactive, move while running, security access. MMDO provides C++ implementation of Aglet CORBA object for server, optimizes running efficiency of server object, and it also keeps the same JAVA function and supports dynamic immigration of server object. We can program the agent application directly but don't need to modify local codes.

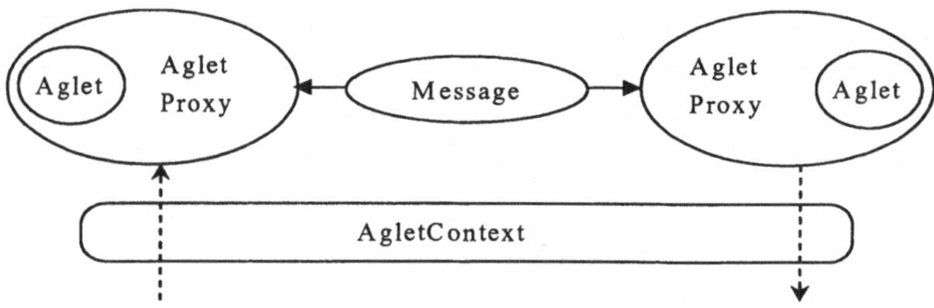

Fig. 3. Aglet logical model

Aglet can do communication interaction by exchanging message object which is constituted by a type string and a message body of task object.

The system structure of Aglet can be divided into two layers. Runtime layer implements basic model specified above, and provides basic function of creation, management and movement. Kernel framework is comprised of persistent manager, buffer manager and security manager, and provides basic methods about Aglet, such as Aglet serialization and deserialization, class loader and transmission, reference management and garbage recollection. MMDO communication layer supports two interoperation communication protocols: TCP/IP、 UDP.

3.2.4 Distributed Resources Discovery Service (DRDS)

Depending on local directory service and distributed resource discovery methods, DRDS is running at the node of domain control. DRDS also needs the support of GMAP platform layer. Mobile application can register resources in the DRDS, or require the DRDS for resources in local domain or in other domain.

To simplify the design, we have assumed that the domain control node is statically deployed and steady. As for the domain member, it can be dynamically changed. Domain control node maintains the following: domain member list、 adjacent domain control node list, and resource tree. So all the resources (include resource in the domain or out) are organized in uniform classification. To support CORBA, J2EE naming service, domain control node also supports the method of service registration, cancel, and discovery which is compatible with the standard.

4 Result of Simulation Test

This article compares the performance result in different mobile application supporting environment and using multiplex communication protocol. It proves that the mobile platform based on Java-C++ resolves the performance of the platform based on JAVA RMI well and has high disposing capability of data. Supporting multiplex communication protocol improves adaptation to the different mobile network environment. So we design the simulation model according with the following points:

(1) The comparison is in the same host or the same local area network. There are some factors which influencing the performance: T_{enc}, T_{dec}, $T_{dispose}$, T_{send}, T_{recv}, $T_{fragment}$. At the same conditions T_{enc}, T_{dec} and $T_{dispose}$ is decided by computer language, T_{send} and T_{recv} is decided by the communication protocol and the network environment.

(2) T_{oneway} equals the time from sending the same size datagram to receiving the response: $T_{oneway} = 2T_{enc} + 2T_{dec} + T_{dispose} + T_{send} + T_{recv} + T_{other}$

(3) $T_{sum} = \sum_{i=1}^{1000} T_{oneway}$

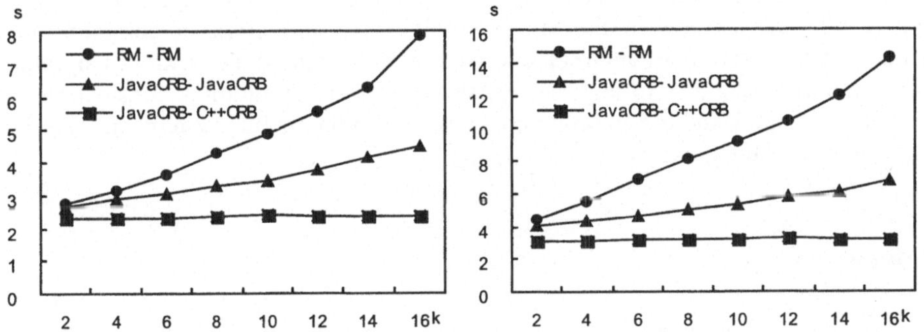

Fig. 4. Performance comparison at the same host and local area network

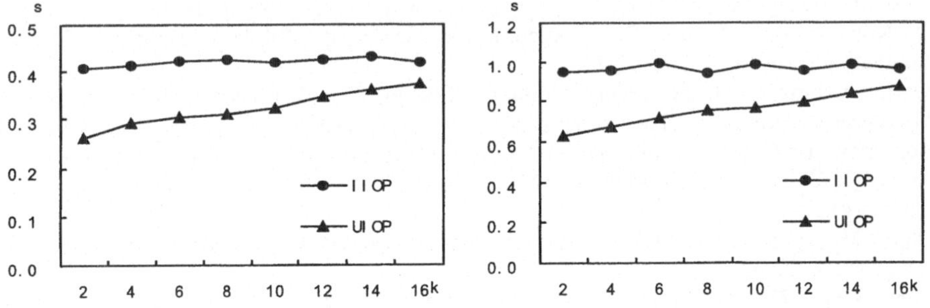

Fig. 5. Performance comparison at the same host and local area network

From the simulation test result, we can conclude that the mobile platform based on JavaORB-C++ ORB improve the efficiency of system communication, CORBA fragment enlarged the system transmit capability. The multiplex communication protocol supported by MMDO improves the system flexibility. Client can flexibly choose communication protocol for the special application environment.

5 Summary and Future Work

For the limitations of the current mobile middleware research, this article proposes a mobile middleware MMDO based on distributed object technology. It efficiently resolves the JAVA performance based on RMI technology, and provides some special mobile service function and a flexible communication protocol support for the mobile environment. DCB is the basic platform of distributed object communication and is suitable for mobile environment; Asynchronous message service supports message "store and forward". GMAP provides management and running environment of agent lifecycle、movement and security; DRDS is a general resource service towards mobile environment with different scope, and provides location of mobile terminal. The mobile middleware in the article resolves the limitation of communication resource and the variety of environment in the mobile computing. Next we can import collaboration mechanism to improve system adaptation. In addition, considering that the resource is lack and the environment is various in the mobile system, an important task is to ensure the quality of service (QoS).

References

1. Aline Baggio, Adaptable and Mobile-Aware Distributed Objects, PhD Thesis, Université Pierre & Marie Curie, June 1999
2. George H. Forman, John Zahorjan, The Challenges of Mobile Computing, UW CSE Tech Report # 93-11-03, ftp://ftp.cs.washington.edu, March 9, 1994
3. E. Kovacs, K. Rohrle, M. Reich, "Integration Mobile Agents into the Mobile Middleware", Porc. Mobile Agents Int'l Workshop, Springer-Verlag, Berlin, 1998: 124-135
4. D. Kotz et al., "Agent TCL: Targeting the Needs of Mobile Computers", Internet Computing, July/Aug. 1997: 58-67
5. Maria A.Butrico, Henry Chang, Anthony Cocchi, "Gold Rush: Mobile Transaction Middleware with Java-Object Replication", in the Proceedings of the Third USENIX Conference on Object-Oriented Technologies and Systems Portland, Oregon, June 1997
6. Angin, O, Campbell, A.T., Kounavis, M.E., Liao, R.R.-F, IEEE Personal Communications, 1998, 5(4):32-43
7. Object Management Group. The Common Request Broker: Architecture and Specification, Revision2.4, October 2000: 407-543
8. Chen Song, WANG Min-Yi, ZHOU Ming-Tian, Research and Implementation of an Enhanced CORBA/ORB Message Communication Mechanism, Computer Science, 2002, 29 (3): 122-124
9. Chen Song, Research and Implementation of Flexible and High-efficient ORB Core of CORBA middleware, master degree paper of UESTC , 2002

On the Malicious Participants Problem in Computational Grid

Wenguang Chen, Weimin Zheng, and Guangwen Yang

Tsinghua University, Beijing 100084, China

Abstract. Computational Grid allows customers to submit tasks to service providers. To maintain the availability, fairness and performance, it is critical to protect Computational Grid systems from malicious participants. Current solutions to this problem assume that the system would contain either malicious consumers only or malicious service provider only. However, in the real world, both consumers and service providers may be malicious in a single computational grid system. We proposed a solution to this problem by ranking both side of participants.

1 Introduction

Grid computing is evolving very fast now. There are already many protocols, platforms, toolkits and applications of Grid [2,6,7,8]. Among them, Computational Grid is probably the most common application. In Computational Grid, customers can submit tasks to service providers. It can be predicted that a commercial Computational Grid market would be formed in the near future, in which service providers can gain money from providing resources to the Grid, and consumers can get the same service from the Grid with less cost than they have to pay without the Grid.

Key components of commercial Grids are scheduling and billing system. In real life, we may always meet malicious users. So may we in the Grid. For an example, a malicious consumer may send many long tasks to occupy the grid resources. A credit based billing system can prevent this by giving each user only limited credit[1,10]. Credit can be real currency, and can also be translated into anything that makes sense, such as time quotas, and priorities etc. However, malicious users can do much more. A malicious consumer may send a long task to occupy the grid resources, while claiming it is a shorter one. A service provider may accept a task and did not execute it at all. To be a successful scheduling and billing system, it must be able to prevent the malicious participants from damaging the systems availability and performance.

There are several solutions to the malicious participants problem now[4,5,9]. They can be divided into two classes: 1) Assuming that all the service providers are good ones, and there're only malicious consumers in the system. Based on the assumption, if a consumer sends a long task to the grid and claims that it is a short one, it will be identified to be a malicious consumer when the server can not complete the task submitted in the expected time. Another approach is to let

M. Li et al. (Eds.): GCC 2003, LNCS 3032, pp. 839–848, 2004.

consume purchase service in a unit time base, so customers don't need to provide the expected execution time of the submitted task. Customers would be charged based on the real execution time of the task. The malicious customer problem is solved if the assumption is correct[4,9]. 2) Assuming that all the consumers are good ones[5], and there're only malicious service providers in the system. In this case, if a service provider did not complete the task submitted by a consumer within the expected time, it will be identified as a malicious one.

All of the work above are based on the assumption that either all service providers or all consumers are "good" ones. However, it is not a correct assumption in the real world. It is quite likely that malicious service providers and consumers co-exist in a grid system. In this paper, we proposed a ranking process, which can be used by scheduling and billing systems of grid, to solve the malicious participants problem.

2 Problem Definition

Before solving the problem. Let's try to define the problem in more detail. This includes definition of terms, assumptions and the goal of our solution.

2.1 Terms

- Consumer: Who send out tasks and pay for tasks.
- Service Provider: Who receive tasks and get paid from completing tasks.
- Participant: Consumer and Service Provider.
- Opposite Participant: Consumer's opposite participant is Service Provider. Service Provider's opposite participant is Consumer.
- Broker: An independent role in Grid. See section 2.2 for more details about Broker.

2.2 System Assumption

- The broker in the grid system belongs to an independent party. It does not owned by any consumer and service provider. The broker is a fair one, and allow consumer to query service provider's status and history information. Service providers can also query information about a certain user.
- All deals in the grid system are monitored and recorded by the broker if necessary.
- Although there are malicious participants in the system, they are rare. Majority of the system are good participants.

2.3 Goal

The solution should achieve the following goals:

- Any malicious behavior should be recorded and has negative feedback for the participant's future deal.
- Malicious participants can be identified after long enough time.
- Good participants should not be recognized as malicious ones.

3 Using Ranks to Solve the Malicious Participants Problem

3.1 Intuitive Idea

Let's see a similar situation in the real world. In eBay, the online auction web site, a seller is ranked by his/her deal history. In this case, the buyer would know if the seller is an honest one, and can decide if he/she still wants to purchase a certain item from the seller.

The online auction process is simpler than grid computing, because buyers would always pay for the product first and only the sellers are possible malicious ones. So they just need to rank sellers. In the grid computing environment, however, as we have just described in the introduction section, both consumers and service providers can be malicious. So we need to rank both customers and sellers.

Before formally describing the ranking process, let's examine several features of it.

- Who rank whom?
  Customers rank service providers. Service providers rank customers. Brokers maintain the rank result.
- When to rank?
  If a consumer finds that the service provider fails to complete its submitted tasks in its expected time, it can complain to brokers. The broker would know that in this deal, the service provider got a bad rank. If the deal complete normally, the consumer would not complain and the brokers know that the consumer and the service provider complete a deal successfully. The history of successful deal would also be recorded.
  The service provider part would be similar. If it finds that the acquired task is longer than the consumer claimed, it will complain to brokers.
- How does broker know who is correct if a consumer and a service provider complains each other?
  When a malicious consumer is complained by its service provider, because of its malicious task submission, the malicious consumer can also complain the service provider to the broker. How does the broker know which complain is true? Well, the broker does not know this for sure, and it does not need to. Because we assume that the majority of participants are good, the ranking system would accumulate the vote from good participants and suppress the vote from malicious ones.

3.2 System Model and Notation

A grid system contains M consumers $(c_1, c_2, \ldots, c_M)$ and N service providers $(s_1, s_2, \ldots, s_N)$. Each consumer c_i and service provider s_j has a rank, which is calculated by the broker, based on the vote from all the opposite participants.

The first step is to calculate a customer's vote to all service providers and a service provider's vote to all customers. We assume that the rank value of customers and service providers are all between $[0, 1]$, where 0 represents maliciousness and 1 represent goodness. The vote of c_i to s_j is denoted by $vs_{i,j}$. The vote of s_j to c_i is denoted by $vc_{j,i}$. So we get 2 matrices: $VS = [vs_{i,j}]_{M\times N}$ and $VC = [vc_{j,i}]_{N\times M}$.

The rank of c_i is denoted by rc_i. The rank of s_j is denoted by rs_j. We get 2 vectors $RC = [rc_i]_M$ and $RS = [rs_j]_N$:

$$rc_i = \sum_{1\leq j\leq N} vc_{j,i} \tag{1}$$

$$rs_j = \sum_{1\leq i\leq M} vs_{i,j} \tag{2}$$

So the rank of a participant is simply the sum of all votes to it.

3.3 Limitations of Vote

To limit the right of a single participant, we let each participant have the equal vote right, which is distributed among its opposite participants. We normalize the total vote right of a participant to 1. To express this limitation formally, we have:

$$\forall 1 \leq i \leq M, \sum_{1\leq j\leq N} vs_{i,j} \leq 1 \tag{3}$$

$$\forall 1 \leq j \leq N, \sum_{1\leq i\leq M} vc_{j,i} \leq 1 \tag{4}$$

It should be noted that the total vote of a participant may be less than 1, which means that the participant gives up part of its vote right, because of lacking of knowledge to make decision. Now let's consider how the vote should be distributed. For an example, in a system with 2 customers and 2 service providers, which are all good ones, c_1 should distribute its vote 1 evenly among s_1 and s_2, we get $vs_{1,1} = 0.5$ and $vs_{1,2} = 0.5$. We can calculate other elements in VS and VC in the same way and we get:

$$VS = \begin{bmatrix} 0.5 & 0.5 \\ 0.5 & 0.5 \end{bmatrix} VC = \begin{bmatrix} 0.5 & 0.5 \\ 0.5 & 0.5 \end{bmatrix}$$

However, the above limitation is still not enough. In the last example, if c_1 is a malicious customer and s_1 is a malicious service provider. Both s_1 and c_1 did not act maliciously in getting tasks and executing tasks. So for c_2 and s_2 they are good participants. But they act maliciously in the voting stage. We may get a VS and VC like following:

$$VS = \begin{bmatrix} 1.0 & 0.5 \\ 0.0 & 0.5 \end{bmatrix} VC = \begin{bmatrix} 1.0 & 0.5 \\ 0.0 & 0.5 \end{bmatrix}$$

We can calculate the ranks of participants by definition: $rs_1 = 1.5$ and $rs_2 = 0.5$. $rc_1 = 1.5$ and $rc_2 = 0.5$. The rank of malicious participants, c_1 and s_1 are much higher than the rank of good participants, c_2 and s_2. What's more, their ranks are even larger than 1, which means they are super good. This would make the ranking system fail, because the purpose of the ranking system is to find out malicious participants. The reason for this result is that the malicious participants can distribute its vote right in an unreasonably uneven way. In order to avoid this, we need to introduce a more strict limitation to the distribution of vote right. Each consumer should distribute at most $1/N$ vote right to a service provider and each service provider should distribute $1/M$ vote right to a consumer at most.

$$\forall 1 \leq i \leq M, 1 \leq j \leq N, vs_{i,j} \leq \frac{1}{M} \text{ and } vc_{j,i} \leq \frac{1}{N} \tag{5}$$

This limitation would greatly reduce the malicious vote's effect to the rank. In the above example, we would get a VS and a VC as following:

$$VS = \begin{bmatrix} 0.5 & 0.5 \\ 0.0 & 0.5 \end{bmatrix} VC = \begin{bmatrix} 0.5 & 0.5 \\ 0.0 & 0.5 \end{bmatrix}$$

The ranks are: $rs_1 = 1.0$ and $rs_2 = 0.5$. $rc_1 = 1.0$ and $rc_2 = 0.5$. No ranks are larger than 1 now. Besides, the effect of malicious vote is reduced to $\frac{1}{M}$ or $\frac{1}{N}$ of its original value respectively, where $M = 2$ and $N = 2$ in this example. When there're more participants, which means M and N is larger, the limitation would be more helpful to maintain the correctness of the rank values.

3.4 Initial Vote

Now let's consider how to vote to a participant which has no deals record with the voter. This determines the initial distribution of the vote right. If c_i does not have any deals with s_j, then $vs_{i,j}$ should in $(0, \frac{1}{N})$ and $vc_{j,i}$ should in $(0, \frac{1}{M})$. Let's assume there at most M_m malicious consumers and N_m malicious service providers in the system. Then we get

$$vs_{i,j} = \frac{(N - N_m)/N}{N} = \frac{N - N_m}{N^2} \tag{6}$$

$$vc_{i,j} = \frac{(M - M_m)/M}{M} = \frac{M - M_m}{M^2} \tag{7}$$

3.5 Vote Calculation with History of Deals

In the above section, we described the rules that voting should follow. In this section, we describe the rules to calculate the vote. Instead of letting each participant determine its own vote distribution by itself, we use the broker to calculate the vote value. The benefit of this approach is that the broker would use a uniform rule to calculate vote distribution, further reduce the possibility of malicious vote, e.g. a malicious consumer vote 0 to a service provider which it does not have any deal with.

If a consumer thinks it met a malicious service provider in a deal, it will complain it to the broker. So will service providers. If neither side complains the deal, the deal is considered as a successful one. We assume all deals are visible to the broker. Thus the broker keeps track of all successful deals and failed deals. We use 3 matrices to record the history of deals:

$$SD = [sd_{i,j}]_{M\times N}$$

where $sd_{i,j}$ is the number of successful deals between c_i and s_j

$$FDCC = [fdcc_{i,j}]_{M\times N}$$

where $fdcc_{i,j}$ is the number of failed deals between c_i and s_j which are complained by c_i

$$FDCS = [fdcs_{i,j}]_{M\times N}$$

where $fdcs_{i,j}$ is the number of failed deals between c_i and s_j which are complained by s_j.

$$1 \le i \le M \ and \ 1 \le j \le N$$

The broker can then calculate the rank of consumers with these data matrices.

$$vs_{i,j} = \begin{cases} \frac{N-N_m}{N^2} & , \text{ if } sd_{i,j} = 0 \text{ and } fdcc_{i,j} = 0 \\ \frac{sd_{i,j}}{(sd_{i,j}+fdcc_{i,j})N} & , \text{ otherwise} \end{cases} \tag{8}$$

$$vc_{i,j} = \begin{cases} \frac{M-M_m}{M^2} & , \text{ if } sd_{i,j} = 0 \text{ and } fdcs_{i,j} = 0 \\ \frac{sd_{j,i}}{(sd_{i,j}+fdcs_{i,j})M} & , \text{ otherwise} \end{cases} \tag{9}$$

4 An Example of the Ranking Process

In this section, we use an example to demonstrate the ranking process described in section 3. We assume that there are 4 consumers and 4 service providers in the system. The N_m and M_m are set to 1. Assume s_1 and c_1 are malicious. Other participants are all good.

4.1 Initial Stage

Because there's no deal information yet, all elements in SD, $FDCC$ and $FDCS$ are 0. VS and VC are calculated with estimated N_m and M_m.

$$SD = \begin{bmatrix} 0&0&0&0 \\ 0&0&0&0 \\ 0&0&0&0 \\ 0&0&0&0 \end{bmatrix} FDCC = \begin{bmatrix} 0&0&0&0 \\ 0&0&0&0 \\ 0&0&0&0 \\ 0&0&0&0 \end{bmatrix} FDCS = \begin{bmatrix} 0&0&0&0 \\ 0&0&0&0 \\ 0&0&0&0 \\ 0&0&0&0 \end{bmatrix}$$

$$VS = \begin{bmatrix} 3/16 & 3/16 & 3/16 & 3/16 \\ 3/16 & 3/16 & 3/16 & 3/16 \\ 3/16 & 3/16 & 3/16 & 3/16 \\ 3/16 & 3/16 & 3/16 & 3/16 \end{bmatrix} VC = \begin{bmatrix} 3/16 & 3/16 & 3/16 & 3/16 \\ 3/16 & 3/16 & 3/16 & 3/16 \\ 3/16 & 3/16 & 3/16 & 3/16 \\ 3/16 & 3/16 & 3/16 & 3/16 \end{bmatrix}$$

$$RS = \begin{bmatrix} 3/4 & 3/4 & 3/4 & 3/4 \end{bmatrix} RC = \begin{bmatrix} 3/4 & 3/4 & 3/4 & 3/4 \end{bmatrix}$$

4.2 A Good Consumer c_2 and a Good Service Provider s_2 Had a Successful Deal

A successful deal between a consumer and a service provider increased their ranks.

$$SD = \begin{bmatrix} 0 & 0 & 0 & 0 \\ 0 & 1 & 0 & 0 \\ 0 & 0 & 0 & 0 \\ 0 & 0 & 0 & 0 \end{bmatrix} FDCC = \begin{bmatrix} 0 & 0 & 0 & 0 \\ 0 & 0 & 0 & 0 \\ 0 & 0 & 0 & 0 \\ 0 & 0 & 0 & 0 \end{bmatrix} FDCS = \begin{bmatrix} 0 & 0 & 0 & 0 \\ 0 & 0 & 0 & 0 \\ 0 & 0 & 0 & 0 \\ 0 & 0 & 0 & 0 \end{bmatrix}$$

$$VS = \begin{bmatrix} 3/16 & 3/16 & 3/16 & 3/16 \\ 3/16 & 1/4 & 3/16 & 3/16 \\ 3/16 & 3/16 & 3/16 & 3/16 \\ 3/16 & 3/16 & 3/16 & 3/16 \end{bmatrix} VC = \begin{bmatrix} 3/16 & 3/16 & 3/16 & 3/16 \\ 3/16 & 1/4 & 3/16 & 3/16 \\ 3/16 & 3/16 & 3/16 & 3/16 \\ 3/16 & 3/16 & 3/16 & 3/16 \end{bmatrix}$$

$$RS = \begin{bmatrix} 3/4 & 13/16 & 3/4 & 3/4 \end{bmatrix} RC = \begin{bmatrix} 3/4 & 13/16 & 3/4 & 3/4 \end{bmatrix}$$

4.3 A Malicious Consumer c_1 and a Good Service Provider s_3 Had a Deal

s_3 complained c_1 because it found s1 to be malicious. However, c_1 also complains s_3. Both of their ranks reduced.

$$SD = \begin{bmatrix} 0 & 0 & 0 & 0 \\ 0 & 1 & 0 & 0 \\ 0 & 0 & 0 & 0 \\ 0 & 0 & 0 & 0 \end{bmatrix} FDCC = \begin{bmatrix} 0 & 0 & 1 & 0 \\ 0 & 0 & 0 & 0 \\ 0 & 0 & 0 & 0 \\ 0 & 0 & 0 & 0 \end{bmatrix} FDCS = \begin{bmatrix} 0 & 0 & 1 & 0 \\ 0 & 0 & 0 & 0 \\ 0 & 0 & 0 & 0 \\ 0 & 0 & 0 & 0 \end{bmatrix}$$

$$VS = \begin{bmatrix} 3/16 & 3/16 & 0 & 3/16 \\ 3/16 & 1/4 & 3/16 & 3/16 \\ 3/16 & 3/16 & 3/16 & 3/16 \\ 3/16 & 3/16 & 3/16 & 3/16 \end{bmatrix} VC = \begin{bmatrix} 3/16 & 3/16 & 3/16 & 3/16 \\ 3/16 & 1/4 & 3/16 & 3/16 \\ 0 & 3/16 & 3/16 & 3/16 \\ 3/16 & 3/16 & 3/16 & 3/16 \end{bmatrix}$$

$$RS = \begin{bmatrix} 3/4 & 13/16 & 9/16 & 3/4 \end{bmatrix} RC = \begin{bmatrix} 9/16 & 13/16 & 3/4 & 3/4 \end{bmatrix}$$

4.4 A Malicious Consumer c_1 and a Malicious Service Provider s_1 Had a Deal

Malicious participants in the system may cooperate to increase their ranks. The deal between them is considered as a successful deal and both of their ranks increased.

$$SD = \begin{bmatrix} 1&0&0&0 \\ 0&1&0&0 \\ 0&0&0&0 \\ 0&0&0&0 \end{bmatrix} \quad FDCC = \begin{bmatrix} 0&0&1&0 \\ 0&0&0&0 \\ 0&0&0&0 \\ 0&0&0&0 \end{bmatrix} \quad FDCS = \begin{bmatrix} 0&0&1&0 \\ 0&0&0&0 \\ 0&0&0&0 \\ 0&0&0&0 \end{bmatrix}$$

$$VS = \begin{bmatrix} 1/4 & 3/16 & 0 & 3/16 \\ 3/16 & 1/4 & 3/16 & 3/16 \\ 3/16 & 3/16 & 3/16 & 3/16 \\ 3/16 & 3/16 & 3/16 & 3/16 \end{bmatrix} \quad VC = \begin{bmatrix} 1/4 & 3/16 & 3/16 & 3/16 \\ 3/16 & 1/4 & 3/16 & 3/16 \\ 0 & 3/16 & 3/16 & 3/16 \\ 3/16 & 3/16 & 3/16 & 3/16 \end{bmatrix}$$

$$RS = \begin{bmatrix} 13/16 & 13/16 & 9/16 & 3/4 \end{bmatrix} \, RC = \begin{bmatrix} 5/8 & 13/16 & 3/4 & 3/4 \end{bmatrix}$$

4.5 Two Good Consumers, c_2 and c_3 Have One Deal with a Malicious Service Provider s_1 Respectively

By far, the ranking process seems not quite successful. For the consumer side, the c_1 has the least rank now, which identifies its maliciousness. However the malicious service provider is not identified correctly. But it's not the fault of the ranking process. Because the malicious service provider did not act maliciously enough yet. So let's examine what happened after c_2 and c_3 had deals with s_1.

$$SD = \begin{bmatrix} 1&0&0&0 \\ 0&1&0&0 \\ 0&0&0&0 \\ 0&0&0&0 \end{bmatrix} \quad FDCC = \begin{bmatrix} 0&0&1&0 \\ 1&0&0&0 \\ 1&0&0&0 \\ 0&0&0&0 \end{bmatrix} \quad FDCS = \begin{bmatrix} 0&0&1&0 \\ 1&0&0&0 \\ 1&0&0&0 \\ 0&0&0&0 \end{bmatrix}$$

$$VS = \begin{bmatrix} 1/4 & 3/16 & 0 & 3/16 \\ 0 & 1/4 & 3/16 & 3/16 \\ 0 & 3/16 & 3/16 & 3/16 \\ 3/16 & 3/16 & 3/16 & 3/16 \end{bmatrix} \quad VC = \begin{bmatrix} 1/4 & 0 & 0 & 3/16 \\ 3/16 & 1/4 & 3/16 & 3/16 \\ 0 & 3/16 & 3/16 & 3/16 \\ 3/16 & 3/16 & 3/16 & 3/16 \end{bmatrix}$$

$$RS = \begin{bmatrix} 7/16 & 13/16 & 9/16 & 3/4 \end{bmatrix} \, RC = \begin{bmatrix} 5/8 & 5/8 & 9/16 & 3/4 \end{bmatrix}$$

4.6 A Malicious Consumer c_1 and a Good Service Provider s_2 Had a Deal

Deals between s_1 and c_2 and c_3 reduce the rank of s_1 enough. So it can be identified as malicious already. Because even if c_1 votes 0 for all other service providers other than s_1, all other service providers would have their rank no less than 9/16. If they have successful deals with good consumers, their ranks will be greater. So the malicious service provider problem has already been solved for the example till now. Let's see how to identify the malicious consumer. Examine the changing of ranks after c1 had a deal with s_2.

$$SD = \begin{bmatrix} 1&0&0&0\\ 0&1&0&0\\ 0&0&0&0\\ 0&0&0&0 \end{bmatrix} \; FDCC = \begin{bmatrix} 0&1&1&0\\ 1&0&0&0\\ 1&0&0&0\\ 0&0&0&0 \end{bmatrix} \; FDCS = \begin{bmatrix} 0&1&1&0\\ 1&0&0&0\\ 1&0&0&0\\ 0&0&0&0 \end{bmatrix}$$

$$VS = \begin{bmatrix} 1/4 & 0 & 0 & 3/16\\ 0 & 1/4 & 3/16 & 3/16\\ 0 & 3/16 & 3/16 & 3/16\\ 3/16 & 3/16 & 3/16 & 3/16 \end{bmatrix} \; VC = \begin{bmatrix} 1/4 & 0 & 0 & 3/16\\ 0 & 1/4 & 3/16 & 3/16\\ 0 & 3/16 & 3/16 & 3/16\\ 3/16 & 3/16 & 3/16 & 3/16 \end{bmatrix}$$

$$RS = \begin{bmatrix} 7/16 & 9/16 & 9/16 & 3/4 \end{bmatrix} RC = \begin{bmatrix} 7/16 & 5/8 & 9/16 & 3/4 \end{bmatrix}$$

The rank of c_1 is 7/16 now. With similar analysis to service providers, we should know that it is lower than any possible rank of good consumers. So we also identified the malicious consumer with ranking process successfully.

5 Conclusion and Future Works

Malicious participants problem is an important problem in Computational Grid. In this paper, we propose a ranking process to solve the problem. We show effectiveness of the process with an example. The result is still preliminary and can be extended in some aspects:1) More quantitative analysis to the current ranking process.2) Improved ranking process that can handle the situation where good participants are not the majority.

Acknowledgement. We would like to thank Professor Deng Xiaotie for discussion on related topics, and to thank Dr. Wu Yongwei for his help on finding some useful references and formatting this paper.

References

1. Amir, Y., Awerbuch, B. et.al.: A cost-benefit framework for online management of a metacomputing system. Proceedings of the First International Conference on Computation Economics (1998)
2. Anderson, David P., Cobb J. et.al.: SETI@home: An Experiment in Public-Resource Computing. Communications of the ACM **45**(11) (2002) 56–61.
3. Brin, S., Page L.: The Anatomy of a Large-Scale Hypertextual Web Search Engine. http://www-db.stanford.edu/ backrub/google.html
4. Cappello, P., Cristiansen, O. B., et.al.: Market-Based Massively Parallel Internet Computing. Third working conference on Massively Parallel Programming Models (1997).

5. Chun, B. N., Culler, D. E.: Use-centric Performance Analysis of Market-based Cluster Batch Schedulers. Proceedings of the 2nd IEEE/ACM International Symposium on Cluster Computing and the Grid (2002) 22–30
6. Foster, I.,Kesselman, C.: Globus: A Metacomputing Infrastructure Toolkit. Intl J. Supercomputer Applications, **11**(2) (1997) 115–128
7. Foster, I., Kesselman, C., editors: The Grid:Blueprint for a New Computing InfraStructure. Morgan Kaufmann. (1999)
8. Foster, I., Kesselman, C., et.al.: Grid Services for Distributed System Integration. Computer, **35**(6) (2002) 37–46
9. Kakarontzas G.,Lalis S.: A Market-based Protocol with Leasing Support for Globally Distributed Computing. Proceedings of the First IEEE/ACM International Symposium on Cluster Computing and the Grid (2001) 562–567
10. Stiller, B., Gerke, J., et.al. Charging Distributed Services of a Computational Grid Architecutre. Proceedings of the First IEEE/ACM International Symposium on Cluster Computing and the Grid (2001) 596–601

Certificate Validation Scheme of Open Grid Service Usage XKMS

Namje Park, Kiyoung Moon, Sungwon Sohn, and Cheehang Park

Information Security Research Division
Electronics and Telecommunications Research Institute (ETRI)
161 Gajeong-Dong, Yuseong-Gu, Daejeon, 305-350, Korea
{namjepark, kymoon, swsohn, chpark}@etri.re.kr

Abstract. Current Grid Security Infrastructure using PKI based on SSO. Trust is hard to establish in a service-oriented grid architecture because of the need to support end user SSO and dynamic transient service. Open Grid Service (OGS) Security Infrastructure in Global Grid Forum will extend use of Grid system or services up to business area using XML Web Service security technology. This paper describes a novel security approach on Open Grid Service to validate certificate based on current Globus Toolkit environment using XKMS and SAML, XACML in XML Security. Our security model is based on XKMS, an implementation of the Java component and international standard specification.

1 Introduction

Grid technologies are increasingly becoming the platform of choice for developing and deploying distributed computation and data intensive application across large virtual organizations. A computational grid is a hardware and software infrastructure that provides dependable, consistent, pervasive and inexpensive access to high-end computational capabilities. Typically the grid resources are provided by various organizations and are used by people from diverse sets of organizations. A Grid is a collection of distributed computing resources available over a local or wide area network that appear to an end user or application as one large virtual computing system. The vision is to create virtual dynamic organizations through secure, coordinated resource sharing among individuals, institutions, and resources. Grid computing is an approach to distributed computing that spans not only locations but also organizations, machine architectures and software boundaries to provide unlimited power, collaboration and information access to everyone connected to a Grid [3].

The different resources in a Grid may have different access policies, including how they authenticate and authorize users. However, if there are no common or overlapping authorizations among the resources, they do not form a usable grid. And in order to access shared resources, security is an essential component. Users, hosts and services need to be able to authenticate themselves in the Grid environment. Experience in using grids for remote computations has demonstrated the need for unattended user authentication in addition to interactive authentication.

M. Li et al. (Eds.): GCC 2003, LNCS 3032, pp. 849–858, 2004.

Grid service requests can span multiple security domains. Trust relationships among these domains play an important role in the outcome of such end-to-end traversals. A service needs to make its access requirements available to interested client entities, so that they understand how to securely request access to it. Trust between end points can be presumed, based on topological assumptions or explicit, specified as policies and enforced through exchange of some trust-forming credentials. In a Grid environment, presumed trust is rarely feasible due to the dynamic and distributed nature of virtual organizations relationships. Trust establishment may be a one-time activity per session or it may be evaluated dynamically on every request. The dynamic nature of the Grid in some cases can make it impossible to establish trust relationships among sites prior to application execution [3]. Given that the participating domains may have different security infrastructures it is necessary to realize the required trust relationships through some form of federation among the security mechanisms.

Furthermore, Open Grid Service Infrastructure (OGSI) in Global Grid Forum (GGF) will extend use of the Grid technology or services up to business area using Web Service technology [4]. Therefore differential resource access is a necessary operation for users to share their resources securely and willingly. Therefore, this paper describes a novel security approach on Open Grid Service to validate certificate based on current Globus Toolkit environment using XKMS (XML Key Management Specification) [1] and SAML (Security Assertion Markup Language) [5], XACML (eXtensible Access Control Markup Language) in XML Security [4].

This paper is organized as follows. First, we propose a design of security system platform for open grid service and explain experimented XKMS model for certificate validation service. Finally, we explain function of system and then we conclude this paper.

2 Secure OGS Framework Based on XML Security

In this section, we define secure Open Grid Service framework based on XML Security and describe its components. We also discuss XKMS system platform in framework.

2.1 XKMS Architecture in Secure OGS Framework

The Open Grid Services Architecture (OGSA) aims to define a new common and standard architecture for grid-based applications. OGSA defines what Grid Services are, what they should be capable of, what types of technologies they should be based on, but doesn't give a technical and detailed specification (which would be needed to implement a Grid service) [4]. OGSA is based on XML Web Service.

Figure 1 illustrates the layering of existing security technologies and standards and shows how these fit into the Open Grid Security model. Moving from the machine and OS security on the bottom to the applications and server environment at the top, one can identify different layers that either are built and depend on their lower neighbors, or are a level up in abstraction.

The same or similar functions can be implemented at different levels, with different characteristics and tradeoffs. For example, security can be an inherent part of a network and binding layer. In the case of the network layer, it can be provided via IPSec or SSL/TLS. In the case of the binding layer, it can be provided by HTTPS and in the case of IIOP, by CSIv2 [4]. In a messaging environment, the message provider (e.g., MQ) can provide end-to-end message security. Given the increasing use of XML, the security standards in the XML space play an important role here: XML Signature, XML Encryption, XML Key Management Service (XKMS), and Assertion Languages (e.g., SAML). Built on top of XML standards are the Web services standards, including WSDL.

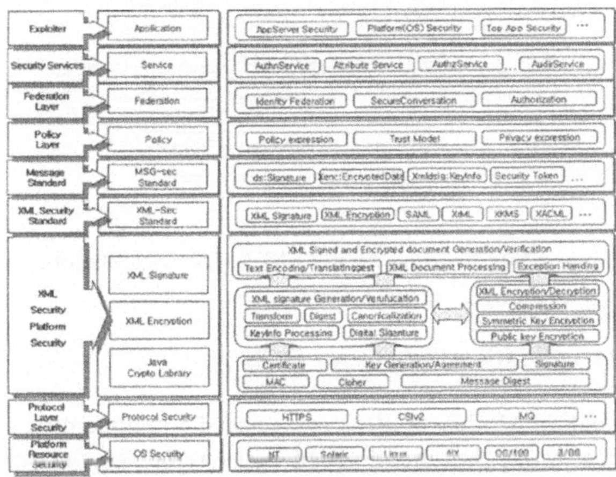

Fig. 1. Security Layer blocks for OGSA based on XML Web Security

This framework supports extensibility because it has been developed based on international standards such as WS-Security, XKMS, XML Encryption, and XML Signature specification.

XKMS service platform is a framework for the approaches about function of XKMS system and work for development based on Java platform. XML Security API is expressed by structure of java crypto library and XML parser, XSLT processor [9]. And It includes service provide mechanism. SOAP security API supplies XML Web Service security. And XML Security API and SOAP security API supports key exchange and encryption. It supports XML Signature and XML Encryption function. Based on this, XKMS service platform is composed. So, XKMS service application program are achieved by component of service platform that is constructed by each function. Other than system application, many XML web application security can be provided using the XML Security API and Library that is provided from the XKMS service platform. Figure 2 illustrates the architecture of XKMS service system platform. Major components of XKMS service platform are java crypto library, XML Security API, SOAP security API, XML Signature API, XML Encryption API.

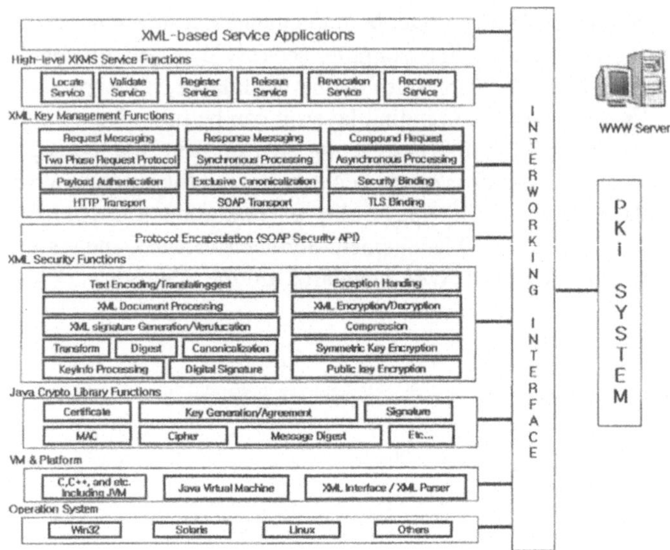

Fig. 2. Architecture of XKMS Service Platform

2.2 Certificate Validation Service for OGS

Certificate Validation Module (CVM) is a service component that offloads certificate validation process from the client. CVM consists of six components such as three components for the validating certificate, two components for upgrading efficiency and a component for managing certificate policies and policy mapping information. Figure 3 show that CVM architecture and protocols used by CVM and show the structure of Certificate Validation Service Model.

CVM in XKMS system perform path validation on a certificate chain according to the local policy and with local PKI (Public Key Infrastructure) facilities, such as certificate revocation (CRLs) or through an Online Certificate Status Protocol (OCSP) [2]. In the CVM, a number of protocols (OCSP, SCVP, and LDAP) are used for the service of certificate validation. For processing the XML client request, certificate validation service from OCSP, LDAP, SCVP protocols in XKMS based on PKI are used.

The XKMS client generates an 'XKMS Validate' request. This is essentially asking the XKMS server to go and find out the status of the Server's certificate. The XKMS server receives this request and performs a series of validation tasks e.g. X.509 certificate path validation. Certificate status is determined. An XKMS server replies to client application with status of the server's certificate and application acts accordingly. Using the OCSP protocol, the CVM obtained certificate status information from other OCSP responders or other CVMs. Using the LDAP protocol, the CVM fetched CRL (Certificates Revocation Lists) from the repository. And CA DB connection protocol (CVMP;CVM Protocol) is used for the purpose of that the server obtains real-time certificate status information from CAs. The client uses OCSP and SCVP. With

XKMS, all of these functions are performed by the XKMS server component. Thus, there is no need for LDAP, OCSP and other registration functionality in the client application itself.

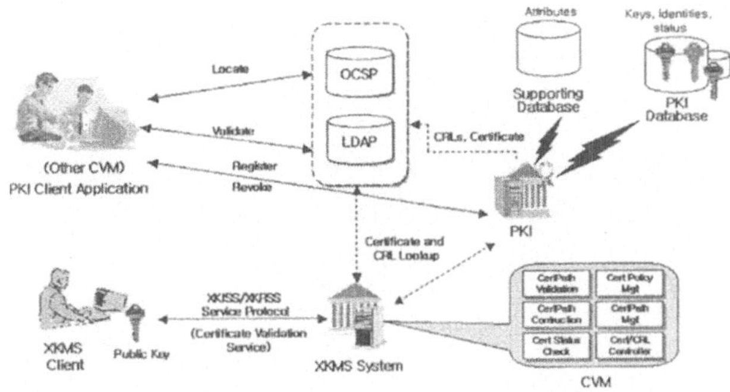

Fig. 3. Certificate Validation Service Model for OGS

3 Flow of CVM for OGS Based on XKMS

3.1 Process of XKMS Service Components

XKMS supports two services. Locate service resolves a <ds:KeyInfo> element but does not require the service to make an assertion concerning the validity of the binding between the data in the <ds:KeyInfo> element. The Validate service provides all the functions of locate but returns a trusted key binding that has been validated in accordance with the policy of validate service [1].

Locate service retrieves and provides information concerning keys. In Locate service of figure 4 begins with an incoming XML Signature. The <ds:Signature> element is parsed for the <ds:KeyInfo> element that contains a <ds:KeyName> element including the odd key identifier. We are assuming the signature processing application doesn't understand this identifier and must delegate the processing to a key Location service. This key locate service processes the key identifier and makes a database query that matches it to an X.509 certificate. This certificate is then formatted as a <ds:KeyInfo> element and passed back to the signature processing application. At this point the signature processing application has enough information to perform cryptographic validation of the signature processing application [8]. At this point the signature processing application has enough information to perform cryptographic validation of the signature. It now has a public key, whereas before it only had a single key identifier. The signature processing application may now choose to perform path validation on its own, or it may decide to delegate this action to a service as well. The key Location service is the first tier of XKMS, which is called the locate service. In addition to passing off <ds:KeyInfo> element, the signature processing application may also pass off a <ds:RetrievalMethod> element if the signature processing application doesn't have access to the necessary network or server location.

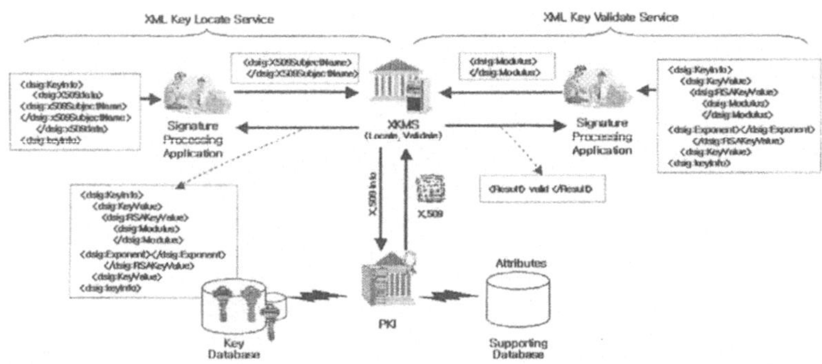

Fig. 4. Locate and Validate service of XKMS

The second tier is called the Validate service and is responsible for asserting trust over the binding of a name and a public key. The Validate service is a superset of the Locate service. This means that in addition to providing name key assertions, it can also locate public key values. In Validate service of figure 4 we have a situation similar to the one presented in Locate service of figure 4. In Validate service of figure 4 we are passing a <ds:X509Data> element to the Validate service with the expectation of a status result and an indication of the key binding. Validate service gives us the name and public key from the queried certificate as well as make en assertion regarding the binding between the name in the certificate and the public key.

In current Globus middleware Toolkit, there is no mechanism of differential resource access. To establish such a security system we are seeking, a standardized policy mechanism is required. Fortunately, Globus Toolkit 3.0 is implemented using the XML Web Service technology, which uses XML formatted documents for interfacing among middleware services. We employ the XACML specification to establish the resource policy mechanism that assigns differential policy to each resource (or service). SAML also has the policy mechanism but it is very limited to use for Grid, while XACML provides very flexible policy mechanism enough to apply to any resource type [8]. For our implementing model, SAML provides a standardized method to exchange the authentication and authorization information securely by creating assertions from output of XKMS (e.g. Assertion Validation Service in XKMS). XACML replaces the policy part of SAML as shown in Figure 5.

Once the three assertions are created and sent to the protected resource, there is no more verification of the authentication and authorization at the visiting site [6]. This, Single-Sign-On (SSO), is a main contribution of SAML in distributed security systems.

Figure 5 shows the flow of SAML and XACML integration for differential resource access. Once assertions are done from secure identification of the PKI trusted service, send the access request to the policy enforcement point (PEP) server (or agent) and send to the context handler. Context handler parses the attribute query and sends it to

PIP (policy information point) agent. The PIP gathers subject, resource and environment attributes from local policy file, and the context handler gives the required target resource value, attribute and resource value to PDP (policy decision point) agent. Finally, the PDP decides access possibility and send context handler so that PEP agent allow or deny the request.

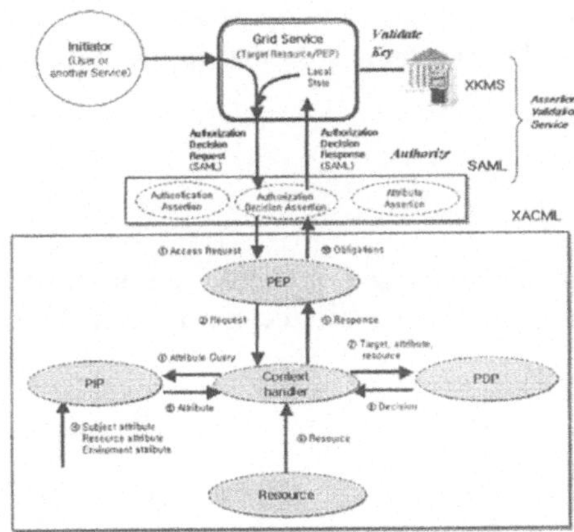

Fig. 5. SAML/XACML Message Flow using XKMS

3.2 Flow of Certificate Validation Service

Certification path validation verifies the binding among the subject identity, the subject public key, and subject attributes that may be present in the certification path. Constraints in certification path limit the possible identity values and the possible attribute values. And certification path validation determines whether certificates in chain are revoked or not revoked [7]. The algorithm of the validation is as follows.

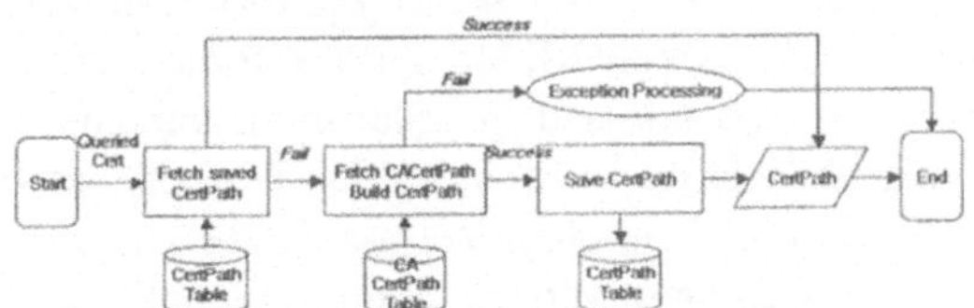

Fig. 6. Certification Path Validation Sequence

First, client generates the certification path validation request. The request may optionally include the client's trust anchor or certification policy. This information is used for validating chain. And, The server builds certification paths using certification path construction module. If the trust anchor in the request is present, the server must build the certification path that start from the trust anchor certificate. Second, certification paths and optional certification policy. If building certification path succeeded and certification policy is present, the server verifies certification path using certification policy constrains and also performs checking certificate status. If building certification path succeeded and certification policy is not present, the validating process is performed by only checking certificate status. Because the current certification path was already verified in first step.

If the previous step succeeded and the verified path was obtained, the verified path is saved in certification path DB table for next request. If the previous step failed or the verified path was not obtained, the server processes an exception handling and makes a fail response. Also the fail reason is recorded in the log file. Finally, Verified certification path.

4 Experiment

XKMS has been implemented based on the design described in previous section. The figure for representing Testbed Architecture of XKMS component is as follows Figure 7.

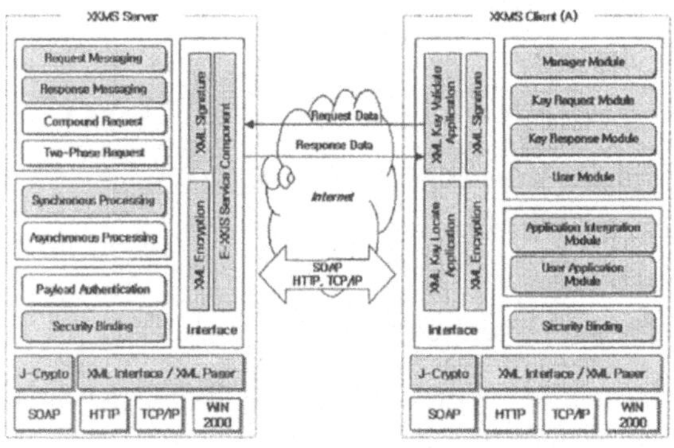

Fig. 7. Testbed Architecture of XKMS Component for Open Grid

Components of the XKMS are XML Security platform library, service components API, application program. Although XKMS service component is intended to support XML applications, it can also be used in order environments where the same management and deployment benefits are achievable. Testbed has been implemented in Java and it runs on JDK ver 1.3 or more. We use Testbed system of windows PC environment to simulate the processing of various service protocols. And the message format is based on specification of W3C.

The manner in which the various XKMS service builds upon each other and consumes each other's services is shown in the following diagram.

The arrow reflects the primary relationship between the security services. The first (Alphabet) path shows alternative ways of checking the security of a SOAP message secured using Web Security service. Second (Number) path is the same except Web Service security delegates signature checking in its entirety to a Digital Signature Service. Table 1 summarizes function of XKMS service system component for CVM.

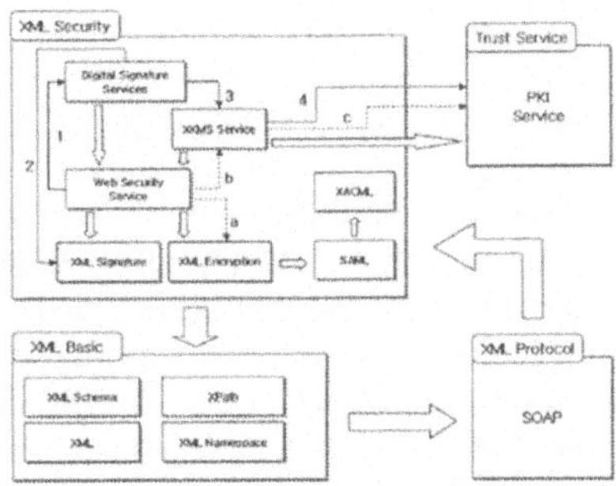

Fig. 8. Interrelation of XKMS Service in Open Grid environment

Table 1. Function of XKMS System Component for CVM

Service & Protocol	XKMS System					
	Tier 0	Tier 1	Tier 2	Tier 3	Tier 4	
Register Service	*	*	*	*	*	KRSS
Locate / Validate Service	M	M	* / M	O	O	KISS
Recovery / Revoke Service	*	*	*	*	*	KRSS
Compound Request Protocol	O	O	O			-
Synchronous Processing	*	M	M	*	*	-
Asynchronous Processing	*	O	O	*	*	-
Two-Phase Request Protocol	*	O	O	*	*	-
Payload Authentication	*	O	O	*	*	-
HTTP / SOAP 1.1 Transport	M	M	M	M	M	-
Cert Path Validation	*	*	M	*	*	-
Cert Status Check	*	*	M	*	*	-

(M:Mandatory, O:Optional, *:No Recommendation)

5 Conclusion

The Grid technology extends its use from meta-computing for researchers to business areas for companies by employing XML Web Service technology. The current GSI needs to apply the current mechanism to OGSI. We propose a novel security approach on open grid service to validate certificate based on current Grid security environment using XKMS and SAML, XACML in XML Security.

This service model allows a client to offload certificate handling to the server and enable to provide central administration of XKMS polices. In order to obtain timely certificate status information, the server uses several methods such as CRL, OCSP etc. Our approach will be a model for the future security system that offers security of Open Grid Security.

References

1 XML Key Management Specification Version 2.0 (W3C Working Draft), April-2003
2. Certificate Management Protocol, RFC2510, March-1999
3. Global Grid Forum: http://www.globalgridforum.org/
4. GWD-1: OGSA Security Roadmap: GGF OGSA Security WorkingGroup, July-2002
5. Assertions and Protocol for the OASIS SAML: OASIS Standard (2002)
6. Euinam Huh, Jihye Kim, Hyeju Kim, Kiyoung Moon: Policy based on grid security infrastructure implementation for differential resource access: ISOC 2003 (2003)
7. Jonghyuk Roh, et al.: A model of Certification Validation Server: ICOIN 2003 (2003)
8. Blake Dournaee: XML Security: RSA Press (2002)
9. Namje Park, Kiyoung Moon, Sungwon Sohn: A Study on Key Information Service Protocol for Secure XML Web Service: The KIPS Transaction, Part C, V(10-C) No 6 (2003)

Distributed IDS Tracing Back to Attacking Sources*

Wu Liu [1,2,3], Hai-Xin Duan [2], Jian-Ping Wu[2], Ping Ren[3,4], and Li-Hua Lu[5]

[1] Chengdu Institute of Computer Applications, Chinese Academy of Sciences 610041 Chengdu, China
liuwu@ccert.edu.cn

[2] Network Research Center of Tsinghua University 100084 Beijing, China

[3] Sichuan Agricultural University, Dujiangyan, 611830, Sichuan, China

[4] Business Management School of Sichuan University, Chengdu 610064, China

[5] Electronic Science and Technical College ,National University of Defense Technology, Changsha, 410073, China

Abstract. In this paper we present robust algorithms of transmission and reconstruction of attacking path(s) in IDS for providing traceback information in IP packets without requiring interactive operational support from Internet Service Providers, which is based on IP address compression techniques, polynomial theory and techniques from algebraic coding theory. Our best scheme has improved robustness over previous combinatorial approaches, both for noise elimination and multiple-path re-construction. Another key advantage of our schemes is that they will automatically benefit from any improvement in the underlying mathematical techniques, for which progress has been steady in recent years.

1 Introduction

A DoS (denial of service) attack is designed to prevent legitimate access to a resource which have become more prevalent recently due to their near intractability and relative ease of execution [7, 14, 17]. Also, the availability of tools such as Stacheldraht [15] and TFN [16] greatly simplify the task of coordinating hundreds or even thousands of compromised hosts to attack a single target. These attacks are so difficult to trace because the only hint a victim has as to the source of a given packet is the source address, which can be easily forged1. Also, many attacks are launched from compromised systems so finding the source of the attacker's packets may not lead to the attacker. Disregarding the problem of finding the person responsible for the attack, if a victim was able to determine the path of the attacking packets in near real-time, it would be much easier to quickly stop the attack. Even finding out partial path information would be useful because attacks could be throttled at far routers.

* This work is supported by grants from the National Natural Science Foundation of China (Grant No. #60203004 & #2001AA142080)

M. Li et al. (Eds.): GCC 2003, LNCS 3032, pp. 859–866, 2004.

This paper presents a new scheme for providing this traceback information by having routers embed information randomly into packets. This is similar to the technique used by Savage, et al [13], with the major difference being that our schemes are based on IP address compression techniques and algebraic coding theory, which has the advantage of providing a scheme that offers more flexibility in design and more powerful techniques that can be used to filter out attacker generated noise and separate multiple paths. Our schemes share similar backwards compatibility and incremental deployment properties to the previous work.

2 Overview

2.1 Definitions

Figure 1 depicts the network as seen from a victim V. For the purposes of this paper, V may be a single host under attack, or a network border device such as a firewall or intrusion detection system that represents many such hosts. Every potential attack origin A_i is a leaf in a tree rooted at V and every router R_i is an internal node along a path between some A_i and V. The attack path from A_i is the unique ordered list of routers between A_i and V. For instance, if an attack originates from A_1 then the true path is $R_1R_4R_7R_9$, which we call ***attack path***. We call any of the suffixes of the full path a ***virtual path***. As for the path $R_1R_4R_7R_9$, $R_1R_4R_7$, R_4R_7, and R_7 are all virtual paths.

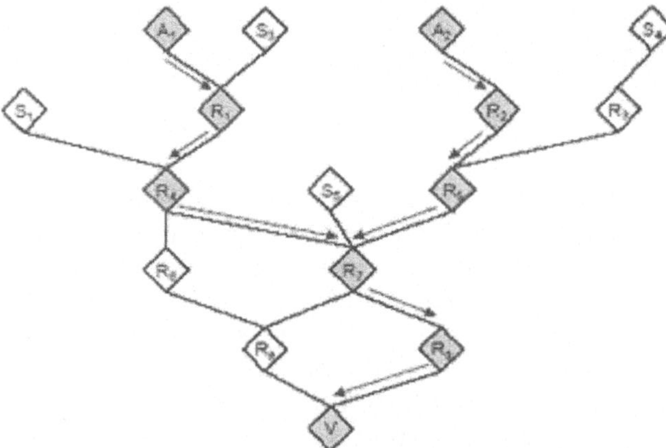

Fig. 1. The Attacking Path

2.2 Input Debugging

One of router's features called input debugging is that it allows an operator to filter particular packets on some egress port and determine which ingress port they arrived on. We will use this feature to mark the attack path.

2.3 Bits Available in IP Header of a Packet

To mark and reconstruct attack paths, we must first append the IP address of the router at attack path into the attack packets, but not take too much spaces or cause more fragments. A good idea is to compress all or part of the router's IP address into the header of the attack packets along attack paths. To allow for practical deployment requires that we "overload" existing header fields in a manner that will have minimal impact on existing users. This is a difficult task, especially given that even after prodigious effort we require 25 bits of space [9, 10, 11, 12, 8], which is shown in Fig. 2.

Version	H. Length	Type of Service (8-bit)	Total Length
Fragment ID (16-bit)		(1-bit) Flags	Fragment Offset
Time to Live		Protocol	Header Checksum
Source IP Address			
Destination IP Address			

Fig. 2. THe IP Header. Darkened areas are available bits (25 bits).

2.4 Algebraic Based IP Traceback

We will now present the basic principles of algebraic approach for encoding traceback information. All of these schemes are based on the principal of reconstructing a polynomial in a prime field.

Theorem 1 If both $f(x)$ and $g(x)$ are polynomials with degree $\leq$ n. If $\exists$ n+1different numbers $x_1, x_2, \cdots x_{n+1}$, such that $f(x_k) = g(x_k)$, $k = 1,2,\cdots n+1$, then $f(x) \equiv g(x)$ [1].

We see from theorem 1 that, for any polynomial $f(x)$ of degree d in the prime field $GF(p)$, we can recover $f(x)$ given $f(x)$ evaluated at (d+1) unique points.

Let $A_1, A_2, \cdots A_n$ be the 32-bit IP addresses of the routers on Path P.

Let $f_p(x) = A_n x^{n-1} + A_{n-1} x^{n-2} + \cdots + A_2 x + A_1$. We associate a packet id x_j with the j th packet. We then somehow evaluate $f_p(x_j)$ as the packet travels along the path, accumulating the result of the computation in a running total along the way. When enough packets from the same path reach the destination, $f_p(x)$ can be reconstructed by interpolation. The interpolation calculation might be a simple set of linear equations, if all of the packets received at the destination traveled the same path. Otherwise, we will need to employ more sophisticated interpolation strategies that succeed even in the presence of incorrect data or data from multiple paths [2, 4, 6].

The simplest scheme that uses this algebraic technique encodes an entire path. At the beginning of a path, let $FullPath_{0,j} = 0$. Each router i on the path calculates $FullPath_{i,j} = (FullPath_{i=1,j} \cdot x_j + A_i) \bmod p$ where x_j is a random value passed in each packet, A_i is the router's IP address and p is the smallest prime larger than $2^{32} - 1$. The value $FullPath_{i,j}$ is then passed in the packet, along with x_j, to the next router. At the packet's destination $FullPath$ will equal $A_n x^{n-1} + A_{n-1} x^{n-2} + \cdots + A_2 x + A_1 \bmod p$, which can be reconstructed by solving the following matrix equation over $GF(p)$:

$$\begin{pmatrix} 1 & x_1 & x_1^2 & \cdots & x_1^{n-1} \\ 1 & x_2 & x_2^2 & \cdots & x_2^{n-1} \\ \vdots & \vdots & \vdots & \ddots & \vdots \\ 1 & x_n & x_n^2 & \cdots & x_n^{n-1} \end{pmatrix} \begin{pmatrix} A_1 \\ A_2 \\ \vdots \\ A_n \end{pmatrix} = \begin{pmatrix} FullPath_{n,1} \\ FullPath_{n,2} \\ \vdots \\ FullPath_{n,n} \end{pmatrix}$$

As long as all the x_i 's are distinct, the matrix is a Vandermonde matrix and is solvable in $O(n^2)$ field operation [18].

Assuming that we get a unique x_j in each packet, we can recover a path of length d with only d packets. The downside, however, is that this scheme would require $\log_2 p + [\log_2 d]$ bits per packet (the first term is the encoding of the running FullPath and the second term is the encoding of the x_j's). Even for modest maximum path lengths of 16, the space required (36 bits) far exceeds the number of bits available to us in an IP header. There does exist some solutions to this problem [3].

Theorem 2 (Sudan) : If we have N total packets, it allows us to recover all virtual paths of length d for which we have at least $\sqrt{N(d-1)}$ packets. [2]

For example, if we assume that we analyze 10000 packets at a time and want to recover all virtual paths of length 17 or less, we would need to ensure that we receive 400 packets from each virtual path.

Theorem 3 : $p(1-p)^{d-1} > \sqrt{N(d-1)} / N$, where p is the marking probability, d is the distance from attacker to the victim, and N is total packets sent from attacker to the victim. [3]

3 Algorithms for IP Traceback

For every IDS, there are three components in principle: the Data Collection module which is usually called Agent(s), the analysis module and the Alert module. Here we add a new module called the Traceback module to trace back to the real attack sources, and therefore the corresponding IDS is called the Intrusion Detection Traceback System (IDTS). In this section we will mainly discuss the Data Collection Module (DCM, in section 3.1 and 3.2), and the Traceback Module (TM, in section 3.3). Notice that, victim hereafter is referred to the IDS running TM, and TM can also be deployed at a router.

3.1 Marking Algorithms at Each Router

The Marking Algorithms presented here are in fact distributed Data Collection modules, which can be incrementally deployed.

At each router R:

$Z_1 \leftarrow$ the first 16 bits of R's IP address
$Z_2 \leftarrow$ the last 16 bits of R's IP address
for each packet *pt*
Let r be a random number from $[0 \cdot\cdot 1)$
if r<p then
  Let x be a random number from $\{0,1\}$
  get the upper router's IP address R' carrying packet p
  $Y_1 \leftarrow$ the first 16 bits of R''s IP address
  $Y_2 \leftarrow$ the last 16 bits of R''s IP address
  pt.addr$\leftarrow Z_1 \oplus Y_1 + (Z_2 \oplus Y_2) \cdot x$
  pt.distance$\leftarrow$0
else
pt.distance$\leftarrow$ *pt*.distance+1

3.2 Analysis of Marking Algorithms

At each Router R, we separate its IP address into two parts Z_1 and Z_2, each has 16 bits. For each packet *pt* passing through R, we marking it with probability p, through hundreds of thousands of experiments and from correlative calculates, we choose p=1/25 (at each router), which is optimal.

When a Router decides to mark a packet, it first get the upper router's IP address Y carrying the packet by Input Debugging feature, and split it into two 16 bits Y_1 and Y_2. Then XOR with R's IP address fragments respectively. Finally get the compressed IP address fragment $Z_1 \oplus Y_1 + (Z_2 \oplus Y_2) \cdot x$, We call the resulting value the ***edge-id*** for the edge between Z and Y. The edge-id is written into the identification field of the packet's IP header, which takes 16 bits, where x equals to 0 or 1. So x takes 1 bit, we store it in the highest bit of the TOS field of the packet's IP header. When enough packets is sent from a attacker to the same victim, he will receive both:

$$Z_1 \oplus Y_1 + (Z_2 \oplus Y_2) \cdot 0 = Z_1 \oplus Y_1 \quad (1)$$

and $Z_1 \oplus Y_1 + (Z_2 \oplus Y_2) \cdot 1 = Z_1 \oplus Y_1 + (Z_2 \oplus Y_2)$ (2)

(2) – (1) will get $Z_2 \oplus Y_2$, and will get Z and Y easily.

Finally, we employ another parameter *distance* for many purposes. It takes the 7 lower bits of the TOS field in the packet's IP Header, which can tracebak attack paths of length 2^7-128. In fact the length of attack paths seldom exceeds 32 and is between

20 and 25 in average. So, in the future we can store the *distance* in 5 bits of the TOS field.

When a packet decide to mark a packet, it will set *distance*=0, otherwise it just increase value of *distance* by one. At the victim this value will be used to decide the distance between the router and the victim, and help to reconstruct the router's IP address. Another function of this parameter is to prevent any attacker from forging virtual paths that are closer than its actual distance from the victim.

We only need to have our degree 1 polynomial evaluated at 2 points in order to recover it, this should not cause us any trouble as long as all routers agree on the change, because the coupon collector's problem tells us that we would expect to get all 6 values in far fewer packets than are required by our multiple path reconstructor. Even the smallest routers should be able to precompute and store the 6 possible values that would need to be inserted when they are in marking mode (these values require only 12 bytes of storage).

3.3 Path Reconstruction Algorithms at Victim(s)

At the victim v:
Let *path_tbl* be a table of tuples (addr, x, distance)
Let G be a tree with root v
Let edges in G be tuples (start, end, distance)
maxd←0
last← v
last_frist←the first 16 bits of v
last_last←the last 16 bits of v
For each packet *pt* from attacker
  path_tbl.Insert(*pt* .addr, *pt*. x, *pt*.distance)
  if *pt*.distance > maxd then
  maxd← *pt*.distance
  for d=0 to maxd
    if *pt*. x =0 then
  A1← *pt* .addr
  If *pt* .addr =1 then
  A2← *pt* .addr;
  IP_first←A1;
  IP_last←A2-A1;
  IP_first← IP_first ⊕ last_frist;
  IP_last← IP_ last ⊕ last_ last;
  Let *IP_addr* be the IP address composed by IP_first and IP_last;
  Insert edge (last, *IP_addr*, *pt*.distance);
  Last← *IP_addr*;
Remove any edge (x,y,d) with d ≠ distance from x to v in G;

4 Experiments

We implemented this scheme under RedHat Linux 8.0 on a Pentium IV running at 1.4 GHz and Simulated by Opnet [20]. Using RC4 [19] as the random number generator, the scheme executed in less than 30 clocks per packet. When routing packets across a 100 Mbit/sec Ethernet, there was no measurable difference in throughput between the modified and unmodified kernels (more than 95 Mbit/sec worth of packets were routed in both cases). From Fig. 3, one can see that for the length 25 of attack path, after the attack sent 1000 packets we can reconstruct the attack path, so trace back to the attack, while In recent denial of service attacks, Yahoo reported receiving over 1 gigabyte of data per second. Even if every packet was of the largest possible size, Yahoo would have received more than enough packets in less than 2 seconds.

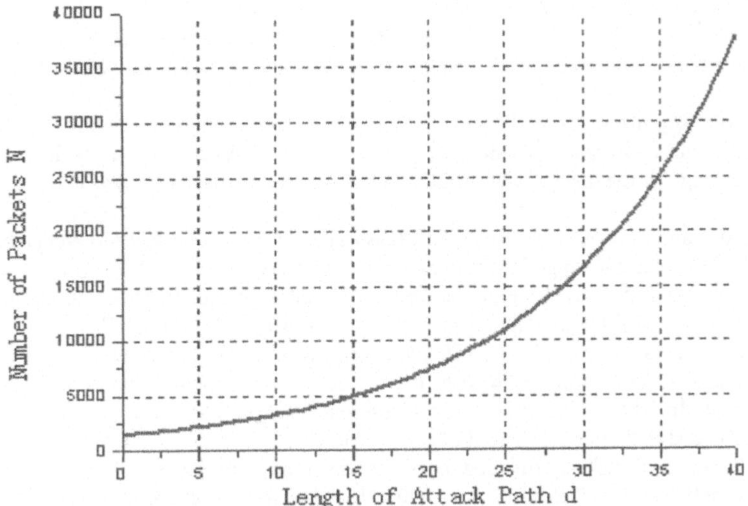

Fig. 3. Number of packets needed to reconstruct the attack path

5 Conclusion

We have presented a new approach in IDS for providing traceback information in IP packets, which is based on mathematical techniques, encoding theory and other skills such as XOR and hash operations. Our best scheme has improved robustness over previous combinatorial approaches, both for noise elimination and multiple-path reconstruction. Another key advantage of our schemes is that they will automatically benefit from any improvement in the underlying mathematical techniques, for which progress has been steady in recent years.

References

[1] Lu Yang, Jing-Zhong Zhang and Xiao-Rong Hou, Nonlinear Algebraic Equation System and Automated Theorem Proving. Shanghai Scientific and Technological Education Published House, SHANGHAI, 1996

[2] V. Guruswami and M. Sudan. Improved decoding of Reed-Solomon and algebraic-geometric codes. IEEE Transactions on Information Theory, 45:1757–1767, 1999.

[3] Drew Dean, Matt Franklin, and Adam Stubblefield, An Algebraic Approach to IP Traceback. In Network and Distributed System Security Symposium, NDSS '01, February 2001.

[4] M. Sudan. Decoding of Reed Solomon codes beyond the error-correction bound. Journal of Complexity, 13(1):180–193, Mar. 1997.

[5] W. H. Press, B. P. Flannery, S. A. Teukolsky, and W. T. Vetterling. Numerical Recipes in FORTRAN: The Art of Scientific Computing. Cambridge University Press, 1992.

[6] E. Berlekamp and L. Welch. Error correction of algebraic block codes. United States Patent 4,490,811, Dec. 86.

[7] Liu Wu, Duan Haixin, et al, Wavelet-Based Analysis of Network Security Databases, International Conference of Communication Technology, 9-11 Apr. 2003, Beijing, P372-377

[8] F. Baker. Requirements for IP Version 4 Routers. RFC 1812, June 1995.

[9] I. Stoica and H. Zhang. Providing Guaranteed Services Without Per Flow Management. In Proceedings of the 1999 ACM SIGCOMM Conference, pages 81–94, Boston, MA, Aug. 1999.

[10] K. Claffy and S. McCreary. Sampled Measurements from June 1999 to December 1999 at the AMES Inter-exchange Point. Personal Communication, Jan. 2000.

[11] C. Kent and J. Mogul. Fragmentation Considered Harmful. In Proceedings of the 1987 ACM SIGCOMM Conference, pages 390–401, Stowe, VT, Aug. 1987.

[12] J. Mogul and S. Deering. Path MTU Discovery. RFC 1191, Nov. 1990.

[13] S. Savage, D.Wetherall, A. Karlin, and T. Anderson. Practical network support for IP traceback. In 2000 ACM SIGCOMM Conference, Aug. 2000.

[14] CERT coordination center denial of service attacks. http://www.cert.org/tech_tips/denial_of_ service.html, Feb. 1999.

[15] D. Dittrich. The "stacheldraht" distributed denial of service attack tool. http://staff.washington. edu/dittrich/misc/stacheldraht. analysis.txt, Dec. 1999.

[16] D. Dittrich. The "Tribe Flood Network" distributed denial of service attack tool. http://staff.washington. edu/dittrich/misc/tfn.analysis, Oct. 1999.

[17] Wu Liu, Haixin Duan, Ping Ren et al, WAVELET BASED DATA MINING AND QUERYING IN NETWORK SECURITY DATABASES, International Conference on Machine Learning and Cybernetics 2003, 2-5 Nov. 2003, Xian, China.

[18] S. M. Bellovin. ICMP traceback messages. http://search.ietf.org/internet-drafts/draft-bellovin-itrace- 00.txt, Mar. 2000.

[19] B. Schneier. Applied Cryptography, Second Edition. John Wiley and Sons, 1996.

[20] http://www.opnet.com.

The Study on Mobile Phone-Oriented Application Integration Technology of Web Services [1]

Luqun Li[1, 2], Minglu Li [1], and Xianguo Cui [2]

[1] Department of Computer Science of Shanghai Jiaotong University, 1954 Huashan Road, Shanghai, China 200030

[2] Shandong university of Science and Technology, Daizong Street 223, Taian, Shandong, China
liluqun@263.net

Abstract. Application integration technology of Web Services is a challenge research area in web application area. Till now, many research works on web service have been done on the platform of desktop PC, however little work is done on the hardware platform of Java phone. By analysis on web services architecture and exploring Java mobile phone, this paper puts forward the realization architecture for mobile phone-oriented application integration technology of web services.

Keywords: Java, J2ME, Web Service, KSOAP, XML

1 Preface

Web Service has become an integral part of many web applications in nowadays. Platform-independent, ubiquitous and easy access web services using common standardized protocol SOAP, Web Services Description Language (WSDL), Universal Description as well as Discovery and Integration (UDDI), has been one of the principal drivers behind this success[1]. For desktop computer, there are near mature software develop SDK and models to build, or access the web service. However, things are not the same for mobile phone, due to resource constraints of mobile phone, such as memory and bandwidth[2], web service specification on these devices is still in the procession of Java Community Process (JSR-172) version[3]. By exploring the engine of web service realization and identify the performance of existing technologies, this article puts forward the realization architecture for mobile phone-oriented application integration technology of web services.

---

[1] This paper is supported by 973 project (No.2002CB312002) of China, grand project (No.03dz15027) and key project (No.025115033) of the Science and Technology Commission of Shanghai Municipality.

M. Li et al. (Eds.): GCC 2003, LNCS 3032, pp. 867–874, 2004.

2 Analysis on Web Services Architecture

A web service is a software module performing a discrete task or set of tasks that can be found and invoked over a network including and especially the World Wide Web. The developer can create a client application that invokes a series of web services through remote procedure calls (RPC) or a messaging service to provide some or most of the application's logic. A published web service describes itself so that developers can locate the web service and evaluate its suitability for their needs [4].

The web services architecture has three distinct roles (See Fig.1): a provider, a requestor, and a broker. The provider creates the web service and makes it available to clients who want to use it. A requestor is a client application that consumes the web service. The requested web service can also be a client of other web services. The broker, such as a service registry, provides a way for the provider and the requestor of a web service to interact.

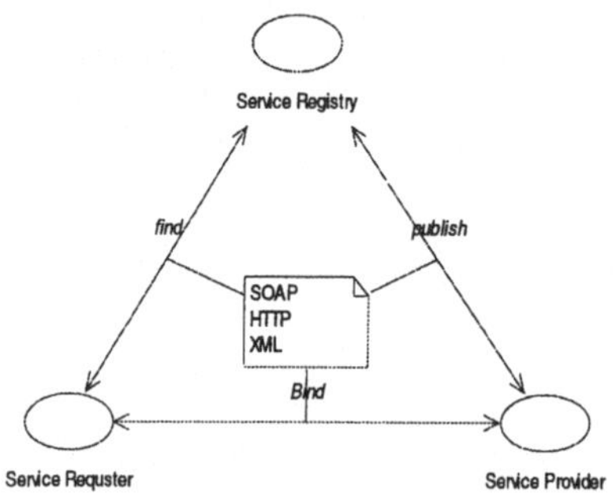

Fig. 1. Service-oriented architecture

Web services use SOAP (Simple Object Access Protocol) for the XML payload and uses a transport such as HTTP to carry the SOAP messages back and forth. SOAP messages are actually XML documents that are sent between a web service and the calling application.

The web services architecture permits the development of web services that encapsulate all levels of business functionality. The three roles of provider, requestor, and broker interact with each other through the operations of publish, find, and bind. A provider informs the broker about the existence of the web service by using the broker's publish interface to make the service accessible to clients. The information published describes the service and specifies where the service is located. The requestor consults the broker to locate a published web service. With the information it gained from the broker about the web service, the requestor is able to bind, or invoke, the web service.

In the common model of web service above, XML with SOAP protocol is shared among the three roles in Web Service. XML-based messaging is at the heart of the current Web Services technology. XML's self-describing nature has significant advantages, especially in platform-independent web application, however XML-based messages are larger and require more processing than existing protocols such as RMI, RMI/IIOP or CORBA/IIOP: data is represented inefficiently, and binding requires more computation. processing and sending XML messages can not avoid coming at the price of bandwidth and performance5.Under the environment of desktop computer and wired wide internet network, the defects of XML mentioned above are not in evidence, almost the three roles in web services accept the fact that if worth of sacrificing some efficiency to get better web application architecture. However the things are different to wireless mobile intelligent terminals, see Java mobile phone.

3 Exploring the Java Mobile Phone

Now the computer science and technology have come into the era of Pervasive Computing. A distinct character of pervasive computing is some distributed works which have been done by the desktop PC have separated from PC, and the works will be processed in two ways, the first one is some of distributed works will be finished by the server, usually the server is a part of enterprise in internet or intranet, web service is a trademark of this one, the second on is some of works will be distributed to much portable intelligent devices, the work can be finished by the portable devices or by the inter-operation of portable device and the server in the internet through wireless internet, usually it is called mobile computing. So the mobile phone-oriented application integration technology of web services has much significance, because people owned the device can access the web service anytime, anywhere. As for the mobile intelligent device, here the author will only highlight on Java mobile phone.

Java mobile phone is a typical member in Java Micro Edition family. Till now most JVM in Java mobile phone are built at least including MIDP1.0 standard. There are many Java mobile phone can be seen in the market today.

Based on CLDC and MIDP, Java phone provide GUI, network (usually Http protocol), data persist storage, etc. support in JVM. Above anything all, all Java phone support Http protocol which is the basic protocol to access web service. Obviously, as for the limited computing ability of Java mobile phone, usually it only acts as the roles of a service consumer in web service.

It can be deduced from the web service architecture that besides CLDC and MIDP1.0, Java phone must use some extended API or a web service gateway to access the web service.

4 Access Web Service from Java Mobile Phone

Access web service from Java mobile phone is a challenge thing, for till now web service on J2ME is still in the procession of Java Community Process (JSR-172) version[3].However the third party open source solution for Java mobile phone to access web service is available. Ksoap and KXML are the options. Besides these, developing no-standard protocol for Java mobile phone can also make Java phone access the web service indirectly.

4.1 Access Web Service Directly

To keep with existing Web Services standards and APIs so that there is minimal impact on the developers. A developer should not have to maintain two code bases with different APIs for the same Web Service, nor should he have to define two different Web Service contracts for any particular service. The right way is keep the web service provider in standard form and the service consumer also in standard form.

However, one thing must be noted, neither KSOAP nor J2ME web service (at least in JRS-172) supports the web service finding engine[3], the programmer will act as the roles for finding web service in the system, hence the architecture web service for Java mobile phone will change into Fig.2, the programmer is also an actor.

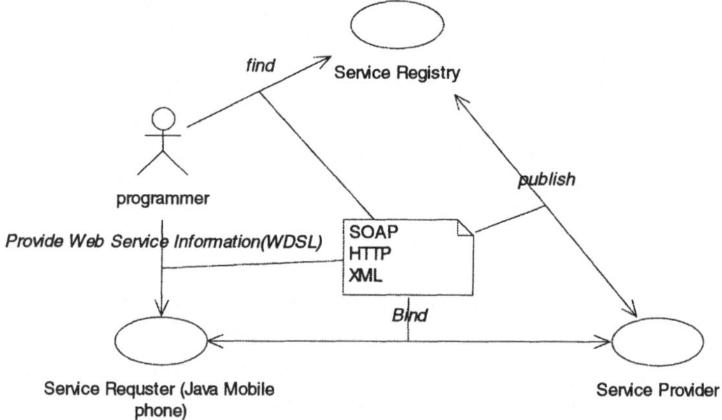

Fig. 2. Service-oriented architecture for Java Mobile Phone

In Section 2, the author pointed that XML-based messages are larger and require more processing, so in the architecture above, due to the limited computing ability of Java mobile phone, additional API and SOAP &XML message parsing will be slow, obviously.

To avoid the low efficiency of Java mobile phone parsing SOAP &XML, Java mobile phone can access web service by gateway or service proxy, in short accessing web service indirectly.

4.2 Access Web Service Indirectly

Gateway and proxy are common words in nowadays. They act as the role between two networks or different protocols. So web service gateway can also act as the role between Java mobile phone no-standard protocols and standard protocols. Web service gateway is service provider as well as service consumer. It can be depicted by Fig.3.

The communication between web service gateway and Java mobile phone can be defined by the programmer in much efficient way, hence KSOAP and KXML is necessary for Java mobile phone. The web service request sent by the Java mobile phone can be in binary code, or in SMS format, the response from the web service gateway can be in any accepted form, see, binary code, text, SMS, MMS, etc. The Java mobile phone can access web service in much efficient way.

The defect of using web service gateway is it needing additional programming work, and the Java mobile phone client side developing will in multi-form.

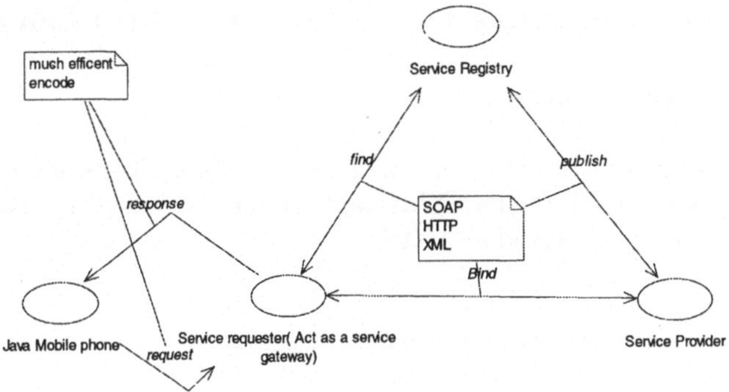

Fig. 3. Service Gateway for Java Mobile Phone in Service-oriented architecture

4.3 Using Fast Web Service

Fast web service is a new project for Sun Microsystems, aimed at eliminating the low efficient of SOAP and XML encode, fast web service uses another protocol ASN.1(See Figure.6). Sun Microsystems in conjunction with OSS Nokalva (a leading ASN.1 tools vendor) has initiated a new work item at the joint ITU-T/ISO body, provisionally entitled "ASN.1 Support for SOAP, Web Services and the XML Information Set" and referred to as X.695. This aims to define a number of proposed specifications to ensure that X.694 and X.691 (or other alternative ASN.1 encoding rules) can be used in Web service environments.X.695 consists of the following sub-specifications: ASN.1 Schema for SOAP ASN.1 Schema for the XML information set Fast annotations for WSDL(See Fig.4).

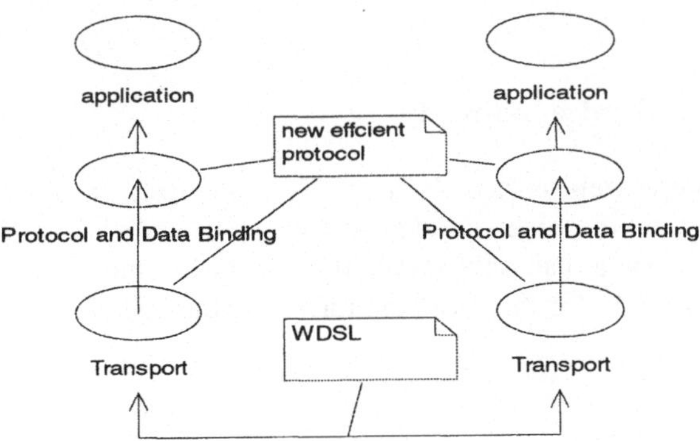

Fig. 4. Fast web service principle

Using fast web service, the Java phone can access web service in a much efficient way, however fast web service is now a not standard protocol now.

5 Experiment on Accessing Web Service from Java Mobile Phone

5.1 Access Web Service Directly

To realize accessing web service from Java mobile phone, Tomcat5.0+AXIS, Java wireless develop kit 1.4 +KSOAP+KXML and Motorola SDK3.1 are used. The following simple service is deployed in AXIS.

```
Hello.jws
public class Hello{
public String say(String s){
return "AXIS says: Hello "+s;
}
}
```

in the Java mobile phone client side, the core code are used:

```
....
SoapObject objResult = (SoapObject) callService(String,
" say");
..
result = " AXIS says: Hello " + objResult.getProperty()
Object callService(String words, String methodName) {
Object result = null;
try {
transport = new HttpTransport(serviceUrl,  methodName);
..
transport.setClassMap(classMap);
request = new SoapObject(serviceNamespace, methodName);
result = transport.call(request);
```

The result can be seen in Fig.5.

5.2 Access Web Service Indirectly

To access the same web service (Hello.JWS) above from Java Mobile phone by web Service gateway. As for this method is very easy, the code is omitted.

The Java mobile phone use only standard protocol to send the request string and get the response string! As for this work is rather easy the code is omitted!

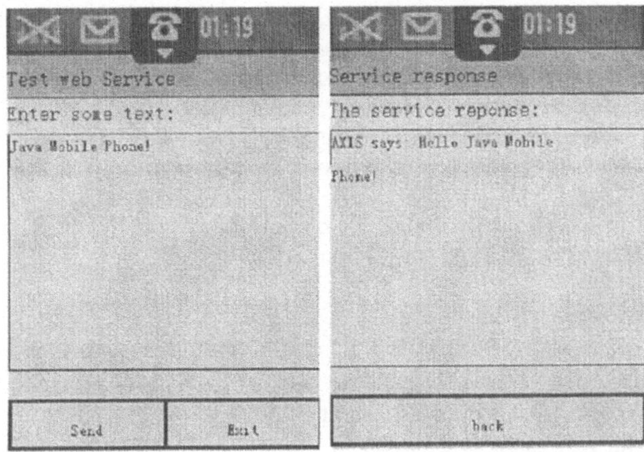

Fig. 5. Web Service accessed by Java Mobile phone by Ksoap

Table 1. Result of Java Mobile phone (the Emulator) accessing web Service

Item	Java phone API	Time to access the web Service (Seconds)
Access Web Service Directly	MIDP1.0+KSOAP+KXML	22
Access Web Service Indirectly	MIDP1.0	12

The time of Java phone to access the web service includes the emulator start time, and application running time, as well as the net web service deploying time on the Axis server. Results above show that Java mobile phone accessing web service by web service gateway is much faster than using KSOAP protocol.

6 Conclusion

The Java mobile phone can access web service by KSOAP protocol. To get much efficient use web service, web service gateway technology can be used. However, addition code on both Java mobile phone and the service side is also needed. As for accessing web service from Java phone is still a new research area and web service standards on it is still under JSR172, the efficiency of accessing web service from Java mobile phone must be taken into account.

References

1. Steve Graham. Building Web Services with Java [M].China Machine Press, Beijing, China. Jan, 2003, P40~70.
2. Li luqun. The Study on Mobile GIS [PH.D dissertation].Shandong university of Science and technology.2002.6, P46~59.

3. Jon Ellis & Mark Young. J2ME Web Services 1.0, Sun Microsystems. July, 2003,P24~45.
4. Mach Hendricks, Ben Galbraith. Programming Guide on Java Web Service [M]. Publishing Hose of Electronics Industry, Beijing, China. Oct, 2002,P32~67..
5. Paul Sandoz, Santiago Pericas-Geertsen. Fast Web Services. Sun Microsystems http://developer.java.sun.com/developer/technicalArticles/WebServices/fastWS/index.html, 11, Sep, 2003,
6. Bill Brogden. Programming Guide on SOAP and Java [M].Publishing House of Electronics Industry. Beijing, China. March, 2002,P59~79.

About the Author:

Li luqun, associate-professor, post-PhD in Computer Department Shanghai Jiaotong University. His main research interests are Web Service and network application study and development. liluqun@263.net

Li Minglu, professor, vice-dean of Computer Department of Shanghai Jiaotong University, His main research area is Griding Computing, Web Service etc.

Cui Xianguo, professor, in Shandong University of Science and Technology, his main research interests are GIS and database.

Group Rekeying Algorithm Using Pseudo-random Functions and Modular Reduction

Josep Pegueroles[1], Wang Bin[2], Miguel Soriano[1], and Francisco Rico-Novella[1]

[1] Telematics Engineering Department. Technical University of Catalonia
c/ Jordi Girona 1-3 Campus Nord 08034 Barcelona, Spain
{josep,soriano,telfrn}@entel.upc.es

[2] Department of Electronic Engineering. Shangai Jiaotong University.
1954 HuaShan Rd. Shanghai, Peoples Republic of China
xiaobinw@yahoo.com

Abstract. The grid is one of the most evident examples of cooperation between a group of network entities. If secure transactions want to be supported within this group a secret key shared by all these entities is needed. The session key should be sent to all authorized users and updated every time the grid group changes. This is the only way of achieving perfect forward and backward secrecy. Traditionally these actions are performed by a centralized trusted third party called the Key Server (KS). Different works for minimizing the storage need for KS and reducing the required bandwidth for updating keys have been presented. We present a method for group rekeying using pseudo-random functions and modular reduction. This method minimizes the number of keys to store by the KS and reduces the required bandwidth for updating the keying material.

1 Introduction

The grid has revealed to be the way of optimizing the use of the three fundamental assets in our networked world: information, bandwidth and computing power. Many applications can take advantage of the grid power: distributed supercomputing, high throughput and on-demand computing, data-intensive and collaborative computing... As in every scenario where e-business takes place, security is a mandatory requirement [1].

When adding security features to group communications a secret shared by all the group members is needed. The shared key provides group secrecy and source authentication. This key must be updated peridiocally, this action is usually known as rekeying. If rekeying is done for every group membership change, Forward and Backward Secrecy (FS and BS) are provided. Traditionally the update is performed by a centralized trusted third party called the Key Server (KS). The most important parameters when performing group rekeying are: number of keys to store by the KS, number of keys to store by each member,

M. Li et al. (Eds.): GCC 2003, LNCS 3032, pp. 875–882, 2004.

number of keys to deliver in the initialization stage, bandwidth required for updating the keys and latency for updating the session key [2].

In this work we propose a new technique based on the usage of pseudo-random functions with modular reduction. This technique performs a good behavior in terms of number of keys to store by the KS and bandwidth needed for rekeying.

The rest of this paper is organized as follows. Section 2 presents state of the art in the group rekeying. Logical Key Tree basis are also discussed and, as an example, LKH is shown as the most widely accepted method for secret group communications. Section 3 introduces the technique to minimize key storage in the server side. This technique is based on the usage of pseudo-random functions. Section 4 explains how this method can be used in combination with modular reduction in order to perform a more efficient group rekeying. The security analysis of the method is presented en Section 5. Finally, conclusions are presented in Section 6.

2 State of the Art

In group security field, several works prevent new group members or leaving members from accessing data sent before they joined or after they leave. The simplest way the KS can deliver a new session key to the members is through a secret unicast connection with each of the remaining members of the group [3]. This solution presents the worst behavior respecting efficiency parameters. All figures have a dependency on the number of members in the group (N), so we say that these problems are order N ($O(N)$).

2.1 Logical Key Tree Schemes

In [4,5,6] logical key tree based schemes were presented as the way of reducing number of messages for rekeying (and bandwidth) to $O(log_2(N))$, where N is the number of members in the group.

Key tree based schemes use two types of encryption keys: Session Encryption Keys (SEK) and Key Encryption Keys (KEK). SEKs are used to cipher the actual data that groups exchange. KEKs are used to cipher the keying material that members need in order to get the SEK. Usually, KEKs are structured in logical binary trees. All users know the root of the key tree and the leaf nodes are users' individual keys.

We will adopt the next criterion as naming convention for the rest of the paper. Tree nodes will be referenced as *(level number, position at level)*, so we will refer to root node as *(1,1)*; sons of root node will be *(2,1)* and *(2,2)* and so on. Key in node (X,Y) will be noted as $K_{(X,Y)}$. Group members are located at leaf nodes. Keys in the leaves are only known by single users.

2.2 Logical Key Hierarchy (LKH)

The simplest logical key tree management scheme is LKH [4]. Consider a group and a centralized group controller (KS). Each member must store a subset of the controller's keys. This subset of KEKs will allow the member to get the new SEK when it changes. A generic member (Mj) stores the subset of keys in the path from the leaf where he is to the root.

Managing Joinings. When a new member joins the group he must contact the KS via a secure unicast channel. Then they negotiate a shared key that they will use in later interactions. This action can be done following any of the well known key agreement algorithms, as Diffie-Hellman. After that, the controller must update every KEK in the path from the leaf, where new member is located, to the root. See Fig 1 in which new keys are noted with quotes. If these keys were not updated the joining member could decipher an eventual recording of the group comunication previous to his joining.

Then, the KS has to reveal the updated keys to the corresponding users. He uses the existing key hierarchy, along with reliable multicast, to efficiently distribute them as follows. He sends two messages containing the whole set of updated keys, one to each of the members in nodes *(4,7)*[1] and *(4,8)*, via a unicast channel and using their individual keys. After that, he constructs and sends a multicast message containing $K_{(2,2)}$ and $K_{(1,1)}$ ciphered with $K_{(3,3)}$, so only members in nodes *(4,5)* and *(4,6)* can decipher it. Finally, he also constructs and sends a multicast message containing new root key $K_{(1,1)}$ and ciphered with $K_{(2,1)}$, so members in nodes *(4,1)* to *(4,4)* can decipher it. At this point, the 8 members in the group know the new subset of keys from their leaves to the root. Every member knows the root key, so this is used to cipher a multicast message containing the new session key (SEK), that also has to be updated.

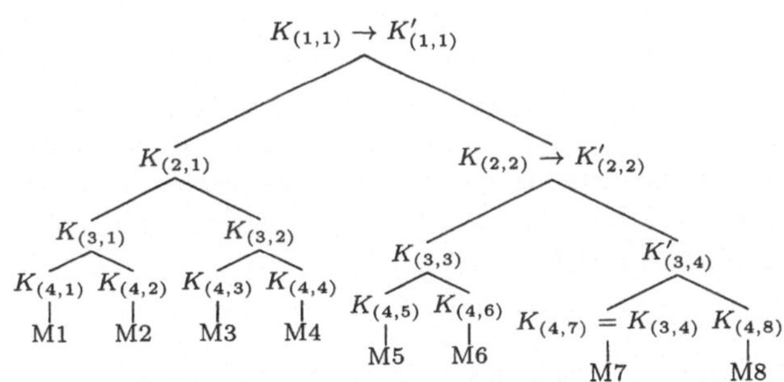

Fig. 1. Example of LKH joining

Following the example it is easy to see how the binary tree-based key management scheme can update keys using $O(log_2(N))$ messages, where N is the number of members in the group. On the contrary the KS has to store of the order of $2N$ keys to maintain the tree.

[1] M7 now is located at node (4,7) and his individual Key now is named $K_{(4,7)}$

3 Optimal Key Storage

Next a variation of the logical key tree method is presented in order to reduce the number of keys that the KS has to store. This technique reduces the key storage requirement of the group controller by constructing the keys in tree nodes by means of a pseudo-random function only known by the KS. When rekeying is needed, the KS does not send the updated key themselves but the required information that single users need in order to update them. A simple example is explained next.

Consider the binary tree in which keys in node *(i,j)* are generated according to expression (1).

$$K_{(i,j)} = F_{r1}(2^i + j) \oplus r \tag{1}$$

F_{r1}denotes a pseudo-random function with random seed $r1$ and r is another random number needed for updating the key. The symbol $\oplus$ is the XOR function. When membership changes, the KS sends to all the members that need to update their keys the following parameter.

$$P = r \oplus r' \tag{2}$$

Using P, each single member, only has to compute (3) in order to update his keys.

$$K'_{(i,j)} = K_{(i,j)} \oplus P = F_{r1}(2^i + j) \oplus r' \tag{3}$$

As neither $F_{r1}(2^i + j)$ nor r is known by anyone but the KS, past and future keys cannot be computed with the only knowledge of *(i,j)* or P. P can be delivered to the remaining members according to LKH rules. In the Optimal Key Storage (OKS) method, the length of the rekeying messages can be shorter than the LKH messages but the number of messages needed for rekeying is $O(log_2 N)$. Besides that, the KS only has to store two random seeds plus the session key, that is to say *r1*,r and SEK.

4 Combination with Modular Reduction

4.1 Initialization Stage

Now, consider a dynamic group of size *N*. A Key Server who shares a secret with each of the members in the group manages the communication. The KS constructs a LKH-like logical tree of keys following the next rules. Each node in the tree is a different pseudo-random number generated according to expression (1). As in LKH, each member is located at the leaves of the tree and knows every number (key) from his leaf to the root.

4.2 Multicasting Stage

When a new key must be agreed. The KS computes a public parameter according to the expression (4)

$$P = r_2 \prod_{i \subset S} rnd_i + (r \oplus r') \tag{4}$$

$r_2$is the result of a pseudo random function, different to F_{r1}, and used to avoid collusion attacks of authorized members, we will discuss about it in section 5. $\prod_{i \subset S} rnd_i$ denotes the product of all random numbers in the subset S. S is the subset of all sibling nodes of the updated path. $(r \oplus r')$ is the blinded parameter that remaining users will use to compute the updated tree. As an example, consider that M3 in Fig.1 leaves the group. The parameter P will look as in expression (5)

$$P = r_2 \cdot rnd_{11} \cdot rnd_4 \cdot rnd_3 + (r \oplus r') \tag{5}$$

4.3 Recovery Stage

When recovering the key, each member will do a modular reduction of P modulo one of the random numbers in his path to the root. As this random number will be included in the product of random numbers, the operation performed by the authorized user will lead to the secret $(r \oplus r')$. See expression (6).

$$P = r_2 \cdot rnd_{11} \cdot rnd_4 \cdot rnd_3 + (r \oplus r') \; mod \; rnd_4 = (r \oplus r') \tag{6}$$

With this parameter each user can compute the updated tree as in Optimal Key Storage, following expression (3).

5 Security Analysis

Group rekeying algorithms have three possible attackers: a rejected member, a collusion of members and an authorized member during successive rekeyings. In our proposal, the only way for the system to be broken is finding one factor of the blinding product of the rekeying message. If a not authorized member finds one of these factors (or an authorized member finds one factor not belonging to his path from his location to the root) he will be able to do the modular reduction of the rekeying message and could obtain the delivered secret.

5.1 Attacks and Attackers

Rejected Member. A single rejected member does not know any factor since, by definition, none of the numbers of his set of secret keys are included in the rekeying message. Moreover, the secrets he knew while he was an authorized member of the group will no longer be used in any future rekeying message. We have to remember that all the remaining secrets of the tree are updated, every time a joining or leaving takes place, by means of applying the updating parameter $(r \oplus r')$ to the remaining keys.

Collusion of Rejected Members. A collusion of rejected members cannot learn anything about the factors since they are already rejected and their secrets are not used to construct the rekeying message.

Collusion of Authorized Members. The trivial way that an authorized member can act maliciously is by revealing any of the numbers in his secret set of keys to another member. This is obviously also a security flaw in LKH. No protection can be provided against this misbehaviour. The only way an eventual system could protect himself against it is by using traitor tracing schemes. The study of this possibility is beyond the scope of this study.

Another authorized members attack is the possibility for two authorized attackers to find a factor not belonging to their sets of secrets. This is avoided by the introduction of the parameter r_2 in the blinding product.

Again, imagine M3 is leaving the group. Suppose $r_2$is not included in expression (5). Two colluding members, e.g. M1 and M4, may cooperate to know rnd_3 through the rekeying message. See the following steps:

1. M1 obtains the secret $(r \oplus r')$ by reducing modulo rnd_4
2. M1 obtains $\prod_{i \subset S} rnd_i$ by subtracting $(r \oplus r')$ from $P = r_2 \cdot rnd_{11} \cdot rnd_4 \cdot rnd_3 + (r \oplus r')$
3. M1 divides rnd_4 from $\prod_{i \subset S} rnd_i$ and gives the result $rnd_{11} \cdot rnd_3$ to M4.
4. M4 divides $rnd_{11}$from the data given by M1 and obtains rnd_3.

As M1 and M4 know the secret $(r \oplus r')$, they could update rnd_3 and be prepared to decipher the rekeying message when they leave the group.

This security flaw is overcome by the introduction of the random number r_2 in expression (5). Then the only way M4 has to know rnd_3 is by factorizing $rnd_3 \cdot r_2$ that it is considered a hard problem if they have prime factors large enough. Of course, $r_2$shall be different for every rekeying message. If not, two products containing $r_2$will discover the factor

Members through Successive Rekeyings. Another relevant threat in our system is what an authorized member could learn about factors during successive rekeyings. If random numbers were reused for different messages an authorized user could easily find a factor by just using great common divisor (gcd()) algorithm. See an example in expression (8).

- Message 1 (member 3 rejected in Fig 1):

$$P = r_2 \cdot rnd_{11} \cdot rnd_4 \cdot rnd_3 + (r \oplus r') \tag{7}$$

- Message 2 (member 2 rejected in Fig 1):

$$P = r_2' \cdot rnd_8 \cdot rnd_5 \cdot rnd_3 + (r \oplus r') \tag{8}$$

Every authorized user during these two messages can easily compute $r_2 \cdot rnd_{11} \cdot rnd_4 \cdot rnd_3$and $r_2' \cdot rnd_8 \cdot rnd_5 \cdot rnd_3$by simply finding the secret $(r \oplus r')$

and subtracting it from P. As $r_2 \neq r'_2$, using these two products it is easy to find rnd_3 as gcd($r_2 \cdot rnd_{11} \cdot rnd_4 \cdot rnd_3$,$r'_2 \cdot rnd_8 \cdot rnd_5 \cdot rnd_3$).

For this reason, all the random numbers in the key tree should be updated every time a rekeying is done. If only LKH mechanisms were used to update these numbers a critical increase in the bandwidth requirement of the system will occur. To avoid this the Optimal Key Storage (OKS) update mechanism is used. In OKS the entire tree is updated every rekeying and all random numbers are recomputed. Two different messages for different rekeyings will have different factors in the message and gcd() algorithm cannot be used. Moreover, the update mechanism for OKS delegates the update of the tree to individual users by only delivering a new secret parameter to them so only one updating message for all members is involved.

5.2 Parameters Restrictions

With all the previous considerations, the proposed method requires some restrictions over the parameters to work properly.

First of all, $r \oplus r' mod rnd_i = r \oplus r'$ implies $r \oplus r' < rnd_i$ for every random number rnd_i. This condition should be easily assured by many simple mechanisms, for instance, setting the length in number of bits of the updating parameter less than the length of the random numbers rnd_i.

In the other hand, as previously stated, random numbers rnd_ishould be composed by large prime numbers. This condition makes factorization of $\prod_{i \subset S}$ a difficult problem. It is important to note that our method does not require rnd_i numbers to be large primes. If they are not prime, the system could even be more secure because the factorization of $\prod_{i \subset S}$ would not reveal anything about rnd_i but their factors, and the finding of rnd_i could only be done by means of the testing of combinations of these factors. In any case [7] gives many information of how can be assured that a large random number is composed by primes of a certain bit length with a chosen probability.

Finally, the avoidance of small factors in $\prod_{i \subset S}$would be also beneficial for our system.

6 Conclusions and Future Work

We have presented a new method for rekeying in group environments. It is based on the use of logical binary trees of keys (generated by means of pseudo-random functions) that are updated using a single rekeying message. This message is constructed using modular reduction properties to selectively choose the receivers that can decipher it.

The proposed method reduces bandwidth required for updating the key tree and number of keys to be stored by the Key Server. The key tree is entirely updated every time a rekeying is done by xoring an updating parameter to every key in the tree. Security analysis of the proposal has also been presented.

The extension of this proposal to batch rekeying techniques is pointed out as the next work to be done.

References

1. Foster, The Grid. Blueprint for a new computing infrastructure. Morgan Kaufmann Publishers, Inc. 1999.
2. Canetti, Garay, Itkis, Micciancio, Naor, Pinkas. Multicast Security: A Taxonomy and Efficient Constructions. INFOCOMM'99 1999
3. Harney, Muckenhirn. Group Key Management Protocol Architecture. IETF RFC2094. 1997
4. Harney, Harder. Logical Key Hierarchy Protocol (LKH). IETF I-D. Harney-sparta-lkhp-sec-00. 1999
5. Balenson, McGrew, Sherman. Key Management for Large Dynamic Groups: One-Way Function Trees and Amortized Initialization. IETF I-D. Irtf-smug-groupkeymgmt-oft-00. 2000
6. Canetti, Malkin, Nissim. Efficient Communication Storage Tradeoffs for Multicast Encryption. Eurocrypt'99. 1999
7. Menezes, Oorschot , Vanstone. Handbook of Applied Cryptography. CRC Press. 1996. ISBN 0-8493-8523-7

Semantics and Formalizations of Mission-Aware Behavior Trust Model for Grids

Minglu Li, Hui Liu, Lei Cao, Jiadi Yu, Ying Li, Qi Qian, and Wei Jin

Department of Computer Science and Engineering,
Shanghai Jiaotong University, 200030 Shanghai, China
{li-ml,liuhui}@cs.sjtu.edu.cn

Abstract. Trust model is an important component of gird security model and can be classified as mission-unaware identity trust model, mission-aware identity trust model, mission-unaware behavior trust model and mission-aware behavior trust model. All of them could be regarded as projections of mission-aware behavior trust model, by which authorization depends on not only the trust but also the cost and quantity of the mission. This paper proposes a formal description of this trust model by using abstract state machine (ASM). It will facilitate us understanding its semantics and accurate definitions, and bridging the gaps between de facto industry standards and this trust model. These formalizations are vertical refinements of the ASM based ground model for grids and could be easily jointed on it.

1 Introduction

The underlying concept of grids is coordinated resources sharing, problem solving or services outsourcing in dynamic, multi-institutional virtual organizations. Of course, all these accessibility are conditional: the provider must own the privilege to make such infrastructure available, constrain when, where, what it can be done. Therefore, building security into grids is inevitable and of great importance.

The security problems of grids are quite different from that of traditional distributed systems [1]. In order to provide standardized ways to implement grids security, a grid security model is proposed by GGF OGSA Security Workgroup [2]. Among those components, trust model is used to define and establish the trust relationships in grids. Its description is based on WS-trust specification [3].

As a mapping of the conceptual level trust model [4], computational level trust models could be classified as mission-unaware identity trust model, mission-aware identity trust model, mission-unaware behavior trust model and mission-aware behavior trust model [5]. If a trust model possesses relatively static end policies, it can be termed as identity trust model. If some end policies evolve their values or contents

[1] Supported by the National Grand Fundamental Research 973 Program of China (No.2002CB312002), the Grand Project (No.03dz15027) and Key Project (No.025115033) of the Science and Technology Commission of Shanghai Municipality.

M. Li et al. (Eds.): GCC 2003, LNCS 3032, pp. 883–890, 2004.

according to the behavior histories, trust model can be correspondingly termed as behavior trust model. On the other hand, if authorization is directly depending on the characteristics of the mission, such as cost, Qos, etc., it becomes mission-aware trust model. Otherwise, it falls into mission-unaware trust model.

The rest of this paper is organized as follows. Section 2 presents current situations of the security solutions for grids. Semantics of trust model are mapped from conceptual level to both software semantics and specification level, which are discussed in section 3. Section 4 proposes an ASM based formal description for mission-aware behavior trust model and section 5 concludes this paper.

2 Backgrounds on Security of Grids

GSI offers secure single sign on and preserves site control over access policies and local security. Its significant features are using of X.509, SSLv3, delegation and GSS-API [6]. GT3 and GSI3 provide the first implementation of OGSA mechanisms. It itemizes numerous security services, including credential processing, authorization, credential conversion, identity mapping and audit [7].

The Legion project also has goals similar to GT3. Its services are in the form of tools. Therefore, the high-level security model defined by Legion could also be implemented by using GT3 [8].

Nowadays, the security model of GSI, GT3 and Legion are still mission-unaware identity trust model though this kind of security model is the ground of other trust models. The first trust aware resource management system (TRMS) for grids suggests that the trust and reputation should decay with time [9]. The mathematical functions used in TRMS are different from that in literature [10], which suggests that recommender weights should be employed to reduce the computing cost of reputation. Trust model also shows great potential value in e-commerce systems, such as risk analysis using trust models [11]. This model uses fuzzy logic based on transaction costs and histories to evaluate the risk of a certain transaction. Among these trust models, the first two could be regarded as mission-unaware behavior trust models while the last one could be classified as mission-aware behavior trust model.

Common shortcomings of current behavior trust models include 1) there does not exist a uniform formal description of this kind of trust model; 2) there exists a gap between de facto industry standards, such as OGSA and WS-trust specification, and this kind of trust model; 3) there does not exist a means that could guide us to describing this kind of trust model as part of grids. In the remainder of this paper, we use trust model to stand for mission-aware behavior trust model unless explicitly stated.

3 Semantics of Trust Model

McKnight and Chervany have built a theoretical, conceptual view of trust. It comprises four constructs based on the real world social properties of trust, including disposition to trust, institution based trust, trusting believes and trusting intention [4].

In order to bring it into reality, this paper will map the conceptual trust model onto software semantic and WS-trust specification.

Software semantic of faith in humanity is mapped onto security level [5]. When an entity has high faith in humanity, it can setup to a low security level, which means the entity assume that others generally deserve trusts or it does not need too much protection. In terms of specification, it could be mapped onto claim requirements. The higher the security level is, the more claim requirements are needed. Similarly, software semantic of trusting stance is mapped onto access control policies. In terms of specification, it could be mapped onto web service endpoint policy.

Software semantic of institution-based trust is mapped onto delegation or proxy. In terms of specification, it could be mapped onto intermediaries. As for structural assurance and situation normality, they are mechanisms to make delegation or proxy legalization and could be mapped onto proof-of-possession used by intermediaries.

Software semantic of trusting believes is mapped onto trust and reputation. Trust comes from direct contact with other entity while reputation is propagated by means of word-of-mouth. Four sub-constructs of trusting believes could be used to evaluate trust and reputation [5]. For example, the ability to provide promised resources can be mapped onto competence, leaving behind data and not doing garbage collection after using the resources is a behavior violating benevolence, delivering intact information and keeping private information secure are needs of integrity, consuming more resources than requested is not accurate in predictability, etc. In terms of specification, all of them could be mapped onto different claims and/or subjects.

Software semantic of trusting intention is that we should take both trust beliefs and characteristics of a mission into account to perform the action of authorization. For example, let cost reflects resources usages, time consumed, Qos of a mission, we could still accept certain number of little cost missions from entity that has not enough trust believes. The principle of trusting intention is that a careful provider gives more thought to expensive missions and might not worry about the risk on certain number of missions of negligible cost, especially in the environment of grids. In terms of specification, trusting intention and its sub-constructs could also mapped onto different claims and/or subjects.

As a whole, the semantic of mission-aware behavior trust model is that it calculates overall trust through a weighted balance of both direct trust and reputation, if overall trust provided is not qualified for security requirement, authorization still could be inducted from the analysis of mission cost and mission quantity.

4 ASM Based Formalizations of Trust Model

The semantics of trust model only focuses on its characteristics and its mapping onto industry standards. Thus far, most trust models have been entirely informal and written in specific mathematical functions [4, 5, 10, 11]. On the other hand, an abstract state machine (ASM) [12, 13] based ground model for grids is proposed to facilitate the analysis of existing grids and the design of new ones with rigor and precision [14]. For the same purpose, this paper refines this ground model vertically to make it support the semantics of trust model.

4.1 Security Consideration in the Ground Model for Grids

According to the evolving thoughts to define the ground model for grids [14], security consideration shapes into different universes, signatures and rules. Universes of the ground model are APPLICATION, PROCESS, USER, ARESOURCE (i.e., abstract resource), PRESOURCE (i.e., physical resource), NODE, TASK (i.e., running processes), ATTR (i.e., attribute) and MESSAGE.

Related signatures of the ground model are 'canLogin', 'canUse', 'globalUser', 'handler', 'installed', 'localUser', 'location', 'mapped', 'mappedResource', 'request', 'task', 'type', 'userMapping', 'uses'. Directly related rules are 'users mapping' and 'resource grant'. Detail information could be found in literature [14].

4.2 Defining the Trust Model

Newly introduced universes of trust model are TOKEN, TRUST, REPUTATION, TIME, CONTEXT, ACCEPTRATIO and COST.

TOKEN stands for security tokens, including both singed and unsigned security tokens [3]. TRUST and REPUTATION stands for the value of trust and reputation, which can be either discrete or continuous. TIME and CONTEXT stands for time and context respectively. The value of ACCEPTRATIO ranges from 0 to 1, which indicates that only part of the 'untrustworthy' missions could be accepted at a given period and its acceptable probability is not more than the acceptable ratio assigned. COST is a composite measurement of mission, which can be either discrete or continuous. It may reflect cpu cycles of computing missions, system resources usage of memory-sharing missions, constrains demands of data-mining missions, Qos of general missions, etc. These universes could be implemented by using claims and subjects.

Newly introduced signatures of trust model are 'acceptRatio : TRUST × COST × CONTEXT × TIME → ACCEPTRATIO', 'adjustReputation : REPUTATION ×...× REPUTATION → REPUTATION', 'authorization : TOKEN × TOKEN × COST × CONTEXT × TIME → BOOLEAN', 'directTrust : TOKEN × TOKEN × TIME × CONTEXT → TRUST', 'evaluateTrust : TOKEN × TOKEN × CONTEXT → TRUST', 'getRecommendation : TOKEN × CONTEXT → TOKEN × REPUTATION', 'hasReputation : TOKEN × TOKEN × CONTEXT → BOOLEAN', 'hasTrust : TOKEN × TOKEN × CONTEXT → BOOLEAN', 'missionAnalysis : TRUST × COST × CONTEXT → BOOLEAN', 'overallReputation : TOKEN × TOKEN × TIME × CONTEXT → REPUTATION', 'overallTrust : TRUST × REPUTATION → TRUST', 'reputation : TOKEN × TOKEN × TIME × CONTEXT → REPUTATION', 'updateReputation : TRUST × REPUTATION → REPUTATION', 'updateTrust : TRUST × TRUST × ACCEPTRATIO → TRUST'. Their explanations could be found in that of the rules.

Rule 1. Obtaining direct trust (directTrust)
Direct trust represents one entity's belief in another entity's trustworthiness within a certain context at a given time based on their direct behavior history. Because trust decays with time, time is also a parameter. In our previous example, trust is divided into six levels that range from very low to extremely high trust level and time is used to construct a decay function that is a multiplying factor of trust [5].

```
s1,s2 ↦  ∀s∈TOKEN ∧ s1≠s2 ∧ c∈CONTEXT ∧ t∈TIME
if hasTrust(s1,s2,c) = true then
  directTrust(s1,s2,t,c)
else
  directTrust(s1,s2,t,c) := default value∈TRUST
  hasTrust(s1,s2,c) := true
```

Rule 2. Calculating overall reputation (overallReputation)
Reputation indicates indirect trust based on recommendations, which is what other entities think about a specific entity. Because reputation is a subjective judgment, recommender's evaluation about one entity might be quite different from our own evaluation about the same entity. Therefore, this rule is used to obtain 'what I think the recommender means from what the recommender said'. The signature of adjustReputation defines how to amend reputation value. In our previous example, adjustReputation is a weighted function to gain average reputation [5].

```
repSet := {}
n := 0
if ∀s∈TOKEN ∧ hasReputation(s,s2,c) = false
  do in-parallel
    getRecommendation(s2,c)
    ...
    getRecommendation(s2,c)
  enddo
do forall s : s∈TOKEN ∧ hasReputation(s,s2,c) = true
  repSet := {reputation(s,s2,t,c)} + repSet
  n := n + 1
enddo
adjustReputtion(repSet.item1,...,repSet.itemn)
```

Rule 3. Calculating overall trust (overallTrust)
Overall trust is depended on both direct trust and reputation. However, direct trust and reputation may have no influence on the overall trust. In our previous example, overall trust is a weighted balance of both direct trust and reputation [5].

```
overallTrust(td↦directTrust(s1,s2,t,c),
r↦overallReputation(s1,s2,t,c))
```

Rule 4. Analyzing mission (missionAnalysis)
Mission analysis means authorization depends on not only the trust, but also the cost and quantity of mission. If the trust provided had not satisfied the trust required, only part of the 'untrustworthy' missions could be authorized at a given period and its acceptable probability is not more than the acceptable ratio assigned. In our previous example, acceptable ratio is kept in the trusting intention probability matrix, where its column means the difference between the trust provided and required and its row represents the cost of mission. The quantity of mission could be controlled by the parameter of time [5].

```
to := overallTrust(td ↦directTrust(s1,s2,t,c),
r↦overallReputation(s1,s2,t,c))
tr := ∃ trust_required ∈ TRUST
```

```
if to-tr ≥ 0 ∨ acceptRatio(to-tr,cost,c,t) ≤ threshold
∈ ACCEPTRATIO then
  authorization(s1,s2,cost,c,t) := true
else
  authorization(s1,s2,cost,c,t) := false
```

Rule 5. Updating direct trust (updateTrust)
After finishing current mission, direct trust could be evaluated to amend original direct trust. Because 'untrustworthy' missions may be authorized at certain acceptable ratio, the suggested philosophy used to update direct trust is that if trust were risen, we regard it as only one successful mission; otherwise, we conclude that all 'untrustworthy' missions, including those had been rejected for the reason of acceptable ratio, are failure too. For example, if acceptable ratio is equal to 1/50, one harmful 'untrustworthy' mission has the same bad influence as that of 50 harmful 'untrustworthy' missions.

```
directTrust(s1,s2,t,c) := updateTrust(td↦directTrust(s1,
s2,t,c),te↦evaluateTrust(s1,s2,c), ∃ threshold ∈
ACCEPTRATIO)
```

Rule 6. Updating reputation (updateReputation)
Similarly, after finishing current mission, direct trust could be evaluated to amend related reputations. This kind of amending could be used to adjust the recommenders' reliabilities, i.e., what the recommender means from what it said. In our previous example, such an amending affects adjustment factors of reputation [5].

```
do forall s : s∈TOKEN ∧ hasReputation(s,s2,c) = true
  reputation(s,s2,t,c) := updateReputa-
tion(te↦evaluateTrust(s1,s2,c),
r↦reputation(s,s2,t,c))
enddo
```

Rule 7. Obtaining recommendation (getRecommendation)
If no reputation were available, an entity could obtain recommendations with this rule. It indicates that there must be a mechanism for entity to publish, discover, locate and retrieve reputations.

```
reputationStore := {(s1,s2,c,r)| s1,s2∈TOKEN ∧
c∈CONTEXT ∧ r∈REPUTATION}
choose (s,s2,c,r) : (s,s2,c,r) ∈ reputationStore
  getRecommendation(s2,c) := (s,r)
endchoose
```

According to the characteristics of ASM, universes, signatures and rules above are high-level abstraction of trust model. Concrete mathematical functions and programming schemes are of no concern at this abstract level and could be regarded as different instantiations of this abstraction. In other words, mathematical functions and programming schemes are vertical refinement and horizontal decomposition of this ASM based trust model.

4.3 Jointing the Trust Model on the Ground Model

In the ground model for grids, two signatures are directly related to security, including 'canUse' and 'canLogin'. These two signatures are authorization functions at two different levels. 'canUse' indicates whether a global user can use a mapped resource while 'canLogin' indicates whether a local user can create and own a process to provide the resource required. According to the design pattern of ASM, trust model is a vertical refinement of the ground model. Therefore, we must joint it on the ground model. For this purpose, new signatures must be introduced.

Newly introduced signatures are 'mappedToken : {USER, PRESOURCE, NODE} → TOKEN', 'mappedContext : {USER, PRESOURCE, NODE} → CONTEXT', 'combinedContext : CONTEXT × ... × CONTEXT → CONTEXT', 'cost : CONTEXT → COST'.

Among them, 'mappedToken' and 'mappedContext' map USER, PRESOURCE and NODE onto corresponding TOKEN or CONTEXT, 'combinedContext' combines different CONTEXT into one CONTEXT, 'cost' retrieve COST from CONTEXT. By means of these signatures, 'canUse' and 'canLogin' could be finally translated into authorization and other related signatures. On the other hand, because entities may want to update direct trust and reputation after each contact, some new mechanisms must be employed. This kind of signatures could be regarded as another refinement of current trust model. Now you see, ASM based model combines abstraction with rigor, legibility and evolution.

5 Discussions and Conclusions

Being an extension of current popular mission-unaware identity trust model, mission-aware behavior trust model is not an artifact. It has been embodied in social activities for centuries and this paper only disinters it from subconsciousness and describes it formally with abstract state machine.

Mission-aware behavior trust model inherently supports single sign on and concise management of large and frequently changing user population, large and rapidly changing resources pool and a dynamic group of processes throughout lifetime. Trust could be used to authenticate IP address, personal identity, (mobile) phone number, membership identity, credit card, UDDI, etc. By means of certain authentication mechanism, trust could become widely acceptable legal token or electronic passport throughout virtual organizations.

Changing access control policies according to behavior histories and taking risk to accept several suspect transactions had been employed by several real systems. However, they may be done manually or scattered around audit, account modules or parts. This trust model is going to establish a systemic view for developers to understand, implement and integrate these functionalities in a more natural, feasible and automatic manner.

Generally speaking, the research on mission-aware behavior trust model is just kicked off; both opportunities and challenges are watching explorers' time. We hope the ASM based trust model could be leverages for the security of grids and could bridge the gaps between researchers and developers.

References

1. Foster, I., Kesselman, C., Tsudik, G., Tuecke, S.: A Security Architecture for Computational Grids. In: Gong, L, Reiter, M. (eds.): Proc. of the 5th ACM Conf. on Computer and Comm. Sec. ACM Press, New York (1998) 83–92
2. Nagaratnam, N., Janson, P., Dayka, J., Nadalin, A., Siebenlist, F., Welch, V., Tuecke, S., Foster, I.: Security Architecture for Open Grid Services. GWD-I Document, GGF OGSA Security Workgroup (2003)
3. A Joint White Paper from IBM Corporation and Microsoft Corporation: Security in a Web Services World: A Proposed Architecture and Roadmap. (2002)
4. McHnight, D., Chervany, N.: Conceptualizing Trust: A Typology and E-Commerce Customer Relationships Model. In: Dennis, E. (ed.): Proc. of the 34th Ann. Hawaii Int. Conf. on Sys. Sci. IEEE Press, Hawaii (2001) 2352–2361
5. Hui, L., Qinke, P., Junyi S., Baosheng, H.: A Mission-Aware Behavior Trust Model for Grid Computing Systems, In: Yanbo, H. (ed.): Proc. of the 2002 Int. Workshop on Grid and Cooperative Computing. Electronics Industry, Hainan, China (2002) 897–909
6. Butler, R., Welch, V., Engert, D., Foster, I., Tuecke, S., Volmer, J., Kesselman, C.: A National-Scale Authentication Infrastructure. IEEE Computer. 33 (2000) 60–66
7. Welch, V., Siebenlist, F., Foster, I., Bresnahan, J., Czajkowski, K., Gawor, J., Kesselman, C., Mederl, S., Pearlman, L., Tuecke S.: Security for Grid Services. http://www.globus.org/ Security/GSI3/GT3-Security-HPDC.pdf
8. Natrajan, A., Humphrey, M., Grimshaw, A.: The Legion Support for Advanced Parameter-Space Studies on a Grid. Fut. Generation Computer Sys. 18 (2002) 1033–1052
9. Azzedin, F., Maheswaran, M.: Evolving and Managing Trust in Grid Computing Systems. In: Kinsner, W., Sebak, A., Ferens. K., (eds.): Proc. of the IEEE Canadian Conf. on Electrical & Computer Eng. Vol.3. IEEE Press, Manitoba, Canada (2002) 1424–1429
10. Abdul-Rahman A., Hailes, S.: Supporting Trust in Virtual Communities. In: Ralph, H., Sprague, J. (eds.): Proc. of the 33rd Ann. Hawaii Int. Conf. on Sys. Sci. IEEE Press, Hawaii (2000) 1769–1777
11. Manchala R.: E-Commerce Trust Metrics and Models. IEEE Internet Computing. 4 (2000) 36–44
12. Börger, E.: The Origins and Development of the ASM Method for High Level System Design and Analysis. J. of Univ. Computer Sci. 8 (2002) 2–74
13. Gurevich, Y.: May 1997 Draft on the ASM Guide. http://www.eecs.umich.edu/gasm/ papers/guide97.html.
14. Zsolt N., Vaidy S.: Characterizing Grids: Attributes, Definitions and Formalisms. J. of Grid Computing. 1(2003) 9–23

Study on a Secure Access Model for the Grid Catalogue*

Bing Xie, Xiao-Lin Gui, and Qing-Jiang Wang

Department of Computer Science and Technology, Xi'an Jiaotong University, 710049, Xi'an, China
xiexiebing@sohu.com
xlgui@mail.xjtu.edu.cn
qjwang@mailst.xjtu.edu.cn

Abstract. To solve the security of access to meta-data in computational Grids, by modifying model BLP, a secure access model named GBLP is introduced to support access control to Grid catalogue. In the computational Grid, resources and users can be endowed with different secure levels. Because Grid catalogue is a logic map of all physical resources, and then, when different secure levels are assigned to different users for catalogue access, the secure access control of Grid resources can be implemented by controlling the access security of Grid catalogue. In an experiment Grid (Wader Grid), the hierarchical access control for Grid catalogue is implemented by using secure model GBLP.

1 Introduction

Computational Grids [1] are usually used to solve the wide-area computational problems in heterogeneous systems interconnected by Internet. Except for dealing with the computational problem, Grids can also provide services for users to share computational data. In fact, most resources on Grids are open. Therefore, either in large-scale parallel computing or in access to resources, the problem about security is inevitable. For example, by cheating Grid Server, an untrusted user is able to login and acquire computing resources, then run applications with virus. Under this condition, Grid system may be put into confusedness. Another more serious situation is that untrusted users utilize these resources to do illegal activities. These activities may result in the loss of benefit of country and collective. Therefore, implementing a secure and stable Grid system is very important.

Grid resources are usually geographically distributed and heterogeneous, a single-image name space is introduced to support uniform access to these resources. Setting secure access level for these resources is essential. Let different users access different resources can prohibit resources from breakdown. The present security mechanism on Grids includes two aspects: identity authentication and access control of Grid

* This work was sponsored by the National Science Foundation of China(NSFC) under the grant No.60273085 and the state High-tech Research and Development project(863) under the grant No.2001AA111081.

M. Li et al. (Eds.). GCC 2003, LNCS 3032, pp. 891–898, 2004.

resources. The former responsibility is mainly to restrict whether users have rights to login system and which rights they have. The latter is responsible for restricting different users to use different rights to access to corresponding resources. At present, there are lots of studies on security mechanism of identity authentication, and some of them are accepted secure and valid. Such as, a method on identity authentication, which is based on safe approach and coupled with SSL, is very popular. But for resource access control, no model is accepted as a secure and reliable one at the present time.

Designing a secure model in new systems is quite difficult. Compared with designing a new model, modeling by improving an existing and widely used model is much easier and more feasible to satisfy the demand of new systematic security. As the logic map of users and resources, Grid meta-data catalogue (Grid catalogue) can implement secure access to resources by controlling the security of access to Grid catalogue. For guaranteeing the secure access to catalogue, a secure model named GBLP is introduced in this paper. This model modified from secure model BLP [2] is used to support secure access to Grid catalogue.

This paper introduces this model's theoretic framework and simply shows its application. This application is implemented using the hierarchical access control for the Grid catalogue in an experiment Grid (Wader Grid [3]).

2 Grid Catalogue

Based on certain data model, meta-data catalogue as a database is used to save and manage objects. And because of its importance, it is also deemed to the core of sharing data in Grid. With Grid catalogue, services can be supported by using some valid methods on its management. For managing objects in Grid catalogue, some operations including store, remove, and delete are usually used, and to manage sub directories in it, replicate and refer are also used.

In every system, there must be some information about itself. And this information's security concerns the security of whole system, hence it's more important than other common files. Therefore, these two kinds of data should be managed in different ways. Grid catalogue also includes these two kinds of data, how to manage these data securely and efficiently is the emphasis of catalogue security. Supporting a secure catalogue service is the base of system security. If catalogue service is insecure, system security is difficult to ensure. For example, when users login a system with bugs, the condition that the users not belonging to system acquire the information about the resources sizes and positions is likely to happen. Once it happens, the resources security is potentially threatened. If catalogue framework is not close enough, and maybe there are even covert channels in it, users in Grid can acquire the information about resources beyond their rights. Under this condition, the whole system's security is threatened and this may even bring disaster to system.

In Wader Grid, catalogue service is supported by standard protocol LDAP[4]. As the standard of the Client/Server protocol, LDAP is usually implemented for organizing and managing data catalogue. It supports protocol TCP/IP without large upper layer protocol as OSI, so it is applied widely. LDAP service also supports multi-language edition of API in its client-side, and its server-side implements GDBM which is a document data base based on index. Therefore, the research in LDAP is very efficient. Fig. 1 shows the meta-data catalogue (part) about Wader Grid. In Wader Grid, catalogue service includes supporting parallel computing and the catalogue's framework with sharing computing data.

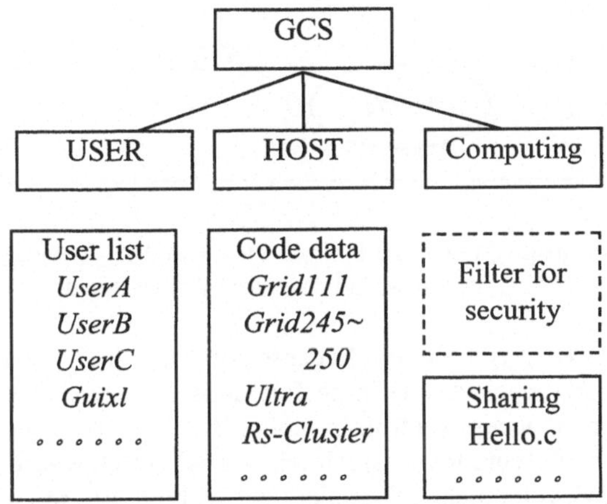

Fig. 1. Part of meta-data catalogue on Wader Grid. In this figure,"/GCS" shows sub catalogue's root in computational Grid, "/GCS/HOST" records all users' information, "/GCS/HOST" expresses the information about all usable computers in Wader Grid, "/GCS/Computing" maps all shared functions in system

3 Model BLP

In 1973, David Bell and Leonard La Padula introduced model BLP for safeguarding the systematic privacy, and now it has become an example in secure models. Model BLP formally defines the states of internal system and constitutes a series of mandatory orders to restrict the transformation among different states. In model BLP, it is believed that system security can be proved by mathematical theorization. In this model, data, users and the other elements of system are all thought as abstract entities. These entities are divided into two types, one is the set of subjects, which can operate actions as read and write etc., and the other is the set of objects, which can accept the actions operated by subjects.

Model BLP assigns certain secure level to entities and defines a series of axioms to ensure the normal transformations among different systematic states. Fig. 2 shows the simple description of secure model BLP, and the following two axioms are the most important in BLP-related theories.

1. *Simple Security*: When a subject wants to access to an object, subject's secure level must be at least equal with the object's.
2. **.- property*: Prohibit data transformation from high secure levels to low ones.

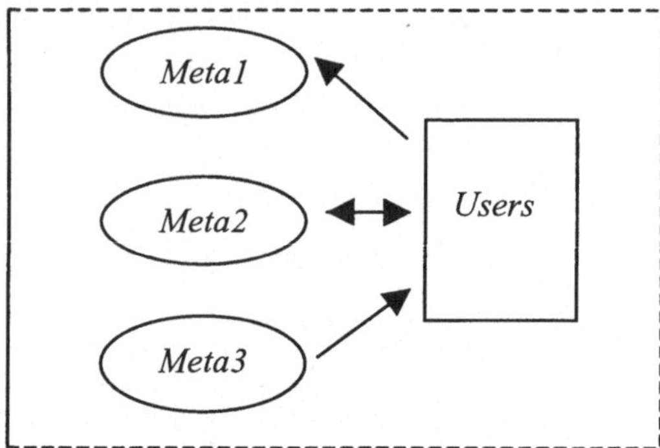

Fig. 2. In this sketch map of model BLP, from *Meta3* to *Meta1,* the security of meta-data is gradually hoisted. And along the arrowhead's set, data is transferred

In nature, model BLP is a model of access control, which is based on secure level. It implements secure access by defining functions of secure classes and constituting the matrix on rights of access control. In model BLP, the basic security element is that subjects' functions of secure levels are at least equal with the accessed objects'.

While with the development of science and technology, model BLP can't satisfy the demand of actual application any more. That is,

1. BLP introduces the concept of authentic subjects. And for guaranteeing systematic movements and management, these users aren't restricted by **.- property*. But their rights are too high to satisfy the theorem of *minimum privilege*[1].
2. BLP permits data transfer from low secure levels to high ones, while this upward transfer may leads to the time-domain covert channel[5]] appears in system, and this is very harmful for system security.

For making model BLP satisfy the demand of secure access control of Grid catalogue, this model should be improved and modified.

4 Framework of Secure Model GBLP and Its Application

4.1 Framework

Definition 1[2] Let L be a set of entities with $L = S \cup O$, S is the set of subjects, O is the set of objects, and $S = S_a \cup S_u$, where S_a is the set of administrators, S_u is the set of usual users, $S_a = S_1 \cup S_2 ... \cup S_n$, and $S_1 \cap S_2 ... \cap S_n = \Phi$, where S_i is a kind of classification of administrators. $O = O_s \cup O_f$, where $O_s \cap O_f = \Phi$, O_s is the set of systematic data, O_f is the set of common

---

[1] A theorem that guarantees the privileges in system are distributed enough.

files. Let A be the set of access' rights, including the following elements: c (compare), s (search), r (read), w (write), a (append), d (delete), re (refer), co (copy). S composes set B together with O and A, where set B is the present access set. And $B \subseteq (S \times O \times A)$.

Definition 2[2] Let M be the set of access control where $M = \{m_{ij} | m_{ij} \in A,\ m_{ij}$ shows S_i has right to access $O_j\}$. Let F be the set of functions of secure level, where f_o is the level of O_j, f_s is the present level of S_u, Let H be the current construction of objects' catalogue. B composes set V together with M, F, H, and set V is the set of systematic states where $V = (B \times M \times F \times H)$, and for $\forall v = (b, M, f, H) \in V$,($b = (s_i, o_j, q) \in B$, $q \in A$ and $f = (f_s, f_o) \in F$).

Definition 3 Let K be the set of functions of properties, $K = \{k_i | k_i$ is the attribute of O, and if $i \neq j$, then $k_i \neq k_j\}$.

Definition 4 Let C be the set of functions of identities, $C = \{c_i | c_i$ shows the special function of S_a, and if $i \neq j$, then $c_i \neq c_j\}$

Definition 5 Let W be the map from C to K, in another words, for $\forall o \in O$, if $\exists c_i(o) \in C$ such that $w(c_i(o)) = k_j$.

Axiom 1 (simple security) For $\forall (s, o, q) \in B$, if $s \in S_u$, and if and only if $f_s(s) \geq f_o(o)$
Then

$$q = c \text{ or } q = s \text{ or } q = r \qquad (1)$$

Axiom 2 (special function) For $\forall (s, o, q) \in B$, if $s \in S_a, o \in O_a$, if and only if $\exists w_l$, such that $w_l(c_m(s)) = k_n(o)$
Then

$$\begin{aligned} &(\mathrm{I})\ q = c \text{ or } q = s \text{ or } q = r \\ &(\mathrm{II})\ q = w \text{ or } q = a \text{ or } q = d \text{ or } q = re \text{ or } q = co \end{aligned} \qquad (2)$$

Axiom 3 (functional division) For $\forall(s,o,q)\in B$, $(s_i \in S_i, i\in N)$, $\exists w_l$[2], such that $w_l(c_m(s_i)) = k_n(o_{i'})$, where $o_{i'} \in O_i \subset O_a, O_1 \cup O_2 ... \cup O_n = O_a$, and $O_1 \cap O_2 ... \cap O_n = \Phi$.

Axiom 4 (compatible property) In model, the tree structure of objects (H) is preserved. In another words,

$$\forall o_j \in H(o_i),\ f_o(o_j) \geq f_o(o_i) \tag{3}$$

Theorem 1 In management of S_u, model GBLP satisfies the basic secure axiom in model BLP.

Proof At first, Axiom 1 is exactly the application[3] of basic secure axiom in model BLP. Secondly, the axiom of *special function* (Axiom 2) describes when the characteristic attributes are compatible to the objects operation write can be applied. It means, only the authenticated subjects can operate as write. Axiom 2 is the special condition of **.- property* (*.-axiom permits to write upward.)

From the above two conditions (and they are all conditions in this system), it is easy to see that model GBLP satisfies the basic secure axiom in model BLP.

Theorem 2 Model GBLP satisfies the theorem of *minimum property*.

Proof The framework divides administrators into $S_1, S_2,...S_n$ by their different characteristic attributes. The set of functions C endow $S_1, S_2,...S_n$ with differently special functions. Axiom 3 shows, for $\forall S_i, \exists O_i$, such that $W: C(S_i) \rightarrow K(O_i)$, with the same reason, for $\forall S_j, \exists O_j$, such that $W: C(S_j) \rightarrow K(O_j)$, where $O_i \cup O_j = O_a$, $O_i \cap O_j = \Phi$. It shows through classifying subjects by different attributes, the objects are also classified accordingly. Therefore, the rights of administrators are separated, and the theorem of *minimum property* is satisfied.

Theorem 3 There is no time-domain covert channel in model GBLP.

Proof Time-domain covert channels mainly occur with the operation "write upward". To usual users, they have no right to write upward, and to administrators, they belong to privilege users (described in detail in Theorem 1), so the problem on writing upward does not exist. Therefore, time-domain covert channel can't exist in model GBLP.

---

[2] Since administrators functions must be operated on objects, w_l 's existence is necessity,

[3] It is simply applied in the management of usual users.

4.2 Experimentation in Wader Grid

Model GBLP is introduced for better solving the secure problem in Grid. By observing the following two aspects, the unity between model GBLP and the strategy of secure access control in computational Grid can be seen obvious.

4.2.1 Set of Systematic States

Model GBLP defines system state set $V = (B \times M \times F \times H)$. In Grid, processes, users are both subjects[4]. Objects include files, catalogue, system information (shown with the file too), etc. LDAP supports users to append attributes, and also to store secure level as attributes. Therefore, for implementing the imperative access control in Grid, processes and users can be endowed with certain secure levels. Equally, resources are endowed with secure levels for management. It means set of functions (F) expresses secure levels and imperatively restricts access control in Grid. For operation actions (A), GBLP is compatible to the demand of catalogue service in Grid. For example, there are the same operations in Grid as compare, search, read, write, append, delete, refer and copy. Among these operations, only the first four are offered to usual users. It indicates that the set of present access states in Grid system can be shown as the same as set $B = (S \times O \times A)$ in model GBLP. When meta-data catalogue implements secure access control, its matrix of access control is shown by ACL form in LDAP, which applies access control with attributes. This matrix in Wader Grid is exactly the matrix of access control in Grid catalogue $M = \{m_{ij} | m_{ij} \in A,$ where m_{ij} expresses that S_i have rights to access to $O_j\}$. By adding the current tree structure of meta-data catalogue, the system state of current system is formed, which is shown by set $V = (B \times M \times F \times H)$.

4.2.2 Access Control

1. By assigning users certain identities, LDAP supports the strategy of identity authentication, which is compatible with the Definition 3 and 4 in model GBLP.
2. In management of usual users, GBLP guarantees access security of common files by referring the properties of model BLP (described in detail in Theorem 1).
3. In management of administrators, GBLP refers concept *authentic subjects* from BLP, and improves it by more dividing the differently special functions. In Wader Grid, administrators are partitioned into two parts, which are named S_1 and S_2, where S_1 and S_2 manages resources information specially and respectively. Assigning identities and dividing special functions are guaranteed by Theorem 2 and 3. From the above, secure system information is ensured, and the principle of *minimum privilege* is satisfied in the management of administrators'.
4. In management of subjects, usual users and administrators are managed in different ways. It means implementing different methods to manage these two kinds of users

[4] These subjects can operate the actions such as "register", "acquire resources", etc.

(described in detail in Axiom 1, 2). In Wader Grid, users and administrators also login system with different entries. Actually, the condition that usual users operate actions beyond their rights is impossible by these double separations.

5. According to the actual demand of catalogue management, model GBLP endows only administrators with write right. This eliminates the bug of time-domain covert channel in model BLP. (described in detail in Theorem 3).

The above principles of operation control in GBLP point to the defects of model BLP and improve them to satisfy Grid catalogue's demand. All these principles point to the management of Wader Grid's catalogue directly, in another words, secure model GBLP suits for the demand of secure management of Grid catalogue.

5 Conclusion

Security and reliability are focal points on Grid study. Grid system can span different regions and systems, so implementing LDAP protocol to construct Grid catalogue makes catalogue management become comparatively easier. In Grid, all kinds of resources are implemented single-image by Grid catalogue, so resources security has a close relationship with catalogue security. Through ensuring secure access control of Grid catalogue logically, model GBLP implements secure access control of physical resources. This paper mainly introduces a method about how to securely manage logic resources in Grid, and the problem concerning how to guarantee the security of access control of physical resources can be solved by local OS. How to combine the secure accesses of logical and physical resources organically is the next study direction.

References

[1] Kaneda, K., Taura, K., Yonezawa, A. Virtual Private Grid: a Command Shell for Utilizing Hundreds of Machines Efficiently. Cluster Computing and the Grid 2nd IEEE/ACM International Symposium (CCGRID2002), May 2002:198-205.

[2] Bell, E. D. and LaPadula, L. J. Secure Computer Systems: Mathematical Foundations. Mitre Report ESD-TR-73-278 (Vol. I--III), Mitre Corporation, Bedford, MA, 1973/1974.

[3] Gui Xiao-lin, Qian De-pei, He Ge. Design and Implementation of a Campus-Wide Metacomputing System (WADE). Journal of Computer Research and Development, 2002, 39(7): 888~894.

[4] Johner, H, Brown, L, Hinner, F.S. et al. Understanding LDAP, International Technical Support Organization, http://www.redbooks.ibm.com, June 1998.

[5] Wang Wei , The Time-Domain Security Analysis Of Bella Padula Model , Journal Of Computer Research And Development, 1997, 34(2): 149 ~152.

Modeling Trust Management System for Grids[1]

Baiyan Li, Wensheng Yao, and Jinyuan You

Department of Computer Science and Engineering, Shanghai Jiao Tong University, Shanghai 200030, China
{li-by, yao-ws, you-jy}@cs.sjtu.edu.cn

Abstract. Grid computing has been widely accepted as a promising paradigm for large-scale resources sharing in recent years. However, the general authorization mechanism, called *trust management system*, for grids is not well-understood. The purpose of this paper is to provide a logic-based formal approach to modeling authorization mechanisms of grids. We develop a logic-based language, called Trust Logic, to represent policies, credentials, and requests in distributed authorization. We give the inference rules of the logic as well as a logic-based *compliance-checking* algorithm for trust management in grids. In our formalism, the compliance-checking problem of trust management is equal to constructing a logical proof, which indicates whether a request is a logical consequence of a set of credentials and policies.

1 Introduction

Grid computing has been widely accepted as a promising paradigm for large-scale resources sharing in recent years [1, 2]. While the security architectures of specific grids such as Globus [3, 4, 5], are well-understood, the general authorization framework for shared resources in grids is not. The purpose of this paper is to provide a formal, logic-based approach to modeling such an authorization system for grids.

The authorization in central systems is based on the *closed-world* assumption [6] i.e., all authorized entities are known and trusted. In the dynamic environment such as grids, however, all entities often are unknown to each other. They have to use information from third parties (e.g. certification authorities) they trust. This makes the authorization in grids different from traditional access control.

The *trust management* [7] problem in open, distributed environments can be described as following: A requester submits a request with a set of credentials, e.g. signed certificates, issued by entities in distributed systems, to an authorizer, who controls the requested resources. The authorizer then decides whether to authorize this request by answering the *proof-of-compliance* [8] question: "Do these credentials prove that a request complies with my local policy?"

Several trust management systems, including PolicyMaker, KeyNote, REFEREE and SPKI/SDSI [6], have been proposed in recent years. But none of them is suitable

[1] This paper is supported by the Shanghai Science and Technology Development Foundation under Grant No. 03DZ15027.

M. Li et al. (Eds.): GCC 2003, LNCS 3032, pp. 899–906, 2004.

for modeling trust management systems of grids for lack of formal models. The SRC logic [9, 10], which uses a "speaks for" relationship of principals as its core concept, seems to be an attractive basis for constructing a system. However, it is designed mainly for authentication; its total delegation has too coarse a granularity for authorization [11].

In our view, the grid is a dynamic "virtual organization" consisting of a large number of entities connected by networks for resources sharing. These entities may be hosts, services, user proxies, or even public keys. In this paper we use the multi-agent Kripke model [12] to characterize the grid. All the entities in a grid are regarded as agents in a Kripke structure based on the possible-worlds semantics [13]. The primitive propositions such as "read file foo", "k_A is a key of agent A", form the world about which we wish to reason. We develop a specific logic, called Trust Logic, to represent the belief of agents with logical formulas based on modal logic $\mathbf{K_n}$ [12]. The core concept of our logic is a well-defined "trusts regarding" relation among agents. The underlying idea is that an agent would believe the statements made by another if he trusts that agent regarding these statements. In our formalism, the compliance-checking problem of trust management is equal to constructing a logical proof, which indicates whether a request is a logical consequence of a set of credentials and policies.

The rest of this paper is organized as follows. In Section 2, we introduce the syntax and semantics of modal logic of belief. In Section 3, we give a theory of trust. In Section 4, we formalize a well-known grid security system and propose a basic compliance-checking algorithm for trust management system of the grid based on our logic. Finally, we give the conclusion of this paper in Section 5.

2 Modal Logic of Belief

There are two logic-based approaches, *syntactic approach* [11] and *modal logic* approach [12], to modeling belief in the literature. The syntactic approach suffers several drawbacks. For example, a minor syntactic difference of two problems may lead to independent solution. On the other hand, the modal logic approach, which uses *possible-worlds* semantics [13], is a customizable semantic approach i.e., with little effort a theory can be derived from some existing logic [14]. We now adopt the latter in this paper.

A logic of any kind needs a language to define its *well formed formulas* (WFFs). Given a nonempty set $\mathbf{\Phi}$ of primitive propositions, which we typically label $p, q, \ldots$, and a set of n agents whose names are denoted $A_1, A_2, \ldots, A_n$, we define a modal language $\mathbf{L}_n(\mathbf{\Phi})$ to be the least set of formulas containing $\mathbf{\Phi}$, closed under negation, conjunction, and modal operators $B_1, B_2, \ldots, B_n$. In other words, the formulas of $\mathbf{L}_n(\mathbf{\Phi})$ are given by rule $\phi ::= p \mid \neg\phi \mid \phi\wedge\phi \mid B_i\phi$ where p ranges over elements of $\mathbf{\Phi}$ and i=1, …, n. We use $\varphi\vee\psi$ for $\neg(\neg\varphi\wedge\neg\psi)$ and $\varphi\supset\psi$ for $\neg\varphi\vee\psi$. We take *true* to be an abbreviation of some valid formulas such as $p\vee\neg p$, and define *false* as the negation of *true*. The formula $B_i\phi$ is read as "agent A_i *believes* ϕ". In this paper, the formulas $B_i\phi$ and A_i *believes* ϕ are semantic equivalence. They can be used alternatively for convenience.

Definition 1: A *frame* for $\mathbf{L_n}(\mathbf{\Phi})$ is a tuple $\mathbf{\Gamma}=(S, K_1,\dots, K_n)$ where S is a nonempty set, and K_i is accessibility relation on S for $i=1, \dots, n$. A *model* for $\mathbf{L_n}(\mathbf{\Phi})$ is a pair $M=(\mathbf{\Gamma}, \pi)$, where $\mathbf{\Gamma}$ is a frame, and π is a truth assignment to the primitive propositions in $\mathbf{\Phi}$ for each states $s\in S$ (i.e., $\pi(s)$: $\Phi\rightarrow\{true, false\}$ for each state $s\in S$).

The model M, usually denoted $M=(S, \pi, K_1, \dots, K_n)$, is a typical Kripke structure for n agents [12]. The accessibility relation K_i, $i=1, \dots, n$, is a binary relation on S which may be serial, transitive or Euclidean [14]. Intuitively, $(s, t)\in K_i$ if in state s, agent A_i considers state t possible. In other words, agent A_i is not able to distinguish the two states by his existing local information. The conditions on K_i enforce certain axioms associated with belief. For example the fact that K_i is serial means that agent A_i always considers some world possible and cannot believe in falsehood. By modifying those conditions, one can get different axioms for belief. A formula in $\mathbf{L_n}(\mathbf{\Phi})$ is *true at a state s in a model M* can be defined as following:

$(M, s) \models p$ iff $\pi(s)(p)=true$ (for $p\in\mathbf{\Phi}$)
$(M, s) \models \varphi\wedge\psi$ iff both $(M, s) \models\varphi$ and $(M, s) \models\psi$
$(M, s) \models\neg\varphi$ iff $(M, s) \mid \varphi$
$(M, s) \models B_i\varphi$ iff $(M, t) \models\varphi$ for all t such that $(s, t)\in K_i$

The first three definitions correspond to the standard clauses in the definition of truth for propositional logic. The last definition formalizes the idea that agent A_i believes φ in global state s exactly iff φ is *true* in all the global states that A_i consider possible in state s.

Formally, we say that a formula φ is valid in M, and write $M \models\varphi$, if $(M, s) \models\varphi$ for every state $s\in S$; we say that φ is satisfiable in M if $(M, s) \models\varphi$ for some state $s\in S$. We say φ is valid with respect to a class $\mathbf{M}$ of structures and write $\mathbf{M} \models\varphi$, if φ is valid in all structures in $\mathbf{M}$, and say φ is satisfiable with respect to $\mathbf{M}$ if it is satisfiable in some structure in $\mathbf{M}$. We use $\mathbf{M_n}$ to denote the class of all Kripke structures for n agents.

We now adopt $\mathbf{K_n}$ here for its low requirements to agent's abilities. Halpern and others have proven the soundness and completeness of $\mathbf{K_n}$ with respect to $\mathbf{M_n}$ in [12].

3 Theory of Trust

There is no a widely accepted definition for "trust" in the literature [15, 16]. We now give the "trust" a precise definition and develop a theory of trust based on $\mathbf{K_n}$.

Definition 2: Let $M=(S, \pi, K_1, \dots, K_n)$ be a multi-agent Kripke structure; A_i and A_j (1 i, j n) be arbitrary agents in M. Let $\mathbf{\Phi}$ be a set of primitive propositions, and $R\subseteq\mathbf{\Phi}$. We say A_i *trusts* A_j *regarding* R, denoted $A_i\succ_R A_j$, iff A_i believes that A_j could determine the truth value of every proposition in R. Formally, $A_i\succ_R A_j\equiv (B_j\, p\supset B_i\, p)\wedge(B_j\neg p\supset B_i\neg p)$ for each $p\in R$.

In this way, we defined restricted "trust" with "belief". We use "$\succ$" as abbreviation of "$\succ_R$" in time of $R=\mathbf{\Phi}$. We define a "speaks-for-regarding" relation symmetrically.

Definition 3: A_i *speaks for* A_j *regarding* R, denoted $A_i\overset{R}{\Rightarrow} A_j$, iff $A_j\succ_R A_i$.

The completeness and soundness of $\mathbf{K_n}$ with respect to $\mathbf{M_n}$ indicate that $\mathbf{K_n}$ can be used to characterize agents' situation in model $\mathbf{M_n}$. But it is not always the case that an agent's situation can be characterized by a collection of axioms. For example, if an agent believes φ in state s, he may be really interested in determining whether ψ is also *true in state s*, rather than $\varphi \supset \psi$ is *true in all states*. In order to properly deal with such situation, we introduce a *logical consequence* concept to reason about belief and trust in this paper.

Definition 4: Let Σ be a set of formulas in a modal language $\mathbf{L_n}(\mathbf{\Phi})$ and φ a single formula of $\mathbf{L_n}(\mathbf{\Phi})$. We say φ is a logical consequence of Σ, denoted $\Sigma \vdash \varphi$, if φ is valid in every $\mathbf{L_n}(\mathbf{\Phi})$ structure M in which every $\psi \in \Sigma$ is valid.

If we represent beliefs of an agent with a set of formulas, then a logical consequence of the set formulas is a derived belief of that agent.

Theorem 1: Let Σ be a set of formulas in a modal language $\mathbf{L_n}(\mathbf{\Phi})$, φ and ψ be formulas of $\mathbf{L_n}(\mathbf{\Phi})$, then $\Sigma \cup \{\varphi\} \vdash \psi$ if $\Sigma \vdash \varphi$ and $\varphi \vdash \psi$.

The notion logical consequence provides us an approach to infer new valid formulas from existing ones with respect to some models. We now propose the inference rules for reasoning about belief. The rules are given in form of theorems based on $\mathbf{K_n}$.

Theorem 2: Let $\mathbf{\Phi}$ be a set of primitive propositions, A_i and A_j be agents. If $R \subseteq \mathbf{\Phi}$ then $\{A_i \succ_R A_j\} \cup \{B_j p\} \vdash B_i p$ for each $p \in R$.

Theorem 3: Let $\mathbf{\Phi}$ be a set of primitive propositions; let A_i, A_j, and A_k (1 i, j, k n) be agents. If R, $V \subseteq \mathbf{\Phi}$ then $\{A_k \succ_R A_i\} \cup \{B_i(A_i \succ_V A_j)\} \vdash B_k(A_i \succ_{R\cap V} A_j)$ for each $p \in R \cap V$.

Theorem 4: Let $\mathbf{\Phi}$ be a set of primitive propositions; let A_i, A_j, and A_k (1 i, j, k n) be agents. If R, $V \subseteq \mathbf{\Phi}$ then $\{ A_i \succ_R A_j \} \cup \{ A_j \succ_V A_k \} \vdash A_i \succ_{R\cap V} A_k$.

Theorem 5: Let $\mathbf{\Phi}$ be a set of primitive propositions; let A_i, A_j, and A_k (1 i, j, k n) be agents. If $R \subseteq \mathbf{\Phi}$ then $\{ A_i \overset{R}{\Rightarrow} A_k \} \cup \{ B_i (A_j \overset{V}{\Rightarrow} A_i)\} \vdash B_k(A_j \overset{R\cap V}{\Rightarrow} A_i)$.

Theorem 6: Let $\mathbf{\Phi}$ be a set of primitive propositions; let A_i, A_j, and A_k (1 i, j, k n) be agents. If $R \subseteq \mathbf{\Phi}$ then $\{A_i \overset{R}{\Rightarrow} A_j\} \cup \{A_j \overset{V}{\Rightarrow} A_k\} \vdash (A_i \overset{R\cap V}{\Rightarrow} A_k)$.

Theorem 7: Let $\mathbf{\Phi}$ be a set of primitive propositions; let A_i, A_j, and A_k (1 i, j, k n) be agents. If φ is a WFF of modal language $\mathbf{L_n}(\mathbf{\Phi})$ then $\{A_i \succ A_j\} \cup \{ B_j \varphi\} \vdash B_i \varphi$.

In a distributed system, no agent is omniscient. So we are intended to model belief from the view of individuals. We define the view of an agent as a collection of beliefs of that agent.

Definition 5: Let $M=(S, \pi, K_1,\ldots,K_n)$ be a Kripke structure for n agents including A_i. The view of agent A_i, denoted $View_i$, is a subset of $\mathbf{L_n}(\mathbf{\Phi})$ that A_i believes in M.

4 Modeling the Trust Management System

In our context, credentials refer to various signed certificates issued by entities in grids. We usually use $k_A=(k_A^{+1}, k_A^{-1})$ to represent the public-key pair of agent A where k_A^{+1}, k_A^{-1} are public and private parts. We regard a public key as an agent that speaks for the agent who owns it. So, if k_A is a public key of agent A, we certainly have $k_A \Rightarrow A$ as a valid formula. We usually use $k_A \Rightarrow A$ to represent the primitive proposition k_A *is a public key of A* as in [10] for that their truth values always are the same. Thus, if a Certification Authority (CA), say *CA1,* signs a certificate to bind k_A with agent *A* using k_{CA1}^{-1}, we acquire certificate $[k_A \Rightarrow A]_{k_{CA1}^{-1}}$ and formula k_{CA1} *believes* $k_A \Rightarrow A$ encoded in our logic.

We adopt the Lampson's method [9] to deal with certificate expiration. We assume that an agent will never issue a negative credential such as k_A *is not a public key of agent A*. This assumption ensures the monotonicity of our reasoning system. If a CA cancels some certificate, we just treat the certificate as a time expired one. We encode basic privileges such as "read file foo", as primitive propositions. We use formula $A \succ_R B$ to represent that entity *A* delegates a set of privileges, denoted *R*, to entity B.

We refer policy to the conventional belief of agent. If agent *A* regards *CA1* as trusted CA, we can encode the fact as $A \succ_{\text{ID-Key}} CA1$ where the ID-Key is defined as follows.

Definition 6: ID-Key={ $k_X \Rightarrow X$ | *X* represents the identifier of agent, k_X represents public key} is the set of primitive propositions that represent identity-key bindings.

4.1 Modeling GSI

The Grid Security Infrastructure (GSI) [3] is the primary security mechanism of Globus Toolkit [5], which uses the standard PKI technologies (e.g., x.509 and SSL/TLS). We now formalize its trust management mechanism using the Trust Logic via a simple but typical scenario as follows.

In our scenario, there are three hosts, denoted A, B, C respectively, and a CA, denoted GCA. The GCA is the CA that issues a *user certificate* to a user UA of host A and two *server certificates* to B and C. All the hosts and users in the scenario trust GCA, and know that k_{GCA} is a public key of GCA. UA has a public key pair k_{UA}= (k_{UA}^{+1}, k_{UA}^{-1}) stored in the host A where k_{UA}^{-1} is protected by a pass-phrase. Host C controls a resource RC which only allows the access from some one with the privileges at least *R*. Now the user UA wants to access RC on host C via host B. The typical access procedure of our scenario in GSI can be described as following:

1. A trusted communication is created between A and B (by authentication).
2. UA requests B to create a proxy, denoted PB, to delegate its authority.
3. B creates the request for UA's proxy certificate and sends it back to A.
4. UA signs the request to create a proxy certificate using its private key and sends it back to B.
5. A sends UA's certificate to B.
6. A trusted communication is created between B and C (by authentication).
7. Proxy PB sends its certificate and UA's certificate to C.
8. Proxy PB encrypts a request message using its private key and sends it to C.
9. C starts a procedure of compliance-checking using these credentials and policies.

The procedure of *compliance-checking* for a request $r \in R$ in our scenario can be formalized as follows in our logic.

Local policies of host C (conventional beliefs of agent RC)

(1) $RC \succ_{\text{ID-Key}} GCA$ (CA configuration)

(2) $k_{GCA} \Rightarrow GCA\ (GCA \succ k_{GCA})$ (CA configuration)

(3) $RC \succ_{R} UA$ (Access Control List (ACL))

Credentials (certificates):

(a) $[k_{UA} \Rightarrow UA]\, k_{GCA}^{-1}$ (ID certificate of UA)

(b) $[UA \succ_{R} k_{PB},\ k_{PB} \Rightarrow PB]\, k_{UA}^{-1}$ (delegated certificate of UA)

(c) $[r]\, k_{PB}^{-1}$ (request of PB)

Objectives to obtain: *RC believes r*

The procedure of compliance-checking for request r:

(4) k_{GCA} believes $k_{UA} \Rightarrow UA$ (from ID certificate (a))

(5) GCA believes $k_{UA} \Rightarrow UA$ (apply theorem 7 to (2) and (4))

(6) $k_{UA} \Rightarrow UA \quad (UA \succ k_{UA})$ (apply theorem 2 to (1) and (5))

(7) k_{UA} *believes* $UA \succ_{R} k_{PB}$ (from delegation certificate (b))

(8) *UA believes* $UA \succ_{R} k_{PB}$ (apply theorem 7 to (6), (7))

(9) $UA \succ_{R} k_{PB}$ (apply theorem 3 to (3) and (8))

(10) $RC \succ_{R} k_{PB}$ (apply theorem 4 to (3) and (9))

(11) k_{PB} *believes r* (from request message (c))

(12) *RC believes r* (apply theorem 2 to (10) and (11))

The formulas above are formalized beliefs of RC ($View_{RC}$), which come from three sources: convention beliefs, credentials and logical consequence of existing beliefs. Although the proof is simple, it can reveal some weaknesses of the trust management of SGI. For example, the delegation certificates don't contain any information about the identifiers of delegated hosts (e.g. host B) [17]. This makes it hard to trace or audit the resources access.

4.2 A Basic Compliance-Checking Algorithm

We now give a general algorithm of compliance-checking for trust management systems of the grid based on our logic. We now start with representing credentials and local policies with 4-tuples defined as follows.

In our context, credentials and policies can be translated into a 4-tuple of the form (X, Y, Z, R) where X, Y, and Z are agents; R is a set of propositions. The 4-tuple is corresponding to a logical formulas $B_X(Y \succ_R Z)$. Thus, we can translate the theorem 2, 3, 4, and 7 into following rules (the symbol p, φ, and $\mathbf{\Phi}$ have the same meanings as in previous sections; the symbol ϕ represents the empty set here):

1. From $(X, \_, \_, \{p\})$ and (Z, Z, X, R) $(\{p\} \subseteq R)$ infer $(Z, \_, \_, \{p\})$
2. From $(X, X, Y, R1)$ and $(Y, Y, Z, R2)$ $(R1 \cap R2 \ \ \phi)$ infer $(X, Y, Z, R1 \cap R2)$
3. From $(W, X, Y, R1)$ and $(W, Y, Z, R2)$ $(R1 \cap R2 \ \ \phi)$ infer $(W, X, Z, R1 \cap R2)$
4. From $(X, \_, \_, \{\varphi\})$ and $(Z, Z, X, \mathbf{\Phi})$ infer $(Z, \_, \_, \{\varphi\})$

Definition 7: Let Ω be a set of 4-tuples that have same value in first field. The transitive closure of Ω, denoted Closure(Ω), can be computed by following mean: If a 4-tuple $\sigma \in \Omega$, then $\sigma \in$ Closure(Ω); if 4-tuples $(W, X, Y, R1) \in \Omega$, $(W, Y, Z, R2) \in \Omega$, and $R1 \cap R2 \quad \phi$, then $(W, X, Z, R1 \cap R2) \in$ Closure(Ω).

Algorithm 1

Input: A series of 4-tuples translated from credentials and policies related to *owner* who controls the resource only allowing access from agent with privileges at least *R*.

Output: *Owner* accepts or rejects a request *r*.

1. Remove useless 4-tuples.
2. Initialize $View_{owner}$ with 4-tuples of the form (*owner*, *owner*, *X*, *R*), and initialize Ω with the remainder.
3. For each tuple of the form (*owner*, *owner*, *X*, *R*) in $View_{owner}$, if there exists a tuple σ_1 of the form $(X, \_, \_, \{p\})$ in Ω where $\{p\} \subseteq R$, the algorithm adds tuple $(owner, \_, \_, \{p\})$ into $View_{owner}$.
4. For each tuple of the form (*owner*, *owner*, *X*, *R1*) in $View_{owner}$, if there exists a tuple of the form $(X, X, Y, R2)$ in Ω where $R1 \cap R2 \quad \phi$, the algorithm adds tuple $(owner, X, Z, R1 \cap R2)$ into $View_{owner}$.
5. For each tuple of the form $(owner, X, Y, \mathbf{\Phi})$ in $View_{owner}$, if there exists a tuple of the form $(Y, \_, \_, \{\varphi\})$ in Ω, the algorithm adds tuple $(X, \_, \_, \{\varphi\})$ into Ω; if there exists a tuple of the form $(Y, \_, \_, \{\varphi\})$ in $View_{owner}$, the algorithm adds tuple $(X, \_, \_, \{\varphi\})$ into $View_{owner}$.
6. $View_{owner}$:=Closure($View_{owner}$).
7. If there exists a tuple of the form (*owner*, *owner*, *requester*, *R*) in $View_{owner}$ where $r \in R$, then the algorithm accepts the request *r*.
8. Repeat step 3–7 until no new tuples are created in $View_{owner}$, then the algorithm rejects the request *r*.

5 Conclusion

In this paper, we introduce a logic-based framework for modeling and reasoning about trust management systems of the grid. The framework consists of a logic language, a set of rules for representing credentials and policies, and a compliance-checking algorithm. Our logic it is based on a solid foundation and able to represent restricted authorization delegation. It can encode various authorization related certificates and policies in a uniform form. So our framework provides a general logic-based approach to making authorization decision for the trust management system of grids that rely on diverse security mechanisms and certificates.

References

1. Foster, I., Kesselman, C.(eds.).: The Grid: Blueprint for a New Computing Infrastructure. Morgan Kaufmann (1999).

2. Foster, I., Kesselman, C., Tuecke S.: The Anatomy of the Grid: Enabling Scalable Virtual Organizations. International Journal of High Performance Computing Application, 15(3) (2001) 200–222.
3. Foster, I., Kesselman, C., Tsudik, G., Tuecke S.: A Security Architecture for Computational Grids. Proc. 5th ACM Conference on Computer and Communications Security Conference. (1998) 83–92.
4. Welch,W., Siebenlist,F., Foster, I., Bresnahan, J., Czajkowski, K., Gawor, J., Kesselman, C., Meder, S., Pearlman, L., Tuecke, S.: Security for Grid Services. Twelfth International Symposium on High Performance Distributed Computing. Seattle Washington (2003), 48-57.
5. Foster, I., Kesselman, C., Intl J.: Globus: A Metacomputing Infrastructure Toolkit. Supercomputer Applications. 11(2) (1997) 115–128.
6. Weeks, S.: Understanding Trust Management Systems. Proceedings of the IEEE Symposium on Security and Privacy. Oakland (2001).
7. Blaze, M., Feigenbaum, J., Lacy, J.: Decentralized Trust Management. In Proceedings of the Symposium on Security and Privacy. Los Alamitos (1996) 164–173.
8. Blaze, M., Feigenbaum, J., Strauss, M.: Compliance Checking in the PolicyMaker Trust Management System. Lecture Notes in Computer Science, vol. 1465. Springer-Verlag, Ber-lin Heidelberg New York (1998).
9. Abadi, M., Burrows, M., Lampson, B. and Plotkin, G.: A Calculus for Access Control in Distributed Systems. ACM Transactions on Programming Languages and Systems, 15(4) (1993) 706–734.
10. Lampson, B., Abadi, M., Burrows, M., Wobber, E.: Authentication in Distributed Systems: Theory and Practice. ACM Transactions on Computer Systems, Vol. 10(4) (1992) 256–310.
11. Li, N., Grosof, B. N., Feigenbaum, J.: Delegation Logic: A Logic-based Approach to Distributed Authorization. ACM Transactions on Information and System Security (TISSEC), Vol. 6 (1) (2003).
12. Halpern J.Y. and Moses, Y.: A Guide to Completeness and Complexity for Modal Logics of Knowledge and Belief. Artificial Intelligence, 54 (1992) 319-379.
13. Hughes,G. E., Cresswell, M. J.: A New Introduction to Modal Logic. Routledge (1996).
14. Rangan, P.: An Axiomatic Basis of Trust in Distributed Systems. In Proceedings of the IEEE CS Symposium on Research in Security and Privacy, (1988) 204–211.
15. Grandison, T., Sloman, M.: A Survey of Trust in Internet Applications. IEEE Communica-tions Surveys (2000).
16. Chuchang,Li, Maris, O. A.: Trust in Secure Communication Systems-The Concept, Representations and Reasoning Techniques. 15th Australian Joint Conference on Artificial Intelli-gence. Canberra Australia (2002) 60–70.
17. Tuecke, S., Engert, D., Foster, I., Thompson, M., Pearlman, L., Kesselman, C.: Internet X.509 Public Key Infrastructure-Proxy Certificate Profile Internet Draft, http://www.ietf.org/internet-drafts/draft-ietf-pkix-proxy-01.txt (2001).

Avoid Powerful Tampering by Malicious Host

Fangyong Hou, Zhiying Wang, Zhen Liu, and Yun Liu

Department of Computer Science and Technology,
National University of Defense Technology,
Changsha, 410073, P.R.China
fyhou@eatng.com

Abstract. This paper indicates a potential security threat which may do harm to distributed computing security. As the program is distributed to run in the remote nodes, adversary may use simulator to produce false results to do tampering. Some sophisticated simulator can give powerful tampering ability to adversary, with the reason explained in this paper. In order to solve this security problem, Real Processor Proving algorithm is applied. This algorithm use some special behavior characteristics of real processor to determine whether the program is running on a real processor in the remote node or just running on a simulator, so that it can detect the using of simulator to avoid this kind of powerful tampering.

1 Introduction

The rapid development of computer network has led people to use distributed computing, such as mobile computing and grid computing. Wide applying of them requires solid security guarantee. Although we can use many mechanisms to provide security, there exists a particular security problem hardly to be solved. This security problem is how to protect distributed program against remote malicious host.

Both mobile agents systems and grid computing systems have one common characteristic, that is, programs are distributed across the network. As host can be malicious, it can attack programs that run on it to subvert their code and data. The problem of protection against malicious host is intrinsically more difficult, because host has full control over program execution. As we give a survey on most of such existing techniques, we find that many main prominent approaches [1], such as in mobile agents system, are all software solutions. The validity of them is to increase the complexity of analyzing code and data for malicious hosts. If adversary has enough time or enough advanced tools, he can breach these software protection mechanisms at end.

Now, adversary has a possible advanced tool to gain more powerful tampering ability. Here, we present a new threat that has not aroused important attentions, while it is truly a potential threat to distributed computing security. As the program is distributed to run on remote hosts, adversary may use simulator to produce false results to do tampering. With sophisticated or advanced simulator, malicious host can have more possibility to do any kind of attacks to compromise the security of distributed program.

M. Li et al. (Eds.): GCC 2003, LNCS 3032, pp. 907–915, 2004.

In this paper, we try to find a valid way to solve this problem, that is, to distinguish a real computer system from a simulated one. We give our technique the name of Real Processor Proving. It is software tampering detecting approach, utilizing some special characteristics that only a real processor can possess, to find using of simulator. Because IA-32 processor is the most popular processor in computer system, we mainly discuss how to distinguish a real physical IA-32 processor from a simulated virtual or false IA-32 processor.

The rest of this paper is organized as follows. Section 2 describes simulator and shows why it can do severe harm to the security of distributed program. Section 3 analyzes which special characteristics can be used to distinguish real processor from simulator. Section 4 describes the realization of Real Processor Proving, and gives some testing results. Section5 concludes this paper.

2 Powerful Tampering with Simulator

Simulator is very useful development tool for software, firmware, and hardware. For IA-32 processor, there exist many available simulators with greatly different capabilities. Some only simulate the user level instructions, while other superior simulator can simulate the system level instructions, as well as full system. Virtutech Simics [2] is an advanced system level instruction set architecture simulator and a full system simulation platform, which provides a controlled, deterministic, and fully virtualized environment. System level implies it can control full supervisor state, emulating the hardware components that are typically only used by the operating system, i.e. it can run unmodified operating systems.

In order to avoid tampering by malicious hosts, the most important things are protecting data integrity and confidentiality, protecting computing integrity and privacy, as well as authentication. Simulator will give help to breach these protections.

Virtutech Simics simulator [3] implements a virtual computer system environment. A virtual system has advantages over real hardware systems in flexibility, controllability, and visibility. You can run whatever software you want, making it do what you want, while being able to see what every component is up to in the degree of detail you chooses. Here are several examples to show its powerful capabilities for tampering.

- It is more easily to understand code action and disclose secret data. Simics simulator can profile code to show every single taken branch and exactly executing of code. It can use various types of esoteric breakpoint to debug. It is fully deterministic, observable and scriptable, allowing you to narrow down the location that you are focusing on. It can cause the exact event flow to be repeated. It exactly knows how and where the data structures are allocated, also knows every accessing to these data and can log these accesses. These tracing and statistics can be of great value when debugging or trying to understand what is really happening in a software inner loop. It can attach whatever filtering and searching software might be helpful for any purpose. With these advantages, adversary gains more power to spying the code, tracing the action, watching the data, and understand the whole program.

- It is more easily to destroy time-limited security measure. Some security mechanisms rely on time limiting. These mechanisms give a specific protection interval, during which adversary has too little time to understand program's behavior. Using simulator, adversary can extend this short protection interval to an arbitrary long interval to have enough time to analyze the program. Program itself cannot detect this transformation of time, because simulator can report all timing referencing base, includes hardware processor clock, with false value.
- It is more easily to masquerade. Simulator gives possibility of cloning systems trivially; even pretend to have some non-existing hardware. It supports independent user modifications to the instruction set, architectural performance models, and devices. Like the reason of 1, it has more opportunity to tampering the process of identity authentication also. So, it is more easily to masquerade as some certain or trusted system.

As we go deep into the simulator, we can find other abilities to convenience tampering. So, we should say that this kind of advanced simulator takes potential powerful tampering utility to adversary.

3 Characteristics Utilized for Real Processor Proving

In this section, we discuss how to distinguish simulator from real processor to avoid such tampering. Mainly discuss what special characteristics of a real processor can be utilized for our Real Processor Proving.

Possibly thorough solution to this question is using special hardware component as the trusted computing base, for example, a special secure processor that have a unique private secret key and can create a unique certification to make proving. The private secret key cannot be disclosed to the outer world of processor and the certificating result can only be calculated in the inner of processor. Because any simulator cannot produce same certificating result without knowing the secret key, we can tell whether a simulator or a real processor executes the program. But most of the computer system have not equipped with this kind of mechanism. At this point, the solution to this security problem should rely on utilizing of some special characteristics that only real processor can possess.

Simulator simulates the instruction set architecture (ISA) of processor. No matter user-level or system-level instruction set architecture simulation, it is very difficult to simulate the micro-architecture of processor. This difficulty with simulation is the critical factor for proving the existence of real processor. Our proving algorithm is basing on it and compares the difference of the results from simulator and real processor. Of course, our proving algorithm is also consisted of instructions that can all be simulated by simulator. Although the value of the execution result will be same, that is, the function between them will has no difference, the character of the execution behavior can be different if we design the proving algorithm carefully. Below, we will discuss what differences we can utilize basing on IA-32 processor.

As we give a survey of IA-32 processor [4] [5] [6] [7] [8], we have found some special things can possibly be applied for our Real Processor Proving algorithm. The standard of our selections relies on three points: validity, capability, and practicability. Validity means it can give different result between real processor and simulator. Capability means it has some degree of resistance against tampering. Practicability means it is suitable or easy to use.

3.1 Processor Identifications and Features

For IA-32 processor, it provides some sophisticated means with which you can identify the processor and determine its features. We can utilize two of them.

The first thing is processor signature. Returned parameters include processor family, type, model and some extended parameters. The second is clock frequency. In order to get proper clock frequency of remote host's processor, we should use a combination of system's timer to measure elapsed time and the Time Stamp Counter (TSC) to measure processor core clocks. That is, we should build a reference period and get beginning time and ending time of it based on system's timer; then read the TSC at the beginning and ending of this reference period. So the clock frequency equals *(Ending TSC – Beginning TSC) / (Ending Time – Beginning Time).*

- Validity. Evaluating the rationality of these identifications and features, we can judge whether a real processor exists. For example, if the frequency reported by remote processor is 100MHz while the reported type is Pentium4, we can reasonably think that remote host cheats us; because we know commonly that P4 processor should operate on 1GHz above.
- Capability. It is not very reliable or it is weak to resist tampering. Because returned parameters, referring to system's timer, and returned TSC values are all under the control of simulator. Only when adversary makes self-contradictory tampering, we can find something wrong. For example, if adversary only modifies TSC with a shorter one, the clock frequency value will be unusual. If he forges all of them carefully to report a reasonable value, we cannot see his tampering actions. But at the same time, this careful tampering will take some difficulties to adversary, requiring imitating all of these features with very high fidelity. So, at some degree, proving method basing on processor identifications and features can be treated as an available approach while not very reliable.
- Practicability. This method is simple to use. We only need to gather enough feature data of processor, for example, collect many reasonable working frequency of Pentium4 CPU in advance.

3.2 Relative Time

Relative time is one timing base that refers to remote processor. The number of clocks of remote processor can measure the length of relative time. We can make judgment by checking the difference of needed number of clocks.

To compare relative time, we execute some instructions on local host and get the number of clocks needed to accomplish these instructions. Then we run these same instructions on remote host to get the number of clocks consumed. If local processor and remote processor are same family with nearly same features, these two numbers should be consistent.

- Validity. Most simulators only give the functional same result as real processor, rarely highly cycle-accurate ones. It is very difficult to produce the clock number as accurate as real processor. For example, because simulator has no special hardware unit to support SSE2 instructions, it will consume much more clocks to simulate execution of SSE2 instructions.
- Capability. This kind of judgment is not very reliable also. The reason is that cycle-accurate simulator can give accurate relative time like real processor, although this requires more sophisticated simulator.
- Practicability. Relative time is easy to use. We only need to gather enough sample data in advance, for example, collect the number of clocks to complete some instructions on Pentium4 CPU.

3.3 Absolute Time

Absolute time is one timing base that refers to real physical time. In order to compare absolute time, we run some instructions on local host and remote host separately, but measure the elapsed time all according to a trusted time reference, such as local host's system timer.

- Validity. Although some advanced commercial simulator such as Simics can accurately simulate the cycle behavior of instruction execution, it will spend longer absolute time than only simulating the functional execution. Even if simulator only simulates function of instruction execution, it will certainly take more absolute time than real processor. This difference can be detected through our proving algorithm.
- Capability. Absolute time difference is an important and unavoidable difference. We can see this from some contrast data. For the best commercial simulator, such as Virtutech Simics, when measured on an Intel PIII 933MHz host with 512 Mbytes of RAM and Linux operate system, simulates P4 CPU, the speed is about 2.1MIPS (it will be more slower in cycle-accurate mode). While a real system with Intel P4 1.7GHz and 256 Mbytes of RAM can reach 3173MIPS of ALU and 960/2087 MFLOPS of FPU/SSE2. This difference is very marked and couldn't be remedied by any simulator. As simulator in remote host can never accomplish execution of instructions as quickly as real processor, result returning from remote processor will have a notable longer latency than from real processor. Unreasonable latency means it is not real processor. Because this difference is unavoidable, method basing absolute time has very high resistance to tampering by simulator.
- Practicability. Absolute time is easy to use. We only need to gather enough sample data in advance, for example, collect the absolute time to complete some instructions. Another important reason is that there is no limitation exists on the use of absolute time, while others will require the proving code to run on high privilege level (e.g., getting TSC is only possible for software operating in real mode or protected

mode with ring 0 privilege), which is rarely fulfilled for a distributed program. Not like those two methods described above, as well as other possible methods below, method basing absolute time can always take effect. So, absolute time is the most important characteristic to detect whether remote host runs on simulator.

Behavior of the memory subsystem and processor performance monitoring values can also be helpful to identify real processor. But they are not suitable for our proving program, because they are difficulties to analyze and our proving program cannot always get the appropriate privilege to collect them. Additionally, some data of them are under the control of simulator, which can be tampered.

Basing these discussions, we can see that processor identifications and features, relative time, absolute time should be appropriate characteristics to be utilized for our Real Processor Proving algorithm. Among them, absolute time is the best way.

4 Realization of Real Processor Proving

In this section, we describe realization of our Real Processor Proving algorithm, and give some experiment results.

4.1 Constructing Proving Objects

Proving object is special code segment, which can get the needed parameters and make a judgment. We have designed three kinds of proving objects.

- Proving Object 1- Rationality of Features Appraiser. This is to utilize processor identifications and features. Relative code segment are executed on remote host (here, we don't take account of those limitations mentioned above) to get the features of remote processor, such as its family, type, model, clock frequency, etc. Then, we evaluate the rationality of them. This is a straightforward proving means that will take effects in simple case. Simulator can easily cheat it (the reason has been explained in section 3).
- Proving Object 2- Relative Time Comparator. This is to utilize relative time. Such code segment should include simple instruction (such as integer instruction) as well as complex instructions (such as FPU and SSE2 instruction). Consumed number of clocks to accomplish this code segment is returned. Then it makes a judgment by comparing it with reference value. Also, adversary can breach this proving object, but he has to pay out more effort, such as knowing what the right values should be before doing cheating.
- Proving Object 3- Absolute Time Comparator. This is to utilize absolute time. Such code segment is executed on remote host to get elapsed time that is measured by a trusted time reference (here, we use local host's system timer). Then, we evaluate whether the execution latency is reasonable. Not like proving object 1 and 2, difference about absolute time can never be exactly imitated. Absolute time can also give evidence when proving object 1 and 2 fail to work. Although, the absolute execution time returned from remote host may be confused by the network latency,

we can use some way to estimate the network latency to eliminate this influence, such as the typical operation of PING.

Except rationality of features appraiser, design of another two kinds of proving objects has five requirements:

- They should execute longer enough to make the consumed time measurable; for example, OS seldom give ns (nanosecond) as event occurring interval.
- Size of them should be short enough to avoid being swapped out of cache to introduce unpredictable miscount. Cache miss will bring a long delay and we will confuse this delay with execution time of processor.
- Proving object should not contain system memory or I/O accessing instructions, with same reason above.
- Proving object should be dynamical created. If they are always the same, adversary may keep copies of them and have enough time to get the right results (e.g., running them on another host with real processor to get needed right parameters). Next time, he can cheat us with these pre-calculated results.
- Execution of proving object should interlaces and repeats many times with variable repeat cycle to smooth testing error that can be introduced by the computing circumstance.

4.2 Building Reference Repository

As proving objects must have some certain reference values to make judgment, we should collect enough sample data to build a reference repository in advance. The sample data should include: identifications and features of processors (e.g., processor family, type, model, clock frequency, etc.), number of the clock to accomplish some specific instructions for specific processors, absolute time to accomplish some specific instructions for specific processors. These sample data should cover a wide range of possible situations. When comparing the results returned from remote host, we get the values that they ought to be from this reference repository.

4.3 Implementing Proving

After construction of proving objects and preparation of reference repository, we embed these proving objects into the program that will be distributed to remote host. Returned results are collected and compared with the results that we get from reference repository. A certain degree of mismatching means that remote processor is not real processor.

This process of implementing Real Processor Proving is: Three kind of proving objects are contained in the code of the distributed program. They will randomly start to execute on remote host with irregular repeat cycle, so execution of them is interlaced with one another. After enough needed data returned, local host can compare them with the reference values to make a judgment that whether remote host's processor is a real processor?

4.4 Testing Results

In order to verify the availability and feasibility of our Real Processor Proving algorithm, we build a simple experiment platform. Machine-A is a standard personal computer system, with Pentium4 1.4GHz and 256MB DDR SDRAM. Virtutech Simics is installed on machine-A to simulate a PIII system. Machine-B is equipped with real PIII 667MHz and 128MB SDRAM. These two machine lie in one local network. Machine-B represents local host, while machine-A is remote host.

Experiment result is shown in fig.1.

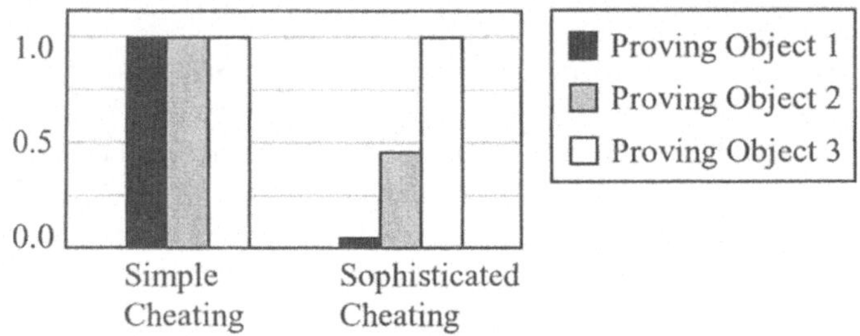

Fig. 1. Normalized recognition of Real Processor Proving. It means the probability to find simulator. Simple cheating means that adversary pay no attention to avoid being found, while sophisticated cheating means that he try to circumvent these testing mechanisms. The result of proving object 2 is typically influenced by the ability of adversary; here, we test some common cases. Additionally, we give required privilege to proving object 1 and 2 to let them take effect.

From fig.1 we can see that all of these three kinds proving objects can be applied to proving the facticity of remote processor. Among them, proving object 3 (absolute time comparator) is the most available and feasible method. It is a robust method when confronted with sophisticated adversary, because adversary has no means to produce reasonable results to cheat it. Proving object 1 (rationality of features appraiser) can become invalid when adversary carefully tampering those returning results. Proving object 2 (relative time comparator) can also become invalid, although it requires more superior ability of adversary.

Besides its robustness, absolute time comparator can hide itself deeply in the code body of distributed program. For other two proving objects, they all contain specific instructions to return processor signature or TSC, or dealing with system's timer. So, adversary can easily be aware of these two proving objects. Absolute time comparator doesn't contain noticeable instructions; adversary cannot clearly know its special purpose.

5 Conclusions

This paper investigates a potential threat to the distributed computing security. As adversary on remote host can use simulator to breach the security of distributed programs, we must find some approaches to protect against this powerful tampering means. To solve this security problem, we try to design a mechanism to prove that it is a real processor in remote host to execute distributed program. Because no special instructions that cannot be simulated by some advanced simulator, we must use special behavior characteristics of processor to find the difference between real processor and simulator. Some characteristics, especially absolute time characteristic, can reveal the differences. We utilize these to design our Real Processor Proving algorithm. This paper explains why these characteristics are special and how to use them to recognize difference to tell the existence of real processor. As we have discussed and the experiment results have shown, our Real Processor Proving is an available approach to avoid such powerful tampering by remote malicious host with sophisticated simulator.

References

1. W. Jansen: Countermeasures for Mobile Agent Security. Computer Communications, Special Issue on Advances in Research and Application of Network Security (2000)
2. Virtutech, Inc.: Introduction to Simics Full-System Simulator without Equal (2002) http://www.virtutech.com/simics/VirtutechSimicsIntroduction.pdf
3. Peter S. Magnusson, et al.: Simics: A Full System Simulation Platform. IEEE Computer (2002) 50-58
4. Intel, Inc.: Intel Processor Identification and the CPUID Instruction (2003) http://developer.intel.ru/download/design/Xeon/applnots/24161823.pdf
5. Intel,Inc.: IA-32 Intel Architecture Software Developer's Manual Volume 1: Basic Architecture (1999) http://developer.intel.com/design/pentium4/manuals/24547012.pdf
6. Intel, Inc.: Intel Architecture Software Developer's Manual Volume 2: Instruction Set Reference (1999) http://developer.intel.com/design/pentium4/manuals/24547112.pdf
7. Intel, Inc.: Intel Architecture Software Developer's Manual Volume 3: System Programming (1999) http://developer.intel.com/design/pentium4/manuals/24547212.pdf
8. Intel, Inc.: P6 Family of Processors Hardware Developer's Manual (1998) http://www.intel.com/design/pentiumII/manuals/24400101.pdf

Secure Grid-Based Mobile Agent Platform by Instance-Oriented Delegation[1]

Tianchi Ma and Shanping Li

College of Computer Science, Zhejiang University, Hangzhou, P.R. China
mtc@cad.zju.edu.cn, shan@cs.zju.edu.cn

Abstract. An instance-oriented security mechanism is proposed to deal with security threats in building a general-purpose mobile agent middleware in Grid environment. The proposed solution imports security instance, which is an encapsulation of one set of authorizations and their validity specifications with respect to the agent's specific code segments, or even the states and requests. Study shows this mechanism can inject large flexibility and scalability into the security framework, and can avoid the inefficiency and potential damages obscuring in a conventional linear delegation model.

1 Introduction

Grid has provided a loose coupling scenario for large numbers of Virtual Organizations (VO) over the network. Each VO will have its own statues flow and working mechanism. Besides of that, the network whether and trust relationships also keep in frequently changing. Therefore, a centralized or hierarchical architecture will be non-adaptive in many large-scale applications. Instead, mobile agents (MA) are imported to enable a further decomposition and distribution of the task, and provide context-aware executions [1][2].

Since security is an essential issue in MA system, many research works have been done on tackling security threats from agents to hosts, or from hosts to agents [2]. However, most of them were designed for special-purpose MA systems, and can hardly be replanted into the general-purpose platform due to their non-adaptation on the Grid's physiology. We then consider about the trust mechanism, which is about authorizations binding on identities. Trust mechanism is widely used in internet security systems. Also there are well-rounded trust mechanisms adopted in current Grid Security Infrastructure ([3], GSI). However, the trust mechanism will fall into awkwardness when it is dealing with MA systems, because too many hosts and parties are involved in a single trip of the agent. Usually, the main problem that a trust mechanism will encounter is the contradiction between its scalability and stability. That is, the more hosts a trust mechanism is overspreading, the greater probability for security holes' occurrence and the larger damage brought by possible attacks. User

[1] This paper is sponsored by Zhejiang Provincial Natural Science Foundation of China (No. 602032)

M. Li et al. (Eds.): GCC 2003, LNCS 3032, pp. 916–923, 2004.

may want to setup a delegation chain to protect all his agent's behaviors are under trust. However, the Grid's scenario determines that there exists the probability of a host losing its trust-worthness suddenly by some irregular reasons (for example, be hacked). There will be dangerous of delegation abusing in this occasion, except the agent's possible privileges has been strictly specified in detail, at its launch time. However, not all the possible resource access can be predicted in the agent's launch time. A delegation with overfull authorization will greatly burden the agent.

To improve that, an instance-oriented security framework is then proposed in this paper. Different from the original host-oriented policy, we define *security instances*. A security instance is an encapsulation of one set of authorizations and their respective validity specifications. User and applications can define several kinds of security instances and their possible operations, according to the application's own logics. The instances are signed by its creator and recorded into the mobile agent's delegation document. A strict-protected *trace list* is adopted for validity computing and intrusion detection. These constitute the delegation document together.

There is always a critical section in each delegation document, which is protected under someone's signature and will act as a read-only proof. In conventional host-oriented delegation, the target host's public key is claimed in the critical section. Different from that, the instance-oriented delegation moves the detail specifications of the agent's privileges into the critical section. So the delegation document can be transferred everywhere with no security hole left, because any host has no privilege to sign a further delegation. Thus the delegation abusing can be successfully avoided. One may argue that the instance-oriented mechanism is no deferent from the signed code mechanism [4]. In fact, the instance can be a code, and can also be other states and requests. They are more complex than the code, because their states and validity will keep changing during the trip. The generalized instance model can provide a broader sense of compatibility, which can be concluded from following sections.

The paper is organized as follows. In section 2, we give an overview to our Everest MA platform. The delegation profile is described in section 3. Section 4 gives the detail of how to charge a security framework by adopting the proposed delegation model. Related works are compared in section 5. At last, in section 6, we give a brief conclusion.

2 The Everest Architecture

The core modules implemented in Everest are shown in Figure 1. We follow the "gatekeeper-backend servers" architecture. The system is depended on Globus Toolkit 2.2. We define each gatekeeper as a simulated Grid site (host), and select some of them to act as the exchange servers.

In the Everest system, the code maintenance and migration are all processed on the gatekeeper of each host, while the job manager and the backend server need only to deal with the mobile agent like normal jobs. While the agent is under migration, the preliminary procedures are handled by the migration daemon on the gatekeeper. An execution daemon on each backend server will then start to save the code's current execution states and transfer it to the target backend server directly without passing the two gatekeepers.

The migration daemon is in charge of the code migration (i.e., handover operation). Also it will send delegation-updating requests to the exchange server, when a delegation document is found falling into invalidation.

The exchange server is composed of a code daemon and several code maintainers. The code daemon is in charge of obtaining request from hosts. Then it forwards those requests to the corresponding code maintainer. Each agent has a code maintainer in the exchange server, to maintain and monitor its current states. When a code asks for a delegation document renew, it is the maintainer who will solve these requests. For other requests like resource reservation, the maintainer will ask the code daemon to contact the corresponding resource provider, and transfer the requests to it. Besides, the code maintainer should have enough knowledge to carry on a client side validation check on the request delegation documents.

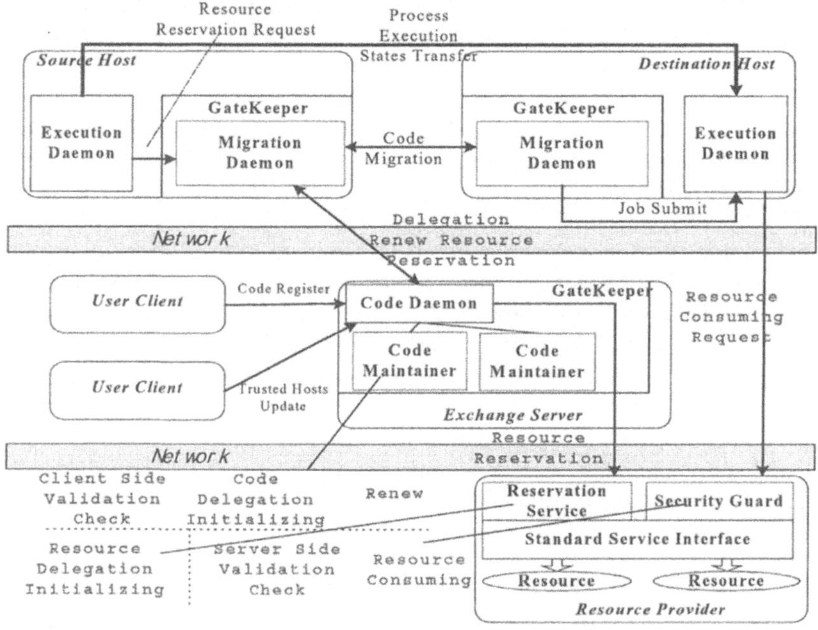

Fig. 1. The core modules of the Everest mobile agent platform

There are two modules covering on the resource provider's standard service interface. The *reservation service* module has the privilege of signing a resource instance delegation document. Actually, the real reservation operation will be done under the standard service interface, while the reservation service cares only those businesses concerning about the delegation document. Another module is the *security guard*, which is used to deal with the resource requests. The security guard will first make a server side validation check on the coming delegation document, and then establish a connection between the remote agents and the standard service interface.

3 Delegation Profile

3.1 The Structure of the Delegation Document

An instance-oriented delegation can have one or multiple instances. Each instance-oriented delegation document is composed of two parts (as it is shown in Figure 2).

The first part is *instance details*. For each instance, there must be an instance detail recorded. An instance detail records the instance's properties, operating rules, and specifications about its validity. The instance detail can only be filled and modified on the initialization of the instance's delegation or in `renew` operations. Otherwise, it is read-only. Both the consumer and the holder of the delegation document should declare their approval of the contents that is recorded in the instance detail. At the bottom of the instance detail, the signature of the delegation's original creator or last modifier (maybe an exchange server) on the instance detail should be attached, in order to prove the detail's validity. And the original creator's certificate list could also be attached on, to prove the validity of its signature (this is not necessary, because the certificate list can be retrieved from other place).

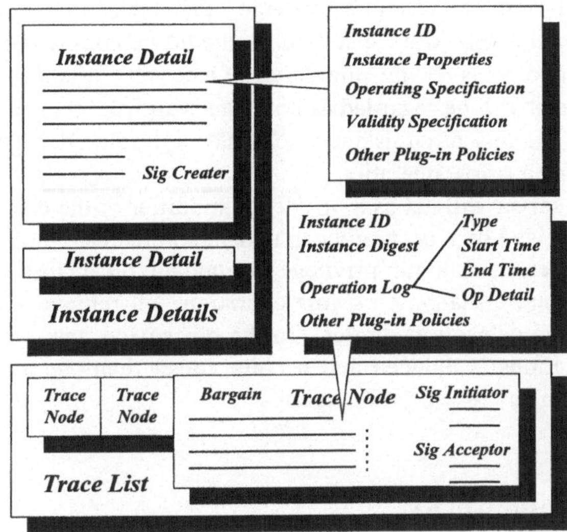

Fig. 2. Instance-oriented delegation profile

The second part is a *trace list*, which is an array including records of all historical operations on the corresponding instances. Each item of the array is called a *trace node*, in which a single operation is recorded. An instance-oriented delegation document can only have one trace list, in which trace nodes for all its instances are linked together. A single trace node is divided into two sections: bargain *content* and a *signature pair*. In the bargain content, first the instance detail's content's digest or a *global instance ID* will be recorded to prove that the bargain is relative to exactly the corresponding instance. Here multiple instances' ID or digest can be put together for a batch operation. After the digest or global instance ID, there should be an operation log, in which the detail information of the corresponding operation should be recorded. The operation log can include the start and end time of the operation, its returning result, and exceptions. The signature pair is the second section of the trace node. It is comprised of both the Initiator and the Acceptor's signatures on the bargain, to show their approval on the bargain's contents. Both the Initiator and the Acceptor will hold a copy of the signed trace node. It can be shown as evidence when the opposing party tries to deny one or more historical operations in the future. The trace list maintains a rigorous order of the trace nodes, by inducting a self-increasing number.

3.2 General Operations

All instances have a common operation -- `handover`. In general, this operation can be performed by all instances, by transferring the instance delegation from one host to another. In a `handover` operation, an instance's states will not be changed. Only its current location is changed. Once a delegation migration is carried between hosts, there must be one or more `handover` operations performed. To prevent from the unlimited diffusion of a potential damage, the max times of performing the `handover` operation should be specified. It should be considered as an issue when an instance's validity is being measured. Once an instance reaches the max `handover` times, it will be regarded as no longer valid and thus no operations can be performed on it. In this circumstance, to make a further delegation, the instance should request for a `renew` operation.

The exchange server will act as a privileged modifier of the delegation documents. Always it is authorized by a user, and can update and recreate the instances issued by that user. However, it has no privilege to update other instances in the same delegation document. Usually, a `renew` operation will remove some obsolete trace nodes and make the delegation shorter. On the other hand, the recorded times of the `handover` operations is reduced and become lower than the specified max times. Thus the delegation can resume valid again.

4 Security Frameworks

For a MA system, two types of instances are inducted in this paper: *code* and *resource request*. There will be a detailed discussion towards each in followed two subsections, with a brief introduction of how to build a systemic security framework on the top of these instances.

4.1 Code Instance

An `execute` operation refers to a period of execution of the corresponding code instance. It must be noticed, even if the code stops at certain host on its trip, it may not perform an execution on the host. Thus the `execute` operation is defined as a process, by which the code's execution states are changed.

For an `execute` operation, its trace node must record the execution's start time and end time on the operation log. Besides that, the digests of the code's execution states on the start and end time should be also recorded. When an Acceptor is trying to check the code's validity, it should retrieve all the trace nodes of `handover` and `execute` operations that were performed on the current code from the current delegation document. It then queues them by the order acquitted from the delegation document's trace list. The continuity on each pair of the two adjoining trace nodes in the queue will be checked.

The code's `renew` can be implemented by a verification on the delegation document and then a regeneration of the document, the sequence of verifications and delegation document regenerations on the exchange server. When a host finds the current code to be invalid, it will act as a *requestor* of the code's `renew`, and send the current delegation document of the code to the exchange server. The exchange server should first make verification on the trace list's validity. If all are correct, the exchange server will clear some of the historical trace nodes and make the delegation document to be valid again. Here a chance of a full-scale verification on the code's execution states is provided.

4.2 Resource Instance

Mobile agents may need to access remote resources frequently during its trip over multiple Grid sites managed by different VOs. Many existing Grid infrastructures have provided efficient and stable resources accessing mechanisms. However, the remote resource provider usually cares more about the security threats that may occur during the resource accessing, that is, whether the resource request is illegal or even vicious, that may cause their local system being crashed.

In the proposed trust framework, the privilege of acquiring a resource accessing is granted only to exchange servers that can be firm-trusted by the users. They will act as a *resource reservation proxy* for the code instances they've issued before. On performing the resource reservation, the exchange server will check the resource request sent from the host who is currently holding the code instance. If the resource request is regarded as a legal one, and strictly needed in the code's task, the exchange server will then admit the deputation and forward the resource request to the resource provider. In a Grid system, it is always hard to deliver security policies to all hosts simultaneously. That is because the hosts are belonged to multiple VOs, thus one can hardly ensure all their stability and trust worthiness. Choosing some security proxies and delivering policies only among them will be a feasible solution, for it can avoid a lot of work on maintenance and consistency.

Basically, a resource instance can be described using a *resource-action* structure. The *Resource* is an abstract type of instance, while an *Action* refers to a single resource call. Besides the handle that is used to access the resource directly (such as URL/URI/RSL/GSR), an action also includes properties such as resource name, action name, parameters (always be a digest), allowable number for access, and which code instance it currently belongs to. Using the two-level structure can provide a more flexible space for user to write their security policies in multiple granularities

The resource reservation can be implemented according to the draft proposed by GGF [5], and the API of creating and modifying a reservation should be updated, to add on some security portions proposed in this paper.

5 Related Works

In the past, several researches have been carried towards the security problem of MA system [6, 7, 8, 9, 10, 11, 12].

In [6], a voting policy is adopted to authenticate the agents. However, this method will cause each step of the agent being executed for multiple times, thus a large overhead will be arisen on the verification.

Bytecode checking [7] is to directly trace the agent's code and execution states (usually Java bytecode), to see if the agent's current state is legal. Proof-Carrying Code (PPC) technologies [8] make the agent to carry some proofs of the validity on its execution states. However, in most times, the calculating will be very time-consuming and the agent's launcher must have certain technologies to write down his security policy in specified formats. Besides, not all attacks can be checked by this way. Some attackers may not crack the current host, instead, it will use some permitted interfaces to crack other hosts (for example, sending vicious email).

Special hardware [9] is inducted in many works to enhance the performance of calculating and checking the agent's validity. However, in most circumstance, applications and users would rather suffer from a time-consuming checking than to buy expensive hardware.

In [10], agents are written and will be run in an entirely cryptography way. However, using this approach, the hosts can hardly know how the code is organized and how it is put into running, thus they will not have ability to modify the code in malice. This seems to be a good solution to prevent any vicious cracks. However, the applications' complexity makes this mechanism less compatible, and could only be used in some simple applications.

The work in [12] introduces a trust infrastructure on the Restina model of general-purpose MAS it designed to provide solid protection on the agents, platforms and message channels. However, all the work there is toward a weak-migration agent. That is, the agent will not change its execution states during the trip.

We've inspired from [11] for the exchange server model. However, in [11], the agent is encrypted and can only be decrypted and executed on the trusted hosts. This greatly restricts the agent's behavior

6 Conclusions

In this paper, a new instance-oriented security framework is proposed to provide the Grid-based MA system a more flexible and stable solution, on its security problems. There are several advantages of the instance-oriented delegation model.

As discussed, this allows applications to configure their own security policy by instantiating the proposed delegation model and embedding their preferred security policies into it, which makes it compatible for heterogeneous platforms, thus to be more appropriate for Grid environment.

The instance-oriented delegation document solves some problems in the original host-oriented delegation document successfully. It prevents the hosts from abusing the delegation document to damage the resource provider, and prevents the system from the unlimited diffusion of damages, which is caused by some potential crisis that will never be check out in conventional trust systems. This makes the delegation model appropriate to the MA systems. And then, a general solution is given on using the instance-oriented delegation document to build security framework in MA systems.

References

1. J. Cao, S. A. Jarvis, S. Saini, D. J. Kerbyson and G. R. Nudd. "ARMS: an Agent-based Resource Management System for Grid Computing", Scientific Programming, Special Issue on Grid Computing, 10(2), 135-148, 2002.
2. H. N. Lin Choi Keung, J. Cao, D. P. Spooner, S. A. Jarvis and G. R. "Grid Information Services Using Software Agents", *Nudd. Proc. 18th Annual UK Performance Engineering Workshop*, Glasgow, UK, 187-198, 2002.
3. I. Foster, C. Kesselman, G. Tsudik, and S. Tuecke. "A Security Architecture for Computational Grids", Proc. 5th ACM Conference on Computer and Communications Security Conference, pp. 83-92, 1998.
4. N. Karnik, "Security in Mobile Agent Systems", Ph.D. Dissertation, Department of Computer Science, University of Minnesota, October 1998
5. V. Sander and A. Roy. "Advanced Reservation API, GFD-E.5", GGF Scheduling Working Group, Scheduling Working Document 9.4
6. F. B. Schneider. "Towards Fault-Tolerant and Secure Agentry", Proceedings 11th International Workshop on Distributed Algorithms, Saarbucken, Germany, September 1997.
7. A. Chander, J. C. Mitchell and I. Shin. "Mobile code security by Java bytecode instrumentation", DARPA Information Survivability Conference & Exposition (DISCEX II), June, 2001.
8. G. Necula and P. Lee. "Proof-Carrying Code", Proceedings of the 24th ACM SIGPLAN-SIGACT Symposium on Principles of Programming Languages (POPL '97)
9. U. G. Wilhelm, S. Staamann, and L. Buttyàn. "Introducing trusted third parties to the mobile agent paradigm", Secure Internet Programming: Security Issues for Mobile and Distributed Objects, J. Vitek and C. Jensen (Eds.), pp. 471-491. Springer-Verlag, 1999.
10. T. Sander and C. F. Tschudin. "Protecting Mobile Agents Against Malicious Hosts", G. Vigna (Ed.): Mobile Agents and Security, pp. 44-60. Springer-Verlag, 1998
11. N. Islam, et al.. "A Flexible Security System for Using Internet Content", IEEE Software, September 1997, pp. 52-59.
12. H. C. Wong and K. Sycara. "Adding Security and Trust to Multi-Agent Systems", Proceedings of Autonomous Agents '99 (Workshop on Deception, Fraud and Trust in Agent Societies). May 1999, Seattle, Washington, pp. 149-161.

Authenticated Key Exchange Protocol Secure against Offline Dictionary Attack and Server Compromise

Seung Bae Park[1], Moon Seol Kang[2], and Sang Jun Lee[3]

[1] Department of Computer Science, Chodang University, 419 SungnamLi, MuanEup, MuanGun, JeonlanamDo, Korea
sbpark@chodang.ac.kr

[2] Department of Computer Science & Engineering, Gwangju University, 592-1 JinwolDong, NamGu, Gwangju, Korea
mskang@hosim.gwangju.ac.kr

[3] Department of Computer Information Communication, Seonam University, 720 GwangchiDong, Namwon, JeonlabukDo, Korea
sjlee@seonam.ac.kr

Abstract. This paper introduces a new scheme, called Augmented Password AKE (APAKE), for authenticated key exchange protocols. In APAKE, a password is represented by a pair of values that is randomly selected in a huge space.

We present an APAKE protocol. The protocol is secure against the attacks including off-line dictionary attack and server compromise allowing for subsequent off-line dictionary attack. The protocol has a pass number of two, and it requires minor computational amounts. We also present a EKE protocol designed by simple modification of the APAKE protocol while preserving the security of the APAKE protocol.

1 Introduction

Two entities, who only share a password and are communicating over an insecure network, want to authenticate each other and agree on a large session key to be used for protecting their subsequent communication. This is called the password Authenticated Key Exchange (AKE) problem.

The attacks which must be guarded in the AKE protocols are for obtaining secret information such as passwords and session keys at the outside of the system and line eavesdropping within the system. The following is well-known attacks guarded in the AKE protocol:

(1) Replay: The attacker records messages which were sent in past communications and re-sends them at a later time;

(2) Pre-play: The attacker records messages sent in past communications and determines a message from the recorded messages for current communication;

(3) Eavesdropping: The attacker listens to messages on the line and tries to learn some useful information from the ongoing communication;

(4) Man-in-the-middle: The attacker intercepts the messages sent between the parties and replaces them with its own messages;

M. Li et al. (Eds.): GCC 2003, LNCS 3032, pp. 924–931, 2004.

(5) Password guessing attacks: The attacker is assumed to have access to a relatively small dictionary containing common choices of passwords. There are primarily two ways in which the attacker can use this dictionary, via on-line dictionary attacks or off-line dictionary attacks. In the off-line dictionary attack, the attacker records past communication, and then examines the dictionary in search of a password that is consistent with the recorded communication. If such a password is found, the attacker concludes that this password is applicable in an attack [1, 8, 9]. In the on-line dictionary attack, the attacker repeatedly chooses a password from the dictionary and tries to use it in order to impersonate as the user. If the impersonation fails, the attacker eliminates this password from the dictionary and tries again with a different password. We do not consider this attack, because there are practical ways of preventing the attack [4, 10];
(6) Server compromise: The attacker acquires sensitive data which is supposed to be kept secret at the server to impersonate as a user [4, 10].

Traditional password protocols are susceptible to off-line dictionary attacks: Many users choose passwords of relatively low entropy, so adversaries are able to compile a dictionary of provable passwords.

The first protocol that has been resistant to off-line dictionary attack is presented in [13]. The protocol assumed that the client had the server's public key. Other protocols for this scenario were developed in [3, 8, 9]. The EKE protocol [2] is the first protocol that does not require the user to know the server's public key. Following EKE, other protocols without requirements for user knowledge of the server's public key were proposed in [1, 4, 10, 11]. Some of the protocols following EKE have been broken [16], while some other protocols including [1, 4] have proven to be secure.

Most protocols do not consider server compromise, and almost protocols do not consider server compromise allowing for subsequent off-line dictionary attack. Furthermore, no schemes for AKE or EKE protocols have been suggested.

In this paper, we define a new scheme for the AKE protocols called *Augmented Password AKE* (APAKE). In APAKE, a password is represented by a value that is selected in random in a space such that the size of the space is greater than the size of the space for determining a private key of the public key cryptosystem. For estimating the security of a protocol based on APAKE, we also define a measure, called *powerfully secure*, considering both the attacks for obtaining a password from the messages in past communications and the security of the public key cryptosystem concurrently.

We present an APAKE protocol using RSA and a symmetric key cipher. In the protocol, a client uses the server's public key to encrypt the value representing a password, and the server uses the symmetric key cipher to encrypt the integers used to generate a session key. The protocol is secure against off-line dictionary attacks and server compromise allowing for subsequent the off-line dictionary attack, and powerfully secure against attacks such as pre-play and Man-in-the-Middle attacks. The protocol has a pass number of two, and it requires minor computational amounts. We present a EKE protocol designed by modification of the APAKE protocol while preserving the security of the APAKE protocol.

We define APAKE in Section 2 and present the APAKE protocol using RSA and symmetric key cipher in Section 3. Our protocol is analyzed in Section 4.

2 Augmented Password AKE Scheme for AKE Protocols

The Augmented Password AKE (APAKE) is defined in Definition 1.

Definition 1 An AKE protocol is APAKE protocol if it consists of the following steps:

Participant *A*
Input: password *P* and *B*'s public key.
(1) Step determining a value representing *P*: chooses an integer *x* in random and then determines *y* so that $x\square y=P$ or $x\square_1 y\square_2 z=P$ where $\square$, $\square_1$ and $\square_2$ denote the operations, and *z* is a shared value between the participants;
(2) Step generating a message sent to *B*: encrypts *x* and *y* by using *B*'s public key and then sends the ciphertexts;
(3) Step verifying *B*: check whether *B* decrypts the ciphertexts, sent at step (2), correctly;
(4) Step generating a session key: cryptographic function or algorithm processes the value(s) recovered from the received message from *B* to produce a session key.
Participant *B*
Input: private key and a processed result of a value representing *P* by cryptographic function or algorithm.
(1) Step for verifying *A*: get *x* and *y* from a message received from *A* by using a private key, and then check whether *A* inputs *P* such that $x\square y=P$ or $x\square_1 y\square_2 z=P$;
(2) Step for generating message sent to *A*: generates the ciphertext(s) corresponding to the random integer(s) by using cryptographic algorithm with key (*x*, *y*);
(3) Step for generating a session key: uses cryptographic function or algorithm to processes the random integer(s) of Step (2).

Fig. 1. APAKE: A scheme for authenticated key exchange

An APAKE protocol can use the public key cryptosystems presented in [6, 12, 17]. In the input of *B*, a cryptographic function can be a trapdoor one way function [5, 15] or one way hash function such as SHA-1 [7], and the cryptographic algorithm can be a symmetric key cipher such as Triple-DES [14]. In steps for generating a session key, the cryptographic function can be one way hash function, and the cryptographic algorithm includes a symmetric key cipher. In Step (4) of Participant *A* and Step (3) of Participant *B*, a secret parameter includes a random integer such as a challenge.

In an APAKE protocol, the securities against attacks for obtaining a password by using messages from past communications and by the cryptanalysis for the public key cryptosystems have to be considered.

Definition 2 An APAKE protocol is *powerfully secure* against an attack if the security for the attack depends on the security of the public key cryptosystem.

3 APAKE Protocol Using RSA and Symmetric Key Cipher

Our protocol is depicted in Fig. 2 and the notations used in the protocol are shown in the follows:

A, B: System participants.
P: A shared password between A and B.
p, q: Primes suitable for RSA.
N, $\Phi(N)$: $N=pq$ and $\Phi(N)=(p-1)(q-1)$.
e, d: Integers such that e is relatively prime to $\Phi(N)$ and $ed\equiv 1 \bmod \Phi(N)$.
x_1, x_2, y_1, y_2: Elements of $\{1, 2, \ldots, N-1\}$.
t: Timestamp.
H: One way hash function.
SK: Session key shared between the participants after completion of the protocols.
$\|$: Concatenation of two operands.
c_1, c_2: Random integers.
$x_i(X)$: X that is encrypted by a symmetric key cipher with a key x_i for 1 i 2.

A		B
e, N, P		$d, (p, q), N, y_1^2 \bmod N, y_2^2 \bmod N$
Pick x_1 in random Get x_2 so that x_1-x_2=P and t Compute $(x_1+t)^e \bmod N$, $x_2^e \bmod N$		
	$A, t, (x_1+t)^e \bmod N, x_2^e \bmod N$ →	
		Get $x_1=(x_1+t)^{ed}-t \bmod N$, $x_2=x_2^{ed} \bmod N$ Check $(x_1-x_2)^2 \bmod N=(y_1-y_2)^2 \bmod N$ Get c_1 and c_2 Compute $x_1(c_1\|H(c_1))$, $x_2(c_2\|H(c_2))$
	← $B, x_1(c_1\|H(c_1)), x_2(c_2\|H(c_2))$	
Decrypt $x_1(c_1\|H(c_1))$, $x_2(c_2\|H(c_2))$ Check hash values $SK=H(c_1\| c_2)$		$SK=H(c_1\| c_2)$

Fig. 2. APAKE protocol using RSA and a symmetric key cipher

In RSA, it is well known that $m^{ed} \bmod N\equiv m$ for an integer m [17]. In our protocol, B authenticates A correctly: B can obtain x_1 and x_2 from $(x_1+t)^e \bmod N$ and $x_2^e \bmod N$ by using a private key d. B knows that $(x_1-x_2)^2 \bmod N=(y_1-y_2)^2 \bmod N$ because $x_1-x_2=y_1-y_2$. Therefore, B accepts A only when $((y_1^2 \bmod N)(y_2^2 \bmod N)) \bmod N=4^{-1}C^2 \bmod N$ where $C=x_1^2+x_2^2-2x_1x_2-y_1^2 \bmod N-y_2^2 \bmod N$. Also, A authenticates B correctly: A can recover $c_1\|H(c_1)$ and $c_2\|H(c_2)$ from $x_1(c_1\|H(c_1))$ and $x_2(c_2\|H(c_2))$ by using x_1 and x_2. Therefore, A can verify B by checking whether B produces the correct hash values.

4 Analysis of APAKE Protocol

We analysis the security of APAKE protocol in Subsection 4.1 and present performance of the protocol in Subsection 4.2 and a EKE protocol in Subsection 4.3.

4.1 Security

In the protocol presented in Fig. 2, a timestamp makes this message of current communication different from the messages of past communications. Therefore, the protocol is secure against replay attack.

Most AKE protocols do not consider server compromise, and furthermore, allmost of the AKE protocols do not consider server compromise allowing subsequent off-line dictionary attack. Why it is so difficult to design AKE protocol such that the protocol is secure against off-line dictionary attack and server compromise with/without having performed off-line dictionary attacks? This is likely due to the fact that all of the presented protocols have unique candidates for representing a password.

Property 1. In the protocol presented in Fig. 2, there are the N-1 candidates for (x_1, x_2).

Theorem 2. The protocol presented in Fig. 2 is powerfully secure against the pre-play and man-in-the-middle.

Proof: In the APAKE protocol, the secret parameter in communications is (x_1, x_2). From property 1, there are the N-1 candidates for (x_1, x_2), and x_1 is selected in random in $\{1, 2, \ldots, N\text{-}1\}$. Furthermore, the number of the elements in $\{1, 2, \ldots, N\text{-}1\}$ is greater than the size of a space for determining two primes p and q for the given N. Therefore, the security of the APAKE protocol depends on the security of RSA.

The APAKE protocol is secure against off-line dictionary attacks, because the size of a space to determine whether an attacker of this attack has guessed the password correctly is greater than the size of a space for determining two primes p and q for the given N.

A function f from a set X to a set Y is called a one way hash function if $f(x)$ is easy to compute for all $x \in X$. Yet, for most elements $y \in \text{Image}(f)$ it is computationally infeasible to find any $x \in X$ such that $f(x)=y$ [14]. A trapdoor one way function is a one way function $f{:}X \rightarrow Y$ with an additional property that given some extra information it becomes feasible to find for any given $y \in \text{Image}(f)$, an $x \in X$ such that $f(x)=y$ [14]. In RSA, for the given composite integer n of unknown two primes p and q, a problem finding p and q from n is well known integer factorization problem and a source of many trapdoor one way functions [14].

Theorem 3. The APAKE protocol presented in Fig. 2 is secure against server compromise allowing for subsequent off-line dictionary attacks.

Proof: The square root modulo n (SQROOT) problem is to find a square root of a modulo n for the given composite integer n and quadratic residue a modulo n. If both factor p and q are unknown, then the integer factorization problem of n is reduced to SQROOT problem in polynomial time, and SQROOT problem is also reduced to the integer factorization problem of n in polynomial time. This means that the integer factorization and SQROOT problems are computationally equivalent [14]. Therefore, it is computationally infeasible to determine a value (y_1, y_2) from the stored value at the verifier. From Theorem 2, we can see that it is computationally infeasible to determine whether the attacker has guessed (y_1, y_2) correctly even if the attacker has stolen the value stored at the server.

4.2 Performance

In the off-line state, B obtains RSA parameters once and selects y_1 in random and performs two modular square multiplications. The performance of our protocol for the on-line state is shown in Table 1.

Table 1. The performance of the APAKE protocol

Estimations for the performance	A	B
Pass	1	1
Random number generation	1	2
RSA encryption or decryption	2	2
Modular multiplication	0	1
Hash function	2	2
Symmetric key cipher encryption or decryption	2	2

4.3 Modification of APAKE Protocol to EKE Protocol

The APAKE protocol is simply modified to EKE protocol (See Fig. 3).

The protocol presented in Fig. 3 is a EKE protocol because the protocol does not require the client to know the server's public key. We do not analyze the security of the protocol presented in Fig. 3 because the approaches analyzing the security of the protocol presented in Fig. 2 can be applied to the protocol presented in Fig . 3.

5 Conclusions

We have defined a scheme for the AKE protocols called the APAKE. APAKE utilizes an important fact that there are large numbers of candidates that can be used to represent a password even if the password is human memorable. We have also defined a measure, called powerfully secure, for estimating the security against the attacks guarded in the APAKE protocols.

We have presented an APAKE protocol that uses RSA and symmetric key cipher. We have described why the protocol is secure against the replay attacks. We have proven that the protocol is powerfully secure against replay and Man-in-the-Middle. We have describe why the protocol is secure against off-line dictionary attacks. We have also proven that the protocol is secure against server compromise attack with having performed off-line dictionary attacks.

In the aspect of the performance, our protocol requires only two pass, and furthermore, it requires minor computational amounts. We have presented an EKE protocol designed by simple modification of the APAKE protocol.

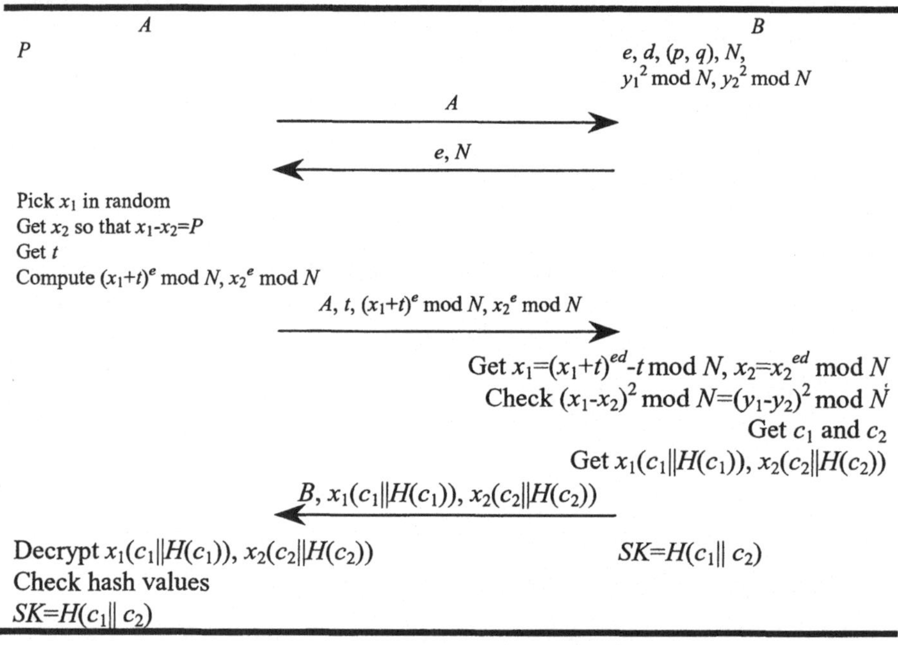

Fig. 3. EKE protocol using RSA and a symmetric key cipher

References

1. Bellare, M., Pointcheaval, D., Rogaway, P.: Authenticated key exchange secure against dictionary attacks. Advances in Cryptology Eurocrypt'00, LNCS Vol. 1807. Springer-Verlag (2000) 139-155
2. Bellovin, S. M., Merrit, M.: Encrypted key exchange: Password-based protocols secure against dictionary attack. In Proceedings of IEEE Security and Privacy (1992) 72-84
3. Boyarsky, M.: Public key cryptography and password protocols: The multi-user case. In ACM Security (CCS'99) (1999) 63-72

4. Boyko, V., MacKenzie, P., Patal, S.: Probably secure password authenticated key exchange using Diffie-Hellman. Advances in Cryptology Eurocrypt'00, LNCS Vol. 1807. Springer-Verlag (2000) 156-171
5. Diffie, W., Hellman, H. E.: New directions in cryptography. IEEE Transactions on Information Theory, 22. (1976) 644-654
6. ElGamal, T.: A public-key cryptosystem and a signature scheme based on discrete logarithms. IEEE Transactions on Information Theory, Vol. IT-31, No. 4. (1985) 469-472
7. FIPS 180-1: Secure hash standards. Federal Information Processing Standards Publication 180-1, US Department Commerce/NIST, National Technical Information Service, Springfield, Virginia (1995)
8. Gong, L., Lomas, T. M. A., Needham, R. M., Saltzer, J. H.: Protecting poorly chosen secrets from guessing attacks. IEEE Journal on Selected Areas in Communications, Vol. 11, No. 5. (1993) 648-656
9. Halevi, S., Krawczyk, H.: Public key cryptography and password protocols. In ACM Security (CCS'98) (1998) 122-131
10. Jablon, D.: Strong password-only authenticated key exchange. ACM Computer Communication Review, ACM SIGCOMM, Vol. 26, No. 5. (1996) 5-20
11. Katz, J., Ostrovsky, R., Yung, M.: Efficient password authenticated key exchange using human memorable passwords. Advances in Cryptology Eurocrypt'01, LNCS Vol. 2045. Springer-Verlag (2001) 475-494
12. Koblitz, N.: Eliptic curve cryptosystems. Mathematics of Computation, Vol. 48, No. 177. (1987) 203-209
13. Lomas, T. M. A., Gong, L., Saltzer, J. H., Needham, R. M.: Reducing risks from poorly chosen keys. ACM Operating Systems Review, Vol. 23, No. 5. (1989) 14-18
14. Menezes, A. J., van Oorschot, P. C., Vanstone, S. A.: Applied Cryptography. CRC press (1997)
15. Merkle, R. C.: Secrecy, Authentication, and Public Key Systems. UMI Research Press, Ann Arbor, Michigan (1979)
16. Patal, S.: Number theoretic attacks on secure password schemes. In proceedings of IEEE Security and Privacy (1997) 236-247
17. Rivest, R. L., Shamir, A., Adleman, L. M.: A method for obtaining digital signatures and public-key cryptosystems. Communications of the ACM, Vol. 21, No. 2 (1978) 120-126

StarOTS: An Efficient Distributed Transaction Recovery Mechanism in the CORBA Component Runtime Environment

Yi Ren, Jianbo Guan, Yan Jia, Weihong Han, and Quanyuan Wu

School of Computer Science,
National University of Defence Technology,
Changsha 410073, China
starots@sohu.com

Abstract. Two Phase Commit (2PC) protocol can be used to guarantee atomicity and durability of global transactions in distributed environment. In this paper, we adopt optimized 2PC protocol (O2PC), which reduces the number of messages between transaction participants and the coordinator. Based on the protocol, an object-oriented transaction recovery manager, StarOTS is implemented as a CORBA service running on top of a given ORB. We discuss how StarOTS is designed and implemented to ensure atomicity and durability of distributed transactions and how it is integrated with the CORBA component environment to meet the requirements of interoperability, efficiency and reliability. Further, we have constructed a novel dynamic management tool offering flexible control and management to the running transactions without modifying StarOTS. The CORBA component model prototype we implemented and StarOTS integrated together help developers quickly design and implement mission critical distributed transactional applications.

1 Introduction

In the late 1990's, it becomes one of the most remarkable progresses in the computer area that the business computing applications changed from traditional centralized to distributed environment. Consequently, distribution, scalability and heterogeneousness turn to be main features of modern business computing systems. People begin to realize that the efficiency of distributed application development turns to be one of the key factors contributing to the success of this kind of applications.

As a result, distributed component technologies and standards come into being. Such as the CORBA Component Model (CCM) [1], Distributed Component Object Model (DCOM) and Enterprise Java Bean (EJB). EJBs are used in Java environment and DCOM is used in MS-Windows environments. CCM takes interoperability into account. Components can be developed in various languages for various OSs, and used upon various CCM platforms. It takes the advantages of platform and language independence features of CORBA and provides higher portability and reusability.

Based on CCM specification, we have built a component model prototype. CCM itself is not sufficient for easy construction of distributed business logics. For

M. Li et al. (Eds.): GCC 2003, LNCS 3032, pp. 932–939, 2004.

distributed applications that becomes more and more complex in size, functionality and quality of service, how to solve the recovery problem and maintain the integrity of crucial data? To solve this problem, we implement StarOTS based on optimized two-phase commit (O2PC) protocol to meet the requirement when failures occur. It guarantees the “all-or-nothing” feature of mission critical applications. At the same time, it marries the merits of both object-oriented and distributed processing technologies. In order to monitor and control the transactions in process, we constructed a novel dynamic management tool OTSMC, which offers flexible control and management of running transactions without modifying StarOTS. StarOTS and the tool are implemented as CORBA services running on top of a given ORB.

Integrating with the application server, StarOTS provides an efficient, reliable way of developing interoperable transactional business applications in distributed heterogeneous environment. It enables the separation of evolving business logic from relatively fixed transaction management logic. This, in turn, simplifies business logic and business application programming. It also allows business logic to evolve without awareness of how to uses transactional data. We believe that the use of StarOTS together with OTSMC offers potential economics and engineering advantages.

2 The CORBA Component Model

CCM is a server side component framework that intends to ease the development of distributed applications made of heterogeneous components. In addition, CCM standard allows software reuse and provides greater flexibility for dynamic configuration of CORBA applications.

CCM Components are the basic building blocks in CCM. Component developers implement components using tools supplied by CCM providers. The resulting component can then be packaged into an assembly file and linked dynamically. Finally, a deployment mechanism supplied by a CCM provider is used to deploy the components in a *component server* by loading their assembly files. Thus, components execute in component servers and are available to client requests.

A CCM container provides the runtime environment for a component. A container's runtime environment provides services, such as transaction, notification, persistence and security, to the managed component. Each container manages components and is responsible for initializing the managed component and connecting it to other components and ORB services.

A component server is indeed an application server which can provides environment for multiple containers to manage the components. It stands between the clients and DBMS in the 3-tier architecture and upon which the business logic is executed as components managed by specific containers.

CCM extends the CORBA object model by defining features and services that enable application developers to implement, manage, configure and deploy components and integrate commonly used CORBA services. In this paper, the transaction recovery mechanism is implemented based on Object Transaction Service [2] of OMG, but further extensions are also added to improve the flexibility and the performance.

3 StarOTS

First, we will summarize key features of CORBA OTS and give a short overview of which part of the service are supported by StarOTS and the interfaces that are essential for using it. The design and implementation of the StarOTS will be discussed later.

3.1 CORBA OTS

OTS can be thought of as a framework to manage transactional contexts and to orchestrate 2PC processing between potentially remote recoverable servers. A CORBA recoverable server object must agree upon a convention of registering *Resources* with the OTS *Coordinator*. The latter drives the 2PC through the invocation of *Resource* methods. *Resources* participate in the voting phase of the commit processing and impact the outcome of global transactions.

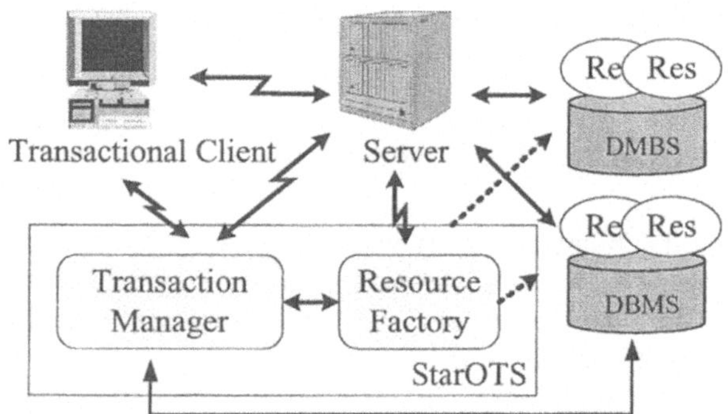

Fig. 1. Structure of StarOTS application system

3.2 StarOTS Overview

StarOTS supports efficient transaction management and control API for transactional applications. It provides a robust and full-featured platform on which to build large-scale distributed applications that require absolute transactional integrity.

Some highlights of StarOTS are:

- Supporting distributed applications and being object-oriented
- Hung on ORB as a removable module
- Supporting optimized two-phase commit protocol
- Supporting explicit and implicit transaction context propagation
- Offer dynamic management of transactions

StarOTS and its application system are illustrated in figure 1. It consists of Transaction Manager, Resource Factory and transactional application. Transaction Manager implements O2PC and guarantees atomicity of operations over resources participating in a transaction. Resource Factory comprises of *ResourceFactory*, *Resources* and DBMSs. *Resource* is in fact a logical abstract of DBMS databases. When transactional client sends a transactional request to the server, transaction context can be propagated to the server.

3.3 Implicit Transaction Context Propagation

In distributed environments, transactional client and server have to share common information, i.e., transaction context, in order to be involved in same transaction.

Explicit transaction context propagation means that the application takes the responsibility to get this context from the transaction manager server and to propagate it between transactional client and server. *Implicit* transaction context propagation means that application developers need not care about the way to get it and propagate it. The advantage of implicit mode is transparency. Existing non-transactional applications thus can be easily extended to be transactional. CCM container managed transaction uses implicit transaction context propagation mode. Under implicit mode, the propagation is invisible to the application programmer. So the responsibility of adding and extracting transaction context is up for the ORB to take. But if implicit mode is directly implemented as part of the ORB kernel, ORB products offered by different vendors will not be interoperable.

So we adopt standard portable interceptor technology [3] to implement implicit transaction context propagation in StarOTS. We implement one client interceptor, one server interceptor and one IOR interceptor. They are registered into the ORB dynamically. When the request information is passing between the client and the server, the interceptors in the request path capture it. Then thread relevant transaction context is added in or extracted out for analyzing.

3.4 Seamless Integration with the DBMSs

StarOTS adopts O2PC protocol [4] to orchestrate participated resources of global transactions. *Resources* managed by StarOTS are presented as objects with standard APIs. They are registered dynamically with StarOTS (*Coordinator*) to participate in global transactions. Application programmers may build their own *Resource* Object which implements OTS specified *Resource* interface.

Furthermore, if StarOTS cannot work with mainstream DBMSs, its usage will be significantly limited. Fortunately, most database products support X/Open XA interface [5]. In order to simplify the use of database, XA interfaces are integrated with *Resource*. StarOTS drives *Resources* to complete the transaction, and *Resources* control databases through XA interfaces. As a bridge between DBMSs and StarOTS, *Resources* integrate them seamlessly.

The CCM prototype uses PostgreSQL as one of its DBMSs. PostgreSQL is open-sourced. It provides only centralized recovery management and doesn't support 2PC protocol. We did delicate changes to PostgreSQL7.2.1 and make it provide the APIs such as prepare and recovery after prepare. Therefore, application developers create *Resources* through *ResourceFactory*. *Resources* are registered to *Coordinator*, which implement the O2PC to ensure atomicity and durability of global transactions.

4 Integration with CCM Runtime Environment

4.1 Overview

CCM provides a framework for building, assembling, and deploying plug-and-play CORBA components. The CCM prototype we implemented is illustrated in figure 2.

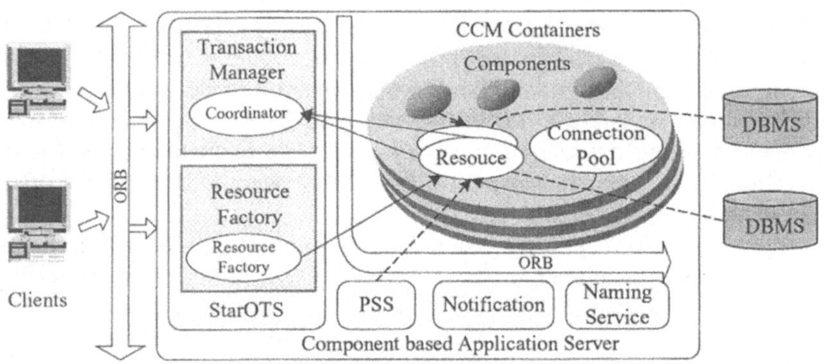

Fig. 2. CCM prototype and StarOTS

4.2 Problems

Integrating StarOTS with CCM runtime environment is not an easy job, since transaction management modes, transaction policies and database connection management must be considered.

CORBA components may support either *self-managed transactions* (SMT) or *container-managed transactions* (CMT). Choosing SMT or CMT is component-level specific. When CMT is selected, additional transaction policies are to be defined in the component's deployment descriptor and transactions are to be automatically demarcated and managed by the container. Components and its containers will act differently under different transaction management modes and different policies.

CCM service integration includes not only StarOTS but also PSS. CORBA components may use StarOTS. At the same time, it may also be used by PSS to make component states persistent. Both PSS and CCM container will use StarOTS. So how to manage the database connection is another problem.

4.3 Solution

In order to implement CMT, the container must be able to intervene into request path from clients to components. In our design, *ServantLocator* is used to take this task. It is activated before and after the requests. Then it delegates its responsibilities to *ExecutorInvoker* in the methods *preinvoke* and *postinvoke*, in which *ExecutorInvoker* will find the component *Executor* and set the context for it. And responsibility of transaction management is delegated to *TxnInterceptor*. The container will take over the transaction context and manage the transactions according to the transaction properties in the component configuration file. And all the synchronized transactional components will be registered into *SyncronizationManager*. *SyncronizationManager* will be invoked at particular transaction demarcation points. The invocation is performed by callback interface *Synchronization* defined in StarOTS.

To resolve the problem of database connection management, *Resource* described in section 3.4 is used. As known, *Resource* in StarOTS is a CORBA object that encapsulates corresponding APIs of DBMSs and it supports O2PC. In order to make the management of database connections easier to implement, we encapsulate the connection and SQL APIs of the DMBS into Resource, too. So the owner of *Resources* can use them to connect to the databases, to query and update the data and at the same time to join a global transaction. A connection pool is created in CCM container that can be used to produce different types of *Resources* for the components or for PSS. And the creation of *Resource* is delegated to *ResourceFactory*.

5 Optimized 2PC Protocol

Centralized recovery protocols are used to ensure local atomicity. For distributed environment, other protocols are needed. 2PC [6] is used in StarOTS. There are 4 messages between the coordinator and the participator. In order to reduce the communication cost and enhance the performance of distributed applications, researchers tried to decrease the number of messages and optimize 2PC protocol [4].

- Read-only

If a local transaction is read only, then whether the transaction will be committed or rollbacked, the DBMS doesn't make any responses to the commands of the coordinator. Usually, a considerable proportion of local transactions in a global transaction only query the business data instead of updating them. In other words, read-only method can help improve the efficiency of 2PC protocol.

- One-Phase Commit

If transaction manager finds that only one local transaction participates, it will hand over the control of the global transaction to the participator. Under this kind of situation, the coordinator sends the one-phase commit command to the participator. The latter just commits the local transaction and returns the result to the coordinator.

Assume that the mean cost of a communication message is C_{2PC} and the proportion of the transactions that vote Rollback or Read-only in the local transactions is t. We also assume that the number of participators is N_{local}. Then if there is only one local transaction, the communication cost of the O2PC is $2C_{2PC}$, else the cost is:

$$4 * (1 - t) * N_{local} * C_{2PC} + 2 * t * N_{local} * C_{2PC}$$

Figure 3 shows the comparison of the communication cost between the 2PC and O2PC. Assume that there are 10 local participators in the global transaction. We conclude that if the number of local transactions is fixed, with the increase of t, the cost the 2PC protocol remains a constant, while the cost of optimized 2PC reduces linearly, as figure 3(a) shows. This is a theoretic analysis. Figure 3(b) shows the mean communication cost according to tests when the number of local participators varies from 1 to 10. It is evident that O2PC reduces the cost comparing with 2PC protocol.

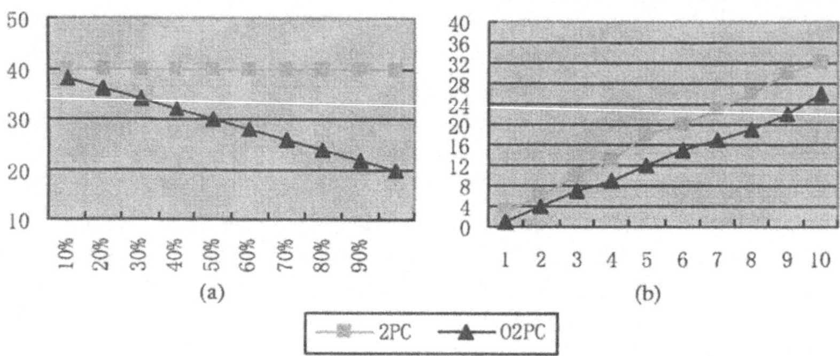

Fig. 3. Comparison of the communication cost

6 Dynamic Management of Transactions

In many existing transaction management systems, administrators can only statically control the processing of transactions by configuring corresponding properties before system start up. Therefore, how to manage the distributed transaction system in a dynamic, flexible and efficient way turns to be a valuable problem to crack. Based on StarOTS, we design and implement an object-oriented transaction service management console OTSMC, which offers the capability of dynamic control and management of all the transactions in a transaction management domain.

OTSMC provides StarOTS users a friendly and natural way to manage transactions. It is transparent to the business transactional applications. And how to make it independent of the application and how to integrate it seamlessly with StarOTS must be considered. We first extend StarOTS to meet the demands of OTSMC. The definition of abstract transaction and abstract transaction service is extended. The extension is designed not to influence the portability and efficiency of StarOTS. At the same time, a few new IDL interfaces are defined and the functions of some interfaces defined in the OMG *CosTransactions* module are extended.

OTSMC can be used to query the status of any global transactions orchestrated by StarOTS, to look over the status of *Resources* related to particular transactions, to examine *Synchronization* resources (if there is any) registered in a transaction, to force rollback of a transaction, to remove a *Resource* from a transaction and to shut down the StarOTS server in a transaction management domain.

7 Summary and Future Work

The most mature distributed programming environment designed for transactional applications is *TP Monitor*. Popular products are exemplified by CICS [7], Tuxedo [8], and Encina [9]. These products support transaction service over heterogeneous platforms. They are, however, built with traditional programming paradigm instead of object-oriented programming paradigm. StarOTS inherits the advantages of CORBA technology. And it marries the merits of both object-oriented and distributed processing technologies to support the atomicity and the durability of distributed transaction. It has been become an efficient method of distributed transaction management and has achieved features as distribution, efficiency, flexibility, interoperability and reliability.

We found that many current component-base software architecture or products do not support any other transaction model except for the flat model, including the CORBA component architecture. This is very limiting since today's applications are often long running and require a higher level of transaction cooperation. So we will conduct research work on how to extend the transaction model in the current open distributed heterogeneous loosely coupled environment.

Acknowledgements. This work is supported by National Natural Science Foundation of China Under grant NO. 90104020 and China National Advanced Science & Technology (863) Plan under Contract No. 2001AA113020.

References

1. Object Management Group. CORBA Components, v3.0, formal. Available online at http://www.omg.org/technology/documents/corba_spec_catalog.htm#ccm (2002)
2. Object Management Group. Transaction Service Specification, v1.3, formal. Available online at http://www.omg.org/technology/documents/corbaservices_spec_catalog.htm (2002)
3. Object Management Group. Portable Interceptors: Joint Revised Submission. Available online at http://www.omg.org/docs/formal (2002)
4. Gerhard Weikum, Gottfried Vossen. Transactional Information Systems: Theory, Algorithms, and the Practice of Concurrency Control and Recovery. Morgan Kaufmann Publishers, San Francisco, USA (2001)
5. X/Open Company Ltd. Distributed Transaction Processing: The XA Specification. Available online at http://www.opengroup.org/pubs/catalog/c193.htm (1991)
6. Jia Yan, Wang Zhiying, Han Weihong, Li Lin. Technology of Distributed Database (In Chinese). Beijing: Publishing Company of Defense Industry (2000)
7. S. Andrade, M.T. Carges, K.R. Kovach. Building a Transaction Processing System on Unix Systems. UniForum Conference Proceedings (1989)
8. A. Dwyer. Enterprise Transaction Processing. UniForum Conference Proceedings (1991)
9. A. D. Wolfe. Transaction Encina, Distributed Computing Monitor, Vol. 7, NO. 11, (1992)

Web Services Testing, the Methodology, and the Implementation of the Automation-Testing Tool[1]

Ying Li, Minglu Li, and Jiadi Yu

Department of Computer Science and Engineering,Shanghai Jiao Tong University, Shanghai 200030, China
{liying, li-ml, jdyu}@cs.sjtu.edu.cn

Abstract. Web Services testing is essential to achieve the goal of scalable, robust and successful Web Services especially in business environment where maybe exist hundreds of Web Services working together. In this paper, we give detailed explanation about the Web Services testing methodology and skill, which are very helpful to the testers. Compared with tradition programming testing, the Web Services testing has its own feature such as performance, authorization, and security. Based on the knowledge of the aspects of Web Services, we design and implement a testing tool to perform some tests automatically.

1 Introduction

With the growing of using XML Web Services [1,2,3], we find that the Web Services testing technique should be enhanced in the Web Service developing cycle. Although Web Services are web application [4], we could use tradition web testing methods, but it has own feature. Testing is essential to achieve the goal of scalable, robust and successful Web Services, testers should concentrate in some key points of Web Services testing in order to design test cases specific to the task. In this paper, we give the basic concepts for the Web Services testing and implement an automatic test tool for some testing.

2 Web Services Testing Methodology

The Web Services are modular, self-described and self-contained applications [5]. With the open standards, Web Services enable developers to build applications based on any platform with any component modular and any programming language.

More and more corporations now are exposing their information as Web Services and what's more, it is likely that Web Services are used in mission critical roles, there-

[1] This paper is supported by 973 project (No.2002CB312002) of China, grand project (No.03dz15027) and key project(No.025115033) of the Science and Technology Commission of Shanghai Municipality.

M. Li et al. (Eds.): GCC 2003, LNCS 3032, pp. 940–947, 2004.

fore performance matters. Consumers of web services will want assurances that Web Services won't fail to return a response in a certain time period. So the Web Services testing is more important to meet the consumers' needs.

2.1 Unit Testing

Unit testing is much more like tradition program test. We could apply this technical into web service's unit test.

2.2 Functional Testing

Functional testing ensures that the functionality of Web Services are as expected. In functional testing, we should not only examine the basic input/output, bounds testing, error checking and so on, but also include the basic security/authorization examination, and test if the service should support all the communications protocols it applied which is also very important to Web Services.

Although Web Services have no user interface, but they provide web methods to invoke, which provide us a way to use automatic script to test them.

2.3 Performance Testing

Performance testing is often to determinate the relevant product statistics. For example: How many messages per second? How many simultaneous users of a service are acceptable? There are basically three ways to conduct performance testing: Ad hoc performance testing; Observational testing; Measured testing.

Compared with tradition program and web program, there exist variety factors to effect the performance of Web Services, which include: Differentiated Web Services solutions; System model; Workload model [6], Transaction model [5], or even Security model.

There are some key parameters to determine Web Services performance; we can use tradition web testing parameters to describe the efficiency or ability of Web Services. These common performance measurements include: MCs(Megacycles), Memory footprint, BoW(bytes over wire, TTLB(time to last byte), user-perceived response time, and the TTFB(time to first byte).

In paper [6], SLA (service level agreement) will rule the relationship between users and services providers. It is very important for testers.

2.4 Load/Stress Testing

The aim of Load/Stress testing is to find out the Web Services' scalability in the growing of the number of the clients invoke them. Load/Stress testing can be applied with performance testing together.

Through Load/Stress testing, the typically bugs would be found more easily than other testing methods, such as:

- Memory leaks: Memory leak would be common in tradition programs. In Web Services, the programming language such as Java, C# is designed to automatic de-allocate memory when objects are no longer used. But it is still possible that the objects would not be de-allocated, such as in java's programming using JDBC. Memory leaks not only appeared in programming language in Web Services, but also in some circumstances in database server. If too many connections appeared at the same time, the database server would not release the cursor in time in some circumstances. The memory leak is extremely difficult to detect. With few use of Web Services, memory leaks are very rarely found since the test does not generate enough usage of the product before it completes. Even through Load/Stress testing, few memory leaks still cannot be found.
- Concurrency and Synchronization: In Load/Stress testing, the testing program will generate many threads to act as virtual users to invoke Web Services, while Web Services can be invoked by others. In such complex circumstance, many different code paths and timing conditions will be performed. In general, the more code paths performed, the more error would be shown.

The load/Stress testing is ideal for automatic testing [7]. The implementation of the testing tools will be introduced at section 3.

2.5 Security Testing

Generally, there are two kinds of Web Services, the Web Services are used in Intranet and the Web Services are used in Internet. Both of them face the security risk since message could be stolen, lost, or modified. The information protection is the complex of means directed on information safety assuring. In practice it should include maintenance of integrity, availability, confidentiality of the information and resources that used for data input, saving, processing and transferring. The complex character of this problem emphasizes that for it solution should be realizing the combination of legislative, organizational and software-hardware measures [8]. So, it is very difficult to test these automatically, but testers should carefully design the test cases according to the real environments and the protocols. The WS-Security 1.0 specification provides varieties ways for Web Services security, such as XML DIGSIG, XML Encryption [9].

The information protection is just one aspect of the security. In Web Services, the main challenge we faced is to consider the protection of resources such as data and applications so that this important information should be only accessed by the appropriate entities. That calls authorization.

2.6 Authorization Testing

In real world, one Web Services would invoke another Web Services, In EAI, there exist thunders of Web Services that could be used together. Not every one could access these services. So testing the authorization is very important to protect the invaluableness data.

Authorization denotes granting authority, in practice, we often use access control list (ACL) or role-based access control (RBAC) to map from the entities to resources in order to assign rights for each resource.

Table 1[10] shows the principal Web Services from an existing trade faire web sites as well as the categories of target users for each service (Table 2)[10].

Authorization testing should test each entity (user categories) to Web Services to get an access table to determine if the authorization is assigned correctly.

We designed a semiautomatic tool to perform the authorization test, which will be discussed later.

Table 1. Principal services offered by existing trade fair Web sites.

Task	Description
T01	To obtain information on how to get to the fair (transportation, ticket costs, time schedule, etc.)
T02	To consult the calendar of the appointments and conventions
T03	To obtain detailed information on the exhibitors
T04	To obtain detailed information on the exhibited products
T05	To consult the map of the fair
T06	To have information on job offering in the fair
T07	To buy ticket on-line
T08	To buy fair catalogue on-line
T09	To obtain information on the receptive structures near the fair (possibly to make reservation)
T10	To consult the call for tender for service providers
T11	To consult the official news
T12	To contact the administrative secretariat
T13	To watch the fair through a webcamera
T14	To watch the fair in 3D vision
T15	To buy advertising banner in the fair web site
T16	User registration for user profiling

Table 2. Distribution of service targets for the user categories within fair trade business

	T01	T02	T03	T04	T05	T06	T07	T08	T09	T10	T11	T12	T13	T14	T15	T16
Organizer																X
Exhibitor	X				X							X		X	X	X
Professional visitor	X	X	X	X	X		X	X	X			X		X		X
Generic Visitor	X	X			X		X	X	X				X	X		X
Service Visitor	X									X		X			X	X
Press	X	X	X	X	X		X	X	X		X	X	X	X		X
Fair Worker	X					X			X			X				X

3 The Design of the Automatic Web Services Testing Tool (AWSTT)

3.1 Related Work

The nunit.org [11] developed an open-source unit-testing tool for all dot net languages. Some primary developing environments provide the functional testing tools, such as Visual studio .NET, IBM WebSphere Studio Application Developer, Weblogic workshop. But they're basic functional tools, none of them provides full functional testing mentioned in 2.2. Few companies develop third party Load/Stress tools, but some tools just use http post and get to simulate the user request, none of them provides security or authorization testing environment.

3.2 The Framework of AWSTT

Since there exist good unit and functional test tools, we put our focus on the design of the 2.3,2.4,2.6. Figure 3 shows the framework of AWSTT. Detail information will be discussed later.

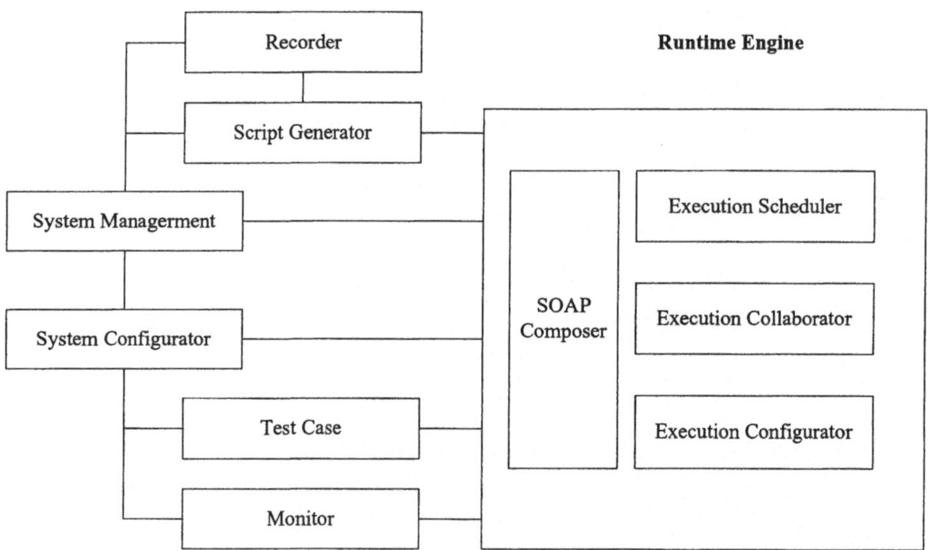

Fig. 1. The framework of AWSTT

3.3 Performance and Load/Stress Testing

Lots of Load/Stress automatic testing tools perform several tests at the same time, for example calling a number of Web Services on the same server simultaneously. The tools first record user's action, then change the action into scripts; the runtime engine executes the script concurrently.

Some Load/Stress tools' capture programs catch all the http requests URL and then concurrently simulate number of users to open the URL, using http post get request to simulate the virtual user, whereas in production most Web Services will be invoked directly using the Simple Object Access Protocol (SOAP)[12]. Here we use JavaScript as the script language to record the action that user invokes Web Services from browser. After record, the SOAP Composer transfers the http post request from the script to SOAP message and save as a configure file to let runtime engine to process. Because one Web Services can provide more than one web method, and one server can hold more than one Web Services, we consider Load/Stress testing includes two aspects:

- Repetition testing. Repetition testing is the basic testing for one function or web method. That means running one Web Services over and over again. Functional test is to examine if the Web Services are working well, while repetition test is to justify if the Web Services could continue to work repeatedly.
- Concurrency testing. Repetition testing is to test one special web method; the aim of concurrency testing is to simulate the real world of the using of Web Services, it performs several operations simultaneously. With the concurrency testing, we can find some problems like thread safety, transaction problems and so on. We designed the runtime engine which can simulate up to 120 users concurrency, with each one can call one or more Web Services according to the configure file.

The performance testing can be a part of Load/Stress testing. The tradition way to analyze the performance is to use the site's log data by using web mining technique [13], or use cookies to analyze user's visiting [14]. But these are not very suitable for Web Services. We currently use SOAP extension to catching SOAP message [15]. A SOAP message is composed by three major parts: a SOAP envelope, a SOAP header and a SOAP body [12]. We apply a new SOAP extension to Web Services to catch the SOAP message and log it to a text file for testing analysis.

Analyzing these data should be very important. In the concurrency testing, Web Services might have transaction; some Web Services would be broken by another Web Services, or even cannot be executed. Currently, we do not provide such analyze tools to help testers to found such problems.

3.4 Authorization Testing

The authorization testing using AWSTT currently cannot be performed automatically, because there exist many authorization methods. In different organizations, there may exist different authorization models such as LADP, authorization services. We cannot get the users' or roles' information from these authorizations directly.

In AWSTT, we can simulate authorization in these ways:

- Invoke and record all Web Services manually through the recorder. That can reuse the test case of the Load/Stress testing. Or we can get such information from UDDI.
- Manually assign users' (roles') rights in authorization server with same token or password. The users' rights should be cover all the Web Services and there are no two users have exactly the same rights.
- Export the users' name form the authorization server and import them to AWSTT
- AWSTT uses the each username, password to assemble a SOAP message, to invoke each Web Services and recorder the state.
- Generate the report.

The SOAP message assemble must be modified by hand, because we cannot prognosticate what encryption method Web Services are used.

4 Summaries and Future Work

In this paper, we give some methods for the Web Services testing. Web Services testing includes unit testing, functional testing, performance testing, Load/Stress testing, security testing and authorization testing. We give detailed information about the key points of the Web Services testing. And designed an automatic testing tool for some of these testing.

The automatic testing tool we currently used has some features, such as SOAP-based log analysis, Repetition and Concurrency Load/Stress testing, and the authorization testing. But it also has some weakness; some features will be implemented in next version:

- Web Services navigation diagram. The Web Services navigation diagram can show how Web Services invoke other Web Services. Given one Web Service, we can get the special one's navigation diagram to other services. If we test all Web Services, then we can get a clear picture of how the Web Services are interacting.
- Transaction monitor and analyze. In EAI, transaction is a critical factor, which affects the Web Services performance deeply. The analysis of the transaction can help optimize the performance of Web Services.

References

[1] Carolyn McGregor, Santhosh Kumaran, Business Process Monitoring using Web Services in B2B e-Commerce , Proceedings of the International Parallel and Distributed Processing Symposium (IPDPS 02)

[2] M. Aoyama, E. Kawaguchi, Intelligent Software Services over the Internet, Information Modeling and Knowledge Bases, IX, IOS Press, Feb. 2000, pp. 128-135.

[3] P. Brereton, et al., The Future of Software, CACM, Vol. 42, No. 21, Dec. 1999, pp. 78-84.

[4] Yuichi Nakamur, Satoshi Hada and Ryo Neyama, Towards the Integration ofWeb Services Security on Enterprise Environments, Proceedings of the 2002 Symposium on Applications and the Internet (SAINT 02w).

[5] Akhil Sahai, Jinsong Quyang, vijay Machiraju, End –to-End Transaction Management for Composite Web based Services, 2001, IEEE.

[6] Valeria Cardellini, Emiliano Casalicchio, Michele Colajanni A Performance Study of Distributed Architectures for the Quality of Web Services, Proceedings of the 34th Hawaii International Conference on System Sciences – 2001.

[7] Alan Booth, Andrew Citron, Stress testing your software without stressing your testers: Automation is the key.
http://www-106.ibm.com/developerworks/webservices/library/ibm-stress/

[8] V.P. Shyrotchin, V.Ye. Mukhin, MEANS AND METHODS FOR THE INFORMATION PROTECTION IN THE GLOBAL NETWORK INTERNET, ies2000

[9] Web Services Security (WS-Security) Version 1.0 05 April 2002.

[10] Claudio Muscogiuri, Gerald Jaeschke, Aldo Paradiso, Matthias Hemmje, FAIRWIS: An Integrated System offering Trade Fair Web-based Information Services – A R&D Case Study, Proceedings of the 35th Hawaii International Conference on System Sciences - 2002

[11] www.nunit.org

[12] Simple Object Access Protocol (SOAP) ,http://www.w3.org/TR/soap12/

[13] Sankar, K.P., Varun, T., Pabitra, M.. Web Mining in Soft Computing Framework: Relevance, State of the Art and Future Directions. IEEE Transactions on Neural Networks, 2002, 13(5) 1163~1177.

[14] Cooley, R., Mobasher, B., Srivastava J.. Data Preparation for Mining World Wide Web Browsing Patterns. Knowledge and Information Systems, 1999, 1 1(1) 5~32.

[15] A.Sahai, V.machiraju, J.Ouyang, K. Wurster Message Tracking in SOAP-Based Web Services, 0-7803-7382-0/02 IEEE 2002

Composing Web Services Based on Agent and Workflow

Jian Cao, Minglu Li, Shensheng Zhang, and Qianni Den

Grid Research Center, Computer Science& Technology Department, Shanghai Jiaotong University
200030, Shanghai, P. R. China,
{cao-jian, li-ml, sszhang, den-qn}@cs.sjtu.edu.cn

Abstract.. Although web service has been regarded as a basic technology to support the next generation web, there are some deficiencies in this technology. A challenge to web service is how to compose several web services according to the business requirements. A web service composition framework WASC is proposed in the paper. In the WASC, different plans are defined as ECA rule set in the service agent and each plan can include several web service invoking activities. After receiving a request, service agent can determine to invoke which service so that the service independent plan will be turned into a service dependent plan by rewriting ECA rules. At the same time, workflow is used to coordinate the actions of service agents. The structures of WASC and service agent are discussed in the paper.

1 Introduction

Web service has been regarded as a basic technology of the next generation web by researchers coming from academy and industry [1]. Comparing with the requirements of the next generation web, web services technology is not capable to play its role so far [2]. One way to overcome some shortcomings of web services is to apply agent technology [3].

To apply agent to web service has been gained more and more attentions. Michael N. Huhns compared difference between web service and agent in web application and he believes the future web service is agent [4]. But he did not put out any methodology in [4]. Many researchers of semantic web putted some methods to enhance the representation capability of service description language in order to make the software agent can inquiry and make use of web service autonomously, for example DAML-S [5].

Some efforts have been recently started to integrate the software agent and the web service communities. The FIPA services group has initiated a specification that enables FIPA agents to use web services infrastructure (e.g. the message transport service), and propose to extend the web services model with the benefits of agent technology [6]. Similarly, AgentCities has established a working group to integrate web services architecture into their AgentCities framework [7]. This working group is exam-

M. Li et al. (Eds.): GCC 2003, LNCS 3032, pp. 948–955, 2004.

ining the complexity of service descriptions and the dynamic composition of web services in open environments. But Mercedes Amor concluded that the web service community does not seem to be interested in integrating agent technology into its infrastructure so far.

Mercedes Amor proposed to integrate web service and software agent technologies through component-based architecture for developing software agents [3], where agent behavior is provided by different plug-ins components. The composition between agent internal components is performed at runtime, allowing the reconfiguration and adaptation of agent behavior to support new interactions, for instance with web services. But in this method, agent can not makes use of a group of web service to react the request from the environment.

In the paper, a service composition framework called WASC based on agent and workflow is presented. The service agents play the main roles in WASC. ECA rules are adopted to describe the mental state of the service agent. Service invoking is modeled as an activity of agent plan. Service agent will turn the general plan to the concrete plan by selecting appropriate web services and executing it autonomously at run time. At the same time, workflow is used to coordinate service agents.

The paper is organized as follows: section 2 gives an overview of WASC. Section 3 defines service agent. The plan of service agent is discussed in detail in section 4. The last section concludes the whole paper and points out some future works briefly.

2 WASC-A Framework Supporting Web Service Composition Based on Agent and Workflow

The framework we proposed is called WASC (**W**orkflow and **A**gent based **S**ervice **C**omposition), see figure 1. The framework is divided into two layers: design& deployment layer (DD layer) and executing& monitoring layer (EM layer).

In DD layer, there are altogether three tools. By using service agent design tool, different agents can be produced as a specification in XML and stored in an agent library. Because service invoking will be defined as an activity of agent plan, the tool will be able to access UDDI to obtain the information about a set of selected web services. The user can also model different business processes as workflows through workflow design tool in a graphical interface. Activities in a workflow will be assigned to persons or agents. Agents can be deployed to different computers by service agent deployment tool.

In the EM layer, process instantiated from workflow model will be driven by workflow engine. Tasks will be allocated to persons or service agents through a message-oriented middleware (MOM). Service agents run in the containers, which is called service agent running environment. After accepting a task assignment, service agent will invoke certain web services according to the requirements autonomously. For each service agent running environment, there is a monitor tool through which user can start, pause and terminate an agent and trace the messages exchanged among agents and workflow engine.

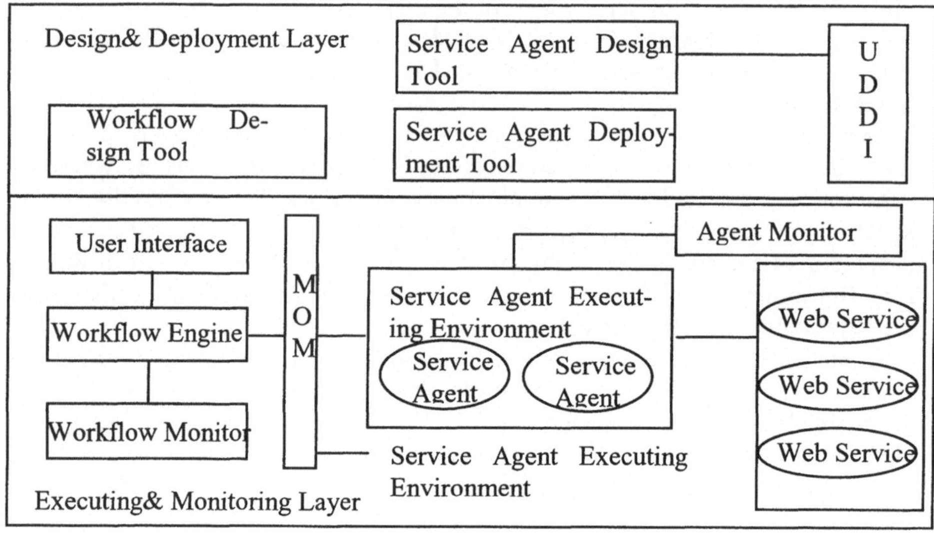

Fig. 1. WASC Framework

3 Definition of Service Agent

The concept of agent is now broadly used not only as a model for computer programming units displaying certain kinds of characteristics but also in a more abstract and general way, as a new metaphor for the analysis, specification, and implementation of complex software system [8].

The structure of service agent is like figure 2. Belief, capability, intention and commitment are four fundamental parts of agent mental model. Intention is achieved by plan. Plan is a partial ordered set of activities that is a unit of action executing. Through executing and monitoring component of agent, agent will communicate with the environment and react to the environment autonomously.

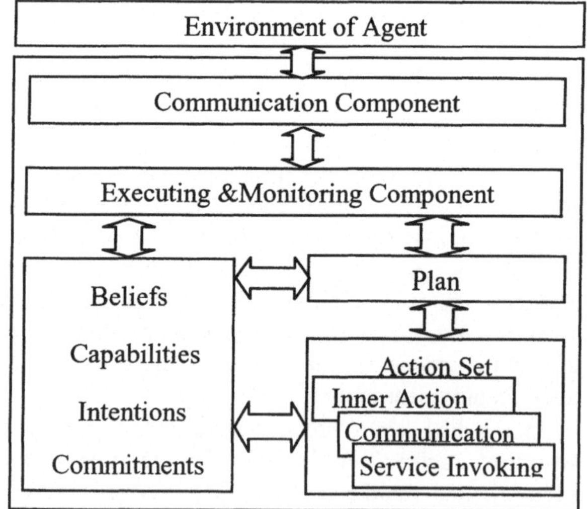

Fig. 2. The Structure of Service Agent

The mental model of service agent is defined based on ontology and ECA rules.

Definition 1: Suppose BS is the belief structure set, BI is the instance set of belief structure, i.e., belief body set. The belief model BM is composed of belief structure set and belief body set, i.e., BM=<BS, BI>. Further more, the belief structure BS can be represented by BS=<CS, R_{cs}>, where CS is the concept class set of domain of an agent, R_{cs} stands for the relationship among concept classes.

The concept classes in BS come from ontology p that is defined for specific domain and the relationships among these concept classes also come from domain ontology. If BM is defined under ontology p, it can be denoted as ^{p}BM. If x is an instance of concept class c, then it is represented by $x=\prod(c)$

$^{p}c_i$ specializes $^{p}c_j$ if and only if any instance of $^{p}c_i$ is always the instance of $^{p}c_j$ and this relationship is represented as $^{p}c_i \leq^{p} c_j$. Obviously specialization (generalization) is a kind of transitive relationship.

Capability, commitment and intention are relating to the behavior of an agent and these behaviors usually happen under certain conditions. In the paper, behavior rule is represented by ECA rules [9].

Definition 2: ECA rule can be defined as $R_{eca}=<e, C_{on}, A_c>$, where e is an event to trig the rule, C_{on} is the condition set to reflect the status of the system and environment and A_c is the action set. An ECA rule states that if e happens and the condition set C_{on} can be satisfied then all the actions of A_c will be executed.

Events can be composed through composing operators to reflect complex states. Some basic composing operators are as follows:

1) AND: e_1 AND e_2 means e_1 and e_2 both happened.
2) OR: e_1 OR e_2 means at least one of e_1 and e_2 happened.

Any thing happened that can be detected directly by the system will be mapped to an atom event. Through composing operators, complex event can be constructed and detected. The commitment of agent is the fact that if an event happened and condition set of an ECA rule can be satisfied, the action defined in the rule will be executed definitely. The intention of agent can be defined as $I_i=<e_i, C_i, p_i>$, where e_i is an event, C_i is a condition set and p_i is a plan. Thus the intention of an agent is the fact that a plan will be executed to respond a specific event under certain conditions.

4 The Plan of Service Agent

Generally, agent will execute a series of actions to achieve a goal. The execution of actions can be organized as activities. Thus a plan can be regarded as a partial ordered activity network.

Definition 3: Plan model can be represented by PM=<A_t, RA>, where A_t is the activity set of a plan; RA is the relationship among these activities. RA=DF∪LF, where DF is the data flow set among activities while LF is the logic relationship among activities. DF and LF are both represented by ECA rules.

Activity has several states. These states include waiting (W), ready (R), executing (E), completed (C), overtime (T) and abort (A). When an activity changes its state from one to another, an event happens. ECA rules are also applied to define the inner behavior of an activity.

Through LF represented by ECA rules, a complex plan can be constructed. The activity of a plan can be decomposed, i.e., an activity can be defined as a sub-plan. If an activity is not divided any more, it is called atom activity; otherwise it is called complex activity.

There are altogether three types of action for service agent:

1) *Inner Actions*: including belief updating, information format transforming and activity status changing;
2) *Communication Actions*: including sending, receiving, parsing and generating messages;
3) *Service Invoking Actions*: invoking a specific web service.

In order to react to a request coming from environment, service agent should take actions according to a plan. The plan can be created on the fly or defined in advance. If agent should make a new plan to each request, on the one hand, this agent must be intelligent enough so that it will be very complicated and difficulty to design, on the other hand, the efficiency of agent will be too low due to planning is a search process and costs space and time. But if plans are fixed in advance, the ability to adapt to the environment of agent will be reduced greatly.

In the paper, Service Independent plans (SI plan) will be defined firstly. When an agent is running, the SI plan will be turned into a Service Dependent plan (SD plan) by rewriting ECA rules.

Firstly, we build the simplest SI plan for a Single Service Invoking plan (SSI plan) like Table 1. After a plan is initialized (a_1), the belief of agent is changed to the input data format (a_2). Then the service is invoked (a_3). The result of service invoking may be success, overtime or failure. If invoking process is success, output data will be transformed into belief of agent (a_4) and the plan will be ended (a_5). If invoking process is overtime or failure, the plan is ended directly (a_5).

When a specific web service will be invoked, the SSI plan should be rewritten into a SD plan by replacing the $<D_1, D_2, C_1, C_2, WS>$ of SSI plan with the corresponding parts of specific web service.

For a web service ws$_i$, a service description can be defined as $C_{s\ i}=<I_{s\ i}, O_{s\ i}, CI_{s\ i}, CO_{s\ i}, Q_oS_{min\ i}, Q_oS_{max\ i}>$. $I_{s\ i}$, and $O_{s\ i}$ are the input and output parameter set respectively and they are represented using believe structure of agent. $CI_{s\ i}$ is the transforming rule for agent beliefs to input parameters of web service which is in XSLT format. $CO_{s\ i}$ is the transforming rule for output parameters of web service to agent beliefs which is also in XSLT format. $Q_oS_{min\ i}$ and $Q_oS_{max\ i}$ are the worst Q_oS and the best Q_oS level of this web service.

Currently, there are different definitions for Q_oS of web service and it generally includes time, cost and reliability. Therefore Q_oS is a multi dimension vector. But if we give each factor a weight and sum up their weighted values then Q_oS can be regarded as a single dimension factor.

Table 1. The SI Plan for Service Invoking

Activity List: a_1: logic start activity a_2: data transforming activity 1 a_3: service invoking a_4: data transforming activity 2 a_5 logic end activity **Data Set and Transformation:** D_1: input data set of service (in XML format) D_2: output data set of service (in XML format) C_1: Transforming Rule for Belief to D1 (in XSLT format) C_2: Transforming Rule for D2 to Belief (in XSLT format)	**Action List:** End( ): the action turning the state of activity to complete TransformBelief(): action transforming belief to input data TransformData( ): action transforming output data to belief Invoke(): service invoking action DataFlow(): input data to an activity **Event List:** Transformed( ): event indicating data has been transformed StartOf( ): event indicating activity status changing from waiting to ready TimeOut(): event indicating an action is over time **WS:** web service
<EndOf(a_1), Null, Initialize(a_2)> <StartOf(a_2), Null, TransformBelief(D_1, C_1)>	<Transformed(D_1), Null, EndOf(a_2)> <EndOf(a_2), Null Initialize(a_3)>
<StartOf(a_3), Null, Invoke(WS)> <Invoked(WS), Null, End(a_3)>	<EndOf(a_3), If "IsSucess"=True, Initialize(a_4)> <TimeOut(WS), Null Initialize(a_5)>
<EndOf(a_3), If "IsSucess"=False, Initialize(a_5)> <StartOf(a_4), Null,TransformData(D_2, C_2)>	<Transformed(D_2), Null, Initialize(a_5)> <EndOf(a_2), Null, DataFlow(D_1, a_3)>
<EndOf(a_3), Null, DataFlow(D_2, a_4)> <StartOf(a_1), Null, End(a_1)>	<StartOf(a_5), Null, End(a_5)>

The SI plan to response a request of environment usually should include several **W**eb **S**ervice **I**nvoking activities (WSI activity). In a SI plan, candidate web services will be defined for each WSI activity a_{wsj} and denoted by $\Gamma(a_{wsj})$. According to the data available, output requirement and Q_oS requirement, appropriate services can be selected.

Suppose there are two parameter sets S_1 and S_2. For $\forall x \in S_1 \cap x \neq Null \cap x\prod({}^{P}cs_1)$, if always $\exists y \in S_2 \cap y \neq Null \cap y\prod({}^{P}cs_2) \cap {}^{P}cs_1 \leq {}^{P}cs_2$, then we call set S_1 specify set S_2 and denote it as $S_1 \leq S_2$. If $S_1 \leq S_2$ and $S_2 \leq S_1$, then $S_1 = S_2$.

According to this concept, if the data set available is DS_a, output data set required is DS_r and Q_oS requirement is Q_oS_r. Then the services which can be invoked in activity a_{wsj} is $\{WS_i | (I_{s\,i} \leq DS_a) \cap (DS_r \leq O_{si}) \cap (Q_oS_{min\,i} \leq Q_oS_r) \cap (ws_i \in \Gamma(a_{wsj}))\}$

Each WSI activity should be expanded by a SSI plan by rewriting SI plan before this plan is executed.

In WASC, service agent plays roles in business processes. As a role, agent should have some qualifications to undertake tasks. The qualification is realized by SI plan.

Suppose web service set relating to a SI plan is WS, ws_i is a specific web service in WS. We have $I_{pmax} = \cup I(ws_i)$, $O_{pmin} = \cap O(ws_i)$. (I ( ) is a function to get the input parameter set of a web service, while O ( ) is a function to get the output parameter set of a web service.) When a request is received by an agent, it can be turned into a service requirement SR=<I_r, O_r>, where I_r is the input data available and O_r is the output data requested. If $I_{pmax} \leq I_r$ and $O_r \leq O_{pmin}$, then the request can be realized. Under other conditions, whether request can be realized or not will depends on the planning result.

In this paper, when we consider whether a service request can be realized by a plan or not, Q_oS requirement for the plan is not included due to the total Q_oS of a plan is difficult to calculate. Although simulation or building a mathematical model to calculate Q_oS is possible, if another web service is selected for a WSI activity, then the whole Q_oS of the plan will be changed and should be calculated again. Thus, we do not consider the Q_oS requirement for the whole plan so far.

If an agent receives a request, it will start a dynamic planning process to make a SD plan. Suppose the BI is the believe body of an agent, note that the value of BI will be changed during the executing process. K is a sequence set. The following algorithm is to make the agent be capable to generate a SD plan for a request :

Algorithm 1:

Suppose *t*, *m* represent the ids of any two activities in a plan, ψ is the activity set with their states are "Ready".

(1) Executing ECA rules and refresh ψ ;

(2) Take out an activity from τ, suppose it is a_t ;

(3) If a_t is a logical end activity, judge whether O≤BI is satisfied:

If it is not satisfied, then go to (6);

Else the planning process is ended; go to (8);

If a_t is a WSI activity then turn to (4);

If a_t is other activity then execute it and return to (1) ;

(4) $\gamma_t=\{ws_i | ws_i \in \Gamma(a_{wst}) \cap I_{s\ i} \leq BI\}$,

If $\gamma_t = \Phi$, then go to (6);

Else add <a_t, γ_t, Null > to the tail of K, go to (7);

(5) $\gamma_t = \gamma_t \setminus \{ws_t\}$:

If $\gamma_t = \Phi$, then go to (6);

Else go to (7);

(6) Judge whether K is empty or not:

If it is empty, then planning process is failure, go to (8);

Else take out the last element of K, suppose it is <a_m, γ_m, ws_m> , let $t=m$, turn back to (5) ;

(7) From γ_t, choice a web service ws_t whose $\alpha_n=(Q_oS_{min\ n}+Q_oS_{max\ n})/2$ is the largest in γ_t , replace the <a_t, γ_t, *> with <a_t, γ_t, ws_t>, execute this activity, return (1);

(8) End.

From the algorithm described above, the planning process of agent is to choice the web service for each WSI activity of the SI plan according to the logic flow of activities. It reduces the complexity than setting up a plan from scratch. But planning process is still a time-consuming task even using this method. We can use case based reasoning technology to reduce the planning load of agent. This method will not be discussed in the paper.

5 Conclusions and Future Work

To compose a group of web services is very important to construct a service based system. How to compose different web services automatically and dynamically according to the changing requirements is a challenging problem. In the paper, a framework named WASC based on workflow and agent is introduced. Web service invoking is designed as an activity of the agent plan. When agent receives a request, the SI plan will be turned into a SD plan by selecting appropriate web services by agent itself. Since the plan is represented by ECA rules, on the one hand the plan of agent can be very complex, on the other hand turning SI plan to SD plan can be realized by rewriting ECA rules.

In the paper, the services to be integrated into agent plan are defined in advance so that the data transforming method can also be defined in advance. It reduces the complexity of dynamical service composing. Now we are trying to extend the service agent ability so that it can search the service automatically.

Acknowledgements. This research is supported by two Chinese high technology plans ("863" plan) (Granted Number: 2001AA415310 and 2001AA412010) and Chinese 973 project (No.2002CB312002).

References

1. McIlraith, S. A., Son, T. C. and Zeng, H.(2002) Semantic Web Services, IEEE Intelligent Systems. Sp. Issue on The Semantic Web, 16(2), p.46-53
2. M. N. Huhns, Agents as Web Services, IEEE Internet Computing, July/August 2002
3. Mercedes Amor, Lidia Fuentes, and José María Troya, Putting Together Web Services and Compositional Software Agents, J.M. Cueva Lovelle et al. (Eds.): ICWE 2003, LNCS 2722, pp. 44–53, 2003.
4. Michael N.Huhns, Software Agents: The Future of Web Services, R. Kowalczyk et al. (Eds.): Agent Technology Workshops 2002, LNAI 2592, pp. 1–18, 2003.
5. DAML Services. The DARPA Agent Markup Language Homepage. http://www.daml.org /services /. 2002
6. FIPA Services. http://www.fipa.org.docs/input/f-in-00050/f-in-00050.html
7. AgentCities Web Services Working Group. http://www.agentcities.org / Activities/ WG/ WebServices
8. Oliveira Eugénio; Fischer Klaus; Stepankova Olga, Multi-agent systems: which research for which applications, Robotics and Autonomous Systems Volume: 27, Issue: 1-2, April 30, 1999, pp. 91-106
9. A.Goh, et.al. ECA Rule-based Support for Workflows, Artificial Intelligence in Engineering, 15(2001), pp37-46

Structured Object-Z Software Specification Language*

Xiaolei Gao[1, 2], Huaikou Miao[1], and Yihai Chen [1]

[1] School of Computer Engineeing and Science, Shanghai University, Shanghai, 200072, China.
gaoxiaolei@163.net, {hkmiao, yhchen}@mail.shu.edu.cn
[2] Xu zhou Normal University, Xuzhou, 221116, China

Abstract. In this paper, we review and compare strengths and weakness of the structure methods, object-oriented methods and formal methods. In order to overcome the disadvantages of each kind of methods and combine the advantages of these three kinds of methods, we propose a new software development methodology named SOFM that attempts to integrate structure method, object-oriented method and formal method. SOZRSL(Structured Object-Z Software Specification Language) is a language to support SOFM. The core of this language is Predicate Data Flow Diagram. We combine PDFD with Object-Z notation to define SOZRSL syntax and the related structures.

1 Introduction

It is well known that the current status of software development is unsatisfactory at large [1][2]. Currently, it seems still difficult to improve this situation in the industrial setting, because there is no better choice for practitioners. Although many formal notations, such as Z [4], VDM-SL [5], LOTOS [6], OBJ [7], and Larch [8], are available in literature, they are seldom used in large-scale software development projects, for formal specifications are not easy to write and read by practitioners either, although for different reasons (e.g., highly abstract mathematical expressions, practical constraints)[3].

One way to address this problem is notation and method integration. Many integrated notations and methods have been reported in literatures, such as VDM++ [9], Z++[10], Object-Z[11], COOZ[12], and SOFL[1][3], but only SOFL emphasizes the coherent use of both graphical notation and textual formal notation with the aim to achieve great comprehensibility of specifications. Although SOFL had gained some acceptance by the academics, but SOFL emphasis the structure method at the design stage and the object-oriented method at the coding stage; the formal method is used throughout the analysis, design and coding stage, so development process of SOFL seems inconsistent and incoherent. In order to solve this problem, we proposed a new method, named Structure Method + Object-Oriented Method + Formal Methods, SOFM for short. Based on the idea of it, We have designed a formal language, called

* This work is supported by China National Natural Science Foundation (No. 60173030)

M. Li et al. (Eds.): GCC 2003, LNCS 3032, pp. 956–963, 2004.

SOZRSL (Structured Object-Z Software Specification Language), for software development. The primary technique for writing specifications using SOZRSL is to use formalized data flow diagrams, called Predicate Data Flow Diagrams (PDFD), to define the architectures of software systems, while using Object-Z notation to define their components. In this paper we first describe the SOFM, then define the SOZRSL that support SOFM. Finally, we proposed how to integrate SOZRSL into software development life cycle.

2 The Idea of SOFM

Structure method provides system developers with a suitable abstract and system decomposing mechanism; it is used to abstract level of software development. But on the other hand, since object-oriented method has the characters of encapsulation and inheritance, it is convenient to reuse, maintain and manage software; formal method can be applied to provide precise specifications, refinements, and verifications of various stages of the system. SOFM is a new software development method; its idea is to integrate the structure method, object-oriented method and formal method into the method that can be used with consistent style in the whole process of software development, such as requirement analysis, design and coding. At the design stage, abstract specification is refined into abstract program. At final stage, abstract program can be further refined into concrete program code automatically or manually.

Structure methods and object-oriented methods are two different kinds of methods. The general way to integrate the two methods is to adopt different methods at various software development stages. The integration method we proposed is to adopt the consistent method at the different stage of software development process; the way that they are integrated is illustrated in Fig.1. In it we view structured method as a two-dimension plane, while the object-oriented method is the third dimension. By this way, object-oriented method can be embedded into structured methods naturally and seamlessly, this also in accordance with the principle of "Big structure and small object" in modern software architecture; in order to guarantee the preciseness of specification and facilitate the formal refinement and validation, it is naturally to integrate formal methods with structure methods and object-oriented methods. In the meantime, we have noticed that programming language, such as C++, is both procedure oriented and object-oriented, so the software requirement specification developed by SOFM method can refined into this kind of code.

Just as many things can't happen in two-dimension world, but it will probably happen in three dimension world. The problems that can't be solved with simply structure method and simply object-oriented method can be solved in SOFM. This requires SOFM developers analyze the problem on a higher altitude; treat the system being developed with a new perspective. It requires the developers utilize object-oriented method during the structure analysis process, layout the rational distribution of objects in software structure and properly deal with the control structure in software objects.

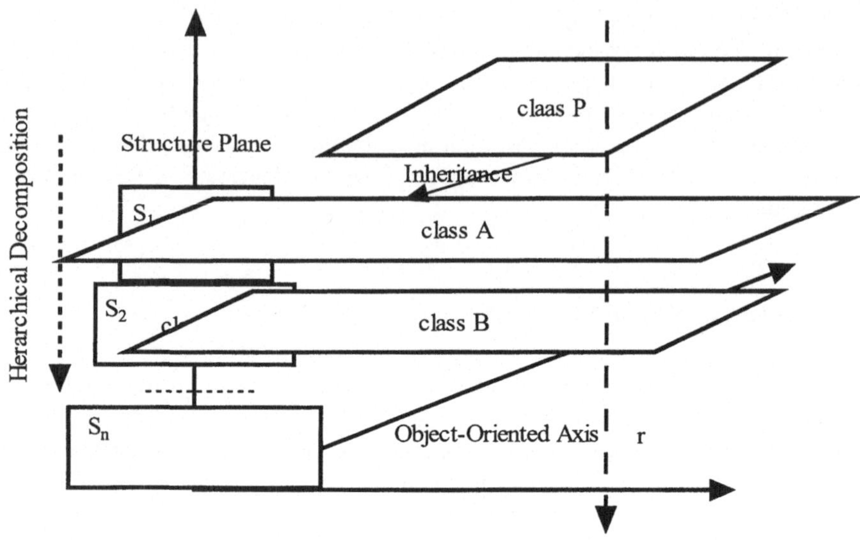

Fig. 1. The illustration diagram of integration of Structure method and Object-oriented Method

3 The SOZRSL

SOZRSL is a new specification language, which supports the SOFM method. SOZRSL is an extension of Object-Z in which the PDFD is introduced to facilitate specification in an SOFM style. The word "extension" means that SOZRSL is based on another language, namely Object-Z, and rather than modifying or adapting its definition, SOZRSL extends it. Therefore, any Object-Z specification is also an SOZRSL specification. The word "facilitate" is purposely chosen to reflect the fact that SOZRSL doesn't enforce any particular style of specification. Indeed, we have just seen that any Object-Z specification is also a SOZRSL specification. SOZRSL does, however, extend Object-Z with constructs which help the specifier, if he or she wishes, to specify systems in a particular fashion.

3.1 Predicate Data Flow Diagram

A predicate data flow diagram, short for PDFD, is a directed graph composed of predicate operations, short for PO. A predicate operation's function is described by Object-Z predicate. Each high level predicate operation is further decomposed into another PDFD according to its constraint at predicate part. Decomposed PDFD depicts how high level predicate operation is implemented by low level predicate operations.

- *Predicate Operation(PO)*

A predicate Operation (short for PO) transforms its input data to output data. This transformation can only accomplished when the predicate Operation satisfies its input data and executes this Operation. So we can define a four tuple <I, Pred, POname, O). *I* denotes input data flow, *O* denotes output data flow, *I* and *O* can be empty; PO-name denotes the name of PO; Pred denotes predicates, which constraint the *I* and *O* of the predicate operation. It can be depicted by Fig.2. All *I* or *O* variables flow into a small rectangle. The predicate constraint will be recorded at the corresponding predicate operation.

If a predicate operation only contains input *I* variables, we call it input predicate operation; if it only contains output *O* variables, it is an output predicate operation.

- *Predicate Data Flow Diagram(PDFD)*

A PDFD is a directed graph $< V, P_c, R >$ where V is a set of declared variables, P_c is a set of PO whose *I* and *O* variables are in V, and R is a collection of directed arcs representing data flows between the PO in P_c. An arc is always associated with a variable. Graphically, we put variable beside the arc. A PDFD can be either connected or disconnected graph. An example of a PDFD is shown in Fig.2.

- *Data Flow*

Suppose $< V, P_c, R >$ is a PDFD, $P_1, P_2 \in P_c$, then directed arc from P_1 to P_2 is a three tuple $< P_1, x, P_2 >$, here $x \in V$, x is the output variable of P_1 and the input variable of P_2. Directed arc denotes data flow from P_1 to P_2 through variable x.

- *Decomposition Rule*

System analysis using PDFD is commonly a successive decomposition process and each decomposition may realize more functions than its high-level predicate operation. It is very unnatural and difficult to make a high level predicate operation capture all of the necessary input and output data flows. Instead, it is natural and easy to let high level predicate operations capture as many input and output data flows as possible for its potential functionality and gradually add more input or output data flows in its decomposed PDFD. Of course, decomposed PDFDs should have more input or output data flows than their higher level predicate operation because, otherwise, the decomposed PDFD would not realize some behaviors required by the high level predicate operation.

Definition 1. Let po be a predicate operation and pdfd a PDFD. Then we define the following terms:

- Input (po)=the set of all the input data flows of predicate operation.
- Output (po)=the set of all the output data flows of predicate operation.
- Input (pdfd)=the set of all the data flows coming into pdfd
- Output (pdfd)=the set of all the data flows going out of pdfd.

Definition 2. If a po is decomposed into a pdfd and the following two predicates are satisfied,

- Input (po)$\subseteq$ Input (pdfd)
- Output (po)$\subseteq$ Output (pdfd)

Then we say po is structurally consistent with pdfd.

To check the structural consistency for a given predicate operation and its decomposed PDFD, we only need to list all of the input and output data flows of the operation and the PDFD, and to compare whether the input and output data flows of the predicate operation are the subsets of those of the decomposed PDFD

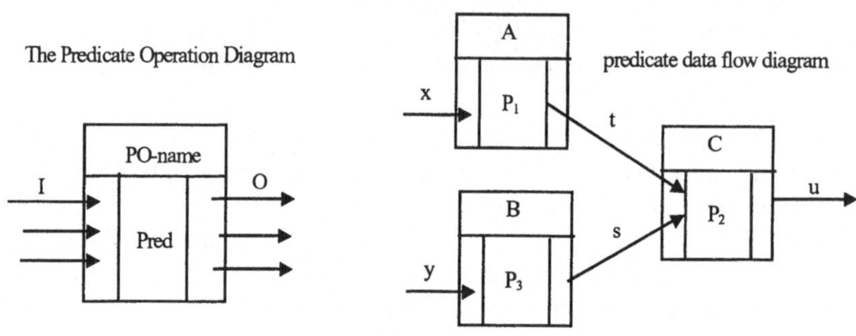

Fig. 2. Representation diagram of PO and PDFD

3.2 The Structure of SOZRSL Specification

A SOZRSL specification is organized as a sequence of modules(S-module) corresponding to a hierarchical PDFD. S-module can be used as textual view of the PDFD, and it may include constant declarations, type declarations, class declaration, variable declarations, and functional specification of predicate operation. The structure of a SOZRSL specification is defined as

S::=S-module{;S-module}

S-module ::= Module-name :PDFD-name[/Module-name, PO-name]
Module-body

Module-name ::= Identifier
PDFD-name ::= Identifier
PO-name ::= Identifier

A SOZRSL specification is a sequence of S-modules. An S-module starts with the module name, after the colon is the related PDFD, here we use name of the associated PDFD name. In this way, the link between an S-module and its corresponding PDFD is established. Since an S-module represents a PDFD that may be the decomposition of a high-level predicate operation. In order to improve the readability of SOZRSL specifications, we can add the high level S-module name and predicate operation name (PO-name) after the PDFD-name, then this predicate operation name (PO-name) describes the PDFD corresponding to this low level module is derived from this predicate operation.

Module-body ::= Paragraph ; … ; Paragraph
Paragraph ::= |BasicTypeDefinition
|AxiomaticDefinition
| GenericDefintion
|AbbreviationDefinition
| FreeTypeDefinition
|SchemaExpression
| Class
| Predicate

In order to illustrate the system structure clearly, in this section we first introduce the PO schema, the reminder will be discussed in detail at following sections.

PO Schema ::= [SchemaHeader [:PO-name /Deco-name]
Declaration
PredicateList]

| SchemaHeader □ SchemaExpression
| SchemaHeader □ SchemaName [FormalParameters]

Deco-name ::= Module-name

An PO schema is consisted of schema name, the name of predicate operation, module name, declaration part and predicate part. The name of PO represents the predicate operation, which defined by operation schema. The S-module name represents the module (Deco-name) corresponding to the PDFD, and this PDFD is decomposed from the PO. A PO corresponds to an PO schema, the input and output data flow of a PO must relate to the declaration part of the PO schema. Each PO must correspond to an PO schema, and each PO schema must be defined in an S-module.

An S-module encapsulates the textual definition of the PO at the PDFD and the PDFD diagram illustrates the relationship between the predicate operations.

The others parts of our SOZRSL is quite similar to Object-Z specification language, for the reason of simplicity, we will not illustrate in detail. Interested reader can refer to related Object-Z books[11].

4 The Process of SOZRSL Software Development

The software development process of SOZRSL is based on successive refinement and decomposition. Fig.3. shows an abstract model of the SOZRSL development process. The phases of the model that are addressed by the SOZRSL development methodology are specification, refinement, and implementation. The main steps are as follows:

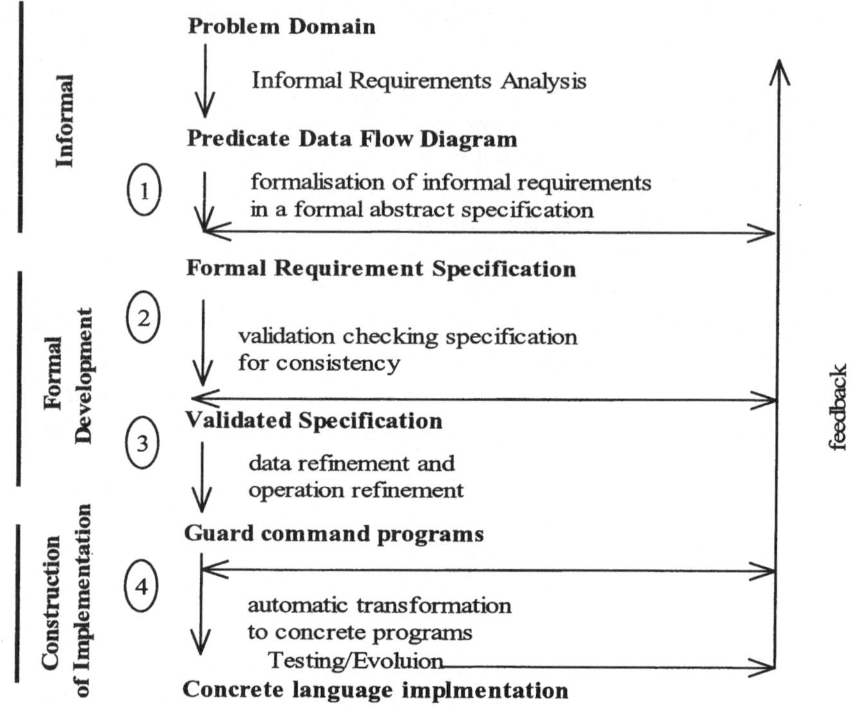

Fig. 3. A model of SOZRSL development process

- constructing a hierarchical predicate data flow diagram.
- describing formal requirements specification in SOZRSL.
- validating these specification by proof.
- refining the more detailed designs into comcrete programming language.
- testing whether the final program satisfies the specification.

5 Conclusions

In this paper, we introduce a new software development method SOFM and its supporting language SOZRSL. We also improve the predicate data flow diagram notation and adapted it to the constructing process of SOZRSL and define the syntax of SOZRSL. Our future research work will focus on defining the formal semantics of SOZRSL based on the syntax defined in this paper.

References

1. Shaoying Liu, A Formal Definition of FRSM and Applications, International Journal of Software Engineering and Knowledge Engineering, Vol. 8, No. 3, September 1998, pp. 253-281
2. Miao Huaikou, Gao Xiaolei and Li Gang, The Comparison and Combination of Structured Methodology, Object-Oriented Methodology and Formal Methods. Computer Engineering & Science, Vol.21,No.4, 1999
3. Shaoying Liu, A Jeff. Offutt, Chris Ho-Stuart, Yong Sun, Mitsuru Ohba, SOFL: A Formal Engineering Methodology for Industrial Applications, IEEE Transactions on Software Engineering, Special issue on Formal Methods, IEEE Computer Society Press, Vol. 24, No. 1, January 1998, pp. 24-45
4. Antoni Diller, Z An Introduction to Formal Methods. London. John Wiley & Sons 1990
5. John Dawes, The VDM-SL Reference Guide. Pitman, 1991
6. T. Bolognesi, E. Brinksm, Introduction to the ISO specification language LOTOS, in The Formal Description Technique LOTOS, P. H. J. van Eijk, C. A. Vissers, and M. Diaz, Eds., pp. 23--73. Elsevier Science Publishers North-Holland, 1989
7. J. A. Goguen, T. Winkler, J. Meseguer, K. Futatsugi, and J.-P. Jouannaud, Introducing OBJ, October 1993
8. John V. Guttag, James J. Horning, K.D. Jones S.J. Garland, A. Modet, and J.M. Wing, Larch: Languages and tools for formal specification. Texts and Monographs in Computer Science. Springer-Verlag, 1993
9. Swapan Mitra, Object-oriented specification in VDM++. In Lano and Haughton
10. Lano K, Z++, An Object-Orientated Extension To Z. Z User Workshop. Oxford 1990
11. Graceme Smith, The Object-Z. Kluuer Academic Publishers, 2000, America
12. Yuan Xiaodong, Zheng Guoliang, COOZ: Complete Object-Oriented Extension to Z. Journal of Software, Vol. 8, No. 9, 1997

Ontology-Based Intelligent Sensing Action in Golog for Web Service Composition

Zheng Dong [1], Cong Qi [2], and Xiao-fei Xu [1]

[1]School of Computer Science and Engineering, Harbin Institute of Technology
{dongzheng, xiaofei}@hit.edu.cn
[2]Department of Information Systems, City University of Hong Kong
laurel0210@sina.com

Abstract. Sensing actions in Golog, which depend so much on the interaction and conversion with users, are the bottleneck of the current approaches of semantic web. By employing ontology as the additional information, we propose an intelligent method for the implementation of sensing actions. A sensing job is changed into the problem of finding the set of instances of an arbitrary concept. Several aspects associated with this idea are discussed in this paper.

1 Introduction

Web Service Composition (WSC) received much attention recently in the field of semantic web. McIlraith proposed a theoretical foundation of WSC [1,2], in which a task is expressed as a high-level generic program in Golog [7,8], and WSC is achieved by the process of goal driven back-chaining reasoning on top of the space of web services. To get actions well planed, sensing is unavoidable. But current Golog has no built-in logics to deal with situations when information is incomplete. Many conversations and interactions with users have to be involved in the process of action planning, which not only decreases the efficiency of the system, but also impedes the exertion of the system's intelligence.

We employ ontology as the sources of additional information, which may be consumed automatically by the Golog interpreter, to make the sensing actions accomplished in an automatic or semi-automatic way. DAMLJessKB [10,11] is used as the ontology inference tool. A sensing problem is changed into the problem of finding the instances of an arbitrary concept in the ontology.

2 Uniform Process of Sensing

Given a domain theory ***Th*** and Golog program δ, a program execution must find a sequence of actions $\vec{a}$ such that: $Th \models Do(\delta, S_0, do(\vec{a}, S_0))$. This denotes that the Golog program δ, starting execution in situation S_0, will legally terminate in situation $do(\vec{a}, S_0)$, where $do(\vec{a}, S_0)$ abbreviates $do(a_n, do(a_{n-1}, ..., do(a_1, S_0)))$.

M. Li et al. (Eds.): GCC 2003, LNCS 3032, pp. 964–971, 2004.

Golog programs are high-level generic procedures with a set of its own operators [7]. Golog program δ and axioms in domain theory ***Th*** are translated into Prolog rules and a Golog interpreter is largely a Prolog interpreter. In current Golog, sensing jobs are implemented as external function calls, which are used to determine the truth value of certain fluents. This can be embodied into the successor state axiom of a fluent $F(\vec{x})$:

```
holds(f(X), do(A(X), S)):- exec(A(x), S).
exec(A, S):- A.                                                        (1)
ex_get_driving_time(Origin, Dist, Time):-
    oaa_Solve(get_directions(Origin, ' ', Dist, ' ', 0, X), [ ]), drvTime(X, Time).
```

Each sensing action 'A' in exec(A, S) needs to be mapped to a specific function in the OAA broker agent. This approach makes it difficult for Golog programming and makes the program less adaptive to a constantly changing environment. We argue that all the sensing actions can be grouped into only two categories.

Functional-fluents-sensing. Each functional fluent $F(\vec{x},s)=\vec{y}$ is translated into a Prolog rule $f(X,Y,S)$. Different from Mcllraith's solution, we propose sensingFFluent as a uniform sensing method for all functional fluents (see (2), (3)).

```
holds(driveTime(O, D, T, do(E2,S)):-                                   (2)
    E2=sensingFFluent(driveTime(O, D, T)).
sensingFFluent(A):- testValid(A); <algorithm acting on arbitrary f-fluent 'A'>.   (3)
```

Parameters-sensing. Golog assumes that the input parameters of actions are always available. But this is not always true. For example, when a user want to eat at a certain time, he launch a 'eat' action, but may not provide information about where and what he want to eat. We propose parameters-sensing to have the vacant parameters sensed automatically, provided there's a background ontology system. The details of parameters-sensing is encapsulated inside the predicate of sensingParams (see (4), (5)). We insure that a sensing action must be launched after it has got a complete set of input values. This is achieved by putting sensingParams predicate in the precondition axiom of the sensing action to sense the input parameters (see (6)).

```
poss(buyAirTicket(O, D, DT)):- sensingParams(buyAirTicket(O, D, DT)),   (4)
    not ownAirTicket(O, D, DT, S), ticketAvail(O, D, DT, S).
sensingParams(B):- testValid(B); <algorithm acting on arbitrary WAA 'B'>.   (5)
poss(buyAirTicket(O, D, DT)):- sensingParams(buyAirTicket(O, D, DT)),   (6)
    not ownAirTicket(O, D, DT, S), ticketAvail(O, D, DT, S).
```

3 Ontology, Concepts, and Sensing Objectives

3.1 Extending DAML from 2-Arity to n-Arity

In any specific field of application (e.g. an enterprise), there may be a stable ontology system covering the whole information space of the field. DAML [6] is the ontology language designed for Semantic Web. Powerful as DAML is, it only supports binary relations, or in other words, a property in DAML is only used to connect two concepts. But in real world, most relations have arbitrary arities.

On the base of DAML, we define, in a new NameSpace 'daml-2', an n-arity property ---- MDProperty. The main part of this property is a set of slots, which further includes some items. Also, global items such as '<Value>' are included in this property. dirveTime(O,D,Time) can be presented by MDProperty as Fig.1(a). Fig.1 (b) is the same property illustrated in a graph mode.

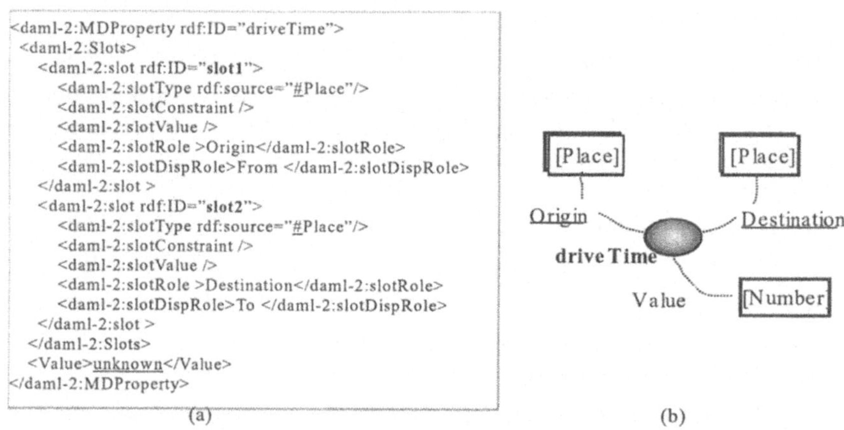

Fig. 1. Drivetime(O,D,T) presented by MDProperty (a) and illustrated in graph mode (b).

MDProperty can be presented formally in such way: suppose ***R*** be a relation of arbitrary dimension, then [$*RoleName*]***R*** represents a dimension of ***R*** identified by the role name. For instance, [$*Origin*]dirveTime represents slot1 of driveTime relation. Further, we use ([$*RoleName*]***R***)^{I} to represent the set of instances of the concept presented by [$*RoleName*]***R***.

3.2 Concepts as Sensing Objects

In an n-ary property, one concept can be constrained by the values of other related concepts and the constrains can be given in a nested way (see Fig.2).

Both f-fluent-sensing and parameters-sensing deal with relations of arbitrary arities. For example, the f-fluent driveTime(O,D,T) and the action buyAirTicket(O, D, DT) are all relations of 3-arity. In driveTime(O,D,T), the concept 'T' is the objective of sensing. If the system does not know the value of 'O' and 'D', then these two concepts become the objective of sensing prior to 'T'. Similarly, the concepts O, D, DT are all objectives of sensing before the action buyAirTicket can be launched.

The above analysis shows us this fact: the objective of any kinds of sensing is to get the proper instances of the concepts involved in the n-arity relations of functional fluents and actions, or more concisely, sensing objectives are concepts.

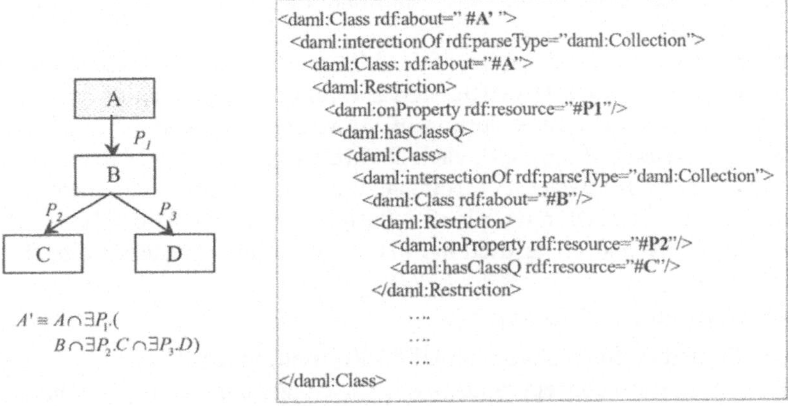

Fig. 2. Concepts with nested constraints

Parts of the parameters (concepts) may be supplied by users, but others need to be sensed. Each uninstantiated concept in an n-arity relation is an objective for sensing. For example, in Fig.3, if concepts 'a' and 'b' in relation R are not supplied by user, the system constructs sensing objectives for them respectively. Note, there may be constraints among vacant concepts, which is discussed in detail in the next section.

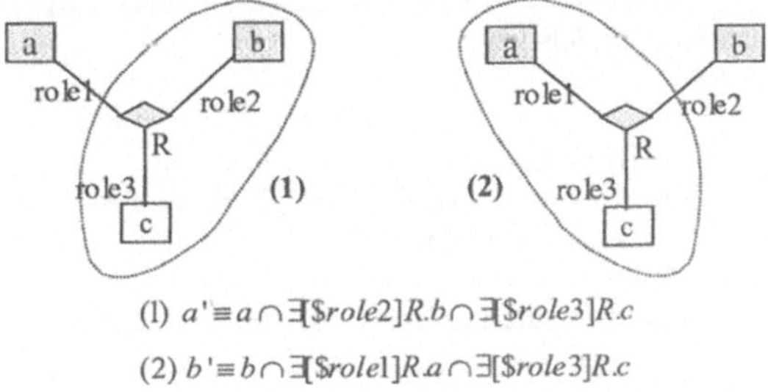

Fig. 3. Each uninstantiated concept is a sensing objective

4 Sensing Implementation Based on Ontology

sensingFFluent(A) and sensingParams(B) are the entrances to the algorithms for accomplishing sensing tasks. Following, we discuss the mayor parts involved in the algorithms.

4.1 Finding the Instances of Concepts

The objective of a sensing job is a constrained concept. The aim of sensing job is to find the instances of the concept from background ontology. Formally, given a concept *Cncpt*, find the maximal set *INST* from ontology, which satisfies: *INST*={inst | instOf(inst, Cncpt)}.

Because of the knowledge nature of DAML, we employ DAMLJessKB [10,11] system as the inference tool. DAMLJessKB is a rule-based production system on the java platform supporting a large portion of DAML semantics. Because DAML is a language on the basis of RDF(S)[9], each DAML statement is translated into a triple by the DAML(or a RDF) parser. For example, the class definition statement of the assembly in Fig.2 is translated into triple (7). Further, because ' #Assembly' is the intersection of Class '#A' and a 'Restriction', (7) can be further translated into the triple (8).

(rdf:type #Assembly rdfs:Class) (7)

(rdf:type (PropertyValue #intersectionOf #A Restriction) rdfs:Class) (8)

Clearly, a constrained concept in DAML is parsed into a nested triple, which acts as a fact in production system like CLIPS (Jess [11] is a CLIPS engine in java environment used by DAMLJessKB).

At the same time, the semantics of DAML is expressed in the form of rules. Fig.4 is a rule implementing basic notion of subclass-instances.

```
(defrule subclass-instances
  (PropertyValue
    http://www.w3.org/2000/01/rdf-schema#subClassOf
    ?child ?parent)
  (PropertyValue
    http://www.w3.org/1999/02/22-rdf-syntax-ns#type
    ?instance ?child)
=>
  (assert
    (PropertyValue
      http://www.w3.org/1999/02/22-rdf-syntax-ns#type
      ?instance ?parent)))
```

Fig. 4. A rule implementing subclass-instances

Provided with facts like (8), the left-hand-sides (LHS) of rules may be triggered, and then the right-hand-sides (RHS) of the rules are asserted. DAMLJessKB provides a rich set of rules. Given a concept, simple or nested, DAMLJessKB will find the instances of it within the scope of ontology.

4.2 Pre-constraining on Concepts

For a given n-arity relation ***R****([role1],[role2],...[rolen])*, all the roles should be constrained, to the best of the ability of Golog interpreter, before the unconstrained roles are launched for sensing. We call this operation 'Pre-constraining'. Then, what information can be used to do Pre-constraining, and what's the process for doing this?

The following information may be used to do pre-constraining: (a) User's assignments; (b) User's personal rules; (c) F-fluent computation; (d) Other relations related to current relation; (e) Current system status (available fluents). Golog interpreter should try these five kinds of information to do pre-constraining. The order of the list also indicates the priority of the information to be used by Golog. (1) User's assignment to the value of a role has the highest priority. Generally, if there's a user's assignment, there's no need to do any further pre-constraining and sensing for this role. (2) User's personal rule can be looked upon as an additional set of axioms of in Golog theory ***Th***. For example, if a person asserts that he prefers western-style-food at every weekend, then when he launches the action 'eat' at weekend, the role of 'subject' of the eat action would be assigned to be 'western-style-food' automatically. Both the launched action in the action ontology and the user rules are in the form of Fig.1. The user's rules can be applied by simply combining itself to the launched action. We do not discuss this in detail in this paper. (3) It's possible for sensingParams(B) to encounter some parameters that are functional fluents. So, sensingFFluent(A) predicate is needed to get the values of these parameters. (4) The values of the roles of a relation R can also be constrained by other relations related to R. see next section for this case.

4.3 Relations with Multiple Unconstrained Roles

Functional fluent (f-fluent) sensing is, in fact, a special case of parameters-sensing. F-fluent sensing is always launched when the input parameters of the fluent are already known. Or in other words, f-fluent sensing is a parameters-sensing with only one role unconstrained. With pre-constraining operations introduced in section 4.2, some parameters-sensing jobs can be changed into simpler jobs like that of f-fluent sensing. But in a general situation, a relation may have multiple unconstrained roles need to be sensed concurrently.

In Fig.5, **'eat'** is a 4-arity relation and **'offer'** is a 2-arity relation. Suppose a user launched the **'eat'** action at a weekend. The pre-constraining operations first populate the roles of 'sb' and 'time' to be 'me' and 'weekend' respectively. Further, the role of 'sth' is confined to be 'west food', which is a sub-class of 'Food' in the background ontology. But the instances of roles 'sth' and 'place' are still unknown. This means that the relation **'eat'** has two unconstrained roles to be sensed concurrently.

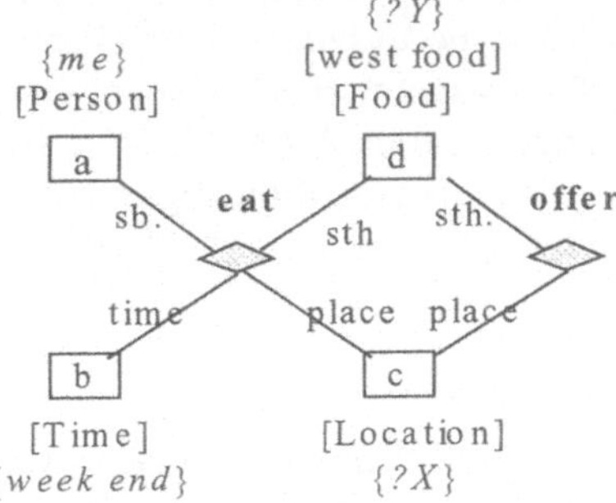

Fig. 5. A relation with multiple unconstrained roles

We add another set of axioms, called 'association', into the Golog theory ***Th***. Each association rule is a relation connected to another relation, providing additional constrains on the slots of the linked relation. For example, '**offer**' is a relation associated to '**eat**'. The rule is in the form of (9).

association (eat, offer, (sth, place)) (9)

With this constraint, '?X' may be represented as:

$$\{?X\} \equiv [Location]\ \text{eat} \cap \exists [\$sb]\text{eat}.\{\text{me}\} \cap \exists [\$time]\text{eat}.\{\text{weekend}\} \cap \exists [\$place]\text{eat}.\{?X\} \cap \exists [\$X]\text{offer}.\{?Y\}. \quad (10)$$

In (10), the unknown concept {?X} contains another unknown concept {?Y}. We take a two-step method to solve this problem. First, every {?Y} in (10) is replaced by the concept '[west food]'. This makes {?X} to be the set of places that offer west food. Second, use the set of {?X} to constrain {?Y} with the following statement:

$$\{?Y\} \equiv [\text{west food}] \cap \exists [\$\text{food}]\text{offer}.\{?X\} \quad (11)$$

This two-step method can be extended to relations with arbitrary unconstrained roles. We do not give out the formal algorithm in this paper. The details of the algorithm, along with the proof of its correctness and its efficiency in running will be presented in another paper.

5 Conclusions

In this paper, we study in detail the structure of sensing actions in Golog, and distinguish the sensing actions into functional-fluent-sensing and parameters-sensing. By altering the axioms and rules in the theory ***Th*** of Golog, a uniform process of sensing is achieved. The basic spirit of our approach is to employ ontology information as the background knowledge, which may be consumed automatically by the Golog interpreter to make the sensing actions accomplished in an automatic or semi-automatic way. 2-arity relations in traditional ontology are extended into n-arity relations, which are more suitable for our problem. Our approach makes use of information as much as possible to constrain the unconstrained roles of a relation with least intervention of users. DAMLJessKB is selected as the ontology inference tool. A sensing problem is changed into the problem of finding the instances of an arbitrary concept of the ontology.

Our study will make the action planning in semantic web more intelligent and friendly. But there still much to do to before the realization of this vision. Although there's no need to altering the reasoning mechanism of Golog interpreter, the structure of ontology has to be extended. And the DAMLJessKB system needs some modifications to fit our requirement. The details of the algorithms in several parts of the system need to be studied in a much formal way, which are not included in this paper.

References

1. Sheila A. Mcllraith, Tran Cao Son. Semantic Web Services [J]. IEEE Intelligent Systems, Vol.16, No.2, 2001, 46-53.
2. S. Mcllraith, T.C. Son. Adapting Golog for Programming the Semantic Web [C]. Proc. 5th Symposium On Logical Formalizations of Commonsense Reasoning, 2001, 195-2002.
3. J.Hendler. Agents and the Semantic Web [J]. IEEE Intelligent Systems, Vol.16, No.2, 2001.3/4,30-37.

4. T. Berners-Lee, M. fischetti, and T. M. Dertouzos, Weaving the Web: the Original Design and Ultimate Destiny of the World Wide Web by its Inventor, San Francisco, 1999.
5. U. Shah et al., "Information Retrieval on the Semantic Web," Proc. ACM Conf. Information and Knowledge Management,ACM Press, 2002.
6. DAML. DAML Web Site. http://www.daml.org/services, 2002.
7. G De Giacomo, Y. Lesperance, H. Levesque. ConGolog, a Concurrent Programming Language Based on the Situation Calculus[J]. Artificial Intelligence, Vol 1-2, no. 121, 2000.8, 109-169.
8. GDe Giacomo and H. Levesque. Projection using regression and sensors. In IJCAI'99, 160-165, 1999.
9. W3C. Resource Description Framework (RDF) model and syntax specification. http://www.w3.org/ TR/1999/REC-rdf-syntax-19990222/, 1999.
10. Joseph Kopena , William C. Regli. DAMLJessKB: A Tool for Reasoning with the Semantic Web [J]. IEEE Intelligent System, Vol.18, No.3, 2003, 74-77.
11. E. Friedman-Hill, Jess: The Rule Engine for the Java Platform, 1995, http://herzberg.ca.sandia.gov/jess.

The Design of an Efficient Kerberos Authentication Mechanism Associated with Directory Systems

Cheolhyun Kim[1], Yeijin Lee[2],, and Ilyong Chung[2]

[1] Department of Computer Science, Hongsung Technical College, Hongsung, Chungnam, Korea
[2] Dept. of Computer Science, Chosun University, Kwangju, Korea
iyc@chosun.ac.kr

Abstract. Since any suggestion to regional services are not described in Kerberos, authentication between regions can be performed via PKINIT (Public Key Cryptography for Initial Authentication)[1] presented by IETF CAT working group.
In this paper, an efficient Kerberos authentication mechanism associated with directory systems is presented by employing X.509 protocol. A new protocol is better than the authentication mechanism proposed by IETF CAT Working group in terms of communication complexity.

1 Introduction

Development of computer communications creates various information services. In order to provide them with users reliably and safely, security services should be concerned. Among them, authentication is the most important, because all other security services depend upon it, which gives confidence that people or things are who or what they claim to be. In recent years, researches on authentication mechanisms[2]-[4] in distributed environment have been very active. Kerberos, the model implemented for MIT's Project Athena, is an add-on system/protocol that allows users to authenticate themselves through the services of a secure server[5]-[6]. It uses DES algorithm to distribute sensitive information on open network. As information is encrypted, it is not susceptible to eavesdropping or misappropriation. Since Kerberos is originally designed on local area network, it accomplishes authentication process nicely in the local realm, however, it doesn't offer services on remote realm. In order to solve this problem on Kerberos described above, integration of the X.509 authentication mechanism[7] into Kerberos system for inter-realm services has been employed. X.509 authentication mechanism, a part of X.500 describing directory services, defines a framework of directory services for authentication process based on asymmetric cryptography and digital signature. IETF working group suggests that Kerberos authentication mechanism between regions is performed via PKINIT, which utilizes ephemeral

* Corresponding Author : Ilyong Chung(iyc@chosun.ac.kr)

M. Li et al. (Eds.): GCC 2003, LNCS 3032, pp. 972–979, 2004.

Diffie-Hellman keys in combination with DSA keys as the primary. It enables access to Kerberos-secured services based on initial authentication utilizing public key cryptography. In this paper, an efficient Kerberos authentication mechanism associated with X.509 and Domain Name System(DNS)[8]-[9] is presented. In order to implement this protocol, authentication between regions is accomplished by the connected chain obtained from X.509 and DNS. According to the authentication mechanism by IETF, local KDC(Key Distribution Center) finds out an address of remote realm, and then gives information on location of realm and initial authentication of client and remote KDC to client. Client requests this service to remote KDC as an original Kerberos mechanism does. However, in our protocol local KDC provides client with information on authentication of client and remote TGS, instead of authentication of client and remote KDC. Therefore, it is better than the authentication mechanism proposed by IETF CAT Working group in terms of communication complexity. This paper is organized as follows. An efficient Kerberos authentication mechanism associated with X.509 and DNS is proposed and then is evaluated in Section 2. The paper concludes with Section 3.

2 The Design of an Efficient Kerberos Authentication Mechanism Applying X.509 and DNS

PK_C : Client's Public key
SK_C : Client's Private key
K_C : Client's Secret key
CS : Certificate Serial Number certified by KDC
AP : Issuer's Public key
A_I : Algorithm Identifier
$K_{I,J}$: Session Key to permit secure exchange between I and J
{M}K : Encrypt information M with key K
ID_C : Client's ID
AD_C : Client's Network Address(Client's IP)
KDC $\ll C \gg$: Client's Certificate issued by KDC
KDC_l : Local KDC
KDC_r : Remote KDC
KDC_s : Remote server
KDC_c : Local Client
cusec : INTEGER (for replay prevention as in RFC1510)
ctime : KerberosTime (for replay prevention as in RFC1510)
nonce : INTEGER (binds responce to the request)

2.1 Design of an Efficient Kerberos Authentication Mechanism

When a user requests a service, KDC looks into location of service, and if it needs connection between realms, then it accomplishes this process by employing X.509 and DNS. First, a user in the realm of CS.MIT must be authenticated by its local KDC, which examines user's lifetime, intrusion by interception and replay attack, etc. Figure 4 illustrates that local connection is performed in user's realm.

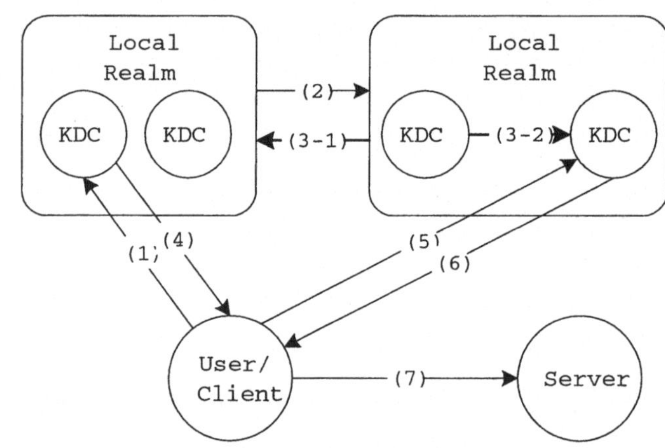

Fig. 1. Authentication process between client and remote server

Since Kerberos verifies information related only to user's identity, it does not require that this information is encrypted with KDC' public key. Otherwise, KDC decrypts all the message that are transmitted in this process and it is forced to overload the system.

A user sends user's ID and content of a requested service to its local KDC. KDC searches information in database, authenticates it and investigates whether or not the service is located in local realm. If it is located in local realm, inter-realm authentication is of no use. In case that this service is located in remote realm, connection from CS.MIT.EDU to IFS.UMICH.EDU is shown in Figure 3. A user in CS.MIT.EDU would like to request a service in IFS.UMICH.EDU. In order to do this, the chain of connections is established between CS.MIT.EDU and MIT.EDU, MIT.EDU and EDU, EDU and UMICH.EDU, UMICH.EDU and IFS.UMICH.EDU. A directory server is responsible only for connecting to neighboring realms, but has no function of authentication. Everything related to authentication is up to KDC. The forward and reverse certificates are obtained from two chains of certificates - CS.MIT.EDU≪MIT.EDU≫MIT.EDU≪EDU≫EDU ≪UMICH.EDU≫UMICH.EDU≪IFS.UMICH.EDU≫ and IFS.UMICH.EDU≪ UMICH.EDU≫UMICH.EDU ≪EDU≫EDU≪MIT.EDU≫MIT.EDU≪ CS.MIT .EDU ≫,respectively. Since connection between two realms is done, the process certificating these counterparts is needed. Local KDC knows public key

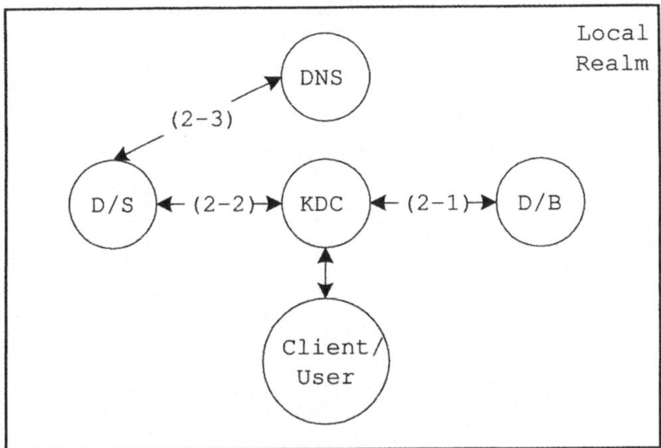

Fig. 2. The process searches location of remote KDC

of IFS.UMICH.EDU, so it transmits message encrypted with this public key. After receiving message from CS.MIT.EDU, remote KDC decrypts message with its private key. Then, remote KDC gives local KDC information requisite to communicate between remote TGS and client, which is decrypted with public key of local KDC. Later, local KDC transmits information related to client in order directly to communicate with remote TGS.

Client sends authentication information encrypted with session key obtained from local KDC, to remote TGS. Remote TGS decrypts the received message with its secret key, finds out session key of client and remote TGS and then transmits message encrypted with this session key, which contains session key of client and server, and ticket for service. Client finds out session key and ticket required to communicate with server, which is used during session. The following algorithm is designed based on contents describing above that show exchanges of authentication information between client and server in remote realm.

KerbInit_Authentication Algorithm

(1) A client requests a service located in remote realm.
$\mathrm{KDC\_}c \rightarrow \mathrm{KDC\_}l : \mathrm{ID}_C, \mathrm{KDC\_}r$

(2) Local KDC looks into whether or not a client is legal by examining client's status, investigates a realm of the requested service. If in remote realm, X.509 and DNS are employed for searching location of a realm. Then it transmits information for connecting with remote realm.
$\mathrm{KDC\_}l \rightarrow \mathrm{KDC\_}r :$
$\{\mathrm{Auth{-}Pack}, \{\mathrm{SigAuth{-}Pack}\}\mathrm{SK}_C,$
$\mathrm{User{-}type}, \mathrm{KDC\_}l \ll C \gg, \mathrm{CS}\}\mathrm{PK}_{KDC\_r}$

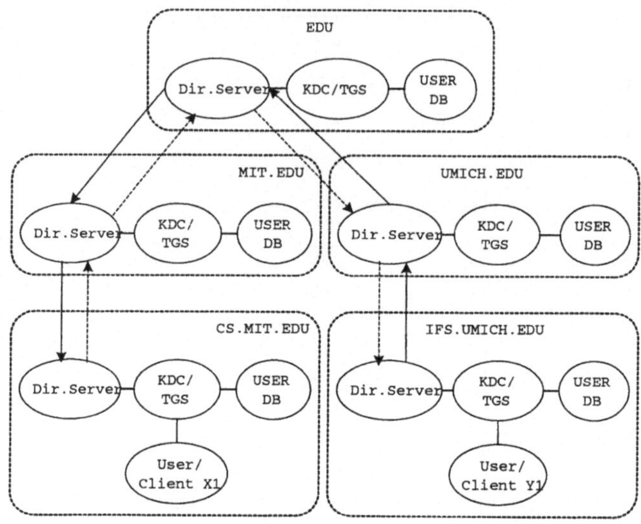

Fig. 3. Authentication paths between two directories

SigAuth−Pack : $\{A_I, PK_C\}$,
Auth−Pack : {KDC, Realm, cusec, ctime, nonce, A_I, AP},
User−type : X.509V3 (DER encoding)
PGP (PGP specification)
PKIX (PKCS #6)

(3) Remote KDC gives local KDC information requisite to communicate between remote TGS and client, which is decrypted with public key of local KDC.

KDC_r $\rightarrow$ KDC_l :
{V, KDC−cert, nonce, kdcPublicValue,
$\{K_{C,TGS}$, TGS, TS, nonce$\}PK_C$,
$\{K_{C,TGS}$, ID_C,AD_C, TGS, TS, nonce$\}K_{TGS}$,
User−Type$\}PK_{KDC_l}$

V : Version
kdcPublicValue : $\{A_I$, AP$\}$,
User−type : X.509V3 (DER encoding)
PGP (PGP specification)
PKIX (PKCS #6)
KDC-cert : Issuer
SerialNumber

(4) Local KDC transmits information encrypted with client's secret key. This information contains session key of client and remote TGS, and ticket for

remote TGS.
KDC_l → KDC_c :
{Auth−Pack, V, A_I, User−type,
TGS, TS, nonce, $K_{C,TGS}$}K_C,
{$K_{C,TGS}$, ID_C, AD_C, TGS, TS, nonce}K_{TGS}

(5) A client sends authentication information encrypted with session key obtained from local KDC, to remote TGS and requests a ticket for server.
KDC_c → TGS_r :
KDC_ s, {$K_{C,TGS}$, ID_C,
AD_C, TGS, TS, nonce}K_{TGS},
{ID_C, AD_C, TS}$K_{C,TGS}$

(6) Remote TGS decrypts the received message with its secret key and finds out session key of client and itself. Then transmits message encrypted with this session key, which contains session key of client and server, and ticket for service.
TGS_r → KDC_c :
{$K_{C,S}$, KDC_s, TS, nonce}$K_{C,TGS}$,
{$K_{C,S}$, ID_C, AD_C, TS, KDC_s, nonce}K_S

(7) A client send this ticket and authentication information encrypted with session key.
KDC_c → KDC_s :
{$K_{C,S}$, ID_C, AD_C, TS, KDC_s, nonce}K_S
{ID_C, AD_C, TS}$K_{C,S}$

2.2 Analysis of the KerbInit_Authentication Algorithm

According to KerbInit_Authentication_Algorithm, authentication protocol is divided into three phases. The first phase consisting of (1) (4) steps in the Algorithm is for connecting two realms and then for receiving the ticket granting ticket(TGT) from remote KDC, the second composed of (5) (6) steps in the Algorithm for obtaining a service granting ticket from remote TGS, and the third for authentication between client and server. In the first phase, X.509 and DNS are employed in order for two KDCs to do mutual authentication. Local KDC and remote KDC communicate each other securely since they transmit information encrypted counterpart's public key. In step (4) local KDC sends to client the message encrypted with secret key of client. Therefore, the first phase are secure. The rest of two phases of the Algorithm should be also secure since it follows the mechanism an original Kerberos performs. Efficiency of this algorithm is now analyzed in terms of communication complexity. According to IETF protocol, a client communicates with remote KDC for requesting a ticket. However, our protocol skips this step since remote KDC has already transmitted information containing this ticket to local KDC in Step (3) of the Algorithm. Therefore, a new authentication mechanism decreases two communication steps even if degree of security is the same. Figure 4 shows that the algorithm presented by IETF and our method are compared.

3 Conclusion

Since Kerberos is originally designed on local area network, it accomplishes authentication process nicely in local realm, however, it doesn't offer services on remote realm. In order to solve this problem, integration of the X.509 authentication mechanism into Kerberos system for inter-realm services has been employed. The mechanism presented utilizes the two distinct key management systems - Kerberos based on symmetric cryptography, while X.509 based on asymmetric cryptography for authenticating inter-realm services. Efficiency of this algorithm has been analyzed in terms of communication complexity. Compared with IETF protocol, our authentication mechanism decreases two communication steps even if degree of security is the same.

Process	PKINIT Algorithm	KerbInit_Authentication Algorithm
Local KDC <=> Remote KDC	- Local KDC encrypts Local KDC's ID and Client's information with Remote KDC's public key and then transmits them to Remote KDC via PKINIT. - Remote KDC produces random value, which is able to authenticate Client and Realm KDC, and then transmits information including this value to Local KDC.	- Local KDC employs DNS to find out a location of Remote KDC and X.509 for mutual authentication. - Remote KDC transmits Remote TGS ticket and session key in order to communicate with Client and Remote TGS.
Local KDC <=> Local Client	- Local KDC decrypts information received from Remote KDC and then transmits Remote KDC's information and random value to Client.	- Local KDC decrypts information received from Remote KDC and then transmits Remote TGS ticket and session key to Client.
Local Client <=> Remote KDC	- Remote KDC checks whether or not the random value received from Client is the same as an original value, and then transmits TGS ticket and session key to Client, if correct.	- the step.
Local Client <=> Remote TGS	- Local Client requests a ticket for the service by using TGS ticket and session key obtained from Remote KDC.	- the same.

Fig. 4. Comparison of the two algorithms

References

1. RFC 1510, Public Key Cryptography for Initial Authentication in Kerberos, draft-ietf-cat-kerberos-pk-init-09.txt, IETF, 1999.
2. A.Dharmadhikari et al, SIM based WLAN Authentication for Open Platforms, Proc. of Conf. on Security and management, CSREA Press, pp. 99-104, 2003.

3. T. Parker, A Secure European System for application in a Multi-vendor Environment, Proc. of the 14th National Computer Security Conf., 1991.
4. A. Levi and M. Caglayan, An Efficient, Dynamic and Trust Preserving Public Key Infrastructure, IEEE Symposium on Security and Privacy, IEEE, pp. 203-214, 2000.
5. The Kerberos Network Authentication Service (V5) draft-ietf-krb-wg-kerberos-clarifications-04.txt, IETF, 2003.
6. K. Lee, The Authentication Mechanism using Kerberos on Digital Library , Proc. Korean Inst. Info. Secu. & Crypt., pp. 13-18, Apr. 1996.
7. M. Lee, Implementation of Real-time Wireless Remote Control System Based on Public Key Infrastructure, Korea Inst. Info. Secu. & Crypt., vol. 13, no. 3, pp. 71-80, June 2003.
8. DNS Security Introduction and Requirements draft-ietf-dnsext-dnssec-intro-05, IETF, 2003.
9. D. Comer, Computer Networks and Internets with Internet Applications, 3rd Edition, Prentice-Hall, 2001.

A Multi-agent Based Architecture for Network Attack Resistant System

Jian Li, Guo-yin Zhang, and Guo-chang Gu

College of Computer Science and Technology,
Harbin Engineering University,
Harbin 150001, P.R. China
Lijian@hrbeu.edu.cn

Abstract. Network Attack Resistant is a highlighted topic of network security research in recent years, it offers real-time protection to systems and is considered as the second important method in network security defense beside firewall. But the existing intrusion detection system architectures have a number of problems that limit their scalability and efficiency. Firstly, this paper introduces the classification of network attack and the key technologies of IDS in the information security field, secondly discusses the agent technologies. On the basis of discussion, a multi-agent based architecture for network attack resistant system is proposed. This architecture can be easily extended and maintained, supporting the network attack resistant system. In addition, it can greatly enhance the whole system efficiency. Then we present the system implementation and experiments of the approach. Finally, we can draw the conclusion that this architecture has the advantage of intelligent attack detection capability and better scalability, and future work is discussed.

1 Introduction

With the rapid development of computer and network technologies, new form attacks are emerging endlessly. Network attack resistant technologies should be studied in greater depth in order to ensure the security of network-based application systems.

Attack detection system forms the last line of defense against the attackers in the security architecture of a computer. Detecting intrusion in a distributed environment requires the components of IDS to spread across different network and gather and process information in different network localities. As a result, the security of these components itself becomes a great concern. Protecting these components is necessary for the proper functioning of the Distributed Intrusion Detection System.

Multi-agent technique is being increasingly used in a range of networking security applications. In this research we proposed an attack resistant architecture using multi-agent technique. We plan to develop multi-agent based internal component so that it could be incorporated into any network attack resistant system and provide attack resistance capability. Developers could conveniently customize and extend the multi-agent architecture to their personal needs.

M. Li et al. (Eds.): GCC 2003, LNCS 3032, pp. 980–983, 2004.

2 Intrusion Detection and Agent Technologies in Network Security

Intrusion detection technology is an active security technology that can prevent the network components from being attacked by hackers. It cannot only help coping with external attacks but also detect the misuse of the legitimate users. Network attacks can be divided into three groups: attack on the lower layers of the network protocol stack, host-based attacks, and attacks on network applications layer. Many kinds of techniques can be found in the current research of intrusion detection.

Many detection approaches can be found in the current research of intrusion detection. They are Expert Systems, Artificial Neural Network, State Transition Analysis, Classification and Clustering Statistical Measures, Genetic Algorithm, Colored Petri-Net, Computer Immunity, Bayesian Network, Fuzzy Logic, Hidden Markov Model, Pattern Matching and so on.

There are some common problems in the current studies of intrusion detection, which are reflected on the unstable performance. The main measures of the performance of intrusion detection are the false alarm rate and hit rate. The performance is only good when the hit rate is high and the false alarm rate is low. Many techniques can only give a good performance on the data including known intrusions, or on the data in which the intrusion and normal sessions are clearly separated. When they work in a real world environment, their performances degrade.

Agent-based detection systems are based on a set of agents hosted on distributed machines, which monitor separately, communicate and cooperate with each other. The agent can be extremely simple or complex. The agent can be anomaly-based or signature-based. Then the unified system is a hybrid one. The advantage of this approach arises automatically from its design structure. It is capable of detecting attacks spanning in time domain and space domain. The system has scalability to detect general attacks or a specific attack. Nonetheless, it is difficult to design the cooperation mechanism. The failing of one agent will make the whole detection system untrustworthy.

This network attack resistant system using the agent technology has several advantages. They can be added or removed from the system without altering other system components. This is because they are running independently. The agents can be reconfigured or upgraded to newer versions without disturbing the rest of the system as long as their external interface remains the same. An agent may be a member of a group of agents that perform different simple functions, but the agent can exchange information and derive more complex results than any one of them may be able to obtain on their own.

3 System Design

We present a multi-agent based architecture for network attack resistant system. The model makes use of the following layers: 1)Data Cleaning and Formatting, 2)Data Gathering, Base Classification, and Basic Data Mining, 3)Mediators, 4)Data Fusion and Data Mining, 5)Database, 6)User Interface and Feedback.

This module and extensible approach to building a system helps solve the complex problems in an attack resistant system. It divides the problem into the problem of information retrieval, classification, collaboration, and compilation. Agent has been developed for this system that retrieve information from distributed systems, classifies the data and stores the data in a database.

At the bottom of the tiered architecture, the system log routers and system activity agents read log files and monitor the operation of the system. The routers feed into the distributed data cleaning agents which previously registered their interest in particular events. Targeted data cleaning agents process data obtained from the routers and activity agents. They render the data into common data formats.

In the middle of the architecture, the low level, mobile agents form the first line of attack detection. They periodically travel to each of their associated data cleaning agents, obtain the recently-gleaned information, and classify the data to determine whether singular intrusions have occurred.

The low level agents are managed by mediators which control the systems visited by the agents, obtain the classified data from the agents, and route the data into the local database and to the user interface. As the system is developed, the mediators will apply data mining algorithms to the data in the database to connect individual events into a cohesive view of the elements involved in an attack.

The architecture for this Multi-Agent based system has the following advantages: 1) The implementation of agent is efficient; 2) Layered system is easy be designed and modified; 3) It provides platform indecency.

As we further build the system, multiple departmental-level systems can be monitored. Data ware housing can be used to combine the knowledge and data from the individual departments into an organization-wide view of attacks. The agent system is targeted to run at the departmental level of an organization. To provide enterprise-wide information about intrusions, the data from each departmental agent system will feed into a data warehouse. Because the data warehouse will provide a global view of the intrusion detection systems, it supports not only the identification of attacks but also helps administrators discover new attacks, makes system administrators find how attacks are mounted on their systems, and identifies weak points in the enterprise information systems.

4 System Implementation and Experiments

Our system was entirely designed using the Java language. The choice of Java was mainly due to the association between Aglets and Java (Aglet is a Java-based mobile agent). Windows platforms were used to run the Aglets servers. The Linux based machines were used to run the Network Intrusion Detection tool, and were responsible for monitoring functions.

For the purpose of testing and to generate some tangible results, we implemented a version of the Graph based Intrusion Detection system (GrIDS). The GrIDS generates different shapes of graphs for a period of time that is an indication of a large scale distributed attack. The nodes and the links of the graph represent the compromised machines and the connection between the machines respectively. The further propagation of the attack to other machines leads the way to the growth of the tree. This tree representation is then summarized to produce results that are compared with threshold values for an indication of an attack.

In our system the mobile agents, we used Aglets Software Development Kit (ASDK), for the development of Java based mobile agents, as its easy availability over the Internet. ASDK, developed by IBM, is a Java-based framework for implementing mobile agents. The Aglet runtime layer provides functionality for creating, dispatching and disposing a mobile agent. The leaf nodes of DIDS could have range of functionality varying from packet filtering to host based or network based intrusion detection. For our system we opted for Snort, we used it to detect any network wide port scans and log the details of the port scans. These alert logs are routinely sent as multicast transmissions to the agent for the generation of attack trees. We used Nmap to simulate a scanning attack.

We carried out a simulation of our system. We carried out a TCP connect port scan on sub networks using Nmap's TCP half-open (SYN) scan option for few open ports on the hosts of the subnet (21:ftp, 22:ssh, 23:telnet, 80:http, 111:sunrpc). A typical calculation may involve counting the number of machines and the ports that were scanned by the attacker and comparing it to see whether a predefined threshold has been reached.

5 Conclusions

In this paper, common network attacks are discussed. A survey on current intrusion detection systems is given, and the agent technology is briefly addressed. Based on the above knowledge, a multi-agent based architecture for network attack resistant system is proposed. This architecture has the advantage of intelligent attack detection capability and better scalability.

In the future works, we'll research on the intelligent method of attack detection to raise system's detection efficiency and reduce the rate of false negative alarm and false positive alarm. By using standard agent communication language, the intrusion detection system can be utilized in a large distributed environment. This modification would also provide a better framework for information sharing between agents and interoperability of various intrusion detection systems.

References

1. Gerhard Weiss.: Multi-agent System: A modern approach to distributed artificial intelligence. The MIT press, Cambridge (2000)
2. Lee, V., Stankovic, J.A., Son, S.H.: Intrusion detection in real-time database systems via time signatures. Proceedings of Sixth IEEE real time Technology and Applications Symposium (RTAS 2000) 124-133
3. Malkin, M., Wu, T., Boneh, D.: Building intrusion tolerant applications. Proceedings of DARPA Information Survivability Conference and Exposition (DISCEX 2000) 74-87

Design and Implementation of Data Mapping Engine Based on Multi-XML Documents[1]

Yu Wang[1], Liping Yu[2], Feng Jin[1], and Yunfa Hu[1]

[1]Department of Computer and Information Technology
Fudan University, Shanghai, 200433, P.R.China
[2]Department of Computer Science
Wuhan University, Wuhan, 430061, P.R.China
leowangyu@263.net, fishylp@163.net, wosjf@etang.com,
yufahu@fudan.edu.cn

Abstract. How to describe the data mapping relations between multi-XML documents and automatically achieve mapping operation is one of the key problems of the web based XML data exchange platform. An engine of data mapping based on multi-XML documents, named MXDME, is designed and realized in this paper, which is the key part of the e-Government Interoperability Platform and has been turned into operation in Shanghai.

1 Introduction

More and more integration platforms for the heterogeneous system have resorted to XML as the solution to store ,exchange and distribute information[1]. The XML-based heterogeneous system have strong attributes of opening and extensibility .The XML-based heterogeneous system generally need to perform some data mapping operations, such as converting source XML documents to the destination XML document. How to describe the data mapping relation between source xml documents and the destination xml document and automatically achieve XML-based data mapping operation is one of the key problems. At present, the XSLT [2] is used to conduct the format converting of xml documents by some system such as the XML data exchanging middle-ware BizTalk of Microsoft [3]. But there exists some problems such as the complexity of XSLT grammar and the lacking of visualized modeling tool. Aiming at these problems in XSLT, we design and implement a Multi-XML Documents Mapping Engine, which is the key part of the e-Government Interoperability Platform and has been turned into operation in Shanghai.

[1] This paper is funded by China National 863 High-Tech Projects (No. 2002AA1Z6707).

M. Li et al. (Eds.): GCC 2003, LNCS 3032, pp. 984–987, 2004.

2 The Architecture of MXDEM

Figure 1 illustrates the Architecture of MXDEM.

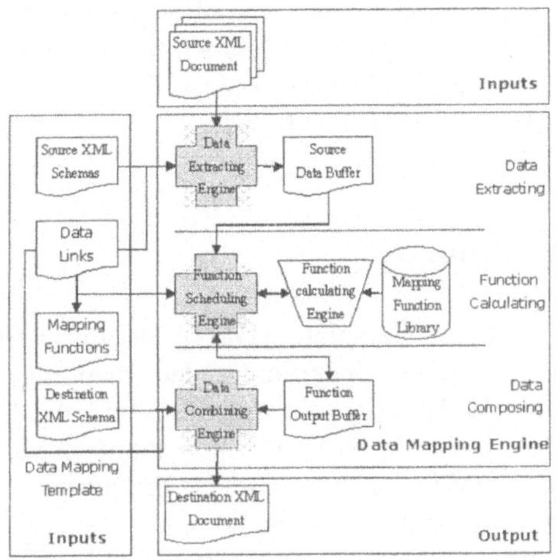

Fig. 1. The Architecture of MXDME

As indicated in figure 1, the Data Extracting Engine (DEE), the Function Scheduling Engine (FSE) and the Data Combining Engine (DCE) are in corres-pondence to the three sub-stages in the data mapping operation. Source Data Buffer (SDB) is used to store the middle results extracted from the source XML documents by DEE, and the results will be offered to FSE as parameters in function calculating. FCE is responsible for operating mapping function compiled by OOP and returning the results to FSE. The outputs of mapping functions are stored in the FOB. These outputs will be used as inputs for other mapping functions by FSE repeatedly. In the MXDEM, an integrated data mapping operation is divided into three stages.

1. Data Extracting. According to the source schemas and data links in DMT, MXDEM extracts the data required by the data mapping operation from source xml documents and stores them in the SDB.
2. Function Calculating. After data extraction, MXDEM calculates each mapping function in this mapping operation one by one.
3. Data Composing. After all mapping functions are calculated, the outputs of mapping functions got in the last stage will be composed to the destination xml document by MXDEM.

3 Mapping Function

A mapping function is a basic calculating unit of MXDEM. An complete data mapping operation in MXDEM is decomposed into a couple of combinations of calculation of mapping functions , with each mapping function performing a single basic data mapping operation, such as Sum ,Average, AddAttribut or DeleteAttribute.

While calculating mapping functions, MXDEM needs to extract relevant information about mapping functions from two respects: mapping function template (MFT) and mapping function instance (MFI).MFT is a standard XML document, storing basic meta-information about mapping functions such as the types and number of input parameters of the mapping functions, the type of output parameter, source code of the mapping functions, etc. MFI keeps the instance information of the mapping function such as its name and coordinate position in the visualized designing tool. The information in MFI will be kept in DMT as sub nodes.

4 Data Mapping Template

MXDEM uses data mapping template (DMT) as the unit to store the meta-information of the dada mapping operation. a data mapping template is a standard XML file, corresponding to data mapping operation one at a time. When performing data mapping, MXDME firstly loads DMT, then source XML documents and mapping functions defined in DMT, and then conducts the successor operation.

DMT consists of the following four parts:

1. Source XML Schemas. This part defines the Schemas of the source XML documents. Different form XSLT, which can have only one source xml document, a DMT can define a couple of source XML documents.
2. Destination XML Schema. This part defines Schema of the destination XML document. There is only one destination XML Schema for each DMT.
3. Data Links. This part defines, in the course of data mapping, the beginning /ending nodes and the type of the data flow.
4. Mapping Functions. This part defines the mapping functions to be calculated in the data mapping operation.

5 Conclusion

How to describe the data mapping relations between multi-XML documents and automatically achieve them is one of the key problems of the heterogeneous integration system based on XML. In this paper, an engine of data mapping based on multi-XML documents, which names MXDME, is designed and implemented. MXDEM has the following outstanding advantages compared with XSLT.

1. Promote the developing efficiency. Through visualized DMT designing tools, users just need to draw and lay mapping functions and set parameters such as data links to built DMT quickly .In compare with the heavy coding of XSLT using complicated grammar, the designing efficiency gets promotion.
2. Strong extensibility. MXDEM can not only extract data from source XML documents, but also extract data from database through mapping functions. Users can even write some mapping functions to implement particular function of data mapping.

At present stage, the main mapping functions offered by MXDEM include string processing, mathematics calculating, accessing data from database, XML nodes processing etc. In our further work, we will continue to enrich mapping function templates in MXDEM and provide it with the function of remote data accessing based on multi-protocols.

References

1. W3C. Extensible Markup Language (XML) 1.0. http://www.w3.org/TR/ 1998/REC-XML - 9980210
2. W3C. XSL Transformations (XSLT) Version 1.0[EB/OL]. http://www.w3.org/TR/ 1999/ REC-xslt/ 1999
3. Microsoft. Information about BizTalk. http://www.microsoft.com/biztalk/

Research on the Methods of Search and Elimination in Covert Channels[1]

Chang-da Wang, Shiguang Ju, Dianchun Guo, Zhen Yang, and Wen-yi Zheng

School of Computer Science and Telecommunication Engineering, Jiangsu University, Zhenjiang, Jiangsu Province, China 212013
changda@21cn.com, jushig@ujs.edu.cn

Abstract. Covert channels can leak the confidential information under the supervision of security model, so its threat is serious. The working principle of covert channels was formalized and the least condition of its existence was also represented. Based on it, the taxonomy for the methods of search and elimination in covert channels was given. Furthermore, there are three prospect directions that can be used to search and eliminate covert channels were also discussed in this paper.

1 Introduction

In 1973, B.W. Lampson represented the concept of "covert channel" firstly. For a covert channel is a communication channel that it is neither designed nor intended to transfer information at all [1], so it can leak the confidential information under the supervision of security model. Generally, the type of covert channels can be classified as "storage channels" and "timing channels". Whether an external clock has been used is the flag to distinguish them [2].

Statistics show that most of Trojan programs were used covert channels to leak confidential information [3]. Though covert channels violate the security policy, it can pass the security model's monitor. So not as the violated invasions can be easily detected by administrators, covert channels cannot be detected automatically if it only depends on the inherent security mechanism.

In the first twenty years while covert channel was proposed, quite a few excellent researchers were attracted to research on it. They have proposed some effective methods for searching and eliminating covert channels against special environment. The following methods are influential in searching covert channels, there are *information-flow analysis*, *shared resource matrix*, *covert flow tree*, *non-interference analysis*, and *source code analysis*, etc. The following methods are influential in eliminating covert channels, there are *store and forward protocol*, *pump protocol*, *fuzzy time protocol* and *isolation protocol* etc.

---

[1] This work was supported by **National Natural Science Foundation of China** (No.60373069) and **Jiangsu Natural Science Foundation** (No.BK200204).

M. Li et al. (Eds.): GCC 2003, LNCS 3032, pp. 988–991, 2004.

2 The Working Principle of Covert Channels

According to present knowledge, covert channel's working principle is that by means of preconcerted code to modify the attributes of shared object and let the subject with lower security level to be aware of this change, then the subject with higher security level can transfer information under the supervision of security model, which violated the security policy of the system (Fig.1). Shared object in storage channels is non-time attribute source such as a file or variable etc, on the contrary, shared object in timing channels is the response time of system.

Axiom 1: Time is a kind of object in covert channels.

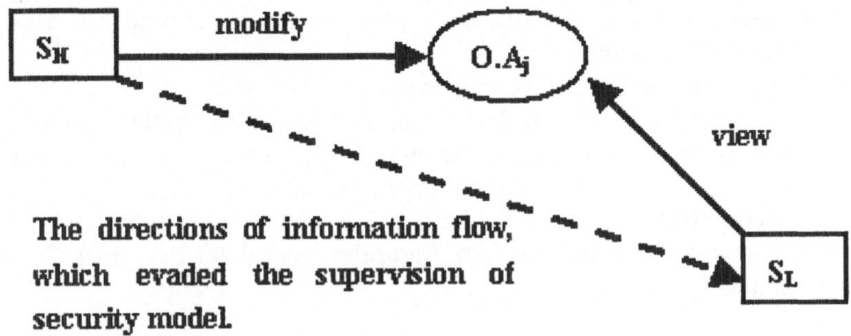

Fig. 1. The working principle of covert channels

It is worth pointing out that all of the operations and information flows denoted by solid-line arrowhead in Fig.1 were valid, but two valid operations lead to an invalid information flow as denoted by dotted-line arrowhead in Fig.1. Based on it, we can get the following conclusion.

Axiom 2: If there is a covert channel, it must be satisfied the following four conditions synchronously.

1) Sender and receiver subjects must be able to access the same attribute of shared object.

2) There is a method by which sender subject with higher security level can modify the shared attribute of object.

3) There is a method by which receiver subject with lower security level can detect this change.

4) Communication in right order between sender and receiver subjects must be ensured.

3 Taxonomy for Search and Elimination Methods

Under the frame of *Axiom 2*, we can classify the methods of search and elimination for covert channels intuitively as following.

- **Taxonomy for search methods**

1) Search the sender and receiver subjects in pairs

Shared resource matrix and *covert flow trees* proposed by Richard A. Kemmerer, etc belong to this kind of method.

2) Search the shared attributes of object

Non-interference analysis proposed by CHII-REN TSAI, etc and *source code analysis* proposed by C. R. Tsai, etc belong to this kind of method.

3) Check the directions of information flow

Information-flow analysis proposed by Jingsha He, etc belongs to this kind of method.

- **Taxonomy for elimination methods**

1) Eliminate the shared attributes of object

Isolation method proposed by P. M. Melliar-Smith, etc belongs to this method.

2) Break the synchronization between the sender and receiver subjects

Store and forward protocol proposed by Nick Ogurtsov, etc, *pump protocol* proposed by M. H. Kang, etc and *fuzzy time protocol* proposed by Wei-Ming Hu belong to this kind of method.

3) Restrict subject to send and/or receive

Under such taxonomy, we can know that all kinds of the search methods have an example. But as for the elimination methods, only *"restrict subject to send and/or receive"* has not an example. Based on it, we had represented an algorithm to eliminate covert channels by restrict both sender and receiver subjects. More details please refer to our paper named "An Algorithm Based on Processes Schedule for Covert Channels Elimination".

4 New Methods for Search and/or Eliminate Covert Channels

Nowadays, it is difficult for the methods of search and elimination in covert channels to make a progress while the frame defined by *Axiom 2* is becoming more and more mature. We believe that it's the exact reasons why the research on these methods has low its step in the past ten years, so it is necessary to introduce new methods in a more wide range when compared with *Axiom 2*. Now, the following three research directions have been adopt by our group.

1) Cut down the living space of covert channels to eliminate it

For covert channels can leak the confidential information under the supervision of security model, moreover its existence is also banned by security policy, so the living space of covert channels can be described as $SM \cap \overline{SP}$, here, SM and SP are the sets covered by security model and security policy respectively. So, for any covert channel CC_i in security system, $CC_i \in SM \cap \overline{SP}$ must be true, so $\bigcup_{i \in N} CC_i \subseteq SM \cap \overline{SP}$. As a result, if we can improve security model constantly so as to fully meet the security policy's request, i.e. under ideal circumstance, SM=SP, then $SM \cap \overline{SP} = \phi$, at this time, $\bigcup_{i \in N} CC_i \subseteq \Phi$, viz. $\bigcup_{i \in N} CC_i = \Phi$, thus, there must be no covert channels in the security system.

2) Use the probability theory to search covert channels

For security model can be looked as a finite state machine, so the main idea of this method is that we can conjecture the covert channels emerge by observe the sequence of event emerge if we mapped the covert channels to a event list. The bedrock of this method is *Bayes' Theorem.*

3) Use AI to search and/or eliminate covert channels

One the one hand, expert system was adopted. The characters of covert channels that had been known by man were stored into the database of an expert system firstly, after that it could be used as a basis to search and eliminate covert channels by roboticized tools. If some covert channels cannot be eliminated automatically, the roboticized tools will give a piece of advice to its user.

On the other hand, MAS (Multi-agent system) was adopted. For agent can be looked as an autonomous subject with belief, desire and intention, so each agent was designated a security level and embedded it in the security system, then these agents can be used to search covert channels and/or interfere the communications of covert channels by their collaboration.

5 Conclusions

The main contributions of this paper are as following. Firstly, the taxonomy for the methods of search and elimination in covert channels was given on the basis of *Axiom 2*. We were also concluded that only few problems needed to do further research under the frame of *Axiom 2*. Secondly, time was defined as a kind of object in covert channels, it was unified the research work of "storage channels" and "timing channels" at the level of working principle. Finally, three prospect directions can be used to search and/or eliminate covert channels were represented.

In this paper, the taxonomy for the methods of search and elimination is not absolutely, for some methods have mixed characters. According to TCSEC, searching and eliminating "storage channels" and "timing channels" in a security system are required to carry out at B2 and B3 level respectively, so under some circumstance, the collaboration between different methods of search and elimination are also needed.

References

1. B.W. Lampson.: A note on the confinement problem. CACM, October 1973, 16(10): 613-615
2. Paul A. Karger and John C. Wray.: Storage Channels in Disk Arm Optimization. IEEE 1991: 52-61
3. John McHugh.: Covert Channel Analysis: A Chapter of the Handbook for the Computer Security Certification of Trusted Systems. Portland State University, December 1995

Design and Performance of Firewall System Based on Embedded Computing

Yuan-ni Guo and Ren-fa Li

Computer and Communication Department
Hunan University, Changsha, China,410082

Abstract. Conventional firewall has failed to resist the attack from the inside network and distributed firewall excessively relies on the host operation system, therefore embedded firewall become the focus of the current network security research. The paper discusses the design and implementation of firewall system based on embedded computing. In addition, it presents architecture of embedded firewall, analyses the implementation mechanism of dynamic packet filter module and network address translation module in the embedded firewall system. Finally, it gives the performance testing results of the embedded firewall.

1 Introduction

With the rapid development of Internet, network security has become a key issue of recent research. Conventional firewall fails to resist the attack from inside the protected network, which is considered as the great danger in the network recently. Besides, it relies on the network topology and can not support the mobile hosts [1]. The host-based distributed firewall can provide a high degree security from the inside network, but it also falls short if it executes on an untrusted operation system and easily meets with the DoS attack [3]. Therefore, it calls for a hardware firewall system based on the embedded computing, which the breakdown of host operation system has no effect on the firewall system. Embedded firewall based on network interface card (NiC) can meet this requirement, but it has no support of embedded operation system and hence is restrained on the scheduling the multiple tasks, using the system resource and calling the system functions [2]. Consequently, the real time and correctness performance of the embedded firewall system can't be guaranteed.

This paper discusses the design and implementation of firewall system based on the embedded computing. The paper is organized as follows: Section 2 presents architecture of embedded firewall system, Section 3 analyses the implementation mechanism of dynamic packet filter module and network address translation (NAT) module in the embedded system. Finally, the performance testing result is included in Section 4 and the result shows that the embedded firewall system is sensitive to the transmission rate and the number of the rules.

M. Li et al. (Eds.): GCC 2003, LNCS 3032, pp. 992–995 2004.

2 Architecture of Embedded Firewall System

In order to assure the real time and security performance of the embedded firewall system, the paper presents Architecture of embedded firewall system based on embedded Linux, that is, we design our firewall software on the embedded operation system. The embedded firewall system is managed by the embedded Linux and we design the dynamic packet filter module and network address translation module in the network layer in the Linux kernel. The protected host by the embedded firewall directly sends the network socket packets to the embedded firewall system using system call. Then the packet is flowed back into the Internet after it is processed by the NAT and dynamic filter module loaded in the embedded firewall. Another interface of the firewall is connected to the policy management server in the network, which is in charge of creating and distributing the firewall policies to each embedded firewall system.

3 Design and Implementation of Embedded Linux Firewall System

Netfilter is the firewall framework inside Linux 2.4 kernel which enables to extend the new network property. Netfilter is a set of hooks inside the Linux 2.4 kernel's network stack which allows kernel modules to register callback functions called every time a network packet traverses one of those hooks [6]. The embedded firewall system in the paper wants to implement the network address translation (NAT) module and dynamic packet filter module in the Linux 2.4 kernel by making use of netfilter firewall framework.

3.1 Dynamic Packet Filter Module

Dynamic packet filter refers to check on the outgoing IP packets from a computer and then allow incoming packets to get through the packet filter if the packets are from the same computer as the outgoing packets were sent to [5]. It is a stateful packet filter according to the static packet filter. So as to implement dynamic packet filter, we should fulfill the connection tracking module in the Linux kernel first. Connection tracking refers to the ability to maintain state information about a connection in memory tables, such as source and destination IP address and port number pairs, protocol types, connection state and timeouts. Connection tracking module is registered at the four hooks in the netfilter framework except NF_IP_FORWARD hook.

After the module is achieved in the Linux kernel, we can make use of user space tool iptables to define our own firewall rulesets. After we design Statefule packet filter rules according to three different protocols (TCP, UCP, ICMP), the dynamic packet filter module is in a certain sense fulfilled. For example, for the three-way handshake of the TCP connection, my iptables rule is designed as follows:
iptables –A INPUT –p tcp –m state –state ESTABLISHED –j ACCEPT
iptables –A OUTPUT –p tcp –m state –state ESTABLISHED, NEW –j ACCEPT
Under such circumstances, the firewall can only accept new TCP packet combined with SYN flag and packets already included in the connection tracking table.

3.2 Network Address Translation Module

Network address translation would alter the source or destination of the packet as it passes through. Due to the limitation of the valid IP address, we can send packets with any source address we want and only replies to packets with one valid IP address assigned to you by using the NAT technology. Based on the previous implemented connection tracking module, NAT module registers at the three hooks: NF_IP_PRE_ROUTING, NF_IP_POST_ROUTING and NF_IP_LOCAL_OUT and translate three different protocols (TCP, UDP, ICMP) separately. When the module is finished in the kernel, we can also use iptables to perform SNAT , that is , allowing the private network (such as 192.168.1.0 subnet) to access the Internet after passing through the our embedded firewall.
iptables –t nat –A POSTROUTING –o eth0 –j SNAT –to 210.43.107.174

4 Performance of Embedded Firewall System

Most previous researchers have focused on analyzing the latency and throughput of router firewalls. Different from such approach, the paper focuses on studying the performance impact and sensitivity of the embedded firewall system [4]. In order to measure the performance, we designed such firewall performance test topology as shown in fig. 1 by using NetIQ Chariot network performance testing platform .

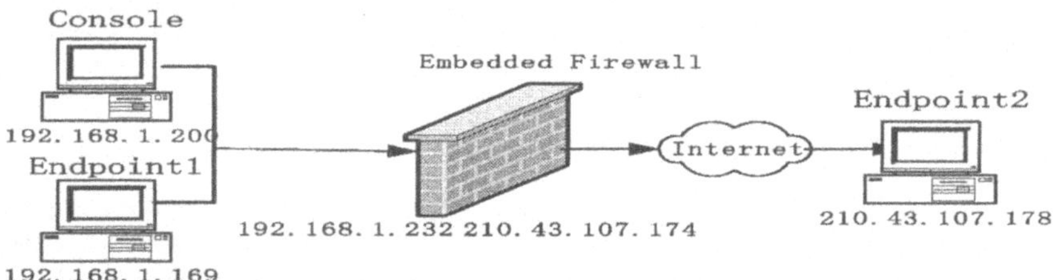

Fig. 1. The performance test topology of embedded firewall

After the embedded firewall fulfilled the dynamic packet filter and NAT functions, the private network (such as 192.168.1.0 subnet) is capable of accessing the Internet . In that the firewall is used NAT, in order to test the correct performance of the firewall, we should place console and endpoint1 both on the 'secure' side of the firewall.
The results of the performance tests demonstrate that the embedded firewall is sensitive to the transmission rate and the number of rules. The paper designs two different tests. The first test wants to find the relationship between throughput and response time under different transmission rates. The second test intends to discover how the number of rules can affect the throughput and response time of firewall.

As shown in Fig. 2, the response time of the embedded firewall decreases as the throughput increases for different transmission rates. Noticed in the Fig. 3, the response time of the embedded firewall increases as the number of the rules increase, but the throughput decreases as the number of rules increase. The change slope between response time and throughput is maximum from the 25 rules to 30 rules in the

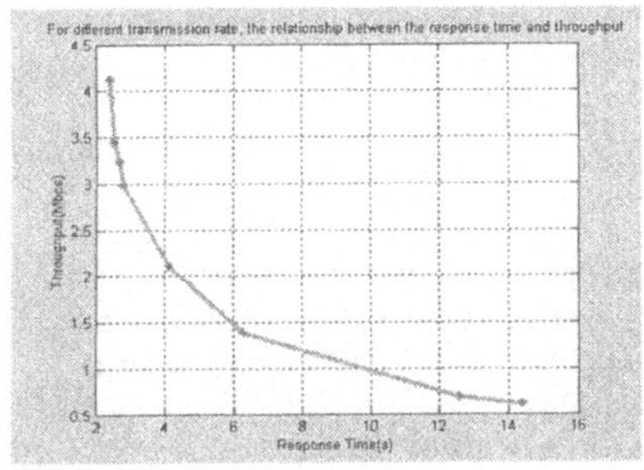

Fig. 2. For different rate, the relationship between the throughput and response time

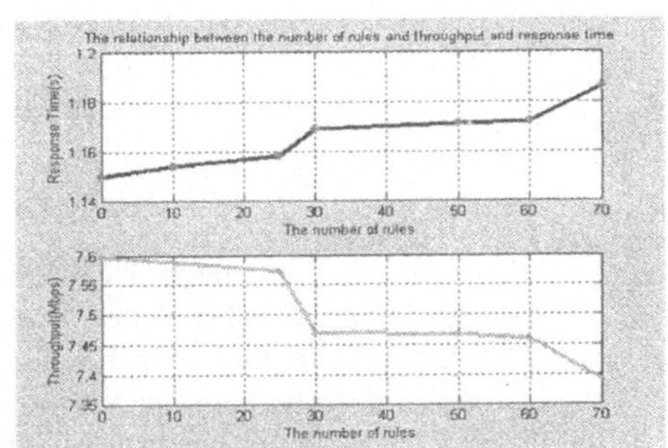

Fig. 3. The relationship between the number of rules and throughput and response time

fig. 3, while the slope changes more slowly in the rule interval [0,10] and [30,60]. However, for rule interval [0, 10], such limited number of rules is impossible to protect the network efficiently though it has obtained good firewall performance. But for interval [30, 60], good secure policy will compensate for the worse firewall performance. Consequently, the rule interval [25, 30] is the optimum number of rules, which can both protect network properly and afford better embedded firewall performance.

5 Conclusion

The paper arrives at a solution of embedded firewall system design and the performance test results explain that the firewall is sensitive to the transmission rate and the number of the rules. This work will lay a basis for future work of designing the policy server of the embedded firewall system.

References

[1] David Friedman. Building Firewalls with Intelligent Network Interface Cards May 2001
[2] Charles Payne. Architecture and Application for a Distributed Embedded Firewall 2001
[3] Steven M.Bellovin Distributed Firewalls July 1999
[4] James Harris Performance analysis of the Linux firewall in a host June 2002
[5] Heikki Julkumen Enhance Network Security with Dynamic Packet Filter 1998
[6] http://www.netfilter.org Netfilter How to

OGSA Security Authentication Services

Hongxia Xie and Fanrong Meng

College of Computer Science and Technology, China University of Mining And Technology
XuZhou, JiangSu 221008 P.R.China
{xiehx,mfr}@cumt.edu.cn

Abstract. Grid computing is concerned with the sharing and coordinated use of diverse resources in distributed "virtual organizations (VOs)." The dynamic and multi-institutional nature of these environments introduces challenging security issues that demand new technical approaches. This paper reflects the challenges and requirements we have identified thus far in an OGSA environment and we proposes a strategy for addressing security within the Open Grid Services Architecture (OGSA) and the OGSA Authentication Services based on the defined architecture.

1 Introduction

Research and development efforts within the Grid community have produced protocols, services, and tools that address the challenges arising when we seek to build scalable VOs. Security is one of the characteristics of an OGSA-compliant component. The basic requirements of an OGSA security model are that security mechanisms be pluggable and discoverable by a service requestor from a service description. This functionality then allows a service provider to choose from multiple distributed security architectures supported by multiple different vendors and to plug its preferred one(s) into the infrastructure supporting its Grid services [1]. OGSA security must be seamless from edge of network to application and data servers, and allow the federation of security mechanisms not only at intermediaries, but also on the platforms that host the services being accessed.

2 Grid Security Model

Industry efforts have rallied around Web services (WS) as an emerging architecture, which has the ability to deliver integrated, interoperable solutions. Ensuring the integrity, confidentiality and security of Web services through the application of a comprehensive security model is critical, both for organizations and their customers – which is the fundamental starting point for constructing VOs. The secure interoperability between VOs demands interoperable solutions using heterogeneous systems. The security of a Grid environment must take into account the security of various aspects involved in a Grid service invocation. This is depicted in the Table 1.

M. Li et al. (Eds.): GCC 2003, LNCS 3032, pp. 996–999, 2004.

Table 1. Components of Grid Security Model

Intrusion Detection	Secure Conversation	Credential and Identity Translation (Single Logon)	Access Control Enforcement	Audit & Non-repudiation		
Anti-virus Management	Service/End point Policy	Mapping Rules	Authorization Policy	Privacy Policy	Trust Model	Secure Logging
Policy Management (authorization privacy federation)	Policy Expression and Exchange					
Intrusion Detection	Bindings Security (Transport, protocol, message security)					
Intrusion Detection						

The set of bindings to be considered includes SOAP and IIOP bindings. The security of a binding is based the set of bindings to be considered includes SOAP and IIOP bindings. The security of a binding is based on the security characteristics of the associated protocol and message format. If new protocols or message formats are introduced, care should be taken to address security requirements in those bindings so that, at a minimum, suitable authentication, integrity, and confidentiality can be achieved [2].

Policy expression and exchange facilities will address the Grid security requirements to exchange policy between participating end points, securing the OGSI infrastructure and play a critical part to achieve secure association between the end points. The bindings and exchange layers discussed so far allow service requestor and service provider to discover one another's policy.

A service requester and a service provider are likely to exchange more messages and submit requests subsequent to an initial request. In order for messages to be securely exchanged, policy may require service requester and service provider to authenticate each other. In that case, a mechanism is required so that they can perform authentication and establish a security context. This security context can be used to protect exchange of subsequent messages.

A Grid environment consists of multiple trust and security domains. Operations between entities in different domains will typically require mutual authentication. However the assumption that all domains may share a global user registry is unrealistic. Hence when operations between entities cross real domain as well as VO boundaries, the identity of service requestors and providers, as well as their respective credentials as expressed in their home domain may not be syntactically or even semantically meaningful in their communication partner's domain [3]. Enabling interoperation will thus require "federating" the involved domains and their respective security mechanisms, for example a Kerberos and a PKI domain.

Policies required in the Grid security model also include authorization policies. Authorization is a key part of a security model and requires special mention. Each domain will typically have its own authorization service to make its own access decisions. In an Internet environment, authorization is typically associated with a service provider such that it controls access to a resource based on the identity of the service requestor [4]. Clients, or service requestors, typically trust the server, or service provider. In case they do not, service provider authentication through SSL is one mechanism to establish service requestor trust in the service provider. In a Grid environment, or even a B2B environment, more stringent rules apply from the service requestor's side. Service requestors evaluate their relationship with the service provider's environment prior to deciding whether to trust the service provider to handle the request.

Maintaining anonymity or the ability to withhold private information is important in certain service environments. Organizations creating, managing, and using Grid services will often need to state their privacy policies and require that incoming service requests make claims about the service provider's adherence to these policies. The WS-Privacy specification will describe a model for how a privacy language may be embedded into WS-Policy descriptions [5]. The Grid security model should adopt WS-Privacy in addition to WS-Policy to enforce privacy policies in a Grid environment.

The Grid trust model should be based on the web services WS-Trust specification. Importantly, due to the dynamic nature of Grids, trust relationships might also need to be established dynamically using trust proxies that act as intermediaries. Trust can be established and enforced based on trust policies defined either a-priori or dynamically.

The Grid security model explicitly calls for secure logging functionality as the necessary foundation for many higher-level audit-related services. Similar to trust model and security management, secure logging is a basic service that is applicable to other components in the model.

The Grid security model groups all security management functions applicable to various aspects of binding, policy and federation. These include key management for cryptographic functions, user registry management, authorization and privacy and trust policy management and management of mapping rules which enables federation. It may also include the management of intrusion detection, anti-virus services and assurance information enabling service requestors to discover what security mechanisms and assurances a hosting environment can offer.

3 OGSA Security Authentications and Management

OGSA must support multiple authentication mechanisms, including Public Key Infrastructure (PKI) and Kerberos. It will be desirable for OGSA implementations to support multiple mechanisms concurrently in order to support bridging of authentication domains. We want to enable OGSA implementations to work with different PKI variants. An OGSA implementation has to be able to adhere to local certificate path validation policies in order to function in environments where PKI systems are already deployed [6]. Kerberos uses its own message format and protocol for authentication and ticket requests. To facilitate the use of Kerberos in the OGSA context, we can wrap Kerberos protocol messages for authentication and ticket requests in OGSA WS protocols, so that client-to-Kerberos server communications use the same wire protocol, routing capabilities, and discovery mechanisms as client-to-PKI server communications. Certificate Validation Service Specification is one standard that may meet the listed goals for a Certificate Validation Service is XKMS. XKMS has the potential to bind attribute to Public Keys as well as to Kerberos principals [7]. OGSA-Kerberos Services Specifications defines OGSA services to enable the tunneling of Kerberos authentication protocols.

It is desirable from a deployment and management perspective that an authorization service be pluggable: i.e., that it can be integrated into applications via a well-defined interface.

A number of services will have authorization policy that can be managed by traditional site administrators and, particularly in the case of transient services, by users. It should be noted that in addition to emerging WS-Policy specifications there is an effort in the larger OGSA community on general policy management. Work on authorization policy management should build on this effort as much as possible and strive to provide feedback on any missing requirements. Grained Authorization Policy Management Specification defines mechanisms for managing coarse-grain authorization policy imposed by an OGSA service on a requestor.

4 Summaries

As Grid services are adopted and applied widely, awareness of the threats organizations face becomes better understood, the need for security architecture within OGSA grows clear. This paper reflects the challenges and requirements we have identified thus far in an OGSA environment. Based on those requirements, the proposed security architecture, by extending and leveraging existing security technology and assets, will enable businesses and organizations to more rapidly develop secure, interoperable Grid services.

References

1. The Security Architecture for Open Grid Services, http://www.ggf.org/ogsa-sec-wg
2. Foster, I., C. Kesselman, J. Nick, S. Tuecke, "The Physiology of the Grid: An Open Grid Services Architecture for Distributed Systems Integration," Open Grid Service Infrastructure WG, Global Grid Forum, June 22, 2002.
3. Simple Public Key Infrastructure, http://www.ietf.org/html.charters/spkicharter. html
4. Security in a Web Services World: A Proposed Architecture and Roadmap, http://www-106.ibm.com/developerworks/library/ws-secmap/
5. The Global Grid Forum, www.gridforum.org
6. Grid Service Specification, http://www.gridforum.org/ogsi-wg/
7. The Kerberos Network Authentication Service (V5), RFC 1510

Detecting Identification of a Remote Web Server via Its Behavioral Characteristics[1]

Ke-xin Yang and Jiu-bin Ju

College of Computer Science and Technology, Jilin University,
Changchun 130012, China
kexinyang@hotmail.com

Abstract. All successful cyber attacks begin with successful information gathering. Now more and more web servers no longer show their product tokens in the "Server" header field of the responses indiscreetly, and they want to protect the system information from reconnaissance by hiding their banners. Web servers have some unique characteristics because of different implementations and those characteristics can be used to detect the identification of remote web servers. Web behavioral characteristics are analyzed in this paper.

1 Introduction

Information gathering always plays an important role in wars. It is the same in the world of network security. In a cyber warfare at first the attackers usually cast about for the intelligence of the targets, such as the vendors and versions information about the operating systems and services running on them, so they can get everything ready beforehand and exploit the vulnerabilities efficiently to perform a precision bombing.

Now more and more web servers no longer show their product tokens in the "Server" header field of the responses indiscreetly. They want to give an obstacle in attackers' way by hiding their banners.

However that is not sufficient to protect the information. It is proved by our experiments that there still exist many clues that suggest a web server's vendor and version. Each kind of software has some unique characteristics because of different implementations. This paper describes how to obtain the evidence from web server's behavioral characteristics to discriminate it from others.

The rest of the paper is structured as follows: Section 2 describes the methodology we used, and Section 3 discusses some relative work. Finally we summarize our conclusions in Section 4.

[1] This work was supported by National Natural Science Foundation of China under Grant No.90204014

M. Li et al. (Eds.): GCC 2003, LNCS 3032, pp. 1000–1003, 2004.

2 Methodology

2.1 Active Observation

It seems that all kinds of web servers are identical to most people, but in fact each kind is special in its interior implementation. To collect these unique characteristics remotely, observing the behavior of the web server is a good approach. There are two methods we can use to observe a target. One is passive observation by observing the communications of a web server. It is based on sniffing traces from the target and its effect depends on its capability to deal with network throughput and its location to gather all traffic of the target. In general this method is difficult to glean enough characteristics to fingerprint accurately a web server. The other method is active observation by communicating with a web server using a purpose made client that can perform a more comprehensive search in a short time.

2.2 Discovering Behavioral Characteristics

The communications between a web server and a client is typically a client-server interaction. In this model, a web server awaits a request from a client, receives and interprets it, performs corresponding service, and returns the response. Each request is a stimulus and a response is its reaction. To fingerprint a web server, we need to generate ample stimuli to provoke enough responses for the analysis of behavioral characteristics. It should be noted that we do not want to show all behavioral characteristics in detail here, and only some of the more representative ones will be discussed.

These behavioral characteristics that can be provoked by the stimuli, i.e. the trail-made requests, can be grouped under three heads: compliant, stylistic and accessional.

2.2.1 Compliant

The characteristics are the symptoms of incompliance of web servers. Though HTTP specifications [1, 2] describe the criterions for compliance, there are still many incompliant implementations, even in the MUST level. Since a request generally includes two parts: request-line and headers, the compliant characteristics will be subdivided into two categories.

2.2.1.1 Compliance in Dealing with Request-Line

A request-line begins with a method token, followed by the Request-URI and the protocol version. Each element will be checked for the behavioral characteristics.

The Method

All the methods implemented must keep to the semantics specified in HTTP RFCs. Any incompliance in a server will conduct an abnormal behavior. For instance, the HEAD method is identical to GET except that the server must not return a message-body in the response, but Microsoft IISs violate it when there comes a HEAD request for a CGI script.

The Request-URI

The Request-URI is a Uniform Resource Identifier and identifies the resource upon which to apply the request. The absolute URI form is required in HTTP/1.1, but Apache/1.3.12 fails to recognize it and downgrades with response "HTTP/1.0 404 Not Found".

The protocol version

The protocol versioning policy is intended to allow the sender to indicate the format of a message and its capacity for understanding further HTTP communication. Right response to a client of HTTP/0.9 will not contain status-line and headers, but IISs do not keep to it when they receive a HTTP/0.9 request with a nonexistent URI. If a space follows the URI, Netscape-Enterprise/6.0 will get into trouble.

2.2.1.2 Compliance in Dealing with Headers

Some new headers were added in HTTP/1.1. For these headers can be combined freely, they can also be used as an ample source to identify a web server. For example, HTTP/1.1 allows a client to request that only part the response entity be included within the response using the Range header field. When the range cannot be satisfied, the web server should report error "416 Requested Range Not Satisfiable", but in fact a web server has different attitude for the same error. If a 10 bytes page is requested with header "Range: bytes=100-200", IIS/5.0 and Apache/2.0.46 will report error, while Apache/1.3.12 still serve the request and respond "200 OK". If the header is "Range: bytes=4-2", only Apache/2.0.46 can deal with it right.

2.2.2 Stylistic

The stylistic characteristics attribute to some factors such as design capability, programming skill, individual style, and so on. They do not affect the functions of web servers and just show the individuation of implementers [3].

Reason Phrase

The reason-phrase is intended to give a short textual description of the status-code for human users. They are often different among different web servers. For the status-code of "304", IISs explain as "Not Modified" whereas a Netscape-Enterprise explains as "Use local copy".

Headers

Most of stylistic characteristics hide in the headers. For example, the boundary of range in IIS/5.1 is in the format of "[lka9uw3et5vxybtp87ghq23dpu7djv84nhls9p]" and Netscape-Enterprise/6.0's is like "9052244116003". Furthermore, the items in the lists of "Public" header and "Allow" header order differently among web servers. An "Allow" header of Apache/2.0.46 is "GET, HEAD, POST, OPTIONS, TRACE" and the header in Netscape-Enterprise/6.0 is "HEAD, GET".

Message-body

The differences in the format of message bodies created automatically by web servers are easily distinguishable. These bodies usually are appended to the "3xx", "4xx" or "5xx" status-lines and written in HTML. These characteristics are very stable for web administrators seldom change these default messages and the "3xx" messages can't be changed unless the code was modified.

2.2.3 Accessional

To be friendlier, some servers usually provide some features that others do not have. For example, when an Apache server received an unknown method request, it will introduce its available methods to the client in an "Allow" list besides 501 error. Another example is to handle some known problems within browser implementations. Apache servers modify their normal HTTP response behavior when the "User-agent" field of a client matches a known browser such as "Mozilla/2".

3 Relative Work

HMAP is a program that can automatically fingerprint web server [4]. HMAP uses mainly some lexical and syntactic characteristics to identify a web server, but most of the characteristics can be changed in the same way of modifying the banner. HMAP depends on sending requests containing odd URL or very large URL to test web servers, that is harmful to the target and if the server arms with some security tools like URLchecker to hinder these URL, these methods will be useless. On the contrary, our method identifies web servers using normal HTTP requests and observes their difference in HTTP implementation to distinguish them.

4 Conclusion

Although security cannot depend on obscurity, information leaking is really a very serious problem. To protect a web server from being probed, we can use the knowledge mentioned above to detect some probing. Another tool, called URLchecker, we developed can find odd requests and normalize them, but it is still very difficult to defeat probing drastically for these test data are very similar to normal web traffic. Compliance in implementation is the root that brings so many behavioral characteristics and reveals so much security information.

References

1. R. Fielding, J. Gettys, J. C. Mogul, H. Frystyk, L. Masinter, P. Leach, and T. Berners-Lee. Hypertext Transfer Protocol - HTTP/1.1. RFC 2616, IETF, June 1999.
2. R. Fielding, J. Gettys, J. Mogul, H. Frystyk, and T. Berners-Lee. Hypertext Transfer Protocol - HTTP/1.1. RFC 2068, IETF, January 1997.
3. Ivan Krsul and Eugene Spafford. Authorship analysis: Identifying the author of a program. In Proceedings of the 18th National Information Systems Security Conference, pages 514–524. October 1995.
4. Dustin William Lee. HMAP: A Technique and Tool For Remote Identification of HTTP Servers, Master's thesis. http://seclab.cs.ucdavis.edu/papers/hmap-thesis.pdf

Access Control Architecture for Web Services

Shijin Yuan and Yunfa Hu

Department of Computer Information and Technology, Fudan University, Shanghai 200433, China
ysjysj1975@yahoo.com.cn, yfhu@fudan.edu.cn

Abstract. Efforts that solve problems regarding the access control for web services are just in their beginning. This paper proposes access control architecture for web services. Rather than basing access solely on the identity of a client the access control decision also takes into account the roles that the client currently holds. The access control architecture is able to discover dynamically what type of authorization is required to access a particular resource; can find all authorizations about a single resource by authorization indexing techniques and can perform the merge and override of multiple authorizations referred to the same object.

1 Introduction

WS-Security [1] is a solution to secure web services at the application level to implement integrity and confidentiality. However, efforts that solve problems regarding the access control for web services are just in their beginning[2]. We present access control architecture for web services based on WS-Security and the OASIS role based access control model [3].

The contributions of this paper are: (1) Rather than basing access solely on the identity of a client the decision also takes into account the roles that the client currently holds. (2) Proposes a set of formal definitions and notations of SOAP extensions for role. (3) Constructs the rational of access control decision maker.

The organization of this article is sketched as follows. We present access control architecture for web services. We then describe the access control decision maker and SOAP extension for role. Finally, we draw our conclusion and discuss a summary of additional work that remains to be undertaken.

2 Access Control Architecture

Fig.1. shows the procedure of securing web services invoke. All web services in a web service provider share a role entry and certificate validation. Every web service maintains a role policy, credential records, access control policy and has an access control decision maker that is essentially a web service method.

M. Li et al. (Eds.): GCC 2003, LNCS 3032, pp. 1004–1007, 2004.

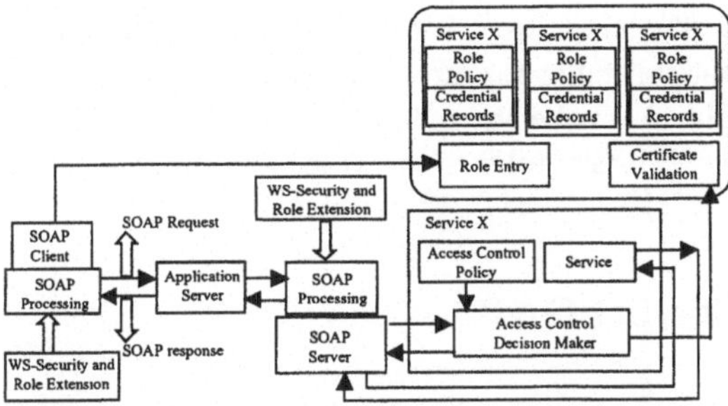

Fig. 1. Access control architecture for web services

Before invoking a web service, a client firstly must request entry to a role by presenting a web services server with the prerequisite credentials. If the server is satisfied it grants the client entry to the requested role by returning a role membership certificate (RMC) which may subsequently be presented to a web service as part of the invoke process.

When a client requests a web service object, he composites a SOAP message securing it by encryption and signature based on WS-Security. Moreover, he must add some role information to make access control for subsequent invoke. The application server listens on the message and hands the SOAP message to SOAP server. Before arriving at the SOAP server, the message is intercepted to process integrity and confidentiality by decryption and validation based on WS-Security. The client may be able to discover dynamically what type of authorization is required to access a particular resource because SOAP server firstly invokes access control decision maker when invoking any methods. According to the response of access control decision maker, SOAP server invokes the methods or not.

Among the component, role policy, role entry, auxiliary credentials, credential records and certificate validation are similar to [3]. Access control policy may be made by XACML[4].

3 Access Control Decision Maker

Every web service provides a method for making access control decision, which is access control decision maker. Every web method has an access control policy list. Access control decision maker has MethodName and AuthorizationList as parameters. MethodName is the URN of being invoked method. AuthorizationList is the list for authorization resources, which can be merged to a single parameter.

If a client of a web service want to invoke a method, SOAP server will first automatically invoke access control decision maker before invoking the method, passes two parameters (i.e. MethodName, AuthorizationList) to it along with RMC in SOAP request. Once the certificates and client have been verified access control decision maker uses the identity of the client, the certified role, any parameters included in the certificate and access control policy list to determine whether or not to grant the access requested. If authorized, it returns a response that indicates accepted, otherwise returns a response that contains what authorization information or credentials are needed to access that particular resource and SOAP response is sent back to the client. If the client has right to invoke the method, SOAP server will invoke the method. In the subsequent process, it is similar to the process without access control.

4 Role Extension in SOAP

We propose formal definitions and notations of SOAP extensions for role by add RolenameToken, BinaryRoleToken and RoleTokenReference sub-elements to security element in [1] that can be used when building secure web services to implement access control. The XML schemas for them are beyond the scope of this paper.

4.1 RolenameToken Element

<RolenameToken> proves a rolename and optional password information. The following is the syntax, attributes and elements of this element.

<RolenameToken Id="...">
    <Rolename>...</Username>
    <Password Type="...">...</Password>
</RolenameToken>

/RolenameToken: This element is used for sending basic role information.
/RolenameToken/@Id: A string label for this role token.
/RolenameToken/Rolename: This required element specifies the rolename of the requester.
/RolenameToken/Password: This optional element provides password information.
/RolenameToken/Password/@Type: This optional attribute specifies the type of password being provided including wsse:PasswordText and wsse:PasswordDigest.

4.2 Encoding Binary Role Tokens

The BinaryRoleToken element defines a role token that is binary encoded. The following is the syntax, attributes and elements.

<BinaryRoleToken Id=...
EncodingType=...
ValueType=.../>

/BinaryRoleToken: This element is used to include a binary-encoded Role token.

/BinaryRoleToken/@Id: An optional string label for this Role token.

/BinaryRoleToken/@ValueType: The ValueType attribute allows a qualified name that defines the value type and space of the encoded binary data including wsse:SPKI and wsse:RMC.

/BinaryRoleToken/@EncodingType: The EncodingType attribute is used to indicate the encoding format of the binary data including wsse:Base64Binary and wsse:HexBinary.

4.3 RoleTokenReference Element

The <RoleTokenReference> element provides an extensible mechanism for referencing Role tokens. The following is the syntax and elements of this element.

```
<RoleTokenReference Id="...">
  <Reference URI="..."/>
</RoleTokenReference>
```

/RoleTokenReference: This element provides a reference to a Role token.

/RoleTokenReference/@Id: A string label for this Role token reference.

/RoleTokenReference/Reference: This element is used to identify a URI location for locating a Role token.

/RoleTokenReference/Reference/@URI: This attribute specifies a URI for where to find a Role token.

5 Conclusion and Future Work

We introduced access control architecture for web services. The key of the proposed access control architecture is SOAP extension for role and access control decision maker. In our architecture, clients can automatically discovery authorization information about a resource; can find all authorizations about a single resource by authorization indexing techniques and solves the merge and override of multiple authorizations referred to the same object.

It will be interesting to develop a prototype and integrate it into a major web service implementation having implementing WS-Security. A single role-on is desirable because of service aggregation. It will be interesting to design a discovery protocol in which information can be safely revealed that clients can extract to foster automatic processing.

References

1. WS-Security. http://msdn.microsoft.com/library/default.asp?url=/library/en-us/dnglobspec/html/ws-security.asp. last accessed: 23/9/2003.
2. XACML http://www.oasis-open.org/committees/xacml/repository/oasis-xacml-1.0.pdf. last accessed: 23/9/2003.
3. John H. Hine, Walt Yao, Jean Bacon, and Ken Moody. An architecture for distributed OASIS services. In Middleware, volume LNCS 1795, pages 104--120. Springer-Verlag, 2000.

Formalizing Web Service and Modeling Web Service-Based System Based on Object Oriented Petri Net[1]

Xiaofeng Tao [1,2] and Changjun Jiang [1,2]

[1] Dept. of Computer Engineering & Technology,Tongji University, 200092, Shanghai, China
[2] Tongji Branch, National Engineering & Technology Center of High Performance Computer, 200092, Shanghai, China
taoxiaofeng@163.com
cjjiang@online.sh.cn

Abstract. Recently Web Service has become a hot spot. Its main idea is to integrate a group of services to construct new value-added Web Service-based systems, which run on the World-Wide-Web. It's necessary to get formalizing and modeling techniques and graphic tools for reliable Web Service and its application construction. In this paper, an approach to formalizing Web Service and modeling its application system based on Object Oriented Petri net (OOPN) is proposed. By means of this approach, a formal description of Web Service based on OOPN can be obtained, and control flow of Web Service-based system can be modeled. Furthermore, this approach is on the top of WSDL, so it's of practicality for application.

1 Introduction

To quickly develop Web Service-based distributed application, there is a need for a kind of technique to abstract, formalize, model, and analyze it at the design time. Presently Business Process Execution Language for Web Services (BPEL4WS) [3] is a complex procedural language for Web Service integration, which is based on the stack of WSDL, SOAP, and UDDI. However, it only describes the business process with a kind of XML-based document, and doesn't provide a formal validation.

In this paper, an approach based on OOPN is proposed for describing Web Service and modeling control flow of Web Service-based application. There are some good features in this approach. Firstly, this approach is on the stack of WSDL. Through the relationship between WSDL and OOPN, it's easy to describe Web Service based on OOPN. So it's valuable for engineering application. Secondly, because of the object-oriented conception, this approach can capture the necessary semantics of Web Serv-

[1] This work is support partially by projects of National 863 Plan (2002AA1Z2102A), Excellent Ph.D. Paper Author Foundation of China (199934), Foundation for University Key Teacher by the Ministry of Education, Shanghai Science & Technology Research Plan(03DZ15029,03JC14071).

M. Li et al. (Eds.): GCC 2003, LNCS 3032, pp. 1008–1011, 2004.

ice. Thirdly, the reliable control flow can be graphically model based on OOPN. Furthermore, the modeled system is based on formal description, so it can be easily analyzed.

The remainder of this paper is organized as follows. Some basic conceptions are presented in Section 2. Section 3 is devoted to the mapping relationship between Web Service and OOPN, as well as construction of a formal Web Service based on OOPN. Section 4 gives steps for modeling control flow of Web Service-based system. Section 5 discusses the analysis and verification of Web Service-based system. Section 6 provides some concluding remarks.

2 Basic Conception

2.1 Web Service

Considered components for describing Web Service in WSDL, without regard to the concrete protocol and property of Web Service, a formal definition of Web Service can be expressed as follows. Notablely,this definition is just used to describe its structure for modeling, not a complete definition.

Definition 1: a Web Service is a 6-tuple,WebService=(Message, Operation, Interface, Binding, Endpoint, Service) where Message is a finite set of messages, Operation is a finite set of operations, Interface is a set of {Operations, Message, F}where F is a relationship between Message and Operation, Binding is a function mapping a concrete protocol to an Interface,Endpoint is a function mapping a concrete endpoint to a bound Interface, Service is a set of endpoints.

2.2 OOPN

OOPN, a high level Petri net, is a kind of modeling language for engineering application, strictly defined by object-oriented conception. OOPN is made up of external object structure, internal object structure and control structure.

Definition 2[2]: an OOPN system is a 4-tuple,OOPNS=(O , G , P , F),where O is a finite set of object place nodes, G is a finite set of message-passing transition nodes, P is a finite set of message-synchronization place nodes, and F is a finite set of directed arcs.

Definition 3[2]: OOPN object is a 6-tuple, O= (Method, Status, Property, OM, IM, F) ,where Method is a finite set of method transition nodes that represent an subnet of OOPN, Status is a finite set of dynamic state place nodes, Property is a finite set of still state place nodes, IM is a finite set of input message place nodes, OM is a finite set of output message place nodes, F is a finite set of directed arcs.

3 Mapping Relationship between Web Service and OOPN

Since WSDL has been a standard of Web Service description, it's more significative to map the components of WSDL into the ones of OOPN for engineering. That's, the approach in this paper is on the top of WSDL (A in Figure 1 illustrates the protocol stack). In **Definition 1** and **Definition 3,** five mapping relations can be obtained as follows (all the proofs are omitted).

$$\exists \text{Message} \rightarrow \{\text{IM} \text{ , OM}\} \quad \text{(E1)}$$

$$\exists \text{Operation} \rightarrow \text{Method} \quad \text{(E2)}$$

$$\exists \text{Interface} \rightarrow \text{O} \quad \text{(E3)}$$

$$\exists F_{WS} \rightarrow F_{OOPN} \quad \text{(E4)}$$

$$\exists \text{Service} \rightarrow \{o\} \text{ where o is an instance set of OOPN object} \quad \text{(E5)}$$

Based on the above five mapping relationship expressions, some conclusion can be obtained as follows.

Definition 4: an OOPN-described Web Service is a 2-tuple, WS={O, o} where O is an Interface object, and o is an instance of the Interface object.

Theorem 1: an Interface in a formalizing Web Service described by OOPN is a sub object net of OOPN.

Theorem 2: a Service in a formalizing Web Service described by OOPN is a concrete instance of a sun object net.

4 Modeling Web Service-Based System

Once an OOPN description of Interface has been got from a WSDL document of Web Service by means of mapping relationship, then a service is just a concrete instance of this Interface. Thus, a group of services described by OOPN can be integrated into the control flow model of Web Service-based system by OOPN rules. B in Figure 1 illustrates the modeling step.

5 Web Service-Based System Analysis

Analyzing the behavioral feature of the control flow model can be used to verify the business logic of the Web Service-based system. For the convenience of analysis, it's necessary to reduce the complexity of the model into a behavior-equivalence modal based on general Petri net. As a matter of fact, a "Port" and an operation of a Web Service represent the same process in a system model, so a service subnet is redundant for the behavioral feature of a model. Pruning the service subnet, the old net can be changed into a general Petri net. With the help of reachable diagram, the business logic of the system can be verified, and in the meanwhile, the deadlock of the model can be checked. The detailed way to analyzing the model performance based on Petri net can be found in [5].

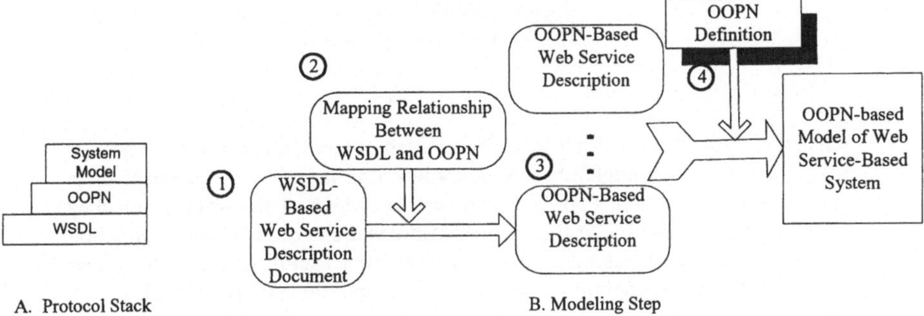

Fig. 1. (A) Illustration of the protocol stack of this approach, (B) Illustration of the modeling step of this approach

6 Conclusion

This paper has proposed an approach to formalizing Web Service and modeling control flow of Web Service-based system based on OOPN. By means of this approach, Web Service described by WSDL can be mapped into the one described by OOPN. And then the control flow of Web Service-based application system can be modeled by OOPN. Future work includes verifying the model and evaluating dynamic performance of the system.

References

1. Chinnici, R., Gudgin M., etc.: Web Services Description Language (WSDL) Version 1.2 Part 1: Core Language, http://www.w3.org/TR/wsdl12/#Service (2003)
2. Tao, X.F., Jiang,C.J., Duan J.T.: Construction of a Kind of Object-Oriented Petri Net and its Application, Mechanical Science and Technology, Vol. 22, No.5 (2003)
3. Andrews, T., Curbera, F., Dholakia, H., etc.: Specification: Business Process Execution Language for Web Services Version 1.1. http://www-106.ibm.com/developerworks/library/ws-bpel (2003)
4. Hamadi, R., Benatallah, B.: A Petri Net-based Model for Web Service Composition, In Proc. Fourteenth Australasian Database Conference (ADC2003) ,Vol. 17 (2003)
5. Tadao, M.: Petri Nets: Properties,Analysis and Applications, Proceeding of IEEE, Vol 77, No. 4 (1989) 541-560

Report about Middleware

Beibei Fan, Shisheng Zhu, and Peijun Lin

Department of Computer Science, Shantou University
515063 Shantou, China
g_bbfan@stu.edu.cn

Abstract. With the development of distributed computing, information needed by people spread throughout various applications in different platforms or is spread across networks. People would like to access all the information they need in a transparent and seamless way. Middleware could connect information to applications and customers in a consistent and useful manner. This paper discusses the history, definition, and category of middleware technology.

1 History of the Evolution of Separate Middleware Services

Some of the earliest conceptualizations of middleware originated with the distributed operating research of the late 1970s and early 1980s, and was further advanced by the I-WAY project at SC'95. The I-WAY linked high performance computers nationwide over high performance networks such that the resulting environment functioned as a single high performance environment. As a consequence of that experiment, the researchers involved re-emphasized the fact that effective high performance distributed computing required distributed common computing and networking resources, including libraries and utilities for resource discovery, scheduling and monitoring, process creation, communication and data transport.

Subsequent research and development through the Globus project of such middleware resources demonstrated that their capabilities for optimizing advanced application performance in distributed domains.

Stimulated by the growth of network-based applications, middleware technologies are taking an increasing importance. They cover a wide range of software systems, including distributed objects and components, message-oriented communication, and mobile application support.

2 Definition of Middleware

Middleware is a new layer between standard or COTS systems and enterprise applications, for networked computers in a distributed processing environment, to provide infrastructure, business-logic-services, data, etc.

M. Li et al. (Eds.): GCC 2003, LNCS 3032, pp. 1012–1016, 2004.

Middleware is used to facilitate communication between developers of both collaboration based and high-performance distributed computing applications and developers of the network infrastructure. Generally, in advanced networks, middleware consists of services and other resources located between both the `applications and the underlying packet forwarding and routing infrastructure.

Middleware is an unstructured, often orthogonal, collection of components (such as resources and services) that could be utilized either individually or in various subsets.

The definition of middleware was dependent on the subjective perspective of those trying to define it. Perhaps it was even dependent on when the question was asked, since the middleware of yesterday (e.g., Domain Name Service, Public Key Infrastructure, and Event Services) may become the fundamental network infrastructure of tomorrow.

Application environment users and programmers see everything below the API as middleware. Networking gurus see anything above IP as middleware. Those working on applications, tools, and mechanisms between these two extremes see it as somewhere between TCP and the API, with some even further classifying middleware into application-specific upper middleware, generic middle middleware, and resource-specific lower middleware. The point was made repeatedly that middleware often extends beyond the "network" into the compute, storage, and other resources that the network connects.

It's transparent to users but provide new capabilities, security, and privacy. It's more about hiding technology from the user than showing it, performing important functions seamlessly and invisibly. With this transparency, new applications can be enabled through simple use of powerful middleware groundwork, making both development and cooperation of new programs much easier.

3 Category of Middleware

Middleware may have components and services that only exist in the persistent infrastructure, but it will also have components that enable and support end-to-end (i.e. application to application or host to host) interaction across multiple autonomous administrative domains.

3.1 Utility-Oriented Middleware

A set of core persistent middleware services is required to support the development of a richer set of middleware services which can be aggregated or upon which applications will be based (e.g., an onion or layered model). This set of core middleware services will help applications leverage the services and capabilities of the underlying network infrastructure, along with enabling applications to adjust in changes to the network. The particular set of such services utilized by an application or process will be a function of the requirements of the application field or affinity group (e.g., network management or high energy physics applications) wishing to utilize the network or distributed data/computation infrastructure.

The basic and core middleware services, which include, but are not limited to: directories, name/address resolution services, security services (i.e., authentication, authorization, accounting, and access control), network management, network monitoring, time servers, and accounting.
As an example, Grid computing is a utility-oriented middleware. Grid computing is a distributed computing infrastructure for advanced science and engineering, distinguished from conventional distributed computing by its focus on large-scale resource sharing, innovative application, and, in some cases, high-performance orientation. Grid problem means flexible, secure, coordinated resource sharing among dynamic collections of individuals, institutions, and resources----what we refer to as virtual organizations. Grid Architecture identifies fundamental system components, specifies the purpose and function of these components, and indicates how these components interact with one another. It identifies and defines the protocols, services, APIs and SDKs.

3.2 Networking-Oriented Middleware

Below the core middleware services, at the boundary of the network layer, lie a number of services that are enabling infrastructure services upon which middleware will be built or which middleware may use and manage. It includes network level capabilities, such as multicast and Differentiated Services.

As an example, OMG's (Object Management Group) open, vendor-independent architecture and infrastructure that computer applications use to work together over networks---CORBA (Common Object Request Broker Architecture) is such a middleware. CORBA is an emerging open distributed object computing infrastructure being standardized by the OMG. CORBA automates common network programming tasks such as object registration, location, and activation; request demultiplexing; framing and error-handling; parameter marshalling and demarshalling; and operation dispatching. Using the standard protocol IIOP, a CORBA-based program from any vendor, on almost any computer, operating system, programming language, and network, can interoperate with a CORBA-based program from the same or another vendor, on almost any computer, operating system, programming language, and network. CORBA is useful in many situations. Because of the easy way that CORBA integrates machines from so many vendors, with sizes ranging from mainframes through minis and desktops to hand-helds and embedded systems, it is the middleware of choice for large (and even not-so-large) enterprises. One of its most important, as well most frequent, uses is in servers that must handle large number of clients, at high hit rates, with high reliability. CORBA works behind the scenes in the computer rooms of many of the world's largest websites; ones that you probably use every day. Specializations for scalability and fault-tolerance support these systems.

3.3 Application-Oriented Middleware

A second level of important middleware services, which builds upon these core set of services, may be called application-oriented middleware or upperware.

It may include accounting/billing, resource managers, single sign-on services, globally unique names, metadata servers, and locators.

This kind of middleware provides interfaces to a wide variety of applications. It might be a service that enables running a legacy system through a thin-client browser or a service that enables the execution of multiple application functions from an integrated user interface.

As an example, Java 2 Platform, Enterprise Edition (J2EE) is a set of coordinated specifications and practices that together enable solutions for developing, deploying, and managing multi-tier server-centric applications. It provides value by significantly reducing the cost and complexity of developing and deploying multi-tier solutions, resulting in services that can be rapidly deployed and easily enhanced. J2EE simplifies enterprise applications by basing them on standardized, modular components, by providing a complete set of services to those components, and by handling many details of application behavior automatically, without complex programming. As a single standard that can sit on top of a wide range of existing enterprise systems—database management systems, transaction monitors, naming and directory services, and more—J2EE breaks the barriers inherent between current enterprise systems. The unified J2EE standard wraps and embraces existing resources required by multi-tier applications with a unified, component-based application model. This enables the next generation of components, tools, systems, and applications for solving the strategic requirements of the enterprise.

3.4 Data-Oriented Middleware

Data-oriented middleware enables applications to communicate with one or more local or remote databases. It includes directory, metadata, and access services.

A directory may be described as a specialized database of lists. Directories serve a wide variety of functions in a computing environment and are used by applications including email, security, and naming services. Lightweight Directory Access Protocol enables extensible access to directories. Two additional related directory standards are: Domain Naming Services—a distributed directory service that may be used on the Internet, and Global Directory Service.

Metadata is all the descriptive information that lets us make sense of the data. Extensible Markup Language is a popular method for formatting data message exchange over the Internet.

Database access services include ODBC. It is often used to refer in a general way to a group of middleware database connectivity drivers and services. This method is commonly used for reporting programs to access application tables and for lookups in other databases or obtaining data to extract or import into another database.

References

1. RFC 2768. Network Policy and Services: A Report of a Workshop on Middleware
2. Middleware Architecture Report: "A Middleware Framework for Delivering Business Solutions". http://www.cots.state.va.us/ea/documents/MidArchApproved.doc
3. The Anatomy of the Grid. http://middleware.internet2.edu/

Grid Security Gateway on RADIUS and Packet Filter

Jing Cao and BingLiang Lou [1]

Computer and Communication School, Hohai University, JiangSu Province 210024, China
Cao Jing, wellindustry@sina.com

Abstract. RADIUS specified by RFC2865 and RFC2866 is used widely for remote dial-in user authentication and authorization. Packet filter such as Linux Netfilter is a primary toolkit to develop firewall or intrusion detection system. Modeling RADIUS client and packet filter together, a security gateway for grid computing is developed as an embedded or a proxy system. To reinforce the flexibility of the gateway, a negotiation process to select self-defined attributes of RADIUS between users and the gateway is discussed under public-key or multi-public-key encryption algorithm

1 Introduction

1.1 RADIUS

RADIUS [1](Remote Authentication Dial-in User Service) is introduced by Steve Willens and published by IETF in 1997. Now, its specifications are RFC2865 and RFC2866 in June, 2000.

RADIUS works on a Client/Server architecture. When NAS (Network Access Server) receives a connection request promoted by remote users and contained with username, password and other user information, it creates an Access-Request packet and sends it to RADIUS Server. The secret, which is shared by RADIUS server and client only and never send on the network, is put through a one-way MD5 hash algorithm with a 16 octet random number, which is called the Request Authenticator, to create a digest value. The digest is xored with the user password and then placed in the User-Password field of the request packet.

Once RADIU server receives an Access-Request packet, it tries to find a matched record indexed by the username in its user files or database, compute the MD5 digest the same as NAS, check whether the digest is equal to the User-Password field of the request packet or not. If it is true, the RADIUS server sends an Access-accept packet to its client. Otherwise, it sends an Access-reject one.

When NAS receives the accept packet, it establishes a link to Internet for the user according to the services type such as WWW and starts the monitor and audit process.

[1] This article is supported by The Science & Technology Funds of Hohai University

M. Li et al. (Eds.): GCC 2003, LNCS 3032, pp. 1017–1020, 2004.

1.2 Packet Filter

Packet filter such as Netfilter of Linux kernel 2.4 can be used to develop security gateway such as firewall or intrusion detection. It have five main hook modules as NF_IP_{PRE_ROUTING, POST_ROUTING, FORWARD, LOCAL_IN and LOCAL_OUT}. A lot of rules such as protocol type, IP address or port number of source or destination, have been defined for the filtering operation. The first hook module, PRE_ROUTING, checks the in-packets and decide weather to DROP, ACCEPT or QUEUE them on they satisfies the predefined rules or not. The accept packets will be forwarded to its destination by the FORWARD hook and the queued ones will be send to user space by LOCAL_IN waiting for further security check of user application process asynchronously. If the packets meet the further requirement, they will be LOCAL_OUT and POST_ROUTING to its destination. The rules defined in user space may be more complex than in kernel.

2 Grid Security Gateways on RADIUS and Packet Filter

Grid computing has received a considerable amount attention recently and is becoming available that allow businesses to utilize and reap the advantage of it [2].

Security is necessary to protect grid resources such as intelligent machine such as CT, database and so on from Internet attack. Sun ONE, .NET and Globus toolkit provide authentication, authorization, and confidentiality and other security services as components such as SSL/TLS, Public Key Infrastructure, Portal and so on.

In this section, a SGG(Security Grid Gateway) on RADIUS and packet filter is developed.

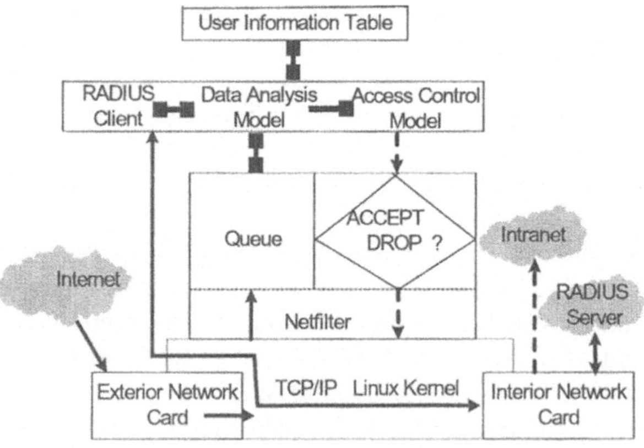

Fig. 1. Logic Architecture of SGG

The SGG may reside on a EMPU(Embedded Micro Processor Unit) or running on a personnel computer with three Ethernet interfaces connected to Internet, RADIUS server and Grid system respectively as user proxy similar to GSI(Grid Security Infrastructure)[3] of Globus.

2.1 Architecture of SGG on RADIUS and Netfilter

In Figure 1, there are three software components in user space. When the packet from LOCAL-IN comes, the ACM(Access Control Model) checks that user information out from the UIT (User Information Table). If the user is a new coming, RADIUS client creates an Access-Request packet and ask its server to authenticate and authorize for the user. If the user is a legitimate one, its authority will be written to user information table. When the user has its record in UIT and the packet acts within its authority, DAM(Data Analysis Model) with intelligence or fuzzy logic will do some statistic and analysis about the frequency user visiting the grid resource, the repeating probability of the same packet, confidential degree of the IP address and other assistant complicate security strategy from application logic to exclude attacks from internet. So, RAD(RADIUS client, Access control and Data analysis models) layer makes itself a kernel and Netfilter a toolkit of the SGG.

2.2 Flexibility of SGG

All transactions between RADIUS client and server depend on one kind of linked list whose elements are 3-tuples like "attribute, length, value". To insert a new attribute, it needs not any change to the software. If the operation system of the client and server supports file system and all attributes are stored in a dictionary file inserting one link to the list is enough. It is also convenient to configure the software and users by inserting, deleting and changing records in the user information file. So, RAD is flexible to do user authentication and configuration. RADIUS supports user self-defined attributes that value from 64 to 255. RAD also supports them and makes them stored in a dictionary the same as RADIUS server. By using of them, RAD is flexible to meet user's special security requirement. For example, if the Service-Type is specified as MDLC(MOTOROLA data link control protocol), WWW and other internet services will not allowed to pass through. Another flexibility of RAD is that the MD5 algorithm can be replaced with a new developed one.

3 Negotiations of Self-Defined Attributes

GRM(Global Resource Manager) is a trusted third partier in the grid system including KDC[4](Key Distributed Center), identity server, MDS [3](Metacomputing Directory Service)and so on.

Identity server, KDC and MDS are responsible for user account and confidential degree management, secret key distribution, online and dynamic resource management. MDS deals with grid resource such as data, computing ability, services and so on and provides searching, enrollment, query, update and other elementary operations [3].

3.1 Negotiations of Self-Defined Attributes

With a little change to the protocol proposed on by Woo and Lam[4], services provider selection and self-defined attribute negotiation can be implemented.

1. A→KDC: $ID_A || ID_B$; 2. KDC→A: $E_{KRauth}[ID_B || KU_b]$
3. A→B: $E_{KUb}[N_a || ID_A]$; 4. B→KDC: $ID_B || ID_A || E_{KUauth}[N_a]$
5. KDC→B: $E_{KRauth}[ID_A || KU_a] || E_{KUb}[E_{KRauth}[N_a || K_s || ID_B]]$
6. B→A: $E_{KUa}[E_{KRauth}[N_a || K_s || ID_B] || N_b || LSA]$
7. A→B: $E_{Ks}[N_b || LSA']$

Where ID*i*, N*i*, KU*i* and KR*i* are the identity, nonce, public key and private key of node *i*, E is the public encryption algorithm, LSA and SAL' are the list of self-defined attributes generated by RAD of B and negotiated or changed by A

3.2 Public- Multi-key Cryptography (PMKC)

An encryption scheme is unconditionally secure if the cipher text generated by the scheme does not contain enough information to determine uniquely the corresponding plaintext, no matter how much cipher text is available [4].

PMKC is a kind of public-key cryptography but its public and private keys may be two or more. If the PMKC is also unconditionally secure, the algorithm is called unconditionally secure PMKC; it also can be used to negotiate the self-defined attributes

5' KDC→B: $E_{KRauth}[ID_A || KU1'_a || KU2'_a]$
$|| E_{KUb}[E_{KRauth}[N_a || K_s || ID_B]]$

6' B→A: $E_{KU1'a}[E_{KRauth}[N_a || K_s || ID_B] || N_b || LSA]$

B→KDC: $E_{KUauth}[E_{KU2'a}[E_{KRauth}[N_a || K_s || ID_B] || N_b || LSA]]$

KDC →A: $E_{KU2'a}[E_{KRauth}[N_a || K_s || ID_B] || N_b || LSA]]$

Where $KU1'_a$ and $KU2'_a$ are the two PMKC public keys of A

References

1 RFC2138、RFC2139、RFC2865、RFC2866
2. Luis F.,Viktors B. et el, Introduction to Grid Computing with Globus, IBM Red Book, Dec. 2002
3. Ian Foster and Carl Kesselman, The Grid: Blueprint for a New Computing Infrastructure, 1998
4. William Stallings, Cryptography and Network Security: Principles and Practice 2nd ed.,Prentice-Hall,Inc

A Security Policy Implementation Model in Computational GRID[1]

Feng Li and Junzhou Luo

Department of Computer Science and Technology, Southeast University
Nanjing, 210096, P.R.China,
libaifeng@netease.com, jluo@seu.edu.cn

Abstract. This paper analyzes the necessity of building a security policy implementation model in the Computational GRID. By choosing and establishing the functional entity in the model, defining the mutual course, stipulating the warrants used in the mutual course, we finally put forward a feasible security policy implementation model.

1 Introduction

The goal of this paper is to set up such a security policy implementation model (SPIM for short) in a computational GRID environment. This process is similar to the responsibility assigning process in real society. We set up police force and the court to ensure the civil order and defend the law; we set up entrance guard to register the visitors, allocate power to the visitors according to registration result. Which entities should be responsible for implementing a certain kind of security policies? What is a secure mutual course? What should other entities in the GRID system do to help the implementation of security policies? In this paper, we will discuss these issues.

2 Design of the Implementation Model

A computational GRID is set up for the sharing of computational resources. This sharing is, necessarily, highly controlled, with resource providers and consumers defining clearly and carefully just what is shared, who is allowed to share, and the conditions under which sharing occurs[2]. A virtual organization has been defined as a dynamic collection of users and resources for one common purpose. Due to this definition, a VO can span several administrative domains.

Therefore we need to introduce a thought of multi-level management. We should separate VO's global security policies (GSP for short) and administrative domain's local security policies (LSP for short). This bears an analogy to the relationship between party constitutions and laws in reality. VO's global policies are just like party constitutions while administrative domain's local policies are like regional laws and regulations. We introduce the design of SPIM through following steps.

---

[1] This work is supported by National 973 Fundamental Research Program at China (G1998030402) and National Natural Science Foundation of China (90204009)

M. Li et al. (Eds.): GCC 2003, LNCS 3032, pp. 1021–1025, 2004.

2.1 Define the Ranges of the Global and Local Security Policies

The GSP generally two aspects: On one hand they may define which CA the VO believes in. On the other hand, some of the GSP should clarify how to allocate power to VO's members. LSP are policies about how to protect the security of the resources. Also, their contents generally cover two aspects.

2.2 Establish the Functional Entities

In real world, party constitutions and laws and regulations must be judged and executed by different bodies. Since in computational GRID, security policies are divided into two categories, we should assign policy implementation duty to two different kinds of entities. So at first, we plan to set up one functional entity per VO responsible for executing the VO's GSP. We call this VO's global security policies execution center ("GSPEC" for short)

Our SPIM choose to build at least one local security policies execution center (LSPEC for shoot) in every administrative domain, use this center to execute LSP uniformly. We can combine this centre with resource allocation server or the resource router. Resource allocation server or the resource router requires LSPEC to see whether the user satisfy LSP' requirements. The formulation and execution of the local security policies are relatively unanimous; the audit result of the resource host can be synthesized; users can know whether it is qualified to use corresponding resources at the time of inquiring or requiring resource allocation.

There is another kind of entity that is essential to realize our model: CA. CA is the source of our trust chain. No matter it is a GSPEC or a LSPEC, it authenticates the user or other entities based on its trust to the issuer CA. And as we introduce proxy mechanism from the thought of Globus Toolkits, we will finally have these entities:

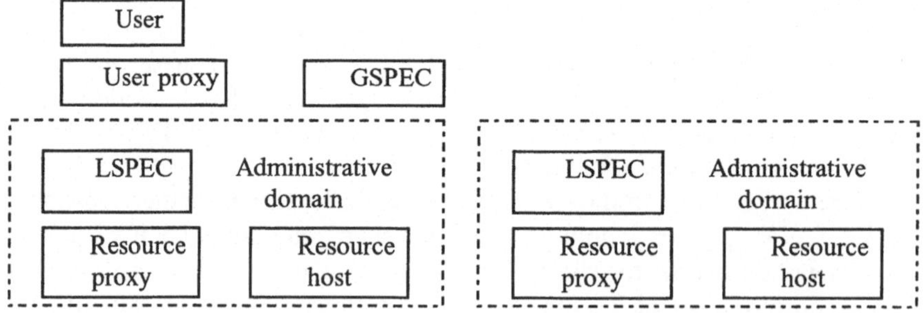

Fig. 1. Entities in the Security Policy Implementation Model

2.3 Mutual Course

Let us observe a mutual course :

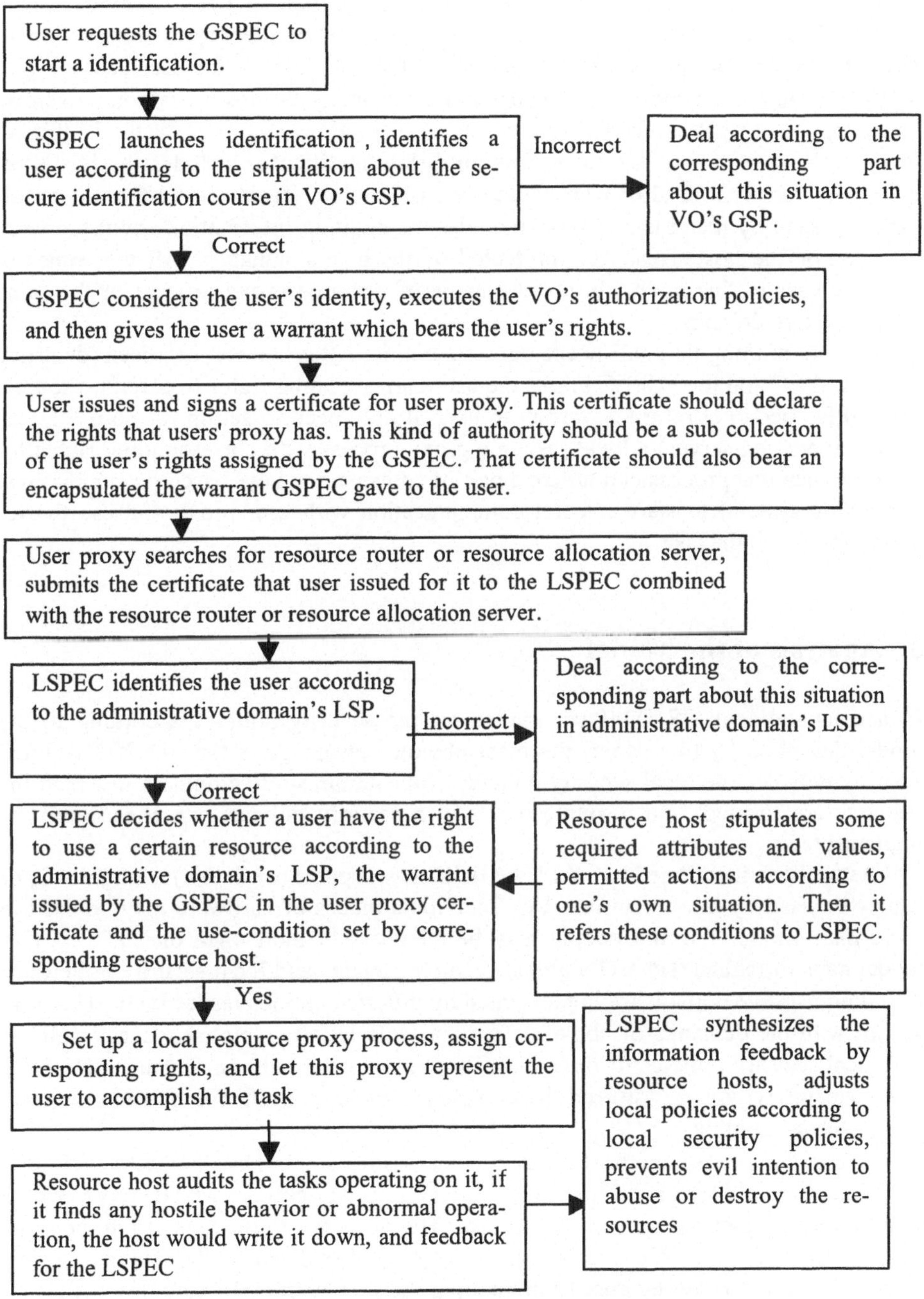

User requests the GSPEC to start a identification.

GSPEC launches identification , identifies a user according to the stipulation about the secure identification course in VO's GSP.

Incorrect

Deal according to the corresponding part about this situation in VO's GSP.

Correct

GSPEC considers the user's identity, executes the VO's authorization policies, and then gives the user a warrant which bears the user's rights.

User issues and signs a certificate for user proxy. This certificate should declare the rights that users' proxy has. This kind of authority should be a sub collection of the user's rights assigned by the GSPEC. That certificate should also bear an encapsulated the warrant GSPEC gave to the user.

User proxy searches for resource router or resource allocation server, submits the certificate that user issued for it to the LSPEC combined with the resource router or resource allocation server.

LSPEC identifies the user according to the administrative domain's LSP.

Incorrect

Deal according to the corresponding part about this situation in administrative domain's LSP

Correct

LSPEC decides whether a user have the right to use a certain resource according to the administrative domain's LSP, the warrant issued by the GSPEC in the user proxy certificate and the use-condition set by corresponding resource host.

Resource host stipulates some required attributes and values, permitted actions according to one's own situation. Then it refers these conditions to LSPEC.

Yes

Set up a local resource proxy process, assign corresponding rights, and let this proxy represent the user to accomplish the task

Resource host audits the tasks operating on it, if it finds any hostile behavior or abnormal operation, the host would write it down, and feedback for the LSPEC

LSPEC synthesizes the information feedback by resource hosts, adjusts local policies according to local security policies, prevents evil intention to abuse or destroy the resources

Fig. 2. A mutual course in the SPIM

2.4 Warrant Type

As we have showed above, in our model, we need several kinds of warrant to bring information between functional entities in the mutual course of a computational GRID system. They are: **Identity warrant**, entities prove their identity to others with it; **Global right certificate**, bears the rights that GSPEC assigns for user according to VO's GSP and user's identity; **User proxy certificate**, indicates proxy could exercise some appointed rights on behalf of the user, also could be a warrant for the LSPEC to identify the user proxy; **Resource use-condition certificate**, includes the host's requirements on what kind of user could use its resource; **Resource host audit result notice,** issued by the resource host, includes the auditing information about the tasks operated on the host's resource, protected by the host's signature. All the names of resource user in this audit file are the name of resource proxy process in the same administrative domain.

One more thing that still needs our attention is: After the user has been identified by the LSPEC and the LSPEC grants the user corresponding rights to certain resource, the LSPEC need not return a warrant to user. It only need to set up (or notify the resource allocation server) a local resource proxy process with corresponding rights for the user, then this process can utilize a pair of conversation key(based on symmetrical encryption system) to start a secret communication with user proxy and use the resources to finish the task.

3 Analysis of the Model

In a computational GRID, if we implement the security policies according to the model described by this paper, the most obvious advantage is that the VO's global security policies, the local security policies of the administrative domain in which the resource are located, and resource host's own security policies can consistently be implemented.

As we have mentioned before: " A GRID may support (or define) a single VO, or it may be used by more than one VO. Individual pieces of hardware may be used in more than one GRID, and people may be members of more than one VO [4]" Our model aims to realize that VO's global security policies and local security policies of the administrative domain are implemented by different entities respectively. This is in accord with the demands of above definition while let VO's global security policies and local security policies of the administrative domain could be formulated and revised separately, greatly lowered the complexity of the formulation and implementation of security policy.

In a mutual course, the host offering resources does not know the users' real identity. What he could see is just the name of resource proxy process which represents the user to use the resources to complete a task. The process and the host are in the same administrative domain. The user's real identity is only known by the resource proxy. This may prevent resource host from auditing the user with evil intent, protect user's privacy of normal behavior. But contemporarily, the model offers the resource host a way to prevent specific user from using its resource. The host could submit a resource use-condition certificate to the LSPEC which outlines limits on specific user's access to the resources.

4 Future Work

We plan future research activities in regard to our Security Policy Implementation Model, and here are some of them: First, we should improve this model considering the computational GRID's systematic operation efficiency. Secondly, as we have mentioned, the resource host would feedback its auditing information to the LSPEC, LSPEC synthesizes the information, adjusts the local security policies according to the result. We think this is an embryonic form of GRID IDS. After the attacks against the computational GRID appeared, we can analyze those attacks, define how the LSPEC synthesize the auditing information it received, adjust security policies according to certain rules and prevent the attack from recurring.

References

1. I.Foster, C.Kesselman, G.Tsudik, S.Tuecke, "A Security Architecture for Computational Grids", Proc.5th ACM Conference on Computer and Communication Security Conferece, 83-92, 1998
2. I.Foster, C.Kesselman, and S.Tuecke, "The Anatomy of the Grid: Enabling Scalable Virtual Organizations", www.globus.org/research/papers/anatomy.pdf , 2002
3. L.Pearlman,V.Welch,I.Foster,C.Kesselman,S.Tuecke, "A Community Authorization Service for Group Collaboration: Status and Future", http://www.globus.org/security/CAS/Papers/ CAS_update_CHEP_03-final.pdf , 2003
4. Mary R.Thompson, Doug Olson, Robert Cowles, Shawn Mullen, Mike Helm, "CA-based Trust Issues for Grid Authentication and Identity Delegation", http://www.gridforum.org/documents/GFD/GFD-I.17.pdf, 2003
5. S. S. Mudumbai, W. Johnston, M. R. Thompson, A. Essiari, G. Hoo, K. Jackson, "Akenti – A Distributed Access Control System", http://www-itg.lbl.gov/Akenti

An Approach of Building LinuxCluster-Based Grid Services

Yu Ce, Xiao Jian, and Sun Jizhou

IBM New Technology Center, Tianjin University, Tianjin 300072, P.R.China,
yuce@twtmail.tju.cn

Abstract. In the framework of Open Grid Service Architecture, this paper presents the design of LinuxCluster-Based Grid Services. Using Cluster System Management , General Parallel File System and openMosix, LinuxCluster-Based Grid Services have good performance. Then the paper introduces the Component model to Grid service, and builds Grid Component Service. Grid Component technology will greatly improve the reusability and transplantation of Grid applications.

Keywords: Linux Cluster, Grid Computing, Grid Component

1 Introduction

As a variation of distributed computing, Grid Computing is to organize the distributed computing power resources and make it appear as a single, open, virtual computing power resource, like the electric power Grid. Once a complete Grid Computing environment is constructed, we will be able to access infinity information, computing power and application resources, wherever we are. That is still a "Utopia", though, with the development of the related technologies, Grid Computing is getting more and more powerful and popular.[FO1][DU1]

A Cluster is a set of high performance computers connected with high speed networks and working as a single computing resource. "Linux Cluster" indicates a type of Cluster on which the operating system is Linux. For its high rate of performance/price, high scalability, open source and many other advantages, Linux Cluster is supported by more and more investors, governments, research departments, and the other organizations which need high performance computing. Our recently research focuses on the LinuxCluster-based Grid service architecture, which will be described in detail in the following sections.

2 Analysis on the Development of Grid Technology

Nowadays more and more applications require high performance computing. The vital limitation of the traditional high performance computing systems is that most of these systems are belong to only one organization respectively, thus the computing capability of each organization is finite, no matter what super computing systems it owns. Furthermore, the data information and other resources

M. Li et al. (Eds.): GCC 2003, LNCS 3032, pp. 1026–1029, 2004.

can't be shared. The emergence of Grid Computing technology makes all these changed. With Grid computing technology, we can integrate the entire network into an immense Super Computer, then, computing, storage, data, information, knowledge and other resources, can easily be shared.

The development of Grid Computing can be divided into three progressive stages, namely Data Grid, Computing Capability Grid and Application Grid. Most of current researches focus on Data Grid, and some others on Computing Capability Grid. To approach the final object: Application Grid, there are still a number of problems to be solved, such as architecture, resource management, security, task migration, load balancing, protocols, etc.

3 Build and Publish Grid Service on Linux Cluster

From the view of architecture there are two important types of Grid, one type is based on traditional layered architecture and the other type is base on OGSA (Open Grid Service Architecture). The layered architecture consists of a set of the protocols, while the kernel of OGSA is "Service".[DU1] OGSA itself can not bring us any "Grid", but only provides an "architecture". The actual Grid Services only exist in the Grid application implementations.

Our research is to design an architecture of LinuxCluster-Based Grid Service following the OGSA philosophy. The computing system of our architecture is a Linux Cluster, which can provide adequate computing capability. To implement Grid Services, we installed Globus Toolkits and MPICH-G on the Linux Cluster. Then based on the Linux Cluster and the Grid toolkits, we can implement the practical Grid Services.[RB1][W3C1] See Fig 1.

3.1 Build the Linux Cluster

Hardware architecture and configuration. A Linux Cluster has at least two types of nodes, namely managing nodes and computing nodes. If necessary, one or more storage nodes may be added to the Cluster. In our Linux Cluster, the managing node and computing nodes are IBM eServer xSeries 345 and 335 respectively, which are designed specially for building Linux Cluster.

We connected all the managing node and computing nodes with three separated networks, namely management, Cluster and computing network.

The management network consists of ISMP (Integrated Systems Management processor) on the main board of each node, RSA (Remote Supervise Adapter), Cabal Chain, Terminal Server and switch/VLAN. Via the management network, The managing node can get full control (such as power on/off or restart any computing node, get remote console, etc) of any computing node.

The Cluster network is a common ether network used to implement the Cluster software management, such as installing OS, Cluster middleware and application software, updating system and software, etc. It doesn't participate in the computing data exchanging between the computing nodes.

The computing network is a high speed network which is especially for massive data exchanging between the computing nodes.

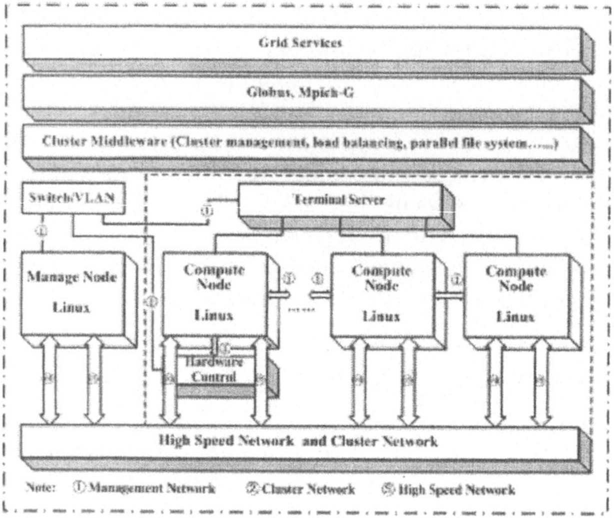

Fig. 1. LinuxCluster-Based Grid Service Architecture

Operating system and Cluster middleware. The operating system of the managing node and computing nodes is RedHat Linux 7.3. We use CSM (Cluster System Management) to manage the Cluster, use GPFS (General Parallel File System) as our parallel file system, use openMosix as the load balancer.[RB2]

With the help of CSM, almost all the Cluster management work can be done on the managing node, such as the installation of the OS and CSM, updating of the configuration files, system kernel, CSM client and other RPM software, alteration of power status of the computing nodes, etc.

GPFS provides file system services to support both parallel and serial applications. GPFS allows parallel applications simultaneously access to the same files, or different files, from any node in GPFS node group while managing a high level of control over all file system operations.

We use openMosix as the load balancer of the Cluster. Thus the Cluster can automatically balance the load between different nodes, then the Cluster itself tries to optimize utilization at any time. The nodes can join or leave the running Cluster without disruption of the service.

In this way, a high performance and automatic load balancing Cluster environment is built, and the next steps are building the Grid environment and implementing the Grid services.

3.2 Grid Tools

The Globus Toolkit is the virtual Grid platform, and it is an open source software toolkit used for building Grids.[GB1] In the LinuxCluster-Based Grid Service Architecture, Globus Core Tools are installed on each managing node. The managing node receives submitted Grid jobs, then with the help of CSM and openMosix, it assigns the actual computing jobs to the computing nodes, transparently. To get higher performance and security, Web Service application servers and certificate authority server run in separate sites, and the Web Service application servers provide interfaces for Grid users.

3.3 Grid Services

GT3 provides most core services, including security (GSI), remote job submission and control (GRAM), Reliable File Transfer (RFT), Replica Location Service (RLS) and consistent interfaces to system and service information (MDS). [GB1] OGSA and OGSI also provide a common framework for developing new Grid services. Some special Grid applications have been built up based on Globus Toolkit, such as SFExpress, Nimrod and MM5 etc.

Though provides many Grid services, GT3 is still under development. When the Grid application developers are building special application, they may find little reusable practical components. The LinuxCluster-Based Grid Service Architecture introduces a Grid Component service, providing Grid Component running and deploying environment. It combines closely with Globus core services. The Grid Component container is regarded as a resource of Grid platform. Just as other resources, it is under the charge of Globus resource management service, and as other popular containers, the Grid Component container also provides the life cycle management of Components. The Component location and discovery mechanism is implemented on the base of MDS service.

By introducing the Component technology into Grid platform, the architecture will greatly improve the reusability and transplantation of Grid applications. Moreover, transparent Component deployment and migration mechanism will increase Grid system's fault tolerance and load balance capability.

4 Future Work

We have been devoted to the research and development of Globus-based Grid Component technology for nearly one year, the coming work is to define Grid Component interface and Component container's specification, then develop a sample container and a user access gateway for further research.

References

[FO1] I. Foster, C. Kesselman: Marching Cubes: The Grid: Blueprint for a New Computing Infrastructure. Morgan Kaufmann (1998)

[RB1] IBM Redbooks: Enabling Applications for Grid Computing with Globus(2003)

[RB2] IBM Redbooks: Linux Clustering with CSM and GPFS(2002)

[DU1] Du Zhihui, Chen Yu, Liu Peng: Grid Computing. Beijin (2002)

[GB1] http://www.globus.org

[W3C1] w3c: Web Service Architecture. (2003)

Dynamic E-commerce Security Based on the Web Services

Gongxuan Zhang and Guowei Zuo

Computer Department of Science and Technology, Nanjing University of Science and Technology,China 20094
gongxuan@mail.njust.edu.cn

Abstract. Web service technology is a new technology for the Internet in recent years, and is extensively taken as the important technology in the next generation dynamic e-commerce. But the dynamic e-commerce's development speed is affected by itself security, that's the web service security. In this paper, the backgrounds and concepts of dynamic electronic commerce are introduced, and then its security is discussed. After that, the web service security protocol (WS-Security) is described with an example.

1 Introduction

Along with the technical development of Internet, electronic commerce (E-Commerce) based on Internet has been developed continuously. The web services technique, a kind of new technique of Internet has let E-Commerce make unprecedented development, and is extensively granted as the core technique of dynamic E-Commerces in the next generation [4]. The dynamic E-Commerce, In which services and requesters can discover each other, compared with the traditional E-Commerce, overcomes the latter's static and inflexible problems. Someone descended a simple concept to dynamic E-Commerces: Putting great emphasis on the B2B to constitute the next generation E-Commerce with the foundation facilities, to make the best benefit for a enterprise inner and outer computations by regulating Internet standard and facilities [2].

For Internet with the dynamic E-Commerce, business entities can communicate within them or trade partners. From discovering new partners to integrating other business entities, the dynamic E-Commerce emphasizes the exchanges among programs, but the earlier B2C did the exchanges between clients and programs [4].

2 Security of Dynamic E-commerce and Web Services

Up to now, there are many security protocols like SSL, SET, etc. SET, developed by Visa and MasterCard and used for bank safe credit card in Internet, primarily provides authentications for customers and banks, guarantees that Internet data deliver with

M. Li et al. (Eds.): GCC 2003, LNCS 3032, pp. 1030–1033, 2004.

safety, integrity, reliability and no-renouncement. It adopts public key system and X.509 digital certification standard, and is a typical application of PKI and has become an international trade security standard in Internet. SSL is an Internet security protocol established by Netscape. The security is a complicated problem in web services. SOAP (Simple Object Access Protocol) messages wrapped in HTTPS can be delivered by SSL and avoid being listened, and clients and servers can verify the identification each other. Though HTTPS mask the messages, it can't satisfy the Web services requirement of higher and special customers in security authentication. The followings are the possible problems of SOAP security requirement.

1. **End-to-End messaging:** SOAP messages can be bound with different transport protocols, and delivered in middlewares. If malicious damages happened in SOAP messages, the application can insert a series of elements into SOAP heads, and then pass them to next middleware, so received SOAP messages are quite different from the original ones. SSL can't guarantee the End-to-End messaging with safety.
2. **Middleware independence and Transport independence:** At the End-to-End messaging application layer, plaint texts are attacked when delivered, so the texts must be encrypted with encryption algorithms that receivers must understand. On the other hand, it is sophisticated and mistakable when safe messages are delivered between up-down two protocol layers. It is quite necessary to build a standard, safe, independent, transparent transport layer. The common way is to make appropriate safety expansion in SOAP for the middleware application layer independence.
3. **Permanent information security:** If the messages continue to deliver forward, it is very important to keep the permanent (stored) information safety. For instance, in E-Commerce, customers are usually asked to fill in the account number with the password, usually reserved in local COOKIE. Therefore the permanent information must be encrypted and realized with the SOAP safety expansion.

Web services security, as one of core techniques for a dynamic E-Commerce, has five aspects: Confidentiality, Authorization, Data integrity, Proof of Origin and Non-repudiation. The important problem is the safety of SOAP messages based on XML.

Web services are on-line applied businesses for enterprises, and others can access the businesses. Web services can be taken as a kind object component on websites, providing remote services invocation mechanism based on XML and SOAP protocol over Internet [3]. At first, the provider gives his services definitions and builds the module's interfaces by WSDL (Web Services Description Language), and publishes them on Internet. And then, the service requester invokes the remote procedures (web services) by names and parameters described in the WSDL document, the web services accept and execute the invocation, and return the results to the requester. SOAP has four parts: SOAP envelop that describes a framework with what the messages are, who sends them, who accepts them; SOAP encoding rules that are used for the data type instances; SOAP RPC representation that describes the agreements for the remote procedure call and return; SOAP binding that describes the lowest layer messages exchange agreements [3]. SOAP consists of the following elements:< Envelope>,< Header>,< body>, < Fault> and so on.

3 The WS-Security Standard and an Example

A current way is to lead security mechanisms on the message layer for the SSL security problems by expanding the SOAP message heads [1]. But there are not uniform standards for realizing the head expansion. For this reason, in 2002 April, IBM, Microsoft and Verisign Company, announced the WS- Security Standard, which provides three abilities to describe the SOAP messages expansions: The permission delivery, messages integrity and messages confidentiality. For the description of WS- Security later, the following signs are useful.

L[X]	The permission of Entity X
L[X→ Y]	The permission of communication between Entity X and Y
T[X]	The certification of Entity X
K[X]	The key of Entity X
{M}(E=x)	Encrypt Message m with key x
{M}(S= x && E= y)	Sign with key x, Encrypt Message M with key y
{M}(S=x&&E= y/ z)	Conjunction of {M}(S= x&& E= y) with { y}(E= z)

The most simple form of safe message communication can be described with which Message M1 is sent from Node A to Node B and Message M2 back as response;

A→B:{M1}(S=T[A]&&E=K[B])&& L[A];B→A:{M2}(S=T[B]&&E=K[A]) &&L[B]

Here is a simple example that the two permissions are based on public key.

1. Alice starts a safe conversation with Bob according to the following steps:

1) She uses the key K[B] from Bob's permission. With WS-Security standard, she signs message M while producing the message abstract and attaching the encrypted message abstract to message M. At the same time, she encrypts the message abstract with her certification T[A] and puts her key in her permission L[A].
2) And then, she encrypts the bodies of message M with WS-Security standard and attaches her permission to the message with the header of credentials. For reducing the cost of encryption, Alice can use a symmetry key K [X] to encrypt message M and then use K[B] to encrypt K[X], and attach it to the message

2. For Bob, the followings are what he needs to do when he received the message:

1) He checks the message by searching XML Encryption Tag. When finding the XML tag, he decrypts the message bodies with his own certification T[B]. Especially, he decrypts K[X] with T[B], and does the message with K[X] at the same time.
2) He checks the message by searching the message header, gets the key from the XML signature section, verifies the decrypted message with the header, and makes decision whether he should believe Alice's permission or not.

There are two solutions if Alice wants to make a private conversation with Bob and doesn't want to encrypt messages with the public key every time. One is that Alice produces a conversation key and passes it to Bob through the current channel. Another one is that she may create a new permission and publish it to the other members, so as to use the symmetry key based on the framework of WS-Security.

For the second solution, a new permission L[B→A] and a new certification T[B→A] is sent to Bob. For the symmetry key, all keys are K[B→A]. T[B→A] is signed with Alice's certification T[A] and encrypted with K[B]. When receiving the message, Bob can obtain this new certification, and then he signs and publishes the new permission L[A→B] to Alice. At the same time, Bob signs T[A→B] with his certification T[B] and encrypts T[A→B] with the received K[B→A]. In later messages, Alice will use the new permission L[A→B]. This process may be redefined as below in mathematics:

A. Exchange initialization

Alice→Bob:{M1}(S=T[A]&&E=K[X]/K[B])L[A]&&L[B→A]&&{T[B→A]}(S= T[A] &&E=K[B])

Bob→Alice:{M2}(S=T[B]&&E=K[B→A])&&L[B]&&L[B→A]&&L[A→B] &&{T[A→ B]}(S= T[B] && E= K[B→ A])

B. Succeed Exchange

Alice→ Bob: { M3}(S= T[A] &&E= K[A→ B]) && L[A] && L[A→ B]

Bob→ Alice: { M4}(S= T[B] &&E= K[B→ A]) && L[B] && L[B→ A]

4 Conclusion

Besides WS-Security, there are a few higher models such as WS- Policy, WS- Trust, and WS- Privacy. These are initial infrastructures for building safe, interoperable web services, and can construct higher infrastructures like WS- SecureConversation, WS-Federation and WS- Authorization [1]. So we have the reason to believe that dynamic E-Commerce based on Web Services will further be developed at great speed.

References

1. Weipeng Shi, Xiaohu Yang.: Web Services Security Base on SOAP Protocol. Application Research of Computers, Vol. 20. Chengdu (2003) 100-105
2. Hong Jiang, qingsong Yu.: Electronic Commerce Research Base on Web Service. Computer Engineering, Vol. 29. Shanghai (2003) 195-197.
3. Wenbin Zhang, Hongyun Ye, Sihong Chen.: B2B Electronic Commerce Environment Construction Based on Web Service. Computer Engineering, Vol. 28. Shanghai (2002) 67-71.
4. Jing Li. Web Services of Dynamic Electronic Commerce. TsingHua University Publishing House, Beijing (2002)

Standardization of Page Service Using XSLT Based on Grid System

Wanjun Zhang, Yi Zeng , Wei Dong, Guoqing Li, and Dingsheng Liu

China Remote Sensing Satellite Ground Station, China Academy of Science,
100086 Beijing China
wjzhang@ne.rsgs.ac.cn

Abstract. User interface can be used to display the result of grid computing [1]. How to provide a friendly user interface and make it visual and clear is crucial important in grid research. In our Spatial Information Grid (SIG)[1] research project, we integrate page registration and display together as Page Service. In this paper, we present an investigation of applying XSLT to standardize Page Service, which can improve the display technology of grid computing results and makes them more convenient to be used in practice. The paper focuses on the page transform and technological process. In the end, we show some test result of our research. The experiments software can be found at http://159.226.224.51/app.

1 Introduction

The main application areas of Grid Computing are scientific computing, business computing and information service [1]. However, they are always accompanied with tremendous data. Obviously, the data is hard for man to comprehend and not easy to use by human's work. If we can present the grid computing results by a friendly user interface with visual information, the way for grid users to understand and analysis data will be much smooth. So how to provide it and build the interaction dynamically becomes an essential problem. In our Spatial Information Grid (SIG) research project, we addresses this problem by using XSLT.

The latest architecture of the current grid system is Open Grid Service Architecture (OGSA) [2], which is based on Web Service technology. In many Web Service applications, eXtensible Markup Language (XML) [3] is widely used as a flexible text format to express data and information, and it also playing an increasingly important role in grid research. As its companion, the eXtensible Stylesheet Language for Transformations (XSLT) [4], which is a language for transforming XML, is widely implemented. When put through an XSLT processor, the information in the XML source document will be evaluated, rearranged, and then reassembled. The end product is

[1] Supported by the High Technology Research and Development 863 Program of China (No. 2002AA-13-10-50) and the main research was conducted by the Open Lab of China Remote Sensing Ground Station.

M. Li et al. (Eds.): GCC 2003, LNCS 3032, pp. 1034–1038, 2004.

flexible source information that can be easily added to, modified, or reordered. This course can definitely be designed in the user interface of grid systems, and becomes a part of standardization of page service.

Compared to general grid systems, the visualizing of data and image is a crucial important problem in spatial grid systems. Why they are credibly depended on display technology? Because users need to process the spatial data and image directly. In our SIG research project, we present the user interface by using Page Service, which integrates page registration and display together as a service. Even users are scattered in different locations, they can easily use web browser to access our grid system, which is interconnected by wide-area network. We integrate several templates to present all kinds of spatial information, such as metadata, remote sensing image, GIS information and so on. We employ some popular technologies such as XSLT and XML data flow to run the applications in SIG project.

This paper focus on how to applying XSLT to design the user interface, and the procedure of how the proposed method works.

2 Introduction to XSLT

XSLT is the most important part of the XSL Standard [5]. It is the part of XSL that is used to transform an XML document into another, or another type of document that is recognized by a browser. One such format is XHTML. Normally XSLT does this by transforming each XML element into an XHTML element. XSLT can also add new elements into the output file, or remove elements. It can rearrange or sort elements, test or make decisions about which element to display, and a lot more. A common way to describe the transformation process is to say that XSL uses XSLT to transform an XML source tree into an XML result tree.

In the transformation process, XSLT uses XPath to define parts of the source document that match one or more predefined templates. When a match is found, XSLT will transform the matching part of the source document into the result document. The parts of the source document that do not match a template will end up unmodified in the result document.

3 XSLT Templates Lib in SIG

XSLT templates lib is a set of display templates we designed in our SIG research project. The purpose is to make the spatial data or image visual and dynamic to load and store. In the following subsections we will describe some capability this lib can provide.

3.1 Be Compatible with GAPL[2] and GARE[3]

GAPL is a workflow language we defined in SIG project. It can connect the grid services by their logical relations based on workflow. However, when these services run, the complete course of an application should have user's participation, for example, users must input the data for some certain step, users have to check the mid-result to determine the next step. Therefore, some pages should be shown in user's browser. As a workflow language, GAPL not support JSP or HTML, but can be compatible with XSLT templates. GAPL combine data flow and page template together, and then transform as HTML or JSP, which can be shown out in browser.

3.2 Adapt to Middle Data Format

Currently, for large amount of spatial data, they are used metadata structure and XML format to describe. In out SIG project, the data transmitted between grid services are also XML format. The applying of XSLT template can change XML data flow to HTML pages directly. Moreover, this method considers the interaction of dissimilar data set, such as data set from different database servers.

3.3 Dynamical Extension

The method of using XSLT templates lib is convenient for the dynamical extension of user interface. If we promise the uniform of the XML format, these templates can reuse many times through the transmission course. Even if one template changes, it will not affect another. In this method, all the data visualization is depended on XSLT templates lib, so we conclude that this templates lib is the basis for the display of information.

4 Mechanism

According to the different locations to transform XML document, there are two mechanisms for XSLT templates' running. The first is to run at the client side. The script program is conducted on client browser and transform XML document to HTML document. The second way is to run at the server side. The server import the Java package, and call the scriptlets to process XML document.

Consider the last method in details, we found that the server side process the documents and templates firstly, and then send HTML stream to the client. This method

---

[2, 3] GAPL (Grid Application Programming Language), GARE (Grid Application Runtime Environment) is a language of grid workflow designed by the research team of the High Technology Research and Development 863 Program of "Key Technology of Spatial Information Grid".

has no relationship with the configuration of the browser, and what display to customers are common web pages. Based on these reason, we adopt the last mechanism in our project design.

5 Key Technology

We give some description of the work procedure in Fig 1.

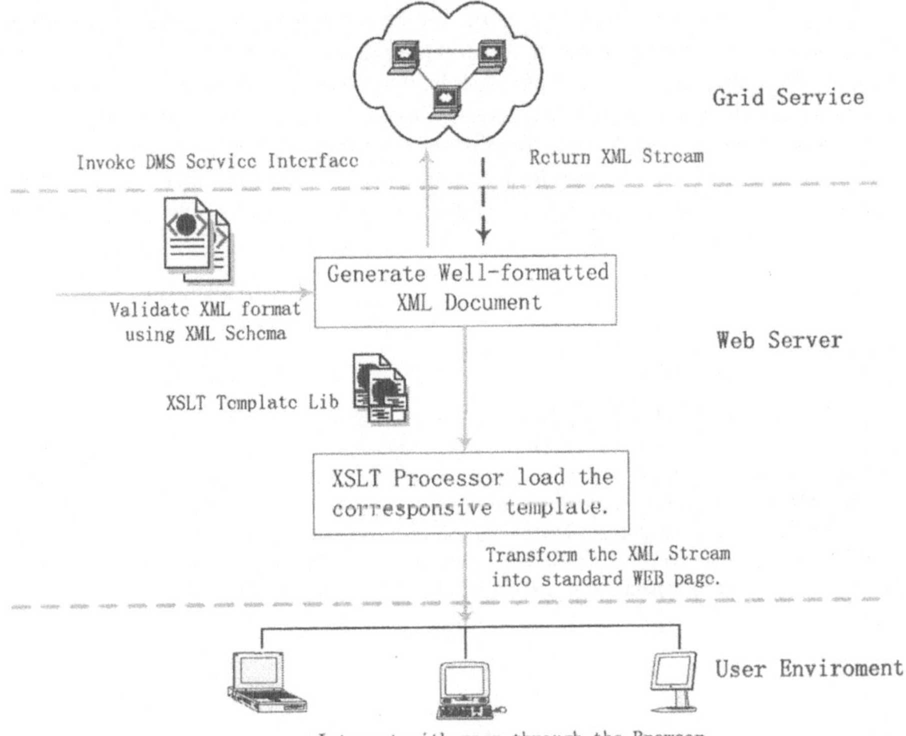

Fig. 1. The chart flow of page service by using XSLT

From the chart, we can see that users can view the data of the SIG by web browser and at the same time interact with the system. The page post the users' require parameter to the web server. At the server side, it load different XSLT template by the different format and requirement. Then users' requirements will be transformed to well-formatted XML stream. The page service will invoke the Interface of DMS[4] to get the result XML stream. The grid service of the SIG will process the requirement and return as a predefined XML data. This mechanism shows excellent capability of person-to-grid interaction.

[4] DMS (Data Mining Service) is a grid service designed by the research team of the High Technology Research and Development 863 Program of "Spatial Information Grid", which function is to manage and retrieve the spatial data and images.

6 Experiments and Conclusion

This paper studies the issue of display technology in grid computing environment, providing a mechanism of applying XSLT to standardize page service. We have conducted some experiments and tested the proposed mechanism. Our team developed a serials of templates, including data search template for users to input kinds of spatial data parameter, data list template to show result data users queried, metadata list template to present metadata information of remote sensing images, parameter input template for users to input parameter for computing, and remote sensing image display template to embed plug-in to show images. This XSLT templates lib has shown excellent standardization, rich interactions and dynamical extension capability.

Moreover, the proposed mechanism is not only for spatial grid systems, but can apply in the user interface of any grid systems. So we conclude that this investigation will improve the display technology of grid computing results and makes them more convenient to be used in practice.

References

1. Du Zhihui, Chen Yu, Liu Peng: Grid Computing. Tsinghua University Press (2002) 8–11
2. Ian Foster, Carl Kesselman, Jeffrey M Nick, Steven Tuecke: The physiology of the grid, an Open Grid Services Architecture for Distributed Systems Integration. At: http://www.globus.org/research/papers
3. Extensible Markup Language (XML): At: http://www.w3c.org/xml
4. XSL Transformations (XSLT): At: http://www.w3.org/TR/xslt
5. The Extensible Stylesheet Language Family (XSL): At: http://www.w3.org/Style/XSL/

Secure Super-distribution Protocol for Digital Rights Management in Unauthentic Network Environment

Zhaofeng Ma and Boqin Feng

Department of Computer Science and Technology,
Xi'an Jiaotong University, Xi'an, 710049, China
supermzf@mail.china.com

Abstract. In this paper, a new and secure super-distribution protocol based on dynamic master/slavery license is proposed to solve the problem of multimedia and software rights management in a uniform view. In the protocol copyrights are authorized and revoked by the dynamic license created according the rights entity and its run-time hardware entity together, the license can be used in master/slavery mode thus it supports super-distribution of copyright hierachically in network domain environment. To resist possible attack and counterfeit, a third part credible authentication center is adopted to ensure the fairness, while data encryption and digital signature technology is used for integrity and security during the authentication procedure. Analysis manifests the proposed schema is feasible, secure and flexible.

1 Introduction

Copyrights are the rights to information and culture against outright coping, in which multimedia and software are the most important entity types to take into account [1]. Digital watermark, secure container et al. as the most famous technologies for multimedia copyright protection have been studied much more, and SafeDisk, SecROM et al. are solutions to software rights management [2]. However balancing the trade-off between easy utilization and strong security is a difficult issue [3]. In this paper, a Secure Super-Distribution Protocol (SSDP) for Digital Rights considering multimedia and software entity in a uniform view is proposed as a generic solution for trusted rights management in unauthentic network environment.

2 The Secure Super-Distribution Protocol of Digital Rights

2.1 Description of SSDP Protocol

Before describing the Secure Super-Distribution Protocol (SSDP) for digital rights management, we firstly give the symbols that will used in the following section (see Table 1).

M. Li et al. (Eds.): GCC 2003, LNCS 3032, pp. 1039–1042, 2004.

Table 1. Symbols of SSDP Protocol

Param	Description	Param	Description
U	User or user Agent	*DID*	Digital Identity kept by U
HID	Hardware Identity from U	*DID'*	Digital Identity kept by AS
HID'	Hardware Identity AS kept	*AS*	Authentication Server
CS	Certificate Server	*DS*	Database Server
V	Server(or goal) Program	*L*	License for DID
T_{start}	the time U request L	T_{curr}	Current Time
P_{lfg}	Logoffing Password	R_{lgf}	Result of logoff operation
K_{AB}	Key shared by A, B	E_K, D_K	En/Derytion by key K
$Sig_K(m)$	Signature of m by key K	$Ver_K(s)$	Verification of signature
Nonce	Random Number.	S_{Lic}	Status of License

The SSDP protocol for digital rights management can be described as following:

(1) At the beginning SSDP, SP provides DID to U and CA (a third part credible authentication center [4]) independently.

(2) U commits the DID and HID to CA to request License;

(3) CA validates DID and the digital entity usage status s. If the DID and *s* is valid, then CA create the license for U dynamically according to the DID and HID (maybe related with amount N for slavery licenses), Otherwise if the DID is invalid, or the case the DID is valid but the HID is not match HID', CA denies to release license.

(4) If necessary, U can use the single license as master one and then decompose the master license into multiple slavery ones to re-distribute the rights hierachically.

(5) When U needs to transfer the service enviroment he must first logoff the license that he got from CA (now the slavery license is automatically locked) and request new licenses again as above.

2.2 Secure Authentication of SSDP

Stage I: Authentication of Master License

(A) Authorization of Master License

Step1: U commits request vector to AS:

$$\text{U->AS: R'}= E_{K_{U,AS}}(\text{DID}||\text{HID}||\text{Nonce}).$$

Step2: AS authenticates the validity of the information from U, AS decrypt the R', $DK_{U,AS}(R')$, if DID $\neq$ DID', then deny the request and return, otherwise go to step3.

Step3: AS commits R=[DID||HID||Nonce] to CS to decide whether to release the License or not:

(1) If S_{Lic}=NOT_RELEASED (here HID=NULL), then CS creates L and $K_{U,V}$ dynamically, and then signs and encrypts it to U:

①CS: Creates L, L= E_{Kv} (DID||HID||P_{run}||T_{start}||Lifetime||N_M), where P_{run}=S_E||R, S_E is the signencryption with rights version, R is the vector for program V to run;

② AS->U: Nonce':=Nonce+N_0 , and then sign L and encrypt it to U:

$$L'= E_{K_{U,AS}}(\text{Nonce'}||L||K_{U,V}||Sig_{Ku'}(L));$$

③ DS : set S_{Lic}=RELEASED, and wirte the T_{start} , Lifetime and P_{run} into DS.

(2) If S_{Lic}=RELEASED or WAITING, then it manifests the license for DID has already been released or the case that it has been loggoffed but waiting for the logoffing result code, CS verifies HID:

①If HID = HID'(the case that the same digital entity runs on the same computer), then CS releases L for U according to (1).

② If HID ≠ HID', CS refuses to release license for the request, which is viewed as multiple copies of one digital entity running on different machines or the same digital entity running on different machines.

(B) Registering the Service

The registering agent U gets license L from AS and verifies the signature, then decrypts L and registers the goal digital entity V to get its services.

Step4: U: $D_{K_{V'}}(L)=D_{K_{V'}}(E_{K_V}$ (DID || HID || P_{un} || |T_{start} ||Lifetime|| N_M)), and then computes whether T_{cur}-T_{start}<Lifetime is satisfied, if the condition is true, then go to step5 to register in V, otherwise deny to register for U.

Step5: U registers the goal digital entity V through $K_{U,V}$ and L,during this procedure U need to connect to AS to validate the timestamp T_{cur}:

①U->V: $Authenticator_u=E_{K_{u,v}}(HID_C||DID_C)$, where DID_C and HID_C represent DID and HID that U committed respectively.

② V: $D_{K_{V'}}(L)=D_{K_{V'}}(E_{K_V}$ (DID || HID || P_{run} || T_{start} ||Lifetime|| N_M)) ,

$D_{K_{u,v}}(Authenticator_u)=D_{K_{u,v}}(E_{K_{u,v}}(HID_C||DID_C)$.

③ If T_{cur}-T_{start}<Lifetime, go to ④ , otherwise manifests that the license has already expired, then refuse to register.

④ If HID=HID_C and DID=DID_C, then goto ⑤ , otherwise refuses to register.

⑤ Input P_{run} to register the goal digital entity V , and gets services from it, then logging the registering procedure in cipher mode.

Stage II: Authorization of Slavery License

In the re-distribution stage, the requested license L is used as master license, and L is used as the Local CA (so called LCA) instead to re-distribute slavery licenses.

Step1: Client user U_{net} of the domain Server S_{Domain} commits request vector to LCA:

$$R' = E_{K_{U,AS}}(DID_i \,||\, I_{net} \,||\, Nonce).$$

Step2: LCA authenticates the request R' from U_{net}, then check whether current released slavery license count reaches its threshold N_M ,that is, if the following is true

$$IsValidate(R_{client} \in S_{Domain} \,\&\&\, N_S < N_M)$$

then LCA releases slavery license L_S:

$$L_S = E_{LCA,C}(I_{net}||DID_i \,||\, P_{run} \,||\, T_{start} \,||Lifetime)$$

Step3: LCA updates Nonce':=Nonce+N_0, and then sign L_S and encrypt it to U_{net}:

$$L' = E_{K_{U,AS}}(\,Nonce'||L_S||\, K_{U,V}||Sig_{K_{U'}}(L_S));$$

Step4: And then Set N_M:= N_M–1;

Step5: In the end, LCA updates S_{Lic}=RELEASED, and record the T_{start} , Lifetime and P_{run} into Local DS in cipher mode.

On the other hand, in the case when U wants to migrate the digital entity to run on another hardware equipment, he must first logoff the current license that he had got from CA, after the whole logoff procedure finishes in a transaction way, he can then get another license to get service as the first time, so does the procedure during re-distribution stage.

2.3 Analysis of SSDP

Theorem 1: The SSDP Protocol can control copyright in a uniform for the reason that the Master/Slavery License is efficient, feasible and secure for trusted rights management in unauthentic network environment.
Proof: In Stage I, when U requesting for master L, he commits Req= $E_{K_{U,AS}}$ (DID || HID || Nonce),CA released L for U if and only if the following condition is satisfied:

$$((DID = DID' \wedge HID = NULL \wedge s = UNRELEASED) \vee (DID = DID' \wedge HID = HID')$$

Once the License L for DID is released, then any other requests can't get another valid license again. So does the slavery license in Stage II. Thus the master /slavery license Mechanism is atomic and efficient in distribution and re-distribution stages.
During Each step in SSDP, all the data transforms in cipher format, U can get L safely if only the cryptography algorithm is secure enough, and according to the hypothesis that if AS is credible, then L is trusted with high security and integrity.
Considering possible attacks, if U tries to adjust his local timer to get another L, but he can't modify the timestamp from AS, thus the replay attack is invalid, thus SSDP protocol is immune to replay attack.
In a word, the proposed SSDP is secure, efficient and trusted for digital rights management in unauthentic network environment.

3 Conclusion

Trusted rights management is an important issue in the Unauthentic Network Environment. The proposed SSDP provides a novel and secure solution not only for multimedia but also for software entity in a uniform protection mode. However, with the development of computing technologies how to enhance the rights in mobile computing environment is a new subject to take into account.

References

1. Milagros DC. Copyright in the Digital Environment. International Information and Library Review, Vol.29 (1997) 201~204
2. Foroughi A, Albin M, Gillard S. Digital Rights Management: a Delicate Balance between Protection and Accessibility. Information Science, 28 (2002) 389~395
3. Depoorter, B, Parisi, F. Fair Use and Copyright Protection: a Price Theory Explanation. International Review of Law and Economics. 21 (2002) 453~473
4. Schneier B. Applied Cryptography-Protocols, Algorithm and Source Code in C. John Wiley & Sons Inc., New York (1996)

X-NIndex: A High Performance Stable and Large XML Document Query Approach and Experience in TOP500 List Data

Shaomei Wu, Xuan Li, and Zhihui Du

Department of Computer Sci. & Tech.
Tsinghua University, Beijing, P. R. C, 100084
wusm@mails.tsinghua.edu.cn

Abstract. This article describes X-NIndex, a novel approach for large XML documents with stable structure. The definition for the large XML document with stable structure is given while the concept of XML document tree coordinate(X-DTC) is introduced. The significant advantage of X-NIndex to other XML query schemas is shown and the experimental results are present.

1 Introduction

Extensive Markup Language (XML) [1] is emerged as the dominant standard for representing and exchanging data over Internet. However, as an organization of data with various semistructures, it is more difficult to store and query various XML documents, especially those consisted with a large amount of data.

To address this problem, there has been much work done on building XML database system, which lead to a research on schema design in the database for storage and query problem in XML. At present, several models have been advanced include XML-QL [8], XML-GL [3], Quilt [7], XPath [4], X-Rel [9], XQuery [6], and XML Indexed Structure with RRC [5]. They process XML data by changing XML document into different data schemas and do query on the schemas.

In our work, we found that much of these approaches are not very efficient in operation of large XML documents, and to solve such problem, we propose a new query structure named X-NIndex (XML Node Index Structure), which is proved to be able to improve query performance greatly.

The features of X-NIndex are: 1) for the XML document with large data amount and stable structure; 2) great efficient in query performance with such XML documents; 3) index structure and the XML document Tree Coordinate (X-DTC).

The rest of this paper is organized as follows: Section 2 describes the new approach of X-NIndex, including the definition of large XML document with stable structure, the concept of X-DTC and the exact process of X-NIndex; Section 3 compares the query performances in X-NIndex and other query structures, presents an example of processing Top500 computers data; Section 4 gives the conclusion of our work.

M. Li et al. (Eds.): GCC 2003, LNCS 3032, pp. 1043–1046, 2004.

2 X-NIndex Query Structure

In this Section, we will give out more details about X-NIndex, including the exact definition of Large XML document with stable structure, the concept of X-DTC and the process of X-NIndex.

2.1 The Definition of Large XML Document with Stable Structure

Here we adopt the XML document to be presented as a rooted tree with several node types such as Element, Attribute, Text, etc, the structure of it is shown in Fig. 1.

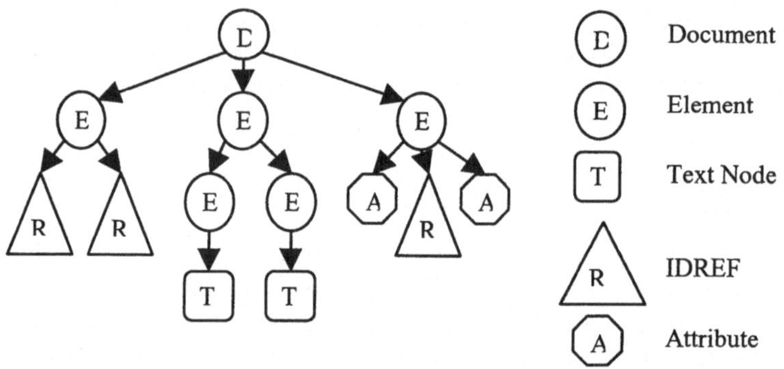

Fig. 1. The Rooted Structured Tree of XML Document

Especially, our discussion is base on a particular type of XML document, large XML Document with stable Structure, and we give the exact definition below:

Definition 1: Large XML Document with Stable Structure has such features: 1) it has a relative stable structure, which means, we do our query on the structure pre-known and the structure of it will not change once during the query; 2) it is consisted by a great amount of records as children of the root document element, and other parts of the document are all the attributes or descendants of such record elements; 3) each record has the same structure; 4) the number of attributes (or children attributes) is much smaller than the number of records.

If not mention clearly, all our study below is considered with such special XML document, for example, the Top500 XML ranking data documents.

2.2 XML Document Tree Coordinate (X-DTC)

To get the location of each node of XML document quickly, we introduce a new concept called X-DTC (XML Document Tree Coordinate). For the characteristic of stable structure, we assume that the children number of each node is given already.

First, we express the document in a tree as in Fig.1, and record each node's children number. Then, we add x and y coordinate into the tree and evaluate each node with a coordinate value, as shown in Fig. 2. Here, the coordinate x is the order of it in its compeers and y is valued with the order of level in the document tree. We prescribe, the document is in level 0 and all the records are in level 1.

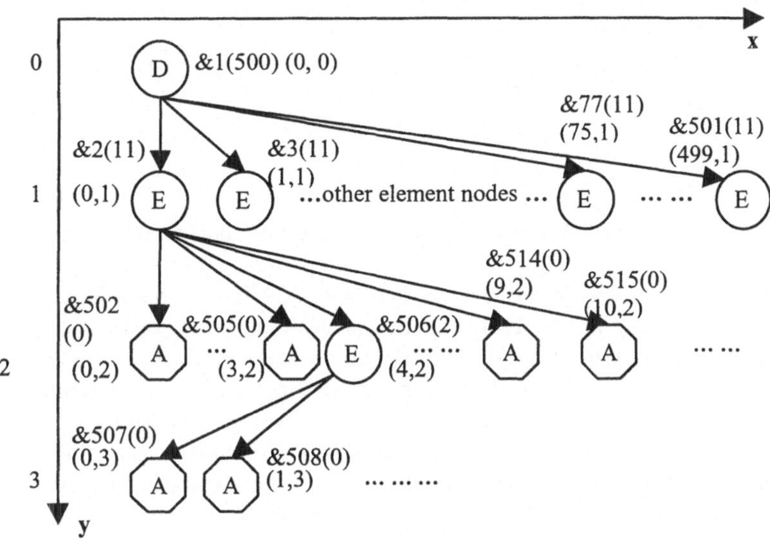

Fig. 2. Document Tree with X-DTC

2.3 The Process of X-NIndex Query Structure

From the analysis above, now we give the process of X-NIndex approach sketchily:
(1) Analyze the original XML document, present it into X-DTC form;
(2) Translate the data nodes of XML document into several indexed tables, do queries on the indexed tables with ordinary search method, for example, binary search;
(3) Using the coordinate data to compute and locate the record we search for in X_DTC, return the results set, which will be found from level 2 to level 3 or below.

3 A Performance Study of X-NIndex

To assess the effectiveness of the X-NIndex approach, we use JAXP and SAX to analyze the Top 500 XML documents. The query performances are compared and reported. It is important to notify that all our experiments are base on the large XML document with stable query, as we defined and referred before.

All experiments were conducted on a 1.60GHz PC with 256MB RAM, 30G hard disk. The experiment is to do different queries on the same sample of Top500 XML document. Results are shown in Fig 3, unit of y-axis is millisecond.

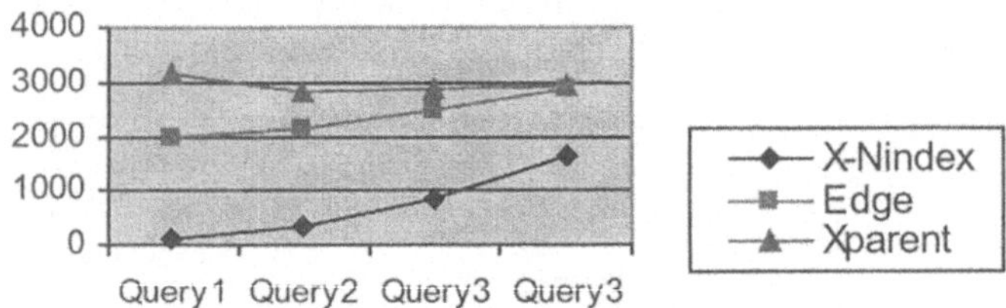

Fig. 3. Results for different queries in the same XML document sample

From the results we could see clearly that with X-NIndex, the effectiveness improved a lot of querying in the XML documents. Although it is not as stable as other approaches, as the efficient of X-NIndex may decrease more obviously with the scale of results set, but there is a limit of efficient descending reached by X-NIndex which is not significant more than the advantage of it in the average condition.

Such good results come from the special stable structure of our study objects, which make it possible to have much work pre-done during parsing the XML document, and much information is collected and helps to direct our queries.

4 Conclusion and Future Work

In this paper, we proposed a new coordinate-index approach called X-NIndex, the features of our work include the pre-analysis of stable XML document and the coordinate installation which helps to increase the efficiency a lot in the query afterward.

As some problems still exist with X-NIndex, for instance, the instability of it with increase of result set, in our future work, we will investigate the improvement with X-NIndex in such cases and conduct some new methods or concepts into this problem.

References

1. W3C Extensible Markup Language XML1.1 in www.w3.org/TR/xml11/.
2. W3C XML Schema 1.1, in www.w3c.org/xml/schema.
3. Ceri, S., Comai, S., Damiani, E., and Fraternali, P. (1999). XML-GL: a graphical language querying and restructuring XML documents 1. in WWW8.
4. Clark, J. and DeRose, S., 1999, XML Path Language (XPath).
5. Dao Dinh Kha, Masatoshi Yoshikawa, Shunsuke Uemura, An XML Indexing Structure with Relative Region Coordinate in ICDE'01.
6. D. Chamberlin, XQuery: An XML query language in IBM System Journal, 2002.
7. Don Chamberlin, Jonathan Robie, Daniela Florescu , Quilt: An XML Query Language for Heterogeneous Data Source.
8. Deutsch, A., Fernandez, M., Suciu, D.(1999b).Storing Semistructured Data in Relations.
9. M. Yoshikawa, T. Amagasa, T. Shimura, S. Uemura,. XRel: A Path-Based Approach to Storage and Retrieval of XML Documents Using Relational Databases, 2001.

The Analysis of Authorization Mechanisms in the Grid[1]

Shiguang Ju, Zhen Yang, Chang-da Wang, and Dianchun Guo

Jiangsu University, Zhen Jiang, 212013, China
jushig@ujs.edu.cn, yangzhen_7@163.com

Abstract. The characteristics of grid are outlined to point out that the traditional authorization mechanisms cannot satisfy the requirement of the grid security. Then the authorization mechanisms employed in five prevalent Grid Security Architectures are compared in terms of granularity assessment, flexibility of rights control, and achievement approach. Based on these, we propose several approaches that can enhance the authorization in grid. The strongpoint and possible problems of each approach are also put forward.

1 Introduction

Grid breaks the limitation on traditional sharing and cooperation. Distinguished from traditional client-server applications, this sharing may involve not only file exchange but also direct access to computers, software, data, and other resources, which is required by a range of collaborative problem-solving and resource-brokering strategies emerging in industry, science, and engineering.

In a Grid environment, since both the resource pool and the user pool are large and change dynamically, the traditional mode of authorization which checks whether a user is acting within static prescribed parameters and needs a centralized administrative entity is no longer satisfactory.

The goal of our work is to compare prevalent Grid Security Architectures. Furthermore, we present several approaches to enhance the authorization in the grid.

2 The Authorization Mechanisms in the Prevalent Grid Security Architectures

Authorization is a key part of a security model and requires special mention. There are several efforts investigating authorization in the Grid environment. In the following, we describe five widespread Grid authorization mechanisms.

1) Grid Security Infrastructure

The Grid Security Infrastructure (GSI) emphasis on a fusion of the present security technologies of distributed systems and supports the notion of local policy. To

[1] This work is supported by **National Natural Science Foundation of China** (No.60373069) and **Jiangsu Natural Science Foundation** (No.BK200204).

M. Li et al. (Eds.): GCC 2003, LNCS 3032, pp. 1047–1050, 2004.

achieve this, GSI provides mechanisms for translating a user's GSI identity to a local identity. Once translated, the local identity can be used to enforce local policy decisions, such as file access, disk quotas, and CPU limits.

In brief, the authorization in GSI is relied on proprietary access control lists (ACLs) and focuses primarily on creating temporary credentials for users and for processes executing on a user's behalf.

2) Community Authorization Services –CAS

The Community Authorization Service [1] augments the existing local policy enforcement mechanisms provided by GSI. It is works with GSI identities and uses restricted proxy certificates to delegate rights. The CAS authorization mechanism supplies policy information from this database in the form of signed credentials to the user, which in turn groups them with his request to a resource. Authorization mechanisms at the resources need to enforce the stated policies.

3) Legion

Legion [2] is object oriented. In Legion every object is identified by a unique Legion object ID (LOID). The LOID contains a X.509 certificate that includes the public key for this object. As the public key is an integral part of the objects identifier, a centralized CA is not needed.

Legion runs on top of existing operating systems and does not undermine the native security mechanisms of the host OS. The Legion system runs in user space on the grid resources to ensure that the resource owner has the final authority over the use of his resources.

4) CRISIS

CRISIS [3] is the security subsystem for WebOS. The authorization of requests in the CRISIS architecture is accomplished by a hybrid of an access control list scheme and a capability list scheme. Certification Authorities (CA) takes requests for creating identity certificates. The CA maintains a reference monitor with the list of principals authorized to create, modify, or invalidate identity certificates. The entity provides its identity plus its capabilities and the resource combines these capabilities with its access control list. Only actions that are permissible by both policies will be admitted.

5) Akenti

Akenti [4] is an access control system for widely distributed resources. Akenti uses public-key certificates for identification, authentication and authorization. Three types of certificates are used: identity certificates, use-condition certificates and attribute certificates.

Authorization of a request to a resource is handled by the Akenti policy engine, which compares attributes of the authenticated user to use-conditions specified by the resource owners. Attribute certificates convey attributes to user identities and use-condition certificates specify the conditions that must be satisfied before a request is granted. Repositories are used to store certificates. An authority configuration file is used to make the resource user learn what repositories need to be queried, which certificate authorities they trust, and who is a stakeholder.

3 The Comparison of Prevalent Authorization Mechanisms

As described above, all of these authorization mechanisms allow for multiple policies sources, but have significant differences, both in terms of requirement to lay emphasis upon and achievement approach.

In this part, we will compare the five authorization mechanisms above in the granularity assessment, flexibility of rights control, and achievement approach.

1) The granularity assessment of authorization

In a typical grid environment, the meaning of the resource allocation in a coarse-grained manner is to concern about how many resources can use as a whole, but not concern about how allocation is used.

In the GSI, both the authorization of user job startup and authorization on job management are coarse-grained. For fine-grained authorization decisions the Generic Authorization and Access Control API (GAA-API) is employed. CAS enabled applications have to use the security context of this API.

2) Flexibility of privilege control

Greater flexibility is required in the authorization of the Grid because a given user may receive and combine components from many different sources.

In the Legion system, flexibility is the primary goal of the security architecture. This goal is satisfied by the grid middleware. The resource owner has the final authority over the use of its resources by specifying usage policies for the access control mechanisms.

The CAS addresses the problems of scalability, flexibility, but lack of policy hierarchy. Compared with other authorization systems such as Akenti, CAS provides mechanisms for distributing administration that are critical for solving the issues of scalability and flexibility.

The GSI is layered securely on top of existing systems and to provide uniform credentials and certification infrastructure. The layering approach comes at the price of limited control over access rights through GSI mechanisms, the need for local user accounts for possible large numbers of grid users.

3) Achievement approach

In the Legion, the authorization mechanism is designed by grid middleware. As a result, Grid middleware systems that implement their own security authorization mechanism provide the functionality necessary to provide such support. The approach in CRISIS can be viewed as one implementation of security for Legion objects.

In contrast the GSI provides only functionality for authentication of global users and their mapping to local user accounts at resources. It requires the existence of a local user account.

4 Improvement Approaches

The analysis and comparison above presents the requirements for authorization mechanisms on grid environments that provides finer grained and more flexible control of rights than that can be available currently. These requirements for fine-grained delegation and restriction of rights can be implemented in the following approaches.

1) Using the grid middleware

This is one of the approaches to satisfy these requirements. But it will pose a problem, that is, Grid middleware systems that implement their own security authorization mechanism provide the functionality necessary to provide such support.

2) Operating system security extension

The above access authorizations are left completely to the underlying resource's operating system. Extensions to the authorization mechanisms provided by such operating systems need to be in place to enforce complex usage policies stated in restricted proxy certificates and to grant rights that are conveyed through privilege management credentials, for example attribute certificates.

A more promising approach is the use of security extensions built into the operating system to achieve necessary flexibility and granularity for authorization.

3) Incorporation of existing security infrastructures

Each of the authorization mechanisms mentioned above have its merits. Therefore, they can be cooperated to improve present authorization mechanisms. The use of proxy certificates and similar approaches is a preliminary step for incorporation.

To sum up, all the methods above could enhance the authorization of the grid. But a common problem to satisfy the requirements is that a considerable overhead is placed on the often compute intensive applications found in grid environments if the necessary control over processes is provided.

5 Conclusions

To assure the privacy and integrity of the communication between the subjects in the grid, it is significant to highly control this sharing between resource providers and consumers. In this paper, we expatiate on the authorization mechanisms in the prevalent Grid Security Architectures for comparison. According to the analysis above, several approaches to enhance the authorization of the Grid are brought forward and will be the topic of subsequent research in this area.

References

1. L. Pearlman, V.W., I. Foster, C. Kesselman, S. Tuecke.: A Community Authorization Service for Group Collaboration. in submitted to IEEE Workshop on Policies for Distributed Systems and Networks. (2002)
2. W. A. Wulf, C. Wang, and D. Kienzle.: A New Model of Security for Distributed Systems. University of Virginia CS Technical Report CS-95-34, August (1995)
3. E. Belani, A. Vahdat, T. Anderson, and M. Dahlin.: The CRISIS Wide Area Security Architecture, In Proceedings of the USENIX Security Symposium, San Antonio, Texas, January (1998)
4. Thompson, M. et al.: Certificate based Access Control for Widely Distributed Resources, Proceedings of the 8th Usenix Security Symposium (1999)

Constructing Secure Web Service Based on XML

Shaomin Zhang[1,2], Baoyi Wang[2], and Lihua Zhou[1]

[1] School of computer science and technology, Xidian University, xi'an 710071, China
[2] School of computer, North China Electric Power University, Baoding 071003, China
zhangshaomin@126.com

Abstract. The paper discusses XML security key technologies related with security of Web service. Based on these discussions, Web service is integrated with some mature security architectures such as PKI. A new Web service layer security model is proposed, and its characteristics are described. Finally, the paper focuses on the implementation of the security services sub-layer XKMS, and describes its design methodology, architecture and realization in detail.

1 Intrduction

As defined by the World Wide Web Consortium, Web services are[1]:

(1) identified by URIs';

(2) accessible via standard Web protocols;

(3) Capable of sending, receiving, and acting on XML-based message;

(4) Capable of interacting with applications and programs that are not directly human-driven user interface.

So XML technology has become a basic architecture in Web applications.

2 Related XML Security Technology[2,3,4]

Related XML security technology is as follows:

(1) XML Signature. It provides a syntax for representing signatures on digital content along with procedures for computing and verifying such signatures.

(2) XML Encryption. SSL always secures the whole document, but with XML encryption you can encrypt only parts of the document.

(3) XKMS. The XKMS enable application developers to outsource the processing of key management to trust services accessed through the Internet. These protocols do not require any particular underlying public key infrastructure but are designed to be compatible with such infrastructures.

(4) SAML. It provides a standard way to define user authentication, authorization, entitlements, and profile information in XML documents.

(5) XACML. XACML allow developers to describe access control policies for each XML element or tag (four action types: read, write, create, and delete).

M. Li et al. (Eds.): GCC 2003, LNCS 3032, pp. 1051–1054, 2004.

3 Constructing Secure Web Service Layer Model Based on XML

At present, PKI and Kerberos play important roles in solving the conventional security threaten problems. Base on the ideas of integrating Web service with mature security models, a new Web service layer security model is proposed.

3.1 The Web Service Layer Security Model

The structure of Web service layer security model is shown as Fig. 1.

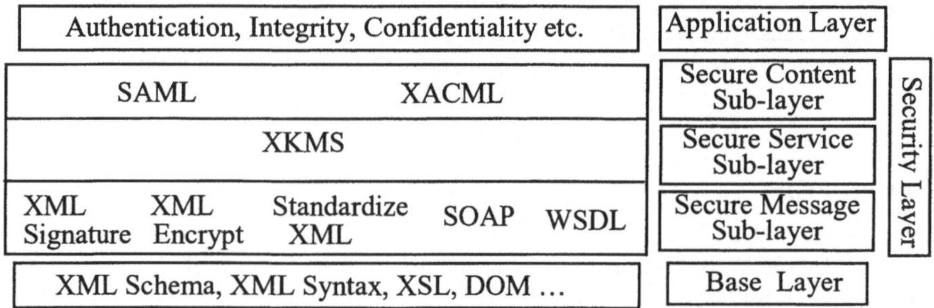

Fig. 1. The structure of Web service layer security model

The model includes three big layers: base layer, security layer and application layer. The base layer provides basic service for the realization of security layer. Security layer performs various security strategy and measures. The security of the application layer depends on the support of the security layer. Further, the security layer is divided into three sub-layers: secure message sub-layer, secure content sub-layer and secure service sub-layer.

3.2 The Characteristic of the Security Layer Model

The characteristics of the security layer model are as follows:

(1) It integrates many matured security models and deduces the realization risk if a Web service wants to provide secure and dependable service;

(2) It is a discrete layer relationship, we can combine different security components to a specific system to reduce its complexity and cost;

(3) It is a dynamic, developing model. Various security techniques and specifications arising recently can be integrated into it according to its characteristic.

4 The Realization of Secure Service Sub-layer

The secure service sub-layer is driven by XKMS: Place signature processing in trust server on Web, simplify authentication and signature management by separating them from application programs.

The function of secure service sub-layer is shown as Fig. 2.

In it, users call XKMS service by X-KISS and X-KRSS, X-KRSS functions as register public key, escrow service, client/server side generating key, revoking key etc., and X-KISS performs key location, key gaining, documents encryption, signature verification, overtime etc. After a basic processing in X-KISS and X-KRSS, the operation is committed to operation transform processing module. The key generation module generates pair keys, and key operation module functions as encryption, decryption, signature, signature verification.

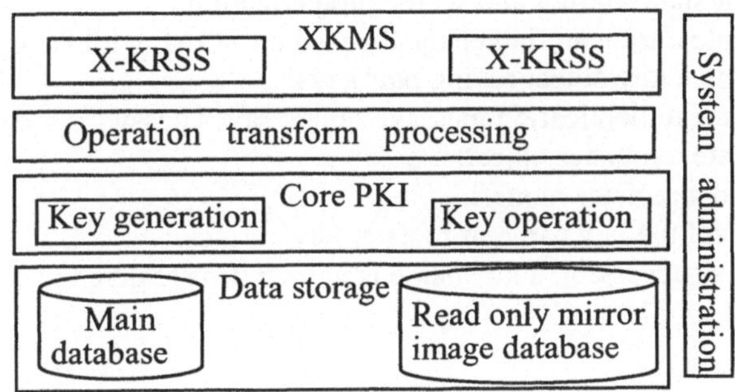

Fig. 2. The function of secure service sub-layer

4.1 The Design of Architecture

In practical application, most of the requesting services to XKMS is to access X-KISS, a little to X-KRSS, so we put X-KISS and X-KRSS to different servers. Its architecture is shown as Fig. 3.

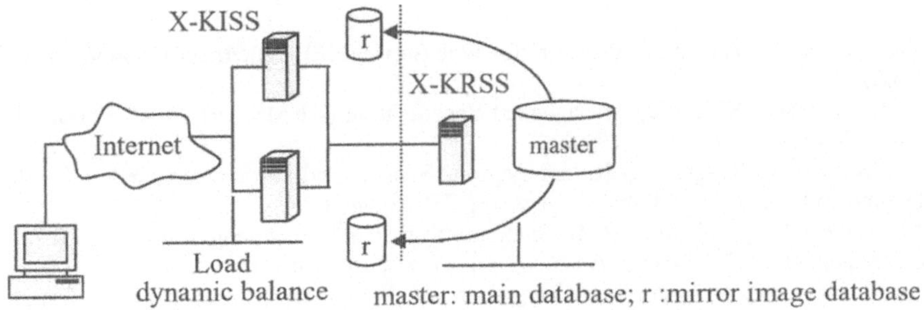

Fig. 3. X-KISS and X-KRSS distribution architecture

The advantages of this architecture are:

(1) If X-KISS or X-KRSS is overload, we can add it to balance load freely.

(2) As X-KISS server's using efficiency is high, so it is ahead of X-KRSS, and can answer client's request rapidly, and functions as buffer and isolation to X-KRSS .

4.2 The Realization of Secure Service Sub-layer

The functions of secure service sub-layer are divided into two parts: the realization layer of XKMS service and key base supporting layer. now I'll illustrate how X-KRSS server performs key register.

In order to ensure every step in X-KRSS server is identified and secure, the X-KRSS server do not accept verification request without signature. A key which is used to signature verification request must be registered. The key can be generated in client side or server side. Now we'll illustrate how the client side generates key and register key by the data sharing and secret authentication.

Step 1: To create a transmitting channel based on SOAP with URL,

Step2: To create a key object saving pair keys.

Step3: Create an authentication message object saves passwords and sharing secret.

Step 4: To create a register object;

Step 5: To send a register request;

Step 6: To accept the key name of register key.

If the register is successful, a key name is gained. It is realized in Java.

5 Conclusion

PKI is a base and core of network security solution. When It is integrated into Web service, a Web service layer security model is proposed. The paper focuses on the implementation of the security services sub-layer XKMS, it would facilitate to the Web application of PKI. Our long-term goal is to create a software system that supports the implementation of trusted Web service in E-government and E-business.

References

1. Doug Lea, Stove Vinoski: Middleware for Web Service. IEEE Internet Computing, vol. 7(1) (2003) 28-29
2. P Hallam-Baker: XML Key Management Specification (XKMS 2.0). W3C Working Draft (2002), http://www.w3.org/TR/xkms2/
3. D Eastlake, J Reagle: XML Encryption Syntax and Processing W3C Candidate Recommendation (2002), http://www.w3.org/TR/xmlenc-core/
4. D Eastlake, J Reagle, D Solo: XML-Signature Syntax and Processing W3C Recommendation (2001). http://www.w3.org/TR/xmldsig-core/
5. Yuichi Nakamur: Towards the Integration of Web Services Security on Enterprise Environments. 2002 symposium on Applications and Internet (SAINT) Workshops (2002) 166-177

ECC Based Intrusion Tolerance for Web Security

Xianfeng Zhang, Feng Zhang, Zhiguang Qin, and Jinde Liu

College of Computer Science and Engineering
University of Electronic Science and Technology of China
Chengdu, 610054, P.R. China
{Zhangxf, Ibmcenter, Qinzg, Jdliu}@uestc.edu.cn

Abstract. The threshold cryptography provides a new approach to building intrusion tolerance applications. In this paper, a threshold decryption scheme based the Menezes-Vanstone elliptic curve cryptosystem is presented. Based on the scheme, the architecture of an intrusion-tolerant Web security system is presented. Performance analysis shows that the architecture is characterized by excellent security as well as high efficiency.

1 Introduction

The threshold cryptography provides new methodology for developing intrusion tolerance system. Generally, threshold encryption and threshold decryption are based on the homomorphic cryptography algorithms. The homomorpohic property is necessary in order to generate shares of the key so that partial cryptograms can be combined into a cryptogram for the correct message [1]. Therefore, nearly all projects about threshold cryptography techniques focused on the homomorphic algorithm. Among these, the ITTC project developed by Stanford University is notable, which researched and developed the intrusion tolerance threshold RSA based application [2].

Currently, ECC (Elliptic Curve Cryptography) is regarded as an attractive cryptography that can provide greater strength, higher speed and smaller keys than other cryptography systems [3,4]. Therefore, the research on threshold ECC and its applications deserves great attention. In the past years, Kazuo Takaragi, Kunihiko Miyazaki, et al study the ECC based threshold signature scheme [5]. However, there are no any research results on ECC based threshold schemes, especially on ECC-based decryption scheme and intrusion tolerant application reported currently. In this paper, we present an ECC based threshold decryption scheme and apply it in building intrusion tolerant Web security system.

2 ECC Based Threshold Decryption Scheme

Throughout this paper, Let $p>3$ be a prime number and let $E(\mathrm{F}_p)$ be an Elliptic Curve group over F_p. Let H be a cyclic subgroup of $E(\mathrm{F}_p)$ such that the discrete logarithm

M. Li et al. (Eds.): GCC 2003, LNCS 3032, pp. 1055–1058, 2004.

problem is intractable over H. Let g be a generator for H. Based on the Menezes-Vanstone Elliptic Curve Cryptosystem [6], plaintext could be any pair $X=(x1, x2)$ of integer from F_p. The public key for the system consists of the elements g, h of $E(F_p)$, whereas the private key consists of an integer d. Here, $d \in [1, p\text{-}1]$ and $h = dg$.

Let A be the sender, B be the receiver. B' private key d is broken up into t pieces of shares $d_1, d_2, \ldots, d_t$ [7] and stored across t share servers, $C_1, C_2, \ldots, C_t$. B doesn't keep d but $d_i g$ $(1 \leq i \leq t)$. Let one combination of d is:

$$d = d_1 + d_2 + \ldots + d_t \tag{1}$$

Encryption

1. A selects a random integer $k < |H|$, and computes

$$Y = kg \bmod p \tag{2}$$

$$(c_1, c_2) = kh \bmod p \tag{3}$$

2. A computes $s1 = c_1 x1 \bmod p$ and $s2 = c_2 x2 \bmod p$. Then the encrypted form of X is $(y, s1, s2)$. And A sends $(y, s1, s2)$ to B.

Decryption

1. B receives the ciphertext $(y, s1, s2)$ and broadcasts y to $C_1, C_2, \ldots, C_t$.
2. Each share server C_i $(i \in [1,t])$ computes Q_i and sends Q_i back to B.

$$Q_i = d_i y \bmod p \tag{4}$$

3. After getting all Q_i $(i \in [1,t])$, B computes Q (suppose $Q=(q_1, q_2) \bmod p$).

$$Q = \sum_{j=1}^{t} Q_j \bmod p \tag{5}$$

4. B computes $b_1 = s_1 q_1^{-1} \bmod p$ and $b_2 = s_2 q_2^{-1} \bmod p$.

The decrypted form of (y, s_1, s_2) is (b_1, b_2).

Proof

$Q = \sum_{j=1}^{t} Q_j \bmod p$ (by equation (5)) $= \sum_{j=1}^{t} d_j y \bmod p$ (by equation (4))

$= \sum_{j=1}^{t} d_j kg \bmod p$ (by equation (2)) $= dkg \bmod p$ (by equation (1))

$= (c_1, c_2) \bmod p$ (by equation (3))

Hence, $(b_1, b_2) = (x_1, x_2) \bmod p$.

3 Application

To enable secure connections to a Web server, a user often connects to the server by SSL. During the negotiation of SSL session key, users need send encrypted premaster key to the server. Then the server would decrypt the premaster key with its private key. To protect the private key, The web server break it up into t pieces shares and stored across t different share servers out of the n share servers based on t-out-of-n sharing [2]. The Web server store each d_i's ($1 \leq i \leq t$) public key $d_i g$ and some other public information, such as dg, g, p and $E(F_p)$.

After receiving the encrypted information (y, s_1,s_2) from a user, the Web server will specify t share servers from the n share servers. The selection of the t share servers can be based on the current workload of the n servers, to balance every server's load. The selected t share servers correspond to a combination of d. In term of the combination, each of the t servers can independently decide which d_i it should apply. Then system can decrypt the ciphertext by the ECC-based threshold decryption scheme presented in section 2.

4 Performance Analysis

Our scheme is based on threshold ECC. We will analysis its performance by comparing it with the ITTC Web security scheme, which is based on threshold RSA.

4.1 Security

In our decryption scheme, if a hacker wants to attack the scheme, he has to work out d_i from $d_i y$, but this is an ECDLP. Analogically, In ITTC scheme, a hacker attacking the scheme has to face a large integer factorization problem. Currently, ECDLP is believed to be harder than the integer factorization problem. From this point, our scheme is more secure than the ITTC scheme.

4.2 Efficiency

An elliptic curve $E(F_p)$ with a 160-bit prime order $g \in E(F_p)$ offers approximately the same level of security as RSA with a 1024-bit modulus N [8]. So, let the g's order be a 160-bit prime in our scheme and modulus N be 1024-bit in ITTC scheme. And we suppose the plaintext W to be encrypted is 1024-bit in the two schemes.

According to section 2, W should be encoded into 4 integer pairs in our scheme. And the ciphertext of W should be 4 640-bit triplets, such as (y, $s1_j$, $s2_j$) ($1 \leq j \leq 4$). To decrypt the 4 640-bit triplets, the communication cost is about $320(t+1)$ bits. While in ITTC scheme, to decrypt the ciphertext of *W*, the total communication cost is about 1024(t+1) bits. Therefore, the communication bandwidth our scheme costs is about 31.2% of that the ITTC scheme costs.

Additionally, in ITTC scheme, the system needs to perform t times of $M^{d_i} \bmod N$ operation and (t-1) modular multiplications (M is the ciperhertext of W). Therefore, the total computation cost is (241t-1) modular multiplications modulo N. While in our scheme, to decrypt 4 triplets, the system needs to perform t scalar multiplication, (t-1) point additions, 2 field inversion operations and 8 field multiplications over F_p. According to [8], the computation cost of ITTC scheme is equal to (9881t-41) times field multiplications over F_p, and the computation cost of our scheme is equal to 1205t+9 field multiplications over F_p. So the computation cost of the ITTC is about 9.64 times greater than that of our scheme.

5 Conclusions

Our web security system provides high threshold availability and threshold confidentiality. In our scheme, more than t correct servers can reconstruct secret d. And it is infeasible for up to t-1 servers to reconstruct d. Our system is designed to be easy to embed into existing applications. An outsider communicating with the web server is unaware that the corresponding private key is stored in shared form.

We haven't described implementation details here. In the near future, we will develop a prototype system based on threshold ECC.

References

1. J.C. Benaloh. Secret sharing homomorphisms: keeping shares of a secret secret. Proc. Crypto'86. LNCS Vol. 263, Springer
2. Michael Malkin, Thomas Wu, Dan Boneh. Building Intrusion Tolerance Applications. 8th USENLX Security Symposium.
3. Xu Qiuliang, Li Daxing. Elliptic curve cryptosystems[J]. Journal of Computer Research and Development, 1999, Vol. 36, No. 11, pp. 1281~1288
4. Zhang Xianfeng, Qin Zhiguang, Liu Jinde. An analysis of the security and efficiency on elliptic curve cryptosystems. Journal of university of electronic science and technology of China, 2001, Vol. 30, No. 2, pp.144~147
5. Kazuo Takaragi, Kunihiko Miyazaki, et al. A threshold digital signature issuing scheme without secret communication http://grouper.ieee.org/groups/1363/StudyGroup/contributions/th-sche.pdf
6. Zhu Wenyu, Sun Qi. The application fundament of computer cryptography. Science Press. 2000, pp.174~175
7. Y. Frankel. A practical protocol for large group oriented network. Eurocrypt 89, pp. 56~61
8. Neal Koblitz, Alfred Menezes, Scott Vanstone. The State of Elliptic Curve Cryptography. Designs, Codes and Cryptography, 19, 2000, pp.173~193

Design for Reliable Service Aggregation in an Architectural Environment*

Xiaoli Zhi and Weiqin Tong

School of Computer Engineering and Science, Shanghai University, Shanghai 200072,China
{xlzhi}@mail.shu.edu.cn

Abstract. How to construct a reliable service aggregation is an important issue in service oriented computing. The paper introduces a design environment to improve the consistence of a service aggregation by cost-effectively using the model checking technique in a software architecture framework.

1 Introduction

The Web Service and grid computing technology promotes the direction of service oriented computing [1]. Service aggregation deals with choosing and composing several component Web Services as a composite service. Many work has been done to make services work together. But the checking problem of whether the aggregated services can behave consistently as expected is left less unnoticed. This work will address this problem in a software architecture-based framework.

Software architecture is claimed to be a fundamental approach to improve software reliability [2]. Among various architecture description languages (ADL), Acme [3] gained a popular attention serving as an interchange ADL. We will complement Acme with behavioral semantic support with Promela. The extended system is called BlueStar. Promela is the input language of the popular model checker Spin. Spin has been demonstrated in several case studies (e.g., [4]) that it is an adequate tool for behavioral analysis of distributed software architecture.

2 The Design Environment BlueStar

BlueStar is an extension work on the basis of AcmeStudio (Acme visual editor); Armani, Acme's type checking library. Fig.1 shows BlueStar's function modules.

* This work is partly sponsored by Shanghai Municipal Science and Technology committee Project No. 03dz15026

M. Li et al. (Eds.): GCC 2003, LNCS 3032, pp. 1059–1062, 2004.

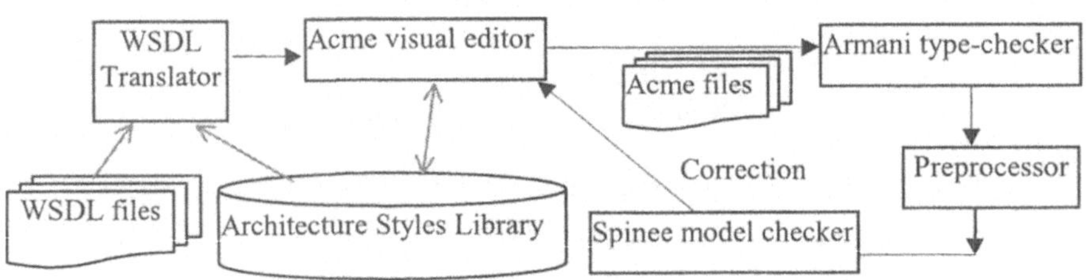

Fig. 1. Functional modules in BlueStar

2.1 Architecture Description and Typecheck

Acme uses seven constructs to specify a system's architectural structure [3] (Refer fig.2 for the graphical notation of six of these constructs). BlueStar describes a design entity's behavioral model with Promela through Acme's extension mechanism, that is, a specific property 'behavior' of type 'behaviorDesT'.

To facilitate the reuse of architectural designs, an ASL (Architecture Styles Library) is developed to maintain architectural types and styles which can be referenced in a system design. BlueStar predines some typical styles and types in ASL.

Considering the behavioral semantics, BlueStar adds another constraint to Arnamni's subtyping to maintain the substitutability: the external behavior of the subtype should be included in that of the supertype, written T´£trace T (refer to next subsection).

2.2 Model checker Spinee

System evolvability is a key aspect of architecture-based design. In most cases, it is necessary to ensure that the detailed system is actually a 'correct' version of the abstract one. The correctness can be determined by establishing their behavioral trace semantics relations [5] based on traces of external events exposed by the two systems to be compared.

Promela does not provide an explicit mechanism to distinguish between external and internal behavior. BlueStar defines two types of external event sources: send/receive operations on external channels indicated through the entity's property 'behavior'; the write operation on global variables specified in the entity's property 'behavior'.

A Promela model defines a global state machine---a finite Labeled Transition System (LTS). Deciding trace relations between two Promela models corresponds to verifying the trace relation for the initial states in their synchronized product LTS. Let σ, ρ be states of the LTS, traces(σ) denote the set of all finite external execution traces of σ. If σ has an infinite internal computation, then σ is divergent, written $\sigma\uparrow$. Otherwise, σ is convergent, written $\sigma\downarrow$. Let s any sequence of external actions. If σ becomes divergent after some prefix of s, write $\sigma\uparrow s$ otherwise $\sigma\downarrow s$. Define must(σ,s) as the set of the external actions each of which is the first actions in any external trace of σ', which is reachable from σ after s. Then:

Trace equivalence ($\equiv_{trace}$): $\sigma \equiv_{trace} \rho$ iff traces(σ) = traces(ρ).

Trace inclusion ($\leq_{trace}$): $\sigma \leq_{trace} \rho$ iff traces(σ) $\subseteq$ traces(ρ).

Testing equivalence ($\sigma \equiv_{test}$): $\sigma \equiv_{test} \rho$ if for all s, we have:

i) $\sigma\uparrow s$ iff $\rho\uparrow s$;

ii) traces(σ) = traces(ρ); and

iii) $\sigma\downarrow s$ implies must(σ,s) = must(ρ,s).

The above three relations checking is implemented by a tool Spinee, which inherits all the analysis capability of Spin. Spinee uses a polynomial algorithm to translate the two input LTS's to weighted directed graphs and obtain their relation by deciding their isomorphism. More details on the Spinee will present in another paper for space limit.

2.3 Translating Service Specification to Architecture Description

The translation templates for a Web Service WSDL specification assume a framework of the representation in BlueStar as follows:

- Map a service to an Acme component and a corresponding Promela process
- Map a port type of WSDL to an Acme port of the service component and some lines of Promela codes in that component's Promela process
- Map an endpoint of WSDL to an Acme connector and a corresponding Promela process
- Map the message identifications in WSDL operations to a series of Promela integer while abstracting away message content information. These constants instead of their string names will be used during model checking. A WSDL operation has no more than three kinds of messages: input, output, and fault. Their different combinations result in four valid types of operation primitives realized by WSDL. They have different behavior abstractions briefly explained in Table 1.

Table 1. Operation primitives and their behavior abstraction

Operation primitive	Behavior
One-way	receive an input message identification (mid)
Request-response	receive an input mid and send back an output mid or a fault mid
Solicit-response	send an output mid then wait to receive an input mid or a fault mid
Notification	send an output mid

Based on the translation template and service behavioral templates, the WSDL translator will take the WSDL specification files and generate skeleton architecture descriptions. Fig.2 shows an example WSDL specification and the structural view generated by the WSDL translator.

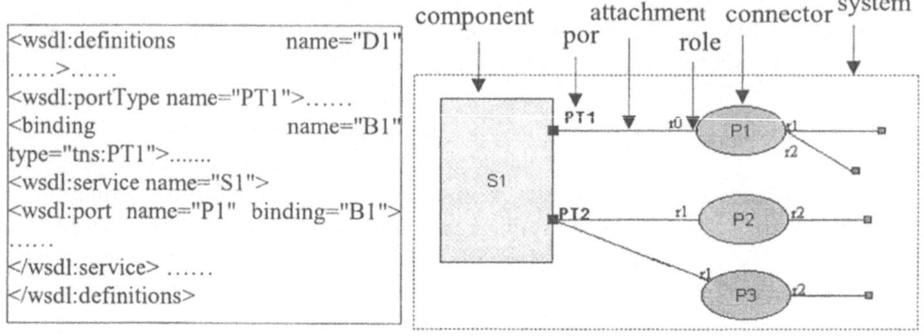

Fig. 2. An example WSDL specification and its architectural structure view

3 Conclusions

To construct a reliable service aggregation, this paper introduced an architecture-based design environment BlueStar. It can describe and analyze a composite service at the architectural level from both the structural and behavioral aspects to gain some measure of confidence in its consistence. On the one hand, BlueStar extend the Acme/Armani with the support of behavior semantics. On the other hand, BlueStar also extends Spin to Spinee with behavioral relation checking capability.

References

1. Zirpins C, Baier T, Lamersdorf W. A Blueprint of Service Engineering. Iin First European Workshop on Object Orientation and Web Service (EOOWS), Darmstadt, Germany, 2003
2. Garlan D, Shaw M. An Introduction to Software Architecture, January 1994, CMU-CS-94-166
3. Garlan D, Monroe R T, Wile D. ACME: An architecture description interchange language. In Proc. of CASCON 97, Toronto, Ontario, November 1997, pp. 169-183.
4. Nakajima S, Tamai T. Behavioural Analysis of the Enterprise JavaBeansTM Component Architecture. In M.B.Dwyer(Ed.):Spin 2001, LNCS 2057, pp.163-182.
5. Erdogmus H, Johnston R, Cleary C. Formal Verification Based on Relation Checking in SPIN: A Case Study. In Proc. of the First Workshop on Formal Methods in Software Practice. San Diego, CA. Jan., 1996. NRC 39183.

The Anatomy of Web Services*

Hongbing Wang[1,2], Yuzhong Qu[2], and Junyuan Xie[1]

[1]Department of computer science and technology, Nanjing University, 210093 Nanjing, China
jyxie@nju.edu.cn
[2] Department of computer science and engineering, Southeast University, 210096 Nanjing, China
{hbw, yzqu}@seu.edu.cn

Abstract. With WSDL, SOAP and UDDI, Web services are becoming popular with Web application. However, current Web services architecture is confronted with a few intractable problems. We shall give an overview of these problems and current efforts. Finally, we set an eye on the amalgamation of Web services and Grid technologies.

1 Introduction

Web services are a new breed of Web application. They are self-contained, self-describing, modular applications that can be published, located, and invoked across the Web. Web services perform functions, which can be anything from simple requests to complicated business processes. Once a Web service is deployed, other applications (and other Web services) can discover and invoke the deployed service.

The key to Web services is software creation through the use of loosely coupled, reusable software components. The Web services framework [1] is divided into three areas — communication protocols, service descriptions, and service discovery — and specifications are being developed for each.

However, current Web services specifications (SOAP, WSDL, and UDDI) meet only lowest requirements, to develop the complete potential of Web services, there are more issues which have to be resolved.

2 The Problems and Current Efforts

SOAP , WSDL, and UDDI are important steps in the direction of a Web populated by services. However, they only address part of the overall stack that needs to be

* This work is jointly supported by NSFC with grant no. 60173036 and JSNSF with grant no. BK2003001.

M. Li et al. (Eds.): GCC 2003, LNCS 3032, pp. 1063–1066, 2004.

available in order to achieve Web services' full Web-wide and global potential. Web services would have to address following problems: security, composition, and semantics

2.1 Security

Of course though, at the most basic level the problems that are likely to affect Web services are the same as for more conventional Web-based systems. Many of these have been discussed at length in past articles. Certainly though the following depiction sums up the current situation:

Security is critical to the adoption of Web services by enterprises, but, as it stands today, the Web services framework doesn't meet basic security requirements.

In the Web services context security means that the recipient of a message should be able to verify the integrity of the message to make sure that it has not been modified, receive a message confidentially so that unauthorized users can't read it, determine the identity of the sender by authenticating them and determine whether or not the center is authorized to carry out the operation requested in the message. These are usually met by encrypting messages.

On the other hand, Web services allow all your systems, both internally and externally, to communicate on HTTP ports so you gain the flexibility. Thereby you inevitably open up the application servers to "application level" attacks.

There are some standards coming to alleviate the former however, such as WS Security (http://www.oasis-open.org/committees/wss/) and various other initiatives (mostly from the major vendors and PKI suppliers, see The XML Signature specification (http://www.w3.org/Signature/), W3C's XML Encryption specification (http://www.w3.org/Encryption/2001/), Security Assertion Markup Language (SAML) (http://www.oasis-open.org/committees/security/), eXtensible Access Control Markup Language (XACML) (http://www.oasis-open.org/committees/xacml/)) towards enabling digital signatures on XML messages and transactions. But the latter was concerned hardly.

2.2 Composition

Early work in Web services composition included eCo (http://www.commerce.net/), WSCL (WSCL, http://www.w3.org/TR/wscl10/), XLANG (http://www.gotdotnet.com/team/xml_wsspecs/xlang-c/default.htm), and WSFL (WSFL, http://www-3.ibm.com/software/solutions/webservices/pdf/WSFL.pdf).

The Web services workflow specifications outlined by XLANG and WSFL have recently been superseded by a new specification from IBM, Microsoft, and BEA called BPEL4WS (Business Process Execution Language for Web Services, http://www-106.ibm.com/developerworks/webservices/library/ws-bpel/). BPEL4WS is a specification that models the behavior of Web services in a business process interaction. The Web Services Choreography Interface (WSCI, http://www.sun.com/software/xml/developers/wsci/wsci-spec-10.pdf) is a specification from Sun, SAP, BEA, and Intalio that defines an XML-based language for Web services collaboration. The Business Process Management Language (BPML) is a meta-language for describing business processes (http://www.bpmi.org/specifications.esp). Business Process Management Initiative, an independent organization chartered by Intalio, Sterling Commerce, Sun, CSC, and others, developed the specification.

Besides above efforts to constitute Web services composition standards [2], many researchers do some helpful works in Web services' composition [3,4]

2.3 Semantics

Most researchers hope now that the Semantic Web vision of a next-generation Web that computers can unambiguously interpret addresses precisely semantic problem of the Web services [5].

Why Web services framework need supports from semantic Web? We should note that current Web services standards, such as SOAP, WSDL, XLANG, WSFL, BPEL4WS, WSCI and BPML, all describe Web service content in terms of XML syntax. Unfortunately, XML alone lacks both a well-defined semantics and sufficient expressive power to realize the vision of diverse Web services having wide-scale interoperability. Seamless interoperability between services that have not been predesigned to work together requires programs to describe their own capabilities and understand other services' capabilities. To realize this vision, we must describe Web content, particularly Web service content and capabilities, in a language that goes beyond XML. The Semantic Web vision of a next-generation Web that computers can unambiguously interpret addresses precisely this problem.

The Semantic Web services vision is to describe Web services' capabilities and content in a computer-interpretable language and improve the quality of existing tasks, including Web service discovery, invocation, composition, monitoring and recovery [6-8].

Initial attempts have already been made to apply semantic Web services technology to a few applications.

A key element of semantic Web services is the creation of a description language. DAML-S, an ontology created by DAML-S Coalition (http://www.daml.org/services/members.html) with support from DARPA, is such a description language. Comprehensive discussions on DAML-S could be found at this Website (http://www.daml.org/services/pub-archive.html).

3 Amalgamations of Web Services and Grid Technologies

A research topic deserving attention to Web services is Grid services. The Open Grid Services Architecture (OGSA, http://www.globus.org/ogsa/) represents an evolution towards a Grid system architecture based on Web services concepts and technologies.

The OGSA integrates key Grid technologies [9] with Web services mechanisms to create a distributed system framework based on the Open Grid Services Infrastructure (OGSI, http://www-unix.globus.org/toolkit/draft-ggf-ogsi-gridservice-33_2003-06-27.pdf). A Grid service instance is a service that conforms to a set of conventions, expressed as Web Service Definition Language (WSDL) interfaces, extensions, and behaviors, for such purposes as lifetime management, discovery of characteristics, and notification. Grid services provide for the controlled management of the distributed and often long-lived state that is commonly required in sophisticated distributed applications. OGSI also introduces standard factory and registration interfaces for creating and discovering Grid services. Grid service instances are made accessible to (potentially remote) client applications through the use of a Grid Service Handle and a Grid Service Reference. An important issue is how OGSI interfaces are likely to be invoked from client applications. OGSI exploits an important component of the Web services framework: the use of WSDL to describe multiple protocol bindings, encoding styles, messaging styles, and so on for a given Web service.

As we known, Grid services have been concerned by many international conferences. An interesting topic is semantic grid services (http://www.semanticgrid.org). The visions of the grid and the semantic Web have much in common but can perhaps be distinguished by a difference of emphasis: the Grid is traditionally focused on computation, while the goal of the Semantic Web take it towards inference, proof and trust. We think that The Grid we are now building is heading towards Semantic Grid.

References

1. Francisco Curbera, Matthew Duftler, Rania Khalaf, William Nagy, Nirmal Mukhi, and Sanjiva Weerawarana , Unraveling the Web Services Web, IEEE Internet Computing, March/April(2002)86-93
2. Wil van der Aalst, Don't Go with the Flow: Web Services Composition Standards Exposed, IEEE intelligent systems, January/February (2003)72-76.
3. Jianwen Su, Richard Hull, Tevfik Bultan, Xiang Fu, Conversation Specification: A New Approach to Design and Analysis of E-Service Composition, Proc. THE TWELFTH INTERNATIONAL WORLD WIDE WEB CONFERENCE (WWW2003), May 20–24, Budapest, Hungary, 2003.
4. Liangzhao Zeng, Boualem Benatallah ,Marlon Dumas, Quality Driven Web Services Composition, Proc. THE TWELFTH INTERNATIONAL WORLD WIDE WEB CONFERENCE (WWW2003), May 20–24, Budapest, Hungary, 2003.
5. S. McIlraith, T.C. Son, and H. Zeng, Semantic Web Services, IEEE Intelligent Systems, vol. 16, no. 2, Mar./Apr.2001, pp. 46–53.
6. Massimo Paolucci, Takahiro Kawamura, Terry R. Payne, and Katia Sycara, Semantic Matching of Web Services Capabilities, Proc. First International Semantic Web Conference (ISWC2002), Sardinia, Italy, June 9-12, 2002.
7. A. Ankolekar et al, DAML-S: Web Service Description for the Semantic Web, Proc. First International Semantic Web Conference (ISWC2002), Sardinia, Italy, June 9-12, 2002.
8. Daniel J. Mandell and Sheila A. McIlraith, A Bottom-Up Approach to Automating Web Service Discovery, Customization, and Semantic Translation, In The Proceedings of the Twelfth International World Wide Web Conference Workshop on E-Services and the Semantic Web (ESSW '03). Budapest, 2003
9. I. Foster,C. Kesselman,S. Tuecke.The Anatomy of the Grid: Enabling Scalable Virtual Organizations.International J.Supercomputer Applications, 15(3), 200-222, 2001

Automated Vulnerability Management through Web Services

H.T. Tian, L.S. Huang, J.L. Shan, and G.L. Chen

Department of Computer Science, University of Science and Technology of China, Hefei, Anhui, China
tht@mail.ustc.edu.cn

Abstract. Vulnerability management plays a key role in the security area, but it is now too time-consuming, and error-prone. Based on a machine-readable vulnerability description language CVML, this paper proposes an automated vulnerability management framework through web services, which alleviates the burden of administrators and improves the security of systems dramatically.

1 Introduction

Flaws in systems that could subvert security mechanisms, called vulnerabilities, are prerequisite in each computer intrusion, so vulnerability management plays a key role in security area. However most of vulnerability information from different sources is now ambiguous, text-based description, which makes vulnerability management a manual process that is very time-consuming and error-prone. This paper presents a new framework for automated vulnerability management through web services, based on an XML-based vulnerability description language. In the framework, various web services are developed to share vulnerability knowledge among different parties (such as databases, security tools), to check and remedy vulnerabilities of systems. This paper is organized as follows: in section 2 the background and related work are reviewed, then a new machine-readable vulnerability representation is introduced in section 3, Section 4 explains the framework, and Finally it goes to conclusions.

2 Background and Related Work

Vulnerability management means discovery, disclosing, remediation, and publication of vulnerabilities in their whole life cycle. But now lack of a precise, machine-readable representation of vulnerabilities makes vulnerability management far too manual, time-consuming, and error-prone. It also embarrasses automated vulnerability assessment, interaction of different security products and tools, combination and refining of vulnerability information from different sources. In fact, system administrators in general are swamped by the flood of vulnerabilities and related patches being released. Various research initiatives have revealed that most breaches occur through

M. Li et al. (Eds.): GCC 2003, LNCS 3032, pp. 1067–1070, 2004.

known vulnerabilities that are not properly fixed by administrators, which indicates that current vulnerability management should be improved.

Most of research on vulnerabilities has focused on how to discover specific vulnerabilities and how to fix them. To our knowledge, there is not a machine-readable language to precisely express vulnerabilities now, and accordingly there is not any systematical research on automated vulnerability management. But some work[3,4] is towards the right direction of automated vulnerability management.

3 XML-Based Vulnerability Representation

Common Vulnerability Markup Language[1] provides a unified and machine-readable way to describe vulnerabilities using XML. Due to limit of space, we only give a high-level view here. It is mainly composed of four sections: evaluation, check-existence, solution, and exploit.

Evaluation section evaluates the vulnerability with three attributes: direct impact, total cost of exploit (TCE) and general rating. The 'direct impact' tells the direct result caused by the vulnerability such as root access, user access, system down, disclosure of sensitive data etc. TCE means the total resources (such as hardware, software, time) and skills (such as the ability of programming with assembly on certain system) needed to exploit the vulnerability. General rating gives the severity of the vulnerability. Generally speaking vulnerabilities with more severe direct impact and less TCE are more serious. Accurate evaluation of vulnerabilities is important for risk assessment and we should take cost-effective measure to treat vulnerabilities.

The part of check-existence explains how to check for the presence of vulnerability on a computer system. It includes three parts: affected platform, affected software, and affected file to indicate where the vulnerability exists. Information here is used to check existence of vulnerabilities.

The section of solution contains information about how to correct the vulnerability. It consists of workaround and patch. Workaround provides operations taken in the absence of patching to correct the vulnerability. 'Patch' gives the patch name, a short note and the update URL pointing to a download site or a web service to fix the vulnerability, which can enable automatic update or hot-fix for system security. The element patch-trace specifies how to check whether the patch has been installed on the target system. It can include an entry in registry for MS Windows, it also can refer to some specific entry in a specific file such as "inetd.conf" in Solaris.

The exploit part is from the view of attackers and designed to support automatic attack generation. We can model attacks with 2-layer topology: functionality-level referring to concrete vulnerability exploit and concept-level referring logical description for illation. The exploit contains three child elements: precondition and post-condition that contribute to concept level description while procedure represents the functionality level. Precondition and post-condition give the privilege required or got on the target system for exploiting the vulnerability, and high-level concepts in any form (such as attack description languages[2]). A successful computer intrusion consists of a few phases. An attacker increases his privilege on the target system in each phase until he gets the ultimate goal: super user privilege or absolute control of the system. Detail about definition and ratiocination of vulnerabilities in concept level is beyond the scope of this paper. Procedure gives functionality-level steps taken in any attack description languages or source code in programming language such as c, c++, Perl etc. Compilation and execution of this part by the attacker will exploit the vulnerability.

4 Automated Vulnerability Management through Web Services

Web services have emerged as the next generation of web-based technology for exchanging information. Based on open standards, web services enable you to build web-based applications using any platform, object model, and programming language that you require. Web services together with CVML provide a new security interoperability standard for vulnerability management. We have implemented a prototype of automatic vulnerability management framework shown in Fig.1.

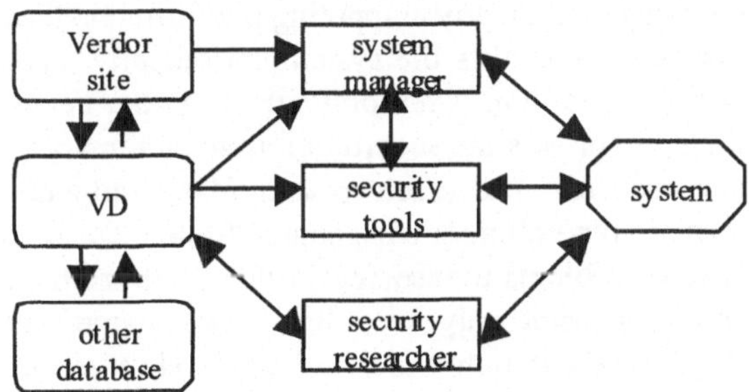

Fig. 1. Vulnerability Management through Web Services

We build a vulnerability database (VD) in format of CVML, and three web services have been developed now: issuer, scanner and attacker.

Any clients (such as agents of other vulnerability databases, security assess tools etc.) can ask the 'issuer' for customized vulnerability information in CVML. 'Issuer' can also provide subscription service in which updates of customized vulnerabilities will be sent to clients timely. Due to the nature of machine-readability of CVML, all kinds of security tools and vulnerability databases could interact with one another automatically and exchanging of vulnerability knowledge could fulfill efficiently without human intervention.

According to a survey by SecurityFocus[5], system administrators spend an average of 2.1 hours/day hunting for security information relevant in all kinds of security bulletins or mailing lists, then download and install patches. It is important to make this manual procedure automatic. In our framework, the agent system manager (SM) is in charge of the vulnerability management systems. Ideally we expect in future all software installed on systems could register with SM of security related information (such as the version, the update sites etc). Currently SM will scan the system periodically to get related information of all software (such as hardware type, OS version, services running, third-party applications etc). Then SM sends the system profile to the web service ‘Scanner’ and it returns all possible vulnerabilities on the system in CVML. According to rules made by system administrators and the ‘solution’ section in CVML, SM will take some action accordingly (such as downloading and installing the patch automatically or only warning).

The web service ‘attacker’ can be used in aid of penetration test. It is based on the system profile or system scanning results. We have implemented in the prototype the privilege chaining process and some concept-level ratiocination of known vulnerabilities for automated generation of attack sequence. When the clients ask the ‘attacker’ for a penetration test, it will return the attack sequence of exploiting vulnerabilities or practice the sequence correspondingly.

5 Conclusions and Future Work

In our framework the agent System Manager as client of web services running on servers, which can be installed on any computing platform (such as PC, mobile phone, PDA etc), scans, assesses, and tests the system periodically, update vulnerable software automatically when possible. It not only alleviates the heavy burden of security administrators, but also improves the security of systems remarkably. We are working on developing more web services (such as authorized vulnerability submission to database) for automated vulnerability management through the Internet.

There are also a few problems unresolved in this field, such as how to check vulnerabilities more precisely (not only according to the name, version of software)? How to make CVML representation widely adopted? How to ensure trustworthiness of the web services? These are all in our future work.

References

1. H.T.Tian, L.S.Huang etc.: Common Vulnerability Markup Language. In: Proceedings of 1st International Conference on Applied Cryptography and Network Security. Lecture Notes in Computer Science, Vol. 2846, Springer (2003)
2. Cuppens, F., Ortalo, R.: Lambda: A Language to Model a Database for Detection of Attacks. In: Proceedings of the Third International Workshop on the Recent Advances in Intrusion Detection (RAID’2000)
3. R.A.Martin, Managing vulnerabilities in networked systems. Computer, Vol.34, Issue:11, (2001) 32-38
4. R.Steinberger.: Vulnerability Management in Unix Environments. Information Security Technical Report, Vol.7, No. 1(2002) 26-36
5. http://www.securityfocus.com

Optimizing Java Based Web Services by Partial Evaluation*

Lin Lin, Linpeng Huang, and Yongqiang Sun

Dept. of Computer Science Shanghai Jiao Tong University
Shanghai, 200030, China
linker_lin03@hotmail.com
{huang-lp, sun-yq}@cs.sjtu.edu.cn

Abstract. Recently, web service is growing more and more popular. Java is a representative language to implement web based services. But its platform independency slows its running speed. Partial evaluation can be used to improve Java bytecode efficiency. In this paper, we present a distributed Java bytecode partial evaluation architecture to accelerate Java based web service running speed by optimizing service according to certain context or, if possible, localizing remote service. Our distributed partial evaluator is based on SOAP message passing. Finally our experiment result of a RMI service shows that the partial evaluator can optimize Java based web services as we have expected.

1 Introduction

Partial evaluation is a program optimization technology. Generally speaking, partial evaluation uses a kind of algorithm which, when given a program and some of its input data (called static inputs), produces a residual program. The residual program must meet the constraint that when running it on the remaining input data (called dynamic inputs), we will get the same result as running the original program on all its input data (including both static and dynamic inputs).

Though partial evaluation technology has been applied to lots of languages, such as logic languages, imperative languages, etc, it is used in object oriented languages, especially Java, only within a few years. Shultz and Lawall have constructed a partial evaluator called Jspec[1], which utilizes Harissa and Tempo[2]. Masuhara and Yonezawa from Tokyo University proposed Bytecode Specialization[3], which specialize program of JVML subset at run-time.

In software engineering, many software architectures are presented to aid software developing. They accelerate software development, but lead to low efficiency of software running. By applying partial evaluation to software engineering, software developer can optimize software architecture under certain context so that they can obtain both developing speed and running speed. Because of the great computing potential of network, more and more software applications are based on internet. They

* Supported by the National High Technology Development Program of China under Grant No. 2001AA113160

M. Li et al. (Eds.): GCC 2003, LNCS 3032, pp. 1071–1074, 2004.

are constructed by distributed software architecture. These web services themselves have the potential to be optimized.

This paper presents a partial evaluation method to optimize Java based web services. Section 2 describes Java base web service specialization opportunities. Section 3 presents a distributed online Java partial evaluation architecture. Then, section 4 gives a simple web service experiment result. Section 5 is the conclusion of this paper.

2 Java Base Web Service Specialization Opportunities

Web service software contains two main parts, which are service and service consumer. Service consumer uses certain mechanism to locate the remote service. It then invokes service methods to achieve its goal. Here can we see some specialization opportunities. Firstly, using known service invocation context, we can optimize the service method. Hereafter, whenever a same context service invocation is performed, we can provide service with the newly optimization produced method. Secondly, if the service method does not use any resources on the service host, we can just send the optimized service back to service consumer machine. So that each time we need a service, we need not get service on a remote machine. All that we need to do is call for the localized service.

Next, we will present a distributed Java bytecode partial evaluator to illustrate our Java based web service specialization idea and to show some perspective results.

3 Distributed Bytecode Partial Evaluator

3.1 System Architecture

The partial evaluator is based on SOAP. Each host in the network has a partial evaluator copy, which contains a dispatcher and a local partial evaluator-Jmix[4], which is developed by ourselves. In the network is also a name server, which contains a service table recording all the relevant information of a service. Fig. 1 illustrates the system architecture. Each dotted arrow represents a SOAP message passing process.

At a certain time, software on a certain computer may call for either local service or remote service. So there are accordingly two situations in partial evaluation. On the one hand, if dispatcher finds a local service invocation, it just makes Jmix optimize the service. On the other hand, if dispatcher (for instance, dispatcher 1 on host 1 in figure 1) finds a remote service invocation, it looks up the service table on name server to get the service information which includes which host the service runs on. If service is on host 2, dispatcher 1 sends a soap message, which encapsulates invocation context, to dispatcher 2 on host 2. Then dispatcher 2 uses the context information distilled from the message to call Jmix 2 to optimize service. If service is localizable, a message containing the specialized service is sent back. Otherwise, only a success message is returned.

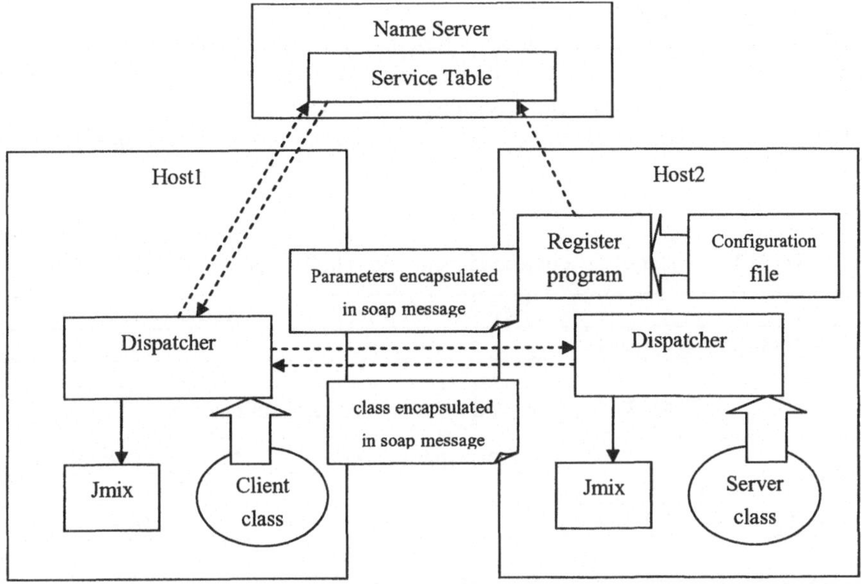

Fig. 1. System architecture

3.2 Implementation of a Distributed Partial Evaluator-DJmix

Let us consider a simple service example. We use remote method invocation to get current time which can be localized. According to this Java RMI service, we will implement our idea previously described. In this section, we will present how to implement DJmix and some experiment results.

3.2.1 Implementation Detail

On the name server, there resides a service table. When service class is deployed, for instance, on host2, there is a configuration file describing information associated with it. Before partial evaluation, content of this file should be filled into the service table, which is called the registering, by a register program.

In Fig. 1, dispatcher 1 on host 1gets the remote service name from Java bytecode. Dispatcher 1 then constructs a SOAP message which contains the service name and sends it to looking up service on name server. Looking up service gets the information node of the service from the service table. Then a message containing this information is returned to dispatcher 1 to perform the partial evaluation request.

Dispatcher 1 constructs a message containing service invocation context according to the information got from last section and sends it to dispatcher 2. Then dispatcher 2 uses the context information distilled from the message to specialize service, and constructs a returning message.

3.2.2 Experiment Result

Partial evaluation is done only once. After that we can get the localized service as many times as possible. So we omit the partial evaluation time in get current time many times situation. Since each remote service call has been optimized to be a localized call, as number of remote service increases, more time to perform remote call is saved.

Table 1. Number of Java bytecode instructions before and after specialization

	Before specialization	After specialization
Number of instructions	19	16

Table 2. Time consuming before and after optimization

	Before specialization	After specialization
Ask for service 10 times	20	10
Ask for service 100 times	171	30

As experiment result shows, after optimization, Java bytecode length is diminished and program runs more efficiently.

4 Conclusions and Future Work

In this paper, we analyze the Java base web service specialization opportunities. Then we propose a distributed partial evaluator which can utilize these specialization opportunities to optimize web service programs. After that, we implement a distributed Java bytecode partial evaluator, called DJmix, based on SOAP message passing. At last, we apply DJmix to a Java RMI service instance, and get some expected results.

References

1. Schultz,U.P., Lawall,J., Consel,C., Muller,G.: Toward Automatic Specialization of Java Programs. Proceedings of 13th European Conference on Object-Oriented Programming (1999) 367-390
2. Consel, C. and Noel, F.: a general approach to run-time specialization and its application to C. Proceedings 23rd ACM SIGPLAN-SIGACT Symposium on Principals of Programming Languages (1996) 145-156
3. Masuhara, H. and Yonezawa, A.: Generating Optimized Residual Code in Run-Time Specialization. Technical Report of PE Day'99 (1999)
4. Hou Yiming: the Design and Implementation of Jmix-a Java Partial Evaluator. Graduate thesis, SJTU, China (2002)

An XML Based General Configuration Language: XGCL[1]

Huaifeng Qin and Xingshe Zhou

Computer Science Department, Northwestern Polytechnical University
{qinhf, zhouxs}@mail.nwpu.edu.cn

Abstract. Contemporary embedded operating systems are built from rich set of components. To address the problem of configuration management, we design an XML based language for configurable embedded system. XGCL takes advantage of the legible and flexible features of XML. It is special designed to provide a common interface for all the embedded operating systems. The paper outlines the architecture of XGCL and gives an implementation instance.

1 Introduction

Most of the contemporary embedded operating systems are built from many components. To fit application need, they must be custom tailed or configed. However most of the configuration technologies existing focus too much on the ability of configuration, and ignore the sophistication of configuration management. Suppose an embedded operating system which can provide thousands of configuration points but can not arranges them properly. It will be a disaster for the developers who work on this platform. In this paper, we introduce a special designed language –XGCL– to provide an efficient way of configuration management.

2 A Brief Survey

Basically, all the system is built with the presence of an appropriate makefile. It is makefile decided which components can be included and compiled. For the configurable system, makefile is often generated dynamically. System configuration could help generating the makefile. To find out the ways existing systems be configed, we selected some typical operating systems and made a simple survey. Parts of these operating systems are common used in embedded system; others are special in design. The survey is carried out by investigating these systems' configuration ability, user interface for configuration and the facility of configuration.

VxWorks: VxWorks [1] provides scalable runtime software. Individual modular of the operating system is scalable and can be tailored according to the need. Tornado is

[1] Supported by the Doctorate Foundation of Northwestern Polytechnical University

M. Li et al. (Eds.): GCC 2003, LNCS 3032, pp. 1075–1078, 2004.

an excellent tool VxWorks provided for the configuration. The configuration mode of VxWorks is based on the templates. Different modular is located in different directory with head files specifying it. Though most of the options can be configed in Tornado, special functions may sometimes be configed by modify the head file manual.

Linux: Because of its low development cost, in recent years Linux has been widely used in embedded systems. Besides modular mechanism, Linux also provides limited source code level configuration ability. Linux provide command line based or X Window based configuration utilities. Configuration options are predefined in file config.in. After the configuration finished, Linux will create files .config and autoconf.h. The file .config is used for generating makefile; the file autoconf.h defined many macros to record configed parameters.

μCOS: μCOS [2] is a special designed mini real-time embedded operating system. μCOS is designed configurable, but it does not provide special configuration user interface. One can simply specify the features needed by modifying the macros defined in configuration file OS_CFG.H.

eCos: eCos(embedded Configurable operating system) [3] is a special designed configurable embedded operating system. Packages are coarse grained configuration units. The individual components within the packages are also configurable. eCos provides a graphical configuration interface – Configuration Tool. Specially, eCos apply a Component Definition Language (CDL) describing the packages and components as well as their configuration option. The integration of CDL and ConfigTool not only facilitate the configuration but also ease the port of third part software.

More or less, all the operating systems surveyed provide the configuration ability and most of them provide a user interface. Theoretically, they are all configed by defining macros in head files. However the human intelligences involved are different. The existence of efficient configuration management mechanism determines their performance.

3 Framework of XGCL

Taking one with another, the configuration mode of eCos is advisable, however the CDL eCos employed is so specific that it is not appropriate for applying it to all the other embedded operating systems. To provide the efficient configuration management mechanism and carry out the configuration work in a more standard manner, it is sound to design a uniform configuration language.

XML (Extensible Markup Language) is a simple, very flexible text format derived from SGML, the Standard Generalized Markup Language [4]. The design goal of XML is to make it be straightforwardly usable over the Internet, be human-legible, be formal and concise, and be easy to create, etc. XML is just a markup specification language. The information it described can be processed by a program. But on its own, XML document does not do anything.

The extensible and legible features of XML make it be the nature prototype language for describing components and the options of various embedded operating systems. Based on the XML, we put forward the idea of a special design configuration language: the XML based General Configuration Language, which is abbreviated to XGCL.

The design intention of XGCL is to take advantage of the extensibility of XML to organize and present different embedded operating system's component in an utmost similar way. Figure 1 shows the framework of XGCL.

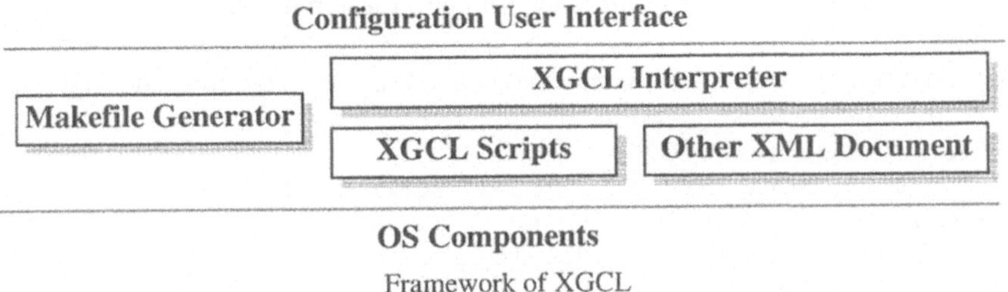

Framework of XGCL

Fig. 1. Roughly, XGCL includes 4 main parts. XGCL Scrip is the base of XGCL. All the OS components are described by XGCL scripts. Other XML Documents include all the other related XML documents needed by the XGCL interpreter. One important document of these is DTD. XGCL interpreter is the core of XGCL. The main work of makefile generator is defining macros, creating headfiles, and generating top-level makefile needed by compiler.

A configurable embedded operating system using XGCL would work as the way below. When initializes a new configuration session, XGCL interpreter read XGCL scripts and other XML documents first, then process them. Configuration user interface gets the information processed and displays them in properly manner.

At the beginning of the configuration, many headfiles will be created. Most of them are copied directly from the source code (or object file) directory; others are system defined headfiles for saving configuration parameters. When saving configuration, makefile generator will inquire XGCL interpreter reading makefile generating rules which is defined in advance in XGCL script. Then based on the current configuration, create a well formed makefile. After finished configuration, a result file would be created. This is a XGCL style file which record user's selections for later use.

4 An Implementation of XGCL

eCos provides well defined configuration system structure. To ease the work, we select eCos as the base operating system to implement XGCL. The configuration system of eCos consists of source code, CDL scripts, package database and Configuration Tool. Our implementation rewrites all the CDL scripts using XGCL and replaces the CDL interpreter of Configuration Tool with XGCL interpreter.

As the organization of elements in CDL presents a hierarchical structure [5], the definition of DTD refers to this structure. There four CDL-related 'commands' in CDL script: cdl_package, cdl_component, cdl_option and cdl_interface. cdl_package and cdl_component can also have nested 'commands' in their bodies. Corresponding to CDL, there are 4 main elements: PACKAGE, COMPONENT, INTERFACE and

OPTION defined in DTD. Each of them is made up of a name and some properties while PACKAGE and COMPONENT can nest other elements.

We select Xerces-C++ [6] parsing XGCL script. Xerces-C++ is a validating XML parser written in a portable subset of C++. It provides a shared library for parsing, generating, manipulating, and validating XML documents. Xerces-C++ also provides source code which enable us tailor it according to the actual needs.

Below shows a piece of XGCL script fragment which is ported from the CDL script

```
<?xml version="1.0"?>
<!DOCTYPE XGCL SYSTEM "dtds/codedtd.dtd">
<XGCL>
  <PACKAGE Name= "CYGPKG_IO_TVGA">
    <Compile>
           <Library>libextras.a</Library>
           <File>tvga.c</File>
    </Compile>
    <Display>Trident Driver</Display>
    <Description>
            This provides Trident 8900C ISA video card
            driver
    </Description>
    <Requires>CYGPKG_ERROR</Requires>
</PACKAGE>
```

5 Conclusion

This paper presented an approach to use XML based language in configurable embedded operating system. XML is one kind of computing language close to the nature language very much. As a language based on XML, XGCL would not only innovate the way for operating system component description but also forward a new mode for the development of configurable embedded operating system.

References

1. Wind River http://www.windriver.com
2. Micrium http://www.ucos-ii.com/
3. eCos http://sources.redhat.com/ecos/
4. Extensible Markup Language http://www.w3.org/XML/
5. Bart Veer, John Dallaway. The eCos Component Writer's Guide. Red Hat Inc, 2001.
6. The Apache XML Project http://xml.apache.org/

Modification on Kerberos Authentication Protocol in Grid Computing Environment

Rong Chen[1], Yadong Gui[2], and Ji Gao[1]

[1] Zhejiang University Computer College Zhejiang China 310017,
[2] Shanghai[1] Supercomputer Center, Shanghai China, 201203

Abstract. The Kerberos is applied widely in OS and grid computing environment. The Kerberos system isn't secure enough for symmetrical encryption. The paper describes a method that transform symmetrical key into asymmetric encryption on the basis of keeping symmetrical key of one side changeless. The algorithm strengthens the security of Kerberos protocol through proofing.

1 Introduction

Authentication is technology that verifies communication object I.D. The most useful protocol is Kerberos basing on the transform of Needlham-Schroeder. Initially developed for the Athena, which adapted symmetrical cryptosystem. Kerberos authentication system has been used in all kinds of the distributed system [1], Grid computing system [2]. For many drawbacks [3], many researchers have modificated the protocol.

Literature [4] put forward advance authentication mechanism to prevent offline dictionary assault. The test result illuminate that this method can weaken the dictionary assault and largely strengthen the security of system. At present, Kerberos v5 has adapted this research result. Literature [5] modifies the Kerberos protocol and algorithm, and introduces the Yaksha system basing on the RSA public cryptosystem.

Differing with the RSA, it divide the private key into two keys-----$d_{aa}*_{ay}=d_a$ mod n [6]. *day* is put into the cryptosystem management system and d_{aa} is sent to user. This system is not only strengthening system cryptosystem management system security but also effectively prohibit the dictionary assault. But the method needs to have a big modification to Kerberos protocol.

This paper describes a kind of Kerberos authentication mechanism that keeps the protocol and transforms the symmetric key in the AS server into the public keys. At the same time on the side of user, symmetry key is transformed into the private key. This has no effect on the public customers, but it has strengthened the security of cryptographic management system. It won't disclose the private key even if the AS server is invaded.

Section 2introduces the authentication protocol basing on elliptic curve. Section 3 introduces the authentication process of the protocol. Section 4 Security proof

[1] Supported by Shanghai information grid. Project No.03dz15026

M. Li et al. (Eds.): GCC 2003, LNCS 3032, pp. 1079–1082, 2004.

2 Modification Authentication Method

In 1985, Neil Kobliz and VictorMiller put forward Elliptic Curve Cryptosystem (ECC). The elliptic curve cryptosystem secure strength not only depends on the discrete logarithm in the elliptic curve but also depends on the curve-selected and system. Presently 200-bit long elliptic curve cryptosystem has a higher strength..

2.1 Mathematics Theorem

1. $E(Fq)\oplus$operation to point form an albel group:

Presume: $p \in E(Fq)$, If the cycle p is very large, and even $p \oplus p \oplus \ldots\ldots \oplus p=\theta$(and has $t\,p$ sum).

The least positive integer t and hope the t very large.

($t=p$ cycle,express as $\pi(p)=t$).

and to $Q \in E(Fq)$, there must be a positive integer m make $Q=m \cdot p= p \oplus p \oplus \ldots\ldots \oplus p$(there are $t\,p$ sum).

Definition 1: *$m=\log_p Q$. The point of elliptic curve form the group E(Fq), and correlative its discrete logarithm is difficult to deal with.*

2.Set up the elliptic curve cryptosystem

The reason that the paper selects ECC is because ECC simple and convenient during the keys converting. Selecting the base domain Fq and the elliptic curve Fq is certain form. In the $E(Fq)$, select the point that period is very large. For example select a point $P=(x_p,y_p)$, its cycle is a big prime number n, mark $\Pi(P)=n$ (prime number)

2.2 Mechanism Implementation

Private key generated

Server manager (maybe an agent) execute as fellow:

(1). Convert 56bit or other data-bits into binary K_{c1}.

(2). Compute the point $Q: = K_{c1}P$ (number d to $\oplus$)

(3). Server gets the public parameter $(E(Fq),p,n,Q)$, and discard the private keys.(On the other side, we know, the user's key is a private key)

AS send the messages

express the m as the domain element $m \in Fq$.

We select the random number k in the area $[1, n-1]$.

Computing point $(x_1,y_1):=kp$ as the AS public key

Computing point $(x_2,y_2):=kQ$. If the $x_2=0$, we come back to the step (2).

Computing $C:=m \bullet x_2$

Transfer the encrypted data (x_1,y_1,C) to user

3.When the user receive the cryptograph (x_1,y_1,C),execute

(1) Convert 56bit or other data-bits K_C into binary K_{c1}.

(2)Use the private key $Kc1$, computing the point (x_2, y_2): $=Kc1\ (x_1, y_1)$, then computing $x_2\text{-}1$ of Fq.

(3)We resume the plaintext m through computing $m:=C\,x_2\text{-}1$

3 Authentication Process of the Protocol

The authentication process as fellow:

1.*C->AS:C,Texp,N*

2.*AS->C:Kcpu[Ks,TGS,Texp,N],* K_{TGS}*[A,Ks]*

3.*C->TGS:Ks[TS],*K_{TGS}*[C,Ks],S,Texp,N*

4.*TGS->C: Ks[*K_{CSE}*,S,Texp,N],KBPA[C,*K_{CSE}*]*

5.*C->SE:*K_{CSE}*[TS],*K_{SEPA}*[A,*K_{CSE}*]*

6.*C->SE:*K_{CSE}*[TS+1]*

Kcpu,K_{SEPU} are the private key of *C,SE,* K_{CPR}*,*K_{SEPR} are the *C* and *SE* the private keys. K_{TGS} is the private key of *TGS,* K_{CSE} is the session private key between *C* and *SE*. The meaning of the symbol as the 2.1.Comparing the Kerberos protocol front and back, we find that the protocol has no change. From the user's view, the authentication process has no change. But we find that the authentication mechanism isn't the traditional symmetric cryptosystem, and is the public cryptosystem.

4 Security Proof

Lemma1: Elliptic curve cryptosystem is a NP problem, under the condition of Q,P known, the problem is in fact unsolvable to the private parameter Ks big enough e.

Theory 2:in the modified scheme, the key management system is secure.

Proof: we can know from this scheme.

K_C is the symmetric key;

Put the Kc into the binary Ks;

If the Ks<e;

Transform the Kc to the e bit

Adapt the difficult discrete logarithm in the elliptic curve.

Q=KsP Q is a public key, P is private key

From the lemma 1 we can know solve the Ks is NP problem.

=>Public key Q is form P1 as the plaintext

And know Ks>e

=>Adapting the Q,P to solve the Ks is NP problem

=>Cryptosystem is secure.

Theory 3: The security of modified Kerberos is higher than the current version.

Proof: Adapting this method hasn't modified the Kerberos

We know that cryptosystem management is secure.

The paper adapts elliptic curve method, and e is secure bit. It can resist against solving this cryptograph.

These two methods are equal. So the security of this mechanism is higher than present version.

5 Conclusion

The number of users is very large; at present many big corporations including the Microsoft Corporation support the Kerberos protocol. From view of business, any big modification must be fit for user's profit. From the view of research, any big modification could produce a new authentication mechanism, and will deviate from the Kerberos authentication system.

Kerberos authentication mechanism is the only one kind of them. We convert the symmetric cryptosystem into the public cryptosystem and make the cryptosystem more secure. And the user's password has no change and even the user can't find any changes.

In the grid computing environment, Kerberos is based on a untrust environment, and the Kerberos system is disclose on the front of a group of untrust man. Kerberos protocol must ensure security, convenient and easy to use.. In the loose and inter-domain grid computing environment, how to strengthen the Kerberos's security is our research in the future.

Referencess

1. G.Bruth and R.Dempsey. Security in Distributed Computing. Pearson Education POD, 1996
2. Foster,C,Kesselman,G.Tsudik,A Security Architecture for computational. ACM Conference on Computer and Communications Security.1998
3. Jospth N.pato. Using pre-authentication to avoid password attack.1993 OSFDCE request for comments 260.
4. Bellovin SM, merritt M, Limitation of the Kerberos authentication system.ACM SIGCOMM Computer Commnication review.
5. Ganesane,R. Augmenting Kerberos with the public key cryptography In:Porceeding of the internet society symposium on the network and distributed security. IEEE Computer Society Press 1995:132-143
6. Ganesane.R, the Yakasha security system. Communications of the ACM 1996.39(3):55-60
7. Gaskell. Integrating Smart Cards into Authentication System. In EdDawson.editor, Proceedings of Cryptosystem:Policy and algorithm Conference. LNCS1029, pages270-281 Springer-Verlag,1995

A Distributed Honeypot System for Grid Security[1]

Geng Yang[1], Chunming Rong[2], and Yunping Dai [1]

[1] Department of Computer Science and Technology
Nanjing University of Posts and Telecommunications, Nanjing 210003, CHINA
yangg@njupt.edu.cn
[2] Department of Electrical and Computer and Engineering
Stavanger University College, P.O.Box 8002, N-4068, NORWAY
chunming.rong@tn.his.no

Abstract. In this paper, we propose a distributed honeypot model for grid computing system security. Based on the IDS Snort and the firewall IPTable, we set up a testing environment and use a simple watching dog to manage capture data. We also discuss implementation of the system and some future research topics.

Keywords: Honeypot, Grid Computing, Distributed System, Network Security

1 Introduction

Computer network security has been focus on passive defense strategies using tools and concepts like Firewall, Intrusion Detection System (IDS). Honeypot is a computer security concept introduced in [1,2]. A Honeypot is essentially a decoy computer system designed to simulate a real legitimate system with little or no defense in order to attract hacker to attack. By analyzing data gathered from one or more Honeypot systems, for example a Honeynet [3,4,5], we may gain more knowledge and intelligence data about the methods, tactics and tools used by the blackhats. Using the information obtained, we may find bugs in computer system or in network system, and then improve the computer or network security in the real computer systems accordingly.

2 Principal of Honeypot

A Honeypot is a program which appears to be a service, set of services, an entire operating system, or even an entire network, but in reality it is a tightly sealed system (like a sandbox) built to lure and contain intruders while the real system and data is safely running apart from the Honeypot. The strategy behind Honeypot is to shut intruders safely from production systems and to obtain intelligent on the intruder by monitoring and logging every actions the intruder makes including access attempts,

[1] This work is supported by The Natural Science Foundation of Jiangsu Province(BK2003106).

M. Li et al. (Eds.): GCC 2003, LNCS 3032, pp. 1083–1086, 2004.

keystrokes, files accessed and modified, and programs executed. Figure 1 shows an example of how Honeypot can be deployed in a network for protection purposes. In this example, Honeypot-A simulates a system without any firewall or Intrusion Detection System (IDS);

00

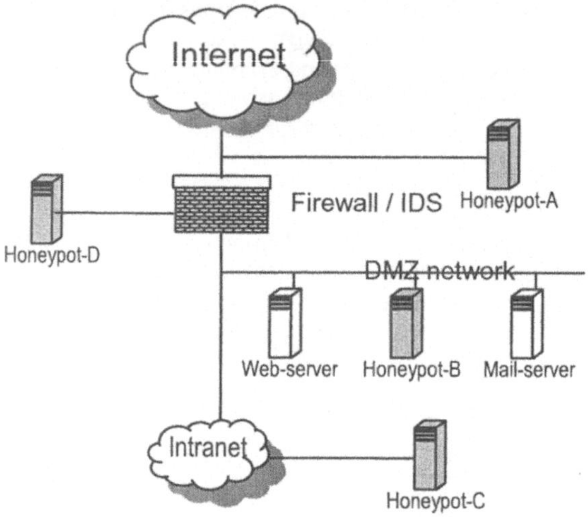

Fig. 1. Example of Honeypots deployment in a network

The most valuable information we gain is by tracking an intruder in a Honeypot and revealing his tactics and maybe ultimately the motives so that the real production system can be better protected using the information gathered. This will give us a early warning on the system vulnerability before they are targeted by blackhats.

3 Honeypot for Grid Security

3.1 Grid Computing Environment

In a grid computing system, facility (or we call services) should be provided for users because those are open sources to public. This probably gives a chance for hacker to enter the system, and finally cause a serious security problem. Hackers could enter the system easily and abuse the sources or use them improperly.. Even though there are some user control mechanism or some other security tools in the system. Security problem is always a big challenge we face, like the same situation as that in LAN. In fact, it could be worse in grid computing networks that in traditional networks, because of sharing resources.

In order to protect grid computing environments, we propose to use a distributed honeypot system as a supplemented security tool to keep away hackers from our real system and trap them into a honeypot.

3.2 A Distributed Honeypot System for Grid Security

A distributed honeypot system is shown in Figure 2. In each source provider, a redirecting module (RM) is run , which is a program module. A source provider could be a computer or a server in a grid computing system. When a suspicious user tries to enter a source provider in a grid computing system, the RM will detect it and redirect it to a fake network, instead of preventing the suspicious user. In the fake local network, many services are available for the user, like FTP, Web, and e-mail services, etc. A management system of the honeypot in the fake network observes actions of the user, collects information and analyzes the data., which gives us useful information about the user, particularly about intention of the user and the services asked.

In a distributed honeypot system, Honeypot are installed in one place only. All suspicious users are redirected into the system. This kind of centralized management makes it effective to collect data and analyze the data. Otherwise, we have to run a honeypot in each source provider in the grid computer system. Computer and human sources are wasted. Moreover, maintaining many Honeypot is difficult than mentioning only one of them.

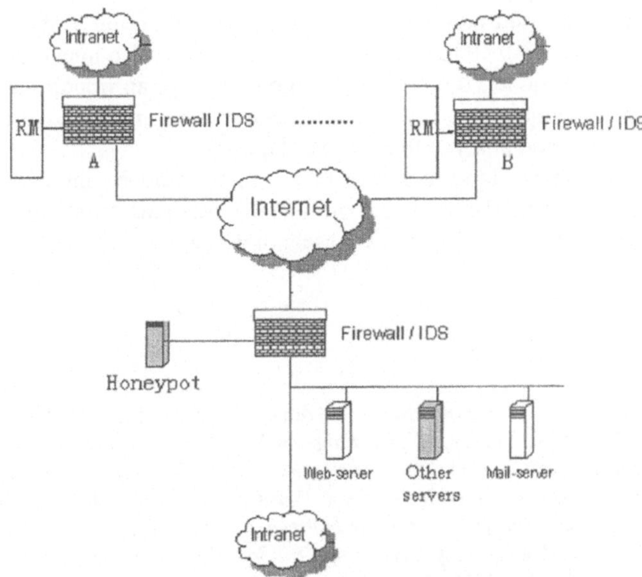

Fig. 2. A distributed honeypot system in network

3.3 Implementation of the Distributed Honeypot System

A honeypot called MagicNet[6] is set based on the IDS Snort, the firewall system IPTables and RedHeat 9.0 Linux system. In order to protect Snort system, no IP address is used for Snort. Data capture is done from three layers. First, Snort captures all data by checking packets and stores the data in system log file syslog which is inserted into a database system MySql. Second, the firewall IPTables records all access in the log files syslog and msyslog which are also merged into the database. Note that if the file syslog is used, the other one msyslog is screened automatically. Finally, the operating system log file is also used to capture data.

The detecting techniques used in IDS is employed to realize the RM module. According some rules, for example checking head data of packets to find out suspicious users, we can redirect them to the honeypot. This program module can be installed in all sources provider in the grid computing system. Moreover, with the developing of mobile agent technology, we could also use an agent to send the RM module to the source provider. This will be another research topic in our future.

The grid computing environment is built based on Globus 3.0. A software swatch (simple watchdog) is used to manage and analyze the data. One a suspicious user enters the system or makes some actions, the watchdog will give an alarm in various ways, such as sending a message to echo or administrator.

4 Conclusions

We proposed a distributed honeypot model for grid computing system. Based on the IDS Snort and the firewall IPTable, we set up a testing environment. Note that in this distributed honeypot model, the redirecting module plays an important role. We took some detecting techniques used in IDS to identify abnormal behavior, and a single watchdog to manage and analyze the capture data.

Many topics could be done in future research. It could be interesting to develop some new algorithms in the RM and some new methods to capture data. A data management system is certainly another research domain.

References

1. L. Spitzner: *Honeypot – Tracking Hackers*, Addison-Wesley (ISBN 0321108957), 2002
2. L. Spitzner: "To build a Honeypot", *Cryptogram Newsletter*, pp. 1-2, June 15, 2001
3. The Honeynet Project: *Know Your Enemy:Revealing the Security Tools, Tactics, and Motives of the Blackhat Community*.Addison-Wesley (ISBN 0201746131), 2001
4. The Honeynet Project, *Know Your Enemy:Honeynets*, April, 2001
5. C. Stoll: *The Cuckoo's Egg, Tracking a Spy Through the Maze of Computer Espionage*,.Pocket Books, 2000
6. Chunming Rong, Geng Yang. Honeypots in Blackhat Mode and its Implications, Proceedings of 4th Int. Conf. On Parallel and Distributed Computing (PDCAT'03), Chengdu, China , 2003:185-188

Web Security Using Distributed Role Hierarchy

Gunhee Lee[1], Hongjin Yeh[1], Wonil Kim[2*], and Dong-Kyoo Kim[1]

[1] Graduate School of Information and Communication, Ajou University, Suwon, Korea
{icezzoco, hjyeh, dkkim}@ajou.ac.kr
[2] College of Electronics & Information Engineering, Sejong University, Seoul, Korea
wikim@sejong.ac.kr

Abstract. Today the Web becomes an essential part of everyday life. In company, school, or public office, people are hooked on computers to connect to the Web. On the other hand, we begin to encounter with web security problems, such as unauthorized access. The access control method such as role-based access control (RBAC) is widely used solution to cope with these problems. In this model, the service provider differentiates services and resources according to the user's attributes such as membership class or job position. Consequently, as the size of the organization increases, users' membership classes and job positions are more complicated, resulting in complex role hierarchy. It is difficult that a centralized role server manages the large and complex role hierarchy. In this paper, we propose a distributed role hierarchy that can manage the role hierarchy effectively and practically to ensure web security. The proposed system employs logically global role hierarchy and physically local role hierarchy. It is managed by distributed role hierarchy modules.

1 Introduction

The Web provides various services depending on the user's membership class or job position. Not only authentication but also authorization is necessary to ensure Web security. Needless to say, implementing reliable access control method is important to ensure Web security.

In the large environment, the relations among users, resources, and cases are too complicated to be managed manually. Therefore, it is very hard to achieve access control consistency for this security system. For example, professor should be able to gain full control of the courses that he/she teaches. While he/she should not gain control of other courses, he/she may read them. In this case, the traditional method has to define many rules for every case. This is a formidable and difficult task. Therefore, the current method can not accommodate these situations properly.

In 1992, David Ferraiolo and Richard Kuhn introduced RBAC (Role-based access control) [1]. In RBAC model, a user has multiple roles and a role has multiple permissions. Permission is represented by the relation of operation and resource.

* Author for Correspondence, +82-2-3408-3795

M. Li et al. (Eds.): GCC 2003, LNCS 3032, pp. 1087–1090, 2004.

Hence the policy is always concerned with what the user's role is [2]. It is much more efficient and time-saving than traditional access control methods [3].

In this paper, we propose an effective and distributed approach to role management in RBAC for secure Web environment. This approach employs decentralized role hierarchy that manages the whole role structure effectively. When a user asks permission for resource, the role hierarchy module checks the availability of managing the related resource. Otherwise, the module sends the request to upper level module. This approach removes burden of centralized role server. Moreover, at the point of the security, proposed approach is more secure than centralized approach, since the role hierarchy has decentralized structure.

This paper is organized as follows. We explain existing RBAC system on the Web and its disadvantages in section 2. In section 3, we describe proposed decentralized approach. This is followed by our conclusions in section 4.

2 Current RBAC on the Web

Currently general RBAC systems use a centralized role server in order to assign role to a user in the Web environment. Before a user requests a resource from the Web server, he or she must acquire the role from the role server. At this time, the role server issues a certificate to the user. User's attributes and roles are in the certificate. After connecting to the Web server, the user client sends the certificate. Next, the server verifies user's attributes and roles and decides user's access. Fig. 1 describes the schematic view of this system [4], [5].

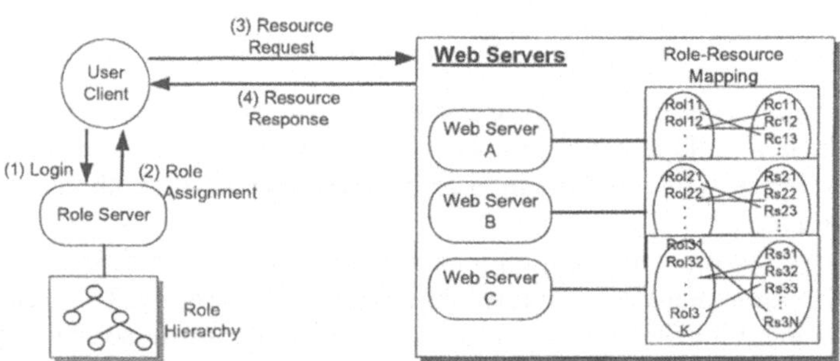

Fig. 1. A schematic view of existing system; the role server has a global role hierarchy.

The complexity of the role hierarchy is too high to manage it effectively with a centralized role server in the large-scale system, since the number of roles and related permissions can be more than thousands. Moreover, in the practical environment, the whole permission-role relation in the hierarchy is related to many distributed web servers. These distributed web servers provide different services and the services are categorized by the level of security or workflow of service. The existing centralized approach is not suitable to the distributed environment. Because all the traffics to obtain role are centralized on the role server, existing approaches cause the vulnerability of security.

3 Proposed Distributed RBAC System

In the proposed system, the global role hierarchy is divided into several local role hierarchies related to services of each web server. Each local web server has own role hierarchy module. A user can initiate a service request from a local web server in the lowest level. When the web server cannot provide requested service due to the limitation of role, it sends a request to a higher-level web server to provide the requested service successfully.

3.1 Distributed Role Hierarchy

We employ two kinds of role hierarchy; global role hierarchy (GRH) and local role hierarchy (LRH). GRH is a logical role hierarchy that describes whole relations among roles in the organization, while LRH is the physical role hierarchy that describes the relations between roles in the categorized role group. The role group is created according to the locality of the service that comes from the relevance and the level of the service. Each LRH is managed by the local role hierarchy module in the web server. The local root role is a bridge to connect with higher level LRH. The right side of Fig. 2 shows the concept of these role hierarchies.

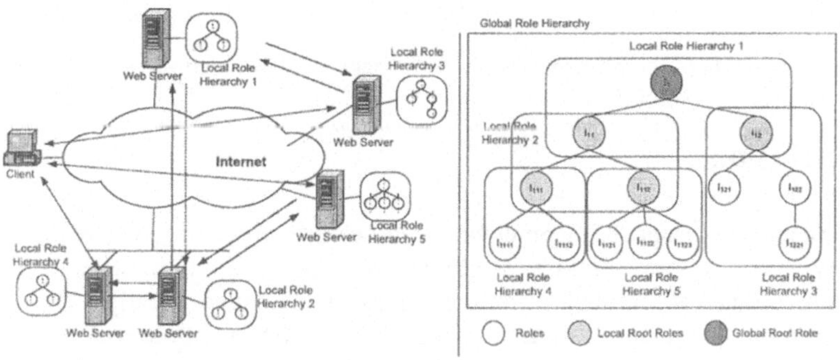

Fig. 2. The schematic of proposed system; a solid line means a user's request, while a dotted line means a traverse of role hierarchy to find available web server. A global role hierarchy is divided into 4 local role hierarchies depending on the role group.

3.2 Proposed Model on the Web

As shown in Fig. 2, several distributed web servers provide services. Actually, these are distributed role hierarchies but conceptually a large role hierarchy. When a user requests a service by connecting to web server, it is sent to a lowest local web server. Role hierarchy module in the given web server checks whether requested service should be handled or not. Handling of the request means that the module can assign the proper role to the user except for the local root role. If it can handle the request, appropriate services are provided. Otherwise, role hierarchy module requests the services to another higher role hierarchy module including own local root role. With the same manner, the higher role hierarchy module checks the availability of handling of the user's request.

Naturally, in some cases, the user's request can be handled by another local web server in equivalent level, not the one in the higher level. In this case, we use reverse traverse method. The requested services can be provided by reverse traverse from a root. When the user's requests are not handled by the highest role hierarchy module, then they traverse again through the alternative route in the global role hierarchy. Fig. 3 shows this case.

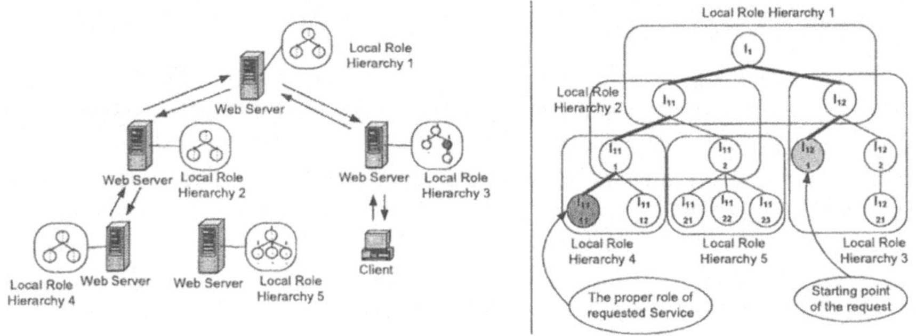

Fig. 3. An example of the reverse traverse that checks available web server in the same level.

4 Conclusions

In this paper, we proposed a practical Web security method using distributed role hierarchy. This system divides a global role hierarchy into several local role hierarchies. Each of divided role hierarchies is managed locally. The proposed method practically enhances security of a system, even against network attack such as DoS. This approach can improve data and resource security of many Web applications, such as e-commerce and work-flow system.

References

1. David Ferraiolo, Richard Kuhn, Role-Based Access Control. Proceedings of 15th National Computer Security Conference (1992)
2. Ravi S. Sandhu, Edward J. Coyne, Hal L. Feinstein, Charles E. Youman, Role-Based Access Control Models. IEEE Computer, IEEE (1996) 38-47
3. D.F.Ferraiolo, R.Sandhu, E.Gavrila, D.R.Kuhn, R.Chandramouli, Proposed NIST Standard for Role-Based Access Control, ACM Transactions on Information and System Security, Vol4, No3 (2001) 224-274
4. Joon S. Park, Ravi Sandhu, RBAC on the Web by Smart Certificates. Proceedings of the 4th ACM workshop on Role-based Access Control, ACM Press, (1999) 1-9
5. Gail-Joon Ahn, Ravi Sandhu, myong Kang, Joon Park, Injecting RBAC to Secure a Web-based Workflow System. Proceedings of the Fifth ACM Workshop on Role-based Access Control (2000) 1-10

User Authentication Protocol Based on Human Memorable Password and Using ECC

Seung Bae Park[1], Moon Seol Kang[2], and Sang Jun Lee[3]

[1] Department of Computer Science, Chodang University, 419 SungnamLi, MuanEup, MuanGun, JeonlanamDo, Korea
sbpark@chodang.ac.kr

[2] Department of Computer Science & Engineering, Gwangju University, 592-1 JinwolDong, NamGu, Gwangju, Korea
mskang@hosim.gwangju.ac.kr

[3] Department of Computer Information Communication, Seonam University, 720 Gwang-chiDong, Namwon, JeonlabukDo, Korea
sjlee@seonam.ac.kr

Abstract. This paper introduces an authentication protocol secure against off-line dictionary attacks and server compromise while processing human memorable password. The protocol uses the fact that there are huge numbers of candidates that can be used to represent a password, even if the password is memorable by humans. The protocol uses ECC to encrypt a value representing a password, but the prover has no need to store a server's public key.

1 Introduction

Authentication is a process whereby a verifier is assured of the identity of a prover involved in a protocol, and that the prover has actually participated.

The well-known attacks which must be guarded in the authentication protocol include: 1) Replay: The attacker records messages sent in past communications and resends them at a later time; 2) Pre-play: The attacker determines a message from the recorded messages in past communications for current communication; 3) Off-line dictionary attack: The attacker records past communications, and then examines a dictionary in search of a password that is consistent with the recorded communication. If such a password is found, the attacker concludes that this password is applicable in an attack [1-4, 5, 6]. 4) On-line dictionary attack: The attacker repeatedly chooses a password from a dictionary and tries to use it in order to impersonate as the user. We do not consider this attack, because there are practical ways of preventing the attack [7, 9]; 5) Server compromise: The attacker acquires sensitive data stored at the verifier to impersonate as a user [7].

Several authentication techniques using a human memorable password, such as one time password [10] and salting technique [11], have been presented. However, the techniques are vulnerable to not only off-line dictionary attacks and server compromise, but even replay attacks and/or pre-play attacks.

M. Li et al. (Eds.): GCC 2003, LNCS 3032, pp. 1091–1094, 2004.

In this paper, we present an authentication protocol that processes human memorable passwords and is secure against the well-known attacks for the authentication protocols. In the protocol, the prover uses ECC to encrypt a value representing the password, but the prover has no necessary to store the verifier's public key.

2 Authentication Protocol Based on Human Memorable Password

Our protocol is depicted in Fig. 1, and the notations used in the protocol are shown in the follows:

p: Prime (p>3).

E: Elliptic curve, defined over Z_p.

a, α, β: a is secret 'exponent' of the verifier and α□E, and β=$a\alpha$.

H: Cyclic subgroup, contained in E, in which the discrete log problem is intractable.

k: Random integer such that k□$Z_{|H|}$ where $|H|$ denotes a number of elements in H.

t, N: t is timestamp, and N=st for primes s and t that are suitable for RSA.

Registering procedure

Input: identity id and a genuine password P.

(1) Get a, α, β, p and choose y_1 in random, and then determine y_2 so that y_1-y_2=P;

(2) Get y_1^2 mod N and y_2^2 mod N, and then store them at id.

Authenticating procedure

Input: id and a password P' inputted as P.

Prover		Verifier
id, P'		a, p, (α, β), y_1^2 mod N, y_2^2 mod N
	id →	
	← (α, β), p	
Pick x_1 in random Determine x_2 so that x_1-x_2=P' Get t and choose k Compute $k\alpha$, $k\beta$=(c_1, c_2) Compute $c_1(x_1+t)$ mod p, and c_2x_2 mod p		
	t, $k\alpha$, $c_1(x_1+t)$ mod p, c_2x_2 mod p →	
		Get $ak\alpha$=(c_1, c_2) Get x_1=$c_1c_1^{-1}(x_1+t-t)$ mod p and x_2=$c_2x_2c_2^{-1}$ mod p Check $(x_1-x_2)^2$ mod N= $(y_1-y_2)^2$ mod N

Fig. 1. Human memorable password based authentication protocol

In the protocol presented in Fig. 1, the verifier authenticates the prover correctly because: the verifier can obtain x_1 and x_2 from $c_1(x_1+t)$ mod p and c_2x_2 mod p by using a private key. The verifier knows that if P=P', then $(x_1+x_2)^2$ mod N=$(y_1-y_2)^2$ mod N because x_1-x_2=y_1-y_2. The verifier accepts the prover only when ((y_1^2 mod N)(y_2^2 mod N)) mod N=$4^{-1}C^2$ mod N where C=x_1^2+x_2^2-$2x_1x_2$-y_1^2 mod N-y_2^2 mod N.

3 Analysis of Protocol

In the protocol presented in Fig. 1, a timestamp makes a message of current communication to be different from messages of past communications. Therefore, the protocol is secure against replay attacks.

Lemma 1. Let 1 x_1, y_1 p, then the size of a space to determine what an integer is selected as (x_1, x_2) or (y_1, y_2) is greater than the size of a space to determine a private key of ECC in the protocol presented in Fig. 1.

Theorem 2. Let 1 x_1 p, then the protocol presented in Fig. 2 is secure against pre-play and off-line dictionary attacks.

A function f from a set X to a set Y is called trapdoor one way function if $f(x)$ is easy to compute for all $x \in X$ but for most elements $y \in \text{Image}(f)$ it is computationally infeasible to find any $x \in X$ such that $f(x)=y$, but it becomes feasible to find for any given $y \in \text{Image}(f)$, an $x \in X$ such that $f(x)=y$ when some extra information is given [8].

In RSA [12], for the given composite integer n of unknown two primes s and t, a problem finding s and t from n is well known integer factorization problem and a source of many trapdoor one way functions [8]. SQROOT problem is to find a square root of a modulo n for the given composite integer n and quadratic residue a modulo n. If both s and t are unknown, then the integer factorization problem of n is reduced to SQROOT problem in polynomial time, and SQROOT problem is also reduced to the integer factorization problem of n in polynomial time. This means that the integer factorization and SQROOT problems are computationally equivalent.

Theorem 3. Let 1 y_1 p, then protocol presented in Fig. 1 is secure against server compromise allowing for subsequent off-line dictionary attack.

Proof: The size of a space to determine (y_1, y_2) is greater than the size of a space to determine a private key of ECC. Therefore, it is computationally infeasible to determine a value (y_1, y_2) from the stored value at the verifier even if the attacker has stolen $y_1^2 \bmod N$ and $y_2^2 \bmod N$.

The number of the passes of our protocol is three. In the Registering procedure, the verifier obtains ECC parameter once, generates a random number once and performs modular square multiplication twice. In the Authenticating procedure, the prover generates a random number once and encrypts (x_1, x_2) by using ECC, and the verifier decrypts a message received from the prover and performs modular multiplication also twice.

4 Conclusions

We have presented an authentication protocol based on human memorable passwords. The protocol is secure against pre-play and off-line dictionary attacks. We have proven that the protocol is secure against server compromise with having performed off-line dictionary attacks. In the aspect of performance, the protocol requires three pass and minor computational amounts.

References

1. Bellare, M., Pointcheaval, D., Rogaway, P.: Authenticated key exchange secure against dictionary attacks. Advances in Cryptology Eurocrypt'00, LNCS Vol. 1807. Springer-Verlag (2000) 139-155
2. Bellovin, S. M., Merrit, M.: Augmented encrypted key exchange: Password-based protocol secure against dictionary attack and password file compromise. In ACM Security (CCS'93) (1993) 244-250
3. Bellovin, S. M., Merrit, M.: Encrypted key exchange: Password-based protocols secure against dictionary attack. In Proceedings of IEEE Security and Privacy (1992) 72-84
4. Boyko, V., MacKenzie, Patal, P. S.: Provably secure password authenticated key exchange using Diffie-Hellman. Advances in Cryptology Eurocrypt'00, LNCS Vol. 1807. Springer-Verlag (2000) 156-171
5. Gong, L.: Optimal authentication protocols resistant to password guessing attacks. In 8th IEEE Computer Security Foundations Workshop (1995) 24-29
6. Gong, L., Lomas, T. M. A., Needham, R. M, Saltzer, J. H.: Protecting poorly chosen secrets from guessing attacks. IEEE Journal on Selected Areas in Communications, 11(5) (1993) 648-656
7. Halevi, S., Krawczyk, H.: Public-key cryptography and password protocols. ACM Security (CCS' 98) (1998) 122-131
8. ISO/IEC 9798-4.: Information technology-Security techniques-Entity authentication-Part 4: Mechanisms using a cryptographic check function. International Organization for Standardization, Geneva, Switzerland (1995)
9. Jablon, D.: Strong password-only authenticated key exchange. ACM Computer Communication Review, ACM SIGCOMM, Vol. 26, No. 5 (1996) 5-20
10. Lamport, L.: Password authentication with insecure communication. Communications of the ACM, Vol. 24 (1981) 770-772
11. Morris, R., Thompson, K.: Password security: a case history. Communications of the ACM, Vol. 22 (1979) 594-597
12. Rivest, R. L., Shamir, A., Adleman, L. M.: A method for obtaining digital signatures and public-key cryptosystems. Communications of the ACM, Vol. 21, No. 2 (1978) 120-126

New Authentication Systems

Seung Bae Park[1], Moon Seol Kang[2], and Sang Jun Lee[3]

[1] Department of Computer Science, Chodang University, 419 SungnamLi, MuanEup, MuanGun, JeonlanamDo, Korea
sbpark@chodang.ac.kr

[2] Department of Computer Science & Engineering, Gwangju University, 592-1 JinwolDong, NamGu, Gwangju, Korea
mskang@hosim.gwangju.ac.kr

[3] Department of Computer Information Communication, Seonam University, 720 Gwang-chiDong, Namwon, JeonlabukDo, Korea
sjlee@seonam.ac.kr

Abstract. This paper introduces a new scheme for authentication system called *Dynamic Authentication System* (DAS). In the DAS, an attacker can learn the user's alphabet only if the attacker knows the entire alphabets which is displayed on the interface in a randomly selected order without replacement in the order. We present two DAS based authentication systems: Increasing DAS and Multi-selecting DAS. These systems enhance the security against shoulder surfing attack while preserving the security against an on-line dictionary attack of the password system.

1 Introduction

The password system is the most widely spread entity authentication system, and the attacks which must be guarded in the input module of the password system include on-line dictionary and shoulder surfing attacks.

In an on-line dictionary attack, an attacker repeatedly picks a password from the dictionary and tries to use it in order to impersonate as a user. One way of preventing such the on-line dictionary attack is limit the number of failed runs [2, 7]. In a shoulder surfing attack, an attacker uses a user's password, obtained by looking over a user's shoulder when the user is typing the password, in order to impersonate as the user [4, 6]. According to our investigation, three password systems have been presented for enhancing the security against the shoulder surfing attack. The first password system requires a password over the fixed length [1]. The second password system displays the alphabets in randomly selected order repeatedly, and a user selects his alphabet in the displayed alphabets [5]. The last system displays an image on the interface, and a user selects his portion on the image repeatedly [3]. The presented password systems, the attacker learns a user's alphabet exactly if only the attacker looks over the user's shoulder when the user inputs the alphabet.

In this paper, we define a new scheme for the authentication systems called *Dynamic Authentication System* (DAS). In the DAS, an attacker of the shoulder surfing attack can learn a user's alphabet only when the attacker has remembered all alphabets

M. Li et al. (Eds.): GCC 2003, LNCS 3032, pp. 1095–1098, 2004.

displayed on the interface in randomly selected order without replacement in the order.

We present two DAS based authentication systems: *Increasing DAS* and *Multi-selecting DAS*. The systems enhance the security against a shoulder surfing attack while preserving the security against an on-line dictionary attack of the password system. The systems have been implemented to obtain the time spent inputting passwords. As a result, the Multi-selecting DAS requires, on average, less time than the time of the password system, and Increasing DAS requires the most reasonable amount of time.

2 Dynamic Authentication System

The *Dynamic Authentication System* (DAS) is defined in Definition 1.

Definition 1 A authentication system is DAS if it satisfies: (1) The security against the on-line dictionary attack is the same as that of the password system; (2) The interface consists of the cells, and each cell contains its own alphabet in randomly selected order without replacement; (3) An attacker of a shoulder surfing attack can learn user's alphabet only if the attacker has remembered all alphabets, contained in the cells, in the order; (4) The performance is to be as near as possible to that of the password system.

In the password system, an attacker of an on-line dictionary attack can hit user's password with a probability $1/(|S|^n\text{-}i+1)$ in the ith attack where S denotes a set of alphabets and $|S|$ a number of the elements in S, and n a length of the password. We think that (2) of Definition 1 is a necessary condition of the authentication system which is more secure than the password system against the shoulder surfing attack.

In the DAS, a shoulder surfing attack is meaningful only when the attacker has remembered the order of the alphabet contained in the cells. For this reason, we rename the shoulder surfing attack to *shoulder memory attack* in which an attacker looks over a user's shoulder when the user inputs his password and then remembers the alphabets contained in the cells to learn the password.

Definition 2 Let $x_1x_2...x_n$ be a password and C a number of the cells in the interface, and assume that an attacker has remembered the order of the C_i alphabets, contained in the C_i cells, when a user inputs x_i $(1\ \ i\ \ n,\ 0\ \ C_i\ \ C)$. An authentication system based on the DAS is called *α-probabilistic secure* against the shoulder memory attack if the attacker can learn a password with the minimum probability in the probabilities C_i/C, and *β-probabilistic secure* with a probability $\text{MIN}(C_1, C_2, ..., C_n)/C$ on the assumption that the attacker has remembered n information beside the C_i alphabets. In *α-probabilistic secure* and *β-probabilistic secure*, C_i is considered as C if C_i=C-1.

A condition (4) is established on the assumption that the password system is excellent in the aspect of performance.

3 Authentication Systems Based on DAS

We describe DAS based authentication systems in Subsection 3.1 and analysis the systems in Subsection 3.2.

3.1 DAS Based Authentication Systems

Let S be a set of the ordered alphabets and C a number of the cells on the interface ($1 \leq C \leq S$) and $x_1 x_2 \ldots x_n$ a password where $x_i \in S$ for $1 \leq i \leq n$. In the Increasing DAS (IDAS), a user and the IDAS interact (1) once, (2) and (3) n times, and (4) and (5) once in the following: (1) A user determines a cell in his heart; (2) The IDAS displays the kth C alphabets in the C cells in randomly selected order without replacement ($1 \leq k \leq n$); (3) Let the user determined the jth cell in (1), and y be an alphabet contained in the jth cell. If $y < x_k$, then a user hits a key x_k-y times to increase all values contained in the C cells as x_k-y, and then the user chooses another key to notify that x_k has been inputted. If $y \geq x_k$, then the user hits a key ($|S|+x_k$-y mod $|S|$) times to increase all values contained in the C cells as $|S|+x_k$-y mod $|S|$ where mod denotes modular operator, and then the user strokes another key to notify that x_k has been inputted; (4) The IDAS displays the (n+1)th C alphabets in the C cells in randomly selected order without replacement; (5) Let y be an alphabet contained in the jth cell. The user hits a key $|S|$-y times to increase all values contained in the C cells as $|S|$-y, and then the user strokes another key to indicate that a password has been inputted. In this step, a special character is contained in the jth cell after the user hit a key $|S|$-y times.

Let S be a set of the alphabets, and each alphabet in the password is an element of S. The interface of the Multi-selecting DAS (MDAS) displays two boards: one board is a cursor consisting of the C cells in which each cell contains its own alphabet in a randomly selected order without replacement, and another board consists of $|S|$+1 cells such that (1) the ith cell contains the ith element of S (1 i $|S|$); (2) the ($|S|$+1)th cell contains a special character. In the MDAS, a user determines any cell in the cursor in his heart, and then selects his alphabet with the cell repeatedly until the special character is finally selected.

3.2 Security and Performance of DAS Based Authentication Systems

Obviously, the security of IDAS and MDAS against an on-line dictionary attack is the same as that of the password system.

In the IDAS, the attacker can learn a password with a probability X/C if he has remembered all alphabets contained in the X cells. Therefore, the IDAS is α-probabilistic secure. In the MDAS, the attacker can learn a password with a probability X/C on the assumption that he has remembered the placement of the cursor. Therefore, MAS is β-probabilistic secure.

The DAS based authentication systems have been implemented in JAVA running on Windows 2000 server on a 700 MHz Pentium III with 384 Mbytes of RAM to obtain the time spent to input the passwords. In the MDAS, the time rigorously dependents on how to design the interface, and we have only considered the interface that requires the least time.

Two hundred people had inputted their passwords, consisting of four decimal numbers, fifty times. The times spent, on the average, are shown in Table 1.

Table 1. Times spent to input passwords

Password system	IDAS	MDAS
1.892	4.968	1.879

4 Conclusions

We have defined a scheme for the authentication systems called the DAS. In the DAS, we have considered the security against both shoulder surfing attacks, renamed to a shoulder memory attacks, and on-line dictionary attacks, as well as the performance.

We have presented two DAS based authentication systems called IDAS and MDAS. Both IDAS and MDAS enhance the security against the shoulder memory attack while preserving the security against the on-line dictionary attack of the password system.

The systems have been implemented with JAVA to obtain the time spent inputting the passwords consisting of four decimal numbers. The experiment's results have shown that the MDAS requires less time, on average, than the time of the password system. The IDAS requires reasonable amount of time.

References

1. Garfinkel, G., Schwartz A., Spafford, G.: Practical Unix & Internet Security. 3rd Edition, O'Reilly & Associates, (2003)
2. Halevi S., Krawczyk, H.: Public-key cryptography and password protocols. ACM Security (CCS' 98). (1998) 122-131.
3. http://www.domainmart.com/news/NYT_symbols-as-passwods.htm
4. http://www.itsecurity.com/dictionary/shoulder.htm
5. http://www.realuser.com/cgi-bin/ru.exe/_/homepages/index.htm
6. http://www.searchsecurity.techtarget.com/sDefinition/0,,sid14_gci802244,00.html
7. Jablon: Strong password-only authenticated key exchange. ACM Computer Communication Review, ACM SIGCOMM, Vol. 26, No. 5. (1996) 5-20

Web Proxy Caching Mechanism to Evenly Distribute Transmission Channel in VOD System

Backhyun Kim[1], Iksoo Kim[1], and SeokHoon Kang[2]

[1]Department of Information and Telecommunication Engineering Univ. of Incheon,
177 Towhadong Namku Incheon, Korea
{hidesky24, iskim}@incheon.ac.kr
[2]Division of Internet Engineering Dongseo University,
San 69-1 Churyedong Sasangku Pusan, Korea
hana@tecace.com

Abstract. The proxy caching technique can significantly reduce server's load but is still suffered from the shortage of the network bandwidth and from the traffic imbalance among proxies. In this paper, we propose the equivalent loaded proxy caching mechanism to minimize the required transmission bandwidth by using the distribution mechanism determined by the request order and by the popularity of videos calculated with the request frequency. In our technique, videos transmitted from the server are fragmented by Switching Agent and are distributively stored among Head-End-Nodes according to the request order, and SA stores some popular videos to reduce the retransmission of an identical video from the server. From simulation results, we acquire that the proposed web caching mechanism has equivalent loaded among HENs and it can reduce VOD server's bandwidth significantly.

1 Introduction

This paper presents equivalent-loaded web caching mechanism to reduce the transmission bandwidth and the load of the server and to prevent an identical video from duplicating among proxies. We have developed an end-to-end client/server architecture called Head-End-Network(HNET). The proposed web caching system consists of a Switching Agent(SA) and Head-End-Nodes(HEN), and resides near to clients. Under the new schemed, requested services are always conveyed from VOD server through SA and HEN to clients, thus the SA and HEN are able to intercept and cache these streams. VOD server delivers a stream for the requested video to clients only once not concerned with the number of requests. SA slices received streams into a equal-sized pieces called segments within the predefined split time and alternatively delivers these segments to HENs in the order of request, therefore HEN dose not store a whole data on an identical video. This paper is organized as follows: In section 2 we describe the proposed equivalent loaded web caching mechanism. In section 3, we present the simulations and analysis of the results. Finally, we give out conclusion in section 4.

M. Li et al. (Eds.): GCC 2003, LNCS 3032, pp. 1099–1102, 2004.

2 Head-End-Network

The proposed web-caching mechanism is a layered proxy structure(HNET) composed of a SA and HENs adopted some caches. In this scheme, the VOD server immediately performs streaming service through the Internet as a source device that provides service of a requested video data and transmits an identical video only once except both SA and HENs take cache miss on it. The HNET operates under the control of SA and shares its information among HNETs.

Switching agent establishes a transmission channel from client to server when a particular video *Vi* is requested first and calculates the request frequency *Dpop* on it. If the requested video has already transmitted and stored among HENs, SA dose not request the transmission for an identical video except it is cache miss both in SA and in HENs. SA stores streams delivered from server depending on the *Dpop* and splits received streams into segments S_{number}, the value of the segment number is equal to Consecutive Value(CV), on an identical video within the predefined split time T_{split} and transmits a segment to one of HENs according to the request order. Thus, different segments of streams on an identical video requested from several HENs are distributively stored at corresponding HENs.

To distribute segments orderly, SA collects the requests on an identical video with Video Identification(VID) within T_{split}, makes the transmission order depending on the request time. And then, SA inserts the CV to each segments' header and transmits them orderly. This information indicates stored segments at each HENs classified by Node Identification(NID) and allows a HEN to find which HEN stores the rest parts of the requested video. To reduce processing time at each HENs, SA makes Multimedia Content Table(MCT) that has three elements; VID, CV and NID. For cache replacement, SA calculates how many segments will be transmitted to each HENs during next T_{split} and inserts this value (number of segments on each HENs: NS_{NID}) to MCT. It periodically transfers MCT to all of HENs within its own HNET. Thus, all HENs under the control of SA can learn what they store and share their stored segments on an identical video.

Stored segments in HEN may be deleted if a HEN's cache has been exhausted and should retransmit to the HEN from VOD server. To minimize the retransmission, HENs need much more cache but this is not cost-effective method. To reduce the capacity of HEN's cache, SA has some caches to store popular videos depending on the request frequency on an identical video content.

HEN locates in between SA and clients as a proxy, accesses VOD server through SA, stores streams delivered from SA and serves them to clients under the control of SA. Also, it accesses the other HENs for acquiring stored video streams on them. HEN knows about the current stored segments on an identical video *Vi* among HENs by the received MCT from SA and, for accurate information on the stored video segments in HEN, notifies the current state of their caches to SA at T_{split} whenever video segments stored in its own cache is changed. When HEN receives the request packet from an attached client, first, it verifies that packet. If it is the request for a stored video segment, the request segment(*VIDrequest*, *CVrequest*) identified as the stored segment(*VIDstored*, *CVstored*), HEN sends the segment(VID, CV) to client. If client requests for not storing segment, HEN searches its MCT for (*VIDrequest*,

CVrequest). If stored at one of the other HENs (HEN_{others}), HEN requests that segment to the accordant HEN($HEN_{other\#}$), but it dose not cache the segment transmitted from $HEN_{other\#}$ to prevent from duplicating among HENs.

3 Simulations and Analysis of the Results

In this section, we show simulation results to demonstrate the benefit of proposed equivalent-loaded web caching mechanism and analyzes on the results of performance using it. The selection of videos is modeled using a Zipf-like distribution [1,2,3] where skew factor z = 0.85[2]. Using the Zipf distribution, if the overall clients' service request rate to the VOD server is λ, the service requesting rate for i'th video is $\lambda i = \lambda P(i)$. We use *P(i)* as a weighting parameter for selection of videos in simulation. The service request rate λ follows Poisson distribution. Our workload and system parameters are summarized in Table. 1. The default values are listed under the *Default* column. We also vary some of these parameters to do sensitivity analysis. The ranges of values used for simulation are given in the third column under the *Range*.

Table 1. Parameters used for the simulation

Parameter	Default	Range
Number of videos	100	N/A
Video length (minutes)	100	N/A
Server bandwidth (streams)	100	80 to 120
HNET bandwidth (streams)	500	100 to 3,000
Number of clients	5,000	N/A
Request rate λ (requests/min)	50	10 to 50
Cache size in SA Σ(request for i/total requests)	0%	0% to 70%
Cache size in HEN (minutes)	100	100 to 1000
Number of HENs	10	2 to 10

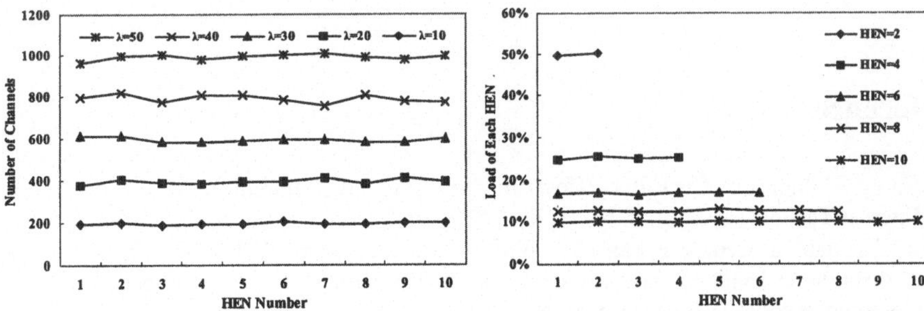

Fig. 1. The number of transmitting channels at each HEN according to request rate λ

Fig. 2. Load of each HEN according to the number of HEN is varying 2 to 10

Fig. 1 shows that the number of transmitting channels needed in each HEN is almost same according to the service request rate λ 10 to 50, and simulation parameters are that HEN is 10; cache size of each HEN is 100 minutes long and the others is the same above. These results are derived from the sum of needed channels in three cases; channels for sending segments to clients, channels for receiving from the other HENs or SA storing requested segments and channels for receiving from VOD server for initial transmission and for retransmitting cache missed segments. From the results, the more the request rate λ increases the more transmission channels are needed. This is due to the fact that an increase of the request rate λ means an increase of clients. We obtain that the number of transmission channels distributes over each HEN evenly. Fig. 2 shows the load of each HEN according to the number of HEN embodied in HNET. In this case, total cache size of HENs was fixed at 1,000 minutes long and the request rate λ was 50. This shows that the number of HENs is the main factor to determine the load of HEN.

4 Conclusion

In this paper, we proposed HNET existing near clients and storing video streams transmitted from VOD server. It makes the load of network evenly distribute over all of configured network. We confirm the loads of distributive HENs composing a HNET are well balanced. With service request frequency, popular videos are stored both in HENs and in SA, and this reduces end-to-end latency. Therefore, cache hit ratio of popular videos is higher than the other videos and the number of transmission channels from VOD server decreases rapidly as videos served to clients are already stored in proxies (SA and HEN). Our simulation results show much better performance to reduce network traffic in the case of popular videos. So, proposed model can improve server's workload, decreases the service blocking probability and serves robust operation in various network environments.

Acknowledgement. This work was supported (in part) by the Korea Science and Engineering Foundation (KOSEF) through the multimedia Research Center.

References

1. Carey Williamson: On Filter Effects in Web Caching Hierarchies. ACM Transactions on Internet Technology. Vol. 2. No. 1, pp 47-77, 2002
2. L. Breslau, P.Cao, L, Fan, G. Phillips, S. Shenker: Web Caching and Zipf-like Distributions: Evidence and Implications. in Proceeding of the Conference on Computer Communications (IEEE Infocom), New York, 1999
3. P. Cao and S. Irani: Cost-aware WWW Proxy Caching Algorithms. In Proc. Of the 1997 USENIX Symposium on Internet Technology and Systems, pp. 193-206, 1997

Author Index

Lecture Notes in Computer Science

For information about Vols. 1–2917

please contact your bookseller or Springer-Verlag

Vol. 3042: N. Mitrou, K. Kontovasilis, G.N. Rouskas, I. Iliadis, L. Merakos (Eds.), NETWORKING 2004, Networking Technologies, Services, and Protocols; Performance of Computer and Communication Networks; Mobile and Wireless Communications. XXXIII, 1519 pages. 2004.

Vol. 3034: J. Favela, E. Menasalvas, E. Chávez (Eds.), Advances in Web Intelligence. XIII, 227 pages. 2004. (Subseries LNAI).

Vol. 3033: M. Li, X.-H. Sun, Q. Deng, J. Ni (Eds.), Grid and Cooperative Computing, Part II. XXXVIII, 1076 pages. 2004.

Vol. 3032: M. Li, X.-H. Sun, Q. Deng, J. Ni (Eds.), Grid and Cooperative Computing, Part I. XXXVII, 1112 pages. 2004.

Vol. 3031: A. Butz, A. Krüger, P. Olivier (Eds.), Smart Graphics. X, 165 pages. 2004.

Vol. 3027: C. Cachin, J. Camenisch (Eds.), Advances in Cryptology - EUROCRYPT 2004. XI, 628 pages. 2004.

Vol. 3026: C. Ramamoorthy, R. Lee, K.W. Lee (Eds.), Software Engineering Research and Applications. XV, 377 pages. 2004.

Vol. 3025: G.A. Vouros, T. Panayiotopoulos (Eds.), Methods and Applications of Artificial Intelligence. XV, 546 pages. 2004. (Subseries LNAI).

Vol. 3024: T. Pajdla, J. Matas (Eds.), Computer Vision - ECCV 2004. XXVIII, 621 pages. 2004.

Vol. 3023: T. Pajdla, J. Matas (Eds.), Computer Vision - ECCV 2004. XXVIII, 611 pages. 2004.

Vol. 3022: T. Pajdla, J. Matas (Eds.), Computer Vision - ECCV 2004. XXVIII, 621 pages. 2004.

Vol. 3021: T. Pajdla, J. Matas (Eds.), Computer Vision - ECCV 2004. XXVIII, 633 pages. 2004.

Vol. 3019: R. Wyrzykowski, J. Dongarra, M. Paprzycki, J. Wasniewski (Eds.), Parallel Processing and Applied Mathematics. XIX, 1174 pages. 2004.

Vol. 3015: C. Barakat, I. Pratt (Eds.), Passive and Active Network Measurement. XI, 300 pages. 2004.

Vol. 3012: K. Kurumatani, S.-H. Chen, A. Ohuchi (Eds.), Multi-Agnets for Mass User Support. X, 217 pages. 2004. (Subseries LNAI).

Vol. 3011: J.-C. Régin, M. Rueher (Eds.), Integration of AI and OR Techniques in Constraint Programming for Combinatorial Optimization Problems. XI, 415 pages. 2004.

Vol. 3010: K.R. Apt, F. Fages, F. Rossi, P. Szeredi, J. Váncza (Eds.), Recent Advances in Constraints. VIII, 285 pages. 2004. (Subseries LNAI).

Vol. 3009: F. Bomarius, H. Iida (Eds.), Product Focused Software Process Improvement. XIV, 584 pages. 2004.

Vol. 3007: J.X. Yu, X. Lin, H. Lu, Y. Zhang (Eds.), Advanced Web Technologies and Applications. XXII, 936 pages. 2004.

Vol. 3006: M. Matsui, R. Zuccherato (Eds.), Selected Areas in Cryptography. XI, 361 pages. 2004.

Vol. 3005: G.R. Raidl, S. Cagnoni, J. Branke, D.W. Corne, R. Drechsler, Y. Jin, C.G. Johnson, P. Machado, E. Marchiori, F. Rothlauf, G.D. Smith, G. Squillero (Eds.), Applications of Evolutionary Computing. XVII, 562 pages. 2004.

Vol. 3004: J. Gottlieb, G.R. Raidl (Eds.), Evolutionary Computation in Combinatorial Optimization. X, 241 pages. 2004.

Vol. 3003: M. Keijzer, U.-M. O'Reilly, S.M. Lucas, E. Costa, T. Soule (Eds.), Genetic Programming. XI, 410 pages. 2004.

Vol. 3002: D.L. Hicks (Ed.), Metainformatics. X, 213 pages. 2004.

Vol. 3001: A. Ferscha, F. Mattern (Eds.), Pervasive Computing. XVII, 358 pages. 2004.

Vol. 2999: E.A. Boiten, J. Derrick, G. Smith (Eds.), Integrated Formal Methods. XI, 541 pages. 2004.

Vol. 2998: Y. Kameyama, P.J. Stuckey (Eds.), Functional and Logic Programming. X, 307 pages. 2004.

Vol. 2997: S. McDonald, J. Tait (Eds.), Advances in Information Retrieval. XIII, 427 pages. 2004.

Vol. 2996: V. Diekert, M. Habib (Eds.), STACS 2004. XVI, 658 pages. 2004.

Vol. 2995: C. Jensen, S. Poslad, T. Dimitrakos (Eds.), Trust Management. XIII, 377 pages. 2004.

Vol. 2994: E. Rahm (Ed.), Data Integration in the Life Sciences. X, 221 pages. 2004. (Subseries LNBI).

Vol. 2993: R. Alur, G.J. Pappas (Eds.), Hybrid Systems: Computation and Control. XII, 674 pages. 2004.

Vol. 2992: E. Bertino, S. Christodoulakis, D. Plexousakis, V. Christophides, M. Koubarakis, K. Böhm, E. Ferrari (Eds.), Advances in Database Technology - EDBT 2004. XVIII, 877 pages. 2004.

Vol. 2991: R. Alt, A. Frommer, R.B. Kearfott, W. Luther (Eds.), Numerical Software with Result Verification. X, 315 pages. 2004.

Vol. 2989: S. Graf, L. Mounier (Eds.), Model Checking Software. X, 309 pages. 2004.

Vol. 2988: K. Jensen, A. Podelski (Eds.), Tools and Algorithms for the Construction and Analysis of Systems. XIV, 608 pages. 2004.

Vol. 2987: I. Walukiewicz (Ed.), Foundations of Software Science and Computation Structures. XIII, 529 pages. 2004.

Vol. 2986: D. Schmidt (Ed.), Programming Languages and Systems. XII, 417 pages. 2004.

Vol. 2985: E. Duesterwald (Ed.), Compiler Construction. X, 313 pages. 2004.

Vol. 2984: M. Wermelinger, T. Margaria-Steffen (Eds.), Fundamental Approaches to Software Engineering. XII, 389 pages. 2004.

Vol. 2983: S. Istrail, M.S. Waterman, A. Clark (Eds.), Computational Methods for SNPs and Haplotype Inference. IX, 153 pages. 2004. (Subseries LNBI).

Vol. 2982: N. Wakamiya, M. Solarski, J. Sterbenz (Eds.), Active Networks. XI, 308 pages. 2004.

Vol. 2981: C. Müller-Schloer, T. Ungerer, B. Bauer (Eds.), Organic and Pervasive Computing – ARCS 2004. XI, 339 pages. 2004.

Vol. 2980: A. Blackwell, K. Marriott, A. Shimojima (Eds.), Diagrammatic Representation and Inference. XV, 448 pages. 2004. (Subseries LNAI).

Vol. 2979: I. Stoica, Stateless Core: A Scalable Approach for Quality of Service in the Internet. XVI, 219 pages. 2004.

Vol. 2978: R. Groz, R.M. Hierons (Eds.), Testing of Communicating Systems. XII, 225 pages. 2004.

Vol. 2977: G. Di Marzo Serugendo, A. Karageorgos, O.F. Rana, F. Zambonelli (Eds.), Engineering Self-Organising Systems. X, 299 pages. 2004. (Subseries LNAI).

Vol. 2976: M. Farach-Colton (Ed.), LATIN 2004: Theoretical Informatics. XV, 626 pages. 2004.

Vol. 2973: Y. Lee, J. Li, K.-Y. Whang, D. Lee (Eds.), Database Systems for Advanced Applications. XXIV, 925 pages. 2004.

Vol. 2972: R. Monroy, G. Arroyo-Figueroa, L.E. Sucar, H. Sossa (Eds.), MICAI 2004: Advances in Artificial Intelligence. XVII, 923 pages. 2004. (Subseries LNAI).

Vol. 2971: J.I. Lim, D.H. Lee (Eds.), Information Security and Cryptology -ICISC 2003. XI, 458 pages. 2004.

Vol. 2970: F. Fernández Rivera, M. Bubak, A. Gómez Tato, R. Doallo (Eds.), Grid Computing. XI, 328 pages. 2004.

Vol. 2968: J. Chen, S. Hong (Eds.), Real-Time and Embedded Computing Systems and Applications. XIV, 620 pages. 2004.

Vol. 2967: S. Melnik, Generic Model Management. XX, 238 pages. 2004.

Vol. 2966: F.B. Sachse, Computational Cardiology. XVIII, 322 pages. 2004.

Vol. 2965: M.C. Calzarossa, E. Gelenbe, Performance Tools and Applications to Networked Systems. VIII, 385 pages. 2004.

Vol. 2964: T. Okamoto (Ed.), Topics in Cryptology – CT-RSA 2004. XI, 387 pages. 2004.

Vol. 2963: R. Sharp, Higher Level Hardware Synthesis. XVI, 195 pages. 2004.

Vol. 2962: S. Bistarelli, Semirings for Soft Constraint Solving and Programming. XII, 279 pages. 2004.

Vol. 2961: P. Eklund (Ed.), Concept Lattices. IX, 411 pages. 2004. (Subseries LNAI).

Vol. 2960: P.D. Mosses (Ed.), CASL Reference Manual. XVII, 528 pages. 2004.

Vol. 2958: L. Rauchwerger (Ed.), Languages and Compilers for Parallel Computing. XI, 556 pages. 2004.

Vol. 2957: P. Langendoerfer, M. Liu, I. Matta, V. Tsaoussidis (Eds.), Wired/Wireless Internet Communications. XI, 307 pages. 2004.

Vol. 2956: A. Dengel, M. Junker, A. Weisbecker (Eds.), Reading and Learning. XII, 355 pages. 2004.

Vol. 2954: F. Crestani, M. Dunlop, S. Mizzaro (Eds.), Mobile and Ubiquitous Information Access. X, 299 pages. 2004.

Vol. 2953: K. Konrad, Model Generation for Natural Language Interpretation and Analysis. XIII, 166 pages. 2004. (Subseries LNAI).

Vol. 2952: N. Guelfi, E. Astesiano, G. Reggio (Eds.), Scientific Engineering of Distributed Java Applications. X, 157 pages. 2004.

Vol. 2951: M. Naor (Ed.), Theory of Cryptography. XI, 523 pages. 2004.

Vol. 2949: R. De Nicola, G. Ferrari, G. Meredith (Eds.), Coordination Models and Languages. X, 323 pages. 2004.

Vol. 2948: G.L. Mullen, A. Poli, H. Stichtenoth (Eds.), Finite Fields and Applications. VIII, 263 pages. 2004.

Vol. 2947: F. Bao, R. Deng, J. Zhou (Eds.), Public Key Cryptography – PKC 2004. XI, 455 pages. 2004.

Vol. 2946: R. Focardi, R. Gorrieri (Eds.), Foundations of Security Analysis and Design II. VII, 267 pages. 2004.

Vol. 2943: J. Chen, J. Reif (Eds.), DNA Computing. X, 225 pages. 2004.

Vol. 2941: M. Wirsing, A. Knapp, S. Balsamo (Eds.), Radical Innovations of Software and Systems Engineering in the Future. X, 359 pages. 2004.

Vol. 2940: C. Lucena, A. Garcia, A. Romanovsky, J. Castro, P.S. Alencar (Eds.), Software Engineering for Multi-Agent Systems II. XII, 279 pages. 2004.

Vol. 2939: T. Kalker, I.J. Cox, Y.M. Ro (Eds.), Digital Watermarking. XII, 602 pages. 2004.

Vol. 2937: B. Steffen, G. Levi (Eds.), Verification, Model Checking, and Abstract Interpretation. XI, 325 pages. 2004.

Vol. 2936: P. Liardet, P. Collet, C. Fonlupt, E. Lutton, M. Schoenauer (Eds.), Artificial Evolution. XIV, 410 pages. 2004.

Vol. 2934: G. Lindemann, D. Moldt, M. Paolucci (Eds.), Regulated Agent-Based Social Systems. X, 301 pages. 2004. (Subseries LNAI).

Vol. 2930: F. Winkler (Ed.), Automated Deduction in Geometry. VII, 231 pages. 2004. (Subseries LNAI).

Vol. 2929: H. de Swart, E. Orlowska, G. Schmidt, M. Roubens (Eds.), Theory and Applications of Relational Structures as Knowledge Instruments. VII, 273 pages. 2003.

Vol. 2926: L. van Elst, V. Dignum, A. Abecker (Eds.), Agent-Mediated Knowledge Management. XI, 428 pages. 2004. (Subseries LNAI).

Vol. 2923: V. Lifschitz, I. Niemelä (Eds.), Logic Programming and Nonmonotonic Reasoning. IX, 365 pages. 2004. (Subseries LNAI).

Vol. 2919: E. Giunchiglia, A. Tacchella (Eds.), Theory and Applications of Satisfiability Testing. XI, 530 pages. 2004.